Oddball
Sports Yearbook
2003

Editor **Peter Nichols**

PUBLISHING

Published in Great Britain by Oddball Publishing Ltd, Brighton, East Sussex
Phone: 01273 722824   Fax: 01273 722824
e-mail: oddball@mistral.co.uk

Text design and layout by Oddball Publishing Ltd
using QuarkXpress on Apple Mac computers
Printed and bound in Great Britain by Biddles Ltd, Guildford and Kings Lynn

A catalogue record for this book is available from the British Library

ISBN 0-9524044-6-X

Introduction

Another suitcase and another town, as Tim Rice so memorably said. The years march on and the Yearbook marches with us, albeit this year in a noticeably different form. Because it was such a monumental year for sport, we ran out of pages somewhere around Table Tennis, and made the decision to add another 48 instantly. However, in order to accommodate the extra pages, we had to make the paper lighter to keep the postage costs down. Hence the book before you.

Even with the added pages, it was still necessary to make cuts, and the sections we savaged were the Review of the Year (yet again) and the Headlines, which has completely disappeared. If its omission has changed your life for the worse, send us a passionate email, and we may re-instate it for the 2004 yearbook.

Thanks, as always, go to those who helped to start the yearbook venture; Penny Dain, Betty Maitland, Pat Molyneux, Chris Sainty, Brian Smith, David Smith, Iain Smith, Anna Wallace and Hugh Wallace. Andrew Haslam and Michael Hughes, as ever, have been indispensible, as has our associate editor Andy Edwards.

Finally, our thanks to you, dear reader, in particular for understanding that an Oddball publication schedule is not always to be taken literally.

Peter Nichols
Editor

• CONTENTS •

For **Will**

Review Of The Year

We always search for a theme in this section, and more often than not (journalism being such), the theme is manufactured. For 2002, the best that we could come up with was that it was a predictable year. After all, in football, England briefly offered hope before adopting a dismal game plan and exiting limping against a class South American side, while Ireland, with the chips down (yes, journalism is about clichés too), played with pride and passion and were unlucky to go out.

In cricket, England lost to Australia in the Ashes series, beaten by a country mile. England, or was it just Nasser Hussain, had been trying a little psychology, talking up England's world ranking based almost entirely on being better than Sri Lanka. The psychological strategy fell apart, though, when the Ashes Tests hoved into view, and England tried to pretend that players who could hardly walk (Darren Gough, Andy Flintoff) were fit enough to frighten the Australians. It smacked of desperation. It was desperation. The Australians went into the First Test with their tails up, and never looked back. So unbalanced was the series that, until the final Test, domestic discussion surrounded the number of Test-match 'days' that England had won, there being no Test victories to discuss. It was, we're afraid, entirely predictable.

Even the England rugby team, a beacon in British sport, capable of not only matching Australia but of beating Australia, fell into its usual habits. The three victories over the southern hemisphere nations were undoubtedly the cause for celebration (especially against the vindictive South Africans), but they still came in the aftermath of yet another Six Nations failure. Is failure too harsh a word? Perhaps it is, but it is also the word that Clive Woodward would use. England's defeat in Paris made it seven straight years (1996-2002) that England had surrendered a possible Grand Slam by losing a single match. You can't get more predictable than that.

Tim Henman (did we hear a sigh at the mention of his name?) is next on the list. There is no doubt that, with regard to Wimbledon, Henman has altered our expectations. No longer do we jump through hoops and balance fish on our noses while clapping our hands if a British player (say, Jeremy Bates) progresses beyond the first round. We don't behave like that anymore, because we have the certain knowledge that Henman will reach the semi-final. For four years out of the last five, Henman, has done just that. The exception, proving the rule, was when he found a fit Mark Philippoussis (and that's a rarity) too much of a handful in a fourth-round encounter in 2000. Prior to that, a brace of semis against Pete Sampras; subsequent to that, defeats by Goran Ivanisevic (his only real chance) and Lleyton Hewitt. Predictable? Nothing less.

Even the Commonwealth Games, the first in England since London in 1934, conformed to our designated theme. Lottery funding; home advantage; the most wonderful supporters ever; yet none of those factors could shake the unwavering inevitability of the outcome. Who would top the medal table? Need you ask? Even the English politicians dared not speak any other name. Australia, as everyone expected, cantered home.

The Games, we should add, were an overwhelming success. Even Jacques Rogge, the president of the International Olympic Committee, who visited Manchester was impressed, and said just that, and before the final syllable had fallen from his lips the odds on London winning the 2012 Olympic Games had shortened considerably. Far be it from us to pour cold water on the possibility (for we would love a London Olympics), but nothing that happened in Manchester is likely to have the slightest influence on London's chances of being awarded the Games.

The Winter Olympics will never come to Britain, however capable the Norfolk Ski Club might be. Rogge would be persuaded immediately if he only visited their dry slopes at Trowse. No, we've got to face the facts here. If the IOC can reject the claims of Britain for 80 years, it isn't likely to change its view in our lifetimes. This despite the fact that we are one of the great Winter Olympic nations, as we proved in Salt Lake City.

This, as you may have gathered, is where our theme is strained to the point of breaking. Or, to be blunt, completely falls apart. From a British viewpoint, the Winter Games was about as unpredictable as you can get. The team arrived in Utah with Alex Coomber having a realistic medal chance in the women's skeleton; the men's team having a prayer (and a small prayer at that) in the curling; and Alain Baxter, in the slalom, generally considered to have a chance reckoned to be between minuscule and none.

Yet the team left Utah with the women's curlers bearing gold medals; Coomber clutching a bronze medal; and Baxter still grinning broadly at winning his bronze medal too. Baxter's smile did not last long for a positive drugs test led to his disqualification and a three-month ban, with the medal going to the fourth-place skier, Austrian Benny Raich. But even the brouhaha surrounding Baxter's Vicks Inhaler *(See Winter Games)* could not lessen the British (and very Scottish) joy of a first Winter Olympic title since Torvill and Dean in 1984.

Rhona Martin, Janice Rankin, Fiona McDonald and Debbie Knox transformed curling from a Scottish sport to a British institution, but even they had a bumpy landing in Scotland (and it wasn't the plane). The Scottish Federation, in its wisdom, insisted that only the national champions could represent Scotland in the forthcoming world championships, so Martin's team had to defend their national title at the Braeside Shopping Centre rink, just a couple of weeks after the Games. They lost, beaten in the final by Jackie Lockhart's team, who then covered themselves in a coating of glory too, by winning the world title.

Britain and Ireland
Highest Earners 2002

Richest Boxer & Top Earner
Lennox Lewis £17.5m

Just the one fight, but the Tyson encounter generated over $100m in pay-per-view
revenue and earned Lewis around £16m. Little wonder the re-match won't go away.

Richest Footballer
David Beckham £12.5m

The year that Beckham coined it. Deals include Castrol, Pepsi, M & S, Police sunglasses
Vodafone, adidas, Rage software, an advance on his 2nd autobiography and a new
£95,000+ Man Utd contract. Even so, his earnings are still regularly inflated and
Brylcreem certainly haven't been paying him the oft-quoted £1m a year.

Richest Driver
Eddie Irvine £6.2m

Irvine's pension; the last year with Jaguar bringing him a handy nest-egg.

Richest Golfer
Padraig Harrington £4.1m

Harrington trained as an accountant and it's increasingly more useful to him:
Over £2.5m on course earnings, and sponsors on every visible part of his anatomy.

Richest Tennis Player
Tim Henman £2.2m

Something of a dip for Henman who just jogged along on about £2.75m for the past
few years. Only £800,000 on court earnings, with injuries taking a toll.

Richest Athlete
Paula Radcliffe £1.85m

Almost half a million in start money for the London and Chicago Marathons, plus world record
and win bonuses for both. Nike, having signed up Radcliffe after Sydney, must be in shock,as all
their bonuses have been achieved, too. The highest annual earnings for a British woman ever.

Richest Basketball Player
John Amaechi £1.4m

All very different from his days with the Sheffield Sharks, Amaechi is now on a four-year
deal worth over $2m per year. Not too many add-ons, but heck that's enough.

Figures for 2002 calendar year, dollars converted at $1.60 to £1 sterling.
Sports shown where richest earned £1.4m or more.

If anything, the band of British world champions is smaller than it usually is, with only four titles won in 2002 in Olympic events; Leanda Cave in the women's triathlon; Ben Ainslie in the Finn Class sailing; Iain Percy and Steve Mitchell in Star Class sailing; and the redoubtable rowers Matthew Pinsent and James Cracknell in the coxless pair.

By our reckoning, Pinsent and Cracknell take the biscuit, even though Ainslie and Percy won world titles in their debut years in the Finn and Star boats. No, the race in Seville was heart-stopping sport. The Australians Drew Ginn and James Tompkins had already established a clear superiority over Pinsent and Cracknell in the World Cup at Lucerne, winning the final by a full three seconds. Had any other crew in world rowing taken such a hammering, that would have been that. But Pinsent and Cracknell are not like any other crew in world rowing; they are beginning to resemble Pinsent and Redgrave, and there is no higher accolade than that. In Seville, they did it in style, intimidating the opposition with a pace so extreme that none dared to match it. It was magnificent rowing.

Though Pinsent and Cracknell are hardly short of a bob or two, rowers don't generally figure in the money lists which we always include at the front of the yearbook. Lennox Lewis was the predictable (here we go again) top earner, amassing almost all his earnings from a single fight, against Mike Tyson. Boxers always earn well, but it was a pretty bleak year generally for British boxers, with Lewis the only world champion amongst the ranks of the WBA, WBC or IBF.

David Beckham has taken his time hitting eight-figure earnings (don't we all), but his astute management team hit the button in World Cup year even if their client was hardly fit enough to do himself justice. The Beckham brand was everywhere and must be worth a small fortune to Manchester United, who finally agreed, in the summer, to a new wage structure for their most famous player. Clearly money isn't everything, though, for the prevailing belief is that Beckham will move on.

Paula Radcliffe has some way to go to catch Beckham in the financial stakes; though over distance above 400m we know who would carry our money. The agreeable Radcliffe switched shoe sponsors (from adidas to Nike) after the Sydney Olympics, and Nike must still be blaming the negotiators of that deal for getting the bonus targets all wrong. How on earth could anyone have predicted the Radcliffe metamorphosis? Just before the deal was announced, Radcliffe had failed to win a medal in the Olympic 10,000m, finishing in the all-too-familiar position of fourth.

For years, the Bedford runner competed at the top level without winning a single major track championship medal. Now, she is not just the best British distance runner, but arguably the greatest ever. If her track season of 2003 matches her road season, she will become a world champion in a new world record (in the 5000m or the 10,000m). It is an awesome transformation and has brought her greater riches in a single year than any British sportswoman ever.

World Cup

Once again, as England had everyone starting to believe that they really could go all the way and win the World Cup (or reach a final for the first time in 36 years, even), it came to nothing. Yes, it took a remarkable free-kick from Ronaldinho. Was it a fluke, or was the Brazilian aware that David Seaman's change-of-direction time is now about a minute? Opinion was divided. Ronaldinho claimed his spectacular chip was deliberate, and who are we to argue? Had victory been snatched from England's grasp, then we might have kicked the cat and called Ronaldinho a lucky bastard, but England delivered such a listless performance, allied to questionable tactics, that you couldn't even gain consolation from the fact that they were beaten by the eventual winners.

England had taken the lead midway through the first half as Michael Owen did what he does best, capitalising on a defensive error (from Lucio, in this instance) to send the watching millions in England, most of whom were dunking soldiers in their boiled eggs (it was that early), wild with jubilation. The optimism proved to be short-lived, for Brazil drew level on the stroke of half-time, Ronaldinho's brilliant burst creating the chance for Rivaldo.

Five minutes into the second half came Ronaldinho's gem, which drew comparisons with Nayim's effort in the 1995 Cup Winners' Cup final. One such goal in a career is unfortunate, two is devastating, and Seaman was devastated. England were unable to rouse themselves despite playing the last 30 minutes against 10 men after Ronaldinho had been sent off for a foul on Danny Mills. In truth, England had looked more comfortable against 11 men than they did against 10, when they found it almost impossible to gain possession.

England's lethargy against Brazil was disappointing as they had progressed to the last eight with a incisive first-half display against Denmark just six days earlier, goals from Rio Ferdinand, Owen and Emile Heskey giving Sven-Goran Eriksson's side an unassailable 3-0 lead by half-time. Denmark was the second most exciting match of the tournament for England supporters, the first coming in the group match against Argentina. David Beckham's little bit of personal revenge was shared by the nation as he scored the only goal of the game from the penalty spot, and a resolute defensive display in the second half gave England a win that was as deserved as it was unexpected

Beckham, though, was evidently some way below full fitness having struggled to make the finals at all after breaking a metatarsal bone in his foot, an obscure injury that bizarrely ended the World Cup hopes of Gary Neville and Danny Murphy as well. Paul Scholes, Nicky Butts, and Michael Owen were also less than fully fit, and Eriksson was confronted with the conundrum of whether to persist with them or draft in lesser, but fitter players.

For Eriksson, the World Cup signalled that the honeymoon was well and truly over. He came in for criticism for his tactics after an unimaginative display against Sweden in the opening match, as well as the performance against Brazil, and the feeling lingers that he will call time on his international career after the finals of EURO 2004, assuming England get there...

The Republic of Ireland's hopes suffered what seemed a significant blow days before the tournament kicked off, when captain Roy Keane left the squad following a surreal outburst at Mick McCarthy after the Ireland manager had called a team meeting that was intended to clear the air. Instead, the air turned blue as Keane ranted, following up his earlier criticisms of training facilities and the attitude of some of the players by questioning McCarthy's birthright. He was inevitably sent home.

After several days of will-he-won't-he, it was confirmed Keane would not be returning, and it seemed Ireland's hopes of making a significant impact had flown home with their one genuine world-class player. Things looked bleak as Cameroon took a first-half lead in Ireland's opening game, but a remarkable second-half fightback and Matt Holland's equaliser earned Ireland a deserved draw, and it got even better against Germany.

Having fallen behind again, Robbie Keane removed his namesake from the headlines, with in a last-minute equaliser, and McCarthy's stance on the other Keane was vindicated as a 3-0 win over Saudi Arabia earned a place in the second round. There they met Spain, and yet again fell behind early as Fernando Morientes headed past Shay Given. It seemed their best chance had gone as Ian Harte squandered a second-half penalty, but Fernando Hierro's attempt to change shirts with Niall Quinn a few minutes early gave Robbie Keane another chance from the penalty spot with seconds left his play, and the striker kept his nerve to send the match into extra time.

The additional 30 minutes was, as is usually the case in these days of the Golden Goal, a nerve-jangling affair, and you were left wondering how different things might have been had someone on the Ireland bench noticed they were playing against 10 men after Spain had used all their substitutes. But they didn't, and the match went to penalties. When Matt Holland, Kevin Kilbane, and David Connolly all failed, it gave Gaizka Mendieta the chance to put Spain into the quarter-finals, which he duly took. Nevertheless, once again, Ireland could leave a tournament with their heads held high.

Spain, having lived by the sword against Ireland, fell by it against Korea in the quarter-finals when they lost on penalties. Spain exited in a petulant manner, calling into question the integrity of the match officials, whom it was alleged were favouring one of the host nations. It mirrored the complaints of the Italians who had been eliminated by the Koreans in the previous round. The Italian complaints were louder and better grounded in fact, but both teams had enough potential footballing quality to win even with a handicap.

It is rare indeed for a World Cup to be marked by so many upsets, with the holders France offering barely a token resistance. The French campaign was undermined before it had even started, as an injury to talismanic playmaker Zinedine Zidane in a pre-tournament friendly ruled the Real Madrid player out of the first two games, and when he did return, he was clearly unfit and unable to exert his usual influence. France looked lethargic in the tournament's opening game, and Senegal (who would go on to become only the second African team in World Cup history to make the quarter-finals) took full advantage, earning a shock 1-0 win with a dynamic display. A goalless draw against Uruguay left the holders on the brink of elimination, and a 2-0 defeat against Denmark sealed their fate. France had just a single point and had not scored a single goal - the worst performance by the holders in World Cup history.

Notwithstanding the Spanish and Italian grouses, the co-hosts' progress was a joy to behold. Guided by the experienced old hand Guus Hiddink and cheered by millions of exuberant supporters in the streets and stadiums, Korea finished top of Group D by virtue of a 1-0 victory over Portugal in the final round of matches. It condemned Luis Figo's side, many people's choice as dark horses of the tournament, to an early exit.

Against Italy, in the second round match, they trailed 1-0 with less than five minutes remaining. Rather than attempting to extend their lead, Italy resorted to type and sought to preserve their lead. Three minutes from time, Seol Ki-Hyeon equalised. Worst was to come for the Italians as Francesco Totti was dismissed in extra time, Ahn Jung-Hwan headed a golden goal. It was a memorable moment for Ahn, who was promptly dismissed by his Italian side Perugia. Although the club president later rescinded his decision, Ahn decided, probably wisely, that his future lay elsewhere.

The United States created a shock, reaching the last eight - to, as ever, widespread apathy back home - having memorably beaten Portugal in the group stages, and were unfortunate to lose 1-0 to Germany, when Torsten Frings escaped without punishment after handling a goal-bound shot off the line. Everyone, with the obvious exception of the Germans, was indignant on the Americans' behalf.

Turkey were another side to perform above expectations, ending Senegal's hopes with another golden goal, this time from Ilhan Mansiz. The Turks enjoyed the best of the draw at the knock-out stage, meeting Japan and Senegal, before a more daunting semi-final (and second match) against Brazil. It was a measure of the radical nature of the tournament that Brazil and Germany, rather than confronting the usual suspects in the semi-finals, met Turkey and Korea.

The Old Order was restored, however, in the semi-finals, with four-time champions Brazil and three-time champions Germany doing just enough to see off the upstart nations.

Neither team was greatly fancied at the start of the World Cup, indeed the German chances had been universally written off. Brazil grew with the tournament and duly claimed their fifth World Cup, winning the final 2-0. Both sides hed been heavily reliant on an inspirational figure to smooth their path to Yokohama, with goalkeeper Oliver Kahn producing a succession of crucial saves as Germany confounded their critics (many of whom were themselves Germans), while Ronaldo somehow shrugged off four injury-plagued years to score six goals prior to the final.

When it mattered most, it was Khan who found inspiration wanting, and it was Ronaldo who was on hand when the giant German keeper spilled Rivaldo's shot. Ronaldo scored the second too, and the farrago of the Stade de France four years earlier, was dispatched to history.

"You were a crap player, you are a crap manager. The only reason I have any dealings with you is that somehow you are manager of my country and you're not even Irish, you English **. You can stick it up your ********"**

Roy Keane, footballer, diplomat and aspirant manager.

"Oh I'd have sent him home all right, but I'd have shot him first"

Brian Clough, Keane's manager at Nottingham Forest.

"I'm leaving the referee to the Koreans. We sacrificed 1,000 soldiers to defend Korea and one Korean has killed 70 million Turks with this decision"

Halak Ulusoy, president of the Turkish FA, on Korean referee Kim Young-Ju. Kim sent off Hakan Unsal after he had kicked the ball which hit Rivaldo's thigh. Rivaldo fell down clutching his face.

"Apart from Kahn, you could put that lot in a bag and beat it with a stick and whoever got hit would deserve it"

Franz Beckenbauer, on the German team which beat Korea 1-0.

"I can buy you, I can buy your house, your family and I can buy that mountain we were running up in training"

Zlatko Zahovic taunting the Slovenia coach Srecko Katanec. Zahovic was sent home.

"That gentleman will never set foot in Perugia again...I have no intention of paying a salary to someone who has ruined Italian football"

Luciano Gaucci, president of Perugia, on Ahn Jung-hwan, who scored against Italy, but played his club football for Perugia.

Group Stage

Group A

Seoul   May 31
FRANCE (0) 0   SENEGAL (1) 1
                         Bouba Diop (30)
France: Barthez, Thuram, Desailly, Leboeuf, Lizarazu, Wiltord (D Cisse 81), Djorkaeff (Dugarry 60), Petit, Vieira, Henry, Trezeguet
Booked: Petit
Senegal: Sylva, A Cisse, Coly, Daf, Diatta, Malik Diop, Diao, Bouba Diop, Fadiga, N'Diaye, Diouf
Booked: Cisse
Attendance: 62,561
Referee: A Bujsaim UAE

Ulsan, Korea   June 1
URUGUAY (0) 1   DENMARK (1) 2
Rodriguez (47)   Tomasson (45, 83)
Uruguay: Carini, Mendez, Montero, Garcia, Rodriguez (Magallanes 87), Guigou, Varela, Silva, Abreu (Morales 88), Sorondo, Recoba (Regueiro 80)
Booked : Mendez
Denmark: Sorensen, Tofting, Henriksen, Laursen, Heintze (Jensen 58), Helveg, Gravesen, Gronkjaer (Jorgensen 70), Tomasson, Sand (Poulsen 89), Rommedahl
Booked : Heintze, Laursen
Attendance: 30,157
Referee: S K Mane KUW

Busan, Korea   June 6
FRANCE (0) 0   URUGUAY (0) 0
France: Barthez, Lizarizu, Vieira, Desailly, Wiltord (Dugarry 93), Henry, Thuram, Petit, Leboeuf (Candela 16), Trezeguet (Cisse 81), Micoud
Booked: Petit
Sent off: Henry
Uruguay: Carini, Lembo, Montero, Garcia, Rodriguez (Guigou 73), Varela, Silva (Magallanes 60), Garcia, Abreu, Sorondo, Romero (De Los Santos 71)
Booked : Garcia, Abreu, Silva, Romero
Attendance: 38,289
Referee: F Ramos Rizo MEX

Daegu   June 6
DENMARK (1) 1   SENEGAL (0) 1
Tomasson (pen 16)   Diao (52)
Denmark: Sorensen, Henriksen, Laursen, Heintze, Helveg, Gronkjaer (Jorgensen 50), Gravesen (Poulsen 62), Tofting, Rommedahl (Lovenkrands 89), Tomasson, Sand
Booked: Sand, Tomasson, Helveg, Poulsen.
Senegal: Sylva, Coly, Daf, Sarr (S Camara 45; Beye 83), Diao, Diouf, Pape Malick Diop, Diatta, Papa Bouba Diop, Fadiga, Moussa N'Diaye (H Camara 45)
Booked: Fadiga, Diao.
Sent Off: Diao
Attendance: 43,500
Referee: C Batres GUA

Incheon   June 11
DENMARK (1) 2   FRANCE (0) 0
Rommedahl (22)
Tomasson (67)
Denmark: Sorensen, Tofting (Nielsen 79), Henriksen, Laursen, Helveg, Niclas Jensen, Gravesen, Poulsen (Bogelund 75), Rommedahl, Jorgensen (Gronkjaer 45), Tomasson
France: Barthez, Candela, Thuram, Desailly, Lizarazu, Makelele, Zidane, Vieira (Micoud 71), Wiltord (Djorkaeff 83), Trezeguet, Dugarry (Cisse 54).
Booked: Dugarry
Attendance: 48,100
Referee: V M Pereira POR

Suwon   June 11
SENEGAL (3) 3   URUGUAY (0) 3
Fadiga (pen 20)   Morales (47)
Bouba Diop (26, 38)   Forlan (69)
                         Recoba (pen 89)
Senegal: Sylva, Coly (Beye 63), Cisse, Diatta, Daf, Henri Camara (Moussa N'Diaye 67), Malick Diop, Bouba Diop, Ndour (Faye 76), Fadiga, Diouf.
Booked: Henri Camara, Daf, Coly, Bouba Diop, Diouf, Fadiga, Beye.
Uruguay: Carini, Lembo, Montero, Sorondo (Regueiro 32), Rodriguez, Varela, Romero (Forlan 46), Garcia, Recoba, Silva, Abreu (Morales 45)
Booked: Carini, Garcia, Rodriguez, Montero.
Attendance: 33,681
Referee: J Wegereef NED

Group B

Busan, Korea   June 2
PARAGUAY (1) 2   SOUTH AFRICA (0) 2
Santa Cruz (39)   T Mokoena (63)
Arce (55)   Fortune (pen 91)
Paraguay: Tavarelli, Gamarra, Caniza, Caceres, Ayala, Arce, Alvarenga (Gavilan 66), Struway (Franco 86), Acuña, Santa Cruz, Campos (Morinigo 72)
Booked: Caceres, Caniza, Tavarelli, Franco
South Africa: Arendse, Radebe,Carnell, Issa (Mukansi 27), Nzama, A Mokoena, Sibaya, Fortune, Zuma, T Mokoena, McCarthy (Koumantarakis 78)
Booked : A Mokoena, Issa, McCarthy, Zuma
Attendance: 25,186
Referee: M Lubos

Gwangju, Korea   June 2
SPAIN (1) 3   SLOVENIA (0) 1
Raul (44), Valeron (74) Cimirotic (82)
Hierro (pen 88)
Spain: Casillas, Juanfran (Romero 82), Puyol, Hierro, Nadal, De Pedro, Luis Enrique (Helguera 73), Valeron, Baraja, Raul, Diego Tristán (Morientes 67)
Booked: Valeron
Slovenia: Simeunovic, Milinovic, Galic, Knavs, Novak (Gajser 77), Ceh, Osterc (Cimirotic 57), Zahovic (Acimovic 63), Pavlin, Rudonja, Karic
Booked : Karic, Cimirotic
Attendance: 25,598
Referee: M Guezzaz MAR

9

Busan   *June 2*
PARAGUAY (1) 2   **SOUTH AFRICA (0) 2**
Santa Cruz (39)   *Struway (og 64)*
Arce (55)   *Fortune (pen 90)*
Paraguay: Tavarelli, Arce, Gamarra, Ayala, Caceres,
Caniza, Alvarenga (Gavilan 66), Acuna, Campos
(Morinigo 72), Struway (Franco 86), Santa Cruz.
Booked: Caceres, Caniza, Tavarelli, Franco
South Africa: Arendse, Nzama, Carnell, A Mokoena,
Radebe, Fortune, Sibaya, T Mokoena, Zuma, Issa
(Mukasi 27), McCarthy (Koumantarakis 78).
Booked: A Mokoena, Issa, Radebe, Zuma
Attendance: 25,186
Referee: L Michel SVK

Jeonju   *June 7*
SPAIN (0) 3   **PARAGUAY (1) 1**
Morientes (53, 69)   *Puyol (og 10)*
Hierro (pen 83)
Spain: Casillas, Puyol, Nadal, Hierro, Juanfran, Baraja,
Luis Enrique (Helguera 45), Valeron (Xavi 85), De Pedro,
Tristan (Morientes 45), Raul
Booked: Baraja
Paraguay: Chilavert, Arce, Gamarra, Ayala, Caceres,
Caniza (Struway 78), Paredes, Gavilan, Acuna, Cardozo
(Campos 63), Santa Cruz.
Booked: Arce, Gavilan, Santa Cruz
Attendance: 24,000
Referee: G Ghandour EGY

Daegu   *June 8*
SOUTH AFRICA (1) 1   **SLOVENIA (0) 0**
Nomvete (4)
South Africa: Arendse, Nzama, Radebe, Aaron
Mokoena, Carnell, Zuma, Sibaya, Tebeho Mokoena,
Fortune (Pule 84), Nomvete (Buckley 71), McCarthy
(Koumantarakis 80)
Booked: Radebe, Tebeho Mokoena
Slovenia: Simeunovic, Milinovic, Vugdalic, Knavs
(Bulajic 60), Novak, Ales Ceh, Pavlin, Karic, Acimovic
(Nastja Ceh 60), Rudonja, Cimirotic (Osterc 41)
Booked: Vugdalic, Ales Ceh, Pavlin
Attendance: 47,226
Referee: A Sanchez Ruzafa ARG

Seogwipo   *June 12*
SLOVENIA (1) 1   **PARAGUAY (0) 3**
Acimovic (45)   *Cuevas (65, 84)*
    Campos (73)
Slovenia: Dabanovic, Milinovic, Tavcar, A Ceh, Bulajic,
Pavlin (Rudonja 40), Novak, Acimovic (N Ceh 63), Karic,
Osterc (Tiganj 77), Cimirotic
Booked: Pavlin, Karic, Rudonja, Milinovic
Sent Off: N Ceh
Paraguay: Chilavert, Arce, Gamarra, Ayala, Caniza,
Alvarenga (Campos 54), Acuna, Paredes, Caceres,
Santa Cruz, Cardozo (Cuevas 61; Franco 90)
Booked: Paredes
Sent Off: Paredes (22)
Attendance: 30,176
Referee: F Ramos Rizo MEX

Daejeon   *June 12*
SOUTH AFRICA (1) 2   **SPAIN (2) 3**
McCarthy (31)   *Raul (4, 56)*
Radebe (53)   *Mendieta (45)*
South Africa: Arendse, Nzama, Radebe (Molefe 80), A
Mokoena, Carnell, Zuma, T Mokoena, Sibaya, Fortune
(Lekgetho 83), Nomvete (Koumantarakis 74), McCarthy
Booked: Nzama, Carnell, Nomvete
Spain: Casillas, Curro Torres, Helguera, Nadal, Romero,
Joaquin, Albelda (Sergio 53), Xavi, Mendieta, Morientes
(Luque 78), Raul (Luis Enrique 82)
Attendance: 31,024
Referee: S K Mane KUW

Group C

Ulsan Mansu   *June 3*
BRAZIL (0) 2   **TURKEY (1) 1**
Ronaldo (50),   *Hasan Sas (45)*
Rivaldo (pen 87)
Brazil: Marcos, Lucio, Roque Junior, Roberto Carlos,
Edmilson, Cafu, Ronaldinho (Denilson 67), Juninho
(Vampeta 72), Gilberto Silva, Ronaldo (Luizao 74),
Rivaldo
Booked: Denilson
Turkey: Rustu, Ozalan, De Pedro, Fatih, Korkmaz
(Mansiz 66), Emre, Tugay (Erdem 89), Bastürk (Curro
Torres 66), Sukur, Sas, Hakan Unsal
Booked: Fatih, Hakan Unsal, Ozalan
Sent Off: Ozalan, Hakan Unsal
Attendance: 33,842
Referee: Kim Y-J KOR

Gwanju, Korea   *June 4*
CHINA (0) 0   **COSTA RICA (0) 2**
    Gomez (61), Wright (65)
China: Jin, Chengying, Fan Zhiyi (Yu Genwei 74), Sun
(Qu Bo 25), Li Tie, Mingyu, Haidong, Li Weifeng, Li
Xiaopeng, Chen (Su Maozhen 66), Xu Yunlong
Booked: Li Tie, Xu Yunlong, Li Xiaopeng
Costa Rica: Lonnis, Marin, Wright, Martinez, Fonseca
(Medford 57), Solis, Wanchope (Lopez 80), Centeno,
Gomez, Wallace (Bryce 70), Castro
Booked : Marin, Solis, Gomez, Centeno
Attendance: 27,217
Referee: K Vassaras GRE

Seogwipo   *June 8*
BRAZIL (3) 4   **CHINA (0) 0**
Roberto Carlos (15)
Rivaldo (32),
Ronaldinho (pen 45)
Ronaldo (55)
Brazil: Marcos, Cafu, Lucio, Roque Junior, Carlos,
Gilberto, Juninho Paulista (Ricardinho 71), Polga,
Ronaldinho (Denilson 46), Rivaldo, Ronaldo (Edilson 72)
Booked: Ronaldinho, Roque Junior
China: Jiang, Wu, Xu, Du, Weifeng Li, Tie Li, Zhao, Ma
(Pu Yang 62), Xiaopeng Li, Qi (Shao 67), Hao (Qu 75).
Attendance: 36,750
Referee: Anders Frisk SWE

Incheon   *June 9*
COSTA RICA (0) 1   **TURKEY (0) 1**
Parks (86)   *Emre (56)*
Costa Rica: Lonnis, Marin, Wright, Martinez, Castro, Solis, Lopez (Parks 77), Wallace (Bryce 77), Centeno (Medford 66), Gomez, Wanchope
Booked: Martinez, Castro
Turkey: Rustu, Asik, Akyel, Ergun, Ozat, Davala, Tugay (Erdem 88), Basturk (Nihat 79), Emre, Sas, Sukur (Mansiz 74)
Booked: Asik, Tugay, Emre
Attendance: 42,299
Referee: C Codjia BEN

Suwon   *June 13*
COSTA RICA (1) 2   **BRAZIL (3) 5**
Wanchope (39)   *Marin (og 10), Ronaldo (13)*
Gomez (56)   *Edmilson (38), Rivaldo (63)*
    Junior (64)
Costa Rica: Lonnis, Marin, Wright, Martinez (Parks 73), Castro, Wallace (Bryce 46), Lopez, Solis (Fonseca 66), Centeno, Gomez, Wanchope
Brazil: Marcos, Cafu, Lucio, Edmilson, Polga, Roque Junior, Juninho Paulista (Ricardinho 60), Gilberto, Rivaldo (Kaka 72), Ronaldo, Edilson (Kleberson 58)
Booked: Cafu
Attendance: 38,524
Referee: G Ghandour EGY

Seoul   *June 13*
TURKEY (2) 3   **CHINA (0) 0**
Sas (6), Korkmaz (9)
Davala (85)
Turkey: Rustu (Omer 35), Asik, Korkmaz, Unsal, Akyel, Tugay (Tayfur 84), Basturk (Mansiz 70), Emre, Davala, Sukur, Sas.
Booked: Asik, Emre, Sas
China: Jiang, Pu Yang, Wu (Shao 46), Weifeng Li, Du, Xu, Tie Li, Zhao, Xiaopeng Li, Hao (Qu 73), Chen Yang (Yu 73).
Booked: Pu Yang, Weifeng Li
Sent Off: Shao (59)
Attendance: 43,605
Referee: O Ruiz COL

Group D

Busan   *June 4*
SOUTH KOREA (1) 2   **POLAND (0) 0**
Hwang (26)   *Bouba Diop (30)*
Yoo (53)
South Korea: Lee Woon-Jae, Kim Tae-Young, Choi, Hong, Kim Nam-Il, Yoo (Lee Chun-Soo 61) , Lee Eul-Yong, Song, Park, Seol (Cha Doo-Ri 90), Hwang (Ahn 50)
Yellow cards: Park Ji-Sung (71), Cha Doo-Ri (90)
Poland: Dudek, Zewlakov, Bak (Klos 51), Hajto, Waldoch, Kozminski, Swierczewski, Kaluzny (Zewlakow 65), Krzynowek, Zurawski (Kryszalowicz 46), Olisadebe
Yellow cards: Krzynowek (32), Hajto (79), Swierczewski (85)
Attendance: 55,982
Referee: Oscar Ruiz COL

Suwon   *June 5*
USA (3) 3   **PORTUGAL (1) 2**
O'Brien (4)   *Beto (40)*
Costa (og 30)   *Agoos (og 71)*
McBride (36)
USA: Friedel, Mastroeni, Sanneh, Pope (Llamosa 80), Agoos, O'Brien, Hejduk, Beasley, McBride, Donovan (Moore 75), Stewart (Jones 45)
Booked: Beasley
Portugal: Baia, Costa (Andrade 73), Couto, Beto, Jorge (Bento 69), Rui Costa (Nuno Gomes 79), Petit, Sergio Conceicao, Figo, Pauleta, Pinto
Booked: Beto, Petit
Attendance: 37,306
Referee: B Moreno ECU

Jeonju   *June 10*
PORTUGAL (1) 4   **POLAND (0) 0**
Pauleta (14,65,77)
Rui Costa (87)
Portugal: Baia, Costa, Couto, Jorge, Figo, Petit, Bento, Frechaut (Beto 63), Sergio Conceicao (Capucho 69), Pauleta, Pinto (Rui Costa 60)
Booked: Frechaut, Costa, Jorge
Poland: Dudek, Kozminski, Waldoch, Hajto, Michal Zewlakow (Rzasa 71), Kryszalowicz, Swierczewski, Kaluzny (A Bak 16), Krzynowek, Olisadebe, Zurawski (Marcin Zewlakow 56)
Booked: Swierczewski, A Bak
Attendance: 31,000
Referee: Hugh Dallas SCO

Daegu   *June 10*
SOUTH KOREA (0) 1   **USA (1) 1**
Ahn (78)   *Mathis (24)*
South Korea: Woon-Jae Lee, Jin-Cheul Choi, Hong, Tae-Young Kim, Yoo (Yong-Soo Choi 69), Song, Eul-Young Lee, Park (Chun-Soo Lee 38), Nam-Il Kim, Hwang (Ahn 56), Seol
Booked: Hong
USA: Friedel, Hejduk, Agoos, Pope, Sanneh, O'Brien, Reyna, Mathis (Wolff 82), Beasley (Lewis 74), McBride, Donovan
Booked: Hejduk, Agoos
Attendance: 60,778
Referee: U Meier SUI

Daejeon   *June 14*
POLAND (2) 3   **USA (0) 1**
Olisadebe (3)   *Donovan (83)*
Kryszalowicz (5)
Marcin Zewlakow (66)
Poland: Majdan, Klos (Waldoch 89), Zielinski, Kozminski, Glowacki, Kucharski (M Zewlakow 64), Kryszalowicz, Murawski, Krzynowek, Zurawski, Olisadebe (Sibik 86)
Booked: Majdan, Kozminski, Kucharski
USA: Friedel, Hejduk, Pope, Agoos (Beasley 36), Sanneh, Mathis, Reyna, O'Brien, Donovan, Stewart (Jones 68), McBride (Moore 58)
Booked: Hejduk
Attendance: 26,482
Referee: Jun Lu CHN

Incheon   *June 14*
PORTUGAL (0) 0   **SOUTH KOREA (0) 1**
        Park (70)
Portugal: Baia, Costa, Beto, Jorge (Xavier 73), Couto, Figo, Bento, Petit (Nuno Gomes 77), Sergio Conceicao, Pinto, Pauleta (Andrade 68)
Booked: Beto, Costa
Sent Off: Pinto, Beto
South Korea: Woon-Jae Lee, Jin-Cheul Choi, Hong, Tae-Young Kim, Nam-Il Kim, Yoo, Yong-Pyo Lee, Park, Song, Seol, Ahn (Chun-Soo Lee 90)
Booked: Tae-Young Kim, Seol, Nam-Il Kim, Ahn
Attendance: 50,239
Referee: A Sanchez Ruzafa ARG

Group E

Niigata, Japan   *June 1*
IRELAND (0) 0   **CAMEROON (1) 1**
Holland (52)   *Mboma (39)*
Ireland: Given, Kelly, Breen, Staunton, Harte (Reid 78), McAteer (Finnan 46), Holland, Kinsella, Kilbane, Duff, Keane
Booked: McAteer, Finnan, Reid
Cameroon: Alioum, Tchato, Kalla, Song, Geremi, Biscal, Foe, Olembe, Wome, Eto'o, Mboma (Suffo 69)
Booked: Mboma, Kalla
Referee: Toru Kamikawa JPN
Attendance: 33,679

Sapporo, Japan   *June 1*
GERMANY (4) 8   **SAUDI ARABIA (0) 0**
Klose (20, 25, 69)
Ballack (40), Jancker (45)
Linke (73), Bierhoff (84)
Schneider (90)
Germany: Kahn, Frings, Linke, Metzelder, Ziege, Schneider, Ramelow (Jeremies 46), Hamann, Ballack, Jancker (Bierhoff 67), Klose (Neuville 77)
Booked: Ziege, Hamann
Saudi Arabia: Al Deayea, Tukeur, Al Dossary, Al Zubromawi, Al Sulaimani, Noor, Al Owairan (Al Shahrani 46), Al Wakad, Al Temyat (Al Khathran 46), Al Jabeer, Al Yami (Al Jumaan 77)
Booked: Noor
Referee: Ubaldo Aquino PAR
Attendance: 32,218

Ibaraki   *June 5*
GERMANY (1) 1   **REP OF IRELAND (0) 1**
Klose (19)   *Keane (90)*
Germany: Kahn, Linke, Ramelow, Metzelder, Frings, Hamann, Ballack, Schneider (Jeremies 90), Ziege, Jancker (Bierhoff 75), Klose (Bode 85)
Rep of Ireland: Given, Finnan, Breen, Staunton (Cunningham 87), Harte (Reid 73), G Kelly (Quinn 73), Holland, Kinsella, Kilbane, Keane, Duff
Attendance: 35,854
Referee: K Nielsen DEN

Saitama   *June 6*
CAMEROON (0) 1   **SAUDI ARABIA (0) 0**
Eto'o (65)
Cameroon: Alioum, Wome (Njanka 84), Tchato, Song, Kalla, Lauren, Foe, Kome (Olembe 45), Geremi, Eto'o, Mboma (N'Diefi 74)
Booked: Wome
Saudi Arabia: Al Daeyea, Al Jahani, Tukar, Zubromawi (A Al Dossari 71), Al Shehri, Sulimani, Al Khathran (Noor 86), Abdallah Al Shahrani, Ibrahim Al Shahrani, Al Temyat, O Al Dossari (Al Yami 35)
Booked: Al Yami
Attendance: 52,328
Referee: T Hauge NOR

Shizuoka   *June 11*
CAMEROON (0) 0   **GERMANY (0) 2**
        Bode (50), Klose (79)
Cameroon: Alioum, Tchato (Suffo 53), Kalla, Song, Wome, Geremi, Olembe (Kome 64), Foe, Lauren, Mboma (Job 82), Eto'o
Booked: Foe, Song, Tchato, Geremi, Olembe, Suffo, Lauren
Germany: Kahn, Linke, Ramelow, Metzelder, Frings, Schneider (Jeremies 80), Hamann, Ballack, Ziege, Klose (Neuville 84), Jancker (Bode 46)
Booked: Jancker, Hamann, Ballack, Ramelow, Kahn, Ziege, Frings
Sent Off: Ramelow
Attendance: 47,085
Referee: A Lopez Nieto ESP

Yokohama   *June 11*
SAUDI ARABIA (0) 0   **REP OF IRELAND (1) 3**
        Robbie Keane (7)
        Breen (62), Duff (87)
Saudi Arabia: Al Daeyea, Al Jahani (Ahmed Al Dossari 78), Tukar, Zubromawi (Abdallah Al Dossari 68), Al Shehri, Sulimani, Al Temyat, Al Khathran (Al Shlhoub 67), Khamis Alowairan Al Dossari, Ibrahim Al Shahrani, Al Yami
Booked: Al Temyat
Rep of Ireland: Given, Finnan, Staunton, Breen, Harte (Quinn 46), Gary Kelly (McAteer 80), Kinsella (Carsley 89), Holland, Kilbane, Keane, Duff
Booked: Staunton
Attendance: 65,320
Referee: Falla Ndoye SEN

Group F

Saitama   *June 2*
ENGLAND (1) 1   **SWEDEN (0) 1**
Campbell (24)   *Alexandersson (59)*
England: Seaman, Mills, A Cole, Ferdinand, Campbell, Beckham (Dyer 63), Scholes, Hargreaves, Heskey, Vassell (J Cole 74), Owen
Booked: Campbell
Sweden: Hedman, Mellberg, Mjallby, Jakobsson, Lucic, Linderoth, Alexandersson, Ljungberg, Magnus Svensson (Anders Svensson 56), Allback (Andreas Andersson 80), Larsson
Booked: Allback, Jakobsson
Attendance: 52,721
Referee: Carlos Simon BRA

Ibaraki   *June 2*
ARGENTINA (0) 1   **NIGERIA (0) 0**
Batistuta (63)
Argentina: Cavallero, Placente, Sorin, Pocchettino,
Samuel, Zanetti, Simeone, Veron (Aimar 78), Ortega,
C Lopez (Gonzalez 45), Batistuta (Crespo 81)
Booked: Samuel, Simeone
Nigeria: Shorunmu, Yobo, Babayaro, Okoronkwo, West,
Sodje (Christopher 73), Ogbeche, Okocha, Lawal, Kanu
(Ikedia 48), Aghahowa
Booked: Sodje
Attendance: 34,050
Referee: G Veissiere FRA

Sapporo   *June 7*
ARGENTINA (0) 0   **ENGLAND (1) 1**
                   Beckham (pen 44)
Argentina: Cavallero, Sorin, Samuel, Pocchettino,
Placente, Zanetti, Simeone, Veron (Aimar 45), Gonzalez
(C Lopez 64), Ortega, Batistuta (Crespo 60)
Booked: Batistuta
England: Seaman, Mills, Ferdinand, Campbell, A Cole,
Beckham, Butt, Hargreaves (Sinclair 19), Scholes,
Heskey (Sheringham 56), Owen (Bridge 80)
Booked: A Cole, Heskey
Attendance: 35,927
Referee: P Collina ITA

Kobe   *June 7*
SWEDEN (1) 2   **NIGERIA (1) 1**
Larsson (35, pen 63)   *Aghahowa (27)*
Sweden: Hedman, Mellberg, Mjallby, Lucic, Jakobsson,
Anders Svensson (Magnus Svensson 84), Linderoth,
Alexandersson, Ljungberg, Allback (Andreas Andersson
64), Larsson.
Booked: Mjallby, Alexandersson
Nigeria: Shorunmu, Yobo, Christopher, Okoronkwo,
West, Babayaro (Kanu 65), Okocha, Ogbeche (Ikedia
71), Udeze, Aghahowa, Utaka
Booked: West
Attendance: 36,194
Referee: R Ortube BOL

Osaka   *June 12*
NIGERIA (0) 0   **ENGLAND (0) 0**
Nigeria: Enyeama, Yobo, Okoronkwo, Udeze,
Christopher, Sodje, Okocha, Opabunmi (Ikedia 86),
Akwuegbu, Obiorah, Aghahowa
England: Seaman, Mills, Ferdinand, Campbell, A Cole
(Bridge 84), Beckham, Scholes, Butt, Sinclair, Heskey
(Sheringham 68), Owen (Vassell 77)
Attendance: 44,864
Referee: B Hall USA

Miyagi   *June 12*
SWEDEN (0) 1   **ARGENTINA (0) 1**
A Svensson (59)   *Crespo (88)*
Sweden: Hedman, Mellberg, Mjallby, Jakobsson, Lucic,
Alexandersson, Linderoth, A Svensson (Jonson 68),
Magnus Svensson, Larsson (Ibrahimovic 88), Allback
(Andersson 45)
Booked: Magnus Svensson, Larsson
Argentina: Cavallero, Zanetti, Samuel, Pocchettino,
Chamot, Ortega, Almeyda (Veron 63), Sorin (Gonzalez
63), Aimar, Claudio Lopez, Batistuta (Crespo 58)
Booked: Chamot, Almeyda, Gonzalez
Sent Off: Caniggia (from bench)
Attendance: 45,777
Referee: A Bujsaim UAE

Group G

Sapporo   *June 3*
ITALY (2) 2   **ECUADOR (0) 0**
Vieri (7, 27)
Italy: Buffon, Panucci, Nesta, Cannavaro, Maldini,
Zambrotta, Doni (Di Livio 64), Di Biagio (Gattuso 69),
Tommasi, Totti (Del Piero 73), Vieri
Booked: Cannavaro
Ecuador: Cevallos, De la Cruz, Hurtado, Guerron,
Poroso, Obregon, Mendez, Edwin Tenorio (Marlon Ayovi
59), Chala (Ascensio 85), Aguinaga (Carlos Tenorio 45),
Delgado
Booked: Poroso, De la Cruz, Chala
Attendance: 31,081
Referee: B Hall USA

Niigata   *June 3*
CROATIA (0) 0   **MEXICO (0) 1**
                   Blanco (pen 61)
Croatia: Pletikosa, Simunic, Tomas, Zivkovic, R Kovac,
Jarni, N Kovac, Prosinecki (Rapaic 45), Soldo, Boksic
(Stanic 67), Suker (Saric 64)
Sent Off: Zivkovic
Mexico: Perez, Vidrio, Marquez, Carmona, Morales,
Torrado, Caballero, Luna, Mercado, Borguetti
(Hernandez 68), Blanco (Palencia 79)
Attendance: 32,239
Referee: Jun Lu CHN

Ibaraki   *June 8*
ITALY (0) 1   **CROATIA (0) 2**
Vieri (56)   *Olic (73), Rapaic (76)*
Italy: Buffon, Panucci, Nesta (Materazzi 23), Cannavaro,
Maldini, Zambrotta, Zanetti, Tommasi, Doni (Inzaghi 79),
Totti, Vieri
Booked: Vieri
Croatia: Pletikosa, R Kovac, Simunic, Saric, Jarni,
Tomas, Rapaic (Simic 79), N Kovac, Soldo (Vranjes 62),
Vugrinec (Olic 57), Boksic
Booked: R Kovac
Attendance: 36,472
Referee: Graham Poll ENG

Miyagi   *June 9*
MEXICO (1) 2   **ECUADOR (1) 1**
Borguetti (28)   *Delgaso (5)*
Torrado (57)
Mexico: Perez, Morales, Vidrio, Marquez, Carmona, Arellano, J Rodriguez (Caballero 87), Torrado, Luna, Borguetti (Hernandez 77), Blanco (Mercado 90)
Ecuador: Cevallos, De la Cruz, Poroso, Hurtado, Guerron, Mendez, Obregon (Aguinaga 58), E Tenorio (M Ayovi 35), Chala, Kaviedes (C Tenorio 53), Delgado
Booked: Kaviedes, Cevallos, Guerron, Carlos Tenorio
Attendance: *45,610*
Referee: *M Daami TUN*

Yokohama   *June 13*
ECUADOR (0) 1   **CROATIA (0) 0**
Mendez (48)
Ecuador: Cevallos, De la Cruz, Hurtado, Guerron, M Ayovi, Mendez, Obregon (Aguinaga 40), Poroso, C Tenorio (Kaviedes 76), Chala, Delgado.
Booked: Chala
Croatia: Pletikosa, Simunic, Tomas, Simic (Vugrinec 52), Robert Kovac, Jarni, Niko Kovac (Vranjes 59), Saric (Stanic 67), Rapaic, Olic, Boksic
Booked: Tomas, Simunic
Attendance: *65,862*
Referee: *W Mattus Vega CRC*

Oita   *June 13*
MEXICO (1) 1   **ITALY (0) 1**
Borguetti (34)   *Del Piero (85)*
Mexico: Perez, Marquez, Vidrio, Carmona, Morales (Garcia 76), Arellano, J Rodriguez (Caballero 75), Luna, Torrado, Blanco, Borguetti (Palencia 80)
Booked: Arellano, Perez
Italy: Buffon, Panucci (Coco 63), Cannavaro, Nesta, Maldini, Inzaghi (Montella 56), Zambrotta, Zanetti, Tommasi, Totti (Del Piero 78), Vieri
Booked: Cannavaro, Panucci, Totti, Zambrotta, Montella
Attendance: *39,291*
Referee: *C Simon BRA*

Group H

Saitama   *June 4*
JAPAN (0) 2   **BELGIUM (0) 2**
Suzuki (59)   *Wilmots (57)*
Inamoto (69)   *Van Der Heyden (75)*
Japan: Narazaki, Matsuda, Morioka (Miyamoto 72), K Nakata, Inamoto, H Nakata, Ono (Alex 64), Toda, Ichikawa, Suzuki (Morishima 70), Yanagisawa
Booked: Toda, Inamoto
Belgium: De Vlieger, Van Meir, Simons, Peeters, Van der Heyden, Van Buyten, Walem (Sonck 70), Verheyen (Strupar 83), Vanderhaeghe, Goor, Wilmots
Booked: Van der Heyden, Verheyen, Peeters, Van Meir
Attendance: *55,256*
Referee: *W Mattus Vega CRC*

Kobe   *June 5*
RUSSIA (0) 2   **TUNISIA (0) 0**
Titov (59), Karpin (pen 64)
Russia: Nigmatullin, Solomatin, Nikiforov, Onopko, Kovtun, Karpin, Semshov (Khokhlov 45), Izmailov (Alenichev 78), Titov, Beschastnykh (Sychev 55), Pimenov
Booked: Semshov, Alenichev
Tunisia: Boumnijel, Trabelsi, Badra (Zitouni 83), Jaidi, Gabsi (Beya 67), Sellimi (Mhadhebi 67), Bouzaine, Mkacher, Bouazizi, Ben Achour, Jaziri
Booked: Gabsi, Jaziri
Attendance: *30,957*
Referee: *P Prendergast JAM*

Yokohama   *June 9*
JAPAN (0) 1   **RUSSIA (0) 0**
Inamoto (51)
Japan: Narazaki, Miyamoto, Matsuda, K Nakata, Myojin, Inamoto (Fukunishi 85), Toda, Ono (Hattori 75), H Nakata, Yanagisawa, Suzuki (Nakayama 72).
Russia: Nigmatullin, Kovtun, Nikiforov, Onopko, Solomatin, Karpin, Smertin (Beschastnykh 57), Izmailov (Khokhlov 52), Semshov, Titov, Pimenov (Sychev 46).
Booked: Pimenov, Solomatin, Nikiforov
Attendance: *66,108*
Referee: *M Merk GER*

Oita   *June 10*
TUNISIA (1) 1   **BELGIUM (1) 1**
Bouzaine (17)   *Wilmots (13)*
Tunisia: Boumnijel, Badra, Jaidi, Gabsi (Sellimi 67), Bouzaine, Ghodbane, Trabelsi, Bouazizi, Melki (Beya 88), Ben Achour, Jaziri (Zitouni 77)
Belgium: De Vlieger, Deflandre, De Boeck, Van Buyten, Van Der Heyden, Simons (Mpenza 74), Verheyen (Sonck 46), Wilmots, Vanderhaeghe, Goor, Strupar (Vermant 46)
Booked: Van Buyten
Attendance: *37,900*
Referee: *M Shield AUS*

Shizuoka   *June 14*
BELGIUM (1) 3   **RUSSIA (0) 2**
Valem (7), Sonck (78)   *Beschastnykh (53)*
Wilmots (82)   *Sychev (89)*
Belgium: De Vlieger, Van Buyten, Van Kerckhoven, Peeters, De Boeck (Van Meir 90), Verheyen (Simons 78), Walem, Vanderhaeghe, Goor, Wilmots, Mpenza (Sonck 70)
Booked: Vanderhaeghe
Russia: Nigmatullin, Kovtun, Solomatin, Onopko, Nikiforov (Sennikov 43), Karpin (Kerzhakov 83), Smertin (Sychev 34), Titov, Khokhlov, Alenichev, Beschastnykh.
Booked: Solomatin, Smertin, Alenichev, Sennikov
Attendance: *46,640*
Referee: *K Nielsen DEN*

Osaka   *June 14*
TUNISIA (0) 0   **JAPAN (0) 2**
                         Morishima (48), Nakata (75)
Tunisia: Boumnijel, Badra, Bouzaiene (Zitouni 78), Jaidi, Ghodbane, Clayton (Mhadhebi 61), Bouazizi, Trabelsi, Ben Achour, Melki (Beya 46), Jaziri
Booked: Bouazizi, Badra
Japan: Narazaki, Matsuda, Koji Nakata, Miyamoto, Myojin, Hidetoshi Nakata (Ogasawara 85), Toda, Ono, Inamoto (Ichikawa 46), Suzuki, Yanagisawa (Morishima 46)
Attendance: 45,213
Referee: G Veissiere (Mediterranee).

Second Round

Seogwipo   *June 15*
GERMANY (0) 1   **PARAGUAY (0) 0**
Neuville (88)
Germany: Kahn, Linke, Metzelder (Baumann 60), Frings, Rehmer (Kehl 46), Ballack, Jeremies, Schneider, Neuville (Asamoah 90), Bode, Klose
Booked: Schneider, Baumann, Ballack
Paraguay: Chilavert, Caniza, Arce, Gamarra, Ayala, Struway (Cuevas 90), Acuna, Bonet (Gavilan 84), Caceres, Santa Cruz (Campos 29), Cardozo.
Booked: Acuna, Cardozo
Sent Off: Acuna
Attendance: 25,176
Referee: C Batres GUA

Niigata   *June 15*
DENMARK (0) 0   **ENGLAND (3) 3**
                         Ferdinand (5)
                         Owen (22), Hesley (44)
Denmark: Sorensen, Helveg (Bogelund 7), Niclas Jensen, Henriksen, Laursen, Rommedahl, Gravesen, Tofting (Claus Jensen 58), Gronkjaer, Sand, Tomasson.
Booked: Tofting
England: Seaman, Mills, Ferdinand, Campbell, Ashley Cole, Beckham, Scholes (Dyer 48), Butt, Sinclair, Heskey (Sheringham 69), Owen (Fowler 46)
Booked: Mills
Attendance: 40,582
Referee: M Merk GER

Oita   *June 16*
SWEDEN (1) 1   **SENEGAL (1) 2**
Larsson (11)   *Camara (37, 104)*
Senegal won on Golden Goal
Sweden: Hedman, Jakobsson, Mellberg, Mjallby, Lucic, Alexandersson (Ibrahimovic 76), Magnus Svensson (Jonson 100), A Svensson, Linderoth, Larsson, Allback (Andersson 64)
Senegal: Sylva, Daf, Coly, Pape Malick Diop (Beye 66), H Camara, Papa Bouba Diop, Cisse, Faye, Diatta, Thiaw, Diouf
Booked: Coly, Thiaw
Attendance: 39,747
Referee: U Aquino PAR

Suwon   *June 16*
SPAIN (1) 1   **REP OF IRELAND (0) 1**
Morientes (8)   *Robbie Keane (pen 90)*
Spain won 3-2 on penalties
Spain: Casillas, Puyol, Helguera, Hierro, Juanfran, Baraja, Valeron, De Pedro (Mendieta 66), Enrique, Raul (Luque 80), Morientes (Albelda 71).
Booked: Juanfran, Baraja, Hierro
Rep of Ireland: Given, G Kelly (Quinn 55), Staunton (Cunningham 50), Breen, Harte (Connolly 82), Finnan, Kinsella, Holland, Kilbane, Duff, Keane
Attendance: 38,926
Referee: A Frisk SWE
Penalty shoot-out
Keane-goal (1-0), Hierro-goal (1-1), Holland-miss (1-1), Baraja-goal (1-2), Connolly-saved (1-2), Juanfran-miss (1-2), Kilbane-saved (1-2), Valeron-miss (1-2), Finnan-goal (2-2), Mendieta-goal (2-3)

Jeonju   *June 17*
MEXICO (0) 0   **USA (1) 2**
                         McBride (8)
                         Donovan (65)
Mexico: Perez, Marquez, Carmona, Vidrio (Mercado 46), Torrado (Garcia Aspe 78), Morales (Hernandez 28), Luna, J Rodriguez, Arellano, Borguetti, Blanco.
Sent Off: Marquez
Booked: Vidrio, Hernandez, Blanco, Carmona, Garcia Aspe
USA: Friedel, Berhalter, Sanneh, Pope, Mastroeni (Llamosa 90), O'Brien, Lewis, Reyna, Wolff (Stewart 59), McBride (Jones 79), Donovan
Booked: Pope, Mastroeni, Wolff, Berhalter, Friedel
Attendance: 36,380
Referee: V M Pereira POR

Kobe   *June 17*
BRAZIL (0) 2   **BELGIUM (0) 0**
Rivaldo (67)
Ronaldo (88)
Brazil: Marcos, Cafu, Lucio, Roque Junior, Edmilson, Carlos, Gilberto, Juninho Paulista (Denilson 57), Rivaldo (Ricardinho 90), Ronaldinho (Kleberson 81), Ronaldo
Booked: Carlos
Belgium: De Vlieger, Van Kerckhoven, Van Buyten, Peeters (Sonck 73), Simons, Wilmots, Goor, Verheyen, Vanderhaeghe, Walem, Mpenza
Booked: Vanderhaeghe
Attendance: 40,440
Referee: P Prendergast JAM

Miyagi   *June 18*
JAPAN (0) 0   **TURKEY (1) 1**
                         Davala (12)
Japan: Narazaki, Matsuda, Miyamoto, K Nakata, Ono, Alex (Suzuki 45), Myojin, Toda, Inamoto (Ichikawa 45; Morishima 86), H Nakata, Nishizawa, Ichikawa
Booked: Toda
Turkey: Rustu, Korkmaz, Akyel, Alpay, Unsal, Tugay, Basturk (Mansiz 90), Davala (Nihat 74), Ergun, Sukur, Sas (Tayfur 85)
Booked: Alpay, Ergun, Sukur
Attendance: 45,666
Referee: P Collina ITA

Daejeon   *June 18*
SOUTH KOREA (0) 2   ITALY (1) 1
Seol (88), Ahn (117)   *Vieri (18)*
South Korea won on Golden Goal
South Korea: Woon-Jae Lee, Jin-Cheul Choi, Hong (Cha 83), Tae-Young Kim (Hwang 62), Nam-Il Kim (Chun-Soo Lee 68), Yoo, Yong-Pyo Lee, Park, Song, Seol, Ahn
Booked: Tae-Young Kim, Song, Chun-Soo Lee, Jin-Cheul Choi
Italy: Buffon, Panucci, Iuliano, Coco, Maldini, Zanetti, Zambrotta (Di Livio 72), Tommasi, Totti, Del Piero (Gattuso 61), Vieri
Sent Off: Totti
Booked: Coco, Totti, Tommasi, Zanetti
Attendance: *38,588*
Referee: *B Moreno ECU*

Quarter-Finals

Shizuoka   *June 21*
ENGLAND (1) 1   BRAZIL (1) 2
Owen (23)   *Rivaldo (45)*
    Ronaldinho (50)
England: Seaman, Mills, Campbell, Ferdinand, A Cole (Sheringham 79), Beckham, Scholes, Butt, Sinclair (Dyer 56), Owen (Vassell 79), Heskey
Booked: Scholes, Ferdinand
Brazil: Marcos, Roque Junior, Lucio, Edmilson, Cafu, Gilberto, Ronaldinho, Kleberson, Carlos, Ronaldo (Edilson 70), Rivaldo
Sent Off: Ronaldinho
Attendance: *47,436*
Referee: *F Ramos Rizo MEX*

Ulsan   *June 21*
GERMANY (1) 1   USA (0) 0
Ballack (39)
Germany: Kahn, Linke, Kehl, Metzelder, Frings, Hamann, Ballack, Schneider (Jeremies 60), Ziege, Neuville (Bode 79), Klose (Bierhoff 87)
Booked: Kehl
USA: Friedel, Sanneh, Mastroeni (Stewart 80), Pope, Berhalter, Hejduk (Jones 65), O'Brien, Reyna, Lewis, Donovan, McBride (Mathis 58)
Booked: Lewis, Pope, Reyna, Mastroeni, Berhalter
Attendance: *37,337*
Referee: *Hugh Dallas SCO*

Gwangju   *June 22*
SENEGAL (0) 0   TURKEY (0) 1
    Mansiz (94)
Turkey won on Golden Goal Rule
Senegal: Sylva, Coly, Diatta, Cisse, Daf, H Camara, Papa Bouba Diop, Pape Malick Diop, Diao, Fadiga, Diouf
Booked: Daf, Diouf
Turkey: Rustu, Korkmaz, Akyel, Alpay, Ergun, Davala, Basturk, Tugay, Emre (Erdem 91), Sukur (Mansiz 67), Sas
Booked: Emre, Mansiz
Attendance: *44,233*
Referee: *O Ruiz COL*

Osaka   *June 22*
SPAIN (0) 0   SOUTH KOREA (0) 0
South Korea win 5-3 on penalties
Spain: Casillas, Puyol, Nadal, Hierro, Romero, Joaquin, Helguera (Xavi 93), Baraja, De Pedro (Mendieta 70), Valeron (Luis Enrique 80), Morientes
Booked: De Pedro, Morientes
South Korea: Woon-Jae Lee, Jin-Cheul Choi, Hong, Tae-Young Kim (Hwang 90), Yoo (Chun-Soo Lee 60), Park, Yong-Pyo Lee, Song, Nam-Il Kim (Eul-Young Lee 32), Seol, Ahn
Booked: Yoo
Attendance: *42,114*
Referee: *G Ghandour EGY*
Penalty shoot-out
Hwang-goal (0-1), Hierro-goal (1-1), Park-goal (1-2), Baraja-goal (2-2), Seol-goal (2-3), Xavi-goal (3-3), Ahn-goal (3-4), Joaquin-saved (3-4), Hong-goal (3-5)

Semi-Finals

Seoul   *June 25*
GERMANY (0) 1   SOUTH KOREA (0) 0
Ballack (75)
Germany: Kahn, Linke, Frings, Metzelder, Ramelow, Hamann, Ballack, Schneider (Jeremies 85), Bode, Neuville (Asamoah 87), Klose (Bierhoff 70)
Booked: Ballack, Neuville
South Korea: Woon-Jae Lee, Jin-Cheul Choi (Min-Sung Lee 56), Hong (Seol 81), Tae-Young Kim, Yoo, Yong-Pyo Lee, Chun-Soo Lee, Park, Song, Hwang (Ahn 54), Cha
Booked: Min-Sung Lee
Attendance: *65,625*
Referee: *U Meier SUI*

Saitama   *June 26*
BRAZIL (0) 1   TURKEY (0) 0
Ronaldo (49)
Brazil: Marcos, Lucio, Roque Junior, Edmilson, Cafu, Kleberson (Belleti 85), Gilberto, Carlos, Rivaldo, Edilson (Denilson 75), Ronaldo (Luizao 67)
Booked: Gilberto
Turkey: Rustu, Akyel, Korkmaz, Alpay, Ergun, Davala (Izzet 73), Basturk (Erdem 88), Tugay, Emre (Mansiz 61), Sas, Sukur
Booked: Tugay, Sas
Attendance: *61,058*
Referee: *K Nielsen DEN*

Third Place Match

Daegu   *June 29*
SOUTH KOREA (1) 2   **TURKEY (3) 3**
Eul-Young Lee(9)   *Sukur (1)*
Song (90)   *Mansiz (13, 32)*
South Korea: Woon-Jae Lee, Hong (Tae-Young Kim
46), Min-Sung Lee, Yoo, Yong-Pyo Lee, Eul-Young Lee
(Cha 64), Chun-Soo Lee, Park, Song, Ahn, Seol (Tae-Uk
Choi 79)
Booked: Eul-Young Lee
Turkey: Rustu, Akyel, Korkmaz, Alpay, Ergun, Davala
(Okan 75), Basturk (Tayfur 85), Tugay, Emre (Unsal 41),
Sukur, Mansiz
Booked: Tugay, Rustu
Attendance: *63,483*
Referee: *S K Mane KUW*

World Cup Final

Yokohama Stadium   *June 30*
GERMANY (0) 0   **BRAZIL (0) 2**
     Ronaldo (67, 79)
Germany: Kahn; Linke, Ramelow, Neuville, Hamann,
Klose (Bierhoff 74), Jeremies (Asamoah 77), Bode (Ziege
81), Schneider, Metzelder, Frings
Booked: Klose
Brazil: Marcos; Cafu, Lucio, Roque Junior, Edmilson,
Carlos, Silva, Ronaldo (Denilson 90), Rivaldo,
Ronaldinho (Juninho 85), Kleberson
Booked: Roque Junior
Attendance: *69,029*
Referee: *P Collina ITA*

World Cup Goalscorers

Alphabetically, by country

8 goals
Ronaldo (Brazil)

5 goals
Rivaldo (Brazil), Miroslav Klose (Germany)

4 goals
Jon Dahl Tomasson (Denmark), Christian Vieri (Italy)

3 goals
Marc Wilmots (Belgium), Michael Ballack (Germany), Pauleta (Portugal), Robbie Keane (Republic of Ireland),
Papa Bouba Diop (Senegal), Fernando Morientes, Raul (Spain), Henrik Larsson (Sweden), Ilhan Mansiz
(Turkey)

2 goals
Ronaldinho (Brazil), Ronald Gomez (Costa Rica), Michael Owen (England), Junichi Inamoto (Japan), Ahn Juny-
Hwan (Korea), Jared Borgetti (Mexico), Nelson Cuevas (Paraguay), Henri Camara (Senegal), Fernando Hierro
(Spain), Umit Davala, Hasan Sas (Turkey), Landon Donovan, Brian McBride (USA)

1 goal
Gabriel Batistuta, Hernan Crespo (Argentina), Wesley Sonck, Peter van der Heyden, Johan Walem (Belgium),
Roberto Carlos, Edmilson, Junior, Samuel Eto'o, Patrick Mboma (Cameroon), Winston Parks, Paulo Wanchope,
Mauricio Wright (Costa Rica), Ivica Olic, Milan Rapaic (Croatia), Dennis Rommedahl (Denmark), Agustin
Delgado, Edison Mendez (Ecuador), David Beckham, Sol Campbell, Rio Ferdinand, Emile Heskey (England),
Oliver Bierhoff, Marco Bode, Carsten Jancker, Thomas Linke, Oliver Neuville, Bernd Schneider (Germany),
Alessandro Del Piero (Italy), Hiroaki Morishima, Hidetoshi Nakata, Takayuki Suzuki (Japan), Hwang Sun-Hong,
Lee Eul-Yong, Park Ji-Sung, Seol Ki-Hyeon, Song Chong-Gug, Yoo Sang-Chul (Korea), Cuauhtemoc Blanco,
Gerardo Torrado (Mexico), Julius Aghahowa (Nigeria), Francisco Arce, Jorge Campos, Roque Santa Cruz
(Paraguay), Pawel Kryszalowicz, Emmanuel Olisadebe, Marcin Zawlakow (Poland), Beto, Rui Costa (Portugal),
Gary Breen, Damien Duff, Matt Holland (Republic of Ireland), Vladimir Beschastnykh, Valery Karpin, Dmitri
Sychev, Egor Titov (Russia), Salif Diao, Khalilou Fadiga (Senegal), Milenko Acimovic, Sebastjan Cimirotic
(Slovenia), Quinton Fortune, Benedict McCarthy, Teboho Mokoena, Siyabonga Nomvethe, Lucas Radebe
(South Africa), Gaizka Mendieta, Juan Carlos Valeron (Spain), Niclas Alexandersson, Anders Svensson
(Sweden), Raouf Bouzaiene (Tunisia), Bulent Korkmaz, Emre Belozoglu, Hakan Sukur (Turkey), Alvaro Recoba,
Diego Forlan, Richard Morales, Dario Rodriguez (Uruguay), Clint Mathis, John O'Brien (USA)

Own goals
Luis Marin (Costa Rica, against Brazil), Estanislao Struway (Paraguay, against South Africa), Jorge Costa
(Portugal, against USA), Carlos Puyol (Spain, against Paraguay), Jeff Agoos (USA, against Portugal)

Commonwealth Games

Manchester set out to confuse us, with six days of glorious sunshine as a backdrop to the athletics programme, for once opening the Games. When the rain did come, a typical unremitting 10-day drizzle, we were all in the pool anyway watching the swimming.

The stadium during that first week set the tone for the Games. If it was wonderful in Helsinki in 1983, glorious in Barcelona in 1992, and sensational in Sydney in 2000; Manchester did not pale in comparison with any of them as an athletics meeting. Arguably, it was better than them all, even if half the Jamaicans didn't want to run, and there were very few events that had any quality in depth.

The reason why it was such a stunning occasion was the audience, the like of which this correspondent has never seen or heard at any sporting event, anywhere. When they were roused, as with Paula Radcliffe's victory in the 10,000m, it was all you could do not to weep. How Radcliffe kept running, we'll never now. Husband Gary, we guess, was ready to scream if she slowed down.

For the most part, the cheers were directed at the English (and in Darren Campbell's case, the Mancunian), but it was not an exclusive roar that made that stadium hum, it belonged to everyone competing.

Radcliffe, naturally, headed the bill. Having spent so many miles in the futile last-lap pursuit of a clutch of Ethiopians, it must have come as some relief to Radcliffe that she had only Kenyans to deal with in Manchester. Well, so we thought. Except the metamorphosis had already happened, the hare was still the hare, but the tempo was now so quick and relentless that there was no-one close to her tail when the last lap bell rang. Radcliffe won the 5000m in 14 minutes and 31.43 seconds, a time just over three seconds slower than the world record set by Jiang Bo in 1997, and which was roundly condemned as a drug-assisted mark.

The athletics also brought a first Commonwealth title for Jonathan Edwards, to go with the Olympic win, the two world championship victories and the European win; the full set, in other words. There was a notable third Commonwealth win for Steve Backley, who was eight metres clear of the rest of the javelin field, but Colin Jackson, seeking to match that, lost.

There were also long faces in the 100m, where both Dwain Chambers and Mark Lewis-Francis pulled up with muscle injuries, leaving the title to Kim Collins, from St Kitts and Nevis. The best competition, though, came in the triple jump where Ashia Hansen and Francoise Mbango, of the Cameroon, had a rare old set to. Hansen took the title by four centimetres on her last jump of the competition, Mbango having jumped her best mark immediately prior.

"I've spoken to my mum and she's still crying. She's proud of me, but there's no way she'll be back. She told me she wasn't doing this again"

Darren Barker, whose mother Jackie watched him fight for the first time when he contested the Commonwealth final, and was still crying two hours later.

"There are aspects of my technique I can still improve upon"

Bob Weir, who took the bronze medal in the discus aged 41, looking to the future.

"He would have been proud, I hope he's smiling up there somewhere"

Jamie Arthur, talking about Howard Winstone, who died in September, 2000. Arthur brought Wales its first Commonwealth boxing gold since Winstone in 1958.

"I wasn't supposed to be the only athlete. There were supposed to be three other guys. I guess they couldn't make it"

Gavin Lee, high jumper, and the entire Montserrat team.

"This is the perfect platform for Athens and I'm certainly not considering the circus now"

Kanukai Jackson, Harrow gymnast, after winning the all-around gymnastics title.

"Ko meutolu toe teu tsgela, Kai tageta, Ti kai tagota, Ka moua e an a koe magonie, Ti-he-he-he, Ti-he-he-he"

The Niuen takola (or haka) chanted before the country's matches in the rugby sevens tournament. The rough translation is: "We are cannibals and we will catch you, tear you apart and eat you"

"During the warm-up, I though I can't come here and not win something after this"

Vivian Chukwuemeka, the Nigerian shotputter. when she arrived at Manchester from California, where she attends college, Chukwuemeka was told she was not on the team, and had to pay for her own accommodation at the Premier Lodge. The Nigerians eventually let her compete and she won the title.

"When I first went back into the water, I felt whole again"

Natalie du Toit, South African swimmer, who lost her left leg in a road accident.

"I have been very impressed with the Commonwealth Games"

Jacques Rogge, offering encouragement for a British Olympic bid (well, he would, wouldn't he?)

Ian Thorpe dominated in the pool, but failed to win seven titles, being not quite up to scratch in the backstroke. That's the cross he has to bear; not being the greatest backstroke swimmer in history. Thorpe broke a world record, in the 400m freestyle, just to illustrate that he wasn't in Manchester to pot hunt, and that he was the greatest freestyle swimmer in history.

The Australians were the most successful team in the pool, which didn't strain anyone's psychic powers to predict. There were, though, a few upsets, mostly courtesy of an England team which has generally re-invented itself since the Australian Bill Sweetenham has taken the helm. Arguably the greatest upset came in the women's 4x200m freestyle, in which event the British team is the reigning world champions.

However, the manner of that victory in Fukuoka - the winning team, Australia, was disqualified when Petria Thomas prematurely leapt back in the pool to celebrate - meant that revenge looked a certainty. Credit then to Karen Legg, Georgina Lee, Joanne Fargus and Karen Pickering, who swam almost three seconds slower than the British team in Fukuoka, but still beat an Australian team that was almost six seconds slower than it's time in the World championships.

Defeat cost Thomas a six-timer of titles for the Australian won all three butterfly events, and figured in the two other Australian relay teams both of which won.

Commonwealth Games

July 26-Aug 4

Final Medal Table

		G	S	B	Ttl
1	Australia	82	62	62	206
2	England	54	51	60	165
3	India	32	21	19	72
4	Canada	31	41	42	114
5	New Zealand	11	13	21	45
6	South Africa	9	20	17	46
7	Cameroon	9	1	2	12
8	Malaysia	7	9	18	34
9	Scotland	6	8	16	30
10	Nigeria	5	4	11	20
11	Wales	4	15	12	31
12	Kenya	4	8	4	16
13	Jamaica	4	6	7	17
14	Singapore	4	2	7	13
15	Bahamas	4	0	4	8
16	Nauru	2	3	10	15
17	Northern Ireland	2	2	1	5
18	Cyprus	2	1	1	4
19	Pakistan	1	3	3	7
20	Fiji	1	1	1	3
20	Zambia	1	1	1	3
22	Zimbabwe	1	1	0	2
23	Namibia	1	0	4	5
24	Tanzania	1	0	1	2
25	Bangladesh	1	0	0	1
25	Guyana	1	0	0	1
25	Mozambique	1	0	0	1
25	St Kitts & Nevis	1	0	0	1
29	Botswana	0	2	1	3
30	Uganda	0	2	0	2
31	Samoa	0	1	2	3
32	Trinidad	0	1	0	1
33	Barbados	0	0	1	1
33	Cayman Islands	0	0	1	1
33	Ghana	0	0	1	1
33	St Lucia	0	0	1	1
33	Lesotho	0	0	1	1
33	Malta	0	0	1	1
33	Mauritius	0	0	1	1

The most impressive winner in the pool, though, was neither English nor Australian. A talented junior, Natalie du Toit had competed at the 1998 Commonwealth Games in Kuala Lumpur as a 14-year-old. Three years later, following a traffic accident, her left leg was amputated above the knee and Du Toit, and everyone connected with her, assumed that her promising swimming career was over.

But back in the water was where Du Toit felt most comfortable and she began training again. In Manchester, the South African was entered in the two disability events and won them both, breaking the world records for her disability class in each of them. She also entered the 800m and, swimming alongside ability athletes, reached the final. "I figured that the leg kick in the long distance freestyle was the least important in all the races," said Du Toit pragmatically.

In the final, the South African was a distant last behind Rebecca Cooke, but the arena kept its loudest roar for Du Toit's touch on the wall. "I don't want to be a role model," she said afterwards, embarrassed by the attention she was receiving, "But if it helps someone else..."

The cycling was disappointing for England, but not for Scotland as Chris Hoy won the race that has become the blue riband of British riding, the 1km time trial. Hoy beat the Olympic champion Jason Queally, and in a time that was genuinely world class - one minute and 1.725 seconds. Nicole Cooke, too, justified the hype with a win in the road race, though our award for the cycling performance of the Games has to go to Clara Hughes, for the Canadian who won the time trial is also an Olympic medallist at speed skating.

The England judo team was rampant; team manager Tony Allcock revived the fortunes of England's lawn bowlers (and they needed reviving); and Kanukai Jackson was a shock winner of the men's all-around title in gymnastics (with Scotland's Steve Frew an even bigger shock on the rings).

Leading the surprises, though, was the English women's hockey team, whose victory over Australia in the semi-final was just about the first in a major competition since they first whittled a hockey stick. All the good work, however, was undone when England lost the final to unfancied India. They lost in bad odour, too, arguing that the referee had ruled out the golden goal when the hooter sounded just before the ball crossed the line. She had too, but the referee, Lynn Farrell, had made a mistake. Penalty corners, from which the goal was scored, have to completed before time can be called. England looked moody for a full half hour after the game before deciding to go home.

Charlotte Kerwood was probably the youngest winner of the Games (what kind of stat is that?), the 15-year-old winning the double trap event, but we took more of a shine to Kaitinano Mwemweta, who finished last in the women's 100m in 13.58 seconds but still broke the Kiribati national record.

Athletics

Men

100m
1 Kim Collins SKN — 9.98
2 Uchenna Emedolu NGR — 10.11
3 Pierre Browne CAN — 10.12

200m
1 Frankie Fredericks NAM — 20.06
2 Marlon Devonish ENG — 20.19
3 Darren Campbell ENG — 20.21

400m
1 Michael Blackwood JAM — 45.07
2 Shane Niemi CAN — 45.09
3 Avard Moncur BAH — 45.12

800m
1 Mbulaeni Mulaudzi RSA — 1:46.32
2 Joseph Mutua KEN — 1:46.57
3 Kris McCarthy AUS — 1:46.59

1500m
1 Michael East ENG — 3:37.35
2 William Chirchir KEN — 3:37.70
3 Youcef Abdi AUS — 3:37.77

5000m
1 Sammy Kipketer KEN — 13:13.51
2 Benjamin Limo KEN — 13:13.57
3 Willy Kiptoo Kirui KEN — 13:18.02

10,000m
1 Wilberforce Talel KEN — 27:45.39
2 Paul Malakwen KEN — 27:45.46
3 John Yuda TAN — 27:45.78

Marathon
1 Francis Naali TAN — 2:11:58
2 Joshua Chelanga KEN — 2:12:44
3 Andrew Letherby AUS — 2:13:23

3000m Steeplechase
1 Stephen Cherono KEN — 8:19.41
2 Ezekiel Kemboi KEN — 8:19.78
3 Abraham Cherono KEN — 8:19.85

110m Hurdles
1 Shaun Bownes RSA — 13.35
2 Colin Jackson WAL — 13.39
3 Maurice Wignall JAM — 13.62

400m Hurdles
1 Chris Rawlinson ENG — 49.14
2 Matthew Elias WAL — 49.28
3 Ian Weakley JAM — 49.69

High Jump
1 Mark Boswell CAN — 2.28m
2 Kwaku Boateng CAN — 2.25m
3 Ben Challenger ENG — 2.25m

Pole Vault
1 Okkert Brits RSA — 5.75m
2 Paul Burgess AUS — 5.70m
3 Dominic Johnson LCA — 5.60m

Long Jump
1 Nathan Morgan ENG — 8.02m
2 Gable Garenamotse BOT — 7.91m
3 K Streete-Thompson CAY — 7.89m

Triple Jump
1 Jonathan Edwards ENG — 17.86m
2 Phillips Idowu ENG — 17.68m
3 Leevan Sands BAH — 17.26m

Shot
1 Justin Anlezark AUS — 20.91m
2 Janus Robberts RSA — 19.97m
3 Carl Myerscough ENG — 19.91m

Discus
1 Frantz Kruger RSA — 66.39m
2 Jason Tunks CAN — 62.61m
3 Robert Weir ENG — 59.24m

Hammer
1 Mick Jones ENG — 72.55m
2 Philip Jenson NZL — 69.48m
3 Paul Head ENG — 68.60m

Javelin
1 Steve Backley ENG — 86.81
2 Scott Russell CAN — 78.98
3 Nick Neiland ENG — 78.63

Decathlon
1 Bernard Claston JAM — 7830
2 Matt McEwen AUS — 7685
3 Jamie Quarry SCO — 7630

20km Walk
1 Nathan Deakes AUS — 1:25:35
2 Luke Adams AUS — 1:26:03
3 David Rotich KEN — 1:28:20

50km Walk
1 Nathan Deakes AUS — 3:52:40
2 Craig Barrett NZL — 3:56:42
3 Tim Berrett CAN — 4:04:25

4x100m
1 England — 38.62
Gardener/Devonish/Condon/Campbell
2 Jamaica — 38.62
3 Australia — 38.87

4x400m
1 England — 3:00.40
Deacon/Baldock/Rawlinson/Caines
2 Wales — 3:00.41
3 Bahamas — 3:01.35

100m Blind (B12/B2)
1 Adekunle Adesoji NGR — **10.76**
2 Hisham Khaironi MAS — 11.53
3 Rory Field RSA — 11.96

Women

100m
1 Debbie Ferguson BAH — 10.91
2 Veronica Campbell JAM — 11.00
3 Sevatheda Fynes BAH — 11.07

200m
1 Debbie Ferguson BAH — 22.20
2 Juliet Campbell JAM — 22.54
3 Lauren Hewitt AUS — 22.69

400m
1 Aliann Pompey GUY — 51.63
2 Lee McConnell SCO — 51.68
3 Sandie Richards JAM — 51.79

800m
1 Maria Mutola MOZ — 1:57.35
2 Diane Cummins CAN — 1:58.82
3 Agnes Samaria NAM — 1:59.15

1500m
1 Kelly Holmes ENG — 4:05.99
2 Hayley Tullett WAL — 4:07.52
3 Helen Pattinson ENG — 4:07.62

5000m
1 Paula Radcliffe ENG — 14:31.42
2 Edith Masai KEN — 14:53.76
3 Iness Chenonga KEN — 15:06.06

10,000m
1 Salina Kosgei KEN — 31:27.83
2 Susan Chepkemei KEN — 31:32.04
3 Susie Power AUS — 31:32.20

Marathon
1 Kerryn McCann AUS — 2:30:05
2 Krishna Stanton AUS — 2:34:52
3 Jackie Gallagher AUS — 2:36:37

100m Hurdles
1 Lacena Golding-Clark JAM — 12.77
2 Vonette Dixon JAM — 12.83
3 Angela Atede NGR — 12.98

400m Hurdles
1 Jana Pittman AUS — 54.40
2 Debbie-Ann Parris JAM — 55.24
3 Karlene Haughton CAN — 56.13

High Jump
1 Hestrie Cloete RSA — 1.96m
2 Susan Jones ENG — 1.90m
3 Nicole Forrester CAN — 1.87m

Pole Vault
1 Tatiana Grigorieva AUS — 4.35m
2 Kym Howe AUS — 4.15m
3 Bridgid Isworth AUS — 4.10m
3 Irie Hill ENG — 4.10m
3 Stephanie McCann ENG — 4.10m

Long Jump
1 Eva Goulbourne JAM — 6.70m
2 Jade Johnson ENG — 6.58m
3 Anju Bobby George IND — 6.49m

Triple Jump
1 Ashia Hansen ENG — 14.86m
2 Francoise Mbango CMR — 14.82m
3 Trecia Smith JAM — 14.32m

Shot
1 Vivian Chukwuemeka NGR — 17.53m
2 Valerie Adams NZL — 17.45m
3 Veronica Abrahamse RSA — 16.77m

Discus
1 Beatrice Faumuina NZL — 60.83m
2 N Jaswant Singh IND — 58.49m
3 Shelley Newman ENG — 58.13m

Hammer
1 Lorraine Shaw ENG — 66.83m
2 Bronwyn Eagles AUS — 65.24m
3 Karyne di Marco AUS — 63.40m

Javelin
1 Laverne Eve BAH — 58.46m
2 Cecilia McIntosh AUS — 57.42m
3 Kelly Morgan ENG — 57.09m

Heptathlon
1 Jane Jamieson AUS 6059
2 Kylie Wheeler AUS 5962
3 Margaret Simpson GHA 5906
20km Walk
1 Jane Saville AUS 1:36:34
2 Lisa Kehler ENG 1:36:45
3 Yuan Yu Fang MAS 1:40:00
4x100m
1 Bahamas 42.44
Clarke/Fynes/Sturrup/Ferguson
2 Jamaica 42.73
3 England 42.84
4x400m
1 Australia 3:25.63
Hewitt/Freeman/Lewis/Pittman
2 England 3:26.73
3 Nigeria 3:29.16
800m Wheelchair
1 Chantal Petitclerc CAN 1:52.93
2 Louise Sauvage AUS 1:53.30
3 Eliza Jane Stankovic AUS 1:54.20

Badminton

Team
1 England
2 Singapore
3 New Zealand
3 Scotland
Final: England bt Singapore 3-0

Men's Singles
1 Muhammad Hafiz Hashim MAS
2 Lee Tsuen Seng MAS
3 Richard Vaughan WAL
3 Wong Choong Hann MAS
Final score: 7-3 7-1 3-7 7-8 7-4

Men's Doubles
1 Chew/Chan MAS
2 Choong/Chang MAS
3 Anderson/Archer ENG
3 Robertson/Clark ENG
Final score: 7-5 4-7 2-7 7-5 7-3

Women's Singles
1 Li Li SIN
2 Tracey Hallam ENG
3 Aparna Popat IND
3 Ng Mee Fen MAS
Final score: 7-5 5-7 8-7 7-0

Women's Doubles
1 Ang/Lim MAS
2 Gordon/Runeston-Petersen NZL
3 Emms/Goode ENG
3 Chin/Wong MAS
Final score: 7-8 7-4 2-7 7-5 7-0

Mixed Doubles
1 Archer/Goode ENG
2 Chew/Chin MAS
3 Clark/Sankey ENG
3 Shirley/Runeston-Petersen NZL
Final score: 0-7 7-5 7-3 7-3

Boxing

-48kg (light-flyweight)
1 Mohammad Qamar IND
2 Darran Langley ENG
3 Mohamad Azizi MAS
3 Taoreed Ajagbe NGR
-51kg (flyweight)
1 Kennedy Kanyanta ZAM
2 Lechadzani Luza BOT
3 Nzimeni Msutu RSA
3 Sebastien Gauthier CAN
-54 (bantamweight)
1 Justin Kane AUS
2 Andrew Kooner CAN
3 Ezekiel Letuka LES
3 Mark Moran ENG
-57kg (featherweight)
1 Haider Ali PAK
2 Som Bahadur Pun IND
3 Joshua Viekko NAM
3 Benoit Gaudet CAN
-60kg (lightweight)
1 Jamie Arthur WAL
2 Denis Zimba ZAM
3 Gilbert Khunwane BOT
3 Andy Morris ENG
-63.5kg (light-welterweight)
1 Darren Barker ENG
2 Mohammed Kayongo UGA
3 Davies Mwale ZAM
3 Davidson Emenogu NGR
-67kg (welterweight)
1 Daniel Geale AUS
2 Kwanele Zulu RSA
3 Daniel Codling NZL
3 Ali Nuumbembe NAM
-71kg (light-middleweight)
1 Jean Pascal CAN
2 Paul Smith ENG
3 Craig McEwan SCO
3 Junior Greenidge BAR
-75kg (middleweight)
1 Paul Miller AUS
2 Steven Birch ENG
3 Jitender Kumar IND
3 Mike Walchuk CAN
-81kg (light-heavyweight)
1 Jegbefumere Albert NGR
2 Joseph Lubega UGA
3 Ben McEachran AUS
3 Daniel Venter RSA
-91kg (heavyweight)
1 Jason Douglas CAN
2 Kertson Manswell TRI
3 Andrew Young SCO
3 Shane Cameron NZL
+91kg (super-heavyweight)
1 David Dolan ENG
2 David Cadieux ENG
3 Gozie Dijeh ZAM
3 Kevin Evans WAL

Cycling
Mountain Bike
Cross-country
Men
1 Roland Green CAN 1:52:48
2 Seamus McGrath CAN 1:53:34
3 Liam Killeen ENG 1:55:34
Women
1 Chrissy Redden CAN 1:32:10
2 Susy Pryde NZL 1:32:26
3 Mary Grigson AUS 1:32:49

Road
Time Trial
Men
1 Cadel Evans AUS 1:00:53.50
2 Michael Rogers AUS 1:02:50.36
3 Nathan O'Neill AUS 1:03:20.69
Women
1 Clara Hughes CAN 34:51.66
2 Anna Millward AUS 35:00.77
3 Lyne Besette CAN 35:10.42

Road Race
Men
1 Stuart O'Grady AUS 4:43:17
2 Cadel Evans AUS 4:45.25
3 Baden Cooke AUS 4:45:45
Women
1 Nicole Cooke WAL 2:35:17
2 Sue Palmer-Komar CAN 2:35:18
3 Rachel Heal ENG 2:35:18

Track
Men
1km Time Trial
1 Chris Hoy SCO 1:01.725
2 Jason Queally ENG 1:01.947
3 Jamie Staff ENG 1:02.456
Sprint
1 Ryan Bayley AUS
2 Sean Eadie AUS
3 Jobie Dajka AUS
Final: Bayley bt Eadie by 2-1
Team Sprint
1 Australia 44.506
Dajka/Eadie/Bayley
2 England 44.772
3 Scotland 44.934
4000m Pursuit
1 Brad McGee AUS 4:16.358
2 Bradley Wiggins ENG
3 Paul Manning ENG 4:21.813
Final: Wiggins was caught
Team Pursuit
1 Australia 3:59.583
Brown/Dawson/Renshaw/Roberts
2 England 4:02.665
Manning/Newton/Wiggins/Steel
3 New Zealand 4:07.824

Points Race
1 Greg Henderson NZL 35
2 Mark Renshaw AUS 27
3 Chris Newton ENG 17
20km Scratch Race
1 Graeme Brown AUS 24:14.660
2 Huw Pritchard WAL
3 Tony Gibb ENG

Women
500m Time Trial
1 Kerrie Meares AUS 35.084
2 Jules Paulding ENG 35.448
3 Lori-Ann Muenzer CAN 35.595
Sprint
1 Kerrie Meares AUS
2 Lori-Ann Muenzer CAN
3 Anna Meares AUS
Final: Meares bt Muenzer by 2-0
3000m Individual Pursuit
1 Sarah Ulmer NZL 3:32.467
2 Katherine Bates AUS 3:34.193
3 Alison Wright AUS 3:40.409
Points Race
1 Katherine Bates AUS 37
2 Rochelle Gilmore AUS 23
3 Clara Hughes CAN 20

Diving
Men
1m Springboard
1 Alexandre Despatie CAN 404.55
2 Tony Ally ENG 386.37
3 Steven Barnett AUS 382.65
3m Springboard
1 Alexandre Despatie CAN 705.69
2 Tony Ally ENG 676.26
3 Robert Newbery AUS 656.64
10m Platform
1 Peter Waterfield ENG 690.30
2 Leon Taylor ENG 689.82
3 Alexandre Despatie CAN 689.79

Women
1m Springboard
1 Irina Lashko AUS 302.82
2 Blythe Hartley CAN 287.04
3 Jane Smith ENG 274.71
3m Springboard
1 Irina Lashko AUS 594.51
2 Emilie Heymans CAN 574.23
3 Jane Smith ENG 556.38
10m Platform
1 Loudy Tourky AUS 538.65
2 Emilie Heymans CAN 527.79
3 Blythe Hartley CAN 490.17

Gymnastics
Men
Team
1 England 162.075
2 Canada 161.350
3 Australia 159.100
All-Around
1 Kanukai Jackson ENG 55.025
2 Philippe Rizzo AUS 53.850
3 Alexander Jelkov CAN 53.650
Floor
1 Kyle Shewfelt CAN 9.637
2 Shu Wai Ng MAS 9.300
3 Philippe Rizzo AUS 9.225
Pommel Horse
1 Philippe Rizzo AUS 9.162
2 Kanukai Jackson ENG 9.087
3 Yik Siang Loke MAS 9.062
Rings
1 Steve Frew SCO 9.462
2 Herodotus Giorgallas CYP 9.462
3 Athol Myhill RSA 9.412
Vault
1 Kyle Shewfelt CAN 9.443
2 Kanukai Jackson ENG 9.281
3 Baz Collie SCO 9.225
Parallel Bars
1 Philippe Rizzo AUS 9.375
2 David Kikuchi CAN 9.150
3 John Smethurst ENG 9.112
High Bar
1 Philippe Rizzo AUS 9.512
2 Damian Istria AUS 9.075
3 Alexander Jeltkov CAN 8.900

Women
Team
1 Australia 111.325
2 England 106.900
3 Canada 106.800
All-Around
1 Kate Richardson CAN 36.750
2 Beth Tweddle ENG 36.387
3 Allana Slater AUS 36.362
Vault
1 Allana Slater AUS 9.268
2 Alexander Croak AUS 9.099
3 Vanessa Meloche CAN 9.093
Uneven Bars
1 Beth Tweddle ENG 9.550
2 Allana Slater AUS 9.537
3 Vanessa Meloche CAN 9.337
Beam
1 Kate Richardson CAN 9.200
2 Allana Slater AUS 9.137
3 Jacqui Dunn AUS 8.912
Floor
1 Sarah Lauren AUS 9.412
2 Becky Owen ENG 9.237
3 Kylie Stone CAN 9.212

Hockey
Men
Semi-finals
New Zealand 7 Pakistan 1
Australia 3 South Africa 1
Bronze Medal Match
Pakistan 10 South Africa 2
Final
Australia 5 New Zealand 2
Women
Semi-finals
England 2 Australia 1
India 2 New Zealand 1
Bronze Medal Match
Australia 4 New Zealand 3
Final
India 3 England 2
Match settled by a golden goal

Judo
Men
-60kg
1 Craig Fallon ENG
2 Akram Shah IND
3 Gary Cole WAL
3 Daniel Simard CAN
-66kg
1 James Warren ENG
2 David Somerville SCO
3 Tim Davies WAL
3 Bhupinder Singh IND
-73kg
1 Tom Hill AUS
2 Chris Christodoulides CYP
3 Lee McGrorty SCO
3 Jean-Francois Marceau CAN
-81kg
1 Graeme Randall SCO
2 Thomas Cousins ENG
3 Luke Preston WAL
3 Tim Slyfield NZL
-90kg
1 Winston Gordon ENG
2 Keith Morgan CAN
3 Steven Vidler SCO
3 Rostand Melaping CMR
-100kg
1 Nicolas Gill CAN
2 Sam Delahay ENG
3 Antonio Felicite MRI
+100kg
1 Nacanieli Qerewaqa FIJ
2 Daniel Sargent ENG
3 Daniel Rusitovic AUS
3 Emeka Onyenachi NGR

Women
-48kg
1 Carolyne Lepage CAN
2 Clare Lynch
3 Alice Livinus NGR
3 Fiona Robertson SCO
-52kg
1 Georgie Singleton ENG
2 Lisa Bradley NIR
3 Karen Cusack SCO
3 Angela Raguz AUS
-57kg
1 Maria Pekli AUS
2 Jenni Brien SCO
3 Luce Baillargeon CAN
3 Sophie Cox ENG
-63kg
1 Karen Roberts ENG
2 Sarah Clarke SCO
3 Bilkisu Ayijimoh Yusuf NGR
3 Claire Scourfield WAL
-70kg
1 Samantha Lowe ENG
2 Catherine Roberge CAN
3 Amanda Costello SCO
3 Sisilia Nasiga FIJ
-78kg
1 Michelle Rogers ENG
2 Jo Melen WAL
3 Jacynthe Maloney CAN
3 Foguing Okodombe CMR
_78kg
1 Simone Callender ENG
2 Angharad Sweet WAL
3 Stephanie Hart SCO
*Only one bronze medal awarded
due to the low entry at this weight*

Netball
Semi-finals
New Zealand 69   Jamaica 51
Australia 49   England 38
Bronze Medal Match
Jamaica 55   England 53
Final
Australia 57   New Zealand 55

Lawn Bowls
Men
Singles
1 Robert Donnelly RSA
2 Jeremy Henry NIR
3 Robert Weale WAL
3 Mike Kernaghan NZL
Pairs
1 Marshall/Sneddon SCO
2 Farish/Morgan ENG
3 Adinall/Baker NZL
3 Aziz/Safuan MAS

Fours
1 England
Ottaway/Skelton/Newman/Holt
2 South Africa
Abrahams/Fraser/Campbell/Burkett
3 Northern Island
Nutt/Graham/Booth/Baker
3 Wales
Slade/Bowen/Greenslade/Wilkins
Disability Triples
1 Scotland
Prior/Heddle/Robertson
2 Wales
Gronow/Dowling/Woolmore
3 Malaysia
Singh/Azmi/Lim
3 Australia
Read/Kearins/Reynolds

Women
Singles
1 Ahmad Siti Zalina MAS
2 Karen Murphy AUS
3 Lorna Trigwell RSA
3 Marlene Castle NZL
Pairs
1 Sims/Edwards NZL
2 Cawker/Hackland RSA
3 Weale/Butten WAL
3 Whitehead/Gowshall ENG
Fours
1 England
Alexander/Page/Mitchell/Duckworth
2 Canada
Fitzpatrick-Wong/Weigand/Ranger/Nivala
3 New Zealand
Jenson/Jorgensen/Khan/Lomas
3 Wales
Sutherland/John/Shipperlee/Miles
Blind Singles
1 Ruth Small ENG
2 Constance Sibanda ZIM
3 Vivian Berkeley CAN
3 Mukri Moira MAS

Rugby Sevens
Quarter-finals
New Zealand 24   Wales 0
Samoa 12   Australia 10
Fiji 7   England 5
South Africa 17   Canada 12
Semi-finals
New Zealand 31   Samoa 12
Fiji 17   South Africa 7
Bronze Medal Match
South Africa 19   Samoa 12
Final
New Zealand 55   Fiji 15

Shooting
Men
10m Air Pistol
1 Michael Gault ENG	675.0	
2 Samresh Jung IND	674.8	
3 Jaspal Rana IND	674.7	

10m Air Pistol Pairs
1 Baxter/Gault ENG   1140
2 Rana/Jung IND   1137
3 Melherbe/Sack NAM   1134
50m Free Pistol
1 Michael Gault ENG   657.5
2 Samrech Jung IND   652.8
3 Daniel van Tonder RSA   644.3
50m Free Pistol Pairs
1 Rana/Jung IND   1088
2 Moore/Quick AUS   1084
3 Van Tonder/Van Tonder RSA 1074
25m Standard Pistol
1 Jaspar Rana IND   574
2 Frederick van Tonder RSA 567
3 Michael Gault ENG   567
25m Standard Pistol Pairs
1 Rana/Jung IND   1130
2 Adams/Quick AUS   1118
3 Van Tonder/Van Tonder RSA 1116
25m Centre Fire Pistol
1 Jaspar Rana IND   583
2 Bruce Quick AUS   579
3 Irshad Ali PAK   577
25m Centre Fire Pistol Pairs
1 Rana/Singh IND   1150
2 Moore/Quick AUS   1149
3 Ali/Ali PAK   1142
25m Rapid Fire Pistol
1 Metodi Igarov CAN   669.3
2 Bruce Quick AUS   667.7
3 Allan McDonald RSA   666.3
25m Rapid Fire Pistol Pairs
1 Kumar/Dhaka IND   1141
2 McDonald/F van Tonder RSA 1131
3 FAvell/Quick AUS   1127
10m Air Rifle
1 Asif Hossain Khan BAN   691.9
2 Abhinav Bindra IND   691.4
3 Timothy Lowndes AUS   690.4
10m Air Rifle Pairs
1 Bindra/Ambekar IND   1184
2 Zakaria/Abdullah MAS   1164
3 Hector/Wallace ENG   1160
50m Rifle Prone
1 Timopthy Lowndes AUS   699.8
2 Mike Babb ENG   699.0
3 Jaco Henn RSA   687.7
50m Rifle Prone Pairs
1 Babb/Day ENG   1189
2 Henn/Thiele RSA   1180
3 Zakari/Din MAS   1173
50m Rifle 3 Positions
1 Charan Singh IND   1251.5
2 Timothy Lowndes AUS   1251.2
3 Samuel Wieland AUS   1248.1

50m Rifle 3 Positions Pairs
1 Lowndes/Wieland AUS 2297
2 Burrage/Hector ENG 2270
3 Singh/Pemmaiah IND 2266

Trap
1 Michael Diamond AUS 148
2 Adam Vella AUS 146
3 Anwer Sultan IND 142

Trap Pairs
1 Diamond/Vella AUS 187
2 Peel/Dean ENG 187
3 Birkett-Evans/Wixey WAL 186

Double Trap
1 Raiyavarthan Singh IND 191
2 William Chetcuti MLT 190
3 Russell Mark AUS 189

Double Trap Pairs
1 Moraad/Singh IND 184
2 Diamond/Mark AUS 184
3 Bellamy/Faulds ENG 182

Skeet Pairs
1 Nicolaides/Kourtellas CYP 194
2 Barton/Cunningham AUS 188
3 Brickell/Harvey ENG 188

Women

10m Air Pistol
1 Lalita Yauleuskaya AUS 479.4
2 Dorothy Hare CAN 477.9
3 Annemarie Forder AUS 476.3

10m Air Pistol Pairs
1 Eagles/Hare CAN 747
2 Chaudhary/Kanungo IND 744
3 Forder/Yauleuskaya AUS 744

25m Sport Pistol
1 Lallita Yauleuskaya AUS 686.8
2 Linda Ryan AUS 682.7
3 Jocelyn Lees NZL 672.4

25m Sport Pistol Pairs
1 Ryan/Yauleuskaya AUS 1150
2 Ng/Maharani MAS 1135
3 Corrigan/Lees NZL 1126

10m Air Rifle
1 Anjali Bhagwat IND 500.8
2 Suma Shirur IND 500.0
3 Louise Minett ENG 494.8

10m Air Rifle Pairs
1 Bhagwat/Shirur IND 795
2 Bowes/Mecredy CAN 781
3 Minett/Eaton ENG 776

50m Rifle Prone
1 Kim Frazer AUS 588
2 Esmari van Reenan RSA 588
3 Juliet Etherington NZL 586

50m Rifle Prone Pairs
1 Dallimore/Brekke WAL 1175
2 Sharp/Jackson SCO 1174
3 Smallbone/Vincent ENG 1167

50m Rifle 3 Positions
1 Anjali Bhagwat IND 678.0
2 Raj Kumari IND 662.2
3 Roslina Bakar MAS 662.2

50m Rifle 3 Position Pairs
1 Bhagwat/Kumari IND 1140
2 McCready/Smith AUS 1131
3 Bowes/Johnson CAN 1123

Trap Singles
1 Cynthia Meyer CAN 95
2 Anita North ENG 94
3 Susan Nattrass CAN 93

Trap Pairs
1 Jenkins/Reeves AUS 90
2 Goddaard/North ENG 89
3 Mayer/Nattrass CAN 86

Double Trap
1 Charlotte Kerwood ENG 141
2 Nadine Stanton NZL 134
3 Cynthia Meyer CAN 132

Double Trap Pairs
1 Borrell/Stanton NZL 137
2 Meyer/Nattrass CAN 136
3 Trindall/Balogh AUS 131

Skeet
1 Lauryn Ogilvie AUS 93
2 Natalie Rahman AUS 93
3 Edith Barnes SCO 87

Skeet Pairs
1 Ogilvie/Rahman AUS 95
2 Bramley/Le Grelle ENG 93
3 Conley/Nattrass CAN 53

Mixed

Full Bore
1 David Calvert NIR 404.62
2 David Dodds RSA 403.53
3 Diane Collings NZL 402.54

Full Bore Pairs
1 Millar/Calvert NIR 590.86
2 Bramley/Dodds RSA 589.85
3 Barnett/Messer ENG 588.84

Squash

Men's Singles
1 Jonathon Power CAN
2 Peter Nicol ENG
3 Stewart Boswell AUS
3 David Palmer AUS
Final: 9-4 4-9 9-3 9-0

Men's Doubles
1 Beachill/Nicol ENG
2 Boswell/Ricketts AUS
3 Palmer/Price AUS
3 Chaloner/Johnson ENG
Final: 15-11 15-12

Women's Singles
1 Sarah Fitz-Gerald AUS
2 Carol Owens NZL
3 Rachel Grinham ENG
3 Cassie Jackman ENG
Final: 9-5 9-0 2-9 10-9

Women's Doubles
1 Owens/Rorani NZL
2 Jackman/Bailey ENG
3 Grinham/Grinham AUS
3 Geaves/Charman ENG
Final: 15-11 5-15 15-13

Mixed Doubles
1 Rorani/Wilson NZL
2 David/Beng Hee MAS
3 Kniepp/Cooper AUS
3 Walker/Geaves ENG
Final: 15-11 15-7

"The best thing about the place is the rear-view mirror as you head for the M6"

Frank Vardanegan, Australian radio reporter, winning friends in Manchester.

"It's hard to breathe and throw up at the same time"

Nicole Hackett, the Australian bronze medallist, describing the swimming stage of the triathlon, held in Salford Quay.

"I honestly just wanted to offer a medal to Australia. I've been there six years and it's a country of love, freedom and peace and I wanted to say thank you"

Youcef Abdi, who migrated to Australia from Algeria in 1996, after winning bronze in the 1500m.

Swimming

Men

50m Free
1	Roland Schoeman RSA	22.33
2	Brett Hawke AUS	22.34
3	Mark Foster ENG	22.47

100m Free
1	Ian Thorpe AUS	48.73
2	Ashley Callus AUS	49.45
3	Ryk Neethling RSA	49.71

200m Free
1	Ian Thorpe AUS	1:44.71
2	Grant Hackett AUS	1:46.13
3	Rick Say CAN	1:49.40

400m Free
1	Ian Thorpe AUS	**3:40.08**
2	Grant Hackett AUS	3:43.48
3	Graeme Smith SCO	3:49.40

1500m Free
1	Grant Hackett AUS	14:54.29
2	Graeme Smith SCO	15:07.19
3	Craig Stevens AUS	15:09.24

50m Back
1	Matt Welsh AUS	25.65
2	Alex Lim MAS	25.67
3	Gerhard Zandberg RSA	25.89

100m Back
1	Matt Welsh AUS	54.72
2	Ian Thorpe AUS	55.38
3	Alex Lim MAS	55.44

200m Back
1	James Goddard ENG	1:59.83
2	Gregor Tait SCO	2:00.55
3	Simon Militis ENG	2:01.04

50m Breast
1	James Gibson ENG	27.72
2	Adam Whitehead ENG	27.79
3	Darren Mew ENG	27.80

100m Breast
1	Adam Whitehead ENG	1;01.13
2	Morgan Knabe CAN	1:01.23
3	James Gibson ENG	1:01.64

200m Breast
1	Jim Piper AUS	2:13.10
2	Terence Parkin RSA	2:13.34
3	Michael Brown CAN	2:13.82

50m Fly
1	Geoff Huegill AUS	23.57
2	Roland Schoeman RSA	23.66
3	Mark Foster ENG	24.11

100m Fly
1	Geoff Huegill AUS	52.36
2	Mike Mintenko CAN	52.80
3	Adam Pine AUS	53.02

200m Fly
1	Justin Norris AUS	1:56.95
2	Steve Parry ENG	1:57.71
3	James Hickman ENG	1:58.55

200m IM
1	Justin Norris AUS	2:01.32
2	Adrian Turner ENG	2:02.10
3	James Goddard ENG	2:02.48

400m IM
1	Justin Norris AUS	4:16.95
2	Brian Johns CAN	4:17.41
3	Adrian Turner ENG	4:18.75

4x100m Free
1	Australia	3;16.42

Callus/Pearson/Hackett/Thorpe

2	South Africa	3:18.86
3	Canada	3:19.39

4x200m Free
1	Australia	7:11.69

Hackett/Dunne/Cram/Thorpe

2	Canada	7;17.17
3	England	7:22.56

4x100m Medley
1	Australia	3:36.05

Welsh/Piper/Huegill/Thorpe

2	England	3:38.37
3	Canada	3:38.91

50m Multi-Disability*
1	Ben Austin AUS	27.59
2	Philippe Gagnon CAN	25.04
3	Benoit Huot CAN	25.07

100m Multi-Disability*
1	Ben Austin AUS	**1:00.21**
2	Philippe Gagnon CAN	55.12
3	Benoit Huot CAN	**1:02.50**

Women

50m Free
1	Alison Sheppard SCO	24.76
2	Jodie Henry AUS	25.37
3	Toni Mills NZL	25.48

100m Free
1	Jodie Henry AUS	55.45
2	Helene Muller RSA	55.60
3	Karen Legg ENG	55.86

200m Free
1	Karen Pickering ENG	1:59.69
2	Karen Legg ENG	1:59.86
3	Elka Graham AUS	2:00.07

400m Free
1	Rebecca Cooke ENG	4:09.49
2	Elka Graham AUS	4:11.47
3	Janelle Atkinson JAM	4:13.24

800m Free
1	Rebecca Cooke ENG	8:28.54
2	Amanda Pascoe AUS	8:34.19
3	Janelle Atkinson JAM	8:36.23

50m Back
1	Dyana Calub AUS	28.98
2	Jennifer Carroll CAN	29.05
3	Sarah Price ENG	29.08

100m Back
1	Sarah Price ENG	1:01.06
2	Dyana Calub AUS	1:01.86
3	Giaan Rooney AUS	1:02.22

200m Back
1	Sarah Price ENG	2:10.58
2	Jo Fargus ENG	2:11.60
3	Katy Sexton ENG	2:12.01

50m Breast
1	Zoe Baker ENG	30.60
2	Sarah Poewe RSA	31.73
3	Tarnee White AUS	31.74

100m Breast
1	Leisel Jones AUS	1:08.74
2	Brooke Hanson AUS	1:09.10
3	Sarah Poewe RSA	1:09.29

200m Breast
1	Leisel Jones AUS	2:25.93
2	Sarah Poewe RSA	2:27.47
3	Kelli Waite AUS	2:28.58

50m Fly
1	Petria Thomas AUS	26.66
2	Nicole Irving AUS	27.13
3	Alison Sheppard SCO	27.30

100m Fly
1	Petria Thomas AUS	58.57
2	Mandy Loots RSA	59.68
3	Jennifer Button CAN	1:00.22

200m Fly
1	Petria Thomas AUS	2:08.40
2	Georgie Lee ENG	2:10.73
3	Margaretha Pedder ENG	2:11.60

200m IM
1	Kirsty Coventry ZIM	2:14.53
2	Jennifer Reilly AUS	2;14.99
3	Marianne Limpert CAN	2:15.07

400m IM
1	Jennifer Reilly AUS	4:43.59
2	Elizabeth van Welie NZL	4:44.56
3	Jessica Abbott AUS	4:47.11

4x100m Free
1	Australia	3:40.41

Mills/Henry/Thomas/Ryan

2	England	3:41.47
3	Canada	3:45.33

4x200m Free
1	England	8:01.39

Legg/Lee/Fargus/Pickering

2	Australia	8:01.91
3	Canada	8:04.66

4x100m Medley
1	Australia	4:03.70

Calub/Jones/Thomas/Henry

2	South Africa	4:05.06
3	England	4:05.65

50m Multi-Disability*
1	Natalie Du Toit RSA	29.68
2	Stephanie Dixon CAN	30.60
3	Danielle Campo CAN	35.02

100m Multi-Disability*
1	Natalie Du Toit RSA	1:02.93
2	Stephanie Dixon CAN	1:05.05
3	Danielle Campo CAN	1:01.76

Placings determined by proximity to class world record

Synchro Swimming

Solo
1	Claire Carver-Dias CAN	93.834
2	Gayle Adamson ENG	87.917
3	Naomi Young AUS	85.834

Duet
1	C-Dias/Letourneau CAN	94.417
2	Adamson/Hooper ENG	88.167
3	Rudder/Young AUS	85.917

Table Tennis

Men's Team
1 England
2 Nigeria
3 India
3 Singapore

Men's Singles
1 Segun Moses Toriola NGR
2 Johnny Huang CAN
3 Chetan Baboor IND
3 Yong Jun Duan SIN
Final: 3-11 11-9 6-11 11-7 12-10 11-9

Men's Doubles
1 Baggaley/Herbet ENG
2 Jenkins/Robertson WAL
3 Subramanian/Baboor IND
3 Duan/Zhang SIN
Final: 11-9 11-3 8-11 11-9 17-15

Women's Team
1 Singapore
2 Australia
3 Canada
3 New Zealand

Women's Singles
1 Li Chunli NZL
2 Li Jia Wei SIN
3 Tan Paey Fern SIN
3 Jing Jun Hong SIN
Final: 11-6 11-9 5-11 11-5 11-8

Women's Doubles
1 Jing/Li SIN
2 Li/Li NZL
3 Miao/Lay AUS
3 Tan/Zhang SIN
Final: 11-3 11-7 10-12 11-4

Women's Wheelchair
1 Sue Gilroy ENG
2 Alette Moll RSA
3 Joy Boyd AUS
3 Cathy Mitton ENG
Final: 11-5 13-11 11-3

Mixed Doubles
1 Duan/Li SIN
2 Clarke/Lay AUS
3 Li/Jackson NZL
3 Zhang/Jing SIN
Final: 9-11 11-9 11-6 11-4

Triathlon

Men
1 Simon Whitfield CAN   1:51:57.94
2 Miles Stewart AUS   1:52:00.27
3 Hamish Carter NZL   1:52:04.29

Women
1 Carol Montgomery CAN 2:03:37.17
2 Leanda Cave WAL   2:03:37.17
3 Nicole Hackett AUS   2:03:42.81

Weightlifting

Men

-56kg Overall
1 Amirul Ibrahim MAS   260.00
2 Thandava Muthu IND   245.00
3 Vickey Batta IND   242.50
-56kg Snatch
1 Amirul Ibrahim MAS   115.00
2 Thandava Muthu IND   112.50
3 M Faizal Baharom MAS   110.00
-56kg Clean & Jerk
1 Amirul Ibrahim MAS   145.00
2 Vickey Batta IND   135.00
3 Thandava Muthu IND   132.50
-62kg Overall
1 Yourik Sarkisian AUS   277.50
2 Marcus Stephen NAU   265.00
3 Terry Hughes NZL   245.00
-62kg Snatch
1 Yourik Sarkisian AUS   125.00
2 Marcus Stephen NAU   117.50
3 Roswadi Rashid MAS   115.00
-62kg Clean & Jerk
1 Yourik Sarkisian AUS   152.50
2 Marcus Stephen NAU   147.50
3 Terry Hughes NZL   135.00
-69kg Overall
1 Teintcheu Dabaya CMR   310.00
2 Muhammad Irfan PAK   310.00
3 Stewart Cruikshank ENG 297.50
-69kg Snatch
1 Teintcheu Dabaya CMR   140.00
2 Muhammad Irfan PAK   140.00
3 Chitradurga Kumar IND   135.00
-69kg Clean & Jerk
1 Teintcheu Dabaya CMR   170.00
2 Muhammad Irfan PAK   170.00
3 Hidayat Hamidon MAS   167.50
-77kg Overall
1 Dave Morgan WAL   305.00
2 Renos Doweiya NAU   290.00
3 Scott McCarthy CAN   290.00
-77kg Snatch
1 Damian Brown AUS   147.50
2 Dave Morgan WAL   145.00
3 Craig Blythman AUS   135.00
-77kg Clean & Jerk
1 Dave Morgan WAL   160.00
2 Renos Doweiya NAU   160.00
3 Scott McCarthy CAN   157.50
-85kg Overall
1 David Matam CMR   340.00
2 Anthony Arthur ENG   330.00
3 Ofisa Ofisa SAM   320.00
-85kg Snatch
1 David Matam CMR   155.00
2 Anthony Arthur ENG   150.00
3 Niusila Opelage SAM   142.50
-85kg Clean & Jerk
1 David Matam CMR   185.00
2 Ofisa Ofisa SAM   180.00
3 Anthony Arthur ENG   180.00

-94kg Overall
1 Alex Karapetyn AUS   365.00
2 David Guest ENG   345.00
3 Julien Galipeau CAN   342.50
-94kg Snatch
1 Alex Karapetyn AUS   167.50
2 David Guest ENG   160.00
3 Tommy Yule SCO   157.50
-94kg Clean & Jerk
1 Alex Karapetyn AUS   197.50
2 Julien Galipeau CAN   192.50
3 Karl Grant ENG   187.50
-105kg Overall
1 Delroy McQueen ENG   375.00
2 Akos Sandor CAN   360.00
3 Edmund Yeo MAS   315.00
-105kg Snatch
1 Delroy McQueen ENG   165.00
2 Akos Sandor CAN   165.00
3 Gurbinder Cheema ENG   160.00
-105kg Clean & Jerk
1 Delroy McQueen ENG   210.00
2 Akos Sandor CAN   195.00
3 Edmund Yeo MAS   170.00
+105kg Overall
1 Nigel Avery NZL   390.00
2 Giles Greenwood ENG   387.50
3 Corran Hocking AUS   380.00
+105kg Snatch
1 Giles Greenwood ENG   180.00
2 Nigel Avery NZL   175.00
3 Chris Rae AUS   175.00
+105kg Clean & Jerk
1 Nigel Avery NZL   215.00
2 Corran Hocking AUS   210.00
3 Giles Greenwood ENG   207.50
Disability Class
1 Solomon Amarakuo NGR 150.40
2 Richard Nicholson AUS   148.50
3 Kon Fatt Cheok MAS   144.10

Women
-48kg Overall
1 Kunjarani Nameirakpam IND 167.50
2 Karine Turcotte CAN   157.50
3 Ebonette Deigaeruk NAU 145.00
-48kg Snatch
1 Kunjarani Nameirakpam IND 75.00
2 Karine Turcotte CAN   70.00
3 Ebonette Deigaeruk NAU 60.00
-48kg Clean & Jerk
1 Kunjarani Nameirakpam IND 92.50
2 Karine Turcotte CAN   87.50
3 Ebonette Deigaeruk NAU 85.00
-53kg Overall
1 Sanamacha Chanu IND   182.50
2 Natasha Barker AUS   175.00
3 Seen Lee AUS   162.50
-53kg Snatch
1 Sanamacha Chanu IND   82.50
2 Natasha Barker AUS   77.50
3 Seen Lee AUS   75.00

-53kg Clean & Jerk
1 Sanamacha Chanu IND 100.00
2 Natasha Barker AUS 97.50
3 Seen Lee AUS 87.50

-58kg Overall
1 Maryse Turcotte CAN 202.50
2 Michaela Breeze WAL 200.00
3 Sunaina IND 192.50

-58kg Snatch
1 Michaela Breeze WAL 87.50
2 Maryse Turcotte CAN 87.50
3 Sunaina IND 85.00

-58kg Clean & Jerk
1 Michaela Breeze WAL 115.00
2 Maryse Turcotte CAN 112.50
3 Sunaina IND 107.50

-63kg Overall
1 Pratima Kumari IND 205.00
2 Prasmita Mangaraj IND 195.00
3 Pascale Dorcelus CAN 185.00

-63kg Snatch
1 Pascale Dorcelus CAN 87.50
2 Pratima Kumari IND 87.50
3 Prasmita Mangaraj IND 85.00

-63kg Clean & Jerk
1 Pratima Kumari IND 117.50
2 Prasmita Mangaraj IND 110.00
3 Pascale Dorcelus CAN 100.00

-69kg Overall
1 Madeleine Yamechi CMR 230.00
2 Neelam Sethi Laxmi IND 205.00
3 Sheba Deireragea NAU 200.00

-69kg Snatch
1 Madeleine Yamechi CMR 100.00
2 Neelam Sethi Laxmi IND 95.00
3 Sheba Deireragea NAU 90.00

-69kg Clean & Jerk
1 Madeleine Yamechi CMR 130.00
2 Neelam Sethi Laxmi IND 110.00
3 Sheba Deireragea NAU 110.00

-75kg Overall
1 Shailaja Pujari IND 222.50
2 Deborah Lovely AUS 202.50
3 Saree Williams AUS 182.50

-75kg Snatch
1 Shailaja Pujari IND 97.50
2 Deborah Lovely AUS 95.00
3 Saree Williams AUS 82.50

-75kg Snatch
1 Shailaja Pujari IND 125.00
2 Deborah Lovely AUS 107.50
3 Saree Williams AUS 102.50

+75kg Overall
1 Reanna Solomon NAU 227.50
2 Caroline Pileggi AUS 225.00
3 Olivia Baker NZL 225.00

+75kg Snatch
1 Caroline Pileggi AUS 100.00
2 Olivia Baker NZL 100.00
3 Reanna Solomon NAU 100.00

+75kg Clean & Jerk
1 Reanna Solomon NAU 127.50
2 Caroline Pileggi AUS 125.00
3 Olivia Baker NZL 125.00

Wrestling
Freestyle only

-55kg
1 Krishnan Kumar IND
2 Mikheil Japaridze CAN
3 Shaun Williams RSA

-60kg
1 Guivi Sissaouri CAN
2 Shokinder Tomar IND
3 Tebe Dorgu NGR

-66kg
1 Ramesh Kumar IND
2 Graham Ewers CAN
3 Fred Jessey NGR

-74kg
1 Daniel Igali CAN
2 Sunday Opiah NGR
3 Rein Ozoline AUS

-84kg
1 Nicholas Ugoalah CAN
2 Anuj Kumar IND
3 Sinivie Boltic NGR

-96kg
1 Dean Schmeichel CAN
2 Anil Kumar Mann IND
3 Muhammad Bashir Bhola PAK

-120kg
1 Palwinder Singh Cheema IND
2 Eric Kirschner CAN
3 Mushtaq Raseem Abdullah AUS

Winter Olympics

Well, at least the curling didn't end in tears. Rhona Martin, Janice Rankin, Fiona McDonald and Debbie Knox; they came, they curled and they conquered. Who could ask for more?

It was not an easy ride, the hurrees were matched the sorrees as they lost their final round robin matches against the USA and Germany. They were practising their farewells to Ogden when Switzerland took to the rink in a match against Germany that meant nothing to the Swiss in terms of the Olympic competition for they had already qualified. But there's always other baggage that comes into the international equation, and the Swiss have never gifted their powerful neighbours any sporting encounter. Germany, on the same points score as Britain, needed a win to qualify, but got hammered 10-4 instead. Thank you, Switzerland, said the British curlers.

The Swedes won their last match against Russia, played alongside the German-Swiss confrontation and suddenly there were three teams on five wins and all to play for. Germany could, at least, sit back and wait while the play-offs for the semi-final began. Having the best record between the three teams at the round robin stage, they were given the bye in the first play-off round.

Perversely, Britain found Sweden harder than Germany, but won both encounters to set up the match of the women's tournament. Forget the final; it was in the semi-final against Canada that the Olympic title was won.

Martin's team were the underdogs by miles; Canada the white-hot tournament favourites. The Canadians were without the captain who had led them to Olympic gold in Nagano, for Sandra Schmirler (Schmirler the curler, what else?) had died of cancer in 2000, at just 36 years of age.

It was Schmirler who had ended British hopes in Nagano, her perfectly delivered stone in the last play of that semi-final settling just one and a half inches closer to the button than that of the British skip Kirsty Hay. Two years later, at the world championships in Glasgow, the Canadians had again ended the British hopes, Martin the Scottish skip on that occasion. And as if that were not history enough, Canada had already enjoyed an untroubled victory in the round robin stage of this tournament. But history, what is history?

In a compelling curling match, the fourth end was crucial, the Canadian skip Kelly Law missing her final shot to give Britain a two-point lead. The Canadians clawed back, Martin re-established the lead, Law countered. Nip and tuck till it was 5-5 going into the final end with Martin, critically, having the final stone. The 35-year-old curler, who almost missed the games through illness, used it well. The frantic brushing was just nervous energy. The shot was perfectly delivered. The score was 6-5 and the British team was in the Olympic final.

Britain and Switzerland are both a long way from Ogden and the final lacked the atmosphere of the semi-final, when the Canadian supporters, much closer to home, had turned out in force. Nevertheless, it was a close-run match with the Swiss taking it to the wire. The scores were three-apiece coming into the tenth and final end, but the hammer (the last delivery) was with Martin and it was just a matter of nerve. Martin's held and the match was won and in the shadow of Ben Lomond (how appropriate can you get?), a Scottish quartet won a British gold medal, the first British Winter Olympic title since Torvill met Dean in perfect unison at Sarajevo 18 years earlier.

Alex Coomber had been touted as Britain's best gold medal chance, the RAF officer was the reigning World Cup champion in the skeleton, but she had twice been beaten into second place in the world championships of this fledgling sport. In a race of just 13 entries, the two American sledders - Tristan Gale and Lea Ann Parsley - came out on top. This was no surprise, the Americans also won the men's skeleton and the women's bobsleigh titles on the same piste, but there was a concern. On the second and final run, the two Americans were the last two competitors on the piste, following Coomber. There was a delay, which was never explained. Time enough, ran the argument, to sweep some of the snow that was falling, from off the course and improve the conditions for Gale and Parsley. We have no convincing evidence either way, but without an explanation from the American officials, it is not hard to construct a conspiracy theory.

Coomber could have complained at the time, but did not, evincing only delight with her bronze medal. Three weeks later, in an article in *The Times* she was saying that it was "all very unfair". Well, too late, Alex, too late. If you do nothing at the time, it sounds only churlish if you introduce your gripe three weeks later. In the same article, Coomber also revealed that she had broken her arm during training at the holding camp in Canada prior to the Games.

All too briefly, there was a third British medal, when Alain Baxter took third place in the slalom. It could have been the first British medal on snow (any snow) since the Winter Games began in 1924 at St Moritz, but it wasn't.

Baxter had not looked an Olympic contender leading up to the Games. His performances were so far below the standard he had set a season earlier that British Ski and Snowboard Federation officials had offered to help raise the money to buy him out of his ski contract with Head skis. Baxter declined the offer, persevering with the Head equipment, and getting it right at the most important moment.

His skiing on the awkward Deer Valley slope was steady rather than inspired and it relied a handful of top skiers losing their nerve to bring Baxter an unexpected bronze medal. The laconic Scot held his post-competition press conference with British journalists under the stairs in a corner of the press centre, and despite his evident joy, he still looked awkward with the media and spoke in a whisper. He didn't act like a man on speed.

The drug test result was released on March 6th, more than a week after the Games had ended. Baxter had been foolish, using a Vicks Inhaler he had brought in the US, rather than one brought in the UK. If you compare the packaging of the two products, there is almost no difference, and Baxter had been using the UK product for some years, for it contained no banned compounds. In the US, though, the Vicks Inhaler contains L-Metamphetamine. It says so on the label, and Baxter should have noted it, but he didn't.

That is the story as Baxter told it, and the detail was accepted by both the IOC and FISA (International Skiing Federation), although he still served a short ban (three months) and lost his Olympic medal. However, nothing was truly resolved, as the IOC refused to re-analyse the sample to determine whether the substance that Baxter ingested was actually L-Metamphetamine (also known as Lev- or Levo- Metamphetamine).

Briefly, L-Metamphetamine has a different structural isomer (or formation) to Metamphetamine, or speed. Also L-Metamphetamine only appears commercially in a single product, the US Vicks Inhaler. Furthermore, the company insists that L-Metamphetamine does not have significant stimulant properties. So, a further test by the IOC would have, firstly, verified Baxter's story and, secondly, given the chemists the opportunity to discuss whether it should be banned at all.

Which is precisely why the IOC accepted Baxter's tale without a re-test of his sample; because the scenario they feared was one that questioned the 'catch-all' nature of their drug rules. That was a road map they didn't want to unfold.

Baxter was our own British controversy, but there were international skirmishes in Salt Lake that dwarfed it. Canadian skaters Jamie Sale and David Pelletier started the mayhem, losing then sharing the Olympic pairs title. There's little doubt that the Canadians should have won the title in the first place, you needed only to look at the confused faces of the two Russians when they were awarded the title to know there had been a dereliction of duty somewhere.

Elena Berezhnaya and Anton Sikharulidze are possibly the only Olympic champions in history to be presented with their gold medals twice in the same week. On the Monday, they stood together on the podium and were booed. On Friday they shared the top tier with Sale and Pelletier and listened to cheers. If the decision to re-assess the marking was the right one, the haste with which it was done was unseemly.

The French judge, Marie-Reine Le Gougne, whose marks had elevated the Russians above the Canadians, was blamed and banned by the International Skating Union, as was the head of the French Federation, Didier Gailhaguet, who was alleged to have colluded with her. The waters were further muddied when, subsequently, the Russian mafia were purported to have been involved. For skating, it meant the end of the much maligned (and rightly so) voting system in which national preferences had long held sway.

The short track programme didn't pass without incident - it never does - with the Korean Kim Dong-Sung disqualified after winning the 1500m. The gold went instead to the American Apolo Anton Ohno, leaving a slightly unpleasant taste in the mouth.

The controversies were counterbalanced by the edifying victories of Janica Kostelic in three alpine events; Alexei Yagudin and Sarah Hughes in the figure skating (though Sasha Cohen is the name to watch out for in the women's event); Simon Ammann in a wonderful ski jumping competition; and by the Canadian women in a stirring ice hockey final against the USA.

Yet it still ended in more tears with cross-country skiers Johann Mühlegg, of Spain, and the Russians Larissa Lazutina and Olga Danilova all disqualified for positive drug tests for Darbopoietin, an EPO-related product. As Mühlegg and Lazutina had won five gold medals between them, it was arguably the biggest drug heist in Olympic history.

"They were the worst possible conditions for me - I had a broken arm and they blatantly closed the track for no reason before the Americans raced"
Alex Coomber, skeleton bronze medallist.

"Mum, we've got a problem"
Alain Baxter, to his mother, Sue Dixon.

"We are not judges, we are only skaters"
Elena Berezhnaya, having just won the Olympic pairs title with Anton Sikharulidze.

"Regrettably for the new leadership, the first time is bound to be a flop"
Vladimir Putin, the Russian president, blaming Jacques Rogge, the IOC president for the apparent anti-Russian sentiment in Salt Lake.

"I obviously wasn't the best skater out there..I was never expecting the whole field to go down and leave me the only one standing...I wasn't exactly sure whether I should believe it or not...I've nearly been killed by the sport a couple of times, I guess this was the day the sport was smiling on me"
Steven Bradbury, the Australian speed skating gold medallist.

"The unbelievable torment to which I was a victim could hide other interests that must at all costs remain in the shadows"
Marie-Reine Le Gougne, French skating judge, who was blamed for the skating debacle in the pairs competition.

Winter Olympic Games

Salt Lake City, Feb 8-24

Medal Table

		G	S	B	Ttl
1	Germany	12	6	7	35
2	Norway	11	7	7	25
3	USA	10	14	11	35
4	Russia	6	6	4	16
5	Canada	6	3	8	17
6	France	4	5	2	1
7	Italy	4	4	4	12
8	Finland	4	2	1	7
9	Netherlands	3	5	0	8
10	Austria	3	4	11	18
11	Switzerland	3	2	6	11
12	Croatia	3	1	0	4
13	China	2	2	4	8
14	Korea	2	2	0	4
15	Australia	2	0	0	2
16	Spain	2	0	0	2
17	Estonia	1	1	1	3
18	Czech Republic	1	0	1	2
19	Great Britain	1	0	1	2
20	Sweden	0	2	4	6
21	Bulgaria	0	1	2	3
22	Japan	0	1	1	2
23	Poland	0	1	1	2
24	Belarus	0	0	1	1
25	Slovenia	0	0	1	1

Alpine Skiing

There are two runs for the technical events; the slaloms and giant slaloms. For combined results, downhill times given first, aggregate slalom times second.

Men

Downhill
1	Fritz Strobl AUT	1:39.13
2	Lasse Kjus NOR	1:39.35
3	Stephan Eberharter AUT	1:39.41

Super-G
1	Kjetil-Andre Aamodt NOR	1:21.58
2	Stephan Eberharter AUT	1:21.68
3	Andreas Schifferer AUT	1:21.83

Giant Slalom
1	Stephan Eberharter AUT (1:11.98/1:11.30)	2:23.28
2	Bode Miller USA (1:12.89/1:11.27)	2:24.16
3	Lasse Kjus NOR (1:12.79/1:11.53)	2:24.32
29	Ross Green GBR (1:15.90/1:13.41)	2:29.31

Slalom
1	Jean-Pierre Vidal FRA	1:41.06	(48.01/53.05)
2	Sebastien Amiez FRA	1:41.82	(50.16/51.66)
3	Benjamin Raich AUT	1:42.41	(49.34/53.07)
21	Noel Baxter GBR	1:49.64	(53.66/55.98)
23	Gareth Traynor GBR	1:50.91	(54.58/56.33)

DQ: Alain Baxter GBR 1:42.32 (50.16/52.16)
Baxter finished third, but was disqualified following a positive test for methamphetamine

Combined
1	Kjetil-Andre Aamodt NOR (1:38.79/1:38.77)	3:17.56
2	Bode Miller USA (1:41.23/1:36.61)	3:17.84
3	Benjamin Raich AUT (1:41.05/1:37.21)	3:18.26
15	Ross Green GBR (1:43.30/1:45.81)	3:29.11

Women

Downhill
1	Carole Montillet FRA	1:39.56
2	Isolde Kostner ITA	1:40.01
3	Renate Goetschl AUT	1:40.39
32	Chimene Alcott GBR	1:45.98

Super-G
1	Daniela Ceccarelli ITA	1:13.59
2	Janica Kostelic CRO	1:13.64
3	Karen Putzer ITA	1:13.86
28	Chimene Alcott GBR	1:17.34

Giant Slalom
1	Janica Kostelic CRO (1:16.00/1:14.01)	2:30.01
2	Anja Paerson SWE (1:16.87/1:14.46)	2:31.33
3	Sonja Nef SUI (1:16.94/1:14.73)	2:31.67
30	Chimene Alcott GBR (1:20.25/1:18.22)	2:38.47

Slalom

1	Janica Kostelic CRO	1:46.10	(52.14/53.96)
2	Laure Pequegnot FRA	1:46.17	(52.32/53.85)
3	Anja Paerson SWE	1:47.09	(52.57/54.52)
19	Emma Carrick-Anderson GBR	1:53.79	(56.25/57.54)

Did Not Finish 1st run: Chimene Alcott GBR

Combined

1	Janica Kostelic CRO	2:43.28
	(1:16.00/1:27.28)	
2	Renate Goetschl AUT	2:44.77
	(1:15.27/1:29.50)	
3	Martina Ertl GER	2:45.16
	(1;16.78/1:28.38)	
14	Chimene Alcott GBR	2:51.34
	(1:19.06/1:32.28)	

Biathlon
Men
10km Sprint

1	Ole Einar Bjoerndalen NOR	24:51.3
2	Sven Fischer GER	25:20.2
3	Wolfgang Perner AUT	25:44.4
71	Jason Sklenor GBR	28:43.4
72	Mark Gee GBR	28:57.8
74	Michael Dixon GBR	28:58.7

12.5km Pursuit

1	Ole Einar Bjoerndalen NOR	32:34.6
2	Raphael Poiree FRA	+43.0
3	Ricco Gross GER	+56.0

20km

1	Ole Einar Bjoerndalen NOR	51:03.3
2	Frank Luck GER	51:39.4
3	Victor Maigourov RUS	51:40.6
48	Jason Sklenor GBR	57:27.2
79	Michael Dixon GBR	1:02:04.9
81	Mark Gee GBR	1:02:10.2

4 x 7.5km Relay

1	Norway	1:23:42.3
	Hanevold/Andresen/Gjelland/Bjoerndalen	
2	Germany	1:24:27.6
	Gross/Sendel/Fischer/Luck	
3	France	1:24:36.6
	Marguet/Defrasne/Robert/Poiree	
19	Great Britain	1:36:06.0
	Sklenor/Gee/Dixon/Pritchard	

Women
7.5km Sprint

1	Kati Wilhelm GER	20:41.4
2	Uschi Disl GER	20:57.0
3	Magdalena Forsberg SWE	21:20.4

10km Pursuit

1	Olga Pyleva RUS	31:07.7
2	Kati Wilhelm GER	+5.3
3	Irina Nikoultchina BUL	+8.1

15km

1	Andrea Henkel GER	47:29.1
2	Liv Grete Poiree NOR	47:37.0
3	Magdalena Forsberg SWE	48:08.3

4 x 7.5km Relay

1	Germany	1:27:55.0
	Apel/Disl/Henkel/Wilhelm	
2	Norway	1:28:25.6
	Skjelbreid/Tjoerhom/Andreassen/Poiree	
3	Russia	1:29:19.7
	Pyleva/Koukleva/Ishmouratova/Akhatova	

Bobsleigh
Men
Two-man

1	Langen/Zimmermann GER	3:10.11
	(47.54/47.52/47.44/47.61)	
2	Reich/Anderhub SUI	3:10.20
	(47.52/47.53/47.45/47.70)	
3	Annan/Hefti SUI	3:10.62
	(47.56/47.64/47.73/47.69)	
10	Johnston/Adam GBR	3:12.27
	(48.04/48.16/48.05/48.02)	
22	Scarisbrick/Bryce GBR	3:14.12
	(48.44/48.46/48.72/48.50)	

Four-man

1	Germany	3:07.51
	Lange/Kuehn/Kuske/Embach	
	(46.71/46.64/46.84/47.32)	
2	USA	3:07.81
	Hays/Jones/Schuffenhauer/Hines	
	(46.65/46.61/47.22/47.33)	
3	USA	3:07.86
	Shimer/Kohn/Sharp/Steel	
	(46.83/46.82/46.98/47.23)	
11	Great Britain	3:09.37
	Scarisbrick/Rider/Goedluck/Ward	
	(47.09/47.05/47.44/47.79)	
14	Great Britain	3:09.77
	Johnston/Harries/McCalla/Attwood	
	(47.06/47.32/47.41/47.98)	

Women

1	Bakken/Flowers USA	1:37.76
	(48.81/48.95)	
2	Prokoff/Holzner GER	1:38.06
	(49.10/48.96)	
3	Erdmann/Herschmann GER	1:38.29
	(49.19/49.10)	
11	Coy/Davies GBR	1:39.55
	(49.77/49.78)	
12	Done/Gautier GBR	1:39.89
	(50.10/49.79)	

Curling

Men

1st Session
Denmark 3 Finland 9; France 5 Germany 9;
USA 10 Sweden 5; Canada 6 Great Britain 4

2nd Session
Norway 4 Switzerland 5; USA 3 Canada 8;
Denmark 8 France 7; Finland 6 Germany 7

3rd Session
Sweden 7 Great Britain 2; Denmark 6 Switzerland 10;
Finland 4 Canada 9; France 2 Norway 9

4th Session
Switzerland 5 Finland 6; Great Britain 6 Norway 7;
Germany 9 USA 8; Denmark 5 Sweden 9

5th Session
Great Britain 7 Germany 6; Canada 8 France 1;
Sweden 7 Switzerland 8; Norway 6 USA 5

6th Session
Canada 5 Sweden 6; Switzerland 2 USA 6;
Denmark 6 Germany 7; Finland 6 France 5

7th Session
France 3 USA 8; Norway 9 Denmark 4;
Great Britain 4 Finland 6; Germany 7 Canada 9

8th Session
Finland 5 Norway 6; Canada 7 Switzerland 2;
France 6 Sweden 9; Great Britain 5 Denmark 6

9th Session
Switzerland 10 Great Britain 4; Finland 4 Sweden 11;
USA 7 Denmark 9; Norway 10 Germany 5

10th Session
Germany 4 Sweden 5; Canada 9 Norway 4;
France 3 Switzerland 7

11th Session
France 3 Great Britain 7; USA 4 Finland 6

12th Session
Denmark 3 Canada 8; Germany 4 Switzerland 10;
Great Britain 7 USA 6; Sweden 8 Norway 9

Standings

		P	W	L
1	Canada	9	8	1
2	Norway	9	7	2
3	Switzerland	9	6	3
3	Sweden	9	6	3
5	Finland	9	5	4
6	Germany	9	4	5
7	Denmark	9	3	6
7	Great Britain	9	3	6
7	USA	9	3	6
10	France	9	0	9

Switzerland ranked ahead of Sweden as the round robin match between them was won by the Swiss

Semi-Finals
Sweden 4 Canada 6; Norway 7 Switzerland 6

Bronze Medal Game
Sweden 3 Switzerland 7

Final
Canada 5 Norway 6

Women

1st Session
Sweden 4 Canada 5; Great Britain 10 Norway 6;
Switzerland 9 Denmark 8; Russia 5 Germany 8

2nd Session
Japan 7 USA 8; Switzerland 7 Russia 6;
Sweden 7 Great Britain 4; Canada 6 Norway 5

3rd Session
Denmark 5 Germany 9; Sweden 5 USA 6;
Canada 7 Russia 6; Great Britain 9 Japan 1

4th Session
USA 4 Canada 6; Germany 5 Japan 3;
Norway 5 Switzerland 7; Sweden 9 Denmark 11

5th Session
Germany 5 Norway 10; Russia 5 Great Britain 8;
Denmark 9 USA 4; Japan 7 Switzerland 8

6th Session
Russia 7 Denmark 5; USA 6 Switzerland 7;
Sweden 10 Norway 3; Canada 9 Great Britain 4

7th Session
Great Britain 7 Switzerland 4; Japan 7 Sweden 8;
Germany 4 Canada 8; Norway 5 Russia 4

8th Session
Canada 9 Japan 4; Russia 4 USA 11;
Great Britain 8 Denmark 6; Germany 7 Sweden 5

9th Session
USA 7 Germany 6; Canada 9 Denmark 4;
Switzerland 7 Sweden 8; Japan 5 Norway 8

10th Session
Norway 9 Denmark 4; Russia 6 Japan 7;
Great Britain 5 USA 6

11th Session
Great Britain 5 Germany 7; Norway 2 USA 11;
Switzerland 7 Canada 6

12th Session
Sweden 9 Russia 6; Germany 4 Switzerland 10;
Denmark 5 Japan 6

Standings

		P	W	L
1	Canada	9	8	1
2	Switzerland	9	7	2
3	USA	9	6	3
4	Germany	9	5	4
4	Sweden	9	5	4
4	Great Britain	9	5	4
7	Norway	9	4	5
8	Japan	9	2	7
8	Denmark	9	2	7
10	Russia	9	1	8

Germany, Sweden and Great Britain played off for the last semi-final place. As Germany had the best record from the round robin games between the three teams, they were given the bye.

Play-off Games
Sweden 4 Great Britain 6; Great Britain 9 Germany 5

Semi-Finals
Switzerland 9 USA 4; Great Britain 6 Canada 5

Bronze Medal Game
USA 5 Canada 9

Final
Switzerland 3 Great Britain 4

Cross Country Skiing

Men

1.5km
1	Tor Arne Hetland NOR	2:56.9
2	Peter Schlickenrieder GER	2:57.0
3	Cristian Zorzi ITA	2:57.2

10km Pursuit
1	Johann Mühlegg ESP	49:20.4
2	Frode Estil NOR	49:48.9
2	Thomas Alsgaard NOR	49:48.9

15km
1	Andrus Veerpalu EST	37:07.4
2	Frode Estil NOR	37:43.4
3	Jaak Mae EST	37:50.8

30km
1	Johann Mühlegg ESP	1:09:28.9
2	Christian Hoffman AUT	1:11:31.0
3	Mikhail Botvinov AUT	1:11:32.3

50km
1	Mikhail Ivanov RUS	2:06:20.8
2	Andrus Veerpalu EST	2:06:44.5
3	Odd-Bjoern Hjelmeset NOR	2:08:41.5

Johann Mühlegg ESP finished first, but was later disqualified after a positive drugs test

4x10km Relay
1	Norway	1:32:45.5
2	Italy	1:32:45.8
3	Germany	1:33:34.5

Women

1.5km
1	Julija Tchepalova RUS	3:10.6
2	Evi Sachenbacher GER	3;12.2
3	Anita Moen NOR	3:12.7

10km Pursuit
1	Olga Danilova RUS	24:52.1
2	Larissa Lazutina RUS	24:59.0
3	Beckie Scott CAN	25:09.9

10km
1	Bente Skari NOR	28:05.6
2	Olga Danilova RUS	28:08.1
3	Julija Tchepalova RUS	28:09.9

15km
1	Stefania Belmondo ITA	39:54.4
2	Larissa Lazutina RUS	39:56.2
3	Katerina Neumannova CZE	40:01.3

30km
1	Gabriella Paruzzi ITA	1:30:57.1
2	Stefania Belmondo ITA	1:31:01.6
3	Anita Moen NOR	1:31:37.3

Larissa Lazutina ESP finished first; but was later disqualified for a drug positive; Olga Danilova who was eighth was also disqualified for a drugs positive

4x5km Relay
1	Germany	49:30.6
2	Norway	49:31.9
3	Switzerland	50:03.6

Figure Skating

Pairs
1	Elena Berezhnaya/Anton Sikharulidze RUS	N/A
1	Jamie Sale/David Pelletier CAN	N/A
3	Shen Xue/Zhao Hongbo CHN	4.5

Berezhnaya and Sikharulidze finished first on the night and were awarded the gold medals. Four days later, following doubts raised concerning the French judge's marking, the ISU Council determined that another pair of gold medals should be awarded to Sale and Pelletier. At the end of April, the ISU Council imposed a three-year suspension on the French judge, Marie Reine Le Gougne, for misconduct.

Men
1	Alexei Yagudin RUS	1.5
2	Evgeni Plushenko RUS	4.0
3	Timothy Goebel USA	4.5

Women
1	Sarah Hughes USA	3.0
2	Irina Slutskaya RUS	3.0
3	Michelle Kwan USA	3.5

Though Hughes and Slutskaya had equal marks, Hughes took the gold medal as she finished ahead in the free programme

Ice Dancing
1	Marina Anissina/Gwenday Peizerat FRA	2.0
2	Irina Lobacheva/Ilia Averbukh RUS	4.0
3	Babara Fusar Poli/Maurizio Margaglio ITA	6.0

Freestyle Skiing

Men

Moguls
1	Janne Lahtela FIN	27.97
2	Travis Mayer USA	27.59
3	Richard Gay FRA	26.91

DNQ: Sam Temple GBR (29th)

Aerials
1	Ales Valenta CZE	257.02	(127.04/129.98)
2	Joe Pack USA	251.64	(129.49/122.15)
3	Alexei Grichin BLR	251.19	(129.71/121.48)

Women

Moguls
1	Kari Traa NOR	25.94
2	Shannon Bahrke USA	25.06
3	Tae Satoya JPN	24.95

DNQ: Joanne Bromfield GBR (28th), Laura Donaldson GBR (29th)

Aerials
1	Alisa Camplin AUS	193.47	(93.72/99.75)
2	Veronica Brenner CAN	190.02	(90.09/99.93)
3	Deirdra Dionne CAN	189.26	(88.98/100.28)

Ice Hockey

Men

In the preliminary round, the teams ranked 7-14 play off in two groups (A & B) with the winners joining the top six ranked teams in the final round. Those eight teams play in two groups (C & D) with the final group placings determining the quarter-final games (1st in group C plays 4th in group D, etc).

Group A
Germany bt Slovakia 3-0; Latvia bt Austria 4-2; Germany bt Austria 3-2; Latvia drew with Slovakia 6-6; Austria bt Slovakia 3-2; Germany bt Latvia 4-1

Group A Table
		P	W	L	D	GF	GA	Pts
1	Germany	3	3	0	0	10	3	6
2	Latvia	3	2	0	1	11	12	3
3	Austria	3	1	2	0	7	9	2
4	Slovakia	3	0	2	1	8	12	1

Group B
Belarus bt Ukraine 1-0; Switzerland drew with France 3-3; Ukraine bt Switzerland 5-2; Belarus bt France 3-1; Switzerland bt Austria 2-1; Ukraine bt France 4-2

Group B Table
		P	W	L	D	GF	GA	Pts
1	Belarus	3	2	1	0	5	3	4
2	Ukraine	3	2	1	0	9	5	4
3	Switzerland	3	1	1	1	7	9	3
4	France	3	0	2	1	6	10	1

Group C
Sweden bt Canada 5-2; Czech Rep bt Germany 8-2; Sweden bt Czech Rep 2-1; Canada bt Germany 3-2; Czech Rep drew with Canada 3-3; Sweden bt Germany 7-1

Group C Table
		P	W	L	D	GF	GA	Pts
1	Sweden	3	3	0	0	14	4	6
2	Czech Republic	3	1	1	1	12	7	3
3	Canada	3	1	1	1	8	10	3
4	Germany	3	0	3	0	5	18	0

Group D
Russia bt Belarus 6-4; USA bt Finland 6-0; Finland bt Belarus 8-1; USA drew with Russia 2-2; USA bt Belarus 8-1; Finland bt Russia 3-1

Group D Table
		P	W	L	D	GF	GA	Pts
1	USA	3	2	0	1	16	3	5
2	Finland	3	2	1	0	11	8	4
3	Russia	3	1	1	1	9	9	3
4	Belarus	3	0	3	0	6	22	0

13/14th Place Game
Slovakia 7   France 1
11/12th Place Game
Switzerland 4   Austria 1
9/10th Place Game
Latvia 9   Ukraine 2

Quarter-finals
Belarus 4	Sweden 3
Russia 1	Czech Rep 0
USA 5	Germany 0
Canada 2	Finland 1

Semi-finals
Canada 7	Belarus 1
USA 3	Russia 2

Bronze Medal Game
Russia 7   Belarus 2

FINAL
Canada 5   USA 2

Women

There were just eight teams in the women's competition playing the first round in two groups (A & B). The top two teams in each group progressed to the semi-finals.

Group A
Canada bt Kazakhstan 7-0; Sweden bt Russia 3-2; Canada bt Russia 7-0; Sweden bt Kazakhstan 7-0; Russia bt Kazakhstan 4-1; Canada bt Sweden 11-0

Group A Table
		P	W	L	D	GF	GA	Pts
1	Canada	3	3	0	0	25	0	6
2	Sweden	3	2	1	0	10	13	4
3	Russia	3	1	2	0	6	11	2
4	Kazakhstan	3	0	3	0	1	18	0

Group B
USA bt Germany 10-0; Finland bt China 4-0; Finland bt Germany 3-1; USA bt China 12-1; USA bt Finland 5-1; Germany drew with China 5-5

Group B Table
		P	W	L	D	GF	GA	Pts
1	USA	3	3	0	0	27	1	6
2	Finland	3	2	1	0	7	6	4
3	Germany	3	0	2	1	6	18	1
4	China	3	0	2	1	6	21	1

Classification Games
Russia 4	China 1
Germany 4	Kazakhstan 0

7/8th Place Game
China 2   Kazakhstan 1
5/6th Place Game
Russia 5   Germany 0

Bronze Medal Game
Sweden 2   Finland 1

FINAL
Canada 3   USA 2

Luge

The men's singles has four runs; the doubles and the women's singles just two runs.

Men
Singles
1 Armin Zoeggeler ITA   2:57.941
(44.546/44.521/44.296/44.578)
2 Georg Hackl GER   2:58.270
(44.614/44.494/44.487/44.675)
3 Markus Prock AUT   2:58.283
(44.698/44.640/44.271/44.674)
25 Mark Hatton GBR   3:01.566
(45.391/45.509/45.107/45.559)

Doubles
1 Leitner/Resch GER   1:26.082
(42.953/43.129)
2 Grimmette/Martin USA   1:26.216
(43.111/43.105)
3 Thorpe/Ives USA   1:26.220
(43.013/43.207)

Women
Singles
1 Sylke Otto GER   2:52.464
(43.356/43.076/42.940/43.092)
2 Bart Niedernhuber GER   2:52.785
(43.346/43.134/43.215/43.090)
3 Silke Kraushaar GER   2:52.865
(43.294/43.224/43.195/43.152)

Nordic Combined

The overall time is given below, plus the points and placing for the jump, and the time and placing for the cross-country skiing. The team event features a K120 jump followed by a 4 x 5km relay.

Men
Individual
1 Samppa Lajunen FIN   39:11.7
(257-3/38:18.7-6)
2 Jaakko Tallus FIN   39:36.4
(267.5-1/39:36.4-20)
3 Felix Gottwald AUT   40:02.5
(235-11/37:23.5-1)

Team
1 Finland   48:42.2
Lajunen/Manninen/Mantila/Tallus
(967.5-1/48:42.2-1)
2 Germany   48:49.7
Ackermann/Hettich/Hoehlig/Kircheisen
(893.5-5/46:58.7-2)
3 Austria   48:53.2
Bieler/Gottwald/Gruber/Stecher
(938.5-2/48:09.2-3)

Sprint
1 Samppa Lajunen FIN   16:40.1
(123.8-1/16:40.1-16)
2 Ronny Ackermann GER   16:49.1
(119.9-2/16:34.1-9)
3 Felix Gottwald AUT   17:20.3
(110.3-11/16:29.3-5)

Skeleton
Men
1 Jim Shea USA   1:41.96 (50.89/51.07)
2 Martin Rettl AUT   1:42.01 (51.02/50.99)
3 Gregor Staehli SUI   1:42.15 (51.16/50.99)
13 Kristan Bromley GBR   1:43.43 (52.17/51.26)

Women
1 Tristan Gale USA   1:45.11 (52.26/52.85)
2 Lea Ann Parsley USA   1:45.21 (52.27/52.94)
3 Alex Coomber GBR   1:45.37 (52.48/52.89)

Snowboard
Men
Parallel Giant Slalom
1 Philipp Schoch SUI
2 Richard Richardsson SWE
3 Chris Klug USA

Halfpipe
1 Ross Powers USA   46.1
2 Danny Kass USA   42.5
3 Jarret Thomas USA   42.1

Women
Parallel Giant Slalom
1 Isabelle Blanc FRA
2 Karine Ruby FRA
3 Lidia Trettel ITA

Halfpipe
1 Kelly Clark USA   47.9
2 Doriane Vidal FRA   43.0
3 Fabienne Reuteler SUI   39.7
17 Lesley McKenna GBR   25.3

Ski Jumping

Jumpers receive points for distance and style, but it is invariably distance which wins competitions. The total points decide the order, as well as the total points below we also show the distance of both jumps and the points totals (distance+style) for each.

Individual K90
1 Simon Ammann SUI   269.0pts
(98m/133.5 + 98.5m/135.5)
2 Sven Hannewald GER   267.5pts
(97m/131 + 99m/136.5)
3 Adam Malysz POL   263.0pts
(98.5m/129.5 + 98m/133.5)
DNQ: Glyn Pedersen GBR 88.0pts (78.5m) 43rd in qlfy

Individual K120
1 Simon Ammann SUI   281.4pts
(132.5m/140.5 + 133m/140.9)
2 Adam Malysz POL   269.7pts
(131m/137.3 + 128m/132.4)
3 Matti Hautamaeki FIN   256.0pts
(127m/129.1 + 125m/126.9)
Glyn Pedersen GBR 56.3pts (91m),48th in qlfy

Team K120
1 Germany   974.1pts
Hannewald/Hocke/Uhrmann/Schmitt
2 Finland   974.0pts
Hautamaeki/Lindstroem/Jussilainen/Ahonen
3 Slovenia   946.3pts
Fras/Peterka/Kranjec/Zonta
Best distance in the team event: Martin Schmitt GER 131.5m

Speed Skating
Long Track
Men
500m

1	Casey Fitzrandolph USA	1:09.23	(34.42/34.81)
2	Hiroyasu Shimizu JPN	1:09.26	(34.61/34.65)
3	Kip Carpenter USA	1:09.47	(34.68/34.79)

1000m

1	Gerard van Velde NED	1:07.18
2	Jan Bos NED	1:07.53
3	Joey Cheek USA	1:07.61

1500m

1	Derek Parra USA	1:43.95
2	Jochem Uytedhaage NED	1:44.57
3	Adne Sondral NOR	1:45.26

5000m

1	Jochem Uytedehaage NED	6:14.66
2	Derek Parra USA	6:17.98
3	Jens Boden GER	6:21.73

10,000m

1	Jochem Uytedehaage NED	12:58.92
2	Gianni Romme NED	13:10.03
3	Lasse Saetre NOR	13:16.92

Women
500m

1	Catriona Lemay Doan CAN	1:14.75	(37.30/37.45)
2	Monique Garbrecht-Enfeldt GER	1:14.94	(37.34/37.60)
3	Andrea Nuyt NED	1:15.19	(37.62/37.57)

1000m

1	Chris Witty USA	1:13.83
2	Sabine Voelker GER	1:13.96
3	Jennifer Rodriguez USA	1:14.24

1500m

1	Anni Freisinger GER	1:54.02
2	Sabine Voelker GER	1:54.97
3	Jennifer Rodriguez USA	1:55.32

3000m

1	Claudia Pechstein GER	3:57.70
2	Renate Groenewald NED	3:58.94
3	Cindy Klassen CAN	3:58.97

5000m

1	Claudia Pechstein GER	6:46.91
2	Gretha Smit NED	6:49.22
3	Clara Hughes CAN	6:53.53

Short Track
Men
500m

1	Marc Gagnon CAN	41.802
2	Jonathan Guilmette CAN	41.994
3	Rusty Smith USA	42.027

Dave Allardice GBR eliminated heats
Leon Flack GBR eliminated heats

1000m

1	Steven Bradbury AUS	1:29.109
2	Apolo Anton Ohno USA	1:30.160
3	Mathieu Turcotte CAN	1:30.563

Nicky Gooch GBR eliminated heats
Flack eliminated semi-finals

1500m

1	Apolo Anton Ohno USA	2:27.155
2	Li Jiajun CHN	2:27.376
3	Marc Gagnon CAN	2:27.611

Flack eliminated heats
Gooch eliminated semi-finals

5000m Relay

1	Canada	6:51.579
	Bedard/Gagnon/Guilmette/Tremblay/Turcotte	
2	Italy	6:56.327
	Antonioli/Carnino/Carta/Franceschina/Rodigari	
3	China	6:59.633
	An/Feng/Guo/Li/Li	

Women
500m

1	Yang Yang (A) CHN	44.930
2	Evgenia Radanova BUL	45.383
3	Wang Chunlu CHN	45.494

Joanna Williams GBR eliminated heats
Sarah Lindsay GBR eliminated quarter-finals

1000m

1	Yang Yang (A) CHN	1:36.391
2	Ko Gi-Hyun KOR	1:36.427
3	Yang Yang (S) CHN	1:37.008

Williams and Lindsay eliminated quarter-finals

1500m

1	Ko Gi-Hyun KOR	2:31.581
2	Choi Eun-Kyung KOR	2:31.610
3	Evgenia Radanova BUL	2:31.723

Williams and Lindsay eliminated heats

3000m Relay

1	Korea	**4:12.793**
	Choi/Choi/Joo/Park	
2	China	4:13.236
	Sun/Wang/Yang/Yang	
3	Canada	4:15.738
	Charest/Drolet/Goulet-Nadon/Kraus/Vicent	

American Football

The Patriots beat the Rams, and you have to go back to 1969 when the New York Jets overturned the Baltimore Colts to find anything comparable. St Louis had won a Super Bowl only two seasons before, and were rated 14 points better than the New England team, and while many of the 72,000 spectators passionately desired a Patriots victory few believed it possible till Adam Vinatieri's field goal sailed over to make it 20-17 with only seconds on the clock.

The Patriots coach Bill Belichick had no compunction in adopting a defensive strategy for this game. The team he was facing in New Orleans had averaged 33 points per game over the past three years. Gambling that the Patriots would get 34 was far too risky a strategy. Besides, Belichick's thoughts have long concerned prevention rather than cure. In 1987 and 1991, he had acted as defensive co-ordinator for the New Yorks Giants in their Super Bowl wins, so he was well versed in the art.

Throughout the game, Belichick shuffled his defensive pack repeatedly; Terry Venables would have been proud of some of the formations he dreamt up. Kurt Warner, apparently confused by the New England defensive patterns, repeatedly clung on to the ball and didn't throw a touchdown pass (and he only threw one) until the game was in its 59th minute. Meanwhile, the Patriots capitalised on mistakes to score two touchdowns in the second period, and with field goals in the first and third period, entered the final phase of the game with a 17-3 lead.

In the fourth quarter, the Patriots could have gone still further ahead, but a 98-yard run from Tebucky Jones was ruled out for illegal holding. Only then did the Rams stir; touchdowns in the 51st and 59th minutes bringing the scores level for about 90 seconds, till Vinatieri settled it.

Tom Brady, the New England quarterback took the MVP award, and in relative terms was probably the poorest paid winner ever, only considered by the management to be worth a paltry $300,000 a year.

Brady had stepped early in the regular season when Drew Bledsoe (salary $10m a year) had punctured an artery in his chest and was sidelined. And tragically, the coach to Brady and Bledsoe, the 45-year-old Dick Rehbein had died at the start of the season. It was a very different mood in the Patriots camp then.

> **"Every kicker knows the Scott Norwood situation. In the last few nights, I woke up sweating..."**
>
> Adam Vinatieri, whose 48-yard field goal in the final seconds gave the Patriots victory in Super Bowl XXXVI. Scott Norwood was the Buffalo Bills kicker in the 1991 Super Bowl who missed a 47-yard kick eight seconds from time, which gifted the game to the New York Giants 20-19. Norwood has said that not a day has passed since without him thinking about that miss.

Super Bowl XXXVI

New England Patriots 20
St Louis Rams 17

Louisiana Superdome, New Orleans
Feb 3
Attendance: 72,922

TEAMS

St Louis	Offense	New England
Torry Holt	WR	Troy Brown
Orlando Pace	LT	Matt Light
Tom Nutten	LG	Mike Compton
Andy McCollum	C	Damien Woody
Adam Timmerman	RG	Joe Andruzzi
Ron Jones	OT-RT	Greg Randall
Ernie Conwell	TE-WR	Jermaine Wiggins
Isaac Bruce	WR	David Patten
Kurt Warner	QB	Tom Brady
James Hodgins	FB	Marc Edwards
Marshall Faulk	RB	Antowain Smith

St Louis	Defense	New England
Cidi Ahanotu	LDE-LE	Bobby Hamilton
Brian Young	LDT-LT	Brandon Mitchell
Jeff Zgonina	RDT-RT	Richard Seymour
Grant Wistrom	RED-RE	Anthony Pleasant
Don Davis	LLB-MLB	Mike Vrabel
London Fletcher	MLB-OLB	Tedy Bruschi
Tommy Polley	RLB-CB	Roman Phifer
Aeneas Williams	LCB	Ty Law
Dexter McCleon	RCB	Otis Smith
Adam Archuleta	SS	Lawyer Milloy
Kim Herring	FS	Tebucky Jones

SUBSTITUTIONS

St Louis
John Baker, Dre Bly, O J Briggance, Jerametrius Butler, Trung Canidate, Mark Fields, Frank Garcia, Willie Gary, Az-Zahir Hakim, Robert Holcombe, Tyoka Jackson, Leonard Little, Brandon Manumaleuna, Sean Moran, Yo Murphy, Ryan Pickett, Ricky Proehl, Jeff Robinson, Nick Sorenson, Cameron Spikes, Ryan Tucker, Jeff Wilkins
Did Not Play: Jamie Martin

New England
Terrell Buckley, Matt Chatham, Je'Rod Cherry, Fred Coleman, Bryan Cox, Kevin Faulk, Antwan Harris, Larry Izzo, Charles Johnson, Ted Johnson, Willie McGinest, Patrick Pass, Lonie Paxton, J R Redmond, Grey Ruegamer, Rod Routledge, Terrance Shaw, Matt Stevens, Adam Vinatieri, Ken Walter, Grant Williams
Did Not Play: Drew Bledsoe, Riddick Parker

MVP: Tom Brady New England QB

Scoring

ST LOUIS	3	0	0	14	17
NEW ENGLAND	0	14	3	3	20

First Quarter
STL: FG Wilkins 50yds, 11:50
Second Quarter
NE: Law 47yd Interception return (Vinatieri kick) 6:11
NE: Patten 8yd pass from Brady (Vinatieri kick) 14:29
Third Quarter
NE: FG Vinatieri 37yds, 13:42
Fourth Quarter
STL: Warner 2yd run (Wilkins kick), 5:29
STL: Proehl 26yd pass from Warner (Wilkins kick), 13:30
NE: FG Vinatieri 48yds, 15:00

Team Statistics

	St Louis	New England
Total First Downs	26	15
Total Net Yardage	427	267
Total Offensive Plays	69	54
- Average Gain	6.2	4.9
Rushes	22	25
- Yards Gained	90	133
Passes Attempted	44	27
- Passes Completed	28	16
- Yards Gained	337	134
Punts	4	8
- Average Distance	39.8	43.1
Punt Returns	3	1
- Return Yardage	6	4
Kickoff Returns	4	4
- Return Yardage	82	100
Penalties	6	5
- Yards Penalised	39	31
Time Of Possession	33:30	26:30

Individual Statistics

PASSING

St Louis	Att	Cp	Yds	TD	IN
K Warner	44	28	365	1	2
New England					
T Brady	27	16	145	1	0

RUSHING

St Louis	No	Yds	Av	TD
M Faulk	17	76	15	0
New England				
A Smith	18	92	17	0

RECEIVING

St Louis	No	Yds	Lg	TD
A Hakim	5	90	29	0
New England				
T Brown	6	89	23	0

NFL Final League Standings 2001

NATIONAL FOOTBALL CONFERENCE

Eastern Division

	W	L	T	Pct	PF	PA
Philadelphia Eagles*	11	5	0	.688	343	208
Washington Redskins	8	8	0	.500	256	303
Arizona Cardinals	7	9	0	.438	295	343
New York Giants	7	9	0	.438	294	321
Dallas Cowboys	5	11	0	.312	246	338

Central Division

	W	L	T	Pct	Pts	OP
Chicago Bears	13	3	0	.812	338	203
Green Bay Packers*	12	4	0	.750	390	266
Tampa Bay Buchs*	9	7	0	.562	324	280
Minnesota Vikings	5	11	0	.312	290	390
Detroit Lions	2	14	0	.125	270	424

Western Division

	W	L	T	Pct	Pts	OP
St Louis Rams	14	2	0	.875	503	273
San Francisco 49ers*	12	4	0	.750	409	282
New Orleans Saints	7	9	0	.438	333	409
Atlanta Falcons	7	9	0	.438	291	377
Carolina Panthers	1	15	0	.063	253	410

AMERICAN FOOTBALL CONFERENCE

Eastern Division

	W	L	T	Pct	PF	PA
New England Patriots	11	5	0	.688	371	272
Miami Dolphins*	11	5	0	.688	344	290
New York Jets*	10	6	0	.625	308	295
Indianapolis Colts	6	10	0	.375	413	486
Buffalo Bills	3	13	0	.188	265	420

Central Division

	W	L	T	Pct	PF	PA
Pittsburgh Steelers	13	3	0	.812	352	212
Baltimore Ravens*	10	6	0	.625	303	265
Tennessee Titans	7	9	0	.438	336	388
Cleveland Browns	7	9	0	.438	285	319
Cincinnati Bengals	6	10	0	.375	226	309
Jacksonville Jaguars	6	10	0	.375	294	286

Western Division

	W	L	T	Pct	Pts	OP
Oakland Raiders*	10	6	0	.625	399	327
Seattle Seahawks	9	7	0	.562	301	324
Denver Broncos	8	8	0	.500	340	339
Kansas City Chiefs	6	10	0	.375	320	344
San Diego Chargers	5	11	0	.312	332	321

Wild card qualifier for play-offs; teams in bold go straight through to Divisional play-offs.

NFL Play-off Games

NATIONAL FOOTBALL CONFERENCE
Wild Card Play-off Games
Jan 12
Green Bay Packers 25   San Francisco 49ers 15
Philadelphia Eagles 31   Tampa Bay Buccaneers 9
Divisional Play-off Games
Jan 19
Philadelphia Eagles 33   Chicago Bears 19
Jan 20
St Louis Rams 45   Green Bay Packers 17
NFC Championship Game
Jan 27
St Louis Rams 29   Philadelphia Eagles 24

AMERICAN FOOTBALL CONFERENCE
Wild Card Play-off Games
Jan 13
Oakland Raiders 38   New York Jets 24
Miami Dolphins 3   Baltimore Ravens 21
Divisional Play-off Games
Jan 19
NE Patriots 16   Oakland Raiders 13
Jan 20
Pittsburgh Steelers 27   Baltimore Ravens 10
AFC Championship Game
Jan 27
NE Patriots 24   Pittsburgh Steelers 17

Football Briefing

Subscriptions:

Trevor Kendall, 2 Drury Close, Waltham, Grimsby DN37 0XP

Regular Season Statistics

AMERICAN FOOTBALL CONFERENCE

Leading Passers	Att	Cp	Pct	Yds	Av	TD
Gannon (Oak)	412	274	66.5	3042	7.38	23
McNair (Ten)	361	222	61.5	2725	7.55	17
Brady (NE)	365	236	64.7	2537	6.95	16
Brunel (Jax)	376	231	61.4	2620	6.97	15
Manning (Ind)	454	287	63.2	3517	7.75	23
Stewart (Pitt)	365	222	60.8	2560	7.01	8

Leading Rushers	Att	Yds	Av	Lg	TD
Holmes (KC)	254	1267	5.0	41	7
C Martin (NYJ)	274	1218	4.4	36	10
Bettis (Pitt)	225	1072	4.8	48	4

Receiving Yards	Yds	No	Av	Lg	TD
R Smith (Den)	1195	98	12.2	65t	10
Harrison (Ind)	1173	83	14.1	68	12
Jimmy Smith (Jax)	1137	92	12.4	35t	7

Touchdowns	TD	Rus	Rec	Ref	X2	Pts
Alexander (Sea)	13	12	1	0	0	78
Harrison (ind)	12	0	12	0	0	72
Dillon (Cin)	11	8	3	0	0	66

Kicking	Pat	FG	Lg	Pts
Elam (Den)	28/28	27/31	50	109
K Brown (Pitt)	23/24	27/39	55	104
Janikowski (Oak)	39/39	21/23	52	102

AMERICAN FOOTBALL CONFERENCE

Leading Passers	Att	Cp	Pct	Yds	Av	TD
Warner (St L)	463	309	66.7	3974	8.58	28
Favre (GB)	424	264	62.3	3300	7.78	27
Garcia (SF)	423	267	63.1	2910	6.88	25
Brooks (NO)	459	256	55.8	3338	7.27	22
McNabb (Phi)	420	241	57.4	2731	6.50	22
Chandler (Atl)	314	188	59.9	2365	7.53	14

Leading Rushers	Att	Yds	Av	Lg	TD
Davies (Was)	275	1116	4.1	32	2
R Williams (NO)	275	1112	4.0	46	6
Green (GB)	243	1103	4.5	83t	6

Receiving Yards	Yds	No	Av	Lg	TD
Boston (Ariz)	1387	86	16.1	52	6
K Johnson (TB)	1196	100	12.0	47	1
Moss (Min)	1180	75	15.7	73t	10

Touchdowns	TD	Rus	Rec	Ret	X2	Pts
Faulk (St L)	14	6	8	0	1	86
Owens (SF)	13	0	13	0	0	78
Moss (Min)	10	0	10	0	0	60

Kicking	Pat	FG	Lg	Pts
Carney (NO)	28/28	26/29	50	106
Wilkins (St L)	43/43	21/24	54	106
Akers (Phi)	32/33	23/25	50	101

World League

Apr 13	
Berlin 24	Frankfurt 27
Rhein Fire 10	Amsterdam 27

Apr 14
Barcelona 17 Claymores 45

Apr 20
Frankfurt 54 Barcelona 14
Amsterdam 24 Berlin 19
Claymores 10 Rhein Fire 13

Apr 27
Amsterdam 27 Barcelona 30
Rhein Fire 20 Berlin 16
Claymores 9 Frankfurt 16

May 3
Berlin 28 Amsterdam 9
Barcelona 3 Rhein Fire 31
Frankfurt 14 Claymores 10

May 11
Claymores 16 Amsterdam 13
Frankfurt 20 Rhein Fire 24

May 12
Barcelona 14 Berlin 24

May 18
Berlin 24 Barcelona 17
Rhein Fire 7 Claymores 17

May 19
Amsterdam 19 Frankfurt 21

May 25
Barcelona 31 Frankfurt 10

May 26
Amsterdam 13 Claymores 17
Berlin 14 Rhein Fire 24

June 1
Rhein Fire 24 Barcelona 21
Frankfurt 20 Amsterdam 13

June 2
Claymores 23 Berlin 31

June 8
Barcelona 31 Amsterdam 45
Rhein Fire 3 Frankfurt 0

June 9
Berlin 24 Claymores 23

June 15
Claymores 27 Barcelona 24
Frankfurt 7 Berlin 27
Amsterdam 28 Rhein Fire 10

Final Table	W	L	T	PF	PA
Rhein Fire	7	3	0	166	156
Berlin Thunder	6	4	0	231	188
Frankfurt Galaxy	6	4	0	189	174
Scot Claymores	5	5	0	197	172
Amsterdam A	4	6	0	218	202
FC Barcelona	2	8	0	202	311

World Bowl 2002

Dusseldorf   June 22
Attendance: 58,572

Berlin Thunder 26
Rhein Fire 20

Scoring	1	2	3	4	OT	
Berlin	13	7	3	3	0	**26**
Rhein	0	0	7	13	0	**20**

Scoring Plays
BT: 1st, 11:32, Boyd 47yd FG
BT: 1st, 5:01, Looker 41yd pass from T.Husak (A.Kruse kick)
BT: 1st, 0:59, Kruse 27yd FG
BT: 2nd, 1:56, Looker 15yd pass from T.Husak (A.Kruse kick)
RF: 3rd, 4:39, Taylor 6yd run (J.Witzcak kick)
BT: 3rd, 0:26, Boyd 45yd FG
RF: 4th, 10:40, Cloman 2yd pass from T.Martin (pass failed)
BT: 4th, 8:00, Boyd 38yd FG
RF: 4, 0:20, Martin 1yd run (M.Burgsmuller kick)

Angling

Fly Fishing

World Championships

Vologne River, La Bresse, France
Aug 13-20
Individual
1   Jerome Brossutti FRA
2   Tomas Starychfojtu CZE
3   Bernard Marguet FRA
8   John Tyzack ENG
20 Ian Jones SCO

Team
1   France
2   Belgium
3   Spain
9   Scotland
10 England
15 Wales

Coarse Fishing

World Championships
MEN
Mondego River, Coimbra, Portugal
Sept 14-15

Individual		kg
1	Juan Blasco ESP	12.060
2	Juan Duran ESP	12.000
3	Stu Conroy ENG	9.222
10	Steve Gardener ENG	9.900

Team		pts
1	Spain	52.5
2	Portugal	55.5
3	Belgium	74
4	England	84
8	Wales	123
21	Ireland	188.5
26	Scotland	215.5
29	Channel Islands	235.5

Six Nations

Furzedon Park Lake, Milton Keynes
Aug 10-11
Team
1   England   22pts
2   France   31
3   Belgium   37
4   Ireland   40
5   Wales   57
6   Scotland   63

National Championships

DIVISION 1, MEN
Basingstoke Canal, Aug 17

Individual		kg
1	Mick Evans (Bury)	11.160
2	Graham Welton (RAF)	8.250
3	Jimmy Byrne (Lymm AC)	6.960
4	Phil Leak (Wigan)	6.860
5	Steve Welford (Browning Hotrods)	6.640
6	P Phillip (Loughborough)	6.350

Team
1   Shakespeare Redditch   592
2   Daiwa Gordon League   589
3   Wigan & District   545
4   Tek-Neek Trabucco   534
5   Oakwood NJC   528
6   Barnsley & District   523

Archery

European Target Championships

Oulu, Finland, July 22-27

Recurve (Olympic)

MEN'S INDIVIDUAL
Qualification Round

1	Ilario di Buo	ITA	678
2	Michele Frangilli	ITA	673
3	Wietse van Alten	NED	667
7	Laurence Godfrey	GBR	657
8	Ian Crowther	GBR	656
15	Roy Nash	GBR	651
40	Simon Needham	GBR	639

1st Round
Simon Needham bt Mitrofanov Guennadi RUS 161-157
Ian Crowther bt Kirt Cahille LUX 154-145
Laurence Godfrey bt Hatava Matti FIN 160-153
Lionel Torres FRA bt Roy Nash 168-156
2nd Round
Simon Needham bt Ian Crowther 160-157
Marklyan Ivashko UKR bt Laurence Godfrey 163-154
3rd Round
Martin Hornak SVK bt Simon Needham 163-158
Semi-Finals
Michele Frangilli ITA bt Wietse van Alten NED 109-101
Balijinima Tsyrempilov RUS bt Ilario di Buo ITA 111-99
Bronze Medal Match
Ilario de Buo ITA bt Wietse van Alten NED 97-91
Final
Michele Frangilli ITA bt B Tsyrempilov RUS 104-91

MEN'S TEAM
Qualification Round

1	Italy	2010
2	Great Britain	1964
	Godfrey/Crowther/Nash	
3	Russia	1955

1st Round
Great Britain bt Bulgaria 248-242
Quarter-Finals
France bt Great Britain 252-245
Semi-Finals
France bt Ukraine 235-235 *Shoot-off*
Netherlands bt italy 245-242
Bronze Medal Match
Italy bt Ukraine 242-239
Final
France bt Netherlands 246-227

WOMEN'S INDIVIDUAL
Qualification round

1	Natalia Valeeva	ITA	671
2	Kateryna Palekha	UKR	655
3	Iwona Marcinkiewicz	POL	654
15	Naomi Folkard	GBR	635
24	Alison Williamson	GBR	619
26	Lana Needham	GBR	617
42	Vlada Priestman	GBR	593

1st Round
Alison Williamson bt Olga Ladigina GEO 164-143
Elif Altinkaynak TUR bt Lana Needham 161-145
Naomi Folkard bt Sabine Mayrhofer AUT 150-145
2nd Round
Alison Williamson bt Wioletta Myszor POL 161-156
Natalia Bolotova RUS bt Naomi Folkard 159-147
3rd Round
Alison Williamson bt Kateryna Serduyk UKR 160-151
Quarter-Finals
Natalia Valeeva ITA bt Alison Williamson 112-98
Semi-Finals
Derya Sarialtin TUR bt Natalia Bolotova RUS 103-99
Natalia Valeeva ITA bt Yustuna Mospinek POL 105-98
Bronze Medal Match
Natalia Bolotova RUS bt Yustuna Mospinek 96-93
Final
Natalia Valeeva ITA bt Derya Sarialtin TUR 94-85

World Target Rankings

As at September 20, 2002
Recurve (Olympic); British shown in top 50

Men

1	Lionel Torres	FRA	168.000
2	Michele Frangilli	ITA	164.500
3	Ilario di Buo	ITA	164.100
4	Baljinima Tsyrempilov	RUS	137.050
5	Yeon Jung-Ki	KOR	130.500
6	Wietse van Alten	NED	113.050
7	Dennis Bager	DEN	112.500
8	Victor Wunderle	USA	111.000
9	Nico Hendrickx	BEL	99.500
10	Park Kyung-Mo	KOR	93.275
12	Simon Needham	GBR	84.113

Women

1	Park Sung-Hyun	KOR	182.000
2	Natalia Valeeva	ITA	167.500
3	Yun Mi-Yin	KOR	160.000
4	Alison Williamson	GBR	151.900
5	Zhang Juan Juan	CHN	136.500
6	Katerina Paleha	UKR	132.950
7	Natalia Nasaridze	TUR	121.200
8	Choi Jin	KOR	115.000
9	He Ying	CHN	112.000
10	Park Hey-Youn	KOR	102.000

WOMEN'S TEAM
Qualification Round

1	Poland	1939
2	Ukraine	1907
3	Turkey	1906
7	Great Britain	1871

1st Round
Great Britain bt Belarus 242-221
2nd Round
Ukraine bt Great Britain 246-237
Semi-Finals
Russia bt Ukraine 239-233
Poland bt Germany 245-236
Bronze Medal match
Ukraine bt Germany 236-222
Final
Russia bt Poland 231-221

Compound

MEN'S INDIVIDUAL
Qualification round

1	Jari Haavisto	FIN	689
4	Chris White	GBR	687
10	Simon Tarplee	GBR	680

1st Round
Chris White bt Dmytro Skvortsov UKR 169-158
Simon Tarplee bt Bato Namsaraev RUS 175-163
2nd round
Chris White bt Terje Röstad NOR 172-166
Morgan Lundlin SWE bt Simon Tarplee 173-172
3rd Round
Anders Malm SWE bt Chris White 175-173
Semi-Finals
Michele Palumbo ITA bt Fred van Zutphen NED 110-109
Björn Andersson SWE bt Anders Malm SWE 114-109
Bronze Medal Match
Fred van Zutphen NED bt Anders Malm SWE 108-99
Final
Michele Palumbo ITA bt Björn Andersson SWE 113-104

MEN'S TEAM
Qualification round

1	Denmark	2041
2	Spain	2033
3	Netherlands	2032

Semi-Finals
Netherlands bt Germany 253-253 *Shoot-off*
Slovenia bt France 255-253
Bronze Medal Match
France bt Germany 251-244
Final
Netherlands bt Slovenia 250-233

WOMEN'S INDIVIDUAL
Qualification round
Top 32 qualify for knock-out rounds

1	Sirkka Sotta-Matikainen	FIN	669
15	Katy Moir	GBR	646
36	Nicola Simpson	GBR	624

1st Round
Katy Moir bt Bettina Thiele GER 163-156
2nd Round
Petra Dortmund GER bt Katy Moir GBR 164-161
Semi-Finals
Petra Dortmund GER bt Catherine Pellen FRA 111-107
Anna-Liisa Tuuttu FIN bt Giorgia Solato ITA 109-107

Bronze Medal Match
Catherine Pellen FRA bt Giorgia Solato ITA 107-99
Final
Anna-Liisa Tuuttu FIN bt Petra Dortmund GER 105-96

WOMEN'S TEAM
Qualification round

1	Finland	1970
2	Germany	1964
3	Russia	1959

Semi-Finals
Russia bt Germany 266-247
Finland bt France 252-245
Bronze Medal Match
France bt Germany 247-238
Final
Russia bt Finland 247-240

European Indoor Target Championships

Ankara, March 13-17

Recurve

MEN'S INDIVIDUAL
Qualification Round
1 Marco Galiazzo ITA 591; 10 Roy Nash GBR 584;
18 Neil Bridgewater GBR 580; 28 Michael Peart GBR 571
1st Round
Michael Peart bt Javier Fernandez ESP 175-174
Neil Bridgewater bt Yaron Kolesnick ISR 174-170
2nd Round
Michael Peart bt Kresimir Strukelj CRO 172-167
Berenger Chailliot FRA bt Neil Bridgewater 177-170
Final Standings
1 Viktor Ruban UKR; 2 Marco Galiazzo ITA;
3 Flavier Pothier FRA

MEN'S TEAM
Final Standings
1 Italy; 2 France; 3 Great Britain

WOMEN'S INDIVIDUAL
Qualification Round
1 Natalia Valeeva ITA 590; 5 Naomi Folkard GBR 579;
23 Lana Needham GBR 561
1st Round
Naomi Folkard bt Elpida Romantzi GRE 171-163
Barbara Kegelmann GER bt Lana Needham 173-169
2nd Round
Naomi Folkard bt Irene Franchini ITA 171-166
3rd Round
Tetyana Berezna UKR bt Naomi Folkard 118-111
Final Standings
1 Natalia Valeeva ITA; 2 Elena Dostai RUS;
3 Tetyana Berezna UKR

WOMEN'S TEAM
Final Standings
1 Ukraine; 2 Georgia; 3 Russia

Compound

MEN'S INDIVIDUAL
Qualification Round
1 Neils Baldur DEN 587; 8 Simon Scott GBR 581;
9 Chris Parkin GBR 581
1st Round
Simon Scott bt Antonio Gonzalez ESP 174-167
Simon Fankhauser SUI br Chris Parkin 174-172
2nd Round
Simon Fankhauser SUI bt Simon Scott 176-174
Final Standings
1 Tevz Grogl SLO; 2 Abu Torrijos ESP;
3 Simon Fankhauser SUI

MEN'S TEAM
Final Standings
1 France; 2 Spain; 3 Slovenia

WOMEN'S INDIVIDUAL
Qualification Round
1 Catherine Debrurck FRA 583;
2 Nicola Simpson GBR 579; 10 Sheila Harris GBR 566
15 Linda Garner GBR 561
1st Round
Almudena de Salvador ESP bt Sheila Harris 166-166 *27-26*
Nicola Simpson bt Linda Garner 170-169
2nd Round
Nicola Simpson bt Almudena de Salvador ESP 117-112
Semi-Final
Giorgio Solato bt Nicola Simpson 113-110
Final Standings
1 Olga Zandvliet NED; 2 Giorgia Solato ITA;
3 Nicola Simpson GBR

WOMEN'S TEAM
Final Standings
1 France; 2 Italy; 3 Great Britain

World Field Championships

Canberra, Sep 9-14
Only final standings given

Men

Recurve
1 Michele Frangilli ITA; 2 Sebastian Rohrberg GER;
3 Alan Wills GBR; 8 Jonathan Shales GBR;
20 Paul Kelly GBR

Compound
1 David Cousins USA; 2 Chris White GBR;
3 Stephane Dardenne FRA

Barebow
1 Martin Ottosson SWE; 2 Twan Cleven NED;
3 Danielle Bellotti ITA; 17 Peter Mulligan GBR;
22 Jeff Williams GBR

Teams
1 Sweden; 2 Germany; 3 Italy; 7 Great Britain

Women

Recurve
1 Laure Barczynski FRA; 2 Cristiana Loriatti ITA;
3 Irene Franchini ITA; 7 Alison Williamson GBR;
19 Gloria Mead GBR; 20 Jacqueline Wilkinson GBR

Compound
1 Catherine Pellen FRA; 2 Karin Teghammar SWE;
3 Anne Laurila FIN; 8 Maryann Richardson GBR;
11 Samantha Stretton GBR; 24 Ann Hartfield GBR

Barebow
1 Reingild Linhart AUT; 2 Monika Jentges GER;
3 Patricia Lovell GBR; 10 Marion Howells GBR;
20 Jane Rees GBR

Team
1 Sweden; 2 Austria; 3 Australia; 6 Great Britain

Association Football

In 1998, England set off for the World Cup with high expectations and came home disappointed; defeated by South American opponents at the knockout stage *(see World Cup review)*. More parallels with four years ago were not hard to find domestically. Then, Arsenal produced a remarkable late surge to overhaul Manchester United at the top of the Premiership and, once again, an extraordinary run of 13 consecutive victories gave Arsène Wenger's side the title and, as in 1998, they also added the FA Cup to their haul.

It was Arsène Wenger's second Double, and justly earned. Chelsea were the victims in the FA Cup Final, matching Arsenal for about 20 minutes, but gradually wilting. Ray Parlour and Freddie Ljungberg scored the goals in the final 20 minutes and Arsenal's defence, marshalled for the last time by Tony Adams, held firm. Adams announced his retirement at the end of the season and is currently studying for a degree in sport science at university, merely the latest stage in a remarkable character transformation.

For a long time, the championship seemed destined for Liverpool or Manchester United, with Arsenal and Newcastle on the fringes of the race. However, following Newcastle's 3-1 win at Highbury on December 18, Arsenal remained unbeaten on the domestic front for the rest of the season, and clinched the title in the best possible way, with Sylvain Wiltord's goal earning a 1-0 win in the penultimate game at Old Trafford in front of 65,000 disgruntled United fans. Nobody could argue that the champions were unworthy; Arsenal scored in all 38 league games and remained unbeaten away from home.

Surprisingly, Liverpool moved above United into second place, as Gerard Houllier's side continued their progress. True, they would run into a number of problems the following season, but that's a story for next year. Michael Owen was in predatory form with 19 league goals, and with a squad based around a nucleus of young English talent, it seemed that Liverpool's time was coming.

United, who used to lead everyone in developing young, home-grown players, found themselves in the unfamiliar position of third place, but Sir Alex Ferguson was typically bullish in defeat. The United manager, who reversed his decision to retire halfway through his farewell season (will he ever go?), had invested heavily the previous summer, and saw his faith in Ruud van Nistelrooy thoroughly vindicated as the Dutch striker returned from a career-threatening injury to score 23 goals in the league and 36 in total, paying back a significant chunk of his £19m transfer fee in the process.

However, Ferguson's decision to sell Jaap Stam and replace him with Laurent Blanc, patently not the player of old, proved a less-successful foray into the market and not until Blanc stepped aside, would the United defence recover.

Juan Sebastian Veron, who was supposed to add an extra dimension to the United midfield, and you'd expect at least one more dimension for £28.1m, simply looked as if the game in England was passing him by. Ferguson would address the defensive shortcomings with the £30m signing of Rio Ferdinand in the World Cup aftermath (just about the last major transfer before the market completely contracted), but doubts about United remained.

There were no such problems for Newcastle, who finished fourth with a squad of talented youngsters, ably guided by old hands Alan Shearer and Gary Speed. The oldest hand of all was on the tiller, Bobby Robson, who has long forgotten where he put his bus pass, but still remembers how to motivate his players.

The Champions League, and more particularly the revenue it generates, was a sore point for Leeds and Chelsea, both of whom suffered financial problems as a result of failing to regain a spot among Europe's elite. After taking the continent by storm and reaching the Champions League semi-finals in 2000/01, Leeds found themselves with the relative indignity of UEFA Cup participation, which brings nothing like the same financial rewards. On the domestic front, Leeds also seemed to be slipping; despite a season, which saw them top of the League on New Year's Day, they could only muster a fifth-placed finish, and a second successive failure to qualify for Europe's biggest club competition spelt the end for David O'Leary. Little were we to know then, that that was the tip of the financial iceberg, and the sale of Ferdinand triggered a succession of high-profile departures. Terry Venables stepped in, but the breach ever-widened and Venables and chairman Peter Ridsdale were soon at odds.

Chelsea's problems were not quite so dramatic, but there was a subtle shift in transfer policy. Having invested so much in experienced overseas stars in previous years, the signing of Frank Lampard - albeit for an inflated £11m - marked a new beginning for Chelsea. Coach Claudio Ranieri's influence became more noticeable, but a sixth-placed finish meant that there would little in the way of further investment.

	FIFA RANKINGS	
	As at December 18	
1	Brazil	856
2	France	787
3	Spain	779
4	Germany	761
5	Argentina	751
6	Netherlands	746
7	England	734
8	Mexico	732
9	Turkey	729
10	USA	723
11	Portugal	710
12	Denmark	707
13	Italy	705
14	Republic Of Ireland	697
15	Czech Republic	687
16	Cameroon	685
17	Belgium	682
18	Paraguay	679
19	Yugoslavia	678
20	Korea	669
21	Costa Rica	652
22	Japan	650
	Russia	650
24	Romania	649
	Sweden	649
26	Norway	648
27	Senegal	646
28	Uruguay	643
29	Nigeria	642
30	South Africa	636
Also		
52	Wales	554
66	Scotland	528
106	Northern Ireland	413

At the other end of the Premiership, Leicester and Derby looked doomed to relegation from early in the season, but Ipswich's fall from grace caught many by surprise. Having finished fifth in 2000/01, there was little inkling of the spectacular collapse that was to follow, as the Tractor Boys struggled to find their form. For a brief spell, it did seem that George Burley's men would become the first side in the history of the Premiership to be bottom at Christmas and escape relegation, but their revival was illusory, and a 5-0 defeat at Liverpool on the final day of the season sent them down, and put Burley on his bike.

Ipswich's demise at least gave Peter Reid's Sunderland a reprieve, though it didn't give a very long one to Reid himself. Sunderland plummeted from ninth on Boxing Day and only missed relegation by four points. They scored just 29 goals in the League all season.

Glenn Hoddle's appointment at Tottenham had been the cause of north London optimism, but progress stalled as they finished only ninth in the League, and lost in the final of the Worthington Cup. Blackburn, moulded into a solid Premiership side by Graeme Souness, kept Hoddle's hand off that Cup, to the particular delight of Andy Cole, un-rated by the Spurs' manager during his term as England manager, but who scored the 69th-minute winner. Hoddle's ability to alienate English international-class footballers remains a very particular talent.

West Ham recovered from an alarming early-season wobble to reach seventh place, while Steve McClaren brought some much-needed stability to Middlesbrough after the turmoil of the Bryan Robson years.

From the Nationwide League, Kevin Keegan guided Manchester City back to the Premiership at the first attempt. In true Keegan style, City went up as champions having scored 108 goals and conceded 52, giving City, by some distance, the best goal difference in the Football League. They look well-positioned to establish themselves in the top flight, but heaven help them if the goals-for count drops to below two a game. The other two promoted clubs had less certain futures, with West Brom basing their success on a solid defence having found goals hard to come by even in the First Division, while Birmingham are a big club but, as Sheffield Wednesday fans will tell you, that guarantees nothing.

At the other end of the table, Barnsley, so recently in the Premiership themselves, were relegated to the second division, where they were joined by Crewe and Stockport, who could not even be saved by the appointment of Carlton Palmer.

Brighton claimed a second successive title to win promotion as champions, although they lost manager Peter Taylor in the close season, and they were joined in promotion by Reading and Stoke. Meanwhile, Plymouth, Luton, Mansfield and Cheltenham were promoted from the Third Division, while Halifax dropped out of the league to be replaced by Boston United.

For the Nationwide League, though, the backdrop was almost more important than the show. The collapse of ITV Digital in the spring left many clubs with serious financial worries. At the time, paying £315m for the right to televise Nationwide League football had looked a hugely risky proposition; particularly as the company itself proved incapable of properly servicing the product. In the first few weeks, it was nigh-on impossible to sign up to the new station (and we know, for Oddball even contacted the ITC over the disarray).

Even with a perfectly-oiled management team, the sale price could never make the deal a viable proposition for the buyer. All the brouhaha about the channel having too weak a signal was a mere digression, but the clubs buried their heads in the sand.

In February the parent companies, Carlton and Granada, confronted the inevitable and announced that ITV Digital would be bankrupted unless the terms of the deal with the Football League were renegotiated. At that stage, the clubs were still owed a total of £178m, and didn't want to accept a penny less, largely because many of them had already spent the money anyway. An offer from ITV of £75m was rejected by David Burns and Keith Harris, respectively chief executive and chairman of the Football League. That decision would cost both their jobs.

Burns and Harris had not negotiated the original deal, so did not have to cover their tracks, but they were under intense pressure from the clubs. Whatever, everyone involved from the side of the Football League mis-read the situation. They got the legal side wrong and the accounts wrong; they didn't have a contract with Carlton or Granada, only the soon-to-be-bankrupted ITV Digital, and (much more crucially) their product couldn't guarantee the sales necessary to generate a profit.

ITV Digital went into administration on March 27th and, after the court case closed on August 1st (without even calling Michael Green and Charles Allen, the heads of Carlton and Granada) with the Football League losing its case, Burns and Harris fell on their swords.

The clubs, greedy to the point of folly, were as guilty as ITV Digital. They tried to claim the high moral ground and their stunts included an attempted boycott of the ITV coverage of the World Cup. Yet somewhere in the rational part of their brains, they might just have heard the argument that there were only three potential buyers for their product in Britain and now they'd reduced it to two. They might have recalled, vaguely, that they lived a market economy, and capitalism was surely a term that rang a bell.

Grown men and women, many of whom had made serious money running healthy and profitable companies lost their marbles when football came into the equation. For God's sake, how many people will pay to see Stockport, Brentford and Grimsby on television on a Friday night. It ain't £315m-worth.

But back to football. In Europe, Real Madrid were another side to repeat their success of four years earlier (yes, we're keeping that theme going), with Zinedine Zidane's sumptuous volley sealing a 2-1 win against Bayer Leverkusen in the Champions League final at Hampden Park. The German side were no one's favourites to reach the final. According to the script, Alex Ferguson would win the Cup for a second time in his native Glasgow and bow out as United manager, but Leverkusen were clearly never sent a copy. Over two semi-final matches, the scores ended level at 3-3, but Leverkusen progressed by virtue of a 2-2 draw in Manchester in the first leg.

Leverkusen had already disposed of Liverpool, thereby preventing a Liverpool-Man United head-to-head, and had also eliminated Arsenal by dint of finishing ahead of them at the group stage (albeit the German team had lost 4-1 at Highbury), so the German club was hardly England's favourite team. As for Arsenal, it really is time they made a significant impact on the continent, although they were able to take some consolation from the domestic front.

As it was, the real final (sorry, Leverkusen) was the semi-final between Real Madrid and Barcelona, with our own Steve McManaman scoring one of the goals and Zinedine Zidane the other as Real effectively settled the tie in the first leg, winning 2-0 at the Neu Camp. A draw at the Bernebau saw Real into the final.

British interest in the UEFA Cup ended early, with both Leeds and Rangers falling at the fourth round stage to PSV Eindhoven and Feyenoord respectively. Rangers' conquerors went on to lift the trophy, although they did have home advantage for the final, a 3-2 victory against Borussia Dortmund, which was played in Rotterdam.

On the international front, Europe took a deep breath and started another qualifying tournament. For starters: England were lacklustre against Slovenia and Macedonia; Scotland were poor *(see page 76)*; Mick McCarthy's Ireland suffered successive defeats and the manager departed; and Northern Ireland snatched a precious point against Ukraine.

Wales, though, deserve a paragraph or two of their own. Not since Ivor Allchurch and John Charles have they had anything worthwhile to celebrate (don't knock it, they only went out of the 1958 World Cup in the quarter-finals to a goal from the 17-year-old Pele), and they've hardly had a world-class player since whose wanted to play for them. But Giggs has changed his mind, because he knows and trusts Sparky and suddenly a team vying with Northern Ireland as the worst in the British Isles is now the best. Well, think about it, could England beat Italy? Mark Hughes (or Sparky) has recruited all the best talent and (far more importantly) motivated them as well. Ryan Giggs, Craig Bellamy, Gary Speed, John Hartsen and even Robbie Savage, who doesn't blow his nose anymore. As the Welsh say, "Mae'n hanner awr wedi naw", or "Good luck". Actually, it doesn't mean "Good luck", it means "It's half past nine", but it's the only Welsh we know.

Euro 2004 Qualifiers

Group 1

Ljubljana | Sep 7
SLOVENIA (1) 3 | **MALTA (0) 0**
Debono (og, 37)
Siljak (59), Cimirotic (90)

Nicosia | Sep 7
CYPRUS (1) 1 | **FRANCE (1) 2**
Okkas (14) | Cisse (39), Wiltord (51)

Stade de France | Oct 12
FRANCE (2) 5 | **SLOVENIA (0) 0**
Vieira (10), Marlet (35, 64)
Wiltord (79), Govou (86)

Ta' Qali | Oct 12
MALTA (0) 0 | **ISRAEL (0) 2**
| Balili (56), H Revivo (76)

Ta' Qali | Oct 16
MALTA (0) 0 | **FRANCE (2) 4**
| Henry (26, 36), Wiltord (59)
| Carriere (84)

Nicosia | Nov 20
CYPRUS (0) 2 | **MALTA (0) 1**
Rauffmann (50) | M Mifsud (90)
Okkas (74)

Group 2

Oslo | Sep 7
NORWAY (0) 2 | **DENMARK (1) 2**
Riise (54), Carew (90+) | Tomasson (22, 72)

Sarajevo | Sep 7
BOSNIA (0) 0 | **ROMANIA (3) 3**
| Chivu (7), D Munteanu (8)
| Ganea (27)

Copenhagen | Oct 12
DENMARK (0) 2 | **LUXEMBOURG (0) 0**
Tomasson (pen 52)
Ebbe Sand (72)

Bucharest | Oct 12
ROMANIA (0) 0 | **NORWAY (0) 1**
| Iversen (83)

Oslo | Oct 16
NORWAY (2) 2 | **BOSNIA (0) 0**
Lundekvam (7) Riise (27)

Luxembourg | Oct 16
LUXEMBOURG (0) 0 | **ROMANIA (4) 7**
| Moldovan (2, 5), Radol (25)
| Contra (45+, 47, 86)
| Ghioane (81)

Group 3

Vienna | Sep 7
AUSTRIA (2) 2 | **MOLDOVA (0) 0**
Herzog (pen 24, pen 29)

Eindhoven | Sep 7
NETHERLANDS (2) 3 | **BELARUS (0) 0**
Davis (35), Kluivert (37)
Hasselbaink (73)

Chisinau | Oct 12
MOLDOVA (0) 0 | **CZECH REP (0) 2**
| Jankulovski (pen 69)
| Rosicky (79)

Minsk | Oct 12
BELARUS (0) 0 | **AUSTRIA (0) 2**
| Schopp (58), Akagundoz (88)

Vienna | Oct 16
AUSTRIA (0) 0 | **NETHERLANDS (3) 3**
| Seedorf (15), Cocu (20)
| Makaay (30)

Teplice | Oct 16
CZECH REP (2) 2 | **BELARUS (0) 0**
Poborsky (6), Baros (23)

Group 4

Serravalle | Sep 7
SAN MARINO (0) 0 | **POLAND (0) 2**
| Kaczorowski (75), Kukielka (88)

Riga | Sep 7
LATVIA (0) 0 | **SWEDEN (0) 0**

Solna | Oct 12
SWEDEN (0) 1 | **HUNGARY (1) 1**
Ibrahimovic (76) | Kenesel (5)

Warsaw | Oct 12
POLAND (0) 0 | **LATVIA (1) 1**
| Laizans (30)

Budapest | Oct 16
HUNGARY 3 | **SAN MARINO 0**
Gera (49, 60, 85)

Serravalle | Nov 20
SAN MARINO (0) 0 | **LATVIA (0) 1**
| Valentini (og 89)

Group 5

Toftir | Sep 7
FAROE ISLAND 2 | **SCOTLAND 2**
Petersen (7, 13) | Lambert (62), Ferguson (83)

Faroes: Knudsen; Johannesen, J K Hansen, Thorsteinsson, J R Jacobsen, Elttor (Lakjuni 89), Benjaminsen, Johnsson, Borg, Petersen (Flotum 80), C H Jacobsen (R Jacobsen 75)
Scotland: Douglas; Ross (Alexander 75), Crainey, Dailly, Weir, Ferguson, Dickov (Crawford 46), Dobie (Thompson 84), Kyle, Lambert, Johnston
Referee: Jacek Granat POL
Attendance: 4,000

Kaunus   *Sep 7*
LITHUANIA (0) 0   **GERMANY (1) 2**
Ballack (27)
Stankevicius (og 59)

Reykjavik   *Oct 12*
ICELAND (0) 0   **SCOTLAND (1) 2**
Dailly (6), Naysmith (63)

Iceland: Arason, Porsteinsson, Vioarson, Gunnarson, Sigurdsson, Kristinsson, Hreidarsson, Ingimarsson, Gudjohnsen, Sigurdsson, Gudnason
Scotland: Douglas, Ross, Wilkie, Pressley, Dailly, Ferguson, McNamara (Davidson 34), Crawford (Severin 89), Thompson, Lambert*, Naysmith (Anderson 90)
Attendance: 7,000
Referee: Alain Sars FRA

Kaunus   *Oct 12*
LITHUANIA (2) 2   **FAROE ISLANDS (0) 0**
Razanauskas (pen 23)
Poskus (37)

Hanover   *Oct 16*
GERMANY (1) 2   **FAROE ISLANDS (1) 1**
Ballack (pen 2)   *Friedrich (og 45)*
Klose (59)

Reykjavik   *Oct 16*
ICELAND (0) 3   **LITHUANIA (0) 0**
H Helgason (50)
Gudjohnsen (61, 74)

Group 6
Albacete   *Oct 12*
SPAIN (1) 3   **NORTHERN IRELAND (0) 0**
Baraja (19, 89), Guti (59)

Spain: Casillas; Bravo, Puyol, Salgado, Baraja, Guti (Capi 82), Helguera, Jaoquin (Mendieta 76), Vicente, Xavi, Raul (Morientes 62)
N Ireland: Taylor; Hughes, McCartney, Murdock (Hughes 65), Taggart, Gillespie, Horlock, Johnson, Lomas, Mulryne, McVeigh (Healy 65)
Attendance: 14,000
Referee: Michel Lubos SVK
Windsor Park   *Oct 16*
N IRELAND (0) 0   **UKRAINE (0) 0**

Northern Ireland: Taylor; Hughes, McCartney, Gillespie, Horlock, Hughes, Johnson (Murdock 84), Lomas, Mulryne (McCann 90), Healy, McVeigh (Kirk 65)
Ukraine: Reva; Luzhny, Starostyak, Tymoschuk, Husin, Radchenko, Voronin, Vorebey (Melashchenko 75), Zubov, Kalynychenko (Rebrov 53), Kormiltsev (Lysytskyy 88)
Attendance: 14,000
Referee: Cosimo Bolognino ITA

Athens   *Sep 7*
GREECE (0) 0   **SPAIN (1) 2**
Raul Gonzalez (8)
Valeron (77)

Yerevan   *Sep 7*
ARMENIA (0) 2   **UKRAINE (2) 2**
Petrosyan (73)   *Serebrennikov (2)*
Sarkisyan (90+)   *Zubov (33)*

Kiev   *Oct 12*
UKRAINE (0) 2   **GREECE (0) 0**
Vorobey (51)
Voronin (90+)

Athens   *Oct 16*
GREECE (1) 2   **ARMENIA (0) 0**
Nikolaidis (2, 59)

Group 7
Bratislava   *Oct 12*
SLOVAKIA (1) 1   **ENGLAND (0) 2**
Nemeth (23)   *Beckham (64), Owen (82)*

Slovakia: Hlinka; Karhan, Petras, Zeman, Dzurik, Nemeth, Vittek (Reiter 81), Janocko (Mintel 89), Leitner, Pinte (Kozlej 89), Konig
England: Seaman; Cole, G Neville, Southgate, Woodgate, Beckham, Butt, Gerrard (Dyer 77), Scholes, Heskey (A Smith 90), Owen (Hargreaves 86)
Attendance: 30,000
Referee: Domenico Messina ITA

St Mary's, Southampton   *Oct 16*
ENGLAND (2) 2   **MACEDONIA (2) 2**
Beckham (13)   *Sakiri (10), Trajanov (24)*
Gerrard (35)

England: Seaman; Bridge (Vassell 59), Campbell, Cole, G Neville, Woodgate, Beckham, Gerrard (Butt 56), Scholes, Owen, A Smith
England: Milosevski; Petrov, Sedloski, Vasoski, Grzdanoski, Mitrevski, Popov, Sakiri, Sumulikoski, Trajanov (Stojanovski 90), Toleski (Pandev 62)
Attendance: 32,095
Referee: Arturo Dauden Ibanez ESP

Istanbul   *Sep 7*
TURKEY (2) 3   **SLOVAKIA (0) 0**
Akin Serhat (14)
Arif Erdem (44, 65)

Vaduz   *Sep 7*
LIECHTENSTEIN (0) 1   **FYR MACEDONIA (1) 1**
M Stocklasa (90+)   *Hristov (8)*

Skopje   *Oct 12*
MACEDONIA (1) 1   **TURKEY (1) 2**
Grozdanovski (2)   *Okan Buruk (29)*
Nihat Kahveci (53)

Istanbul   *Oct 16*
TURKEY (3) 5   **LIECHTENSTEIN (0) 0**
Okan Buruk (7)
Davala (14), Ilhan (23)
Akin Serhat (81, 90)

Group 8

Brussels
BELGIUM (0) 0

Sep 7
BULGARIA (1) 2
Jankovic (17)
Stilian Petrov (63)

Osljek
CROATIA (0) 0

Sep 7
ESTONIA (0) 0

Andorra La Vella
ANDORRA (0) 0

Oct 12
BELGIUM (0) 1
Sonck (61)

Sofia
BULGARIA (2) 2
Stilian Petrov (22)
Berbatov (37)

Oct 12
CROATIA (0) 0

Tallin
ESTONIA (0) 0

Oct 16
BELGIUM (1) 1
Sonck (2)

Sofia
BULGARIA (1) 2
Chilikov (37)
Balakov (58)

Oct 16
ANDORRA (0) 1
Antonio Lima (80)

Group 9

Helsinki
FINLAND (0) 0

Sep 7
WALES (0) 2
Hartson (30), Davies (72)

Finland: Niemi; Nylund (Johansson 70), Hyppia, Saarinen (Kopteff 76), Tihinen, Litmanen, Riihilahti, Kolkka, Kuqi, Nurmela (Kottila 90), Tainio
Wales: Delaney; Gabbidon, Melville, Pembridge, Davies, Giggs, Johnson (Bellamy 70), Jones, Savage, Speed, Hartson
Attendance: 35,833
Referee: Konrad Plautz AUT

Millennium Stadium
WALES (1) 2
Davies (11)
Bellamy (70)

Oct 16
ITALY (1) 1
Del Piero (31)

Wales: Delaney; Gabbidon, Melville, Davies, Giggs, Jones, Pembridge, Savage, Speed, Bellamy (Blake 90), Hartson
Italy: Buffon; Cannavaro, Nesta, Panucci, Ambrosini, Di Biagio (Gattuso 54, Marazzina 85), Pirio, Tommasi, Zauri, Del Piero, Montella (Maccarone 69)
Attendance: 70,000
Referee: Gilles Veissiere FRA

Baku
AZERBAIJAN (0) 0

Nov 20
WALES (1) 2
Speed (10), Hartson (68)

Italy: Buffon; Cannavaro, Nesta, Panucci, Ambrosini, Di Biagio (Gattuso 54, Marazzina 85), Pirio, Tommasi, Zauri, Del Piero, Montella (Maccarone 69)
Wales: Delaney; Gabbidon, Melville, Davies, Giggs, Jones, Pembridge, Savage, Speed, Bellamy (Blake 90), Hartson
Attendance: 8,000
Referee: Luc Huyghe BEL

Baku
AZERBAIJAN (0) 0

Sep 7
ITALY (1) 2
Akhmedov (og 33)
Del Piero (65)

Naples
ITALY (1) 1
Del Piero (36)

Oct 12
YUGOSLAVIA (1) 1
Mijatovic (27)

Helsinki
FINLAND 3
Agaev (og 14)
Tihinen (60), Hyypia (72)

Oct 12
AZERBAIJAN 0

Belgrade
YUGOSLAVIA (0) 2
Kovacevic (55)
Mihajlovic (pen 84)

Oct 16
FINLAND (0) 0

Group 10

Moscow
RUSSIA (2) 4
Karyaka (20)
Bestchstnykh (24)
Kerzhakov (71)
Babb (og, 88)

Sep 7
REPUBLIC OF IRELAND (0) 2
Doherty (69), Morrison (76)

Russia: Ovchinnikov; Ignashevitch, Nizhegorodov, Onopko, Aldonin, Gusev (Solomatin 29), Loskov, Semak (Khokhlov 76), Yanovsky, Bestchastnykh (Kerzhakov 46), Karyaka
Ireland: Given; Breen, Cunningham, Harte, Duff (Morrison 18), Finnan, Holland, Kilbane (Babb 84), Kinsella, McAteer (Doherty 63), Keane
Attendance: 22,000
Referee: Claude Colombo FRA

Lansdowne Road, Dublin
IRELAND (0) 1
Magnin (og 78)

Oct 16
SWITZERLAND (1) 2
Yakin (45), Celestina (87)

Ireland: Given; Breen, Cunningham, Harte (Doherty 87), Kelly, Duff (Butler 82), Healy, Holland, Kilbane (Morrison 62), Kinsella, Keane
Switzerland: Stiel; Haas, Magnin, M Yakin, Cabanas, Muller, Vogel, Wicky (Cantaluppi 84), H Yakin (Celestini 84), Chapuisat, Frei
Attendance: 40,000
Referee: Rune Pedersen

Basel
SWITZERLAND (1) 4
Frei (37),
H Yakin (62)
Muller (74), Chapuisat (81)

Sep 7
GEORGIA (0) 1
Arveladze (62)

Tirana
ALBANIA 1
Murati (79)

Oct 12
SWITZERLAND 1
M Yakin (37)

Volgograd
RUSSIA 4
Kerzhakov (3)
Semak (42, 55)
Onopko (52)

Oct 16
ALBANIA 1
Duro (13)

Other Internationals

Amsterdam 13 Feb
HOLLAND (1) 1 **ENGLAND (0) 1**
Kluivert (26) *Vassell (61)*
Holland: Van Der Sar; Ricksen, Reiziger, F De Boer
(Paauwe 67), Van Bronckhorst, Van Bommel (Davids
46), R De Boer (Sikora 59), Cocu (Boateng 46),
Overmars (Makaay 88), Van Nistelrooy (Hasselbaink 64),
Kluivert
England: Martyn (James 46), G Neville (P Neville 77),
Bridge (Powell 46), Ferdinand, Campbell (Southgate 46),
Beckham, Gerrard (Lampard 77), Scholes (Butt 77),
Vassell (J Cole 77), Heskey, Ricketts (Phillips 46)
Attendance: 48,500
Referee: Duhamel FRA

Elland Road Mar 27
ENGLAND 1 **ITALY 2**
Fowler 63 *Montella (66, pen 90)*
England: Martyn (James 46); Mills (P Neville 46), Bridge
(G Neville 46), Campbell (King 46), Southgate (Ehiogu
46), Beckham (Murphy 46), Butt (Hargreaves 46),
Lampard (J Cole 46), Sinclair (Sheringham 70), Heskey
(Fowler 46), Owen (Vassell 46)
Italy: Buffon; Panucci (Coco 74), Materazzi (Iuliano 57),
Nesta (Adani 82), Cannavaro, Zambrotta, Doni (Tomassi
74), Di Biagio (Gattuso 57), Zanetti (Albertini 57), Totti
(Montella 46), Delvecchio (Maccarone 74)
Attendance: 36,635
Referee: Fandel GER

Anfield 17 Apr
ENGLAND (1) 4 **PARAGUAY (0) 0**
Owen (4), Murphy (47)
Vassell (54), Ayala (og 77)
England: Seaman; G Neville (Carragher 68), Bridge (P
Neville 68), Southgate (Sheringham 68), Keown (Murphy
46), Dyer (Fowler 46), Gerrard (Hargreaves 46), Butt
(Sinclair 46), Scholes (Mills 46), Vassell (Lampard 68),
Owen (J Cole 46)
Paraguay: Tavarelli; Arce, Ayala, Gamarra (Caceres 81),
Caniza, Gavilan (Sarabia 57), Bonet (Morinigo 82),
Struway, Paredes, Cardozo (Baez 60), Santa Cruz
Attendance: 42,713
Referee: Bolognino ITA

Jeju 21 May
SOUTH KOREA 1 **ENGLAND 1**
Park Ji-Sung (51) *Owen (26)*
Korea: Lee Woon-Jae, Song Chung-Gug, Hong Myung-
Bo, Choi Jin-Chul, Kim Nam-Il, Choi Tae-Uk, Lee Young-
Pyo, Yoo Sang-Chul, Park Ji-Sung, Seol Ki-Hyeon (Ahn
Jung-Hwan), Lee Chun-Soo
England: Martyn (James 46), Mills (Brown 68), Campbell
(Southgate 45), Ferdinand (Keown 45), A Cole (Bridge
45), Murphy (J Cole 45), Hargreaves, Scholes (Sinclair
45), Heskey, Owen (Sheringham 45), Vassell

Kobe 26 May
ENGLAND 2 **CAMEROON 2**
Vassell (11) *Eto'o (4), Geremi (56)*
Fowler (90)
England: Martyn (James 45); Brown, Campbell
(Southgate 45), Ferdinand (Keown 45), Bridge, J Cole,
Hargreaves, Scholes (Sinclair 45), Heskey (Mills 45),
Vassell (Fowler 75), Owen (Sheringham 45)
Cameroon: Alioum (Songo'o 78); Song (Ndo 69), Kalla
(Mettomo 56), Tchato, Geremi (Alnoudji 66), Wome
(Njanka 61), Lauren (Suffo 60), Foe (Djemba-Djemba
53), Olembe (Ngom Kome 53), Eto'o (Epale 60), Mboma
(Ndiefi 66)
Attendance: 42,000
Referee: Katayama JPN

Villa Park 7 Sept
ENGLAND 1 **PORTUGAL 1**
A Smith (40) *Costinha (79)*
England: James; Mills (Hargreaves 46), Ferdinand
(Woodgate 46), Southgate, A Cole (Bridge 46), Bowyer
(Sinclair 62), Gerrard (Dunn 46), Butt (Murphy 62),
Heskey, Owen (J Cole 62), A Smith
Portugal: Baia (Ricardo 46); Beto (Nuno Gomes 46),
Meira (Silva 78), Couto (Ferreira 46), Conceicao (Valente
46), Petit (Vidigal 65), Rui Costa (Boa Morte 46), Rui
Jorge (Capucho 46), Figo (Viana 46), Simao (Constinha
54), Pauleta (Santos 46)
Attendance: 40,058
Referee: Ovrebo NOR

Stade de France Mar 27
FRANCE 5 (4) **SCOTLAND (0) 0**
Zidane (12)
Trezeguet (21, 41)
Henry (31), Marlet (87)
France: Barthez, Candela (Karembeu 58), Leboeuf
(Christanval 64), Desailly (Silvestre 46), Lizarazu, Vieira
(Makelele 46), Petit, Zidane (Djorkaeff 81), Wiltord
(Marlet 58), Henry, Trezeguet (Carriere 74)
Scotland: Sullivan, Weir, Crainey, Lambert, Dailly,
Caldwell, Freedman (Gemmill 46), Matteo, Crawford
(Thompson 63), Cameron (Holt 45, McNamara 74),
McCann
Attendance: 80,000
Referee: Jacek Granat POL

Aberdeen Apr 17
SCOTLAND (1) 1 **NIGERIA (1) 2**
Dailly (7) *Aghahowa (41, 67)*
Scotland: Douglas, Stockdale (Alexander 46), Crainey,
Lambert, Weir, Dailly, McNaughton, Williams (Stewart
64), Thompson (O'Connor 75), Gemmill (Caldwell 46),
McCann (Johnston 78).
Nigeria: Ejide, Yobo, Kanu, Okoronkwo, Utaka (sub
Ikedia 54), Ogbeche, Okocha, Christopher (sub Adepoju
78), Sodje (sub Ifeajigwa 85), Aghahowa, Ejiofor
Attendance: 20,465
Referee: Tom Henning Ovrebo NOR

ASSOCIATION FOOTBALL

Busan   *May 16*
SOUTH KOREA 4 (1)   **SCOTLAND 1 (0)**
Lee Chun-Soo (15)   *Dobie (75)*
Ahn (57, 87), Yoon (67)
South Korea: Kim Byung-Hong; Myong-Bo (Yoon Jong-Hwan, 65), Choi Jin-Cheul (Lee Min-Sung, 46), Kim Tae-Lee, Young-Lee, Eul-Yong, Yoo Sang-Chul, Song Chung-Lee, Chun-Soo (Cha Doo-Ri, 72), Hwang Sun-Hong (Ahn Jung-Hwan, 46), Park Ji-Sung (Choi Tae-Uk, 72)
Scotland: N Sullivan; M Ross, C Dailly, D Weir, G Alexander (Stockdale 62), A Johnston (Kyle, 66), G Caldwell, S Gemmill, G O'Connor (Williams, 46), M Stewart (Severin, 46), S Dobie
Attendance: 60 000
Referee: Nagalingam SIN

Hong Kong   *May 20*
SOUTH AFRICA (1) 2   **SCOTLAND (0) 0**
Mokoena (32)
Koumantarakis (90)
South Africa: Vonk, Aaron Mokoena (Nzama 62), Radebe, Issa, Carnell, Zuma (Koumantarakis 82), Sibaya, Fortune (Buckley 84), Pule (Arendse 69), McCarthy, Tebeho Mokoena
Scotland: Douglas, Stockdale (Neil Alexander 69), Gary Caldwell (Wilkie 46), Dailly, Weir, Ross, Gemmill (Stewart 86), Williams (Severin 78), Dobie, Kyle, Johnston (McFadden 62)
Attendance: 3,007
Referee: Chan Siu Kee HKG

Hampden Park   *Aug 21*
SCOTLAND (0) 0   **DENMARK (1) 1**
     Sand (8)
Scotland: Douglas; Ross, Naysmith (Johnston 71), Weir (Severin 77), Dailly, Ferguson, McNaughton (Crainey 46), Stockdale (Alexander 71), Kyle, Lambert (McInnes 81), Thompson (Dobie 55)
Denmark: Sorensen, Bogelund (Gronkjaer 46), Henriksen (Lustu 83), Laursen (Wieghorst 68), N Jensen, Poulsen, Gravesen (C Jensen 46), Lovenkrands (Silberbauer 71), Tomasson, Rommedahl (Michaelsen 46), Sand
Attendance: 28,766
Referee: Leslie Irvine NIR

Easter Road   *Oct 15*
SCOTLAND (1) 3   **CANADA (1) 1**
Crawford (11, 73)   *De Rosario (pen 9)*
Thompson (49)
Scotland: Gallacher, Ross (Davidson 45), Wilkie (Murray 75), Pressley, Dailly, Anderson, Alexander, Crawford (Kyle 90), Thompson (McFadden 80), Gemmill (Severin 65), Devlin
Canada: Hirschfeld, Fenwick, Hastings, McKenna, Pozniak, Imhof (Xausa 81), Stalteri, Nsaliwa, Radzinski, De Rosario, De Guzman
Attendance: 16,207
Referee: Luc Huyghe BEL

Braga   *Nov 20*
PORTUGAL (2) 2   **SCOTLAND (0) 0**
Pauleta (7, 18)
Portugal: Quim (Nelson 89), Fernando Couto, Rui Jorge (Ribeiro 58), Fernando Meira, Ricardo Rocha, Figo (Ferreira 46), Rui Costa (Mendes 58), Sergio Conceicao, Simao (Neca 78), Tiago (Assis 83), Pauleta (Nuno Gomes 46).
Scotland: Douglas, Anderson (McInnes 23), Ross (Devlin 46), Pressley, Dailly, Wilkie (Severin 83), G. Alexander, Crawford, Dobie (Kyle 78), Lambert (Williams 68), Naysmith
Attendance: 8,000
Referee: Vierol Anghelieni ROM

Millennium Stadium   *Feb 13*
WALES (1) 1   **ARGENTINA (0) 1**
Bellamy (34)   *Cruz (61)*
Wales: Jones (Crossley 45); Delaney, Page, Melville, Speed, Davies , Savage, Pembridge (C Robinson 90), Giggs (J Robinson 61), Bellamy, Hartson
Argentina: Saja, Vivas, Chamot, Placente, Veron, Husain, Sorin, Kily Gonzalez, Caniggia (Galletti 90), Cruz (Saviola 73), Riquelme (Aimar 73)
Attendance: 63,000
Referee: Paul McKeon IRL

Millennium Stadium   *Mar 27*
WALES (0) 0   **CZECH REPUBLIC (0) 0**
Wales: Ward; Delaney, Page, Melville, Gabbidon, Koumas, S Davies, Savage, J Robinson, Hartson, Blake
Czech Rep: Fukal, Ujfalusi, Novotny, Jankulovski (Holenak 82), Poborsky, Galasek, Rosicky, Smicer, Stajner, Lokvenc
Attendance: 19,200
Referee: Claus Bo Larsen DEN

Millennium Stadium   *May 14*
WALES (0) 1   **GERMANY (0) 0**
Earnshaw (46)
Wales: Crossley, Delaney, Page, Melville, Speed, S Davies, Savage, Pembridge, Giggs, Hartson, Earnshaw (Coleman 90)
Germany: Kahn, Linke, Metzalder, Heinrich, Ziege (Asamoah 63), Jeremies, Hamann (Kehl 72), Frings, Deisler (Bode 63), Klose, Bierfhoff (Janker 72)
Attendance: 36,920
Referee: Roy Helge Olsen NOR

Varazdin   *Aug 21*
CROATIA (0) 1   **WALES (0) 0**
Petric (79)   *Davies (11)*
Croatia: Pletikosa, Zivkovic, Tapalovic, Simunic, R Kovac, N Kovac, Saric, Vugrinec, Vlaovic, Rapaic, Maric
Wales: Jones, Delaney, Barnard, Melville, Gabbidon, Pembridge, Earnshaw, Johnson, Hartson, S Davies, C Robinson
Attendance: 3000
Referee: Lutz-Michael Frolich GER

Limassol   *Feb*
N IRELAND (1) 1   **POLAND (2) 4**
Lomas 18   *Kryszalowicz (6, 67)*
    Kaluzny (11), Zewlakov (69)
N Ireland: Taylor; Lomas, A Hughes, Griffin (McCartney 46), Kennedy (Duff 82), Gillespie, Magilton (McCann), Mulryne (Lennon 46), Johnson (McVeigh 66), M Hughes, Healy (Elliott 46)
Poland: Majdan (Bledrzewski 90); Kozminski, J Bak, Waldoch, Iwan (Smolarek 46), Kaluzny (A Bak 46), Swierczewski (Zdebel 46), Krznowek, Kryszalowicz (Zielinski 82), Olisadebe (Zewlakov 46, Rzasa 60)
Attendance: 221   Referee: Tassos Papaioannou CYP

Vaduz   *Mar 27*
LIECHTENSTEIN (0) 0   N IRELAND (0) 0
Liechtgenstein: Jehle; Tesler, Hasler, Zech, Michael Stocklassa, Gigon, Nigg (Burgmeier 72), Martin Stocklassa, M Beck, T Beck, Buchel
N Ireland: Taylor (Carroll 46); Lomas, Williams, McCartney, McCann (Holmes 69), Gillespie, Mulryne, Magilton, Johnson, Healy (Elliott 83), Feeney (M Hughes 57)
Attendance: 1,080   Referee: K Rogalia SUI

Belfast   *Apr 18*
N IRELAND (0) 0   **SPAIN (1) 5**
    Raul (23, 54), Baraja (47)
    Puyol (69), Morientes (49)
N Ireland: Taylor (Carroll 46); Nolan, Williams, McCartney, A Hughes, Gillespie (McCourt 77), Johnson, Horlack, Elliott, Healy, Feeney (McEvilly 63)
Spain: Canizares; (Casillas 74) Puyol, Hierro (Sergio 74), Nadal (Torres 46), Juanfran, Joaquim (Helguera 46), Baraja, Albeida (Mendieta 46), De Pedro (Valeron 46), Raul, Morientes
Attendance: 11,105
Referee: H Clark SCO

Windsor Park   *Aug 21*
N IRELAND (0) 0   **CYPRUS (0) 0**
N Ireland: Taylor; Griffin (Duff 46), Murdock, Williams, McCartney, Kennedy, Gillespie (Feeney 87), Johnson, Healy, Quinn, Horlock. Subs: Ingham, Duff, McCann, Feeney, Robinson.
Cyprus: Panayiotou (Siimitras 89); Konnafis, Spyrou, Dasalakis (Nicolauo 46), Nikolaou (Michael 42), Okkarides, Theodotou, Elefteriou (Christodoulou 70), Ioannios Okkas (Kaiafas 66), Satsias, Yiasoumi (Agathocleous 60)
Attendance: 6922   Referee: S Jones WAL

Lansdowne Road   *Feb 13*
REP IRELAND 2   **RUSSIA (0) 0**
Reid (3), Robbie Keane (20)
Ireland: Given (Kiely 46); Finnan (McAteer 72, Quinn 90), Harte (Staunton 72), Roy Keane (Holland 86), O'Brien (Dunne 46), Cunningham (Breen 46), Reid (G Kelly 46), Healy (Carsley 46), Robbie Keane (Sadlier 72), Kilbane (Kennedy 46), Duff (Morrison 46)
Russia: Nigmatulin, Khlestov (Daev 90), Onopko, Nikiforov (Chugainov 68), Kovtun, Khokhlov (Izmailov 53), Mostovoi, Titov, Karpin, Alenitchev (Sernak 72), Beschastnykh
Atendance: 44,000
Referee: Dermot Gallagher ENG

Lansdowne Road   *Mar 28*
REP IRELAND (1) 3   **DENMARK (0) 0**
Harte (19)
Robbie Keane (54)
Morrison (90)
Rep Ireland: Kiely (Colgan 46); Kelly, Cunningham, Staunton, Harte, McAteer (Reid), Holland, Kinsella (Healy 65), Duff, Robbie Keane, Morrison
Denmark: Sorensen (Kjaer 46); Rytter, Laursen, Henriksen, Heintze (Jensen 81), Poulsen, Nilsen, Gronkjaer, Nielsen (Madsen 46), Rommedahl (Lovenkrands 69), Sand
Attendance: 42,000   Referee: Brian Lawlor WAL

Lansdowne Road   *Apr 17*
REP IRELAND (1) 2   **USA (1) 1**
Kinsella (6)   *Pope (34)*
Doherty (83)
Ireland: Given; Finnan (G Kelly 46), Breen (Doherty 71), O'Brien (Cunningham 46), Harte (Staunton 46), Delap, Kinsella (Holland 46), Healy, Kilbane (Reid 46), Robbie Keane (Morrison), Duff (Connolly 46)
USA: Freidel (Keller 46); Sanneh, Pope, Berhalter (Vanney 46), Agoos, Reyna (Heiduk 71), Stewart (Lewis 46), Armas, O'Brien (Donovan 46), McBride (Moore 46), Mathis (Woolf 64)
Attendance: 39,000   Referee: Philippe Leuba SUI

Lansdowne Road   *May 16*
REP IRELAND (0) 1   **NIGERIA (1) 2**
Reid (69)   *Agahowa (13)*
    Dodje (47)
Ireland: Given; Finnan, Cunningham, Staunton, Harte, McAteer (Reid 46), Roy Keane (Kinsella 64), Holland, Kilbane (G Kelly 60), Robbie Keane (Morrison 60), Duff (Connolly 60)
Nigeria: Shorumnu; West, Yobo, Okoronkwo, Sodje, Ikedia, Opabunmi, Ogbeche, Kanu, Okocha (Oruma 66), Agahowa
Attendance: 42,655   Referee: A Costa POR

Helsinki   *Aug 21*
FINLAND (0) 0   **REP OF IRELAND 3**
    Robbie Keane (12)
    Healy (75), Barrett (82)
Finland: Jaaskelainen, Pasanen, Saarinen, Hyypia, Tihinen, Jari Ilola, Nuorela, Tainio, Johansson, Litmanen, Kolkka
Ireland: Kiely (Given 76), Kelly, Harte (Barrett 76), Cunningham (Doherty 46), Breen, Carsley (Holland 86), McAteer (McPhail 46), Kinsella (Healy 46), Duff (Delap 46), Robbie Keane (Goodwin 83), Butler (Kilbane 46)
Referee: Rune Pederson NOR

Athens   *Nov 20*
GREECE (0) 0   **REP OF IRELAND (0) 0**
Greece: Nikopolidis, Seitaridis, Fyssas, Dabizas, Kyrgiakos, Basinas, Giannakopoulos, Karagounis, Charisteas, Tsartas, Themistoklis
Greek substitutes not available (nine subs were made)
Ireland: Given, Finnan, Dunne, O'Shea, Cunningham, Carsley, Healy, Holland, Doherty, McPhail, Crowe (Rory Delap 86)
Attendance: 5000   Referee: A Trentalange ITA

English Football

FA Carling Premiership 2001-2002

		P	W	D	L	GF	GA	W	D	L	GF	GA	GD	Pts
1	Arsenal	38	12	4	3	42	25	14	5	0	37	11	43	87
2	Liverpool	38	12	5	2	33	14	12	3	4	34	16	37	80
3	Manchester United	38	11	2	6	40	17	13	3	3	47	28	42	77
4	Newcastle United	38	12	3	4	40	23	9	5	5	34	29	22	71
5	Leeds United	38	9	6	4	31	21	9	6	4	22	16	16	66
6	Chelsea	38	11	4	4	43	21	6	9	4	23	17	28	64
7	West Ham United	38	12	4	3	32	14	3	4	12	16	43	-9	53
8	Aston Villa	38	8	7	4	22	17	4	7	8	24	30	-1	50
9	Tottenham Hotspur	38	10	4	5	32	24	4	4	11	17	29	-4	50
10	Blackburn Rovers	38	8	6	5	33	20	4	4	11	22	31	4	46
11	Southampton	38	7	5	7	23	22	5	4	10	23	32	-8	45
12	Middlesboro	38	7	5	7	23	26	5	4	10	12	21	-12	45
13	Fulham	38	7	7	5	21	16	3	7	9	15	28	-8	44
14	Charlton Athletic	38	5	6	8	23	30	5	8	6	15	19	-11	44
15	Everton	38	8	4	7	26	23	3	6	10	19	34	-12	43
16	Bolton Wanderers	38	5	7	7	20	31	4	6	9	24	31	-18	40
17	Sunderland	38	7	7	5	18	16	3	3	13	11	35	-22	40
18	Ipswich Town	38	6	4	9	20	24	3	5	11	21	40	-23	36
19	Derby Town	38	5	4	10	20	26	3	2	14	13	37	-30	30
20	Leicester City	38	3	7	9	15	34	2	6	11	15	30	-34	28

ONE2ONE FA CHARITY SHIELD

Millennium Stadium, Aug 12th 2001

MANCHESTER UNITED 1
(Van Nistleroy 51)

LIVERPOOOL 2
(McAllister 2 pen, Owen 16)

Manchester United: Barthez, Irwin, Silvestre, Neville G, Keane, Stam, Beckham, Butt (Yorke), Van Nistleroy, Scholes Giggs

Liverpool: Westerveld; Babbel, Riise (Carragher), Hamann, Henchoz, Hyypia, Murphy (Berger), McAllister, Heskey, Owen, Barmby (Biscan)

Referee: Andy D'Urso

Attendance: 70,227

Goalscorers

In order of League golas scored

	Lg	Cps	Other	Total
Thierry Henry (Arsenal)	24	1	7	32
Ruud van Nistleroy (Man U)	23	2	11	36
Jimmy F Hasselbaink (Chels)	23	6	0	29
Alan Shearer (Newcastle)	23	4	0	27
Michael Owen (Liverpool)	19	2	6	27
Ole Gunnar Solskjaer (Man U)	17	1	7	25
Robbie Fowler (Leeds)	15	0	1	16
Includes three League goals for Liverpool				
Eidar Gudjohnsen (Chels)	14	6	3	23
Marian Pahars (Southampton)	14	2	0	16
Frederik Ljundberg (Arsenal)	12	2	3	17
Michael Ricketts (Bolton)	12	1	2	15
Juan Angel (Aston Villa)	12	0	2	14
James Beattie (Southampton)	12	2	0	14
Darius Vassell (Aston Villa)	12	0	0	12
Mark Viduka (Leeds)	11	2	3	16
David Beckham (Man U)	11	0	5	16
Jason Euell (Charlton)	11	2	0	13
Kevin Phillips (Sunderland)	11	2	0	13
Frederic Kanoute (West Ham)	11	1	0	12

	Arsenal	Aston Villa	Blackburn Rvrs	Bolton W	Charlton Ath	Chelsea	Derby County	Everton	Fulham	Ipswich Town	Leeds United	Leicester City	Liverpool	Manchester Utd	Middlesbrough	Newcastle Utd	Southampton	Sunderland	Tottenham H	West Ham Utd
Arsenal	****	3-2	3-3	1-1	2-4	2-1	4-3	4-1	4-1	2-0	1-1	4-0	1-1	1-1	2-1	1-1	2-1	1-1	1-1	2-0
Aston Villa	1-2	****	2-0	3-2	1-1	1-0	2-1	3-2	0-0	2-0	2-0	1-2	0-2	1-2	1-1	3-0	1-3	2-2	3-1	2-1
Bradford	2-3	3-0	****	1-0	4-1	0-0	0-3	1-2	2-0	0-3	1-2	0-1	4-0	2-3	2-1	1-1	2-0	1-1	1-0	2-0
Charlton Ath	0-2	3-2	1-1	****	0-0	2-2	1-0	3-1	1-0	3-1	1-0	1-1	1-1	0-0	0-1	3-3	3-1	0-0	3-1	4-4
Chelsea	0-3	1-2	0-2	5-1	0-0	0-0	2-1	1-0	1-2	2-2	1-3	0-2	2-2	3-3	2-1	2-2	4-1	4-0	0-3	5-1
Coventry C	1-1	1-3	0-0	0-0	0-0	****	1-0	1-0	1-1	0-0	1-1	0-2	4-0	0-2	0-2	1-2	0-2	0-3	0-1	2-1
Derby C	0-2	3-1	2-0	1-0	2-2	2-1	****	3-0	2-0	3-0	3-1	0-3	3-0	0-2	2-3	3-4	1-1	1-0	1-1	5-0
Everton	0-1	3-2	1-2	3-1	0-0	2-1	3-4	****	2-0	0-1	0-0	2-2	3-2	0-2	0-2	0-0	0-1	1-1	1-3	1-0
Ipswich T	1-3	0-0	2-0	3-0	3-1	1-1	0-1	2-1	****	1-0	0-1	0-0	1-0	1-1	2-1	3-1	1-2	0-0	0-2	7-1
Leeds Utd	0-2	1-1	1-2	1-0	0-1	1-1	1-2	0-1	1-0	****	1-1	2-0	0-0	1-2	0-1	0-1	1-3	0-2	1-1	3-0
Leicester C	1-1	3-1	3-1	0-0	0-1	2-3	1-3	0-0	0-1	1-1	****	1-2	2-0	1-1	2-1	0-1	2-1	1-0	3-0	2-3
Liverpool	1-3	2-2	2-1	1-1	0-0	0-0	2-0	3-2	0-0	2-3	1-2	****	1-1	2-2	2-0	1-2	3-1	0-4	1-0	0-1
Man City	1-2	1-3	4-3	1-1	2-2	2-3	2-0	2-0	2-2	2-0	2-2	0-2	****	4-0	3-0	2-2	1-3	0-1	1-0	1-1
Man Utd	1-3	1-0	2-1	1-2	0-0	0-0	1-0	4-1	0-1	4-3	3-1	0-3	2-0	****	1-1	4-3	1-1	2-2	3-1	0-1
Middlesbro'	0-4	2-1	1-3	1-1	0-1	1-2	2-1	1-1	0-0	3-0	0-0	0-1	0-1	1-0	****	3-0	1-0	1-1	1-0	2-0
Newcastle U	0-2	3-0	2-1	3-2	3-1	1-2	1-0	2-0	0-1	1-3	0-0	1-3	1-1	0-2	3-0	****	1-1	1-1	1-1	3-1
So'ton	0-2	1-3	1-2	0-0	0-3	0-2	1-1	0-1	1-2	3-1	1-3	2-1	0-2	5-0	1-0	3-1	****	2-0	2-1	2-1
Sunderland	1-1	1-2	1-0	0-0	1-0	0-0	1-1	1-3	0-0	5-0	1-0	2-0	2-1	2-1	1-1	2-1	3-1	****	1-2	1-0
Tottenham	1-1	0-0	1-1	3-2	3-2	0-1	1-0	1-0	2-0	1-2	0-2	0-2	3-1	3-1	0-0	2-0	0-2	2-0	****	1-0
West Ham U	1-1	1-1	2-0	2-1	2-0	2-1	4-0	1-0	1-0	3-0	3-0	0-1	1-1	0-1	2-0	3-1	2-0	2-0	1-0	****

Nationwide League 2001-2002

Division One

		P	W	D	L	GF	GA	W	D	L	GF	GA	GD	Pts
1	Manchester City	46	19	3	1	63	19	12	3	8	45	33	+56	99
2	West Bromwich Albion	46	15	4	4	36	11	12	4	7	25	18	+32	89
3	Wolverhampton W	46	13	4	6	33	18	12	7	4	43	25	+33	86
4	Millwall	46	15	3	5	43	22	7	8	8	26	26	+21	77
5	Birmingham City	46	14	4	5	44	20	7	9	7	26	29	+21	76
6	Norwich City	46	15	6	2	36	16	7	3	13	24	35	+9	75
7	Burnley	46	11	7	5	39	29	10	5	8	31	33	+8	75
8	Preston North End	46	13	7	3	45	21	7	5	11	26	38	+12	72
9	Wimbledon	46	9	8	6	30	22	9	5	9	33	35	+6	67
10	Crystal Palace	46	13	3	7	42	22	7	3	13	28	40	+8	66
11	Coventry City	46	12	4	7	33	19	8	2	13	26	34	+6	66
12	Gillingham	46	12	5	6	38	26	6	5	12	26	41	-3	64
13	Sheffield United	46	8	8	7	34	30	7	7	9	19	24	-1	60
14	Watford	46	10	5	8	38	30	6	6	11	24	26	+6	59
15	Bradford City	46	10	1	12	41	39	5	9	9	28	37	-7	55
16	Nottingham Forest	46	7	11	5	26	21	5	7	11	24	30	-1	54
17	Portsmouth	46	9	6	8	36	31	4	8	11	24	41	-12	53
18	Walsall	46	10	6	7	29	27	3	6	14	22	44	-20	51
19	Grimsby Town	46	9	7	7	34	28	3	7	13	16	44	-22	50
20	Sheffield Wednesday	46	6	7	10	28	37	6	7	10	21	34	-22	50
21	Rotherham United	46	7	13	3	32	29	3	6	14	20	37	-14	49
22	Crewe Alexander	46	8	8	7	23	32	4	5	14	24	44	-25	49
23	Barnsley	46	9	9	5	37	33	2	6	15	22	53	-27	48
24	Stockport County	46	5	1	17	19	44	1	7	15	23	58	-60	26

Play-offs

SEMI-FINALS (over 2 legs)
Birmingham City 1 (B Hughes 56)
Millwall 1 (Dublin 80)

Millwall 0
Birmingham City 1 (John 90)
Birmingham won 2-1 on aggregate

Norwich City 3 (Rivers 56, McVeigh 73, Mackay 90)
Wolverhampton W 1 (Sturridge 22)

Wolverhampton W 1 (Cooper 77)
Norwich City 0
Norwich City won 3-2 on aggregate

FINAL
Millennium Stadium   May 12
BIRMINGHAM CITY 1   NORWICH CITY 1
(Horsfield 102)   (I Roberts 91)
aet: Birmingham won 4-2 on penalties

Birmingham: Vaesen; Kenna, Grainger, B Hughes, Vickers (Carter), M Johnson, Devlin, Tebily, Horsfield (A Johnson), John, Mooney (Lazaridis)
Norwich: Green; Kenton, Drury, Mackay, Fleming, Holt, Rivers (Notman), Mulryne, McVeigh (Sutch), Nielsen (I Roberts), Easton
Referee:
Att: 71,597

Goalscorers

	Lg	Cps	Other	Total
Shaun Goater (Man City)	28	4	-	32
Clint Morrison (C Palace)	22	2	-	24
Darren Huckerby (Man City)	20	6	-	26
Stern John (B'ham)	20	1	1	22
(includes 13 league & 1 cup for Nottm F)				
Doug Freeman (C Palace)	20	1	-	21
Dean Sturridge (Wolves)	20	-	1	21
Peter Crouch (Portsmouth)	18	1	-	19
David Connolly (Wimbledon)	18	-	-	18
Marlon King (Gillingham)	17	3	0	20
Steve Claridge (Millwall)	17	1	-	18
Gareth Taylor (Burnley)	16	-	-	16
Mark Robins (Rotherham)	15	1	0	16
Bruce Dyer (Barnsley)	14	4	-	18
Richard Sadler (Millwall)	14	3	-	17
Lee Hughes (Coventry)	14	-	-	14
Eoin Jess (Bradford)	14	-	-	14
Richard Cresswell (Preston)	13	3	-	16
Tommy Mooney (Birmingham)	13	2	-	15

	Barnsley	Birmingham	Bradford C	Burnley	Coventry	Crewe A	Crystal P	Gillingham	Grimsby T	Man City	Millwall	Norwich C	Nottm Forest	Portsmouth	Preston NE	Rotherham	Sheff Utd	Sheff Wed	Stockport Co	Walsall	Watford	WBA	Wimbledon	Wolves
Barnsley	****	1-3	3-3	1-1	1-1	2-0	1-4	4-1	0-0	0-3	1-1	0-2	2-1	1-4	2-1	1-1	1-1	3-0	2-2	4-1	1-0	3-2	1-1	1-0
Birmingham	1-0	****	4-0	3-3	2-0	3-1	1-4	4-1	0-0	1-2	1-2	2-1	1-1	1-1	2-1	2-1	2-0	2-3	2-2	0-3	3-2	0-1	2-0	2-2
Bradford C	4-0	1-3	****	1-1	2-1	2-0	1-2	5-1	0-0	1-3	1-0	2-0	2-1	2-0	3-1	3-1	2-2	1-0	1-0	2-2	0-0	1-0	0-2	3-1
Burnley	3-3	2-3	2-1	****	2-1	3-3	1-0	2-0	3-2	1-1	0-0	2-1	3-3	2-0	2-0	2-0	3-0	0-2	0-2	1-2	0-0	0-0	0-1	3-0
Coventry C	4-0	1-1	4-0	2-3	****	1-0	1-6	1-0	2-1	4-3	0-1	1-0	3-0	2-0	2-0	3-0	2-1	3-0	2-1	0-1	0-1	0-1	0-1	3-1
Crewe Alex	2-0	0-1	2-0	3-3	1-0	****	4-1	2-1	4-0	0-1	0-0	1-1	3-1	2-0	3-1	2-0	1-0	1-0	2-1	0-1	1-0	2-0	0-1	2-3
Crystal P	1-0	3-1	0-1	3-1	1-3	4-1	****	3-1	4-1	1-2	0-0	1-1	1-1	2-0	2-1	2-2	1-3	1-3	0-1	2-2	0-1	2-0	1-1	0-1
Gillingham	3-0	1-1	0-4	2-2	1-2	2-1	0-0	****	5-1	2-1	4-0	4-0	1-0	0-0	2-1	0-1	0-0	0-0	0-0	2-3	0-1	1-0	0-0	1-1
Grimsby T	1-0	3-0	3-1	5-1	0-1	0-1	2-0	2-1	****	2-3	1-2	4-0	2-1	2-0	2-0	3-0	2-1	3-1	3-3	3-3	2-0	0-1	2-1	0-1
Man City	5-1	3-0	3-1	3-1	4-2	0-1	2-3	1-3	0-2	****	0-0	0-2	1-0	2-6	3-1	2-2	1-3	2-1	1-3	0-1	2-1	2-1	1-0	1-0
Millwall	3-1	1-1	3-1	0-2	3-2	5-2	1-0	1-2	4-0	0-2	****	2-0	3-3	1-0	2-2	0-0	1-1	1-3	0-4	0-1	2-2	2-2	1-0	1-0
Norwich City	2-1	0-1	1-4	2-1	2-0	2-1	2-1	2-2	0-0	1-3	2-2	****	1-0	1-0	2-0	0-0	3-1	1-1	3-1	0-1	0-0	3-1	2-1	2-0
Nottm Forest	0-0	1-0	1-0	1-0	2-0	2-0	2-1	0-0	3-1	0-0	1-0	4-0	****	2-1	1-1	1-0	2-1	0-2	0-0	1-3	2-1	2-0	0-1	0-2
Portsmouth	4-4	0-1	0-1	2-3	2-1	4-2	4-2	2-1	0-0	2-6	3-0	1-2	1-0	****	4-0	0-1	1-1	0-0	4-3	0-0	2-1	2-1	1-1	1-4
Preston NE	2-2	1-0	1-1	1-1	4-0	2-2	2-1	0-2	0-0	1-3	0-0	4-0	2-0	2-3	****	0-0	1-0	2-2	1-0	3-3	2-0	2-0	1-1	2-1
Rotherham	1-1	2-2	1-1	3-0	0-0	0-0	2-3	3-2	3-3	1-1	3-2	1-1	1-0	2-1	1-0	****	2-1	0-0	2-2	3-2	1-0	1-0	2-1	1-2
Sheff Utd	1-1	4-0	2-2	0-1	0-1	1-0	1-3	0-0	2-1	1-0	0-0	2-1	2-0	2-0	2-1	0-0	****	0-0	0-0	1-2	0-3	2-0	2-0	0-1
Sheff Wed	1-1	0-1	1-0	0-2	3-0	1-0	1-3	0-0	3-1	2-1	1-3	1-1	0-2	0-0	2-2	0-0	0-0	****	1-1	0-3	1-1	1-1	1-1	3-0
Stockport Co	1-3	0-3	1-0	0-2	2-1	2-1	0-1	0-0	3-3	1-3	0-4	0-5	1-3	2-3	2-0	3-2	3-0	3-0	****	1-0	4-0	3-2	4-0	1-4
Walsall	2-1	1-2	2-2	1-2	0-1	0-1	2-2	1-1	4-0	2-1	0-2	2-1	0-2	1-2	1-2	3-2	1-2	2-0	5-0	****	0-2	4-0	2-2	0-3
Watford	3-0	3-3	0-0	1-2	1-0	4-1	0-1	2-3	2-0	2-1	0-2	3-1	3-1	0-0	2-0	1-2	2-1	2-1	3-0	0-2	****	1-0	1-2	1-1
WBA	3-1	1-0	1-0	1-0	1-0	2-0	2-0	1-0	0-1	0-2	2-2	0-0	0-1	3-1	5-0	1-0	1-1	0-3	3-2	2-1	0-3	****	1-2	0-1
Wimbledon	0-1	3-1	1-2	0-0	0-1	2-0	1-1	3-1	2-1	2-1	2-1	2-1	0-0	2-1	1-1	1-0	1-1	1-2	6-0	1-2	1-2	0-0	****	0-1
Wolves	4-1	2-1	3-1	3-0	3-1	0-1	0-1	2-0	0-1	0-3	1-0	0-2	2-1	0-2	2-3	2-1	3-2	0-3	2-2	1-4	3-0	1-0	0-1	****

Nationwide League 2001-2002

Division Two

		P	W	D	L	GF	GA	W	D	L	GF	GA	GD	Pts
1	**Brighton & Hove Albion**	46	17	5	1	42	16	8	10	5	24	26	+24	**90**
2	**Reading**	46	12	7	4	36	20	11	8	4	34	23	+27	**84**
3	**Brentford**	46	17	5	1	48	12	7	6	10	29	31	+34	**83**
4	**Cardiff City**	46	12	8	3	39	25	11	6	6	36	25	+25	**83**
5	**Stoke City**	46	16	4	3	43	12	7	7	9	24	28	+27	**80**
6	**Huddersfield Town**	46	13	7	3	35	19	8	8	7	30	28	+18	**78**
7	**Bristol City**	46	13	6	4	38	21	8	4	11	30	32	+15	**73**
8	**Queens Park Rangers**	46	11	10	2	35	18	8	4	11	25	31	+11	**71**
9	**Oldham Athletic**	46	14	6	3	47	27	4	10	9	30	38	+12	**70**
10	**Wigan Athletic**	46	9	6	8	36	23	7	10	6	30	28	+15	**64**
11	**Wycombe Wanderers**	46	13	5	5	38	26	4	8	11	20	38	-6	**64**
12	**Tranmere Rovers**	46	10	9	4	39	19	6	6	11	24	41	+3	**63**
13	**Swindon Town**	46	10	7	6	26	21	5	7	11	20	35	-10	**59**
14	**Port Vale**	46	11	6	6	35	24	5	4	14	16	38	-11	**58**
15	**Colchester United**	46	9	6	8	35	33	6	6	11	30	43	-11	**57**
16	**Blackpool**	46	8	9	6	39	31	6	5	12	27	38	-3	**56**
17	**Peterborough United**	46	11	5	7	46	26	4	5	14	18	33	+5	**55**
18	**Chesterfield**	46	9	3	11	35	36	4	10	9	18	29	-12	**52**
19	**Notts County**	46	8	7	8	28	29	5	4	14	31	42	-12	**50**
20	**Northampton Town**	46	9	4	10	30	33	5	3	15	24	46	-25	**49**
21	**Bournemouth**	46	9	4	10	36	33	1	10	12	20	38	-15	**44**
22	**Bury**	46	6	9	8	26	32	5	2	16	17	43	-32	**44**
23	**Wrexham**	46	7	7	9	29	32	4	3	16	27	57	-33	**43**
24	**Cambridge United**	46	7	7	9	29	34	0	6	17	18	59	-46	**34**

Play-offs

Semi-finals *(over 2 legs)*
Huddersfield Town 0   Brentford 0

Brentford 2   Huddersfield Town 0
(Powell 14, Owusu 46)
Brentford won 2-0 on aggregate

Stoke City 1   Cardiff City 2
(Burton 84)   *(Earnshaw 12,
                               Fortune-West 59)*

Cardiff City 0   Stoke City 2
                               *(O'Connor 90,
                               Oulare 115)*
Stoke won 3-2 aggregate - aet

FINAL

Millennium Stadium   May 11
Brentford 0   Stoke City 2
                               (Burton 16, Burgess 45 og)
Brentford: P Smith; Dobson, Anderson, Ingimarsson,
Powell, Sidwell, Evans, Rowlands (O'Connor),
Owusu, Burgess (McCammon), Hunt
Stoke: Cutler, Thomas, Clarke, Handyside, Shtanyuk,
Dinning (Brightwell), Gudjonsson, O'Connor, Burtn,
Gunnlaugsson (Van Deurzen), Iwelumo (Cooke)
aet

Attendance: 42,523

Goalscorers

	Lg	Cps	Other	Total
Bobby Zamora (Brighton)	28	4	-	32
Andy Thomson (QPR)	21	-	-	21
Lloyd Owusu (Brentford)	20	1	1	22
Danny Allsop (Notts Co)	19	6	3	28
Nicky Forster (Reading)	19	-	-	19
Leon McKenzie (Peterborough)	18	1	1	20
Andy Liddell (Wigan)	18	-	-	18
Ben Burgess (Brentford)	17	1	-	18
Jamie Forrester (Northampton)	17	1	-	18
Tony Thorpe (Bristol City)	16	1	1	18
Leon Knight (Huddersfield)	16	1	-	17
Lee Peacock (Bristol City)	15	-	2	17
Jamie Cureton (Reading)	15	1	-	16
Scott McGleish (Colchester)	15	1	-	16
Simon Haworth (Tranmere)	15	1	-	16

Home \ Away	Blackpool	Bournemouth	Brentford	Brighton	Bristol C	Bury	Cambridge	Cardiff C	Chesterfield	Colchester	Huddersfield	Northampton	Notts County	Oldham	Peterboro	Port Vale	QPR	Reading	Stoke City	Swindon T	Tranmere	Wigan Ath	Wrexham	Wycombe W
Blackpool	****	4-3	1-3	2-2	5-1	0-1	1-1	1-1	1-0	2-1	1-2	1-2	0-0	0-2	2-2	0-1	2-0	0-2	2-2	1-0	1-1	3-1	3-0	2-2
Bournemouth	0-1	****	0-2	1-0	0-2	1-0	1-1	0-2	1-3	1-0	1-0	2-0	2-0	2-2	1-0	0-0	1-1	2-2	2-0	1-0	0-0	0-0	2-1	1-1
Brentford	2-0	1-0	****	4-0	1-2	0-2	0-1	0-0	3-1	1-0	2-1	1-0	0-0	2-2	1-1	0-0	2-1	0-0	3-1	2-0	0-0	1-0	0-3	5-3
Brighton	4-0	2-1	4-0	****	4-0	1-1	1-0	0-2	1-0	3-0	3-1	2-3	1-0	2-0	2-0	2-1	1-0	1-1	2-0	0-3	0-1	0-2	1-2	1-1
Bristol City	2-1	1-0	1-2	1-3	****	2-2	1-3	3-2	2-1	1-0	1-0	1-0	2-0	0-3	2-1	4-1	0-2	3-3	3-1	3-1	0-0	2-1	3-0	2-1
Bury	1-1	2-1	5-1	3-2	2-1	****	0-1	0-1	1-2	2-0	1-0	2-1	4-0	1-2	4-0	1-0	3-0	1-0	3-0	1-1	3-0	1-1	3-0	0-2
Cambridge U	1-1	0-3	0-2	4-3	2-1	2-0	****	2-1	2-0	4-1	2-0	2-0	2-1	2-1	2-0	5-0	0-0	1-2	1-0	1-1	2-2	2-2	2-1	2-0
Cardiff	2-2	2-2	3-1	0-0	1-0	2-1	2-1	****	2-1	3-1	1-2	3-3	0-0	1-2	0-2	1-1	0-1	1-0	1-0	0-3	0-1	0-2	2-1	0-1
Chesterfield	2-1	2-1	0-1	1-1	3-0	5-1	2-0	3-0	****	4-1	2-0	1-3	1-0	1-1	0-0	4-1	0-0	3-1	2-0	1-0	1-1	2-0	2-1	0-0
Colchester U	1-1	1-2	1-4	0-0	2-1	3-2	4-3	1-1	1-2	****	2-1	2-1	2-0	0-3	2-1	3-1	2-2	2-3	3-3	4-0	2-1	0-0	5-1	0-0
Huddersfield	2-4	1-0	1-1	1-2	0-0	0-1	2-1	2-2	2-0	3-6	****	3-3	3-2	2-1	2-1	1-1	3-2	2-1	0-1	1-0	0-1	0-2	2-1	2-4
Northampton	1-3	1-0	1-1	2-0	0-3	2-0	3-1	1-0	0-0	1-1	3-3	****	2-0	0-3	0-3	2-0	0-1	2-0	2-0	1-0	4-1	1-3	4-1	2-1
Notts County	1-0	2-0	0-0	2-0	2-0	1-0	5-1	0-4	1-1	1-2	1-1	0-2	****	0-2	3-3	0-1	0-1	0-1	0-2	3-1	3-0	0-2	2-2	0-0
Oldham Ath	2-1	1-0	3-2	1-0	0-1	2-0	2-2	1-2	0-2	2-3	1-2	2-2	0-2	****	0-2	4-1	1-1	3-4	1-2	3-0	4-1	1-1	0-2	0-0
Peterborough	3-2	6-0	1-1	2-1	4-1	2-1	2-0	0-0	2-1	3-1	0-1	0-1	4-2	0-2	****	2-0	4-1	2-0	2-0	1-2	2-0	0-2	2-3	0-1
Port Vale	1-1	0-0	2-1	1-0	1-0	4-0	2-1	1-2	1-1	3-1	1-1	2-0	0-1	2-1	0-2	****	4-1	0-1	1-1	0-2	0-2	2-0	3-1	2-1
QPR	2-0	1-1	0-0	3-0	0-0	1-2	4-3	2-1	1-1	4-1	1-2	0-1	3-2	0-0	2-0	4-1	****	1-0	1-0	1-0	2-0	1-1	3-2	2-0
Reading	3-0	2-2	1-2	1-1	1-0	1-0	1-1	0-3	2-1	1-1	3-2	5-1	1-0	3-4	0-1	1-1	1-0	****	1-0	2-0	0-3	1-0	2-0	1-0
Stoke City	2-0	2-0	3-2	0-0	0-0	3-0	5-0	0-3	0-0	3-0	1-1	3-0	0-0	0-2	2-0	5-0	1-0	1-0	****	0-3	4-1	3-1	0-1	2-0
Swindon Town	1-0	0-0	2-0	3-1	1-0	1-0	2-0	0-1	1-0	3-0	0-1	3-0	1-0	2-2	2-2	1-0	4-0	0-2	0-3	****	2-0	1-0	3-0	1-1
Tranmere	4-0	0-0	1-1	1-1	1-2	2-1	6-1	1-3	3-1	2-2	1-1	2-1	4-2	0-0	2-1	3-1	1-2	4-1	2-2	2-2	****	1-2	3-1	2-1
Wigan Athletic	0-1	0-0	1-0	3-0	1-0	1-1	4-1	4-0	1-1	1-1	1-0	1-2	1-1	1-1	0-0	2-2	1-1	2-0	6-1	0-0	2-2	****	2-3	1-0
Wrexham	1-1	2-1	0-3	1-2	0-2	1-0	5-0	1-3	2-1	1-1	1-0	5-1	4-1	0-2	2-3	2-3	1-3	4-1	0-1	3-1	5-0	2-0	****	0-0
Wycombe W	1-4	1-1	5-3	1-1	2-1	0-2	2-0	0-1	0-0	0-0	2-4	2-1	0-0	0-0	0-1	2-1	2-0	1-0	2-0	1-1	2-1	1-0	0-0	****

Nationwide League 2001-2002
Division Three

		P	W	D	L	GF	GA	W	D	L	GF	GA	GD	Pts
1	**Plymouth Argyle**	46	19	2	2	41	11	12	7	4	30	17	+43	102
2	**Luton town**	46	15	5	3	50	18	15	2	6	46	30	+48	97
3	**Mansfield Town**	46	17	3	3	49	24	7	4	12	23	36	+12	79
4	**Cheltenham Town**	46	11	11	1	40	20	10	4	9	26	29	+17	78
5	**Rochdale**	46	13	8	2	41	22	8	7	8	24	30	+13	78
6	**Rushden & Diamonds**	46	14	5	4	40	20	6	8	9	29	33	+16	73
7	**Hartlepool United**	46	12	6	5	52	23	8	5	10	21	25	+26	71
8	**Scunthorpe United**	46	14	5	4	43	22	5	9	9	31	34	+18	71
9	**Shrewsbury Town**	46	13	4	6	36	19	7	6	10	28	34	+11	70
10	**Kidderminster Harriers**	46	13	6	4	35	17	6	3	14	21	30	+9	66
11	**Hull City**	46	12	6	5	38	18	4	7	12	19	33	+6	61
12	**Southend United**	46	12	5	6	36	22	3	8	12	15	32	-3	58
13	**Macclesfield Town**	46	7	7	9	23	25	8	6	9	18	27	-11	58
14	**York City**	46	11	5	7	26	20	5	4	14	28	47	-13	57
15	**Darlington**	46	11	6	6	37	25	4	5	14	23	46	-11	56
16	**Exeter City**	46	7	9	7	25	32	7	4	12	23	41	-25	55
17	**Carlisle United**	46	11	5	7	31	21	1	11	11	18	35	-7	52
18	**Leyton Orient**	46	10	7	6	37	25	3	6	14	18	46	-16	52
19	**Torquay United**	46	8	6	9	27	31	4	9	10	19	32	-17	51
20	**Swansea City**	46	7	8	8	26	26	6	4	13	27	51	-24	51
21	**Oxford United**	46	8	7	8	34	28	3	7	13	19	34	-9	47
22	**Lincoln City**	46	8	4	11	25	27	2	12	9	19	35	-18	46
23	**Bristol Rovers**	46	8	7	8	28	28	3	5	15	12	32	-20	45
24	**Halifax Town**	46	5	9	9	24	28	3	3	17	15	56	-45	36

Play-offs
Semi-finals *(over 2 legs)*

Hartlepool 1   Cheltenham Town 1
(Williams 45)   *(Grayson 89)*

Cheltenham Town 1   Hartlepool 1
(Williams 26)   *(Arnison 17)*
2-2 on aggregate
aet; Cheltenham won 5-4 on pens

Rushden & D 1   Rochdale 2
(Wardley 34,   *(McEvilly 8, Simpson 57)*
Butterworth 73)

Rochdale 1   Rushden & D 2
(Peters 65, og)   *(Lowe 67, Hall 76)*
Leyton Orient won 2-1 on aggregate
Rushden won 4-3 on aggregate

FINAL
Millennium Stadium   May 26
Cheltenham Town 3   Rushden & Diamonds 1
(Devaney 27,   (Hall 28)
Alsop 49, Finnigan 80)
Cheltenham: Book; Griffin, Victory, Williams, Walker, Duff, Finnigan, Devaney (Grayson), Alsop, Naylor, Yates
Rushden: Turley; Mustafa, Underwood, Butterworth, Peters, Tillson, Hall, Wardley, Partridge (Angell), Lowe, Gray (Brady)

Attendance: 24,368

Goalscorers

	Lg	Cps	Other	Total
Steve Howard (Luton)	24	-	-	24
Luke Rogers (Shrewsbury)	22	-	-	22
Chris Greenacre (Mansfield)	21	7	-	28
Julian Alsop (Cheltenham)	20	4	2	26
Onandi Lowe (Rushden)	19	-	1	20
Gordon Watson (Hartlepool)	18	-	-	18
Gary Alexander (Hull)	17	3	3	23
Nathan Ellington (Bristol R)	15	4	2	21
Ian Clark (Darlington)	15	-	-	15
(includes 2 league goals for Hartlepool)				
Dean Crowe (Luton)	15	-	-	15
Richie Foran (Carlisle)	14	1	1	16
Kevin Townson (Rochdale)	14	-	1	15
Michael Proctor (York)	14	-	-	14
Martin Carruthers (Scunthorpe)	13	3	1	17
Steve Torpey (Scunthorpe)	13	-	2	15
Paul Moody (Oxford)	13	-	-	13
Lee Nogan (York)	13	-	-	13
Lee Thorpe (Lincoln)	13	-	-	13

	Barnet	Blackpool	Brighton HA	Cardiff City	Carlisle Utd	Cheltenham	Chesterfield	Darlington	Exeter City	Halifax Town	Hartlepool U	Hull City	K'mister	Leyton O	Lincoln City	Macclesfield	Mansfield T	Plymouth A	Rochdale	Scunthorpe	Shrewsbury	Southend U	Torquay	York
Bristol Rovers	****	0-0	1-2	1-0	0-0	0-1	1-1	2-1	2-1	5-3	1-2	3-2	1-1	1-1	3-1	1-2	0-2	0-3	1-0	2-1	1-1	4-1	1-0	2-2
Carlisle United	1-0	****	0-0	1-3	1-3	0-0	0-2	1-0	1-0	6-1	2-2	0-2	1-0	4-1	2-3	1-2	0-2	0-3	0-2	3-3	2-1	3-1	2-0	2-1
Cheltenham	0-0	2-0	****	1-0	3-1	2-1	3-0	2-1	0-0	1-1	1-1	1-1	0-1	2-3	3-0	2-0	4-1	3-0	0-1	1-0	1-1	2-2	1-2	4-0
Darlington	1-0	2-2	0-2	****	0-0	2-1	0-1	2-0	1-0	3-1	2-1	0-2	4-1	0-1	0-0	0-1	0-0	3-1	0-1	1-0	1-1	0-2	1-0	2-1
Exeter City	1-0	1-0	4-2	4-2	****	4-0	5-0	1-3	2-1	0-0	2-2	0-2	0-1	4-1	0-1	0-1	1-1	1-1	0-4	2-2	3-3	0-3	1-3	0-0
Halifax Town	0-0	2-2	4-1	2-2	1-1	****	0-0	1-0	0-2	1-1	3-0	2-4	1-2	1-0	1-0	2-0	1-2	2-4	0-4	2-2	1-0	2-2	0-0	1-1
Hartlepool Utd	1-1	3-1	0-1	1-2	2-0	3-0	****	0-1	3-1	6-1	1-1	1-1	0-4	4-1	4-1	2-3	1-1	5-1	0-1	2-2	5-1	2-1	1-0	3-0
Hull City	0-0	0-1	5-1	2-0	3-0	3-0	1-1	****	0-1	3-1	1-1	2-4	1-2	1-1	3-0	0-1	1-2	2-4	3-2	0-1	1-1	0-3	4-1	1-1
Kidderminster	2-0	202	0-0	1-0	3-1	2-0	3-2	1-1	****	0-1	0-2	0-2	0-1	1-1	3-0	0-0	1-1	5-1	0-1	0-4	1-1	3-1	1-0	4-1
Leyton Orient	3-1	0-0	0-2	0-0	1-1	1-2	2-0	0-1	1-3	****	0-0	1-0	2-0	0-0	0-0	2-0	0-1	1-2	2-1	1-2	2-1	0-2	1-2	1-2
Lincoln City	0-1	3-1	0-2	1-1	0-0	2-0	2-2	0-1	0-1	2-1	****	0-1	1-0	0-1	1-1	0-1	1-0	0-1	0-1	0-1	2-1	2-1	0-0	1-3
Luton Town	3-0	1-1	2-1	5-2	3-0	5-0	2-2	3-0	1-0	5-3	5-0	****	1-0	5-3	4-2	2-0	1-1	2-4	2-3	1-0	1-0	3-0	5-1	2-1
Macclesfield T	2-1	1-0	1-0	1-1	1-2	2-1	3-0	0-2	0-1	3-0	4-1	4-1	****	0-1	0-1	1-1	3-1	0-0	4-3	3-1	2-0	0-2	0-1	2-1
Mansfield T	2-0	2-0	4-2	4-2	0-1	1-1	4-2	0-1	1-2	2-1	1-2	4-1	4-0	****	4-2	2-0	1-2	1-4	2-1	2-1	0-1	3-0	2-0	1-1
Oxford United	0-0	0-1	1-0	1-2	2-0	3-0	1-2	1-0	2-1	3-0	3-0	1-0	2-0	1-0	****	1-3	1-2	1-0	2-1	1-0	0-1	3-0	1-1	1-2
Plymouth A	1-0	3-0	2-0	1-0	3-0	6-1	2-1	2-0	3-0	1-0	3-0	2-0	2-0	3-2	4-2	1-3	1-1	****	2-2	3-0	0-1	2-0	2-2	1-0
Rochdale	2-1	1-1	2-2	3-1	2-0	2-4	0-0	3-3	3-0	3-1	3-1	1-0	0-1	3-1	3-1	2-3	****	0-0	2-2	1-0	0-1	2-0	2-0	3-0
Rushden & D	3-1	3-1	1-0	2-1	2-1	2-1	0-1	1-0	3-2	3-0	3-1	2-4	1-2	3-1	0-1	2-3	1-1	****	0-2	3-3	0-1	4-0	2-0	5-4
Scunthorpe U	1-2	2-1	1-2	7-1	3-4	0-1	1-1	0-2	2-1	4-1	0-2	0-1	1-0	1-0	2-1	2-1	2-1	1-1	****	3-1	0-2	2-2	1-0	3-0
Shrewsbury T	0-1	1-0	2-1	3-0	0-1	3-0	1-3	4-0	3-0	1-0	0-2	2-2	1-1	3-0	1-0	3-1	1-0	0-3	3-1	****	0-2	3-0	0-1	3-2
Southend U	2-1	3-2	0-1	1-0	3-1	4-1	0-0	2-0	1-0	1-0	0-1	2-2	2-0	1-0	2-2	0-1	0-0	4-2	0-2	0-2	****	4-2	1-0	0-1
Swansea C	2-1	0-0	2-2	1-0	4-2	0-2	1-3	1-0	0-1	3-1	0-0	1-2	0-1	2-0	2-2	0-1	0-1	4-2	2-2	3-3	3-2	****	2-1	0-3
Torquay U	2-1	2-1	0-1	2-1	0-2	2-4	1-0	1-1	1-4	0-0	1-1	5-1	1-2	3-1	0-0	1-2	3-0	0-0	0-0	2-1	2-1	1-2	****	1-1
York City	3-0	3-0	1-3	2-0	2-3	1-0	1-0	2-1	2-1	1-2	1-0	2-1	1-0	3-1	1-0	1-2	0-1	0-1	0-2	1-1	2-1	1-0	0-3	****

English Non-League Football

Nationwide Conference

	P	W	D	L	F	A	Pts
Boston United	42	25	9	8	84	42	84
Dagenham & Redbridge	42	24	12	6	70	47	84
Yeovil Town	42	19	13	10	66	53	70
Doncaster Rovers	42	18	13	11	68	46	67
Barnet	42	19	10	13	64	48	67
Morecambe	42	17	11	14	63	67	62
Farnborough Town	42	18	7	17	66	54	61
Margate	42	14	16	12	59	53	58
Telford United	42	14	15	13	63	58	57
Nuneaton Borough	42	16	9	17	57	57	57
Stevenage Borough	42	15	10	17	57	60	55
Scarborough	42	14	14	14	55	63	55
Northwich Victoria	42	16	7	19	57	70	55
Chester City	42	15	9	18	54	51	54
Southport	42	13	14	15	53	49	53
Leigh R'way Mechs Inst.	42	15	9	19	56	58	52
Hereford United	42	14	10	18	50	53	52
Forest Green Rovers	42	12	15	15	54	76	51
Woking	42	13	9	20	59	70	48
Hayes	42	13	5	24	53	80	44
Stalybridge Celtic	42	11	10	21	40	69	43
Dover Athletic	42	11	6	25	41	65	39

Leading Scorers (League & Cup): Daryl Clare (Boston) 24; Mark Stein (Dagenham) 24

Unibond League

Premier Division	P	W	D	L	F	A	Pts
Burton Albion	44	31	11	2	106	30	104
Vauxhall Motors	44	27	8	9	86	55	89
Lancaster City	44	23	9	12	80	57	78
Worksop Town	44	23	9	12	74	51	78
Emley	44	22	9	13	69	54	75
Accrington Stanley	44	21	9	14	89	64	72
Runcorn FC Halton	44	21	8	15	76	53	71
Barrow	44	19	10	15	75	59	67
Altrincham	44	19	9	16	66	58	66
Bradford Park Avenue	44	18	5	21	77	76	59
Droylsden	44	17	8	19	65	78	59
Blyth Spartans	44	14	16	14	59	62	58
Frickley Athletic*	44	16	11	17	63	69	58
Gateshead	44	14	14	16	58	71	56
Whitby Town	44	15	8	21	61	76	53
Hucknall Town	44	14	9	21	49	68	51
Marine	44	11	17	16	62	71	50
Burscough	44	15	5	24	69	86	50
Gainsborough Trinity	44	13	10	21	61	76	49
Colwyn Bay	44	12	11	21	49	82	47
Bishop Auckland	44	12	8	24	46	68	44
Hyde United	44	10	10	24	61	87	40
Bamber Bridge	44	7	10	27	38	88	30

Deducted one point for fielding an ineligible player

Leading Scorers: Terry Fearns (Vauxhall) 36; Paul Mullin (Accrington) 34; Rod Thornley (Altrincham) 33

Dr Martens League

Premier Division	P	W	D	L	F	A	Pts
Kettering Town	42	27	6	9	80	41	87
Tamworth	42	24	13	5	81	41	85
Havant & Waterlooville	42	22	9	11	74	50	75
Crawley Town	42	21	10	11	67	48	73
Newport County	42	19	9	14	61	48	66
Tiverton Town	42	17	10	15	70	63	61
Moor Green	42	18	7	17	64	62	61
Worcester City	42	16	12	14	65	54	60
Stafford Rangers	42	17	9	16	70	62	60
Ilkeston Town	42	14	16	12	58	61	58
Weymouth	42	15	11	16	159	67	56
Hinckley United	42	14	13	15	64	62	55
Fokestone Invicta	42	14	12	16	51	61	54
Cambridge City	42	12	16	14	60	70	52
Welling United	42	13	12	17	69	66	51
Hednesford Town	42	15	6	21	59	70	51
Bath City	42	13	11	18	56	65	50
Chelmsford City	42	13	11	18	63	75	50
Newport (IOW)	42	12	12	18	38	61	48
King's Lynn	42	11	13	18	44	57	46
Merthyr Tydfil	42	12	8	22	53	71	44
Salisbury City	42	6	8	28	36	87	26

Leading Scorers: Paul Kiely (Stafford) 29; James Taylor (Havant) 28; David Laws (Weymouth) 25

Ryman League

Premier Division	P	W	D	L	F	A	Pts
Gravesend & Northfleet	42	31	6	5	86	27	99
Canvey Island	42	27	8	7	79	41	89
Aldershot Town	42	22	13	7	73	40	79
Braintree Town	41	21	11	9	73	39	74
Purfleet	42	22	6	14	78	51	72
Grays Athletic	42	22	5	15	63	46	71
Chesham United	42	18	13	11	74	60	67
Hendon	41	18	13	10	62	54	67
Billericay Town	42	18	12	12	73	60	66
St Albans City	42	18	5	19	72	69	59
Hitchin Town	42	14	13	15	55	55	55
Sutton United	40	16	6	18	62	62	54
Heybridge Swifts	41	14	11	16	73	70	53
Kingstonian	42	15	5	22	50	69	50
Boreham Wood	42	14	8	20	49	68	50
Maidenhead United	42	15	2	25	47	63	47
Bedford Town	42	12	10	20	55	77	46
Basingstoke Town	42	12	9	21	48	74	45
Enfield	41	10	11	20	62	91	41
Hampton & Richmond	42	10	9	23	40	62	39
Harrow Borough	42	10	6	26	40	85	36
Croydon	42	4	10	28	33	84	22

Leading Scorers: Lee Boylan (Canvey) 31; Nicky Simpson (Braintree) 25; Simon Martin (St Albans) 24; Craig Maskall (Hampton) 24; Kevin Slinn (Bedford) 24

FA Challenge Cup 2001-2002

First Round

Aldershot Town 0
Bristol Rovers 0

Bristol Rovers 1 *(Astafjevs)*
Aldershot Town 0

Altrincham 1 *(Thornley pen)*
Lancaster C 1 *(Whittaker)*

Lancaster C 1 *(Mayers)*
Altrincham 4 *(Poland 3, 1 pen, Thornley pen)*

Barnet 0
Carlisle United 0

Carlisle United 1 *(Soley)*
Barnet 0

Bedford Town 0
Peterborough U 0

Peterborough U 2 *(A Clarke, Fenn)*
Bedford Town 1 *(Slinn)*

Blackpool 2 *(Jaszczun, MacKenzie)*
Newport C 2 *(Hughes og, Clark)*

Newport C 1 *(Rose)*
Blackpool 4 *(Ormerod 2, Murphy, Benton og)*

Bournemouth 3 *(Hughes, Hayter, S Fletcher)*
Worksop T 0

Brentford 1 *(Gibbs)*
Morecambe 0

Brighton & H 1 *(Zamora)*
Shrewsbury T 0

Bristol City 0
Leyton Orient 1 *(Watts)*

Cambridge U 1 *(Tudor)*
Notts County 1 *(Allsopp)*

Notts County 2 *(Allsopp, Owers)*
Cambridge U 0

Colchester U 0
York City 0

York City 2 *(Brass, Potter)*
Colchester U 2 *(McGleish, Duguid)*
aet York won 3-2 on pens

Carlisle Utd 5 *(Stevens 4, Dobie)*
Woking 1 *(West)*

Dagenham & Red 1 *(Stein)*
Southport 0

Doncaster R 2 *(Tierney, Watson)*
Scunthorpe 3 *(Hodges,Carruthers, Calvo-Garcia)*

Exeter City 3 *(Curran, Tomlinson, Roscoe)*
Cambridge City 0

Grays Athletic 1 *(Lock)*
Hinckley 2 *(Hunter, Lenton)*

Halifax T 2 *(Middleton, Wood)*
Farnborough T 1 *(C Piper)*

Hayes 2 *(Warner 36, Clark 41, pen, D Warner 85)*
Wycombe 4 *(Rammell 24, 73, Currie 45, 82)*

Hereford U 1 *(Wright)*
Wrexham 0

Huddersfield T 2 *(Moses, Knight)*
Gravesend & N *(Clarke 2og)*

Kettering Town 1 *(Norman)*
Cheltenham Town 6 *(Naylor 2, Alsopp 2, Howells, Devaney)*

Kidderminster Harriers 0
Darlington 1 *(Campbell)*

Lewes 0
Stoke 2 *(Handyside, Gunnarsson)*
played at Stoke

Lincoln 1 *(Holmes)*
Bury 1 *(Seddon)*

Bury 1 *(Singh)*
Lincoln 1 *(Cameron)*
aet Lincoln won 3-2 on pens

Macclesfield Town 2 *(Lambert 2)*
Forest Green Rovers 2 *Meechan, Cooper pen)*

Forest Green Rovers 1 *(Cooper)*
Macclesfield Town 1 *(Greene)*
aet Macclesfield won 11-10 on pens

Mansfield Town 1 *(Greenacre)*
Oxford United 0

Northwich Victoria 2 *(Blundell, Mike)*
Hull City 5 *(Johnsson, Matthews, Dudfield, Alexander, Barnard og)*

Oldham Ath 1 *(Duxbury)*
Barrow 1 *(Housham)*

Barrow 0
Oldham Ath 1 *(Eyres)*

Port Vale 3 *(Burgess, Cummins, Brooker)*
Aylesbury U 0

Reading 1 *(Cureton)*
Welling U 0

Southend U 3 *(Rawle, Bramble 2)*
Luton Town 2 *(Forbes, Brkovic)*

Stalybrige Celtic 0
Chesterfield 3 *(Beckett, Scott og, D'Auria)*

Swansea C 4 *(Williams, Cusack, Sidibie, Watkin)*
QPR 0

Swindon T 3 *(Ruddock pen, Invincible, Heywood)*
Hartlepool U 1 *(Clarke)*

Reading 4 *(Hodges, Cureton, Butler, Jones)*
Grays Athletic 0

Tamworth 1 *(Wilson)*
Rochdale 1 *(Doughty)*

Rochdale 1 *(Oliver)*
Tamworth 0

Tiverton Town 1 *(Nancekivell)*
Cardiff C 3 *(Brayson, Hamilton, Earnshaw)*

Torquay U 1 *(Hill)*
Northampton T 2 *(Gabbiadini 2)*

Tranmere R 4 *(Navarro, Price 2 Flynn)*
Brigg Town 1 *(Leech)*

Whitby Town 1 *(Gildea)*
Plymouth Argyle 1 *(Phillips)*

Plymouth A 3 *(Bent, Stonebridge, Phillips)*
Whitby Town 2 *(Burt, Robinson)*

Wigan Athletic 0
Canvey island 1 *(Gregory)*

Worcester City 0
Rushden & D 1 *(Hanlon)*

Second Round

Altrincham 1 *(Maddox)*
Darlington 2 *(Chillingworth, Wainwright)*

Blackpool 2 *(J Murphy, Simpson)*
Rochdale 0

Brighton & H 2 *(Zamora, Cullip)*
Rushden & D 1 *(Hanlon pen)*

Canvey Island 1 *(Gregory)*
Northampton Town 0

Cardiff C 3 *(Earnshaw, G Gordon, Fortune-West)*
Port Vale 0

Chesterfield 1 *(Beckett)*
Southend U 1 *(Bramble)*

Southend U 2 *(Whelan, Belgrave)*
Chesterfield 0

Exeter City 0
Dagenham & Redbridge 0

Dagenham & R 3 (Janney,
            MacDougald, Charlery)
Exeter City 0

Halifax Town 1 (Harsley)
Stoke City 1 (Cooke)

Stoke City 3 (Gudjohnsson,
            Iwelumo, Gunnarsson)
Halifax Town 0

Hinckley United 0
Cheltenham Town 2 (Naylor, Alsop)

Hull City 2 (Dudfield, Alexander)
Oldham A 3 (Sheridan, Eyres,
            Duxbury)

Leyton Orient 2 (Ibehre, Watts)
Lincoln City 1 (Hamilton)

Macclesfield T 4 (Byrne 2, Glover 2
Swansea City 1 (Cusack)

Mansfield 4 (Greenacre 3, Cordon)
Huddersfield Town 0

Peterborough U 1 (Danielsson)
Bournemouth 0

Plymouth Argyle 1 (Wootton)
Bristol Rovers 1 (Walters

Bristol Rovers 3 (Ommel, Hogg,
            Ellington)
Plymouth Argyle 2 (Friio 2)

Scunthorpe United 3 (Carruthers 2
            Calvo-Garcia)
Brentford 2 (Dobson, Burgess)

Swindon Town 3 (Invincible,
            P Edwards, Howe)
Hereford T 2 (G Williams, Wright)

Tranmere 6 (Price, Koumas 3
            Barlow pen, Yates)
Carlisle 1 (Foran)

Wycombe W 3 (Bulman, Walker,
            Currie)
Notts County 0

York City 2 (Richardson, Potter)
Reading 0

Third Round

Aston Villa 2 (Taylor, P Neville og)
Manchester Utd 3 (Solskjaer,
            Van Nistleroy 2)

Barnsley 1 (Barnard)
Blackburn Rovers 1 (Hignett)

Blackburn R 3 (Grabbi, Dunn pen,
            Johansson)
Barnsley 1 (Dyer)

Brighton & Hove 0
Preston NE 2 (Skora, Macken)

Burnley 4 (Little, I Moore 3
Canvey Island 1 (Boylan)

Cardiff 2 (Kavanagh, Young)
Leeds United 1 (Viduka)

Charlton A 2 (Stuart pen, Euell)
Blackpool 1 (Hills)

Cheltenham Town 2 (Naylor 2)
Oldham Athletic 1 (Eyres)

Coventry City 0
Tottenham H 2 (Poyet, Ferdinand)

Crewe Alexander 2 (Rix, Foster)
Sheffield Wed 1 (Hamshaw)

Dagenham & R 1 (McDougald)
Ipswich Town 4 (Peralta 2,
            Magilton, Stewart)

Darlington 2 (Wainwright, Conlon)
Peterborough United 2 (Farrell,
            Ballard pen)

Peterborough 2 (McKenzie,
            A Clarke)
Darlington 0

Derby 1 (Ravenelli)
Bristol Rovers 3 (Ellington 3)

Grimsby Town 0
York City 0

York City 1 (Neilson og)
Grimsby Town 0

Leicester City 2 (Scowcroft 2)
Mansfield Town 1 (Greenacre)

Liverpool 3 (Owen 2, Anelka)
Birmingham 0

Macclesfield Town 0
West Ham 3 (Defoe 2, Cole)

Man City 2 (Wanchope, Horlock)
Swindon Town 0

Millwall 2 (Sadlier 2)
Scunthorpe U 1 (McCombe)

Newcastle U 2 (Shearer, Acuna)
Crystal Palace 0

Norwich City 0
Chelsea 0

Chelsea 4 (Stanic, Lampard, Zola,
            Forssell)
Norwich City 0

Portsmouth 1 (Smith og)
Leyton Orient 4 (Smith, Watts, Gray,
            Christie)

Rotherham 2 (Barker, Mullin)
Southampton 1 (Pahars pen)

Sheff United (Brown)
Nottingham Forest 0

Southend 1 (Belgrave)
Tranmere R 3 (Allison, Price, Flynn)

Stockport Co 1 (Daly pen)
Bolton 4 (Bergsson, Norris,
            Pederson, Ricketts)

Stoke City 0
Everton 1 (Stubbs)

Sunderland 1 (Phillips)
WBA 2 (Clement pen, Johnson)

Walsall 2 (Bennett, Angell)
Bradford C 0

Watford 2 (Noel-Williams, Gayle)
Arsenal 4 (Henry, Ljundberg, Kanu,
            Bergkamp)

Wimbledon 0
Middlesborough 0

Middlesborough 2 (Whelan,
            Cunningham og)
Wimbledon 0

Wolverhampton W 0
Gillingham 1 (Shaw)

Wycombe W 2 (Brown pne,
McSporran)
Fulham 2 (Legwinski, Marlet)

Fulham 1 (Hayles)
Wycombe W 0

Fourth Round

Arsenal 1 (Bergkamp)
Liverpool 0

Charlton Athletic 1 (Stuart)
Walsall 2 (Leitao 2)

Chelsea 1 (Hasselbaink)
West Ham 1 (Kanouote)

West Ham 2 (Defoe 2)
Chelsea 3 (Hasselbaink, Forssell,
            Terry)

Cheltenham 2 (Milton, Alsop)
Burnley 1 (A Moore)

Everton 4 (McGhee og, Ferguson
            Campbell 2)
Leyton Orient 1 (Canham)

Gillingham 1 (Jones og)
Bristol Rovers 0

Ipswich Town 1 (M Bent)
Man City 4 (Berkovic, Goater 2,
Huckerby)

Middlesbrough 2 (Whelan,
Campbell)
Manchester United 0

Millwall 0
Blackburn Rovers 1 (Cole)

Peterborough 2 (O'Brien og, Farrell)
Newcastle U 4 (O'Brien, McClen,
            Shearer pen, Hughes)

Preston NE 2 *(Cresswell,*
Alexander pen)
Sheffield U 1 *(Ndlovu)*

Rotherham 2 *(Mullin, Warne)*
Crewe Alex 4 *(Thomas, Ashton 2,*
Vaughan)

Tottenham H 4 *(Anderton pen,*
Iverson, Etherington,
Barness og)
Bolton W 0

Tranmere 3 *(Rideoout, Flynn,*
Koumas
Cardiff City 1 *(Kavanagh pen)*

WBA 1 *(Clement pen)*
Leicester City 0

York City 0
Fulham 2 *(Malbranque, Marlet)*

Fifth Round

Arsenal 5 *(Wiltord 2, Kanu, Adams,*
Parlour)
Gillingham 2 *(King, Gooden)*

Chelsea 3 *(Gudjohnsen,*
Hasselbaink, Forssell)
Preston NE 1 *(Cresswell)*

Everton 0
Crewe Alexander 0

Crewe Alexander 1 *(Ashton)*
Everton 2 *(Radzinski, Campbell)*

Middlesbrough 1 *(Ehiogu)*
Blackburn 0

Newcastle United 1 *(Solano)*
Manchester City 0

Tottenham H 4 *(Ziege, Poyet 2,*
Sheringham)
Tranmere 0

Walsall 1 *(Byfield)*
Fulham 2 *(Bennett og, Hayles)*

WBA 1 *(Dichio)*
Cheltenham Town 0

Sixth Round

Newcastle U 1 *(Robert)*
Arsenal 1 *(Edu)*

Arsenal 3 *(Pires, Bergkamp,*
Campbell)
Newcastle U 0

Middlesbrough 3 *(Whelan, Nemeth,*
Ince)
Everton 0

Tottenham H 0
Chelsea 4 *(Gallas, Gudjohnsen 2*
Le Saux)

WBA 0
Fulham 1 *(Marlet)*

Semi-finals

Fulham 0
Chelsea 1 *(Terry)*
(at Villa Park)

Middlesbrough 0
Arsenal 1 *(Festa og)*
(at Old Trafford)

FINAL

Millennium Stadium, Cardiff

May 4

Arsenal (0) 2
(Parlour 70, Ljungberg 80)

Chelsea (0) 0

Arsenal: Seaman, Lauren, Cole,
Vieira, Campbell, Adams, Wiltord
(Keown), Parlour, Henry (Kanu),
Bergkamp (Edu), Ljungberg

Chelsea: Cudicini, Melchior
(Zenden), Babayaro (Terry), Petit,
Gallas, Desailly, Gronkjaer,
Lampard, Hasselbaink (Zola),
Gudjohnsen, Le Saux

Referee: Mike Riley
Attendance: 73,963

"Misses no corners"
Jeff Astle's motto. Astle, the WBA and England striker, died in January.

"I managed to put David Johnson through, as well as the other guy whose name I can't remember"
Paul Gascoigne, while playing for Burnley.

"That's a word you don't hear around football training grounds any more - mortgage"
Niall Quinn.

"Anyone found not to be singing will be removed from the ground and forced to watch England"
Announcer at the Millennium Stadium, during the Wales v Italy match.

"It wasn't that difficult"
Frank Lampard, after beating his dad's tally of England caps. Frank Lampard senior won two.

Worthington Cup 2001-2002

First Round

Barnsley 2 *(Tinkler, Dyer)*
Halifax Town 0

Birmingham 3 *(Mooney 2, 1 pen,*
      Whelan og)
Southend United 0

Blackpool 3 *(Ormerod 3)*
Wigan Ath 2 *(Brannan, Haworth)*

Bournemouth 0
Torquay 2 *(Graham, Brandon)*

Brentford 1 *(O'Connor)*
Norwich 0

Brighton & H 2 *(Zamora 2)*
Wimbledon 1 *(Williams)*

Bristol C 2 *(Amankwaah, Jones)*
Cheltenham T 1 *(Grayson)*

Burnley 2 *(A Moore, McGregor)*
Rushden & D 3 *(Peters, Mustafa,*
      Derby)

Bury 1 *(Reid pen)*
Sheff Wed *(Ekoku, Maddix,*
      McLaren)

Cambridge U 1 *(Alcide)*
WBA 1 *(Dobie)*
aet; WBA won 5-3 on pens

Darlington 0
Sheffield U 1 *(D'Jaffo)*

Exeter City 0
Walsall 1 *(Herivelto)*

Grimsby T 2 *(Jevons, Rowan)*
Lincoln City *(Battersby)*

Hartlepool U 0
Nottingham Forest 2 *(John,*
      Bart-Williams)

Huddersfield 0
Rochdale 1 *(Ford)*

Kidderminster 2 *(Bird 2)*
Preston NE *(Macken, Gallacher*
      Jackson)

Leyton Orient 2 *(Minton, Houghton)*
Crystal Palace 4 *(Morrison 2,*
      Black 2)

Macclesfield T 1 *(Glover)*
Bradford C 2 *(Todd, McCall)*

Mansfield T 3 *(Greenacre 18, 43,*
      White 60)
Notts Co 4 *(Allsopp 20, 25, 31,*
      Mildenhall 34)

Millwall 2 *(Sadlier 24, Claridge 61*
      pen)
Cardiff C 1 *(Earnshaw 45)*

Northampton T 2 *(Forrester,*
      McGregor)
QPR 1 *(Evatt og)*

Oxford U 1 *(Scott 41)*
Gillingham 2 *(King pen,*
aet   Onuora)

Port Vale 2 *(McPhee 2)*
Chesterfield 1 *(Rowland)*

Portsmouth 1 *(Crouch)*
Colchester 2 *(Stockwell, Izzet)*

Reading 4 *(Henderson 2,*
      Parkinson, A Smith)

Stockport C 3 *(Kuqi,Taylor 2)*
Carlisle U 0

Stoke 0
Oldham 0
aet; Oldham won 6-5 on pens

Swansea C 0
Peterborough 2 *(Fenn ,A Clarke)*

Tranmere 3 *(Henry, Flynn, Barlow)*
Shrewsbury T 1 *(Jemson)*

Watford 1 *(Gayle)*
Plymouth A 0

Wolverhampton 1 *(Dinning)*
Swindon T 2 *(Howe,*
      O'Halloran pen)

Wrexham 2 *(Faulconbridge,*
      Russell)
Hull C 3 *(Whitmore, Greaves,*
      Alexander)

Wycombe W 0
Bristol R 1 *(Hiiller)*

York C 2 *(Bullock, Brass)*
Crewe A 2 *(Little, Richards)*

Second Round

Blackpool 0
Leicester C 1 *(Akinbiyi)*

Blackburn 2 *(Jansen, Dunning)*
Oldham A 0

Bolton 4 *(Ricketts 68, Holdsworth,*
      Nishizawa, Pedersen)
Walsall 3 *(Wrack, Byfield, Barras)*
aet

Brighton 0
Southampton 3 *(Beattie ,*
      Svensson 2)

Bristol C 2 *(Clist, Thorpe)*
Watford 3 *(Gayle pen, Vega, Hyde)*

Bristol Rovers 0
Birmingham 3 *(A Johnson,*
      M Johnson, Hughes)

Charlton 2 *(Fortune, Konchesky)*
Port Vale 0

Colchester 1 *(Keith)*
Sheffield Wednesday 0

Crewe 2 *(Walton, S Smith pen)*
Rushden & D 0
aet

Derby 3 *(Burton 2, Kinkladze)*
Hull 0

Everton 1 *(Ferguson pen)*
C Palace 1 *(Freedman pen)*
aet; C Palace won 5-4 on pens

Gillingham 2 *(King, Nethercott og)*
Millwall 1 *(Moody)*

Grimsby 3 *(Broomes, Jeffrey, Allen)*
Sheffield Utd 3 *(Devlin, Ndlova,*
      Suffo)
aet; Grimsby won 4-2 on pens

Middlesbrough 3 *(Murphy, Nemeth,*
      Wilson)
Northampton 1 *(Parkin)*

Newcastle 4 *(Ameobi, Bellamy 3)*
Brentford 1 *(Owusu)*

Nottm Forest 1 *(Lester)*
Stockport Co 1 *(Taylor)*
aet; Nottm Forest won 8-7 on pens

Notts Co 2 *(Allsopp pen, Stallard)*
Man City 4 *(Shuter, Goater, Dickov,*
aet   Huckerby)

Peterborough 2 *(Forsyth, Hedman*
      og)
Coventry 2 *(Thompson, Carsley)*
aet; Coventry won 4-2 on pens

Reading 0
West Ham 0
aet; Reading won 6-5 on pens

Rochdale 2 *(Townson 2)*
Fulham 2 *(Boa Morte, Brevett)*
aet; Fulham won 6-5 on pens

Rotherham 0
Bradford C 3 *(Blake 2, 1 pen, Tod,*
      Lawrence)

Sheff Wed 4 *(Ekoku, Morrison pen,*
Di Piedi, Bonvin)*
Sunderland 2 *(Phillips, Laslandes)*

Tottenham 2 *(King, Ferdinand)*
Torquay U 0

Tranmere 4 *(Flynn, Koumas,*
      Barlow, Mellon)
Preston NE 1 *(Cresswell)*

WBA 2 *(Dobie, Jordao)*
Swindon T 0
aet

Third Round

Arsenal 4 *(Wiltord 3, 1 pen, Kanu pen)*
Man Utd 0

Aston Villa 1 *(Dublin)*
Reading 0

Barnsley 0
Newcastle 1 *(Bellamy)*

Blackburn 2 *(Hignett, Short)*
Middlesbrough 1 *(Nemeth)*

Bolton W 1 *(Wallace)*
Nottingham Forest 0

Coventry C 0
Chelsea 2 *(Gudjohnsen, Forssell)*

Crewe 2 *(Hulse, Brammer)*
Ipswich 3 *(Reuser 2, Armstrong)*

Fulham 5 *(Hayles, Legwinski, Collins, Saha, Malbranque pen)*
Derby 2 *(Burley, Ravanelli)*

Gillingham 0
Southampton 2 *(Beattie pen, Pahars)*

Leicester City 0
Leeds 6 *(Keane 3, Bakke, Viduka, Kewell)*

Liverpool 1 *(McAllister pen)*
Grimsby T 2 *(Broomes, Jevon)*

Man City 6 *(Huckerby 4, Luntala og, Goater)*
Birmingham City 0

Sheff Wed 2 *(Westwood, Crane)*
C Palace 2 *(Rodger, Riihilahti)*
aet; Sheff Wed won 3-1 on pens

Tranmere Rovers 0
Tottenham 4 *(Sheringham pen, Anderton, Poyet, Rebrov)*

Watford 4 *(Hyde, Noel-Williams 2, Vega)*
Bradford C 1 *(Ward pen)*

WBA 0
Charlton Athletic 1 *(Euell pen)*

Fourth Round

Arsenal 2 *(Edu, Wiltord)*
Grimsby Town 0

Aston Villa 0
Sheff Wed 1 *(Ekoku)*

Blackburn 2 *(Johansson, Johnson)*
Manchester City 0

Bolton 2 *(Holdsworth pen, Ricketts)*
Southampton 2 *(Davies, El Khalej)*

Fulham 1 *(Hayles)*
Tottenham 2 *(Rebrov, Davies)*

Leeds 0
Chelsea 2 *(Gudjohnsen 2)*

Newcastle U 4 *(Robert, Ameobi, Shearer 2)*
Ipswich Town 1 *(Bent)*

Watford 3 *(Vernazza, Robinson, Helguson)*
Charlton 2 *(Brown, Robinson)*
aet

Fifth Round

Blackburn 4 *(Jansen 3, Hughes)*
Arsenal 0

Chelsea 1 *(Hasselbaink)*
Newcastle 0

Sheff Wed 4 *(Sibon, Hamshaw, O'Donnell, Solvedt)*
Watford 0

Tottenham 6 *(Davies, Ferdinand 3, Barness og, Iversen)*
Bolton Wanderers 0

Semi-finals

Chelsea 2 *(Hasselbaink 2)*
Tottenham 1 *(Ferdinand*

Tottenham 5 *(Iversen, Sherwood, Sheringham, Davies, Rebrov)*
Chelsea 1 *(Forssell)*
Tottenham won 6-3 on agg

Sheff Wed 1 *(Ekoku)*
Blackburn 2 *(Hignett, Cole)*

Blackburn 4 *(Jansen, Duff Cole, Hignett)*
Sheff Wed 2 *(Ekoku pen, Soltvedt)*
Blackburn won 6-3 on aggregate

FINAL
Millennium Stadium, Feb 24

BLACKBURN ROVERS (1) 2
(Jansen 25, Cole 69)
TOTTENHAM HOTSPUR (1) 1
(Ziege 33)

Blackburn: Friedel; Taylor, Bjornbye, Dunn, Berg, Johansson, Gillespie (Hignett), Jansen (Yordi), Cole, Hughes, Duff

Tottenham: Sullivan, Taricco (Davies), Ziege, Thatcher, Perry, King, Anderton, Sherwood, Ferdinand, Sheringham, Poyet (Iverson)

Referee: Graham Poll
Attendance: 72,500

LDV Vans Trophy 2001-2002

First Round

Barnet 2 *(Sawyers, Essandoh)*
Bournemouth 1 *(Kandol)*

Blackpool 3 *(Parkinson, Caldwell
J Murphy)*
Stoke 2 *(Iwelumo, Neal pen)*

Bristol City 1 *(Peacock)*
Torquay 0

Cardiff 7 *(Bonner, Gordon 5, Giles)*
Rushden & D 1 *(Hall)*

Cheltenham 2 *(Victory, Alsop)*
Plymouth 1 *(Friio)*

Colchester 1 *(Izzet)*
Swindon 0

Dagenham 3 *(Heffer 2, Goodwin)*
L Orient 2 *(Smith, McLean)*

Darlington 2 *(Brumwell, Riddler og)*
Macclesfield 1 *(Glover pen)*

Doncaster 0
Kidderminster 1 *(Larkin)*

Exeter 1 *(Fleming og)*
Cambridge 2 *(Chillingworth, One)*

Hartlepool 0
Bury 1 *(Newby)*

Huddersfield 0
Halifax 0
aet; Huddersfield won 4-3 on pens

Leigh 2 *(Heald, Maamria pen)*
Scarborough 1 *(Pounder)*
aet; Leigh won on golden goal

Northampton 2 *(Hunt, McGregor)*
Oxford United 0

Notts Co 2 *(Allsop, Hackworth pen)*
York City 0

Port Vale 2 *(Armstrong, Brooker)*
Carlisle 1 *(Foran)*

Rochdale 2 *(Platt, Jones pen)*
Southport 0

Scunthorpe 3 *(Torpry, Beagrie 2)*
Lincoln 1 *(Cameron)*

Shrewsbury 0
Chesterfield 1 *(D'Auria)*

Stevenage 1 *(Sigere)*
Southend 4 *(Bramble, Rawle,
Hutchings, Webb)*

Swansea 1 *(Coates)*
Brighton 2 *(Lehmann, Steele)*

Wrexham 5 *(Trundle 2, Morrell 2
Thomas)*
Wigan 1 *(Hill og)*

Wycombe W 1 *(Emblen)*
Brentford 0

Yeovil T 3 *(Giles 2, Grant)*
QPR 0

Second round

Brighton 2 *(Pitcher, Melton)*
Wycombe 1 *(Holligan)*

Bristol Rovers 1 *(Cameron pen)*
Yeovil Town 1 *(McIndoe)*
aet; Bristol R won 5-4 on pens

Bury 2 *(Lawson, Swailes)*
Notts Co 3 *(Caskey, Allsopp 2)*

Cambridge 1 *(One)*
Cheltenham 1 *(Naylor)*

Cardiff 1 *(Nugent pen)*
Peterborough 3 *(Bullard pen,
McKenzie, Green)*

Chesterfield 1 *(Reeves)*
Kidderminster 0

Dagenham 3 *(McGaven, Ovendale
og, Vickers)*
Luton 2 *(Brennan, Thompson)*

Hull 3 *(Alexander 3, 1 pen)*
Leigh 0

Mansfield 0
Blackpool 4 *(MacKenzie 2, 1 pen,
Ormerod 2)*

Northampton Town 0
Barnet 1 *(Flynn)*

Oldham 2 *(Eyre, Richards)*
Tranmere 0

Reading 2 *(N Smith, Henderson)*
Colchester 1 *(Stockwell)*

Rochdale 1 *(Townson)*
Port Vale 2 *(Burton pen, Armstrong)*

Scunthorpe 3 *(Hodges, Carruthers
McCombe)*
Darlington 0

Southend 0
Bristol C 2 *(Amankwaah, Peacock)*

Wrexham 0
Huddersfield T 1 *(Holland)*

Quarter-finals

Barnet 4 *(Strevens 2, Arber, Berkley)*
Reading 1 *(Henderson)*

Bristol C 2 *(Murray, Thorpe)*
Peterborough 1 *(Bullard)*

Bristol R 4 *(Hogg, Ellington 2,
Ommel)*
Dagenham 1 *(Charlery)*

Cambridge 2 *(Kitson, One)*
Brighton & H 1 *(Melton)*

Chesterfield 0
Blackpool 3 *(Edwards og, J Murphy,
Bullock)*

Huddersfield 4 *(Schofield 2, Hay
Booth)*
Scunthorpe 1 *(Torpey)*

Hull 2 *(Whittle, Whitmore)*
Port Vale 1 *(McPhee)*

Notts County 0
Oldham Athletic 1 *(Smart)*

Semi-finals

North
Hull City 0
Huddersfield T 1 *(Booth)*

Oldham A 2 *(Duxbury, Eyres)*
Blackpool 5 *(Walker 3, J Murphy,
Bullock)*

South
Cambridge Utd 2 *(Tudor, Guttridge)*
Barnet 0

Bristol City 3 *(Matthews 2, Bell)*
Bristol Rovers 0

Northern Final

Blackpool 3 *(Wellens, J Murphy
Taylor)*
Huddersfield T 1 *(Schofield)*

Huddersfield T 2 *(Wijnhard pen,
Schofield)*
Blackpool 1 *(Bullock)*
*Blackpool won 3-1 on aggregate,
after golden goal*

Southern Final

Cambridge United 0
Bristol City 0

Bristol City 0
Cambridge United 2 *(One 2)*
Cambridge won 2-0 on aggregate

FINAL

BLACKPOOL (1) 4 *(J Murphy,
Clarke, Hills, Taylor)*

CAMBRIDGE (1) 1 *(Wanless pen)*

Blackpool: Barnes; O'Kane,
Jaszczun, collins, Clarke, Marshall
(Hughes) Wellens (Simpson),
Bullock, Murphy, J Taylor (Walker)
Hills
Cambridge: Perez; Angus
(Goodhind), Murray, Duncan, Tann,
Ashbee, Wanless, Tudor
(Jackman), Kitson (One), Young,
Gutteridge
Referee: R Furnandiz

Attendance: 20,287bb

"I never try to make a right decision. I make a decision and then try to make it right"
Martin O'Neill, Celtic manager.

"The League must be totally restructured. It's archaic and amateurish and needs to get professional. It's a billion-pound business - but if I had a kebab shop, I wouldn't let them run it"
Theo Paphitis, Millwall chairman, after the Football League lost its court case against ITV Digital.

"Sometimes, I think he thinks he's Alex Ferguson"
Jason McAteer, on Roy Keane.

"It's a top club, but it's not a top, top, top club"
Jimmy Floyd Hasselbaink, on Chelsea.

"There's an unprofessional culture at this club and I've smelt it since the beginning"
Steve Parkin, Barnsley manager.

"People have got this pre-conceived idea of me as a fat bastard"
Andy Goram.

"They can't be monks - we don't want them to be monks, we want them to be football players because a monk doesn't play football at this level"
Bobby Robson, after disciplinary problems at Newcastle.

"A hundred goals scored and fifty conceded, I guess you could say it's my style"
Kevin Keegan, Manchester City manager.

"I haven't got big ears. I've got a very small head"
Gary Lineker.

"The world will hate it when America wins the World Cup"
Daniel Henninger, in the *Wall Street Journal*.

"It's always dangerous to think football 24 hours a day. Tord Grip has played his accordion and Dave Sexton has been singing to us - he's excellent. We try to have a laugh. Life is fun"
Sven-Goran Erikkson, preparing for the World Cup.

Scottish Football

Martin O'Neill's Celtic continued to dominate, and had the title all but wrapped up by December, having defeated Rangers twice and only dropped two points out of a possible 54. Until the appointment of Alex McLeish, Rangers rarely looked capable of mounting a sustained challenge, and Celtic eventually ran out champions by 18 points, the single loss, remarkably, not against Rangers but Aberdeen. They were denied another Double, however, by Peter Lovenkrands' last-minute winner for Rangers in a thrilling Scottish Cup final, which the Ibrox club won 3-2. Rangers also took the Scottish League Cup with a comfortable 4-0 win over Ayr United. Livingston proved the season's big surprise, finishing third in the table, while St Johnstone finished bottom of the standings by a long, long way and could have considered themselves lucky not to have been relegated directly to the Second Division.

On the international front, Berti Vogts, got his feet under the management table, but it wasn't a comfy chair he was sitting in. Seven friendly matches during the calendar year resulted in just a single victory, against mighty Canada, but by that time, Vogts had already looked over the edge of the precipice.

When Scotland went two down to the Faroe Islands after 13 minutes of their opening Euro 2004 qualifier five weeks earlier, Berti got the mobile out and was on the phone to the booking desk at Lufthansa (we reckon). Around an hour later, Berti rang the German airline back to see if he could switch flights, as Barry Ferguson had just equalised. That was as good as it got in Toftir; a two-all draw against a country (or a part of Denmark as it technically is) whose total population was increased by over 2% with the arrival of just 1050 Scottish supporters.

To add a little sea salt to the Scottish wounds, the first goal for the visitors, from Paul Lambert, took two lucky deflections, and the Faroese manager, Henrik Larsen (now that name sounds familiar) could afford to say after the game that he felt as if: "We have lost two points rather than gained one."

Before you ask, of course it got better. How could it not? Iceland were next, and Scotland knew no fear. They walloped the sporting leviathan 2-0 with goals from Gary Naysmith and Christian Dailly and the ecstatic Vogts said "It has been a great weekend for Scottish football", and those of us left in the real world wondered what it had come to when a great weekend for Scottish football came about because of a two-goal victory over a team which has never in its history qualified for either the World Cup or the European championships, and which probably never will.

Bob Wilson, Danny McGrain, Alan Hansen, Frank McLintock, Frank Gray, Charlie Cooke, Graeme Souness, Dave Mackay, Gordon Strachan, Denis Law, Kenny Dalglish and George Graham, get your boots out.

Bell's Scottish Premier League 2001-2002

	P	W	D	L	GF	GA	W	D	L	GF	GA	PTS	GD
1 Celtic	38	18	1	0	51	9	15	3	1	43	9	103	+76
2 Rangers	38	14	4	1	42	11	11	6	2	40	16	85	+55
3 Livingston	38	9	5	4	23	17	7	5	8	27	30	58	+3
4 Aberdeen	38	12	2	5	31	19	4	5	10	20	30	55	+2
5 Hearts	38	8	3	8	30	27	6	3	10	22	30	48	-5
6 Dunfermline Athletic	38	9	4	6	25	24	3	5	11	16	40	45	-23
7 Kilmarnock	38	7	6	6	24	26	6	4	9	20	28	49	-10
8 Dundee United	38	6	5	8	18	30	6	5	8	20	29	46	-21
9 Dundee	38	8	5	6	23	24	4	3	12	18	31	44	-14
10 Hibernian	38	6	6	7	35	30	4	5	10	16	26	41	-5
11 Motherwell	38	8	5	6	30	25	3	2	14	19	44	40	-20
12 St Johnstone	38	2	3	15	11	32	3	3	12	13	30	21	-38

	Aberdeen	Celtic	Dundee	Dundee U	Dunferm'	Hearts	Hibernian	Kilmarnock	Livingston	Motherwell	Rangers	St Johnstone
Aberdeen	****	2-0	0-0	2-1	3-2	3-2	2-0	2-0	0-3	4-2	0-3	1-0
	****	0-1	****	4-0	1-0	2-3	****	1-1	3-0	1-0	0-1	****
Celtic	2-0	****	3-1	5-1	3-1	2-0	3-0	1-0	3-2	2-0	2-1	3-0
	1-0	****	****	1-0	5-0	2-0	****	****	5-1	****	1-1	2-1
					5-0							
Dundee	1-4	0-4	****	1-1	2-2	1-1	2-1	1-2	1-0	3-1	0-0	1-1
	2-3	0-3	****	0-1	****	****	1-0	2-0	2-0	2-0	****	1-0
Dundee U	1-1	0-4	2-2	****	3-2	0-2	3-1	0-2	0-0	1-1	1-6	2-1
	****	****	1-0	****	0-2	****	1-2	0-2	****	1-0	0-1	0-0
							2-1					
Dunfermline	1-0	0-4	1-0	1-1	****	0-1	1-0	0-2	1-2	5-2	1-4	2-1
	0-0	****	2-0	****	****	1-1	1-1	****	2-0	1-0	3-1	2-4
											1-1	
Hearts	1-0	0-1	3-1	1-2	1-1	****	1-1	2-0	1-3	3-1	2-2	3-0
	3-1	1-4	2-0	1-2	2-0	****	****	****	2-3	****	0-2	1-3
Hibernian	2-0	1-4	1-2	0-1	5-1	2-1	****	2-2	0-3	1-1	0-3	4-0
	3-4	1-1	2-2	****	1-1	1-2	****	2-2	****	4-0	****	3-0
Kilmarnock	3-1	0-1	0-1	2-0	0-0	1-0	0-0	****	1-5	2-0	2-2	2-1
	****	0-2	3-2	2-2	****	3-3	1-0	****	1-1	1-4	****	0-1
Livingston	2-2	0-0	1-0	2-0	0-0	2-1	1-0	0-1	****	3-1	0-2	2-1
	0-0	1-3	****	1-1	4-1	2-0	0-3	****	****	****	2-1	****
Motherwell	3-2	1-2	4-2	0-0	1-0	2-0	1-3	2-2	0-0	****	2-2	1-2
	****	0-4	2-1	2-0	****	1-2	4-0	2-0	1-2	****	****	1-1
Rangers	2-0	0-2	2-0	3-2	4-0	3-1	2-2	3-1	0-0	3-0	****	1-0
	2-0	1-1	2-1	****	****	2-1	1-1	5-0	3-0	3-0	****	****
St Johnstone	1-1	1-2	0-2	0-1	0-2	0-2	0-0	1-0	2-2	2-3	0-2	****
	0-1	****	0-1	1-4	0-1	****	0-1	0-3	3-0	0-2	0-2	****

League divided into two divisions after 33 games

Goalscorers

	Lg	Cups	Total		Lg	Cups	Total
Henrik Larsson (Celtic)	29	2	31	Shota Arveladze (Rangers)	11	6	17
John Hartson (Celtic)	19	5	24	Juan Sara (Dundee)	11	1	12
Tore Andre Flo (Rangers)	17	2	19	Stuart Elliott (Motherwell)	10	1	11
Robbie Winters (Aberdeen)	13	1	14	James McFadden (Motherwell)	10	-	10

First Division 2001-2002

		P	W	D	L	GF	GA	W	D	L	GF	GA	Pts	GD
1	Partick Thistle	36	12	6	0	38	15	7	3	8	23	23	**66**	+23
2	Airdrieonians	36	8	6	4	31	19	7	5	6	28	21	**56**	+19
3	Ayr United	36	8	6	4	25	16	5	7	6	28	28	**52**	+9
4	Ross County	36	10	2	6	33	21	4	8	6	18	22	**52**	+8
5	Clyde	36	8	6	4	27	21	5	4	9	24	35	**49**	-5
6	Inverness Caledonian T	36	11	3	4	47	22	2	6	10	13	29	**48**	+9
7	Arbroath	36	9	3	6	22	28	5	3	10	20	31	**48**	-17
8	St Mirren	36	6	8	4	19	19	5	4	9	24	34	**45**	-10
9	Falkirk	36	5	5	8	24	36	5	4	9	25	37	**39**	-24
10	Raith Rovers	36	7	5	6	31	25	1	6	11	19	37	**35**	-12

Second Division 2001-2002

		P	W	D	L	GF	GA	W	D	L	GF	GA	Pts	GD
1	Queen Of The South	36	12	2	4	33	19	8	5	5	31	23	**67**	+22
2	Alloa Athletic	36	8	8	2	35	17	7	6	5	20	16	**59**	+22
3	Forfar Athletic	36	8	3	7	25	25	7	5	6	26	22	**53**	+4
4	Clydebank	36	8	4	6	25	23	6	5	7	19	22	**51**	-1
5	Hamilton Academicals	36	9	5	4	26	15	4	4	10	23	29	**48**	+5
6	Berwick Rangers	36	6	4	8	19	28	6	7	5	25	24	**47**	-8
7	Stranraer	36	7	5	6	27	25	3	10	5	21	26	**45**	-3
8	Cowdenbeath	36	5	8	5	27	28	6	3	9	22	23	**44**	-2
9	Stenhousemuir	36	3	8	7	15	25	5	4	9	18	32	**36**	-24
10	Morton	36	3	8	7	20	28	4	6	8	28	35	**35**	-15

Third Division 2001-2002

		P	W	D	L	GF	GA	W	D	L	GF	GA	Pts	GD
1	Brechin City	36	12	4	2	38	14	10	3	5	29	24	**73**	+29
2	Dumbarton	36	10	4	4	30	22	8	53	7	29	26	**61**	+11
3	Albion Rovers	36	8	5	5	28	23	8	6	4	23	19	**59**	+9
4	Peterhead	36	9	4	5	36	26	8	1	9	27	26	**56**	+11
5	Montrose	36	9	2	7	25	20	7	5	6	18	19	**55**	+4
6	Elgin City	36	9	3	6	26	20	4	5	9	19	27	**47**	-2
7	East Stirlingshire	36	8	1	9	27	27	4	3	11	24	31	**40**	-7
8	East Fife	36	6	4	8	23	26	5	3	10	16	30	**40**	-17
9	Stirling Albion	36	6	4	8	23	29	3	6	9	22	39	**37**	-23
10	Queen's Park	36	4	6	8	17	21	5	2	11	21	32	**35**	-15

Goalscorers

Division 1	Lg	Cp	Ttl
Coyle (Airdrie)	23	4	27
Novo (Raith Rovers)	19	4	23
Wyness (Inverness CT)	18	4	18
Ritchie (Inverness CT)	15	3	18
Annand (Ayr U)	14	7	21
Hislop (Ross County)	14	3	17
Roberts (Airdrie)	12	4	16
Britton (Partick T)	12	3	15
Hardie (Partick T)	11	5	16
Hinds (Clyde)	11	-	11
Miller (Falkirk)	11	-	11

Division 2	Lg	Cp	Ttl
Tosh (Forfar)	19	4	23
O'Neil (QOTS)	19	2	21
Brown (Cowdenbeath)	17	-	17
Harty (Stranraer)	16	3	19
Weatherson (QOTS)	15	-	15
Hutchinson (Alloa)	14	2	16
Moore (Hamilton)	12	1	13
Byers (Forfar)	9	2	11
Wood (Berwick)	9	1	10
Wright (Cowdenbeath)	9	1	10
Burke (Clydebank)	9	-	9

Division 3	Lg	Cp	Ttl
Stewart (Peterhead)	19	2	21
Flannery (Dumbarton)	18	1	19
Johnston (Peterhead)	18	-	18
Williams (Stirling A)	17	5	22
Templeton (Brechin)	15	1	16
Laidlaw (Montrose)	13	3	16
Gilzean (Elgin C)	12	1	13
McManus (East Fife)	11	4	15
McLean (Albion R)	11	2	13
Gordon (E Stirlingshire)	11	-	11
Grant (Brechin)	10	3	13

Tennent's Scottish Cup

First Round

Albion Rovers 0
Elgin City 0

Elgin City 0
Albion Rovers 1 (McLean)

Alloa A 3 (Little, Evans, Hutchison)
Dumbarton 1 (McKeown)

Brechin C 4 (Fotheringham,
O'Boyle 2, Grant)
Stenhousemuir 0

Clydebank 1 (Paton)
Peterhead 0

Morton 1 (Aitken)
Queen Of The South 2 (O'Neil 2)

Stirling A 2 (Williams, Munro)
Buckie Thistle 1 (Holmes)

Tarff Rovers 1 (Lamont)
Montrose 4 (Laidlaw 3, Lowe)

Wick A 2 (MacDonald, MacKenzie)
Threave Rovers 3 (Cochrane,
Hudson, Adams)

Second Round

Alloa Athletic 1 (G Evans)
Queen Of The South 0

Berwick Rangers 1 (Feroz)
Cowdenbeath 0

Brechin City 0
Albion Rovers 1 (Harty)

Clydebank 0
Stranraer 1 (Harty)

Deveronvale 0
Spartans 0

Spartans 1 (Samuel)
Deveronvale 2 (Brown, Chisholm)

E Stirlingshire 1 (Lyle)
Forres Mechanics 1 (Brown)

Forres Mechanics 3 (Main 2, Ross)
E Stirlingshire 1 (McDonald)

Forfar Athletic 2 (Byers, Sellars)
Threave Rovers 0

Gala Fairydean 1 (Lindsay)
Stirling Albion 0

Hamilton A 4 (Callaghan, McPhee,
McNiven, McFarlane)
Montrose 0

Queen's Park 0 (Walker, Harty)
East Fife 0

East Fife 2 (McManus 2)
Queen's Park 2 (Jackson 2)
aet; East Fife won 4-2 on pens

Third Round

Albion Rovers 0
Livingston 0
Match abandoned; floodlights failed

Albion Rovers 1 (McLean)
Livingston 4 (Wilson, Bingham 2,
Fernandez)

Alloa Athletic 0
Celtic 5 (Balde, Wieghorst,
Maloney, Petta, Sylla)

Arbroath 0
Inverness CT 2 (Robson, Ritchie)

Berwick Rangers 0
Rangers 0

Rangers 3 (Amoruso, Konterman,
Arveladze)
Berwick Rangers 0

Clyde 1 (Fraser)
St Mirren 0

Deveronvale 0
Ayr United 6 (Annand 2, Sheerin,
McGinley, Crabbe, Grady)

Dundee 1 (Milne)
Falkirk 1 (Rodges)

Falkirk 0
Dundee 2 (Zhiyi)

Dundee United 3 (Aljofree 2, Miller)
Forres Mechanics 0

Dunfermline 3 (Crawford 2,
S M Thompson)
Motherwell 1 (Elliott)

East Fife 2 (McManus, Bailey)
Partick T 4 (Walker 2, McLean,
Hardy

Gala Fairydean 0
Forfar 5 (Tosh 2, Yardley, Sellars,
Byers)

Hamilton A 1 (McPhee)
Raith Rovers 0

Hearts 2 (Fuller 2)
Ross County 1 (Perry)

Kilmarnock 3 (Mitchell, Sanjuan,
Canero)
Airdieonians 0

St Johnstone 0
Aberdeen 2 (Thornley,
Darren Young)

Stranraer 0
Hibernian 0

Hibernian 4 (Luna, Zitelli pen,
Smith, Hurtado)
Stranraer 0

Fourth Round

Aberdeen 2 (Winters, McAllister)
Livingston 0

Ayr U 3 (Grady, MacPherson og,
Robertson)
Dunfermline A 0

Clyde 1 (Mensing)
Forfar A 2 (Tosh, Sellars)

Dundee United 4 (Winters,
Thompson 2, Aljofree)
Hamilton 0

Hearts 1 (Wales)
Inverness CT 3 (Tokely, Wyness,
Bagan)

Kilmarnock 0
Celtic 2 (Hay og, Larsson)

Partick Thistle 1 (McLean)
Dundee 1 (Torres)

Dundee 1 (Sara)
Partick T 2 (Britton, Gibson)

Rangers 4 (Flo 2, Lovenkrands,
Dodds)
Hibernian 1 (Brebner)

Quarter-finals

Aberdeen 0
Celtic 2 (Hartson, Petrov)

Dundee United 2 (Winters, Easton)
Ayr United 2 (Crabbe, McGinlay)

Forfar Athletic 0
Rangers 6 (Dodds 3, Arveladze 2,
Kanchelskis)

Partick T 2 (Hardie, Paterson)
Inverness CT 2 (Wyness 2)

Inverness CT 0
Partick T 1 (Paterson)

Semi-finals

Ayr United 0
Celtic 3 (Larsson, Thompson 2)

Rangers 3 (Nerlinger 2, Ferguson)
Partick Thistle 0

FINAL
Hampden Park, May 4

CELTIC (1) 2 *(Hartson, Balde)*

RANGERS (1) 3

Celtic: Douglas, Mjallby, Sutton, BAlde, Thompson, Petrov, Lennon, Lambert (McNamara), Agathe, Larsson, Hartson

Rangers: Klos, Ricksen, Amoruso, Moore, Numan, Ross, Ferguson, Lovenkrands, De Boer, Caniggia (Arveladze), McCann

Referee: Hugh Dallas

Attendance: 51,138

CIS Cup
First Round
Airdrieonians 3 *(James, Roberts, MacFarlane)*
Morton 0

Albion Rovers 0
Inverness CT 2 *(Richie 2)*

Alloa A 4 *(Little, Curran, Walker, Thompson)*
Peterhead 0

Berwick Rangers 0
Partick T 3 *(Lennon, McLean, McDowell)*

Clyde 2 *(Crawford 2)*
Stenhousemuir 2 *(Abbott, Ferguson)*
aet; Clyde won 4-2 on pens

Dumbarton 2 *(Brown, Flannery)*
Clydebank 0

East Fife 1 *McManus)*
Arbroath 0

E Stirlingshire 0
Queen Of The South 3 *(Feroz 3)*

Elgin City 2 *(McGlashan, Gilzean)*
Stranraer 3 *(Shaw, Harty, Finlayson)*

Forfar Athletic 1 *(Tosh)*
Falkirk 2 *(Lawrie, Craig)*

Queen's Park 0
Hamilton A 1 *(Moore)*

Raith Rovers 1 *(Henderson)*
Montrose 0

Ross Co 3 *(Boukraa, Bone 2)*
Brechin City 0

Stirling A 3 *(Williams 3)*
Cowdenbeath 2 *(Wilson, Wright)*

Second Round
Airdrieonians 2 *(Coyle pen, Lasley og)*
Motherwell 1 *(Kelly)*

Ayr U 4 *(Grady, Teale, Sharp, Annand)*
Stranraer 0

Clyde 1 *(A Kane)*
St Johnstone 2 *(MacDonald 2)*

Dundee U 3 *(Thompson, Easton Griffin)*
Dumbarton 0

Dunfermline A 3 *(Nicholson, Mason 2)*
Alloa Athletic 0

Falkirk 0
Raith Rovers 2 *(Novo, A Smith)*

Hamilton 0
Dundee 2 *(Millne, Boylan)*

Inverness 3 *(Teasdale, Robson 2)*
Partick T 3 *(Hardie, Lennon, McLean)*
aet; Inverness won 4-2 on pens

Livingston 3 *(Caputo 2, Tosh)*
East Fife 0

Queen Of The South 1 *(Feroz)*
Aberdeen 2 *(Dadi, Thornley)*

Ross County 0
Hearts 0
aet; Ross won 5-4 on pens

Stirling A 2 *(Williams, Munro)*
St Mirren 1 *(Quitongo)*

Third Round
Aberdeen 1 *(Mackie)*
Livingston 6 *(Wilson 2, Caputo 2, Lovell, Bingham)*

Ayr United 0
Kilmarnock 0
aet; Ayr won 5-4 on pens

Celtic 8 *(Hartson 2, Maloney 4, Tebily, Healey)*
Stirling A 0

Dundee United 3 *(Thompson, Hamilton, Paterson)*
St Johnston 2 *(Hartley, Dods)*

Dunfermline 1 *(Hampshire)*
Inverness CT 1 *(Bavidge)*
aet; Inverness won 4-1 on pens

Raith Rovers 0
Hibernian 2 *(Brewster 2)*

Rangers 3 *(Arveladze 2, Numan)*
Airdrieonians 0

Ross County 2 *(Irvine, Boukraa)*
Dundee 1 *(Caballero)*

Quarter-finals

Ayr U 5 *(Grady, Robertson, McGinlay, Annand 2)*
Inverness CT 1 *(Tokely)*

Hibernian 2 *(McManus, Luna)*
Dundee U 0

Livingston 0
Celtic 2 *(Balde, Hartson)*

Ross County 1 *(Mackay)*
Rangers 2 *(Arveladze, Reyna)*

Semi-finals
Rangers 2 *(Lovenkrands, Konterman)*
Celtic 1 *(Balde)*

Hibernian 0
Ayr United 1 *(Annand)*

FINAL
Hampden Park

Mar 17

RANGERS (1) 4
(Flo, Ferguson pen, Caniggia 2)
AYR UNITED (0) 0

Rangers: Klos; Ricksen, Vidmar (Hughes), Amoruso, Numan, Konterman, Ferguson, Latapy (Dodds), Caniggia, Flo, Lovenkrands (McCann)

Ayr United: Nelson; Robertson, Lovering, Duffy, Hughes, Craig, Wilson (Chaplain), McGinlay, McLaughlin (Kean), Grady, Sheerin

Referee: Hugh Dallas

Attendance: 50,049

Bell's League Challenge

First Round

Airdrieonians 2 *(McPherson, Taylor)*
Queen Of The South 0

Albion Rovers 2 *(Hamilton, McMullen)*
Montrose 0

Berwick R 3 *(Ritchie, Glancy, Wood)*
Elgin City 0

Brechin C 4 *(Templeman, Fotheringham 2, 1 pen, Smith)*
Stirling A 1 *(Henderson pen)*

Cowdenbeath 0
Ross County 2 *(Hislop 2)*

East Fife 2 *(McManus, Graham)*
Raith R 3 *(Novo 2, Dennis)*

East Stirling 0
Alloa A 1 *(Hamilton)*

Falkirk 4 *(Kerr, Watson 2, 1 pen Craig)*
Arbroath 1 *(Brownlie)*

Inverness CT 3 *(Christie, Bavidge, Ritchie)*
Forfar 2 *(Tokely og, Moffatt)*

Morton 1 *(O'Connor)*
Clyde 3 *(Ross 2, Convery)*

Partick T 5 *(Lennon 2, Britton 2, Hardie)*
Queen's Park 0

Peterhead 2 *(Stewart 2)*
Hamilton A 0

St Mirren 1 *(Yardley)*
Ayr U 3 *(Teale, Sheerin, Annand)*

Stenhousemuir 1 *(Mooney)*

Stranraer 4 *(Gaughan, Wright, Johnstone, Gallagher)*

Second Round

Albion R 1 *(Bonar)*
Aidrieonians 4 *(Taylor, Roberts, Coyle, James)*

Alloa A 3 *(G Evans, Irvine, Little)*
Inverness CT 2 *(Ritchie, Wyness)*

Brechin C 4 *(Grant, Smith 2, Bain)*
Peterhead 0

Clyde 5 *(A Kane 2, Mitchell, Keogh, McCusker)*
Berwick Rangers 0

Dumbarton 0
Ross County 2 *(McQuade, Hislop)*

Falkirk 0
Clydebank 0
aet; Clydebank won 5-4 on pens

Raith R 3 *(Matheson, Novo, Zoco)*
Partick T 5 *(McDowell, McCallum, Fleming 2, Hardie)*

Stranraer 3 *(Finlayson, Harty, Wright)*
Ayr U 2 *(Bradford, McGinlay)*

Quarter-Finals

Alloa A 4 *(Fisher, Little, Hamilton Curran)*
Stranraer 3 *(Gallagher 2, Jenkins)*

Clyde 1 *(Keogh)*
Partick Thistle 0

Clydebank 1 *(Burke)*
Airdrieonians 2 *(McPherson, Coyle)*

Ross County 0
Brechin C 2 *(Grant, Kernaghan)*

Semi-Finals

Airdrieonians 1 *(Roberts)*
Brechin City 1 *(Fotheringham)*
aet; Airdrie won 4-3 on pens

Clyde 0
Alloa Athletic 1 *(Hutchison)*

FINAL

Broadwood Stadium

Oct 14

AIRDRIEONIANS (0) 2
(Coyle, Roberts)
ALLOA ATHLETIC (0) 1
(Evans)

Airdrieonians: Ferguson; Armstrong, McPherson, Stewart, McManus, James, Gardner (Dunn), MacFarlane, Coyle, Taylor, Roberts

Alloa Athletic: Soutar; Knox (Curran), Seaton, Watson, Thomson, Valentine, Hamilton, Fisher (Christie), Walker (Evans), Hutchison, Little

Referee: Michael McCurry

Attendance: 4548

Welsh Football
League of Wales 2001-2002

	P	W	D	L	GF	GA	Pts
Barry Town	34	23	8	3	82	29	77
Total Network Solutions	34	21	7	6	65	33	70
Bangor City	34	21	6	7	83	38	69
Caersws	34	18	4	12	65	44	58
Afan Lido	34	18	4	12	42	36	58
Rhyl	34	17	5	12	53	45	56
Cwmbran Town	34	17	4	13	66	53	55
Connah's Quay Nomads	34	14	9	11	56	46	51
Aberystwyth Town	34	14	9	11	53	48	51
Carmarthen Town	34	13	9	12	51	37	48
Caernarfon Town	34	12	8	14	64	64	44
Port Talbot Town	34	12	7	15	44	55	43
Newtown	34	9	11	14	35	44	38
Flexsys Cefn Druids	34	8	8	18	49	79	32
Llanelli	34	8	7	19	41	64	31
Oswestry Town	34	8	6	20	39	55	30
Haverfordwest County	34	6	10	18	47	76	28
Rhayader	34	3	6	24	29	89	15

Welsh Cup Final
Aberysthwyth   *May 5*
Barry Town 4   **Bangor City 1**

Northern Irish Football
Smirnoff Irish League 2001-2002

PREMIERSHIP	P	W	D	L	GF	GA	Pts
Portadown	**36**	**22**	**9**	**5**	**75**	**34**	**75**
Glentoran	36	21	11	4	63	23	74
Linfield	36	17	11	8	64	35	62
Coleraine	36	19	2	15	64	58	59
Omagh Town	36	15	9	12	55	55	54
Cliftonville	36	9	11	16	37	46	38
Glenavon	36	9	9	18	37	57	36
Newry Town	36	8	12	16	40	62	36
Crusaders	36	9	7	20	41	65	34
Ards	36	6	9	21	30	71	27

FIRST DIVISION	P	W	D	L	GF	GA	Pts
Lisburn Distillery	36	24	4	8	64	26	76
Institute	36	22	8	6	76	35	74
Dungannon Swifts	36	17	8	11	55	42	59
Larne	36	14	11	11	51	42	53
Ballymena United	36	14	11	11	59	56	53
Bangor	36	10	12	14	40	45	42
Limavady United	36	10	7	19	49	67	37
Carrick Rangers	36	9	9	18	34	55	36
Ballyclare Comrades	36	7	12	17	40	73	33
Armagh City	36	8	8	20	40	67	32

Due to expansion, was no relegation from the Premiership, and the top two teams from the first division were promoted.

Nationwide Irish Cup Final
Windsor Park
Linfield 2   **Portadown 1**

European Leagues 2001-2002

BELGIUM

	P	W	D	L	GF	GA	Pts
Genk	**34**	**20**	**12**	**2**	**85**	**43**	**72**
Club Brugge	34	22	4	8	74	41	70
Anderlecht	34	18	12	4	71	37	66
Gent	34	16	10	8	62	51	58
Standard Liege	34	15	12	7	57	38	57
Mouscron	34	17	5	12	68	40	56
Lokeren	34	15	10	9	43	33	55
St Truiden	34	16	5	13	52	47	53
Beerschot	34	11	16	7	68	51	49
Molenbeek	34	13	5	16	50	59	44
La Louviere	34	12	8	14	41	52	44
Charleroi	34	11	6	17	40	63	39
Lommel	34	10	9	15	54	66	39
Westerlo	34	9	9	16	49	61	36
Lierse	34	9	8	17	55	65	35
Royal Antwerp	34	7	10	17	47	67	31
Aalst	34	4	9	21	32	73	21
Beveren	34	2	8	24	30	91	14

Cup Final: Mouscron 1 Club Brugge 3
Top Scorer: Sonck (Genk) 30

FRANCE

	P	W	D	L	GF	GA	Pts
Lyon	**34**	**20**	**6**	**8**	**62**	**32**	**66**
Lens	34	18	10	6	55	30	64
Auxerre	34	16	11	7	48	38	59
Paris St Germain	34	15	13	6	43	24	58
Lille	34	15	11	8	39	32	56
Bordeaux	34	14	8	12	34	31	50
Troyes	34	13	8	13	40	35	47
Sochaux	34	12	10	12	41	40	46
Marseille	34	11	11	12	34	39	44
Nantes	34	12	7	15	35	41	43
Bastia	34	12	5	17	38	44	41
Rennes	34	11	8	15	40	51	41
Montpelier	34	9	13	12	28	31	40
Sedan	34	8	15	11	35	39	39
Monaco	34	9	12	13	36	41	39
Guingcamp	34	9	8	17	34	57	35
Metz	34	9	6	19	31	47	33
Lorient	34	7	10	17	43	64	31

Cup Final: Bastia 0 Lorient 1
Top scorer: Cisse (Auxerre) & Pauleta (Bordeaux) 22

GERMANY

	P	W	D	L	GF	GA	Pts
Borussia Dortmund	**34**	**21**	**7**	**6**	**62**	**33**	**70**
Leverkusen	34	21	6	7	77	38	69
Bayern Munich	34	20	8	6	65	25	68
Hertha	34	18	7	9	61	38	61
Schalke	34	18	7	9	52	36	61
Werder Bremen	34	17	5	12	54	43	56
Kaiserslautern	34	17	5	12	62	53	56
Stuttgart	34	13	11	10	47	43	50
Munich 1860	34	15	5	14	59	59	50
Wolfsberg	34	13	7	14	57	49	46
Hamburg	34	10	10	14	51	57	40
Moenchengladbach	34	9	12	13	41	53	39
Cottbus	34	9	8	17	36	60	35
Hansa Rostock	34	9	7	18	35	54	34
Nuremburg	34	10	4	20	34	57	34
Freiburg	34	7	9	18	37	64	30
Cologne	34	7	8	19	26	61	29
St Pauli	34	4	10	20	37	70	22

Cup Final: Schalke 4 Leverkusen 2
Top scorers: Amoroso (Borussia Dortmund) & Max (Munich 1860) 18

IRELAND

	P	W	D	L	GF	GA	Pts
Shelbourne	**33**	**19**	**6**	**8**	**50**	**28**	**63**
Shamrock Rovers	33	17	6	10	54	32	57
St Patrick's Athletic	33	20	8	5	59	29	53
Bohemians	33	14	10	9	57	32	52
Derry City	33	14	9	10	42	30	51
Cork City	33	14	7	12	48	39	49
UCD	33	12	12	9	40	39	48
Bray Wanderers	33	12	10	11	54	45	48
Longford Town	33	10	10	13	41	51	40
Dundalk	33	9	12	12	37	46	39
Galway United	33	5	4	24	28	73	19
Monaghan United	33	2	6	25	19	85	12

St Patricks had nine points deducted for fielding an illegible player.

Cup Final: Bohemians 1 Dundalk 2

ITALY

	P	W	D	L	GF	GA	Pts
Juventus	**34**	**20**	**11**	**3**	**64**	**23**	**71**
Roma	34	19	13	2	58	24	70
Internazionale	34	20	9	5	62	35	69
AC Milan	34	14	13	7	47	33	55
Chievo	34	14	12	8	57	52	54
Lazio	34	14	11	9	50	37	53
Bologna	34	15	7	12	40	40	52
Perugia	34	13	7	14	38	46	46
Atalanta	34	12	9	13	41	50	45
Parma	34	12	8	14	43	47	44
Torino	34	10	13	11	37	39	43
Piacenza	34	11	9	14	49	43	42
Brescia	34	9	13	12	43	52	40
Udinese	34	11	7	16	41	52	40
Verona	34	11	6	17	41	53	39
Lecce	34	6	10	18	36	56	28
Fiorentina	34	5	7	22	29	63	22
Venezia	34	3	9	22	30	61	18

Cup Final: Juventus 2 Parma 0
Parma 1 Juventus 0
Juventus won 2-1 on aggregate
Top scorer: Hubner (Piacenzo) & Trezeguet (Juventus) 24

NETHERLANDS

	P	W	D	L	GF	GA	Pts
Ajax	**34**	**22**	**7**	**5**	**73**	**34**	**73**
PSV Eindhoven	34	20	8	6	77	32	68
Feyenoord	34	19	7	8	68	29	64
Heerenveen	34	17	9	8	57	27	60
Vitesse	34	16	12	6	45	34	54
NAC Breda	34	15	9	10	55	52	51
Utrecht	34	14	9	11	60	51	48
RKC Waalwijk	34	14	6	14	49	44	48
NEC Nijmegen	34	13	6	15	38	59	45
AZ	34	12	7	15	43	45	43
Willem II	34	10	13	11	54	61	43
Twente	34	10	12	12	41	41	42
Roda JC	34	11	8	15	33	45	41
De Graafschap	34	10	7	17	43	55	37
Groningen	34	10	7	17	40	59	37
Den Bosch	34	8	9	17	40	55	33
Sparta	34	4	12	18	26	75	24
Fortuna Sittard	34	3	8	23	27	71	17

Cup Final: Utrecht 2 Ajax 3
Top scorer: Von Hooijdonk (Feyenoord) 24

PORTUGAL

	P	W	D	L	GF	GA	Pts
Sporting Lisbon	**34**	**22**	**9**	**3**	**74**	**25**	**75**
Boavista	34	21	7	6	53	20	70
Porto	34	21	5	8	66	34	68
Benfica	34	17	12	5	66	37	63
Belenenses	34	17	6	11	54	44	57
Maritimo	34	17	5	12	49	35	56
Uniao Leiria	34	15	10	9	52	35	55
Pacos	34	12	10	12	41	44	46
Guimaraes	34	11	9	14	35	41	42
Braga	34	10	12	12	43	43	42
Beira Mar	34	10	9	15	48	56	39
Gil Vicente	34	10	8	16	42	56	38
Setubal	34	9	11	14	40	46	38
Santa Clara	34	9	10	15	32	46	37
Varzin	34	8	8	18	27	55	32
Salgueiros	34	8	6	20	29	71	30
Farense	34	7	7	20	29	63	28
Alverca	34	7	6	21	39	67	27

Cup Final: Leixoes 0 Sporting Lisbon 1
Top scorer: Jardel (Sporting Lisbon) 42

RUSSIA

	P	W	D	L	GF	GA	Pts
Spartak Moscow	**30**	**17**	**9**	**4**	**56**	**30**	**60**
Lokomotiv Moscow	30	16	8	6	53	24	56
Zenit	30	16	8	6	52	35	56
Torpedo Moscow	30	15	7	8	53	42	52
Krylia Sovekov	30	14	7	9	38	23	49
Saturn	30	13	8	9	45	22	47
CSKA Moscow	30	12	11	7	39	30	47
Sokol	30	12	5	13	31	42	41
Dynamo Moscow	30	10	8	12	43	51	38
Volgograd	30	8	8	14	38	42	32
Vladikavkaz	30	8	8	14	31	47	32
Rostelmash	30	8	8	14	29	43	32
Anzhi	30	7	11	12	28	34	32
Torpedo ZIL	30	7	10	13	22	35	31
Fakel	30	8	4	18	30	53	28
Chernomorets	30	5	8	17	19	54	23

Cup Final: CSKA Moscow 1 Zenit 0

SPAIN

	P	W	D	L	GF	GA	Pts
Valencia	**38**	**21**	**12**	**5**	**51**	**27**	**75**
Deportivo La Coruña	38	20	8	10	65	41	68
Real Madrid	38	19	9	10	69	44	66
Barcelona	38	18	10	10	65	37	64
Celta Vigo	38	16	12	10	64	46	60
Real Betis	38	15	14	9	42	34	59
Alaves	38	17	3	18	41	44	54
Sevilla	38	14	11	13	51	40	53
Athletico Bilbao	38	14	11	13	54	66	53
Malaga	38	13	14	11	44	44	53
Rayo Vallecano	38	13	10	15	46	52	49
Valladolid	38	13	9	16	45	58	48
Real Sociedad	38	13	8	17	48	54	47
Espanyol	38	13	8	17	47	56	47
Villareal	38	11	10	17	46	55	43
Mallorca	38	11	10	17	40	52	43
Osasuna	38	10	12	16	36	49	42
Las Palmas	38	9	13	16	40	50	40
Tenerife	38	10	8	20	32	58	38
Zaragoza	38	9	10	19	35	54	37

Cup Final: Real Madrid 1 La Coruna 2
Top scorer: Diego Tristan (La Coruna) 24

SWEDEN

	P	W	D	L	GF	GA	Pts
Hammarby	**26**	**14**	**6**	**6**	**45**	**28**	**48**
Djurgaarden	26	13	8	5	36	24	47
AIK Stockholm	26	12	9	5	45	29	45
IFK Gothenburg	26	12	8	6	41	31	44
Helsingborg	26	11	9	6	47	29	42
Orgryte	26	10	9	7	36	33	39
Halmstad	26	10	8	8	50	31	38
Orebro	26	8	9	9	48	44	33
Malmo	26	9	5	12	39	46	32
Elfsborg	26	9	3	14	31	51	30
Sundsvall	26	7	8	11	28	37	29
Norrkoping	26	7	8	11	29	40	29
Hacken	26	5	9	12	35	50	24
Trelleborg	26	3	5	18	25	62	14

Top scorer: Selakovic (Halmstad) 15

European Cup Competitions 2001-2002

European Cup
First Qualifying Round

Araks 0
Serif 1 *(Barburos)*

Serif 2 *(Comlenoc, Dadu)*
Araks 0

Barry Town 2 *(York, French)*
Shamkir 0

Shamkir 0
Barry Town 1 *(Phillips)*

Bohemians 3 *(Maher, Crowe 2, 1 pen)*
Levadia 0

Levadia 0
Bohemians 0

F91 Dudelange 1 *(Cicchirillo)*
Skonto Riga 6 *(Verpakovskis,
   Miholaps 2, Kolesnicenko 2,
   Zemlinskis)*
Skonto Riga 0
F91 Dudelange 1 *(Cicchirillo)*

KR Reykjavik 2 *(Benediktsson,
   S Olafsson)*
Vilaznia 1 *(Duro)*

Vilaznia 1 *(Duro)*
KR Reykjavik 0
2-2: Vilaznia won on away goal

Levski 4 *(Terziev, Ivanov 2, 1 pen
   Markov)*
Zeljeznicar 0

Zeljeznicar 0
Levski 0

Linfield 0
Torpedo Kutaisi 0

Torpedo Kutaisi 1 *(Ashvetia)*
Linfield 0

Sloga 0
Kaunus 0

Kaunus 1 *(Papeckys)*
Sloga 1 *(Nuhiji)*
1-1: Sloga won on away goals

Valetta 0
Haka 0

Haka 5 *(Torkkeli, Kovacs 3, Pogioli)*
Valetta 0

VB Vagur 0
Slavia Mozyr 0

Slavia Mozyr 5 *(Jacobsen og,
   Stripeikis 3, 1 pen, Rybackov)*
VB Vagur 0

Second Qualifying Round

Anderlecht 4 *(Crasson 2,
   De Boeck 2)*
Serif 0

Serif 1 *(Boret)*
Anderlecht 2 *(Iachtchouk, De Boeck)*

Bohemians 1 *(Crowe)*
Halmstad 2 *(Jonsson, Selakovic)*

Halmstad 2 *(Jonsson, Selakovic)*
Bohemians 0

Ferencvaros 0
Hajduk Split 0

Hajduk Split 0
Ferencvaros 0
aet; Split won 5-4 on pens

Galatasaray 2 *(Karan, Kaya)*
Vilaznia 0

Vilaznia 1 *(Sinani)*
Galatasaray 4 *(Umit, Arif, Hakan
   Sas, Serkan)*

Haka 0
Maccabi Haifa 1 *(Zano)*

Maccabi Haifa 4 *(Rosso, Katan 3)*
Haka 0
*Haifa fielded an ineligible player; tie
awarded to Haka*

Levski 0
Brann 0

Brann 1 *(Walltin)*
Levski 1 *(Ivanov*
1-1; Levski won on away goal

Maribor 0
Rangers 3 *(Flo 2, Nerlinger)*

Rangers 3 *(Flo, Caniggia 2)*
Maribor 1 *(Starcevic)*

Omonia 1 *(Thiebaut)*
Red Star Belgrade 1 *(Pjanovic)*

Red Star Belgrade 2 *(Lerinc,
   Acimovic)*
Omonia 1 *(Kaiafas)*

Porto 8 *(Pena 3, Deco 3, Sodestrom
   Capucho)*
Barry Town 0

Barry Town 3 *(Phillips, Flynn,
   Lloyd pen)*
Porto 1 *(Dias)*

Shakhjor Donetsk 3 *(Bakharev,
   Tymoschuk, Vorobei)*
Lugano 0

Lugano 2 *(Gaspoz, Rossi)*
Shakhjor Donetsk 1 *(Aghahowa)*

Skonto Riga 1 *(Korgalidze)*
Wisla 2 *(Glowacki, Zurawski)*

Wisla 1 *(Zurawski)*
Skonto Riga 0

Slavia Mozyr 0
Inter Bratislava 1 *(Kunzo)*

Inter Bratislava 1 *(Lembakoali)*
Slavia Mozyr 0

Steaua 3 *(Raducanu 2, Trica)*
Sloga 0

Sloga 1 *(Nuhiji)*
Steaua 2 *(N'Gassam, Raducanu)*

Torpedo Kutaisi 1 *(Ashvetia)*
FC Copenhagan 1 *(Zuma)*

FC Copenhagan 3 *Zuma, Lonstrup,
   Fernandez)*
Torpedo Kutaisi 1 *(Kutateladze)*

Third Qualifying Round

Ajaz 1 *(Arveladze)*
Celtic 3 *(Petta, Agathe, Sutton)*

Celtic 0
Ajax 1 *(Wamberto)*

FC Copenhagen 2 *(Laursen pen,
   Fernandez)*
Lazio 1 *(Crespo)*

Lazio 4 *(Crespo 2, Lopez, Fiore)*
FC Copenhagen 1 *(Zuma)*

Galatasaray 2 *(Karan, K Bulent)*
Levski 1 *(Ivanov)*

Levski 1 *(Pantelic)*
Galatasaray 1 *(Aykut)*

Hajduk Split 1 *(Bilic)*
Mallorca 0

Mallorca 2 *(Eto'o, Luque)*
Hajduk Split 0

Haka 0
Liverpool 5 *(Heskey, Owen 3,
   Hyypia)*

Liverpool 4 *(Fowler, Redknapp,
   Heskey, Wilson og)*
Haka 1 *(Kovacs)*

Halmstad 2 *(Svensson, Selakovic)*
Anderlecht 3 *(Seol, Hasi, Mornar)*

Anderlecht 1 *(De Boeck)*
Halmstad 1 *(Jonsson)*

Inter Bratislava 3 *(Lembakoali 2, Drobnjak)*
Rosenborg 3 *(Brattbakk, Skammelsrud pen, Kunzo og)*

Rosenborg 4 *(Jonhsen, Rushfeldt, Skammelsrud, Strand)*
Intern Bratislava 0

Lokomotiv Moscow 3 *(Lecgetho, Izmailov, Ignashevic)*
Tirol Innsbruck 1 *(Kirchler)*

Tirol Innsbruck 0
Lokomotiv Moscow 1 *(Maminov)*

Parma 0
Lille 2 *(Bassir, Ecker)*

Lille 0
Parma 1 *(Sensini)*

Porto 2 *(Parades, Helder)*
Grasshoppers 2 *(Nunez, Petric)*

Grasshoppers 2 *(Petric, Chapuisat)*
Porto 3 *(Clayton, Capucho, Deco)*

Rangers 0
Fenerbahce 0

Fenerbahce 2 *(Revivo, Serhat)*
Rangers 1 *(Ricksen)*

Red Star Belgrade 0
Leverkusen 0

Leverkusen 3 *(Neuville 2, Kirsten)*
Red Star Belgrade 0

Shakhjor Donetsk 0
Borussia Dortmund 2 *(Ricken, Oliseh)*

Borussia Dortmund 3 *(Koller 2, Amoroso)*
Shakhjor Donetsk 1 *(Aghahowa)*

Slavia Prague 1 *(Kuka)*
Panathinaikos 2 *(Liberopoulos, Karagounis)*

Panathinaikos 1 *(Basinas pen)*
Slavia Prague

Steaua 2 *(Trica 2)*
Dynamo Kiev 4 *(Belkevich 2, 1pen, Idahor, Melaschenko)*

Dynamo Kiev 1 *(Melaschenko)*
Steaua 1 *(Neaga)*

Wisla 3 *(Pater 2, Frankowski)*
Barcelona 4 *(Rivaldo 3, 1 pen, Kluivert)*

Barcelona 1 *(Luis Enrique)*
Wisla 0

Champions League
First Group Stage

Where teams end up on equal points, group positions are determined by which team has the better record in matches between the equally placed teams.

Group A

Lokomotiv Moscow 1 *(Maminov)*
Anderlecht 1 *(Hendrikx)*

Roma 1 *(Totti pen)*
Real Madrid 2 *(Figo, Guti)*

Andeerlecht 0
Roma 0

Real Madrid 4 *(Munitis, Figo pen, Roberto Carlos, Savio)*
Anderlecht 1 *(Dindane)*

Roma 2 *(Chugainov og, Totti)*
Lokomotiv Moscow 1 *(Obradovic)*

Anderlecht 0
Real Madrid 2 *(Raul, McManaman)*

Lokomotiv Moscow 0
Roma 1 *(Cafu)*

Anderlecht 1 *(Ilic)*
Lokomotiv Moscow 5 *(Izmailov, Sennikov, Pimenov, Buznikin 2)*

Real Madrid 1 *(Figo pen)*
Roma 1 *(Totti)*

Lokomotiv Moscow 2 *(Buznikin, Cherevchanko)*
Real Madrid 0

Roma 1 *(Delvecchio)*
Anderlecht 1 *(Mornar)*

Final Table	P	W	D	L	F	A	Pts
Real Madrid	6	4	1	1	13	5	13
Roma	6	2	3	1	6	5	9
Lokomotiv	6	2	1	3	9	9	7
Anderlecht	6	0	3	3	4	13	3

Group B

Dynamo Kiev 2 *(Melaschenko, Idahor)*
B Dortmund 2 *(Koller, Amoroso)*

Liverpool 1 *(Owen)*
Boavista 1 *(Silva)*

Boavista 3 *(Sanchez, Silva, Duda)*
Dynamo Kiev 1 *(Gioane)*

B Dortmund 0
Liverpool 0

Boavista 2 *(Silva, Sanchez)*
B Dortmund 0

Liverpool 1 *(Litmanen)*
Dynamo Kiev 0

B Dortmund 2 *(Ricken, Koller)*
Boavista 1 *(Goulart)*

Dynamo Kiev 1 *(Gioane)*
Liverpool 2 *(Murphy, Gerrard)*

Boavista 1 *(Silva)*
Liverpool 1 *(Murphy)*

B Dortmund 1 *(Rosicky)*
Dynamo Kiev 0

Dynamo Kiev 1 *(Melaschanko)*
Boavista 0

Liverpool 2 *(Smicer, Wright)*
B Dortmund 0

Final Table	P	W	D	L	F	A	Pts
Liverpool	6	3	3	0	7	3	12
Boavista	6	2	2	2	8	7	8
B Dortmund	6	2	2	2	6	7	8
Dynamo Kiev	6	1	1	4	5	9	4

Group C

Mallorca 1 *(Engonga pen)*
Arsenal 0

Schalke 0
Panathinaikos 2 *(Vlaovic, Basinas)*

Arsenal 3 *(Ljungberg, Henry 2, 1 pen)*
Schalke 2 *(Van Hoogdalem, Mpenza)*

Panathinaikos 2 *(Vlaovic, Konstantinou)*
Mallorca 0

Panathinaikos 1 *(Karagounis)*
Arsenal 0

Schalke 0
Mallorca 1 *(Eto'o)*

Arsenal 2 *(Henry 2, 1 pen)*
Panathinaikos 1 *(Olisadebe)*

Mallorca 0
Schalke 4 *(Van Hoogdalem, Hajto pen, Asamoah, Sand)*

Arsenal 3 *(Pires, Bergkamp, Henry)*
Mallorca 1 *(Novo)*

Panathinaikos 2 *(Olisadebe, Konstantinou)*
Schalke 0

Mallorca 1 *(Biagini)*
Panathinaikos 0

Schalke 3 *(Mulder, Vermant, Moller)*
Arsenal 1 *(Wiltord)*

Final Table	P	W	D	L	F	A	Pts
Panathinaikos	6	4	0	2	8	3	12
Arsenal	6	3	0	3	9	9	9
Mallorca	6	3	0	3	4	9	9
Schalke	6	2	0	4	9	9	6

Group D

Galatasaray 1 (Karan)
Lazio 0

Nantes 4 (Andre, Quint pen,
        Dalmat, Vahirua)
PSV Eindhoven 1 (De Jong)

Lazio 1 (Couto)
Nantes 3 (Fabbri, Armand, Ziani)

PSV Eindhoven 3 (Bruggink,
        Fabeer, Kezman)
Galatasaray 1 (Karan)

Nantes 0
Galatasaray 1 (Yalcin)

PSV Eindhoven 1 (Hofland)
Lazio 0

Galatasaray 0
Nantes 0

Lazio 2 (Fiore, Lopez-pen)
PSV Eindhoven 1 (Kezman)

Lazio 1 (Stankovic)
Galatasaray 0

PSV Eindhoven 0
Nantes 0

Galatasaray 2 (Yalcin, Arif)
PSV Eindhoven 0

Nantes 1 (Andre)
Lazio 0

Final Table	P	W	D	L	F	A	Pts
Nantes	6	3	2	1	11	8	11
Galatasaray	6	3	1	2	5	4	10
Eindhoven	6	2	1	3	6	9	7
Lazio	6	2	0	4	4	7	6

Group E

Juventus 3 (Trezeguet 2,
        Amoroso-pen)
Celtic 2 (Petrov, Larsson-pen)

Rosenborg 1 (Rushfeldt)
Porto 2 (Pena, Deco)

Celtic 1 (Larsson)
Porto 0

Rosenborg 1 (Skammelsrud-pen)
Juventus 1 (Del Piero)

Celtic 1 (Thompson)
Rosenborg 0

Porto 0
Juventus 0

Porto 3 (Clayton 2, Mario Silva)
Celtic 0

Juventus 1 (Trezeguet)
Rosenborg 0

Juventus 3 (Del Piero, Montero,
        Trezeguet)
Porto 1 (Clayton)

Rosenborg 2 (Brattbakk 2)
Celtic 0

Celtic 4 (Valgaeren, Sutton 2,
        Larsson-pen)
Juventus 3 (Del Piero, Trezeguet 2)

Porto 1 (Pena)
Rosenborg 0

Final Table	P	W	D	L	F	A	Pts
Juventus	6	3	2	1	11	8	11
Porto	6	3	1	2	7	5	10
Celtic	6	3	0	3	8	11	9
Rosenborg	6	1	1	4	4	6	4

Group F

Fenerbahce 0
Barcelona 3 (Kluivert, Saviola,
        Andersson)

Lyon 0
Leverkusen 1 (Kirsten)

Fenerbahce 0
Lyon 1 (Delmotte)

Leverkusen 2 (Basturk, Neuville)
Barcelona 1 (Luis Enrique)

Barcelona 2 (Kluivert, Rivaldo-pen)
Lyon 0

Leverkusen 2 (Lucio, Ballack)
Fenerbahce 1 (Revivo)

Barcelona 2 (Kluivert, Luis Enrique)
Leverkusen 1 (Ramelow)

Lyon 3 (Govou, Carriere, Delmotte)
Fenerbahce 1 (Derelioglu)

Fenerbahce 1 (Derelioglu)
Leverkusen 2 (Schneider, Kirsten)

Lyon 2 (Luyindula, Carriere)
Barcelona 3 (Kluivert, Rivaldo,
        Gerard)

Barcelona 1 (Rivaldo)
Fenerbahce 0

Leverkusen 2 (Sebescen, Berbatov)
Lyon 4 (Carriere 2, Nee, Govou)

Final Table	P	W	D	L	F	A	Pts
Barcelona	6	5	0	1	12	5	15
Leverkusen	6	4	0	2	10	9	12
Lyon	6	3	0	3	10	9	9
Fenerbahce	6	0	0	6	3	12	0

Group G

La Coruna 2 (Fran, Valeron)
Olympiakos 2 (Giannakopoulos,
        Oforiquaye)

Man United 1 (Beckham)
Lille 0

La Coruna 2 (Pandiani, Naybet)
Man United 1 (Scholes)

Lille 3 (Bakhari, Cheyrou, Tafforeau)
Olympiakos 1 (Giannakopoulos)

Lille 1 (Olufade)
La Coruna 1 (Valeron)

Olympiakos 0
Man United 2 (Beckham, Cole)

Man United 2 (Van Nistelrooy 2)
La Coruna 3 (Sergio, Diego Tristan 2)

Olypiakos 2 (Alexandris,
        Niniadis)
Lille 1 (Bassir)

La Coruna 1 (Diego Tristan-pen)
Lille 1 (Cheyrou-pen)

Man United 3 (Solskjaer, Giggs,
        Van Nistelrooy)
Olympiakos 0

Lille 1 (Cheyrou)
Man United 1 (Solskjaer)

Olympiakos 1 (Alexandris)
La Coruna 1 (Capdevila)

Final Table	P	W	D	L	F	A	Pts
D La Coruna	6	2	4	0	10	8	10
Man United	6	3	1	2	10	6	10
Lille	6	1	3	2	7	7	6
Olympiakos	6	1	2	3	6	12	5

Group H

Bayern Munich 0
Sparta Prague 0

Spartak Moscow 2 (Robson,
        Bestchastnykh)
Feyenoord 2 (Bosvelt, Tomasson)

Sparta Prague 4 (Hartig, Labant-
        pen, Kinci, Michalik)
Feyenoord 0

Spartak Moscow 1 (Baranov)
B Munich 3 (Salihamidzic, Elber 2)

Feyenoord 2 (Van Hooijdonk,
        Tomasson)
Bayern Munich 2 (Elber 2)

Sparta Prague 2 (Kinci, Sionko)
Spartak Moscow 0

B Munich 5 (Pisarro 2, Elber 2,
        Zickler)
Spartak Moscow 1 (Bestchastnykh)

Feyenoord 0
Sparta Prague 2 (Jarosik, Novotny)

B Munich 3 (Van Gobbel og,
        Santa Cruz 2)
Feyenoord 1 (Elmander)

Spartak Moscow 2 (Robson,
        Bestchastnykh)
Sparta Prague 2 (Holub, Babnik)

Feyenoord 2 (Tomasson, Elmander)
Spartak Moscow 1 (Bestchastnykh)

Spartak Prague 0
Bayern Munich 1 *(Novotny-og)*

Final Table	P	W	D	L	F	A	Pts
B Munich	6	4	2	0	14	5	14
S Prague	6	3	2	1	10	3	11
Feyenoord	6	1	2	3	7	14	5
S Moscow	6	0	2	4	7	16	2

Second Group Stage

Group A

Bayern Munich 1 *(Sergio)*
Man United 1 *(Van Nistelrooy)*

Boavista 1 *(Sanchez)*
Nantes 0

Man United 3 *(Van Nistelrooy 2,
    Blanc)*
Boavista 0

Nantes 0
Bayern Munich 1 *(Sergio)*

Boavista 0
Bayern Munich 0

Nantes 1 *(Moldovan)*
Man United 1 *(Van Nistelrooy-pen)*

Bayern Munich 1 *(Santa Cruz)*
Boavista 0

Man United 5 *(Beckham, Solskjaer 2,
    Silvestre, Van Nistelrooy-pen)*
Nantes 1 *(Da Rocha)*

Man United 0
Bayern Munich 0

Nantes 1 *(Moldovan)*
Boavista 1 *(Martelinho)*

Bayern Munich 2 *(Jeremies, Pizarro)*
Nantes 1 *(Ahamada)*

Boavista 0
Man United 3 *(Blanc, Solskjaer,
    Beckham-pen)*

Final Table	P	W	D	L	F	A	Pts
Man United	6	3	3	0	13	3	12
B Munich	6	3	3	0	5	2	12
Boavista	6	1	2	3	2	8	5
Nantes	6	0	2	4	4	11	2

Group B

Galatasaray 1 *(Perez)*
Roma 1 *(Emerson)*

Liverpool 1 *(Owen)*
Barcelona 3 *(Kluivert, Rochemback,
    Overmars)*

Barcelona 2 *(Saviola 2)*
Galatasaray 2 *(Karan, Fleurquin)*

Roma 0
Liverpool 0

Barcelona 1 *(Kluivert)*
Roma 1 *(Panucci)*

Liverpool 0
Galatasaray 0

Galatasaray 1 *(Niculescu)*
Liverpool 1 *(Heskey)*

Roma 3 *(Emerson, Montella, Tomassi)*
Barcelona 0

Barcelona 0
Liverpool 0

Roma 1 *(Cafu)*
Galatasaray 1 *(Karan)*

Galatasaray 0
Barcelona 1 *(Luis Enrique)*

Liverpool 2 *(Litmanen-pen, Heskey)*
Roma 0

Final Table	P	W	D	L	F	A	Pts
Barcelona	6	3	2	1	7	7	9
Liverpool	6	1	4	1	4	4	7
Roma	6	1	4	1	6	5	7
Galatasaray	6	0	5	1	5	6	5

Group C

Panathinaikos 0
Porto 0

Sparta Prague 2 *(Michalik, Sionko)*
Real Madrid 3 *(Zidane, Moreintes 2)*

Porto 0
Sparta Prague 1 *(Sionko)*

Real Madrid 3 *(Helguera, Raul 2)*
Panathinaikos 0

Real Madrid 1 *(Elber)*
Porto 0

Sparta Prague 0
Panathinaikos 2 *(Karagounis,
    Konstantinou)*

Panathinaikos 2 *(Konstantinou 2)*
Sparta Prague 1 *(Klein)*

Porto 1 *(Capucho)*
Real Madrid 2 *(Solari, Helguera)*

Porto 2 *(Deco, Pena)*
Panathinaikos 2 *(Kolkka)*

Real Madrid 3 *(Solari, Guti, Savio)*
Sparta Prague 0

Panathinaikos 2 *(Liberopoulos,
    Goumas)*
Real Madrid 2 *(Morientes, Portillo)*

Sparta Prague 2 *(Sionko, Jarosik)*
Porto 0

Final Table	P	W	D	L	F	A	Pts
Real Madrid	6	5	1	0	14	5	16
Panathinaikos	6	2	2	2	7	8	8
S Prague	6	2	0	4	6	10	6
Porto	6	1	1	4	3	7	4

Group D

Juventus 4 *(Trezeguet 2, Del Piero,
    Tudor)*
Leverkusen 0

La Coruna 2 *(Makaay, Diego Tristan)*
Arsenal 0

Arsenal 3 *(Ljungberg 2, Henry)*
Juventus 1 *(Taylor-og)*

Leverkusen 3 *(Ze Roberto, Neuville,
    Ballack)*
La Coruna 0

Juventus 0
La Coruna 0

Leverkusen 1 *(Kirsten)*
Arsenal 1 *(Pires)*

Arsenal 4 *(Pires, Henry, Vieira,
    Bergkamp)*
Leverkusen 1 *(Sebescen)*

La Coruna 2 *(Diego Tristan,
    Djalminho)*
Juventus 0

Arsenal 0
La Coruna 2 *(Valeron, Naybet)*

Leverkusen 3 *(Butt-pen, Brdaric,
    Babic)*
Juventus 1 *(Tudor)*

La Coruna 1 *(Diego Tristan)*
Leverkusen 3 *(Ballack, Schneider,
    Neuville)*

Juventus 1 *(Zalayeta)*
Arsenal 0

Final Table	P	W	D	L	F	A	Pts
Leverkusen	6	3	1	2	11	11	10
La Coruna	6	3	1	2	7	6	10
Arsenal	6	2	1	3	8	8	7
Juventus	6	2	1	3	7	8	7

Quarter-finals

Bayern Munich 2 *(Effenberg, Pizarro)*
Real Madrid 1 *(Geremi)*

Real Madrid 2 *(Helguera, Guti)*
Bayern Munich 0
Real Madrid won 3-2 on aggregate

La Coruna 0
Man United 2 *(Beckham,
    Van Nistelrooy)*

Man United 3 *(Solskjaer 2, Giggs)*
La Coruna 2 *(Blanc-og, Djalminho)*
Man United won 5-2 on aggregate

Liverpool 1 *(Hyypia)*
Leverkusen 0

Leverkusen 4 *(Ballack 2, Berbatov,
    Lucio)*
Liverpool 2 *(Xavier, Litmanen)*
Leverkusen won 4-3 on aggregate

Panathinaikos 1 *(Basinas-pen)*
Barcelona 0

Barcelona 3 *(Luis Enrique 2,*
Saviola)
Panathinaikos 1 *(Konstantinou)*
Barcelona won 3-2 on aggregate

Semi-finals
Barcelona 0
Real Madrid 2 *(Zidane,*
McManaman)

Real Madrid 1 *(Raul)*
Barcelona 1 *(Helguera-og)*
Real Madrid won 3-1 on aggregate

Man United 2 *(Zivkovic-og,*
Van Nistelrooy-pen)
Leverkusen 2 *(Ballack, Neuville)*

Leverkusen 1 *(Neuville)*
Man United 1 *(Keane)*
3-3; Leverkusen won on away goals

FINAL
Hampden Park, Glasgow   May 15

LEVERKUSEN (1) 1
(Lucio 14)

REAL MADRID (2) 2
(Raul 8, Zidane 45)

Leverkusen: Butt; Sebescen
(Kirsten 65), Placente, Ramelow,
Zivkovic, Lucio (Babic 90),
Schneider, Ballack, Neuville,
Basturk, Brdaric (Berbatoc 39)
Real Madrid: Cesar (Casillas 68);
Michel Salgado, Roberto Carlos,
Makelele (Conceicao 73), Hierro,
Helguera, Figo (McManaman 61),
Morientes, Raul, Zidane, Solari

Referee: Urs Meier *SUI*

Attendance: 52,000

UEFA Cup
British and Irish Clubs only until quarter-finals

Qualifying Round
Brondby 2 *(Jonson, Bagger)*
Shelbourne 0

Shelbourne 0
Brondby 3 *(Bagger, Jorgensen Madsen)*

Cwmbran Town 0
Slovan Bratislava 4 *(Mojic, Obzera, Vittek, Sobona)*

Slovan Bratislava 1 *(Meszaros)*
Cwmbran Town 0

Glenavon 0
Kilmarnock 1 *(Innes)*

Kilmarnock 1 *(Mitchell)*
Glenavon 0

Longford Town 1 *(O'Connor)*
Liteks 1 *(Yurukov)*

Liteks 2 *(Jankovic 2, 1 pen)*
Longford Town 0

Midtjylland 1 *(Pimpong)*
Glentoran 1 *(Glendinning)*

Glentoran 0
Midtjylland 4 *(Skoubo 2, From, Pimpong)*

Polonia 4 *(Tarachulski 2, Moskal 2)*
Total Network Solutions 0

Total Network Solutions 0
Polonia 2 *(Bak, Bartczak)*

First Round
AEK Athens 2 *(Tsartas, pen, Nikolaidis)*
Hibernian 0

Hibernian 3 *(Luna 2, Zitelli)*
AEK Athens 2 *(Tsartas 2)*

Anzhi 0
Rangers 1 *(Konterman)*
Tie decided over one game - in Warsaw

Aston Villa 2 *(Angel 2)*
Varteks 3 *(Bjelanovic 2, Karic)*

Varteks 0
Aston Villa 1 *(Hadji)*
Villa won on away goals

Chelsea 3 *(Gudjohnsen 2, Lampard)*
Levski 0

Levski 0
Chelsea 2 *(Terry, Gudjohnsen)*

Ipswich Town 1 *(Bramble)*
Torpedo Moscow 1 *(Vyazmikin)*

Torpedo Moscow 1 *(Vyazmikin)*
Ipswich Town 2 *(George, Stewart, pen)*

Kilmarnock 1 *(Dargo)*
Viking 1 *(Sanne)*

Viking 2 *(Sanne, Nevland)*
Kilmarnock 0

Maritimo 1 *(Bruno)*
Leeds 0

Leeds 3 *(Keane, Kewell, Bakke)*
Maritimo 0

Second Round
Hapoel Tel Aviv 2 *(Gershon, pen, Kleschenco)*
Chelsea 0

Chelsea 1 *(Zola)*
Hapoel Tel Aviv 1 *(Osterc)*

Ipswich Town 0
Helsingborg 0

Helsingborg 1 *(Eklund)*
Ipswich Town 3 *(Hreidarsson, Stewart 2)*

Leeds 4 *(Viduka 2, Bowyer 2)*
Troyes 2 *(Loko 2)*

Troyes 3 *(Anzine, Hamed, Rothen)*
Leeds 2 *(Vikuka, Keane)*

Rangers 3 *(Amoroso, Ball, De Boer)*
Dynamo Moscow 1 *(Gusev)*

Dynamo Moscow 1 *(Gusev)*
Rangers 4 *(De Boer, Khonutovsky, og, Flo, Levonkrands)*

Third Round
Grasshoppers 1 *(Chapuisat)*
Leeds 2 *(Harte, Smith)*

Leeds 2 *(Kewell, Keane)*
Grasshoppers 2 *(Nunez 2)*

Ipswich Town 1 *(Armstrong)*
Internazionale 0

Internazionale 4 *(Vieri 3, Kallon)*
Ipswich Town 1 *(Armstrong, pen)*

Rangers 0
Paris St Germain 0

Paris St Germain 0
Rangers 0
aet; Rangers won 4-3 on pens

Valencia 1 *(Vicente)*
Celtic 0

Celtic 1 *(Larsson)*
Valencia 0
aet: Valencia won 5-4 on pens

Fourth Round
PSV Eindhoven 0
Leeds United 0

Leeds United 0
PSV Eindhoven 1 *(V of Hesselink)*

Rangers 1 *(Ferguson, pen)*
Feyenoord 1 *(Ono)*

Feyenoord 3 *(Van Hooijdonk 2, Kalou)*
Rangers 2 *(McCann, Ferguson, pen)*

Quarter-finals
Hapoel Tel Aviv 1 *(Cleswcenko)*
AC Milan 0

AC Milan 2 *(Rui Costa, Gershon)*
Hapoel Tel Aviv 0

Internazionale 1 *(Materazzi)*
Valencia *(Rufete)*

Valencia 0
Internazionale 1 *(Ventola)*

Liberec 0
Borussia Dortmund 0

Borussia Dortmund 4 *(Amoroso, Koller, Ricken, Ewerthon)*
Liberec 0

PSV Eindhoven 1 *(Kezman)*
Feyenoord 1 *(Van Hooijdonk)*

Feyenoord 1 *(Van Hooijdonk)*
PSV Eindhoven 1 *(Van Bommel)*
aet; Feyenoord won 5-4 on pens

Semi-finals
Borussia Dortmund 4 *(Amoroso 3, 1 pen, Heinrich)*
AC Milan 0

Internazionale 0
Feyenoord 1 *(Cordoba, og)*

FINAL
Rotterdam, May 8

FEYENOORD (2) 3
(Van Hooijdonk 33, pen, 40, Tomasson 50)

BORUSSIA DORTMUND (0) 2
(Amoroso 47, pen, Koller 58)

Feyenoord: Zoetebier; Gyan, Rzasa, Ono (De Haan 75), Van Wonderen, Paauwe, Bosvelt, Kalou (Elmander 75), Van Hooijdonk, Van Persie (Leonardo 62), Tomasson
Dortmund: Lehmann; Evanilson, Dede, Ricken (Heinrich 69), Worns, Kohler, Reuter, Ewerthon (Addo 61), Koller, Amoroso, Rosicky
Referee: Vitor Manuel Pereira POR
Attendance: 45,000

Women's Football

World Cup Qualifiers

Uefa countries were allocated five places for the 2003 World Cup in China. The gropup winners qualified directly, the runners-up played-off for the final place.

GROUP 1	P	W	D	L	F	A	Pts
Norway	**6**	**5**	**1**	**0**	**21**	**3**	**16**
France	6	4	0	2	11	9	12
Ukraine	6	2	1	3	9	12	7
Czech Rep	0	0	6	6	6	23	0

GROUP 2	P	W	D	L	F	A	Pts
Sweden	**6**	**5**	**0**	**1**	**27**	**4**	**15**
Denmark	6	5	0	1	21	5	15
Switzerland	6	1	0	5	2	18	3
Finland	6	1	0	5	4	24	3

GROUP 3	P	W	D	L	F	A	Pts
Russia	**6**	**3**	**2**	**1**	**10**	**6**	**11**
Iceland	6	2	3	1	8	9	9
Italy	6	2	1	3	7	7	7
Spain	6	2	0	4	8	11	6

GROUP 4

England matches only given; no scorers for 2001 games

Kassel, Sep 27,2001
Germany 3   **England 1**

Blundell Park, Nov 4, 2001
England 0   **Netherlands 0**

Aveira, Nov 24, 2001
Portugal 1   **England 1**

Portsmouth, Feb 24
England 3   **Portugal 0**
Williams,, K Smith 2

The Hague, Mar 23
Netherlands 1   **England 4**
Griffioen   *Chapman, Burke,*
                     K Smith, Walker

Selhurst Park, May 19
England 0   **Germany 1**
                   Unitt, og

GROUP 4	P	W	D	L	F	A	Pts
Germany	**6**	**6**	**0**	**0**	**30**	**1**	**18**
England	6	2	2	2	9	6	8
Netherlands	6	1	1	4	6	16	4
Portugal	6	1	1	4	4	26	4

Play-offs

Reykjavik, Sep 16
Iceland 2   **England 2**
Faerseth,   *Walker 2*
Hendrksdottir

St Andrews, Sep 22
England 1   **Iceland 0**
Barr
England won 3-2 on aggregate

Selhurst Park, Oct 17
England 0   **France 1**
                   Pichon

St Etienne, Nov 16
France 1   **England 0**
Diacre
France won 2-0 on aggregate and qualifed for World Cup

FA Women's Premier League

NATIONAL DIVISION

	P	W	D	L	GF	GA	Pts
Arsenal	**18**	**16**	**1**	**1**	**60**	**15**	**49**
Doncaster Belles	18	13	2	3	57	21	41
Charlton Athletic	18	10	1	7	4-	24	31
Leeds United	18	7	5	6	36	37	26
Everton	18	8	2	8	30	31	26
Tranmere Rovers	18	7	3	8	31	36	24
Brighton & Hove	18	7	3	8	19	33	24
Southampton Saints	18	5	3	10	19	34	18
Barry Town	18	2	3	13	19	49	9
Sunderland	18	1	5	12	15	46	8

NORTHERN DIVISION

	P	W	D	L	GF	GA	Pts
Birmingham	**22**	**16**	**3**	**1**	**68**	**21**	**51**
Wolverhampton	22	11	4	5	39	27	37
Oldham Curzon	22	10	6	4	39	22	36
Ilkeston Town	22	9	6	5	43	27	33
Liverpool	22	8	6	6	41	27	30
Bangor City	22	7	7	6	35	36	28
Aston Villa	22	7	5	8	42	34	26
Sheffield Wednesday	22	6	7	7	33	38	25
Garswood Saints	22	4	6	10	21	47	18
Manchester City	22	4	4	12	13	45	16
Coventry City	22	0	2	18	8	64	2

SOUTHERN DIVISION

	P	W	D	L	GF	GA	Pts
Fulham	**22**	**22**	**0**	**0**	**234**	**6**	**66**
Bristol Rovers	22	14	2	6	72	35	44
Millwall Lionesses	22	14	1	7	55	55	43
Chelsea	22	13	2	7	59	51	41
Langford	22	12	1	9	53	48	37
Wimbledon	22	11	3	8	41	55	36
Ipswich Town	22	8	4	10	43	52	28
Barking	22	7	2	13	40	79	23
Newport County	22	6	3	13	37	60	21
Barnet	22	5	6	11	27	75	18
QPR	22	3	5	14	19	60	14
Berkhamsted	22	1	3	18	10	116	6

AXA FA Women's Cup Final

Selhurst Park   *May 6*
FULHAM 2   **DONCASTER 1**
Yankey 55,   *Handley 61*
Chapman 20

Women's League Cup Final

Wycombe   *Apr 7*
FULHAM 7   **BIRMINGHAM CITY 1**

Athletics

As transitions go, few in sport have been more remarkable. Paula Radcliffe, for so long the athlete without a sprint, became the athlete who didn't need one. When you run the rest into the ground, as Radcliffe did in London, Manchester, Munich and Chicago a sprint becomes surplus to requirements.

It was the performance in the London Marathon which set the tone for the summer to come. No one expected Radcliffe to dawdle round the streets of London, but the second-half sequence of mile splits, with not a challenger in sight, was phenomenol. Almost everyone watching, including the race founder, Chris Brasher, thought that Radcliffe's reach had exceeded her grasp long before she crossed the line on The Mall for the second fastest time in history. The slowest mile of the last 13 was just five minutes and 16 seconds, while the fastest was the 25th mile which Radcliffe covered in just five minutes and six seconds. Khalid Khannouchi, on his way to breaking the men's world record, a little later, was only 11 seconds faster. Seventeen years earlier, along almost the same streets, Ingrid Kristiansen had set a world record that stood for 13 years, and for arguably the first time since, the suspension of disbelief, as Radcliffe went about her business, was almost palpable. Six months later, on a windless day in the windy city, Radcliffe duly claimed the world record, but by then we expected nothing less. In London, we witnessed a revolution.

Radcliffe's first London would be Brasher's last. On February 28th 2003, he died of pancreatic cancer. Brasher was an immensely complex human being, who could and did offend people as easily as he could charm them. Brasher didn't take to half measures. His genius was his ability to make things happen and the philosophical cornerstone was the gold medal he won in the 1956 Olympic steeplechase. Roger Bannister and Chris Chataway had the talent, but Brasher had the mindset. Bannister and Chataway won everything but an Olympic gold medal; Brasher won only an Olympic gold medal.

London Marathon
Mile Splits

Mile	Radcliffe	Khannouchi
1	5:17	4:47
2	5:27	4:47
3	5:21	4:39
4	5:31	4:47
5	5:29	4:45
6	5:38	4:51
7	5:35	4:47
8	5:21	4:47
9	5:25	4:50
10	5:22	4:51
11	5:17	4:49
12	5:22	4:46
13	5:26	4:49
Half	1:11:05	1:02:47
14	5:07	4:45
15	5:08	4:39
16	5:11	4:43
17	5:14	4:45
18	5:12	4:48
19	5:16	4:47
20	5:11	4:44
21	5:16	4:54
22	5:08	4:52
23	5:13	4:52
24	5:09	4:53
25	5:06	4:55
End	2:18:56	2:05:38

To Brasher, it proved that commitment was everything, that all the prizes were there to be won. So, he chased them; as sports editor of the Observer, television producer at the BBC, co-founder of the British Orienteering federation, millionaire owner of Reebok UK, and co-founder of the London Marathon in 1981, with John Disley. He couldn't have started London without Disley for when you inflict wounds, on a casual basis, you need an emollient.

The first London Marathon was inspirational; Dick Beardsley and Inge Simonson crossing the finish line together, hands held. It has never been less than inspirational since. For those of us who worked under Brasher on the event, we expected him to outlive us all, expected him to continue with new campaigns, new causes into his nineties, to quietly refuse the Queen's telegram on his 100th birthday, because he didn't want it noticed. For a public man, he could be very private.

On the Sunday before he died, Pat Collins ran a tribute in The Mail On Sunday. On the morning of his death, the bush telegraph spread the news faster even than the agencies. "It's the end of an era," said Tom Knight, of the Daily Telegraph, almost whispering down the phone. And so it is, and so it was.

Radcliffe's summer was spent listening to adulation. In Manchester, in front of 38,000 uproarious supporters, she threatened the world record for 5000m *(see Commonwealth Games section)*, and nine days later broke the European record for the 10,000m in dreadful conditions at Munich. Manchester was her first major track title, Munich her second. In the European championships, the Bedford athlete's dominance was such that Sonia O'Sullivan, who can run a bit herself, was over three-quarters of a minute behind in second place. "I knew I was capable of running 30 minutes in perfect conditions," said Radcliffe, who would surely have run even faster than that without the rain.

WORLD OUTDOOR RECORDS 2002

Men

100m	9.78	**Tim Montgomery**	USA	Paris	September 14
Marathon	2:05:38	**Khalid Khannouchi**	USA	London	April 14
3000m Steeplechase	7:53.17*	**Brahim Boulami**	MAR	Zurich	August 16
10km Road	27:02**	**Haile Gebrselassie**	ETH	Doha	December 11

Women

25km	1:27:05.9	**Tegla Loroupe**	KEN	Mengerskirchen	September 21
Marathon	2:17:18	**Paula Radcliffe**	GBR	Chicago	October 13
3000m Steeplechase	9:16.51	**Alesya Turova**	TUR	Gdansk	July 27
5000m Walk	20:02.60	**Gillian O'Sullivan**	IRL	Dublin	July 13
10km Road	30:29**	**Asmae Leghzaoui**	MAR	New York	June 8

* Awaiting ratification
** Defined by the IAAF as a World Best rather than a World Record

British athletes took six other titles in Munich, the old men taking the most credit. Colin Jackson's final international outdoor season saw him win a fourth hurdles gold medal, making the 35-year-old the first track athlete in the history of the European championships to win four titles in the same event. Steve Backley, a couple of years younger than Jackson, matched his achievement, winning his fourth javelin title on his fifth throw (something of a rarity for a man who usually starts with his best throw). Backley is not unique, though, for the Latvian Jan Lusis, who presented Backley with his gold medal, won the title four times between 1962 and 1971 while competing for the Soviet Union.

Dwain Chambers found redemption in 100m, recording a healthy 9.96 into a 0.3m headwind. Chambers needed a victory, following the debacle of Manchester, where his start was so poor that he couldn't have won the race even without his injury.

Chambers also led the 100m sprint quartet to victory, while Daniel Caines anchored the 400m sprint team to victory, the fifth successive win by Britain in the event. To say it was not a vintage 4x400m relay is something of an understatement. Britain's winning time was just three minutes, 2.97 seconds. In each of the previous four wins, the British team had run under three minutes.

Ashia Hansen won the triple jump, replaying the drama of Manchester with a last-leap win, but Jonathan Edwards could not make it a triple jump double, winning only a bronze behind the Swede Christian Olsson. Konstadinos Kenderis should be mentioned, his 200m win in 19.85 was the equal of Radcliffe's run.

Away from Munich, the season's highlights included a British men's victory in a depleted European Cup event and a world record in the 100m at the Grand Prix Final in Paris. Seldom, it must be said, has a world 100m record made so little an impact. Tim Montgomery is certainly not blessed with an excess of charisma (nor intelligence, given his liaison with Ben Johnson's old coach Charlie Francis) and the stadium it was run in was almost empty. Maybe it was a great run a year too early. Paris 2003 would have been better.

The Fastest Man In History

THE 100M AT THE GRAND PRIX FINAL

1	**Tim Montgomery** USA	**9.78** (0.104)	World Record
2	**Dwain Chambers** GBR	**9.87** (0.140)	European Record
3	**Jon Drummond** USA	**9.97** (0.131)	
4	**Kim Collins** SKN	**9.98** (0.158)	National Record
5	**Francis Obikwelu** POR	**10.03** (0.200)	
6	**Bernard Williams** USA	**10.05** (0.180)	
7	**Abdul Aziz Zakari** GHA	**10.20** (0.163)	
8	**Coby Miller** USA	**10.21** (0.197)	

Reaction times in brackets

European Championships

Munich, Germany, Aug 6-11

Men

100m				
(-0.3)	1	Dwain Chambers	GBR	9.96
	2	Francis Obikwelu	POR	10.06
	3	Darren Campbell	GBR	10.15

Jason Gardener GBR 10.28 in 2nd rd, elim in s-f

200m				
(-0.5)	1	Konstadinos Kenderis	GRE	19.85
	2	Frances Obikwelu	POR	20.21
	3	Marlon Devonish	GBR	20.24
	4	Christian Malcolm	GBR	20.30

Darren Campbell GBR 20.66 in 1st rd dq in 2nd rd; Gary Ryan IRL 20.93 in 1st rd, elim s-f; Paul Hession IRL 21.28 & Paul Brizzel IRL 21.32, both elim 1st rd

400m				
	1	Ingo Schultz	GER	45.14
	2	David Canal	ESP	45.24
	3	Daniel Caines	GBR	45.28

Tim Benjamin GBR 46.07 in s-f, withdrew injured from final; Sean Baldock 46.62 elim 1st rd; Paul McKee IRL 45.92 elim s-f; Robert Daly IRL 46.67 elim 1st rd; David McCarthy IRL 47.30 elim 1st rd

800m				
	1	Wilson Kipketer	DEN	1:47.25
	2	Andre Bucher	SUI	1:47.43
	3	Nils Schumann	GER	1:47.60

Anthony Whiteman GBR 1:50.60 elim 1st round
James McIlroy GBR 1:47.67 elim in s-f

1500m				
	1	Mehdi Baala	FRA	3:45.25
	2	Reyes Estevez	ESP	3:45.25
	3	Rui Silva	POR	3:45.43
	4	Michael East	GBR	3:46.30
	9	Anthony Whiteman	GBR	3:47.10
	12	John Mayock	GBR	3:48.41

James Nolan IRL 3:48.48 elim 1st rd

5000m				
	1	Alberto Garcia	ESP	13:38.18
	2	Ismail Sghyr	FRA	13:39.81
	3	Sergy Lebed	UKR	13:40.00
	6	Mark Carroll	IRL	13:42.87
	9	Sam Haughian	GBR	13:50.75

10,000m				
	1	Jose Manuel Martinez	ESP	27:47.65
	2	Dieter Baumann	GER	27:47.87
	3	Jose Rios	ESP	27:48.29
	5	Karl Keska	GBR	28:01.72
	16	Seamus Power	IRL	29:43.65

Mar				
	1	Janne Holman	FIN	2:12:14
	2	Pavel Loskutov	EST	2:13:18
	3	Julio Rey	ESP	2:13:21

3000msc				
	1	Antonio Jimenez	ESP	8:24.34
	2	Simon Vroeman	NED	8:24.45
	3	Luis Martin	ESP	8:24.72

110mh				
(+0.4)	1	Colin Jackson	GBR	13.11
	2	Stanislavs Olijars	LAT	13.22
	3	Artur Kohutek	POL	13.32

Tony Jarrett GBR 13.63 in 1st rd, dq in semi-finals; Damian Greaves GBR 13.90 elim 1st round; Peter Coghlan IRL 13.96 elim 1st rd

400mh				
	1	Stephane Diagana	FRA	47.58
	2	Jiri Muzik	CZE	48.43
	3	Pavel Januszewski	POL	48.46

Chris Rawlinson GBR 49.48, dnf final; Matt Elias GBR 50.18 elim 1st rd; Tony Borsumato GBR 49.37 elim s-f

HJ				
	1	Yaroslav Rybakov	RUS	2.31m
	2	Stefan Holm	SWE	2.29m
	3	Staffan Strand	SWE	2.27m

Ben Challenger GBR 2.15m elim qualifying;
Dalton Grant GBR elim qfy no mark

PV				
	1	Alex Averbukh	ISR	5.85m
	2	Lars Borgeling	GER	5.80m
	3	Tim Lobinger	GER	5.80m

LJ				
	1	Olexy Lukashevich	UKR	8.08m
	2	Sinisa Ergotic	CRO	8.00m
	3	Yago Lamela	ESP	7.99m
	6	Chris Tomlinson	GBR	7.78m

TJ				
	1	Christian Olsson	SWE	17.53m
	2	Charles Friedek	GER	17.33m
	3	Jonathan Edwards	GBR	17.32m
	5	Phillips Idowu	GBR	16.92m

Idowu 17.54m in qualifying. Despite press reports, this mark was not a best-ever mark in qualifying. Tosin Oke GBR no mark in final, 16.48m in qfy

SP				
	1	Yury Bilonog	UKR	21.37m
	2	Joachim Olsen	DEN	21.16m
	3	Ralf Bartels	GER	20.58m

DT				
	1	Robert Fazekas	HUN	68.83m
	2	Virgilijus Alekna	LTU	66.62m
	3	Michael Mollenback	GER	66.37m

Bob Weir GBR 58.37m elim qfy

HT				
	1	Adrian Annus	HUN	81.17m
	2	Vladyslav Piskunov	RUS	80.39m
	3	A Papadimitriou	GRE	80.21m

JT				
	1	Steve Backley	GBR	88.54m
	2	Sergey Makarov	RUS	88.05m
	3	Boris Henry	GER	85.33m
	10	Mick Hill	GBR	76.12m

Terry McHugh IRL no mark in qualifying; Nick Neiland GBR 71.92m elim qfy; Mick Hill GBR 78.38m elim qfy

Dec				
	1	Roman Sebrle	CZE	8800
	2	Erki Nool	EST	8438
	3	Lev Lobodin	RUS	8390

20kmW				
	1	Francois Javier Fernandez	ESP	1:18:37
	2	Vladimir Andreyev	RUS	1:19:56
	3	Juan Molina	ESP	1:20:36
	8	Robert Heffernan	IRL	1:21:10

Andrew Drake GBR dq

50kmW				
	1	Robert Korzeniowski	POL	3:36:39
	2	Aleksey Voyevodin	RUS	3:40:16
	3	Jesus Angel Garcia	ESP	3:44:33

Jamie Costin IRL dq

4x100m			
1	Great Britain		38.19
	Malcolm/Campbell/Devonish/Chambers		
2	Ukraine		38.53
3	Poland		38.71

4x400m			
1	Great Britain		3:01.25
	Deacon/Elias/Baulch/Caines		
2	Russia		3:01.34
3	France		3:02.76
5	Ireland		3:03.73
	Daly/McKee/Burke/McCarthy		

ATHLETICS

Women

100m 1 Ekaterini Thanou GRE 11.10
(-0.7) 2 Kim Gavaert BEL 11.22
3 Manuela Levorato ITA 11.23
6 Abiodun Oyepitan GBR 11.41
*Oyepitan 11.33 in semi-final; Joice Maduaka GBR 11.60
elim 1st round*

200m 1 Muriel Hurtis FRA 22.43
2 Kim Gevaert BEL 22.53
3 Manuela Levorato ITA 22.75
*Shani Anderson GBR 23.42 1st rd, elim s-f;
Ciara Sheehy IRL 23.25 (1st rd) elim s-f; Sarah Reilly
IRL 24.03 elim 1st rd*

400m 1 Olesya Zykina RUS 50.45
2 Grit Breuer GER 50.70
3 Lee McConnell GBR 51.02
*McConnell 51.24 in heat; Catherine Murphy GBR dnf 1st
rd; Karen Shinkins IRL 52.50 elim 1st rd*

800m 1 Jolanda Ceplak SLO 1:57.65
2 Mayte Martinez ESP 1:58.86
3 Kelly Holmes GBR 1:59.83
*Jo Fenn GBR 2:02.91 1st rd, elim in s-f; Adrienne McIvor
IRL 2:05.01 elim 1st rd*

1500m 1 Sureyya Ayhan TUR 3:58.79
2 Gabriela Szabo ROM 3:58.81
3 Tatyana Tomashova RUS 4:01.28
*Maria Lynch IRL 4:14.41 elim 1st rd;
Geraldine Hendricken IRL 4:18.13 elim 1st rd;
JKelly Holmes GBR 4:08.11 elim; Helen Pattinson GBR
4:09.66 elim; Hayley Tullett GBR 4:10.68, all elim 1st rd*

5000m 1 Marta Dominguez ESP 15:14.76
2 Sonia O'Sullivan IRL 15:14.85
3 Yelena Zadorozhnaya RUS 15:15.22
5 Joanne Pavey GBR 15:18.70
15 Una English IRL 16:19.36
18 Hayley Yelling GBR 16:21.21
19 Maria McCambridge IRL 17:00.15

10,000m 1 Paula Radcliffe GBR 30:01.09
2 Sonia O'Sullivan IRL 30:47.59
3 L Biktasheva RUS 31:04.00
17 Marie Davenport IRL 32:35.11
20 Liz Yelling GBR 32:44.44
26 Anne Keenan Buckley IRL 33:19.94

Mar 1 Maria Guida ITA 2:26:05
2 Luminata Zaituc GER 2:26:58
3 Sonja Oberem GER 2:28:45

100mh 1 Glory Alozie ESP 12.73
2 Olena Krasovska UKR 12.88
3 Yana Kasova BUL 12.91
5 Diane Allahgreen GBR 13.07
*Allahgreen 13.10 in heat;
Derval O'Rourke IRL 13.41 elim 1st rd; Allagreen 12.92
in semi-final*

400mh 1 Ionela Tirlea ROM 54.95
2 Heike Meissner GER 55.89
3 Anna Olichwierczuk POL 56.18
7 Natasha Danvers GBR 56.93
8 Sinead Dudgeon GBR 59.39
*Danvers 56.55 in 1st rd; Dudgeon 56.91 in 1st rd;
Tracey Duncan GBR 57.54 elim in 1st rd*

HJ 1 Kajsa Bergqvist SWE 1.98m
2 Marina Kuptsova RUS 1.92m
3 Olga Kaliturina RUS 1.89m
=7 Susan Jones GBR 1.89m
Jones 1.90m in qfy

LJ 1 Tatyana Kotova RUS 6.85m
2 Jade Johnson GBR 6.73m
3 Tunde Vaszi HUN 6.73m
Johnson won silver on count-back (6.72-6.57)

TJ 1 Ashia Hansen GBR 15.00m
2 Heli Koivula FIN 14.83m
3 Yelena Oleynikova RUS 14.54m

SP 1 Irina Korzhanenko RUS 20.64m
2 Vita Pavlysh UKR 20.02m
3 Svetlana Krivelyova RUS 19.56m

DT 1 Ekaterini Voggoli GRE 64.31m
2 Natalya Sadova RUS 64.12m
3 Anastasia Kelesidou GRE 63.92m
11 Shelley Newman GBR 57.38m

HT 1 Olga Kuzenkova RUS 72.94m
2 Kamila Skolimowska POL 72.46m
3 Manuela Montebrun FRA 72.04m
*Lorraine Shaw GBR 61.50m dnq;
Eileen O'Keefe IRL 59.64m dnq;*

JT 1 Mirela Manjani GRE 67.47m
2 Steffi Nerius GER 64.09m
3 Mikaela Ingberg FIN 63.50m
12 Kelly Morgan GBR 53.89m
Morgan 56.90m in qualifying

Hept 1 Carolina Kluft SWE 6542
2 Sabine Braun GER 6434
3 Natalya Sazanovich BLR 6341
Julie Hollman GBR dnf

20kmW 1 Olimpiada Ivanova RUS 1:26:42
2 Yelena Nikolayeva RUS 1:28:20
3 Erica Alfridi ITA 1:28:33
4 Gillian O'Sullivan IRL 1:28:46
13 Olive Loughnane IRL 1:33:08

4x100m 1 France 42.46
Combe/Hurtis/Felix/Sidibe
2 Germany 42.54
3 Russia 43.11
*Great Britain 44.45, elim in s-f
Maduaka/Anderson/Forrester/Oyepitan*

4x400m 1 Germany 3:25.10
Ekpo-Umoh/Rockmeier/Marx/Breuer
2 Russia 3:25.59
3 Poland 3:26.15
4 Great Britain 3:26.65
Karagounis/Frost/Purkiss/McConnell

European Championships Medal Table

1	Russia	7	9	8	24
2	Great Britain	7	1	6	14
3	Spain	6	3	6	15
4	France	4	1	2	7
5	Greece	4	-	2	6
6	Sweden	3	1	1	5
7	Germany	2	9	7	18
8	Ukraine	2	4	1	7
9	Hungary	2	-	1	3
10	Poland	1	1	5	7
11	Finland	1	1	1	3
12	Czech Republic	1	1	-	2
12	Denmark	1	1	-	2
12	Romania	1	1	-	2
15	Italy	1	-	3	4
16	Israel	1	-	-	1
16	Slovenia	1	-	-	1
16	Turkey	1	-	-	1
19	Portugal	-	2	1	3
20	Belgium	-	2	-	2
20	Estonia	-	2	-	2
20	Ireland	-	2	-	2
23	Croatia	-	1	-	1
23	Latvia	-	1	-	1
23	Lithuania	-	1	-	1
23	Netherlands	-	1	-	1
23	Switzerland	-	1	-	1
28	Belarus	-	-	1	1
28	Bulgaria	-	-	1	1

"Don't call me the greatest. I was washing dishes in a Brooklyn restaurant when Gebrselassie and Tergat were winning world titles. They are the greatest and have been my inspiration. It was a privilege to be in the same race as them today"

Khalid Khannouchi, in London.

"I did it cleanly and fairly. There was no way of catching her. Without saying too much...take your own guesses"

Kelly Holmes, after finishing third in the 800m at Munich. Now what could she possibly mean?

My father was cross with me because I was doing athletics and my country was going through a famine in which millions died. All I had was running. I just ran and ran all the time and got better"

Haile Gebrselassie.

"I practised every other day for three weeks"

Everett Hosack, a 100-year-old from Chagrin Falls, Ohio, who broke the world record for his age-group (the over 100s presumably) in the 100m dash for Over 75s at the Penn Relay meeting in April. Hosack was last of the seven runners, which was hardly surprising given that he was conceding over 20 years to most of the runners. Hosack's time was 43 seconds, which knocked 10 seconds off the old record.

World Cup

Madrid, Sep 20-21

Men

100m	1	Uchenna Emedolu	AFR/NGR	10.06		**SP**	1	Adam Nelson	USA	20.80m
(-0.3)	2	Kim Collins	AME/SKN	10.06			2	Justin Anlezark	OCE/AUS	20.77m
	3	Francis Obikwelu	EUR/POR	10.09			3	Ralf Bartels	GER	20.67m
	5	Dwain Chambers	GBR	10.16			7	Carl Myerscough	GBR	19.13m

200m	1	Francis Obikwela	EUR/POR	20.18		**DT**	1	Robert Fazekas	HUN	71.25m
(-0.6)	2	Frank Fredericks	AFR/NAM	20.20			2	Frantz Kruger	AFR/RSA	66.78m
	3	Marlon Devonish	GBR	20.32			3	Mario Pestona	ESP	64.64m
							7	Robert Weir	GBR	58.91m

400m	1	Michael Blackwood	AME/JAM	44.60		**HT**	1	Adrian Annus	EUR/HUN	80.93m
	2	Ingo Schultz	GER	44.86			2	Koji Murofushi	ASI/JPN	80.08m
	3	Fawzi Al-Shammari	ASI/KUW	45.14			3	Karsten Kobs	GER	78.44m
	7	Tim Benjamin	GBR	45.80			8	Michael Jones	GBR	66.92m

800m	1	Antonio Manuel Reina	ESP	1:43.83		**JT**	1	Sergey Makarov	EUR/RUS	86.44m
	2	Djabir Said-Guerni	AFR/ALG	1:44.03			2	Boris Henry	GER	81.60m
	3	David Krummenacker	USA	1:45.14			3	Emeterio González	AME/CUB	79.77m
	8	James McIlroy	GBR	1:48.43			4	Steve Backley	GBR	79.39m

1500m	1	Bernard Lagat	AFR/KEN	3:31.20
	2	Reyes Estévez	ESP	3:33.67
	3	Mehdi Baala	EUR/FRA	3:38.04
	6	Michael East	GBR	3:41.88

4x100m
1 USA 37.95
Drummond/Smoots/Conwright/Miller
2 Americas 38.32
Mayola/Collins/Williams/Demeritte
3 Africa 38.63
Sanou/Emedolu/Zakari/Fredericks
6 Great Britain 39.23
Barbour/Devonish/Malcolm/Plummer

3000m	1	Craig Mottram	OCE/AUS	7:41.37
	2	José David Galvan	AME/MEX	7:47.43
	3	Roberto García	ESP	7:53.96
	5	Tony Whiteman	GBR	8:03.33

4x400m
1 Americas 2:59.19
Sanchez/Francique/McDonald/Blackwood
2 USA 2:59.21
Carter/Byrd/Herring/Pettigrew
3 Africa 3:01.69
Hecini/Ladibi/Augustin/Milazar
5 Great Britain 3:03.34
Deacon/Baulch/Benjamin/Elias

5000m	1	Alberto García	ESP	13:30.04
	2	Paul Kosgei	AFR/KEN	13:31.71
	3	Ismail Sghyr	EUR/FRA	13:32.82
	5	John Mayock	GBR	13:38.63

3000msc	1	Wilson Boit Kipketer	AFR/KEN	8:25.34
	2	Luis Miguel Martín	ESP	8:26.35
	3	Khamis A Saifeldin	ASI/QAT	8:30.66
	8	Stuart Stokes	GBR	8:43.38

FINAL MEN'S STANDINGS
1. Africa 134pts; 2. USA 199; 3. Europe 115;
4. Americas 111; 5. Spain 94; 6. Germany 86.5;
7. Great Britain 86; 8. Asia 80; 9. Oceania 62.5

110mh	1	Anier Garcia	AME/CUB	13.10
(-2.2)	2	Allen Johnson	USA	13.45
	3	Stanislav Olijars	EUR/LAT	13.58

DQ: Colin Jackson GBR (fell)

400mh	1	James Carter	USA	48.27
	2	Mubarak Faraj Al-Nubi	ASI/QAT	48.96
	3	Chris Rawlinson	GBR	49.18

HJ	1	Yaroslav Rybakov	RUS	2.31m
	2	Mark Boswell	CAN	2.29m
	3	Ben Challenger	GBR	2.20m

PV	1	Okkert Brits	AFR/RSA	5.75m
	2	Jeff Hartwig	USA	5.70m
	3	Lars Börgeling	GER	5.40m
	7	Tim Thomas	GBR	5.00m

LJ	1	Savante Stringfellow	USA	8.21m
	2	Iván Pedroso	AME/CUB	8.19m
	3	Yago Lamela	ESP	8.11m
	6	Chris Tomlinson	GBR	7.85m

TJ	1	Jonathan Edwards	GBR	17.34m
	2	Walter Davis	USA	17.23m
	3	Christian Olsson	EUR/SWE	17.05m

Women

100m	1	Marion Jones	USA	10.90
(-0.3)	2	Tayna Lawrence	AME/JAM	11.06
	3	Susanthika Jayasinghe	ASI/SRI	11.20

200m	1	Debbie Ferguson	AME/BAH	22.49
(-0.8)	2	Murial Hurtis	EUR/FRA	22.78
	3	Myriam Leonie Mani	AFR/CMR	22.81

400m	1	Ana Guevara	AME/MEX	49.56
	2	Jearl Miles Clark	USA	50.27
	3	Olesya Zykina	RUS	50.67
	4	Lee McConnell	EUR/GBR	50.82

800m	1	Maria Mutola	AFR/MOZ	1:58.60
	2	Mayte Martínez	ESP	1:59.24
	3	Jolanda Ceplak	SLO	1:59.42

1500m	1	Süreyya Ayhan	EUR/TUR	4:02.57
	2	Tatyana Tomashova	RUS	4:09.74
	3	Kathleen Friedrich	GER	4:10.20

3000m	1	Berhane Adere	AFR/ETH	8:50.88
	2	Gabriela Szabo	EUR/ROM	8:50.89
	3	Yelena Zadorozhnaya	RUS	8:50.93

5000m	1	Olga Yegorova	RUS	15;18.15
	2	Marta Domínguez	ESP	15:19.73
	3	Jo Pavey	EUR/GBR	15:20.10

100mh	1	Gail Devers	USA	12.65
(-0.8)	2	Bridgette Foster	AME/JAM	12.82
	3	Glory Alozie	ESP	12.95

400mh	1	Yulia Pechonkina	RUS	53.74
	2	Sandra Glover	USA	54.46
	3	Jana Pittman	OCE/AUS	55.15

HJ	1	Hestrie Cloete	AFR/RSA	2.02m
	2	Kajsa Bergqvist	EUR/SWE	2.02m
	3	Marina Kuptsova	RUS	2.00m

PV	1	Annika Becker	GER	4.55m
	2	Svetlana Feofanova	RUS	4.40m
	3	Dana Cervantes	ESP	4.30m

LJ	1	Tatyana Kotova	RUS	6.85m
	2	Maurren Higa Maggi	AME/BRA	6.85m
	3	Concepción Montaner	ESP	6.68m
	4	Jade Johnson	EUR/GBR	6.41m

TJ	1	François Mbango	AFR/CMR	14.37m
	2	Ashia Hansen	EUR/GBR	14.32m
	3	Carlota Castrejana	ESP	14.13m

SP	1	Irina Korzhanenko	RUS	20.20m
	2	Yumileidi Cumbá	AME/CUB	19.14m
	3	Astrid Kumbernuss	GER	19.11m

DT	1	Beatrice Faumuina	OCA/NZL	62.47m
	2	Ekaterini Voggoli	EUR/GRE	61.77m
	3	Natalya Sadova	RUS	61.30m

HT	1	Gu Yuan	ASI/CHN	70.75m
	2	Yipsi Moreno	AME/CUB	69.65m
	3	Olga Kuzenkova	RUS	66.98m

JT	1	Osleidys Menéndez	AME/CUB	64.41m
	2	Tatyana Shikolenko	RUS	60.11m
	3	Mikaela Ingberg	EUR/FIN	60.08m

4x100m	1	Americas	41.91
		Lawrence/Campbell/McDonald/Ferguson	
	2	USA	42.05
		Gaines/Jones/Miller/Devers	
	3	Africa	42.99
		Odozor/Mani/Sanganoko/Ojokolo	

4x400m	1	Americas	3:23.53
		Richards/Pernia/Amertil/Guevara	
	2	USA	3:24.67
		Collins/Cox/Reid/Hennagan	
	3	Russia	3:26.59
		Antyukh/Pechonkina/Nazarova/Zykina	
	5	Europe	3:29.21
		Prokopek/Yefremova/Usovich/McConnell	

FINAL WOMEN'S STANDINGS
1. Russia 126pts; 2. Europe 123; 3. Americas 110;
4. USA 105; 5. Africa 99; 6. Germany 79.5;
7. Asia 75; 8. Spain 74.5; 9. Oceania 59

European Cup

Super League

Annecy, France, June 22-23

Men

100m	1	Dwain Chambers	GBR	10.04
	2	Aime Nthepe	FRA	10.27
	3	Kostyantyan Rurak	UKR	10.31
200m	1	Marlon Devonish	GBR	20.27
	2	Marcin Urbas	POL	20.45
	3	Marco Torrieri	ITA	20.65
400m	1	Daniel Caines	GBR	45.14
	2	Ingo Schultz	GER	45.33
	3	Marek Plawgo	POL	45.35
800m	1	Yury Borzakovsky	RUS	1:46.58
	2	Nils Schumann	GER	1:46.99
	3	Pawel Czapiewski	POL	1:47.92
	5	Simon Lees	GBR	1:48.43
1500m	1	Mehdi Baala	FRA	3:47.21
	2	Michael East	GBR	3:48.26
	3	Pawel Czapiewski	POL	3:48.77
3000m	1	Driss Maazouzi	FRA	7:53.41
	2	Mikhail Yeginov	RUS	7:54.05
	3	Jan Fitschen	GER	7:54.92
	4	Tony Whiteman	GBR	8:00.31
5000m	1	Dmitry Maksimov	RUS	14:09.92
	2	Sam Haughian	GBR	14:11.60
	3	Ismail Sghyr	FRA	14:14.00
3000msc	1	Bouabdallah Tahri	FRA	8:30.22
	2	Damian Kallabis	GER	8:32.04
	3	Roman Usov	RUS	8:34.10
	7	Stuart Stokes	GBR	8:48.69
110m	1	Colin Jackson	GBR	13.15
	2	Mike Fenner	GER	13.33
	3	Andrea Giaconi	ITA	13.35
PV	1	Tim Lobinger	GER	5.75m
	2	Denis Yurchenko	UKR	5.65m
	3	Giuseppe Gibilisco	ITA	5.65m
	6	Tim Thomas	GBR	5.05m
LJ	1	Chris Tomlinson	GBR	8.17m
	2	Nicola Trentin	ITA	8.15m
	3	Salim Sdiri	FRA	8.03m
TJ	1	Jonathan Edwards	GBR	17.19m
	2	Fabrizio Donato	ITA	17.17m
	3	Charles Friedek	GER	17.11m
SP	1	Yury Bilonog	UKR	20.55m
	2	Ville Tiisanoja	FIN	20.29m
	3	Paolo Dal Soglio	ITA	19.87m
	6	Carl Myerscough	GBR	19.41m
DT	1	Michael Möllenbeck	GER	66.82m
	2	Dmitry Shevchenko	RUS	62.03m
	3	Olgierd Stanski	POL	60.88m
	8	Glen Smith	GBR	54.77m
HT	1	Olli-Pekka Karjalainen	FIN	79.25m
	2	Andry Skvaruk	UKR	79.04m
	3	Maciej Palyszko	POL	78.25m
JT	1	Sergey Makarov	RUS	88.24m
	2	Steve Backley	GBR	85.03m
	3	Boris Henry	GER	83.90m
4x100m	1	Great Britain		38.65
		Devonish/Lewis-Francis/Malcolm/Condon		
	2	Germany		38.88
	3	Italy		38.89
4x400m	1	Great Britain		3:00.57
		Deacon/Benjamin/Baulch/Caines		
	2	Germany		3:00.80
	3	France		3:00.92

FINAL SCORES: 1 Great Britain 111.0, 2 Germany 107.0, 3 France 105.0, 4 Russia 94.0, 5 Italy 89.5, 6 Poland 85.0, 7 Ukraine 63.5, 8 Finland 60.0

Women

100m	1	Muriel Hurtis	FRA	10.96
(+0.4)	2	Manuela Levorato	ITA	11.20
	3	Yulia Tabakova	RUS	11.24
	6	Shani Anderson	GBR	11.38
200m	1	Muriel Hurtis	FRA	22.51
	2	Manuela Levorato	ITA	22.76
	3	Sina Schielke	GER	22.91
	4	Vernicha James	GBR	22.94
400m	1	Antonina Yefremova	UKR	50.70
	2	Grazyna Prokopek	POL	51.34
	3	Francine Landre	FRA	51.78
	6	Helen Karagounis	GBR	52.03
800m	1	Irina Mistyukevich	RUS	1:59.76
	2	Elisabeth Grousselle	FRA	1:59.95
	3	Ivonne Teichmann	GER	2:00.07
	4	Kelly Holmes	GBR	2:00.33
1500m	1	Maria Cioncan	ROM	4:03.74
	2	Lidia Chojecka	POL	4:04.84
	3	Tatyana Tomashova	RUS	4:05.14
	4	Helen Pattinson	GBR	4:05.20
3000m	1	Gabriela Szabo	ROM	8:38.03
	2	Yelena Zadorozhnaya	RUS	8:39.84
	3	Lidia Chojecka	POL	8:49.95
	5	Kathy Butler	GBR	9:09.36
5000m	1	Olga Yegorova	RUS	16:04.26
	2	Jo Pavey	GBR	16:06.65
	3	Fatima Yvelain	FRA	16:08.21
3000msc	1	Justyna Bak	POL	9:43.38
	2	Cristina Casandra-Iloc	ROM	9:49.51
	3	Melanie Schulz	GER	9:49.79
	4	Tara Krzywicki	GBR	10:23.21
100mh	1	Patricia Girard	FRA	12.64
	2	Kirsten Bolm	GER	12.85
	3	Maria Koroteyeva	RUS	12.94
	4	Dinae Allahgreen	GBR	13.11
HJ	1	Iryna Mikhalchenko	UKR	1.95m
	2	Oana Pantelimon	ROM	1.93m
	3	Kathryn Holinski	GER	1.93m
	=4	Susan Jones	GBR	1.90m
PV	1	Svetlana Feofanova	RUS	4.70m
	2	Yvonne Buschbaum	GER	4.60m
	3	Vanessa Boslak	RA	4.45m
	5	Janine Whitlock	GBR	4.10m
LJ	1	Tatyana Kotova	RUS	7.42m
	2	Cristina Nicolau	ROM	6.65m
	3	Bianca Kappler	GER	6.64m
	5	Jade Johnson	GBR	6.42m

SP	1	Svetlana Krivelyova	RUS	19.63m
	2	Astrid Kumbernuss	GER	19.61m
	3	Krystyna Zabawska	POL	18.52m
	8	Julie Dunkley	GBR	15.85m
DT	1	Natalya Sadova	RUS	65.91m
	2	Nicoleta Grasu	ROM	63.05m
	3	Franka Dietzsch	GER	59.30m
	6	Shelley Newman	GBR	57.89m
HT	1	Olga Kuzenkova	RUS	73.07m
	2	Manuela Montebrun	FRA	68.53m
	3	Irina Sekachova	UKR	66.88m
	7	Lorraine Shaw	GBR	63.09m
JT	1	Tatyana Shikolenko	RUS	64.61m
	2	F Moldovan	ROM	61.59m
	3	Steffi Nerius	GER	59.98m
	6	Kelly Morgan	GBR	56.55m
4x100m	1	France		42.41
		Girard/Hurtis/Félix/Sidibé		
	2	Germany		42.49
	3	Russia		43.11

DNF: Great Britain

4x400m	1	Great Britain		3:27.87
		Murphy/Frost/Karagounis/McConnell		
	2	Germany		3:28.72
	3	Italy		3:29.14

FINAL SCORES: 1 Russia 122.5, 2 Germany 103.0, 3 France 89.0, 4 Romania 88.0, 5 Great Britain 84.5, 6 Poland 75.5, 7 Ukraine 72.5, 8 Italy 72.0

First League
Group A
Banska Bystrica, Slovakia, June 22-23
FINAL STANDINGS
Men
1 Greece 124; 2 Czech Rep 107; 3 Hungary 101; 4 Belgium 85; 5 Slovakia 82; 6 Norway 79; 7 Romania 74; 8 Lithuania 61
Women
1 Greece 133; 2 Hungary 107; 3 Czech Rep 107; 4 Bulgaria 104.5; 5 Finland 99.5; 6 Slovakia 63; 7 Norway 59; 8 Turkey 46
Greece promoted, Lithuania and Turkey relegated

Group B
Seville, June 22-23
FINAL STANDINGS
Men
1 Spain 132; 2 Sweden 122; 3 Netherlands 100; 4 Portugal 91; 5 Slovenia 77; 6 Denmark 77; 7 Switzerland 70; 8 Austria 48
Women
1 Spain 128; 2 Sweden 111; 3 Belarus 106.5; 4 Portugal 88.5; 5 Slovenia 88; 6 Netherlands 73; 7 Switzerland 72.5; Latvia 81.5
Spain promoted, Austria and Latvia relegated

Second League
Group A
Tallinn, June 22-23
FINAL STANDINGS
Men
1 Belarus 127; 2 Estonia 118; 3 Ireland 114.5; 4 Latvia 94; 5 Cyprus 87.5; 6 Iceland 74; 7 Georgia 48; 8 Luxembourg 47
Women
1 Ireland 129; 2 Lithuania 124; 3 Estonia 112; 4 Denmark 106; 5 Cyprus 95; 6 Iceland 75; 7 Georgia 40; 8 Luxembourg 35
Belarus and Ireland promoted, Luxembourg relegated

Group B
Belgrade, June 22-23
FINAL STANDINGS
Men
1 Bulgaria 173; 2 Israel 167.5; 3 Croatia 157; 4 Moldova 150; 5 Turkey 149.5; 6 Yugoslavia 140; 7 Bosnia 111; 8 Armenia 83; 9 Small States 62; 10 FYR Macedonia 59; 11 Albania 49
Women
1 Belgium 173; 2 Yugoslavia 163; 3 Austria 145.5; 4 Croatia 136.5; 5 Moldova 117; 6 Israel 107; 7 Albania 82.5; 8 Bosnia 52; 9 FYR Macedonia 44; 10 Small States 38
Bulgaria and Belgium promoted

Combined Events
Super League
Bydgoszcz, Poland, June 29-30
Decathlon Team: 1 Germany 23,750; 2 Finland 22,798; 3 Russia 22,621; 4 Ukraine 22,424; 5 Austria 22,272; 6 France 21,818; 7 Netherlands 21,660; 8 Hungary 17,457
Individual: 1 Maczey GER 8104
Heptathlon Team: 1 Germany 17,940; 2 Russia 17,449; 3 Ukraine 17,381; 4 Poland 17,327; 5 Czech Rep 17,190; 6 Belarus 16,801; 7 Italy 16,531; 8 Great Britain 16,376
Individual: 1 Ertl GER 6017; 12 Sotherton GBR 5794

First League
Riga, Latvia, June 29-30
Decathlon Team: 1 Czech Rep 22,524; 2 Italy 22,442; 3 Spain 21,907; 4 Switzerland 21,795; 5 Latvia 21,745; 6 Poland 21,203; 7 Belarus 20,631
Individual: 1 Podebradsky CZE 7883
Heptathlon Team: 1 France 17,321; 2 Greece 16,860; 3 Finland 16,680; 4 Netherlands 16,460; 5 Sweden 16,214; 6 Estonia 16,150; 7 Switzerland 16,131
Individual: 1 Kluft SWE 6272

Second League
Maribor, Slovenia, June 29-30
Decathlon Team: 1 Estonia 22,178; Great Britain 21,154; 3 Norway 20,996; 4 Sweden 20,854; 5 Slovenia 20,668; 6 Slovakia 19,681; 7 Lithuania 19,350; 8 Denmark 19,319
Individual: 1 Kallas EST 7529; 3 Sawyer GBR 7271
Heptathlon Team: 1 Lithuania 16,857; 2 Portugal 16,041; 3 Spain 16,022; 4 Hungary 14,782; 5 Austria 14,382; 6 Slovenia 13,349
Individual: 1 Skujyke LTU 6155

IAAF Golden League and GP Final

Exxon Mobil Bislett Games
Oslo, June 28

Men *GP*100m(-0.1): Dwain Chambers GBR 10.05; *GP*400m: Leonard Byrd USA 45.75; *GP*Mile: Hicham El Guerrouj MAR 3:50.12; *GP*5000m: Benjamin Limo KEN 12:57.50; *GP*400mh: Felix Sanchez DOM 48.91; *GP*HJ: Tomas Janku CZE 2.28m; *GP*PV: Tim Mack USA 5.70m; *GP*TJ: Jonathan Edwards GBR 17.51m; JT: Boris Henry GER 85.42m

Women *GP*100m(-1.0): Marion Jones USA 10.96; *GP*400m: Ana Guevara MEX 50.45; 800m Zulia Calatayud CUB 2:00.26; *GP*1500m: Maria Cioncan ROM 4:03.55; *GP*5000m: Gabriela Szabo ROM 14:46.86; *GP*100mh: Gail Devers USA 12.53; JT: Osleidys Menendez CUB 63.51m

Meeting Gaz de France
St Denis, July 5

Men *GP*100m(+0.4): Maurice Greene USA 9.99; 800m: David Krummenacker USA 1:44.83; *GP*1500: Hicham El Guerrouj MAR 3:29.96; *GP*5000m: Benjamin Limo KEN 13:02.34; 3000msc: Ezekiel Kemboi KEN 8:10.11; 110mh(0.0): Anier Garcia CUB 13.14; *GP*400mh: Felix Sanchez DOM 47.91; *GP*PV: Romain Mesnil FRA 5.65m; *GP*TJ: Jonathan Edwards GBR 17.75m

Women 100m(+0.1): Marion Jones USA 10.89; 200m(0.0): Kelli White USA 22.56; *GP*400m: Ana Guevara MEX 50.00; *GP*1500m: Nicole Teter USA 4:05.52; *GP*3000m: Gabriela Szabo ROM 8:31.88; *GP*100mh(0.0): Gail Devers USA 12.56; 400mh: Jana Pittman AUS 54.58; HJ: Kajsa Bergqvist SWE 1.97m; *GP*JT: Tatyana Shikolenko RUS 64.59m

Golden Gala
Rome, July 12

Men *GP*100m(+0.9): Maurice Greene USA 9.89; 200m(+0.6): Frank Fredericks NAM 19.99; *GP*400m: Michael Blackwood JAM 44.99; 800m: David Krummenacker USA 1:45.24; *GP*Mile: Hicham El Guerrouj MAR 3:48.28; *GP*5000m: Salah Hissou MAR 12:55.85; *GP*400mh: Felix Sanchez DOM 47.73; *GP*HJ: Mark Boswell CAN 2.35m; *GP*PV: Tim Lobinger GER 5.85m; *GP*TJ: Walter Davis USA 17.33m; *GP*HT: Igor Astapkovich BLR 80.79m

Women *GP*100m(+0.7): Marion Jones USA 10.89; *GP*400m: Ana Guevara MEX 49.51; *GP*1500m: Maria Mutola MOZ 4:01.50; *GP*5000m: Edith Masai KEN 14:53.77; *GP*100mh(+0.6): Gail Devers USA 12.51; TJ: Huang Qiuyan CHN 14.47m; SP: Astrid Kumbernuss GER 19.43m; *GP*JT: Osleidys Menendez CUB 63.91m

Herculis Monaco
Monaco, July 19

Men *GP*100m(+0.1): Maurice Greene USA 9.97; 800m: Wilson Kipketer DEN 1:43.76; *GP*1500m: Hicham El Guerrouj MAR 3:27.34; *GP*3000m: Benjamin Limo KEN 7:34.72; 3000msc: Brahim Boulami MAR 7:58.09; 110mh Larry Wade USA 13.19; *GP*400m: Felix Sanchez DOM 47.86; *GP*PV; Jeff Hartwig USA 5.80m; TJ: Christian Olsson SWE 17.63m

Women *GP*100m(+0.3): Marion Jones USA 10.84; *GP*400m: Ana Guevara MEX 49.25; 800m: Zulia Calatayud CUB 1:56.09; *GP*1500m: Alesya Turova BLR 4:01.01; *GP*3000m: Gabriela Szabo ROM 8:21.42; 100mh(0.0): Gail Devers USA 12.42; PV: Svetlana Feofanova RUS 4.69m; JT: Tatyana Shikolenko RUS 65.08m

Weltklasse
Zurich, Aug 16

Men *GP*100m(-1.3): Tim Montgomery USA 9.98m; 800m: Joseph Mutua KEN 1:43.33; *GP*1500m: Hicham El Guerrouj MAR 3:26.89; *GP*5000m: Sammy Kipketer KEN 12:56.99; 3000msc: Brahim Boulami MAR 7:53.17 WR; *GP*400mh: Felix Sanchez DOM 47.35; *GP*HJ: Stefan Holm SWE 2.35m; *GP*PV: Lars Borgeling GER 5.80m; Tim Lobinger GER 5.80m; *GP*TJ: Jonathan Edwards GBR 17.63m; DT: Robert Fazekas HUN 66.81m

Women *GP*100m(-0.5): Marion Jones USA 10.88; *GP*400m: Ana Guevara MEX 49.16; 800m: Maria Mutola MOZ 1:57.24; *GP*1500m: Gabriela Szabo ROM 3:58.78; *GP*3000m: Berhane Adere ETH 8:32.76; *GP*100mh(-0.8): Glory Alozie ESP 12.63; *GP*LJ: Maurren Higa Maggi BRA 6.84m; *GP*JT: Tatyana Shikolenko RUS 64.72m

Ivo Van Damme Memorial
Brussels, Aug 30

*GP*100m(+0.3): Tim Montgomery USA 9.91; 200m(+0.5): Coby Miller USA 20.07; 800m: Wilson Kipketer DEN 1:42.74; *GP*1500m: Hicham El Guerrouj MAR 3:29.95; *GP*3000m: Abderrahim Goumri MAR 7:35.77; 10,000m: Sammy Kipketer KEN 26:49.38; 3000msc: Ezekiel Kemboi KEN 8:06.65; *GP*400mh: Feliz Sanchez DOM 47.99; *GP*PV Aleksander Averbukh ISR 5.80m; TJ: Walter Davis USA 17.40m; JT: Boris Henry GER 83.76m

Women *GP*100m(+1.0): Marion Jones USA 10.88; 200m(-0.3): Jones USA 22.11; *GP*400m: Ana Guevara MEX 49.69; 1000m: Maria Mutola MOZ 2:30.12; *GP*1500m: Sureyya Ayhan TUR 3:57.75; *GP*3000m: Berhane Adere ETH 8:26.14; 100mh(+0.5): Gail Devers USA 12.49; HJ: Kajsa Bergqvist SWE 1.99m; *GP*JT Nikolett Szabo HUN 63.25m

ISTAF 2002
Berlin, Sep 6

Men *GP*100m(+0.3): Dwain Chambers GBR 10.02; *GP*400m: Michael Blackwood JAM 44.87; 800m: Wilfred Bungei KEN; *GP*1500m: Hicham El Guerrouj MAR 3:30.00; *GP*5000m: Luke Kipkosgei KEN 13:10.41; 400mh: Felix Sanchez DOM 48.05; *GP*PV: Aleksander Averbukh ISR 5.80m; *GP*TJ Christian Olsson SWE 17.40m; JT: Boris Henry GER 85.82m

Women *GP*100m(+0.3): Marion Jones USA 11.01; *GP*400m: Ana Guevara MEX 49.91; *GP*1500m: Sureyya Ayhan TUR 3:58.43; *GP*5000m: Berhane Adere ETH 14:41.43; *GP*100mh(+0.4): Bridgette Foster JAM 12.62; LJ: Heike Drechsler GER 6.45m; *GP*JT: Osleidys Menendez CUB 64.45m

Grand Prix Final
Paris, Sept 14
Grand Prix Final
Men *GP*100m(+2.0): Tim Montgomery USA 9.78 WR; *GP*400m: Michael Blackwood JAM 44.72; *GP*1500m: Hicham El Guerrouj MAR 3:29.27; *GP*3000m: Abraham Chebii KEN 8:33.42; *GP*400mh: Felix Sanchez DOM 47.62; *GP*HJ: Stefan Holm SWE 2.31m; *GP*PV: Jeff Hartwig USA 5.75m; *GP*TJ: Christian Olsson SWE 17.48m; *GP*SP: Adam Nelson USA 21.34m; *GP*HT: Koji Murofushi JPN 81.14m
Women *GP*100m(+1.4): Marion Jones USA 10.88; *GP*400m: Ana Guevara MEX 49.90; *GP*1500m: Yelena Zadorozhnaya RUS 4:00.63; *GP*3000m: Gabriela Szabo ROM 8:56.29; *GP*100mh: Gail Devers USA 12.51; *GP*LJ: Maurren Higa Maggi BRA 7.02m; *GP*DT: Natalya Sadova RUS 65.79m; *GP*JT: Osleidys Menendez CUB 65.69m

Overall Grand Prix Standings
Men

1	Tim Montgomery USA	116
2	Hicham El Guerrouj MAR	116
3	Felix Sánchez DOM	116
4	Christian Olsson SWE	102
5	Jonathan Edwards GBR	96
6	Bernard Lagat KEN	91
7	Jeff Hartwig USA	89
8	Benjamin Limo KEN	89
9	Tim Lobinger GER	84
10	Stefan Holm SWE	81.5

GBR: 25 Dwain Chambers 68; 68 Chris Rawlinson 36; 69 Phillips Idowu 36; 105 Mark Lewis-Francis 18; 141 Tony Whiteman 11; 147 Daniel Caines 10; 153= Larry Achike 9; 196= Mick Jones & John Mayock 6; 246= Jason Gardener 4; 289= Darren Campbell, Tony Borsumato & Andy Graffin 3

Women

1	Marion Jones USA	116
2	Gail Devers USA	111
3	Ana Guevara MEX	108
4	Osleidys Menéndez CUB	106
5	Tatyana Shikolenko RUS	101
6	Berhane Adere ETH	100
7	Bridgette Foster JAM	99
8	Gabriela Szabo ROM	98
9	Lorraine Fenton JAM	97
10	Tayna Lawrence JAM	93

GBR: 60 Jo Pavey 33; 86 Kelly Holmes 18; 110= Jade Johnson 14; 124= Paula Radcliffe 10; 129= Helen Pattinson & Catherine Murphy 9; 157 Lee McConnell 6; 193= Shelley Newman 4; 240= Joice Maduaka 2; 277= Kathy Butler, Abi Oyepitan & Julie Pratt 1

Grand Prix I
Grand Prix Brasil de Atletismo
Rio de Janeiro, May 5
Men *GP*100m(-0.5): Kim Collins SKN 10.18; 200m(+0.9): Uchenna Emedolu NGR 20.81; *GP*400m: Leonard Byrd USA 44.45; 800m: Nicholas Wachira KEN 1:46.29; *GP*1500m: Hudson Santos BRA 3:36.56; *GP*400mh: Eric Thomas USA 48.36; HJ: Mark Boswell CAN 2.25m; *GP*PV: Derek Miles USA 5.70m; *GP*TJ: Kenta Bell USA 17.00m; *GP*SP: Kevin Toth USA 20.78m
Women *GP*100m: Mercy Nku NGR 11.27; 200m: Aparecida de Moura Lucimar BRA 23.67; *GP*400m: Michelle Collins USA 50.43; 1500m: Mardrea Hyman JAM 4:12.03; *GP*100mh: Bridgette Foster JAM 12.64; *GP*LJ: Maurren Higa Maggi BRA 6.90m; *GP*JT: Valeriya Zabruskova RUS 58.88m

IAAF Grand Prix in Osaka 2001
Osaka, May 11
Men *GP*100m(+1.8): Shawn Crawford USA 9.94; *GP*400m: Antonio Pettigrew USA 44.72; *GP*1500m: Abdelkader Hachlaf MAR 3:40.36; 5000m: Zakayo Ngatho KEN 13:18.96; 3000msc: Yasunori Uchitomi JPN 8:41.52; 110mh(+1.1): Mark Crear USA 13.48; *GP*400m: James Carter USA 49.21; *GP*HJ: Mark Boswell CAN 2.24m; *GP*PV: Timothy Mack USA 5.60m; LJ: Savante Stringfellow USA 8.49m; *GP*HT: Adrian Annus HUN 80.10m
Women *GP*100m(+2.5): Susanthika Jayasinghe SRI 11.11; *GP*400m: Kaltouma Nadjina CHA 52.20; 800m: Charmaine Howell JAM 2:03.25; *GP*5000m: Benita Johnson AUS 15:01.44; *GP*100mh: Melissa Morrison USA 12.81; *GP*LJ: Olga Rublyova RUS 6.73m; *GP*JT: Ha Xiaoyan CHN 58.90m

Qatar Athletic Grand Prix
Doha, May 15
Men *GP*100m(0.0): Bernard Williams USA 10.08; *GP*400m: Fawzi Al-Shammari KUW 44.93; *GP*1500m: Noah Ngeny KEN 3:33.02; *GP*3000m: Paul Bitok KEN 7:37.53; 3000msc: Wilson Boit Kipketer KEN 8:05.98; *GP*400mh: Faraj Al-Nubi Mubarak QAT 48.41; *GP*HJ: Stefan Holm SWE 2.28m; LJ: James Beckford JAM 8.21m; *GP*SP: Gheorghe Guset ROM 20.27m; DT: Robert Fazekas HUN 69.13m; *GP*HT: Koji Murofushi JPN 83.33m
Women *GP*100m(+0.4): Chandra Sturrup BAH 11.01; *GP*400m: Christine Amertil BAH 50.82; *GP*1500m: Judit Varga HUN 4:09.04; *GP*3000m: Leah Malot KEN 9:11.43 *GP*100mh(+0.5): Bridgette Foster JAM 12.76; PV: Krisztian Molnar HUN 4.42m; *GP*LJ: Tatyana Kotova RUS 6.99m; *GP*DT: Vera Pospisilova CZE 63.66m

Prefontaine Classic
Eugene, USA, May 26
Men *GP*100m(+3.5): Tim Montgomery USA 9.97; *GP*400m: Angelo Taylor USA 44.85; *GP*Mile: Hicham El Guerrouj MAR 3:50.89; *GP*5000m: Abraham Chebii KEN 13:13.53; 110mh(+1.7): Allen Johnson USA 13.16; *GP*HJ: Charles Clinger USA 2.35m; *GP*PV: Timothy Mack USA 5.84m; *GP*SP: Kevin Toth USA 22.19m
Women *GP*100m(+1.8): Marion Jones USA 10.90; *GP*400m: Michelle Collins USA 50.87; *GP*1500m: Nicole Teter USA 4:12.93; *GP*3000m: Marla Runyan USA 8:39.36; *GP*100mh(+2.7): Gail Devers USA 12.29; PV: Stacy Dragila USA 4.72m; *GP*DT: Aretha Hill USA 63.48m

Oracle US Open
Palo Alto, USA, June 8

Men *GP*100m(+3.0): Kim Collins SKN 10.18; *GP*400m: Felix Sanchez DOM 45.24; 800m: Derrick Peterson USA 1:47.18; *GP*Mile: William Chirchir KEN 3:55:40; *GP*5000m: Luke Kipkosgei KEN 13:17.46; *GP*HJ: Matt Hemingway USA 2.25m; *GP*PV: Timothy Mack USA 5.55m; LJ: Miguel Pate USA 8.28m; *GP*TJ: Timothy Ruslan USA 17.17m; *GP*SP: John Godina USA 21.38m; JT: Ty Sevin USA 74.86m

Women *GP*100m(-2.7): Marion Jones USA 11.20; *GP*400m: Jearl Miles-Clark USA 50.45; *GP*1500m: Regina Jacobs 4:11.35; *GP*100mh(-0.7): Gail Devers USA 12.81; HJ: Trisha Waller USA 1.93m; PV: Stacey Drgaila USA 4.32m; *GP*DT: Suzanne Powell USA 64.39m

Athens Grand Prix Tsiklitiria
Athens, June 10

Men *GP*100(-0.2): Maurice Greene USA 9.97; 200m: Bernard Williams USA 20.19; *GP*1500m: Noah Ngeny KEN 3:36.87; 3000msc: Stephen Cherono KEN 8:17.31; 400mh: Joey Woody USA 48.61; *GP*HJ: Mark Boswell CAN 2.33m; *GP*PV: Jeff Hartwig USA 5.90m; *GP*TJ: Christian Olsson SWE 17.40m; *GP*HT: Andriy Skvaruk UKR 81.71m

Women *GP*100m(+0.9): Zhanna Pintusevic-Block UKR 11.02; *GP*400m: Lorraine Fenton JAM 51.49; 800m: Jolanda Ceplak SLO 2:00.16; *GP*3000m: Berhane Adere ETH 8:55.67; *GP*100mh(+3.4): Olena Krasovska UKR 12.73; *GP*LJ: Tatyana Kotova RUS 6.90m; *GP*DT: Natalya Sadova RUS 66.56m; *GP*JT: Osleidys Menendez CUB 66.18m

Athletissima 2002
Lausanne, July 2

Men *GP*100m(-0.3): Francis Obikwela POR 10.09; 200m(+0.2): Obikwela POR 20.26; 800m: Djabir Said-Guerni ALG 1:44.70; *GP*1500m: Bernard Lagat KEN 3:32.24; *GP*3000m: Benjamin Limo KEN 7:36.02; 3000msc: Ezekiel Kemboi KEN 8:10.32; 110mh(+1.1); Anier Garcia CUB 13.03; *GP*400mh: Chris Rawlinson GBR 48.21; *GP*PV: Jeff Hartwig USA 5.85m; *GP*PV: Walter Davis USA 17.39m

Women *GP*100m: Marion Jones USA 11.04; *GP*400m: Lorraine Fenton JAM 50.39; 800m: Maria Mutola MOZ 1:56.25; *GP*1500m: Maria Cioncan ROM 4:03.11; *GP*100mh: Gail Devers USA 12.40; HJ: Kajsa Bergqvist SWE 2.04m; *GP*JT: Osleidys Menendez CUB 67.40m

DN Galan
Stockholm, July 16

Men *GP*100m(-0.1): Tim Montgomery USA 10.08; *GP*400m: Alvin Harrison USA 44.57; *GP*1500m: Bernard Lagat KEN 3:31.38; *GP*5000m: Abderrahim Goumri MAR 13:00.76; 3000msc: Wilson Boit Kipketer KEN 8:00.56; 110mh: Anier Garcia CUB 13.13; *GP*HJ: Andrey Chubsa BLR 2.32m; *GP*TJ: Jonathan Edwards GBR 17.78m; JT: Sergey Makarov RUS 87.73m

Women *GP*100m: Zhanna Pintusevich-Block UKR 10.91; *GP*400m: Lorraine Fenton JAM 50.13; 800m: Nicole Teter USA 1:58.13; *GP*5000m: Edith Masai KEN 15:05.31; *GP*100mh: Gail Devers USA 12.42; HJ: Kajsa Bergqvist SWE 2.00m; PV: Svetlana Feofanova RUS 4.78m: LJ: Tatyana Kotova RUS 7.02m

Norwich Union British Grand Prix
Crystal Palace, Aug 23

Men

100m-GP
1	Dwain Chambers GBR	9.98
2	Tim Montgomery USA	10.05
3	Maurice Greene USA	10.06

200m
1	Darvis Patton USA	20.25
2	Ramon Clay USA	20.34
3	Marlon Devonish GBR	20.43

400m-GP
1	Felix Sanchez DOM	45.14
2	Alvin Harrison USA	45.31
3	Ingo Schultz GER	45.46

800m
1	Yuriy Borzakovsky RUS	1:44.78
2	David Krummenacker USA	1:44.87
3	Joseph Mutua KEN	1:45.02

Mile-GP
1	Hicham El Guerrouj MAR	3:50.86
2	Cornelius Chirchir KEN	3:51.68
3	Rui Silva POR	3:52.21

3000m-GP
1	Benjamin Limo KEN	7:50.29
2	Paul Bitok KEN	7:50.54
3	Luke Kipkosgei KEN	7:50.68

110m Hurdles
1	Allen Johnson USA	13.23
2	Larry Wade USA	13.26
3	Colin Jackson GBR	13.37

400m Hurdles-GP
1	Felix Sanchez DOM	48.08
2	James Carter USA	48.09
3	Hadi S Al-Somaily KSA	48.62

Triple Jump-GP
1	Walter Davis USA	17.33m
2	Phillips Idowu GBR	17.29m
3	Jonathan Edwards GBR	17.21m

Javelin
1	Sergey Makarov RUS	86.70m
2	Eriks Rags LAT	85.32m
3	Alexandr Ivanov RUS	83.78m

Women

100m-GP
1	Marion Jones USA	10.97
2	Zhanna Pintusevich-Block UKR	11.11
3	Chryste Gaines USA	11.12

800m
1	Maria Mutola MOZ	1:59.06
2	Jolanda Ceplak SLO	1:59.61
3	Mayte Martinez ESP	2:00.54

5000m-GP
1	Berhane Adere ETH	14:33.65
2	Gabriela Szabo ROM	14:34.29
3	Sonia O'Sullivan IRL	14:46.97

110m Hurdles-GP
1	Bridgette Foster JAM	12.65
2	Gail Devers USA	12.71
3	Glory Alozie ESP	12.84

High Jump
1	Hestrie Cloete RSA	1.97m
2	Marina Kuptsova RUS	1.97m
3	Inha Babakova UKR	1.94m

Pole Vault
1	Svetlana Feofanova RUS	4.62m
2	Monika Pyrek POL	4.62m
3	Yelena Belyakova RUS	4.52m

Long Jump
1	Maurren Higa Maggi BRA	6.78m
2	Tunde Vaszi HUN	6.70m
3	Jade Johnson GBR	6.60m

Grand Prix II

Melbourne Track Classic
Melbourne, Mar 7
Men 100m(-1.9): Everton Evelyn BAR 10.64;
200m(-1.3): Alvin Harrison USA 20.63; 400m: Harrison
45.77; 800m: Kris McCarthy AUS 1:47.21; 1500m:
Cornelius Chirchir KEN 3:38.98; *GP*5000m: Stephen
Cherono KEN 13:11.55; 110mh: (-1.4): Tim Ewen AUS
14.09; 400mh: Michael Hazel AUS 50.90; HJ: Nick
Moroney AUS 2.19m; *GP*PV: Paul Burgess AUS 5.50m;
LJ: John Thornell AUS 7.87m; TJ: Andrew Murphy AUS
16.62m; SP: Justin Anlezark AUS 19.82m; *GP*HT: Stuart
Rendell AUS 78.01m; JT: Andrew Currey AUS 83.97m
Women 100m (-3.4): Lauren Hewitt AUS 11.81; 200m:
Hewitt 23.20; 400m: Jane Arnott NZL 53.11; 800m:
Tamsyn Lewis AUS 2:02.30; *GP*5000m: Hayley
McGregor AUS 15:32.17; 100mh (-0.4): Jacqui Munro
AUS 13.43; 400mh: Sonia Brito AUS 57.90; PV: Kym
Howe AUS 4.30m; *GP*LJ: Bronwyn Thompson AUS
7.00m; *GP*DT: Beatrice Faumuina NZL 61.13m; HT:
Bronwyn Eagles AUS 69.18m

Engen Grand Prix
Pretoria, South Africa, Apr 12
Men *GP*100m: Tim Montgomery USA 9.94; 200m:
Shawn Crawford USA 19.85; *GP*400m: Marcus La
Grange RSA 44.65; 800m: Mbulaeni Mulaudzi RSA
1:45.52; 3000m: Norman Dlomo RSA 8:04.16; 110mh:
Stanislav Olijars LAT 13.15; *GP*400mh: Llewellyn Herbert
RSA 48.02; HJ: Jacques Freitag RSA 2.34m; LJ: Martin
McClintock RSA 7.49m; SP: Karel Potgeiter RSA
18.75m; DT: Lars Riedel GER 66.72m; *GP*HT: Chris
Harmse RSA 80.19m; JT: Eriks Rags LAT 84.69m
Women 100m (0.0): Dikeledi Moropane RSA 11.42;
400m: Heide Seyerling-Quinn RSA 51.77; 800m: Agnes
Samaria NAM 2:04.31; 400mh: Tetiana Tereschuk-
Antipova UKR 54.71; HJ: Vita Palamar UKR 1.90m; PV:
Krisztima Molnar HUN 4.26m; *GP*LJ: Tunde Vaszi HUN
6.60m; *GP*JT: Moonika Aava EST 55.43m

Adidas Oregon Track Classic
Portland, May 18
Men 100m(+1.4): Coby Miller USA 9.98; *GP*400m:
Michael Blackwood Jam 45.29; 1000m: David
Krummenacker USA 2:15.97; Mile: David Lelei KEN
3:55.49; 3000m: Abraham Chebii KEN 7:44.86; 3000msc:
Brahim Boulami MAR 8:04.51; *GP*HJ: Matt Hemingway
USA 2.32m; *GP*SP: Adam Nelson USA 22.51m
Women *GP*400m: Kaltouma Nadjiina CHA 51.58; 800m:
Nicole Teter USA 2:00.52; 5000m: Tirunesh Dibaba ETH
15:13.78; *GP*100mh(+1.1): Miesha McKelvy USA 12.73;
PV: Mary Sauer USA 4.62m; *GP*DT: Beatrice Faumuina
NZL 63.51m

Fanny Blankers-Koen Games
Hengelo, June 2
Men 200m(-3.1): Caimin Douglas AHO 20.92; 800m:
Hezekiel Sepeng RSA 1:44.89; *GP*3000m: Richard Limo
KEN 7:41.38; 3000msc: Reuben Kosgei KEN 8:05.87;
110mh: Duane Ross USA 13.65; PV: Aleksandr
Averbukh ISR 5.60m; *GP*SP: Yury Bilonog UKR 20.94m;
*GP*HT: Karsten Kobs GER 78.84m
Women 100m (-2.2): Endurance Ojokolo NGR 11.45;
800m: Sandra Stals BEL 2:01.32; 1500: Kelly Holmes

GBR 4:03.93; *GP*5000m: Elvan Abeylegesse TUR
15:00.49; 400mh: Sandra Glover USA 55.70; *GP*LJ:
Lyudmila Galkina RUS 6.69m; *GP*DT: Natalya Sadova
RUS 63.75m

Atletisimo Sevilla 2002
Seville, June 8
Men 100m (-2.0): Simon Maestra ESP 10.69; 400m:
Greg Haughton JAM 44.75; 800m: Antonio Manuel Reina
ESP 1:47.80; *GP*1500: Bernard Lagat KEN 3:36.52;
5000m: Benjamin Maiyo KEN 13:14.05; 3000msc:
Antonio Jimenez ESP 8:18.09; 400mh: Periklis Iakovakis
GRE 49.91; PV: Nick Hysong USA 5.50m; LJ: Savante
Stringfellow USA 8.01m; *GP*SP: Manuel Martinez ESP
20.91m; DT: Robert Fazekas HUN 68.67; *GP*HT: Adrian
Annus HUN 81.09m
Women 100m(-1.5): Henrieta Ajaegbu NGR 11.96;
400m: Norfalia Carabali ESP 53.32; 800m: Kelly Holmes
GBR 2:00.46; 3000m: Marta Dominguez ESP 8:57.44;
*GP*100mh(-2.5): Bridgette Foster JAM 12.76; PV: Tanya
Koleva BUL 4.15m; *GP*LJ: Niurka Montalvo ESP 6.38m;
*GP*JT: Noraida Bicet CUB 61.88m

Cena Slovenska Slovak Gold
Bratislava, June 12
Men 100m(+2.1): Leo Settle USA 10.26; 400m: Marc
Raquil FRA 45.96; 800m: Werner Botha RSA 1:47.05;
*GP*HJ: Toni Huikuri FIN 2.31m; *GP*SP: Yury Bilonog UKR
21.13m
Women 100m(+1.0) Vernicha James GBR 11.40; 400m:
Grazyna Prokopek POL 52.69; 800m: Natalya
Khrushchelyova RUS 2:02.04; 100mh(+0.8): Haydy Aron
FRA 13.00; 400mh: Marina Shiyan RUS 55.76; *GP*LJ:
Irina Yermolayeva RUS 6.56m; *GP*DT: Vera Pospisilova
CZE 63.38m

Norwich Union Classic
Sheffield, June 30
Men 100m(+2.7): Dwain Chambers GBR 9.95; 200m:
Frank Fredericks NAM 20.29; *GP*400m: Daniel Caines
GBR 45.67; 1500m: Hicham El Guerrrouj MAR 3:40.20;
*GP*3000m: Mohammed Amyn MAR 7:57.83;
110mh(+1.2): Larry Wade USA 13.36; 300mh: Chris
Rawlinson 34.48 WR; PV: Denys Yurchenko UKR 5.65m;
*GP*TJ: Phillips Idowu GBR 17.34m; JT: Sergey Makarov
RUS 92.61m
Women 100m(-0.7): Tayna Lawrence JAM 11.09;
*GP*400m: Kaltouma Nadjina CHA 51.92; 800m: Maria
Mutola MOZ 2:00.84; *GP*3000m: Sonia O'Sullivan IRL
8:44.02; 400mh: Yulia Pechonkina RUS 54.54; TJ:
Yelena Oleynikova RUS 14.58m; *GP*DT: Ellina Zvereva
BLR 66.16m

Zagreb 2002
Zagreb, July 8
Men 100m: Bernard Williams USA 10.14; 200m: Abdul
Aziz Zakari GHA 20.43; 1500m: Cornelia Chirchir KEN
3:35.49; 110mh(+1.0): Larry Wade USA 13.18;
*GP*400mh: Eric Thomas USA 48.27; *GP*HJ: Mark Boswell
CAN 2.27m; LJ: Savante Stringfellow USA 8.06m; *GP*SP:
Adam Nelson USA 21.28m
Women 100m(0.0): Kelli White USA 11.26; 200m(+0.7):
White USA 22.53; *GP*400m: LaTasha Colander-
Richardson USA 51.21; 1500m: Alesya Turova BLR
4:05.41; *GP*100m(-2.5): Anajette Kirkland USA 12.82; HJ:
Hestrie Cloete RSA 2.00m; *GP*DT: Nicoleta Grasu ROM
64.90m; HT: Manuela Montebrun FRA 70.83m

Asics GP
Helsinki, Aug 13
Men 100m(-1.3): Darvis Patton USA 10.20; 200m(-1.8): Patrick Johnson AUS 21.09; 800m: Mbulaeni Mulaudzi RSA 1:45.29; 3000m: Samuli Vasala FIN 7:46.95 110mh(-0.8): Colin Jackson GBR 13.23; *GP*400mh: Llewellyn Herbert RSA 48.83; *GP*HJ: Yaroslav Rybakov RUS 2.29m; LJ: Dwight Phillips USA 8.27m; *GP*SP: Kevin Toth USA 21.15m; JT: Sergey Makarov RUS 89.98m
Women 100m(-1.1): Chryste Gaines USA 11.23; *GP*400m: Maria Mutola MOZ 51.55; 800m: Agnes Samaria NAM 1:59.69; *GP*3000m: Sentayehu Ejigu ETH 8:52.88; 100mh: Johanna Halkoaho FIN 13.66; TJ: Magdelin Martinez ITA 14.37m; *GP*JT: Tatyana Shikolenko RUS 64.17m

Raiffeisen Gugl - Meeting Linz
Linz, Aug 19
Men 100m(-0.4): Frank Fredericks NAM 10.19; 200m(+0.4): Fredericks NAM 20.15; 800m Michael Rotich KEN 1:47.52; 3000msc: Wilson Boit Kipketer KEN 8:19.52; 100mh(-0.3): Colin Jackson GBR 13.38; *GP*400mh: Hadi Soua'an Al-Somaily KSA 48.18; *GP*HJ: James Nieto USA 2.30m; PV: Tim Lobinger USA 5.80m; LJ: Dwight Phillips USA 8.38m; *GP*SP: Adam Nelson USA 20.67m
Women 100m: Tayna Lawrence JAM 11.15; 200m: Debbie Ferguson BAH 22.63; 1000m: Maria Mutola MOZ 2:38.08; *GP*3000m: Meseret Defar ETH 8:48.13; *GP*100mh: Vonette Dixon JAM 12.85; 400mh: Ionela Tirlea ROM 54.61; *GP*DT: Ellina Zvereva BLR 62.91m

Rieti 2002
Rieti, Italy, Sep 8
Men 100m(+0.7): Uchenna Emedolu NGR 10.10; 200m(+0.4): Emedolu NGR 20.31; 800m Wilson Kipketer KEN 1:42.32; 1500m: Hicham El Guerrouj MAR 3:26.96; 3000m: Patrick Ivuti KEN 7:38.69; 110mh: Allen Johnson USA 13.29; *GP*400mh: Joey Woody USA 48.96; *GP*HJ: Stefan Holm SWE 2.29m; *GP*SP: Paolo dal Soglio ITA 20.50m
Women 200m(+0.7): Myriam Leonie Mani CMR 22.91; 400m: Olabisi Afolabi NGR 51.94; *GP*1500m: Suzy Favor Hamilton USA 3:59.43; *GP*100mh(+0.9): Anjanette Kirkland USA 12.85; PV: Annika Becker GER 4.53m; TJ: Magdelin Martinez ITA 14.73m; *GP*JT: Sonia Bicet CUB 61.53

World Junior Championships
Kingston, Jamaica, July 18-22
Men 100m(-0.6): Darrel Brown TRI 10.09; 200m(+0.9): Usain Bolt JAM 20.61; 400m: Darold Williamson USA 45.37; 800m: Alex Kipchirchir KEN 1:46.59; 1500m: Yassine Bensghir MAR 3:40.72; 5000m: Hillary Chenonge KEN 13:28.30; 10,000m: Geber-Egziabher Gebremariam ETH 29:02.71; 3000m: Michael Kipyego KEN 8:29.54 (12th Steve Murphy GBR 9:05.80); 110m: Antwon Hicks USA 13.42; 400mh: Louis van Zyl RSA 48.89 (4th Steve Green GBR 51.14); HJ: Andra Manson USA 2.31m (10th Martyn Bernard GBR 2.14m); PV: Maksim Mazuryk UKR 5.55m; LJ: Ibrahim Abdulla Al-Waleed QAT 7.99m; TJ: David Giralt CUB 16.68m; SP: Edis Elkasevic CRO 21.47m; DT: Wu Tao CHN 64.51m; HT: Werner Smit RSA 76.43m; JT: Igor Janik POL 74.16m; 10kmW: Vladimir Kanaykin Rus 41:41.40 (DQ: Dominic King GBR); Decathlon: Leonid Andreev UZB 7693pts; 4x100m: USA 38.92; 4x400m: USA 3:03.71
Women 100m(-0.2): Lauryn Williams USA 11.33; 200m(-0.2): Vernicha James GBR 22.93 (7th Amy Spencer GBR 23.76); 400m: Monique Henderson USA 51.10 (5th Lisa Miller GBR 53.20); 800m: Janeth Jepkosgei KEN 2:00.80 (4th Jemma Simpson GBR 2:04.11); 1500m: Viola Kibiwot KEN 4:12.57 (4th Lisa Dobriskey GBR 4:14.72); 3000m: Meseret Defar ETH 9:12.61; 5000m: Meseret Defar ETH 15:54.94; 100mh: Anay Tejeda CUB 12.81; 400mh: Lashinda Demus USA 54.70; HJ: Vlasic Blanka CRO 1.96m; PV: Floe Kuhnert GER 4.40m (7th Kate Dennison GBR 4.00m); LJ: Adina Anton ROM 6.46m; TJ: Mabel Gay CUB 14.09m; SP: Valerie Adams NZL 17.73m; DT: Ma Xuejin CHN 58.85m (9th Claire Smithson GBR 50.85m); HT: Ivana Brkljacic CRO 65.39m; JT: Linda Brivule LAT 55.35m; 10kmW: Fumi Mitsumaura JPN 46:01.51; 4x100m: Jamaica 43.30 (3rd Great Britain 44.22 Jade Lucas-Read/Jeanette Kwakye/Amy Spencer/Vernicha James); 4x400m: USA 3:29.95 (2nd Great Britain 3:30.46 Kim Wall/Amy Spencer/Vernicha James/Lisa Miller); Heptathlon: Carlina Kluft SWE 6470

Domestic Events
European Championships
Trials
Birmingham, July 12-14

Men

100m	1	Mark Lewis-Francis	Birchfield	10.06
	2	Darren Campbell	Belgrave	10.11
	3	Jason Gardener	Bath	10.13
200m	1	Marlon Devonish	Coventry	20.18
	2	Darren Campbell	Belgrade	20.26
	3	Christian Malcolm	Cardiff	20.29
400m	1	Tim Benjamin	Cardiff	45.73
	2	Sean Baldock	Belgrave	45.84
	3	Jared Deacon	Border Harriers	45.89
800m	1	James McIlroy	WSEH	1:50.09
	2	Neil Speaight	Belgrave	1:50.71
	3	Alasdair Donaldson	NEB	1:50.80
1500m	1	Tony Whiteman	Shaftesbury	3:38.24
	2	John Mayock	Barnsley	3:38.97
	3	Michael East	NEB	3:39.18
5000m	1	Jon Wild	Sale	13:52.59
	2	Rob Denmark	Basildon	13:53.18
	3	Matthew Smith	Tipton	13:53.47
3000msc	1	Benedict Whitby	WSEH	8:40.12
	2	Christian Stephenson	Cardiff	8:44.31
	3	Patrick Davoren	Phoenix	8:47.92
110mh	1	Colin Jackson	Brecon	13.40
	2	Tony Jarrett	Enfield/H'gay	13.52
	3	Damien Greaves	NEB	13.54
400mh	1	Chris Rawlinson	Belgrave	48.68
	2	Anthony Borsumato	Sale	48.90
	3	Matt Elias	Cardiff	49.79
HJ	1	Dalton Grant	Woodford	2.20m
	2	Ben Challenger	Belgrave	2.20m
	3	Mark Mandy	Birchfield (IRL)	2.10m
PV	1	Nick Buckfield	Crawley	5.35m
	2	Mark Davis	Birchfield	5.20m
	3	Christian North	Woodford G	5.20m
LJ	1	Darren Ritchie	Sale	7.93m
	2	Christopher Tomlinson	NEB	7.82m
	3	Mark Awanah	Blackheath	7.46m
TJ	1	Phillips Idowu	Belgrave	17.02m
	2	Tosin Oke	Cambridge	16.60m
	3	Steven Shalders	Cardiff	16.09m
SP	1	Mark Proctor	NEB	18.54m
	2	Emeka Udechuku	Woodford	17.19m
	3	Scott Rider	Harrow	17.19m
DT	1	Bob Weir	Birchfield	58.22m
	2	Glen Smith	Birchfield	56.38m
	3	Emeka Udechuku	Woodford	56.28m
HT	1	Mick Jones	Belgrave	72.26m
	2	Paul Head	NEB	67.61m
	3	Mike Floyd	Sale	66.33m
JT	1	Mick Hill	Leeds	77.86m
	2	Mark Roberson	NEB	74.23m
	3	Nick Nieland	Shaftesbury	73.20m
5kmW	1	Steve Hollier	Wolves	20:41.29
	2	Donald Bearman	Steyning	21:55.07
	3	Nathan Adams	Sheffield	23:11.68

Women

100m	1	Joice Maduaka	Woodford	11.31
	2	Abi Oyepitan	Shaftesbury	11.42
	3	Diane Allahgreen	Trafford	11.44
200m	1	Shani Anderson	Shaftesbury	23.03
	2	Joice Maduaka	Woodford	23.21
	3	Ellena Ruddock	Rugby	23.41
400m	1	Lee McConnell	Shaftesbury	51.59
	2	Catherine Murphy	Shaftesbury	52.10
	3	Helen Karagounis	Birchfield	52.45
800m	1	Susan Scott	Glasgow	2:03.89
	2	Jo Fenn	Woodford	2:04.12
	3	Emma Davies	Belgrave	2:05.52
1500m	1	Kelly Holmes	Southall	4:06.02
	2	Helen Pattinson	Preston	4:06.98
	3	Hayley Tullett	Swansea	4:08.23
5000m	1	Hayley Yelling	WSE	16:11.23
	2	Catherine Dugdale	Swansea	16:25.14
	3	Debbie Sullivan	Havering	16:28.27
2000msc	1	Tara Krzywicki	Charnwood	6:31.77
	2	Claire Entwistle	Wigan	6:54.92
	3	Ursula Counsell	Bristol	7:04.94
100mh	1	Diane Allahgreen	Trafford	13.00
	2	Julie Pratt	Woodford	13.27
	3	Rachel King	Belgrave	13.34
400mh	1	Natasha Danvers	Shaftesbury	56.14
	2	Sinead Dudgeon	Edinburgh	56.88
	3	Tracey Duncan	Woodford	57.51
HJ	1	Susan Jones	Trafford	1.92m
	2	Debbie Marti	Bromley	1.75m
	3	Julie Crane	Sale	1.75m
PV	1	Janine Whitlock	Trafford	4.35m
	2	Irie Hill	WSE	4.15m
	3	Tracey Bloomfield	Guildford	4.05m
LJ	1	Jade Johnson	Herne Hill	6.52m
	2	Sarah Claxton	Belgrave	6.17m
	3	Donita Benjamin	Army	6.08m
TJ	1	Ashia Hansen	Shaftesbury	14.50m
	2	Yamile Aldama	(CUB)	14.40m
	3	Michelle Griffith	WSE	13.18m
SP	1	Myrtle Augee	Bromley	16.16m
	2	Julie Dunkley	Shaftesbury	15.89m
	3	Joanne Duncan	Woodford	15.71m
DT	1	Philippa Roles	Sale	56.32m
	2	Shelley Newman	Belgrave	54.08m
	3	Emma Carpenter	Exeter	53.28m
HT	1	Lorraine Shaw	Sale	64.97m
	2	Liz Pidgeon	Woodford	62.08m
	3	Zoe Derham	Birchfield	59.89m
JT	1	Kelly Morgan	WSE	64.87m
	2	Goldie Sayers	Belgrave	56.96m
	3	Karen Martin	RAF	56.34m
5kmW	1	Lisa Kehler	Wolves	21:42.51m
	2	Sharon Tonks	Bromsgrove	24:05.49m
	3	Estle Viljoen	Wimbledon	24:26.11m

Aqua Pura Commonwealth Games Trials
Manchester, June 15-16

Men

100m	1	Dwain Chambers	Belgrave	10.03
	2	Mark Lewis-Francis	Birchfield	10.07
	3	Chris Lambert	Belgrave	10.28
200m	1	Marlon Devonish	Coventry	20.36
	2	Chris Lambert	Belgrave	20.41
	3	Graham Beasley	Belgrave	20.76
400m	1	Daniel Caines	Birchfield	45.32
	2	Jared Deacon	Border Harriers	45.57
	3	Sean Baldock	Belgrave	46.47
800m	1	Simon Lees	Solihull	1:47.89
	2	Neil Speaight	Belgrave	1:48.48
	3	Curtis Robb	Liverpool	1:48.50
1500m	1	Michael East	NEB	3:46.89
	2	Tony Whiteman	Shaftesbury	3:47.28
	3	Tom Mayo	Cannock	3:47.56
5000m	1	Sam Haughian	WSE	13:42.80
	2	Michael Power	Australia	13:44.32
	3	Matt O'Dowd	Swindon	13:46.24
10,000m	1	Rob Denmark	Basildon	28:43.42
	2	Jon Wild	Sale	28:43.82
	3	Andres Jones	Cardiff	28:43.93
3000msc	1	Stuart Stokes	Sale	8:35.6
	2	Benedict Whitby	WSE	8:38.0
	3	Donald Naylor	Swansea	8:39.0
110mh	1	Damian Greaves	NEB	13.73
	2	Mensah Elliott	Blackheath	13.95
	3	Dominic Girdler	Charnwood	13.95
400mh	1	Matthew Elias	Cardiff	49.46
	2	Tony Borsumato	Manchester	49.52
	3	Matt Douglas	Belgrave	49.76
HJ	1	Ben Challenger	Belgrave	2.23m
	2	Richard Aspden	Belgrave	2.14m
	3	Luke Crawley	Solihull	2.14m
PV	1	Viktor Chistyakov	Australia	5.60m
	2	Tim Thomas	Swansea	5.20m
	3	Paul Williamson	Belgrave	5.20m
LJ	1	Chris Tomlinson	NEB	7.98m
	2	Darren Ritchie	Sale	7.76m
	3	Mark Awanah	Blackheath	7.70m
TJ	1	Steven Shalders	Cardiff	16.41m
	2	Tosin Oke	Cambridge H	16.33m
	3	Larry Achike	Shaftesbury	16.32m
SP	1	Carl Myerscough	Blackpool	19.82m
	2	Mark Proctor	NEB	17.75m
	3	Emeka Udechuku	Woodford	17.48m
DT	1	Carl Myerscough	Blackpool	61.22m
	2	Glen Smith	Birchfield	58.32m
	3	Emeka Udechuku	Woodford	57.97m
HT	1	Mick Jones	Belgrave	72.16m
	2	Paul Head	NEB	69.61m
	3	Mike Floyd	Sale	67.74m
JT	1	Nick Nieland	Shaftesbury	80.05m
	2	Mark Roberson	NEB	78.80m
	3	Mick Hill	Leeds	78.15m

Women

100m	1	Debbie Ferguson	Bahamas	11.25
	2	Shani Anderson	Shaftesbury	11.51
	3	Amanda Forrester	Stoke	11.57
200m	1	Vernicha James	Belgrave	22.95
	2	Shani Anderson	Shaftesbury	23.32
	3	Emily Freeman	Wakefield	23.43
400m	1	Maria Mutola	Mozambique	52.03
	2	Helen Karagounis	Birchfield	52.17
	3	Carey Easton	Edinburgh	53.11
800m	1	Jo Fenn	Woodford	2:00.24
	2	Agnes Samaria	Namibia	2:00.26
	3	Tamsin Lewis	Australia	2:00.73
1500m	1	Helen Pattinson	Preston	4:08.66
	2	Susan Scott	Glasgow	4:09.79
	3	Sarah Jamieson	Australia	4:09.89
5000m	1	Catherine Berry	Kingston	15:32.32
	2	Natalie Harvey	Australia	15:38.25
	3	Hayley Yelling	WSE	15:38.30
10,000m	1	Sonia O'Sullivan	Ireland	31:33.19
	2	Sabrina Mockenhaupt	Germany	32:27.63
	3	Elana Meyer	South Africa	32:36.15
100mh	1	Diane Allahgreen	Trafford	13.07
	2	Natasha Danvers	Shaftesbury	13.20
	3	Julie Pratt	Woodford	13.33
400mh	1	Natasha Danvers	Shaftesbury	56.44
	2	Tracey Duncan	Woodford	56.53
	3	Katie Jones	Trafford	57.71
HJ	1	Susan Jones	Trafford	1.88m
	2	Stephanie Higham	Border Harriers	1.85m
	3	Debbie Marti	Bromley	1.82m
PV	1	Janine Whitlock*	Trafford	4.41m
	2	Tatyana Grigorieva	Australia	4.25m
	3	Irie Hill	WSE	4.15m
LJ	1	Jade Johnson	Herne Hill	6.45m
	2	Ann Danson	Sale	6.38m
	3	Kelly Sotherton	Birchfield	6.21m
TJ	1	Ashia Hansen	Shaftesbury	14.03m
	2	Michelle Griffith	WSE	12.99m
	3	Tanisha Scanlon	Ireland	12.69m
SP	1	Julie Dunkley	Shaftesbury	16.37m
	2	Myrtle Augee	Bromley	15.87m
	3	Joanne Duncan	Woodford	15.85m
DT	1	Shelley Newman	Belgrave	57.99m
	2	Emma Carpenter	Exeter	56.63m
	3	Phillipa Roles	Sale	56.52m
HT	1	Lorraine Shaw	Sale	65.34m
	2	Zoe Derham	Birchfield	62.27m
	3	Suzanne Roberts	Wakefield	59.75m
JT	1	Kelly Morgan	WSE	63.03m
	2	Karen Martin	Derby	55.02m
	3	Goldie Sayers	Belgrave	54.59m

* Whitlock, who set a British record at the CG Trials above, subsequently tested positive for the steroid methandionone and was dropped from the England team for Manchester

Great Britain v Russia v USA
Glasgow, Aug 18
Men 100m: Dwain Chambers GBR 10.28secs;
200m:Darvis Patton USA 20.16; 400m: Antonio Pettigrew
USA 46.13; 1500m: Michael East GBR 3:55.15secs; LJ:
Savante Stringfellow USA 8.20m; 110mh: Larry Wade
USA 13.24; 400mh: Joey Woody USA 49.14; JT: Sergey
Makarov RUS 87.99m; TJ: Jonathan Edwards GBR
17.54m; 4x100m: Great Britain 39.48
Women 100m: Chryste Gaines USA 11.12; 200m: Joice
Maduaka GBR 23.37; 400m: Jearl Miles Clark USA
51.65; 1500m: Tatyana Tomashova RUS 4:09.64;
100mh: Gail Devers USA 12.79; TJ: Ashia Hansen GBR
13.96m; HT: Olga Kuzenkova RUS 71.73m; PV: Svetlana
Feofanova RUS 4.62m; 4x100m: Russia 43.99
Final Standings: 1 USA 144pts, 2 Great Britain 117pts, 3
Russia 116pts

Great Britain v Cuba v Yugoslavia v Catalunya
Barcelona, Sep 6
Men 100m(-0.6): Daniel Plummer GBR 10.64; 400m:
Tim Benjamin GBR 46.39; 800m: Miguel Quesada CAT
1:49.24; 1500m: Reyes Estevez CAT 3:43.37; 3000m:
José Rios CAT 8:05.81; 110mh: Yoel Hernandez CUB
13.89; HJ: Raul Touset CUB 2.15m; LJ: Luis Melis CUB
8.00m; SP: Alexis Paumier CUB 17.60m; JT: Emeterio
Gonzalez CUB 81.95m; Swedish Relay
(400x200x200x100): Great Britain 1:50.22
Women 100m: Amanda Forrester GBR 11.55; 400m:
Melanie Purkiss GBR 54.52; 800m: Susan Scott GBR
2:02.93; 3000m: Sonja Stolic YUG 9:00.13; 100mh(+1.4):
Anay Tejada CUB 13.26; PV: Tracey Bloomfield GBR
3.92m; TJ: Biljana Mitrovic YUG 13.67; SP: Yumileidi
Cumba CUB 18.88m; JT: Sonia Bicet CUB 63.27m;
Swedish Relay: Great Britain 2:08.67

Final Standings: 1 Great Britain 221; 2 Yugoslavia 165;
3 Cuba 154; 4 Catalunya 144

Lynn Loses Record At Last

For most of the 34 years that Lynn Davies held the British long jump record, set at altitude in Mexico in 1968 (but not at the Olympics) there was never any likelihood that a British jumper would go further. We haven't got an accurate account of how many seasons the leading British mark was under eight metres, but rest assured it was a good few.

Stewart Faulkner, Mark Forsythe and Nathan Morgan, in that progression, came closest, with the powerful Faulkner just eight centimetres adrift. However, it was eventually surpassed in sunny Florida, by an athlete who, if he were a horse, would almost be described as unbroken.

Chris Tomlinson was training in Tallahassee with Jonathan Edwards, and in a local competition leapt 8.27m to better Davies' record by four centimetres. The performance took place on Saturday afternoon, April 13th too late for the national papers on Sunday and, by Monday, had been relegated to an in-brief below the London Marathon reports. So poor Tomlinson, having broken the oldest record in the book, hardly got the credit he deserved.

As it happens, Davies may have lost his record, but he gained a job, replacing David Hemery as the new president of UK Athletics.

Indoor Athletics

European Championships

Vienna, March 1-3

Men

60m
1	Jason Gardener	GBR	6.49
2	Mark Lewis-Francis	GBR	6.55
3	Anatoliy Dovgal UKR 6.62		

Akinola Lashore GBR eliminated semi-finals

200m
1	Marcin Urbas	POL	20.64
2	Christian Malcolm	GBR	20.65
3	Robert Mackowiak	POL	20.77
4	Daniel Caines	GBR	21.14

Doug Turner GBR eliminated semi-finals

400m
1	Marek Plawgo	POL	45.39
2	Jimisola Laursen	SWE	45.59
3	Ioan Vieru	ROM	46.17

800m
1	Pawel Czapiewski	POL	1:44.78
2	Andre Bucher	SUI	1:44.93
3	Antonio Reina	ESP	1:45.25

1500m
1	Ruis Silva	POR	3:49.93
2	Juan Higuero	ESP	3:50.08
3	Michael East	GBR	3:50.52

Angus MacLean GBR eliminated heat

3000m
1	Alberto Garcia	ESP	7:43.89
2	A Jimenez	ESP	7:46.49
=3	Jesus Espana	ESP	7:48.08
=3	John Mayock	GBR	7:48.08

60mh
1	Colin Jackson	GBR	7.40
2	Eimar Lichtenegger	AUT	7.44
3	Yevgeny Pechonkin	RUS	7.50

DamienGreaves elim 1st round

HJ
1	Steffan Strand	SWE	2.34m
2	Steffan Holm	SWE	2.30m
3	Yevgeny Rybakov	RUS	2.30m

PV
1	Tim Lobinger	GER	5.75m
2	P Kristiansson	SWE	5.75m
3	Lars Borgeling	GER	5.75m

Nick Buckfield GBR eliminated qualifying

LJ
1	Raul Fernandez	ESP	8.22m
2	Yago Lamela	ESP	8.17m
3	Petar Datchev	BUL	8.17m

TJ
1	Christian Olsson	SWE	17.54m
2	Marian Oprea	ROM	17.22m
3	A Glavatskity	RUS	17.05m

SP
1	Manuel Martinez	ESP	21.26m
2	J Olsen	DEN	21.23m
3	Mikulas Konopka	SVK	20.87m

Hept
1	Roman Sebrle	CZE	6280
2	Tomas Dvorak	CZE	6165
3	Erki Nool	EST	6084

4x400m
1	Poland	3:05.50
2	France	3:06.42
3	Spain	3:06.60

Women

60m
1	Kim Gevaert	BEL	7.16
2	Marina Kislova	RUS	7.18
3	Georgia Kokloni	GRE	7.22

Joice Maduaka GBR eliminated heats

200m
1	Muriel Hurtis	FRA	22.52
2	Karin Ayr	AUT	22.70
3	Gabi Rockmeier	GER	23.05

400m
1	Natalya Antukh	RUS	51.65
2	Claudia Marx	GER	52.15
3	Karen Shinkins	IRL	52.17
6	Catherine Murphy	GBR	52.98

800m
1	Jolanda Ceplak	SLO	1:55.82	**WR**
2	Stephanie Graf	AUT	1:55.85	
3	E Grousselle	FRA	2:01.46	

Jennifer Meadows GBR DNF heat

1500m
1	Y Puzanova	RUS	4:06.30
2	Elena Iagar	ROM	4:06.90
3	Alesya Turova	BLR	4:07.69
9	Hayley Tullett	GBR	4:17.14

3000m
1	Marta Dominguez	ESP	8:53.87
2	Carla Sacramento	POR	8:53.96
3	Yelena Zadorozhnaya	RUS	8:58.36

60mh
1	Glory Alozie	ESP	7.84
2	Linda Ferga	FRA	7.96
3	Kirsten Bolm	GER	7.97
7	Diane Allahgreen	GBR	8.06

Rachel King GBR elim heat

HJ
1	Marina Kuptsova	RUS	2.03m
=2	Kajsa Bergqvist	SWE	1.95m
=2	Dora Gyorffy	HUN	1.95m
5	Susan Jones	GBR	1.90m

PV
1	Svetlana Feofanova	RUS	4.75m	**WR**
2	Yvonne Buschbaum	GER	4.65m	
3	Monika Pyrek	POL	4.60m	

Janine Whitlock GBR eliminated qualifying

LJ
1	Niki Xanthou	GRE	6.74m
2	Olga Rublyova	RUS	6.74m
3	Lyudmila Galkina	RUS	6.68m

TJ
1	Tereza Marinova	BUL	14.81m
2	Ashia Hansen	GBR	14.71m
3	Y Oleynikova	RUS	14.30m

SP
1	Vita Pavlysh	UKR	19.76m
2	A Legnante	ITA	18.60m
3	Lieja Koeman	NED	18.53m

4x400m
1	Belarus	3:32.24
2	Poland	3:32.45
3	Italy	3:36.49

Pent
1	Yelena Prokhorova	RUS	4622
2	Naide Gomes	POR	4595
3	Carolina Kluft	SWE	4535

European Indoor Championships Medal Table

	G	S	B	Total
Spain	5	3	3	11
Russia	5	2	5	12
Poland	4	1	2	7
Sweden	2	4	1	7
Great Britain	2	3	2	7
Germant	1	2	3	6
France	1	2	1	4
Portugal	1	2	0	3
Czech Republic	1	1	0	2
Belarus	1	0	2	3
Bulgaria	1	0	1	2
Greece	1	0	1	2
Ukraine	1	0	1	2
Belgium	1	0	0	1
Slovenia	1	0	0	1
Austria	0	3	0	3
Romania	0	2	1	3
Italy	0	1	1	2
Denmark	0	1	0	1
Hungary	0	1	0	1
Switzerland	0	1	0	1
Estonia	0	0	1	1
Ireland	0	0	1	1
Netherlands	0	0	1	1
Slovak Republic	0	0	1	1

AAA Indoor Championships
Cardiff, Feb 2-3
Men 60m: Jason Gardener 6.52; 200m: Doug Turner 21.24; 400m: Robert Daly IRL 47.58; 800m: James McIlroy 1:51.10; 1500m: Anthony Whiteman 3:52.44; 3000m: Michael East 8:18.41; 60mh: Colin Jackson 7.60 3000mW: Robert Heffernan IRL 11:10.02; PV: Nick Buckfield 5.50m; HJ: Ben Challenger 2.17m; LJ: Gable Garenamotse BOT 8.01m; TJ: Tosin Oke 15.95m; SP: Erik van Vreumingen NED 17.38m
Women 60m: Joice Maduaka 7.33; 200m: Amy Spencer 23.74; 400m: Catherine Murphy 52.54; 800m: Jenny Meadows 2:05.07; 1500m: Nathalie Lewis 4:25.49; 60mh: Diane Allahgreen 8.01; 3000mW: Gillian O'Sullivan IRL 12:17.56; PV: Janine Whitlock 4.20m; HJ: Susan Jones 1.90m; LJ: Kelly Sotherton 6.22m; TJ: Ashia Hansen 13.53m; SP: Helena Engman SWE 16.27m

Air Force Millrose Games
New York, Feb 2
Men 60m: Shawn Crawford USA 6.49; 800m: David Krummenacker USA 1:52.30; Mile: Laban Rotich KEN 3:57.04; 60mh: Larry Wade USA 7.60m; HJ: Charles Clinger USA 2.31m; PV: Jeff Hartwig USA 5.87m
Women 60m: Chandra Sturrup BAH 7.11; 800m: Jolanda Ceplak SLO 1:59.98; Mile: Regina Jacobs USA 4:34.60; 60mh: Miesha McKelvy USA 8.04; HJ(Speed Comp): Tisha Waller USA 1.95m; Weight Throw: Anna Norgren USA 23.56m; PV: Stacy Dragila USA 4.55m

Ge Galan
Stockholm, Feb 6
Men 60m Morne Nagel RSA 6.53; 400m: Daniel Caines GBR 46.35; 800m: Glody Dube BOT 1:47.21; 3000m: Luke Kipkosgei KEN 7:40.70; 60mh: Yevgeniy Pechonkin RUS 7.54; HJ: Staffan Strand SWE 2.35m; TJ: Christian Olsson SWE 17.28m
Women 400m: Catherine Murphy GBR 53.44; 800m: Stephanie Graf AUT 1:59.51; 1500m: Berhane Adere ETH 4:05.54; HJ: Marina Kuptsova RUS 1.97m; PV: Svetlana Feofanova RUS 4.72m

Energiser Indoor - Vlaanderen
Ghent, Feb 10
Men 60m: Morne Nagel RSA 6.53; 200m: Ingo Schultz GER 20.97; 400m: Bastian Swillims GER 46.94; 800m: Andre Bucher SUI 1:45.80; 1500m: Mehdi Baala FRA 3:37.19; 3000m: Monder Rizki BEL 8:06.70; 10,000m: Mark Bett KEN 27:50.29; 60mh: Colin Jackson GBR 7.49; LJ: Savante Stringfellow USA 8.12m
Women 60m: Chioma Ajunwa NGR 7.15; 200m: Muriel Hurtis FRA 22.96; 800m: Stephanie Graf AUT 1:56.85; HJ: Dora Györffy HUN 1.92m; PV: Svetlana Feofanova RUS 4.73m

Norwich Union Indoor Grand Prix
Birmingham, Feb 17
Men 60m: Morne Nagel RSA 6.50; 200m: Shawn Crawford USA 20.30; 400m: Daniel Caines GBR 46.06; 800m: André Bucher SUI 1:47.48; 1500m: Mehdi Baala FRA 3:40.08: Two miles: Salah Hissou MAR 8:15.60; 60m: Colin Jackson GBR 7.44; LJ: Kevin Dilworth USA 8.18m
Women 60m: Chioma Ajunwa NGR 7.06; 400m: Natalia Antyukh RUS 51.17; 800m: Stephanie Graf AUT 1:57.61; 3000m: Berhane Adere ETH 8:32.88; HJ: Marina Kuptsova RUS 1.96m; PV: Svetlana Feofanova RUS 4.64m; TJ: Tereza Marinova BUL 14.59m

Meeting Gaz de France du Pas de Calais
Lievin, France, 24 Feb
Men 60m: Morne Nagel RSA 6.50; 200m: Christian Malcolm GBR 20.71; 400m: Marek Plawgo POL 46.01; 800m: André Bucher SUI 1:45.08; 1500m: Rui Silva POR 3:35.26 ; 60mh: Allen Johnson USA 7.52; HJ: Mark Boswell CAN 2.33m
Women 200m: Murielle Hurtis FRA 22.51; 800m: Maria Mutola MOZ 1:58.83; 60mh: Olga Shishigina KZK 7.89; Mile: Carla Sacramento POR 4:23.00; PV: Svetlana Feofanova RUS 4.74m **WR**; TJ: Tereza Marinova BUL 14.71m

Cross-Country

IAAF World Championships

Dublin, Mar 23-24

SENIOR MEN (4.27km)
Individual

1	Kenenisa Bekele	ETH	12:11
2	Luke Kipkosgei	KEN	12:18
3	Hailu Mekonnen	ETH	12:20

GBR
23 John Mayock 12:44; 30 Philip Mowbray 12:50;
39 Spencer Barden 12:53; 42 Ben Noad 12:54;
72 Rob Whalley 13:10; 79 Benedict Whitby 13:13
IRL
25 Gareth Turnbull 12:45; 63 Robert Connolly 13:04;
84 Paul Reilly 13:19; 93 Paul McNamara 13:26;
94 Mark Kenneally 13:26; 107 Gareth Coughlan 13:55
Teams
1 Kenya 20; 2 Ethiopia 32; 3 Spain 57;
4 Morocco 78; 5 USA 113; 6 France 117;
7 Great Britain 120; 8 Australia 120; 9 Italy 123;
10 Algeria 129; 12 Ireland 190
(19 teams)

SENIOR MEN (12.07km)
Individual

1	Kenenisa Bekele	ETH	34:52
2	John Yuda	TAN	34:58
3	Wilberforce Talel	KEN	35:20

GBR
43 Sam Haughian 36:53; 49 Allen Graffin 37:10;
60 Matthew Smith 37:32; 68 Ian Hudspith 37:38;
69 Glynn Tromans 37:40; 102 Matt O'Dowd 38:41
IRL
44 Peter Matthews 36:59; 48 Mark Carroll 37:09;
64 Seamus Power 37:36; 92 Fiachra Lombard 38:21;
111 John Burke 39:06; 123 Martin McCarthy 40:22
Teams: 1. Kenya 18; 2. Ethiopia 43; 3. Morocco 58;
4. France 71; 5. USA 107; 6. Spain 121; 7. Eritrea 141;
8. Tanzania 146; 9. Portugal 166; 10. Great Britain 173;
15. Ireland 190
(20 teams)

JUNIOR MEN (7.87km)
Individual

1	Gebre-E Gebremarian	ETH	23:18
2	Abel Cheruiyot	KEN	23:19
3	Boniface Kiprop	KEN	23:28

GBR
31 Tom Sharland 25:15; 68 Matthew Lole 26:05;
82 Steven Ablitt 26:27; 84 Matthew Bowser 26:29;
95 David Jones 26:50; 105 Chris Watson 27:26;
IRL
87 Mark Christie 26:38; 90 William Harty 26:40;
103 Joseph Sweeney 27:12; 111 Alan McCormack 27:59;
112 Eoin Higgins 28:13
Team: 1 Kenya 18; 2 Ethiopia 24; 3 Uganda 37;
4 Japan 77; 5 Morocco 89; 6 Zambia 94; 7 USA 113;
8 Algeria 131; 9 Sudan 143; 10 South Africa 146;
11 Great Britain 176; 17 Ireland 252
(18 teams)

SENIOR WOMEN (4.27km)
Individual

1	Edith Masai	KEN	13:30
2	Werknesh Kidane	ETH	13:36
3	Isabella Ochichi	KEN	13:39

GBR
22 Helen Pattinson 14:18; 35 Lucy Elliott 14:28;
60 Amanda Wright-Allen 14:48; 75 Sonia Thomas 15:01;
78 Emma Ward 15:04; 80 Jane Potter 15:10
IRL
7 Sonia O'Sullivan 13:55; 10 Anne Keenan-Buckley 14:03;
19 Rosemary Ryan 14:14; 62 Maria McCambridge 14:49;
64 Valerie Vaughan 14:50; 92 Maureen Harrington 15:30
Teams
1 Ethiopia 32; 2 Kenya 34; 3 Ireland 85; 4 Russia 86;
5 Australia 86; 6 USA 90; 7 Portugal 108; 8 Morocco 133;
9 Romania 158; 10 Tanzania 158; 11 Great Britain 160
(17 teams)

SENIOR WOMEN (7.87km)
Individual

1	Paula Radcliffe	GBR	26:55
2	Deena Drossin	USA	27:04
3	Colleen De Reuck	USA	27:17

GBR
18 Liz Yelling 28:07; 20 Kathy Butler 28:12;
42 Hayley Yelling 29:00; 46 Angela Mudge 29:07;
59 Jenny Brown 29:52
IRL
45 Marie McMahon 29:07; 58 Orla O'Mahoney 29:42;
63 Pauline Curley 30:04; 68 Teresa Duffy 31:02;
71 Geraldine Hendricken 31:40;
74 Margaret Danagher 32:25
Teams: 1 Ethiopia 28; 2 USA 38; 3 Kenya 41;
4 Japan 67; 5 Great Britain 69; 6 Portugal 84;
7 Spain 104; 8 France 121; 9 Italy 125; 10 Belgium 159;
12 Ireland 171
(13 teams)

JUNIOR WOMEN (6.07km)
Individual

1	Viola Kibiwot	KEN	20:13
2	Tirunesh Dibaba	ETH	20:14
3	Vivian Cheruiyot	KEN	20:22

GBR
31 Charlotte Dale 22:01; 45 Henrietta Freeman 22:15;
46 Faye Fullerton 22:16; 53 Jessica Nugent 22:27;
63 Freya Murray 23:01; 68 Lisa Dobriskey 23:10
IRL
72 Fionnuala Britton 23:21; 87 Linda Byrne 24:15;
89 Michelle Gallagher 24:21; 100 Lisa Marie Coohill
25:26; 101 Ava Hutchinson 25:35
Team: 1 Kenya 13; 2 Ethiopia 24; 3 Japan 63;
4 Australia 77; 5 USA 87; 6 Russia 106; 7 France 128;
8 Great Britain 130; 9 South Africa 139; 10 Eritrea 144
16 Ireland 248
(18 teams)

European Cross Country Championships

Medulin, Croatia, Dec 8

SENIOR MEN (9.83km)
Individual
   1 Sergey Lebed   UKR   28:58
   2 Mustapha Essaid   FRA   29:03
   3 Fabian Roncero   ESP   29:03
GBR
19 Allen Graffin 29:40; 21 Jon Brown 29:41;
23 Glynn Tromans 29:45; 30 Spencer Barden 29:53;
63 Ben Noad 31:18; 71 Dominic Bannister 31:44
IRL
8 Alistair Cragg 29:13; 26 Fiachra Lombard 29:50;
32 Seamus Power 29:55; 37 Gareth Turnbull 30:08;
47 Mark Kenneally 30:39
Teams
1 Spain 31; 2 France 43; 3 Portugal 57; 4 Great Britain 93;
5 Ukraine 99; 6 Ireland 103; 7 Belgium 113; 8 Italy 129;
9 Sweden 167; 10 Austria 212
(13 teams)

JUNIOR MEN (6.17km)
Individual
   1 Evgeny Rybakov   RUS   18:16
   2 Anatoly Rybakov   RUS   18:18
   3 Halil Akkas   TUR   18:23
GBR
19 Luke Beevor 19:12; 25 Edward Pritchett 19:19;
30 Mohamed Farah 19:25; 45 Tom Humphries 19:41;
46 J Blackledge 19:41; DNF Tom Sharland
IRL
17 Colm Rooney 19:10;
Teams
1 Russia 37; 2 France 57; 3 Italy 92; 4 Romania 104;
5 Turkey 105; 6 Spain 111; 7 Great Britain 119;
8 Ukraine 143; 9 Belgium 153; 10 Yugoslavia 153
(18 teams)

SENIOR WOMEN (6.17km)
Individual
   1 Helena Javornik   SLO   20:16
   2 Galina Bogomolova   RUS   20:18
   3 Elva Abeylegesse   TUR   20:19
GBR
5 Hayley Tullett 20:25; 14 Hayley Yelling 20:49;
20 Liz Yelling 21:00; 41 Sharon Morris 21:34;
51 Louise Damen 21:53; 56 Diane Henaghan 22:02
IRL
18 Anne Keenan-Buckley 20:53; 29 Breeda Dennehy-Willis 21:14; 39 Valerie Vaughan 21:28; 47 Sinead Delahunty 21:42; 57 Maria McCambridge 22:08; 58 Annette Kealy 22:09
Teams
1 Russia 48; 2 Portugal 54; 3 Great Britain 80;
4 France 82; 5 Spain 116; 6 Ireland 133; 7 Poland 169;
8 Italy 179; 9 Belgium 191; 10 Turkey 196
(12 teams)

JUNIOR WOMEN (3.73km)
Individual
   1 Charlotte Dale   GBR   12:26
   2 Elina Lindgren   FIN   12:27
   3 Galina Egorova   RUS   12:28
GBR
7 Freya Murray 12:40; 8 Danielle Barnes 12:40;
11 Rachael Nathan 12:44; 12 Lisa Dobriskey 12:45;
26 Katrina Wootton 13:00
IRL
49 Fionnuala Britton 13:20
Teams
1 Great Britain 27; 2 Russia 35; 3 Belgium 105;
4 Netherlands 109; 5 Turkey 117; 6 Ukraine 131;
7 Hungary 138; 8 Germany 144; 9 France;
10 Spain 186
(17 teams)

Road Racing/Walking

OSAKA MARATHON
Jan 27
Women
1 Lornah Kiplagat   KEN 2:23:55
2 Harumi Hiroyama   JPN 2:24:34
3 Haruko Okamoto   JPN 2:27:01

TOKYO MARATHON
Feb 9
Men
1 Eric Wainaina   KEN 2:08:43
2 Alberto Juzdado   ESP 2:08:59
3 Julio Rey   ESP 2:11:14

LAKE BIWA MARATHON
Mar 3
Men
1 Ryuji Takei   JPN 2:08:35
2 Mohamed Ouaadi   FRA 2:09:00
3 Fred Kiprop   KEN 2:09:08

NAGOYA MARATHON
Mar 10
Men
1 Mizuko Noguchi   JPN 2:25:35
2 Hiromi Ominami   JPN 2:27:29
3 Megumi Tanaka   JPN 2:28:10

PARIS MARATHON
Apr 7
Men
1 Ben Zwierzchiewski   FRA 2:08:18
2 Pavel Loskutov   EST 2:08:53
3 Migidio Bourifa   ITA 2:09:07
Women
1 Marleen Renders   BEL 2:23:04
2 Rie Matsuoka   JPN 2:24:33
3 Esther Kiplagat   KEN 2:25:32

BOSTON MARATHON
Apr 15
Men
1 Rodgers Rop   KEN 2:09:02
2 Chris Cheboiboch   KEN 2:09:05
3 Fred Kiprop   KEN 2:09:45
Women
1 Catherine Ndereba   KEN 2:23:53
2 Malgorzata Sobanska POL 2:26:42
3 Lyubov Morgunova   RUS 2:27:18

ROTTERDAM MARATHON
Apr 21
Men
1 Simon Biwott   KEN 2:08:39
2 Kenneth Cheruiyot   KEN 2:09:43
3 José-M Martinez   ESP 2:09:55
Women
1 Takemi Ominami   JPN 2:23:43
2 Masako Chiba   JPN 2:25:11
3 Junko Akagi   JPN 2:37:36

NEW YORK MINI MARATHON
June 8 (10km)
Women
1 Asmae Leghzaoui   MAR 30:29
2 Lornah Kiplagat   KEN 30:44
3 Sonia O'Sullivan   IRL 31:22
World Best by Leghzaoui

GREAT SOUTH RUN
Portsmouth, Sep 8 (10 Miles)
Men
1 Kasamili   KEN 47:27
Women
1 Sonia O'Sullivan   IRL 51:00
World Best by O'Sullivan

DAM TO DAM
Amsterdam-Zaandam, Sep 22
(10 Miles)
Women
1 Lornah Kiplagat   KEN 50:54
World Best by Kiplagat

EUROPEAN 100KM
CHAMPIONSHIPS
Winschoten, Netherlands
Sep 14
Men
1 Pascal Fetizon   FRA 6:34:16
2 Denis Zhalybin   RUS 6:36:19
3 Oleg Karitonov   RUS 6:41:16
Women
1 Elvira Kolpakova   RUS 7:24:52
2 Monica Casiraghi   ITA 7:33:14
3 Danielle Sanderson   GBR 7:47:29

BERLIN MARATHON
Sept 29
Men
1 Raymond Kipkoech   KEN 2:06:47
2 Simon Biwott   KEN 2:06:49
3 Vincent Kipsos   KEN 2:06:52
Women
1 Naoko Takahashi   JPN 2:21:49
2 Adriana Fernandez   MEX 2:24:11
3 Hellen Kimutai   KEN 2:26:10

GREAT NORTH RUN
Oct 6 (Half Marathon)
Men
1 Paul Kosgei   KEN 59:58
2 John Yuda   TAN 60:02
3 Rodgers Rop   KEN 61:40
Women
1 Sonia O'Sullivan   IRL 67:19
2 Susie Power   AUS 67:56
3 Joyce Chepchumba   KEN 68:34

CHICAGO MARATHON
Oct 13
Men
1 Khalid Khannouchi   USA 2:05:56
2 Daniel Njenga   KEN 2:06:16
3 Toshinari Takaoka   JPN 2:06:16
Women
1 Paula Radcliffe   GBR 2:17:18
2 Catherine Ndereba   KEN 2:19:26
3 Yoko Shibui   JPN 2:21:22
World Record by Radcliffe

AMSTERDAM MARATHON
Oct 20
Men
1 B Kimutai Kosgei   KEN 2:07:26
1 Simon Bor   KEN 2:07:55
3 Stephan Cheptot   KEN 2:07:59
Women
1 Gete Wami   ETH 2:22:10
2 Constantina Dita   ROM 2:23:52
3 Stine Larsen   NOR 2:27:06

BEIJING MARATHON
Oct 20
Men
1 Li Zhuhong   CHN 2:13:09
Women
1 Wei Yanan   CHN 2:20:23

NEW YORK MARATHON
Nov 3
Men
1 Rodgers Rop   KEN 2:08:07
2 Chris Cheboiboch   KEN 2:08:17
3 Laban Kipkemboi   KEN 2:08:39
Women
1 Joyce Chepchumba   KEN 2:25:56
2 Lyubov Denisova   RUS 2:26:17
3 Olivera Jevtic   YUG 2:26:44

TOKYO MARATHON
Nov 17
Women
1 Banuelia Mrashani   TAN 2:24:59
2 Rie Matsuoka   JPN 2:25:02
3 Timofeyeva   RUS 2:26:45

FUKUOKA MARATHON
Dec 1
Men
1 Gezehegne Abera   ETH 2:09:13
2 Tsuyoshi Ogata   JPN 2:09:15
3 Eric Wainaina   KEN 2:10:08

Flora London Marathon

The London Marathon will never know another day like this one; Khalid Khannouchi broke the world record and yet only had a bit part in the day's proceedings. The star of the show was an athlete who had trouble winning races only a year or two before. Paula Radcliffe ran her first marathon in a manner that suggested that she never once considered defeat; though one could argue that until 2002 she ran her track races in a similar fashion and invariably she was defeated. Her progress in her first marathon was inexorable, with mile times getting faster rather than slower. Her second half race split was 67:51, in other words she was a full three minutes quicker over the second half of the race than the first. The mile splits for the Tower of London, aided by a day when the wind hardly drew its breath, caused universal astonishment. Radcliffe didn't break the world record, but she did break every other record in the book, and the world record would only be six months away anyway. Radcliffe's 2:18:56 in London was a British record by over six minutes, a European record by over two minutes, was over four minutes faster than the marathon debut record, and almost three minutes faster than the womens-only world marathon record. The next three runners were all under 2:23, a world-class marathon time. No one will remember Svetlana Zakharova, Lyudmila Petrova or Reiko Tosa, even though each ran faster than any other woman in London except Radcliffe and Ingrid Kristiansen, in 1985. Khannouchi achieved more than Radcliffe, but was inevitably recognised less. The one-time Moroccan, now an American, broke his own world record set in Chicago in 1999 by four seconds. Paul Tergat was second again, but much faster than a year earlier. Indeed, only one man has ever run a marathon faster than Tergat and that man is Khannouchi. Haile Gebrselassie ran the fastest-ever marathon debut, finishing third in 2:06:35, but by his inimitable standards, and on this inimitable day, it was almost a run of the mill achievement.

Blackheath-The Mall
Apr 14

	Men				Women		
1	Khalid Khannouchi	USA	2:05:38	1	Paula Radcliffe	GBR	2:18:56
2	Paul Tergat	KEN	2:05:48	2	Svetlana Zakharova	RUS	2:22:31
3	Haile Gebrselassie	ETH	2:06:35	3	Lyudmila Petrova	RUS	2:22:33
4	Abdelkader El Mouaziz	MAR	2:06:52	4	Reiko Tosa	JPN	2:22:46
5	Ian Syster	RSA	2:07:06	5	Susan Chepkemei	KEN	2:23:19
6	Stefano Baldini	ITA	2:07:29	6	Joyce Chepchumba	KEN	2:26:53
7	Antonio Pinto	POR	2:09:10	7	Silvia Skvortsova	RUS	2:27:07
8	Mark Steinle	GBR	2:09:17	8	Zinaida Semyonova	RUS	2:27:45
9	Tesfaye Jifar	ETH	2:09:50	9	Derartu Tulu	ETH	2:28:37
10	Mohammed El Hattab	MAR	2:11:50	10	Shitaye Gemechu	ETH	2:28:58

World Half Marathon
Brussels, May 5
MEN
Individual

1	Paul Kosgei	KEN	1:00:39
2	Jaouad Gharib	MAR	1:00:42
3	John Yuda	TAN	1:00:57

Teams
1 Kenya 3:04:42; 2 Japan 3:07:12; 3 Ethiopia 3:07:25

WOMEN
Individual

1	Berhane Adere	ETH	1:09:06
2	Susan Chepkemei	KEN	1:09:13
3	Jelena Prokopcuka	LAT	1:09:15
14	Sonia O'Sullivan	IRL	1:10:04
47	Amanda Wright-Allen	GBR	1:14:53

Teams
1 Kenya 3:28:22; 2 Russia 3:30:05; 3 Ethiopia 3:30:58

World Race Walking Cup
Turin, Oct 12-13

Men
20km
Individual

1	Jefferson Perez	ECU	1:21:26
2	Vladimir Andreyev	RUS	1:21:50
3	Alejandro Lopez	MEX	1:22:01

Teams
1 Russia 24; 2 Belarus 28; 3 Italy 34;
4 Ecuador 61; 5 China 63; 6 Spain 82;
7 Portugal 82; 8 Slovakia 91; 9 Czech Rep 99;
10 Germany 127

50km
Individual

1	Aleksey Voyevodin	RUS	3:40:59
2	German Skurygin	RUS	3:42:08
3	Tomasz Lipiec	POL	3:45:37

Teams
1 Russia 7; 2 France 59; 3 China 78;
4 Australia 81; 5 Italy 85; 6 Sweden 93;
7 Latvia 101; 8 Japan 101; 9 Portugal 118;
10 Belarus 125

Women
20km

1	Erica Alfridi	ITA	1:28:55
2	Olimpiada Ivanova	RUS	1:28:57
3	Natalya Fedoskina	RUS	1:28:59

Teams
1 Russia 9; 2 Italy 26; 4 Romania 42; 4 Belarus 44;
5 Mexico 57; 6 Spain 64; 7 Portugal 73; 8 China 86;
9 Germany 111; 10 Ukraine 134

Badminton

The European badminton players look forward to their continental championships in much the same way as the cross country runners do. The runners sigh with deep-seated relief that they do not have to face the Africans, while the badminton players sleep easier in the knowledge that the Asians, by and large, will be absent. Well, that's the theory anyway. Unfortunately, as Africans have been recruited for running by the European nations, so have the Asians been signed up for badminton. We would sit on the high moral ground here, if there is one, except that Wales now has Edy Irwansyan, once Indonesian, is now in their team and England have not been idle, courting Eng Hian and Flandi Limpele, also Indonesian, who play in shirts with England on their backs, even though they are still ineligible for major championships.

Anyway, the other problem with the European badminton scene is the Danes. We don't want to get too personal about this - and since Denmark won the 1992 European Football Championships, they haven't had much more to celebrate than an Olympic handball title - but their presence came close to spoiling the European event in Malmo for anyone who wasn't Danish.

Peter Rasmussen won the men's singles, defeating his compatriot Kenneth Jonasssen in the final; Daniel Eriksen and Martin Lungaard Hansen won the men's doubles; Jane Bramsen and Ann-Lou Jorgensen took the women's doubles; and Jens Eriksen and Mette Schjoldager won the mixed doubles. The sweep of titles was only resisted in the women's singles where Mia Audina, of the Netherlands by way of Indonesia, claimed the title.

The best domestic performance came, predictably, from Nathan Robertson and Gail Emms who reached the final of the mixed doubles. Robertson and Emms would go on to claim the Malaysian Open title in July, and reach the final in Singapore a month later. Unfortunately, the most important event of their year fell between those two competitions and wasn't such an edifying experience *(See Commonwealth Games)*.

In the team event at Malmo, England eased through their group matches to meet Denmark in the final, where they were defeated 3-1. As England had also encountered the Danish team in the Uber Cup semi-final in February (yes, they lost there too), they must have been feeling heartily sick of everything Danish by that stage.

Finally, we note that Park Joo-Bong not only coached the Malaysian men to victory in the Thomas Cup, but the Korean was (as Americans would say) inducted into Badminton's Hall of Fame. Park, the former Olympic doubles champion, was once coach to the English team a few years back, but we never did persuade him to play for us.

European Championships

Baltiska Hallen, Malmo, Sweden, Apr 13-20

Men's Singles

1st round
Ville Kinnunen FIN bt Graham Simpson SCO 7/0 7/2 7/2
Mark Constable ENG bt Vedran Ciganovic CRO 7/1 7/1 7/1
Richard Vaughan WAL bt Nicolai Nicolaenko RUS 7/1 8/6 7/1
Aamir Ghaffar ENG bt Jürgen Koch AUT 7/5 7/3 7/2
Niels Christian Kaldau DEN bt Graeme Smith SCO 7/2 7/4 7/1
Jan Fröhlich CZE bt Ciaran Darcy IRL 1/7 7/6 6/8 7/1 7/2
Peter Rasmussen DEN bt Colin Haughton ENG 7/3 7/3 7/2
Edy Irwansyah WAL bt Arturo Ruiz ESP 7/3 7/1 7/0
Christian Unternaehrer SUI bt Alistair Casey SCO 5/7 7/1
3/7 7/4 7/3
Andrew South ENG bt Ruud Kuijten BEL 7/5 2/7 5/7 7/1 7/5
2nd Round
Mark Constable bt Hayik Misakyan ARM 7/0 7/1 7/3
Richard Vaughan bt Andrei Malioutin BLR 7/3 7/0 7/1
Rasmus Wengberg SWE bt A Ghaffar 7/3 7/8 4/7 7/1 7/2
Edy Irwansyah bt Daniel Eriksson SWE 7/2 3/7 7/5 7/3
Anders Boesen DEN bt Andrew South 7/1 7/1 7/5
3rd Round
Björn Joppien GER bt Mark Constable 7/0 7/5 7/5
Richard Vaughan bt Antti Viitikko FIN 1/7 7/4 7/3 7/2
Edy Irwansyah bt Vladislav Druzchenko UKR 7/3 7/1 7/2
Quarter-finals
Rasmus Wengberg bt Richard Vaughan 7/5 1/7 8/6 3/7 7/0
Semi-finals
Peter Rasmussen bt Anders Boesen 5/7 7/5 5/7 7/4 7/5
Kenneth Jonassen DEN bt Rasmus Wengberg 7/1 8/7 7/4
Final
Peter Rasmussen bt Kenneth Jonassen 0/7 7/5 3/7 7/5 7/2

Women's Singles

1st round
Camilla Martin DEN bt Kate Ridler WAL w/o
Susan Hughes SCO bt Kati Tolmoff EST 7/1 7/3 5/7 2/7 7/2
Katja Wengberg SWE bt Liz Cann ENG 7/2 1/7 8/6 4/7 7/5
Julia Mann ENG bt Maria Väisänen FIN 7/4 7/0 7/0
Tracey Hallam ENG bt Bing Huang IRL 7/2 7/1 7/2
Fiona Sneddon SCO bt Simone Prutsch AUT 7/1 3/7 2/7
7/3 7/5
Kelly Morgan WAL bt Natalia Golovkina UKR 7/2 7/0 7/1
Juliane Schenk GER bt Kathryn Graham SCO 7/0 7/3 7/3
Rebecca Pantanay ENG bt Natalia Esipenko UKR 7/1 6/8
7/0 7/0
2nd Round
Camilla Martin bt Susan Hughes 7/0 7/2 7/3
Julia Mann bt Joanna Szleszynska POL 7/0 7/2 7/4
Tracey Hallam bt Nadezdha Kostioutchik BLR 8/6 7/2 7/3
Kelly Morgan bt Fiona Sneddon 7/0 7/0 7/3
Mia Audina NED bt Rebecca Pantanay 7/3 7/0 7/0
3rd Round
Julia Mann bt Elodie Eymard FRA 7/4 6/8 7/4 5/7 8/6
Brenda Beenhakker NED bt Tracey Hallam 7/0 7/3 8/6
Kelly Morgan bt Petra Overzier GER 7/3 7/4 7/0
Quarter-finals
Jie Yao NED bt Julia Mann 7/2 7/1 7/1
Brenda Beenhakker bt Kelly Morgan 7/2 6/8 4/7 7/2 7/1
Semi-finals
Jie Yao bt Camilla Martin 0/7 2/7 7/0 7/3 7/1
Mia Audina bt Brenda Beenhakker 7/1 8/6 7/1
Final
Jie Yao bt Mia Audina 8/6 7/3 7/1

Men's Doubles

1st Round
All British/Irish entries received byes
2nd Round
Clark/N Robertson ENG bt Herout/Gaspar CZE
7/2 7/1 7/4
Hughes/Lewis WAL bt Ruiz/Escartin ESP
6/8 7/5 2/7 7/3 7/4
Hopp/Tesche bt Gatt/C Robertson SCO 7/3 7/1 7/5
Eriksen/Lundgaard Hansen DEN bt Hogg/Smith SCO
7/1 7/2 7/4
Archer/Hurrell ENG bt Crespo/Llopis ESP
0/7 8/6 7/4 4/7 7/4
3rd Round
Clark/Robertson bt Hughes/Lewis 7/2 7/2 7/3
Logosz/Mateusiak POL bt Archer/Hurrell
7/2 4/7 7/5 5/7 7/3
Quarter-finals
Clark/Robertson bt Nicolaenko/Nicolaenko RUS
7/8 7/2 7/2 7/4
Semi-finals
Clark/Robertson bt Paaske/Rasmussen DEN 7/3 1/7 7/1
8/6
Eriksen/Lundgaard bt Logosz/Mateusiak 7/1 8/6 7/1
Final
Eriksen/Lundgaard bt Clark/Robertson
7/4 1/7 7/3 2/7 7/3

Women's Doubles

1st Round
Emms/Goode ENG bt Engauer/Fastenbauer AUT
7/1 7/0 7/1
2nd Round
Watt/Wemyss SCO bt Rasmussen/Ruohonen FIN
7/2 7/1 7/4
Karosaite/Milikuskaite LTU bt Ashworth/Ridler WAL w/o
Augustyn/Kostioutchik POL/BLR bt Gallup/Muggeridge
WAL 7/4 7/2 4/7 7/5
Miles Sankey ENG bt Martinez/Tavero ESP
7/1 7/0 7/0
McEwan/Middlemiss SCO bt Akchundova/Mekchtiyeva
AZE w/o
Bramsen/Jorgensen DEN bt Huang/Ashworth IRL/WAL
7/2 7/1 7/0
3rd Round
Watt/Weymss bt Karosaite/Milikuskaite 7/0 7/3 7/0
Emms/Goode bt Bergblom/Persson 7/1 8/6 7/3
Miles/Sankey bt Eymard/Vattier FRA 7/5 7/0 7/5
McEwan/Middlemiss bt Weckström/Weckström FIN
7/5 7/1 7/2
Quarter-finals
Grether/Pitro GER bt Watt/Weymss 2/7 8/6 7/4 7/5
Harder/Schjoldager DEN bt Emms/Goode 7/4 7/2 7/0
Sankey/Miles bt Ananina/Russkikh RUS 8/7 7/5 6/8 7/3
Semi-finals
Harder/Schjoldager bt Grether/Pitro 7/1 3/7 7/4 2/7 7/1
Bramsen/Jorgensen bt Sankey/Miles 2/7 7/4 7/0 7/0
Final
Bramsen/Jorgensen bt Harder/Schjoldager 7/4 7/1 7/5

Mixed Doubles

1st Round
Blair/Munt ENG bt Nikolaenko/Rusljakova RUS
3/7 7/5 6/8 7/1 8/6
Lewis/Rasmussen WAL/FIN bt Tolstopyatov/Griga UKR w/o
Smith/Middlemiss SCO bt Navickas/Karosaite LTU
7/0 7/0 7/3
Archer/Goode bt Mamedaliev/Akhundova AZE w/o
Crespo/Marco ESP bt C Robertson/Weymss SCO
7/2 7/2 7/0
Hogg/McEwan SCO bt Cassel/Mette GER 7/4 7/5 8/6
Clark/Sankey ENG bt Bircher/Baumeyer SUI 7/1 7/2 7/4
Pohar/Pohar SLO bt Hughes/Ashworth WAL
7/5 7/3 3/7 1/7 7/1
2nd Round
Dobrev/Nedeltcheva BUL bt Blair/Munt 7/4 7/4 7/2
Siegemund/Pitro GER bt Lewis/Rasmussen 7/1 7/0 7/5
Smith/Middlemiss bt Van Dahn/Alfredsson LTU/SWE
1/7 6/8 7/3 7/4 8/7
Bruil/Jonathans NED bt Archer/Goode 7/5 8/6 1/7 7/5
Hogg/McEwan bt Misakyan/Nazaryan ARM 7/0 7/0 7/2
Robertson/Emms bt Gaspar/Gasparova CZE 7/0 7/0 7/1
Clark/Sankey bt Silva/Lamy POR 7/3 7/2 7/2
3rd Round
Siegemund/Pitro bt Smith/Middlemiss 7/3 7/4 7/0
Robertson/Emms bt Hogg/McEwan 7/2 7/0 7/4
Bergström/Karlsson bt Clark/Sankey 7/1 7/5 7/4
Quarter-finals
Robertson/Emms bt Lamp/Joergensen DEN 7/4 2/7 8/6 7/1
Semi-finals
Eriksen/Schjoldager DEN bt Bruil/Jonathan NED
6/8 7/3 2/7 7/3 7/2
Robertson/Emms bt Sogaard/Olsen DEN 6/8 7/2 7/1 7/5
Final
Eriksen/Schjoldager bt Robertson/Emms 7/5 7/3 7/1

Team

Group A
Denmark bt Sweden 5-0; Denmark bt Germany 5-0;
Denmark bt Finland 5-0; Germany bt Sweden 3-2;
Sweden bt Finland 5-0; Germany bt Finland 5-0

Group A Table	P	W	L	Games	Pts
Denmark	3	3	0	45-6	6
Germany	3	2	1	27-25	4
Sweden	3	1	2	25-30	2
Finland	3	0	3	7-43	0

Group B
England bt Netherlands 3-2; England bt Ukraine 4-1;
England bt Russia 3-2; Netherlands bt Ukraine 4-1;
Netherlands bt Russia 5-0; Ukraine bt Russia 3-2

Group B Table	P	W	L	Games	Pts
England	3	3	0	36-22	6
Netherlands	3	2	1	36-18	4
Ukraine	3	1	2	15-34	2
Russia	3	0	3	23-36	0

Group C
Poland bt Bulgaria 3-2; Poland bt Scotland 3-2;
Poland bt Czech Rep 4-1; Bulgaria bt Scotland 5-0;
Bulgaria bt Czech Rep 4-1; Scotland bt Czech Rep 4-1

Group C Table	P	W	L	Games	Pts
Poland	3	3	0	32-22	6
Bulgaria	3	2	1	37-16	4
Scotland	3	1	2	24-30	2
Czech Rep	3	0	3	13-38	0

Group D
Wales bt France 4-1; Wales bt Spain 4-1;
Wales bt Portugal 4-1; Spain bt France 3-2;
Spain bt Portugal 4-1; France bt Portugal 5-0

Group C Table	P	W	L	Games	Pts
Wales	3	3	0	38-15	6
Spain	3	2	1	27-30	4
France	3	1	2	29-29	2
Portugal	3	0	3	20-40	0

CLASSIFICATION MATCHES
15/16th Place Play-off
Portugal bt Czech Republic 4-1
13/14th Place Play-off
Scotland bt France 3-0
11/12th Place Play-off
Bulgaria bt Spain 3-2
9/10th Place Play-off
Poland bt Wales 3-1
7/8th Place Play-off
Russia bt Finland 4-0
5/6th Place Play-off
Sweden bt Ukraine 4-1
3rd/4th Place Play-off
Netherlands bt Germany 3-1
Final
Denmark bt England 3-1

Final Standings: 1 Denmark; 2 England; 3 Netherlands;
4 Germany; 5 Sweden; 6 Ukraine; 7 Russia; 8 Finland;
9 Poland; 10 Wales; 11 Bulgaria; 12 Spain; 13 Scotland;
14 France; 15 Portugal; 16 Czech Rep

IBF WORLD RANKINGS
As at August 29, 2002

Men's Singles

1	Wong Choong Hann	MAS	250.01
2	Xia Xuanze	CHN	249.00
3	Bao Chunlai	CHN	237.75
4	Lee Hyun-Il	KOR	234.90
5	Lin Dan	CHN	220.43
6	Shon Seung-Mo	KOR	216.15
7	Kenneth Jonassen	DEN	210.43
8	Ong Ewe Hock	MAS	203.18
9	James Chua	MAS	198.92
10	Hong Chen	CHN	195.08
23	Richard Vaughan	WAL	145.20
40	Edy Irwansyah	WAL	113.07
42	Colin Haughton	ENG	108.35

Women's Singles

1	Camilla Martin	DEN	356.19
2	Zhou Mi	CHN	294.49
3	Wang Chen	HKG	267.87
4	Mla Audina	NED	249.88
5	Zhang Ning	CHN	245.72
6	Going Ruina	CHN	243.19
7	Konako Yonekura	JPN	239.18
8	Kim Kyeung-Ran	KOR	238.63
9	Xie Xingfang	CHN	230.46
10	Yao Jie	NED	218.44
15	Kelly Morgan	WAL	163.76
21	Tracey Hallam	ENG	141.75
22	Julie Mann	ENG	138.74
47	Susan Hughes	SCO	93.31

Men's Doubles

1	Ha/Kim	KOR	314.78
2	Eriksen/Lungaard Hansen	DEN	295.80
3	Chew/Chan	MAS	242.42
6	Hian/Limpele	ENG	221.03
8	N Robertson/Clark	ENG	189.02

Women's Doubles

1	Huang/Yang	CHN	289.73
2	Ra/Lee	KOR	270.38
3	Zhang/Wei	CHN	260.63
11	Sankey/Miles	ENG	173.89
17	Watt/Wemyss	ENG	146.51
19	Muggeridge/Gallup	WAL	129.99
24	Goode/Emms	ENG	115.16

Mixed Doubles

1	Kim/Ra	KOR	298.69
2	N Robertson/Emms	ENG	265.07
3	Sogaard/Olsen	DEN	238.57
15	Archer/Goode	ENG	122.66
17	Hogg/McEwan	SCO	116.44
20	Blair/Munt	ENG	105.42

Thomas & Uber Cup Finals
Guangzhou, May 9-19
The Thomas Cup is a men's team competition; the Uber Cup is the women's equivalent.

Thomas Cup
Semi-finals
Malaysia bt China 3-1
Indonesia bt Denmark 3-0
Final
Indonesia bt Malaysia 3-2

Uber Cup
Semi-finals
China bt Hong Kong 3-0
Korea bt Netherlands 3-2
Final
China bt Korea 3-1

Yonex All England Open
Birmingham, Mar 5-10
Men's Singles
Chen Hong CHN bt B Santoso INA 7/4 7/5 7/1
Women's Singles
Camilla Martin DEN bt Gong Zhichao CHN 7/5 8/6 7/3
Men's Doubles
Ha/Kim KOR bt Hian/Limpele ENG* 7/2 7/2 1/7 7/3 15-13 7-15 15-7
Women's Doubles
Gao/Huang CHN bt Wei/Zhang CHN 7/3 7/5 8/7
Mixed Doubles
Kim/Ra INA bt Eriksen/Schjoldager DEN 7/3 7/3 7/0
*Still technically Indonesian players

Swiss Open
Basel, Mar 12-17
Men's Singles
Marleve Mainaky INA bt James Chua MAS
Women's Singles
Mia Audina NED bt Zeng Yaqiong CHN
Men's Doubles
Lee/Yoo KOR bt Eriksen/Lundgaard DEN
Women's Doubles
Ra/Lee KOR bt Jonathans/Emms NED/ENG
Mixed Doubles
Kim/Ra KOR bt J Rasmussen/Bramsen DEN

Korean Open
Yeosu City, Mar 26-31
Men's Singles
Lin Dan CHN bt Shon Sheung Mo KOR 1/7 7/3 7/3 7/5
Women's Singles
Zhang Ning CHN bt Gong Rui Na CHN 7/0 5/7 7/1 7/2
Men's Doubles
Ha/Kim KOR bt Lee/Yoo KOR 8/7 4/7 8/7
Women's Doubles
Gao/Huang CHN bt Chen/Jiang CHN 7/2 7/3 5/7 7/3
Mixed Doubles
Kim/Ra KOR bt Sogaard/Olsen DEN 7/1 7/3 7/5

Yonex Open Japan
Tokyo, April 2-7
Men's Singles
Lee Hyun Il KOR bt Dai Yun CHN 7/1 7/0 7/1
Women's Singles
Zhou Mi CHN bt Gong Ruina CHN 7/1 7/0 7/1
Men's Doubles
Chew/Chan MAS bt Choong/Lee MAS w/o
Women's Doubles
Ra/Lee KOR bt Gao/Huang CHN 7/5 1/7 7/2 6/8 7/1
Mixed Doubles
Kim/Ra KOR bt Widianto/Vita INA 7/3 7/2 7/2

Proton-Eon Malaysian Open
Penang, June 25-30
Men's Singles
James Chua MAS bt Ong Ewe Hock MAS 15/10 15/6
Women's Singles
Hu Ting CHN bt Camilla Martin DEN 11/8 11/6
Men's Doubles
Liu/Chen CHN bt Choong/Chan MAS 17/14 15/3
Women's Doubles
Huang/Yang bt CHN bt Zhang/Zhao CHN 11/5 11/5
Mixed Doubles
N Robertson/Emms ENG bt Zhang/Wang CHN 11/9 11/4

Yonex-Sunrise Singapore Open
Aug 19-25
Men's Singles
Chen Hong CHN bt Ronald Susilo SIN 15/4 15/1
Women's Singles
Zhou Mi CHN bt Zhang Ing CHN 11/6 11/3
Men's Doubles
Hian/Limpele ENG* bt Ha/Kim KOR 15/8 11/15 17/14
Women's Doubles
Huang/Yang CHN bt Hwang/Lee KOR 11/1 11/8
Mixed Doubles
Kim/Ra KOR bt Robertson/Emms ENG 11/2 13/10

Sanyo Indonesian Open
Jakarta, Aug 26-Sep 1
Men's Singles
Taufik Hidyat INA bt Chen Hong CHN 15/12 15/12
Women's Singles
Gong Ruina CHN bt Zhang Ning CHN 11/6 11/7
Men's Doubles
Lee/Yoo KOR bt Hian/Limpele ENG* 15/10 15/11
Women's Doubles
Gao/Huang CHN bt Ekmongkolpaisarn/Thungthongkam THA 11/4 11/5
Mixed Doubles
Suprianto/Timur INA bt Widianto/Vita INA 11/7 11/3

Realkredit Danish Open
Farum, Oct 29-Nov 3
Men's Singles
Chen Hong CHN bt Kenneth Jonassen DEN
15/9 9/15 15/6
Women's Singles
Camilla Martin DEN bt Gong Ruina CHN 11/5 3/11 11/7
Men's Doubles
Ha/Kim KOR bt Chan/Chew MAS 15/4 15/8
Women's Doubles
Wei/Zhao CHN bt Audina/Jonathans NED 11/3 6/11 11/9
Mixed Doubles
Kim/Hwang KOR bt Widianto/Vita INA 11/9 13/10

Baseball

It's been almost 50 years since the Giants loaded the furniture van and left New York for San Francisco. The move came just four years after the Giants had won the 1954 World Series. The contest against the Anaheim Angels was their third World Series since, and they lost again. Back in the New York, you can be sure, there were a few old-stagers saying it was just desserts.

Up until the World Series, it had not proved the most edifying of seasons. The players, having shorter memories than amoebas, came close to a salary strike. The fans, having longer memories, would almost certainly have voted with their feet had the close-down happened, as they did when the players came back from the 1994 strike.

There were numerous tales of impending financial disasters, and one mid-season estimate suggested that the collective debt of the Major League clubs amounted to $3.5 billion. According to the owners, the cause of the debt was the high salaries of the players. But the players, to be fair, needed their fat wage packets (average annual pay $2.3m) to pay for the drugs, which helped to muscle them up so they could score the regular home runs, which the fans wanted so much to see. It was Catch 22 really. Would you believe it too, the players actively argued against drug-testing because it infringed their rights.

Which brings us neatly to Barry Bonds, who has never touched a steroid in his life (he says), despite the chants of opposing supporters throughout the season. Bonds, as the holder of the most magical number of all - the 73 home runs hit in 2001 - was hoping that this World Series would be the icing on an already illustrious career.

The Angels did not appear to be the most formidable of opponents. They had never made a World Series, were a team without stars and Disney had put the franchise up for sale because the club wasn't making enough money. Furthermore, they were cursed. In 1966, the club had built a new stadium at Anaheim on an old native American burial ground, which had damned them.

Bonds did all he could to win, but the Angels wouldn't give him the ball. Nine times during the series, they walked him, and though Bonds hit four homers, and his team led 3-2 with two to play, the Giants still lost the Series.

"Somewhere, Gene Autry is smiling right now"

Bud Selig, baseball commissioner. It was Autry, the singing cowboy, who established the Angels in 1961, and later sold the club to the Disney Corporation. Autry died in 1998, aged 91.

2002 World Series
San Francisco Giants v Anaheim Angels

GAME 1
Oct 19

	1	2	3	4	5	6	7	8	9	R	H	E
Giants*	0	2	0	0	0	2	0	0	0	4	6	0
Angels	0	1	0	0	0	2	0	0	0	3	9	0

GAME 2
Oct 20

	1	2	3	4	5	6	7	8	9	R	H	E
Angels	5	2	0	0	1	1	0	2	X	11	16	1
Giants	0	4	1	0	4	0	0	0	1	10	12	1

GAME 3
Oct 22

	1	2	3	4	5	6	7	8	9	R	H	E
Angels	0	0	4	4	0	1	0	1	0	10	16	0
Giants	1	0	0	0	3	0	0	0	0	4	6	2

GAME 4
Oct 23

	1	2	3	4	5	6	7	8	9	R	H	E
Giant	0	0	0	0	3	0	0	1	X	4	12	1
Angels	0	1	2	0	0	0	0	0	0	3	10	1

GAME 5
Oct 24

	1	2	3	4	5	6	7	8	9	R	H	E
Giants	3	3	0	0	0	2	4	4	X	16	16	0
Angels	0	0	0	0	3	1	0	0	0	4	10	2

GAME 6
Oct 26

	1	2	3	4	5	6	7	8	9	R	H	E
Angels	0	0	0	0	0	0	3	3	X	6	10	1
Giants	0	0	0	0	3	1	1	0	0	5	8	1

GAME 7
Oct 27

	1	2	3	4	5	6	7	8	9	R	H	E
Angels	0	1	3	0	0	0	0	X		4	5	0
Giants	0	1	0	0	0	0	0	0	0	1	6	0

Anaheim Angels won the series 4-3

* home team shown first

Division Series

American League
Oakland Athletics v Minnesota Twins
Athletics 5 Twins 7; Athletics 9 Twins 1; Twins 3
Athletics 2; Twins 11 Athletics 6; Twins 5 Athletics 4
Twins won series 3-2

Anaheim Angels v New York Yankees
Angels 5 Yankees 8; Yankees 6 Angels 8;
Yankees 6 Angels 9; Yankees 5 Angels 9
Angels won series 3-1

National League
Atlanta Braves v San Francisco Giants
Braves 5 Giants 8; Giants 3 Braves 7; Giants 2
Braves 10; Braves 3 Giants 8; Braves 1 Giants 3
Giants won series 3-2

Arizona Diamondbacks v St Louis Cardinals
Diamondbacks 2 Cardinals 12; Diamondbacks 1
Cardinals 2; Diamondbacks 3 Cardinals 6
Cardinals won series 3-0

Championship Series

American League
MINNESOTA TWINS V ANAHEIM ANGELS

Minnesota Twins 2	Anaheim Angels 1
Minnesota Twins 3	Anaheim Angles 6
Anaheim Angels 2	Minnesota Twins 1
Anaheim Angels 7	Minnesota Twins 1
Anaheim Angels 13	Minnesota Twins 5

Angels won series 4-1

National League
ST LOUIS CARDINALS V SAN FRANCISCO GIANTS

St Louis Cardinals 6	San Francisco Giants 9
St Louis Cardinals 1	San Francisco Giants 4
San Francisco Giants 4	St Louis Cardinals 5
San Francisco Giants 4	St Louis Cardinals 3
San Francisco Giants 2	St Louis Cardinals 1

Giants won series 4-1

American League standings

EAST	Won	Lost	PCT	GB	Home	Road	East	Central	West	Nat Lge
New York Yankees	103	58	.640	-	52-28	51-30	46-29	29-7	17-15	11-7
Boston Red Sox	93	69	.574	10.5	42-39	51-30	51-25	19-17	18-14	5-13
Toronto Blue Jays	78	84	.481	25.5	42-39	36-45	41-35	16-16	12-24	9-9
Baltimore Orioles	67	95	.414	36.5	34-47	33-48	26-50	18-14	14-22	9-9
Tampa Bay Devil Rays	55	106	.342	48.0	30-51	25-55	25-50	13-19	10-26	7-11

CENTRAL	Won	Lost	PCT	GB	Home	Road	East	Central	West	Nat Lge
Minnesota Twins	94	67	.584	-	54-27	40-40	15-17	50-25	19-17	10-8
Chicago White Sox	81	81	.500	13.5	47-34	34-47	18-14	40-36	15-21	8-10
Cleveland Indians	74	88	.457	20.5	39-42	35-46	19-17	37-39	12-20	6-12
Kansas City Royals	62	100	.383	32.5	37-44	25-56	10-22	33-43	14-22	5-13
Detroit Tigers	55	106	.342	39.0	33-47	22-59	11-25	29-46	9-23	6-12

WEST	Won	Lost	PCT	GB	Home	Road	East	Central	West	Nat Lge
Oakland Athletics	103	59	.636	-	54-27	49-32	23-22	32-9	32-26	16-2
Anaheim Angels[†]	99	63	.611	4.0	54-27	45-36	28-13	30-15	30-28	11-7
Seattle Mariners	93	69	.574	10.0	48-33	45-36	25-20	23-18	34-24	11-7
Texas Rangers	72	90	.444	31.0	42-39	30-51	25-16	18-27	20-38	9-9

National League standings

EAST	Won	Lost	PCT	GB	Home	Road	East	Central	West	Nat Lge
Atlanta Braves	101	59	.631	-	52-28	49-31	47-28	24-12	15-16	15-3
Philadelphia Phillies	83	79	.512	19.0	49-32	34-47	37-39	21-15	13-19	12-6
New York Mets	80	81	.497	21.5	40-40	40-41	34-41	22-14	14-18	10-8
Florida Marlins	79	83	.488	23.0	46-35	33-48	36-40	18-18	15-17	10-8
Montreal Expos	75	86	.466	26.5	38-43	37-43	35-41	20-15	10-22	10-8

CENTRAL	Won	Lost	PCT	GB	Home	Road	East	Central	West	Nat Lge
St Louis Cardinals	97	65	.599	-	52-29	45-36	11-19	57-33	21-9	8-4
Houston Astros	84	78	.519	13.0	47-34	37-44	16-14	49-41	14-16	5-7
Cincinnati Reds	78	84	.481	19.0	38-43	40-41	12-18	50-40	14-16	2-10
Pittsburgh Pirates	72	89	.447	24.5	38-42	34-47	16-13	43-47	10-20	3-9
Chicago Cubs	67	95	.414	30.0	36-45	31-50	12-18	36-54	13-17	6-6
Milwaukee Brewers	56	106	.346	41.0	31-50	25-56	7-23	35-55	12-18	2-10

WEST	Won	Lost	PCT	GB	Home	Road	East	Central	West	Nat Lge
Arizona Diamondbacks	98	64	.605	-	55-26	43-38	21-11	23-13	43-33	11-7
San Francisco Giants[†]	95	66	.590	2.5	50-31	45-35	17-14	23-13	47-29	8-10
Los Angeles Dodgers	92	70	.568	6.0	46-35	46-35	20-12	20-16	40-36	12-6
Colorado Rockies	73	89	.451	25.0	47-34	26-55	18-14	17-19	31-45	7-11
San Diego Padres	66	96	.407	32.0	41-40	25-56	16-16	13-23	29-47	8-10

[†] Wild card qualifiers

Basketball

F or the third consecutive year, the US post-season programme was about one player. Shaquille O'Neal carried the LA Lakers to an NBA championship three-peat, clocking up a record 145 points for a four-game championship, as the Lakers waltzed past the hapless New Jersey Nets. Almost to a man, the Nets bleated that the 7ft 1in O'Neal was unstoppable, and they were probably right.

O'Neal wasn't even properly fit. An arthritic big toe had hampered the player for much of the season. If big toe injuries sound trivial, they are not, especially when the toe in question is bearing a payload of 338lb which is what happens when O'Neal takes his other foot off the ground to shoot. O'Neal's feet are substantial, they have to be, he takes a US size 22 (UK 21) shoe. His big toe alone is the size of a small boy's foot. Perhaps we are dwelling too much on his toe, here, but it may be the only hope for the rest. If he stays fit, there can only be more NBA titles; and more MVP awards which go hand-in-hand with them.

Almost as scary as a fit O'Neal, who is 30 this year and may have only a couple of years left at the top, is the fact the Lakers have arguably the second best player in the NBA as well. Kobe Bryant has been happy to leave the limelight to his teammate, but when all the Davids swarm around Goliath, Bryant steps out from the shadows, as he did in the third game against the Nets, to show just how good he is too. Bryant scored 36 points in that game, the three-point victory effectively burying New Jersey's remaining faint hopes. It was Bryant, after the fourth win had sealed the championship, who spoke casually about 'dreaming of a fourth'. At that point, he hadn't even celebrated the third.

Phil Jackson has nine titles and has equalled the coaching record of Red Auerbach. Jackson wins in threes; two hattricks with Chicago Bulls, and now one with the Lakers. Jackson has been gifted with the best two pair-ups of recent years; Michael Jordan-Scottie Pippin at the Bulls, and O'Neal-Bryant at the Lakers. But Bryant won no pennants at Orlando, and only started winning at LA after Jackson arrived, so you could hardly call it luck.

Jordan had a patchy old year, scoring just two points for the Wizards in one game against the Lakers. By all accounts, though, he should never had been on court, struggling with a long-standing knee injury.

NBA Earnings 2001-2		
1 Kevin Garnett	Minn	$22.40m
2 Shaquille O'Neal	LA-L	$21.43m
3 Alonzo Mourning	Miami	$18.76m
4 Juwan Howard	Dallas	$18.75m
5 Scottie Pippin	Portland	$18.10m
6 Karl Malone	Utah	$17.50m
7 Rasheed Wallace	Portland	$14.40m
8 Dikembe Mutombo	Phil	$14.32m
9 Gary Payton	Seattle	$12.93m
10 Allan Houston	NY-K	$12.75m
10 Chris Webber	Sac	$12.75m

The USA could have done with O'Neal in the world championships, held on home territory at Indianapolis. They could have done with Bryant, Allen Iverson, Kevin Garnett, Jason Kidd and Vince Carter as well. They could even have done with Jordan, dodgy knee and all, for defeats by Argentina and Yugoslavia left the USA battling it out with Spain for the distinction of being the fifth best team in the world. Spain, though, wanted it more, and America was sixth. It wasn't such a shock that they finished behind Yugoslavia, with five NBA stars in the team, and even Argentina. Yet even playing with "arrogance and selfishness' (As Rick Telander in the Chicago Sun-Times reported it), the US team would not have expected to finish behind a New Zealand team which, before Indianapolis, had only ever won one game in a world championship finals. The New Zealanders, though, played team basketball.

If the England team had qualified for the world championships, they probably would taken the wrong kit, or lost the plane tickets, or gone by boat and missed the entire event. One or all of those catastrophes would have been visited upon the England team because that's how the sport has been run in England in recent years. It wasn't so long ago that coach Laszlo Nemeth had no money for players' food on an away trip (to Belarus) because the administrators couldn't afford it.

This time, they found the answer to that problem; leave the players at home, then you don't need to feed them. That is precisely what happened when England played Russia in Moscow in a European championships semi-final match.

The administrators forgot to get visas for four key players and only seven players could go. The seven were duly walloped 94-42, but were saved from an Australian cricket score by the fact that the Russians treated the match more as a training exercise.

Perhaps therein lies the future of English basketball; no real matches, just acting as punchbags for properly organised teams which need a bit of practice.

> ## How Good is Shaq?
>
> **"They throw it into him, and he doesn't even have to dribble. It's just a dunk. We don't have anybody like that. Not only us, but there's 27 other teams that don't have anybody like that either"**
> Byron Scott, Nets' coach.
>
> **"I don't have the answer and I think there's 28 coaches who haven't come up with the answer, either"**
> Jason Kidd, Nets' guard.
>
> **"When he wants to get to the basket, there is no one in this league who can stop him, and there won't be for a long time"**
> Scott, again.
>
> **"You can't lose with Shaq"**
> Kobe Bryant.
>
> **"Shaq is a Goliath"**
> Bryant, again.
>
> **"He's a monster. that's all I can say about him"**
> Scott, once more.

N B A

Regular Season Standings

EASTERN CONFERENCE

Atlantic Division

	W	L	Pct	GB	Home	Road
New Jersey Nets	52	30	.634	-	33-8	19-22
Boston Celtics	49	33	.598	3	27-14	22-19
Orlando Magic	44	38	.537	8	27-14	17-24
Philadelphia 76ers	43	39	.524	9	22-19	21-20
Washington Wizards	37	45	.451	15	22-19	15-26
Miami Heat	36	46	.439	16	18-23	18-23
New York Knicks	30	52	.366	22	19-22	11-30

Central Division

	W	L	Pct	GB	Home	Road
Detroit Pistons	50	32	.610	-	26-15	24-17
Charlotte Hornets	44	38	.537	6	21-20	23-18
Toronto Raptors	42	40	.512	8	24-17	18-23
Indiana Pacers	42	40	.512	8	25-16	17-24
Milwaukee Bucks	41	41	.500	9	25-16	16-25
Atlanta Hawks	33	49	.402	17	23-18	10-31
Cleveland Cavaliers	29	53	.354	21	20-21	9-32
Chicago Bulls	21	61	.256	29	14-27	7-34

WESTERN CONFERENCE

Midwest Division

	W	L	Pct	GB	Home	Road
San Antonio Spurs	58	24	.707	-	32-9	26-15
Dallas Mavericks	57	25	.695	1	30-11	27-14
Minnesota TW	50	32	.610	8	29-12	21-20
Utah Jazz	44	38	.537	14	25-16	19-22
Houston Rockets	28	54	.341	30	18-23	10-31
Denver Nuggets	27	55	.329	31	20-21	7-34
Memphis Grizzlies	23	59	.280	35	15-26	8-33

Pacific Division

	W	L	Pct	GB	Home	Roa
Sacramento Kings	61	21	.744	-	36-5	25-16
L A Lakers	58	24	.707	3	34-7	24-17
Portland Trailblazers	49	33	.598	12	30-11	19-22
Seattle Supersonics	45	37	.549	16	26-15	19-22
L A Clippers	39	43	.476	22	25-16	14-27
Phoenix Suns	36	46	.439	25	23-18	13-28
Golden State Warriors	21	61	.256	40	14-27	7-34

Regular Season Statistics

Leading Scorers

	P	FG	FT	Pts	PPG
1 Paul Pierce (Boston)	82	707	520	2144	26.1
2 Tim Duncan (SAS)	82	764	560	2089	25.5
3 Kobe Bryant (LA-L)	80	749	488	2019	25.2
4 Tracy McGrady (Orlando)	76	715	415	1948	25.6
5 Allen Iverson (Phi)	60	665	475	1883	31.4
6 Shaquille O'Neal (LA-L)	67	665	475	1822	27.2
7 Gary Payton (Seattle)	82	737	267	1815	22.1
8 Antoine Walker (Boston)	81	666	240	1794	22.1
9 Karl Malone (Utah)	80	635	509	1788	22.4
10 Dirk Nowitzki (Dallas)	76	600	440	1779	23.4

Rebounds (by average)

	P	Off	Def	Total	Ave
1 Ben Wallace (Detroit)	80	318	721	1039	13.0
2 Tim Duncan (SAS)	82	268	774	1042	12.7
3 Kevin Garnett (Minn)	81	243	738	981	12.1
4 Danny Fortson (GSW)	77	290	609	899	11.7
5 Elton Brand (LA-C)	80	396	529	925	11.6

Field Goal Percentage

	P	FG	Att	FG%
1 Shaquille O'Neal (LA-L)	67	712	1229	.579
2 Elton Brand (LA-C)	80	532	1010	.527
3 Donyell Marshall (Chicago)	58	343	661	.519
4 Pau Gasol (Memphis)	82	551	1064	.518
5 John Stockton (Utah)	82	401	775	.517

3pt Field Goal Percentage

	P	3FG	Att	%
1 Steve Smith (SAS)	77	116	246	.472
2 Jon Barry (Detroit)	82	121	258	.469
3 Eric Piatkowski (LA-C)	71	111	238	.466
4 Wally Szczerbiak (Minn)	82	87	191	.455
5 Steve Nash (Dallas)	82	156	343	.455

Free Throw Percentage

	P	FT	Att	%
1 Reggie Miller (Indiana)	79	296	325	.911
2 Richard Hamilton (Detroit)	63	300	337	.890
3 Darrell Armstrong (Orlando)	82	182	205	.888
4 Damon Stoudamire (Portland)	75	174	196	.888
5 Steve Nash (Dallas)	82	260	293	.887

Assists (by average)

	P	Ass	Ave
1 Andre Miller (LA-C)	81	882	10.9
2 Jason Kidd (New Jersey)	82	808	9.9
3 Gary Payton (Sea)	82	737	9.0
4 Baron Davis (Charlotte)	82	698	8.5
5 John Stockton (Utah)	82	674	8.2

Steals (by average)

	P	Stl	Ave
1 Allen Iverson (Phi)	60	168	2.80
2 Ron Artest (Indiana)	55	141	2.56
3 Jason Kidd (NJN)	82	175	2.13
4 Baron Davis (Charlotte)	82	172	2.10
5 Doug Christie (Sac)	81	160	1.98

Blocks (by average)

	GP	Blk	Ave
1 Ben Wallace (Detroit)	80	278	3.47
1 Raef LaFrentz (Indiana)	78	213	2.73
3 Alonzo Mourning (Miami)	75	186	2.48
4 Tim Duncan (SAS)	82	203	2.48
5 Dikembe Mutombo (NJN)	80	190	2.38

Minutes (by average)

	P	MIN	MPG
1 Allen Iverson (Phi)	60	2622	43.7
2 Cuttino Mobley (Houston)	74	3116	42.1
3 Antoine Walker (Boston)	81	3406	42.0
4 Steve Francis (Houston)	57	2343	41.1
5 Latrell Sprewell (NYK)	81	3326	41.1

Play-offs
EASTERN CONFERENCE
New Jersey Nets v Indiana Pacers
New Jersey 83 Indiana 89; Indiana 79 New Jersey 95;
Indiana 84 New Jersey 85; New Jersey 74 Indiana 97;
Indiana 109 New Jersey 120 (2 OT)
New Jersey won series 3-2
Detroit Pistons v Toronto Raptors
Toronto 63 Detroit 85; Toronto 91 Detroit 96;
Detroit 84 Toronto 94; Detroit 83 Toronto 89;
Toronto 82 Detroit 85
Detroit won series 3-2
Boston Celtics v Philadelphia 76ers
Philadelphia 82 Boston 92; Philadelphia 85 Boston 93;
Boston 103 Philadelphia 108; Boston 81 Philadelphia 83;
Philadelphia 87 Boston 120
Boston won series 3-2
Charlotte Hornets v Orlando Magic
Orlando 79 Charlotte 80; Charlotte 103 Orlando 111 (OT);
Orlando 100 Charlotte 110 (OT); Orlando 85 Charlotte 102
Charlotte won series 3-1

WESTERN CONFERENCE
Sacramento Kings v Utah Jazz
Utah 86 Sacramento 89; Sacramento 86 Utah 93;
Utah 87 Sacramento 90; Utah 86 Sacramento 91
Sacramento won series 3-1
San Antonio Spurs v Seattle Supersonics
Seattle 89 San Antonio 110; San Antonio 90 Seattle 98;
Seattle 75 San Antonio 102; San Antonio 79 Seattle 91;
Seattle 78 San Antonio 102
San Antonio won series 3-2
Los Angeles Lakers v Portland Trailblazers
Portland 87 Los Angeles 95; Portland 96 Los Angeles 103;
Portland 91 Los Angeles 92
Los Angeles won series 3-0
Minnesota Timberwolves v Dallas Mavericks
Minnesota 94 Dallas 101; Minnesota 110 Dallas 122;
Minnesota 102 Dallas 115
Dallas won series 3-0

Conference Semi-finals
EASTERN CONFERENCE
New Jersey Nets v Charlotte Hornets
Charlotte 93 New Jersey 99; Charlotte 88 New Jersey 102;
New Jersey 97 Charlotte 115; Charlotte 79 New Jersey 89;
Charlotte 95 New Jersey 103
New Jersey won series 4-1
Detroit Pistons v Boston Celtics
Boston 84 Detroit 96; Detroit 77 Boston 85;
Detroit 64 Boston 66; Detroit 79 Boston 90;
Detroit 81 Boston 90
Boston won series 4-1

WESTERN CONFERENCE
Sacramento Kings v Dallas Mavericks
Dallas 91 Sacramento 108; Sacramento 102 Dallas 110;
Dallas 119 Sacramento 125; Dallas 113 Sacramento 115
(OT); Dallas 101 Sacramento 114
Sacramento won series 4-1
Los Angeles Lakers v San Antonio Spurs
San Antonio 80 LA 86; LA 85 San Antonio 88;
San Antonio 89 LA 99; San Antonio 85 LA 87;
San Antonio 87 LA 93
Los Angeles won series 4-1

Conference Finals
EASTERN CONFERENCE
New Jersey Nets v Boston Celtics
Game 1: Boston 97 New Jersey 104
Game 2: New Jersey 86 Boston 93
Game 3: New Jersey 90 Boston 94
Game 4: Boston 92 New Jersey 94
Game 5: Boston 92 New Jersey 103
Game 6: Boston 88 New Jersey 96
New Jersey won series 4-2

WESTERN CONFERENCE
Sacramento Kings v Los Angeles Lakers
Game 1: Sacramento 99 Los Angeles 106
Game 2: New Jersey 86 Boston 93
Game 3: Los Angeles 90 Sacramento 103
Game 4: Sacramento 99 Los Angeles 100
Game 5: Los Angeles 91 Sacramento 92
Game 6: Sacramento 102 Los Angeles 106
Game 7: Sacramento 106 Los Angeles 112 (OT)
Los Angeles won series 4-3

NBA Finals
LA Lakers v New Jersey Nets

Game 1: *Los Angeles, June 5*
LA Lakers 99 New Jersey Nets 94
Shaquille O'Neal issued a warning to the Nets, with 36 points, 16 rebounds and four blocks. "It seemed just like a regular season game," said Lakers guard, Brian Shaw.

Game 2: *Los Angeles, June 7*
LA Lakers 106 New Jersey Nets 83
Lakers at a gallop, with O'Neal completely dominating proceedings, with 40 points, 12 rebounds and eight assists.

Game 3: *East Rutherford, June 9*
New Jersey Nets 103 LA Lakers 106
The Nets finally slow down O'Neal (only 35 points), but leave the door open for Kobe Bryant to score 36 points. Even so, scores were equal after the third quarter and the Nets were ahead until three minutes from time.

Game 4: *East Rutherford, June 12*
New Jersey Nets 107 LA Lakers 113
Another 34 points gave O'Neal a record tally of 145 for a four-game series, and ensured that Lakers recorded the seventh sweep in NBA history, and the first since 1995.

LA LAKERS WON SERIES 4-0
MVP: Shaquille O'Neal - LA Lakers

International Men

World Championships

Indianapolis, Aug 29-Sep 8

1st Group Stage

The top three teams in each group progress

Group A

Spain 71 Yugoslavia 69; Spain 88 Angola 55;
Spain 85 Canada 54; Yugoslavia 113 Angola 63;
Yugoslavia 87 Canada 71; Angola 84 Canada 74

Group A Table	P	W	L	F	A	Pts
Spain	3	3	0	244	178	6
Yugoslavia	3	2	1	269	205	5
Angola	3	1	2	202	275	4
Canada	3	0	3	199	256	3

Group B

Brazil 90 Puerto Rico 86; Brazil 88 Turkey 86;
Brazil 102 Liberia 73; Puerto Rico 78 Turkey 75;
Puerto Rico 99 Liberia 77; Turkey 107 Liberia 80

Group B Table	P	W	L	F	A	Pts
Brazil	3	3	0	280	245	6
Puerto Rico	3	2	1	263	242	5
Turkey	3	1	2	268	246	4
Liberia	3	0	3	230	308	3

Group C

USA 104 Germany 87; USA 84 China 65;
USA 110 Algeria 60; Germany 88 China 76;
Germany 102 Algeria 70; China 96 Algeria 82

Group C Table	P	W	L	F	A	Pts
USA	3	3	0	298	212	6
Germany	3	2	1	277	250	5
China	3	1	2	237	254	4
Algeria	3	0	3	212	308	3

Group D

Argentina 112 New Zealand 85; Argentina 100 Russia 81;
Argentina 107 Venezuela 72; New Zealand 90 Russia 81;
New Zealand 98 Venezuela 85; Russia 86 Venezuela 69

Group D Table	P	W	L	F	A	Pts
Argentina	3	3	0	319	238	6
New Zealand	3	2	1	273	278	5
Russia	3	1	2	248	259	4
Venezuela	3	0	3	226	291	3

2nd Group Stage

Matches carried forward from 1st stage are listed again

Group E

Puerto Rico 73 Spain 65; Puerto Rico 85 Yugoslavia 83;
Puerto Rico 86 Brazil 90; Puerto Rico 78 Turkey 75;
Puerto Rico 89 Angola 87; Spain 71 Yugoslavia 69;
Spain 84 Brazil 67; Spain 87 Turkey 64; Spain 88 Angola 55;
Yugoslavia 90 Brazil 69; Yugoslavia 110 Turkey 78;
Yugoslavia 113 Angola 63; Brazil 88 Turkey 86;
Brazil 86 Angola 83; Turkey 86 Angola 66

Group E Table	P	W	L	F	A	Pts
Puerto Rico	6	5	1	510	477	11
Spain	6	5	1	480	382	11
Yugoslavia	6	4	2	552	437	10
Brazil	6	4	2	502	502	10
Turkey	6	2	4	496	509	8
Angola	6	1	5	438	536	7

Group F

Argentina 87 USA 80; Argentina 86 Germany 77;
Argentina 112 New Zealand 85; Argentina 100 Russia 81;
Argentina 95 China 71; USA 104 Germany 87;
USA 110 New Zealand 62; USA 106 Russia 82;
USA 84 China 65; Germany 84 New Zealand 64;
Germany 103 Russia 85; Germany 88 China 76;
New Zealand 90 Russia 81; New Zealand 94 China 88;
Russia 95 China 68

Group F Table	P	W	L	F	A	Pts
Argentina	6	6	0	587	466	12
USA	6	5	1	594	443	11
Germany	6	4	2	541	485	10
New Zealand	6	3	3	493	560	9
Russia	6	2	4	510	536	8
China	6	1	5	464	538	7

Quarter-finals

Spain 62	Germany 70
Brazil 67	Argentina 78
Puerto Rico 63	New Zealand 65
Yugoslavia 81	USA 78

Classification Games

Places 13-16

Canada 91 Lebanon 67; Algeria 83 Venezuela 98;
Lebanon 70 Algeria 100; Canada 98 Venezuela 97

Places 9-12

Angola 66 Russia 77; Turkey 94 China 86;
China 84 Angola 96; Turkey 91 Russia 86

Places 5-8

Spain 105 Brazil 89; Puerto Rico 74 USA 84;
Puerto Rico 91 Brazil 84; USA 75 Spain 81

Semi-finals

Germany 80	Argentina 86
New Zealand 78	Yugoslavia 89

3rd-Place Playoff

New Zealand 94   Germany 117

Final

YUGOSLAVIA (41) 84   ARGENTINA (39) 77

Final Rankings: 1 Yugoslavia; 2 Argentina; 3 Germany;
4 New Zealand; 5 Spain; 6 USA; 7 Puerto Rico; 8 Brazil;
9 Turkey; 10 Russia; 11 Angola; 12 China; 13 Canada;
14 Venezuela; 15 Algeria; 16 Lebanon

BASKETBALL

European Championships 2003

Semi-Final Round

Final Tables only; plus England and Ireland results. The top two teams in each Group have qualified for the finals in Sweden in September

Group A Table

	P	W	L	F	A	Pts
Lithuania	10	9	1	1001	765	19
Turkey	10	7	3	810	733	17
Ukraine	10	7	3	834	794	17
Bulgaria	10	5	5	857	877	15
Switzerland	10	2	8	658	812	12
Netherlands	10	0	10	712	891	10

Group B Table

	P	W	L	F	A	Pts
Greece	10	9	1	889	637	19
Spain	10	9	1	866	685	19
Israel	10	5	5	738	707	15
Romania	10	4	6	657	804	14
Belgium	10	3	7	663	751	13
Denmark	10	0	10	603	832	10

Group C Ireland matches

Nov 21, 2001
Germany (44) 85   Ireland (24) 77

National Basketball Arena, Nov 24, 2001
Ireland (42) 76   Croatia (42) 78

National Basketball Arena, Nov 28, 2001
Ireland (22) 75   Macedonia (38) 68

Limassol, Jan 23
Cyprus (28) 67   Ireland (27) 74

ESB Arena, Dublin, Jan 26
Ireland (26) 59   Bosnia (40) 74

ESB Arena, Dublin, Nov 20
Ireland (30) 71   Germany (40) 80

Zagreb, Nov 23
Croatia (37) 87   Ireland (33) 69

Ohrid, Nov 27
Macedonia (44) 83   Ireland (30) 72

Cork, Jan 22, 2003
Ireland (50) 104   Cyprus (36) 99 (OT2)

Sarajevo, Jan 25, 2003
Bosnia (57) 94   Ireland (31) 77

Group C Table

	P	W	L	F	A	Pts
Germany	10	9	1	833	709	19
Croatia	10	8	2	834	724	18
Bosnia Herzogovina	10	6	4	826	748	16
FYR Macedonia	10	4	6	816	810	14
Ireland	10	3	7	754	815	13
Cyprus	10	0	10	645	902	10

Group D Table

	P	W	L	F	A	Pts
France	10	8	2	843	734	18
Latvia	10	6	4	878	854	16
Hungary	10	5	5	829	804	15
Estonia	10	5	5	815	810	15
Belarus	10	3	7	673	798	13
Poland	10	3	7	805	843	13

Group E England matches

Roseti degli Abruzzi, Nov 21, 2001
Italy (43) 99   England (27) 63

Coventry Skydome, Nov 23, 2001
England (37) 73   Slovenia (27) 70

Opava, Nov 28, 2001
Czech Republic (42) 74 England (48) 87

Coventry Skydome, Jan 23
England (40) 51   Russia (39) 80

Terceira, Azores, Jan 26
Portugal (37) 74   England (35) 70

Coventry Skydome, Nov 20
England (23) 39   Italy (51) 97

Letiga, Nov 23
Slovenia (60) 104   England (30) 71

Aston Events Centre, Nov 27
England (37) 68   Czech Republic (37) 74

Moscow, Jan 22, 2003
Russia (55) 94   England (19) 42

Aston Events Centre, Jan 25, 2003
England (52) 92   Portugal (35) 84

Group E Table

	P	W	L	F	A	Pts
Italy	10	8	2	874	669	18
Slovenia	10	7	3	826	771	17
Russia	10	6	4	852	742	16
Czech Republic	10	4	6	821	879	14
England	10	3	7	656	850	13
Portugal	10	2	8	804	922	12

Euroleague

Final
PalaMalaguti, Italy, May 5
Panathanaikos 89   Kinder Bologna 83

London Towers played 14, lost 14 in the Group B qualifying stage.

International Women

World Championships

Zhangjiang, China, Sep 14-25

1st Group Stage

Group A

Australia 73 Spain 58; Australia 85 Argentina 53;
Australia 98 Japan 53; Spain 97 Argentina 55;
Spain 100 Japan 63; Argentina 74 Japan 65

Group A Table	P	W	L	F	A	Pts
Australia	3	3	0	256	164	6
Spain	3	2	1	255	191	5
Argentina	3	1	2	182	247	4
Japan	3	0	3	181	272	3

Group B

Brazil 85 China 73; Brazil 86 Yugoslavia 75;
Brazil 93 Senegal 52; China 72 Yugoslavia 65;
China 81 Senegal 63; Yugoslavia 94 Senegal 66

Group B Table	P	W	L	F	A	Pts
Brazil	3	3	0	264	200	6
China	3	2	1	226	213	5
Yugoslavia	3	1	2	234	224	4
Senegal	3	0	3	181	268	3

Group C

USA 89 Russia 55; USA 105 Lithuania 48;
USA 80 Taipei 39; Russia 97 Lithuania 61;
Russia 83 Taipei 46; Lithuania 92 Taipei 80

Group C Table	P	W	L	F	A	Pts
USA	3	3	0	274	142	6
Russia	3	2	1	235	196	5
Lithuania	3	1	2	201	282	4
Taipei	3	0	3	165	255	3

Group D

France 90 South Korea 80; France 92 Cuba 61;
France 131 Tunisia 35; South Korea 78 Cuba 71;
South Korea 124 Tunisia 70; Cuba 90 Tunisia 65

Group D Table	P	W	L	F	A	Pts
France	3	3	0	313	176	6
South Korea	3	2	1	282	231	5
Cuba	3	1	2	222	235	4
Tunisia	3	0	3	170	345	3

2nd Group Stage

Matches carried forward from 1st stage are listed again

Group E

Brazil 75 Australia 74; Brazil 85 China 73;
Brazil 68 Spain 78; Brazil 86 Yugoslavia 75;
Brazil 85 Argentina 39; Australia 101 China 72;
Australia 73 Spain 58; Australia 93 Yugoslavia 82;
Australia 85 Argentina 53; China 72 Spain 59;
China 72 Yugoslavia 65; China 102 Argentina 55;
Spain 81 Yugoslavia 67; Spain 97 Argentina 55;
Yugoslavia 83 Argentina 76

Group E Table	P	W	L	F	A	Pts
Brazil	6	5	1	492	391	11
Australia	6	5	1	524	393	11
China	6	4	2	472	428	10
Spain	6	4	2	473	398	10
Yugoslavia	6	2	4	466	474	8
Argentina	6	1	5	352	517	7

Group F

USA 89 Russia 55; USA 101 France 68;
USA 91 South Korea 53; USA 105 Lithuania 48;
USA 87 Cuba 44; Russia 74 France 59;
Russia 92 South Korea 47; Russia 97 Lithuania 61;
Russia 81 Cuba 66; France 90 South Korea 80;
France 71 Lithuania 63; France 92 Cuba 61;
South Korea 76 Lithuania 70; South Korea 78 Cuba 71;
Lithuania 63 Cuba 60

Group F Table	P	W	L	F	A	Pts
USA	6	6	0	553	307	12
Russia	6	5	1	482	368	11
France	6	4	2	511	414	10
South Korea	6	3	3	458	484	9
Lithuania	6	2	4	397	489	8
Cuba	6	1	5	392	466	7

Quarter-finals

Brazil 70	South Korea 71
China 70	Russia 86
Spain 55	USA 94
Australia 78	France 52

Classification Games

Places 13-16

Japan 91 Senegal 89; Taipei 107 Tunisia 70;
Senegal 87 Tunisia 52; Japan 76 Taipei 61

Places 9-12

Yugoslavia 74 Cuba 76; Argentina 71 Lithuania 65;
Yugoslavia 62 Lithuania 83; Cuba 92 Argentina 71

Places 7/8

Brazil 74	France 65

Places 5/6

China 72	Spain 91

Semi-finals

South Korea 53	Russia 70
Australia 56	USA 71

3rd Place Play-off

South Korea 63	Australia 91

Final

USA (48) 79	Russia (35) 74

Note: some play-off matches appear to be missing from official results

British & Irish

British Basketball League

Northern Conference

		P	W	L	For	Ag	Pts
1	Chester Jets	32	24	8	3156	2846	48
2	Sheffield Sharks	32	21	11	2854	2644	42
3	Newcastle Eagles	32	17	15	3063	3001	34
4	Edinburgh Rocks	32	13	19	2603	2728	26
5	Leicester Riders	32	11	21	2766	2893	22
6	Derby Storm	32	3	29	2525	3080	6

Southern Conference

		P	W	L	For	Ag	Pts
1	London Towers	32	21	11	2876	2799	42
2	Brighton Bears	32	21	11	2775	2662	42
3	Milton Keynes Lions	32	16	16	2723	2612	32
4	London Leopards	32	16	16	2859	2788	32
5	Birmingham Bullets	32	15	17	2822	2880	30
6	Thames Valley Tigers	32	14	18	2790	2888	28

BBL Championships Play-offs

Top four teams in each Conference qualify

Round 1
Coventry Skydome, Apr 6
Newcastle Eagles 94   London Leopards 88
Milton Keynes Lions 69   Edinburgh Rocks 64

Quarter-Finals
Coventry Skydome, Apr 7
Sheffield Sharks 85   Milton Keynes Lions 81
Brighton Bears 102   Newcastle Eagles 101

Semi-Finals
Coventry Skydome, Apr 14
Sheffield Sharks 104   London Towers 87
Brighton Bears 82   Chester Jets 95

BBL Championship Final
Wembley Arena, Apr 27
Chester Jets 84   Sheffield Sharks 82

NTL National Cup

Final
Sheffield Arena, Jan 13
Chester Jets 112   Birmingham Bullets 105

BBL Trophy

Final
NEC Arena, Birmingham, Mar 16
Chester Jets 90   Milton Keynes Lions 89

National Basketball League

NBL Conference

		P	W	L	For	Ag	Pts
1	Teeside Mohawks	18	17	1	1920	1564	34
2	Plymouth Raiders	18	14	4	1680	1561	28
3	Solent Stars	18	11	7	1695	1583	22
4	Kingston Wildcats	18	10	8	1464	1542	20
5	Manchester Magic	18	9	9	1637	1548	18
6	Worthing Thunder	18	9	9	1718	1680	18
7	Reading Rockets	18	7	11	1603	1590	14
8	InterBasket London	18	5	13	1352	1592	10
9	Coventry Crusaders	18	4	14	1483	1584	8
10	Sutton Pumas	18	4	14	1465	1773	8

Championship Play-off Final

Coventry Skydome, May 12
Teeside Mohawks 127   Solent Stars 117

Division One

		P	W	L	For	Ag	Pts
1	Derbyshire Arrows	22	20	2	2013	1571	40
2	Ealing Tornadoes	22	19	3	2029	1750	38
3	Ware Rebels	22	16	6	2012	1789	32
4	Oxford Devils	22	16	6	1924	1554	32
5	Kingston/Hull Icebergs	22	12	9	1792	1744	25
6	Westminster Warriors	22	11	10	1562	1654	23
7	North London Lords	22	7	14	1582	1718	15
8	North West London	22	7	15	1584	1781	14
9	Worcester Wolves	22	7	15	1642	1895	14
10	Mansfield Express	22	6	15	1639	1743	13
11	Cardiff Clippers	22	6	16	1551	1826	12
12	Liverpool	22	3	19	1590	1895	6

Championship Play-off Final

Coventry Skydome, May 12
Derbyshire Arrows 83   Ealing Tornadoes 81

Division One Women

		P	W	L	For	Ag	Pts
1	Sheffield Hatters	16	14	2	1259	872	28
2	Rhondda Rebels	16	14	2	1323	903	28
3	Nottingham Wildcats	16	12	4	1095	886	24
4	Thames Valley Tigers	16	11	5	1078	1050	22
5	Spelthorne Acers	16	8	8	1024	1070	16
6	UWIC Stealers	16	5	11	931	1106	10
7	Wandsworth Sting	16	3	13	870	1091	6
8	Doncaster Panthers	16	3	13	862	1118	6
9	NW London Wolverines	16	2	14	779	1125	4

Championship Play-off Final

Coventry Skydome, May 12
Sheffield Hatters 76   Rhondda Rebels 60

ESB Superleague, Ireland

		P	W	L	Pts
1	Waterford Crystals	26	21	5	42
2	Frosties Tralee Tigers	26	20	6	40
3	Burger King Limerick	26	18	8	36
4	DART Killester	26	18	8	36
5	Neptune	26	15	11	30
6	Esat Blue Demons	26	15	11	30
7	St Vincents	26	14	12	28
8	Sx3 Star of the Sea	26	12	14	24
9	Hibernian UCD	26	12	14	24
10	Big Al's Notre Dame	26	11	15	22
11	Killarny Lakers	26	10	16	20
12	Tolka Rovers	26	8	18	16
13	Abbey Foods Sligo	26	7	19	14
14	Tyrone Towers	26	1	25	2

Championship Play-off Final

Tralee Tigers 78   DART Killester 69

Irish Cup
Limerick 89   Star of the Sea 83

Billiards

World Professional Championship

Centurion Hotel, Midsomer Norton, May 18-24
Round 1
Lee Lagan bt Mark Hurst 848-335
Marrtin Spoormans bt Brian Dix 428-424
David Nichols bt Gary Rogers 379-268

Round 2	Round 3	Q-finals	S-finals	FINAL
Clive Everton ENG Lee Lagan ENG	Lee Lagan 529-421 Peter Gilchrist ENG	Peter Gilchrist 1298-770	Peter Gilchrist 1403-768	
Ian Williamson ENG Martin Spoormans ENG	Nalin Patel IND Ian Williamson 413-298	Nalin Patel 762-6338		Peter Gilchrist 1767-851
Peter Sheehan ENG David Nichols ENG	Chris Shutt ENG Peter Sheehan 546-516	Peter Sheehan 1163-1146	Geet Sethi 1091-911	
Ashok Shandilya IND Pankai Advani IND	Geet Sethi IND Ashok Shandilya 645-551	Geet Sethi 1475-939		
Devendra Joshi IND Alok Kumar IND	David Causier ENG Devendra Joshi 858-394	David Causier 1291-1168	David Causier 1024-656	**Mike Russell 2251-1273**
Paul Bennett ENG Rom Surin IND	Robbie Foldvari AUS Paul Bennett 681-188	Robbie Foldvari 783-513		Mike Russell 2456-1094
Manoj Kothari IND Sushrut Pandia IND	Roxton Chapman ENG Manoj Kothari 459-429	Manoj Kothari walkover	Mike Russell 2167-402	
Arun Agrawal IND Dhruv Sitwala IND	Mike Russell ENG Dhruv Sitwala 647-287	Mike Russell 1702-695		

World Matchplay Championship

Centurion Hotel, Midsomer Norton, Feb 26-Mar 2
Semi-Final
Chris Shutt ENG bt David Causier ENG 1773-1122
Roxton Chapman ENG bt Davendra Joshi IND 1553-642
FINAL
Chris Shutt bt Roxton Chapman 2431-1025

Women's World Championship

Swindon   April 20
Semi-finals
Kelly Fisher ENG bt Caroline Walch ENG 289-123
Emma Bonney ENG bt Sarah Kingwell ENG 215-121
FINAL
Emma Bonney bt Kelly Fisher 227-196

Bobsleigh

World Cup, Men

FINAL STANDINGS
Drivers only given
Two-Man

1	Martin Annen SUI	220
2	Pierre Lueders CAN	193
3	Christian Reich SUI	190
4	Todd Hays USA	164
5	Gunther Huber ITA	164
6	Wolfgang Stampfer AUT	160
14	Lee Johnston GBR	112
29	Neil Scarisbrook GBR	44
41	Peter Donohoe IRL	4

Four-Man

1	Martin Annen SUI	206
2	Andre Lange GER	201
3	Christian Reich SUI	170
4	Bruno Mingeon FRA	168
5	Arend Glas NED	153
6	Bruno Thomas FRA	152
15	Neil Scarisbrook GBR	105
16	Lee Johnston GBR	87

Combined

1	Martin Annen SUI	426
2	Christian Reich SUI	360
3	Andre Lange GER	356
4	Pierre Lueders CAN	335
5	Wolfgang Stampfer AUT	306
6	Todd Hays USA	299
14	Lee Johnston GBR	199
20	Neil Scarisbrook GBR	149
52	Peter Donohoe IRL	4

World Cup, Women

FINAL STANDINGS
Drivers only given
Two-Woman

1	Susi Erdmann GER	272
2	Sandra Prokoff GER	264
3	Jean Racine USA	232
4	Francoise Burdet SUI	227
5	Bonny Warner USA	220
6	Jill Bakken USA	202
13	Cheryl Done GBR	141
17	Michelle Coy GBR	108
26	Lesley Fitzgerald IRL	30

Skeleton World Cup

FINAL STANDINGS
Men

1	Gregor Stahli SUI	245
2	Chris Soule USA	218
3	Martin Rettl AUT	157
4	Jeff Pain CAN	155
5	Jim Shea USA	151
6	Duff Gibson CAN	139
15	Kristan Bromley GBR	90
16	Steve Anson GBR	86
18	Clifton Wrottesley IRL	75
23	Adrian Collins GBR	49
33	Tim Cassin IRL	9

Women

1	Alex Coomber GBR	115
2	Maya Pedersen SUI	114
3	Lindsay Alcock CAN	109
4	Lea Ann Parsley USA	105
5	Michelle Kelly CAN	90
6	Steffi Hanzlik GER	69
16	Emma Stewart GBR	30

Bowls

Devon won the counties title for the first time in 43 years and the secretary of the EBA resigned (though not because of it), but the headlines at Worthing came with the re-appearance of the old dog David Bryant, who qualified with his Clevedon partner Mike Langley for the pairs competition. Bryant was once the wunderkind of bowls, in the days when pipe-smoking was an almost radical indulgence. He made his debut at Worthing in 1953, when he was just 21 and already puffing, and the reception for his return, after a 13-year break, showed just how revered in the sport the 70-year-old still is. Bryant and Langley had a brief moment of glory, running out 21-17 winners against Alec Hay and Eric Bigley, from Oxhey, but in the next round, they met Welford's Martin Timms and Trevor Francis who had the temerity to beat them. Not that Bryant needed another trophy to polish. We started to count the ones he does have but gave up after the three outdoor world titles (the only person ever), the three indoor world titles (the only person ever), the four successive Commonwealth singles titles (the only person ever)...

The first weekend of the EBA Championships overlapped the last weekend of the EWBA event, the women's championships coming hard on the heels of the Commonwealth Games. It was just one long bowls party. At Leamington, Tracey Powell and Linda Smith became the first sisters to win the pairs event. They wore trousers, too, which was an acceptable fashion item for women in about 1950, but took another 52 years to earn the approval of the EWBA.

Outdoor

EBA Championships

Worthing, Aug 18-30
Men only

Singles Final
Martyn Sekyar (Southampton) bt
Andrew Briden (Herts) 21-2

Pairs Final
Peter Picknell/Keith Hawes (Iver Heath) bt
Marc Stones/Grant Burgess (Gilt Edge) 17-13

Triples Final
Banbury (Gary Lucas/Alan Prew/Greg Moon) bt
Cavaliers (Michael Bowley/David Baird/Phil Dickens)
23-17

Fours Final
Siemens (Nick Cammack/Michael Owen/Duncan
Robinson/Brett Morley) bt Carnon Downs (Gary
Watkins/Tim Phillips/Mark Foster/Steven Lawer) 25-12

Champion Of Champions Singles
Mick Sharpe bt Steve Farish 21-17

Middleton Cup Final (Inter County Champs)
Devon bt Essex 122-113

EWBA Championships

Leamington, Aug 5-17
Women only

Singles Final
Helen Wall (S Derby) bt Jayne Christie (Henlow) 21-13

Pairs Final
Linda Smith/Tracey Powell (Leominster) bt
Liz Tunn/Brenda Brown (Colchester) 22-14

Triples Final
Blackwell bt Spalding Town 16-14

Fours Final
Consett Park (Robson/Gowland/Stokoe/Jones) bt
Penryn (Daniel/Swadling/Jose/Reynolds) 30-10

Champion Of Champions
J Baxter-Avison (Notts) bt E Alexander (Cambs) 21-12

National Express Johns Trophy
Warwicks bt Devon 127-107

Walker Cup
Durham bt Huntingdon 40-35

Indoor

World Singles Championships
Hopton-on-sea, Norfolk, Jan 10-20
3rd Round
Paul Foster SCO bt Adam Jeffery AUS 5-9 12-0 2-0
Gary McCloy ENG bt Stephen Rees WAL 11-4 10-1
Tony Allcock ENG bt Jason Greenslade WAL
10-5 8-6
Jonathan Ross ENG bt John Price WAL 5-8 10-9 2-0
Alex Marshall SCO bt Andy Thompson ENG 10-3 9-4
Richard Corsie SCO bt Noel Kennedy HKG 6-6 7-9
Mark McMahon ENG bt Simon Skelton ENG
10-4 3-11 2-1
Ian Bond ENG bt David Gourlay SCO 10-8 12-0
Quarter-finals
Paul Foster bt Gary McCloy 11-6 8-4
Tony Allcock bt Jonathan Ross 9-5 3-10 2-0
Richard Corsie bt Alex Marshall 11-6 8-8
Ian Bond bt Mark McMahon 11-6 11-9
Semi-finals
Tony Allcock bt Paul Foster 9-3 6-6 (93 mins)
Richard Corsie bt Ian Bond 9-4 3-7 2-0 (95 mins)
FINAL
Tony Allcock bt Richard Corsie 8-3 9-4 (80 mins)

World Pairs Championship
Hopton-on-sea, Norfolk, Jan 24-27
1st Round
Les Gillett/Mark McMahon ENG bt Alan Mathias/Philip
Rowlands WAL 10-4 9-4
Graham Robertson/Greg Harlow SCO/ENG bt Jimmy
Chiu/Jacky Wong HKG 14-3 9-4
Robert Weale/Jason Greenslade WAL bt Joey
Strickland/George Sneddon SCO 7-8 7-5 2-1
David Gourlay/Alex Marshall SCO bt Rowan
Brassey/Kerry Chapman NZL 13-1 9-1
Mark Casey/Adam Jeffrey AUS bt Stephen Rees/John
Price WAL 10-5 6-8 2-0
Ian McClure/Jeremy Henry NIR bt Gary Smith/Andy
Thompson ENG 6-8 8-3 2-0
John Leeman/Alan Theobald ENG bt David Holt/Tony
Allcock ENG 3-10 12-2 2-1
Hugh Duff/Paul Foster SCO bt Duanne Abrahams/Donny
Piketh RSA 10-7 9-2
Quarter-finals
Robertson/Harlow bt Gillett/McMahon 10-2 9-2
Gourlay/Marshall bt Weale/Greenslade 9-2 5-8 2-0
McClure/Henry bt Casey/Jeffrey 8-4 10-2
Duff/Foster bt Leeman/Theobald 11-3 10-7
Semi-finals
Robertson/Harlow bt Gourlay/Marshall 94 8-4 (97 mins)
Duff/Foster bt McClure/Henry 4-9 6-5 2-1 (135 mins)
Final
Duff/Foster bt Robertson/Harlow 5-8 10-8 2-1 (130 mins)

BUPA Care Homes Open
Blackpool, Nov 4-11, 2001
Quarter-finals
Alan Thurlow AUS bt Andy Thompson ENG 1-8 6-4 1-0
Greg Harlow ENG bt Mark McMahon ENG 6-5 4-5 1-0
Ian Bond ENG bt John Price WAL 5-3 2-7 1-0
Jason Greenslade WAL bt Robert Weale WAL
5-2 5-10 1-0
Semi-finals
Greg Harlow bt Alan Thurlow 10-1 8-6
Ian Bond bt Jason Greenslade 11-2 6-8 1-0
Final
Ian Bond bt Greg Harlow 7-4 8-6 1-0

Scottish Masters
Kelvin Hall, Glasgow, Dec 4-7, 2001
MEN'S SINGLES
Semi-finals
Darren Burnett SCO bt David Gourlay SCO 8-6 8-6
Mike Prosser WAL bt David Harding WAL 9-4 7-6
Final
Darren Burnett bt Mike Prosser 5-7 13-3 2-0

WOMEN'S SINGLES
Semi-finals
Julie Forrest SCO bt Caroline Brown SCO 12-3 9-1
Cheryl Northall ENG bt Betty Morgan WAL 4-10 6-8 2-0
Final
Julie Forrest bt Cheryl Northall 10-2 10-5

Welsh Masters
Llanelli, Jan 30-Feb 1
Semi-finals
Les Gillett ENG bt John Price WAL 1-6 9-3 2-1
Robert Weale WAL bt Mike Prosser WAL 4-5 10-4 2-0
Final
Les Gillett bt Robert Weale 11-4 6-12 2-1

Boxing

In the months, or should it be years, preceding the Mike Tyson - Lennox Lewis fight, the old warriors queued up to patronise Lewis. Larry Holmes and Evander Holyfield were to the fore, averring that the reigning champion had neither the power nor the spirit to deal with Tyson. They were wrong, having paid no heed to time, for the Tyson they fought (Holyfield twice), though even then in decline, was not the Tyson that Lewis fought, a boxer running on empty.

Lewis must take some credit, for his weight of punch had determined the outcome of the fight by the third round. Standing six inches taller and almost a stone heavier at a mighty 17st 11lb, it would have needed more than just a glimpse of the old Tyson to unsettle him. Instead, the jab pummelled away at Tyson's face until only despair was written amongst the splattered blood upon it. Tyson was but a shadow of the once fierce combatant, a timorous beastie. In the eighth round, the other Lewis fist, the right one, ended it.

The defeated Tyson was contrite. Far from suggesting lunching on anyone's babies, Tyson cuddled Lewis like a baby himself. It was hard to imagine that this was the same boxer whose mindless rampage at a press conference in January had ended with him taking a bite at Lewis' leg. In the post-contest euphoria, Tyson asked for another bout (not bite), oh so politely, which should have been declined there and then. But the pay-per-view figures had worked out much better than expected for the television promoters with around £67m in revenue, enough to pay both boxers handsomely and leave plenty of profit. Tyson still needs the money (whatever does he do with it?) and Lewis, with no demons left, does not appear to be about to retire, so the return match lingers.

Quite who else Lewis might fight is another matter. Chris Byrd beat Evander Holyfield (whose continued presence confirms how weak the heavyweight division currently is) and had been pencilled in as the reserve for the Lewis bout if Tyson had strayed off the straight and narrow yet one more time. A contest against Byrd, though, would excite less pay-per-view interest than nordic skiing, and Lewis surely isn't hanging around, at 36, for just another £2m fight.

John Ruiz succumbed to Roy Jones (we are straying into 2003 here), but the exemplary Jones, as good as he is, would have to concede five stones to Lewis. The only realistic opponent for Lewis at this stage is the Ukrainian academic (he has a masters in sports science) Vitali Klitschko. Standing 6ft 8in and weighing in at 17st 7lb, Klitschko is one of the few boxers around who could enter the ring on equal physical terms with Lewis. A record of 33 wins, without a single fight going the distance, looks good on the CV as well.

Tyson may still get in ahead of Klitschko, but beware of the marketing. To sell the next fight, he may have to eat Lewis' mother, Violet.

Only one other British boxer fought for one of the three most vaunted belts, Clinton Woods taking on Jones for the undisputed light-heavyweight crown. The bout took place because the American had been threatened by the WBC that he would be stripped of the title, if it didn't take place. If Woods' advisers, who helped to lever the process, were at the fight, one hopes they found it difficult viewing. For all his courage, and there was plenty, Woods was in the wrong ring. Jones hit him 122 times in six brief rounds before Denis Hobson, Woods' manager, lay a white towel on the ropes. It was folly.

Johnny Nelson and Joe Calzaghe defended their respective WBA titles, but neither defence enhanced the belts they wore. Nelson was judged fortunate to earn a draw against the Panamanian Guilermo Jones at Derby in November, while Calzaghe ended up fighting Tocker Pudwill, a stand-in for Thomas Tate, who once took Sven Ottke to 12 rounds. "The plan was to utilize boxing skills, counter punch a little bit and see what Calzaghe was going to bring to the table," said the American, who changed his mind on his strategy when he got off the stool and decided to slug his way to victory. Pudwill was down twice in the first round and lasted 39 seconds of the second round.

Naseem Hamed was sited, too, booed as he struggled to win against an unknown Spaniard Marco Calvo. In this cruellest of sports, Hamed is reaping the reward for his early arrogance. Humility is a necessary part of the rebuilding process.

"When he said he wanted to eat Lennox Lewis's children, he was copying Napoleon, who said he would defeat his foes and then eat them"
Stacy McKinley, Tyson's sparring partner, explaining the former world champion's threats to Lennox Lewis made in 2000 after Tyson stopped Lou Savarese in Glasgow.

"Deep down in his heart, I think he really he is a nice guy, a very personable person, a real sweetheart. But some guys just don't know how to show it"
Tommy Brooks, Tyson's former trainer.

"I wanted to complete my legacy as the best fighter on the planet. I showed boxing who is the best in the world. I can adapt to any style. Nobody gets away from my jab. It's been a long road but I finally have what I wanted"
Lennox Lewis, after beating Tyson

"He was just splendid, a masterful boxer"
Tyson to Violet, Lewis' mother, after the fight.

"If you could give me one more chance I would appreciate it"
Tyson to Lewis after the fight.

"People will want to see if it was a fluke or if it was real"
Shelley Finkel, Tyson's manager, applying suspect logic in his argument for a Lewis-Tyson rematch.

Professional Boxing

Results given for WBA, IBF, and WBC. When all three are held by one boxer, it is an undisputed title

HEAVYWEIGHT

IBF/WBC

Memphis, June 8
Lennox Lewis GBR bt
Mike Tyson USA
KO, round 8

IBF

Atlantic City, Dec 14
Chris Byrd USA bt
Evander Holyfield USA
unanimous pts

WBA

Las Vegas, July 27
John Ruiz USA bt
Kirk Johnson USA
DQ, round 10

CRUISERWEIGHT

WBA

Marseille, Feb 23
Jean-Marc Mormeck FRA bt
Virgil Hill USA
TKO, round 9

Marseille, Aug 10
Jean-Marc Mormeck FRA bt
Dale Brown CAN
TKO, round 8

IBF

Phoenix, Feb 1
Vassily Jirov USA bt
Jorge Castro ARG
unanimous pts

LIGHT-HEAVYWEIGHT

WBC/IBF

Miami, Feb 2
Roy Jones USA bt
Glenn Kelly AUS
KO, round 10

Miami, Sep 7
Roy Jones USA bt
Clinton Woods GBR
TKO, round 6

WBA

Levallois, May 23
Bruno Girard FRA bt
Thomas Hansvoll
unanimous pts

Palaval-Les-Flots, July 13
Bruno Girard FRA bt
Lou del Valle USA
majority pts

SUPER-MIDDLEWEIGHT

WBA

Las Vegas, July 27
Byron Mitchell USA bt
Julio Cesar Green DOM
TKO, round 4

IBF

Magdeburg, Mar 16
Sven Ottke GER bt
Rick Thornberry AUS
unanimous pts

Magdeburg, June 1
Sven Ottke GER bt
Thomas Tate USA
unanimous pts

Leipzig, Aug 24
Sven Ottke GER bt
Joe Gatti CAN
TKO, round 9

Nuremburg, Nov 16
Sven Ottke GER bt
Rudy Markussen DEN
unanimous pts

WBC

Mashantucket, Mar 1
Eric Lucas CAN bt
Vinny Pazienza USA
unanimous pts

Montreal, Sep 6
Eric Lucas CAN bt
Omar Sheika USA
unanimous pts

MIDDLEWEIGHT

IBF/WBC
Reading, Pennsylvania, Feb 2
Bernard Hopkins USA bt
Carl Daniels USA
TKO, round 10

WBA
Tokyo, Feb 2
Willliam Joppy USA bt
Naotaka Hozumi JPN
TKO, round 10

SUPER-WELTERWEIGHT

WBA/WBC
Las Vegas, Sep 14
Oscar de la Hoya USA bt
Fernando Vargas
TKO, round 11

IBF
Miami, Feb 2
Ronald Wright USA bt
Jason Papillion USA
TKO, round 5

Portland, Sep 7
Ronald Wright USA bt
Bronco McKart USA
DQ, round 8

WELTERWEIGHT

WBA
Reading, Pennsylvania, Mar 30
Ricardo Mayorga NCA bt
Andrew Lewis GUY
TKO, round 5

IBF
Campione d'Italia, Apr 13
Michele Piccirillo ITA bt
Cory Spinks USA
unanimous pts

WBC
New York City, Jan 26
Vernon Forrest USA bt
Shane Mosley USA
unanimous pts

Indianapolis, July 20
Vernon Forrest USA bt
Shane Mosley USA
unanimous pts

SUPER-LIGHTWEIGHT

IBF/WBC
Las Vegas, May 18
Kostya Tszyu AUS bt
Ben Tackie GHA
unanimous pts

WBA
San Juan, Puerto Rico, May 11
Diobelys Hurtado CUB bt
Randall Bailey USA
KO, round 7

Houston, Oct 19
Vivian Harris GUY bt
Diobelys Hurtado CUB
TKO, round 2

LIGHTWEIGHT

WBA
San Antonio, Jan 5
Leonard Dorin ROM bt
Raul Balbi ALG
majority pts

Bucharest, May 31
Leonard Dorin ROM bt
Raul Balbi ALG
unanimous pts

IBF
Pittsburgh, Mar 9
Paul Spadafora USA bt
Angel Manfredy USA
unanimous pts

Chester, W Virginia, Nov 9
Paul Spadafora USA bt
Dennis Holbaek DEN
unanimous pts

WBC
Las Vegas, Apr 20
Floyd Mayweather USA bt
Jose Luis Castillo MEX
unanimous pts

Las Vegas, Dec 7
Floyd Mayweather USA bt
Jose Luis Castillo MEX
unanimous pts

SUPER-FEATHERWEIGHT
WBA
Las Vegas, Jan 12
Acelino Freitas BRA bt
Joel Casamayor CUB
unanimous pts

Phoenix, Aug 3
Acelino Freitas BRA bt
Daniel Attah USA
unanimous pts

IBF
Tecmecula, Aug 18
Steve Forbes USA bt
David Santos USA
majority pts
Forbes stripped of title for failing to make the weight; title vacant

WBC
Tokyo, Aug 24
Sirimongkol Singmanassak THA bt Kengo Nagashima JPN
KO, round 2

FEATHERWEIGHT
WBA
Tampa, Aug 24
Derrick Gainer USA drew with
Daniel Seda PUR
Gainer retained title

IBF
New York City, Apr 27
Johnny Tapia USA bt
Manuel Medina MEX
unanimous pts

WBC
Las Vegas, Feb 17
Marco Antonio Barrera MEX bt
Erik Morales MEX
unanimous pts
Barrera did not accept the title

Las Vegas, Nov 16
Erik Morales MEX bt
Paulie Ayala USA
unanimous pts

SUPER-BANTAMWEIGHT
WBA
Thailand, Feb 21
Yoddamrong Sithyodthong THA bt Yober Ortega VEN
unanimous pts

Saitama, Japan, May 18
Osamu Sato JPN bt
Yoddamrong Sithyodthong THA
KO, round 8

Tokyo, Oct 9
Salim Medjkoune FRA bt
Osamu Sato JPN
unanimous pts

IBF
Memphis, June 8
Manny Pacquiao PHI bt
Jorge Julio COL
TKO, round 2

Davao City, Oct 26
Manny Pacquiao PHI bt
Fahrakorb Rakkiat Gym THA
TKO, round 1

WBC
Tokyo, Feb 5
Willie Jorin USA drew with
Osamu Sato JPN
Jorin retains title

Sacramento, Nov 1
Oscar Larios MEX
Willie Jorin USA
TKO, round 1

BANTAMWEIGHT
WBA
Copenhagen, Apr 19
Johnny Bredahl DEN bt
Eidy Moya VEN
TKO, round 9

Copenhagen, Nov 8
Johnny Bredahl DEN bt
Leo Gamez VEN
unanimous pts

IBF
Las Vegas, July 27
Tim Austin USA bt
Adan Vargas MEX
TKO, round 10

WBC
Bangkok, Jan 11
Veeraphol Sahaprom THA bt
Sergio Perez MEX
unanimous pts

Nonthaburi, May 1
Veeraphol Sahaprom THA bt
Julio Coronell COL
unanimous pts

SUPER-FLYWEIGHT
WBA
Tokyo, Mar 8
Alexander Munoz bt
Celes Kobayashi JPN
TKO, round 8

Osaka, July 31
Alexander Munoz VEN bt
Eiji Kojima JPN
KO, round 2

IBF
Reading, Pennsylvania, Mar 30
Felix Machado VEN bt
Martin Castillo USA
RSC round 6 following accidental headbutt, Machado retained title

WBC
Yokohama, Mar 23
Masamori Tokuyama JPN bt
Ryuko Kazuhiro JPN
KO, round 9

Tokyo, Aug 26
Masamori Tokuyama JPN bt
Eric Lopez MEX
TKO, round 7

Osaka, Dec 20
Masamori Tokuyama JPN bt
Gerry Penalosa PHI
majority pts

FLYWEIGHT
WBA
Anaheim, Oct 12
Eric Morel PUR bt
Denkaosaen Kaowitch THA
TKO, round 11

IBF
El Paso, Nov 29
Irene Pacheco COL bt
Alejandro Montiel
unanimous pts

WBC
Konkaen, Thailand, Apr 19
**Pongsaklek Wonjongkam THA bt
Daisuke Naito JPN**
KO, round 1

Bangkok, Sep 6
**Pongsaklek Wonjongkam THA bt
Jesus Martinez**
unanimous pts

Osaka, Nov 26
**Pongsaklek Wongjongkam THA
bt Hidenobu Honda JPN**
unanimous pts

JUNIOR-FLYWEIGHT
WBA
Miami, Jan 19
**Rosenda Alvarez NCA bt
Pitchit Siriwat THA**
tko, round 12

IBF
Las Vegas, Aug 9
**Miguel Barrera COL bt
Roberto Leyva MEX**
unanimous pts

WBC
Chiba, Japan, Feb 23
**Choi Yo-Sam KOR bt
Shingo Yamaguchi JPN**
ko, round 10

Seoul, July 6
**Jorge Arce MEX bt
Choi Yo-Sam KOR**
TKO, round 6

Las Vegas, Nov 16
**Jorge Arce MEX bt
Augustin Luna MEX**
TKO, round 3

STRAW-WEIGHT
WBA
Yokohama, Jan 29
**Keitaro Hoshino JPN bt
Joma Gamboa PHI**
unanimous pts

Yokohama, July 28
**Noel Arambulent VEN bt
Keitaro Hoshino JPN**
majority pts

Osaka, Dec 20
**Noel Arambulent VEN bt
Keitaro Hoshino JPN**
majority pts

IBF
title vacant

WBC
Villahermosa, Mexico, Feb 2
**Jose Antonio Aguirre MEX bt
Juan Palacious**
unanimous pts

"I feel that ethically and morally I can no longer be a part of boxing"

Dr George O'Neill, who resigned from his job with the British Board of Boxing Control, after the governing body cleared the former world bantamweight champion Wayne McCullough to box again.

"They just don't understand the art and craft of boxing"

Naseem Hamed, booed by the crowd after defeating the lowly-ranked Spaniard Manuel Calvo.

"I've always said the first time he comes home with two black eyes, swollen lips and cuts all over his face, that's it, he can take up golf"

Mandy Calzaghe, on husband Joe.

"I once took her to a show in Bristol and she hated every second of it. She had to leave halfway through because she couldn't stand the sight of blood"

Dean Francis, talking about his girlfiend, actress Jan Anderson...who plays a nurse in Casualty.

A m a t e u r B o x i n g

European Championships
Perm, Russia, July 12-21

Because of the proximity of these championships to the Commonwealth Games, there was only a single boxer representing England and Scotland and none at all representing Northern Ireland and Wales. The Irish team had a dreadful championships, their seven boxers failing to win a single bout.

Light Flyweight (-48kg)
1 Sergey Kazakov   RUS
2 Gojan Vyacheslav   MDA
3 Rudolf Dydy   SVK
3 Eugen Tanassie Sorin ROM
Final: RSCO (3)
John Paul Kinsella IRL lost to Vyacheslav in his first bout

Flyweight (-51kg)
1 Georgy Balakshin   RUS
2 Alexander Vladimirov BUL
3 Thomas Jerome   FRA
3 Igor Samoilenko   MDA
Final: 28-18
Darren Campbell IRL lost to Alexandrov BUL in his first bout

Bantamweight (-54kg)
1 Khawazhi Khatsygov   BLR
2 Gennady Kovalyov   RUS
3 Waldemar Cucereanu   ROM
3 Ali Allab   FRA
Final: 17-8
Damien McKenna IRL lost to Dalakliev BUL in his first bout

Featherweight (-57kg)
1 Raimkul Malakhbekov   RUS
2 Shakhin Imranov   AZE
3 Simion Vyorel   ROM
3 Konstantin Kupatadze GEO
Final: RSCO (2)
David Mulholland ENG bt Torunen FIN in his first bout, lost to Kupatadze in the q-finals

Lightweight (-60kg)
1 Alexander Maletin   RUS
2 Boris Georgiev   BUL
3 Mikele Di Rocco   ITA
3 Aidyn Selchuk   TUR
Final: KO
Andrew Murray IRL lost to Vidas LTU in his first bout

Light Welterweight (-63.5kg)
1 Dimitar Panayotov   BUL
2 Willy Bley   FRA
3 Dmitry Pavlyuchenkov RUS
3 Zamora Brunet   ITA
Final: 18-11
Michael Kelly IRL lost to Kravets UKR in his first bout
Barry Morrison SCO lost to Brunet ITA in his first bout

Welterweight (-67 kg)
1 Timur Gaidalov   RUS
2 Al-Dr Bokalo   UKR
3 Dorel Simion   ROM
3 Sebastian Zbik   GER
Final: 29-15
James Moore IRL lost to Spas BUL in his first bout

Light Middleweight (-71kg)
1 Andrey Mishin   RUS
2 Lukash Vilashek   GER
3 Ivan Gaivan   MDA
3 Marian Simion   BUL
Final: RSCO (2)
John Duddy lost to Rolandas LTU in his first bout.

Middleweight (-75kg)
1 Oleg Mashkin   UKR
2 Karoli Baljay   HUN
3 Yani Rauhala   FIN
3 Mamadou Djambang   FRA
Final: 31-17

Light Heavyweight (-81kg)
1 Mikhail Gala   RUS
2 John Dovi   FRA
3 Viktor Perun   UKR
3 Istvan Syoch   HUN
Final: 27-15

Heavyweight (-91kg)
1 Evgeny Makarenko   RUS
2 Vyacheslav Uzelkov   UKR
3 Marat Tovmasian   ARM
3 Victor Zuev   BLR
Final: 20-16

Super Heavyweight (+91kg)
1 Alexandere Povetkin   RUS
2 Roberto Cammarelle   ITA
3 Sebastian Kober   GER
3 Artyom Tsarikov   UKR
Final: 20-16

ABA Champions
Super-heavyweight (+ 91kg) - Matt Grainger
Heavyweight (-91kg) - David Dolan
Cruiserweight (-86kg) - James Dolan
Light-heavyweight (-81kg) - Tony Marsden
Middleweight (-75kg) - Neil Perkins
Light-middleweight (-71kg) - Paul Smith

Welterweight (-67kg) - Michael Lomax
Light-welterweight (-63.5kg) - Lenny Daws
Lightweight (-60kg) - Andrew Morris
Featherweight (-57kg) - David Mulholland
Bantamweight (-54kg) - Derry Matthews
Flyweight (-51kg) - Duncan Barriball
Light-flyweight (-48kg) - Darran Langley

Canoeing

At Sydney, Tim Brabants did what no other Briton had done before and won an Olympic medal, a bronze in the K1000m. In another Olympics, Brabants would have been the cause for considerable celebration, but in Sydney success for Britain was a currency that was traded on a daily basis, and Brabants, whose event was held out in the country, at Lake Penrith, had hardly a writer present to record his considerable achievement.

Two years down the line and Brabants was the groundbreaker again, or should it be the lakebreaker, becoming the first Briton to win a European title in a flatwater event, appropriately in the very heartland of the sport, at Szeged in Hungary. Once the European championships were the world's pre-eminent event. They were discontinued, then revived, but with Europe still by far the strongest paddling region on the planet (17 of the 19 world titles at Seville went to European paddlers) there is no question of the value of a European crown.

For Brabants, now qualified as a doctor in Nottingham and undertaking his year as a junior houseman, it was a miracle enough that he could find the time to train, let alone win a title. For British paddling, it was a giant leap for not only was there a title to savour, but Rachel Train (of the ubiquitous Trains) won a bronze medal in the K1 200m as well.

Hopes were high for the world championships, held little more than a month later, but once you've run up one hill, the next is always a touch harder. Train made a respectable sixth in her 200m final, but the good doctor did not even reach his final, and ended with a modest second place in the B Final.

Britain's other European champion was more expected, Paul Ratcliffe having made a habit of winning most titles going, with the exception of those you get at world championships and Olympic Games. So, one could call it a typical Ratcliffe season for the Olympic silver medallist from Sydney duly collected the European title in Bratislava with a brilliant second run that took him from fourth to first, finishing ahead of his old adversary Helmut Oblinger. Then at Bourg St Maurice five weeks later he failed to clear the first hurdle, eliminated in qualifying.

To Ratcliffe's credit, though, he never exits a competition with a whimper, always the bang. In the Olympics, he tried to paddle a significant part of the course underwater, in Bourg St Maurice he ducked through two pairs of gates and was rewarded with two 50-second penalties. As that more than doubled his points score (taking him from 3rd to 74th), it made qualifying a touch difficult. Not being there (nor seeing the race on TV), we can't comment on why the British team chose not to appeal the penalties, but if there was a smidgeon of doubt then it is surely their responsibility to do so. Anyway, 50 seconds is way too big a penalty for the crime.

F l a t w a t e r   (s p r i n t)

World Championships

Seville, Aug 29-Sep 1
British and Irish results shown where B Finals reached

MEN

K1 200m

1	Ronald Rauhe	GER	35.134
2	Anton Ryahov	UZB	35.414
3	Romas Petrukanecas	LTU	35.660

K1 500m

1	Nathan Baggaley	AUS	1:39.901
2	Petar Merkov	BUL	1:40.207
3	Anton Ryahov	UZB	1:40.560

Paul Darby-Dowman GBR, 3rd in B Final

K1 1000m

1	Erik Veras-Larsen	NOR	3:27.586
2	Javier Correa	ARG	3:28.273
3	Adam Seroczynski	POL	3:28.400

Tim Brabants GBR, 2nd in B Final

K2 200m

1	Duonela/Balciiunas	LTU	32.401
2	Wysocki/Twardowski	POL	32.554
3	Rauhe/Wiskotter	GER	32.781

K2 500m

1	Rauhe/Wiskotter	GER	1:31.915
2	Wysocki/Twardowski	POL	1:32.468
3	Kammerer/Storcz	HUN	1:32.795

Sabbertson/Almasi GBR, 4th in B Final

K2 1000m

1	Oskarsson/Nilsson	SWE	3:21.625
2	Veras-Larsen/Fjeldhein	NOR	3:13.691
3	Vereckei/Vereb	HUN	3:14.438
8	Darby-Dowman/Wynne	GBR	3:17.377

Fleming/Maloney IRL, 7th in B Final

K4 200m

1	Slovakia	30.154
2	Spain	30.154
3	Hungary	30.374

Ireland (Strevens/Pringle/Strevens/Egan) 8th B Final

K4 500m

1	Slovakia	1:22.892
2	Belarus	1:23.219
3	Spain	1:23.659

G Britain (Wilson/Johnson/Moule/Foulgher) 9th B Final

K4 1000m

1	Slovakia	2:52.837
2	Germany	2:52.910
3	Bulgaria	2:52.990

C1 200m

1	Maxim Opalev	RUS	39.257
2	Dmitro Sablin	UKR	39.477
3	Andrzej Jezierski	POL	39.843

C1 500m

1	Maxim Opalev	RUS	1:50.596
2	Gyorgy Kolonics	HUN	1:51.636
3	Andreas Dittmer	GER	1:51.843

C1 1000m

1	Andreas Dittmer	GER	3:49.031
2	Maxim Opalev	RUS	3:49.644
3	Stephen Giles	CAN	3:50.737

C2 200m

1	Rojas/Balceiro	CUB	37.027
2	Fuksa/Netusil	CZE	37.100
3	Vartolomei/Averian	ROM	37.240

C2 500m

1	Rojas/Balceiro	CUB	1:43.467
2	Popescu/Simiocencu	ROM	1:43.960
3	Ulegin/Kostoglod	RUS	1:44.280

C2 1000m

1	Kobierski/Sliwinski	POL	3:32.456
2	Rojas/Balceiro	CUB	3:33.676
3	Dalton/Scarola	CAN	3:33.969

C4 200m

1	Russia	33.650
2	Czech Republic	33.964
3	Romania	24.237

C4 500m

1	Romania	1:34.758
2	Russia	1:35.231
3	Poland	1:35.338

C4 1000m

1	Poland	3:17.794
2	Canada	3:18.127
3	Belarus	3:18.421

WOMEN

K1 200m

1	Teresa Portela	ESP	40.693
2	Caroline Brunet	CAN	41.426
3	Elzbieta Urbanczyk	POL	41.713
6	Rachel Train	GBR	42.320

K1 500m

1	Katalin Kovacs	HUN	1:52.116
2	Caroline Brunet	CAN	1:52.483
3	Josefa Idem	ITA	1:53.069

Anna Hemmings GBR, 5th in B Final 1:55.106

K1 1000m

1	Katalin Kovacs	HUN	3:53.340
2	Katrin Wagner	GER	3:53.920
3	Josefa Idem	ITA	3:54.770
7	Tricia Davey	GBR	4:01.579

K2 200m

1	Molanes/Manchon	ESP	37.670
2	Pastuszka/Skowron	POL	37.830
3	Pindzeva/Dacheva	BUL	37.897
6	Hemmings/Train	GBR	38.930

K2 500m

1	Szabo/Bota	HUN	1:43.607
2	Wagner/Mucke	GER	1:44.693
3	Molanes/Manchon	ESP	1:45.253

Cattle/Hardy GBR, 7th in B Final 1:52.883

K2 1000m

1	Szabo/Bota	HUN	3:37.259
2	Opgen-Rhein/Mucke	GER	3:38.572
3	Gafni/Pessakhovitch	ISR	3:42.165

K4 200m

1	Hungary	34.480
2	Spain	34.647
3	Germany	35.854

K4 500m

1	Hungary	1:35.724
2	Germany	1:37.171
3	Spain	1:37.331

Great Britain (Davey/Train/Cattle/Hardy) 4th in B Final

K4 1000m

1	Poland	3:17.007
2	China	3:17.194
3	Hungary	3:18.487

European Championships
Szeged, Hungary, July 19-21

MEN

K1 200m
1	Ronald Rauhe	GER	35.201
2	Vince Fehervari	HUN	35.441
3	Romas Petrukanecas	LTU	35.621

K1 500m
1	Akos Vereckei	HUN	1:36.868
2	Petar Merkov	BUL	1:36.924
3	Jovino Gonzalez	ESP	1:37.440
5	Paul Darby-Dowman	GBR	1:38.304

K1 1000m
1	Tim Brabants	GBR	3:34.148
2	Adam Seroczynski	POL	3:34.226
3	Lutz Liwowski	GER	3:34.616

K2 200m
1	Fehervari/Hegedus	HUN	32.382
2	Rauhe/Wieskotter	GER	32.546
3	Twardowski/Wysocki	POL	32.554

K2 500m
1	Rauhe/Wieskotter	GER	1:26.971
2	Kammerer/Storcz	HUN	1:27.047
3	Oskarsson/Nilsson	SWE	1:27.263

DNQ: Almasi/Sabberton GBR 5th in semi-final

K2 1000m
1	Oskarsson/Nilsson	SWE	3:11.931
2	Kadnar/Erban	SVK	3:13.545
3	Larsen/Fjeldheim	NOR	3:13.665
6	Darby-Dowman/Wynne	GBR	3:15.933

K4 200m
1	Slovakia	30.414
2	Spain	30.482
3	Hungary	30.518

K4 500m
1	Slovakia	1:19.650
2	Hungary	1:20.278
3	Italy	1:20.350

DNQ: GBR (Johnson/Foulger/Moule/Hobrough) 7th in s-f

K4 1000m
1	Slovakia	2:51.446
2	Hungary	2:52.748
3	Bulgaria	2:52.754

DNQ: GBR (R Darby-D/Fowler/Eldridge/Wilson), 7th in s-f

C1 200m
1	Maxim Opalev	RUS	39.904
2	Andrzej Jezoerski	POL	40.748
3	Sandor Malomsoki	HUN	40.988

C1 500m
1	Maxim Opalev	RUS	1:45.614
2	Andreas Dittmar	GER	1:46.826
3	Martin Doktor	CZE	1:48.038

C1 1000m
1	Andreas Dittmar	GER	3:58.103
2	Maxim Opalev	RUS	3:58.979
3	Stanimir Atanasov	BUL	4:00.893

C2 200m
1	Buzal/Vegh	HUN	36.899
2	Fuksa/Netusil	CZE	36.971
3	Vartolomei/Averian	ROM	37.011

C2 500m
1	Ulegin/Kostoglod	RUS	1:38.502
2	Simiocencu/Popescu	ROM	1:39.650
3	Wylenzek/Gille	GER	1:40.866

C2 1000m
1	Simiocencu/Popescu	ROM	3:38.607
2	Kobierski/Sliwinski	POL	3:38.727
3	Ulegin/Kostoglod	RUS	3:38.859

C4 200m
1	Russia	33.854
2	Hungary	33.886
3	Czech Republic	34.322

C4 500m
1	Hungary	1:29.956
2	Russia	1:30.424
3	Romania	1:30.640

C4 1000m
1	Hungary	3:18.790
2	Romania	3:20.146
3	Russia	3:20.674

WOMEN

K1 200m
1	Teresa Portela	ESP	40.319
2	Aneta Pastuszka	POL	40.563
3	Rachel Train	GBR	41.227

K1 500m
1	Katalin Kovacs	HUN	1:47.343
2	Josepha Idem	ITA	1:48.703
3	Elzbieta Urbanczyk	POL	1:49.963

DNQ: Anna Hemmings GBR, 5th in s-f

K1 1000m
1	Katalin Kovacs	HUN	3:55.298
2	Josefa Iden	ITA	3:57.842
3	Katrin Wagner	GER	3:59.432
7	Tricia Davey	GBR	4:05.144

K2 200m
1	Amanchon/Molanes	ESP	37.145
2	Pastuszka/Skowron	POL	37.529
3	Poryvaeva/Gouli	RUS	37.637
9	Hemmings/Train	GBR	38.613

K2 500m
1	Pastuszka/Skowron	POL	1:37.987
2	Szabo/Bota	HUN	1:39.087
3	Manchon/Molanes	ESP	1:39.795

DNQ: Hardy/Cattle GBR 8th in s-f

K2 1000m
1	Szabo/Bota	HUN	3:38.282
2	Skowron/Bialkowska	POL	3:39.968
3	Mucke/Opgen-Rhein	GER	3:40.172

K4 200m
1	Spain	34.317
2	Hungary	34.521
3	Russia	35.165

K4 500m
1	Hungary	1:30.765
2	Spain	1:32.049
3	Poland	1:33.077

DNQ: GBR (Hardy/Rachel Train/Davey/Cattle) 5th in s-f

K4 1000m
1	Hungary	3:21.280
2	Romania	3:23.674
3	Poland	3:26.500

S l a l o m

World Championships
Bourg St Maurice, France, Aug 22-25
GBR non-qualifying places shown
MEN
K1

1	Fabien Lefevre	FRA	184.89
2	Miha Terdic	SLO	189.94
3	Ivan Pisvejc	CZE	190.10

DNQ: Campbell Walsh (17th in s-f); Anthony Brown (39th in s-f); Paul Ratcliffe (77th in qfy), all GBR
Note: Ratcliffe led after 1st run, but incurred 100 seconds of penalties on his second run

K1 Team

1	Germany	214.11
2	Italy	216.64
3	France	218.25
5	Great Britain	218.68

Ratcliffe/Walsh/Brown

C1

1	Michal Martikan	SVK	192.92
2	Jan Benzien	GER	199.29
3	Patrice Estanguet	FRA	199.32

DNQ: 12 Stuart McIntosh (12th s-f); 20 Dan Goddard (20th s-f); David Florence (35th s-f)

C1 Team

1	Czech Rep	224.27
2	Germany	226.55
3	Slovenia	236.59

C2

1	Hochschorner/Hochschorner	SVK	206.21
2	Luquet/Luquet	FRA	209.41
3	Jiras/Mader	CZE	209.53
6	Bowman/Smith	GBR	213.91

DNQ: Roden/Roden (16th s-f); Burt/Nicoll (21st s-f)

C2 Team

1	France	239.09
2	Germany	257.07
3	Poland	265.80
4	Great Britain	265.90

Bowman/Smith Roden/Roden Burt/Nicoll

WOMEN
K1

1	Rebecca Giddens	USA	216.09
2	Mandy Planert	GER	218.11
3	Cristina Giai Pron	ITA	222.46
6	Laura Blakeman	GBR	227.80
9	Helen Reeves	GBR	232.68

DNQ: Heather Corrie (12th s-f); Fiona Pennie (37th s-f)

K1 Team

1	France	294.73
2	Czech Rep	298.78
3	Great Britain	306.24

Reeves/Blakeman/Corrie

European Championships
Bratislava, Slovakia, July 12-14
MEN
K1

1	Paul Ratcliffe	GBR	199.51
2	Helmut Oblinger	AUT	200.56
3	Peter Cibak	SVK	201.74
4	Campbell Walsh	GBR	202.52

DNQ: Neil Buckley (14th s-f)

C1

1	Mariusz Wieczorek	POL	206.17
2	Tony Estanguet	FRA	208.70
3	Jan Benzien	GER	211.50

DNQ: Robert Turner (12th s-f); David Florence (14th s-f); Stuart McIntosh (18th s-f)

C2

1	Hochschorner/Hochschorner	SVK	214.73
2	Jirak/Mader	CZE	215.58
3	Volf/Stepanek	CZE	219.27

DNQ: 14 Smith/Bowman (14th s-f); Burt/Nicoll (16th qlfy)

WOMEN
K1

1	Elena Kaliska	SVK	219.50
2	Irena Pavelkova	CZE	223.15
3	Stepanka Hilgertova	CZE	225.62

DNQ: Nerys Rowlands (11th s-f); Antya Jayes (17th s-f)

World Cup Final
Tibagi, Brazil, Sep 13-15
MEN

K1
1 David Ford CAN 197.85
2 Fabien Lefevre FRA 197.97
3 Anthony Brown GBR 199.76
13 Campbell Walsh GBR 109.26
14 Tim Baillie GBR 109.36
C1
1 Stefan Pfanmuller GER 219.89
2 Stanislav Jezek CZE 221.91
3 Justin Boocock AUS 223.19
C2
1 Hochschorner/Hochschorner SVK 266.71
2 Quemerais/Le Pennec FRA 270.92
3 Walter/Henze GER 275.25
7 Burt/Nicoll GBR 358.90
WOMEN
K1
1 Mandy Planert GER 275.78
2 Irena Pavelkova CZE 277.48
3 Elena Kaliska SVK 280.92
9 Anyta Jayes GBR 474.71

Slalom

World Cup Final Standings

MEN
K1

1	Fabien Lefevre	FRA	110.5
2	David Ford	CAN	91.0
3	Benoit Peschier	FRA	88.5
7	Anthony Brown	GBR	51.0
24	Campbell Walsh	GBR	22.0
30	Tim Baillie	GBR	17.5
34	Tim Morrison	GBR	15.0
52=	Etienne Stott	GBR	9.0
73=	Richard Hounslow	GBR	5.0

C1

1	Stefan Pfannmoeller	GER	106.0
2	Stanislav Jezek	CZE	91.5
3	Justin Boocock	AUS	79.0
21=	Stuart McIntosh	GBR	24.0
39=	Andrew Hamilton	GBR	12.0
42	Rob Wylie	GBR	11.0

C2

1	Hochschorner/Hochschorner	SVK	123.0
2	Walter/Henze	GER	96.0
3	Kuban/Olejnik	SVK	84.0
13	Burt/Nicoll	GBR	39.5
24	Bowman/Smith	GBR	17.0
31=	Roden/Roden	GBR	7.0
31=	Green/Green	GBR	7.0

WOMEN
K1

1	Mandy Planert	GER	120.0
2	Irena Pavelkova	CZE	111.5
3	Elena Kaliska	SVK	83.0
16	Heather Corrie	GBR	28.0
20	Anyta Jayes	GBR	25.5
22=	Helen Reeves	GBR	22.0
28	Nerys Rowlands	GBR	18.0
35=	Helen Barnes	GBR	14.0
43=	Fione Pennie	GBR	10.0
43=	Laura Blakeman	GBR	10.0
53	Kimberly Walsh	GBR	8.0

Marathon

World Championships

Zamora, Spain, Sep 27-29
These championships were originally scheduled for Tyn in August, but due to extensive flooding in the Czech Republic, were moved to Spain

MEN
K1

1	Manuel Busto Fernandez	ESP	2:32:55.470
2	Torsten Tranum	DEN	2:32:56.050
3	Atila Jambor	HUN	2:32.56.660
10	Ivan Lawler	GBR	2:35:40.120
13	Steven Baker	GBR	2:35:41.800

K2

1	Veras-Larsen/Fjeldheim	NOR	2:23:30.260
2	De Nijs/Te Linde	NED	2:23:31.520
3	Busto/Martinez	ESP	2:23:33.160
7	Johnson/Golder	GBR	2:24:27.070
18	Slater/Prestwood	GBR	2:32:20.280

C1

1	Pavel Bednar	CZE	2:57:18.710
2	Lionel Dubois	FRA	2:57:20.480
3	Pedro Areal Abreu	ESP	2:58:44.930

C2

1	Csabia/Gyore	HUN	2:45:47.280
2	Jirasky/Machac	CZE	2:46:25.940
3	Gilanyi/Kolozsvari	HUN	2:46:28.590

WOMEN
K1

1	Elisabetta Introini	ITA	2:51:22.520
2	Maria Santos Garcia	ESP	2:51:28.060
3	Marianne Fjeldheim	NOR	2:51:37.100
5	Jenny Spencer	GBR	2:55:24.200

K2

1	Csay/Szonda	HUN	2:34:58.040
2	Schuck/Pontzen	GER	2:41:31.960
3	Przybylska/Michalak	POL	2:41:33.110

Nations Points

1	Spain	109
2	Hungary	105
3	Czech Republic	72
10=	Great Britain	43

Canoe Sailing

World Championships

Bristol, Rhode Island, USA, Aug 25-29

1	Steve Clark USA	10pts
2	Anders Petterson SWE	15pts
3	Erich Chase USA	26pts
6	Mark Goodchild GBR	33pts
7	John Ellis GBR	36pts

Canoe Polo

World Championships

Essen, Germany, Sep 8-15
Men

1 Great Britain
2 Netherlands
3 Germany

Women

1 Germany
2 France
3 Australia
5 Great Britain

Cricket

Now, not for one minute do we want to instigate a witch-hunt, but can anyone explain how Nasser Hussain and Duncan Fletcher ride the waves so well, are so apparently immune to criticism, when the only Test successes for England in two years and eight series have come against the Sri Lankans, while against Pakistan, New Zealand and India, there have been three drawn series and a defeat, and against Australia, two almighty thrashings.

The accepted wisdom has been that teams controlled by the Hussain/Fletcher axis do not lose as easily as English teams once did. That's a tricky argument to sustain when England lose the first four Tests against Australia in a series for only the third time ever and the first time in 51 years. When that happens the defence has to change, and so it has, for we are now dealing with the greatest team in sporting history, and England did well to get that close.

Oh please, as Joan Rivers might say, the Australians have only one genuinely scary bowler, Brett Lee, who was not available for the first two Tests. Their second strike bowler, Jason Gillespie, was struggling for fitness, and the much-lauded Glen McGrath is now totally reliant on line and length, the quicker balls ever more scarce. Their leg-spinner of genius can now no longer bowl a wrong-'un (well, he can't bowl at all at the minute, but that's leaking into next year), and their stand-in bowler, Andy Bichel, wasn't even number one at Worcester last year. So, what's the big deal?

To be even-handed about this, we are prepared to admit that they can bat in depth, but England still had the batsman of the series and if we can't build on that what chance have we? John Buchanan, the Australian coach, was just about right in his famous leaked missive, when he argued that England's problems are largely psychological.

The simple fact is that England has the largest blooding pool of new talent in the world, but is singularly loathe to develop and use that talent in a rational manner. Instead, they cling on to those cricketers deemed to be 'Test Class' even though they have actually achieved very little.

It will not be long now before Alec Stewart has to start holding the book he's reading a little further from his eyes. Yet, England still calls on him at every opportunity, on the grounds that the 40-year-old is a genuine batsman/wicket-keeper. Well, the last time Stewart scored a century for England was against mighty Zimbabwe in May 2000, and the only reason that his average against Australia in the Ashes' series was a respectable 44.66 was because he scored 109 runs in the final Test. His first five innings in the series (when the tone was set) brought just 93 runs, at an average of 18.6.

Mark Butcher is, apparently, another cricketer avowed of 'Test Class', who has twice taken the Australian attack to the sword in Test matches. Butcher was single-handedly responsible for the win at Headingley in 2001 with a brilliant 173 not out, but the series had by then been decided. Butcher's average up to that point was a less-than-sensational 32.8. In Australia, Butcher again made a singular contribution when the series had been lost, scoring 124 in England's first innings in the final Test. To that point, his series average was just 20.0.

Hussain, himself, had only a passable time with the bat, a top score of 75 from 10 completed innings being nowhere near good enough. But it's as a captain, not as a batsmen that Hussain has looked more exposed.

Mike Atherton's body language on the field always militated against his ability as a captain; his gestures would be closed rather than open, and would not impart confidence to his players. Hussain has a more open body posture, but has begun to display his irritation with on-field events far too openly. It signals a loss of control.

That Hussain remains captain of the Test side seems largely down to the inability of the selectors to find anyone else for the job. Michael Vaughan is an obvious candidate, but they are terrified that it could affect his batting, and at the moment that's about all that England can count on.

There has, at least, been some progress with the bowling, with Steve Harmison and James Anderson showing some promise, and Simon Jones being dreadfully unfortunate at Brisbane.

Michael Vaughan

Coming Of Age

England v Sri Lanka

1st Test (2nd Innings)
Lord's, May 16-20

115

England v India

1st Test (2nd Innings)
Lord's, July 25-29

100

England v India

2nd Test (1st Innings)
Trent Bridge, Aug 8-12

197

England v India

4th Test (1st Innings)
The Oval, Sep 5-9

195

England v Australia

2nd Test (1st Innings)
Adelaide, Nov 21-24

177

England v Australia

4th Test (2nd Innings)
Melbourne, Dec 26-30

145

England v Australia

5th Test (2nd Innings)
Sydney, Jan 2-6, 2003

145

Tests in 2002
1414 runs at an
average of 64.27

Ashes Series 2002-03
633 runs at an
average of 63.30

Even so, the desire to include both Darren Gough and Andrew Flintoff in the Ashes party did the remainder of the England team no favours. Gough's knee injury was career-threatening, and it's difficult to get out of bed with a double hernia, let alone play cricket. So, the desperation of the selectors to include both of them was a negative signal to the other players, and their replacements.

It's South Africa and Zimbabwe this summer; the former in disarray, the latter just having lost their only world-class player, Andy Flower now retired. Bangladesh and Sri Lanka follow, so there has never been a better time to blood new Test players. On the other hand, they could give that bloke Mark Ramprakash another go, Graeme Hick is a genuine world-class player, and Phil de Freitas is a model of consistency.

"The last positive thing England did for cricket was invent it"
Ian Chappell.

"Australia haven't seen the best of English cricket in a long while and it's up to us to put that right"
Nasser Hussain, on the eve of the Ashes series.

"There was swing and excessive bounce, but maybe that confused us a little bit about the length we had to bowl"
Duncan Fletcher, the England coach, explaining why his bowlers struggled against India in the Third Test at Headingley. Presumably, without the bounce and the swing, England would have bowled India out for 30, then?

"I don't think anyone can be compared to him. Bradman was not a normal person - he scored a century every three innings and that's something one can only dream of"
Sachim Tendulkar, on reaching 30 Test centuries (at Headingley) to place second in the all-time list, one ahead of Bradman, and four behind Sunil Gavaskar.

"I never was any good at cricket"
John Bunton, 65-year-old retired schoolteacher who attempted to catch a Ganguly six at Headingley. The ball hit Bunton square on the forehead.

"I have absolutely no interest in cricket now"
Garry Sobers.

"How can England improve? Bat, bowl and field better, that would be a start"
Mark Waugh, offering a little advice.

Australia v England

As Nasser Hussain might say, it doesn't matter if you bat first, second, or put them in twice before you bat, scoring 79 is still not enough to win a Test Match. It's not enough to win a Sunday pub match against the White Horse at Ditchling, who probably applied for Test status as soon as they saw the second-innings score of England.

Psychologically, though, Hussain's decision to put the Australians in had sent a message to the England batsmen that was hard to misinterpret. Especially as the team's best strike bowler, Darren Gough, was already on the plane home. It didn't sink in immediately, for on the second day the English batsmen mustered some resistance. It was on Sunday, the fourth day of the Test, that the captain's mistrust of his players' ability reaped the inevitable reward. They lost the will to resist, dismissed for the lowest Test total by England in Australia for 98 years.

Hussain alone was not to blame; Duncan Fletcher was sitting in the dressing room. They both should have resigned on the spot, for it was the worst tactical decision by an England captain since Ian Botham accepted the job in 1980. Fletcher and Hussain stayed and it got worse, despite the best Test performance by an English batsmen in Australia since Wally Hammond. We should introduce a modicum of perspective here for Hammond scored 905 runs at an average of 113.12 in the 1928-9 series, and Michael Vaughan isn't at that level yet.

Vaughan may be a few divisions below Hammond, but in the Second Test he proved that he is about the same distance above the other English cricketers with a quite exemplary 177 in the first innings. Hussain had won the toss again at the Adelaide Oval and this time had to bat, not least because his third-best strike bowler, Simon Jones, had ruptured his anterior cruciate ligament in a sliding tackle of the ball in the First Test and was ruled out for nine months.

Vaughan's resistance was solitary, though, and England lost by a mammoth innings and 51 runs. It was much better in the Third Test, when we only lost by an innning and 48 runs. In the fourth Test, it was better still, for we only went down by five wickets. Yes, sarcasm, and Vaughan, is all we have left.

Of the other England batsmen, the least said the better. In the first four Tests only Vaughan reached the century mark. The second highest England score in those matches was Craig White's 85 not out at Melbourne. When Mark Butcher scored 124 at Sydney, it was already a dead rubber, and that has a familiar ring to it, too.

If the batting fell short (one English batsmen averaging over 50, against five Australians), so did the bowling, with only Steve Harmison taking his wickets, just the five, for less than 25 runs apiece, while Glen McGrath, Shane Warne and Jason Gillespie took 53 wickets between them at exactly 23 runs each. Oh dear.

CRICKET

First Test
Woolloongabba, Brisbane, Nov 7-10

AUSTRALIA - First Innings

				balls	4/6
J Langer	c Stewart	b Jones	32	38	6/0
M Hayden	c Stewart	b Caddick	197	268	25/2
R Ponting		b Giles	123	195	12/2
D Martyn	c Trescothick	b White	26	100	2/0
S Waugh*	c Crawley	b Caddick	7	37	0/0
D Lehmann	c Butcher	b Giles	30	61	2/0
A Gilchrist†	c Giles	b White	0	2	0/0
S Warne	c Butcher	b Caddick	57	65	8/0
A Bichel	lbw	b Giles	0	1	0/0
J Gillespie	not out		0	20	0/0
G McGrath	lbw	b Giles	0	2	0/0
Extras (B1, LB11, W1, NB7)			20		
Total (130.2 overs, 587 mins)			492		

Fall of Wickets: 1-67 (Langer, 14.3 overs), 2-339 (Ponting, 75.4), 3-378 (Hayden, 92.5), 4-399 (Martyn, 103.3), 5-408 (Waugh, 106.6), 6-415 (Gilchrist, 109.1), 7-478 (Lehmann, 122.3), 8-478 (Bichel, 122.4), 9-492 (Warne, 129.2), 10-492 (McGrath, 130.2)

Bowling: Caddick 35-9-108-3 (1nb); **Hoggard** 30-4-122-0 (1nb, 1w); **Jones** 7-0-32-1; **White** 27-4-105-2 (5nb); **Giles** 29.2-3-101-4; **Butcher** 2-0-12-0

AUSTRALIA - Second Innings

J Langer	c Stewart	b Caddick	22	25	4/0
M Hayden	c & b Giles		103	152	13/1
R Ponting	c Trescothick	b Caddick	3	11	0/0
D Martyn	c Hussain	b Giles	64	120	6/0
A Gilchrist†	not out		60	59	4/2
S Waugh*	c Trescothick	b Caddick	12	42	0/0
D Lehmann	not out		20	21	0/0
Extras (B3, LB5, NB4)			12		
Total (5 wickets dec, 71 overs, 307 mins)			296		

Did Not Bat: S Warne, A Bichel, J Gillespie, G McGrath

Fall of Wickets: 1-30 (Langer, 6.5 overs), 2-39 (Ponting, 10.1), 3-192 (Hayden, 48.4), 4-213 (Martyn, 52.2), 5-242 (Waugh, 63.1)

Bowling: Caddick 23-2-95-3 (3nb); Hoggard 13-2-42-0; White 11-0-61-0 (1nb); Giles 24-2-90-2

ENGLAND - First Innings

M Trescothick	c Ponting	b McGrath	72	158	12/1
M Vaughan	c Gilchrist	b McGrath	33	36	4/0
M Butcher	c Hayden	b McGrath	54	126	4/0
N Hussain*	c Gilchrist	b Gillespie	51	111	4/1
J Crawley	not out		69	144	8/0
A Stewart†		b Gillespie	0	2	0/0
C White		b McGrath	12	19	2/0
A Giles	c Gilchrist	b Bichel	13	25	1/0
A Caddick	c Ponting	b Bichel	0	3	0/0
M Hoggard	c Hayden	b Warne	4	23	0/0
S Jones	absent hurt				
Extras (B2, LB8, NB7)			17		
Total (106.5 overs, 451 mins)			325		

Fall of Wickets: 1-49 (Vaughan, 12.1 overs), 2-170 (Butcher, 52.1), 3-171 (Trescothick, 52.6), 4-268 (Hussain, 85.6), 5-270 (Stewart, 87.2), 6-283 (White, 92.6), 7-308 (Giles, 99.5), 8-308 (Caddick, 101.2), 9-325 (Hoggard, 106.5)

Bowling: McGrath 30-9-87-4 (1nb); **Gillespie** 18-4-51-2; **Bichel** 23-4-74-2 (5nb); **Warne** 26.5-4-87-1; **Waugh** 4-2-5-0; **Lehmann** 5-0-11-0

ENGLAND - Second Innings

M Trescothick	c Gilchrist	b Gillespie	1	6	0/0
M Vaughan	lbw	b McGrath	0	2	0/0
M Butcher	c Ponting	b Warne	40	76	5/0
N Hussain	c Ponting	b McGrath	11	45	1/0
J Crawley	run out (Langer/Gilchrist)		0	2	0/0
A Stewart	c Hayden	b Warne	0	1	0/0
C White	c Hayden	b McGrath	13	19	2/0
A Giles	c Gilchrist	b McGrath	4	11	1/0
A Caddick	c Lehmann	b Warne	4	7	1/0
M Hoggard	not out		1	5	0/0
S Jones	absent hurt				
Extras (lb 1, nb 4)			5		
Total (28.2 overs, 127 mins)			79		

Fall of Wickets: 1-1 (Vaughan, 0.3 overs), 2-3 (Trescothick, 1.5), 3-33 (Hussain, 15.6), 4-34 (Crawley, 16.3), 5-35 (Stewart, 16.5), 6-66 (White, 23.1), 7-74 (Giles, 25.6), 8-74 (Butcher, 26.2), 9-79 (Caddick, 28.2)

Bowling: McGrath 12-3-36-4 (2nb); **Gillespie** 6-1-13-1; **Warne** 10.2-3-29-3 (2nb)

Toss: England
Umpires: **Steve Bucknor** WI and **R Koertzen** RSA
TV Umpire: **S Taufel**

Man of the Match: **Matthew Hayden** AUS
AUSTRALIA WON BY 384 RUNS

Second Test
Adelaide Oval, Nov 21-24

ENGLAND - First Innings

M Trescothick		b McGrath	35	54	4/0
M Vaughan	c Warne	b Bichel	177	306	22/3
R Key	c Ponting	b Warne	1	23	0/0
N Hussain*	c Gilchrist	b Warne	47	120	6/0
M Butcher	c Gilchrist	b Gillespie	22	51	3/0
A Stewart†	lbw	b Gillespie	29	72	1/0
C White	c Bichel	b Gillespie	1	12	0/0
R Dawson	lbw	b Warne	6	39	0/0
A Caddick		b Warne	0	4	0/0
M Hoggard	c Gilchrist	b Gillespie	6	21	0/0
S Harmison	not out		3	1	0/0
Extras (lb 7, nb 8)			15		
Total (115.5 overs)			342		

Fall of Wickets: 1-88 (Trescothick, 21.2), 2-106 (Key, 30.6), 3-246 (Hussain, 72.4), 4-295 (Vaughan, 89.3), 5-295 (Butcher, 92.4), 6-308 (White, 96.6), 7-325 (Dawson, 108.6), 8-325 (Caddick, 110.4),9-337 (Stewart, 115.1), 10-342 (Hoggard, 115.5)

Bowling: McGrath 30-11-77-1 (2nb); **Gillespie** 26.5-8-78-4; **Bichel** 20-2-78-1 (4nb); **Warne** 34-10-93-4 (2nb); **Waugh** 5-1-9-0

ENGLAND - Second innings

M Trescothick	lbw	b Gillespie	0	8	0/0
M Vaughan	c McGrath	b Warne	41	95	2/1
M Butcher	lbw	b McGrath	4	4	1/0
N Hussain*		b Bichel	10	30	1/0
R Key	c Lehmann	b Bichel	1	6	0/0
A Stewart†	lbw	b Warne	57	101	5/0
C White	c sub (Lee)	b McGrath	5	50	0/0
R Dawson	c Gilchrist	b McGrath	19	30	4/0
M Hoggard		b McGrath	1	12	0/0
S Harmison	lbw	b Warne	0	10	0/0
A Caddick	not out		6	18	1/0
Extras (b 3, lb 4, nb 8)			15		
Total (59.2 overs)			159		

Fall of Wickets: 1-5 (Trescothick, 1.4), 2-17 (Butcher, 2.3), 3-36 (Hussain, 11.2), 4-40 (Key, 13.3), 5-114 (Vaughan, 36.2), 6-130 (White, 47.6), 7-130 (Stewart, 48.1), 8-132 (Hoggard, 51.1), 9-134 (Harmison, 52.6), 10-159 (Dawson, 59.2)

Bowling: McGrath 17.2-6-41-4 (4nb); **Gillespie** 12-1-44-1; **Warne** 25-7-36-3 (4nb); **Bichel** 5-0-31-2

AUSTRALIA - First innings

J Langer	c Stewart	b Dawson	48	59	7/0
M Hayden	c Caddick	b White	46	73	6/1
R Ponting	c Dawson	b White	154	269	9/0
D Martyn	c Hussain	b Harmison	95	229	7/0
S Waugh*	c Butcher	b White	34	40	2/0
D Lehmann	c sub (A Flintoff) b White		5	22	0/0
A Gilchrist†	c Stewart	b Harmison	54	67	4/2
S Warne	c & b Dawson		25	38	2/0
A Bichel		b Hoggard	48	56	8 0
J Gillespie	not out		0	1	0/0
Extras (b 1, lb 17, w 7, nb 18)			43		
Total (9 wkts dec, 139.2 overs)			552		

Did Not Bat: GD McGrath

Fall of Wickets: 1-101 (Hayden, 18.3), 2-114 (Langer, 21.4), 3-356 (Martyn, 99.5), 4-397 (Ponting, 105.1), 5-414 (Lehmann, 111.4), 6-423 (Waugh, 113.4),7-471 (Warne, 124.5), 8-548 (Bichel, 138.5), 9-552 (Gilchrist, 139.2)

Bowling: Caddick 20-2-95-0 (5nb, 2w); **Hoggard** 26-4-84-1; **Harmison** 28.2-8-106-2 (6nb, 1w); **White** 28-2 -106-4 (7nb); Dawson 37-2-143-2

Toss: **England**
Umpires: **S Bucknor** WI and **R Koertzen** RSA
TV Umpire: **S Davies**

Man of the Match: **Ricky Ponting** AUS
AUSTRALIA WON BY AN INNINGS AND 51 RUNS

Third Test
WACA Ground, Perth, Nov 29-Dec 1

ENGLAND - First Innings

M Trescothick	c Gilchrist	b Lee	34	44	7/0
M Vaughan	c Gilchrist	b McGrath	34	79	2/0
M Butcher	run out (Waugh)		9	15	1/0
N Hussain*	c Gilchrist	b Lee	8	12	1/0
R Key		b Martyn	47	108	5/1
A Stewart†	c Gilchrist	b McGrath	7	25	1/0
C White	c Martyn	b Lee	2	19	0/0
A Tudor	c Martyn	b Warne	0	11	0/0
R Dawson	not out		19	51	3/0
C Silverwood	c Hayden	b Gillespie	10	14	1/0
S Harmison		b Gillespie	6	15	0/0
Extras (lb 2, nb 7)			9		
Total (64.2 overs)			**185**		

Fall of Wickets: 1-47 (Trescothick, 12.4), 2-69 (Butcher, 18.5), 3-83 (Hussain, 20.6), 4-101 (Vaughan, 29.3), 5-111 (Stewart, 37.6), 6-121 (White, 43.3), 7-135 (Tudor, 46.6), 8-156 (Key, 52.5), 9-173 (Silverwood, 60.1), 10-185 (Harmison, 64.2)

Bowling: McGrath 17-5-30-2 (2nb); **Gillespie** 17.2-8-43-2; **Lee** 20-1-78-3 (5nb); **Warne** 9-0-32-1; **Martyn** 1-1-0-1

ENGLAND - Second Innings

M Trescothick	c Gilchrist	b Lee	4	18	0/0
M Vaughan	run out (Lee/Gilchrist/McGr)		9	53	0/0
R Dawson	c Waugh	b Gillespie	8	21	1/0
M Butcher	lbw	b McGrath	0	7	0/0
N Hussain*	c Gilchrist	b Warne	61	170	7/0
R Key	lbw	b McGrath	23	106	2/0
A Stewart†	not out		66	83	10/0
C White	st Gilchrist	b Warne	15	25	1/0
A Tudor	retired hurt		3	11	0/0
S Harmison	b Lee		5	10	1/0
C Silverwood	absent hurt				
Extras (b 8, lb 5, w 1, nb 15)			29		
Total (82.1 overs)			**223**		

FAll of Wickets: 1-13 (Trescothick, 6.4), 2-33 (Dawson, 12.6), 3-34 (Vaughan, 15.5), 4-34 (Butcher, 15.6), 5-102 (Key, 50.6), 6-169 (Hussain, 69.4), 7-208 (White, 77.5), 8-223 (Harmison, 82.1)

Bowling: Lee 18.1-3-72-2 (8nb, 1w); **McGrath** 21-9-24-2; (3nb); **Gillespie** 15-4-35-1; **Warne** 26-5-70-2; **Martyn** 2-0-9-0

AUSTRALIA - First Innings

J Langer	run out (Silverwood/Stewart)		19	19	2/0
M Hayden	c Tudor	b Harmison	30	42	5/0
R Ponting		b White	68	82	10/1
D Martyn	c Stewart	b Tudor	71	158	13/0
D Lehmann	c Harmison	b White	42	61	7/1
S Waugh*		b Tudor	53	89	10/0
A Gilchrist†	c Tudor	b White	38	28	7/1
S Warne	run out (Harmison/Tudor)		35	56	5/0
B Lee	c Key	b White	41	40	5/1
J Gillespie		b White	27	26	4/1
G McGrath	not out		8	9	1/0
Extras (b 4, lb 5, nb 15)			24		
Total (99.1 overs)			**456**		

Fall of Wickets: 1-31 (Langer, 5.3), 2-85 (Hayden, 12.6), 3-159 (Ponting, 34.2), 4-226 (Lehmann, 51.2),5-264 (Martyn, 62.6), 6-316 (Gilchrist, 72.1), 7-348 (Waugh, 81.2), 8-416 (Warne, 92.4), 9-423 (Lee, 95.2), 10-456 (Gillespie, 99.1)

Bowling: Silverwood 4-0-29-0; **Tudor** 29-2-144-2 (11nb); **Harmison** 28-7-86-1 (1nb); **White** 23.1-3-127-5 (3nb); **Butcher** 10-1-40-0; Dawson 5-0-21-0

Toss: **England**
Umpires: **S Bucknor** WI and **R Koertzen** RSA
TV Umpire: **D Harper**

Man of the Match: **Damien Martyn** AUS
AUSTRALIA WON BY AN INNINGS AND 48 RUNS

Fourth Test
Melbourne Cricket Ground, Dec 26-30

ENGLAND - First Innings

J Langer	c Caddick	b Dawson	250	407	30/1
M Hayden	c Crawley	b Caddick	102	149	10/3
R Ponting		b White	21	32	3/0
D Martyn	c Trescothick	b White	17	30	3/0
S Waugh*	c Foster	b White	77	117	15/0
M Love	not out		62	141	4/0
A Gilchrist†		b Dawson	1	6	0/0
Extras (LB11, W5, NB5)			21		
Total (6 wickets dec, 146 overs)			551		

Did Not Bat: B Lee, J Gillespie, S MacGill, G McGrath

Fall of Wickets: 1-195 (Hayden, 44.2), 2-235 (Ponting, 53.5), 3-265 (Martyn, 63.6), 4-394 (Waugh, 103.3), 5-545 (Langer, 143.5), 6-551 (Gilchrist, 145.6)

Bowling: Caddick 36-6-126-1 (3nb, 1w); **Harmison** 36-7-108-0 (1nb); **White** 33-5-133-3 (1nb); **Dawson** 28-1-121-2; **Butcher** 13-2-52-0 (4w)

AUSTRALIA - Second Innings

J Langer	lbw	b Caddick	24	56	1/0
M Hayden	c sub (Tudor)	b Caddick	1	2	0/0
R Ponting	c Foster	b Harmison	30	35	3/1
D Martyn	c Foster	b Harmison	0	3	0/0
S Waugh*	c Butcher	b Caddick	14	25	2/0
M Love	not out		6	14	0/0
A Gilchrist†	not out		10	13	2/0
Extras (b 8, lb 5, nb 9)			22		
Total (5 wickets, 23.1 overs)			107		

Did Not Bat: B Lee, J Gillespie, S MacGill, G McGrath

Fall of Wickets: 1-8 (Hayden, 2.1), 2-58 (Ponting, 11.2), 3-58 (Martyn, 11.5), 4-83 (Waugh, 18.1), 5-90 (Langer, 18.5)

Bowling: Caddick 12-1-51-3 (2nb); **Harmison** 11.1-1-43-2 (7nb)

ENGLAND - First Innings

M Trescothick	c Gilchrist	b Lee	37	75	6/1
M Vaughan		b McGrath	11	17	2/0
M Butcher	lbw	b Gillespie	25	78	3/0
N Hussain*	c Hayden	b MacGill	24	58	3/0
R Dawson	c Love	b MacGill	6	18	1/0
R Key	lbw	b Lee	0	2	0/0
J Crawley	c Langer	b Gillespie	17	45	2/0
C White	not out		85	134	9/3
J Foster†	lbw	b Waugh	19	76	0/0
A Caddick		b Gillespie	17	30	1/1
S Harmison	c Gilchrist	b Gillespie	2	14	0/0
Extras (B3, LB10, NB14)			27		
Total (89.3 overs)			270		

Fall of Wickets: 1-13 (Vaughan, 6.2), 2-73 (Trescothick, 22.4), 3-94 (Butcher, 32.1), 4-111 (Dawson, 37.6), 5-113 (Key, 38.4), 6-118 (Hussain, 41.6), 7-172 (Crawley, 54.2), 8-227 (Foster, 76.5), 9-264 (Caddick, 85.5), 10-270 (Harmison, 89.3)

Bowling: McGrath 16-5-41-1 (2nb); **Gillespie** 16.3-7-25-4 (1nb); **MacGill** 36-10-108-2; **Lee** 17-4-70-2 (7nb); **Waugh** 4-0-13-1

ENGLAND - Second Innings (following on)

M Trescothick	lbw	b MacGill	37	46	5/1
M Vaughan	c Love	b MacGill	145	218	19/3
M Butcher	c Love	b Gillespie	6	29	0/0
N Hussain*		c & b McGrath	23	70	3/0
R Key	c Ponting	b Gillespie	52	109	7/0
J Crawley		b Lee	33	105	3/0
C White	c Gilchrist	b MacGill	21	62	3/0
J Foster†	c Love	b MacGill	6	13	1/0
R Dawson	not out		15	45	2/0
A Caddick	c Waugh	b MacGill	10	19	1/0
S Harmison		b Gillespie	7	15	1/0
Extras (B3, LB21, W2, NB6)			32		
Total (120.4 overs)			387		

Fall of Wickets: 1-67 (Trescothick, 15.6), 2-89 (Butcher, 24.6), 3-169 (Hussain, 48.5), 4-236 (Vaughan, 69.4), 5-287 (Key, 81.1), 6-342 (Crawley, 104.5), 7-342 (White, 105.3), 8-356 (Foster, 109.5), 9-378 (Caddick, 117.5), 10-387 (Harmison, 120.4)

Bowling: McGrath 19-5-44-1; **Gillespie** 24.4-6-71-3; **MacGill** 48-10-152-5; **Lee** 27-4-87-1 (6nb, 2w); **Waugh** 2-0-9-0

Toss: **Australia**
Umpires: **D Orchard** RSA and **R Tiffin** ZIM
TV Umpire: **D Hair**

Man of the Match: **Justin Langer** AUS
AUSTRALIA WON BY FIVE WICKETS

Fifth Test
Sydney Cricket Ground, Jan 2-6

ENGLAND - First Innings

Batsman			R		
M Trescothick	c Gilchrist	b Bichel	19	40	2/0
M Vaughan	c Gilchrist	b Lee	0	7	0/0
M Butcher		b Lee	124	275	19/0
N Hussain*	c Gilchrist	b Gillespie	75	149	8/0
R Key	lbw	b Waugh	3	27	0/0
J Crawley	not out		35	142	3/0
A Stewart†		b Bichel	71	86	15/0
R Dawson	c Gilchrist	b Bichel	2	9	0/0
A Caddick		b MacGill	7	29	0/0
M Hoggard	st Gilchrist	b MacGill	0	5	0/0
S Harmison	run out (Langer/MacGill)		4	4	1/0
Extras	(B6, LB3, NB13)		22		
Total	(127 overs)		362		

Fall of Wickets: 1-4 (Vaughan, 3.1), 2-32 (Trescothick, 13.5), 3-198 (Hussain, 67.5), 4-210 (Key, 75.6), 5-240 (Butcher, 85.6), 6-332 (Stewart, 113.1), 7-337 (Dawson, 115.3), 8-348 (Caddick, 122.4), 9-350 (Hoggard, 124.3), 10-362 (Harmison, 126.6)

Bowling: Gillespie 27-10-62-1 (1nb); **Lee** 31-9-97-2 (2nb); **Bichel** 21-5-86-3 (4nb); **MacGill** 44-8-106-2 (5nb); **Waugh** 4-3-2-1

AUSTRALIA -First Innings

Batsman			R		
J Langer	c Hoggard	b Caddick	25	44	3/0
M Hayden	lbw	b Caddick	15	11	2/0
R Ponting	c Stewart	b Caddick	7	6	1/0
D Martyn	c Caddick	b Harmison	26	71	4/0
S Waugh*	c Butcher	b Hoggard	102	135	18/0
M Love	c Trescothick	b Harmison	0	6	0/0
A Gilchrist†	c Stewart	b Harmison	133	121	18/0
A Bichel	c Crawley	b Hoggard	4	9	0/0
B Lee	c Stewart	b Hoggard	0	1	0/0
J Gillespie	not out		31	83	2/1
S MacGill	c Hussain	b Hoggard	1	5	0/0
Extras	(b 2, lb 6, w 2, nb 9)		19		
Total	(80.3 overs)		363		

Fall of Wickets: 1-36 (Hayden, 5.6), 2-45 (Ponting, 7.2), 3-56 (Langer, 11.3), 4-146 (Martyn, 34.2), 5-150 (Love, 36.2), 6-241 (Waugh, 52.5), 7-267 (Bichel, 58.2), 8-267 (Lee, 58.3), 9-349 (Gilchrist, 78.3), 10-363 (MacGill, 80.3)

Bowling: Hoggard 21.3-4-92-4 (5nb); **Caddick** 23-3-121-3 (2nb); **Harmison** 20-4-70-3 (2nb, 2w); **Dawson** 16-0-72-0

ENGLAND - Second innings

Batsman			R		
M Trescothick		b Lee	22	21	4/0
M Vaughan	lbw	b Bichel	183	278	27/1
M Butcher	c Hayden	b MacGill	34	66	4/0
N Hussain*	c Gilchrist	b Lee	72	181	9/0
R Key	c Hayden	b Lee	14	26	1/0
J Crawley	lbw	b Gillespie	8	15	1/0
A Stewart†	not out		38	82	3/0
R Dawson		c & b Bichel	12	35	1/0
A Caddick	c Langer	b MacGill	8	26	1/0
M Hoggard		b MacGill	0	10	0/0
S Harmison	not out		20	23	4/0
Extras	(b 9, lb 20, w 2, nb 10)		41		
Total	(9 wickets dec, 125.3 overs)		452		

Fall of Wickets: 1-37 (Trescothick, 5.5), 2-124 (Butcher, 28.6), 3-313 (Hussain, 85.5), 4-344 (Key, 93.5), 5-345 (Vaughan, 94.2), 6-356 (Crawley, 98.6), 7-378 (Dawson, 108.5), 8-407 (Caddick, 116.4), 9-409 (Hoggard, 118.6)

Bowling: Gillespie 18.3-4-70-1; **Lee** 31.3-5-132-3 (5nb, 1w); **MacGill** 41-8-120-3; **Bichel** 25.3-3-82-2 (5nb, 1w); **Martyn** 3-1-14-0; **Waugh** 6-2-5-0

AUSTRALIA - Second Innings

Batsman			R		
J Langer	lbw	b Caddick	3	8	0/0
M Hayden	lbw	b Hoggard	2	6	0/0
A Bichel	lbw	b Caddick	49	58	8/0
R Ponting	lbw	b Caddick	11	16	2/0
D Martyn	c Stewart	b Dawson	21	79	2/0
S Waugh*		b Caddick	6	11	1/0
M Love		b Harmison	27	50	3/0
A Gilchrist†	c Butcher	b Caddick	37	29	7/0
B Lee	c Stewart	b Caddick	46	32	9/1
J Gillespie	not out		3	36	0/0
S MacGill		b Caddick	1	2	0/0
Extras	(b 6, lb 8, w 3, nb 3)		20		
Total	(all out, 54 overs, 240 mins)		226		

Fall of Wickets: 1-5 (Langer, 1.6), 2-5 (Hayden, 2.2), 3-25 (Ponting, 5.6), 4-93 (Bichel, 21.4), 5-99 (Waugh, 25.3), 6-109 (Martyn, 32.2), 7-139 (Love, 39.4), 8-181 (Gilchrist, 43.3), 9-224 (Lee, 53.2), 10-226 (MacGill, 53.6)

Bowling: Hoggard 13-3-35-1 (1nb); **Caddick** 22-5-94-7; **Harmison** 9-1-42-1 (2nb, 2w); **Dawson** 10-2-41-1

Toss: England
Umpires: **D Orchard** RSA and **R Tiffin** ZIM
TV Umpire: **S Taufel**

Man of the Match: **Michael Vaughan ENG**
ENGLAND WON BY 225 RUNS

Man of the Series: MICHAEL VAUGHAN

England v Australia Test Averages

England

BATTING

	M	I	NO	Rns	HS	Av	100	50
M Vaughan	5	10	0	633	183	63.30	3	-
A Stewart	4	8	2	268	71	44.66	-	3
J Crawley	3	6	2	162	69*	40.50	-	1
N Hussain	5	10	0	382	75	38.20	-	4
M Butcher	5	10	0	318	124	31.80	1	1
M Trescothick	5	10	0	261	72	26.10	-	1
C White	4	8	1	154	85*	22.00	-	1
R Key	4	8	0	141	52	17.62	-	1
R Dawson	4	8	2	87	19*	14.50	-	-
J Foster	1	2	0	25	19	12.50	-	-
C Silverwood	1	1	0	10	10	10.00	-	-
A Giles	1	2	0	17	13	8.50	-	-
S Harmison	4	8	2	47	20*	7.83	-	-
A Caddick	4	8	1	52	17	7.42	-	-
A Tudor	1	2	1	3	3*	3.00	-	-
M Hoggard	3	6	1	12	6	2.40	-	-
S Jones	1	0						

BOWLING

	M	O	M	R	W	Av	BB
S Harmison	1	49	12	120	5	24.00	3-57
A Giles	1	53.2	5	191	6	31.83	4-101
S Jones	1	7	0	32	1	32.00	1-32
A Caddick	4	171	28	690	20	34.50	7-94
C White	4	122.1	14	532	14	38.00	5-127
S Harmison	4	132.3	28	455	9	50.55	3-70
M Hoggard	3	103.3	17	375	6	62.50	4-92
A Tudor	1	29	2	144	2	72.00	2-144
R Dawson	4	96	5	398	5	79.60	2-121
C Silverwood	1	4	0	29	0	-	-
M Butcher	5	25	3	104	0	-	-

Australia

BATTING

	M	I	NO	Rns	HS	Av	100	50
M Hayden	5	8	0	496	197	62.00	3	-
J Gillespie	5	5	4	61	31*	61.00	-	-
A Gilchrist	5	8	2	333	133	55.50	1	2
J Langer	5	8	0	423	250	52.87	1	-
R Ponting	5	8	0	417	154	52.12	2	1
M Love	2	4	2	95	62*	47.50	-	1
D Martyn	5	8	0	320	95	40.00	-	3
S Warne	3	3	0	117	57	39.00	-	1
S Waugh	5	8	0	305	102	38.12	1	2
D Lehmann	3	4	1	97	42	32.33	-	-
B Lee	3	3	0	87	46	29.00	-	-
A Bichel	3	4	0	101	49	25.25	-	-
G McGrath	4	2	1	8	8*	8.00	-	-
S MacGill	2	2	0	2	1	1.00	-	-

BOWLING

	M	O	M	R	W	Av	BB
G McGrath	4	162.2	53	380	19	20.00	4-36
S Waugh	5	25	8	43	2	21.50	1-2
D Martyn	5	6	2	23	1	23.00	1-0
J Gillespie	5	181.5	53	492	20	24.60	4-25
S Warne	3	131.1	29	347	14	24.78	4-93
A Bichel	3	94.3	14	351	10	35.10	3-86
S MacGill	2	169	36	486	12	40.50	5-152
B Lee	3	144.4	26	536	13	41.23	3-78
D Lehmann	3	5	0	11	0	-	-

England v India

India may have one of the most demanding Test Match schedules, but their team still managed to last the distance better than England, coming from behind to draw this batsmen-donimated series one apiece. Raul Dravid and Michael Vaughan shared the men of the series awards; with Dravid (602 runs) staying longer and Vaughan (615) scoring faster. In total 5,151 runs were scored in the four Test matches at an average of 45.99 per wicket. It was lusty stuff.

England started well, with Nasser Hussain, John Crawley and Michael Vaughan striking centuries in the opening Test. Had Ajit Agarkar not dug in his heels in the Indian's second innings for an unbroken 109, the margin of victory would have been considerably more than the 170 which went into the record books. Hussain was even named man of the match. Had the England captain ever known such unalloyed joy?

When England responded to India's 357 in the Second Test with a healthy total of 657, Vaughan scoring an imperious 197, there was not a cloud in the English sky, metaphorically and literally. One hopes that Hussain found deep joy and contentment in that moment, for that was as good as it got. Dravid, Tendulkar (with a flurry) and Ganguly dropped the Indian anchor and the Test was drawn.

On a fruity wicket at Headingley in the Third Test, it was perversely a batsman, Dravid, who took the Test by the throat. He didn't rush, taking five and a half hours on the opening day to reach 110, largely by picking and chosing the balls to play. The England bowlers, thrilled to see both movement and bounce, forgot the old adage about making the batsmen play the ball. Of Caddick's 130 balls on day one, 57 of them passed by untouched.

On the second day, Tendulkar and Ganguly took over where Dravid left off, keeping the scoreboard ticking over steadily. Tendulkar's century came up first; it was his 30th in Test cricket, and left him just four short of Sunil Gavaskar's Test record. That was the most notable landmark, until the 500 beckoned. With the light dimming, the umpires offered the Indian captain a return to the pavilion. Ganguly politely declined, as you would at 488-3, and it was the catalyst for a remarkable last hour, which saw 96 runs scored from the final 67 balls of the day. Ganguly lost his wicket just before stumps, but the partnership had already reached 249, a record against England, and the match was set up for India. Hussain's resistance notwithstanding, England lost by an innings to level the series.

it was honours even at the Oval, Dravid and Vaughan again to the fore, before the rain washed away the last vestiges of the series. It was September 9th and almost winter anyway, and time to dwell on Australia.

First Test
Lord's, July 25-29

ENGLAND - First Innings

				balls	4/6
M Butcher	c Jaffer	b Kumble	29	86	4/0
M Vaughan	lbw	b Khan	0	5	0/0
N Hussain*	c Ratra	b Agarkar	155	331	25/0
G Thorpe		b Khan	4	8	1/0
J Crawley	c Dravid	b Sehwag	64	126	9/0
A Stewart†	lbw	b Khan	19	65	1/0
A Flintoff	c Ratra	b Agarkar	59	62	10/1
C White	st Ratra	b Kumble	53	75	4/1
A Giles		b Nehra	19	26	3/0
S Jones	c Dravid	b Kumble	44	43	7/1
M Hoggard	not out		10	34	2/0
Extras (B11, LB11, W2, NB7)			31		
TOTAL (all out, 142.2 overs, 587 mins)			487		

Fall of Wickets: 1-0 (Vaughan, 1.5), 2-71 (Butcher, 26.4), 3-78 (Thorpe, 29.5), 4-223 (Crawley, 72.2), 5-263 (Stewart, 93.1), 6-356 (Flintoff, 111.6), 7-357 (Hussain, 113.1), 8-390 (Giles, 120.3), 9-452 (Jones, 130.6), 10-487 (White, 142.2)

Bowling: Nehra 30-4-101-1 (5nb, 2w), **Khan** 36-13-90-3, **Agarkar** 21-3-98-2, **Kumble** 42.2-9-128-3, **Ganguly** 3-1-16-0 (1nb), **Sehwag** 10-0-32-1 (1nb)

ENGLAND - Second Innings

M Butcher	lbw	b Kumble	18	33	2/0
MP Vaughan	c Jaffer	b Nehra	100	141	11/0
N Hussain*	c Ratra	b Agarkar	12	25	1/0
GP Thorpe	c Ganguly	b Kumble	1	6	0/0
JP Crawley	not out		100	132	8/0
A Flintoff	c Tendulkar	b Nehra	7	12	1/0
A Stewart†	st Ratra	b Kumble	33	39	4/0
C White	not out		6	4	1/0
Extras (B5, LB14, NB5)			24		
TOTAL (6 wkts dec, 64.4 overs, 280 mins)			301		

Did Not Bat: A Giles, M Hoggard, S Jones

Fall of Wickets: 1-32 (Butcher, 8.5), 2-65 (Hussain, 17.6), 3-76 (Thorpe, 20.3), 4-213 (Vaughan, 50.1), 5-228 (Flintoff, 52.5), 6-287 (Stewart, 63.2)

Bowling: Nehra 14-1-80-2 (4nb), **Khan** 11-1-41-0 (1nb), **Kumble** 24-1-84-3, **Agarkar** 11.4-1-53-1, **Tendulkar** 2-0-14-0, **Sehwag** 2-0-10-0

INDIA - First Innings

W Jaffer		b Hoggard	1	4	0/0
V Sehwag		b Giles	84	96	10/1
R Dravid	c Vaughan	b Hoggard	46	162	6/0
A Nehra	lbw	b Flintoff	0	8	0/0
S Tendulkar	c Stewart	b White	16	61	2/0
S Ganguly*	c Vaughan	b Flintoff	5	32	0/0
V Laxman	not out		43	68	5/0
A Ratra†	c Stewart	b Jones	1	24	0/0
A Agarkar	c Flintoff	b Jones	2	9	0/0
A Kumble		b White	0	11	0/0
Z Khan	c Thorpe	b Hoggard	3	24	0/0
Extras (B4, LB8, NB8)			20		
TOTAL (all out, 81.5 overs, 375 mins)			221		

Fall of Wickets: 1-2 (Jaffer, 0.5), 2-128 (Sehwag, 33.6), 3-130 (Nehra, 36.4), 4-162 (Dravid, 53.3), 5-168 (Tendulkar, 56.2), 6-177 (Ganguly, 62.4), 7-191 (Ratra, 69.3), 8-196 (Agarkar, 71.2), 9-209 (Kumble, 74.4), 10-221 (Khan, 81.5)

Bowling: Hoggard 16.5-4-33-3, **Flintoff** 19-9-22-2 (1nb) **Giles** 9-1-47-1, **Jones** 21-2-61-2 (6nb), **White** 16-3-46-2 (1nb)

INDIA - Second Innings

W Jaffer	c Hussain	b Vaughan	53	79	7/0
V Sehwag		b Jones	27	42	5/0
R Dravid		b Giles	63	112	10/0
S Tendulkar		b Hoggard	12	35	2/0
S Ganguly*	lbw	b Hoggard	0	1	0/0
V Laxman	c Vaughan	b Jones	74	120	9/0
A Ratra†	c Butcher	b Hoggard	1	11	0/0
A Agarkar	not out		109	190	16/0
A Kumble		c & b Hoggard	15	18	3/0
Z Khan	c Stewart	b White	7	4	1/0
A Nehra	c Thorpe	b White	19	54	2/1
Extras (B4, LB3, W2, NB8)			17		
TOTAL (all out, 109.4 overs, 467 mins)			397		

Fall of Wickets: 1-61 (Sehwag, 12.2), 2-110 (Jaffer, 28.3), 3-130 (Tendulkar, 40.4), 4-140 (Ganguly, 40.5), 5-165 (Dravid, 47.3), 6-170 (Ratra, 50.5), 7-296 (Laxman, 85.2), 8-320 (Kumble, 90.2), 9-334 (Khan, 91.3), 10-397 (Nehra, 109.4)

Bowling: Hoggard 24-7-87-4, **Flintoff** 17-2-87-0 (2nb, 1w) **White** 16.4-2-61-2 (4nb), **Jones** 17-1-68-2 (2nb, 1w), **Giles** 29-7-75-1, **Vaughan** 6-2-12-1

Toss: **England**
Umpires: **R Koertzen** RSA and **R Tiffin** ZIM
TV Umpire: **P Willey** ENG

Man of the Match: **Nasser Hussain**
ENGLAND WON BY 170 RUNS

Second Test
Trent Bridge, Nottingham, Aug 8-12

INDIA - First Innings

W Jaffer		b Hoggard	0	8	0/0
V Sehwag		b White	106	183	18/0
R Dravid	c Key	b Hoggard	13	43	2/0
S Tendulkar		b Cork	34	68	6/0
S Ganguly*	c Stewart	b Hoggard	68	149	11/0
V Laxman	c Key	b Flintoff	22	41	4/0
A Agarkar	c Butcher	b Harmison	34	39	6/0
P Patel†	c Flintoff	b Harmison	0	8	0/0
Harbhajan	c Hussain	b Harmison	54	37	10/0
Z Khan	not out		14	30	3/0
A Nehra	c Stewart	b Hoggard	0	2	0/0
Extras (B1, LB8, W2, NB1)			12		
TOTAL (all out, 101.1 overs, 455 mins)			**357**		

Fall of Wickets: 1-6 (Jaffer, 2.2), 2-34 (Dravid, 16.5), 3-108 (Tendulkar, 38.4), 4-179 (Sehwag, 59.3), 5-218 (Laxman, 71.5), 6-285 (Agarkar, 87.2), 7-287 (Patel, 89.3), 8-295 (Ganguly, 90.1), 9-356 (Harbhajan, 100.3), 10-357 (Nehra, 101.1)

Bowling: Hoggard 35.1-10-105-4 (2w), **Cork** 11-3-45-1, **Harmison** 20-7-57-3, **Flintoff** 27-6-85-1, **White** 8-0-56-1 (1nb)

ENGLAND - First Innings

R Key		b Nehra	17	50	2/0
M Vaughan	c Patel	b Agarkar	197	258	23/0
M Butcher	c Dravid	b Harbhajan	53	115	7/0
N Hussain*	c Patel	b Harbhajan	3	7	0/0
J Crawley	c Jaffer	b Khan	22	34	3/0
A Stewart†		b Khan	87	92	14/0
A Flintoff		b Khan	33	46	6/0
C White	not out		94	119	12/1
D Cork	c Jaffer	b Harbhajan	31	42	7/0
M Hoggard	c Dravid	b Nehra	32	102	3/0
S Harmison	c Jaffer	b Agarkar	3	19	0/0
Extras (B9, LB17, W4, NB15)			45		
TOTAL (all out, 144.5 overs, 646 mins)			**617**		

Fall of Wickets: 1-56 (Key, 16.5), 2-221 (Butcher, 55.2), 3-228 (Hussain, 57.1), 4-272 (Crawley, 66.5), 5-335 (Vaughan, 81.3), 6-432 (Flintoff, 98.1), 7-433 (Stewart, 98.3), 8-493 (Cork, 113.4), 9-596 (Hoggard, 139.4), 10-617 (Harmison, 144.5)

Bowling: Nehra 32-3-138-2 (9nb, 2w), **Khan** 26-4-110-3, **Agarkar** 24.5-3-93-2 (2w), **Harbhajan** 45-3-175-3, **Ganguly** 5-0-42-0 (5nb), **Tendulkar** 6-0-15-0, **Sehwag** 6-1-18-0 (1nb)

INDIA - Second Innings

V Sehwag	lbw	b Hoggard	0	2	0/0
W Jaffer	lbw	b Flintoff	5	5	1/0
R Dravid	lbw	b Cork	115	244	16/0
S Tendulkar		b Vaughan	92	113	17/0
S Ganguly*		b Harmison	99	159	13/0
V Laxman	c White	b Cork	14	33	2/0
A Agarkar	lbw	b Vaughan	32	40	6/0
P Patel†	not out		19	60	1/0
Harbhajan		b Harmison	1	6	0/0
Z Khan	not out		14	40	1/0
Extras (B5, LB12, W4, NB12)			33		
TOTAL (8 wkts dec, 115 overs, 503 mins)			**424**		

Did Not Bat: A Nehra

Fall of Wickets: 1-0 (Sehwag, 0.2), 2-11 (Jaffer, 1.4), 3-174 (Tendulkar, 37.2), 4-309 (Dravid, 78.3), 5-339 (Laxman, 88.6), 6-378 (Ganguly, 94.3), 7-395 (Agarkar, 101.1), 8-396 (Harbhajan, 102.5)

Bowling: Hoggard 23-0-109-1 (2nb), **Flintoff** 22-2-95-1 (1nb, 2w), **Harmison** 29-5-63-2 (1nb, 1w), **Cork** 12-1-54-2 (2nb, 1w), **Vaughan** 21-5-71-2 (6nb), **White** 8-2-15-0

Toss: **India**
Umpires: **R Koertzen** RSA and **R Tiffin** ZIM
TV Umpire: **J Lloyds** ENG

Man of the Match: **Michael Vaughan**
MATCH DRAWN

Third Test
Headingley, Leeds, Aug 22-26

INDIA - First Innings

S Bangar	c Stewart	b Flintoff	**68**	236	10/0
V Sehwag	c Flintoff	b Hoggard	**8**	23	1/0
R Dravid	st Stewart	b Giles	**148**	307	23/0
S Tendulkar	lbw	b Caddick	**193**	330	19/3
S Ganguly*		b Tudor	**128**	167	14/3
V Laxman	c Hussain	b Tudor	**6**	7	1/0
A Agarkar		b Caddick	**2**	7	0/0
P Patel†	not out		**7**	11	0/0
Harbhajan	c Hoggard	b Caddick	**18**	11	4/0
Extras (B14, LB13, W5, NB18)			**50**		
TOTAL (8 wkts dec, 180.1 overs, 760 mins)			**628**		

Did Not Bat: A Kumble, Z Khan

Fall of Wickets: 1-15 (Sehwag, 6.5), 2-185 (Bangar, 74.2), 3-335 (Dravid, 113.4), 4-584 (Ganguly, 173.1), 5-596 (Tendulkar, 174.5), 6-602 (Agarkar, 176.3), 7-604 (Laxman, 177.4), 8-628 (Harbhajan, 180.1)

Bowling: Hoggard 36-12-102-1 (4nb), **Caddick** 40.1-5-150-3 (8nb), **Tudor** 36-10-146-2 (4nb), **Flintoff** 27-6-68-1 (2nb, 1w), **Giles** 39-3-134-1, **Butcher** 1-1-0-0, **Vaughan** 1-0-1-0

ENGLAND - First Innings

R Key	c Laxman	b Khan	**30**	76	6/0
M Vaughan	c Sehwag	b Agarkar	**61**	116	9/0
M Butcher	lbw	b Kumble	**16**	35	2/0
N Hussain	lbw	b Khan	**25**	47	5/0
J Crawley	c Laxman	b Harbhajan	**13**	45	1/0
A Stewart†	not out		**78**	120	11/0
A Flintoff	lbw	b Harbhajan	**0**	1	0/0
A Tudor	c Sehwag	b Agarkar	**1**	23	0/0
A Giles	lbw	b Kumble	**25**	52	4/0
A Caddick		b Harbhajan	**1**	11	0/0
M Hoggard	c Sehwag	b Kumble	**0**	18	0/0
Extras (B1, LB12, NB10)			**23**		
TOTAL (all out, 89 overs, 363 mins)			**273**		

Fall of Wickets: 1-67 (Key, 21.6), 2-109 (Butcher, 32.4), 3-130 (Vaughan, 41.5), 4-140 (Hussain, 47.2), 5-164 (Crawley, 56.3), 6-164 (Flintoff, 56.4), 7-185 (Tudor, 63.1), 8-255 (Giles, 78.5), 9-258 (Caddick, 81.5), 10-273 (Hoggard, 88.6)

Bowling: Khan 19-3-59-2 (2nb), **Agarkar** 15-4 -59-2 (2nb), **Bangar** 4-1-9-0 (1nb), **Kumble** 33-7-93-3 (5nb) **Harbhajan** 18-6-40-3

ENGLAND - Second Innings

R Key	lbw	b Kumble	**34**	81	4/0
M Vaughan	lbw	b Agarkar	**15**	27	2/0
M Butcher	c Dravid	b Bangar	**42**	100	6/0
N Hussain*	c Sehwag	b Kumble	**110**	194	18/1
J Crawley	c Sehwag	b Bangar	**12**	26	2/0
A Stewart†	c Dravid	b Kumble	**47**	134	7/0
A Flintoff	c Dravid	b Khan	**0**	2	0/0
A Tudor	c Sehwag	b Harbhajan	**21**	56	4/0
A Giles	run out (Ganguly/Harbhajan)		**10**	26	1/0
A Caddick	c Ganguly	b Kumble	**3**	18	0/0
M Hoggard	not out		**1**	6	0/0
Extras (B3, LB5, NB6)			**14**		
TOTAL (all out, 110.5 overs, 461 mins)			**309**		

Fall of Wickets: 1-28 (Vaughan, 9.4), 2-76 (Key, 26.5), 3-116 (Butcher, 39.5), 4-148 (Crawley, 47.1), 5-265 (Hussain, 92.6), 6-267 (Flintoff, 93.2), 7-267 (Stewart, 94.2), 8-299 (Giles, 103.6), 9-307 (Tudor, 109.2), 10-309 (Caddick, 110.5)

Bowling: Khan 22-7-63-1 (5nb), **Agarkar** 18-5-59-1, **Bangar** 13-2-54-2, **Kumble** 29.5-12-66-4 (1nb), **Harbhajan** 27-7-56-1, **Sehwag** 1-0-3-0

Toss: India
Umpires: **E A R de Silva** SRI and **D Orchard** RSA
TV Umpire: **P Willey** ENG

Man of the Match: **Raul Dravid**
INDIA WON BY AN INNINGS AND 46 RUNS

Fourth Test
The Oval, Sep 5-9

ENGLAND - First Innings

M Trescothick	c Bangar	b Khan	**57**	76	9/0
M Vaughan	c Ratra	b Khan	**195**	279	290
M Butcher	c Dravid	b Harbhajan	**54**	145	6/0
J Crawley	lbw	b Bangar	**26**	87	4/0
N Hussain*	c Laxman	b Bangar	**10**	43	1/0
A Stewart†	c Ratra	b Harbhajan	**23**	75	2/0
D Cork	lbw	b Harbhajan	**52**	112	8/0
A Tudor	c Dravid	b Harbhajan	**2**	11	0/0
A Giles	c Dravid	b Kumble	**31**	72	3/0
A Caddick	not out		**14**	38	1/0
M Hoggard	lbw	b Harbhajan	**0**	1	0/0
Extras (B12, LB31, W1, NB7)			**51**		
TOTAL (all out, 155.4 overs, 637 mins)			**515**		

Fall of Wickets: 1-98 (Trescothick, 22.5), 2-272 (Butcher, 73.3), 3-349 (Vaughan, 93.2), 4-367 (Crawley, 102.1), 5-372 (Hussain, 106.3), 6-434 (Stewart, 124.4), 7-446 (Tudor, 128.5), 8-477 (Cork, 142.3), 9-514 (Giles, 154.6), 10-515 (Hoggard, 155.4)

Bowling: Khan 28-4-83-2 (4nb), **Agarkar** 24-4-111-0 (1nb), **Bangar** 24-8-48-2, **Harbhajan** 38.4-6-115-5, **Kumble** 35-11-105-1, **Ganguly** 4-1-6-0 (1nb), **Tendulkar** 2-0-4-0

ENGLAND - Second Innings

M Trescothick	not out	**58**	98	9/0
M Vaughan	not out	**47**	75	7/0
Extras (b 4, nb 5)		**9**		
TOTAL (0 wickets, 28 overs, 117 mins)		**114**		

Did Not Bat: M Butcher, N Hussain*, J Crawley, A Stewart, D Cork, A Tudor, A Giles, A Caddick, M Hoggard

Bowling: Khan 5-0-37-0 (4nb), **Bangar** 2-0-6-0, **Kumble** 10-2-28-0 (1nb), **Harbhajan** 7-1-24-0, **Agarkar** 4-0-15-0

INDIA - First Innings

S Bangar	c Butcher	b Hoggard	**21**	84	3/0
V Sehwag	c Cork	b Caddick	**12**	10	2/0
R Dravid	run out (Giles/Stewart)		**217**	468	280
S Tendulkar	lbw	b Caddick	**54**	89	10/0
S Ganguly*	c Stewart	b Cork	**51**	84	8/0
V Laxman	c Giles	b Caddick	**40**	147	3/0
A Agarkar		b Vaughan	**31**	63	3/1
A Ratra†	c Butcher	b Caddick	**8**	38	0/0
A Kumble	c Hussain	b Giles	**7**	22	1/0
Harbhajan		b Giles	**17**	31	3/0
Z Khan	not out		**6**	16	1/0
Extras (b 10, lb 6, nb 28)			**44**		
TOTAL (all out, 170 overs, 709 mins)			**508**		

Fall of Wickets: 1-18 (Sehwag, 3.4), 2-87 (Bangar, 28.1), 3-178 (Tendulkar, 56.1), 4-283 (Ganguly, 86.1), 5-396 (Laxman, 132.1), 6-465 (Agarkar, 151.3), 7-473 (Dravid, 155.6), 8-477 (Ratra, 160.4), 9-493 (Kumble, 163.6), 10-508 (Harbhajan Singh, 169.6)

Bowling: Hoggard 25-2-97-1 (11nb), **Caddick** 43-11-114-4 (3nb), **Giles** 49-12-98-2, **Tudor** 19-2-80-0 (8nb), **Cork** 22-5-67-1 (6nb), **Vaughan** 12-1-36-1

Toss: England
Umpires: **E A R de Silva** SRI and **D Orchard** RSA
TV Umpire: **N Mallender** ENG

Man of the Match: **Raul Dravid**
MATCH DRAWN

Players of the Series: **Michael Vaughan** & **Raul Dravid**
SERIES DRAWN 1-1

England v India Test Averages

England

India

BATTING (England)

	M	I	NO	Rns	HS	Av	100	50
C White	2	3	2	153	94*	153.00	-	1
M Trescothick	1	2	1	115	58*	115.00	-	2
M Vaughan	4	7	1	615	197	102.50	3	1
A Stewart	4	6	1	287	87	57.40	-	2
N Hussain	4	6	0	315	155	52.50	2	-
J Crawley	4	6	1	237	100*	47.40	1	1
S Jones	1	1	0	44	44	44.00	-	-
D Cork	2	2	0	83	52	41.50	-	1
M Butcher	4	6	0	212	54	35.33	-	2
R Key	2	3	0	81	34	27.00	-	-
A Giles	3	4	0	85	31	21.25	-	-
A Flintoff	3	5	0	99	59	19.80	-	1
M Hoggard	4	5	2	43	32	14.33	-	-
A Caddick	2	3	1	18	14*	9.00	-	-
A Tudor	2	3	0	24	21	8.00	-	-
S Harmison	1	1	0	3	3	3.00	-	-
G Thorpe	1	2	0	5	4	2.50	-	-

BOWLING (England)

	M	O	M	R	W	Av	BB
S Harmison	1	49	12	120	5	24.00	3-57
M Vaughan	4	40	8	120	4	30.00	2-71
S Jones	1	38	3	129	4	32.25	2-61
C White	2	48.4	7	178	5	35.60	2-46
A Caddick	2	83.1	16	264	7	37.71	4-114
M Hoggard	4	160	35	533	14	38.07	4-87
D Cork	2	45	9	166	4	41.50	2-54
A Giles	3	126	23	354	5	70.80	2-98
A Flintoff	3	112	25	357	5	71.40	2-22
A Tudor	2	55	12	226	2	113.00	2-146
M Butcher	4	1	1	0	0	-	-

BATTING (India)

	M	I	NO	Rns	HS	Av	100	50
R Dravid	4	6	0	602	217	100.33	3	1
S Tendulkar	4	6	0	401	193	66.83	1	2
S Ganguly	4	6	0	351	128	58.50	1	3
S Bangar	2	2	0	89	68	44.50	-	1
A Agarkar	4	6	1	210	109*	42.00	1	-
V Laxman	4	6	1	199	74	39.80	-	1
V Sehwag	4	6	0	237	106	39.50	1	1
P Patel	2	3	2	26	19*	26.00	-	-
Harbhajan Singh	3	4	0	90	54	22.50	-	1
Z Khan	4	5	3	44	14*	22.00	-	-
W Jaffer	2	4	0	59	53	14.75	-	1
A Kumble	3	3	0	22	15	7.33	-	-
A Nehra	2	3	0	19	19	6.33	-	-
A Ratra	2	3	0	10	8	3.33	-	-

BOWLING (India)

	M	O	M	R	W	Av	BB
S Bangar	2	43	11	117	4	29.25	2-48
Harbhajan Singh	3	135.4	23	410	12	34.16	5-115
A Kumble	3	174.1	42	504	14	36.00	4-66
Z Khan	4	147	32	483	11	43.90	3-90
A Agarkar	4	118.3	20	488	8	61.00	2-59
V Sehwag	4	19	1	63	1	63.00	1-32
A Nehra	2	76	8	319	5	63.80	2-80
S Tendulkar	4	10	0	33	0	-	-
S Ganguly	4	12	2	64	0	-	-

England v Sri Lanka

First Test
Lord's, May 16-20

SRI LANKA - First Innings

M Atapattu	c Trescothick b Cork		185	351	24/0
S Jayasuriya*	run out (Vaughan/Stewart)		18	25	3/0
K Sangakkara†	c Flintoff	b Hoggard	10	17	2/0
D Jayawardene	c Trescothick b Flintoff		107	168	17/0
P de Silva	c Stewart	b Cork	88	225	12/0
R Arnold	c Trescothick b Hoggard		50	87	7/0
H Tillakaratne	not out		17	74	1/0
W Vaas	c Trescothick b Cork		6	17	1/0
D Zoysa	c Stewart	b Flintoff	28	49	2/2
T Fernando	not out		6	22	1/0
Extras (B1, LB13, W1, NB25)			40		
Total (8 wickets dec, 169 overs)			555		

Did not Bat: P Perera.

Fall of Wickets: 1-38 (Jayasuriya, 7.5), 2-55 (Sangakkara, 13.1), 3-261 (Jayawardene, 64.5 ov), 4-407 (Atapattu, 115.6), 5-492 (Arnold, 142.1), 6-492 (de Silva, 143.3), 7-505 (Vaas, 149.4), 8-540 (Zoysa, 162.4)

Bowling: Caddick 38.3-6-135-0 (3nb); **Hoggard** 39-4-160-2 (8nb, 1w); **Cork** 35.3-11-93-3 (6nb); **Flintoff** 39-8-101-2 (4nb); **Butcher** 3-0-17-0; **Vaughan** 14-2-35-0

SRI LANKA - Second Innings

M Atapattu	c Butcher	b Caddick	7	36	0/0
K Sangakkara†	not out		6	29	1/0
D Jayawardene	not out		14	21	1/0
Extras (B5, LB2, NB8)			15		
Total (1 wicket, 13 overs)			42		

Did Not Bat: S Jayasuriya*, P de Silva, R Arnold, H Tillakaratne, W Vaas, D Zoysa, T Fernando, P Perera.

Fall of Wickets: 1-16 (Atapattu, 8.1)

Bowling: Caddick 7-2-10-1 (1nb); **Flintoff** 5-0-18-0 (7nb); **Hoggard** 1-0-7-0

ENGLAND First Innings

M Trescothick	c Jayasuriya b Zoysa		13	12	2/0
M Vaughan	c Zoysa	b Perera	64	148	9/0
M Butcher	c Jayawardene b Fernando		17	25	1/0
N Hussain*	c Sangakkara b Zoysa		57	87	11/0
G Thorpe	lbw	b Perera	27	45	3/0
J Crawley	c Sangakkara b Vaas		31	73	4/0
A Stewart†	run out (sub Chandana)		7	12	0/0
A Flintoff	c Sangakkara b Fernando		12	18	3/0
D Cork	c Sangakkara b Fernando		0	2	0/0
A Caddick	c Sangakkara b Perera		13	30	1/0
M Hoggard	not out		0	2	0/0
Extras (B4, LB7, W9, NB14)			34		
Total (73.1 overs)			275		

Fall of Wickets: 1-17 (Trescothick, 3.4), 2-43 (Butcher, 12.6), 3-149 (Hussain, 37.4), 4-203 (Vaughan, 51.2), 5-203 (Thorpe, 51.3), 6-214 (Stewart, 56.6), 7-237 (Flintoff, 62.4), 8-237 (Cork, 62.6), 9-267 (Caddick, 70.5), 10-275 (Crawley, 73.1)

Bowling: Vaas 21.1-4-51-1 (2nb); **Zoysa** 19-3-82-2 (6nb, 3w); **Fernando** 22-5-83-3 (3nb, 1w); **Perera** 11-0-48-3 (3nb, 1w)

ENGLAND - Second Innings (following on)

M Trescothick	lbw	b Zoysa	76	135	7/0
M Vaughan	c Sangakkara b Perera		115	219	17/0
M Butcher	run out (Vaas/Sangakkara)		105	295	10/0
N Hussain*	lbw	b Perera	68	186	6/1
G Thorpe	c Fernando b de Silva		65	99	7/0
J Crawley	not out		41	154	4/0
A Stewart†	not out		26	79	2/0
Extras (B1, LB9, W1, NB22)			33		
Total (5 wickets dec, 191 overs)			529		

Did Not Bat: A Flintoff, D Cork, A Caddick, M Hoggard.

Fall of Wickets: 1-168 (Trescothick, 48.6), 2-213 (Vaughan, 64.2), 3-372 (Hussain, 128.2), 4-432 (Butcher, 143.6), 5-483 (Thorpe, 163.3)

Bowling: Vaas 44-8-113-0 (1nb); **Zoysa** 34-6-84-1 (8nb, 1w); **Perera** 30-4-90-2 (8nb); **De Silva** 27-7-63-1; **Fernando** 26-1-96-0 (4nb); **Jayasuriya** 25-6-66-0; **Arnold** 4-1-7-0; **Tillakaratne** 1-1-0-0

Toss: Sri Lanka
Umpires: **D Harper** AUS and **S Venkataraghavan** IDN
TV Umpire: **J Lloyds**

Man of the Match: **Marvin Atapattu**
MATCH DRAWN

Second Test
Edgbaston, May 30-June 2

SRI LANKA - First Innings

M Atapattu	c Stewart	b Hoggard	13	30	1/0
S Jayasuriya*	c Stewart	b Caddick	8	24	1/0
K Sangakkara†	c Stewart	b Flintoff	16	42	1/0
D Jayawardene	c Flintoff	b Caddick	47	60	7/0
P de Silva	c Trescothick	b Hoggard	10	12	2/0
H Tillakaratne	lbw	b Tudor	20	53	3/0
R Arnold	c Flintoff	b Caddick	1	13	0/0
W Vaas		b Flintoff	23	52	4/0
D Zoysa	c Hoggard	b Tudor	0	4	0/0
T Fernando	run out (Caddick/Tudor)		13	36	0/0
M Muralitharan	not out		0	1	0/0
Extras (B1, NB10)			11		
Total (52.5 overs)			162		

Fall of Wickets: 1-23 (Atapattu, 7.6), 2-23 (Jayasuriya, 8.4), 3-76 (Sangakkara, 23.3), 4-96 (de Silva, 25.6), 5-100 (Jayawardene, 28.1), 6-108 (Arnold, 32.1), 7-141 (Tillakaratne, 44.1), 8-141 (Zoysa, 44.5), 9-159 (Vaas, 51.5), 10-162 (Fernando, 52.5)

Bowling: Caddick 17-4-47-3 (4nb); **Hoggard** 17-4-55-2 (5nb); **Giles** 4-1-7-0; **Tudor** 9.5-3-25-2 (1nb); **Flintoff** 5-0-27-2

SRI LANKA - Second Innings

M Atapattu		b Hoggard	56	152	5/0
S Jayasuriya*		b Hoggard	12	28	3/0
K Sangakkara†	lbw	b Hoggard	1	7	0/0
D Jayawardene	c Thorpe	b Caddick	59	158	7/0
P de Silva	c Thorpe	b Caddick	47	103	6/0
H Tillakaratne		b Caddick	39	59	6/0
R Arnold	c Giles	b Hoggard	4	5	1/0
W Vaas	st Stewart	b Giles	28	28	3/1
T Fernando		b Hoggard	0	2	0/0
D Zoysa	not out		1	9	0/0
M Muralitharan	absent hurt				
Extras (B4, LB4, NB17)			25		
Total (89.1 overs)			272		

Fall of Wickets: 1-28 (Jayasuriya, 7.5), 2-30 (Sangakkara, 9.2), 3-135 (Atapattu, 51.3), 4-156 (Jayawardene, 58.2), 5-233 (Tillakaratne, 80.6), 6-238 (De Silva, 82.1), 7-247 (Arnold, 83.3), 8-247 (Fernando, 83.5), 9-272 (Vaas, 89.1)

Bowling: Caddick 25-4-67-3 (2nb); **Hoggard** 23-2-92-5 (11nb); **Flintoff** 6-0-23-0 (3nb); **Giles** 26.1-3-57-1; **Tudor** 9-1-25-0 (1nb)

ENGLAND - First Innings

M Trescothick	c Tillakaratne	b Vaas	161	232	23/3
M Vaughan	c Jayasuriya	b Muralitharan	46	64	7/0
M Butcher		b Muralitharan	94	209	13/0
N Hussain*		b Muralitharan	22	45	4/0
G Thorpe	c Vaas	b Fernando	123	229	12/0
A Stewart†	c Tillakaratne	b Muralitharan	7	40	0/0
A Flintoff	c Tillakaratne	b Muralitharan	29	51	6/0
A Tudor	c Tillakaratne	b Zoysa	3	24	0/0
A Giles	c Sangakkara	b Zoysa	0	4	0/0
A Caddick	c Sangakkara	b Zoysa	3	6	0/0
M Hoggard	not out		17	94	1/0
Extras (LB19, W6, NB15)			40		
Total (163.5 overs)			545		

Fall of Wickets: 1-92 (Vaughan, 21.2), 2-294 (Trescothick, 75.5), 3-338 (Butcher, 88.6), 4-341 (Hussain, 90.4), 5-368 (Stewart, 104.2), 6-426 (Flintoff, 122.1), 7-436 (Tudor, 129.3), 8-444 (Giles, 131.1), 9-454 (Caddick, 133.2), 10-545 (Thorpe, 163.5)

Bowling: Vaas 41-3-141-1 (2w); **Zoysa** 24-3-93-3 (9nb); **Muralitharan** 64-12-143-5 (2nb); **Fernando** 21.5-2-92-1 (4nb), **Jayasuriya** 6-2-27-0; **De Silva** 7-0-30-0

Toss: **England**
Umpires: **D Harper** AUS and **S Venkataraghavan** IDN
TV Umpire: **P Willey**

Man of the Match: **Michael Hoggard**
ENGLAND WON BY AN INNINGS AND 111 RUNS

N a t W e s t   S e r i e s

England v Sri Lanka (Match 1)
Trent Bridge, June 27

ENGLAND

M Trescothick	c Sangakkara	b Vaas	26	25	4/0
N Knight	lbw	b Zoysa	20	18	3/0
N Hussain*		b Fernando	32	41	3/0
G Thorpe		b Fernando	18	31	1/0
A Stewart†		b Vaas	83	103	8/0
R Irani	c Jayawardene b Arnold		39	55	1/0
A Flintoff	not out		50	28	5/2
P Collingwood	not out		10	3	2/0
Extras (B4, LB4, W3, NB4)			15		
Total (6 wickets, 50 overs)			293		

Did Not Bat: A Giles, R Kirtley, M Hoggard
Fall of Wickets: 1-39 (Knight, 5.5), 2-47 (Trescothick, 8.1), 3-103 (Hussain, 18.3), 4-104 (Thorpe, 18.6), 5-199 (Irani, 39.1), 6-283 (Stewart, 49.3)
Bowling: Vaas 9-0-58-2; **Zoysa** 7-0-46-1 (3nb); **Fernando** 8-0-46-2 (1nb, 1w); **Chandana** 10-0-43-0 (1w); **Jayasuriya** 10-0-51-0 (1w); **Arnold** 6-0-41-1

Toss: **England**
Umpires: **D Orchard** RSA and **D Shepherd**
TV Umpire: **N Mallender**

SRI LANKA

S Jayasuriya*	c Hussain	b Hoggard	12	17	2/0
R Kaluwitharana†	c Thorpe	b Collingwood	52	64	5/1
M Atapattu	c Irani	b Flintoff	47	58	7/0
D Jayawardene		b Collingwood	29	37	3/0
R Arnold	run out (Hoggard)		29	46	2/0
K Sangakkara	c Kirtley	b Flintoff	22	28	2/0
U Chandana	c Thorpe	b Flintoff	1	4	0/0
M Nawaz	not out		15	22	0/0
W Vaas		b Kirtley	10	14	1/0
D Zoysa		b Kirtley	0	1	0/0
C Fernando	not out		5	13	0/0
Extras (B1, LB10, W10, NB6)			27		
Total (9 wickets, 50 overs)			249		

Fall of Wickets 1-19 (Jayasuriya, 4.2), 2-91 (Atapattu, 18.5), 3-149 (Kaluwitharana, 27.6), 4-152 (Jayawardene, 29.6), 5-214 (Arnold, 40.6), 6-215 (Sangakkara, 41.3), 7-215 (Chandana, 41.5), 8-238 (Vaas, 46.4), 9-238 (Zoysa, 46.5)
Bowling: Hoggard 10-0-49-1 (3nb, 2w); **Kirtley** 10-0-40-2 (1nb, 2w); **Irani** 10-0-39-0; **Flintoff** 10-0-49-3 (1w); **Giles** 5-0-30-0; **Collingwood** 5-0-31-2 (1w)

Man of the Match: **A Flintoff**
ENGLAND WON BY 44 RUNS

England v India (Match 2)
Lord's, June 29

ENGLAND

M Trescothick	c Dravid	b Ganguly	86	78	8/1
N Knight	run out (Tendulkar/Kumble)		31	42	2/0
N Hussain*	st Dravid	b Yuvraj Singh	54	82	3/0
A Flintoff	c Mongia	b Yuvraj Singh	22	20	3/0
G Thorpe	c Sehwag	b Yuvraj Singh	12	15	1/0
A Stewart†	not out		28	35	2/0
R Irani	run out (Kaif/Khan)		12	21	0/0
P Collingwood	c Dravid	b Khan	6	7	1/0
A Giles	not out		2	2	0/0
Extras (B2, ILB6, W8, NB2)			18		
Total (7 wickets, 50 overs)			271		

Did Not Bat: R Kirtley, M Hoggard

Fall of Wickets: 1-86 (Knight, 13.4), 2-153 (Trescothick, 26.3), 3-201 (Flintoff, 33.6), 4-217 (Thorpe, 37.6), 5-222 (Hussain, 39.5), 6-256 (Irani, 47.2), 7-267 (Collingwood, 49.2)
Bowling: Khan 9-0-48-1 (2w); **Agarkar** 8-0-49-0 (2nb); **Harbhajan Singh** 10-0-50-0 (1w); **Kumble** 10-0-46-0; **Ganguly** 6-0-31-1; **Yuvraj Singh** 7-0-39-3

Toss: **England**
Umpires: **S Bucknor** WI and **N Mallender**
TV Umpire: **J Lloyds**

INDIA

S Ganguly*	c Kirtley	b Giles	43	67	4/0
V Sehwag	c Trescothick	b Giles	71	65	9/1
D Mongia		b Giles	1	5	0/0
S Tendulkar	lbw	b Irani	1	9	0/0
R Dravid†	not out		73	86	7/0
Yuvraj Singh	not out		64	65	7/0
Extras (LB12, W3, NB4)			19		
Total (4 wickets, 48.5 overs)			272		

Did not Bat: M Kaif, Harbhajan Singh, Z Khan, A Kumble, A Agarkar

Fall of Wickets: 1-109 (Sehwag, 17.3), 2-111 (Mongia, 19.1, 3-118 (Tendulkar, 22.3), 4-141 (Ganguly, 27.4)

Bowling: Hoggard 8.5-0-62-0 (3nb, 1w); **Kirtley** 10-0-57-0; **Flintoff** 8-0-56-0 (1nb); **Giles** 10-1-39-3 (2w); **Irani** 10-0-33-1; **Collingwood** 2-0-13-0

Man of the Match: **Yuvraj Singh**
INDIA WON BY 6 WICKETS

Sri Lanka v India (Match 3)
The Oval, June 30

SRI LANKA

S Jayasuriya*	c Dravid	b Agarkar	36	38	6/1
Kaluwitharana†	c Dravid	b Agarkar	15	19	2/0
M Atapattu		b Khan	7	14	1/0
D Jayawardene		c & b Khan	62	105	4/0
R Arnold	c Dravid	b Agarkar	6	10	1/0
M Nawaz	c Sehwag	b Ganguly	11	26	1/0
U Chandana	c Kaif	b Nehra	18	42	1/0
W Vaas	not out		26	37	2/0
D Zoysa	c Kaif	b Khan	4	4	1/0
T Fernando	not out		4	6	0/0
Extras (LB8, W4, NB1)			13		
Total (8 wickets, 50 overs)			202		

Did Not Bat: C Fernando
Fall of Wickets: 1-42 (Kaluwitharana, 7.1), 2-65 (Jayasuriya, 11.4), 3-65 (Atapattu, 12.1), 4-78 (Arnold, 15.3), 5-97 (Nawaz, 23.5), 6-140 (Chandana, 38.3), 7-182 (Jayawardene, 46.1), 8-186 (Zoysa, 46.5)

Bowling: Nehra 10-0-29-1 (3w); **Khan** 10-1-48-3 (1w); **Agarkar** 9-2-44-3 (1nb); **Ganguly** 10-1-28-1; **Kumble** 10-0-43-0; **Sehwag** 1-0-2-0

Toss: **Sri Lanka**
Umpires: **D Orchard** RSA and **P Willey**
TV Umpire: **N Mallender**

INDIA

S Ganguly*	lbw	b Vaas	7	10	1/0
V Sehwag	c Jayasuriya	b Vaas	12	20	2/0
D Mongia	c Vaas	b C Fernando	33	55	3/1
S Tendulkar	c Kaluwitharana	b Zoysa	49	70	3/1
R Dravid		b Chandana	8	26	0/0
Yuvraj Singh	c sub (Silva)	b C Fernando	31	44	3/0
M Kaif	not out		38	44	4/0
A Agarkar	not out		7	10	1/0
Extras (LB2, W9, NB7)			18		
Total (6 wickets, 45.2 overs)			203		

Did Not Bat: A Kumble, Z Khan, A Nehra

Fall of Wickets: 1-17 (Ganguly, 2.6), 2-26 (Sehwag, 6.5), 3-97 (Mongia, 20.2), 4-113 (Dravid, 27.3), 5-135 (Tendulkar, 32.3), 6-195 (Yuvraj Singh, 42.6)

Bowling: Vaas 10-1-38-2 (1w); **Zoysa** 10-0-46-1 (6nb, 1w); **C Fernando** 10-0-53-2 (4w); **T Fernando** 3-0-11-0; **Chandana** 10-1-46-1 (1nb, 3w); **Jayasuriya** 2-0-5-0; **Arnold** 0.2-0-2-0

Man of the Match: **A Agarkar**
INDIA WON BY 4 WICKETS

Sri Lanka v England (Match 4)
Headingley, July 2

SRI LANKA

S Jayasuriya*	c Kirtley	b Hoggard	112	87	9/5
Kaluwitharana†	c Hussain	b Gough	7	6	1/0
M Atapattu	c Stewart	b Flintoff	18	36	2/0
Jayawardene	b Flintoff		4	11	1/0
Gunawardene	run out (Hussain)		20	21	3/0
U Chandana	lbw	b Gough	30	13	4/1
R Arnold	not out		17	14	1/0
W Vaas		b Gough	4	6	0/0
K Sangakkara	not out		1	1	0/0
Extras (LB11, W13, NB3)			27		
Total (7 wickets, 32 overs)			240		

Did Not Bat: D Zoysa, C Fernando

Fall of Wickets: 1-26 (Kaluwitharana, 2.1), 2-118 (Atapattu, 16.1), 3-132 (Jayawardene, 18.6), 4-171 (Gunawardene, 24.6), 5-201 (Jayasuriya, 27.3), 6-225 (Chandana, 29.4), 7-233 (Vaas, 31.3)

Bowling: Gough 7-0-45-3 (2nb, 4w); **Hoggard** 4-0-53-1 (1nb, 4w); **Kirtley** 6-1-37-0 (1w); **Flintoff** 7-0-18-2 (2w); **Collingwood** 5-0-49-0 (1w); **Irani** 3-0-27-0

Toss: **England**
Umpires: **S Bucknor** WI and **N Mallender**
TV Umpire: **P Willey**

ENGLAND

M Trescothick	c Vaas	b Jayasuriya	82	60	11/0
N Knight		c & b Vaas	0	3	0/0
R Irani	c Jayawardene	b Vaas	27	28	5/0
A Flintoff	c Jayawardene	b Arnold	20	13	2/1
N Hussain*	c Gunawardene	b Fernando	0	2	0/0
G Thorpe	run out (Sanga/Kalu)		15	13	2/0
P Collingwood		b Fernando	38	36	2/0
A Stewart†	not out		38	31	5/1
D Gough	not out		3	7	0/0
Extras (LB3, W10, NB5)			18		
Total (7 wickets, 31.2 overs)			241		

Did Not Bat: R Kirtley, M Hoggard

Fall of Wickets: 1-1 (Knight, 0.4), 2-69 (Irani, 8.4), 3-97 (Flintoff, 11.6), 4-98 (Hussain, 12.2), 5-126 (Thorpe, 15.4), 6-171 (Trescothick, 21.2), 7-237 (Collingwood, 30.1)

Bowling: Vaas 6-0-39-2 (1w); **Zoysa** 5.2-0-54-0 (4nb); **Arnold** 5-0-42-1 (1w); **Fernando** 6-0-38-2 (1nb, 3w); **Chandana** 5-0-40-0 (2w); **Jayasuriya** 4-0-25-1

Man of the Match: **S Jayasuriya**
ENGLAND WON BY 3 WICKETS

India v England (Match 5)
Riverside Ground, Chester-le-Street, July 4

INDIA

S Ganguly*	lbw	b Gough	0	1	0/0
V Sehwag	c Trescothick	b Kirtley	16	19	2/0
D Mongia	c Flintoff	b Gough	27	38	3/0
S Tendulkar	not out		105	108	8/1
R Dravid†	c Flintoff	b Collingwood	82	117	7/0
Yuvraj Singh	not out		40	19	4/1
Extras (LB8, W5, NB2)			15		
Total (4 wickets, 50 overs)			285		

Did Not Bat: M Kaif, A Agarkar, Z Khan, A Kumble, A Nehra.

Fall of Wickets: 1-0 (Ganguly, 0.1), 2-48 (Sehwag, 7.6), 3-52 (Mongia, 10.2), 4-221 (Dravid, 44.3)

Bowling: Gough 10-0-52-2 (2w); **Kirtley** 10-0-77-1 (1nb, 2w); **Flintoff** 10-0-36-0 (1nb); **Irani** 10-1-23-0; **Collingwood** 5-0-48 -1; **Giles** 5-0-41-0 (1w)

Toss: India
Umpires: **D Orchard** RSA and **D Shepherd**
TV Umpire: **J Lloyds**

ENGLAND

M Trescothick	lbw	b Khan	23	26	3/0
N Knight	not out		17	28	3/0
N Hussain*	not out		9	21	0/0
Extras (LB1, W3)			4		
Total (1 wicket, 12.3 overs)			53		

Did Not Bat: M Vaughan, A Stewart, R Irani, A Flintoff, P Collingwood, A Giles, D Gough, R Kirtley

Fall of Wickets: 1-30 (Trescothick, 5.4)

Bowling: Nehra 6-0-21-0 (2w); **Khan** 6-0-31-1 (1w); **Agarkar** 0.3-0-0-0

Man of the Match: **No Award**
NO RESULT

Sri Lanka v India (Match 6)
Edgbaston, July 6

SRI LANKA

S Jayasuriya*		b Nehra	22	33	2/1
Kaluwitharana†	Dravid	b Agarkar	8	21	0/0
M Atapattu		b Kumble	50	73	5 0
Jayawardene	c Nehra	b Kumble	36	64	2 0
Gunawardene	c Yuvraj Singh	b Khan	7	29	0/0
R Arnold	run out (Yuvraj/Kumble)		13	26	1/0
Samaraweera	c Sehwag	b Nehra	3	12	0/0
U Chandana	c Nehra	b Agarkar	4	10	0/0
W Vaas	c Ganguly	b Khan	26	20	4/0
Wickramasinghe	run out (Yuvraj/Khan)		2	4	0/0
C Fernando	not out		2	2	0/0
Extras (B4, LB4, W2, NB4)			14		
Total (all out, 48.2 overs)			187		

Fall of Wickets: 1-33 (Jayasuriya, 8.1), 2-41 (Kaluwitharana, 11.1), 3-125 (Jayawardene, 30.2), 4-129 (Atapattu, 32.4), 5-146 (Gunawardene, 39.2), 6-150 (Samaraweera, 41.5), 7-153 (Arnold, 42.5), 8-182 (Vaas, 46.6), 9-185 (Chandana, 47.4), 10-187 (Wickramasinghe, 48.2)

Bowling: Nehra 10-2-28-2; **Khan** 8.2-0-36-2 (1nb, 1w); **Agarkar** 9-1-31-2; **Ganguly** 6-0-30-0 (3nb); **Tendulkar** 5-0-18-0; **Kumble** 10 -0-36-2 (1w)

Toss: India
Umpires: **S Bucknor** (WI) and **N Mallender**
TV Umpire: **P Willey**

INDIA

V Sehwag		b Vaas	0	1	0/0
S Ganguly*	c Kaluwitharana	b Wickramasinghe	24	51	2/0
D Mongia	c Jayasuriya	b Vaas	5	30	0/0
S Tendulkar	c Atapattu	b Fernando	19	25	3/0
R Dravid†	run out (Fernando)		64	95	5/1
Yuvraj Singh	c Chandana	b Fernando	37	68	4/1
M Kaif	not out		7	16	0/0
A Agarkar	not out		7	8	1/0
Extras (LB3, W17, NB5)			25		
Total (6 wickets, 48.1 overs)			188		

Did Not Bat: A Kumble, Z Khan, A Nehra.

Fall of Wickets 1-0 (Sehwag, 0.1), 2-30 (Mongia, 12.3), 3-33 (Ganguly, 13.4), 4-59 (Tendulkar, 19.1), 5-150 (Yuvraj Singh, 39.6), 6-179 (Dravid, 46.4)

Bowling: Vaas 10-1-26-2 (2w); **Fernando** 10-0-22-2 (3nb, 5w); **Wickramasinghe** 9-0-47-1 (2nb, 2w); **Chandana** 6.1-0-32-0 (2w); **Samaraweera** 10-1-35-0 (2w); **Jayasuriya** 3-0-23-0

Man of the Match: **R Dravid**
INDIA WON BY 4 WICKETS

Sri Lanka v England (Match 7)
Old Trafford, July 7

SRI LANKA

M Atapattu	run out (Collingwood)		34	52	4/0
S Jayasuriya*	c Hussain	b Tudor	23	26	3/0
K Sangakkara†	lbw	b Vaughan	70	79	8/0
Jayawardene	run out (Tudor/Stewart)		42	67	3/0
R Arnold		c & b Snape	6	15	0/0
L Silva	c Collingwood	b Vaughan	9	21	0/0
Samaraweera	st Stewart	b Vaughan	3	7	0/0
U Chandana	c sub (Giles)	b Flintoff	15	18	1/0
W Vaas		b Vaughan	0	2	0/0
D Zoysa	c Knight	b Gough	9	9	2/0
Wickramasinghe	not out		3	3	0/0
Extras	(LB9, W5, NB1)		15		
Total	(all out, 49.4 overs)		229		

Fall of Wickets: 1-59 (Jayasuriya, 11.3), 2-73 (Atapattu, 13.4), 3-162 (Jayawardene, 33.5), 4-185 (Arnold, 38.3), 5-191 (Sangakkara, 41.1), 6-200 (Samaraweera, 43.5), 7-205 (Silva, 45.1), 8-205 (Vaas, 45.3), 9-224 (Zoysa, 48.4), 10-229 (Chandana, 49.4)
Bowling: Gough 10-0-51-1 (3w); **Tudor** 8-1-44-1; **Flintoff** 5.4-0-29-1 (1nb, 1w); **Irani** 10-0-40-0; **Snape** 10-2-34-1; **Vaughan** 6-1-22-4 (1w)

Toss: **Sri Lanka**
Umpires: **D Orchard** RSA and **P Willey**
TV Umpire: **J Lloyds**

ENGLAND

M Trescothick		b Zoysa	27	23	4/0
N Knight		b Zoysa	29	34	4/0
N Hussain*	run out (Atapattu/Sanga)		28	43	2/1
M Vaughan		c & b Chandana	14	15	2/0
A Stewart†	c Chandana	b Samaraweera	8	23	1/0
R Irani	c Zoysa	b Jayasuriya	28	58	1/0
A Flintoff		b Jayasuriya	7	16	0/0
P Collingwood	run out (Jaya/Chandana)		29	36	2/0
J Snape	not out		15	27	1/0
A Tudor	c Atapattu	b Jayasuriya	6	9	0/0
D Gough	run out (Jayawardene)		0	2	0/0
Extras	(B1, LB10, W4)		15		
Total	(47.4 overs)		206		

Fall of Wickets: 1-37 (Trescothick, 5.5), 2-76 (Knight, 12.5), 3-100 (Vaughan, 18.2), 4-108 (Hussain, 20.3), 5-118 (Stewart, 25.6), 6-135 (Flintoff, 32.4), 7-160 (Irani, 38.4), 8-186 (Collingwood, 43.6), 9-200 (Tudor, 46.6), 10-206 (Gough, 47.4)
Bowling: Vaas 6-0-29-0; **Zoysa** 7-0-42-2 (3w); **Wickramasinghe** 1-0-10-0; **Arnold** 5-0-24-0; **Chandana** 9.4-1-25-1 (1w); **Samaraweera** 10-1-27-1 **Jayasuriya** 9-0-38-3

Man of the Match: **K Sangakkara**
SRI LANKA WON BY 23 RUNS

England v India (Match 8)
The Oval, July 9

ENGLAND

M Trescothick		b Kumble	9	24	1/0
N Knight	c Kaif	b Yuvraj	31	38	4/0
R Irani		b Kumble	53	55	2/1
A Flintoff	c Nehra	b Agarkar	51	38	6/1
M Vaughan	c Yuvraj	b Khan	30	17	2/1
N Hussain*	c Kaif	b Khan	6	7	0/0
P Collingwood		b Nehra	9	9	1/0
A Stewart†		b Khan	0	1	0/0
A Tudor	not out		3	2	0/0
D Gough	not out		7	2	0/1
Extras	(LB6, W18, NB6)		30		
Total	(8 wickets, 32 overs)		229		

Did Not Bat: M Hoggard.
Fall of Wickets: 1-52 (Trescothick, 8.1), 2-72 (Knight, 11.5), 3-148 (Flintoff, 22.6), 4-196 (Vaughan, 27.5), 5-202 (Irani, 28.3), 6-219 (Collingwood, 30.6),7-219 (Hussain, 31.1 ov), 8-219 (Stewart, 31.2)

Bowling: Nehra 5-0-28-1 (4w); **Khan** 7-0-53-3 (1nb, 2w); **Kumble** 7-0-39-2 (1w); **Agarkar** 4-0-38-1 (1w); **Yuvraj Singh** 6-0-37-1 (1nb); **Sehwag** 1-0-9-0; **Ganguly** 1-0-10-0; **Tendulkar** 1-0-9-0 (2w)

Toss: **India**
Umpires: **S Bucknor** WI and **P Willey**
TV Umpire: **N Mallender**

INDIA

V Sehwag	c Stewart	b Irani	46	41	8/1
S Ganguly*	c Flintoff	b Tudor	6	10	0/0
V Laxman	c Hoggard	b Collingwood	14	21	1/0
S Tendulkar	c Stewart	b Hoggard	36	29	5/0
Yuvraj Singh	st Stewart	b Irani	5	13	0/0
M Kaif		b Irani	1	8	0/0
A Ratra†	c Stewart	b Irani	2	6	0/0
A Agarkar	c Collingwood	b Irani	0	2	0/0
A Kumble	not out		21	19	2/0
Z Khan	c Gough	b Flintoff	2	7	0/0
A Nehra	c Irani	b Tudor	24	19	2/1
Extras	(LB1, W7)		8		
Total	(29.1 overs)		165		

Fall of Wickets: 1-31 (Ganguly, 5.5), 2-62 (Sehwag, 9.3), 3-78 (Laxman, 14.1), 4-100 (Yuvraj Singh, 17.5), 5-114 (Kaif, 19.5), 6-118 (Ratra, 21.1), 7-118 (Agarkar, 21.3), 8-120 (Tendulkar, 22.1), 9-127 (Khan, 23.6), 10-165 (Nehra, 29.1)

Bowling: Gough 4-0-19-0 (2w); **Tudor** 4.1-0-30-2 (1w); **Flintoff** 4-0-33-1 (1w); **Irani** 7-1-26-5 (2w); **Collingwood** 5-0-31-1 (1w); **Hoggard** 5-0-25-1

Man of the Match: **R Irani**
ENGLAND WON BY 64 RUNS

India v Sri Lanka (Match 9)
County Ground, Bristol, July 11

INDIA

S Ganguly*	run out (Silva/Sangakkara)		9	19	2/0
V Sehwag	run out (Fernando)		39	40	6/0
D Mongia		b Samaraweera	48	63	6/0
S Tendulkar	c Chandana	b Vaas	113	102	12/1
R Dravid†	lbw	b Chandana	13	16	1/0
Yuvraj Singh	lbw	b Samaraweera	8	11	1/0
M Kaif	c Silva	b Zoysa	41	43	3/0
Harbhajan	run out (Jayasuriya)		0	0	0/0
Z Khan		b Fernando	0	1	0/0
A Nehra		b Fernando	3	6	0/0
T Yohannan	not out		5	5	0/0
Extras	(LB6, W12, NB7)		25		
Total	(all out, 50 overs)		**304**		

Fall of Wickets: 1-32 (Ganguly, 6.5), 2-73 (Sehwag, 11.2), 3-172 (Mongia, 27.4), 4-199 (Dravid, 32.1), 5-210 (Yuvraj Singh, 35.1), 6-284 (Tendulkar, 46.1), 7-286 (Harbhajan Singh, 46.3), 8-288 (Khan, 47.2), 9-296 (Kaif, 48.3), 10-304 (Nehra, 49.6)

Bowling: Vaas 10-1-64-1 (2w); **Zoysa** 10-0-66-1 (6nb, 2w); **Fernando** 10-1-55-2 (1nb, 2w); **Chandana** 8-0-44-1; **Jayasuriya** 2-0-14-0 (3w); **Jayawardene** 2-0-16-0

Toss: **India**
Umpires: **D Orchard** (RSA) and **D Shepherd**
TV Umpire: **J Lloyds**

SRI LANKA

S Jayasuriya*	lbw	b Khan	5	4	1/0
M Atapattu	run out (Yuvraj Singh)		53	74	5/0
K Sangakkara†	st Dravid	b Harbhajan	66	47	11/1
Jayawardene	c Nehra	b Yuvraj Singh	31	44	2/0
D Zoysa	c Mongia	b Ganguly	8	9	0/1
R Arnold	run out (Kaif)		8	9	1/0
L Silva	st Dravid	b Harbhajan	30	37	2/0
Samaraweera		b Harbhajan	15	22	1/0
U Chandana	c Nehra	b Harbhajan	1	4	0/0
W Vaas	not out		4	6	0/0
C Fernando	run out (Mongia/Dravid)		3	16	0/0
Extras	(B1, LB5, W5, NB6)		17		
Total	(44.1 overs)		**241**		

Fall of Wickets: 1-11 (Jayasuriya, 1.2), 2-96 (Sangakkara, 12.5), 3-160 (Jayawardene, 25.6), 4-165 (Atapattu, 28.4), 5-171 (Zoysa, 28.6), 6-188 (Arnold, 31.5), 7-210 (Samaraweera, 37.6), 8-221 (Chandana, 39.3), 9-233 (Silva, 41.1), 10-241 (Fernando, 44.1)

Bowling: Nehra 7-0-28-0 (1nb); **Khan** 8.1-0-52-1 (1nb); **Yohannan** 5-0-39-0 (3nb, 2w); **Ganguly** 10-0-40-1 (1nb, 1w); **Harbhajan Singh** 10-0-46-4 (1w); **Yuvraj Singh** 2-0-12-1; **Mongia** 1-0-8-0 (1w); **Sehwag** 1-0-10-0

Man of the Match: **S Tendulkar**
INDIA WON BY 63 RUNS

NATWEST SERIES FINAL
Lord's, July 13

ENGLAND

M Trescothick		b Kumble	109	100	7/2
N Knight		b Khan	14	29	2/0
N Hussain*		b Nehra	115	128	10/0
A Flintoff		b Khan	40	32	2/1
M Vaughan	c Mongia	b Khan	3	5	0/0
P Collingwood	not out		3	4	0/0
R Irani	not out		10	7	0/0
Extras	(B2, LB16, W7, NB6)		31		
Total	(5 wickets, 50 overs)		**325**		

Did Not Bat: A Stewart†, A Tudor, D Gough, A Giles

Fall of Wickets: 1-42 (Knight, 7.4), 2-227 (Trescothick, 36.5), 3-307 (Flintoff, 46.5), 4-312 (Hussain, 47.6), 5-312 (Vaughan, 48.1)

Bowling Nehra 10-0-66-1 (2nb, 1w); **Khan** 10-1-62-3 (1nb, 2w); **Kumble** 10-0-54-1; **Harbhajan Singh** 10-0-53-0 (2w); **Ganguly** 3-0-28-0 (2nb); **Sehwag** 4-0-26-0; **Yuvraj Singh** 3-0-18-0

Toss: **England**
Umpires: **S Bucknor** WI and **D Shepherd**
TV Umpire: **P Willey**

INDIA

V Sehwag		b Giles	45	49	7/0
S Ganguly*		b Tudor	60	43	10/1
D Mongia	c Stewart	b Irani	9	15	1/0
S Tendulkar		b Giles	14	19	1/0
R Dravid	c Knight	b Irani	5	12	0/0
Yuvraj Singh	c Tudor	b Collingwood	69	63	9/1
M Kaif	not out		87	75	6/2
Harbhajan		b Flintoff	15	13	0/1
A Kumble	c Stewart	b Flintoff	0	2	0/0
Z Khan	not out		4	7	0/0
Extras	(B3, LB8, W6, NB1)		18		
Total	(8 wickets, 49.3 overs)		**326**		

Did Not Bat: A Nehra.
Fall of Wickets: 1-106 (Ganguly, 14.3), 2-114 (Sehwag, 15.6), 3-126 (Mongia, 18.3), 4-132 (Dravid, 20.6), 5-146 (Tendulkar, 23.6), 6-267 (Yuvraj Singh, 41.4), 7-314 (Harbhajan Singh, 47.3), 8-314 (Kumble, 47.5)

Bowling Gough 10-1-63-0 (3w); **Tudor** 9-0-62-1 (1nb, 1w); **Flintoff** 7.3-0-55-2 (2w); **Irani** 10-0-64-2; **Giles** 10-0-47-2; **Collingwood** 3-0-24-1

Man of the Match: **M Kaif**
Player of the Series: **M Trescothick**
INDIA WON BY 2 WICKETS

New Zealand v England

Given that the last Test series against New Zealand before this one resulted in an ignominious 2-1 home defeat, and took England close to the very bottom of the world cricket rankings, a drawn series achieved down under has to count as an improvement.

Unfortunately, we are finding it difficult to isolate recent history from past encounters in which the New Zealanders constantly played second fiddle. For 58 years, in fact, during which time the New Zealand team failed to win a single Test Match victory against England. When they finally broke the duck, in 1978, it was almost entirely due to the brilliance of Sir Richard Hadlee, who returned match figures of 10-100.

There was no Hadlee in the team which England met in this three Test series; there was not even Dion Nash, who caused such problems to England in the 1999 series, the quick bowler ruled out through a recurring back injury, which would lead to his retirement later in the year. Excepting an extraordinary four hours when Nathan Astle was Sachin Tendulkar, Stan McCabe and Don Bradman all rolled into one, there was not a single New Zealand player in the series who could be called world class, and plenty who would struggle in the county championship.

Stephen Fleming is one exception, a player of some merit, though not with the bat in this series, his average of 12.66 slightly worse than Ashley Giles. Fleming, though, has been an admirable captain though, managing his limited resources with considerable skill, and salvaging a victory in the final Test to level the series.

England won the first Test, largely because the New Zealand bowling was so ordinary. Graham Thorpe scored a double century, while Nasser Hussain and Andy Flintoff scored centuries, and no other English batsmen reached 35. It was Thorpe and Flintoff in England's second innings who put the match beyond reach, but that didn't deter Astle who hit an astonishing double century in just 153 balls, the second hundred coming in (deep breath here) 39 balls, in a futile , but glorious chase for victory.

The second Test at Wellington petered out into a draw, but the minds of both teams were elsewhere, with a number of players flying out after stumps to Ben Hollioake's funeral in Perth.

On a portable wicket at Auckland for the Third Test, England had the home team reeling at 4-19 after nine overs, but that was as good as it got. Only one English batsman reached a half century and Andy Caddick and Matthew Hoggard were out-bowled by Chris Drum and Darryl Tuffey and English heads that were low already were lower still when the game was lost.

First Test
Jade Stadium, Christchurch, Mar 13-16

ENGLAND - First Innings

M Trescothick	c Parore	b Cairns	0	3	0/0
M Vaughan	c Parore	b Cairns	27	31	2/2
M Butcher	c Butler	b Cairns	0	2	0/0
N Hussain*	lbw	b Drum	106	244	14/0
G Thorpe	c Fleming	b Drum	17	42	1/1
M Ramprakash	c Parore	b Astle	31	55	6/0
A Flintoff	lbw	b Astle	0	14	0/0
J Foster†	lbw	b Drum	19	75	4/0
A Giles	c Drum	b Butler	8	11	2/0
A Caddick	lbw	b Butler	0	12	0/0
M Hoggard	not out		0	8	0/0
Extras (B1, LB10, NB9)			20		
Total (81.2 overs)			228		

Fall of Wickets: 1-0 (Trescothick, 0.3), 2-0 (Butcher, 0.5), 3-46 (Vaughan, 10.4), 4-83 (Thorpe, 22.6), 5-139 (Ramprakash, 41.1), 6-151 (Flintoff, 47.1), 7-196 (Foster, 70.5), 8-214 (Giles, 74.2), 9-226 (Caddick, 78.3), 10-228 (Hussain, 81.2)

Bowling: Cairns 15-4-58-3 (3nb); **Drum** 20.2-8-36-3; **Butler** 16-2-59-2 (4nb); **Astle** 18-10-32-2; **Vettori** 9-1-26-0 (1nb); **McMillan** 3-1-6-0 (1nb)

ENGLAND - Second Innings

M Trescothick	c Vettori	b Butler	33	44	5/0
M Vaughan		b Butler	0	5	0/0
M Butcher	hit wicket	b Butler	34	50	3/0
N Hussain*	c Parore	b Drum	11	27	0/0
G Thorpe	not out		200	231	28/4
M Ramprakash		b Drum	11	25	2/0
A Flintoff	c sub (McKenzie) b Astle		137	163	23/3
J Foster†	not out		22	44	5/0
Extras (B6, LB4, NB10)			20		
Total (6 wickets dec, 96.4 overs)			468		

Did Not Bat: A Giles, A Caddick, M Hoggard.

Fall of Wickets: 1-11 (Vaughan, 3.2), 2-50 (Trescothick, 11.5), 3-81 (Hussain, 20.4), 4-85 (Butcher, 21.1), 5-106 (Ramprakash, 28.4), 6-387 (Flintoff, 79.3)

Bowling: Drum 32-6-130-2 (2nb); **Butler** 23-2-137-3 (3nb); **Cairns** 4-0-8-0; **McMillan** 10-0-66-0 (2nb); **Astle** 5.4-0-20-1 (1nb); **Vettori** 22-3-97-0 (2nb)

NEW ZEALAND - First Innings

M Richardson	lbw	b Hoggard	2	19	0/0
M Horne	c Thorpe	b Hoggard	14	59	2/0
D Vettori	c Foster	b Hoggard	42	57	7/0
L Vincent		b Hoggard	12	33	2/0
S Fleming*	c Giles	b Caddick	12	59	2/0
N Astle	lbw	b Hoggard	10	8	1/0
C McMillan	c Vaughan	b Hoggard	40	48	7/1
C Cairns	c Flintoff	b Caddick	0	3	0/0
A Parore†	lbw	b Caddick	0	1	0/0
C Drum	not out		2	27	0/0
I Butler	c Hussain	b Hoggard	0	2	0/0
Extras (LB5, NB8)			13		
Total (51.2 overs)			147		

Fall of Wickets: 1-4 (Richardson, 3.4), 2-50 (Horne, 19.2), 3-65 (Vettori, 23.5), 4-79 (Vincent, 31.1), 5-93 (Astle, 33.1), 6-117 (Fleming, 43.1), 7-117 (Cairns, 43.4), 8-117 (Parore, 43.5), 9-146 (McMillan, 49.4), 10-147 (Butler, 51.2)

Bowling: Caddick 18-8-50-3 (3nb); **Hoggard** 21.2-7-63-7 (2nb); **Flintoff** 12-2-29-0 (3nb)

NEW ZEALAND - Second Innings

M Richardson	c Foster	b Caddick	76	136	13/0
M Horne	c Foster	b Caddick	4	53	0/0
L Vincent	c Butcher	b Caddick	0	3	0/0
S Fleming*	c Foster	b Flintoff	48	109	7/0
N Astle	c Foster	b Hoggard	222	168	28/11
C McMillan		c & b Caddick	24	31	3/0
A Parore†		b Caddick	1	4	0/0
D Vettori	c Flintoff	b Giles	12	22	3/0
C Drum	lbw	b Flintoff	0	7	0/0
I Butler	c Foster	b Caddick	4	15	1/0
C Cairns	not out		23	29	3/1
Extras (B9, LB11, W1, NB16)			37		
Total (93.3 overs)			451		

Fall of Wickets: 1-42 (Horne, 16.6), 2-53 (Vincent, 18.5), 3-119 (Richardson, 42.4), 4-189 (Fleming, 54.2), 5-242 (McMillan, 66.1), 6-252 (Parore, 68.1), 7-300 (Vettori, 77.1), 8-301 (Drum, 78.3), 9-333 (Butler, 82.4), 10-451 (Astle, 93.3)

Bowling: Caddick 25-8-122-6 (8nb, 1w); **Hoggard** 24.3-5-142-1 (5nb); **Giles** 28-6-73-1; **Flintoff** 16-1-94-2 (2nb)

Toss: **New Zealand**
Umpires: **B Bowden** and **E de Silva** SL
TV Umpire: **D Quested**

Man of the Match: **G Thorpe**
ENGLAND WON BY 98 RUNS

Second Test
Basin Reserve, Wellington, Mar 21-25

ENGLAND - First Innings

M Trescothick	c Vincent	b Vettori	37	68	7/0
M Vaughan	c Fleming	b Drum	7	20	1/0
M Butcher	c Astle	b Drum	47	88	4/0
N Hussain*	c Astle	b Vettori	66	160	7/0
G Thorpe	c Fleming	b Martin	11	33	1/0
M Ramprakash		b Butler	24	70	4/0
A Flintoff	c Drum	b Butler	2	5	0/0
J Foster†	not out		25	45	2/1
A Giles	c McMillan	b Butler	10	12	1/0
A Caddick	c Richardson	b Martin	10	27	1/0
M Hoggard	c Parore	b Butler	7	21	0/0
Extras (B4, LB2, W6, NB22)			34		
Total (88.3 overs)			280		

Fall of Wickets: 1-26 (Vaughan, 7.6), 2-63 (Trescothick, 19.5), 3-133 (Butcher, 37.3), 4-163 (Thorpe, 48.6), 5-221 (Ramprakash, 70.4), 6-221 (Hussain, 71.1), 7-223 (Flintoff, 72.3), 8-238 (Giles, 76.1), 9-250 (Caddick, 80.4), 10-280 (Hoggard, 88.3)

Bowling: Butler 18.3-2-60-4 (10nb); **Drum** 24-6-85-2 (3nb, 2w); **Martin** 17-3-58-2 (2nb); **Vettori** 25-3-62-2 (3nb); **Astle** 1-0-1-0; **McMillan** 3-0-8-0

NEW ZEALAND - First Innings

M Richardson	c Giles	b Caddick	60	180	5/0
M Horne		b Caddick	8	30	1/0
L Vincent	c Thorpe	b Giles	57	153	6/0
S Fleming*	c Thorpe	b Caddick	3	6	0/0
N Astle	c Hussain	b Giles	4	15	0/0
C McMillan	lbw	b Caddick	41	58	4/1
A Parore†	c Ramprakash	b Giles	0	4	0/0
D Vettori	c Thorpe	b Caddick	11	21	1/0
C Drum	c Trescothick	b Giles	2	28	0/0
I Butler	c Foster	b Caddick	12	35	2/0
C Martin	not out		0	6	0/0
Extras (B2, LB9, NB9)			20		
Total (88.3 overs)			218		

Fall of Wickets: 1-16 (Horne, 8.2), 2-135 (Vincent, 57.1), 3-138 (Fleming, 58.2), 4-143 (Richardson, 62.3), 5-147 (Astle, 65.2), 6-149 (Parore, 65.6), 7-178 (Vettori, 72.3), 8-201 (McMillan, 80.3), 9-207 (Drum, 85.1), 10-218 (Butler, 88.3)

Bowling: Caddick 28.3-8-63-6 (2nb); **Hoggard** 13-5-32-0 (1nb); **Giles** 37-3-103-4; **Flintoff** 10-4-9-0 (2nb)

ENGLAND - Second Innings

M Trescothick	c Richardson	b Vettori	88	129	10/2
M Vaughan	c Drum	b Vettori	34	72	2/1
M Butcher	c Martin	b Drum	60	111	9/0
A Flintoff		c & b Vettori	75	44	9/2
N Hussain*	not out		13	33	0/0
G Thorpe	not out		1	3	0/0
Extras (B5, LB13, NB4)			22		
Total (4 wickets dec, 65 overs)			293		

Did Not Bat: M Ramprakash, J Foster†, A Giles, A Caddick, M Hoggard

Fall of Wickets: 1-79 (Vaughan, 21.1), 2-194 (Butcher, 50.5), 3-209 (Trescothick, 53.1), 4-291 (Flintoff, 63.4)

Bowling: **Butler** 6-0-32-0; **Drum** 16-2-78-1 (3nb); **Vettori** 24-1-90-3 (1nb); **Astle** 9-4-18-0; **Martin** 7-1-40-0; **McMillan** 3-0-17-0

NEW ZEALAND - Second Innings

M Richardson	c Thorpe	b Giles	4	38	1/0
M Horne	c Foster	b Flintoff	38	80	3/0
L Vincent	lbw	b Hoggard	71	170	7/0
S Fleming*		b Hoggard	11	108	0/0
N Astle	not out		11	58	1/0
C McMillan	not out		17	51	3/0
Extras (B3, LB1, NB2)			6		
Total (4 wickets, 84 overs)			158		

Did Not Bat: A Parore†, D Vettori, C Drum, I Butler, C Martin

Fall of Wickets: 1-28 (Richardson, 14.3), 2-65 (Horne, 29.1), 3-128 (Vincent, 63.5), 4-131 (Fleming, 67.4)

Bowling: Caddick 17-6-31-0 (1nb); **Hoggard** 13-4-31-2; **Giles** 33-11-53-1; **Flintoff** 16-6-24-1 (1nb); **Vaughan** 5-1-15-0

Toss: **New Zealand**
Umpires: **R Dunne** and **D Hair** AUS
TV Umpire: **E Watkin**

Man of the Match: **A Caddick**
MATCH DRAWN

Third Test
Eden Park, Auckland, Mar 30-Apr 3

NEW ZEALAND - First Innings

M Richardson		b Caddick	5	10	0/0
L Vincent		b Caddick	10	25	2/0
S Fleming*	c Ramprakash	b Hoggard	1	10	0/0
C Harris	lbw	b Flintoff	71	185	11/0
N Astle	c Thorpe	b Caddick	2	4	0/0
C McMillan	lbw	b Caddick	41	59	8/0
A Parore†	c sub (Afzaal)	b Flintoff	45	129	5/1
D Vettori	lbw	b Hoggard	3	14	0/0
A Adams	c Giles	b Flintoff	7	10	1/0
D Tuffey	c Butcher	b Hoggard	0	7	0/0
C Drum	not out		2	4	0/0
Extras (LB10, NB5)			15		
Total (75.2 overs)			202		

Fall of Wickets: 1-12 (Richardson, 4.1), 2-17 (Fleming, 7.2), 3-17 (Vincent, 8.1), 4-19 (Astle, 8.5), 5-86 (McMillan, 27.4), 6-172 (Harris, 66.3), 7-191 (Vettori, 71.4), 8-198 (Parore, 72.3), 9-200 (Adams, 74.3), 10-202 (Tuffey, 75.2)

Bowling: Caddick 25-5-70-4 (2nb); **Hoggard** 28.2-10-66-3 (1nb); **Flintoff** 16-6-49-3 (2nb); **Butcher** 5-3-6-0; **Giles** 1-0-1-0

ENGLAND - First Innings

M Trescothick	lbw	b Tuffey	0	2	0/0
M Vaughan	c Parore	b Adams	27	53	3/0
M Butcher	c Richardson	b Tuffey	0	3	0/0
N Hussain*	c Fleming	b Drum	2	9	0/0
G Thorpe		b Tuffey	42	89	5/0
M Ramprakash	c Parore	b Tuffey	9	14	0/1
A Flintoff	c Parore	b Adams	29	29	5/1
J Foster†	not out		16	33	2/0
A Giles	lbw	b Tuffey	0	7	0/0
A Caddick		b Tuffey	20	35	3/0
M Hoggard	c Fleming	b Adams	0	4	0/0
Extras (B1, LB11, NB3)			15		
Total (45.4 overs)			160		

Fall of Wickets: 1-0 (Trescothick, 0.2), 2-0 (Butcher, 0.5), 3-11 (Hussain, 5.1), 4-60 (Vaughan, 17.2), 5-75 (Ramprakash, 20.5), 6-118 (Flintoff, 31.2), 7-122 (Thorpe, 34.3), 8-124 (Giles, 36.3), 9-159 (Caddick, 44.4), 10-160 (Hoggard, 45.4)

Bowling: Tuffey 19-6-54-6 (2nb); **Drum** 10-3-45-1; **Adams** 15.4-2-44-3 (1nb); **McMillan** 1-0-5-0

NEW ZEALAND - Second Innings

M Richardson	c sub (Afzaal)	b Butcher	25	105	4/0
A Parore†	c Thorpe	b Hoggard	36	66	4/0
S Fleming*		b Hoggard	1	5	0/0
C Harris	lbw	b Butcher	43	78	5/0
N Astle	c Butcher	b Flintoff	65	51	8/2
C McMillan	not out		50	51	3/3
A Adams		b Flintoff	11	10	2/0
D Vettori	c Foster	b Flintoff	0	2	0/0
L Vincent	c Giles	b Hoggard	10	14	1/0
D Tuffey		b Hoggard	5	6	1/0
Extras (B3, LB9, W1, NB10)			23		
Total (9 wickets dec, 63.1 overs)			269		

Did Not Bat: C Drum

Fall of Wickets: 1-53 (Parore, 21.5), 2-55 (Fleming, 23.1), 3-91 (Richardson, 35.2), 4-166 (Harris, 47.1), 5-217 (Astle, 52.6), 6-232 (Adams, 54.6), 7-235 (Vettori, 56.4), 8-262 (Vincent, 61.5), 9-269 (Tuffey, 63.1)

Bowling: Caddick 11-3-41-0 (2nb, 1w); **Hoggard** 19.1-3-68-4; **Flintoff** 23-1-108-3 (8nb); **Butcher** 9-2-34-2; **Giles** 1-0-6-0

ENGLAND - Second Innings

M Trescothick		b Drum	14	19	2/0
M Vaughan	c Fleming	b Drum	36	42	5/1
M Butcher	c sub (Walker)	b Astle	35	68	6/0
N Hussain*		c & b Adams	82	119	13/1
G Thorpe	c Parore	b Tuffey	3	6	0/0
A Flintoff		b Tuffey	0	2	0/0
M Ramprakash		b Tuffey	2	15	0/0
J Foster†	c Parore	b Adams	23	62	4/0
A Giles	not out		21	27	4/0
A Caddick	c Vettori	b Drum	4	15	1/0
M Hoggard	c Astle	b Adams	2	5	0/0
Extras (B1, LB8, NB2)			11		
Total (63 overs)			233		

Fall of Wickets: 1-23 (Trescothick, 5.5), 2-73 (Vaughan, 14.1), 3-122 (Butcher, 27.4), 4-125 (Thorpe, 28.4), 5-125 (Flintoff, 28.6), 6-155 (Ramprakash, 36.1), 7-204 (Foster, 54.4), 8-207 (Hussain, 56.4), 9-230 (Caddick, 61.5), 10-233 (Hoggard, 62.6)

Bowling: Tuffey 16-3-62-3 (1nb); **Drum** 10-0-52-3 (1nb); **Adams** 16-3-61-3; **Astle** 19-6-44-1; **Vettori** 2-0-5-0

Toss: New Zealand
Umpires: **D Cowie** and **S Venkataraghavan** IND
TV Umpire: **A Hill**

Man of the Match: **D Tuffey**
NEW ZEALAND WON BY 78 RUNS

SERIES DRAWN 1-1

England v New Zealand Test Averages

England

BATTING	M	I	NO	Rns	HS	Av	100	50
G Thorpe	3	6	2	274	200*	68.50	1	-
N Hussain	3	6	1	280	106	56.00	1	2
J Foster	3	5	3	105	25*	52.50	-	-
A Flintoff	3	6	0	243	137	40.50	1	1
M Butcher	3	6	0	176	60	29.33	-	1
M Trescothick	3	6	0	172	88	28.66	-	1
M Vaughan	3	6	0	131	36	21.83	-	-
M Ramprakash	3	5	0	77	31	15.40	-	-
A Giles	3	4	1	39	21*	13.00	-	-
A Caddick	3	4	0	34	20	8.50	-	-
M Hoggard	3	4	1	9	7	3.00	-	-

BOWLING	M	O	M	R	W	Av	BB
A Caddick	3	124.3	38	377	19	19.84	6-63
M Butcher	3	14	5	40	2	20.00	2-34
M Hoggard	3	119.2	34	402	17	23.64	7-63
A Flintoff	3	93	20	313	9	34.77	3-49
A Giles	3	100	20	236	6	39.33	4-103
M Vaughan	3	5	1	15	0	-	-

New Zealand

BATTING	M	I	NO	Rns	HS	Av	100	50
N Astle	3	6	1	314	222	62.80	1	1
C Harris	1	2	0	114	71	57.00	-	1
C McMillan	3	6	2	213	50*	53.25	-	1
M Richardson	3	6	0	172	76	28.66	-	2
L Vincent	3	6	0	160	71	26.66	-	2
C Cairns	1	2	1	23	23*	23.00	-	-
A Parore	3	5	0	82	45	16.40	-	-
M Horne	2	4	0	64	38	16.00	-	-
D Vettori	3	5	0	68	42	13.60	-	-
S Fleming	3	6	0	76	48	12.66	-	-
A Adams	1	2	0	18	11	9.00	-	-
I Butler	2	3	0	16	12	5.33	-	-
C Drum	3	4	2	6	2*	3.00	-	-
D Tuffey	1	2	0	5	5	2.50	-	-
C Martin	1	1	0	0	0*	-	-	-

BOWLING	M	O	M	R	W	Av	BB
D Tuffey	1	35	9	116	9	12.88	6-54
A Adams	1	31.4	5	105	6	17.50	3-44
C Cairns	1	19	4	66	3	22.00	3-58
N Astle	3	52.4	20	115	4	28.75	2-32
I Butler	2	63.3	6	288	9	32.00	4-60
C Drum	3	112.2	25	426	12	35.50	3-36
C Martin	1	24	4	98	2	49.00	2-58
D Vettori	3	82	8	280	5	56.00	3-90
C McMillan	3	20	1	102	0	-	-

First One-day International
Jade Stadium, Christchurch, Feb 13 (d/n)

ENGLAND

M Trescothick†	lbw	b Butler	1	4	0/0
N Knight	c Adams	b Tuffey	73	70	11/0
N Hussain*	c Nevin	b Adams	35	38	6/0
G Thorpe	run out (McMillan)		41	52	6/0
A Flintoff	c Vincent	b Cairns	12	15	0/1
P Collingwood	c Tuffey	b Vettori	9	15	1/0
C White	c Cairns	b Vettori	0	4	0/0
J Foster†	c Vincent	b Vettori	3	10	0/0
A Giles	c Harris	b Cairns	2	8	0/0
A Caddick	c Harris	b Adams	2	14	0/0
D Gough	not out		5	13	0/0
Extras (LB6, W6, NB1)			13		
Total (40.2 overs)			196		

Fall of Wickets: 1-2 (Trescothick, 0.5), 2-84 (Hussain, 11.5), 3-156 (Knight, 26.4), 4-170 (Thorpe, 28.4), 5-181 (Collingwood, 31.5), 6-181 (Flintoff, 32.2), 7-183 (White, 33.3), 8-189 (Foster, 35.4), 9-189 (Giles, 36.1), 10-196 (Caddick, 40.2)

Bowling: Butler 5-0-37-1 (2w); **Tuffey** 8-0-48-1 (4w); **Cairns** 9-1-43-2 (1nb); **Adams** 6.2-1-25-2; **Astle** 1-0-9-0; **Harris** 3-0-11-0; **Vettori** 8-1-17-3

Toss: **England**
Umpires: **A Hill** and **E Watkin**
TV Umpire: **D Quested**

NEW ZEALAND

C Nevin†	c Collingwood	b Flintoff	55	63	5/1
N Astle	not out		67	105	8/0
S Fleming*		c & b White	10	15	1/0
C McMillan	c Foster	b Gough	15	15	2/0
C Cairns		b Gough	8	4	2/0
L Vincent	c Flintoff	b Gough	0	1	0/0
C Harris	c Foster	b Gough	0	5	0/0
A Adams	not out		28	23	2/2
Extras (LB9, W6)			15		
Total (6 wickets, 38.3 overs)			198		

Did Not Bat: D Vettori, D Tuffey, I Butler

Fall of Wickets: 1-99 (Nevin, 18.4), 2-111 (Fleming, 22.5), 3-136 (McMillan, 28.1), 4-144 (Cairns, 28.5), 5-144 (Vincent, 28.6), 6-144 (Harris, 30.5)

Bowling: Gough 9-1-44-4 (3w); **Caddick** 7.3-0-51-0 (1w); **Flintoff** 8-0-30-1 (2w); **White** 5-0-36-1; **Giles** 9-1-28-0

Man of the Match: N Astle
NEW ZEALAND WON BY 4 WICKETS

Second One-day International
Wellington, Feb 16

NEW ZEALAND

C Nevin[†]		c & b Gough	21	20	3/0
N Astle	lbw	b Gough	7	16	0/0
B McCullum	c Trescothick	b Flintoff	9	15	1/0
S Fleming*	c Shah	b Hoggard	40	61	4/1
C McMillan	c Flintoff	b White	69	91	3/1
L Vincent		b Hoggard	36	57	1/0
C Cairns	c Flintoff	b White	11	6	0/1
C Harris	c Knight	b Gough	14	19	0/0
A Adams	not out		25	18	2/0
D Vettori	not out		0	0	0/0
Extras (LB5, W3, NB4)			12		
Total (8 wickets, 50 overs)			244		

Did Not Bat: D Tuffey.

Fall of Wickets: 1-25 (Astle, 4.6), 2-34 (Nevin, 6.3), 3-52 (McCullum, 11.4), 4-110 (Fleming, 26.3), 5-194 (McMillan, 42.3), 6-198 (Vincent, 43.2), 7-206 (Cairns, 44.2), 8-243 (Harris, 49.5)

Bowling: Gough 10-0-47-3; **Hoggard** 8-1-36-2 (3nb, 2w); **Flintoff** 10-0-46-1 (1w); **White** 10-1-53-2 (1nb); **Giles** 8-0-40-0; **Collingwood** 4-0-17-0

Toss: England
Umpires: **R Dunne** and **D Quested**
TV Umpire: **A Hill**

ENGLAND

M Trescothick[†]	c Nevin	b Adams	0	7	0/0
N Knight		b Adams	9	20	0/0
N Hussain*	c Fleming	b Tuffey	3	13	0/0
G Thorpe	lbw	b Adams	10	14	2/0
O Shah	c Fleming	b Cairns	7	39	0/0
P Collingwood	c Vettori	b Astle	0	11	0/0
A Flintoff	c McCullum	b Astle	26	57	1/1
C White	lbw	b Harris	11	27	1/0
A Giles	c Vettori	b Harris	12	40	1/0
D Gough		b Astle	0	3	0/0
M Hoggard	not out		0	0	0/0
Extras (LB2, W2, NB7)			11		
Total (37.2 overs)			89		

Fall of Wickets: 1-1 (Trescothick, 1.2), 2-13 (Hussain, 6.1), 3-18 (Knight, 7.2), 4-28 (Thorpe, 11.5), 5-35 (Collingwood, 15.6), 6-40 (Shah, 18.1), 7-65 (White, 26.4), 8-89 (Giles, 36.4), 9-89 (Flintoff, 37.1), 10-89 (Gough, 37.2)

Bowling: Tuffey 8-3-23-1 (4nb); **Adams** 7-0-13-3 (1w); **Cairns** 4-1-11-1 (1nb, 1w); **Astle** 2.2-0-4-3; **Vettori** 7-0-18-0; **Harris** 9-2-18-2 (2nb)

Man of the Match: **A Adams**
NEW ZEALAND WON BY 155 RUNS

Third One-day International
McLean Park, Napier, Feb 20

ENGLAND

M Trescothick[†]	c Harris	b Cairns	41	50	6/0
N Knight	c Nevin	b Cairns	80	129	4/0
N Hussain*		b Harris	24	48	3/0
G Thorpe	c Astle	b Cairns	52	53	4/0
A Flintoff	c Vincent	b Adams	19	21	1/0
P Collingwood	not out		9	7	2/0
O Shah	not out		0	0	0/0
Extras (B1, LB5, W5, NB8)			19		
Total (5 wickets, 50 overs)			244		

Did Not Bat: C White, A Giles, D Gough, M Hoggard

Fall of Wickets: 1-71 (Trescothick, 12.6), 2-127 (Hussain, 28.4), 3-192 (Knight, 42.4), 4-231 (Thorpe, 48.1), 5-240 (Flintoff, 49.2)

Bowling: Butler 4-0-21-0 (5nb); **Tuffey** 10-0-39-0 (2nb, 3w); **Cairns** 10-1-51-3 (1nb); **Adams** 9-1-49-1 (2w); **Vettori** 10-0-49-0; **Harris** 7-0-29-1

Toss: New Zealand
Umpires: **B Bowden** and **D Cowie**
TV Umpire: **R Dunne**

NEW ZEALAND

C Nevin[†]	c sub (Hollioake)	b Hoggard	21	18	4/0
N Astle	c Trescothick	b Gough	2	7	0/0
S Fleming*	not out		76	112	6/0
C McMillan	c Collingwood	b Hoggard	14	33	1/0
L Vincent	c White	b Collingwood	29	49	0/1
C Cairns	c Flintoff	b Collingwood	7	17	0/0
C Harris	lbw	b Collingwood	3	14	0/0
A Adams	c Shah	b Collingwood	2	6	0/0
D Vettori	lbw	b Giles	9	9	1/0
D Tuffey		b Giles	1	10	0/0
I Butler		b Gough	3	6	0/0
Extras (B 2, LB15, W15, NB2)			34		
Total (46.3 overs)			201		

Fall of Wickets: 1-10 (Astle, 2.1), 2-31 (Nevin, 5.3), 3-70 (McMillan, 15.5), 4-128 (Vincent, 29.4), 5-140 (Cairns, 33.6), 6-152 (Harris, 37.3), 7-168 (Adams, 39.6), 8-180 (Vettori, 42.1), 9-186 (Tuffey, 44.2), 10-201 (Butler, 46.3)

Bowling: Gough 8.3-0-21-2 (3w); Hoggard 10-0-44-2 (2nb, 3w); Flintoff 7-0-34-0 (3w); White 3-0-15-0; Giles 10-1-32-2; Collingwood 8-0-38-4 (3w)

Mn of the Match: **P Collingwood**
ENGLAND WON BY 43 RUNS

Fourth One-day International
Eden Park, Auckland, Feb 23

ENGLAND

M Trescothick†	c Cairns	b Tuffey	0	3	0/0
N Knight	run out (Tuffey/Vettori/Nevin)		38	60	4/1
N Hussain*	lbw	b Cairns	17	34	3/0
G Thorpe	not out		59	67	4/0
M Vaughan	run out (Vettori)		59	53	8/1
A Flintoff	c Astle	b Cairns	2	7	0/0
P Collingwood	st Nevin	b Harris	4	12	0/0
C White	not out		3	4	0/0
Extras (B4, LB6, W1)			11		
Total (6 wickets, 40 overs)			**193**		

Did Not Bat: A Giles, D Gough, M Hoggard

Fall of Wickets: 1-0 (Trescothick, 0.3), 2-40 (Hussain, 10.5), 3-78 (Knight, 19.1), 4-167 (Vaughan, 33.3), 5-170 (Flintoff, 34.6), 6-185 (Collingwood, 38.4)

Bowling: Tuffey 8-1-32-1; **Adams** 8-1-36-0; **Cairns** 8-0-39-2 (1w); **Vettori** 8-0-31-0; **Harris** 4-0-23-1; **Astle** 4-0-22-0

Toss: England
Umpires: **D Cowie** and **A Hill**
TV Umpire: **B Bowden**

NEW ZEALAND

C Nevin†	c Trescothick	b Hoggard	8	8	1/0
N Astle	c Gough	b Flintoff	23	48	3/0
B McCullum	c Vaughan	b Hoggard	5	9	1/0
S Fleming*	c Vaughan	b Gough	8	11	1/0
C McMillan	c Knight	b Flintoff	10	17	1/0
L Vincent	c Giles	b Flintoff	7	25	0/1
C Cairns		b Collingwood	58	56	4/2
C Harris	c Flintoff	b White	23	28	1/1
A Adams	not out		26	14	3/1
D Vettori	c Hoggard	b Gough	4	4	0/0
D Tuffey		b Flintoff	5	7	0/0
Extras (LB7, W5)			12		
Total (38 overs)			**189**		

Fall of Wickets: 1-9 (Nevin, 1.6), 2-16 (McCullum, 5.1), 3-42 (Fleming, 8.6), 4-58 (McMillan, 14.5), 5-60 (Astle, 16.2), 6-86 (Vincent, 22.4), 7-153 (Harris, 33.3), 8-167 (Cairns, 34.6), 9-181 (Vettori, 36.2 ov), 10-189 (Tuffey, 37.6)

Bowling: Gough 7-1-33-2 (1w); **Hoggard** 8-1-27-2; **Flintoff** 7-1-17-4 (2w); **Collingwood** 6-0-43-1 (1w); **White** 8-0-44-1; **Giles** 2-0-18-0 (1w)

Man of the Match: **A Flintoff**
ENGLAND WON BY 33 RUNS

Fifth One-day International
Dunedin, Feb 26

ENGLAND

M Trescothick†	c Harris	b Tuffey	5	12	1/0
N Knight	c Harris	b Tuffey	24	25	4/0
N Hussain*	c Cairns	b Tuffey	50	80	6/0
G Thorpe		b Adams	9	17	1/0
O Shah	lbw	b Cairns	57	81	6/0
P Collingwood	c Fleming	b Cairns	21	34	1/0
A Flintoff		b Cairns	1	8	0/0
C White	c Astle	b Adams	17	22	1/0
A Giles	not out		21	23	1/0
D Gough	not out		2	2	0/0
Extras (LB4, W3, NB4)			11		
Total (8 wickets, 50 overs)			**218**		

Did Not Bat: M Hoggard

Fall of Wickets: 1-8 (Trescothick, 2.3), 2-43 (Knight, 8.4), 3-62 (Thorpe, 13.2), 4-133 (Hussain, 31.5), 5-170 (Shah, 38.6), 6-172 (Flintoff, 40.4), 7-183 (Collingwood, 44.1), 8-214 (White, 49.2)

Bowling: Tuffey 9-1-42-3; **Adams** 10-0-50-2; **Cairns** 10-0-32-3 (2nb, 1w); **Vettori** 9-0-48-0 (1nb); **Harris** 10-0-35-0 (1nb, 1w); **Astle** 2-0-7-0 (1w)

Toss: **England**
Umpires: **R Dunne** and **D Quested**
TV Umpire: **E Watkin**

NEW ZEALAND

C Nevin†	c Trescothick	b Flintoff	15	27	1/0
N Astle	not out		122	150	12/5
B McCullum		b White	7	10	1/0
S Fleming*	c Knight	b White	1	12	0/0
C McMillan	lbw	b Gough	44	69	4/1
C Cairns	c Hussain	b Gough	0	3	0/0
L Vincent	not out		20	27	1/0
Extras (LB4, W5, NB5)			14		
Total (5 wickets, 48.5 overs)			**223**		

Did Not Bat: C Harris, A Adams, D Vettori, D Tuffey

Fall of Wickets: 1-55 (Nevin, 9.5), 2-77 (McCullum, 12.2), 3-80 (Fleming, 14.4), 4-180 (McMillan, 40.1), 5-180 (Cairns, 40.4)

Bowling: Gough 10-0-42-2 (1nb); **Hoggard** 6-0-41-0 (2nb); **Flintoff** 9.5-0-56-1 (1nb, 3w); **White** 10-0-30-2 (1nb); **Giles** 8-0-37-0 (1w); **Collingwood** 5-0-13-0 (1w)

Man of the Match: **N Astle**
NEW ZEALAND WON BY 5 WICKETS

NEW ZEALAND WON ODI SERIES BY 3-2

Overseas Tests

Dates given are tour dates.
Home teams are given first.

December 2001-January 2002
Bangladesh lost to Pakistan 2-0
(Two Tests)

January-February, Sharjah
Pakistan beat West Indies 2-0
(Two Tests)

January-February
Sri Lanka beat Kenya 3-0
(Three Unofficial Tests)

January-February
India beat Zimbabwe 2-0
(Two Tests)

February-March
South Africa lost to Australia 2-1
(Three Tests)

March-April
West Indies beat India 2-1
(Five Tests)

May
Pakistan beat New Zealand 1-0
(Only one Test, the first Test was cancelled)

June-July
West Indies lost to New Zealand 1-0
(Two Tests)

July
Sri Lanka beat Bangladesh 2-0
(Two Tests)

October
South Africa beat Bangladesh 2-0
(Two Tests)

October, Colombo & Sharjah
Pakistan lost to Australia 3-0
(Three Tests)

October-November
India beat West Indies 2-0
(Three Tests)

November
Zimbabwe lost to Pakistan 2-0
(Two Tests)

December
Bangladesh lost to West Indies 2-0
(Two Tests)

December-January 2003
South Africa beat Pakistan 2-0
(Two Tests)

Champions Trophy

SEMI-FINALS
Colombo, Sri Lanka
Sep 25
India 261-9 (50)
South Africa 251-6 (50)
India won by 10 runs

Colombo, Sri Lanka
Sep 27
Australia 162 (48.4)
Sri Lanka 163-3 (40)
Sri Lanka won by 7 wickets

FINAL
Colombo, Sri Lanka
Sep 29-30
Sri Lanka 244-5 (50)
India 38-1 (8.4)
No result, trophy shared

County Cricket

For the third time in four years, Surrey were crowned champions. Five of their batsmen ended the season with averages of over 50, and they were led with zeal by Adam Hollioake, who returned to the fray in mid-June, following the death of his brother and the birth of his daughter, Bennaya, named after Ben. Hollioake is now the fourth most successful Surrey captain in history. Stuart Surridge still the leader with his five titles in the fifties, but Hollioake, at 31, has time enough to catch him.

Surrey were confirmed champions on September 9th, and when it was all academic anyway secured their biggest win of the summer, indeed the biggest win of any summer, against a demoralised Leicestershire side. Chasing 626 in their second innings, Leicester were bowled out for just 142, leaving Surrey winners by 483 runs, the largest winning run-margin in County Championship history, beating the previous mark set in 1913 when Sussex defeated Gloucestershire by 470 runs.

Essex won the Division Two title, settling it with a seven-wicket win over Nottinghamshire, who nevertheless joined them in the promotion stakes. Midllesex, who finished second, also went up, while Hampshire, Somerset and Yorkshire went down. While Rugby Union still struggles to come to terms with promoting/relegating a single club, cricket happily desposes of one third of its Division One clubs every year. It still seems one too many, but the fact that there is no relegation from Division Two does give the counties some stability.

Glamorgan won the Norwich Union National League, while a Matthew Elliot century at Lord's was primarily responsible for Yorkshire winning the C & G Trophy, some consolation for an otherwise dismal summer. The Super Cup, in its last year of tobacco sponsorship (and about time too), was won by Warwickshire, Jim Troughton and Ian Bell setting up the victory with a stand of 84 runs from 72 balls. It was Bob Woolmer's swansong as the Warwickshire county coach.

After 30 years, the Super Cup has been replaced by the Twenty20 Cup which, as the title informs, is a one day match consisting of 20 overs for each side and reckoned to last just under three hours, with the mid-innings break. The matches are timed to start at 5:30pm and the object is to bring a younger audience to the sport. If it succeeds in that, the seven counties who voted against the idea will soon be won over.

The counties have also voted for a return to the system which allowed two overseas players per county, to offset the losses of England-contracted players, and because of the difficulties in securing any overseas player for the entire county season, when the demands for cricketers in all Test-playing countries are now so manifold.

2002 Final Averages
All First-class Matches

	BATTING		BOWLING	
	Minimum 10 innings		*Minimum 20 wickets*	

	M	In	NO	Rns	HS	Avge	100	50		O	M	R	W	Avge	Best
N Knight (Wa)	10	19	3	1520	255*	95.00	5	5	Azhar M (Su)	109.2	27	345	20	17.25	8-61
M Vaughan (Yo)	9	15	2	976	197	75.07	4	3	J Srinath (Le)	179.2	29	561	30	18.70	5-25
M Trescothick (So)	6	11	2	622	161	69.11	2	4	D Cork (De)	403.4	101	1210	64	18.90	6-51
M Hussey (Nor)	13	23	2	1442	310*	68.66	5	4	I Harvey (Glo)	152.2	29	533	28	19.03	6-68
A Hollioake (Su)	9	13	2	738	208	67.09	2	5	R Irani (Es)	227.5	72	591	29	20.37	6-71
D Lehmann (Yo)	10	18	1	1136	216	66.82	3	7	P Martin (La)	452	143	1126	53	21.24	5-54
M Bevan (Le)	9	14	2	697	146	63.36	2	4	R Johnson (So)	307.1	66	914	43	21.25	7-43
Jayawaredene (SL)	6	11	2	567	125*	63.00	3	1	M Saggers (K)	571	111	1786	83	21.51	6-39
I Ward (Su)	17	31	3	1759	168*	62.82	7	7	A Harris (Not)	413.4	93	1475	67	22.01	7-54
K Pietersen (Not)	12	17	3	871	254*	62.21	4	-	J Anderson (La)	326.4	61	1114	50	22.28	6-23
M Di Venuto (De)	15	28	3	1538	230	61.52	4	7	J Stephenson (Es)	295.4	59	1082	48	22.54	7-44
R Irani (Es)	12	19	3	977	207*	61.06	3	1	R Kirtley (Sx)	379	94	1199	53	22.62	6-107
M Ramprakash (M)	15	25	4	1194	218	56.85	4	6	S MacGill (Not)	227.4	37	930	40	23.25	8-111
G Hick (Wo)	18	30	4	1453	315*	55.88	4	6	K Dean (De)	590	148	1951	83	23.50	7-42
M Maynard (So)	13	20	1	1058	151	55.68	3	6	D Maddy (Le)	334.3	78	1025	43	23.83	5-37
M Elliott (Yo)	5	10	1	487	127	54.11	1	4	N Boje (Not)	238	58	671	27	24.85	6-128
J Crawley (La)	15	25	4	1130	272	53.80	2	7	A Richardson (Wa)	300.2	64	951	38	25.02	8-46
A Stewart (Su)	11	16	2	751	123	53.64	1	5	A Bichel (Wo)	297	77	902	36	25.05	9-93
K Barnett (Glo)	8	15	3	641	182*	53.41	3	1	A Noffke (M)	305.1	57	1128	45	25.06	8-24
P Collingwood (Du)	7	12	0	636	190	53.00	1	4	Kabir Ali (Wo)	547.1	129	1781	71	25.08	7-43
S James (Gla)	14	22	1	1111	249	52.90	4	3	A Mullally (Ha)	463.2	145	1156	46	25.13	6-56
S Law (La)	15	26	3	1216	218	52.86	2	6	P Franks (Not)	234.5	53	813	32	25.40	5-51
E Joyce (M)	18	27	3	1267	129	52.79	4	6	M Malik (Not)	146.4	29	562	22	25.54	5-67
P Weekes (M)	18	25	6	990	127*	52.10	4	3	G Welch (De)	486.1	157	1409	55	25.61	6-60
M Gough (Du)	8	14	2	616	103	51.33	1	3	Saqlain M (Su)	488.4	112	1359	53	25.64	6-121
J Troughton (Wa)	14	24	3	1067	131*	50.80	3	6	A Davies (Du)	357.5	106	942	36	26.16	5-61
R Clarke (Su)	10	16	2	711	153*	50.78	2	4	S Pollock (Wa)	301.3	101	733	28	26.17	4-37
A Brown (Su)	16	26	2	1211	188	50.45	5	3	G Smith (Not)	400.1	85	1275	48	26.56	8-53
M Powell (Gla)	16	26	3	1152	135	50.08	3	7	M Kasprowicz (Gla)	418.4	78	1413	53	26.66	6-47
A Flower (Es)	16	29	6	1151	172*	50.04	2	6	A Tudor (Su)	322	74	1124	42	26.76	5-66
P de Silva (SL)	8	12	2	500	88	50.00	-	6	S Cook (M)	367.2	71	1305	48	27.18	8-63
V Sehwag (IND)	8	13	0	640	142	49.23	3	1	A Cowan (Es)	276.1	70	843	31	27.19	5-68
C Spearman (Glo)	17	34	4	1444	180*	48.13	5	7	A Caddick (So)	423.3	87	1313	48	27.35	6-84
A Strauss (M)	17	27	2	1202	141	48.08	3	5	S Jones (Gla)	323.5	53	1101	40	27.52	6-45
S Ganguly (IND)	7	11	1	477	128	47.70	1	4	A Kumble (IND)	212	51	607	22	27.59	4-58
D Maddy (Le)	16	29	4	1187	156	47.48	2	8	Harbhajan (IND)	243.2	43	773	28	27.60	7-83
M Atapattu (SL)	7	12	1	522	185	47.45	2	1	L Wharton (De)	208.5	45	695	25	27.80	6-62
R Blakey (Yo)	16	29	7	1041	103	47.31	1	8	M Mason (Wo)	224.4	55	613	22	27.86	5-50
O Shah (M)	17	26	3	1084	172*	47.13	3	6	G Swann (Nor)	270.5	60	884	31	28.51	6-126
M Butcher (Su)	13	21	1	936	123	46.80	3	5	K Innes (Es)	268.3	65	834	29	28.75	4-41
D Smith (WI-A)	6	10	0	465	181	46.50	1	2	A Sheriyar (Wo)	616.2	160	1905	66	28.86	6-71
S Koenig (M)	18	29	2	1251	141*	46.33	4	7	R Sidebottom (Yo)	380.5	85	1190	41	29.02	5-60
D Nash (M)	15	19	5	646	100	46.14	1	4	Abdur Razzaq (M)	206.3	25	757	26	29.11	7-133
D Robinson (Es)	18	34	2	1474	175	46.06	5	6	C Tremlett (Ha)	336	83	1061	36	29.47	5-57
Tillakaratne (SL)	8	13	5	388	81	45.75	-	2	G Chapple (La)	539.3	128	1594	54	29.51	6-30
U Afzaal (Not)	18	32	4	1275	134	45.53	5	6	A Smith (Glo)	270	55	916	31	29.54	5-69
R Russell (Glo)	17	28	6	991	119*	45.04	3	5	S Harmison (Du)	324.2	75	1001	33	30.33	5-65
C Adams (Sx)	10	19	0	848	217	44.63	3	3	D Malcolm (Le)	477.5	79	1826	60	30.43	7-76
B Smith (Wo)	18	30	3	1202	137	44.51	4	6	J Dakin (Es)	360.2	77	1233	40	30.82	4-17
A Habib (Es)	15	25	3	964	123	43.81	2	8	A Mascarenhas (Ha)	420.5	144	1141	37	30.83	5-87

Frizzell County Championship

FIRST DIVISION

		P	W	L	D	Bt	Bl	Pts
1	Surrey	16	10	2	4	59	48	242.75
2	Warwickshire	16	7	2	7	42	44	198.00
3	Kent	16	7	4	5	48	44	195.50
4	Lancashire	16	6	4	6	33	43	172.00
5	Leicestershire	16	5	5	6	42	46	171.00
6	Sussex	16	3	6	7	43	47	154.00
7	Hampshire	16	2	5	9	35	44	131.00
8	Somerset	16	1	7	8	39	44	126.75
9	Yorkshire	16	2	8	6	35	45	124.75

Surrey (0.25), Kent (0.5), Leicestershire (1.0), Hampshire (8.0), Somerset (0.25) and Yorkshire (3.25) suffered deductions for slow over-rates.

SECOND DIVISION

		P	W	L	D	Bt	Bl	Pts
1	Essex	16	10	3	3	42	46	219.00
2	Middlesex	16	7	3	6	61	43	211.75
3	Nottinghamshire	16	8	5	3	47	48	201.75
4	Worcestershire	16	7	4	5	53	43	200.00
5	Glamorgan	16	5	5	6	41	44	169.00
6	Derbyshire	16	7	7	2	37	48	167.75
7	Northamptonshire	16	5	7	4	46	41	162.50
8	Gloucestershire	16	2	7	7	42	44	136.50
9	Durham	16	1	11	4	21	42	90.75

Essex (1.0), Middlesex (0.25), Nottinghamshire (1.25), Derbyshire (9.25), Northamptonshire (0.5), Gloucestershire (1.5) and Durham (0.25) suffered deductions for slow over-rates.

COUNTY CHAMPIONSHIP STATISTICS

Top Individual Scores

Division 1

272	J Crawley (Lancashire)
255*	N Knight (Warwickshire)

Division 2

315*	G Hick (Worcestershire)
310*	M Hussey (Northamptonshire)

Leading Run Scorers

1	1708	I Ward (Surrey)
	1520	N Knight (Warwickshire)
	1233	E Smith (Kent)
	1216	S Law (Lancashire)
	1211	A Brown (Surrey)
2	1538	M Di Venuto (Derbyshire)
	1388	C Spearman (Gloucestershire)
	1379	M Hussey (Northamptonshire)
	1289	D Robinson (Essex)
	1262	G Hick (Worcestershire)

Best Bowing Return

1	8-46	A Richardson (Warwickshire)
	8-61	Azhar Mahmood (Surrey)
2	9-93	A Bichel (Worcestershire)
	8-24	A Noffke (Middlesex)

Leading Wicket Takers

1	79	M Saggars (Kent)
	68	A Khan (Kent)
	60	D Malcolm (Leicestershire)
	54	G Chapple (Lancashire)
	53	P Martin (Lancashire)
	53	Saqlain Mushtaq (Surrey)
	53	M Bulbeck (Somerset)
2	80	K Dean (Derbyshire)
	63	A Harris (Nottinghamshire)
	60	Kabir Ali (Worcestershire)
	57	D Cork (Derbyshire)
	57	A Sherivar (Worcestershire)

Leading Catchers

1	30	D Fulton (Kent)
2	27	M Di Venuto (Derbyshire)

Leading Wicketkeeper

1	63 (61c/2s)	N Burns (Leicestershire)
2	62 (60c/2s)	C Read (Nottinghamshire)

Norwich Union National League

2002 FINAL TABLES

One-day matches - 45 overs each
(Last year's position in brackets)

Division 1

		P	W	L	NR	T	Pts	RR
1	Glamorgan Dragons (-)	16	12	3	1	0	50	+8.359
2	Worcester Royals (-)	16	11	3	2	0	48	+10.68
3	Warwickshire Bears (3)	16	9	6	1	0	38	+8.412
4	Yorkshire Phoenix (6)	16	8	7	1	0	34	+1.437
5	Kent Spitfires (1)	16	7	8	0	1	30	+5.848
6	Leicester Foxes (2)	16	7	8	1	0	30	+3.521
7	Somerset Sabres (4)	16	5	10	1	0	22	-3.526
8	Durham Dynamos (-)	16	5	11	0	0	20	-21.17
9	Notts Outlaws (5)	16	3	11	2	0	16	-11.28

Division 2

		P	W	L	NR	T	Pts	RR
1	Gloucs Gladiators (-)	16	10	4	2	0	44	+12.74
2	Surrey Lions (-)	16	10	5	1	0	42	+6.529
3	Essex Eagles (7)	16	10	6	0	0	40	+3.934
4	Derby Scorpions (9)	16	8	7	1	0	34	-0.982
5	Lancashire Lightning (6)	16	7	7	2	0	32	-6.960
6	Northants Steelbacks (-)	16	7	8	1	0	30	+7.600
7	Hampshire Hawks (4)	16	6	9	1	0	26	-2.807
8	Sussex Sharks (5)	16	4	10	2	0	20	-7.426
9	Middlesex Crusaders (8)	16	4	10	2	0	20	-12.51

Season's Statistics

Top Scoring Batsmen
Average in brackets

Div 1
B Smith (Worcestershire)   654 (65.40)
D Stevens (Leicestershire)   651 (43.40)
V Solanki (Worcestershire)   555 (39.64)
K Pietersen (Nottinghamshire)   515 (64.37)
I Sutcliffe (Leicestershire)   512 (39.38)

Div 2
S Law (Lancashire)   561 (51.00)
C Spearman (Gloucestershire)   542 (38.71)
M Ramprakash (Middlesex)   537 (44.75)
A Flower (Essex)   506 (50.60)
D Sales (Northamptonshire)   459 (32.78)

Highest Scores

Div 1: 147 K Pietersen (Nottinghamshire)
141* G Hick (Worcestershire)

Div 2: 133 S Law (Lancashire)

Top Wicket-taking Bowlers

Div 1	N Killeen (Durham)	30 (18.73)
	R Croft (Glamorgan)	28 (19.64)
	P Jones (Somerset)	22 (24.18)
	S Pollock (Warwickshire)	21 (13.00)
	Kabir Ali (Worcestershire)	21 (26.52)
	A Davies (Glamorgan)	21 (24.66)
Div 2	E Giddins (Surrey)	30 (14.50)
	A Smith (Gloucestershire)	24 (14.70)
	A Mascarenhas (Hampshire)	24 (21.08)
	A Hollioake (Surrey)	23 (13.86)
	G Welch (Derbyshire)	23 (22.47)

Best Bowling Returns
Div 1: 5-9 D Leatherdale (Worcestershire)

Div 2: 6-31 G Welch (Derbyshire)

Top Wicketkeepers

Div 1	P Nixon (Kent)	26 (20/6)
	A Pratt (Durham)	25 (19/6)
	R Turner (Somerset)	23 (17/6)
	M Wallace (Glamorgan)	23 (17/6)
	R Blakey (Yorkshire)	22 (17/5)
Div 2	R Russell (Gloucestershire)	26 (21/5)
	T Bailey (Northamptonshire)	25 (19/6)
	J Batty (Surrey)	21 (19/2)
	N Porthas (Hampshire)	20 (19/1)
	A Flower (Essex)	20 (16/4)

Top Catchers

Div 1	M Maynard (Somerset)	14
	M Powell (Warwickshire)	11
	K Dutch (Somerset)	10
Div 2	N Johnson (Hampshire)	13
	A Hollioake (Surrey)	9
	T Ambrose (Sussex)	9

Super Cup

Group Stage *50-over competition*

NORTH DIVISION
County Ground, Derby, Apr 28
Lancashire 71-2 (4.3 overs)
Derbyshire did not bat
No result

Trent Bridge, Nottingham, Apr 28
Yorkshire 225 (47.4)
Nttinghamshire 68-3 (13)
Yorkshire won by 2 runs (D/L)

Grace Road, Leicester, Apr 29
Leicestershire 316 (50)
Durham 284 (50)
Leics won by 32 runs

Trent Bridge, Nottingham, Apr 30
Derbyshire 72-7 (10)
Nottinghamshire 75-0 (8.2)
Notts won by 10 wickets (D/L)

Chester-Le-Street, May 1
Durham 166-7 (44)
Lancashire 154 (41)
Durham won by 16 runs (D/L method)

Headingley, Leeds May 1
Leicestershire 221-7 (46)
Yorkshire 214-8 (45)
Leics won by 6 runs (D/L)

Chester-Le-Street, May 2
Yorkshire 271-7 (50)
Durham 147 (44.4)
Yorkshire won by 124 runs

County Ground, Derby, May 3
Leicestershire 119-2 (32)
Derbyshire 51-2 (5.1)
No result

Old Trafford, May 3
Lancashire 297-5 (50)
Nottinghamshire 138 (26)
Lancashire won by 76 runs

County Ground, Derby, May 4
Yorkshire 288-6 (50)
Derbyshire 157 (37.3)
Yorkshire won by 131 runs

Trent Bridge, May 4
Nottinghamshire 224-6 (50)
Durham 219 (49.4)
Notts won by 5 runs

Old Tafford, May 5
Leicestershire 175-9 (50)
Lancashire 158 (47.2)
Leics won by 17 runs

Chester-Le-Street, May 6
Derbyshire 172 (48.2)
Durham 174-6 (46.5)
Durham won by 4 wickets

Grace Road, Leicester, May 6
Nottinghamshire 95 (21.4)
Leicestershire 98-2 (18.1)
Leics won by 8 wickets

Headingley, Leeds, May 6
Yorkshire 81 (27.2)
Lancashire 82-2 (10.5)
Lancashire won by 8 wickets

	W	L	NR	Pts	RR
Leics	4	0	1	9	+0.461
Yorks	3	2	0	6	+0.450
Lancs	2	2	1	5	+1.346
Durham	2	3	0	4	-0.536
Notts	2	3	0	4	-0.709
Derby	0	3	2	2	-1.461

MIDLANDS/WALES/WEST DIV

Northampton, Apr 28
Glamorgan 122 (30.5)
Northamptonshire 124-2 (26.1)
Northants won by 8 wickets

Edgbaston, Apr 28
Warwickshire 263-6 (41)
Somerset 78-5 (19)
Warwicks won by 94 runs (D/L)

New Road, Worcester, Apr 29
Worcestershire 70 (22)
Gloucestershire 71-4 (18.2)
Gloucs won by 6 wickets

County Ground, Bristol, May 1
Gloucestershire 240-6 (43)
Warwickshire 91 (28.4)
Gloucs won by 149 runs

Northampton, May 1
Northamptonshire 232-7 (50)
Worcestershire 233-5 (50)
Worcs won by 5 wickets

Sophia Gardens, Cardiff, May 3
Glamorgan 171-8 (50)
Gloucestershire 173-2 (29.1)
Gloucs won by 8 wickets

Taunton, May 3
Northamptonshire 299-6 (50)
Somerset 154 (34.1)
Northants won by 145 runs

Edgbaston, May 3
Warwickshire 130 (44.4)
Worcestershire 131-7 (48.3)
Worcs won by 3 wickets

County Ground, Bristol, May 5
Gloucester 270-7 (50)
Somerset 231 (45.5)
Gloucs won by 39 runs

Edgbaston, Birmingham, May 5
Narthamptonshire 226 (48.5)
Warwickshire 228-4 (49.1)
Warwicks won by 6 wickets

New Road, Worcester, May 5
Glamorgan 191-8 (50)
Worcestershire 192-5 (39.4)
Worcs won by 5 wickets

Sophia Gardens, Cardiff, May 6
Warwickshire 261-8 (50)
Glamorgan 203 (47)
Warwicks won by 58 runs

Northampton, May 6
Northamptonshire 212-5 (44)
Gloucestershire 94 (24)
Northants won by 118 runs

Taunton, May 6
Somerset 126 (32)
Worcestershire 122-3 (19)
Worcs won by 7 wickets (D/L)

	W	L	NR	Pts	RR
Gloucs	4	1	0	8	+1.326
Worcs	4	1	0	8	-0.059
Northants	3	2	0	6	+1.512
Warwicks	3	2	0	6	+0.006
Glamorgan	0	4	1	1	-1.737
Somerset	0	4	1	1	-2.393

SOUTH DIVISION

Chelmsford, Apr 28
Essex 206-9 (50)
Sussex 120-6 (31)
Essex won by 20 runs (D/L)

Lord's, Apr 28
Surrey 123 (38)
Middlesex 124-2 (30.2)
Middlesex won by 8 wickets

Rose Bowl, Apr 29
Kent 183-8 (50)
Hampshire 115 (37.2)
Kent won by 68 runs

Rose Bowl, Southampton May 4
Surrey 194 (50)
Hampshire 171-9 (50)
Surrey won by 23 runs

Canterbury, May 1
Sussex 282-3 (50)
Kent 156 (41)
Sussex won by 126 runs

The Oval, May 1
Hampshire 243 (50)
Surrey 242-7 (47)
Hampshire won by 1 run

Chelmsford, May 2
Surrey 223 (49.1)
Essex 224-6 (45.2)
Essex won by 4 wickets

Canterbury, May 2
Middlesex 133-6 (19)
Kent 139-3 (18.4)
Kent won by 7 wickets

Hove, May 3
Hampshire 203-9 (50)
Sussex 204-4 (49)
Sussex won by 6 wickets

The Oval, May 4
Surrey 257-9 (50)
Kent 213 (45.3)
Surrey won by 44 runs

Chelmsford, May 5
Hampshire 174 (46.1)
Essex 176-4 (39.4)
Essex won by 6 wickets

Lord's, May 5
Sussex 252-6 (50)
Middlesex 224 (48.3)
Sussex won by 28 runs

The Oval, May 6
Hampshire 237-5 (50)
Surrey 234-9 (50)
Hampshire won by 3 runs

Canterbury, May 6
Kent 231-9 (50)
Essex 234-8 (49.2)
Essex won by 2 wickets

Hove, May 6
Sussex 220 (44.4)
Surrey 220-9 (46)
Sussex won by losing fewer wickets

	W	L	NR	Pts	RR
Essex	4	0	1	9	+0.473
Sussex	4	1	0	8	+0.616
Hampshire	2	3	0	4	-0.025
Kent	2	3	0	4	-0.478
Middlesex	1	3	1	3	+0.369
Surrey	1	4	0	2	-0.290

Quarter-finals

Bristol, May 21
Gloucestershire 203-8 (50)
Worcestershire 204-2 (41.4)
Worcestershire won by 8 wickets

Chelmsford, May 22
Yorkshire 237-9 (50)
Essex 239-3 (45)
Essex won by 7 wickets

Grace Road, May 22
Leicestershire 163-8 (50)
Lancashire 164-6 (47.4)
Lancashire won by 4 wickets

Hove, May 22
Sussex 196-7 (50)
Warwickshire 197-6 (48.4)
Warwickshire won by 4 wickets

Semi-finals

Chelmsford, June 6
Essex 262-9 (50)
(Irani 57, Ali 4-34)
Worcestershire 124 (33.4)
(Irani 3-30)
Essex won by 138 runs

Old Trafford, June 7
Lancashire 211-9 (50)
(Chilton 101, Pollock 4-27)
Warwickshire 213-9 (50)
(Bell 46)
Warwickshire won by 1 wicket

Super Cup Final

Lord's, June 22

ESSEX

				balls	4/6
N Hussain	c Piper	b Pollock	0	2	0/0
D Robinson	c Brown	b Carter	18	36	3/0
G Napier	run out		17	18	2/1
J Stephenson		b Carter	0	1	0/0
A Flower†	c Piper	b Smith	30	44	3/0
R Irani*	c Smith	b Brown	8	33	0/0
A Habib	c Knight	b Giles	19	42	0/0
A Grayson	not out		38	66	0/0
J Dakin	c Powell	b Brown	12	32	0/0
A Cowan	not out		27	28	1/0
Extras (LB4, W4, NB4)			12		
Total (8 wickets, 50 overs)			181		

Fall of wickets: 1-0, 2-33, 3-33, 4-40, 5-61, 6-86, 7-109, 8-134

Bowling: Pollock 10-1-32-1 (1nb), **Carter** 10-1-45-2 (1nb, 1w), **Brown** 10-0-32-2 (1w), **Giles** 10-1-28-1 (1w), **Smith** 10-0-40-1 (1w)

Toss: Warwickshire
Umpires: **J H Hampshire and B Dudleston**
TV Umpire: **B Leadbeater**

WARWICKSHIRE

				balls	4/6
M Powell*	c Flower	b Cowan	11	18	2/0
N Knight	c Flower	b Irani	9	20	0/0
I Bell	not out		65	89	7/0
J Troughton	c Flower	b Napier	37	33	8/0
S Pollock	c Dakin	b Irani	34	31	5/0
T Penney	lbw	b Stephenson	0	3	0/0
D Brown	not out		12	24	0/0
Extras (LB6, W8)			14		
Total (5 wickets, 36.2 overs)			182		

Did Not Bat: N Smith, A Giles, K Piper†, N Carter

Fall of Wickets: 1-19, 2-21, 3-105, 4-158, 5-159

Bowling: Irani 10-2-40-2; **Cowan** 8-0-37-1; **Clarke** 2-0-20-0 (2w); **Dakin** 2-0-22-0 (4w); **Grayson** 4-0-11-0; **Napier** 5.2-0-31-1 (1w); **Stephenson** 5-0-15-1 (1w)

Match Award: **Ian Bell**
WARWICKSHIRE WON BY 5 WICKETS

C & G Trophy

50 overs; Results from Fourth round

Fourth Round

Chelmsford, June 19
Lancashire 166 (46.5)
Essex 167-1 (28.3)
Essex won by 9 wickets

Bristol, June 19
Durham 179 (47.3)
Gloucestershire 180-2 (26)
Gloucs won by 8 wickets

Canterbury, June 19
Kent 328-9 (47.3)
Warwickshire 200 (37.1)
Kent won by 128 runs

Grace Road, Leicester, June 19
Leicestershire 233 (49.1)
Sussex 234-4 (47.3)
Sussex won by 6 wickets

Northampton
Yorkshire 303-3 (50)
Northamptonshire 254 (48.2)
Yorkshire won by 49 runs

Trent Bridge
Nottinghamshire 262-5 (50)
Worcestershire 265-2 (44)
Worcs won by 8 wickets

Taunton
Hampshire 262-5 (50)
Somerset 265-4 (45.1)
Somerset won by 6 wickets

The Oval
Surrey 438-5 (50)
Glamorgan 429 (49.5)
Surrey won by 9 runs

Quarter-finals

Chelmsford, July 16
Essex 283-9 (50)
Yorkshire 283-5 (50)
Yorkshire won by losing fewer wickets

Canterbury, July 16
Gloucestershire 232-8 (50)
Kent 238-5 (44.2)
Kent won by 5 wickets

Taunton, July 17
Worcestershire 271 (49)
Somerset 273-6 (47.3)
Somerset won by 4 wickets

Hove, July 17
Surrey 337-3 (50)
Sussex 323-8 (50)
Surrey won by 14 runs

Semi-finals

Headingley, July 31
Surrey 173-8 (48)
Yorkshire 167-0 (24.1)
Yorkshire won by 10 wickets (D/L)

Taunton, Aug 1
Somerset 344-5 (50)
Kent 339 (49.1)
Somerset won by 5 runs

C & G Trophy Final
July 17

SOMERSET

P Bowler	c Blakey	b Hoggard	67	89	6/0
M Trescothick	c Vaughan	b Hoggard	27	25	4/1
J Cox*	lbw	b McGrath	34	49	5/0
M Burns	lbw	b Hoggard	21	41	2/0
I Blackwell		b Sidebottom	12	16	1/0
K Parsons	c Sidebottom	b Hoggard	41	46	3/0
R Turner†	c White	b Sidebottom	20	26	0/0
R Johnson		b Hoggard	2	3	0/0
K Dutch	not out		13	7	2/0
A Caddick	not out		0	1	0/0
Extras	(B1, LB6, W6, NB6)		19		
Total	(8 wickets, 50 overs)		256		

Did Not Bat: P Jones.
Fall of Wickets: 1-41, 2-122, 3-159, 4-171, 5-191, 6-230, 7-233, 8-250
Bowling: Silverwood 8-1-30-0 (1w); Hoggard 10-0-65-5 (3nb); Sidebottom 9-0-49-2 (3w); McGrath 9-0-37-1; Dawson 10-0-48-0 (1w); Vaughan 4-0-20-0 (1w)
Toss: Somerset
Umpires: **J Holder** and **G Sharp**
TV Umpire: **K Palmer**

YORKSHIRE

C White	c Turner	b Johnson	12	14	1/0
M Wood		b Johnson	19	38	2/0
C Silverwood		b Johnson	0	3	0/0
M Elliott	not out		128	125	16/0
M Vaughan	lbw	b Jones	31	56	0/0
A McGrath	not out		46	53	4/0
Extras	(LB7, W15, NB2)		24		
Total	(4 wickets, 48 overs)		260		

Did Not Bat: G Fellows, R Blakey*†, R Dawson, R Sidebottom, M Hoggard.
Fall of Wickets: 1-19, 2-19, 3-64, 4-157
Bowling: Caddick 9-0-53-0 (1nb, 4w); Johnson 10-2-51-3 (2w); **Parsons** 6-0-31-0 (1w); **Jones** 9-0-45-1 (1w); **Dutch** 8-0-43-0 (2w); **Blackwell** 6-0-30-0 (1w)

Man of the Match: **Matthew Elliott**
YORKSHIRE WON BY SIX WICKETS

Women's Cricket

England in India

FIRST ONE-DAY INTERNATIONAL
Chennai, Jan 6
England 106 (David 4-14)
India 110-2 (Raj 36*)
India won by 8 wickets

SECOND ONE-DAY INTERNATIONAL
Hyderabad, Jan 8
England 71-7 (Goswami 3-8)
India 72-1 (Chopra 37*)
India won by 9 wickets

THIRD ONE-DAY INTERNATIONAL
Hyderabad, Jan 9
India 191-5 (Maben 53*)
England 78 (Raj 3-4)
India won by 113 runs

FOURTH ONE-DAY INTERNATIONAL
Mumbai, Jan 21
England 142 (Thompson 55, David 4-13)
India 143-5 (Chopra 49*)
India won by 5 wickets

FIFTH ONE-DAY INTERNATIONAL
Poona, Jan 24
England 180-6 (Thompson 67, Atkins 51)
India 182-4 (Amrita 78*, Jain 48)
India won by 6 wickets

Tri-Series

One-day competition between England, New Zealand and India

FIRST MATCH (England v India)
St Saviour, Jersey, July 10
India 59 (Harper 4-11)
England 60-4 (Edwards 31*)
England won by 6 wickets

SECOND MATCH (New Zealand v India)
St Saviour, Jersey, July 11
New Zealand 168 (Drumm 56, Kulkarni 4-37)
India 26 (Pullar 5-10)
New Zealand won by 142 runs

THIRD MATCH (England v New Zealand)
St Saviour, Jersey, July 12
Match Abandoned

FOURTH MATCH (England v New Zealand)
Racecourse, Durham, July 16
England 111
New Zealand 113-3 (Drumm 63*)
New Zealand won by 7 wickets

FIFTH MATCH (India v New Zealand)
Racecourse, Durham, July 17
India 95 (Pullar 3-10)
New Zealand 96-5 (David 3-17)
New Zealand won by 7 wickets

SIXTH MATCH (England v India)
Riverside, Chester-le-Street, July 19
Match Abandoned

TRI-SERIES FINAL (England v New Zealand)
New Zealand 161 (Pulford 55)
England 98 (Mason 3-20)
New Zealand won by 63 runs

India in Ireland

FIRST ONE-DAY INTERNATIONAL
Rush Cricket Ground, Dublin, July 24
Ireland 101 (Grealey 32, Paranjpe 4-8)
India 104-2 (Sharma 52)
India won by 8 wickets

SECOND ONE-DAY INTERNATIONAL
Merrion Cricket Ground, Dublin, July 26
India 206-7 (Kirkire 58, Naik 50)
Ireland 62 (Goyal 3-3)
India won by 144 runs

THIRD ONE-DAY INTERNATIONAL
Fox Lodge Cricket Club, Strabane, July 28
Match abandoned

India in England

FIRST TEST
Denis Compton Oval, Shenley, August 8-11
Match Abandoned

SECOND TEST
County Ground, Taunton, August 14-17
England 329 (Newton 98, Godliman 65, David 4-71)
India 467 (Raj 214, Kala 62, Goswami 62)
England 198-6 dec (Edwards 56)
Match Drawn
Mithali Raj's score of 214 was the highest individual score recorded in a women's Test.

ONE-DAY INTERNATIONAL
Beaconsfield, August 11
India 118 (Kala 38, Connor 3-25, Guha 3-28)
England 119-4 (Edwads 54, Leng 46)
England won by 6 wickets

Curling

They came to Braehead in March trailing clouds of glory after two wonderful weeks in Ogden when all the dreams had been realised. Rhona Martin had skipped British team, a quartet of Scots, to the Olympic title, but that cut no ice (to use an appropriate metaphor) with the Scottish selectors who, three weeks later, insisted that the team sent to the world championships in North Dakota in April carried the mantle of Scottish champions.

On the Braehead rink, incongruously sited at the backend of a Clydeside shopping complex, in front of the largest crowd (shall we say 1000?) and the biggest press corps (shall we say four?) for a Scottish championships, Martin's team went through the paces. Unfortunately, the paces were not enough.

Jackie Lockhart, with her team of near novices, displayed far greater hunger than Martin's team who were undergoing their 71st match of the winter season. They made no apologies, though, when the three-match competition went against them. "We were rubbish...the best team won," said Martin, brutally.

Lockhart had not won the Olympic title, but it sounded like it. "If anyone was going to do it, it was me. You can't keep an old dog down," said the euphoric 36-year-old from Aberdeen. Her team took their lead from the skip, but behind the nods and the smiles, you wondered if Sheila Swan, Katriona Fairweather, Ann Laird, and Edith Louden, the reserve, might find it all too much in Bismarck the following month.

The North Dakotans must have been flummoxed when the Scottish women's team arrived for the world championships. A fair few locals would have been at the Games and seen one Scottish crew, albeit in British kit, claim the ultimate prize in the sport. Back in Bismarck, seven weeks later, they saw another turn up to challenge for the world title.

Maybe that was their secret, or maybe they didn't need one. It's impossible to say whether the absence of Lockhart's team from the Olympic Games was an advantage or not, for there is no absolute in curling. You don't have to deliver the perfect stone, you can't even measure it; you only have to deliver a better one than your opponent.

Scotland won the first four games, lost to Sweden, and won the next three games. They were destined to be top of the round robin ranking even before the ninth and final match. The knock-out matches were nail-bitingly close, with both the semi-final against Canada and the final against Sweden settled on the last end. It had taken 24 years, and three defeats in previous finals, before the Scottish women had come home with a gold medal in the world championships. Scotland could celebrate having two best women's teams in the world, and when the men won a bronze, too, Caledonian joy left speech redundant.

World Championships
Brunswick, North Dakota, Apr 6-14

Men
ROUND ROBIN
1st Draw: Norway 5 Denmark 9; Switzerland 6 Scotland 7; Finland 6 Sweden 4; USA 8 Japan 5; Austria 7 Canada 9
2nd Draw: Austria 1 Switzerland 13; Sweden 5 Canada 4; Norway 6 USA 7; Finland 4 Denmark 5; Scotland 8 Japan 1
3rd Draw: Japan 2 Canada 9; Denmark 12 USA 7; Scotland 8 Austria 3; Sweden 5 Norway 7; Finland 5 Switzerland 9
4th Draw: Denmark 9 Scotland 10; Finland 4 Norway 5; Switzerland 4 Canada 11; Japan 10 Austria 6; USA 8 Sweden 3
5th Draw: Finland 8 Austria 2; Scotland 6 Sweden 5; Denmark 5 Japan 8; Switzerland 7 USA 8; Canada 12 Norway 4
6th Draw: Canada 7 USA 8; Norway 8 Japan 4; Sweden 4 Switzerland 8; Scotland 4 Finland 8; Denmark 10 Austria 3
7th Draw: Switzerland 4 Norway 8; Canada 8 Denmark 5; USA 2 Scotland 7; Austria 1 Sweden 11; Japan 3 Finland 7
8th Draw: Sweden 5 Japan 4; USA 10 Austria 1; Canada 7 Finland 6; Denmark 4 Switzerland 9; Norway 8 Scotland 5
9th Draw: USA 1 Finland 7; Japan 3 Switzerland 11; Austria 3 Norway 11; Canada 5 Scotland 6; Sweden 4 Denmark 8

ROUND ROBIN RANKING
		W	L
1	Scotland	7	2
2	USA	6	3
3	Canada	6	3
4	Norway	6	3
5	Switzerland	5	4
6	Denmark	5	4
7	Finland	3	6
8	Sweden	3	6
9	Japan	2	7
10	Austria	0	9

SEMI-FINALS
Scotland 0-2-0-0-0-1-0-0-0-1-0 **4**
Norway 0-0-0-1-0-0-2-0-1-0-1 **5**

USA 0-2-0-2-0-1-0-1-0-0 **6**
Canada 1-0-1-0-2-0-2-0-2-2 **10**

BRONZE MEDAL GAME
USA 0-1-0-1-1-0-1-0-1-0 **5**
Scotland 1-0-1-0-0-2-0-1-0-1 **6**
Rocque/Pfeifer/Ferbey/Nedohin

FINAL
Canada 1-0-2-0-2-1-0-2-1-1 **10**
Maskel/Goodland/Fraboni/Pustovar
Norway 0-2-0-1-0-0-2-0-0-0 **5**
Rocque/Pfeifer/Ferbey/Nedohin

Women
ROUND ROBIN
1st Draw: Switzerland 4 Canada 7; USA 5 Denmark 9; Sweden 7 Korea 3; Norway 6 Germany 4; Scotland 12 Russia 5
2nd Draw: Scotland 9 USA 2; Korea 5 Russia 13; Switzerland 8 Norway 6; Sweden 5 Canada 6; Denmark 8 Germany 7
3rd Draw: Germany 5 Russia 9; Canada 4 Norway 9; Denmark 2 Scotland 8; Korea 5 Switzerland 12; Sweden 2 USA 11
4th Draw: Canada 6 Denmark 9; Sweden 9 Switzerland 5; USA 6 Russia 10; Germany 5 Scotland 6; Norway 11 Korea 2
5th Draw: Sweden 10 Scotland 8; Denmark 7 Korea 6; Canada 3 Germany 9; USA 2 Norway 10; Russia 9 Switzerland 7
6th Draw: Russia 2 Norway 6; Switzerland 12 Germany 3; Korea 7 USA 9; Denmark 7 Sweden 8; Canada 4 Scotland 6
7th Draw: USA 7 Switzerland 6; Russia 7 Canada 8; Norway 9 Denmark 5; Scotland 5 Korea 4; Germany 7 Sweden 4
8th Draw: Korea 4 Germany 8; Norway 6 Scotland 7; Russia 7 Sweden 8; Canada 6 USA 4; Switzerland 7 Denmark 5
9th Draw: Norway 3 Sweden 7; Germany 2 USA 8; Scotland 5 Switzerland 9; Russia 5 Denmark 8; Korea 6 Canada 8

ROUND ROBIN RANKING
		W	L
1	Scotland	7	2
2	Sweden	6	3
3	Norway	6	3
4	Canada	5	4
4	Switzerland	5	4
4	Denmark	5	4
7	Russia	4	5
8	USA	4	5
9	Germany	3	6
10	Korea	0	9

Tiebreakers
Canada placed 1st in the shoot-out draw and had a bye.
Denmark 5 Switzerland 10; Canada 6 Switzerland 5

SEMI-FINALS
Sweden 0-1-0-1-0-1-0-2-0-2 **7**
Norway 0-0-1-0-2-0-1-0-2-0 **6**

Scotland 0-1-0-0-1-0-1-0-1-0-1 **5**
Canada 0-0-1-0-0-1-0-1-0-1-0 **4**

BRONZE MEDAL GAME
Norway 0-1-0-0-1-1-1-1-2-1 **8**
Canada 1-0-3-2-0-0-0-0-0 **6**

FINAL
Sweden 0-0-0-1-0-0-3-0-1-0 **5**
Lindholm/Jornlind/Sigfridsson/Engholm
Scotland 0-0-0-0-0-3-0-2-0-1 **6**
Laird/Fairweather/Swan/Lockhart

European Championships

Vierumäki, Finland, Dec 8-16, 2001

Men

Round Robin Ranking

		W	L
1	Sweden	7	2
2	Switzerland	7	2
3	Norway	6	3
4	Finland	6	3
5	Scotland	5	4
6	Denmark	4	5
7	France	4	5
8	Germany	3	6
9	Czech Rep	2	7
10	Italy	1	8

Semi-finals

Sweden 1-0-1-0-1-0-1-1-2 **7**
Finland 0-1-0-2-0-0-1-0-0-0 **4**

Norway 0-3-0-0-2-1-1-0-0-0-1 **8**
Switzerland 0-0-0-2-0-0-0-2-1-2-0 **7**

Bronze Medal Game

Finland 2-0-1-0-1-0-0-1-1-0 **6**
Norway 0-1-0-1-0-0-2-0-0-0 **4**

Final

Sweden 0-0-0-1-0-0-2-1-0-1 **5**
Switzerland 0-1-0-0-0-1-0-0-2-0 **4**

Women

Round Robin Ranking

		W	L
1	Sweden	7	0
2	Germany	6	1
3	Denmark	5	2
4	Switzerland	4	3
5	Norway	3	4
6	Scotland	2	5
7	Russia	1	6
8	Finland	0	7

Semi-finals

Sweden 1-0-1-0-3-0-0-2-0-1 **8**
Switzerland 0-2-0-3-0-0-1-0-1-0 **7**

Denmark 0-1-0-1-1-0-1-0-1-1 **6**
Germany 0-0-2-0-0-1-0-1-0-0 **4**

Bronze Medal Game

Switzerland 2-0-0-2-0-0-2-1-0-0-1 **8**
Germany 0-0-2-0-1-3-0-0-0-1-0 **7**

Final

Sweden 0-0-0-2-0-3-1-0-0-1 **7**
Denmark 0-0-1-0-1-0-0-1-0-0 **3**

Cycling

For once, we will relegate the Tour de France to the bottom of the page, it's getting predictable anyway. While Lance Armstrong wins his titles by seven minutes (give or take) each year, Chris Hoy takes championship titles by one thousandth of a second. Now that is close; even light only travels 187 miles in that time.

Hoy had a three-timer, too. Armstrong couldn't match that. The first title for the Scot came in Manchester *(see Commonwealth Games section),* the next two in at the world championships in Copenhagen two months later. Having defeated the reigning Olympic champion Jason Queally at the Commonwealth Games, Hoy faced the reigning world champion Arnaud Tournant in the Danish capital.

As title holders do, Tournant went last, chasing the mark set earlier by Hoy of one minute and 1.893 seconds. The Frenchman was almost a third of a second down at the halfway point, but had turned the deficit into an advantage of 0.171 seconds coming into the final 250 metres. At this point, had Hoy been carrying a towel, the instinct would have been to throw it on track, for the Frenchman looked to have the title well within his grasp, but perhaps he raised his head fractionally, or a tiny puff of wind entered the stadium or Tournant cycled over a matchstick. That's all it would have needed. No title has ever been won by a narrower margin.

Hoy's hattrick came in the team sprint. Jason Queally was absent injured, but the reserve, Jamie Staff, had already placed fifth in the kilometre and hardly diminished the undoubted quality of the British trio. In a face-off against the Australia Commonwealth Games champions, the Britons were clear winners.

"At the start of the year I always write down my objectives and I wanted to a medal at the Commonwealth Games and the world championships in the team sprint and a top five in the kilometre...and I've won three World Cup events, gold in the kilometre at the Commonwealth Games and two world titles here. That's way beyond my wildest dreams," said a jubilant Hoy.

The third day of the championships produced a third gold for Briton when Chris Newton won the points race on the day before his 29th birthday. Newton's philosophy was just to stay with the race favourite Bruno Risi and it worked so well that Newton won the race. Risi got nothing. The three titles made it the best-ever performance by British riders in a world championships.

There are only two more hurdles for Lance Armstrong; a fifth Tour de France win to put himself alongside Jacques Anquetil, Bernard Hinault, Eddy Merckx and Miguel Indurain, and a sixth to put himself above them. Even if he stops now, which seems exceedingly unlikely, the Texan will still be unique, as the only rider ever to win four Tours without winning a fifth.

This time around, Armstrong took the yellow jersey in earnest (he'd already held it briefly for stage 1) after the 11th stage, which was two days earlier than in 2001. It was the first day in the mountains and his teammate Roberto Heras set such a scorching pace up the climbs that not only did he dispose of most of the opposition, but at one point was in danger of dropping Armstrong himself, until he was asked by the American to slow down. Heras would get his reward in Spain two months later, when he won the Vuelta, but his job here was to secure the stage for the American, which he duly did. Only Spain's Joceba Beloki hung onto Armstrong's coat tails, but they were long tails, the Spaniard finishing over a minute down. You could say the Tour ended there and then, for Armstrong now has the same air of invincibility that was associated with Miguel Induráin a decade ago.

Richard Virenque won a stage, some rehabilitation for the Frenchman whose liaison with Willy Voet proved so costly to both. Thor Hushovd won a stage, too, becoming the first Norwegian since 1987 to do so. That was on a day when the story should have been the attacks on the race leader, but nobody did attack. The following day Armstrong recorded his eighth time trial victory in four years (from 11 time trials). If he so desired, he could almost have freewheeled from Melun to Paris on the next and final day.

Armstrong's fourth victory has yet to endear him to the French who can't believe he is not using questionable methods and it doesn't help that the American will not distance himself from advisers like Michele Ferrari, under examination by the Italian courts for administering proscribed drugs to athletes.

We eventually got our drama, and of course it was drug-related. It happened on the final day, but not in Paris, at Chamonix where the French customs asked to look in the boot of Madame Rumsiene's car at the start of the Mont Blanc tunnel and discovered a variety of drugs. As Madame Rumsiene is the wife of Raimondas Rumsas, the Lithuanian who had just finished third in the Tour, the police were very interested in the contents of her temperature-controlled boot.

It was history almost repeating itself; exchange one border for another and Rumsiene for Willy Voet and 2002 for 1998.

Raimondas claimed that the drugs were for his mother-in-law, who was suffering from cancer. The drugs included testosterone, growth hormone and EPO, and perhaps as many as 35 other products. Let us just say, it is unusual for a daughter to set about treating her mother's cancer in this fashion.

> **"I am not here to make friends of the crowd who have spent the day drinking while awaiting the race. In three or four years I will be on the beach with my children drinking a cold beer and far from them"**
>
> Lance Armstrong, responding to the boos from the crowd on the Ventoux climb.

Road Racing

Tour de France

Date	Stage	Start-Finish (Distance)	Stage Winner	Overall Leader
July 6	Prologue	Luxembourg (7km)*	**Lance Armstrong USA (US Postal)**	Armstrong
July 7	1	Luxembourg - Luxembourg (192.5km)	**Rubens Bertogliati GER (Telekom)**	Bertogliati
July 8	2	Luxembourg - Saarbrucken (181km)	**Oscar Freire ESP (Mapei)**	Bertogliati
July 9	3	Metz - Reims (174.5 km)	**Robbie McEwen AUS (Lotto-Adecco)**	Zabel
July 10	4	Epernay - Chateau-Thierry (67.5 km)**	**ONCE-Eroski**	Igor Gonzalez
July 11	5	Soissons - Rouen (195km)	**Jaan Kirsipuu EST (Ag2R)**	Igor Gonzalez
July 12	6	Fourges-les-Eaux - Alencon (199.5 km)	**Erik Zabel GER (Telekom)**	Igor Gonzalez
July 13	7	Bagnoles de l'Orne - Avranches (176km)	**Bradley McGee AUS (FDJeux.com)**	Igor Gonzalez
July 14	8	St Martin de Landelles - Plouay (217.5km)	**Karsten Kroon NED (Rabobak)**	Igor Gonzalez
July 15	9	Lanester - Plouay (52km)*	**Santiago Botero COL (Kelme)**	Igor Gonzalez
July 17	10	Bazas - Pau (147km)	**Patrice Halgand FRA (US Postal)**	Igor Gonzalez
July 18	11	Pau - La Mongie (158km)	**Lance Armstrong USA (US Postal)**	Armstrong
July 19	12	Lannenezan - Plateau de Beille (199.5km)	**Lance Armstrong USA (US Postal)**	Armstrong
July 20	13	Lavelanet - Beziers (171km)	**David Millar GBR (Cofidis)**	Armstrong
July 21	14	Lodeve - Mont Ventoux (221km)	**Richard Virenque FRA (Farm Frites)**	Armstrong
July 23	15	Vaison-la-Romaine - Les deux Alpes (226.5km)	**Santiago Botero COL (Kelme)**	Armstrong
July 24	16	Les deux Alpes - La Plagne (179.5)	**Michael Boogerd NED (Rabobank)**	Armstrong
July 25	17	Aime - Cluses (142km)	**Dario Frigo ITA (Tacconi)**	Armstrong
July 26	18	Cluses - Bourg-en-Bresse (176.5km)	**Thor Hushovd NOR (US Postal)**	Armstrong
July 27	19	Regnie - Durette (50km)*	**Lance Armstrong USA (Telekom)**	Armstrong
July 28	20	Melun - Paris (140km)	**Robbie McEwen AUS (Lampre-Daikin)**	Armstrong

*Time Trial   ** Team Time Trial   Total Finishers 153*

Final Classification

General Classification

1	Lance Armstrong USA (US Postal)	82:05:12
2	Joseba Beloki ESP (ONCE-Eroski)	+7:17
3	Raimondas Rumsas LTU (Lampre Daikin)	+8:17
4	Santiago Botero COL (Kelme-Costa Blanca)	+13:10
5	Igor Gonzalez de Galeano ESP (ONCE)	+13:54
6	José Azevedo POR (ONCE-Eroski)	+15:44
7	Francisco Mancebo ESP (iBanesto.com)	+16:05
8	Levi Leipheimer USA (Rabobank)	+17:11
9	Roberto Heras Hernandez ESP (US Postal)	+17:12
10	Carlos Sastre ESP (CSC-Tiscali)	+19:05
11	Ivan Basso ITA (Fassa Bortolo)	+19:18
12	Michael Boogerd NED (Rabobank)	+20:33
13	David Moncoutie FRA (Cofidis)	+21:08
14	Massimiliano Lelli ITA (Cofidis)	+27:51
15	Tyler Hamilton USA (CSC-Tiscali)	+28:36
16	Richard Virenque FRA (Farm Frites)	+28:42
17	Stephane Goubert FRA (Jeann Delatour)	+29:51
18	Unai Osa ESP (iBanesto.com)	+30:17
19	Nicolas Vogondy FRA (FDJeux.com)	+32:44
20	Nicki Sørensen DEN (CSC-Tiscali)	+32:56
68	David Millar GBR (Cofidis)	+1:59:51

Points Standings (Green Jersey)

1	Robbie McEwen AUS (Lotto-Adecco)	280pts
2	Erik Zabel GER (Telekom)	261
3	Stuart O'Grady AUS (Crèdit-Agricole)	208

Mountains (Polka Dot Jersey)

1	Laurent Jalabert FRA (CSC-Tiscali)	262pts
2	Santiago Botero COL (Kelme-Costa B)	178
3	Lance Armstrong USA (US Postal)	159

Young Rider (Under-25)

1	Ivan Basso ITA (Fasso Bortolo)	82:24:30
2	Nicolas Vogondy FRA (FDJeux.com)	+13:26
3	Christophe Brandt BEL (Lotto-Adecco)	+48:32

Teams

1	ONCE-Eroski	246:36:14
2	CSC-Tiscali	+22:49
3	iBanesto.com	+30:17

Giro d'Italia

Groningen-Milan, May 11-June 2

STAGE WINNERS	*Overall*
P J-C Dominguez ESP (Phonak)	Dominguez
(Groningen 6.5km)*	
1 Mario Cipollini ITA (Acqua e Sapone)	Cipollini
(Groningen - Munster 215km)	
2 Stefano Garzelli ITA (Mapei)	Garzelli
(Cologne - Ans/Liege 209km)	
3 Mario Cipollini ITA (Acqua e Sapone)	Garzelli
(Veerviers - Alzette 206km)	
4 Robbie McEwen AUS (Lotto-Adecco)	Garzelli
(Alzette - Strasbourg 232km)	
5 Stefano Garzelli ITA (Mapei)	Garzelli
(Fossano - Limone Piemonte 150km)	
6 Giovanni Lombardi ITA (Acqua e Sapone)	Heppner
(Cuneo - Varazze 190km)	
7 Rik Verbrugghe BEL (Lotto-Adecco)	Heppner
(Circuito della Versilia 159km)	
8 Aitor Gonzalez ESP (Kelme)	Heppner
(Capannori - Orvieto 237km)	
9 Mario Cipollini (Acqua e Sapone)	Heppner
(Tivoli - Caserta 201km)	
10 Robbie McEwen AUS (Lotto-Adecco)	Heppner
(Maddaloni - Benevento 118km)	
11 Gilberto Simoni ITA (Saeco-Longoni)	Heppner
(Benevento - Campitello Matese 140km)	
12 Denis Lunghi ITA (Colpack)	Heppner
(Campobasso - Chieti 200km)	
13 Julio Perez Cuapio MEX (Ceramiche)	Heppner
(Chieti - San Giacomo 190km)	
14 Tyler Hamilton USA (CSC-Tiscali)	Heppner
(Numana 30.3km)*	
15 Mario Cipollini ITA (Acqua e Sapone)	Heppner
(Terme Euganee - Conegliano 156km)	
16 Julio Perez Cuapio MEX (Ceramiche)	Evans
(Conegliano - Corvara 163km)	
17 Pavel Tonkov RUS (Lampre-Daikin)	Savoldelli
(Corvara - Folgaria 222km)	
18 Mario Cipollini ITA (Acqua e Sapone)	Savoldelli
(Rovereto - Brescia 143km)	
19 Aitor Gonzalez ESP (Kelme)	Savoldelli
(Cambiago - Monticello Brinaza 44.3km)*	
20 Mario Cipollini ITA (Acqua e Sapone)	Savoldelli
(Cantù - Milan 181km)	

FINAL CLASSIFICATION

1	Paolo Savoldelli ITA (Index Alexia)	89:22:42
2	Tyler Hamilton USA (CSC-Tiscali)	+1:41
3	Pietro Caucchioli ITA (Alessio)	+2:12
4	Juan Manuel Garate ESP (Lampre-Daikin)	+3:14
5	Pavel Tonkov RUS (Lampre-Daikin)	+5:34
6	Aitor Gonzalez Jimenez ESP (Kelme-Costa)	+6:54
7	Georg Totschnig AUT (Gerolsteiner)	+7:02
8	Fernando Escartin ESP (Team Coast)	+7:07
9	Rik Verbrugghe BEL (Lotto-Adecco)	+9:36
10	Dario Frigo ITA (Tacconi Sport-Emmegi)	+11:50
68	Max Sciandri GBR (Lampre-Daikin)	+1:51:12

Mountains: Julio Perez Cuapio MEX (Ceramiche) 69pts
Points: Mario Cipollini ITA (Aqua e Sapone) 184pts
Team: Alessio 267:57:29

Vuelta a España

Valdencia-Madrid Sept 7-29

STAGE WINNERS	
1 Joseba Beloki ESP (ONCE-Eroski)	Beloki
(Valencia 24.6km)*	
2 Danilo di Luca ITA (Saeco-Longoni)	Beloki
(Valencia - Alcoy 144.7km)	
3 Mario Cipollini ITA (Aqua e Sapone)	Beloki
(San Vicente de Raspeg - Murcia 134.2km)	
4 Mario Cipollini ITA (Aqua e Sapone)	Beloki
(Aguilas - Roquetas De Mar 149.5km)	
5 Guido Trentin ITA (Cofidis)	Zarrabeitia
(El Ejido o Almeira - Sierra Nevada 198km)	
6 Roberto Heras ESP (US Postal)	Sevilla
(Granada - La Pandera 153.1km)	
7 Mario Cipollini ITA (Aqua e Sapone)	Sevilla
(Jaen - Malaga 196.8km)	
8 Aitor Gonzalez (Banesto)	Sevilla
(Malaga - Ubrique 173.6km)	
9 Pablo Lastras ESP (iBanesto.com)	Sevilla
(Córdoba - Córdoba 130.2km)	
10 Aitor Gonzalez ESP (Kelme-Costa)	Sevilla
(Córdoba 36.5km)*	
11 Pablo Lastras ESP (iBanesto.com)	Sevilla
(Alcobendas - Collado Villalba 166.1km)	
12 Alessandro Petacchi ITA (Fasso)	Sevilla
(Segovia - Burgos 210.5km)	
13 Giovanni Lombardi ITA (Acqua e Sap)	Sevilla
(Burgos - Santander 189.8km)	
14 Serguei Smetanine RUS (Jazztel)	Sevilla
(Santander - Gijón 190.2km)	
15 Roberto Heras ESP (US Postal)	Heras
(Gijón - Angliru 176.7km)	
16 Santiago Botero COL (Kelme)	Heras
(Avilés - León 154.7km)	
17 Angelo Furlan ITA (Alessio)	Heras
(Benavente - Salamanca 145.6km)	
18 Santiago Blanco ESP (iBanesto.com)	Heras
(Salamanca - Estación de la Covatilla 193.7km)	
19 José Garcia Acosta ESP (iBanesto)	Heras
(Béjar - Avila 177.8km)	
20 Angelo Furlan ITA (Lampre)	Sevilla
(Avila - Warner Bros Park 141.2km)	
21 Aitor Gonzalez ESP (Kelme)	Casero
(Warner Bros Park - Stadion Bernabeu 41.2km)*	

FINAL CLASSIFICATION

1	Aitor Gonzalez ESP (Kelme-Costa)	75:13:52
2	Roberto Heras ESP (US Postal)	+2:14
3	Joseba Beloki ESP (ONCE-Eroski)	+3:11
4	Oscar Sevilla ESP (Kelme-Costa)	+3:26
5	Iban Mayo ESP (Euskaltel)	+5:42
6	Angel Casero ESP (Team Coast)	+6:33
7	Francesco Casagrande ITA (Fasso)	+6:38
8	Félix Garcia Casas ESP (Bigmat.Auber)	+6:46
9	Manuel Beltran ESP (Team Coast)	+8:29
10	Gilberto Simoni ITA (Saeco-Longoni)	+9:22
109	Charlie Wegelius GBR (Mapei)	+3:03:43

Mountains: Aitor Osa ESP (iBanesto.com) 107pts
Points: Erik Zabel GER (Telekom) 188pts
Team: Kelme-Costa Blanca 225:37:59

World Championships

Hasselt-Zolder, Belgium, Oct 8-13
Where times are not given for a rider, they have the same time as the first timed rider above them.

Men
Road Race (256km)
1 Mario Cipollini ITA   5:30:03
2 Robbie McEwen AUS
3 Erik Zabel GER
DNF: David Millar GBR, Julian Winn GBR

Time Trial
1 Santiago Botero COL   48:08.45
2 Michael Rich GER   +8.23
3 Igor Gonzalez ESP   +17.15
6 David Millar GBR   +35.32
26 Stuart Dangerfield GBR   +2:17.89

Women
Road Race (128km)
1 Susanne Ljungskog SWE   2:59:15
2 Nicole Brandli SUI
3 Joanne Somarriba Arrola ESP
35 Nicole Cooke GBR   +0:27
62 Rachel Heal GBR   +1:30
68 Frances Newstead GBR   +2:02
73 Susan Carter GBR   +3:25
83 Sara Waller GBR   +8:03
DNF: Emma Davies GBR

Time Trial
1 Zoulfia Zabirova RUS   30:02.62
2 Nicole Brandli SUI   +14.70
3 Karin Thurig SUI   +15.65
32 Frances Newstead GBR   +2:12.68

Men's World Cup
FINAL STANDINGS

1 Paolo Bettini ITA (Mapei)   279
2 Johan Museeuw BEL (Domo-Farm)   270
3 Michele Bartoli ITA (Fasso)   242
4 Igor Astarloa ESP (Saeco-Longoni)   183
5 Davide Rebellin ITA (Gerolsteiner)   179
6 Dario Frigo ITA (Tacconi)   156
7 George Hincapie USA (US Postal)   124
8 Peter van Petegem BEL (Cofidis)   121
9 Oscar Freire ESP (Mapei)   111
10 Jo Plankaert BEL (Cofidis)   107
37 Max Sciandri GBR (Lampre)   10

Men's World Cup

Milan-San Remo
Mar 23 (251km)
1 Michele Bartoli ITA (Fassa Bortolo)   6:14:49
2 Davide Rebellin ITA (Gerolsteiner)
3 Oskar Camenzind SUI (Phonak)
54 Max Sciandri GBR (Lampre)   +7:44

Tour Of Flanders
April 7 (264km)
1 Andrea Tafi ITA (Mapei-Quick Step)   6.53.00
2 Johan Museeuw BEL (Domo-Farm)   +0:21
3 Peter Van Petegem BEL (Lotto-Adecco)
51 Maximilian Sciandri GBR (Lampre)

Paris-Roubaix
Apr 14 (261km)
1 Johan Museeuw BEL (Domo-Farm)   6:39:08
2 Steffen Wesemann GER (Telekom)   +3:04
3 Tom Boonen BEL (US Postal)   +3:08
16 Maximilian Sciandri GBR (Lampre)   +8:14

Liège-Bastogne-Liège
Apr 21 (258km)
1 Paolo Bettini ILT (Mapei-Quickstep)   6:39:44
2 Stefano Garzelli ITA (Mapei-Quickstep)
3 Ivan Basso ITA (Fassa Bortola)   +0:15
38 Maximilian Sciandri GBR (Lampre)   +1:27

Amstel Gold Race
Apr 28 (255km)
1 Michele Bartoli ITA (Fassa Bortolo)   6:49:17
2 Serguei Ivanov RUS (Fassa Bortolo)
3 Michael Boogerd NED (Rabobank)

HEW Cyclassics
Aug 4 (253km)
1 Johan Museeuw BEL (Domo-Farm)   5:43:35
2 Igor Astarloa ESP (Saeco)
3 Davide Rebellin ITA (Gerolsteiner)

San Sebastian Classic
Aug 10 (227km)
1 Laurent Jalabert FRA (CSC)   5:47:29
2 Igor Astarloe ESP (Saeco)
3 Gabriele Missaglia ITA (Lampre)
127 Max Sciandri GBR (Lampre)   +12:13

Championnats de Zurich
Aug 18 (237km)
1 Dario Frigo ITA (Tacconi)   5:56:54
2 Paolo Bettini ITA (Mapei)   +1:06
3 Lance Armstrong USA (US Postal)

Paris-Tours
Oct 6 (257km)
1 Jakob Storm Piil DEN (CSC Tiscali)   5:39:11
2 Jacky Durand FRA (FDJeux)
3 Erik Zabel GER (Telekom)   +0:20
45 Jeremy Hunt GBR (Big Mat)
63 Max Sciandri GBR (Lampre)

Giro di Lombardia
Oct 19 (251km)
1 Michele Bartoli ITA (Fassa Bortolo)   6:14:49
2 Davide Rebellin ITA (Gerolsteiner)
3 Oskar Camenzind SUI (Phonak)
54 Max Sciandri GBR (Lampre)   +7:44

Women's World Cup

Cooma-Thredbo
Mar 3 (103km)
1	Petra Rossner GER	3:14:25
2	Rochelle Gilmore AUS	
3	Mirjam Melchers NED	
24	Sue Thomas GBR	+2:00
38	Julie Hooper GBR	+4:50
48	Nicola Bedwell GBR	

Hamilton City
Mar 10 (107km)
1	Petra Rossner GER	2:58:22
2	Rochelle Gilmore AUS	
3	Hanka Kupfernagel GER	

Primavera Rosa
Mar 23 (107km)
1	Mirjam Melchers NED	2:55:31
2	Diana Ziliute LTU	
3	Chantal Beltman NED	
20	Nicole Cooke GBR	+0:14
45	Melanie Sears GBR	+1:01
48	Susan Carter GBR	
93	Sara Symington GBR	+4:32

La Fléche Wallone
Apr 17 (93km)
1	Fabiana Luperini ITA (Edilsavino)	2.33.15
2	Lyne Bessette CAN (Saturn)	+0:12
3	Priska Doppmann SUI (Swiss Team)	
5	Nicole Cooke GBR (Deia-Pragma)	
7	Caroline Alexander GBR (GB Team)	+0:27
31	Sara Symington GBR (GB Team)	+1:30
66	Susan Thomas GBR (GB Team)	+5:23
67	Rachel Heal GBR (GB Team)	+5:28
89	Susan Carter GBR (GB Team)	+6:35

Castilla y Leon
Apr 21 (111km)
1	Regina Schleicher GER (Fanini)	2:55:51
2	Petra Rossner GER (Saturn)	
3	Mirjam Melchers NED (Farm Frites)	
24	Nicole Cooke GBR (Deia-Pragma)	
34	Susan Thomas GBR (GB Team)	+0:17
35	Caroline Alexander GBR (GB Team)	
38	Melanie Sears GBR (GB Team)	+0:24
64	Rachel Heal GBR (GB Team)	+1:12
70	Susan Carter GBR (GB Team)	+2:37
71	Joanne Cavill GBR (GB Team)	

Montreal
June 1 (99km)
1	Deirdre Demet-Barry USA (Talgo)	2:58:16
2	Anna Millward AUS (Saturn)	+0:39
3	Genevieve Jeanson (RONA)	+1:02
8	Sara Symington GBR (GB Team)	+1:11
14	Caroline Alexander GBR (GB Team)	+1:19
25	Rachel Heal GBR (GB Team)	+2:08

GP de Plouay
Aug 25 (115km)
1	Regina Schleicher GER (Franini)	2:52:38
2	Petra Rossner GER (Saturn)	
3	Susanne Ljungskog SWE (Interim)	
36	Frances Newstead GBR (GB Team)	+4:58
37	Melanie Sears GBR (GB Team)	+5:51

GP Suisse Féminin
Sep 8 (119km)
1	Svetlana Boubnenkova RUS (Edilsavino)	3:22:20
2	Simona Parente ITA (Edilsavino)	+0:11
3	Priska Doppman SUI (Swiss Team)	+0:20

DNF: Caroline Alexander, Rachel Heal, Julie Mann, Sara Waller, Penny Edwards, all GBR

Rotterdam Tour
Sep 15 (119km)
1	Petra Rossner GER (Saturn)	3:24:42
2	Regina Schleider GER (Mixed Team)	
3	Debby Mansveld NED (Interim)	
20	Sara Waller GBR	
22	Susan Carter GBR	
32	Melanie Szubrycht GBR	

Women's World Cup

FINAL STANDINGS

1	Petra Rossner GER (Saturn)	345
2	Mijam Melchers NED (Farm Frites)	283
3	Regina Schleicher GER (Fanini)	225
4	Priska Doppmann SUI	155
5	Rochelle Gilmore AUS	111
6	Susanne Ljungskog SWE (Interim)	99
7	Fabiana Luperini ITA (Edilsavino)	98
8	Hanka Kupfernagel GER (Nurnberger)	92
9	Svetlana Boubnenkova RUS (Edilsalvino)	86
10	Simona Parente ITA (Edilsalvino)	84
35	Caroline Alexander GBR	28
36	Nicole Cooke GBR (Deia-Pragma)	28
51	Sara Symington GBR	18
88	Sarah Waller GBR	1

British Champions

Men
Road Race
Rivington, June 30 (211km)
1	Julian Winn (Pinarello)	5:22:30
2	Tom Southam (Team Nijdam)	+0:12
3	Jeremy Hunt (Big Mat)	+0:17

Time Trial
Suffolk, Sep 14
1	Michael Hutchinson (Team MDT)	1:11:26
2	Zak Carr (APIBikes.com)	+0:05
3	Stuart Dangerfield (Camel Valley)	+0:06

Women
Road Race
Rivington, July 14 (211km)
1	Nicole Cooke (Deia-Pragma)	2:56:00
2	Rachel Heal (Powerbar)	+0:12
3	Melanie Sears (Powerbar)	+1:20

Time Trial
Suffolk, Sep 14
1	Frances Newstead (GS Strada)	50:49
2	Emma Davies (Powerbar)	+1:17
3	Rachel Heal (Powerbar)	+0:03

Track Racing

World Championships

Copenhagen, Sep 25-29
Placings given for all British riders; no Irish riders competing

Men

Kilometre Time Trial
1 Chris Hoy GBR   1:01.893
2 Arnaud Tournant FRA   1:01.894
3 Shane Kelly AUS   1:02.128
5 Jamie Staff GBR   1:02.780

Individual Pursuit
1 Brad McGee AUS
2 Luke Roberts AUS
3 Jens Lehmann GER
Final: McGee 4:17.875 - Roberts 4:24.925
Bradley Wiggins GBR, 5th qualifier in 4:24.378, 5th in round 1 (last eight) in 4:22.883

Team Pursuit
1 Australia
   Dawson/Lancaster/Wooldridge/Roberts
2 Germany
   Bach/Fulst/Siedler/Lehmann
3 Great Britain
   Manning/Steel/Wiggins/Newton
Final: AUS 4:00.362 - GER 4:07.384
3rd/4th: GBR 4:02.382 - UKR 4:08.151

Sprint
1 Sean Eadie AUS
2 Jobie Dajka AUS
3 Florian Rousseau FRA
Final: 2-1 (10.575 Eadie/10.787 Dajka/10.602 Eadie)
Jamie Staff GBR led qualifying in 10.130, lost in the q-f to Rousseau FRA, final ranking for Staff 8th

Team Sprint
1 Great Britain
   Staff/Hoy/MacLean
2 Australia
   Bayley/Dajka/Eadie
3 Germany
   Fiedler/Lausberg/Bergemann
Final: GBR 44.370 - AUS 44.508

Points Race (30km)
1 Chris Newton GBR   76pts
2 Franz Stocher AUT   50pts
3 Juan Curuchet ARG   49pts
Newton lapped the field three times

Scratch Race (15km)
1 Franco Marvulli SUI
2 Tony Gibb GBR
3 Stefan Steinweg GER

Madison
1 Neuville/Perque FRA   5pts
2 Garber/Stocher AUT   18 pts (-1 lap)
3 Curuchet/Simon ARG   17pts (-1 lap)
11 Gibb/Steel GBR   0pts (-1 lap)

Keirin
1 Jobie Dajka AUS 10.8
2 Jose Antonio Villanueva ESP
3 Rene Wolff GER
Ross Edgar GBR was fourth in his semi-final

Women

Individual Pursuit
1 Leontien Zijlaard-Van Moorsel NED
2 Olga Slioussareva RUS
3 Katherine Bates AUS
4 Emma Davies GBR
Final: Van Moorsel 3:34.330 - Slioussareva 3:36.188
3rd/4th: Bates 3:36.289 - Davies 3:42.335
Sara Symington GBR eliminated in quarter-finals by Van Moorsel

500m Time Trial
1 Natalia Tsylinskaya BLR 34.838
2 Nancy Contreras Reyes MEX 34.898
3 Kerrie Meares AUS   34.964
7 Julie Paulding GBR   35.542

Sprint
1 Natallia Tsylinskaya BLR
2 Kerrie Meares AUS
3 Katrin Meinke GER
Final: 2-0 (12.597/12.347)
Victoria Pendleton GBR 9th in Qualifying in 11.813, lost to Lindemuth USA in round 1 repechage

Points Race (25km)
1 Olga Slioussareva RUS   35pts
2 Lada Kozlikova CZE   20pts
3 Vera Carrara ITA   20pts
DNF: Sara Symington GBR

Scratch Race (10km)
1 Lada Kozlikova CZE
2 Rochelle Gilmore AUS
3 Olga Slioussareva RUS
DNF: Emma Davies GBR

Keirin
1 Li Na CHN
2 Clara Sanchez FRA
3 Rosalee Hubbard AUS

British Championships

Manchester Velodrome,

MEN
Kilometre TT: Jon Norfolk 1:05.537
Individual Pursuit: Michael Hutchinson 4:35.225
Team Pursuit: VC St Raphael
Sprint: Andy Slater
Team Sprint: Team Athena 46.442
Athena riders: McLean/Hoy/Queally
Scratch Race (20km): Russell Downing
Points Race: Chris Newton
Kierin: Jon Norfolk 12.42
Madison: Taylor/Pritchard 1:05.48

WOMEN
500 TT: Victoria Pendleton 35.765
Individual Pursuit: Emma Davies
Sprint: Victoria Pendleton
Scratch Race: Angela Hunter
Points Race: Angela Hunter

Mountain Bikes

World Championships

Kaprun, Austria, Aug 24-Sep 1

MEN

Cross-Country

1	Roland Green CAN	2:19:02
2	Filip Meirhaeghe BEL	+0:19
3	Thomas Frischknecht SUI	+1:45
23	Nick Craig GBR	+15:27
53	Barrie Clarke GBR	+26:39
59	Zak Toogood GBR	+30:37
DNF: Oli Beckinsale GBR		

Downhill

1	Nicolas Voulloz FRA	5:08.53
2	Steve Peat GBR	+0.54
3	Chris Kovarik AUS	+5.35
13	Crawford Carrick-Anderson GBR	+12.11
25	Rob Warner GBR	+19.91
35	Dan Atherton GBR	+25.74
72	Stuart Hughes GBR	+50.89

Four Cross

1 Brian Lopes USA
2 Cedric Gracia FRA
3 Eric Carter USA
14 Dave Wardell GBR
16 Dale Holmes GBR
22 William Longden GBR
27 Steve Peat GBR
32 Martin Longden GBR

WOMEN

Cross-Country

1	Gunn-Rita Dahle NOR	2:14:05
2	Anna Szafraniec POL	+1:23
3	Sabine Spitz GER	+2:48
13	Caroline Alexander GBR	+13:57
44	Jenny Copnall GBR	+1 lap

Downhill

1	Anne Caroline Chausson FRA	5:45.58
2	Fionn Griffiths GBR	+6.60
3	Missy Giove USA	+10.56
4	Tracy Moseley GBR	+14.61
21	Helen Gaskell GBR	+46.00

Four Cross

1 Anne Caroline Chausson FRA
2 Katrina Miller AUS
3 Sabrina Jonnier FRA

World Cup

Final Standings

First British & Irish shown and any in top 20

MEN

Downhill

1	Steve Peat GBR	1002
2	Cedric Garcia FRA	729
3	Christopher Kovarik AUS	709
23	Crawford Carrick-Anderson GBR	164
79	John Lawlor IRL	16

Cross Country

1	Filip Meirhaeghe BEL	935
2	Christoph Sauser SUI	740
3	Bart Brentjens NED	706
32	Liam Killeen GBR	168

4-Cross

1	Brian Lopes USA	151
2	Cedric Garcia FRA	126
3	Mike King USA	124
8	Steve Peat GBR	65
9	Dale Holmes GBR	57
13	Will Longden GBR	41
20	Scott Beaumont GBR	18

WOMEN

Downhill

1	Anne-Caroline Chausson FRA	1027
2	Sabrina Jonnier FRA	915
3	Tracy Moseley GBR	795
5	Fionn Griffiths GBR	621
13	Helen Gaskell GBR	314

Cross Country

1	Alison Dunlap USA	850
2	Sabine Spitz GER	815
3	Marga Fullana ESP	750
6	Caroline Alexander GBR	350

4-Cross

1	Anne-Caroline Chausson FRA	220
2	Sabrina Jonnier FRA	190
3	Katrina Miller AUS	155
16	Fionn Griffiths GBR	7
20	Joey Gough GBR	4

British Championships

Hopton Castle, nr Ludlow, July 20-21

MEN

Downhill

1 Steve Peat; 2 Stu Hughes; 3 Stu Thompson

Cross-Country

1 Oli Beckinsale; 2 Barrie Clarke; 3 Nick Craig

WOMEN

Downhill

1 Tracy Moseley; 2 Helen Gaskell; 3 Helen Mortimer

Cross-Country

1 Caroline Alexander; 2 Sue Thomas; 3 Jenny Copnall

Cyclo-cross

World Championships

Zolder, Belgium   Feb 2-3

Men

1	Mario de Clercq	BEL	1:01.11
2	Tom Vannoppen	BEL	+0.03
3	Sven Nijs	BEL	+0.06
12	Roger Hammond	GBR	+2.03
36	David Collins	GBR	+4.44
39	Matthew Ellis	GBR	+5.09
43	Stephen Knight	GBR	+5.29

Women

1	Laurence Leboucher	FRA	39.06
2	Hanka Kupfernagel	GER	+1.04
3	Daphny van den Brand	NED	+1.04
20	Victoria Wilkinson	GBR	+5.18
21	Isla Rowntree	GBR	+6.01

World Cup

FINAL STANDINGS

Men

1	Sven Nijs	BEL	282pts
2	Mario de Clercq	BEL	270pts
3	Bart Wellens	BEL	241pts
46	Roger Hammond	GBR	12pts
60	David Collins	GBR	1pt

Nations

1	Belgium	72pts
2	Netherlands	53pts
3	Czech Republic	46pts

BMX

World Championships

Paulinia, Brazil, July 22-28

Elite Men

1 Kyle Bennett USA
2 Randy Stumphauser USA
3 Wade Bootes AUS

Junior Men

1 Pablo Guttierrez FRA
2 Taylor Wells USA
3 Edwin Montoya COL

Elite Women

1 Gabriela Diaz ARG
2 Karine Chambonneau FRA
3 Jana Horakova CZE

Junior Women

1 Willy Kanis NED
2 Cyrielle Convert FRA
3 Analis Diaz ARG

Darts

Number 10 was the easiest yet; Phil Taylor not conceding a set on the way to the final, and then taking barely an hour to dispose of Peter Manley 7-0 for his eighth straight PDC victory, to go with the two BDO titles from way back. Manley, whose nickname is 'One Dart' was shell-shocked. On an old website (from 2000) we discovered that Manley only rated Taylor fifth in his all-time list, behind Eric Bristow, John Lowe, Leighton Rees and Jockey Wilson. Perhaps Taylor saw the site, because 'No Hope' would have been a more suitable monicker for the hapless Manley.

"I was just cruising really. These blokes are not playing their normal game, they are in awe of us. These six-nils and seven-nils are ridiculous. Peter's better than that," said Taylor, who had along the way also broken his own three-dart average for a round, taking it to 111.

For the rest of the year, it was not Manley but John Part who played the supporting role. Perhaps his nickname should be 'Bit' Part, because that's how the Canadian must have felt after losing to Taylor in the finals of both the Stan James World Matchplay and the Paddy Power Grand Prix. Even at Purfleet, he found it impossible to avoid Taylor, going down 6-0 in a quarter-final match.

At least Part was not on the receiving end of Taylor's blitz at Blackpool in an earlier round of the world matchplay. The poor soul on that occasion was Chris Mason, who had held his own with the Stoke licensee for the first four sets of their quarter-final match. Nine-darters are as rare as sightings of the hoopoe, and the last to be televised was that by Paul Lim back in 1991. Stan James, the bookmaker, had offered £100,000 to any player who could repeat the feat, and Taylor in the fifth set did just that. The money was presented in a suitcase. Any other sport would just have given Taylor a cheque, and that would have been that, but darts still can't quite shake off its old trappings.

The parallel world championship, at Frimley Green, was won by Australian Tony David, a haemophiliac who doctors once believed would not live to see his 20th birthday, and even now still walks with a limp, and cannot properly straighten his throwing arm.

David, from Queensland, had been living off a disability pension of about £150 per fortnight, but doubtless had some difficulty claiming it after his victory in the final over England's Mervyn King. For his win, David earned about £48,000, enough to help the 26-year-old to buy his own home.

| **Taylor's Nine** |
| *Scored against Chris Mason in the quarter-finals of the World Matchplay Event* |
| 60 |
| 60 |
| 60 |
| 60 |
| 60 |
| 60 |
| 60 |
| 57 |
| 24 |
| = 501 |

Skol World Championship

Circus Tavern, Purfleet, Dec 28, 2001-Jan 5
First round
Alan Warriner ENG (1) bt Reg Harding ENG 4-2
Colin Lloyd ENG bt Alex Roy ENG (16) 4-2
Dennis Smith ENG (5) bt Paul Lim USA 4-0
Richie Burnett WAL (8) bt Peter Evison ENG 4-1
Ronnie Baxter ENG (12) bt Kevin Painter ENG 4-2
Denis Ovens ENG (9) bt Andy Jenkins ENG 4-3
Peter Manley ENG (4) bt Steve Brown USA 4-1
John Lowe ENG (13) bt Les Fitton ENG 4-1
Shayne Burgess ENG bt Jamie Harvey SCO (15) 4-3
Steve Beaton ENG (18) bt Bob Anderson ENG 4-3
Phil Taylor ENG (2) bt Paul Williams ENG 4-1
Dave Askew ENG (11) bt Chris Mason ENG 4-3
Roland Scholten BEL (6) bt Cliff Lazarenko ENG 4-1
John Part CAN (7) bt Mick Manning ENG 4-2
Rod Harrington ENG (3) bt Keith Deller ENG 4-3
Dennis Priestley ENG (14) bt Matt Chapman ENG 4-1
Second Round
Lloyd bt Warriner 6-4; Burnett bt Ovens 6-4;
Baxter bt Smith 6-1; Manley bt Lowe 6-5
Taylor bt Burgess 6-1; Askew bt Scholten 6-3;
Part bt Beaton 6-0; Priestley bt Harrington 6-3
Quarter-finals
Lloyd bt Burnett 6-4; Askew bt Priestley 6-2;
Manley bt Baxter 6-2; Taylor bt Part 6-0
Semi-finals
Manley bt Lloyd 6-4; Taylor bt Askew 6-0
FINAL
Phil Taylor ENG bt Peter Manley ENG 7-0

BDO World Championship

Lakeside CC, Frimley Green, Jan 5-14
First round
Colin Monk ENG bt Tony O'Shea ENG 3-2
John Walton ENG (1) bt Andy Fordham ENG 3-0
Stefan Nagy SWE bt Gary Anderson SCO 3-0
Wayne Mardle ENG (8) bt Davy Richardson ENG 3-0
Eric Clarys BEL bt Andre Welge GER 3-1
Raymond Barneveld NED (5) bt Bobby George ENG 3-1
Mensur Suljovic BIH bt Vincent van der Voort NED 3-2
Mervyn King ENG (4) bt Russell Stewart AUS 3-1
Steve Coote ENG bt Markus Korhonen SWE 3-1
Martin Adams ENG (2) bt Peter Johnstone SCO 3-0
Wayne Jones ENG bt Tony Eccles ENG 3-2
Ted Hankey ENG (7) bt Jarkko Komula FIN 3-2
Co Stompe NED bt Mike Veitch SCO 3-0
Bob Taylor SCO (6) bt John Ferrell ENG 3-0
Tony David AUS bt Ritchie Davies WAL 3-1
Marko Pusa FIN (3) bt Matt Clark ENG 3-1
Second Round
Monk bt Walton 3-2; Mardle bt Nagy 3-1;
Barneveld bt Clarys 3-0; King bt Suljovic 3-1;
Adams bt Coote 3-1; Jones bt Hankey 3-2;
Taylor bt Stompe 3-1; David bt Pusa 3-1
Quarter-finals
Monk bt Mardle 5-4; King bt Barneveld 5-3;
Adams bt Jones 5-1; David bt Taylor 5-4
Semi-finals
David bt Adams 5-4; King bt Monk 5-1
FINAL
Tony David AUS bt Mervyn King ENG 6-4

Other Events

Women's World Championship
Lakeside CC, Frimley Green, Jan 6-15
Held in conjunction with the BDO men's event
First Round
Trina Gulliver ENG (1) bt Mandy Solomons ENG 2-0
Vicky Pruim BEL (4) bt Jan Robbins WAL 2-0
Francis Hoenselaar NED (2) bt Stacy Bromberg USA 2-0
Sandra Greatbatch WAL bt Crissy Howat ENG 2-0
Semi-finals
Francis Hoenselaar bt Sandra Greatbatch 2-1
Trina Gulliver bt Vicky Pruim 2-1
Final
Trina Gulliver bt Francis Hoenselaar 2-1

Stan James World Matchplay
Blackpool, July 28-Aug 3
Semi-finals
John Part CAN bt Colin Lloyd ENG 17-12
Phil Taylor ENG bt John Lowe ENG 17-15
Final
Phil Taylor bt John Part 18-16
In his quarter-final match against Chris Mason, Taylor achieved a nine-dart finish, earning a £100,000 prize.

Las Vegas Desert Classic
MGM Garden Arena, Las Vegas, July 5-7
Men's Final
Phil Taylor ENG bt Ronnie Baxter ENG 3-0
Women's Final
Deta Hedman ENG bt Carolyn Mars USA 2-1

Paddy Power World Grand Prix
City West Hotel, Dublin, Oct 22-27
Semi-finals
John Part CAN bt Andy Jenkins ENG 6-1
Phil Taylor ENG bt Peter Evison ENG 6-0
Final
Phil Taylor bt John Part 7-3

Winmau World Masters
Bridlington, Nov 1-3
Men's Final
Mark Durbridge ENG bt Tony West ENG 8-4
Women's Final
Trina Gulliver ENG bt Karen Smith ENG 4-1

Equestrianism

I f the International Olympic committee ever carries out its threat to remove eventing from the Olympic programme, British equestrianism would be in absolute despair. For a nation that once excelled at driving and matched the best at jumping now has only eventing left. At Jerez, in the World Equestrian Games, the horse trials were the source of both British medals, the drivers and the jumpers so far down the ranks that they should have got a special thank you for just turning out.

Dermott Lennon, from County Down, won the individual jumping, the blue riband event of the Games. Ireland's Eddie Macken was twice runner-up, in 1974 and 1978, and Gerry Mullins was fourth in 1983, but Lennon became the first ever Irish winner. The 32-year-old cattle farmer's son started cautiously, only 26th after the opening speed round. After three rounds, four combinations reached the final, where the riders exchanged horses. Lennon, in only his first season with the Irish team, was drawn the Swedish mare Utfors Mynta, and won with just a single fence down.

After the dressage, Britain actually led the team competition in the eventing, but the cross-country was disastrous, with Pippa Funnell, William Fox-Pitt and Leslie Law all running into trouble. The team was saved by the performance of Jeanette Brakewell on Over to You, who climbed from 26th to sixth place, and primed herself for that silver medal on the final day. The Australian gifted the team bronze medal to a stunned and delighted British team; Australians bearing sporting gifts of any kind is rare indeed.

Away from Jerez, Nick Skelton, who retired with a neck injury in 2001 after representing his country 137 times, including at four Olympic Games, returned to the fray. With the damaged ligament now healed and his ambition rekindled, Skelton is tilting at the Athens Games on his young horse Arko. Well, if ever his country needed him...

FEI-Gandini World Jumping Rankings

as at 28/2/03

1	Ludger Beerbaum	GER	3676.350
2	Markus Fuchs	SUI	2577.000
3	Rodrigo Pessoa	BRA	2441.173
4	Marcus Ehning	GER	2234.223
5	Otto Becker	GER	2187.270
6	Jos Lansink	BEL	2063.500
7	Lars Nieberg	GER	1867.110
8	Toni Hassmann	GER	1850.118
9	Ludo Philippaerts	BEL	1743.140
10	Sören von Rönne	GER	1577.130
11	Leslie Howard	USA	1412.260
12	Michel Robert	FRA	1400.125
13	Eric Navet	FRA	1360.880
14	M Michaels-Beerbaum	GER	1315.158
15	Gianni Govoni	ITA	1297.700
16	Rolf-Göran Bengtsson	SWE	1257.240
17	McLain Ward	USA	1233.124
18	Jeroen Dubbeldam	NED	1212.130
19	Robert Smith	GBR	1167.630
20	Peter Wylde	USA	1156.105

World Equestrian Games

Jerez, Sep 10-22

Dressage
Individual

1	Nadine Capellmann GER	237.515
	on Farbenfroh	
2	Beatriz Ferrer-Salat ESP	234.385
	on Beauvalais	
3	Ulla Salzgeber GER	233.535
	on Rusty	

No GB qualifiers for GP Special;
GB Placings after Grand Prix

28	Richard Davidson GBR	66.080
	on Ballaseyr Royale	
31	Laura Richardson GBR	65.800
	on Millenium	
50	Emile Faurie GBR	63.160
	on Insterburg	
51	Peter Storr GBR	63.040
	on Gambrinus	

Team

1	Germany	5642
2	USA	5527
3	Spain	5403
10	Great Britain	4876

Davidson/Richardson/Faurie/Storr

Vaulting
Men

1	Matthias Lang GER	8.973
	on Farceur Breceen HN	
2	Gero Meyer GER	8.771
	on Kolumbus	
3	Devon Maitozo USA	8.612
	on Abu Dhabi 2	

No GB qualifiers for the final two rounds;
GB placings after round 2

24	Philip Beasley GBR	7.253
	on W H Bentley	
26	Ricky Davies GBR	6.802
	on Grately Limelight	

GB placings after round 1

28	John McNaly GBR	6.980
	on Bowler II	

Women

1	Nadia Zulow GER	8.835
	on Rubins Universe	
2	Rikke Lauman DEN	8.555
	on Milano	
3	Ines Juckstock GER	8.450
	on Dallmers Little Foot	

No GB qualifiers for the final three rounds;
GB placings after round 1

25	Elizabeth Watson GBR	6.980
	on Bowler II	
37	Sarah Watson GBR	6.357
	on Bowler II	
43	Lucy Bell GBR	6.065
	on Bowler II	

Team

1	Germany	8.199
2	Switzerland	8.042
3	Sweden	7.821
11	Great Britain	6.720

Rogerson/Panter/Eccles/Hall/Smith/Rawlinson/Mulvenna/
Phillips/Johnston

Three-day Event
Individual

1	Jean Teulere FRA	45.80
	on Espoir de la Mare	
2	Jeanette Brakewell GBR	52.00
	on Over To You	
3	Piia Pantsu FIN	52.60
	on Ypaja Karuso	
13	Pippa Funnell GBR	73.00
	on Supreme Rock	
14	William Fox-Pitt GBR	74.00
	on Tamarillo	
18	Leslie Law GBR	80.60
	on Shear H2O	
22	Kristina Cook GBR	85.80
	on Captain Christy	

Team

1	USA	175.40
2	France	192.40
3	Great Britain	199.00

Brakewell/Funnell/Fox-Pitt/Law

Endurance
Individual

1	Sheikh Ahmed Al Maktoum UAE	9:19:29
	on Bowman	
2	Antonio Rosi ITA	9:35:23
	on Alex Raggio Di Sole	
3	Sunny Demedy FRA	9:38:47
	on Fifi Du Bagnas	
18	Rebecca Broughton GBR	11:03:14
	on Murmansk	
45	Pamela James GBR	12:38:57
	on Selim De Ducor	
51	Sarah Kelleway GBR	12:54:58
	on IBN Aswana	

Team

1	France	30:37:01
2	Italy	31:05:52
3	Australia	32:57:47

No British Team completed

Driving
Individual

1	Ijsbrand Chardon	NED	134.30
2	Christoph Sandmann	GER	1:36.07
3	Thomas Eriksson	SWE	140.67
15	James Capstick	GBR	171.90
24	Caren Bassett	GBR	185.00
30	George Bowman	GBR	209.88
33	Richard Lane	GBR	219.85

Team

1	Netherlands	275.01
2	USA	286.52
3	Germany	291.54
8	Great Britain	376.55

Showjumping

Individual

Scores from final round, qualifying score in brackets
In the final round, the riders exchanged horses

1	Dermott Lennon	IRL	4	(13.16)
	on Liscalgot			
2	Eric Navet	FRA	8	(6.29)
	on Dollar du Murier HTS de Seine			
3	Peter Wylde	USA	12	(9.55)
	on Fein Cera			

No British rider qualified for the third day (top 25)
After day 2
35 Tim Stockdale on Fresh Direct Parcival
Did Not Complete Day 2
Geoffrey Bloomfield on Eloise De Semilly
Di Lampard on Abbervail Dream
Scott Smith on Cabri D'Elle
Mark Armstrong on Elise

Team

1	France	13.22
2	Sweden	21.02
3	Belgium	22.68
7	Ireland	30.94

Great Britain in 16th place did not qualify for the second round

Reining

Individual

1	Shawn Florida USA	221.5
	on San Jo Freckles	
2	Tom McCutcheon USA	219.0
	on Conquistador Whiz	
3	Shawna Sapergia USA	219.0
	on Pretty Much Eagle	
11	Douglas Allen GBR	214.0
	on Jays Master Copy	
18	Roseanne Sternberg GBR	212.0
	on Nijomi Sonny Reb	
23	Bob Mayhew GBR	207.5
	on Fast Draw Peppy	
24	Francesca Sternberg GBR	205.5
	on Chuka Chic	

Team

1	USA	657.5
2	Canada	650.0
3	Italy	646.0
5	Great Britain	633.5

5 teams only completed

Dressage

World Cup Final

's-Hertogenbosch, Netherlands, Mar 21-24

Grand Prix

1	Ulla Salzgeber GER	76.98
	on Rusty	
2	Beatriz Ferrer-Salat ESP	72.24
	on Beauvalais	
3	Lars Petersen DEN	71.32
	on Blue Hors Cavan	

Kur to Music

1	Ulla Salzgeber GER	81.57
	on Rusty	
2	Lars Petersen DEN	79.67
	on Blue Hors Cavan	
3	Beatriz Ferrer-Salat ESP	79.12
	on Beauvalais	

World Equestrian Games
Medal Table

1	Germany	5	2	3	10
2	France	4	1	1	6
3	USA	3	3	3	9
4	Netherlands	2	0	0	2
5	Ireland	1	0	0	1
5	UAE	1	0	0	1
7	Italy	0	2	1	3
8	Sweden	0	1	2	3
9	Great Britain	0	1	1	2
9	Spain	0	1	1	2
11	Canada	0	1	0	1
11	Denmark	0	1	0	1
11	Switzerland	0	1	0	1
14	Australia	0	0	1	1
14	Belgium	0	0	1	1
14	Finland	0	0	1	1

Jumping

World Cup Final
Liepzig, May 2-5

1 Otto Becker GER   7 faults
  on Dobel's Cento
2 Ludger Beerbaum GER   8 faults
  on Gladdys S
3 Rodrigo Pessoa BRA   11 faults
  on Balobet du Rouet

Nations Cup Final
Donaueschingen, Aug 24

1 Italy   4
2 Belgium   12
3 France   12

Hickstead Nations Cup
Hickstead, Sussex, July 25

Nations Cup
1 Germany   16 faults
2 Ireland   16 faults
3 Netherlands   20 faults
4 Great Britain   20 faults

British Grand Prix
1 Meredith Michaels-Beerbaum GER 44.71
  Shutterfly
2 Reynald Angot FRA   45.04
  Tlaloc
3 Christian Ahlmann GER   45.62
  Coster

Hickstead Derby Meeting
Hickstead, Sussex, Aug 23-25

The Bunn Leisure Derby
1 Peter Charles IRL
  on Corrada
2 Robert Smith GBR
  on Mr Springfield
3 Duncan Inglis GBR
  on Tougardens Joshuan

The Hasseroder Speed Derby
1 Guy Williams GBR   97.24
  on Be Precise
2 Jens Fredricson SWE   98.16
  on R S Isac
3 Pippa Funnell GBR   100.83
  on The Tourmaliine Rose

Olympia
Olympia, West London, Dec 19-23

Sony Ericsson Grand Prix
1 Toni Hasmann GER   34.08
  on Goldika 559
2 Robert Smith GBR   35.25
  on Mr Springfield
3 Marcus Ehning GER   36.76
  on Anka

Sony Ericsson World Cup Qualifier
1 Robert Smith GBR   50.53
  on Marius Claudius
2 Lars Nieberg GER   53.55
  on Adlantus AS FRH
3 Markus Merschformann GER
  on Camirez B

Kerrygold Horse Show
Dublin, Aug 7-11

Kerrygold International Grand Prix
1 Marc Houtzager NED   45.24
  on HBC Jacomar
2 Philippe Lejeune BEL   45.84
  on Nabab de Reve
3 David O'Brien IRL   46.65
  on Boherdeal Clover

Kerrygold Nations Cup
1 France   232.80
2 Italy   232.53
3 Ireland   225.14
4 Great Britain   224.05

Where There's Muck...

Hugo Simon has won a few events in his 40-odd years in the sport, but you might be surprised at the value put on his earnings by the Austrian tax authorities. They are curious of the whereabouts of 7.7 million Euros which they believe the 60-year-old has not been entirey up-front about. Simon has, according to reports, paid half a million Euros in arrears willingly. Would that we could?

Eventing

Badminton
May 1-4
1 Pippa Funnell GBR
   on Supreme Rock
2 William Fox-Pitt GBR
   on Tamarillo
3 Leslie Law GBR
   on Shear H2O

Punchestown
May 17-19
1 Lucinda Fredericks AUS   50.40
   on Belly Leck Boy
2 Pippa Funnell GBR   55.60
   on Prinmore's Pride
3 Andrew Nicholson NZL   56.40
   on Fenicio

British Open
Championship
(& World Cup round)
Gatcombe Park, Aug 2-5
1 Andrew Nicholson AUS   44.08
   on Mallards Treat
2 Pippa Funnell GBR   50.23
   on Prinmore's Pride
3 William Fox-Pitt GBR   50.41
   on Moon Man

Bramham
June 10-13
1 Pippa Funnell GBR   44.21
   on Walk On Star
2 Jeanette Brakewell GBR   49.41
   on The Busker
3 Sara Algotsson SWE   50.81
   on Robin des Bois

Burghley
Aug 29-Sep 1
1 William Fox-Pitt GBR   51.81
   on Highland Lad
2 Polly Stockton GBR   52.80
   on Word For Word
3 Mary King GBR   52.80
   on King Soloman

Blenheim
Sep 5-8
1 Lucinda Fredericks AUS   55.60
   on Headley Britannia
2 Jean Lou Bigot FRA   59.20
   on Nogency
3 Tim Davies GBR   60.80
   on Quackers

Fencing

World Championships
Lisbon   Aug 8-12

Men
Individual Foil
  1 Simone Vanni ITA
  2 Andre Wessels GER
  3 Piotr Kielpikowski POL
  3 Wu Hanxiong CHN
 49 James Beevers GBR
 62 Ben Montague GBR
 68 David Mansour GBR

Team Foil
  1 Germany
  2 France
  3 Spain
 11 Great Britain

Individual Epée
  1 Pavel Kobolkov RUS
  2 Fabrice Jeannet FRA
  3 Vitaly Zakharov BLR
 50 Gregory Allen GBR
 65 Thomas Cadman GBR
126 Tristan Lane GBR
141 Graham Paul GBR

Team Epée
  1 France
  2 Russia
  3 Korea
 20 Great Britain

Individual Sabre
  1 Stanislav Pozdniakov RUS
  2 Julien Pillet FRA
  3 Luigi Tarantino ITA
  3 Mihai Covaliu ROM
 16 James Williams GBR
 83 Dominic Flood GBR
 96 Christopher Jamieson GBR

Team Sabre
  1 Russia
  2 Italy
  3 Germany
 17 Great Britain

Women
Individual Foil
  1 Svetlana Bojko RUS
  2 Ekaterina Youcheva RUS
  3 Edina Knapek HUN
  3 Aida Mohamed HUN
 57 Eloise Smith GBR
 63 Camille Datoo GBR
 75 Clare Velden GBR

Team Foil
  1 Russia
  2 Poland
  3 Romania
 11 Great Britain

Individual Epée
  1 Hee Hyun KOR
  2 Imke Duplitzer GER
  3 Britta Heidemann GER
  3 Ana Branza ROM
 44 Georgina Usher GBR
 83 Samantha Martin GBR
100 Debbie Catchpole GBR
124 Joanna Beadsworth GBR

Team Epée
  1 Hungary
  2 Estonia
  3 China
 15 Great Britain

Individual Sabre
  1 Tan Xue CHN
  2 Elena Jemaeva AZE
  3 Cecile Argiolas FRA
  3 Elean Netchaeva RUS
  8 Louise Bond-Williams GBR
 28 Chrysgall Nicoll GBR
 49 Tamsyn Tremeer GBR
 51 Charlotte Brown GBR

Team Sabre
  1 Russia
  2 Hungary
  3 Azerbaijan
 10 Great Britain

No medals yet again for Britain in the major championships, but after a world title drought that now extends to 43 years that could hardly be deemed a surprise. Allan Jay's world championship win in the foil was in the same year that Cliff Richard hit number one in the charts with his cryin', talkin', sleepin', walkin' Livin' Doll. There has been, though, a smouldering amongst the ashes in the shape of Laurence Halstead and Richard Kruse, the former winning a European junior title in 2001, Kruse emulating his compatriot's achievement a year later in Coneglio, Italy. The future hums, but not Livin' Doll please.

European Championships

Moscow, July 1-7

Men

Individual Foil

1	Andrea Cassara	ITA
2	Simon Senft	GER
3	Michael Ludwig	AUT

Team Foil

1	Italy
2	France
3	Germany
7	Great Britain

Individual Epée

1	Gabor Boczko	HUN
2	Pawel Kolobkov	RUS
3	Geza Imre	HUN

Team Epée

1	France
2	Poland
3	Ukraine

Individual Sabre

1	Stanislav Podzniakov	RUS
2	Sergey Charikov	RUS
3	Mihai Covaliu	ROM

Team Sabre

1	Russia
2	Italy
3	Hungary

Women

Individual Foil

1	Sylvia Gruchala	POL
2	Laura Carlescu	ROM
3	Svetlana Bojko	RUS

Team Foil

1	Poland
2	Hungary
3	Russia
10	Great Britain

Individual Epée

1	Maureen Nisima	FRA
2	Niki Sidiropoulou	GRE
3	Ljubov Choutova	RUS

Team Epée

1	Hungary
2	Russia
3	Ukraine
14	Great Britain

Individual Sabre

1	Cecile Argiolas	FRA
2	Elena Netchaeva	RUS
3	Irina Bazhenova	RUS

Team Sabre

1	Russia
2	Hungary
3	Azerbaijan
8	Great Britain

Golf

Europe has generally done well with its selection of Ryder Cup captains; Tony Jacklin, Bernard Gallacher and Seve Ballesteros being the three who most readily spring to mind. For those with longer memories, and our Welsh readers, we should not omit Dai Rees from the list either, who not only captained but played in the successful 1957 British team.

Would you swop any of those for Sam Torrance, though? They may have been inspirational, they may have been impassioned (just a bit, eh Seve?), but they never made you feel that you would welcome them as a member of your family. Torrance was your mother's brother, your dad's uncle, your long-lost cousin. He was your friend, your advocate, your closest ally; and that was the message sent to every single member of that team. Torrance cared so much, that the passion almost stilled him.

For three days, on the skirt of every green, Torrance quietly anguished. For two of them, European pairs kept the match perfectly balanced; it stood at eight wins apiece on Saturday night. It was very different from the last European victory in 1997, when the Americans trailed by five points going into the singles, and almost reclaimed the lost ground. Torrance's team had nothing to spare for day three, no fat in the budget.

Curtis Strange, the US captain, proclaimed surprise at Torrance's strategy in the singles on the final day, for the American believed that the big guns would be fired late. I know we have hindsight, but that was never a starter Curtis, just never. Torrance did what he had to when you have faith; he went for the win. Montgomerie drilled in the opening rivet; first out, first in, and first point, with the defeated Scott Hoch convinced that he had never seen the Scot play so well. "I was doing what Sam ordered," said Montgomerie.

Sergio Garcia was at two (we'll come to him), Darren Clarke at three, Bernhard Langer at four, and Padraig Harrington at five; names the Americans were all too familiar with. The strategy worked, with Langer and Harrington, like Montgomerie, closing matches well before the 18th tee. In fact, only two Europeans lost their singles matches, Garcia and Lee Westwood, who in tandem had sparkled in the foursomes and fourballs, losing just one of four. The match of the two Philips settled the contest, with Price of Wales beating Mickelson of California, on the 16th. Paul McGinley didn't win, but after Price's success, needed only a half on the 18th and the Irishman got it.

Torrance could and did celebrate, but this was not Brookline. When a call came through on the mobile from Ballesteros, Torrance took it quietly as, by that time, Jesper Parnevik and Tiger Woods had reached the final green, albeit in a match that counted for little. Torrance was showing simple respect.

If Sergio Garcia had been playing for the US, this would have been the perfect victory for every European supporter could have celebrated the win and claimed the moral high ground as well, but he wasn't. For those of us (and allegiances are being given away here) who had waited three years to see Hal Sutton eat humble pie (what's it taste like, Hal?) having Garcia behave as badly as Sutton had at Brookline was all we needed.

"He doesn't win with class and he doesn't lose with class," said John Burke, who caddies for Davis Love III, after the Spaniard had suffered his first defeat against the American on Saturday afternoon. Well, Burke was right, for having lost with bad grace that day, his antics after the Europeans won on Sunday had even less grace. Just go watch Ernie Els, Sergio.

Until Muirfield, we all thought that Neels and Hettie Els had got it wrong at the Christening, for Ernest was surely a misnomer for their beloved son. Never has a golfer been less earnest at this level. His nickname, the Big Easy, says it all; this is a man who never runs when he can walk, shouts when he can whisper, or cries when he can frown. Yet there he was, third time around on the 18th green on the same final day at Muirfield and winging his hat up in the air while his right leg swung in an angular fashion. Ernest still wasn't being earnest, wasn't being utterly devoured with passion, yet if what he was doing wasn't quite jumping, it was undoubtedly joy he was displaying.

Ryder Cup

The Belfry, Sep 27-29
European players shown first

FOURBALLS
Friday Morning
Clarke/Bjorn bt Woods/Azinger 1up
Garcia/Westwood bt Duval/Love III 4 and 3
Montgomerie/Langer bt Hoch/Furyk 4 and 3
Harrington/Fasth lost to Mickelson/Toms 1up
Europe 3 USA 1

FOURSOMES
Friday Afternoon
Clarke/Bjorn lost to Sutton/Verplank 2 and 1
Garcia/Westwood bt Woods/Calcavecchia 2 and 1
Montgomerie/Langer halved with Mickelson/Toms
Harrington/McGinley lost to Cink/Furyk 3 and 2
Europe 4½ USA 3½

FOURBALLS
Saturday Morning
Fulke/Price lost to Mickelson/Toms 2 and 1
Westwood/Garcia bt Cink/Furyk 2 and 1
Montgomerie/Langer bt Verplank/Hoch 1up
Clarke/Bjorn lost to Woods/Love III 4 and 3
Europe 6½ USA 5½

FOURSOMES
Saturday Afternoon
Fasth/Parnevik lost to Calcavecchia/Duval 1up
Montgomerie/Harrington bt Mickelson/Toms 2 and 1
Garcia/Westwood lost to Woods/Love III 1up
Clarke/McGinley halved with Hoch/Furyk
Europe 8 USA 8

SINGLES
Sunday
Colin Montgomerie bt Scott Hoch 5 and 4
Sergio Garcia lost to David Toms 1up
Darren Clarke halved with David Duval
Bernhard Langer bt Hal Sutton 4 and 3
Padraig Harrington bt Mark Calcavecchia 5 and 4
Thomas Bjorn bt Stewart Cink 2 and 1
Lee Westwood lost to Scott Verplank 2 and 1
Niclas Fasth halved with Paul Azinger
Paul McGinley halved with Jim Furyk
Pierre Fulke halved with Davis Love III
Philip Price bt Phil Mickelson 3 and 2
Jesper Parnevik halved with Tiger Woods

Final Score
Europe 15½ USA 12½

There was good reason, for this title is the oldest, the staunchest of all golfing traditions and the Els are a traditional family. He had come close before, placing second in 1996 and 2000, and third a year earlier. Yet it took an eternity this time, the Claret Jug seemingly locked in a tantalus, while Els wasted every advantage that came his way. Till finally, he found, in the Frenchman Thomas Levet, a man who was as happy as himself to come second in the Open, and he had won. There was a crooked smile from the South African to go with the hop and the thrown hat, but don't expect it next time. As you probably knew all along, Els is not an Ernest at all. That is his middle name, after his grandad. His first name is, in fact, Theodore, and the diminutive for Theodore is Teddy which suits him perfectly. So maybe Neels and Hettie were right all along.

We have left Tiger Woods till late, but sometimes you have to find something different to write about. Had the wind and the rain not taken it upon themselves to shape events on Saturday at Muirfield, we could have even been writing about the first-ever Grand Slam in golfing history, for Woods had two under his belt after his wins at Augusta and Farmingdale and who's to say that with only one to go, sheer intimidation would not have brought about the fourth at Hazeltine.

There's plenty who would be awed in those circumstances, but we doubt that Rich Beem would be one of them. He has been compared to John Daly, who came from nowhere to win the 1991 US PGA. Beem has a similar cavalier approach and admits to enjoying a beer too many, but appears to be more rooted in reality. We hope so, for along with David Duval, who hides an engaging personality behind dark glasses, ranks at the top of our list of favourite Americans.

Amongst the Brits, we should mention Luke Donald, of Beaconsfield, who won his first tournament on the US tour in November at Madison. Already, Donald looks a serious contender for a Major.

"There are 150 people here and nobody saw it, nobody heard it, it wouldn't happen to f**** Tiger Woods"**
Gary Evans after losing his ball in the rough in the Open.

"I can think of a million reasons why"
Tiger Woods on why the American Express championship (worth $1m to the winner) was more important than the Ryder Cup

"Just some days, you're the windshield, some days you're the bug, and of late, I've been the windshield. "
Rich Beem, after winning the US PGA title.

"The money is obviously very wonderful...but forever I'll be known as a former PGA champion and there's not a lot of people that can say that. I'm pretty sure I could sell that to Tom Watson and Arnold Palmer for more than a buck"
Beem again (Watson and Palmer never won the PGA)

The 131st Open Championship

Muirfield   July 18-21

278	**Ernie Els RSA**	70 66 72 70
(-6)	(£700,000)	
	Steve Elkington AUS	71 73 68 66
	Stuart Appleby AUS	73 70 70 65
	Thomas Levet FRA	72 66 74 66
	(£286,666 each)	
	Els won on an extra (5th) play-off hole	
279	Padraig Harrington IRL	69 67 76 67
(-5)	Gary Evans ENG	72 68 74 65
	(£140,000 each)	
280	Sergio Garcia ESP	71 69 71 69
(-4)	Søren Hansen DEN	68 69 73 70
	Peter O'Malley AUS	72 68 75 65
	Scott Hoch USA	74 69 71 66
	Thomas Björn DEN	68 70 73 69
	Retief Goosen RSA	71 68 74 67
	(£77,499 each)	
281	Nick Price ZIM	68 70 75 68
(-3)	Justin Leonard USA	71 72 68 70
	Davis Love III USA	71 72 71 67
	Peter Lonard AUS	72 72 68 69
	(£49,750 each)	
282	Greg Norman AUS	71 72 71 68
(-2)	Scott McCarron USA	71 68 72 71
	Bob Estes USA	71 70 73 68
	Duffy Waldorf USA	67 69 77 69
	(£41,000 each)	
283	Corey Pavin USA	69 70 75 69
(-1)	Mark O'Meara USA	69 69 77 68
	David Duval USA	72 71 70 70
	Toshimitsu Izawa JPN	76 68 72 67
	Justin Rose ENG	68 75 68 72
	Chris Riley USA	70 71 76 66
	(£32,000 each)	
284	Bernhard Langer GER	72 72 71 69
(level)	Des Smyth IRL	68 69 74 73
	Tiger Woods USA	70 68 81 65
	Loren Roberts USA	74 69 70 71
	Jesper Parnevik SWE	72 72 70 70
	Jerry Kelly USA	73 71 70 70
	Pierre Fulke SWE	72 69 78 65
	Bradley Dredge WAL	70 72 74 68
	Niclas Fasth SWE	70 73 71 70
	(£24,000 each)	
285	Ian Woosnam WAL	72 72 73 68
(+1)	Stephen Leaney AUS	71 70 75 69
	Scott Verplank USA	72 68 74 71
	Darren Clarke NIR	72 67 77 69
	Andrew Coltart SCO	71 69 74 71
	Neal Lancaster USA	71 71 76 67
	(£16,916 each)	
286	Trevor Immelman RSA	72 72 71 71
(+2)	Steve Jones USA	68 75 73 70
	Esteban Toledo MEX	73 70 75 68
	Carl Pettersson SWE	67 70 76 73
	(£13,750 each)	
287	Paul Eales ENG	73 71 76 67
(+3)	Rocco Mediate USA	71 72 74 70
	Jeff Maggert USA	71 68 80 68
	(£12,000 each)	
288	Warren Bennett ENG	71 68 82 67
(+4)	Barry Lane ENG	74 68 72 74
	Ian Poulter ENG	69 69 78 72
	Bob Tway USA	70 66 78 74
	Ian Garbutt ENG	69 70 74 75
	Fredrik Andersson SWE	74 70 74 70
	Mikko Ilonen FIN	71 70 77 70
	Shingo Katayama JPN	72 68 74 74
	Craig Perks NZL	72 70 71 75
	(£10,266 each)	
289	Nick Faldo ENG	73 69 76 71
(+5)	Steve Stricker USA	60 70 81 69
	Richard Green AUS	72 72 75 70
	Stewart Cink USA	71 69 80 69
	Joe Durant USA	72 71 73 73
	Paul Lawrie SCO	70 70 78 71
	Kuboya Kenichi JPN	70 73 73 73
	(£9,300 each)	
290	Jarrod Moseley AUS	70 73 75 72
(+6)	Phil Mickelson USA	68 76 76 70
	Chris DiMarco USA	72 69 75 74
	(£8,800 each)	
291	Mike Weir CAN	73 69 74 75
(+7)	Toru Taniguchi JPN	71 73 76 71
	Jim Carter USA	74 70 73 74
	Stephen Ames TRI	68 70 81 72
	Matthew Cort ENG	73 71 78 69
	(£8,516 each)	
292	Sandy Lyle SCO	68 76 73 75
(+8)	Chris Smith USA	74 69 71 78
	(£8,500 each)	
293	Anders Hansen DEN	71 72 79 71
(+9)	Roger Wessels RSA	72 71 73 77
	(£8,500 each)	
294	David Park WAL	73 67 74 80
(+10)	(£8,500)	
295	Mark Calcavecchia USA	74 66 81 74
(+11)	Lee Janzen USA	70 69 84 72
	(£8,500 each)	
297	Colin Montgomerie SCO	74 64 84 75
(+12)	(£8,500)	
298	David Toms USA	67 75 81 75
(+13)	(£8,500)	

The following did not make the cut:
145: Magnus Persson Atlevi SWE 72 73, Eduardo Romero ARG 72 73, Marc Farry FRA 70 75, Jean-Francois Remesy FRA 68 77, Brad Faxon USA 70 75, José Maria Olazábal 73 72, Matt Kuchar USA 75 70, Lee Westwood ENG 72 73, John Bickerton ENG 73 72, Michael Campbell NZL 74 71, Adam Scott AUS 77 68 (£2,954 each); **146:** John Senden AUS 76 70, Choi Kyoung-Ju KOR 73 73, Taichi Teshima JPN 69 77, Craig Parry AUS 72 74, Robert Karlsson SWE 72 74, Billy Mayfair USA 71 75, Alex Cejka GER 73 73, Paul McGinley IRL 72 74, Scott Henderson SCO 78 68, Tom Lehman USA 70 76, Tom Clark RSA 70 76, Tom Whitehouse ENG 75 71, Tim Petrovic USA 73 73 (£2,465 each); **147:** David Howell ENG 73 74,

Raphael Jacquelin FRA 74 73, Tommy Nakajima JPN 75 72, Scott Laycock AUS 73 74, Jim Furyk USA 71 76, Vijay Singh FIJ 72 75, Mathias Grönberg SWE 75 72, Robert Allenby AUS 73 74, Luke Donald ENG 73 74, Simon Young* ENG 76 71 (£2,465 each); **148:** Andrew Oldcorn SCO 79 69, Ian Stanley AUS 76 72, Miguel Angel Jiménez ESP 73 75, Ricardo Gonzalez ARG 76 72, José Coceres ARG 70 78, Greg Owen ENG 76 72, John Kemp* ENG 74 74 (£2,250 each); **149:** Hal Sutton USA 74 75, Phillip Price WAL 75 74, Adam Mednick SWE 75 74, Benn Barham ENG 76 73 (£2,250 each); **150:** Mattias Eliasson SWE 78 72, Darren Fichardt RSA 80 70, Dean Wilson USA 71 79, John Cook USA 74 76, Raymond Russell SCO 71 79, Frank Lickliter USA 74 76, Paul Casey ENG 72 78

(£2,250 each); **151:** Toru Suzuki JPN 79 72, Gary Emerson ENG 75 76, Dudley Hart USA 74 77, Peter Baker ENG 75 76, Fredrik Jacobson SWE 78 73, Patrik Sjöland SWE 75 76, John Daly USA 74 77, Kevin Sutherland USA 73 78 (£2,000 each); **152:** Malcolm McKenzie ENG 76 76, Billy Andrade 77 75, Alejandro Larrazabal ESP 77 75, Angel Cabrera ARG 73 79, John Riegger USA 78 74 (£2,000 each); **155:** Tom Watson USA 77 78, Jamie Spence ENG 77 78 (£2,000 each); **157:** James Kingston RSA 76 81, Paul Mayoh ENG 84 73 (£2,000 each); **159:** Kiyoshi Miyazato JPN (£2,000); **Disqualified:** Roger Chapman ENG 74, Jonathan Kaye USA 74 (£2,000 each) **Withdrawn:** Thongchai Jaidee THA (£2,000) * *Denotes amateur*

Open Championships don't come much closer than this. At the end of the regular competition (as the Americans would doubtless call it) there were four men tied for the lead, three men one shot behind them, and a further six players two shots back. In all, there were 27 players within six shots of the leaders, including such unlikely candidates as Gary Evans and Greg Norman (sorry, Greg), but not including Tiger Woods. Muirfield taught golf how to dispose of Woods; invoke the Gods. After two days of golf, Woods was doing a passable impression of a golfer on the way to a Grand Slam, the Grand Slam. On Saturday, with rain lashing the course and the wind cracking its cheeks, Woods would have been hard pressed to give Bruce Forsyth a game. It was a seminal moment in the golfing career of young Woods, being just about the only examination that he has so far failed. It took the 26-year-old 81 shots, the worst round of his professional career. Given it probably won't ever happen again, we should record every gory detail...

Out: 5(+1), 4, 4, 4(+1), 7(+2), 5(+1), 3, 5(+1), 5   =42 (+6)
In: 5(+1), 4, 5(+1), 5(+2), 5(+1), 4, 3, 4(-1), 4   =39 (+4)

As you can see, there were two double-bogeys, seven bogeys, eight pars, and glory-be a birdie. As disastrous as his round was, however, Woods was still not as bad as Lee Janzen or Colin Montgomerie who, in the face of the same storm, struck 84 shots. No one seemed to mention how Janzen felt, but Montgomerie did go on the record, or rather off it, as he refused to wait for the world's media to finish with Woods and went off in a strop, or not a strop, depending on whether you believe Mrs Doubtfire, as the Americans call him, or not. Meanwhile Els, who had looked a likely winner on day three, looked less likely on day four as the two Australians Stuart Appleby and Steve Elkington, and the Frenchman Thomas Levet all raised their games. In fact, an astonishing 34 players bettered Els score in the final round, but none of them won. Having conceded every inch of ground gained in three rounds, the South African must have grown his finger nails for the last round, so stubbornly did he cling to the rock. Four went into the four-hole play-off and Els needed a birdie to win on the last. He missed and it was down to two, with Levet's bogey on the same hole equally costly. That Els finally won was due to a sweet sand shot on the extra hole. Relief all round.

US Masters

Augusta National Course, Georgia   Apr 11-14
US unless stated

276	**Tiger Woods**	**70 69 66 71**	
(-12)	($1,008,000)		
279	Retief Goosen RSA	69 67 69 74	
(-9)	($604,800)		
280	Phil Mickelson	69 72 68 71	
(-8)	($380,800)		
281	José Maria Olazábal ESP	70 69 71 71	
(-7)	($268,800)		
282	Padraig Harrington IRL	69 70 72 71	
(-6)	Ernie Els RSA	70 67 72 73	
	($212,800)		
283	Vijay Singh FIJ	70 65 72 76	
(-5)	($187,600)		
284	Sergio Garcia ESP	68 71 70 75	
(-4)	($173,600)		
285	Miguel Angel Jiménez ESP	70 71 74 70	
(-3)	Angel Cabrera ARG	68 71 73 73	
	Adam Scott AUS	71 72 72 70	
	($151,200)		
286	Brad Faxon	71 75 69 71	
(-2)	Chris Dimarco	70 71 72 73	
	($123,200)		
287	Nick Faldo ENG	75 67 73 72	
(-1)	Shigeki Maruyama JPN	75 72 73 67	
	Colin Montgomerie SCO	75 71 70 71	
	Davis Love III	67 75 74 71	
	Thomas Björn DEN	74 67 70 76	
	($98,000)		
288	Paul McGinley IRL	72 74 71 71	
(level)	($81,200)		
289	Nick Price ZIM	70 76 70 73	
(+1)	Justin Leonard	70 75 74 70	
	Jerry Kelly	72 74 71 72	
	Darren Clarke NIR	70 74 73 72	
	($65,240)		
290	Jeff Sluman	73 72 71 74	
(+2)	Stewart Cink	74 70 72 74	
	Mike Weir CAN	72 71 71 76	
	Mark Brooks	74 72 71 73	
	Tom Pernice	74 72 71 73	
	($46,480)		
291	Jesper Parnevik SWE	70 72 77 72	
(+3)	Robert Allenby AUS	73 70 76 72	
	Charles Howell III	74 73 71 73	
	($38,080)		
292	Bernard Langer GER	73 72 73 74	
(+4)	Craig Stadler	73 72 76 71	
	Billy Mayfair	74 71 72 75	
	John Daly	74 73 70 75	
	($32,410)		
294	Greg Norman AUS	71 76 72 75	
(+6)	Fred Couples	73 73 76 72	
	Rocco Mediate	75 68 77 74	
	David Toms	73 74 76 71	
	($26,950)		
295	Tom Watson	71 76 76 72	
(+7)	Steve Lowery	75 71 76 73	
	Kirk Triplett	74 70 74 77	
	($22,960)		
296	Scott Verplank	70 75 76 75	
(+8)	($20,720)		
297	Lee Westwood ENG	75 72 74 76	
(+9)	($19,600)		
298	Bob Estes	73 72 75 78	
(+10)	($18,480)		

The following did not make the cut:
148: David Duval 74 74, Scott McCarron 75 73, Larry Mize 74 74, Michael Hoey* NIR 75 73, Joe Durant 74 74, Paul Azinger 75 73, Tom Lehman 76 72, Michael Campbell NZL 74 74, Kevin Sutherland 78 70, Rory Sabbatini RSA 73 75; **149:** Mark O'Meara 78 71, Toshimitsu Izawa JPN 73 76, Mark Calcavecchia 79 70, Paul Lawrie SCO 75 74, Lee Janzen 74 75; **150:** Tom Kite 77 73, Jim Furyk 73 77, Billy Andrade 75 75, Matt Kuchar 73 77, Toru Taniguchi JPN 80 70, Kenny Perry 76 784, Shingo Katayama JPN 78 72, Bubba Dickerson* 79 71; **151:** Steve Stricker 75 76, Scott Hoch 76 75, Niclas Fasth SWE 76 75; **152:** Fuzzy Zoeller 75 77, Craig Perks NZL 81 71; **153:** Raymond Floyd 79 74, José Coceres ARG 74 79; **154:** Sandy Lyle SCO 73 81, Robert Hamilton* 77 77, Tim Jackson* 76 78; **155:** Ian Woosnam WAL 77 78; **156:** Seve Ballesteros ESP 75 81; **157:** Tommy Aaron 79 78; **158:** Gary Player RSA 80 78, Ben Crenshaw 81 77; **159:** Stuart Appleby AUS 80 79; **160:** Chez Reavie* 74 86; **166:** Charles Coody 82 84; **174:** Arnold Palmer 89 85
* Denotes Amateur

Not until the last hole on the third day did Tiger Woods take a share of the lead; this was restraint of the highest order. Until that moment, the South African Retief Goosen held mastery, and apparently his nerve too. Appearances, though, can be mightily deceptive. After leading for the best part of two days, a night of dwelling on possibilities proved too much for Goosen and a three-putt at the first on the final afternoon handed his playing partner the lead. Thereafter Woods could rely as much on the errors made by the posse chasing him, as much as by his own remarkable talent. Goosen conceded first, his lapses costly enough to leave him five shots adrift of Woods by the 13th hole. Goosen recovered his poise and some ground over the final holes, but you don't claw back Woods at Augusta. Ernie Els flattered, but only to deceive, finding water instead of grass twice on the same hole, the reconstructed 13th. "I got greedy. I had been telling myself all week not to get greedy and I did just that," said a disconsolate Els, who ended with an eight for the hole. Vijay Singh dropped his into the water around the same green, but recovered with a chip and a putt to make par. The Fijian's nemesis was at the 15th where he chalked up a nine, more than enough to discount his chances of a third Masters title. Who did score well on the final round? Well, not many. Shigeki Maruyama took just 67 shots, but the Japanese golfer was the only player to duck under 70. José Maria Olazábal managed a steady 71 to finish third, the two-time champion being the first European home, one shot ahead of Ireland's Padraig Harrington. The stage, though, belonged to Woods who, while in no way matching the cavalier style of his first Masters victory in 1997 (a walloping 12-stroke win), still recorded yet another benchmark in a what is already a prodigiuous career, as he became only the third man ever to retain a Masters title, after Jack Nicklaus and Nick Faldo. Furthermore, Woods took his record in Majors to six wins in his last 10 events.

Most Majors

1	**Jack Nicklaus USA**	18
	Openx3, Mastersx6, USOpenx4, USPGAx5	
2	**Walter Hagen USA**	11
	Openx4, USOpenx2, USPGAx5	
3	**Ben Hogan USA**	9
	Openx1, Mastersx2, USOpenx4, USPGAx2	
3	**Gary Player RSA**	9
	Openx3, Mastersx3, USOpenx1, USPGAx2	
5	**Tom Watson USA**	8
	Openx5, Mastersx2, USOpenx1	
5	**Tiger Woods USA**	8
	Openx1, Mastersx3, USOpenx2, USPGAx2	
7	**Robert Tyre (Bobby) Jones* USA**	7
	Openx3, USOpenx4	
7	**Arnold Palmer USA**	7
	Openx2, Mastersx4, USOpenx1	
7	**Gene Sarazen USA**	7
	Openx1, Mastersx1, USOpenx2, USPGAx3	
7	**Sam Snead USA**	7
	Openx1, Mastersx3, USPGAx3	
7	**Harry Vardon ENG**	7
	Openx6, USOpenx1	
12	**Nick Faldo ENG**	6
	Openx3, Mastersx3	
12	**Lee Trevino USA**	6
	Openx2, USOpenx2, USPGAx2	

*amateur

US Open

Bethpage State Park (The Black Course), Farmingdale, New York state   *June 13-16*
US unless stated

277	**Tiger Woods**	**67 68 70 72**	
(-3)	($1,000,000)		
280	Phil Mickelson	70 73 67 70	
(level)	($585,000)		
282	Jeff Maggert	69 73 68 72	
(+2)	($362,356)		
283	Sergio Garcia ESP	68 74 67 74	
(+3)	($252,546)		
285	Nick Faldo ENG	70 76 66 73	
(+5)	Scott Hoch	71 75 70 69	
	Billy Mayfair	69 74 68 74	
	($182,882 each)		
286	Tom Byrum	72 72 70 72	
(+6)	Padraig Harrington IRL	70 68 73 75	
	Nick Price ZIM	72 75 69 70	
	($138,669 each)		
287	Peter Lonard AUS	73 74 73 67	
(+7)	($119,357)		
288	Robert Allenby AUS	74 70 67 77	
(+8)	Justin Leonard	73 71 68 76	
	Jay Haas	73 73 70 72	
	Dudley Hart	69 76 70 73	
	($102,338 each)		
289	Shigeki Maruyama JPN	76 67 73 73	
(+9)	Steve Stricker	72 77 69 71	
	($86,372 each)		
290	Luke Donald ENG	76 72 70 72	
(+10)	Steve Flesch	72 72 75 71	
	Charles Howell III	71 74 70 75	
	Thomas Levet	71 77 70 72	
	Mark O'Meara	76 70 69 75	
	Craig Stadler	74 72 70 74	
	($68,995 each)		
291	Jim Carter	77 73 70 71	
(+11)	Darren Clarke NIR	74 74 72 71	
	Chris DiMarco	74 74 72 71	
	Ernie Els RSA	73 74 70 74	
	Davis Love III	71 71 72 77	
	Jeff Sluman	73 73 72 73	
	($47,439 each)		
292	Jason Caron	75 72 72 73	
(+12)	K.J. Choi KOR	69 73 73 77	
	Paul Lawrie SCO	73 73 73 73	
	Scott McCarron	72 72 70 78	
	Vijay Singh FIJ	75 75 67 75	
	($35,639 each)		
293	Shingo Katayama JPN	74 72 74 73	
(+13)	Bernhard Langer GER	72 76 70 75	
	($31,945 each)		
294	Stuart Appleby AUS	77 73 75 69	
(+14)	Thomas Bjorn DEN	71 79 73 71	
	Niclas Fasth SWE	72 72 74 76	
	Donnie Hammond	73 77 71 73	
	Franklin Langham	70 76 74 74	
	Rocco Mediate	72 72 74 76	
	Kevin Sutherland	74 75 70 75	
	Hidemichi Tanaka JPN	73 73 72 76	
	($26,783 each)		

295	Tom Lehman	71 76 72 76
(+15)	David Toms	74 74 70 77
	Frank Lickliter II	74 76 68 77
	Kenny Perry	74 76 71 74
	Jean Van de Velde FRA	71 75 74 75
	($20,072 each)	
296	Craig Bowden	71 77 74 74
(+16)	Tim Herron	75 74 73 74
	Robert Karlsson SWE	71 77 72 76
	Jose Maria Olazabal ESP	71 77 75 73
	($16,294 each)	
297	Harrison Frazar	74 73 75 75
(+17)	Ian Leggatt	72 77 72 76
	Jesper Parnevik SWE	72 76 69 80
	Corey Pavin	74 75 70 78
	($14,764 each)	
298	Brad Lardon	73 73 74 78
(+18)	($13,988)	
299	John Maginnes	79 69 73 78
(+19)	Greg Norman AUS	75 73 74 77
	Bob Tway	72 78 73 76
	($13,493 each)	
300	Andy Miller	76 74 75 75
(+20)	Jeev Milkha Singh	75 75 75 75
	Paul Stankowski	72 77 77 74
	($12,794 each)	
301	Spike McRoy	75 75 74 77
(+21)	($12,340)	
302	Angel Cabrera ARG	73 73 79 77
(+22)	Brad Faxon	75 74 73 80
	($12,000 each)	
303	Kent Jones	76 74 74 79
(+23)	Len Mattiace	72 73 78 80
	($11,546 each)	
304	John Daly	74 76 81 73
(+24)	Tom Gillis	71 76 78 79
	($11,083 each)	
307	Kevin Warwick	73 76 84 74
(+27)		

The cheers which greeted Tiger Woods and Sergio Garcia as they stood on the first tee for the final round may have had more to do with relief than anything else. They had a contest at last, albeit not as dramatic as the crowd made it sound. Woods started the last day four strokes clear of the Spaniard, who had never before started a Major in the final group. But a day earlier, Woods had already secured a cushion of three shots and apparently was cantering towards yet another Major - his eleventh. Garcia's third-round 67 had a symbolic value; that the rest of the golfing world was not giving up without a fight. How long did the fight last, exactly? Two holes, or thereabouts, Woods surprisingly three-putting on both of them. Woods pulled himself together (doesn't he always) and it was Garcia's turn to wobble on the third, when he missed a six-foot putt. He couldn't find the green on the seventh either, and at the turn the exhuberant shouts at the first tee were just a faint and distant memory, for the contest was over. Garcia still held on to fourth place, for his best result in a Major since he lost by a single shot to Woods in the 1999 US PGA, but the one-time prodigy no longer looks so prodigious. Phil Mickelson stayed on to take second; and it almost goes without saying that he would. Since the Californian turned professional in 1992, he has registered 16 top-10 finishes in Majors, seven times placing second or third, and it was still only his 32nd birthday he was celebrating on the final day at Farmingdale. He has, therefore, plenty of time to collect his first win in a Major, but weren't we saying that about Colin Montgomerie only the other day, and no one says it any more about the Scot. Jeff Maggert was third and Garcia was the first European home. Only just behind him was the first Briton, Nick Faldo, whose fifth place was the Englishman's best finish in a Major since he placed fourth in the 1996 Open Championship. Faldo was not quite the model of consistency he once was, his third round 66 was 10 shots better than his second round, but his performance will surely foster hopes that he can emulate Jack Nicklaus and win a Major after his 45th birthday (Nicklaus was 46 when he won the Masters in 1986, Faldo was 45 in July 2002). British golfers generally under-perform in the US Open, Tony Jacklin's win in 1970 is still the only one in the record books, but there was cause for optimism in the show of Luke Donald who, after a disappointing opening round of 76, strung together three decent rounds (72-20-72) for a final placing of 18th.

US PGA Championship

Hazeltine National GC, Chaska, Minnesota   Aug 15-18
Par 70

USA unless stated

278	**Rich Beem**	72 66 72 68			
(-10)	($990,000)				
279	Tiger Woods	71 69 72 67			
(-9)	($594,000)				
283	Chris Riley	71 70 72 70			
(-5)	($374,000)				
284	Fred Funk	68 70 73 73			
(-4)	Justin Leonard	72 66 69 77			
	($235,000)				
285	Rocco Mediate	72 73 70 70			
(-3)	($185,000)				
286	Mark Calcavecchia	70 68 74 74			
(-2)	($172,000)				
287	Vijay Singh FIJ	71 74 74 68			
(-1)	($159,000)				
288	Jim Furyk	68 73 76 71			
(level)	($149,000)				
289	Robert Allenby AUS	76 66 77 70			
(+1)	Stewart Cink	74 74 72 69			
	Jose Coceres ARG	72 71 72 74			
	Pierre Fulke SWE	72 68 78 71			
	Sergio Garcia ESP	75 73 73 68			
	Ricardo Gonzalez ARG	74 73 71 71			
	Steve Lowery	71 71 73 74			
	($110,714 each)				
290	Stuart Appleby AUS	73 74 74 69			
(+2)	Steve Flesch	72 74 73 71			
	Padraig Harrington IRL	71 73 74 72			
	Charles Howell III	72 69 80 69			
	Peter Lonard AUS	69 73 75 73			
	($72,000 each)				
291	Heath Slocum	73 74 75 69			
(+3)	($57,000)				
292	Michael Campbell NZL	73 70 77 72			
(+4)	Retief Goosen RSA	69 69 79 75			
	Bernhard Langer GER	70 72 77 73			
	Justin Rose ENG	69 73 76 74			
	Adam Scott AUS	71 71 76 74			
	Jeff Sluman	70 75 74 73			
	($44,250)				
293	Brad Faxon	74 72 75 72			
(+5)	Tom Lehman	71 72 77 73			
	Craig Perks NZL	72 76 74 71			
	Kenny Perry	73 68 78 74			
	Kirk Triplett	75 69 79 70			
	($33,500 each)				
294	David Duval	71 77 76 70			
(+6)	Ernie Els RSA	72 71 75 76			
	Neal Lancaster	72 73 75 74			
	Phil Mickelson	76 72 78 68			
	Mike Weir CAN	73 74 77 70			
	($26,300 each)				
295	Chris DiMarco	76 69 77 73			
(+7)	Joel Edwards	73 74 77 71			
	John Huston	74 74 75 72			
	Scott McCarron	73 71 79 72			
	($21,500)				
296	Briny Baird	79 69 73 75			
(+8)	Søren Hansen DEN	73 69 78 76			

	Shigeki Maruyama JPN	76 72 75 73	
	Loren Roberts	77 70 77 72	
	Kevin Sutherland	72 75 71 78	
	($17,000 each)		
297	Angel Cabrera ARG	71 73 77 76	
(+9)	Steve Elkington AUS	72 75 76 74	
	Davis Love III	70 75 76 76	
	Len Mattiace	74 73 76 74	
	Tom Watson	76 71 83 67	
298	Cameron Beckman	74 71 75 78	
(+10)	Tim Clark RSA	72 74 76 76	
	Brian Gay	73 74 78 73	
	Toshimitsu Izawa JPN	72 73 75 78	
	Lee Janzen	70 76 77 75	
	Greg Norman AUS	71 74 73 80	
	Chris Smith	75 73 72 78	
	($11,742 each)		
299	Joe Durant	74 71 79 75	
(+11)	Nick Faldo ENG	71 76 74 78	
	Hal Sutton	73 73 75 78	
	($11,200 each)		
301	JJ Henry	78 70 77 76	
(+13)	($11,000)		
302	Don Berry	76 71 80 75	
(+14)	Matt Gogel	74 73 83 72	
	JP Hayes	73 75 78 76	
	Joey Sindelar	77 71 78 76	
	($10,750 each)		
304	Dave Tentis	76 72 78 78	
(+16)	($10,500)		
305	José Maria Olazábal ESP	73 75 77 80	
(+17)	($10,400)		
309	Pat Perez	77 71 85 76	
(+21)	($10,300)		
310	Thomas Levet FRA	78 70 82 80	
(+22)	($10,200)		

The following did not make the cut ($2,000 each)
149: Ian Leggett CAN 75 74, Nick Price ZIM 72 77, Fuzzy Zoeller USA 76 73, Choi Kyoung-Ju KOR 78 71, Scott Verplank USA 77 72, Larry Nelson 76 73, Darren Clarke NIR 79 70, Thomas Björn DEN 74 75, Paul Lawrie SCO 75 74, Greg Owen ENG 76 73, JL Lewis 76 73
150: Eduardo Romero ARG 73 77, Ian Woosnam WAL 77 73, Jerry Kelly USA 77 73, Bob Tway 74 76, Skip Kendall 74 76, Dean Wilson 74 76, Paul Azinger 76 74, Jay Haas 77 73, Duffy Waldorf 77 73, Spike McRoy 74 76, Chad Campbell 74 76, David Gossett 72 78, Jonathan Kaye 77 73, Sean Farren 74 76, John Rollins 77 73;
151: Mark O'Meara 75 76, Tim Herron 76 75, Taichi Teshima JPN 77 74, John Cook 75 76, David Toms 77 74;
152: Rick Hartmann 79 73, Bruce Zabriski 75 77, Steve Stricker 74 78, Anders Hansen DEN 79 73, Colin Montgomerie SCO 74 78, Billy Andrade 75 77, Matt Kuchar 78 74, Toru Taniguchi JPN 75 77, Craig Parry AUS 75 77, Robert Gamez 76 76, Shingo Katayama JPN 74 78, James Blair III 74 78, Carl Pettersson SWE 77 75, Caul Paulson 73 79;

153: Billy Mayfair 77 76, Peter O'Malley AUS 79 74, Paul McGinley IRL 74 79, John Daly 77 76, Frank Lickliter 77 76, Tim Thelen 75 78, Rob Labritz 78 75;
154: Mark Brooks 75 79, Mike Gilmore 78 76;
155: Jesper Parnevik SWE 82 73, Scott Hoch 80 75, Jeff Maggert 78 77, David Peoples 79 76, Robert Thompson 78 77;
156: Scott Laycock AUS 80 76, Niclas Fasth SWE 79 77, Jeffrey Lankford 80 76, Barry Evans 80 76, Joe Klinchock 79 77;
157: Curtis Strange 81 76, Dudley Hart 82 75, Bob Estes 81 76, Jim Carter 74 83, Craig Stevens 82 75;

158: Lee Westwood ENG 75 83, Tim Fleming 77 81;
159: Phillip Price WAL 76 83, Paul Casey ENG 85 74, Buddy Harston 76 83, Alan Morin 82 77, Tim Weinhart 77 82;
160: Wayne Defrancesco 78 82;
162: Steve Schneiter 86 76;
166: Barry Mahlberg 80 86;
167: Kim Thompson 87 80, Kent Stauffer 87 80;
179: Tom Dolby 85 94

Withdrawn: Stephen Ames TRI 73 74

Hazeltine was the first time that Tiger Woods finished second in a Major; and if that was not enough of a surprise, the name of the winner was. Not even aficionados knew much about Rich Beem, except that, according to the event records he had played in the US PGA once before and had finished 70th. Beem had quit the game in 1995 and earned his living for a year or more selling mobile phones and car stereos for a company called Magnolia Hi-Fi in Bellevue, Seattle. His interest in the sport was re-awakened in 1998 and a year later he joined the PGA Tour. Until Hazeltine, though, Beem's fame had largely been defined by innumerable references in a book devoted to the hedonistic lifestyle of a number of US golfers called "Blood, Sweat and Tees". In the wake of Beem's success, the book shot to number six in the US best-seller list, but the golfer did not profit from the sales. "I didn't even get a free book," he said bitterly. He did get $990,000 though for holding off the charge of the finest golfer in the world to win the PGA title. To start from the end; Wood's charge over the final holes was wondrous, the winner of eight Majors and seeking a ninth, made birdies at each of the final four holes. For most other golfers (including the hundred or so ranked above Beem at the time) such a flourish from Woods would have been enough. Pure unadulterated intimidation. But if the leaderboard got to Beem, he didn't show it. A sensational birdie at the 16th helped to give the former stereo salesman a cushion of three putts at the eighteenth. Beem took two of them, but didn't need the third. Beem was the champion, but a most disarmingly modest one. "I don't discount the fact that I can play with these guys, but to win a major is something special and I don't know if I have it," he had said before the event. Beem was not alone in that belief; when the screw turns in the Majors previous experience is invaluable, but the 31-year-old was only playing in his fourth Major and never had he been close to the high points of the leaderboard in any of them. At Hazeltine, a level-par opener of 72 was followed by an inspired 66, with Beem clattering the balls off the tees and a putt barely missed. Par on the third day, left him two shots down on Jason Leonard, who once won a British Open and was due, perhaps, a PGA title, but not this time. When it came to the final-day hothouse, Leonard crumpled and Beem did not. They are probably still partying in El Paso. You need to go hunting to find the first British finisher. It was Justin Rose who was 14 shots adrift of Beems; or out of sight. it wasn't a bad result for Rose, but it was for British golf.

World Ranking

as at December 4

	Player	Ctry	Average		Player	Ctry	Average
1	Tiger Woods	USA	15.72	51	Len Mattiace	USA	2.26
2	Phil Mickelson	USA	7.72	52	John Cook	USA	2.23
3	Ernie Els	RSA	6.84	53	Loren Roberts	USA	2.17
4	Sergio Garcia	ESP	6.19	54	Tom Lehman	USA	2.14
5	Retief Goosen	RSA	6.16	55	Alex Cejka	GER	2.10
6	David Toms	USA	6.02	56	Dean Wilson	USA	2.05
7	Padraig Harrington	IRL	5.63	57	Mark Calcavecchia	USA	2.05
8	Vijay Singh	FIJ	5.53	58	Tim Clark	RSA	2.05
9	Davis Love III	USA	4.82	59	Jonathan Byrd	USA	1.96
10	Colin Montgomerie	SCO	4.39	60	Anders Hansen	DEN	1.96
11	Jim Furyk	USA	4.18	61	Stephen Leaney	AUS	1.94
12	Chris DiMarco	USA	4.18	62	José Coceres	ARG	1.94
13	Nick Price	ZIM	4.14	63	Bradley Dredge	WAL	1.93
14	Angel Cabrera	ARG	3.70	63	John Rollins	USA	1.93
15	David Duval	USA	3.68	65	Robert Karlsson	SWE	1.93
16	Bernhard Langer	GER	3.58	66	Nick Faldo	ENG	1.91
17	Justin Leonard	USA	3.51	67	Kevin Sutherland	USA	1.89
18	Michael Campbell	NZL	3.48	68	Paul Azinger	USA	1.86
19	Eduardo Romero	ARG	3.47	69	Dudley Hart	USA	1.85
20	Charles Howell III	USA	3.46	70	John Huston	USA	1.84
21	Rich Beem	USA	3.42	71	Tsuneyuki Nakajima	JPN	1.83
22	Scott Hoch	USA	3.40	72	Stewart Cink	USA	1.80
23	Darren Clarke	NIR	3.38	73	Phil Tataurangi	NZL	1.79
24	Bob Estes	USA	3.35	74	Billy Andrade	USA	1.79
25	Robert Allenby	AUS	3.33	75	Ricardo Gonzalez	ARG	1.78
26	Rocco Mediate	USA	3.30	76	Peter O'Malley	AUS	1.78
27	Jerry Kelly	USA	3.20	77	Ian Poulter	ENG	1.77
28	Kenny Perry	USA	3.11	78	Steve Elkington	AUS	1.77
29	Shigeki Maruyama	JPN	3.03	79	Thomas Levet	FRA	1.70
30	Scott McCarron	USA	2.81	80	David Smail	NZL	1.70
31	Craig Parry	AUS	2.79	81	Jesper Parnevik	SWE	1.69
32	Stuart Appleby	AUS	2.74	82	Ian Woosnam	WAL	1.96
33	Scott Verplank	USA	2.73	83	Fredrik Jacobson	SWE	1.69
34	Fred Funk	USA	2.73	84	Chris Smith	USA	1.66
35	Thomas Bjorn	DEN	2.70	85	Matt Kuchar	USA	1.66
36	Steve Lowery	USA	2.66	86	Pat Perez	USA	1.64
37	Justin Rose	ENG	2.65	87	Kirk Triplett	USA	1.63
38	José Maria Olazábal	ESP	2.62	88	Billy Mayfair	USA	1.62
39	Niclas Fasth	SWE	2.61	89	Bob Tway	USA	1.60
40	Adam Scott	AUS	2.58	90	Steve Flesch	USA	1.60
41	Choi Kyoung-Ju	KOR	2.57	91	Rory Sabbatini	RSA	1.59
42	Paul Lawrie	SCO	2.57	92	John Daly	USA	1.54
43	Peter Lonard	AUS	2.52	93	Steve Stricker	USA	1.54
44	Chris Riley	USA	2.51	94	Luke Donald	ENG	1.53
45	Jeff Sluman	USA	2.51	95	Bob Burns	USA	1.53
46	Shingo Katayama	JPN	2.49	96	Soren Hansen	DEN	1.53
47	Mike Weir	CAN	2.47	97	Craig Perks	NZL	1.50
48	Brad Faxon	USA	2.44	98	Scott Laycock	AUS	1.49
49	Toshimitsu Izawa	JPN	2.38	99	Matt Gogel	USA	1.49
50	Toru Taniguchi	JPN	2.38	100	Paul McGinley	IRL	1.49

Averages are shown to two decimal places, where necessary they have been taken to further decimal places to determine final rankings.

European Tour

Date	Tournament	Venue	Winner	Score	1st Prize Euros	Runner(s)-up	Margin
Jan 10 13	Bell's South African Open	The Country Club Durban	**Tim Clark** RSA	269 (-19)	128,052	Steve Webster ENG	2 shots
Jan 17 20	South African PGA	Houghton GC Johannesburg	**Justin Rose** ENG	268 (-20)	128,173	Goosen, Maritz RSA Foster ENG	2 shots
Jan 25 28	Johnnie Walker Classic	Lake Karrinyup Perth, Australia	**Retief Goosen** RSA	274 (-14)	243,640	Pierre Fulke SWE	8 shots
Jan 31 Feb 3	Heineken Classic	Royal Melbourne Victoria	**Ernie Els** RSA	271 (-17)	221,385	Fowler, O'Malley AUS Howell ENG	5 shots
Feb 7 10	ANZ Championship	The Lakes GC Sydney	**Richard S Johnson** AUS	46pts	195,079	Scott Laycock AUS Craig Parry AUS	44pts
Feb 20 24	WGC-Accenture Match Play	La Costa Resort Carlsbad, CAL	**Kevin Sutherland** USA		1,145,476	Scott McCarron USA	1 hole
Feb 21 Feb 24	Caltex Singapore Masters	Laguna National GC Singapore	**Arjun Atwal** IND	274 (-14)	171,855	Richard Green AUS	5 shots
Feb 28 Mar 3	Carlsberg Malaysian Open	Royal Selangor GC Kuala Lumpur	**Alastair Forsyth** SCO	267 (-17)	184,366	Stephen Leaney AUS	play -off
Mar 7 10	Dubai Desert Classic	Emirates GC Dubai	**Ernie Els** RSA	272 (-16)	273,335	Niclas Fasth SWE	4 shots
Mar 14 17	Qatar Masters	Doha GC Qatar	**Adam Scott** AUS	269 (-19)	285,650	Jean-François Remesy FRA	6 shots
Mar 21 24	Madeira Island Open	Santo da Serra, Portugal	**Diego Borrego** ESP	281 (-7)	91,660	Ivo Giner ESP 1 shot Maarten Lafeber NED	
Apr 4 7	Algarve Open de Portugal	Val do Lobo	**Carl Petterson** SWE	142 (-2)	125,000	David Gilford ENG	play -off
Apr 11 14	US Masters	Augusta National Georgia, USA	**Tiger Woods** USA	276 (-16)	1,144,807	Retief Goosen RSA	3 shots
Apr 19 21	The Seve Trophy	Druids Glen Wicklow, Ireland	**GB & Ireland** 10-man team	14½ - 11½	150,000 per player	Continental Europe	
Apr 25 28	Canarias Open de Espana	El Cortijo Gran Canaria	**Sergio Garcia** ESP	275 (-13)	287,000	Emanuele Canonica ITA	4 shots
May 2 5	Novotel Perrier Open de France	Le Golf National Paris	**Malcolm MacKenzie** ENG	274 (-14)	333,330	Trevor Immelman RSA	1 shot
May 9 12	International Open	The De Vere Belfry Sutton Coldfield	**Angel Cabrera** ARG	278 (-10)	294,356	Barry Lane ENG	1 shot
May 17 20	Deutsche Bk Open TPC of Europe	St Leon-Rot Heidelberg	**Tiger Woods** USA	268 (-20)	450,000	Colin Montgomerie SCO	play-off
May 23 26	Volvo PGA Championship	The Wentworth Club, Surrey	**Anders Hansen** DEN	269 (-19)	528,708	Eduardo Romero Colin Montgomerie	5
May 30 June 2	Victor Chandler British Masters	Woburn, Milton Keynes	**Justin Rose** ENG	269 (-19)	329,373	Ian Poulter ENG	1
June 6 9	The Compass English Open	Marriott Forest of Arden, Warwicks	**Darren Clarke** NIR	271 (-17)	208,797	Søren Hansen DEN	3
June 13 16	US Open	Southern Hills CC Tulsa, Oklahoma	**Tiger Woods** USA	277 (-3)	1,058,313	Phil Mickelson USA	3
June 20 23	The Great North Open	De Vere Slaley Hall Northumberland	**Miles Tunnicliff** ENG	279 (-9)	155,960	Sven Strüver GER	4
June 28 July 1	Murphy's Irish Open	Fota Island, Cork	**Søren Hansen** DEN	270 (-14)	266,660	Fichardt RSA play-off Bland ENG, Fasth SWE	

Date	Event	Venue	Winner	Score	Prize	Runner(s)-up	
July 4 7	Smurfit European Open	The K Club Dublin	**Michael Campbell** NZL	282 (-6)	515,584	Harrington, Lawrie Dredge, Goosen	1
July 11 14	Barclays Scottish Open	Loch Lomond Glasgow	**Eduardo Romero** ARG	273 (-11)	573,016	Fredrik Jacobson SWE	play -off
July 18 21	**The 130th Open Golf Championship**	Muirfield East Lothian	**Ernie Els** RSA	278 (-6)	1,095,154 (£700,000)	Steve Elkington Stuart Appleby	play -off
July 25 28	TNT Dutch Open	Hilversumsche GC, Hilversum	**Tobias Dier** GER	263 (-17)	300,000	Jamie Spence ENG	1
Aug 1 4	Volvo Scandinavian Masters	Kungsängen, Stockholm	**Graeme McDowell** NIR	270 (-14)	316,660	Trevor Immelman RSA	1
Aug 8 11	The Celtic Manor Resort Wales Open	The Celtic Manor Resort, Newport	**Paul Lawrie** SCO	272 (-16)	291,432	John Bickerton ENG	5
Aug 15 18	**US PGA Championship**	Hazeltine National Chaska, Minnesota	**Rich Beem** USA	265 (-15)	1,019,144	Tiger Woods USA	1
Aug 15 18	North West of Ireland Open	Ballyliffin GC Co Donegal	**Adam Mednick** SWE	281 (-7)	58,330	Andrew Coltart Constatino Rocca	1
Aug 22 25	WGC-NEC Invitational	Salahee GC Redmond, Wash.	**Craig Parry** AUS	268 (-16)	1,016,673	Fred Funk USA Robert Allenby AUS	4
Aug 22 25	Diageo Scottish PGA Championships	Gleneagles Hotel	**Adam Scott** AUS	262 (-26)	260,461	Raymond Russell SCO	10
Aug 29 Sep 1	BMW International Open	Golfclub Munchen Nord-Eichenried	**Thomas Björn** DEN	264 (-24)	300,000	Berhard Langer John Bickerton	1
Sep 5 8	Omega European Masters	Crans-sur-Sierre Switzerland	**Robert Karlsson** SWE	270 (-14)	250,000	Paul Lawrie SCO Trevor Immelman RSA	4
Sep 12 15	Linde German Masters	Gut Larchenhof Cologne	**Stephen Leaney** AUS	266 (-22)	500,000	Alex Cejka GER	1
Sep 19 22	WGC-American Express Champs	Mount Juliet Kilkenny, Ireland	**Tiger Woods** USA	263 (-25)	1,026,378	Retief Goosen RSA	1
Sep 27 29	**Ryder Cup**	The De Vere Belfry Sutton Coldfield	**Europe beat USA** 15½ - 12½				
Oct 3 6	Links Championship	St Andrews Kingbarns	**Padraig Harrington** IRL	269 (-19)	818,662	Eduardo Romero ARG	play -off
Oct 10 13	Trophee Lancombe	Saint-Nom-La-Breteche, Paris	**Alex Cejka** GER	272 (-12)	239,640	Carlos Rodiles ESP	2
Oct 17 20	Cisco World Match Play Championship*	Wentworth Club, Surrey	**Ernie Els** RSA		395,907	Sergio Garcia ESP	2 & 1 in final
Oct 24 27	Telefonica Open de Madrid	Club de Campo, Madrid	**Steen Tinning** DEN	265 (-19)	233,330	Brian Davis Coltart, Adam Scott	1
Oct 31 Nov 3	Italian Open	Olgiata, Rome	**Ian Poulter** ENG	197 (-19)	183,330	Paul Lawrie SCO	2
Nov 7 10	Volvo Masters	Montecastillo GC, Jerez, Spain	**Langer/Montgomerie**† GER/SCO	281 (-3)	435,648	Dredge O'Malley, Cabrera	1
Nov 21 24	BMW Asian Open**	Westin Resort, Ta Shee, Taiwan	**Padraig Harrington** IRL	273 (-15)	247967	Jyoti Randhawa IND	1
Dec 12 15	WGC:EMC World Cup*	Puerto Vallarta Mexico	**Japan** (Maruyama/Izawa)	252 (-36)	$500,000 each	USA (Mickelson/Toms)	2

* Denotes Approved Special Events
** This event is part of the 2002 Tour
† Langer and Montgomerie agreed a tie when scores were still equal after second sudden death play-off hole

European Tour
Order of Merit 2002

	Player	Ctry	Evts	Euros		Player	Ctry	Evts	Euros
1	Retief Goosen	RSA	22	2,360,127.65	51	Richard Green	AUS	23	449,524.09
2	Padraig Harrington	IRL	22	2,334,655.45	52	Emanuele Canonica	ITA	20	432,406.41
3	Ernie Els	RSA	16	2,251,708.28	53	Rolf Muntz	NED	29	423,767.34
4	Colin Montgomerie	SCO	23	1,980,719.95	54	Andrew Coltart	SCO	31	414,462.91
5	Eduardo Romero	ARG	21	1,811,329.89	55	Jamie Spence	ENG	27	414,075.09
6	Sergio Garcia	ESP	11	1,488,728.30	56	Graeme McDowell	NIR	13	412,203.39
7	Adam Scott	AUS	24	1,361,775.88	57	Sandy Lyle	SCO	16	407,599.12
8	Michael Campbell	NZL	21	1,325,403.70	58	Paul McGinley	IRL	22	401,597.63
9	Justin Rose	ENG	25	1,323,528.84	59	Tobias Dier	GER	30	398,534.65
10	Paul Lawrie	SCO	25	1,151,433.91	60	Simon Dyson	ENG	33	397,290.51
11	Angel Cabrera	ARG	17	1,128,913.46	61	Henrik Bjornstad	NOR	25	388,581.18
12	Thomas Björn	DEN	22	1,110,213.17	62	Joakim Haeggman	SWE	25	386,388.74
13	José Maria Olazábal	ESP	16	1,066,082.90	63	Peter Fowler	AUS	28	384,737.23
14	Trevor Immelman	RSA	30	1,064,085.05	64	Richard S Johnson	SWE	33	383,505.29
15	Stephen Leaney	AUS	24	1,055,029.03	65	Ignacio Garrido	ESP	23	380,108.73
16	Anders Hansen	DEN	26	1,047,920.33	66	Miguel Angel Jiménez	ESP	12	362,452.62
17	Niclas Fasth	SWE	23	982,849.04	67	Søren Kjeldsen	DEN	28	342,578.41
18	Bradley Dredge	WAL	26	961,121.51	68	Steve Webster	ENG	29	336,649.82
19	Bernhard Langer	GER	15	947,232.58	69	Santiago Luna	ESP	21	325,336.98
20	Søren Hansen	DEN	29	932,789.00	70	Roger Chapman	ENG	26	322,283.32
21	Gary Evans	ENG	30	862,656.79	71	Nick O'Hern	AUS	25	321,618.09
22	Darren Clarke	NIR	20	848,023.42	72	Raphaël Jacquelin	FRA	29	319,580.60
23	Alex Cejka	GER	18	846,734.23	73	Richard Bland	ENG	26	318,773.53
24	Ian Poulter	ENG	27	832,559.99	74	David Howell	ENG	22	315,409.48
25	Thomas Levet	FRA	27	821,430.29	75	Lee Westwood	ENG	21	308,338.70
26	Carl Pettersson	SWE	29	806,892.69	76	Raymond Russell	SCO	27	303,749.82
27	Nick Faldo	ENG	19	771,471.76	77	Warren Bennett	ENG	28	298,915.72
28	Ricardo Gonzalez	ARG	21	748,354.12	78	David Lynn	ENG	29	295,737.78
29	John Bickerton	ENG	29	707,012.40	79	Darren Fichardt	RSA	25	290,509.03
30	Fredrik Jacobson	SWE	24	703,400.03	80	Anthony Wall	ENG	32	285,572.43
31	Barry Lane	ENG	29	679,966.21	81	Mark Pilkington	WAL	33	283,758.97
32	Peter O'Malley	AUS	20	668,183.41	82	Ian Garbutt	ENG	30	281,920.74
33	Robert Karlsson	SWE	23	625,087.92	83	Jonathan Lomas	ENG	32	276,028.51
34	Ian Woosnam	WAL	21	598,814.59	84	Mathias Grönberg	SWE	15	270,977.34
35	Pierre Fulke	SWE	21	563,825.75	85	Sam Torrance	SCO	17	268,770.58
36	Nick Dougherty	ENG	32	562,508.57	86	Patrik Sjöland	SWE	28	255,341.77
37	Greg Owen	ENG	27	557,654.95	87	David Carter	ENG	28	235,858.88
38	Jean-Francois Remesy	FRA	30	549,440.34	88	Charlie Wi	KOR	17	234,036.35
39	Brian Davis	ENG	29	548,351.95	89	Arjun Atwal	IND	23	231,642.74
40	Peter Lonard	AUS	11	523,579.89	90	Jamie Donaldson	WAL	30	229,892.78
41	Steen Tinning	DEN	24	519,101.32	91	Roger Wessels	RSA	27	228,055.40
42	Alastair Forsyth	SCO	27	504,442.78	92	Miles Tunnicliff	ENG	14	223,170.50
43	Carlos Rodiles	ESP	23	492,732.05	93	Mark Foster	ENG	29	220,239.97
44	Malcolm Mackenzie	ENG	28	486,446.31	94	Henrik Nystrom	SWE	24	216,222.41
45	Jarrod Moseley	AUS	27	480,416.43	95	Mark Roe	ENG	27	211,859.19
46	Paul Casey	ENG	19	475,848.21	96	Mikael Lundberg	SWE	27	207,480.21
47	Jarmo Sandelin	SWE	24	474,041.75	97	Stephen Gallacher	SCO	28	205,607.17
48	Phillip Price	WAL	21	473,096.01	98	Marc Farry	FRA	30	205,156.38
49	Maarten Lafeber	NED	29	465,943.98	99	Mårten Olander	SWE	25	198,864.71
50	David Gilford	ENG	25	452,157.67	100	Andrew Oldcorn	SCO	24	198,481.87

US PGA Tour

Date	Tournament	Venue	Winner	Score	1st Prize	Runner(s)-up	Margin
Jan 3 6	Mercedes Championship	The Plantation Kapalua, Hawaii	**Sergio Garcia** ESP	274 (-18)	$720,000	David Toms USA	play -off
Jan 10 13	Sony Open in Hawaii	Waialae CC Honolulu, Hawaii	**Jerry Kelly** USA	266 (-14)	$810,000	John Cook USA	1 shot
Jan 16 20	Bob Hope Chrysler Classic	Bermuda Dunes Indian Wells, CA	**Phil Mickelson** USA	330 (-30)	$720,000	David Berganio Jr USA	play -off
Jan 24 27	Phoenix Open	TPC of Scottsdale Arizona	**Chris DiMarco** USA	267 (-17)	$720,000	Kenny Perry USA 1 shot Kaname Yokoo JPN	
Jan 31 Feb 3	AT&T National Pro-Am	Pebble Beach California	**Matt Gogel** USA	274 (-14)	$720,000	Pat Peres USA	3 shots
Feb 7 10	Buick Invitational	Torrey Pines GC La Jolla, California	**José Maria Olazábal** ESP	275 (-13)	$648,000	JL Lewis USA 1 shot Mark O'Meara USA	
Feb 14 17	Nissan Open	Riviera CC, Pacific Palisades, CA	**Len Mattiace** USA	269 (-15)	$666,000	Faxon, McCarron, Sabbatini	1 shot
Feb 21 24	WGC Accenture Match Play	La Costa Carlsbad, CA	**Kevin Sutherland** USA		$1,000,000	Scott McCarron USA	1 hole
Feb 18 24	Touchstone Energy Tucson Open	Omni Tucson Golf Resort, Arizona	**Ian Leggatt** CAN	268 (-20)	$540,000	David Peoples Loren Roberts	2 holes
Feb 28 Mar 3	Genuity Championship	Doral Golf Resort Miami, Florida	**Ernie Els** RSA	271 (-17)	$846,000	Tiger Woods USA	2 shots
Mar 7 10	Honda Classic	TPC at Heron Bay Coral Springs, FL	**Matt Kuchar** USA	269 (-19)	$630,000	Brad Faxon USA, 2 shots Joey Sindelar USA	
Mar 14 17	Bay Hills Invitational	Bay Hill Club Orlando, Florida	**Tiger Woods** USA	275 (-13)	$720,000	Michael Campbell NZL	4 shots
Mar 21 24	THE PLAYERS Championship	TPC at Sawgrass Ponte Vedre, FL	**Craig Perks** USA	280 (-8)	$1.08m	Stephen Ames TRI	2 shots
Mar 28 31	Shell Houston Open	TPC at Woodlands Texas	**Vijay Singh** FIJ	266 (-22)	$720,000	Darren Clarke NIR	6 shots
Apr 4 7	BellSouth Classic	TPC at Sugarloaf Duluth, Georgia	**Retief Goosen** RSA	272 (-16)	$684,000	Jesper Parnevik SWE	4 shots
Apr 11 14	**The Masters Tournament**	Augusta National Georgia	**Tiger Woods** USA	276 (-12)	$1.008m	Retief Goosen RSA	3 shots
Apr 18 21	Worldcom Classic	Harbour Town GL Hilton Head, SC	**Justin Leonard** USA	270 (-14)	$720,000	Heath Slocum USA	1 shot
Apr 25 28	Greater Greensboro Chrysler Classic	Forest Oaks CC Greensboro, NC	**Rocco Mediate** USA	272 (-16)	$684,000	Mark Calcavecchia USA	3 shots
May 2 5	Compaq Classic of New Orleans	English Turn GC New Orleans	**K J Choi** KOR	271 (-17)	$810,000	Dudley Hart Geoff Ogilvy	4 shots
May 9 12	Verizon Byron Nelson Classic	Cottonwood Valley GC, Irving, TX	**Shigeki Maruyama** JPN	266 (-14)	$864,000	Ben Crane USA	2 shots
May 16 19	Mastercard Colonial	Colonial CC Fort Worth, Texas	**Nick Price** ZIM	267 (-13)	$774,000	David Toms USA 5 shots Kenny Perry USA	
May 23 26	Memorial Tournament	Muirfield Village GC Dublin, Onio	**Jim Furyk** USA	274 (-14)	$810,000	John Cook USA 2 shots David Peoples USA	
May 30 June 2	Kemper Insurance Open	TPC at Avenel; Potomac, Maryland	**Bob Estes** USA	273 (-11)	$648,000	Rich Beem USA	1 shot
June 6 9	Buick Classic	Westchester CC Harrison, NY	**Chris Smith** USA	272 (-12)	$630,000	Gossett Peres, Roberts	2 shots

June 13 16	**US Open** **Championship**	Bethpage State Pk Farmingdale, NY	**Tiger Woods** USA	277 (-3)	$1,000,000	Phil Mickelson USA	3 shots
June 20 23	Canon Greater Hartford Open	River Highlands Cromwell, CT	**Phil Mickelson** USA	266 (-14)	$720,000	Jonathan Kaye Davis Love III	1 shot
June 27 30	FedEx St Jude Classic	TPC at Southwind Memphis, Tenn	**Len Mattiace** USA	266 (-18)	$684,000	Tim Petrovic USA	1 shot
July 4 7	Advil Western Open	Cog Hill G & CC Lemont, Illinois	**Jerry Kelly** USA	269 (-19)	$720,000	Davis Love III USA	2 shots
July 11 14	Greater Milwaukee Open	Brown Deer GC Milwaukee, WI	**Jeff Sluman** USA	261 (-23)	$558,000	Tim Herron USA Steve Lowery USA	4 shots
July 18 21	**The Open**	Muirfield East Lothian	**Ernie Els** RSA	274 (-10)	£1,106,140	Elkington Appleby, Levet	Play -off
July 18 21	BC Open	En-Joie GC Endicott, NY	**Spike McRoy** USA	269 (-19)	$378,000	Fred Funk USA	1 shot
July 25 28	John Deere Classic	TPC at Deere Run Silvis, Illinois	**J P Hayes** USA	262 (-22)	$540,000	Robert Gamez USA	4 shots
Aug 1 4	The International	Castle Pines GC Castle Rock, CO	**Rich Beem** RSA	44pts	$810,000	Steve Lowery USA	1 point
Aug 8 11	Buick Open	Warwick Hills CC Grand Blanc, MI	**Tiger Woods** USA	271 (-17)	$594,000	Funk, O'Meara Toledo, Gay	4 shots
Aug 15 18	**PGA Championship**	Hazeltine GC Chaska, Minn	**Rich Beem** USA	278 (-10)	$990,000	Tiger Woods USA	1 shot
Aug 22 25	World Golf Championships	Salahee CC Sammamish, WA	**Craig Parry** AUS	268 (-16)	$1,000,000	Fred Funk USA Robert Allenby AUS	4
Aug 22 25	Reno-Tahoe Open	Montreux G & CC Reno, Nevada	**Chris Riley** USA	268 (-16)	$540,000	Jonathan Kaye USA	play -off
Aug 29 Sep 1	Air Canada Championship	Northview G & CC Surrey BC	**Gene Sauers** USA	269 (-15)	$630,000	Steve Lowery USA	1 shot
Sep 5 8	Bell Canadian Open	Angus Glen GC Markham, Ontario	**John Rollins** USA	272 (-16)	$720,000	Neal Lancaster Justin Leonard	play -off
Sep 12 15	SEI Pennsylvania Classic SEI	Waynesborough CC Paoli, PA	**Dan Forsman** USA	270 (-14)	$594,000	Billy Andrade Robert Allenby AUS	1
Sep 19 22	WGC American Express Champs	Mount Juliet Estate Kilkenny, IRL	**Tiger Woods** USA	263 (-25)	$1,000,000	Retief Goosen RSA	1
Sep 19 22	Tampa Bay Classic	Westin Innesbrook Palm Harbour, FL	**K J Choi** KOR	267 (-17)	$468,000	Glen Day	7
Sep 26 29	Valero Texas Open	LaCantera GC San Antonio, Texas	**Loren Roberts** USA	261 (-19)	$630,000	Fred Couples Fred Funk, Garrett Willis	3
Sep 27 29	Ryder Cup	The Belfry Sutton	**Europe beat USA** 15½ - 12½				
Oct 3 6	Michelob Championship	Kingsmill GC Williamsburg, VA	**Charles Howell III** USA	270 (-14)	$666,000	Scott Hoch Brandt Jobe	1
Oct 10 13	Invensys Classic	Southern Highlands GC, Las Vegas	**Phil Tataurangi** NZL	330 (-30)	$900,000	Jeff Sluman Stuart Appleby AUS	1
Oct 17 20	Walt Disney World Golf Classic	Lake Buena Vista, Florida	**Bob Burns** USA	263 (-25)	$666,000	Chris DiMarco	1
Oct 24 27	Buick Challenge Callaway Gardens	Pine Mountain Georgia	**Jonathan Byrd** USA	261 (-27)	$666,000	David Toms USA	1
Oct 28 Nov 3	THE TOUR Championship	East Lake GC Atlanta, GA	**Vijay Singh** FIJ	268 (-12)	$900,000	Charles Howell III USA	2
Oct 28 Nov 3	Southern Fare Bureau Classic	Annandale GC Madison	**Luke Donald** ENG	201 (-15)	$468,000	Deanne Pappas RSA	1

| Dec | 5 8 | Target World Challenge | Thousand Oaks, California | **Padraig Harrington** IRL | 268 (-20) | $1,000,000 | Tiger Woods | 2 |
| Dec | 12 15 | WGC:EMC World Cup | Puerto Vallarta Mexico | **Japan** (Maruyama/Izawa) | 252 (-36) | $500,000 each | USA (Mickelson/Toms) | 2 |

US PGA Tour Money List

	Player	Ctry	Evts	US$		Player	Ctry	Evts	US$
1	Tiger Woods	USA	18	6,912,625	51	Bob Burns	USA	30	1,199,802
2	Phil Mickelson	USA	26	4,311,971	52	Steve Flesch	USA	32	1,192,341
3	Vijay Singh	USA	28	3,756,563	53	Mark Calcavecchia	USA	25	1,162,509
4	David Toms	USA	27	3,459,739	54	Dudley Hart	USA	26	1,161,080
5	Ernie Els	RSA	18	3,291,895	55	Bob Tway	USA	28	1,160,399
6	Jerry Kelly	USA	29	2,946,889	56	Lee Janzen	USA	29	1,127,740
7	Rich Beem	USA	30	2,938,365	57	Matt Gogel	USA	25	1,089,482
8	Justin Leonard	USA	26	2,738,235	58	Luke Donald	ENG	30	1,088,205
9	Charles Howell III	USA	32	2,702,747	59	Steve Elkington	AUS	23	1,084,535
10	Retief Goosen	RSA	15	2,617,004	60	Jonathan Kaye	USA	27	1,082,803
11	Chris DiMarco	USA	29	2,606,430	61	Joel Edwards	USA	28	1,077,651
12	Sergio Garcia	ESP	21	2,401,993	62	Brandt Jobe	USA	28	972,479
13	Fred Funk	USA	30	2,383,071	63	Jesper Parnevik	SWE	26	964,304
14	Jim Furyk	USA	28	2,363,250	64	Geoff Ogilvy	AUS	27	957,184
15	Jeff Sluman	USA	32	2,250,186	65	J L Lewis	USA	31	957,182
16	Shigeki Maruyama	JPN	24	2,214,794	66	J P Hayes	USA	24	955,271
17	K J Choi	KOR	27	2,204,907	67	Tim Herron	USA	30	954,917
18	Len Mattiace	USA	28	2,194,064	68	Rory Sabbatini	RSA	23	936,664
19	Nick Price	ZIM	18	2,170,912	69	Brian Gay	USA	34	926,735
20	Robert Allenby	AUS	27	2,115,771	70	Ben Crane	USA	30	921,076
21	Davis Love III	USA	26	2,056,160	71	Duffy Waldorf	USA	27	909,003
22	Rocco Mediate	USA	23	2,040,676	72	Cameron Beckman	USA	26	907,740
23	Chris Riley	USA	28	2,032,979	73	Stewart Cink	USA	27	894,212
24	Jose Maria Olazabal	ESP	20	1,987,027	74	Tom Lehman	USA	22	868,632
25	John Rollins	USA	34	1,956,565	75	Billy Mayfair	USA	31	864,745
26	Bob Estes	USA	26	1,934,600	76	Heath Slocum	USA	32	864,615
27	Kenny Perry	USA	27	1,928,598	77	Glen Day	USA	31	859,930
28	Loren Roberts	USA	25	1,919,047	78	Mike Weir	CAN	25	843,890
29	Scott McCarron	USA	28	1,896,714	79	Kirk Triplett	USA	25	843,273
30	Steve Lowery	USA	28	1,882,553	80	David Duval	USA	24	838,045
31	Brad Faxon	USA	25	1,814,672	81	Chad Campbell	USA	34	825,474
32	Stuart Appleby	AUS	28	1,729,459	82	Briny Baird	USA	33	817,514
33	Phil Tataurangi	NZL	28	1,643,686	83	Neal Lancaster	USA	31	813,230
34	Craig Perks	NZL	28	1,632,042	84	Jim Carter	USA	29	812,346
35	John Cook	USA	25	1,624,095	85	Robert Gamez	USA	21	807,892
36	Kevin Sutherland	USA	28	1,569,529	86	Tim Petrovic	USA	31	797,206
37	Craig Parry	AUS	21	1,466,235	87	Joey Sindelar	USA	32	790,750
38	Scott Hoch	USA	21	1,465,173	88	Steve Stricker	USA	22	789,713
39	Jonathan Byrd	USA	32	1,462,713	89	Rod Pampling	AUS	29	776,903
40	Pat Perez	USA	30	1,451,726	90	Paul Azinger	USA	20	769,926
41	Peter Lonard	AUS	24	1,413,113	91	Esteban Toledo	MEX	32	766,463
42	Billy Andrade	USA	31	1,365,707	92	Hidemichi Tanaka	JPN	31	766,423
43	Chris Smith	USA	30	1,361,094	93	Frank Lickliter II	USA	30	740,460
44	Dan Forsman	USA	25	1,305,790	94	Jeff Maggert	USA	27	733,198
45	John Huston	USA	26	1,299,053	95	Mark Brooks	USA	32	731,671
46	Stephen Ames	TRI	28	1,278,037	96	Harrison Frazar	USA	28	731,295
47	Ian Leggatt	CAN	29	1,245,048	97	Mark O'Meara	USA	24	730,132
48	David Peoples	USA	30	1,243,774	98	Jay Haas	USA	24	722,782
49	Matt Kuchar	USA	27	1,237,725	99	Gene Sauers	USA	11	715,605
50	Scott Verplank	USA	26	1,217,022	100	David Gossett	USA	29	676,308

Women's Golf

Usually the Solheim Cup has the stage to itself, but not this year. With the rescheduled Ryder Cup to start only five days after, the competition at Interlachen was always in danger of being viewed as a warm-up. A European victory was the surest way to elevate its profile over here, and during a sweet first session such an ambition looked all too simple to achieve. Laura Davies, playing with Spanish rookie Paula Marti, set the tempo. Julie Inkster and Laura Diaz were no match, and Davies duly entered the record books as the highest-ever points scorer in this competition, with 15. It was a heady old morning with further wins for Europe from Helen Alfredsson and Suzann Pettersen, and Annika Sorenstam and Carin Koch. As the selection of both Davies and Alfredsson had been a matter of considerable controversy, the captain Dale Reid, whose call it was, could at least enjoy her lunch. Tea was another matter.

Koch was part of a winning team in the afternoon, and the Swede, who didn't lose any of her matches in 2000 either, would go on to become the only unbeaten European over the three days. Everywhere else, though, the Americans were tilting the scales back, and despite an extraordinary performance from Davies, who drove 290 yards at the 18th into the water and still holed out for a birdie. But Davies and Marti lost, and at the close of day one, there was no advantage to either side.

Only Sorenstam and Koch could muster a win on Saturday morning, but the afternoon was the high spot of the weekend for the visitors, Europe successful in all the fourball matches. Davies added another to her record tally, and the two Swedes, Sorenstam and Koch again overwhelmed their opponents. If only they could have stopped it there and then, but the American captain Patty Sheehan wasn't about to agree to that.

America always does well in the singles, but not often as well as they did on this particular Sunday. There were moments for Europe; like the magnificent comeback from five down by Suzann Pettersen against Michele Redman. There was Iben Tinning's surprise win against Kelli Keuhne, and Sophie Gustafson's win over Cristie Kerr, but for most of a long, long afternoon, the scoreboard was only one colour, the red of America. From 10 possible points, Europe took just two and a half, and a two-point lead became a three-point defeat and Reid had to go home and face the critics again. Even in Minnesota she could almost hear them sharpening their knives.

> **"It's the difference between men and women in general... women aren't allowed to be jerks"**
> Kelly Robbins, US golfer, on the sexual divide.

For the first time in its history, the British Women's Open was played in Scotland, Turnberry hosting the event. All it needed was a Scot to win it, but there wasn't one near. Kathryn Marshall and Catriona Matthew came closest, but they were a mighty 16 shots behind the winner. As they were also the highest placed Britons, in joint 35th, we believe this may be a record, of sorts. Certainly we can't find any other past performance quite as lamentable (yup, that bad, I'm afraid). Karrie Webb won it, opening and closing her tournament with two very fine rounds of 66. The closing 66 had the higher degree of difficulty, as the 27-year-old had to cope with very Scottish conditions, and did so far better than Tiger had a month earlier. The Australian, who was in her seventh year as a pro, was notching up her fifth major, and her third victory in this event, the first coming in her rookie year of 1995, and the second two years later.

Everything else in golf concerned Annika Sorenstam, who dominated the US LPGA Tour. Sorenstam won 11 Tour events and in an extraordinary end-of season purple patch, was successful in five of the last eight tournaments. Her earnings tally of $2,863,904 was naturally a record, being over a million dollars more than the next woman on the list, Korean Se Ri Pak. Sorenstam now holds or shares almost every record in the LPGA book, and has taken her career earnings to over $11m. It must now be beyond argument that she is the best player the women's game has ever seen. Sorry, Laura.

Solheim Cup

Interlachan Country Club, Minnesota, Sep 20-22
European players shown first

FOURSOMES
Friday Morning
Davies/Marti bt Inkster/Diaz 2up
Tinning/Carriedo lost to Daniel/Ward 1up
Alfredsson/Pettersen bt Robbins/Hurst 4 and 2
Sorenstam/Koch bt Mallon/Kuehne 3 and 2
Europe 3 USA 1

FOURBALLS
Friday Afternoon
Davies/Marti lost to Jones/Kerr 1up
Gustafson/Icher lost to Diaz/Klein 4 and 3
Sorenstam/Hjorth lost to Redman/Mallon 2 and 1
McKay/Koch bt Inkster/Kuehne 3 and 2
Europe 4 USA 4

FOURSOMES
Saturday Morning
Sorenstam/Koch bt Kerr/Redman 4 and 3
Tinning/McKay lost to Klein/Ward 3 and 2
Davies/Marti lost to Mallon/Inkster 2 and 1
Alfredsson/Pettersen lost to Diaz/Robbins 3 and 1
Europe 5 USA 7

FOURBALLS
Saturday Afternoon
Sorenstam/Koch bt Daniel/Ward 4 and 3
Hjorth/Tinning bt Hurst/Kuehne 1up
Davies/Gustafson bt Robbins/Klein 1up
Icher/Garriedo bt Jones/Kerr 1up
Europe 9 USA 7

SINGLES
Sunday
Raquel Carriedo lost to Julie Inkster 4 and 3
Paula Marti lost to Laura Diaz 5 and 3
Helen Alfredsson lost to Emilie Klein 2 and 1
Iben Tinning bt Kelli Kuehne 3 and 2
Suzann Pettersen halved with Michele Redman
Annika Sorenstam halved with Wendy Ward
Maria Hjorth lost to Kelly Robbins 5 and 3
Sophie Gustafson bt Cristie Kerr 3 and 2
Laura Davies lost to Meg Mallon 3 and 2
Mhairi McKay lost to Pat Hurst 4 and 2
Carin Koch halved with Beth Daniel
Karin Icher lost to Rosie Jones 3 and 2

Final Score
Europe 12½ USA 15½

Weetabix British Open

Turnberry (Ailsa Course)   *Aug 8-11*

273	**Karrie Webb AUS**	66	71	70	66
(-15)	(249,007)				
275	Michelle Ellis AUS	69	70	68	68
(-13)	Paula Marti ESP	69	68	69	69
	(136,552 each)				
277	Catrin Nilsmark SWE	70	69	69	69
(-11)	Jeong Jang KOR	73	69	66	69
	Candie Kung TPE	65	71	71	70
	Jennifer Rosales PHI	69	70	65	73
	(67,975 each)				
278	Meg Mallon USA	69	71	68	70
(-10)	Beth Bauer USA	70	67	70	71
	Carin Koch SWE	68	68	68	74
	(40,430 each)				
279	Sophie Gustafson SWE	69	73	69	68
(-9)	Se Ri Pak KOR	67	72	69	71
	(31,728 each)				
280	Pat Hurst USA	69	70	69	72
(-8)	Angela Stanford USA	69	70	69	72
	Natalie Gulbis USA	69	70	67	74
	(26,641 each)				
283	Beth Daniel USA	73	68	68	74
(-5)	Tina Barrett USA	67	70	70	76
	(23,053 each)				
284	Jean Bartholomew USA	71	72	72	69
(-4)	Fiona Pike AUS	72	73	67	72
	Marine Monnet FRA	71	70	70	73
	Wendy Doolan AUS	70	69	71	74
	Jane Geddes USA	71	69	70	74
	Rachel Teske AUS	67	74	68	75
	(19,438 each)				
285	Suzann Pettersen NOR	72	71	72	70
(-3)	Patricia Meunier Lebouc FRA	69	71	69	76
	(16,466 each)				
286	Emilee Klein USA	68	71	72	75
(-2)	Dorothy Delasin USA	70	71	70	75
	Elisabeth Esterl GER	67	71	72	76
	(15,047 each)				
287	Yu Ping Lin TPE	73	69	74	71
(-1)	Kelli Kuehne USA	75	67	71	74
	Brandie Burton USA	71	70	71	75
	Cristie Kerr USA	72	71	69	75
	Iben Tinning DEN	71	69	71	76
	(12,771 each)				
288	Toshimi Kimura JPN	74	70	70	74
(level)	(11,647)				
289	Kathryn Marshall SCO	70	71	76	72
(+1)	Shani Waugh AUS	70	73	74	72
	Catriona Matthew SCO	73	71	70	75
	Kelly Robbins USA	70	75	68	76
	Liselotte Neumann SWE	70	71	71	77
	(10,442 each)				
290	Becky Iverson USA	69	76	72	73
(+2)	Karen Lunn AUS	73	71	72	74
	Helen Alfredsson SWE	70	75	71	74
	Lora Fairclough ENG	71	69	73	77
	Sophie Sandolo ITA	71	74	68	77
	(8,4334 each)				
291	Asa Gottmo SWE	72	72	72	75
(+3)	Mhairi McKay SCO	68	72	75	76
	(7,068 each)				
292	Heather Daly-Donofrio USA	70	71	77	74
(+4)	Tracy Hanson USA	70	73	75	74
	Johanna Head ENG	70	73	74	75

	Federica Dassu ITA	68	72	75	77
	Becky Morgan WAL	72	72	71	77
	Giulia Sergas ITA	73	67	73	79
	(5,783 each)				
293	Suzanne Strudwick ENG	72	72	74	75
(+5)	Heather Bowie USA	78	65	73	77
	Grace Park KOR	73	69	71	80
	(4,364 each)				
294	Wendy Ward USA	73	71	77	73
(+6)	Karen Stupples ENG	73	72	72	77
	Raquel Carrido ESP	70	72	71	81
	(3,614 each)				
295	Betsy King USA	69	76	74	76
(+7)	(3,132)				
296	Vicki Goetze-Ackermann USA	73	72	75	76
(+8)	(2,972)				
297	Charlotta Sorenstam SWE	72	72	77	76
(+9)	Kim Mi-Hyun KOR	68	76	75	78
	(2,731 each)				
298	Tonya Gill USA	72	72	74	80
(+10)	(2,570)				
299	Riikka Hakkarainen FIN	72	73	76	78
(+11)	(2,490)				
301	Marina Arruti ESP	71	72	74	84
(+13)	(2,409)				
302	Ana Larraneta ESP	72	72	75	83
(+14)	(1,606)				

Missed the cut (USA unless stated) 146: Kimberley Williams 73 73, Janice Moodie SCO 72 74, Becky Brewerton WAL 73 73, Lee J-Y KOR 75 71, Lorie Kane CAN 74 72, Maria Hjorth SWE 76 70, Gloria Park KOR 74 72, Jill McGill 72 74, Cecilia Ekelundh SWE 73 73, Nicole Stillig GER 72 74, Silvia Cavalleri ITA 72 74; **147:** Cindy Schreyer USA 71 76, Lynette Brooky NZL 75 72, Laura Diaz 69 78, Danielle Ammaccapane 73 74, Donna Andrews 71 76, Leslie Spalding 73 74, Susan G-Brooker 74 73, Gina Scott NZL 75 72, Kristal P-Manzo 73 74, Vibeke Stensrud NOR 71 76, Wendy Dicks ENG 74 73, Beth Bader 74 73, Karen Weiss USA 73 74, Stephanie Arricau FRA 75 72; **148:** Rosie Jones 75 73, Joanne Mills AUS 74 74, Mihoko Takahashi JPN 76 72, Karine Icher FRA 72 76, Sherri Steinhauer 73 75, Alison Munt AUS 76 72, Laurette Maritz RSA 75 73, Catherine Cartwright 73 75; **149:** Jackie G-Smith 75 74, Laura Davies ENG 74 75, Pearl Sinn 77 72, Dale Reid SCO 71 78, Michelle Estill 76 73; **150:** Orie Fujino JPN 77 73, Annika Sorenstam SWE 73 77, Nancy Scranton 73 77, Cecilie Lundgreen NOR 75 75, Mikino Kubo JPN 74 76, Trish Johnson ENG 78 72, Kris Tschetter 77 73; **151:** Kirsty Taylor ENG 76 75, Michelle McGann 75 76, Joanne Morley ENG 76 75, Hiromi Kobayashi JPN 75 76, Stephanie Keever 80 71; **152:** Nina Karlsson SWE 74 78, Kasumi Fujii JPN 75 77, Samantha Head ENG 78 74, Maria Boden SWE 75 77, Ana Belen Sanchez ESP 78 74, Corinne Dibnah AUS 74 78, Takayo Bando JPN 77 75, Andra Burks 77 75; **153:** Sandrine Mendiburo FRA 78 75, Juli Inkster 75 78, Nicola Moult ENG 76 77; **154:** Sara Eklund SWE 80 74, Nadine Taylor AUS 82 72, Virginie Auffret FRA 77 77, **155:** Alison Nicholas ENG 78 77, Mia Lojdahl SWE 76 79, Emma Weekes* ENG 78 77; **156:** Denise Killeen 77 79; **157:** Hilary Homeyer 76 81; **158:** Georgina Simpson ENG 78 80, Sarah Bennett ENG 77 81; **159:** Cherie Byrnes AUS 77 82; **163:** Ashli Bunch 80 83; **165:** Caroline Grady ENG 85 80; **166:** Vanessa Vignali ESP 85 81; **168:** Pernilla Sterner SWE; **Retired:** Valerie Michaud FRA

European Tour

Date	Tournament	Venue	Winner	Score	1st Prize	Runner(s)-up	Margin
Feb 21 24	ANZ Ladies Masters	Royal Pines Resort Queensland	**Annika Sorenstam** SWE	278 (-10)	74,092	Karrie Webb AUS	play -off
Feb 28 Mar 3	AAMI Women's Australian Open	Yarra Yarra GC Melbourne	**Karrie Webb** AUS	278 (-10)	49,291	Suzann Pettersen NOR	play -off
May 2 5	Tenerife Ladies Open	Golf del Sur Tenerife	**Raquel Carriedo** ESP	292 (+4)	30,000	Johanna Head ENG	1
May 10 12	Ladies Irish Open	Killarny G & FC Lackabane	**Iben Tinning** DEN	214 (-2)	24,750	Suzann Pettersen NOR	play -off
May 16 19	La Perla Italian Open	Poggio dei Medici GCC, Florence	**Iben Tinning** DEN	278 (-14)	28,575	Silvia Cavalleri ITA	1
May 25 26	Open of Costa Azul	Aroeira Portugal	**Kanna Takanashi** JPN	139 (-5)	10,500	Julie Forbes SCO	1
May 30 June 2	Caja Duero Open de Espana	Campo de Golf de Salamanca	**Karine Icher** FRA	277 (-11)	37,500	Raquel Carriedo ESP	1
June12 15	Evian Masters	Evian Masters GC Evian Les Bains	**Annika Sorenstam** SWE	269 (-19)	332,243	Maria Hjorth SWE	4
June 20 23	Open de France Credit Mutuel Nord	Le Golf d'Arras Anzin St Aubin	**Lynnette Brooky** NZL	272 (-16)	41,250	Paula Marti ESP	5
July 6 8	Kellogg's All-Bran British Masters	Mottram Hall GC Cheshire	**Paula Marti** ESP	209 (-10)	£15,000	Raquel Carriedo ESP	1 shot
Aug 1 4	P4 Norwegian Masters	Oslo Golfklubb	**Laura Davies** ENG	283 (-5)	52,800	Ana Larraneta ESP	play -off
Aug 8 11	Weetabix Women's British Open	Ailsa Course Turnberry	**Karrie Webb** AUS	273 (-15)	249.007	Michelle Ellis AUS	2
Aug 15 18	Compaq Open	Vasatorps GC Stockholm	**Annika Sorenstam** SWE	271 (-17)	77,122	Sophie Gustafson SWE	4
Aug 22 25	Wales WPGA Ch'ship of Europe	Royal Porthcawl GC	**Asa Gottmo** SWE	285 (-7	94,740	Maria Hjorth SWE	2
Oct 3 5	Biarritz Ladies Classic	Biarritz Le Phare	**Sophie Gustafson** SWE	200 (-10)	24,750	Mhairi McKay SCO	play -off

European Tour Money List
Final Standing
Only includes players who have contested five events

	Player	Ctry	Evts	Euros		Player	Ctry	Evts	Euros
1	Maria Hjorth	SWE	12	266,066	16	Helen Alfredsson	SWE	6	81,855
2	Paula Marti	ESP	7	222,501	17	Mhairi McKay	SCO	5	79,470
3	Sophie Gustafson	SWE	7	148,741	18	Nicola Moult	ENG	13	73,262
4	Karine Icher	FRA	11	142,471	19	Ana Belen Sanchez	ESP	11	71,503
5	Asa Gottmo	SWE	12	141,108	20	Becky Morgan	WAL	6	55,515
6	Iben Tinning	DEN	12	125,761	21	Kirsty S Taylor	ENG	10	52,903
7	Suzann Pettersen	NOR	12	118,808	22	Corinne Dibnah	AUS	13	52,594
8	Marine Monnet	FRA	13	118,643	23	Samantha Head	ENG	13	51,629
9	Laura Davies	ENG	7	117,136	24	Kathryn Marshall	SCO	5	51,475
10	Lynette Brooky	NZL	12	111,786	25	Ana Larraneta	ESP	10	45,596
11	Catrin Nilsmark	SWE	6	103,183	26	Silvia Cavalleri	ITA	6	45,490
12	Raquel Carriedo	ESP	12	102,740	27	Liselotte Neumann	SWE	5	40,376
13	Elisabeth Esterl	GER	13	101,087	28	Gina Scott	NZL	12	40,293
14	Kirsty Taylor	ENG	13	92,318	29	Shani Waugh	AUS	7	36,416
15	Johanna Head	ENG	8	90,095	30	Trish Johnson	ENG	10	36,010

US LPGA Tour

Date	Tournament	Venue	Winner	Score	1st Prize	Runner(s)-up	Margin
Feb 28 Mar 2	LPGA Takefuji Classic	Kona CC, Kailua-Kona, Hawaii	**Annika Sorenstam** SWE	196 (-14)	$135,000	Lorie Kane USA	play -off
Mar 14 17	PING Banner Health	Moon Valley CC, Phoenix, Arizona	**Rachel Teske** AUS	281 (-7)	$150,000	Annika Sörenstam SWE	play -off
Mar 21 24	Welch's/Circle K Championship	Randolph Park GC, Tucson, Arizona	**Laura Diaz** USA	270 (-18)	$120,000	Juli Inkster USA	1
Mar 28 31	**Nabisco** **Championship**	Mission Hills CC, Rancho Mirage, CA	**Annika Sorenstam** SWE	280 (-8)	$225,000	Liselotte Neumann SWE	1
Apr 5 7	The Office Depot	Tarzana California	**Se Ri Pak** KOR	209 (-7)	$150,000	Annika Sorenstam SWE	1
Apr 18 21	Longs Drugs Challenge	Twelve Bridges GC Lincoln, California	**Cristie Kerr** USA	280 (-8)	$135,000	Han Hee-Won KOR	1
May 3 5	Chick-fil-A Charity Championship	Eagles Landing CC Stockbridge, Georgia	**Juli Inkster** USA	132 (-12)	$187,500	Kelly Robbins USA	2
May 9 12	Electrolux USA Championship	Legends GC, Franklin, Tennessee	**Annika Sorenstam** SWE	271 (-17)	$120,000	Pat Hurst USA	1
May 16 19	Asahi Ryokuken Championship	Mount Vintage North Augusta	**Janice Moodie** SCO	273 (-15)	$187,500	Laura Davies ENG	7
May 23 26	LPGA Corning Classic	Corning CC Corning, New York	**Laura Diaz** USA	274 (-14)	$150,000	Rosie Jones USA	2
May 31 June 2	Kellogg Keebler Classic	Stonebridge CC Aurora, ILL	**Annika Sorenstam** SWE	195 (-21)	$180,000	Redman, McKay Ammaccapane	11
June 6 9	**McDonald's LPGA** **Championship**	DuPont CC, Wilmington, DEL	**Se Ri Pak** KOR	279 (-5)	$225,000	Beth Daniel USA	3
June 12 15	Evian Masters	Royal GC Evian, Evian-les-Bains	**Annika Sorenstam** SWE	269 (-19)	$315,000	Maria Hjorth Kim Mi-Hyun	4
June 20 23	Wegmans Rochester Int.	Locust Hill CC Pittsford, NY	**Karrie Webb** AUS	276 (-12)	$180,000	Kim Mi-Hyun KOR	1
June 28 30	Shoprite LPGA Classic	Marriott Seaview Atlantic City, NJ	**Annika Sorenstam** SWE	201 (-12)	$180,000	Kock, Golden Inkster	3
July 4 7	**US Open** **Championship**	Prairie Dunes CC	**Juli Inkster** USA	276 (-2)	$535,000	Annika Sorenstam KOR	2
July 11 14	Jamie Farr Kroger Classic	Highland Meadows GC, Sylvania, Ohio	**Rachel Teske** AUS	270 (-14)	$150,000	Beth Bauer USA	2
July 18 21	Giant Eagle LPGA Classic	Squaw Creek CC Lake Tahoe	**Kim Mi-Hyun** KOR	202 (-14)	$150,000	Kelly Robbins USA	1
July 25 28	Sybase Big Apple Classic	Wykaygl CC, New Rochelle, New York	**Gloria Park** KOR	270 (-14)	$142,500	Han Hee-Won KOR	play -off
July 29 Aug 4	Wendy's Ch'ship for Children	Tartan Fields Dublin, Ohio	**Kim Mi-Hyun** KOR	208 (-8)	$150,000	Han Hee-Won KOR	1
Aug 8 11	**Weetabix** **British Open**	Turnberry Ayrshire	**Karrie Webb** AUS	273 (-15)	$236,383	Michelle Ellis AUS	2
Aug 15 18	**Bank of Montreal** **Canadian Open**	Summerlea Quebec	**Meg Mallon** USA	284 (-4)	$180,000	Redman, Ellis Matthew	
Aug 22 25	First Union Betsy King Classic	Berkleigh CC Kutztown, Penn	**Se Ri Pak** KOR	267 (-21)	$180,000	Angela Stanford USA	3
Aug 29 Sep 1	State Farm Rail Classic	The Rail GC, Springfield, Illinois	**P Meunier-Lebouc** FRA	270 (-18)	$165,000	Se Ri Pak Kim Mi-Hyun	2

Sep 6 8	Williams Championship	Tulsa CC, Tulsa, Oklahoma	**Annika Sorenstam** SWE	199 (-11)	$150,000	Lorie Kane USA	4
Sep 13 15	Safeway LPGA Championship	Portland Oregon	**Annika Sorenstam** SWE	199 (-17)	$150,000	Kate Golden USA	1
Sep 20 23	**Solheim Cup**	Interlachen CC Edina, Minnesota	**USA bt Europe**	15.5 - 12.5			
Oct 3 6	Samsung World Championship	Vallejo California	**Annika Sorenstam** SWE	266 (-22)	$162,000	Cristie Kerr USA	6
Oct 10 13	Mobile Tournament of Champions	Semmes Alabama	**Se Ri Pak** KOR	268 (-20)	$122,000	Catriona Matthew Carin Kock	4
Oct 25 27	Sports Today Classic	Nine Bridges Resort Jeju, Korea	**Se Ri Pak** KOR	213 (-3)	$225,000	Carin Koch USA	6
Oct 31 Nov 3	Cisco World Ladies Matchplay Ch'ship	Narita, Japan	**Grace Park** KOR		$153,000	Midori Yooneyama JPN	1 up
Nov 8 10	Mizuno Classic	Ohtsu City Japan	**Annika Sorenstam** SWE	201 (-15)	$169,500	Grace Park KOR	2
Nov 21 24	Tyco/ADT Championship	West Palm Beach Florida	**Annika Sorenstam** SWE	275 (-13)	$215,000	Rachel Teske AUS	3

US LPGA 2002 Money List

Final Standing

	Player	Ctry	US$		Player	Ctry	US$
1	Annika Sorenstam	SWE	2,863,904.00	26	Maria Hjorth	SWE	359,194.00
2	Se Ri Pak	KOR	1,722,281.00	27	Shani Waugh	AUS	356,918.00
3	Juli Inkster	USA	1,154,349.00	28	Patricia Meunier-Lebouc	FRA	354,175.00
4	Mi Hyun Kim	KOR	1,049,993.00	29	Laura Davies	ENG	344,232.00
5	Karrie Webb	AUS	1,009,760.00	30	Jenny Rosales	PHI	342,887.00
6	Grace Park	KOR	861,943.00	31	Dorothy Delasin	USA	309,885.00
7	Laura Diaz	USA	843,790.00	32	Liselotte Neumann	SWE	295,225.00
8	Carin Koch	SWE	785,817.00	33	Vicki Goetze-Ackerman	USA	278,166.00
9	Rachel Teske	AUS	779,329.00	34	Jeong Jang	KOR	276,820.00
10	Rosie Jones	USA	722,412.00	35	Emilee Klein	USA	272,036.00
11	Lorie Kane	CAN	685,520.00	36	Candie Kung	TPE	261,044.00
12	Cristie Kerr	USA	685,393.00	37	Heather Bowie	USA	259,995.00
13	Michele Redman	USA	666,849.00	38	Kate Golden	USA	259,143.00
14	Hee-Won Han	KOR	612,747.00	39	Natalie Gulbis	USA	257,310.00
15	Catriona Matthew	SCO	567,394.00	40	Leta Lindley	USA	252,051.00
16	Kelly Robbins	USA	540,146.00	41	Wendy Doolan	AUS	250,838.00
17	Mhairi McKay	SCO	489,384.00	42	Akiko Fukushima	JPN	243,528.00
18	Beth Bauer	USA	480,909.00	43	Pat Hurst	USA	237,682.00
19	Beth Daniel	USA	480,618.00	44	Donna Andrews	USA	229,825.00
20	Meg Mallon	USA	463,731.00	45	Angela Stanford	USA	221,857.00
21	Gloria Park	KOR	460,630.00	46	Karen Stupples	ENG	214,760.00
22	Janice Moodie	SCO	424,238.00	47	Kris Tschetter	USA	213,935.00
23	Kelli Kuehne	USA	405,799.00	48	Joanne Morley	ENG	210,643.00
24	Danielle Ammaccapane	USA	396,280.00	49	Jill McGill	USA	202,375.00
25	Michelle Ellis	AUS	367,843.00	50	Jackie Gallagher-Smith	USA	187,180.00

Amateur Golf

The Curtis Cup

Fox Chapel Country Club, Pittsburgh, Aug 3-4
Great Britain and Ireland listed first

SATURDAY MATCHES
Foursomes
Hudson/Duggleby lost to Duncan/Jerman 4 and 3
Stirling/Laing lost to Fankhauser/Semple Thompson 1up
Smith/Coffey lost to Swaim/Myerscough 3 and 2

Singles
Rebecca Hudson bt Emily Bastel 2up
Emma Duggleby lost to Leigh Anne Hardin 2 and 1
Fame Moore lost to Meredith Duncan 5 and 4
Sarah Jones lost to Angela Jerman 6 and 5
Heather Stirling lost to Courtney Swaim 4 and 2
Vikki Laing bt Mollie Fankhauser 1up

Great Britain & Ireland 2   USA 7

SUNDAY MATCHES
Foursomes
Stirling/Laing bt Hardin/Bastel 3 and 1
Hudson/Smith lost to Myerscough/Swaim 4 and 2
Duggleby/Coffey bt Duncan/Jerman 4 and 2

Singles
Rebecca Hudson bt Mollie Fankhauser 3 and 1
Vikki Laing lost to Carole Semple Thompson 1up
Emma Duggleby bt Leigh Anne Hardin 4 and 3
Heather Stirling lost to Laura Myerscough 2up
Alison Coffey lost to Meredith Duncan 3 and 1
Sarah Jones bt Courtney Jones 5 and 3

Final Score
Great Britain & Ireland 7   USA 11

The Amateur Championship

Royal Porthcawl   June 3-8

Semi-final
Graham Gordon (Newmachar) bt
Martin Sell (Wrag Barn) 1up

Jamie Elson (Kenilworth) bt
Alejandro Larrazabal (Spain) 19th hole

FINAL
Martin Sell beat
Alejandro Larrazabal 1 hole

Gymnastics

One rung at a time makes sense where ladders are concerned, so whose to say it isn't the best way to progress in gymnastics, too? The British women's team work that way, or have done of late, and moved up another rung in when they made their target of sixth place in the European Championships at Patras in April; up from seventh at Paris three years earlier.

Beth Tweddle has not been so constrained in her progress. Only in her second season as a senior, Tweddle became the first British woman ever to win a medal in a European championships when she placed third on the uneven bars. There is some suggestion that Tweddle's capability on the bars dates from an accident at the 1998 British championships when the Liverpool gymnast broke a foot while warming up for competition. Unable to put any weight on her foot while the bone mended, the bars was the only apparatus she could use in training.

If that was the cause, the effect has been remarkable, for Tweddle is now world-class on the apparatus. Prior to Patras, she had won the bars at the Cottbus meeting, and in the autumn was just one place off the podium at the world apparatus championships in Hungary.

The American Courtney Kupets was the surprise winner at Debrecen, with mistakes by Svetlana Khorkina, who had predictably led the qualifying, relegating the Russian to just seventh place. Khorkina is still only 24, but has been ruling the roost on the uneven bars since she won the Olympic title in Atlanta. By the time the Athens Olympic Games comes around, Khorkina will have been competing at the highest level for eight years, which is a decent spell in any Olympic sport, but an eternity in gymnastics. If time has caught up with the Russian in Athens (assuming she even gets there) the uneven bars will be up for grabs and, for the first time ever, a British woman could approach the Olympic Games with a realistic chance of a medal.

Kanukai Jackson matched Tweddle at the European level, winning a vault bronze at Bremen in the men's championships. Jackson had a disappointing world championships, but his success at Manchester *(See Commonwealth Games)* may have made it difficult for the Harrow gymnast to wind himself up again mentally for a third time in the year.

Li Xiaopeng was the dominant gymnast at Debrecen winning both the vault and the parallel bars (surpringly no woman won more than a single medal), but the decision to omit the all-around titles from the championships was anti-climactic. Lots of supporting acts, but no star to celebrate.

> **"By the time you're out of your teens, you body is pleading with you to stop"**
>
> Beth Tweddle, who has just two more years to go, by her own timetable.

Artistic

World Championships

Debrecen, Hungary, Nov 20-24
Individual apparatus only

Men

Floor

1	Marian Dragulescu	ROM	9.712
2	Gervasio Deferr	ESP	9.700
3	Jordan Jovtchev	BUL	9.675

Pommel

1	Marius Urzica	ROM	9.787
2	Xiao Qin	CHN	9.750
3	Takehiro Kashima	JPN	9.687

DNQ: Kanukai Jackson (43rd) GBR

Rings

1	Szilveszter Csollany	HUN	9.725
2	Jordan Jovtchev	BUL	9.675
3	Matteo Morandi	ITA	9.650

DNQ: Jackson (40th), Mark Freeman (41st) both GBR

Vault

1	Li Xiaopeng	CHN	9.818
2	Leszek Blanik	POL	9.675
3	Yang Wei	CHN	9.631

DNQ: Jackson (23rd), Darren Gerrard (33rd) both GBR

Parallel Bars

1	Li Xiaopeng	CHN	9.812
2	Mitja Petkovsek	SLO	9.787
3	Alexei Sinkevich	BLR	9.712

High Bars

1	Vlasios Maras	GRE	9.725
2	Ivan Ivankov	BLR	9.700
3	Aljaz Pegan	SLO	9.700

DNQ: Barry Collie (54th)

Women

Vault

1	Elena Zamolodchikova	RUS	9.443
2	Natalia Ziganshina	RUS	9.393
3	Oxana Chusovitina	UZB	9.387

DNQ: Nicola Willis (18th) GBR

Uneven Bars

1	Courtney Kupets	USA	9.550
2	Andreea Petrovschi	ROM	9.525
3	Lyudmilla Eshova	RUS	9.375
4	Beth Tweddle	GBR	9.312

Beam

1	Ashley Postell	USA	9.537
2	Oana Mihaela Ban	ROM	9.350
3	Irina Yarotska	UKR	9.212

DNQ: Beth Tweddle (17th in qualifying), Rebecca Owen (25th in qualifying) both GBR

Floor

1	Elena Gomez	ESP	9.487
2	Verona van der Leur	NED	9.350
3	Samantha Sheeham	USA	9.325

DNQ: Nicola Willis (19th), Rebecca Owen (26th) both GBR

European Championships

Men

Bremen, May 25-28

Team

1	Romania	168.170
2	Russia	167.098
3	Belarus	166.582
14	Great Britain	155.896

All-Around

1	Dan Potra	ROM	55.710
2	Jordan Jovtchev	BUL	55.623
3	Alexei Bondarenko	RUS	55.612
14	Kanukai Jackson	GBR	51.848

Floor

1	Alexei Nemov	RUS	9.825
2	Jordan Jovtchev	BUL	9.762
3	Marian Dragulescu	ROM	9.687

Pommel

1	Marius Urzica	ROM	9.812
2	Ioan Suciu	ROM	9.662
3	Alberto Busnari	ITA	9.637

Rings

1	Jordan Jovtchev	BUL	9.750
2	Dimosthenis Tampakos	ROM	9.730
3	Szilveszter Csollany	HUN	9.725

Vault

1	Dmitri Kasparovich	BLR	9.656
1	Marian Dragulescu	ROM	9.656
3	Kanukai Jackson	GBR	9.581

Parallel Bars

1	Vasilios Tsolakidis	GRE	9.873
2	Mitja Petkovsek	SLO	9.750
3	Alexei Sinkevich	BLR	9.687

High Bar

1	Vlasios Maras	GRE	9.812
2	Florent Maree	FRA	9.712
3	Igor Cassina	ITA	9.687

European Championships
Women

Patras, Greece   *Apr 18-21*

Team

1	Russia	111.833
2	Netherlands	107.635
3	Italy	105.948
6	Great Britain	102.772

All-Around

1	Svetlana Khorkina	RUS	37.592
2	Verona van der Leur	NED	37.542
3	Alona Kvasha	UKR	36.405
10	Rebecca Owen	GBR	35.198
14	Beth Tweddle	GBR	34.242

DNQ for Final: Katy Lennon GBR

Vault

1	Natalia Ziganshina	RUS	9.443
2	Verona van de Leur	NED	9.387
3	Joanna Petrovschi	ROM	9.131

Uneven Bars

1	Svetlana Khorkina	RUS	9.550
2	Renske Endel	NED	9.450
3	Beth Tweddle	GBR	9.287

Beam

1	Ludmilla Eshova	RUS	9.562
2	Svetlana Khorkina	RUS	9.262
3	Verona van der Leur	NED	9.187
7	Beth Tweddle	GBR	8.550

Floor

1	Alona Kvasha	UKR	9.500
2	Natalia van der Leur	NED	9.450
3	Elena Gomez	ESP	9.362

World Cup Final

Stuttgart, Nov 30-Dec 1

Men

Floor
1 Marian Dragulescu ROM 9.662
Pommel
1 Marius Urzica ROM 9.787
Rings
1 Jordan Jovtchev BUL 9.700
Vault
1 Lu Bin CHN 9.749
Parallel Bars
1 Li Xiaopeng CHN 9.837
High Bar
1 Aljaz Pegan SLO 9.675

Women

Vault
1 Oksana Chusovitina UZB 9.412
Uneven Bars
1 Ioanna Petrovschi ROM 9.500
Beam
1 Sun Xiaojiao CHN 9.487
Floor
1 Verona van der Leur NED 9.412

British Championships
Men

Wigan, Nov 2-3

All-Around

1	Kanukai Jackson (Harrow)		53.150
2	Barry Collie (Hinckley)		52.000
3	Ross Brewer (Sutton)		51.650

Floor

1	Ross Brewer (Sutton)	8.88
2	Barry Collie (Hinckley)	8.65
3	Kirk Zammit (Hendon)	8.45

Pommel

1	Ross Brewer (Sutton)	9.13
2	Barry Collie (Hinckley)	8.80
3	Kanukai Jackson (Harrow)	8.55

Rings

1	David Massam (South Essex)	9.20
2	Kanukai Jackson (Harrow)	9.00
3	Barry Collie (Hinckley)	8.60

Vault

1	David Colvin (Fromeside)	8.93
2	Ross Brewer (Sutton)	8.61
3	Allister Whitehead (Wiltshire)	8.50

Parallel Bars

1	Barry Collie (Hinckley)	8.55
2	Ross Brewer (Sutton)	8.43
3	Kirk Zammit (Hendon)	8.33

High Bar

1	Ross Brewer (Sutton)	9.03
2	Barry Collie (Hinckley)	8.53
3	David Colvin (Fromeside)	7.03

Women

Guildford, July 5-7

All-Around

1	Beth Tweddle (Liverpool)	35.050
2	Nicola Willis (South Essex)	34.550
3	Katy Lennon (Leatherhead)	33.575

Vault

1	Katy Lennon (Leatherhead)	9.062
2	Gayle Campbell (Falkirk)	8.937
3	Beth Tweddle (Liverpool)	8.937

Uneven Bars

1	Beth Tweddle (Liverpool)	9.475
2	Rebecca Mason (Sandbach)	8.800
3	Nicola Willis (South Essex)	8.500

Beam

1	Beth Tweddle (Liverpool)	8.950
2	Nicola Willis (South Essex)	8.350
3	Renay Jones (Swansea)	8.737

Floor

1	Nicola Willis (South Essex)	8.775
2	Katy Lennon (Leatherhead)	8.225
3	Eva Nobbs (Wetherby)	8.050

Rhythmic

European Championships

Granada, Nov 8-10

1	Alina Kabaeva	RUS	110.925
2	Tamara Yerofeeva	UKR	107.700
3	Anna Bessonova	UKR	105.425
19	Hannah McKibbin	GBR	87.800

Team

1	Russia	214.700
2	Ukraine	207.925
3	Bulgaria	195.350
10	Great Britain	161.500

(Hannah McKibbin/Rebecca Jose)

Commonwealth Championships

Slough, Apr 20-21

All-Around

1	Hannah McKibbin	ENG	95.950
2	Rebecca Jose	ENG	95.016
3	Pamela Jewell	CAN	86.834

Rope

1	Rebecca Jose	ENG	23.367
2	Hannah McKibbin	ENG	23.200
3	Belinda Potgieter	RSA	21.517

Hoop

1	Hannah McKibbin	ENG	24.417
2	Tanya Vahala	AUS	22.533
3	Irena Funtikova	CAN	22.367

Ball

1	Rebecca Jose	ENG	23.817
2	Hannah McKibbin	ENG	22.967
3	Pamela Jewell	CAN	21.283

Clubs

1	Hannah McKibbin	ENG	24.933
2	Rebecca Jose	ENG	23.233
3	Pamela Jewell	CAN	22.933

Team

1	England	230.051
2	Australia	208.433
3	Canada	203.184
4	South Africa	181.399
5	Wales	176.809
6	New Zealand	167.101
7	Northern Ireland	41.633

Grand Prix

Final Rankings

Rope

1	Simone Peycheva	BUL	118
2	Zarina Gizikova	RUS	84
3	Alina Kabaeva	RUS	83
20	Hannah McKibbin	GBR	3

Hoop

1	Zarina Gizikova	RUS	129
2	Tamara Yerofeeva	UKR	121
3	Anna Bessonova	UKR	91
26	Hannah McKibbin	GBR	2

Ball

1	Zarina Gizikova	RUS	116
2	Tamara Yerofeeva	UKR	93
3	Anna Bessonova	UKR	92
27	Hannah McKibbin	GBR	2

Clubs

1	Tamara Yerofeeva	UKR	106
2	Zarina Gizikova	RUS	89
3	Simone Peycheva	BUL	81
21	Hannah McKibbin	GBR	4

British Championships

Burton-on-Trent, Dec 7-8

All-Around

1	Rebecca Jose (Spelthorne)	97.050
2	Hannah Walker (Coventry)	86.925
3	Rachel Ennis (Hillingdon)	81.075

Rope

1	Rebecca Jose (Spelthorne)	22.050
2	Hannah Walker (Coventry)	20.300
3	Rachel Ennis (Hillingdon)	18.900

Hoop

1	Rebecca Jose (Spelthorne)	23.125
3	Rachel Ennis (Hillingdon)	20.450
3	Caroline Jackson (Spelthorne)	18.225

Ball

1	Rebecca Jose (Spelthorne)	24.600
2	Hannah Walker (Coventry)	23.275
3	Rachel Ennis (Hillingdon)	18.975

Clubs

1	Rebecca Jose (Spelthorne)	24.100
2	Rachel Ennis (Hillingdon)	21.225
2	Hannah Walker (Coventry)	20.000

Trampoline

European Championships

St Petersburg, Nov 11-16

Men

Trampoline

1	Alexandre Moskalenko	RUS	42.1
2	Guerman Khnytchev	RUS	41.8
3	David Martin	FRA	41.6

Elim in Prelims: Paul Smith (17th), Simon Milnes (25th), Gary Smith (27th), Lee Brearley (32nd), all GBR

Trampoline Synchro

1	Stehlik/Kubicka	GER	50.8
2	Milnes/Alexander	GBR	49.5
3	Moskalenko/Roussakov	RUS	49.2

Elim in Prelims: Brearley/Alexanders (19th) GBR

Trampoline Team

1	Ukraine	122.9
2	Russia	121.6
3	Great Britain	119.6
	Smith/Milnes/Smyth	

Double Mini Tramp

1	Alex Cuenca	ESP	64.0
2	Amadeu Neves	POR	63.5
3	Martin Gromowski	GER	63.2

Elim in Prelims: Glen Rate (16th), Arren Stokes (17th), Toby Eager (19th), all GBR

Tumbling

1	Andrey Dukhno	RUS	74.6
2	Yves Tarin	FRA	73.2
3	Robert Proctor	GBR	71.3
5	Robert Small	GBR	67.7

Elim in Prelims: Damien Walters (13th) GBR

Tumbling Team

1	Russia	111.1
2	France	110.7
3	Great Britain	108.4
	Gibson/Proctor/Small	

Women

Trampoline

1	Natalia Chernova	RUS	39.6
2	Olena Movchan	UKR	39.6
3	Galina Lebedeva	BLR	39.2
6	Kirsten Lawton	GBR	36.3
8	Claire Wright	GBR	5.5

Elim in Prelims: Aurora Necco (16th), Natalie O'Connor (22nd) both GBR

Trampoline Synchro

1	Lebedeva/Petrenia	BLR	47.9
2	Lawton/Wright	GBR	47.8
3	Dogodnadze/Ludwig	GER	47.7

Elim in Prelims: Necco/O'Connor (9th) GBR

Trampoline Team

1	Russia	117.6
2	Ukraine	116.1
3	Great Britain	115.4
	Necco/Lawton/Wright	

Double Mini Tramp

1	Ilse Despriet	BEL	62.7
2	Kathrin Deuner	GER	62.3
3	Katarina Prokesova	SVK	61.4
6	Stephanie Coyte	GBR	60.3

Elim in Prelims: Natalie O'Connor (16th) GBR

Tumbling

1	Elena Bluzhina	RUS	73.1
2	Kathryn Peberdy	GBR	72.4
3	Olena Chabanenko	UKR	69.5
5	Charmaine Sala	GBR	66.0

Elim in Prelims: Julie Cheung (12th), Elizabeth Gough (21st) both GBR

Tumbling Team

1	Ukraine	102.1
2	Great Britain	101.2
	Cheung/Sala/Peberdy	
3	Belarus	99.3

Junior Events

Held at the same venue as the senior events; only British results listed.

Women

Trampoline: 1 Hannah Lewis
Trampoline Synchro: 3 Driscoll/Lewis
Trampoline Team: 1 Great Britain
Tumbling: 1 Samantha Palmer
Tumbling Team; 2 Great Britain

Men

Double Mini Tramp; 3 Dominic Swaffer

British Championships

NEC, Birmingham, July 7-8

Men's Trampoline

1	Paul Smyth (Edgbarrow)	110.6
2	Lee Brearley (Salford)	109.5
3	James Higgins (Northampton)	107.3

Women's Trampoline

1	Claire Wright (Edgbarrow)	105.9
2	Natalie O'Connor (Edgbarrow)	100.3
3	Hannah Lewis (OLGA)	100.3

Sports Acrobatics

World Championships
Riesa, Germany, Sep 27-29

Team

1	Russia	83
2	China	77
3	Ukraine	77
4	Great Britain	68

Men's Pair

1	Li Renjie/Song Min	CHN	17.66
2	Dewulf/Van Vynckt	BEL	17.02
3	Nikolov/Ivanov	RUS	16.93
7	Jones/Morritt	GBR	15.57

Men's Group

1	Russia	17.64
2	Great Britain	16.53
	McKenzie/Scott/Petterson/Hindson	
3	China	16.35

Women's Pair

1	Lopatkina/Mokhova	RUS	17.59
2	Konko/Ukolova	UKR	16.98
3	Wu Jinmei/Shi Danying	CHN	16.59

Women's Group

1	Russia	18.64
2	China	18.18
3	Ukraine	17.83
6	Great Britain	16.59
	Belchamber/Lawton/Drinkald	

Mixed Pair

1	Kirjanova/Trubitsin	RUS	18.76
1	Booth/Davis	USA	18.76
3	Bonner/Hobby	GBR	17.61

Sports Aerobics

World Championships
Klaipeda, Lithuania, July 29-31

Individual Men

1	Jonathan Canada	ESP	19.680
2	Gregory Alcan	FRA	18.150
3	Stanislav Marchenkov	RUS	17.800

Individual Women

1	Yuriko Ito	JPN	18.450
2	Daniela Lacatus	ROM	17.950
3	Tania Pohoata	ROM	17.450

Mixed Pairs

1	Soloviova/Oskner	RUS	18.700
2	Lecis/Satti	ITA	18.350
3	Lacatus/Nicolai	ROM	17.850

Trios

1	Spain	19.061
2	Bulgaria	18.871
3	Chile	17.894

Groups

1	Romania	17.539
2	Russia	16.347
3	Russia 2	16.000

Hockey

This was the year that English hockey went broke, or more accurately, the year that it found out it was broke. It's amazing how many British sports have gone broke in the past few years; treasurers suddenly waking up to the realisation that the numbers shown in brackets on the accounts sheet is money you haven't got.

Someone had to go when the penny dropped. Well, it wasn't penny exactly, it was over £700,000 and that didn't include VAT of half a million. Richard Wyatt, father of international Jon but also the chief executive of the Hockey Association, was the man who went and EHA president Mike Corby, who had experienced similar problems with squash, was put in charge of the rescue operation.

The white knight, it transpired, was a business associate of Corby, who came forward with the irresistible offer of an interest-free loan of £500,000. Steve Newton, president of Brighton & Hockey club, offered the money to set up Hockey England Limited as the new controlling body of the sport. The clubs voted to put in another £75 per team, and English hockey was saved and everyone was overjoyed. Er, except perhaps the creditors of the English Hockey Association, who, at the last count, were expecting 25p in the £1 for the money they were owed.

The England men's team had their World Cup first and flattered to deceive, as ever, defeating India for the first time in 18 years, and only realising how little it meant when everyone else beat them too. Usually England regroup in the later stages of this competition and salvage a place in the 5th/6th place play-off, but not this time. Defeat against Japan was probably the lowest point, and they ended up in seventh overall.

Germany won the men's World Cup, but their women fared less well, humbled by the England team 7-2 in the play-offs. The English women then staged a magnificent comeback against the Koreans - from 3-1 down they levelled and won on penalties - and ended the tournament in a very respectable fifth place, just a place behind the Australians, Argentina the first-time winners.

In domestic hockey, Slough won the women's Premier League, but a week after putting seven goals past Olton in the league, a bemused Slough lost to them in the EHA Cup Final. Reading achieved the men's double, but not without a little subterfuge en route. In their match against Surbiton, an opposition player stood in the shower to try and overhear the team talk of Reading coach Jon Copp. "I am outraged. I think what Surbiton did was disgraceful," said Copp, who moved his team talk to a room upstairs. While Brett Garrard, the player in question, said he often stood in the shower fully clothed. No, he didn't really. To his credit, he said he was sorry.

M e n

World Cup

Kuala Lumpur, Feb 24-Mar 9

Pool A

Pakistan 5 South Africa 0; Spain 2 Belgium 0;
Germany 5 Argentina 2; Netherlands 4 New Zealand 2;
Pakistan 3 Belgium 2; Germany 3 South Africa 0;
Spain 3 New Zealand 1; Netherlands 2 Argentina 1;
Netherlands 5 Belgium 1; Argentina 4 South Africa 1;
Spain 3 Germany 2; Pakistan 2 New Zealand 0;
Spain 1 Netherlands 1; New Zealand 2 South Africa 1;
Argentina 2 Pakistan 1; Germany 3 Belgium 0;
Germany 2 New Zealand 1; Spain 2 South Africa 2;
Argentina 3 Belgium 1; Netherlands 2 Pakistan 1;
Argentina 3 New Zealand 1; Pakistan 2 Spain 0;
South Africa 3 Belgium 0; Germany 1 Netherlands 0;
New Zealand 4 Belgium 3; Germany 3 Belgium 2;
Netherlands 3 South Africa 0; Argentina 3 Spain 1

Pool A Standings

		P	W	D	L	GF	GA	Pts
1	Germany	7	6	0	1	19	8	18
2	Netherlands	7	5	1	1	17	5	15
3	Argentina	7	5	0	2	18	12	15
4	Pakistan	7	4	0	3	16	9	12
5	Spain	7	3	2	2	12	11	11
6	New Zealand	7	2	0	5	9	17	6
7	South Africa	7	1	1	5	7	19	4
8	Belgium	7	0	0	7	7	23	0

Pool B

Korea 6 Cuba 2; England 1 Poland 0; Japan 2 India 2;
Australia 2 Malaysia 0; Korea 2 India 0; Malaysia 1
Japan 0; Australia 1 England 0; Poland 4 Cuba 1;
Malaysia 3 India 2; Australia 5 Poland 1; England 7
Cuba 0; Korea 3 Japan 0; Australia 6 Cuba 0; Japan 2
Poland 1; England 3 India 2; Korea 3 Malaysia 0;
Australia 5 Japan 0; India 4 Cuba 0; Korea 4 Poland 0;
Malaysia 2 England 1; Japan 2 England 1; Malaysia 4
Cuba 2; India 4 Poland 1; Australia 4 Korea 2; Japan 4
Cuba 2; England 2 Korea 0; Australia 4 India 3; Poland 2
Malaysia 2

Pool B Standings

		P	W	D	L	GF	GA	Pts
1	Australia	7	7	0	0	28	6	21
2	Korea	7	5	0	2	20	11	15
3	Malaysia	7	5	0	2	14	13	15
4	England	7	4	0	3	15	7	12
5	India	7	2	1	4	15	15	7
6	Japan	7	3	1	3	10	15	7
7	Poland	7	1	1	5	9	19	3
8	Cuba	7	0	0	7	5	31	0

Places 13-16 Play-offs

South Africa 5   Cuba 1
Belgium 2   Poland 1

Places 15/16 Play-off

Poland 3   Cuba 0

Places 13/14 Play-off

South Africa 5   Belgium 4
South Africa won on golden goal

Places 9-12 Play-offs

India 3   Spain 0
New Zealand 3   Japan 3
New Zealand won 10-9 on penalty strokes

Places 11/12 Play-off

Spain 5   Japan 1

Places 9/10 Play-off

New Zealand 2   India 1

Places 5-8 Play-offs

Argentina 2   England 1
Pakistan 2   Malaysia 1

Places 7/8 Play-off

England 3   Malaysia 2

Places 5/6 Play-off

Pakistan 5   Argentina 3

SEMI-FINALS

Germany 3   Korea 2
Australia 4   Netherlands 1

BRONZE MEDAL MATCH

Netherlands 2   Korea 1
Netherlands won on golden goal

FINAL

Germany 2   Australia 1

Final Standings:

1. Germany; 2. Australia; 3. Netherlands; 4. Korea;
5. Pakistan; 6. Argentina; 7. England; 8. Malaysia;
9. New Zealand; 10. India; 11. Spain; 12. Japan;
13. South Africa; 14. Belgium; 15. Poland; 16. Cuba

Champions Trophy

Cologne, Aug 31-Sep 8

Round Robin Matches

Germany 3 Pakistan 2; India 3 Netherlands 3;
Korea 3 Australia 2; Germany 3 India 2;
Pakistan 4 Korea 1; Netherlands 6 Australia 1;
India 3 Australia 2; Netherlands 3 Pakistan 1;
Germany 2 Korea 1; India 3 Pakistan 2;
Germany 3 Australia 2; Netherlands 4 Korea 2;
Pakistan 2 Australia 0; Netherlands 5 Germany 2;
Korea 4 India 2

Table

		P	W	D	L	GF	GA	Pts
1	Netherlands	5	4	1	0	21	9	13
2	Germany	5	4	0	1	13	12	12
3	India	5	3	0	2	13	14	7
4	Pakistan	5	2	0	3	11	10	6
5	Korea	5	2	0	3	11	14	6
6	Australia	5	0	0	5	7	17	0

Places 5/6 Play-off

Australia 3   Korea 0

BRONZE MEDAL MATCH

Pakistan 4   India 3

FINAL

Netherlands 3   Germany 0

European Club Championship
A Division
Antwerp, Belgium, May 17-20
Pool A Rankings
1. 's-Hertogenbosch NED; 2. Surbiton ENG;
3. WKS Grunwald POL; 4. Stroitel Brest BLR
Pool B Rankings
1. Der Alster GER; 2. Egara ESP;
3. Dragons BEL; 4. Western SCO
Crossover Matches (5th-8th)

| Dragons 3 | Stroitel Brest 2 |
| Grunwald 3 | Western 1 |

3rd/4th Place Play-off

| Egara 3 | Surbiton 2 |

FINAL

| Der Alster 2 | s-Hertogenbosch 2 |

De Alster won 3-0 on penalty strokes
Final Ranking: 1. Der Alster; 2. s-Hertogenbosch;
3. Egara; 4. Surbiton; 5. Dragons; 5. Grunwald;
7. Western; 7. Stroitel Brest
Western and Stroitel relegated to B Division

B Division
Wettingen, Switzerland, May 17-20
FINAL

| Lille FRA 3 | Pembroke IRL 1 |

Final Rankings: 1. Lille; 2. Pembroke;
3. Dinamo Ekaterinaburg RUS; 4. Wettingen SUI;
5 WAC AUT; 5. Slavia Prague CZE;
7. Kolos Vinnitsa UKR; 7. Eagles GIB
LIlle and Pembroke promoted to A Division
Kolos and Eagles relegated to C Division

C Division
Cardiff, Wales, May 16-19
FINAL

| HC Roma ITA 4 | Orient Lygby 3 |

Final Rankings: 1. Roma; 2. Orient Lygby;
3. Whitchurch WAL; 4. Ramaldense POR; 5. HAT 85 FIN;
5. Zelina CRO; 7. Valhalla SWE
Roma and Orient promoted to B Division

European Cup Winners' Cup
A Division
Eindhoven, Netherlands, Mar 29-Apr 1
Final

| Oranje Zwart BEL 1 | Reading ENG 1 |

Oranje won 5-3 on penalty strokes
Final Ranking: 1 Orange; 2. Reading; 3. Rheydter GER;
4 Pocztowiec POL; 5. Zurich SUI; 5. Racing Club FRA;
7. Aberdeen SCO; 7. White Star BEL
Aberdeen and White Star relegated to Division B

B Division
Gibraltar, Mar 29-Apr 1
Final

| Atletica Terrassa ESP 4 | Glenanne IRL 0 |

Terrassa and Glenanne promoted to Division C

English Hockey

Premier Division

		P	W	D	L	GF	GA	Pts
1	Reading	18	16	1	1	61	24	49
2	Surbiton	18	12	2	4	42	24	38
3	Cannock	18	10	3	5	45	30	33
4	Loughborough	18	8	2	8	49	36	26
5	Guildford	18	8	2	8	49	37	26
6	Canterbury	18	7	2	9	52	56	23
7	Teddington	18	5	4	9	28	44	19
8	Hampstead	18	5	2	11	30	41	17
9	Old Loughtonian*	18	4	5	9	25	445	15
10	Southgate	18	1	5	12	19	63	8

* Two points deducted for fielding an ineligible player

Premiership Final
Beeston, May 6

| Reading 3 | Surbiton 2 |

Division One

		P	W	D	L	GF	GA	Pts
1	St Albans	18	13	4	1	53	29	43
2	Doncaster	18	10	4	4	46	33	34
3	Bournville	18	10	3	5	42	33	33
4	Beeston	18	10	2	6	43	33	32
5	Firebrands	18	6	6	6	39	38	24
6	Chelmsford	18	6	4	8	33	35	22
7	Barford Tigers	18	5	2	11	39	49	17
8	Stourport	18	4	5	9	30	42	17
9	Brooklands	18	4	4	10	35	47	16
10	Lewes	18	4	2	12	36	57	14

Division Two

		P	W	D	L	GF	GA	Pts
1	Belper	22	19	1	2	106	26	58
2	Hounslow & Ealing	22	14	3	5	49	32	45
3	East Grinstead	22	11	3	8	53	51	36
4	Havant	22	10	4	8	58	47	34
5	Peterborough	22	8	5	9	41	56	29
6	Indian Gymkhana	22	7	6	9	50	53	27
7	Formby	22	8	3	11	47	55	27
8	Nottingham	22	8	3	11	38	58	27
9	Blueharts	22	7	3	12	37	51	24
10	Oxford Hawks	22	7	2	13	34	48	23
11	Ipswich*	22	6	5	11	44	59	23
12	Bromley	22	6	4	12	35	56	22

* Relegated after play-offs

EHA Cup
Final
Milton Keynes, Apr 7

| Cannock 7 | Belper 0 |

European Nations Cup 2003
Scotland and Ireland, through qualifiers in Poznan and
Dublin respectively, reached the finals of the Nations
Cup, joining England in the 12-nation line-up at
Barcelona in September.

Women

World Cup

Meadow Lea, Perth, Australia, Nov 24-Dec 8

Poll A Matches

China 0 Korea 0; Germany 4 Russia 0;
Argentina 1 New Zealand 0; Ukraine 2 Scotland 1;
New Zealand 3 Russia 1; China 3 Scotland 0;
Korea 3 Germany 1; Argentina 5 Ukraine 1;
Scotland 2 New Zealand 1; Korea 2 Ukraine 2;
Argentina 1 Germany 0; China 2 Russia 1;
Germany 3 Scotland 0; Korea 3 New Zealand 0;
Ukraine 3 Russia 3; Argentina 2 China 0;
Germany 3 New Zealand 1; Argentina 5 Scotland 0;
Korea 5 Russia 0; China 4 Ukraine 1;
New Zealand 3 Ukraine 0; China 3 Germany 1;
Argentina 2 Korea 1; Scotland 3 Russia 1;
Germany 5 Ukraine 2; Korea 6 Scotland 2;
Argentina 1 Russia 0; China 2 New Zealand 0

Pool A Standings

		P	W	D	L	GF	GA	Pts
1	Argentina	7	7	0	0	17	2	21
2	China	7	5	1	1	14	5	16
3	Korea	7	4	2	1	20	7	14
4	Germany	7	4	0	3	17	10	12
5	New Zealand	7	2	0	5	8	12	6
6	Scotland	7	2	0	5	8	21	6
7	Ukraine	7	1	2	4	11	23	5
8	Russia	7	0	1	6	6	21	1

Pool B Matches

Japan 1 Spain 1; England 3 Ireland 0;
Australia 4 USA 0; Netherlands 3 South Africa 0;
Netherlands 2 Japan 0; South Africa 2 England 2;
USA 2 Ireland 1; Australia 1 Spain 0;
Spain 3 South Africa 1; Japan 2 USA 1;
Australia 2 Ireland 1; Netherlands 2 England 1;
South Africa 1 Japan 1; Spain 4 USA 1;
Netherlands 6 Ireland 0; Australia 3 England 1;
South Africa 3 USA 0; Spain 2 Ireland 1;
Japan 1 England 1; Netherlands 3 Australia 1;
England 1 USA 0; Japan 1 Ireland 0;
Spain 1 Netherlands 1; Australia 5 South Africa 0;
Netherlands 5 USA 2; England 3 Spain 0;
South Africa 6 Ireland 0; Australia 1 Japan 1;

Pool B Standings

		P	W	D	L	GF	GA	Pts
1	Netherlands	7	6	1	0	22	5	19
2	Australia	7	5	1	1	17	6	16
3	England	7	3	2	2	12	9	11
4	Spain	7	3	2	2	11	9	11
5	Japan	7	2	4	1	7	7	10
6	USA	7	2	0	5	9	17	6
7	South Africa	7	1	2	4	10	17	5
8	Ireland	7	0	0	7	4	22	0

Places 13-16 Play-offs

South Africa 4   Russia 1
Ukraine 4   Ireland 3

Places 15/16 Play-off

Ireland 1   Russia 0

Places 13/14 Play-off

South Africa 3   Ukraine 1

Places 9-12 Play-offs

Japan 3   Scotland 0
USA 1   New Zealand 0

Places 11/12 Play-off

New Zealand 3   Scotland 0

Places 9/10 Play-off

USA 0   Japan 0
USA won 4-2 on penalty strokes

Places 5-8 Play-offs

England 7   Germany 2
Korea 2   Spain 0

Places 7/8 Play-off

Germany 6   Spain 1

Places 5/6 Play-off

England 3   Korea 3
England won 4-3 on penalty strokes

Semi-finals

Argentina 1   Australia 0
Netherlands 1   China 0

BRONZE MEDAL MATCH

China 2   Australia 0

FINAL

Argentina 1   Netherlands 1
Argentina won 4-3 on penalty strokes

Final Standings:

1. Argentina; 2. Netherlands; 3. China; 4. Australia;
5. England; 6. Korea; 7. Germany; 8. Spain;
9. USA; 10. Japan; 11. New Zealand; 12. Scotland;
13. South Africa; 14. Ukraine; 15. Ireland; 16. Russia

Champions Trophy

Macau, China, Aug 24-Sep 1

Round Robin Matches

Argentina 1 New Zealand 0; Australia 0 Netherlands 0;
China 1 England 1; Argentina 1 Netherlands 1;
New Zealand 5 England 0; China 1 Australia 0;
Australia 3 New Zealand 1; Argentina 4 England 0;
China 1 Netherlands 1; Australia 2 England 0;
Netherlands 2 New Zealand 2; Argentina 1 China 1;
Netherlands 2 England 0; China 1 New Zealand 0;
Argentina 2 Australia 2

Table

		P	W	D	L	GF	GA	Pts
1	China	5	3	2	0	5	3	11
2	Argentina	5	2	3	0	9	4	9
3	Australia	5	2	2	1	7	4	8
4	Netherlands	5	1	4	0	6	4	7
5	New Zealand	5	1	1	3	8	7	4
6	England	5	0	1	4	1	14	1

Places 5/6 Play-off

New Zealand 2   England 0

BRONZE MEDAL MATCH

Netherlands 4   Australia 3 (OT)

FINAL

China 2   Argentina 2
China won 3-1 on penalty strokes

European Indoor Cup

A Division
Les Ponts de Ce, France, Jan 25-27
FINAL
Germany 14   Lithuania 3
Final Standings: 1. Germany; 2. Lithuania; 3. France;
4. Austria; 5. Czech Rep; 6. Russia; 7. Slovakia;
8. Scotland

B Division
Rotterdam, Jan 25-27
FINAL
Netherlands 7   Belarus 3
Final Standings: 1. Netherlands; 2. Belarus; 3. Poland;
4. Switzerland; 5. Finland

European Club Championship

A Division
Terrassa, Spain, May 17-20
Pool A Rankings
1. s-Hertogenbosch NED; 2. Slough ENG;
3. Terrassa ESP; 4. Slavia Praha CZE
Pool B Rankings
1. Kolos Borispol UKR; 2. Gintra LTU;
3. Russelheimer GER; 4. Donchanka RUS
Crossover Matches
Donchanka 3   Terrassa 2
Russelheimer 4   Slavia Praha 2
3rd/4th Place Play-off
Slough 2   Gintra 0
FINAL
s-Hertogenbosch 5   Borispol 0
Final Ranking: 1. Hertogenbosch; 2. Borispol;
3. Slough; 4. Gintra; 5. Donchanka; 5. Russelheimer;
7. Terrassa; 7. Slavia Praha
Terrassa and Praha relegated to B Division

B Division
Vienna, May 17-20
FINAL
Bonagrass SCO 2 Pegasus IRL 0
Final Rankings: 1. Bonagrass Grove; 2. Pegasus;
3. Ritm Grodno BLR; 4. Cambrai FRA; 5. Swansea WAL;
5. Wiener Neudorf AUT; 7. Wettingen SUI;
7. Libertas san Saba ITA
Bonagrass and Pegasus promoted to A Division

European Cup Winners' Cup

A Division
Ourense, Spain, Mar 29-Apr 1
FINAL
Rotterdam NED 3   Leicester ENG 0
Final Standings
l1. Rotterdam; 2. Leicester; 3. Western SCO;
4. Ourense ESP; 5. Moscow RUS; 5. Der Alster GER;
7. Ballymoney IRL; 7. Lorenzoni ITA
Ballymoney and Lorenzoni relegated to B Division

English Hockey

Premier Division

		P	W	D	L	GF	GA	Pts
1	Slough	18	12	3	3	40	22	39
2	Olton & West Warwick	18	9	5	4	52	29	32
3	Fyffes Leicester	18	10	2	6	34	23	32
4	Clifton	18	9	4	5	37	17	31
5	Canterbury	18	7	4	7	30	34	25
6	Chelmsford	18	6	5	7	26	26	23
7	Ipswich	18	6	5	7	34	41	23
8	Hightown	18	5	2	11	29	44	17
9	Sutton Coldfield	18	5	2	11	25	51	17
10	Doncaster	18	4	2	12	23	43	14

Premiership Final
Beeston, May 6
Olton 3   Slough 1

Division One

		P	W	D	L	GF	GA	Pts
1	Trojans	18	11	4	3	30	12	37
2	Wimbledon	18	11	3	4	38	18	36
3	Loughborough	18	9	6	3	40	22	33
4	Harleston	18	6	8	4	23	19	26
5	Liverpool	18	7	4	7	25	29	25
6	Old Loughtonians	18	7	3	8	27	30	24
7	Hounslow & Ealing	18	5	6	7	21	33	21
8	Sunderland	18	4	7	7	23	25	19
9	Woking	18	4	2	12	27	51	14
10	Bradford Newitts	18	3	3	12	14	29	12

Division Two

		P	W	D	L	GF	GA	Pts
1	Reading	18	12	5	1	30	11	41
2	Poynton	18	9	4	5	38	29	31
3	Bedford	18	9	4	5	29	21	31
4	Exmouth	18	8	4	6	32	34	28
5	Leyland Motors	18	8	0	10	34	41	24
6	Deeside Ramblers	18	6	5	7	15	23	23
7	St Albans	18	6	3	9	30	23	21
8	Aldridge	18	6	3	9	18	23	21
9	Rover Oxford	18	4	6	8	31	39	18
10	Bracknell	18	3	4	11	19	32	13

EHA Cup
Final
Milton Keynes, Apr 7
Ipswich 3   Olton 2

Horse Racing

For Mighty Montefalco, a 108-rated hurdler, it was very untaxing afternoon at Uttoxeter. He was already an odds-on shot and, when the second favourite Derring Bridge dug in his hooves at the start and wouldn't race a yard, you could have staked the house on the fact that the favourite wouldn't be beaten. Mighty Montefalco came home a comfortable winner and was surely bemused by the roar of the crowd for winning such a modest little prize.

On his back, and smiling for once, was Tony McCoy who had just ridden his 1700th winner and surpassed the record of Richard Dunwoody. What's more, he had done it in less than half the time and, injuries permitting, could easily add another 1000 or more before any thought of retirement flits across his perpetually furrowed brow. The plaudits post-Uttoxeter were universal; almost the only caveat, the fact that McCoy laughs even less often than Peter Scudamore once did. No one ventured to suggest that the Irishman wasn't just the best jockey in the business now, but the best that there has ever been.

"Whoa!" as you might say to a horse. McCoy has won more races than anyone ever, but if Richard Johnson had been Martin Pipe's stable jockey for the past eight years, or Mick Fitzgerald, or even Seamus Durack, might we not be celebrating their genius rather than McCoy's? Without doubt, each of those jockeys would have been crowned champion for most of the same period.

McCoy's tenacity in a finish is what endears him to backers, though frequently the Irishman has paid scant regard to whatever whip rules have been in operation, with a complicity of stewards (is this the group noun?) applying a two-tier system. One rule for him and one for us, to paraphrase Mick Fitzgerald.

McCoy is good, very good, and 2002 belonged to him, but we still believe that history will judge that others have been better. John Francome would probably sit atop of our list, and Fred Winter wasn't bad either.

McCoy was, at least, a good news story for the year, as was Rock Of Gibraltar, who won seven straight Group One races and was still only rated five pounds better than Terry Mills' Where Or When. Given that the only time they met, the Rock left Where Or When seven lengths behind without a great deal of bother, 10 pounds would be the minimum. The Rock has retired, leaving his half-owner Sir Alex richer still, but Aidan O'Brien needing to find a new champion or two. He will, naturally.

Record Breakers

Most wins by NH jockeys

Stan Mellor 1954-1972	1035
John Francome 1970-1985	1138
Peter Scudamore 1978-1993	1678
Richard Dunwoody 1982-1999	1699
Tony McCoy 1984-2012?	3000?

For most of the rest of the racing year, the stories were less edifying. First, Kenyon Confronts, then Panorama took racing to task. The sport could almost have taken its lead from Ferguson for it instantly adopted a siege mentality; a philosophy that has stood the test of time for Man United. The sport was fine, the media was wrong, was an argument, though, which had a hollow ring. For any neutral watching the Panorama programme, the responses of Kieren Fallon, Jimmy Fitzgerald and Graham Bradley were so emotional, so hostile, that the viewer was left wondering what they had to hide, even though it might have been nothing at all. The Bradley affair rolls on, with the former jockey taking legal action to get his ban lifted so that he can operate as a bloodstock agent.

His fellow jockeys have rallied around Bradley, but the facts are not so kind. In court in 2001, at the trial of another jockey, Bradley admitted to accepting money in exchange for supplying information to a renowned gambler Brian Wright. Nights out, gifts, cash in envelopes were all admitted by Bradley, who wasn't even on trial himself. Showing such a flagrant disregard to the rules of racing should ensure that a continuing Bradley ban goes without saying, but it doesn't. The people who suffer when racing is shown to be corrupt are only the punters, and they (or we) have always been considered expendable.

Internally, the only head that rolled was that of the British Horseracing Board's head of security Jeremy Phipps, who didn't for one moment, apparently, believe that the man who preceded him in the job, Roger Buffham, would tape record his damning comments about his employers. It was Buffham who provided the source for most of the Panorama programme and the industry subsequently set about his character assassination. The wrong call again. Soon no one will remember who Buffham was, but they will still have in their minds an image of a sport that has dirty linen aplenty.

International Ratings
2002

European Two-Year-Olds

1	Oasis Dream (John Gosden)	123
2	Tout Seul (Fulke Johnson Houghton)	122
3	Six Perfections (Pascal Bary FRA)	121
4	Elusive City (Gerard Butler)	119
	Tomahawk (Aidan O'Brien IRL)	119
6	Dalakhani (A de Royer Dupre FRA)	118
	Somnus (Tim Easterby)	118
8	Airwave (Henry Candy)	117
	Hold That Tiger (Aidan O'Brien IRL)	117
	Zafeen (Mick Channon)	117

International Three-Year-Olds

1	Rock Of Gibraltar (Aidan O'Brien IRL)	128
2	High Chaparral (Aidan O'Brien IRL)	126
	Sulamani (Pascal Bary FRA)	126
4	War Emblem (Bob Baffert USA)	124
5	Act One (Jonathan Pease FRA)	123
6	Hawk Wing (Aidan O'Brien IRL)	123
	Where Or When (Terry Mills)	123
8	Came Home (Paco Gonzalez USA)	121
	Medaglia D'Oro (Bobby Frankel USA)	121

International Older Horses

1	Marienbard (Saeed Bin Suroor)	127
2	Golan (Michael Stoute)	126
	Grandera (Saeed Bin Suroor)	126
	Keltos (Carlos Laffon Parais FRA)	126
5	Azeri (Mike Smith USA)	125
	Nayef (Marcus Tregoning)	125
	Volponi (Phil Johnson USA)	125
8	Domedriver (Pascal Bary USA)	124
	Northerly (Fred Kersley AUS)	124
	Orientate (D Wayne Lucas USA)	124
	Street City (Saeed Bin Suroor)	124

Flat Racing

Vodafone Derby Stakes-

Epsom, June 8   3yo c&f   1m 4f 10y   *12 ran*

1 High Chaparral (9-0)	Johnny Murtagh	7/2
Aidan O'Brien IRL	*£800,400*	
2 Hawk Wing (9-0)	Mick Kinane	9/4JF
Aidan O'Brien IRL	*£303,600*	
3 Moon Ballad (9-0)	Jamie Spencer	20/1
Saeed Bin Suroor	*£151,800*	
4 Jelani (9-0)	Fergal Lynch	100/1
Andrew Turnell	*£69,000*	
5 Fight Your Corner (9-0)	Kevin Darley	8/1
Mark Johnston	*£34,500*	
6 Where Or When (9-0)	Jimmy Fortune	66/1
Terry Mills	*£20,700*	
7 Naheef (9-0)	Frankie Dettori	5/1
8 Bandari (9-0)	Richard Hills	9/2
9 Louisville (9-0)	Kieren Fallon	25/1
10 Tholjanah (9-0)	Willie Supple	14/1
11 Frankies Dream (9-0)	Pat Eddery	100/1
F Coshocton (9-0)	Philip Robinson	28/1

Distances: 2, 12, 1, 5, 17, 2, 12, 6, 6
Going: Good to Soft
Time: 2:39.45 (+5.85)
Winning Owners: Michael Tabor & Sue Magnier
Second Owner: Sue Magnier
Third Owner: Godolphin

The Other Classics

Sagitta 2000 Guineas Stakes

Newmarket, May 4   3yo c&f   1m   *22 ran*

1 Rock Of Gibraltar (9-0)	Johnny Murtagh	9/1
2 Hawk Wing (9-0)	Jamie Spencer	6/4F
3 Redback (9-0)	Darryll Holland	14/1

Distances: nk, 1¼   Aidan O'Brien IRL   £174,000

Sagitta 1000 Guineas Stakes

Newmarket, May 5   3yo f   1m   *17 ran*

1 Kazzia (9-0)	Frankie Dettori	14/1
2 Snowfire (9-0)	Pat Eddery	28/1
3 Alasha (9-0)	Johnny Murtagh	6/1

Distances: nk, nk   Saeed Bin Suroor   £174,000

Vodafone Oaks Stakes

Epsom, June 7   3yo f   1m 4f 10y   *14 ran*

1 Kazzia (9-0)	Frankie Dettori	100/30F
2 Quarter Moon (9-0)	Mick Kinane	15/2
3 Shadow Dancing (9-0)	Martin Dwyer	14/1

Distances: ½, 14   Saeed Bin Suroor   £203,000

St Leger Stakes

Doncaster, Sep 14   3yo c&f   1m 6f 132y   *8 ran*

1 Bollin Eric (9-0)	Kevin Darley	7/1
2 Highest (9-0)	Sir Michael Stoute	10/1
3 Bandari (9-0)	Richard Hills	13/8F

Distances: 1¼, 2   Tim Easterby   £240,000

2002 UK Group One Wins By Trainer

Last year's win count in brackets

Aidan O'Brien 6 (10)

2000 Guineas, Derby, Sussex Stakes, St James's Palace
Coronation Stakes, Racing Post Trophy

Saeed Bin Suroor 3 (5)

1000 Guineas, Oaks, Prince Of Wales Stakes

Michael Stoute 3 (3)

King George VI and QE Stakes, Nassau Stakes, Yorkshire Oaks

Henry Candy 2 (-) Nunthorpe, Cheveley Park Stakes

John Gosden 2 (-) Middle Park Stakes, Golden Jubilee Stakes

John Dunlop 1 (-) Spring Cup   **Tim Easterby 1** (-) St Leger

James Fanshawe 1 (-) Fillies Mile   **Barry Hills 1** (-) Champion Stakes

Mark Johnston 1 (-) Gold Cup   **Fulke Johnson Houghton 1** (-) Dewhurst Stakes

Carlos Laffon Parias FRA 1 (-) Lockinge   **Terry Mills 1** (-) Queen Elizabeth II Stakes

David Nicholls 1 (-) July Cup   **Peter Schergen GER 1** (-) Coronation Cup

Marcus Tregoning 1 (-) Juddmonte

Group One

(see also Ascot)

Juddmonte Lockinge Stakes
Newbury, May 18   4yo+ 1m   10 ran
1 Keltos (4-9-0)   Olivier Peslier   9/1
2 Noverre (7-9-0)   Jamie Spencer   5/6F
3 Olden Times (5-9-0)   Mick Kinane   8/1
Distances: 3½, 1½   C Laffon Parias FRA   £99,760

Vodafone Coronation Cup Stakes
Epsom, June 7   4yo+ 1m 4f 10y   6 ran
1 Boreal (4-9-0)   Kieren Fallon   4/1
2 Storming Home (4-9-0)   Michael Hills   7/2
3 Zindabad (6-9-0)   Kevin Darley   9/1
Distances: 3½, 6   Peter Schiergen GER   £159,500

Coral Eurobet Eclipse Stakes
Sandown, July 6   3yo+ 1m 2f 7y   5 ran
1 Hawk Wing (3-8-10)   Mick Kinane   8/15F
2 Sholokhov (3-8-10)   Paul Scallan   14/1
3 Equerry (4-9-7)   Frankie Dettori   4/1
Distances: 2½, 2½   Aidan O'Brien IRL   £188,500

Darley July Cup Stakes
Newmarket, July 11   3yo+ 6f   14 ran
1 Continent (5-9-5)   Darryll Holland   12/1
2 Bahamian Pirate (7-9-5) Richard Hughes   16/1
3 Danehurst (4-9-2)   George Duffield   5/2F
Distances: ½, 1½   David Nicholls   £145,000

King George VI & Queen Elizabeth Stakes
Ascot, July 27   3yo+ 1m 4f   9 ran
1 Golan (4-9-7)   Kieren Fallon   11/2
2 Nayef (4-9-7)   Richard Hills   7/1
3 Zindabad (6-9-7)   Kevin Darley   11/2
Distances: hd, 3½   Sir Michael Stoute   £435,000

Sussex Stakes
Goodwood, July 31   3yo+ 1m   5 ran
1 Rock Of Gibraltar (3-8-13) Mick Kinane   8/13F
2 Noverre (4-9-7)   Frankie Dettori   3/1
3 Reel Buddy (4-9-7)   Richard Hughes   33/1
Distances: 2, 2   Aidan O'Brien   £157,675

Vodafone Nassau Stakes
Goodwood, Aug 3   3yo+ f&m 1m 1f 192y   10 ran
1 Islington (3-8-6)   Kieren Fallon   100/30
2 Sulk (3-8-6)   Richard Hughes   33/1
3 Quarter Moon (3-8-6)   Mick Kinane   9/4F
Distances: 4, ½   Sir Michael Stoute   £78,300

Juddmonte International Stakes
York, Aug 20   3yo+ 1m 2f 85y   7 ran
1 Nayef (4-9-5)   Richard Hills   6/4F
2 Golan (4-9-5)   Kieren Fallon   9/4
3 Noverre (4-9-5)   Frankie Dettori   7/2
Distances: ½, 1½   Marcus Tregoning   £261,000

Aston Upthorpe Yorkshire Oaks
York, Aug 21   3yo+ f&m 1m 3f 195y   11 ran
1 Islington (3-8-8)   Kieren Fallon   2/1
2 Guadalupe (3-8-8)   Andre Suborics   20/1
3 Sulk (3-8-8)   Richard Hughes   16/1
Distances: 5, hd   Sir Michael Stoute   £145,000

Victor Chandler Nunthorpe Stakes
York, Aug 22   2yo+ 5f   17 ran
1 Kyllachy (4-9-11)   Jamie Spencer   3/1F
2 Malhub (4-9-11)   Richard Hills   15/2
3 Indian Prince (4-9-11)   Kieren Fallon   33/1
Distances: ½, ½   Henry Candy   £107,300

Stanley Leisure Sprint Cup Stakes
Haydock, Sep 7   3yo+ 6f   14 ran
1 Invincible Spirit (5-9-0) Johnny Carroll   25/1
2 Malhub (4-9-0)   Richard Hills   11/2
3 Three Points (5-9-0)   Kevin Darley   12/1
Distances: shd, 2   John Dunlop   £116,000

Meon Valley Stud Fillies' Mile Stakes
Ascot, Sep 28   2yo f 1m   10 ran
1 Soviet Song (8-10)   Oscar Urbina   11/10F
2 Casual Look (8-10)   Martin Dwyer   16/1
3 Reach For the Moon (8-10) Mick Kinane   9/1
Distances: 1½, 1½   James Fanshawe   £116,000

Queen Elizabeth II Stakes
Ascot, Sep 28   3yo+ 1m   5 ran
1 Where Or When (3-8-11)   Kevin Darley   7/1
2 Hawk Wing (3-8-11)   Mick Kinane   1/2F
3 Tillerman (6-9-1)   Kieren Fallon   10/1
Distances: 2, 3   Terry Mills   £178,500

Shadwell Stud Middle Park Stakes
Newmarket, Oct 3   2yo c 6f   10 ran
1 Oasis Dream (8-11)   Jimmy Fortune   6/1
2 Tomahawk (8-11)   Mick Kinane   5/1
3 Elusive City (8-11)   Kieren Fallon   6/4F
Distances: 1½, nk   John Gosden   £100,920

Betfair Cheveley Park Stakes
Newmarket, Oct 4   2yo f 6f   6 ran
1 Airwave (8-11)   Chris Rutter   11/2
2 Russian Rhythm (8-11)   Kieren Fallon   8/13F
3 Danaskaya (8-11)   Kevin Manning   25/1
Distances: 1½, ½   Henry Candy   £87,000

Darley Dewhurst Stakes
Newmarket, Oct 19   2yo c&f 7f   16 ran
1 Tout Seul (9-0)   Steve Carson   25/1
2 Tomahawk (9-0)   Mick Kinane   100/30
3 Trade Fair (9-0)   Richard Hughes   11/4F
Distances: 1¼, 1¼   F Johnson Houghton   £153,700

Emirates Airline Champion Stakes
Newmarket, Oct 19   3yo+ 1m 2f   11 ran
1 Storming Home (4-9-2)   Michael Hills   8/1
2 Moon Ballad (3-8-11)   Jamie Spencer   5/2F
3 Noverre (4-9-2)   Frankie Dettori   9/2
Distances: ½, ¾   Barry Hills   £245,920

Racing Post Trophy Stakes
Doncaster, Oct 26   2yo c&f 1m   9 ran
1 Brian Boru (9-0)   Kevin Darley   11/8F
2 Powerscourt (9-0)   George Duffield   6/1
3 Illustrator (9-0)   Pat Eddery   8/1
Distances: 1½, ½   Aidan O'Brien IRL   £120,000

Royal Ascot

Going: June 18 Good; June 19-22 Good to Firm   Royal Ascot extended to five days for Queen's Jubilee

Queen Anne Stakes (Group 2)

June 18		*3yo+ 1m*	*12 ran*
1	No Excuse Needed (4-9-2)	Johnny Murtagh	13/2
2	Tillerman (6-9-2)	Richard Hughes	11/1
3	Tough Speed (5-9-2)	Pat Eddery	12/1
Distances: shd, 3		*Sir Michael Stoute*	*£78,300*

King's Stand Stakes (Group 2)

June 18		*3yo+ 5f*	*15 ran*
1	Dominica (3-8-7)	Martin Dwyer	16/1
2	Continent (5-9-2)	Darryll Holland	16/1
3	Kyllachy (4-9-2)	Jamie Spencer	11/10F
Distances: hd, ½		*Marcus Tregoning*	*£78,300*

St James's Palace Stakes (Group 1)

June 18		*3yo c 1m*	*9 ran*
1	Rock Of Gibraltar (9-0)	Mick Kinane	4/5F
2	Landseer (9-0)	Johnny Murtagh	13/2
3	Aramram (9-0)	Steve Drowne	20/1
Distances: 1¾, 4		*Aidan O'Brien IRL*	*£168,200*

Coventry Stakes (Group 3)

June 18		*2yo 6f*	*16 ran*
1	Statue Of Liberty (8-12)	Mick Kinane	5/2F
2	Pakhoes (8-12)	Pat Smullen	16/1
3	Kawagino (8-12)	Paul Doe	33/1
Distances: nk, 3½		*Aidan O'Brien IRL*	*£34,800*

Duke of Edinburgh Handicap (Class B)

June 18		*3yo+ 1m 4f*	*20 ran*
1	Thundering Surf (5-9-0)	Richard Hughes	11/1
2	Holy Orders (5-9-2)	David Condon (7)	14/1
3	Counsel's Opinion (5-8-10)	Richard Mullen	14/1
4	Red Carnation (4-9-5)	Philip Robinson	20/1
Distances: nk, 2, ¾		*John Jenkins*	*£31,900*

Balmoral Handicap (Class B)

June 18		*3yo 5f*	*28 ran*
1	Zargus (3-8-0)	Martin Dwyer	14/1
2	Fire Up the Band (3-8-2)	Oliver Pears	7/1F
3	Agnetha (3-9-7)	Pat Smullen	20/1
4	Simianna (3-8-10)	Francis Norton	33/1
Distances: nk, ¾, 1		*Bill Muir*	*£29,000*

Jersey Stakes (Group 3)

June 19		*3yo 7f*	*15 ran*
1	Just James (8-11)	Olivier Peslier	20/1
2	Steenberg (8-11)	Ted Durcan	20/1
3	Meshaheer (8-11)	Frankie Dettori	10/1
Distances: nk, ½		*Jeremy Noseda*	*£43,500*

Queen Mary Stakes (Group 3)

June 19		*2yo f 5f*	*19 ran*
1	Romantic Liason (8-8)	Pat Eddery	16/1
2	Never A Doubt (8-8)	Michael Hills	12/1
3	Rag Top (8-8)	Dane O'Neill	6/1F
Distances: 3½, nk		*Brian Meehan*	*£34,800*

Prince of Wales's Stakes (Group 1)

June 19		*3yo+ 1m 2f*	*12 ran*
	Grandera (4-9-0)	Frankie Dettori	4/1
	Indian Creek (4-9-0)	Richard Quinn	25/1
	Banks Hill (4-8-11)	Olivier Peslier	7/2F
Distances: 5, ¾		*Saeed Bin Suroor*	*£145,000*

Royal Hunt Cup Handicap (Class B)

June 19		*3yo+ 1m*	*30 ran*
1	Norton (5-8-9)	Jimmy Fortune	25/1
2	Invader (6-8-3)	Royston French	50/1
3	Beauchamp Pilot (4-8-8)	Eddie Ahern	7/1
4	Morro Castle (4-8-3)	Hiroki Goto	33/1
Distances: ½, ½, hd		*Terry Mills*	*£69,600*

Ascot Stakes Handicap (Class C)

June 19		*4yo+ 2m 4f*	*26 ran*
1	Riyadh (4-9-5)	Kieren Fallon	7/1F
2	Establishment (5-8-7)	Frankie Dettori	12/1
3	Mana D'Argent (5-8-10)	Keith Dalgleish	20/1
4	Random Quest (4-9-7)	Jamie Spencer	33/1
Distances: hd, 1, ½		*Martin Pipe*	*£26,680*

Chesham Stakes (Listed)

June 20		*2yo 7f*	*12 ran*
1	Helm Bank (9-0)	Keith Dalgleish	25/1
2	Tomahawk (9-2)	Mick Kinane	1/2F
3	Celtic Sapphire (8-7)	Kevin Darley	11/1
Distances: shd, nk		*Mark Johnston*	*£23,200*

Ribblesdale Stakes (Group 2)

June 20		*3yo f 1m 4f*	*15 ran*
1	Irresistible Jewel (8-8)	Pat Smullen	12/1
2	Shadow Dancing (8-8)	Martin Dwyer	8/1
3	Red Rioja (8-8)	Jon Egan	20/1
Distances: ¾, ½		*Dermot Weld IRL*	*£78,300*

Norfolk Stakes (Group 3)

June 20		*2yo 5f*	*12 ran*
1	Baron's Pit (8-12)	Richard Hughes	12/1
2	The Bonus King (8-12)	Kevin Darley	10/1
3	Marino Marini (8-12)	Mick Kinane	4/7F
Distances: hd, 3		*Richard Hannon*	*£34,800*

Gold Cup Stakes (Group 1)

June 20		*4yo+ 2m 4f*	*15 ran*
1	Royal Rebel (6-9-2)	Johnny Murtagh	8/1
2	Vinnie Roe (4-9-0)	Pat Smullen	5/2F
3	Wareed (4-9-0)	Frankie Dettori	13/2
Distances: nk, 1		*Mark Johnston*	*£127,600*

King George V Handicap (Class B)

June 20		*3yo 1m 4f*	*19 ran*
1	Systematic (8-12)	Kevin Darley	9/1
2	Highest (8-13)	Johnny Murtagh	11/1
3	Leadership (9-0)	Richard Hughes	7/1JF
4	Shagraan (8-12)	Olivier Peslier	7/1JF
Distances: nk, hd, ½		*Mark Johnston*	*£31,900*

Hampton Court Stakes (Listed)

June 20		*3yo 1m 2f*	*13 ran*
1	Burning Sun (8-11)	Richard Quinn	10/1
2	Izdiham (8-11)	Richard Hills	6/1F
3	Common World (8-11)	Eddie Ahern	25/1
Distances: 1½, hd		*Henry Cecil*	*£29,000*

Royal Ascot

Britannia Stakes Handicap (Class B)
June 20   3yo c&g   1m   31 ran
1 Pentecost (8-5)   Liam Keniry (5)   2 5/1
2 Ghannam (8-13)   Richard Hills   6/1
3 Shot To Fame (9-2)   Mick Kinane   20/1
4 Wing Commander (8-10)   Michael Fenton   40/1
Distances: nk, nk, nk   Ian Balding   £31,900

Wolferton Rated Stakes Handicap (Listed)
June 21   3yo+   6f   17 ran
1 Ullundi (7-9-7)   Richard Hughes   10/1
2 Arabie (4-8-11)   Richard Quinn   7/1
3 Rasm (5-8-10)   Richard Hills   12/1
4 Pole Star (4-8-10)   Johnny Murtagh   17/2
Distances: hd, 2, ½   Paul Webber   £29,000

King Edward VII Stakes (Group 2)
June 21   3yo c&g   1m 4f   7 ran
1 Balakheri (8-8)   Johnny Murtagh 11/4F
2 Bollin Eric (8-8)   Kevin Darley   3/1
3 First Charter (8-8)   Jamie Spencer   25/1
Distances: 1½, hd   Sir Michael Stoute   £78,300

Coronation Stakes (Group 1)
June 21   3yo f   1m   11 ran
1 Sophisticat (9-0)   Mick Kinane   11/2
2 Zenda (9-0)   Richard Hughes   7/1
3 Dolores (9-0)   Richard Quinn   5/1
Distances: nk, 2½   Aidan O'Brien IRL   £145,000

Queen's Vase Stakes (Group 3)
June 21   3yo   2m 45y   14 ran
1 Mamool (8-11)   Frankie Dettori   9/1
2 Mr Dinos (8-11)   Kevin Darley   4/1
3 Anchestor (8-11)   Johnny Murtagh   7/1
Distances: ½, 1   Saeed Bin Suroor   £34,800

Windsor Castle Stakes (Class B)
June 21   2yo   5f   14 ran
1 Revenue (8-11)   Johnny Murtagh   14/1
2 One Last Time (8-13)   Dane O'Neill   7/2
3 Sir Albert (8-13)   Darryll Holland   5/1
Distances: 1½, shd   Michael Bell   £20,300

Buckingham Palace Stakes Handicap (Class B)
June 21   3yo+   7f   27 ran
1 Demonstrate (4-8-6)   Richard Hughes   12/1
2 Lunar Leo (4-8-9)   Martin Dwyer   16/1
3 Kareeb (5-9-0)   Pat Eddery   16/1
4 Point Of Dispute (7-9-2)   Mick Kinane   25/1
Distances: 1, ½, 1½   John Gosden   £29,000

Henry Carnarvon Stakes (Listed)
June 22   2yo   6f   19 ran
1 Duty Paid (8-11)   Richard Quinn   11/1
2 Luvah Girl (8-11)   Kevin Darley   12/1
3 Pearl Dance (8-11)   Frankie Dettori   5/1F
Distances: hd, hd   David Elsworth   £23,200

Hardwicke Stakes (Group 2)
June 22   4yo+   1m 4f   7 ran
1 Zindabad (6-8-12)   Kevin Darley   4/1
2 Storming Home (4-8-9)   Michael Hills   11/4JF
3 Millenary (5-8-9)   Pat Eddery   11/4JF
Distances: 1, shd   Mark Johnston   £84,680

Golden Jubilee Stakes (Group 1)
Formerly Cork & Orrery Stakes
June 22   3yo+   6f   12 ran
1 Malhub (4-9-4)   Kevin Darley   16/1
2 Danehurst (4-9-1)   Seb Sanders   13/2
3 Three Points (5-9-4)   Frankie Dettori   4/1
Distances: 1½, ½   John Gosden   £156,600

Wokingham Stakes Handicap (Class B)
June 22   3yo+   6f   28 ran
1 Capricho (5-8-11)   Richard Quinn   20/1
2 Border Subject (5-9-10)   Steve Drowne   10/1
3 Chookie Heiton (4-9-4)   Mick Kinane   12/1
4 Crystal Castle (4-9-4)   Frankie Dettori   16/1
Distances: 1¼, ¾, 1½   John Akehurst   £58,000

Sandringham Rated Stakes H'cap (Listed)
June 22   3yo   1m   14 ran
1 Tashawak (9-7)   Richard Hills   12/1
2 Chorist (8-7)   Kieren Fallon   6/1F
3 Reefs Sis (8-8)   P Quinn   16/1
Distances: 2, 1½, 1¾   John Dunlop   £29,000

Queen Alexandra Stakes (Class B)
June 22   4yo+   2m 6f 34y   9 ran
1 Cover Up (5-9-0)   Philip Robinson 11/4F
2 Archduke Ferdinand (4-8-12) Francis Norton   9/1
3 Dorans Pride (12-9-0)   Kevin Darley   6/1
Distances: nk, nk   Sir Michael Stoute   £20,300

Leading Jockeys

	1st	2nd	3rd
Richard Hughes	4	2	1
Johnny Murtagh	4	2	1
Kevin Darley	3	3	3
Richard Quinn	3	2	1
Martin Dwyer	2	2	-
Frankie Dettori	2	1	3
Richard Hills	1	2	1
Pat Smullen	1	2	1
Kieren Fallon	1	1	-
Pat Eddery	1	-	3
Keith Dalgleish	1	-	1
Olivier Peslier	1	-	1
Jimmy Fortune	1	-	-
Liam Keniry	1	-	-
Philip Robinson	1	-	-

Leading Trainers

Mark Johnston	4
Aidan O'Brien	3
Sir Michael Stoute	3

Group 2

(see also Ascot)

Attheraces Mile Stakes
Sandown, Apr 27   4yo+ 1m 14y
Swallow Flight (6-9-0)
Darryll Holland   2/1F
Geoff Wragg £34,800

Sagitta Jockey Club Stakes
Newmarket, May 3   4yo+ 1m 4f
Marienbard (5-8-9)
Jamie Spencer   9/1
Saeed Bin Suroor £46,400

Convergent Dante Stakes
York, May 15   3yo 1m2f 85yds
Moon Ballad (8-11)
Jamie Spencer   13/2
Saeed Bin Suroor £84,100

Merewood Yorkshire Cup
York, May 16   4yo+ 1m 5f 194y
Zindabad (6-8-9)
Kevin Darley   2/1F
Mark Johnston £78,300

Bonusprint Henry II Stakes
Sandown, June 3   4yo+ 2m 78y
Akbar (6-9-0)
Richard Hills   16/1
Mark Johnston £34,800

Tripleprint Temple Stakes
Sandown, June 3   3yo+ 5f 6y
Kyllachy (4-9-3)
Jamie Spencer   9/2
Henry Candy £34,800

Kleinwort Benson Cherry Hinton Stakes
Newmarket, July 9   2yo f 6f
Spinola (8-9)
Richard Quinn   7/1
Peter Harris £34,800

Princess Of Wales' Pearl and Coutts Stakes
Newmarket, July 9   3yo+ 1m 4f
Millenary (5-9-2)
Pat Eddery   5/2F
John Dunlop £46,400

Falmouth Stakes
Newmarket, July 10 3yo+ f&m 1m
Tashawak (3-8-6)
Richard Hills   10/1
John Dunlop   £46,400

Gerrard Investment Richmond Stakes
Goodwood, July 30   2yo c&g 6f
Elusive City (8-11)
Kieren Fallon   9/2
Gerard Butler £43,500

J P Morgan Bank Goodwood Cup
Goodwood, Aug 1   3yo+ 2m
Jardines Lookout (5-9-2)
Mick Kinane   10/1
Alan Jarvis £52,200

Stan James Geoffrey Freer Stakes
Newbury, Aug 17   3yo+ 1m 5f 61y
Mubtaker (5-9-3)
Richard Hills   11/8F
Marcus Tregoning £37,700

Great Voltigeur Stakes
York, Aug 20   3yo c&g 1m 3f 195y
Bandari (8-9)
Richard Hills   4/5F
Mark Johnston £87,000

Scottish Equitable Gimcrack Stakes
York, Aug 21   2yo c&g 6f
Country Reel (8-11)
Frankie Dettori   3/1F
David Loder £72,500

Peugeot Lowther Stakes
York, Aug 22   2yo f 6f
Russian Rhythm (9-0)
Kieren Fallon   8/13F
Sir Michael Stoute £50,575

Celebration Mile Stakes
Goodwood, Aug 24   3yo+ 1m
Tillerman (6-9-1)
Richard Hughes   5/1
Amanda Perrett £40,600

Champagne Stakes
Doncaster, Sep 13   2yo c&g 7f
Almushahar (8-10)
Frankie Dettori   8/11F
David Loder £86,400

Polypipe Flying Childers Stakes
Doncaster, Sep 14   2yo 5f
Wunders Dream (8-12)
Michael Fenton   9/2
James Given £45,000

Mill Reef Stakes
Newbury, Sep 20   2yo 6f 8y
Zafeen (8-12)
Steve Drowne   8/11F
Mick Channon £31,900

Hackney Empire Royal Lodge Stakes
Ascot, Sep 28   2yo c&g 1m
Al Jadeed (8-11)
Richard Hills   3/1
John Gosden £69,600

Brunswick Diadem Stakes
Ascot Sep 28   3yo+ 6f
Crystal Castle (4-9-0)
Kieren Fallon   3/1F
John Hammond £58,000

Peugeot Sun Chariot Stakes
Newmarket, Oct 5 3yo+ f&m 1m 2f
Dress To Thrill (3-8-10)
Pat Smullen   11/8F
Dermot Weld £46,400

Victor Chandler Challenge Stakes
Newmarket, Oct 19   3yo+ 7f
Nayyir (4-9-0)
Eddie Ahern   7/1
Gerard Butler £58,000

Owen Brown Rockfel Stakes
Newmarket, Oct 19   2yo f 7f
Luvah Girl (8-9)
Kevin Darley   13/2
Roger Charlton £34,800

Group 3

(see also Ascot)

Shadwell Nell Gwyn Stakes
Newmarket, Apr 16   3yo c&g 7f
Misterah (8-9)
Richard Hills   9/2
Marcus Tregoning £20,300

Earl of Sefton Stakes
Newmarket, Apr 17 4yo+ 1m 110y
Indian Creek (4-8-10)
Richard Quinn   11/1
David Elsworth £23,300

Macau Jockey Club Craven Stakes
Newmarket, Apr 18   3yo c&g 1m
King Of Happiness (8-9)
Kieren Fallon   9/4F
Sir Michael Stoute £23,200

Dubai Irish Village Stakes
Formerly John Porter Stakes
Newbury, Apr 20   4yo+ 1m 4f 5y
Zindabad (6-8-12)
Kevin Darley   7/2
Mark Johnston £23,300

Dubai Duty Free Stakes
Formerly Fred Darling Stakes
Newbury, Apr 20   3yo f 7f
Queen's Logic (9-0)
Steve Drowne   1/3F
Mick Channon £23,200

Lane's End Greenham Stakes
Newbury, Apr 20   3yo c 7f
Redback (9-0)
Darryll Holland   5/1
Richard Hannon £23,200

Heathorn Classic Trial Stakes
Sandown, Apr 26   3yo 1m 2f 7y
Simeon (8-11)
Kevin Darley   6/4
Barry Hills £37,200

attheraces.co.uk
Gordon Richard Stakes
Sandown, Apr 27   4yo+ 1m 2f 7y
Chancellor (4-8-10)
Michael Hills   9/2
Barry Hills   £23,200

Leicestershire Stakes
Leicester, Apr 27   4yo+ 7f
Warningford (8-8-12)
Oscar Urbina   100/30
James Fanshawe   £20,825

Bovi Homes
Sagaro Stakes
Ascot, May 1   4yo+ 2m
Give Notice (5-8-12)
Frankie Dettori   8/1
John Dunlop   £24,360

Victor Chandler
Palace House Stakes
Newmarket, May 4   3yo+ 5f
Kyllachy (4-8-12)
Jamie Spencer   2/1F
Henry Candy   £23,200

Victor Chandler Chester Vase
Chester, May 7   3yo 1m 4f 66y
Fight Your Corner (8-10)
Kevin Darley   9/2
Mark Johnston   £34,800

Betfair.com Ormonde Stakes
Chester, May 9   4yo+ 1m 5f 89y
St Expedit (5-8-11)
Darryll Holland   11/8F
Geoff Wragg   £43,500

attheraces 418
Derby Trial Stakes
Lingfield, May 11   3yo 1m 3f 106y
Bandari (8-7)
Kevin Darley   11/4
Mark Johnston   £34,800

Tattersalls Musidora Stakes
York, May 14   3yo f 1m 2f 85y
Islington (8-8)
Kieren Fallon   5/6F
Sir Michael Stoute   £29,750

Duke Of York Stakes
York, May 16   3yo+ 6f
Invincible Spirit (5-9-5)
Mick Kinane   3/1F
John Dunlop   £34,800

Brigadier Gerard Stakes
Sandown, June 4   4yo+ 1m 2f 7y
Potemkin (4-8-10)
Dane O'Neill   7/2
Richard Hannon   £24,000

Vodafone Diomed Stakes
Epsom, June 8   3yo+ 1m 114y
Nayyir (4-9-4)
Eddie Ahern   5/1JF
Gerard Butler   £43,500

Ante International
Criterion Stakes
Newmarket, June 29   3yo+ 7f
Atavus (5-9-2)
Jamie Mackay   11/4
George Margarson   £20,300

Chipchase Stakes
Newcastle, June 29   3yo+ 6f
Tedburrow (10-9-2)
Dean McKeown   11/1
E Alston   £20,300

Lancashire Oaks Stakes
Haydock, July 6   3yo+ f&m 1m 4f
Mellow Park (3-8-5)
Darryll Holland   13/8F
Jeremy Noseda   £29,000

TNT July Stakes
Newmarket, July 10   2yo c&g 6f
Mister Links (8-10)
Richard Hughes   2/1F
Richard Hannon   £23,200

Sodexho Scottish Classic
Ayr, July 15   3yo+ 1m 2f
Imperial Dancer (4-9-3)
Chris Catlin   7/4
Mick Channon   £27,900

Princess Margaret Stakes
Ascot, July 27   2yo f 6f
Russian Rhythm (8-9)
Kieren Fallon   EvsF
Sir Michael Stoute   £26,100

Peugeot Gordon Stakes
Goodwood, July 30   3yo 1m 4f
Bandari (8-13)
Willie Supple   15/8
Mark Johnston   £34,100

Champagne Vintage Stakes
Goodwood, Jul 31   2yo 7f
Dublin (8-11)
Jamie Spencer   11/1
David Loder   £29,000

Betfair.com
Molecomb Stakes
Goodwood, Aug 1   2yo 5f
Wunders Dream (8-7)
Michael Fenton   8/1
James Given   £26,100

King George Stakes
Goodwood, Aug 1   3yo+ 5f
Agnetha (3-8-7)
Mick Kinane   11/2
Dermot Weld IRL   £29,000

Theo Fennell Lennox Stakes
Goodwood, Aug 3   3yo+ 7f
Nayyir (4-9-4)
Eddie Ahern   9/2
Gerard Butler   £29,000

Rose Of Lancaster Stakes
Haydock, Aug 10 3yo+ 1m 2f 120y
Race Abandoned

Stan James
Hungerford Stakes
Newbury, Aug 17   3yo+ 7f 64y
Reel Buddy (4-8-13)
Richard Quinn   7/2
Richard Hannon   £20,300

Wetherbys Insurance
Lonsdale Stakes
York, Aug 20 3yo+ 1m 7f 195y
Boreas (7-9-1)
Jamie Spencer   13/2
Luca Cumani   £58,000

Winter Hill Stakes
Windsor, Aug 24   3yo+ 1m 2f 7y
Naheef (3-8-6)
Frankie Dettori   6/4F
Saeed Bin Suroor   £26,100

Touchdown in Malaysia
Prestige Stakes
Goodwood, Aug 25   2yo f 7f
Geminiani (8-9)
Michael Hills   3/1F
Barry Hills   £23,200

Iveco Daily Solario Stakes
Sandown, Aug 31   2yo 7f 16y
Foss Way (8-11)
Jimmy Fortune   11/2
John Gosden   £21,750

Milcars September Stakes
Kempton, Sep 7   3yo+ 1m 4f
Asian Heights (4-9-3)
Darryll Holland   5/4F
Geoff Wragg   £26,100

Park Hill Stakes
Doncaster, Sep 11   f&m 3yo+
1m 6f 132y
Alexander Three D (3-8-5)
Michael Hills   7/4F
Barry Hills   £30,000

GNER Park Stakes
Doncaster, Sep 12   3yo+ 1m
Duck Row (7-9-0)
Richard Hughes   8/1
Jim Toller   £30,000

GNER Doncaster Cup
Doncaster, Sep 12   3yo+ 2m 2f
Boreas (7-9-1)
Jamie Spencer   7/2
Luca Cumani   £60,000

May Hill Stakes
Doncaster, Sep 12   2yo f 1m
Summitville (8-9)
Michael Fenton   11/2
James Given   £24,000

Select Stakes
Goodwood, Sep 14   3yo+
1m1f192yds
Moon Ballad (3-8-12)
Jamie Spencer   4/6F
Saeed Bin Suroor   £20,300

International
Newbury, Sep 21   3yo+ 5f 34y
Lady Dominatrix (3-8-9)
Paul Doe   9/1
P Dutfield £26,100

Supreme Stakes
Goodwood, Sep 26   3yo+ 7f
Firebreak (3-8-9)
Frankie Dettori   5/4F
Saeed Bin Suroor £20,300

Old Vic Cumberland Lodge
Ascot, Sep 29   3yo+ 1m 4f
Systematic (3-8-6)
Darryll Holland   1/2F
Mark Johnston £30,940

Somerville Tattersall Stakes
Newmarket, Oct 2   2yo c&g 7f
Governor Brown (8-9)
Richard Quinn   6/1
Paul Cole £35,700

Willmott Cornwallis Stakes
Ascot, Oct 12   2yo 5f
Peace Offering (8-12)
Kevin Darley   8/1
Terry Mills £23,200

Princess Royal Willmott Dixon Stakes
Ascot, Oct 12   3yo+ f&m 1m 4f
Love Everlasting (4-9-0)
Kevin Darley   8/11F
Mark Johnston £31,000

Jockey Club Cup
Newmarket, Oct 19   3yo+ 2m
Persian Punch (9-9-0)
Martin Dwyer   9/2
David Elsworth £29,000

Vodafone Horris Hill Stakes
Newbury, Oct 25   2yo c&g 7f 64y
Makhlab (8-9)
Richard Hills   5/1
Barry Hills £23,200

St Simon Stakes
Newbury, Oct 26   3yo+ 1m 4f
The Whistling Teal (6-9-0)
Darryll Holland   13/2
Geoff Wragg £23,200

Other Major Races

randombet.com Lincoln Handicap
Doncaster, Mar 23   1m
Zucchero (6-8-13)
Simon Whitworth   33/1
David Arbuthnot £62,855

Tote Chester Cup
Chester, May 8   4yo+ 2m 2f 147y
Fantasy Hill (6-8-9)
Pat Eddery   9/2
John Dunlop £58,000

Tote Silver Bowl Handicap
Haydock, May 25 3yo 1m 30yds
Common World (8-13)
Kieren Fallon   7/4F
Gerard Butler £40,600

Vodafone Dash Handicap
Epsom, June 8   3yo+ 5f
Rudi's Pet (8-8-7)
Adrian Nicholls   16/1
David Nicholls £58,000

William Hill Trophy Handicap
York, June 15   3yo 6f
Artie (7-10)
Dale Gibson   25/1
Tim Easterby £49,010

Northumberland Plate
Newcastle, June 29 3yo+ 2m 19y
Bangalore (6-9-5)
Seb Sanders   8/1
Amanda Perrett £98,571

Tote Scoop6 Handicap
Sandown, Jul 6 3yo+ 1m 14yds
Heretic (4-9-6)
Oscar Urbina   7/1
James Fanshawe £58,000

Tote Old Newton Cup
Haydock, July 6 3yo+ 1m 3f 200y
Sun Bird (4-7-12)
J McAuley   40/1
Richard Allan £34,800

John Smith's Cup Handicap
York, July 13   3yo+ 1m 2f 85y
Vintage Premium (5-9-9)
P Hanagan   20/1
Richard Fahey £87,750

Wetherbys Super Sprint
Newbury, July 20   2yo 5f 34y
Presto Vento (8-9)
Eddie Ahern   6/1
Richard Hannon £78,300

Tote International Handicap
Ascot, Jul 28   3yo+ 7f
Crystal Castle (4-8-0)
John Egan   14/1
John Hammond £87,000

Hong Kong JC Handicap
Ascot, July 28   3yo+ 5f
Boleyn Castle (5-9-8)
R Miles (7)   20/1
Terry Mills   £46,400

Tote Gold Trophy
Goodwood, July 31 3yo 1m 4f
Dawn Invasion (9-7)
Richard Hughes   12/1
Amanda Perrett £40,600

William Hill Mile Handicap
Goodwood, Aug 2   3yo+ 1m
Smirk (4-9-5)
Kevin Darley   12/1
Mark Johnston £58,000

Vodafone Stewards' Cup
Goodwood, Aug 3   3yo+ 6f
Bond Boy (5-8-2)
Chris Catlin   14/1
Brian Smart £49,300

Shergar Cup Sprint
Ascot, Aug 10   3yo 6f
Feet So Fast (3-8-12)
Mick Kinane   6/4F
W Musson   £50,000

Tote Ebor Handicap
York, Aug 21   3yo+ 1m 5f 194y
Hugs Dancer (5-8-5)
Dean McKeown   25/1
James Given £120,250

St Leger Yearling Stakes
Doncaster, Sep 11   2yo 6f
Somnus (8-11)
Ted Durcan   10/1
Lionel Cottrell £155,850

Ladbroke Ayr Gold Cup
Ayr, Sep 21   3yo+ 6f
Funfair Wane (3-9-3)
Adrian Nicholls   16/1
David Nicholls £65,000

Courage Best Handicap
Newbury, Sep 21   3yo+ 1m 2f 6y
Solo Flight (5-8-13)
Michael Hills   20/1
Barry Hills £58,000

Tote Trifecta Handicap
Ascot, Sep 28   3yo+ 7f
Millennium Force (4-8-7)
Chris Catlin   14/1
Mick Channon £43,500

Tote Exacta Handicap
Ascot, Sep 29   3yo+ 1m 4f
Scott's View (3-9-3)
Darryll Holland   11/2
Mark Johnston £40,600

Betabet 2YO Trophy
Redcar, Oct 5   6f
Somnus (8-12)
Ted Durcan   11/2
Tim Easterby £97,585

Tote Cambridgeshire
Newmarket, Oct 5   3yo+ 1m 1f
Beauchamp Pilot (4-9-5)
Eddie Ahern   9/1
James Given £69,600

Tattersalls Auction Stakes
Newmarket, Oct 18   2yo 6f
Michelle Ma Belle (7-12)
Chris Catlin   6/1
S Kirk £50,000

Tote Cesarewitch Handicap
Newmarket, Oct 19   3yo+ 2m2f
Miss Fara (7-8-0)
Ryan Moore (5)   12/1
Martin Pipe £69,600

Top Flat Trainers

Turf Only, Listed by Total Money

		1st	2nd	3rd	4th	Total	%	Win Money	Total Money	£1 Stake
1	Aidan O'Brien	20	12	12	11	99	20.2	2,679,994	3,389,908	+21.04
2	Sir Michael Stoute	75	68	52	46	397	18.9	1,262,490	2,135,902	-46.42
3	Saeed Bin Suroor	24	22	5	10	84	28.6	1,108,782	1,935,229	+24.31
4	Mark Johnston	113	89	77	67	760	14.9	1,331,272	1,800,156	-33.80
5	Barry Hills	107	97	90	73	719	14.9	988,498	1,699,938	-112.37
6	Richard Hannon	107	107	110	113	1161	9.2	845,706	1,412,547	-513.83
7	John Dunlop	109	82	73	67	646	16.9	798,362	1,377,904	-142.63
8	Mick Channon	67	87	86	93	803	8.3	480,011	976,021	-451.07
9	Marcus Tregoning	53	36	28	20	219	24.2	719,763	975,600	+32.11
10	Ed Dunlop	74	45	55	49	445	16.6	630,332	879,473	-72.67
11	Tim Easterby	73	78	57	89	800	9.1	531,857	783,902	-245.82
12	Henry Cecil	47	55	32	31	256	18.4	417,967	759,764	-79.21
13	Geoff Wragg	29	20	19	15	159	18.2	442,238	741,661	+3.84
14	John Gosden	55	40	44	38	334	16.5	398,187	735,796	-45.62
15	Michael Jarvis	55	40	20	31	289	19.0	515,153	702,127	+2.63
16	James Fanshawe	38	35	38	26	258	14.7	288,745	662,191	-58.32
17	David Elsworth	36	28	26	32	300	12.0	358,685	646,243	+42.98
18	Paul Cole	55	51	43	39	432	12.7	451,521	629,591	-99.47
19	Ian Balding	36	46	43	33	464	7.8	366,955	613,047	-176.61
20	Brian Meehan	65	50	60	53	527	12.3	322,410	568,217	+59.60
21	Gerard Butler	49	36	41	22	345	14.2	400,729	555,464	-51.00
22	David Nicholls	47	48	47	57	727	6.5	326,617	521,296	-317.26
23	David Loder	42	17	12	7	107	39.3	367,773	512,519	+0.24
24	Luca Cumani	25	29	16	22	225	11.1	348,516	492,670	-96.72
25	Peter Harris	37	36	32	37	425	8.7	248,060	490,005	-91.40

Top Flat Jockeys

Turf Only, Listed by Races Won

		1st	2nd	3rd	4th	Total	%	Win Money	Total Money	£1 Stake
1	Kieren Fallon	166	125	111	92	979	17.0	2,022,357	3,056,914	-188.67
2	Kevin Darley	162	123	115	85	986	16.4	1,705,881	2,409,728	+6.10
3	Pat Eddery	122	81	77	72	792	15.4	1,028,678	1,871,653	-103.18
4	Richard Quinn	116	125	87	87	779	14.9	924,742	1,916,911	-110.29
5	Jamie Spencer	106	88	61	65	686	15.5	876,680	1,336,983	+68.21
6	Darryll Holland	105	66	72	67	630	16.7	882,118	1,285,153	+40.61
7	Frankie Dettori	96	64	44	36	403	23.8	1,885,195	2,952,505	+3.59
8	George Duffield	95	60	70	63	778	12.2	530,154	775,528	-233.54
9	Richard Hughes	90	60	70	55	587	15.3	777,520	1,357,251	+1.37
10	Seb Sanders	83	74	51	42	661	12.6	398,001	595,414	+0.79
11	Francis Norton	82	78	69	68	823	10.0	519,285	776,612	-90.07
12	Richard Hills	79	74	58	46	447	17.7	1,088,019	1,671,688	-19.25
13	Steve Drowne	76	91	82	78	917	8.3	580,916	938,657	-389.67
14	Willie Supple	73	71	64	69	678	10.8	431,272	781,244	-121.88
15	Joe Fanning	71	61	67	59	722	9.8	338,891	505,823	-116.97
16	Jimmy Fortune	71	78	74	86	693	10.2	482,732	939,505	-220.82
17	Chris Catlin	69	69	59	86	837	8.2	297,999	459,391	-124.24
18	Fergal Lynch	64	64	79	78	664	9.6	267,604	430,985	-215.78
19	Michael Fenton	63	80	85	69	811	7.8	343,892	607,751	-355.36
20	Dane O'Neill	63	58	52	55	665	9.5	516,432	723,065	-202.84
21	Ian Mongan	63	68	53	61	656	9.6	210,974	339,550	-213.28
22	Robert Winston	62	71	96	74	832	7.5	348,410	590,856	-287.12
23	Brett Doyle	62	53	59	52	543	11.4	293,060	498,675	-55.99
24	Martin Dwyer	59	63	65	75	736	8.0	426,164	669,848	-248.52
25	Michael Hills	58	53	49	44	485	12.0	587,966	1,249,661	-88.54

Overseas Races

Australia

Cox Plate
Moonee Valley, Oct 26 3yo+
1m 2f 44y
Northerly (6-9-2)

P Payne	3/1JF	
F Kersley	*£711,268*	

Tooheys Melbourne Cup
Flemington, Nov 5 3yo+ 2m
Media Puzzle (5-8-4)

Damian Oliver	11/2	
Dermot Weld IRL	*£871,479*	

Canada

E P Taylor Stakes
Woodbine, Sep 29 3yo+
1m 2f turf
Fraulein (3-8-5)

Kevin Darley	112/10	
Ed Dunlop	*£193,966*	

Canadian International
Woodbine, Sep 29 3yo+
1m 4f turf
Ballingarry (3-8-6)

Mick Kinane	41/10	
Saeed Bin Suroor	*£387,931*	

Dubai

Godolphin Mile
Nad Al Sheba, Mar 23
3yo+ 1m dirt
Grey Memo (5-9-0)

Gary Stevens	7/1	
W Stute	*£410,959*	

UAE Derby
Nad Al Sheba, Mar 23
3yo 1m 2f dirt
Essence Of Dubai (3-8-7)

Frankie Dettori	20/1	
Saeed Bin Suroor	*£821,918*	

Dubai Sheema Classic
Nad Al Sheba, Mar 23
4yo+ 1m 4f turf
Nayef (4-8-11)

Richard Hills	9/4F	
Marcus Tregoning	*£821,918*	

Dubai Golden Shaheen
Nad Al Sheba, Mar 23
4yo+ 6f dirt
Caller One (5-9-4)

Gary Stevens	5/2	
Jimmy Chapman	*£821,918*	

Dubai Duty Free
Nad Al Sheba, Mar 23
4yo+ 1m 1f 195y turf
Terre A Terre (5-8-10)

C Soumillon	5/1	
E Libaud	*£821,918*	

Dubai World Cup
Nad Al Sheba, Mar 23
4yo+ 1m 2f dirt
Street Cry (4-9-0)

Jerry Bailey	7/4JF	
Saeed Bin Suroor	*£2,465,743*	

France

Prix Ganay
Longchamp, Apr 28 4yo+
1m 2f 110y
Aquarelliste (4-8-13)

D Boleuf	3/5F	
Elie Lellouche FRA	*£52,582*	

Poule d'Essai des Poulains
Longchamp, May 12 3yo c 1m
Landseer (9-2)

Mick Kinane	61/10	
Aidan O'Brien IRL	*£122,693*	

Poule d'Essai des Pouliches
Longchamp, May 12 3yo f 1m
Zenda (9-0)

Richard Hughes	63/10	
John Gosden	*£122,693*	

Prix Lupin
Longchamp, May 12 3yo c&f
1m 2f 110y
Act One (9-2)

T Gillet	4/5F	
J E Pearse	*£52,582*	

Prix Saint-Alary
Longchamp, May 19 3yo f 1m 2f
Marotta (9-0)

Thierry Jarnet	192/10	
R Gibson	*£52,582*	

Prix d'Ispahan
Longchamp, May 19
4yo+ c&f 1m 1f 55y
Best Of The Bests (5-9-2)

Frankie Dettori	39/10	
Saeed Bin Suroor	*£52,582*	

Prix Jean Prat
Chantilly, June 2 3yo 1m 1f
Rouvres 17 (9-2)

O Doleuze	84/10	
Criquette Head FRA	*£52,582*	

Prix du Jockey-Club
Chantilly, June 2 3yo c&f 1m 4f
Sulamani (9-2)

Thierry Thulliez	199/10	
P Bary FRA	*£387,973*	

Prix de Diane Hermès
Chantilly, June 9 3yo f
1m 2f 110y
Bright Sky (9-0)

Dominique Boeuf	3/1JF	
Elie Lellouche	*£175,276*	

Grand Prix de Paris
Longchamp, June 23 3yo c&f 1m 2f
Khalkevi (9-2)
Christophe Soumillon   28/10
A de Royer Dupre FRA   £175,276

Grand Prix de Saint-Cloud
Saint-Cloud, June 30 3yo+ 1m 4f
Ange Gabriel (4-9-8)
Thierry Jarnet   16/1
E Libaud FRA   £122,693

Prix Maurice de Gheest
Deauville, Aug 11 3yo+ 6f 110y
May Ball (5-8-13)
Gerard Mosse   119/10
John Gosden   £52,583

Prix du Haras
Deauville, Aug 18 3yo+ c&f 1m
Banks Hill (4-9-1)
Olivier Peslier   17/10F
Andre Fabre FRA   £175,276

Prix Morny
Deauville, Aug 25 2yo c&f 6f
Elusive City (9-0)
Kieren Fallon   3/5
Gerard Butler   £87,638

Prix du Moulin
Longchamp, Sep 8 3yo+ c&f 1m
Rock Of Gibraltar (3-8-11)
Mick Kinane   3/5
Aidan O'Briern IRL   £105,166

Prix Vermeille
Longchamp Sep 15 3yo f 1m 4f
Pearly Shells (9-0)
Christophe Soumillon   19/10F
F Rohaut FRA   £77,595

Prix de Cadran
Longchamp Oct 6 4yo+ 2m 4f
Give Notice (5-9-2)
Jonny Murtagh   9/2JF
John Dunlop   £70,110

Prix de L'Abbaye
Longchamp, Oct 6 2yo+ 5f
Continent (5-9-11)
Darryll Holland   7/1
David Nicholls   £70,110

Prix de l'Opera
Longchamp, Oct 6 3yo+ f 1m 2f
Bright Sky (3-8-12)
Dominique Boeuf   7/4F
Elie Lellouche FRA   £87,638

Prix Marcel Boussac
Longchamp, Oct 6 2yo 1m
Six Perfections (8-11)
Thierry Thulliez   4/6F
P Bary   £87,638

Grand Criterium
Longchamp, Oct 6 2yo 1m
Hold That Tiger (9-0)
Kieren Fallon   9/1
Aidan O'Brien IRL   £122,693

Prix de L'Arc de Triomphe
Longchamp, Oct 6 3yo+ 1m 4f
Marienbard (5-9-5)
Frankie Dettori   10/1
Saeed Bin Suroor   £560,883

Prix de la Foret
Longchamp, Oct 13 3yo+ 7f
Dedication (3-8-11)
O Doleuze   67/10
Criquette Head FRA   £52,582

Prix Royal Oak
Longchamp, Oct 27
3yo+ 1m 7f 110y
Mr Dinos (3-8-9)
Dominique Boeuf
Paul Cole   £52,583

Criterium International
St-Cloud, Nov 2 2yo 1m
Dalkhani (9-0)
Christophe Soumillon   4/5F
A de Royer Dupre FRA   £87,423

Criterium de St-Cloud
St-Cloud, Nov 13 2yo 1m
Ballingarry (9-0)
Jamie Spencer   7/10CF
Aidan O'Brien IRL   £38,797

Germany

BMW Deutsches Derby
Hamburg, July 7 3yo c&f 1m 4f
Next Desert (9-2)
A Starke   26/10F
A Schutz GER   £147,239

WGZ Bank-Deutschlandpreis
Dusseldorf, July 28 3yo+ 1m 4f
Marienbard (5-9-7)
Frankie Dettori   17/10F
Saeed Bin Suroor   £67,485

Grosser Dallmayr Preis
Munich, Aug 4 3yo+ 1m 2f
Kaieteur (3-8-9)
Pat Eddery   44/10
Brian Meehan   £55,828

Credit Suisse Pokal
Cologne, Aug 11 3yo+ 1m 2f
Yavana's Pace (10-9-7)
Keith Dalgleish   99/10
Mark Johnston   £72,393

Grosser Preis Von Baden
Baden-Baden, Sep 1 3yo+ 1m 4f
Marienbard (5-9-6)
Frankie Dettori   28/10
Saeed Bin Suroor   £312,883

Pries von Europa
Cologne, Sep 22 3yo+ 1m 4f
Well Made (5-9-6)
T Hellier   84/10
H Blume GER   £95,092

Hong Kong

Queen Elizabeth II Cup
Sha Tin, Apr 22 3yo+ 1m 2f
Silvano (5-9-0)
Andreas Suborics
Andreas Wohler GER   £488,432

Ireland

Irish 2000 Guineas
Curragh, May 25 3yo c&f 1m
Rock Of Gibraltar (9-0)
Mick Kinane   4/7F
Aidan O'Brien IRL   £145,774

Irish 1000 Guineas
Curragh, May 26 3yo f 1m
Gossamer (9-0)
Jamie Spencer   4/1F
Luca Cumani   £138,411

Tattersall's Gold Cup
Curragh, May 26 4yo+ 1m 2f 110y
Rebelline (4-8-11)
D McDonogh   5/4F
Kevin Prendergast   £98,896

Irish Derby
Curragh, June 30 3yo c&f 1m 4f
High Chaparral (9-0)
Mick Kinane   1/3F
Aidan O'Brien IRL   £457,106

Irish Oaks
Curragh, July 14 3yo f 1m 4f
Margarula (9-0)
K Manning   33/1
J Bolger IRL   £137,457

Heinz 57 Phoenix Stakes
Leopardstown, Aug 11 2yo c&f 6f
Spartacus (9-0)
C O'Donoghue   16/1
Aidan O'Brien IRL   £103,436

Moyglare Stud Stakes
Curragh, Sep 1 2yo f 7f
Mail The Desert (8-11)
Steve Drowne   8/1
Mick Channon   £96,074

Champion Stakes
Leopardstown, Sep 7 3yo+ c&f
1m 2f
Grandera (4-9-4)
Frankie Dettori   5/2
Saeed Bin Suroor   £383,560

Irish St Leger
Curragh, Sep 14 3yo+ 1m 6f
Vinnie Roe (4-9-9)
Pat Smullen   4/7F
Dermot Weld IRL   £107,117

National Stakes
Curragh, Sep 15 2yo c&f 1m
Refuse To Bend (9-0)
Pat Smullen   7/1
Dermot Weld IRL   £112,055

Italy

Premio Presidente della Repubblica
Capannelle , May 12   4yo+ 1m 2f
Falbrav (4-9-2)
V Fargiu
L D'Auria ITA   *£1187,247*

Oaks D'Italia
San Siro, May 19   3yo f 1m 3f
Guadalupe (8-11)
Kieren Fallon
P Schiergen GER   *£173,546*

Derby Italiano
Capannelle, May 26   3yo c&f 1m 4f
Rakti (9-1)
M Demuro
B Grizzetti   *£395,337*

Gran Premio Di Milano
San Siro, June 16   3yo+ 1m 4f
Falbrav (4-9-7)
D Vargiu
L D'Auria ITA   *£123,309*

Premio Vittoria Di Capua
San Siro, Oct 13   3yo+ 1m
Slickly (6-8-13)
Frankie Dettori   51/100F
Saeed Bin Suroor   *£73,555*

Gran Criterium
San Siro, Oct 20   2yo 1m
Spartacus (8-11)
Mick Kinane   13/10F
Aidan O'Brien IRL   *£102,101*

Gran Premio
San Siro, Oct 20   3yo+ 1m 4f
Black Sam Bellamy (3-8-12)
Mick Kinane   64/10
Aidan O'Brien IRL   *£126,391*

Japan

Japan Cup
Nakayama, Nov 24   3yo+ 1m 4f
Falbrav (4-9-0)
Frankie Dettori   195/10
L D'Auria ITA   *£1,328,300*

Singapore

Singapore International Cup
Kranji, May 11   3yo+ 1m 2f
Grandera (4-8-13)
Frankie Dettori
Saeed Bin Suroor   *£663,569*

United States

Kentucky Derby
Churchill Downs, May 4 3yo
1m 2f dirt
War Emblem (9-0)
V Espinoza
Bob Baffert USA   *£599,315*

Preakness Stakes-
Pimlico, May 18 3yo 1m 1f 110y dirt
War Emblem (9-0)
V Espinoza   28/10F
Bob Baffert USA   *£445,205*

Belmont Stakes
Belmont Pk, June 9 3yo 1m 4f dirt
Sarava (9-0)
E Prado
K McPeek USA   £410,959

Arlington Million
Arlington, Aug 17 3yo+ 1m 2f turf
Beat Hollow (5-9-0)
Jerry Bailey
R Frankel USA   *£410,959*

Keeneland Turf Mile
Keeneland, Oct 6   3yo+ 1m
Landseer (3-8-11)
E Prado   34/10
Aidan O'Brien IRL   *£254,795*

Breeders' Cup
Arlington, Oct 26

Distaff
3yo f & m 1m 110y (dirt)   8 ran
1 Azeri (3-8-11)   Mike Smith   18/10F
2 Farda Amiga (3-8-7)   Pay Day   49/10
3 Imperial Gesture (3-8-7) Jerry Bailey 41/10
Distances: 5, hd   Allen E Paulsen USA   £712,329

Juvenile Fillies
2yo 1m 110y (dirt)   10 ran
1 Storm Flag Flying (8-7)   Jose Velazquez 4/5F
2 Composure (8-7)   Mike Smith   7/2
3 Santa Catarina (8-7)   Jerry Bailey   52/10
Distances: ½, 9¾   C McGaughey III USA   £356,164

Mile
3yo+ 1m (turf)   14 ran
1 Domedriver (5-9-0)   Thierry Thulliez 26/1
2 Rock Of Gibraltar (3-8-10) Mick Kinane 4/5F
3 Good Journey (6-9-0)   Pat Day   54/10
Distances: ¾, nse   P Bary FRA   £381,096

Sprint
3yo+ 6f (dirt)   13 ran
1 Orientate (4-9-0)   Jerry Bailey   27/10F
2 Thunderello (3-8-11)   Edgar Prado   49/1
3 Crafty CT (4-9-0)   Pat Valenzuela   165/10
Distances: ½, ½   D Wayne Lucas USA   £406,027

Filly & Mare
3yo+ f & m 1m 3f (turf)   12 ran
1 Starine (5-8-11)   Jose Velazquez 132/10
2 Banks Hill (4-8-11)   Jerry Bailey   38/10
3 Islington (3-8-6)   Kieren Fallon   4/1
Distances: 1½, nk   R J Frankel USA   £480,822

Juvenile
2yo c & g 1m 110y (dirt)   13 ran
1 Vindication (8-10)   Mike Smith   41/10
2 Kafwain (8-10)   Edgar Prado   198/10
3 Hold That Tiger (8-10) Kieren Fallon   11/2
Distances: 2¾, 2¼   B Baffert USA   £381,096

Turf
3yo+ c & g 1m 4f (turf)   8 ran
1 High Chaparral (3-8-9) Mick Kinane   9/10F
2 With Anticipation (7-9-0) Pat Day   87/10
3 Falcon Flight (6-9-0) Pat Valenzuela 123/10
Distances: Adrian O'Brien IRL £861,918

Classic
3yo+ 1m 2f (dirt)   12 ran
1 Volponi (4-9-0)   Jose Santos   435/10
2 Medaglio D'Oro (3-8-9) Jerry Bailey   27/10F
3 Mllwaukee Brew (5-9-0) Edgar Prado   24/1
Distances: 6½, nk   Philip Johnson USA   £1,424,658

National Hunt Racing

2001/2002 Season

Britannia Handicap Chase
Uttoxeter, July 1 *4m 110y*
Race abandoned

Tote Scoop6 Summer Handicap Chase
Market Rasen, July 21 *2m 4f*
Dorans Gold (7-10-0)
Timmy Murphy 7/1
Paul Nicholls *£37,297*

Barbara King Desert Orchid Pattern Handicap Chase
Wincanton, Oct 28 *2m 5f*
Celibate (10-104)
Noel Fehily 5/1
Charlie Mann *£21,000*

Peterhouse Group Charlie Hall Chase
Wetherby, Nov 3 *3m 1f*
Sackville (8-11-5)
David Casey 5/1
Frances Crowley *£29,000*

williamhill.co.uk Haldon Handicap Chase
Exeter, Nov 6 *2m 1f 110y*
Best Mate (6-10-12)
Jim Culloty 8/13F
Henrietta Knight *£21,000*

Badger Brewery H'cap Chase
Wincanton, Nov 10 *3m1f110yds*
Montifault (6-11-3)
Timmy Murphy 11/4F
Paul Nicholls *£26,000*

Tote Silver Trophy Handicap Hurdle
Chepstow, Nov 10 *2m 4f*
Majed (5-10-3)
Tony McCoy 9/4F
Martin Pipe *£22,750*

Sporting Index Cross-country Chase
Cheltenham, Nov 16 *3m 7f*
Lucky Clover (9-11-2)
Joe Tizzard 10/1
Clive Tizzard *£21,157*

Tote Handicap Hurdle
Cheltenham, Nov 17 *3m 1f 110y*
It Takes Time (7-10-10)
Tony McCoy 4/1
Martin Pipe *£27,716*

Thomas Pink Handicap Chase
Cheltenham, Nov 17 *2m 4f 110y*
Shooting Light (8-11-3)
Tony McCoy 9/4F
Martin Pipe *£58,000*

Intervet Handicap Chase
Cheltenham, Nov 17 *3m 3f 110y*
Hati Roy (8-10-13)
Jim Culloty 4/1F
Henrietta Knight *£32,500*

Edward Hanmer Memorial Limited Handicap Chase
Haydock, Nov 18 *3m*
Kingsmark (8-10-12)
David Dennis (3) 11/2
Martin Todhunter *£27,000*

Pricewaterhouse Ascot Hurdle
Ascot, Nov 23 *2m 4f*
Baracouda (6-11-8)
Thierry Doumen 11/10F
Francois Doumen *£15,600*

First National Gold Cup Chase
Ascot, Nov 24 *2m 3f 110y*
Wahiba Sands (8-10-4)
Tony McCoy 4/1
Martin Pip *£30,000*

Tote Becher Handicap Chase
Aintree, Nov 25 *3m 3f*
Amberleigh House (9-10-9)
Warren Marston 33/1
Donald McCain *£29,000*

Peterborough Chase
Huntingdon, Nov 24 *2m 4f 110y*
Edredon Bleu (9-11-10)
Jim Culloty 10/11F
Henrietta Knight *£30,000*

Telebet Novices Chase
Newbury, Nov 30 *3m*
Valley Henry (6-11-9)
Timmy Murphy 15/8F
Paul Nicholls *£17,850*

Ladbrokes Handicap Hurdle
Newbury, Dec 1 *2m 4f*
Cyfor Malta (8-12-0)
Tony McCoy 3/1
Martin Pipe *£20,300*

Hennessy Cognac Gold Cup
Newbury, Dec 1 *3m 2f 110y*
What's Up Boys (7-10-12)
Paul Flynn 14/1
Philip Hobbs *£58,000*

Pertemps Fighting Fifth Hurdle
Newcastle, Dec 1 *2m*
Landing Light (6-11-8)
J Kavanagh 4/5F
Nicky Henderson *£22,200*

John Hughes Rehearsal Chase
Chepstow, Dec 8 *3m*
Arctic Camper (9-10-4)
Norman Williamson 12/1
Venetia Williams *£23,440*

George Stevens Handicap Chase
Cheltenham, Dec 14 *3m 1f 110y*
Royale De Vassy (7-10-0)
Norman Williamson 7/1
Venetia Williams *£28,496*

Tingle Creek Chase
Cheltenham, Dec 15 *2m 110y*
Race Abandoned

Tripleprint Gold Cup Chase
Cheltenham, Dec 15 *2m 5f*
Race Abandoned

Bonusprint Bula Hurdle
Cheltenham, Dec 15 *2m 1f*
Race Abandoned

Tommy Whittle Chase
Haydock, Dec 15 *3m*
Legal Right (8-11-2)
Tony McCoy 5/4F
Jonjo O'Neill *£26,100*

Tote Silver Cup H'cap Chase
Ascot, Dec 22 *3m 110y*
Shooting Light (8-11-6)
Tony McCoy 5/2F
Martin Pipe *£32,500*

Ladbroke Handicap Hurdle
Ascot, Dec 22 *2m 110y*
Marble Arch (5-10-11)
Norman Williamson 7/1
Hugh Morrison *£58,000*

Pertemps Christmas Hdle
Kempton, Dec 26 *2m*
Landing Light (6-11-7)
Mick Fitzgerald 5/4F
Nicky Henderson *£29,750*

King George VI Chase
Kempton, Dec 26 *3m*
Florida Pearl (9-11-10)
Adrian Maguire 8/1
Willie Mullins *£87,000*

Castleford Chase
Wetherby, Dec 26 *2m*
Race Abandoned

Worthington Classic Finale Junior Hurdle
Chepstow, Dec 27 *2m 110y*
Tempo D'Or (3-11-0)
B Gicquel 2/1
G Macaire FRA *£17,400*

Coral Welsh National Handicap Chase
Chepstow, Dec 27 *3m 5f 110y*
Supreme Glory (8-10-0)
Leighton Aspell 10/1
P Murphy *£43,500*

Victor Chandler Handicap Chase
Ascot, Jan 12   *2m*
Turgoenev (7-10-4)
Richard McGrath   9/2
Tim Easterby   *£34,800*

Great Yorkshire Handicap Chase
Doncaster, Jan 26   *3m*
Moor Lane (10-10-4)
Barry Fenton   4/1F
Ian Balding   *£39,871*

Pillar Property Chase
Cheltenham, Jan 26   *3m 1f 110y*
Rince Ri (9-11-10)
Ruby Walsh   9/4
Ted Walsh IRL   *£45,000*

Byrne Bros Cleve Hurdle
Cheltenham, Jan 26   *2m 5f 110y*
Kates Charm (9-11-3)
Mick Fitzgerald   3/1
Robert Alner   *£30,000*

Ladbroke Trophy Chase
Cheltenham, Jan 26   *2m 5f*
Foly Pleasant (8-11-10)
Jim Culloty   4/1
Henrietta Knight   *£32,500*

Agfa Diamond Handicap Chase
Sandown, Feb 2   *3m 110y*
Billingsgate (10-11-1)
Richard Johnson   7/2
Philip Hobbs   *£23,200*

Tote Scoop6 Handicap Hurdle
Sandown, Feb 2   *2m 6f*
Iris Royal (6-9-11)
M Foley (5)   14/1
Nicky Henderson   *£29,000*

National Trial Handicap Chase
Uttoxeter, Feb 2   *3m 4f*
Streamstown (8-11-1)
Adrian Maguire   14/1
Ferdy Murphy   *£40,600*

attheraces.co.uk Game Spirit Chase
Newbury, Feb 9   *2m 1f*
Lady Cricket (8-11-1)
Tony McCoy   15/8
Martin Pipe   *£20,880*

Tote Gold Trophy Hurdle
Newbury, Feb 9   *2m 110y*
Copeland (7-11-7)
Tony McCoy   13/2
Martin Pipe   *£63,800*

Aon Chase
Newbury, Feb 9   *3m*
Bacchanal (8-11-10)
Mick Fitzgerald   5/4F
Nicky Henderson   *£34,800*

Reynoldstown Novice Chase
Ascot, Feb 16   *3m 110y*
Jimmy Tennis (5-10-13)
Norman Williamson   3/1
Venetia Williams   *£20,825*

William Hill Handicap Hurdle
Ascot, Feb 16   *2m 4f*
Ideal Du Bois Beury (6-10-0)
Tom Scudamore   10/1
Martin Pipe   *£18,087*

Ritz Club Ascot Chase
Ascot, Feb 16   *3m 110y*
Tresor De Mai (8-11-7)
Tony McCoy   9/2
Martin Pipe   *£37,700*

Tote Eider National Chase
Newcastle, Feb 16   *4m 1f*
This Is Serious (8-11-2)
Tony Dobbin   4/1F
Charlie Swan   *£37,700*

Axminster Carpets Hurdle
Wincanton, Feb 21   *2m*
Hors La Loi (7-11-2)
Dean Gallagher   9/2
James Fanshawe   *£21,000*

De Vere Gold Cup Chase
Haydock, Feb 23   *3m 4f 110y*
Race abandoned

Racing Post Handicap Chase
Kempton, Feb 23   *3m*
Gunther McBride (7-10-3)
Richard Johnson   5/1
Philip Hobbs   *£52,200*

Sunderland Imperial Cup Handicap Hurdle
Sandown, Mar 9   *2m 110y*
Polar Red (5-11-1)
Tony McCoy   6/4F
Martin Pipe   *£26,100*

Marstons Pedigree Midlands Grand National
Uttoxeter, Mar 16   *4m 2f*
The Bunny Boiler (8-10-0)
Norman Williamson   5/1
Noel Meade IRL   *£49,600*

Weatherbys Hurdle
Ascot, Apr 13   *3m*
Spendid (10-11-2)
Warren Marsten   2/1JF
Alan King   *£17,400*

Mira Silver Trophy Chase
Cheltenham, Apr 17   *2m 5f*
Fadalko (9-11-10)
Mick Fitzgerald   2/1JF
Alan King   *£17,400*

Doubleprint Novice Chase
Ayr, Apr 20   *3m 1f*
Carbury Cross (7-10-10)
Mick Fitzgerald   EvsF
Paul Nicholls   *£24,562*

Gala Casinos Daily Scottish Grand National
Ayr, Apr 20   *4m 1f*
Take Control (8-10-6)
Ruby Walsh   20/1
Martin Pipe   *£60,000*

Masai Hurdle
Sandown, Apr 26   *2m 110y*
Copeland (7-11-6)
Tony McCoy   6/4F
Martin Pipe   *£35,700*

Bet.Watch.Live Hurdle
Sandown, Apr 27   *3m*
It Takes Time (8-11-5)
Tony McCoy   5/6F
Martin Pipe   *£29,000*

Queen Mother Chase
Sandown, Apr 27   *2m*
Cenkos (8-11-6)
Barry Geraghty   8/1
Paul Nicholls   *£44,625*

Attheraces Gold Cup Handicap Chase
Sandown, Apr 27   *3m 5f 110y*
Bounce Back (6-10-9)
Tony McCoy   14/1
Martin Pipe   *£72,500*

Cheltenham Festival
Mar 12-14, Going: Good to Soft

Gerrard Sharp Novices' Hurdle
Mar 12	2m 110y		28 ran
1 Like-A-Butterfly (8-11-3)	Charlie Swan		7/4F
2 Westender (6-11-8)	Tony McCoy		6/1
3 In Contrast (6-11-8)	Richard Johnson		16/1
Distances: nk, 2½, ½	*Christy Roche IRL*		*£52,200*

Irish Independent Arkle Challenge Chase
Mar 12	2m		12 ran
1 Moscow Flyer (8-11-8)	Barry Geraghty		11/2
2 Seebald (7-11-8)	Tony McCoy		5/2F
3 Armaturk (5-11-8)	Tim Murphy		8/1
Distances: 4, 13, ¾	*Jessica Harrington*		*£72,500*

Smurfit Champion Hurdle Trophy
Mar 12	2m 110y		15 ran
1 Hors La Loi III (7-12-0)	Dean Gallagher		10/1
2 Marble Arch (6-12-0)	Ruby Walsh		25/1
3 Bilboa (5-11-9)	Thierry Doumen		14/1
Distances: 3, ½, shd	*Jessica Harrington*		*£72,500*

William Hill National Hunt Handicap Chase
Mar 12	3m 1f		23 ran
1 Frenchman's Creek (8-10-5)	Paul Carberry		8/1
2 Carbury Cross (8-10-2)	Liam Cooper		25/1
3 Ad Hoc (8-11-7)	Ruby Walsh		7/1
4 You're Agoodun (10-11-0)	J Kavanagh		20/1
Distances: 3, 16, ¾	*Hugh Morrison*		*£45,500*

Fulke Walwyn Kim Muir Challenge Cup Amateur Handicap Chase
Mar 12	3m 1f		23 ran
1 The Bushkeeper (8-11-2)	D Crosse		9/2F
2 Ceanannas Mor (8-10-7)	R Fowler (5)		20/1
3 Supreme Charm (8-10-9)	G Elliott		25/1
4 Phar From A Fiddle (9-9-11)	P Gundry		16/1
Distances: 7, 3½, 1	*Nicky Henderson*		*£26,000*

Pertemps Final Handicap Hurdle Final
Mar 12	3m 1f 110y		24 ran
1 Freetown (6-11-2)	Tony Dobbin		20/1
2 Surprising (7-10-4)	Richard Johnson		12/1
3 Montreal (5-10-7)	Ruby Walsh		25/1
4 Native Emperor (6-10-9)	Liam Cooper		10/1
Distances: 4, hd, 5	*Len Lungo*		*£32,500*

Royal & SunAlliance Novices Hurdle
Mar 15	2m 5f		14 ran
1 Galileo (6-11-7)	J Maguire		12/1
2 Over The Bar (6-11-7)	Norman Willliamson		14/1
3 Lanzerac (5-11-7)	Paul Flynn		66/1
Distances: 3½, shd	*Tom George*		*£52,200*

Queen Mother Champion Chase
Mar 15	2m		9 ran
1 Flagship Uberalles (8-12-0)	Richard Johnson		7/4F
2 Native Upmanship (9-12-0)	Norman Williamson		9/1
3 Cenkos (6-12-0)	Tim Murphy		66/1
Distances: 3, ½	*Philip Hobbs*		*£127,600*

Coral Cup Handicap Hurdle
Mar 13	2m 5f		27 ran
1 Ilnamar (6-10-5)	Rod Greene		25/1
2 Joss Naylor (7-10-0)	Liam Cooper		13/2
3 Master Tern (7-10-3)	Tony Dobbin		8/1
4 Stromness (5-10-3)	Robert Thornton		12/1
Distances: 8, 3, 4	*Martin Pipe*		*£42,000*

Royal & SunAlliance Novices' Chase
Mar 13	3m 1f		19 ran
1 Hussard Collonges (7-11-4)	Russ Garritty		33/1
2 Iznogoud (6-11-4)	Tony McCoy		14/1
3 Chives (7-11-4)	Richard Guest		33/1
Distances: 2, 4	*Nicky Henderson*		*£26,000*

National Hunt Chase Challenge Cup
Mar 13	4m		21 ran
1 Rith Dubh (10-11-11)	J McNamara		10/1
2 Timbera (8-12-0)	David Russell		8/1
3 Silver Steel (7-12-0)	A Crowe		12/1
Distances: hd, 13	*Jonjo O'Neill*		*£26,000*

Mildmay Of Flete Challenge Cup H'p Chase
Mar 13	2m 4f 110y		21 ran
1 Blowing Wind (9-10-9)	Richard Johnson		14/1
2 Lady Cricket (8-11-12)	Jimmy McCarthy		13/2F
3 It's Time For A Win (10-10-0)	Robbie Supple		7/1
4 Strong Run (9-10-4)	Barry Fenton		10/1
Distances: 1¼, 1¼, 1	*Martin Pipe*		*£45,500*

Wetherbys Bumper Open NH Flat Race
Mar 13	2m 110y		23 ran
1 Pizarro (5-11-6)	Jamie Spencer		14/1
2 Rhinestone Cowboy (6-11-6)	N Williamson		5/2F
3 Back In Front (5-11-6	Charlie Swan		12/1
Distances: nk, 3½	*Edward O'Grady*		*£18,000*

JCB Triumph Hurdle
Mar 14	2m 1f		28 ran
1 Scolardy (4-11-0)	Charlie Swan		16/1
2 Newhall (4-10-9)	F Flood		8/1
3 Diamond Joshua (4-11-0)	Jim Culloty		66/1
Distances: 11, ¾	*Willie Mullins*		*£52,200*

Bonusprint Stayers' Hurdle
Mar 14	3m 110y		16 ran
1 Baracouda (7-11-10)	Thierry Doumen		13/8F
2 Bannow Bay (7-11-10)	Christy Roche		2/1
3 It Takes Time (8-11-10)	Tony McCoy		12/1
Distances: nk, 13	*Francois Doumen*		*£72,500*

Tote Cheltenham Gold Cup Chase
Mar 14	3m 2f 110y		12 ran
1 Best Mate (7-12-0)	Jim Culloty		7/1
2 Commanche Court (9-12-0)	Ruby Walsh		25/1
3 See More Business (12-12-0)	Joe Tizzard		40/1
Distances: 1¾, 8	*Henrietta Knight*		*£18,000*

Christies Foxhunter Challenge Cup Chase

Mar 14	3m 2f 110y		20 ran
1 Last Option (10-12-0)	F Needham		20/1
2 Gunner Welburn (10-12-0)	R Cope		8/1
3 Torduff Express (11-12-0)	P Gundry		10/1
Distances: ½, ½	R Tate		£26,000

Grand Annual Challenge Cup H'cap Chase

Mar 14	2m 110y		18 ran
1 Fadoudal Du Cochet (9-10-0)	David Casey		6/1
2 Exit Swinger (7-11-0)	Tony McCoy		4/1F
3 Dark 'n Sharp (7-10-0)	Richard Johnson		13/2
4 Logician (11-10-1)	F Keniry		20/1
Distances: ¾, 3, 5	A Moore IRL		£39,000

Cathcart Challenge Cup Chase

Mar 14	2m 5f		11 ran
1 Royal Auclair (5-10-11)	Tony McCoy		2/1F
2 Cregg House (7-11-3)	Ruby Walsh		33/1
3 Davids Lad (8-11-3)	Tim Murphy		5/1
Distances: 1¼, 7	Martin Pipe		£42,000

Vincent O'Brien County Handicap Hurdle

Mar 14	2m 1f		21 ran
1 Rooster Booster (8-11-1)	Richard Johnson		8/1
2 The Gatherer (8-10-6)	Conor O'Dwyer		12/1
3 Ben Ewar (8-10-1)	Barry Fenton		50/1
4 Benbyas (5-10-0)	Tim Murphy		12/1
Distances: nk, 2½, ½	Christy Roche IRL		£52,200

Leading Cheltenham Jockeys

Jockey	1st	2nd	3rd
Richard Johnson	3	1	2
Charlie Swan	3	-	1
Tony McCoy	1	4	1
Jim Culloty	1	-	1
Tony Dobbin	1	-	1

Leading Cheltenham Trainers

Trainer	Winners
Martin Pipe	3
Jessica Harrington	2
Nicky Henderson	2
Christy Roche	2

"In my opinion, the Jockey Club as an institution isn't capable of running racing"

Alan Meale, Labour MP.

"Brad's gone and shot his mouth off, those transcripts are dynamite"

Jeremy Phipps, former head of BHB security, in a taped conversation to Roger Buffham, his predecessor.

"What I have to say to Charlie Mann, I will say to his face. My father once said, `There are only so many breaths in your body. Why waste one of them on somebody who doesn't matter?' "

Martin Pipe, whose horses were tested for EPO in February. Mann had previously been outspoken in his claims that EPO was being used in the sport. Samples from horses at five stables were taken in dawn raids on February 26th, a day when there was no NH racing in the UK. All the tests came back negative. No EPO tests have been undertaken on horses immediately after they have won races; the most likely time to detect any such usage.

"We want a positive and healthy relationship which best serves the interest of racing, newspapers and readers"

Statement from the BHB, who wanted to increase charges to newspapers for using racecard data by 30 times. The policy was dropped after newspapers began to remove sponsors' names from listings.

Martell Grand National

Aintree, Apr 6, 4m 4f, Going: Good

1	**Bindaree** (8-10-4) Jim Culloty *Nigel Twiston-Davies £290,000*	-	20/1
2	**What's Up Boys** (8-11-6) Richard Johnson 1¾ *Philip Hobbs £110,000*		10/1
3	**Blowing Wind** (9-10-6) Tony McCoy *Martin Pipe £55,000*	27	8/1F
4	**Kingsmark** (9-11-9) Ruby Walsh *Mark Todhunter £25,000*	9	16/1
5	**Supreme Charm** (10-10-0) Robert Thornton 17 *Kim Bailey £12,500*		28/1
6	**Celibate** (11-10-3) Noel Fehily *Charlie Mann £7,500*	3½	66/1
7	**You're Agoodun** (10-10-8) J Kavanagh *Martin Pipe*	3½	50/1
8	**Royal Predica** (8-10-8) Jim McCarthy *Kim Bailey*	18	80/1
9	**Streamstown** (8-10-8) J McNamara *Ferdy Murphy*	28	40/1
10	**Birkdale** (11-10-2) J Maguire *Kim Bailey*	13	50/1
11	**Mely Moss** (11-10-2) N Williamson *Ferdy Murphy*	dist	25/1

40 ran
Time: 9:08.60 (Fast by 5.4 secs)
Winning Owner: H Mould
Winning Breeder: Noel King
Second Owner: R J B Partners
Third Owner: P A Deal

TOTE returns:
Win £33.80 ; Places £6.90, £3.60, £2.70, £4.60
Exacta £478.60; CSF £184.14; Tricast £1792.79

Total SP 143%

Non-finishers
The right-hand number shows the fence at which the horse fell or unseated rider. Where the horse has pulled up, the last fence jumped is given.

Carryonharry (8-10-0) R Wakley 66/1	F	1
Goguenard (8-10-0) Warren Marston 66/1	F	1
Inn At The Top (10-10-8) A Smith 40/1	F	1
Logician (11-10-0) Mark Bradbourne 80/1	B	1
Marlborough (10-11-12) Mick Fitzgerald 20/1	F	1
Paris Pike (10-10-13) Richard Guest 10/1	F	1
Red Ark (9-10-0) K Johnson 50/1	U	1
Struggles Glory (11-10-3) Ben Hitchcott 66/1	B	1
Wicked Crack (9-10-5) Conor O'Dwyer 33/1	F	1
Niki Dee (12-10-3) Russ Garritty 66/1	F	4
Samuel Wilderspin (10-10-0) T Doyle 14/1	F	4
Frantic Tan (10-10-5) T Jenks 50/1	U	5
Iris Bleu (6-10-0) P Moloney 100/1	F	5
Alexander Banquet (9-11-11) B Geraghty 22/1	U	6
Gun'n Roses II (8-10-2) M Foley 100/1	F	7
Smarty (9-10-1) Tom Scudamore 16/1	P	8
Beau (9-11-1) Carl Llewellyn 11/1	U	14
Murt's Man (8-10-2) Andrew Thornton 66/1	P	16
Super Franky (9-10-5) P O'Brien 66/1	F	18
Ackzo (9-10-0) Dean Gallagher 25/1	P	19
Lyreen Wonder (9-11-4) B Cash 40/1	U	20
Manx Magic* (9-10-7) G Supple 100/1	F	20
Majed (6-11-10) Barry Fenton 66/1	F	22
The Last Fling* (12-10-6) Richard McGrath 40/1	F	24
Inis Cara (10-10-0) Brian Crowley 66/1	P	24
Djeddah (11-10-0) Thierry Doumen 66/1	U	26
Ad Hoc (8-11-1) Paul Carberry 10/1	B	27
Davids Lad (8-11-1) Tim Murphy 10/1	F	27
Spot Thedifference (9-10-0) David Casey 33/1	U	27

F=Fell, P=Pulled Up, R=Refused, U=Unseated

* Horse died

Other Aintree Festival Races

Martell Handicap Hurdle

Apr 4		*3m 110y*	*14 ran*
1	Sudden Shock (7-10-1)	J Kavanagh	33/1
2	Iris Royal (6-9-12)	M Foley (5)	10/1
3	Freetown (6-11-10)	Tony Dobbin	7/1
4	Old Rouvel (11-10-5)	Robert Thornton	12/1
Distances: ½, 4, ¾		*Jonjo O'Neill*	*£23,200*

Martell Cup Chase

Apr 4		*3m 1f*	*6 ran*
1	Florida Pearl (10-11-12)	Barry Geraghty	5/2
2	Cyfor Malta (9-11-6)	Tony McCoy	6/1
3	Lord Noelie (9-11-2)	Jim Culloty	2/1F
Distances: 11, nk		*Willie Mullins*	*£69,600*

Martell Red Run Handicap Chase

Apr 4		*2m*	*15 ran*
1	Dark 'n Sharp (7-10-8)	Richard Johnson	5/1F
2	Lord York (10-10-9)	Paul Carberry	14/1
3	Glenelly Gale (8-10-0)	David Casey	20/1
4	Batswing (7-9-7)	P Robson (7)	11/1
Distances: 9, ½, 5		*R Phillips*	*£34,800*

Martell Foxhunters Chase

Apr 4		*2m 5f 110y*	*30 ran*
1	Torduff Express (11-12-0)	P Gundry	8/1
2	ASecret Bay (12-12-0)	J Pritchard	7/2F
3	Bells Life (12-12-0)	G Tuer	40/1
Distances: 13, 4, 4		*Paul Nicholls*	*£21,645*

Martell XO Anniversary 4YO Novice Hurdle

Apr 4	2m 110y	17 ran
1 Quazar (11-4)	Tony Dobbin	16/1
2 Abbot (11-0)	Noel Fehily	16/1
3 Newhall (10-13)	F Flood	5/1
Distances: 2½, 1¾	Jonjo O'Neill	£58,000

Martell Novices Handicap Chase

Apr 4	2m 4f	10 ran
1 Spring Margot (6-11-9)	Norman Williamson	16/1
2 Harvis (7-11-0)	Russ Garritty	20/1
3 Mr Bossman (9-10-0)	Dean Gallagher	50/1
Distances: 2½, 19	Philip Hobbs	£29,000

Martell Mersey Novices Hurdle

Apr 4	2m 4f	12 ran
1 Classified (6-11-8)	Tony McCoy	9/2
2 Eternal Spring (5-11-3)	Dean Gallagher	2/1F
3 Boneyarrow (6-11-5)	Ruby Walsh	7/1
Distances: 2½, 6	Martin Pipe	£29,000

Martell V.S. Handicap Chase

Apr 5	3m 1f	14 ran
1 Carbury Cross (8-11-2)	Liam Cooper	3/1F
2 Enrique (7-11-0)	Richard Johnson	7/1
3 Macgeorge (12-11-4)	Robert Thornton	20/1
4 Cadougold (11-10-10)	Tom Scudamore	14/1
Distances: 18, 18, 1½	Jonjo O'Neill	£26,000

Martell Top Novices Hurdle

Apr 5	2m 110y	11 ran
1 In Contrast (6-11-5)	Richard Johnson	5/2
2 Westender (6-11-8)	Tony McCoy	5/4F
3 April Louise (6-10-9)	Rod Greene	66/1
Distances: 8, 16	Philip Hobbs	£29,000

Martell Melling Chase

Apr 5	2m 4f	8 ran
1 Native Upmanship (9-11-10)	Ruby Walsh	100/30JF
2 Wahiba Sands (9-11-10)	Tony McCoy	16/1
3 Fadalko (9-11-10)	Ruby Walsh	8/1
Distances: 1, nk	A Moore IRL	£69,600

John Hughes Handicap Chase

Apr 5	2m 5f 110y	28 ran
1 It's Time For A Win (10-10-12)	Ruby Walsh	10/1
2 Monty's Pass (9-10-11)	Barry Geraghty	10/1
3 Koraker (8-11-1)	D Dennis	10/1
4 Shannon Gale (10-10-4)	P Moloney	20/1
Distances: 6, 3½, 11	Philip Hobbs	£32,500

Martell Sefton Novices Hurdle

Apr 5	3m 110y	15 ran
1 Stromness (5-11-4)	Robert Thornton	8/1
2 Tarxien (8-11-4)	Tony McCoy	6/1
3 Stormez (5-11-4)	Tom Scudamore	14/1
Distances: 4, 2	Alan King	£34,800

Martell Mildmay Novices Chase

Apr 5	3m 1f	9 ran
1 Barton (9-11-9)	Tony Dobbin	3/1F
2 Southern Star (7-11-5)	Andrew Thornton	14/1
3 Japhet (5-11-0)	B Gicquel	7/2
Distances: 10, ½	Tim Easterby	£46,250

Martell Noblige Handicap Hurdle

Apr 5	2m 4f	14 ran
1 Ravenswood (5-10-5)	Tom Scudamore	7/4F
2 Farinel (6-10-8)	Conor O'Dwyer	9/1
3 Indalo (7-10-10)	Norman Williamson	9/1
4 Just In Time (7-10-12)	Ruby Walsh	16/1
Distances: 3½, 2½, 5	Martin Pipe	£23,200

Cordon Bleu Handicap Hurdle

Apr 6	2m 110y	17 ran
1 Intersky Falcon (5-10-0)	Liam Copper	10/1
2 Idaho D'Ox (6-10-9)	Tom Scudamore	20/1
3 Milligan (7-11-9)	Norman Williamson	6/1
4 Dark Shell (7-10-12)	Mick Fitzgerald	8/1
Distances: 15, 3½, 2	Jonjo O'Neill	£23,200

Martell Maghull Novice Chase

Apr 7	2m	5 ran
1 Armaturk (5-11-1)	Tim Murphy	5/2
2 Seebald (7-11-4)	Tony McCoy	EvsF
3 Fondmort (6-11-4)	Mick Fitzgerald	7/2
Distances: 1¼, 19	Paul Nicholls	£46,500

Martell Aintree Hurdle

Apr 6	2m 4f	14 ran
1 Ilnamar (6-11-7)	Ruby Walsh	9/1
2 Grimes (9-11-7)	Charlie Swan	9/2
3 It Takes Time (8-11-7)	Tony McCoy	9/1
Distances: 1¼, 1¾	Martin Pipe	£69,600

Martell Reserves Novices Hunter Chase

Apr 6	3m 1f	16 ran
1 Quetal (9-12-0)	N Harris	9/1
2 Barryscourt Lad (8-12-0)	Joanna Holmes	9/1
3 Garryspillane (10-12-0)	G Hanmer	20/1
Distances: 1½, 1	Laura Young	£10,822

Martell Champion National Hunt Flat Race

Apr 6	2m 1f	20 ran
1 Kickham (6-11-4)	P Fenton	3/1F
2 Iris's Gift (5-11-1)	Ben Hitchcott (3)	8/1
3 Touch Closer (5-11-1)	T Doyle (3)	12/1
Distances: 2½, ½	E O'GRady IRL	£10,822

Overseas

2001/2002 Races

Czech Republic

Velka Pardubicka Ceske Pojistovny Chase
Pardubice, Cze, Oct 14
7yo+ 4m 2f 110y
Chalco (9-10-7)
P Gehm
Josefg Vana Li CZE £36,121

France

Prix La Haye Jousselin Chase
Auteuil, Nov 4   3m 3f 110y
El Paso III (9-10-5)
L Metais
B Secly FRA   £77,595

Prix Maurice Gillois Chase
Auteuil, Nov 1   2m 6f
Double Car (6-10-5)
C Cheminaud
B de Watrigant   £132,515

Grand Prix d'Automne
Auteuil, Nov 1   3m
Magnus (5-10-1)
C Pieux
J Ortet FRA   £67,895

Gras Savoye Grand Steeple-Chase de Paris
Auteuil, May 26   3m 5f
Double Car (6-10-5)
C Cheminaud
B de Watrigant   £132,515

Ireland

Galway Plate Chase
Galway, Aug 1   2m 6f
Grimes (8-10-1)
Conor O'Dwyer   4/1JF
Christy Roche IRL   49,395

Guinness Galway Handicap Hurdle
Galway, Aug 2   2m
Ansar (5-9-9)
Paul Carberry   6/1
Dermot Weld IRL   53,931

Kerry National Handicap Chase
Listowel, Sep 26   3m
More Than A Stroll (9-10-6)
Conor O'Dwyer   14/1
Arthur Moore   48,588

James Nicholson Champion Chase
Down Royal, Nov 10   3m
Foxchapel King (8-11-3)
David Casey   4/1
M Morris   £53,225

Royal Bond Novice Hurdle
Fairyhouse, Dec 2   2m
Like-A-Butterfly (7-11-7)
Charlie Swan   4/7F
Christy Roche IRL   £28,830

Pierse Drinmore Novice Chase
Fairyhouse, Dec 2   2m 4f
Harbour Pilot (6-11-12)
Paul Carberry   7/2
Noel Meade IRL   £31,451

Hattons Grace Hurdle
Fairyhouse, Dec 2   2m 4f
Limestone Lad (9-11-12)
Paul Carberry   5/4F
James Bowe   £31,451

John Durkin Memorial Chase
Punchestown, Dec 9   2m 4f
Florida Pearl (9-11-12)
Paul Carberry   5/1
Willie Mullins IRL   £36,693

Denny Novice Chase
Leopardstown, Dec 26   2m 1f
Moscow Flyer (5-11-10)
Barry Geraghty   5/4F
Mrs J Harrington   £39,314

Paddy Power Chase
Leopardstown, Dec 27   3m
I Can Imagine (6-9-2)
J Elliott (5)   12/1
Robert Tyner IRL   £59,919

Ericsson Chase
Leopardstown, Dec 28   3m
Foxchapel King (8-12-0)
David Casey   9/2
M Morris IRL   £IR65,300

Pierse Leopardstown Handicap Chase
Leopardstown, Jan 13   3m
Lyreen Wonder (9-10-13)
B Cash   100/30
Arthur Moore IRL   £39,877

Pierse Handicap Hurdle
Leopardstown, Jan 13   2m
Adamant Approach (8-11-1)
Ruby Walsh   8/1
Willie Mullins IRL   £48,251

AIG Champion Hurdle
Leopardstown, Jan 27   2m
Ned Kelly (6-11-10)
Norman Williamson   11/8F
Edward O'Grady IRL   £53,374

Powers Irish Grand National
Fairyhouse, Apr 1   3m 5f
The Bunny Boiler (8-9-9)
R Geraghty (5)   12/1
Noel Meade IRL   £65,693

Powers Gold Cup Chase
Fairyhouse, Apr 2   2m 4f
Big-And-Bold (6-11-9)
Ruby Walsh   7/1
G Lyons   £34,168

Powers Hurdle Series Final
Fairyhouse, Apr 2   2m
Anxious Moments (7-9-8)
David Casey   8/1
Charlie Swan   £39,877

BMW Chase
Punchestown, Apr 23   2m
Strong Run (9-12-0)
Paul Carberry   4/1
Noel Meade IRL   £38,159

Evening Herald Champion Novice Hurdle
Punchestown, Apr 23   2m
Scottish Memories (6-11-12)
Paul Carberry   11/4
Noel Meade IRL   £32,233

Menolly Homes Champion Novice Hurdle
Punchestown, Apr 24   2m 4f
Davenport Milenium (6-11-12)
Ruby Walsh   100/30
Willie Mullins IRL   £34,233

Punchestown Heineken Gold Cup
Fairyhouse, Apr 24   3m 1f
Florida Pearl (10-12-0)
Barry Geraghty   13/8F
Willie Mullins IRL   £60,858

Champion 4yo Hurdle
Punchestown, Apr 25   2m
Quazar (4-11-0)
Tony Dobbin   9/2F
Jonjo O'Neill   £41,901

Swordlestown Novice Chase
Fairyhouse, Apr 25   2m
Moscow Flyer (8-11-12)
Barry Geraghty   2/5F
Mrs J Harrington   £32,331

Kevin McManus Champion Stayers Hurdle
Fairyhouse, Apr 25   3m
Limestone Lad (10-11-12)
Paul Carberry   4/6F
James Bowe IRL   £30,429

Emo Oil Champion Hurdle
Punchestown, Apr 26   2m
Davenport Milenium (6-12-0)
Ruby Walsh   11/2
Willie Mullins IRL   £49,693

David Austin Memorial Novice Handicap Chase
Punchestown, Apr 26   3m 1f
It's Himself (10-10-8)
G Tormey   6/1
A Martin IRL   £36,134

NATIONAL HUNT 2001-2002

Top Trainers
Listed by Total Money

		Total Money	Win Money	1st	2nd	3rd	Total	%	£1Stake
1	Martin Pipe	2,692,176	1,901,743	235	132	108	999	23.5	-144.63
2	Paul Nicholls	1,443,207	934,856	136	88	67	547	24.9	+21.72
3	Philip Hobbs	1,359,391	854,666	119	94	83	600	19.8	-105.45
4	Jonjo O'Neill	979,222	698,485	113	63	50	477	23.7	+124.74
5	Nicky Henderson	861,650	585,827	93	63	38	417	22.3	-37.31
6	Henrietta Knight	817,419	516,624	48	50	35	283	17.0	-56.29
7	Nigel Twiston-Davies	593,571	425,331	35	58	45	490	7.1	-280.99
8	Venetia Williams	591,820	395,166	55	32	35	234	23.5	-75.84
9	Mary Reveley	542,666	371,534	90	51	67	553	16.3	-62.79
10	Ferdy Murphy	498,858	319,054	68	66	55	543	12.5	-178.23
11	Len Lungo	326,440	263,576	61	35	33	278	21.9	-0.80
12	Ian Williams	319,574	202,476	48	48	44	408	11.8	-156.48
13	Alan King	310,506	216,343	34	27	26	203	16.7	+21.62
14	Tom George	296,136	222,182	30	32	28	213	14.1	+85.75
15	Charlie Mann	282,315	142,575	35	39	38	270	13.0	-3.02
16	Willie Mullins	268,925	241,300	4	0	2	20	20.0	+20.50
17	François Doumen	261,467	183,435	9	7	6	39	23.1	-10.26
18	Henry Daly	260,795	163,500	28	27	28	241	11.6	-80.76
20	Paul Webber	257,860	160,296	33	32	22	230	14.3	+19.12
21	Robert Alner	256,412	157,425	29	33	37	294	9.9	-97.67
22	Kim Bailey	243,855	163,709	36	31	31	268	13.4	-30.11
23	Tim Easterby	243,248	189,577	19	20	14	134	14.2	-32.11
24	Sue Smith	236,636	148,434	27	38	29	286	9.4	-43.29
25	Hughie Morrison	219,502	134,152	6	2	4	27	2.2	+12.50

Top Jockeys
Listed by races won

		1st	2nd	3rd	4th	Total	%	Win Money	Total Money	£1 Stake
1	Tony McCoy	289	185	132	86	1008	28.7	1,958,944	2,755,779	-76.77
2	Richard Johnson	132	100	86	49	602	21.9	858,347	1,281,210	+9.20
3	Mick Fitzgerald	109	83	49	55	564	19.3	603,138	893,629	-146.21
4	Tony Dobbin	109	54	61	45	537	20.3	639,028	814,622	-11.81
5	Tim Murphy	98	67	65	47	524	18.7	596,485	920,507	+60.31
6	Norman Williamson	82	55	47	36	414	19.8	682,662	946,538	+48.25
7	Graham Lee	58	54	50	34	439	13.2	208,998	322,345	+6.43
8	Robert Thornton	56	61	55	62	543	10.3	304,340	470,439	-178.71
9	Andrew Thornton	54	63	59	51	482	11.2	235,469	402,213	-163.31
10	Adrian Maguire	53	61	55	56	486	10.9	328,821	476,768	-184.04
11	Jim Culloty	51	59	36	35	341	14.7	765,072	973,252	-53.91
12	Henry Oliver	47	45	34	43	462	10.2	175,706	280,431	-31.00
13	Joe Tizzard	44	53	30	33	363	12.1	261,758	426,279	-128.65
14	Alan Dempsey	43	27	34	17	280	15.4	180,950	259,055	-0.34
15	Leighton Aspell	42	56	53	60	480	8.8	234,354	342,949	-166.38
16	Liam Cooper	42	27	21	22	214	19.6	234,354	342,949	+40.97
17	Russ Garritty	40	43	28	34	288	13.9	212,388	297,931	-19.70
18	Warren Marston	39	48	50	62	503	7.8	209,789	328,934	-163.77
19	Mark Bradbourne	38	40	45	39	395	9.6	173,262	305,432	+43.32
20	Rupert Wakley	36	43	41	46	455	7.9	139,910	234,357	-138.65
21	Dave Dennis	36	33	29	23	316	11.4	177,285	243,746	-19.77
22	Noel Fehily	36	31	34	32	308	11.7	143,225	263,268	-6.98
23	Carl Llewellyn	35	51	47	51	557	6.3	152,197	325,700	-326.20
24	Richard McGrath	35	45	49	45	440	8.0	184,578	299,478	-138.88
25	Jimmy McCarthy	35	41	39	43	382	9.2	156,399	283,021	-87.56

Ice Hockey

And then there were seven, making the Superleague the smallest of all the professional sports leagues in the UK for any sport (well, we can't think of a smaller one). The demise of Newcastle brought the number down from eight, leaving the 'magnificent seven' playing each other up to 10 times in a season, without even counting Cup matches. If that didn't devalue the season, the decision to include all the teams in the play-offs was surely a mockery, particularly as the team which finished bottom of the Superleague, Manchester Storm, played in the play-off final. Storm would later run into financial problems and go into administration, which would be the catalyst for the creation of a new professional set-up, but we should leave that to the next book, and concentrate on the positive aspects of the 2001-2002 season.

Which takes us directly to the newest franchise in the Superleague; the Irish team without an Irishman. it didn't matter who they played in the team, though, the Odyssey Arena in Belfast was still the fullest venue in the league. In front of enthusiastic home support, the Giants could do little wrong, winning 14 straight home games, from October to January, to send them clear in the league. The Giants were defending a 19-match unbeaten run, home and away, when they visited Bracknell on January 19th. A two-all draw kept the run going, but more importantly guaranteed the title six weeks before the season's end. For Giants coach Dave Whistle, it was a second title in three years, the previous one coming when he coached the Bees.

The Giants looked set to add the Challenge Cup too, for the final was being played at the Odyssey. In the final, they faced Ayr Scottish Eagles, a team they had already played eight times during the season and had beaten on seven of those occasions; the eighth being drawn. Well, sport being a contrary child, the Eagles won the Challenge Cup handsomely, 5-0.

The Stanley Cup went to the Detroit Red Wings, the Carolina Hurricanes only taking the series to the fifth game. It was the Red Wings' third Cup win in six years, but that statistic rather masks the fact that since they won successive titles in 1997 and 1998, there had been three early exits from the play-offs.

To rectify matters, Mike Ilitch, the Red Wings owner, got the cheque book out. For the legendary goalie Dominic Hasek, he paid $8m for a single season; forward Luc Robitaille cost $4m for the year; and he coughed up another $9m for a two-year deal with Brett Hull. Those deals took the Red Wings payroll for the season to $65m, the highest in the NHL. "That's what you want in ownership. You want an owner that wants to win...Great players demand great money, that's just the way it is," said Hull. At Manchester, Newcastle and Cardiff, they must weep when they hear talk like that.

World Championship

Gothenburg, Karlstad, Jonkoping, April 26-May 11

Preliminary Round

The top three teams in Groups A & D, qualify for Group E; the top three teams in Groups B & C qualify for Group F. Results from the preliminary stage for teams in the same group are carried forward to the Group E/F stage. The top two teams in Groups E & F qualify for the semi-finals.

Group A

Germany 9 Japan 2; Czech Rep 5 Switzerland 0;
Germany 3 Switzerland 0; Czech Rep 5 Japan 3;
Switzerland 5 Japan 1; Czech Rep 7 Germany 5

Standings	P	W	D	L	GF	GA	Pts
1 Czech Republic	3	3	0	0	17	8	6
2 Germany	3	2	0	1	17	9	4
3 Switzerland	3	1	0	2	5	9	2
4 Japan	3	0	0	3	6	19	0

Group B

Slovakia 7 Poland 0; Finland 3 Ukraine 0;
Slovakia 5 Ukraine 4; Finland 8 Poland 0;
Finland 3 Slovakia 1; Ukraine 3 Poland 0

Standings	P	W	D	L	GF	GA	Pts
1 Finland	3	3	0	0	14	1	6
2 Slovakia	3	2	0	1	13	7	4
3 Ukraine	3	1	0	2	7	8	2
4 Poland	3	0	0	3	0	18	0

Group C

Russia 8 Slovenia 1; Sweden 5 Austria 3;
Russia 6 Austria 3; Sweden 8 Slovenia 2;
Austria 5 Slovenia 3; Sweden 2 Russia 0

Standings	P	W	D	L	GF	GA	Pts
1 Sweden	3	3	0	0	15	5	6
2 Russia	3	2	0	1	14	6	4
3 Austria	3	1	0	2	11	14	2
4 Slovenia	3	0	0	3	6	21	0

Group D

USA 5 Italy 2; Canada 4 Latvia 1; Canada 5 Italy 0;
USA 3 Latvia 2; Latvia 4 Italy 1; Canada 2 USA 1

Standings	P	W	D	L	GF	GA	Pts
1 Canada	3	3	0	0	11	2	6
2 USA	3	2	0	1	9	6	4
3 Latvia	3	1	0	2	7	8	2
4 Italy	3	0	0	3	2	14	0

Qualification Round

Group E

Czech Rep 5 Switzerland 0*; Canada 4 Latvia 1*;
Germany 3 Switzerland 0*; USA 3 Latvia 2*;
Czech Rep 7 Germany 5*; Canada 2 USA 1*;
USA 3 Switzerland 0; Canada 3 Germany 1;
Czech Rep 3 Latvia 1; Canada 3 Switzerland 2;
Germany 3 Latvia 2; Czech Rep 5 USA 4;
USA 2 Germany 2; Czech Rep 5 Canada 1;
Switzerland 6 Latvia 4

Result carried forward from preliminary round

Standings	P	W	D	L	GF	GA	Pts
1 Czech Republic	5	5	0	0	25	11	10
2 Canada	5	4	0	1	13	10	8
3 USA	5	2	1	2	13	11	5
4 Germany	5	2	1	2	14	14	5
5 Switzerland	5	1	0	4	8	18	2
6 Latvia	5	0	0	5	10	19	0

Group F

Sweden 5 Austria 3*; Finland 3 Ukraine 0*;
Russia 6 Austria 3*; Slovakia 5 Ukraine 4*;
Finland 3 Slovakia 1*; Sweden 2 Russia 0*;
Finland 3 Austria 1; Slovakia 2 Sweden 1;
Russia 3 Ukraine 3; Slovakia 6 Austria 3;
Sweden 7 Ukraine 0; Finland 1 Russia 0;
Sweden 4 Finland 2; Ukraine 3 Austria 2;
Slovakia 6 Russia 4

Standings	P	W	D	L	GF	GA	Pts
1 Sweden	5	4	0	1	19	7	8
2 Finland	5	4	0	1	12	6	8
3 Slovakia	5	4	0	1	20	15	8
4 Russia	5	1	1	3	13	15	3
5 Ukraine	5	1	1	3	10	20	3
6 Austria	5	0	0	5	12	23	0

Relegation Round

Group G

Slovenia 4 Japan 3; Poland 5 Italy 1;
Slovenia 4 Poland 2; Italy 6 Japan 0;
Slovenia 4 Italy 0; Poland 5 Japan 2

Standings	P	W	D	L	GF	GA	Pts
1 Slovenia	3	3	0	0	12	5	6
2 Poland	3	2	0	1	12	7	4
3 Italy	3	1	0	2	7	11	2
4 Japan	3	0	0	3	7	15	0

Japan and Italy relegated

Play-off Round

Quarter-finals
Finland 3 USA 1; Sweden 6 Germany 2;
Russia 3 Czech Rep 1; Slovakia 3 Canada 2

Semi-finals
Russia 3 Finland 2; Slovakia 3 Sweden 2

3rd/4th place play-off
Sweden 5 Finland 3

FINAL
Slovakia 4 Russia 3 (2-0; 1-1; 1-2)

Final Ranking
1 Slovakia; 2 Russia; 3 Sweden; 4 Finland;
5 Czech Rep; 6 Canada; 7 USA; 8 Germany;
9 Ukraine; 10 Switzerland; 11 Latvia; 12 Austria;
13 Slovenia; 14 Poland; 15 Italy; 16 Japan

Italy relegated to Division I, Japan relegated to Far East Qualifier, which was a single game against China, which Japan won, putting them back in the championship proper for 2003, while the team above them (Italy) had to play in a lower division. We haven't quite worked this logic out!

World Championship Other Divisions

Division I, Group A

Eindhoven, Netherlands, Apr 14-20
Final Standing: 1 Belarus; 2 France; 3 Kazakhstan; 4
Netherlands; 5 Croatia; 6 Korea
*Belarus promoted to the championships proper, Korea
relegated to Division II*

Division I, Group B

Szekesfehervar, Hungary, Apr 14-20
Norway 8 Romania 1; Denmark 5 Great Britain 3;
Hungary 6 China 0; Denmark 12 Romania 2;
Norway 12 China 2; Hungary 4 Great Britain 1;
Denmark 13 China 0; Great Britain 5 Romania 2;
Great Britain 8 China 3; Denmark 4 Norway 3;
Hungary 4 Romania 1; Norway 2 Great Britain 1;
Romania 2 China 2; Denmark 6 Hungary 2

Standings	P	W	D	L	GF	GA	Pts
1 Denmark	5	5	0	0	40	10	10
2 Hungary	5	4	0	1	19	9	8
3 Norway	5	3	0	2	26	11	6
4 Great Britain	5	2	0	3	18	16	4
5 Romania	5	1	0	4	10	31	2
6 China	5	0	0	5	7	43	0

*Denmark promoted to the championships proper, China
relegated to Division II*

Division II, Group A

Cape Town, Mar 31-Apr 6
Final Standing: 1 Estonia; 2 Belgium; 3 Israel;
4 Australia; 5 South Africa; 6 Turkey
*Estonia promoted to Division I, Turkey relegated to
qualification*

Division II, Group B

Novi Sad, Yugoslavia, Mar 25-31
Final Standing: 1 Lithuania; 2 Yugoslavia; 3 Spain;
4 Bulgaria; 5 Iceland; 6 Luxembourg
*Lithuania promoted to Division I, Luxembourg relegated
to qualification*

Division II, Qualifier

Mexico City, Apr 11-13
Final Standing: 1 DPR Korea; 2 Mexico; 3 New Zealand
DPR Korea and Mexico promoted to Division II

British Superleague

		P	W	D	L	GF	GA	Pts
1	Belfast Giants	48	31	8	9	177	119	70
2	Ayr Scottish Eagles	48	20	9	19	136	130	49
3	Sheffield Steelers	48	18	12	18	138	144	48
4	Nottingham Panthers	48	19	9	20	140	141	47
5	Bracknell Bees	48	15	13	20	140	158	43
6	London Knights	48	14	13	21	130	145	41
7	Manchester Storm	48	13	12	23	117	141	38

Superleague Play-offs

Nottingham, Mar 30-31 (Finals Weekend)
Semi-Finals
Manchester Storm 2   Ayr Scottish Eagles 1
Sheffield Steelers 3   London Knights 2
FINAL
Sheffield Steelers 4   Manchester Storm 3

Superleague Challenge Cup

FINAL
Belfast, Mar 3
Belfast Giants 0   Ayr Scottish Eagles 5

British National League

		P	W	D	L	GF	GA	Pts
1	Dundee	44	40	0	4	289	101	80
2	Coventry	44	33	2	9	227	118	68
3	Fife	44	31	1	12	222	110	63
4	Basingstoke	44	24	2	18	201	151	50
5	Guildford	44	24	1	19	198	144	49
6	Hull	44	23	2	19	190	161	48
7	Edinburgh	44	20	1	23	180	212	41
8	Milton Keynes	44	17	4	23	146	160	38
9	Paisley	44	18	1	25	161	259	37
10	Peterborough	44	11	3	30	136	208	25
11	Slough	44	7	4	33	112	216	18
12	Cardiff	44	5	1	38	90	312	11

National League Play-offs

Aggregate scores given; each round two legs.
Semi-finals
Coventry bt Guildford 10-4
Dundee bt Fife 10-3

FINAL
Dundee bt Coventry 8-7

English Premier League

		P	W	D	L	GF	GA	Pts
1	Invicta	28	20	3	5	149	92	43
2	Solihull	28	20	2	6	203	118	42
3	Isle of Wight	28	18	4	6	189	104	40
4	Romford	28	18	2	8	169	79	38
5	Swindon	28	19	1	9	153	98	37
6	England	28	6	0	22	22	120	12
7	Nottingham	28	4	1	23	65	196	9
8	Haringey	28	1	1	26	68	211	3

Play-off Final

Aggregate score given; each round two legs.
Invicta bt Isle of Wight 6-3

National Hockey League (NHL)

Eastern Conference

NORTHEAST DIVISION

	P	W	L	T	Pts
Boston Bruins	82	43	24	15	101
Toronto Maple Leafs	82	43	25	14	100
Ottawa Senators	82	39	27	16	94
Montreal Canadiens	82	36	31	15	87
Buffalo Sabres	82	35	35	12	82

ATLANTIC DIVISION

	P	W	L	T	Pts
Philadelphia Flyers	82	42	27	13	97
New York Islanders	82	42	28	12	96
New Jersey Devils	82	41	28	13	95
New York Rangers	82	36	38	8	80
Pittsburgh Penguins	82	28	41	13	41

SOUTHEAST DIVISION

	P	W	L	T	Pts
Carolina Hurricanes	82	35	26	21	91
Washington Capitals	82	36	33	13	85
Tampa Bay Lightning	82	27	40	15	69
Florida Panthers	82	22	44	16	60
Atlanta Thrashers	82	19	47	16	54

Western Conference

CENTRAL DIVISION

	P	W	L	T	Pts
Detroit Red Wings	82	51	17	14	116
St. Louis Blues	82	43	27	12	98
Chicago Blackhawks	82	41	27	14	96
Nashville Predators	82	28	41	13	69
Columbus Blue Jackets	82	22	47	13	57

PACIFIC DIVISION

	P	W	L	T	Pts
San Jose Sharks	82	44	27	11	99
Los Angeles Kings	82	40	27	15	95
Phoenix Coyotes	82	40	27	15	95
Dallas Stars	82	36	28	18	90
Mighty Ducks of Anaheim	82	29	42	11	69

NORTHWEST DIVISION

	P	W	L	T	Pts
Colorado Avalanche	82	45	28	9	99
Vancouver Canucks	82	42	30	10	94
Edmonton Oilers	82	38	28	16	92
Calgary Flames	82	32	35	15	79
Minnesota Wild	82	26	35	21	73

Conference Quarter-finals

EASTERN CONFERENCE (Best of 7 Series)
Carolina Hurricanes bt New Jersey Devils 4-2
Montreal Canadiens bt Boston Bruins 4-2
Toronto Maple Leafs bt New York Islanders 4-3
Ottawa Senators bt Philadelphia Flyers 4-1

WESTERN CONFERENCE (Best of 7 Series)
Detroit Red Wings bt Vancouver Canucks 4-2
St Louis Blues bt Chicago Blackhawks 4-1
St Jose Sharks bt Phoenix Coyotes 4-1
Colorado Avalanche bt Los Angeles Kings 4-3

Conference Semi-finals

EASTERN CONFERENCE (Best of 7)
Carolina Hurricanes bt Montreal Canadiens 4-2
Toronto Maple Leafs bt Ottawa Senators 4-3

WESTERN CONFERENCE (Best of 7)
Detroit Red Wings bt St Louis Blues 4-1
Colorado Avalanche bt San Jose Sharks 4-3

Conference Finals

EASTERN DIVISION (Best of 7)
Carolina Hurricanes bt Toronto Maple Leafs 4-2

WESTERN DIVISION (Best of 7)
Detroit Red Wings bt Colorado Avalanche 4-3

NHL Stanley Cup Championship

Best of 7 series
Game 1: Detroit Red Wings 2 Carolina Hurricanes 3
Game 2: Detroit Red Wings 3 Carolina Hurricanes 1
Game 3: Carolina Hurricanes 2 Detroit Red Wings 3
Game 4: Carolina Hurricanes 0 Detroit Red Wings 3
Game 5: Detroit Red Wings 3 Carolina Hurricanes 1

Detroit Red Wings won the Stanley Cup 4-1

NHL Leading Scorers

Goals score two points, assists a single point

	Player	Team	GP	G	A	Pts
1	Jarome Iginla	Calgary	82	52	44	96
2	Markus Naslund	Vancouver	81	40	50	90
3	Todd Bertuzzi	Vancouver	72	36	49	85
4	Mats Sundin	Toronto	82	41	39	80
5	Jaromir Jagr	Washington	69	31	48	79
6	Joe Sakic	Colorado	82	26	53	79
7	Pavol Demitra	St Louis	82	35	43	78
8	Adam Oates	Wash-Phi	80	14	64	78
9	Mike Modano	Los-Dallas	78	34	43	77
10	Ron Francis	Carolina	80	27	50	77

NHL Leading Goaltenders

In order of average goals conceded. 10 games+

	Player	Team	GP	Av	%S
1	David Aebischer	Colorado	21	1.88	93.1
2	Jose Theodore	Montreal	67	2.11	93.1
3	Jussi Markannen	Edmonton	14	1.84	92.9
4	Patrick Roy	Colorado	63	1.94	92.5
5	Jamie Storr	LA Kings	19	1.90	92.2
6	Roman Cechmanek	Philadelphia	46	2.05	92.1
7	Marty Turco	Dallas	31	2.09	92.1
8	Nikolai Khabibulin	Tampa	70	2.36	92.0
9	Sean Burke	Phoenix	60	2.29	92.0
10	J-S Gigue	Anaheim	53	2.13	92.0

Ice Skating

Nagano was the forgotten world championships, the scandals of Salt Lake City a month before still occupying the media more, in western Europe at least. The north Americans took a more expansive view, which is not always the case. In world championships, though, Canadian and American representation is always plentiful and the public loves a good skate.

Well, skates don't come much better than those of Alexei Yagudin, who was awarded four perfect scores at Salt Lake City, but surpassed that with six perfects in the compulsories at Nagano, and two more in the free skating. It was Yagudin's fourth world title in five years; his only lapse coming in 2001 when he was second to his compatriot Evgeni Plushenko. Only the American Scott Hamilton, in recent years, can boast a superior record.

Yagudin, who celebrated his 22nd birthday in Nagano, still competes as a Russian, but lives and trains in Newington, Connecticut, under the guidance of his compatriot Tatiana Tarasova. As well as coaching the best male skater in the world, Tarasova now also tutors the most talented female skater around, the diminutive American Sasha Cohen. In July, Cohen dispensed with the services of her veteran English coach, John Nicks, and moved from her base in California to Connecticut. In 1998 in Nagano, Tarasov achieved the unique distinction of coaching skaters in two events (Oksana Gritschuk and Yevgeni Platov in the dance; Ilia Kulik in the men's) to Olympic titles. With Yagudin and Cohen, she could quite possibly repeat the achievement in Turin in 2006.

Irina Sluskaya looked wounded at the marks awarded to her in the Olympics, but there was compensation of sorts for the Russian in Nagano. Sarah Hughes, the unexpected gold medallist from Salt Lake opted out, but Cohen and Michelle Kwan took the stage again.

Cohen is a skater who has few defensive ploys. She throws herself into her jumps with explosive power for her tiny frame. When they all come off, the rest will be nowhere, but in Nagano they didn't. Kwan was foot-perfect, but the four-time world champion does not thrill with her skating, she is perhaps a touch too slow on the ice, and Slutskaya, skating as well as she had all season, could claim her first world title.

Xue Shen and Hongbo Zhao won the pairs title, only the second world championship title for China. Their success, though, came in the absence of both the couples who were the centre of controversy in Salt Lake. The ice dance was won by the Russians Irina Lobacheva and Ilia Averbukh, but yet again the judging came under scrutiny. This time it was the Lithuanian couple, Povilas Vanagas and Margarita Drobiazko, who appealed against their fourth place. "If I was on the ISU's technical committee, I would quit. Everything is decided by which judges are on the panel and it's just unfortunate that the system kills the competitive nature of the sport," said Vanagas. The appeal was turned down.

World Championships

Nagano, Japan, Mar 16-24

FIGURE SKATING

Men

Two elements; technical & free-skating

1	Alexei Yagudin	RUS	2.0
2	Timothy Goebel	USA	4.8
3	Takeshi Honda	JPN	6.0
35	James Black	GBR	

Black did not qualify for free-skating

Women

1	Irina Slutskaya	RUS	2.0
2	Michelle Kwan	USA	4.2
3	Fumie Suguri	JPN	5.0

PAIRS

Two elements; technical & free-skating

1	Xue Shen Hongbo Zhao	CHN	1.5
2	Tatiana Totmianina Maxim Marinin	RUS	3.0
3	Kyoko Ina John Zimmerman	USA	4.5

ICE DANCING

Four elements; two compulsory, original and free dances

			Pts
1	Irina Lobacheva Ilia Averbukh	RUS	2.0
2	Shae-Lynn Bourne Victor Kraatz	CAN	4.0
3	Galit Chait Sergei Sakhnovski	ISR	7.0
14	Marika Humphreys Vitali Baranov	GBR	27.0

European Championships

Lausanne   Jan 14-20

Ice Dancing

1	Marina Anissina Gwendal Peizerat	FRA	2.2
1	Barbara Fusar-Poli Maurizio Margaglio	ITA	3.8
3	Irina Lobacheva Ilia Averbukh	RUS	6.0
11	Marika Humphreys Vitaly Baranov	GBR	22.8

Pairs

1	Tatiana Totmianina Maxim Marinin	RUS	1.5
2	Sarah Abitbol Stephane Bernadis	FRA	3.5
3	Maria Petrova Alexei Tikhonov	RUS	4.0
10	Tiffany Ann Sfikas Andrew Seabrook	GBR	13.5

FIGURE SKATING

Men

1	Alexei Yagudin	RUS	2.0
2	Alexander Abt	RUS	3.6
3	Brian Joubert	FRA	8.6
23	Matthew Davies	GBR	40.4

Women

1	Maria Butyrskaya	RUS	3.0
2	Irina Slutskaya	RUS	3.3
3	Viktoria Volchkova	RUS	5.0

Grand Prix Final

Kitchener, Canada, Dec 12-14 2001

FIGURE SKATING

Men

1	Alexei Yagudin	RUS	3.0
2	Evgeny Plushenko	RUS	3.0
3	Timothy Goebel	USA	6.0

Women

1	Irina Slutskaya	RUS	2.0
2	Michelle Kwan	USA	4.4
3	Sarah Hughes	USA	6.4

PAIRS

1	Jamie Sale David Pelletier	CAN	2.6
2	Elena Berezhnaya Anton Sikharulidze	RUS	3.4
3	Xue Shen Hongbo Zhao	CHN	6.0

ICE DANCING

1	Shae-Lynn Bourne Victor Kraatz	CAN	3.0
2	Marina Anissina Gwendal Peizerat	FRA	3.0
3	Margarita Drobiazko Povilas Vanagas	LTU	6.4

British Championships

Basingstoke, Dec 4-8, 2001

FIGURE SKATING

Men

1	Matthew Davies (Dundee)	1.5
2	James Black (Hull)	3.0
3	David Hartley (Sheffield)	4.5

Women

1	Zoe Jones (Centrum)	2.5
2	Vicki Hodges (Streatham)	3.5
3	Dannielle Guppy (Blackpool)	5.0

PAIRS

1	Tiffany Sfikas (Swindon) Andrew Seabrook	1.5

ICE DANCING

1	Marika Humphreys (Deeside) Vitali Baranov	2.0
2	Pam O'Connor (Nottingham) Jonathon O'Dougherty	4.0
3	Sinead Kerr (Murrayfield) John Kerr	6.0

Judo

Graeme Randall's recent retirement could be a seminal moment for British judo. Britain has only had three world champions in the past 10 years; Nicola Fairbrother, Kate Howey and Randall. With Kate Howey displaced from the Commonwealth team (*see CG section*), and now having to prove her credentials all over again - and the extension of bouts from four to five minutes may not be to her advantage - it is entirely possible that we could be saying goodbye to the last of them at world championship level.

At least in Georgina Singleton, Britain has a player who has the potential to emulate her illustrious compatriots. In what must be considered a slightly disappointing European championships for Briton, largely due to the lack of medals on the men's side, Singleton stood out. The 24-year-old maths teacher had always had talent - she is a former world junior champion - but has not always been given the opportunity.

She began the last Olympic year with a silver medal in the European championships, but was not selected for the Games when Debbie Allan, who usually fought at 57kg, opted to fight at a lower weight. But Allan misjudged badly, failing to make the weight in Sydney, and leaving Britain without a representative in the lightweight category. Singleton watched the debacle unfold from 10,000 miles away and was mortified.

Singleton was back in the British team for both the major events a year later, finishing fifth in the European event, but beaten in both her fights at the world championships. However, not one of the European medallists from that event was present in Maribor, and the German silver medallist from the Munich world championships, Raffaella Imbriani, was also absent. In short, Singleton was never going to get an easier opportunity for a major title.

In the first round, Singleton threw Poland's Barbara Bukowska for ippon and that set the tone. None of her remaining three bouts went to the limit, and only for the final against Spain's Ana Carrascosa was Singleton on the mat for more than two minutes, the Spaniard pinned down for ippon after two minutes and 48 seconds. Karen Roberts added a silver medal in the 63kg class, surprisingly her first-ever medal in a European championships, while the third medal, also a silver, came in the women's team event, Singleton again to the fore.

Randall, who is moving into coaching, will be much missed as a player. The Scot delivered when the British Judo Association most needed it, with a victory in the 81kg class at the world championships in Birmingham in 1999, the first time a British man had won a world title since Neil Adams' win in 1981. Randall looked in good shape in Sydney, too, before negative tactics cost him the bout against the Iranian Kazem Sarikhani in the second round.

European Championships

Maribor, Slovenia, May 16-19

Men

-60kg
1	Yacine Douma	FRA
2	Elchin Ismaylov	AZE
3	Nestor Khergani	GEO
3	Evgeny Stanev	RUS
5	John Buchanan	GBR

-66 Kg
1	Miklos Ungvari	HUN
2	Jozef Krnac	SVK
3	Islam Matsiev	RUS
3	Musa Nastuyev	UKR

James Warren GBR won one bout

-73 Kg
1	Anatoly Laryukov	BLR
2	David Kevkhishvili	GEO
3	Giuseppe Maddaloni	ITA
3	Vsevulods Zeljonis	LAT

Lee Burbridge GBR won two bouts

-81 Kg
1	Irakli Uznadze	TUR
2	Aleksei Budolin	EST
3	Robert Krawczyk	POL
3	Roberto Meloni	ITA

Evan Burton GBR did not win a bout

-90 Kg
1	Valentyn Grekov	UKR
2	Siarhei Kuharenka	BLR
3	Mark Huizinga	NED
3	Zurab Zviadauri	GEO
5	Winston Gordon	GBR

-100 Kg
1	Elco van der Geest	NED
2	Martin Padar	EST
3	Antal Kovacs	HUN
3	Igor Makarov	BLR

Sam Delahay GBR won one bout

+100 Kg
1	Tamerlan Tmenov	RUS
2	Pedro Soares	POR
3	Dennis van der Geest	NED
3	Janusz Wojnarowicz	POL

No British participant

Open
1	Dennis van der Geest	NED
2	Alexander Mikhaylin	RUS
3	Ruslan Shaparov	BLR
3	Pedro Soares	POR

No British participant

Team
1	Georgia
2	Belarus
3	Russia
5	Great Britain

Great Britain lost to Ukraine in the round 1, then beat Hungary and Turkey in the repechage before losing to France in the repechage semi-final

Women

-48 Kg
1	Frederique Jossinet	FRA
2	Tatiana Moskvina	BLR
3	Giuseppina Macri	ITA
3	Laura Moricz-Moise	ROM

Clare Lynch GBR did not win a bout

-52 Kg
1	Georgina Singleton	GBR
2	Ana Carrascosa	ESP
3	Alina Dumitru	ROM
3	Petra Nareks	SLO

-57 Kg
1	Cinzia Cavazzuti	ITA
2	Yvonne Bonisch	GER
3	Isabel Fernandez	ESP
3	Deborah Gravenstijn	NED
7	Sophie Cox	GBR

-63 Kg
1	Lucie Decosse	FRA
2	Karen Roberts	GBR
3	Claudia Heill	AUT
3	Gella Vandecavaye	BEL

-70 Kg
1	Adriana Dadci	POL
2	Edith Bosch	NED
3	Amina Abdellatif	FRA
3	Rasa Sraka	SLO
7	Samantha Lowe	GBR

-78 Kg
1	Celine Lebrun	FRA
2	Lucia Morico	ITA
3	Anastasiya Matrosova	UKR
3	Claudia Zwiers	NED
5	Joanna Melen	GBR

+78 Kg
1	Sandra Koppen	GER
2	Anne Sophie Mondiere	FRA
3	Barbara Andolina	ITA
3	Francoise Harteveld	NED

Simone Callender GBR won one bout

Open
1	Katja Gerber	GER
2	Tea Donguzachvili	RUS
3	Barbara Andolina	ITA
3	Eva Bisseni	FRA
7	Karina Bryant	GBR

Team
1	France
2	Great Britain
3	Netherlands

Great Britain beat Belgium and Slovenia before losing to France in the final

European Championships
Medal Table

1	France	5	1	2	7
2	Netherlands	2	1	6	9
3	Germany	2	1	0	3
4	Belarus	1	3	2	6
5	Russia	1	2	3	6
6	Great Britain	1	2	0	3
7	Italy	1	1	5	7
8	Georgia	1	1	2	4
9	Poland	1	0	2	3
9	Ukraine	1	0	2	3
11	Hungary	1	0	1	2
12	Turkey	1	0	0	1
13	Estonia	0	2	0	2
14	Spain	0	1	1	2
14	Portugal	0	1	1	2
16	Azerbaijan	0	1	0	1
16	Slovakia	0	1	0	1
18	Romania	0	0	2	2
18	Slovenia	0	0	2	2
20	Austria	0	0	1	1
20	Belgium	0	0	1	1
20	Latvia	0	0	1	1

World Team Championships

Basle, Switzerland, Aug 31-Sep 1

Men
Final Standing
1. Japan; 2. Georgia; 3. Italy;
3. France; 5. Iran; 5. Cuba;
7. Brazil; 7. Korea
No British team

Women
Final Standing
1. Japan; 2. Cuba; 3. Italy;
3. China; 5. France; 5. Korea;
7. Great Britain; 7. Netherlands

Paris 'A' Tournament
Bercy, Feb 9-10

Men

-60kg
1	Choi Min Ho	KOR
2	Joao Derly	BRA
3	Ruben Houkes	NED
3	Masato Uchishiba	JPN

-66kg
1	Yordanis Arencibia	CUB
2	Lee Won-Hee	KOR
3	Christophe Besnard	FRA
3	Konstantin Zaretskii	RUS

-73kg
1	Koen Sleeckx	BEL
2	Christophe Massina	FRA
3	Illya Chymchuri	UKR
3	Ferid Kheder	TUN

-81kg
1	Yoshihiro Akiyama	JPN
2	Ahn Dong-Jin	KOR
3	Antony Rodriguez	FRA
3	Nuno Delgado	POR

-90kg
1	Mark Huizinga	NED
2	Lionel Hugonnier	FRA
3	Yuta Yazaki	JPN
3	Zurab Zviadauri	GEO

-100kg
1	Keiji Suzuki	JPN
2	Ihar Makarou	BLR
3	Yuri Rybak	BLR
3	Michele Monti	ITA

+100kg
1	Aythami Ruano	ESP
2	Paolo Bianchessi	ITA
3	Tatsuhiro Muramoto	JPN
3	Tamerlan Tmenov	RUS

Women

-48kg
1	Frederique Jossinet	FRA
2	Giuseppina Macri	ITA
3	Kayo Kitada	JPN
3	Danieska Carrion	CUB

-52kg
1	Salima Souakri	ALG
2	Annabelle Euranie	FRA
3	Yuki Yokosawa	JPN
3	Amarilis Savon	CUB

-57kg
1	Yurisleidis Lupetey	CUB
2	Kie Kusakabe	JPN
3	Sabrina Filzmoser	AUT
3	Cinzia Cavazzuti	ITA

-63kg
1	Gella Vandecaveye	BEL
2	Yan Xuelan	CHN
3	Ylenia Scapin	ITA
3	Danielle Vriezema	NED

-70kg
1	Masae Ueno	JPN
2	Regla Leyen	CUB
3	Anett Boehm	GER
3	Edith Bosch	NED

-78kg
1	Mizuho Matsuzaki	JPN
2	Celine Lebrun	FRA
3	Claudia Zwiers	NED
3	Jenny Karl	GER

+78kg
1	Midori Shintani	JPN
2	Sandra Koeppen	GER
3	Liu Xia	CHN
3	Ivis Duenas	CUB

British Open
Crystal Palace, Apr 20-21

Men

-60kg
1	Craig Fallon	GBR
2	George Kurdlislasvili	MLD
3	John Buchanan	GBR
3	Marlon Boons	NED

-66kg
1	Josef Krnac	SLO
2	Carlos Montero	ESP
3	David Somerville	GBR
3	Oscar Penas	ESP

-73kg
1	Ryan Rezer	USA
2	Lee Burbridge	GBR
3	David Euranie	FRA
3	Ralph Akoto	GER

-81kg
1	Oscar Fernandez	ESP
2	Andre Allard	FRA
3	Johannes Schlabal	GER
3	Valentin Knobzoch	GER

-90kg
1	Sven Helbling	GER
2	Winston Gordon	GBR
3	Thierry Masterbroek	NED
3	Jason Jones	NED

-100kg
1	Henry Hubert	GER
2	Nacer Dahli	FRA
3	Tim Petola	FIN
3	Franz Birkfellner	AUT

+100kg
1	Ernesto Perez	ESP
2	Pedro Soares	POR
3	Sidney Carty	NED
3	Tsuyashi Tsumurai	JPN

Women

-48kg
1	Aurelie Carmao	FRA
2	Nynka Klopstra	NED
3	Donna Robertson	GBR
3	Clare Lynch	GBR

-52kg
1	Georgina Singleton	GBR
2	Veronique Kieffer	FRA
3	Veramarie Konig	GER
3	Kristle Taglman	BEL

-57kg
1	Ellen Wilson	USA
2	Virginie Henry	FRA
3	Sophie Cox	GBR
3	Miren Leon	ESP

-63kg
1	Sarah Clarke	GBR
2	Karen Roberts	GBR
3	Gemma Hutchins	GBR
3	Grace Vividen-Chapman	USA

-70kg
1	Samantha Lowe	GBR
2	Kate Howey	GBR
3	Sandra Garfalo	FRA
3	Amanda Costello	GBR

-78kg
1	Sandra Burdereux	FRA
2	Joanna Melen	GBR
3	Sian Wilson	GBR
3	Estelle Descot	FRA

+78kg
1	Eioda Becquet	FRA
2	Nanouska St Pre	USA
3	Rebbeca Ramanich	FRA
3	Cedrine Portet	FRA

British Closed
Wigan, Dec 1

Men

-60kg: Craig Fallon (Midlands)
-66kg: David Somerville (Scotland)
-73kg: Matthew Purssey (North)
-81kg: Euan Burton (Scotland)
-90kg: Peter Cousins (North)
-100kg: Sam Delahay (West)
+100kg: Danny Sargent (South)

Women

-48kg: Donna Robertson (Midlands)
-52kg: Vicki Dunn (South)
-57kg: Sophie Cox (North-West)
-63kg: Karen Roberts (North)
-70kg: Kate Howey (South)
-78kg: Rachel Wilding (South)
+78kg: Karina Bryant (South)

Modern Pentathlon

Errol Flynn would not have made much of a modern pentathlon; couldn't shoot without a steadying gin and tonic, smoked too much to swim or run any distance (and preferred tennis anyway). He could fence, though. Most actors can; it was once a must-have in the profession.

Maybe Sian Lewis and Georgina Harland should have gone to RADA. As well as giving them a profession to fall back upon (if modern pentathlon is ever thrown out of the Olympics), it could have provided some necessary assistance with their fencing. The cost for Harland over the past two summers has been world championship bronze medals when they should have been silver. At Millfield, in 2001, her fencing score of 692 was so low that only three of the 31 finallists scored fewer points. A year on, in San Francisco, Harland had improved enough to muster 776 points, but it was still 336 points fewer than Bea Simoka, who took the title with a score of just 100 points more than the Briton.

Lewis' fencing of 608 at the world championships was so poor that the only advice we can offer is that she cling on to the pistol next time. Lewis, though, was beset by rather more serious problems than a wayward epee, admitting during the year that she was suffering from anorexia nervosa. Given which, her performance in the European championships, in which she took the bronze medal, was sensational.

Too much criticism of the British women could be construed as a mite churlish, for their efforts over the past five years have brought a rich haul of medals.

For the men, however, there has been nothing to crow about since Richard Phelps won the world title in 1993. The admirable Phelps hit his 42nd birthday during the season, but still ended the year the fourth-ranked British man. At Usti Nad Labem in June, Phelps competed in the men's relay team alongside Matt Barnes and Sam Weale, the latter athlete 22 years his junior. Weale, who won a bronze medal in the European junior championships, and Ben McLean, who is also a junior, offer hope for the future. A future, incidentally, which may include Olympic participation, as the International Olympic Committee chose not to eject any sports at their congress in November.

Medal Mania

The recent world championship record of the British women

1997
Bronze: Relay
1998
Silver: Team
Bronze: Relay
1999
Gold: Relay
Silver: Team
2000
Silver: Team
Silver: Relay
2001
Gold: Stephanie Cook
Gold: Team
Gold: Relay
2002
Bronze: Georgina Harland

World Championships
Stanford University, San Francisco July 16-21
There is no riding phase in qualifying rounds in all
modern pentathlon competitions

Men

Individual		Total
1 Michal Sedlecky	CZE	5640
(1168, 944, 1240, 1088, 1200)		
2 Erik Johansson	SWE	5632
(976, 1028, 1276, 1200, 1152)		
3 Eric Walther	GER	5592
(1084, 804, 1352, 1160, 1192)		
24 Matthew Barnes	GBR	5200
(1048, 636, 1156, 1144, 1216)		

DNQ:
Semi-final A

17 Ben McLean	GBR	4072
(976, 784, 1296, 0, 1016)		

Semi-final B

18 Samuel Weale	GBR	4084
(712, 1096, 1248, 0, 1028)		

Semi-final C

21 Alexander Buirski	GBR	4000
(832, 1280, 748, 0, 1140)		

Team
1 Hungary 16036
Viktor Horvath/Sandor Fulep/Gabor Balogh
2 Czech Republic 15348
Libor Capalini/Sedlecky/Michal Michalik
3 Lithuania 15056
Edvinas Krungolcas/Tadas Zemaitis/Andrejus Zadneprovskis
14 Great Britain 13356
Barnes/Weale/McLean

Relay
1 Germany 5588
Walther/Sebastian Dietz/Carst Niederberger
2 Lithuania 5556
Zadneprovskis/Edvinas Krungolcas/Tadas Zemaitis
3 Poland 5516
Maciej Bogucki/Marcin Horbacz/Andrzej Stefanek
15 Great Britain 4648
Weale/Barnes/McLean

Women

Individual		Total
1 Bea Simoka	HUN	5568
(1120, 1112, 1208, 1172, 956)		
2 Szuzsa Voros	HUN	5508
(1120, 804, 1240, 1200, 1144)		
3 Georgina Harland	GBR	5468
(1000, 776, 1296, 1116, 1280)		
22 Emily Bright	GBR	5064
(964, 692, 1220, 1108, 1080)		
27 Sian Lewis	GBR	4532
(1084, 608, 1100, 540, 1200)		

DNQ
Semi-final Group B (top 16 qualify)

25 Joanna Clark	GBR	3780
(832, 1068, 832, 0, 1048)		

Team
1 Hungary 15660
Simoka/Voros/Csilla Furi
2 Italy 15388
Claudia Corsini/Claudia Cerutti/Federica Foghetti
3 Russia 15172
Marina Kolonina/Tatiana Mouratova/Evdokia Gretchichnikova
4 Great Britain 15064
Lewis/Bright/Harland

Relay
1 Czech Republic 5260
Grolichova/Kalinovska/Volenilkova
2 Italy 5188
Cerutti/Corsini/Bertoli
3 Hungary 5164
Voros/Mathe/Simoka

European Championships
Usti nad Labem, Czech Rep, June 18-22

Men

Individual		Total
1 Libor Capalini	CZE	5804
(1144, 972, 1356, 1200, 1132)		
2 Andrejus Zadneprovskis	LTU	5612
(1120, 860, 1316, 1116, 1200)		
3 Gabor Balogh	HUN	5572
(1132, 860, 1272, 1172, 1136)		

DNQ:
Semi-final Group A

23 Ben McLean	GBR	4000
(964, 808, 1252, 0, 976)		

Semi-final Group B

19 Matthew Barnes	GBR	4072
(892, 808, 1164, 0, 1208)		

Team
1 Hungary 16,348
Balogh/Fulep/Sarfalvi
2 Lithuania 16,328
3 Czech Republic 16,288
No British team

Relay
1 Lithuania 5628
Zadneprovskis/Krungolcas/Zemaitis
2 Belarus 5580
3 Ukraine 5480
14 Great Britain 4708
Barnes/Richard Phelps/Weale

Women

Individual		Total
1 Claudia Corsini	ITA	5548
(1108, 880, 1232, 1200, 1128)		
2 Axelle Guiget	FRA	5476
(1072, 952, 1156, 1200, 1096)		
3 Sian Lewis	GBR	5464
(1132, 736, 1172, 1140, 1284)		
4 Georgina Harland	GBR	5440
(952, 880, 1296, 1012, 1300)		
10 Kate Allenby	GBR	5328
(1060, 832, 1220, 1188, 1028)		
20 Emily Bright	GBR	5200
(976, 736, 1224, 1180, 1084)		

Team

1 Great Britain   16,232
   Lewis/Harland/Allenby
2 Italy   15,952
3 Poland   15,880

Relay

1 Italy   5352
2 Great Britain   5276
   Bright/Harland/Lewis
3 Russia   5264

World Cup Final

Budapest, Aug 11

Men

1 Andrejus Zadneprovskis LTU   5600
   (1108, 972, 1328, 1116, 1076)
2 Libor Capalini   CZE   5544
3 Sergio Salazar Sergio   MEX   5528

No British men

Women

1 Claudia Corsini   ITA   5500
   (1156, 936, 1244, 1088, 1076)
2 Paulina Boenisz   POL   5412
3 Szuzsa Voros   HUN   5352
14 Emily Bright   GBR   5036
   (952, 776, 1208, 1092, 1008)
24 Georgina Harland   GBR   4700
   (832, 808, 1272, 740, 1048)

World Cup Final Standings

Men

1 Niklaus Bruenisholz SUI   132
1 Andrej Shimanovic BLR   132
3 Manuel Pradillo MEX   128

Women

1 Elen Rublevska LAT   150
2 Csilla Furi HUN   120
3 Katalin Partics GRE   115
7 Georgina Harland GBR   106
7 Victoria Hinton GBR   106
15 Kate Allenby GBR   86

British Championships

Bath, Mar 2-3

Men

1 Matthew Barnes   5344
   (940,944,1140, 1100, 1220)
2 Vitali Ibrishim MDA   5252
3 Sam Weale   5227

Women

1 Georgina Harland   5616
   (952, 1056, 1308, 1100, 1200)
2 Sian Lewis   5479
3 Kate Allenby   5288

Motor Cycling

If Max Biaggi ever believed that a change of engine would lead to a change of fortune, he was quickly disabused of the notion by the rider who has plagued his existence. Valentino Rossi, having won the last four races of the 2001 season on a two-stroke 500cc bike, won the first of the 2002 season on a four-stroke 990cc Honda. In the new age of Grand Prix racing, it was very much, plus ça change, c'est la même chose, as the Italians don't say.

'The Doctor', as Rossi calls himself (there appears no rational explanation for this nickname), could not follow up in South Africa a fortnight later, where he was second to Japan's Tohru Ukawa, but won the next seven races with surgical precision. When he stepped off the track at the Sansenring in July, the Italian was 96 points clear in the championship race. Thereafter, no one was bothering to count the points, they were merely noting the wins. By the end of the season, Rossi had matched his tally of a year before with 11 victories from 16 races.

In seven seasons of racing, Rossi has accumulated 50 GP wins, at 23 years old easily the youngest rider ever to reach that tally. He had previously entered the record books as the youngest-ever rider to win world titles in all three classes (he was just a year younger when he achieved that).

Rossi could be diverted from the sport into motor rallying, and the Italian was lured into an attempt on the Network Q Rally in November. It was a brief encounter, Rossi crashing in the forests of Brechfa, minutes into the first stage, apparently blinded by the winter sunlight. It may just persuade the Italian to put his rallying ambitions on hold.

If Rossi continues to be hungry for GP success, it will be difficult to put a limit on what the Knightsbridge-based rider could achieve. Certainly, he will be guided shrewdly, for Mick Doohan is steering the Honda team, and the Australian knows exactly what's needed to put together a string of victories in the heavyweight class (Doohan ran up five in a row).

For most of the Superbike season, Troy Bayliss did a passable impression of Rossi, establishing a 57-point championship lead after the first race of the USA round at the Laguna Seca circuit in July. Bayliss didn't win the second race that day, it went to the American Colin Edwards who finished just over a second clear of the Australian.

It was hardly a crisis for Bayliss, who had won 14 of the first 18 races of the season, including an opening streak of six wins, that had never previously been achieved in the Superbikes. The Australian arrived at Brands Hatch following the Laguna Seca round not only with a substantial lead in the championship, but in sight of Doug Polen's record of 17 wins in a single season. For the self-defined country bumpkin, everything on the farm looked just hunky-dorey.

Counting the Brands Hatch event, there were just eight races left in the season and for Edwards to win the title, he would have to win them all, and he did. Bayliss was second in six of them, but it wasn't enough. Edwards had compiled the finest-ever sequence of victories in the superbikes and one of the greatest comebacks in motorcycle history, and he should have been jumping through hoops, but the Texan wasn't. He had pitched for a ride in the MotoGP championship with the Honda team: "I asked then what were the chances of partnering Valentino Rossi in the GPs next year and they said none. The only thing that matters now is the money you can bring to a team. I'd have thought I was first in line for a GP ride, but the days when Americans like Kenny Roberts can get to the top on merit are gone," he said. In mid-September, Honda Repsol named the young American Nicky Hayden as Rossi's second-string for the 2003 season.

Two weeks later, Edwards sealed the Superbike championship for Honda, then took his leathers elsewhere, signing for the Alice Aprilia team in the MotoGp championship. With Bayliss also switching codes, the Superbike championship for 2003 is up for grabs.

Neil Hodgson was over 200 points adrift of Edwards and Bayliss last season, but in their absence does appear to be a domestic rider with a chance of success. Carl Fogarty has finally got his Petronas team off the ground, but expecting them to fire in their first season is surely asking too much.

As ever, Jeremy McWilliams will ensure there is a British presence in the MotoGP, but most eyes will be on Chaz Davies, the 16-year-old from Presteigne in Wales who, after battling it out for a year in the 125cc class, now moves up to the 250cc machines. With the backing of rally driver Colin McRae, Davies is likely to be given every chance to prove himself.

"I've already beaten Valentino Rossi, but unfortunately only on my computer"
Chaz Davies, 15-year-old Welsh schoolboy, who competed in the 125cc Grand Prix events.

"Because I trained in a cave"
Valentino Rossi, in a list of reasons that he gave for his success.

"It got out of control at times, it's better now..."
Rossi, on his relationship with Max Biaggi.

"I never saw Agostini and my father says the best was Hailwood, but I liked Kevin Schwartz because he was a little crazy"
Rossi, again.

"Unfortunately, I don't have a team myself or I would get him on board straight away"
Bernie Ecclestone, trying to encourage one of the F1 teams to sign up Rossi.

Grand Prix

Japanese GP
Suzuka, Apr 7

500CC (21 laps, total distance 122.241km)
1	Valentino Rossi (Honda)	ITA	49:32.766	25
2	Akira Ryo (Suzuki)	JPN	+1.550	20
3	Carlos Checa (Yamaha)	ESP	+8.353	16

250CC (19 laps, 110.599km)
1	Osamu Miyazaki (Yamaha)	JPN	47:09.454	25
2	Daisaku Sakai (Honda)	ITA	+6.941	20
3	Randy de Puniet (Aprilia)	FRA	+29.020	16

NC: Jay Vincent & Leon Haslam GBR

125CC (18 laps, 104.778km)
1	Arnaud Vincent (Aprilia)	FRA	46:22.971	25
2	Mirko Giansanti (Aprilia)	ITA	+1.164	20
3	Manuel Poggiali (Aprilia)	SMR	+2.558	16

South African GP
Phakisa Freeway, Apr 21

500CC (28 laps, 118.776km)
1	Tohru Ukawa (Honda)	JPN	44:39.467	25
2	Valentino Rossi (Honda)	ITA	+0.932	20
3	Loris Capirossi (Honda)	ITA	+8.259	16

NC: Jeremy McWilliams GBR
Points after round 2: Rossi 45, Checa 27, Ukawa 25

250CC (26 laps, 110.292)
1	Marco Melandri (Aprilia)	ITA	42:52.922	25
2	Franco Battaini (Aprilia)	ITA	+2.962	20
3	Fonsi Nieto (Aprilia)	ESP	+5.213	16
12	Jay Vincent (Honda)	GBR	+47.886	4
15	Leon Haslam (Honda)	GBR	+1:04.093	1

Points after round 2: Battaini & De Puniet 26, Melandri & Miyazaki 25, Alzamora 22, Rolfo 21

125CC (23 laps, 101.808km)
1	Manuel Poggiali (Gilera)	SMR	41:26.120	25
2	Arnaud Vincent (Aprilia)	FRA	+0.270	20
3	Daniel Pedrosa (Honda)	ESP	+0.826	16
21	Chaz Davies (Aprilia)	GBR	+1:08.257	-

Points after round 2: Vincent 45, Poggiali 41

Spanish GP
Jerez de la Frontera, May 5

500CC (27 laps, 119.421km)
1	Valentino Rossi (Honda)	ITA	46:51.843	25
2	Daijiro Katoh (Honda)	JPN	+1.190	20
3	Tohru Ukawa (Honda)	JPN	+2.445	16
16	Jeremy McWilliams (Proton)	GBR	+54.171	-

Points after round 3: Rossi 70, Ukawa 41, Katoh 39, Capirossi 36, Abe 30, Checa 27, Barros 21, Ryo 20

250CC (26 laps, 114.998km)
1	Fonsi Nieto (Aprilia)	ESP	46:03.241	25
2	Roberto Rolfo (Honda)	ITA	+1.987	20
3	Emilio Alzamora (Honda)	ESP	+5.355	16
17	Jay Vincent (Honda)	GBR	+1:06.893	-
19	Leon Haslam (Honda)	GBR	+1:15.733	-

Points after round 3: Nieto 44, Rolfo 41, Battaini 39, Alzamora 38, Porto 28, De Puniet 26

125CC (23 laps, 101.729km)
1	Lucio Cecchinello (Aprilia)	ITA	42:08.107	25
2	Arnaud Vincent (Aprilia)	FRA	+2.274	20
3	Steve Jenkner (Aprilia)	GER	+2.773	16

Points after round 3: Vincent 65, Poggiali 41, Pedrosa 37, Cecchinello 32, Jenkner 30, Sanna 28

French GP
Le Mans, May 19

500CC (21 laps, 87.78km)
1	Valentino Rossi (Honda)	ITA	34:22.335	25
2	Tohru Ukawa (Honda)	JPN	+0.217	20
3	Max Biaggi (Yamaha)	ITA	+1.701	16
10	Jeremy McWilliams (Proton)	GBR	+21.847	6

NC: Jason Vincent GBR
Points after round 4: Rossi 95, Ukawa 61, Capirossi 45, Abe 43, Katoh 39, Barros 29, Aoki 28, Checa 27, Biaggi 23

250CC (26 laps, 108.68km)
1	Fonsi Nieto (Aprilia)	ESP	43:41.140	25
2	Marco Melandri (Aprilia)	ITA	+0.252	20
3	Randy de Puniet (Aprilia)	FRA	+6.431	16
15	Jay Vincent (Aprilia)	GBR	+56.894	1

NC: Leon Haslam GBR
Points after round 4: Nieto 69, Rolfo 52, Alzamora 47, Melandri 45, De Puniet 42, Battaini 39, Porto 36

125CC (24 laps, 100.32km)
1	Lucio Cecchinello (Aprilia)	ITA	42:09.029	25
2	Manuel Poggiali (Gilera)	SMR	+0.076	20
3	Daniel Pedrosa (Honda)	ESP	+0.604	16
18	Chaz Davies (Aprilia)	GBR	1:10.303	-

Points after round 4: A Vincent 78, Poggiali 61, Cecchinello 57, Pedrosa 53, Jenkner 35, Sanna 28

Italian GP
Mugello, June 2

500CC (23 laps, 120.635km)
1	Valentino Rossi (Honda)	ITA	43:40.837	25
2	Max Biaggi (Yamaha)	ITA	+2.404	20
3	Tohru Ukawa (Honda)	JPN	+11.289	16

Points after round 5: Rossi 120, Ukawa 77, Capirossi 55, Abe 52, Biaggi 43, Checa & Barros 40, Katoh 39

250CC (21 laps, 110.145km)
1	Marco Melandri (Aprilia)	ITA	40:42.759	25
2	Roberto Locatelli (Aprilia)	ITA	+0.258	20
3	Fonsi Nieto (Aprilia)	ESP	+0.720	16
15	Jay Vincent (Honda)	GBR	+52.393	1
18	Leon Haslam (Honda)	GBR	+57.737	-

Points after round 5: Nieto 85, Melandri 70, Rolfo 60, Locatelli 55, Alzamora 52, De Puniet 53, Battaini 49

125CC (20 laps, 104.9km)
1	Manuel Poggiali (Gilera)	SMR	40:20.019	25
2	Youichi Ui (Derbi)	JPN	+0.507	20
3	Pablo Nieto (Aprilia)	ESP	+0.512	16
18	Chaz Davies (Aprilia)	GBR	+43.717	-

Points after round 5: Poggiali 86, Vincent 85, Cecchinello 67, Pedrosa 66, Jenkner 43, Borsoi 38

MOTOR CYCLING

Catalan GP
Catalunya, June 15

500CC (25 laps, 118.175km)

1	Valentino Rossi (Honda)	ITA	44:20.679	25
2	Tohru Ukawa (Honda)	JPN	+0.880	20
3	Carlos Checa (Yamaha)	ESP	+8.531	16
12	Jeremy McWilliams (Proton)	GBR	+57.585	4

Points after round 6: Rossi 145, Ukawa 97, Capirossi 65, Biaggi & Checa 56, Abe 52, Barros 51, Katoh 47

250CC (23 laps, 108.721km)

1	Marco Melandri (Aprilia)	ITA	41:40.377	25
2	Roberto Rolfo (Honda)	ITA	+2.193	20
3	Fonsi Nieto (Aprilia)	ESP	+2.689	16
18	Leon Haslam (Honda)	GBR	+1:09.785	-
19	Jay Vincent (Honda)	GBR	+1:17.851	-

Points after round 6: Nieto 101, Melandri 95, Rolfo 80, De Puniet 66, Battaini 60, Alzamora 59, Locatelli 55

125CC (22 laps, 103.994km)

1	Manuel Poggiali (Gilera)	SMR	41:18.211	25
2	Daniel Pedrosa (Honda)	ESP	+0.019	20
3	Steve Jenkner (Aprilia)	GER	+9.888	16
24	Leon Camier (Italjet)	GBR	+1 lap	-

Points after round 6: Poggiali 111, Vincent 90, Pedrosa 86, Cecchinello 80, Jenkner 59, Nieto 45

Dutch GP
Assen, June 29

500CC (19 laps, 114.513km)

1	Valentino Rossi (Honda)	ITA	38:49.425	25
2	Alex Barros (Honda)	BRA	+2.233	20
3	Carlos Checa (Yamaha)	ESP	+9.682	16

Points after round 7: Rossi 170, Ukawa 108, Checa 72, Barros 71, Biaggi 69, Capirossi 65, Abe 59, Katoh 51

250CC (18 laps, 108.486km)

1	Marco Melandri (Aprilia)	ITA	37:48.960	25
2	Tony Elias (Aprilia)	ESP	+4.957	20
3	Roberto Rolfo (Honda)	ITA	+6.672	16
19	Jay Vincent (Honda)	GBR	+1:29.259	-

Points after round 7: Melandri 120, Nieto 112, Rolfo 96, Battaini 67, De Puniet 66, Locatelli 64, Elias 60

125CC (17 laps, 102.459km)

1	Daniel Pedrosa (Honda)	ESP	37:31.974	25
2	Manuel Poggiali (Gilera)	SMR	+2.523	20
3	Joan Olive (Honda)	ESP	+2.716	16
24	Chaz Davies (Aprilia)	GBR	+59.504	-
28	Leon Camier (italjet)	GBR	+1:46.306	-

Points after round 7: Poggiali 131, Pedrosa 111, Vincent 103, Cecchinello 91, Jenkner 69, Nieto 54

British GP
Donington Park, July 14

500CC (30 laps, 120.690km)

1	Valentino Rossi (Honda)	ITA	46:32.888	25
2	Max Biaggi (Yamaha)	ITA	+2.371	20
3	Alex Barros (Honda)	BRA	+5.533	16

Points after round 8: Rossi 195, Ukawa 108, Biaggi 89, Barros 87, Checa & Abe 72, Capirossi 65, Katoh 60

250CC (27 laps, 108.621km)

1	Marco Melandri (Aprilia)	ITA	42:55.815	25
2	Fonsi Nieto (Aprilia)	ESP	+0.717	20
3	Toni Elias (Aprilia)	ESP	+3.493	16
16	Jay Vincent (Honda)	GBR	+1:00.795	-
17	Leon Haslam (Honda)	GBR	+1:03.974	-
21	Andrew Whittley (Aprilia)	GBR	+1 lap	-

Points after round 8: Melandri 145, Nieto 132, Rolfo 107, Battaini 80, De Puniet & Elias 76, Locatelli 67

125CC (26 laps, 104.598km)

1	Arnaud Vincent (Aprilia)	FRA	42:57.387	25
2	Daniel Pedrosa (Honda)	ESP	+0.193	20
3	Manuel Poggiali (Gilera)	SMR	+0.699	16
16	Chaz Davies (Honda)	GBR	+56.261	-
21	Christian Elkin (Honda)	GBR	+1 lap	-
22	Chris Martin (Honda)	GBR	+1 lap	-
24	Leon Camier (Italjet)	GBR	+1 lap	-

Points after round 8: Poggiali 147, Pedrosa 131, Vincent 128, Cecchinello 91, Jenkner 80, Nieto 54

German GP
Sachsenring, July 21

500CC (30 laps, 111.120km)

1	Valentino Rossi (Honda)	ITA	43:32.783	25
2	Max Biaggi (Yamaha)	ITA	+0.730	20
3	Tohru Ukawa (Honda)	JPN	+1.100	16
7	Jeremy McWilliams (Proton)	GBR	+15.438	9

Points after round 9: Rossi 220, Ukawa 124, Biaggi 109, Barros 87, Checa 85, Abe 82, Capirossi 65, Katoh 60

250CC (22 laps, 81.488km)

1	Marco Melandri (Aprilia)	ITA	32:12.725	25
2	Roberto Rolfo (Honda)	ITA	+0.181	20
3	Sebastian Porto (Yamaha)	ARG	+2.150	16
13	Leon Haslam (Honda)	GBR	+1:00.304	3
14	Jay Vincent (Honda)	GBR	+1:00.434	2

Points after round 9: Melandri 170, Nieto 145, Rolfo 122, Battaini 88, Elias 86, Locatelli 78, De Puniet 76, Porto 74

125CC (27 laps, 100.008km)

1	Arnaud Vincent (Aprilia)	FRA	40:40.023	25
2	Alex de Angelis (Aprilia)	SMR	+0.108	20
3	Steve Jenkner (Aprilia)	GER	+9.995	16
20	Chaz Davies (Aprilia0	GBR	+1:03.125	-

Points after round 9: Poggiali 160, Vincent 153, Pedrosa 140, Jenkner 96, Cecchinello 91, Nieto 65, Sanna 58

Czech Republic GP
Brno, August 25

500CC (22 laps, 118.866km)

1	Max Biaggi (Yamaha)	ITA	44:36.498	25
2	Daijiro Katoh (Honda)	JPN	+2.755	20
3	Tohru Ukawa (Honda)	JPN	+7.598	16

Points after round 10: Rossi 220, Ukawa 140, Biaggi 134, Checa 96, Barros 94, Abe 90, Katoh 80, Capirossi 75

250CC (20 laps, 108.060km)

1	Marco Melandri (Aprilia)	ITA	41:41.572	25
2	Sebastian Porto (Yamaha)	ARG	+7.023	20
3	Toni Elias (Aprilia)	ESP	+8.135	16
12	Jay Vincent (Honda)	GBR	+30.805	4
17	Leon Haslam (Honda)	GBR	+1:04.058	-

Points after round 10: Melandri 195, Nieto 158, Rolfo 127, Elias 102, Porto 94, Battaini 88, Locatelli 87

125CC (19 laps, 102.657km)

1	Lucio Cecchinello (Aprilia)	ITA	41:18.287	25
2	Daniel Pedrosa (Honda)	ESP	+0.202	20
3	Arnaud Vincent (Aprilia)	FRA	+0.278	16

Points after round 10: Poggiali 171, Vincent 169, Pedrosa 160, Cecchinello 116, Jenkner 106, Sanna 67

Portuguese GP

Estoril , Sept 8

500CC (28 laps, 117.096km)

1	Valentino Rossi (Honda)	ITA	54:12.962	25
2	Carlos Checa (Yamaha)	ESP	+22.200	20
3	Tohru Ukawa (Honda)	JPN	+24.220	16
9	Jeremy McWilliams (Proton)	GBR	+1 lap	7

Points after round 11: Rossi 245, Ukawa 156, Biaggi 144, Checa 116, Barros 105, Abe 99, Katoh 80

250CC (26 laps, 108.732km)

1	Fonsi Nieto (Aprilia)	ESP	53:58.901	25
2	Marco Melandri (Aprilia)	ITA	+0.684	20
3	Sebastian Porto (Yamaha)	ARG	+7.342	16
7	Leon Haslam (Honda)	GBR	+1:36.634	9

NC: Jay Vincent GBR

Points after round 11: Melandri 215, Nieto 183, Rolfo 140, Porto 110, Elias 105, Locatelli 98, Battaini 88

125CC (24 laps, 100.368km)

1	Arnaud Vincent (Aprilia)	FRA	49:05.300	25
2	Simone Sanna (Aprilia)	ITA	+0.867	20
3	Steve Jenkner (Aprilia)	GER	+2.600	16
11	Chaz Davies (Aprilia)	GBR	+1:54.525	5

Points after round 11: Vincent 194, Poggiali 171, Pedrosa 166, Cecchinello 126, Jenkner 122, Sanna 87

Brazilian GP

Nelson Piquet Circuit, Sep 21

500CC (24 laps, 118.392km)

1	Valentino Rossi (Honda)	ITA	49:09.516	25
2	Max Biaggi (Yamaha)	ITA	+1.674	20
3	Kenny Roberts (Suzuki)	USA	+18.764	16

NC: Jeremy McWilliams GBR

Points after round 12: Rossi 270, Biaggi 164, Ukawa 156, Barros 118, Checa 116, Abe 109, Capirossi 86

250CC (22 laps, 108.526km)

1	Sebastian Porto (Yamaha)	ARG	47:01.307	25
2	Roberto Rolfo (Honda)	ITA	+14.114	20
3	Franco Battaini (Aprilia)	ITA	+15.812	16
10	Leon Haslam (Honda)	GBR	+1:15.478	6

NC: Jay Vincent GBR

Points after round 12: Melandri 228, Nieto 183, Rolfo 160, Porto 135, Elias 116, Battaini 104, Locatelli 98

125CC (21 laps, 103.593km)

1	Masao Azuma (Honda)	JPN	46:28.675	25
2	Arnaud Vincent (Aprilia)	FRA	+1.705	20
3	Manuel Poggiali (Gilera)	SMR	+1.760	16
29	Chaz Davies (Aprilia)	GBR	+2:04.263	-

Points after round 12: Vincent 214, Poggiali 187, Pedrosa 166, Cecchinello 132, Jenkner 122, Sanna 89

Pacific GP

Motegi, Oct 6

500CC (24 laps, 115.224km)

1	Alex Barros (Honda)	BRA	44:18.913	25
2	Valentino Rossi (Honda)	ITA	+1.641	20
3	Loris Capirossi (Honda)	ITA	+7.672	16
10	Jeremy McWilliams (Proton)	GBR	+37.355	6

Points after round 13: Rossi 290, Ukawa 169, Biaggi 164, Barros 143, Checa 127, Abe 117, Capirossi 102

250CC (23 laps, 110.423km)

1	Toni Elias (Aprilia)	ESP	43:52.991	25
2	Marco Melandri (Aprilia)	ESP	+0.175	20
3	Yuki Takahashi (Honda)	JPN	+4.431	16
19	Jay Vincent (Honda)	GBR	+54.765	-

Points after round 13: Melandri 248, Nieto 196, Rolfo 170, Porto 143, Elias 141, Battaini 113, Locatelli 105

125CC (21 laps, 100.821km)

1	Daniel Pedrosa (Honda)	ESP	41:43.377	25
2	Manuel Poggiali (Gilera)	SMR	+8.071	20
3	Steve Jenkner (Aprilia)	GER	+8.701	16
24	Chaz Davies (Aprilia)	GBR	+1:21.111	-

Points after round 13: Vincent 215, Poggiali 207, Pedrosa 191, Jenkner 138, Cecchinello 132, Nieto 102

Malaysian GP

Sepang, Oct 13

500CC (21 laps, 116.508km)

1	Max Biaggi (Yamaha)	ITA	44:01.592	25
2	Valentino Rossi (Honda)	ITA	+0.542	20
3	Alex Barros (Honda)	BRA	+1.572	16
12	Jeremy McWilliams (Proton)	GBR	+45.761	4

Points after round 14: Rossi 310, Biaggi 189, Ukawa 182, Barros 159, Checa 136, Abe 123, Capirossi 109

250CC (20 laps, 110.96km)

1	Fonso Nieto (Aprilia)	ESP	43:28.624	25
2	Toni Elias (Aprilia)	ESP	+0.412	20
3	Roberto Rolfo (Honda)	ITA	+2.947	16
14	Jay Vincent (Honda)	GBR	+49.793	2
17	Leon Haslam (Honda)	GBR	+1:02.950	-

Points after round 14: Melandri 248, Nieto 221, Rolfo 186, Elias 161, Porto 156, Battaini 124, Locatelli 108

125CC (18 laps, 99.864km)

1	Arnaud Vincent (Aprilia)	FRA	40:32.656	25
2	Lucio Cecchinello (Aprilia)	ITA	+0.287	20
3	Daniel Pedrosa (Honda)	ESP	+0.345	16
25	Chaz Davies (Aprilia)	GBR	+1:36.014	-

Points after round 14: Vincent 240, Poggiali 220, Pedrosa 207, Cecchinello 152, Jenkner 148, Nieto 113

Australian GP

Phillip Island Circuit, Oct 20

500CC (27 laps, 120.096km)

1	Valentino Rossi (Honda)	ITA	42:02.041	25
2	Alex Barros (Honda)	BRA	+9.782	20
3	Tohru Ukawa (Honda)	JPN	+11.134	16
10	Jeremy McWilliams (Proton)	GBR	+31.994	6

Points after round 15: Rossi 335, Biaggi 199, Ukawa 198, Barros 197, Checa 141, Abe 123, Capirossi 109, Katoh 104

250CC (25 laps, 111.200km)

1	Marco Melandri (Aprilia)	ESP	39:44.293	25
2	Fonsi Nieto (Aprilia)	ESP	+0.007	20
3	Sebastian Porto (Yamaha)	ARG	+5.766	16
18	Leon Haslam (Honda)	GBR	+1:10.966	-

Points after round 15: *Melandri 273, Nieto 241, Rolfo 199, Elias 172, Porto 172, Battaini 133, Locatelli 108, De Puniet 106, Alzamora 104*

125CC (23 laps, total distance 102.304km)

1	Manuel Poggiali (Gilera)	SMR	38:09.028	25
2	Lucio Cecchinello (Aprilia)	ITA	+0.252	20
3	Pablo Nieto (Aprilia)	ESP	+0.310	16
22	Chaz Davies (Aprilia)	GBR	+1:27.678	-

Points after round 15: *Vincent 253, Poggiali 245, Pedrosa 218, Cecchinello 172, Jenkner 157, Nieto 129, Sanna 104, Azuma 101*

Valencian GP

Comunitat Valencia, Nov 3

500CC (30 laps, 120.150km)

1	Alex Barros (Honda)	BRA	47:22.404	25
2	Valentino Rossi (Honda)	ITA	+0.230	20
3	Max Biaggi (Yamaha)	ITA	+15.213	16
8	Jeremy McWilliams (Proton)	GBR	+1:05.079	8

250CC (27 laps, 108.135km)

1	Marco Melandri (Aprilia)	ITA	43:57.812	25
2	Roberto Rolfo (Honda)	ITA	+4.318	20
3	Emilio Alzamora (Honda)	ESP	+4.538	16
14	Jay Vincent (Honda)	GBR	+44.942	2

125CC (25 laps, total distance 100.125km)

1	Daniel Pedrosa (Honda)	ESP	42:13.044	25
2	Arnaud Vincent (Aprilia)	FRA	+0.100	20
3	Pablo Nieto (Aprilia)	ESP	+2.704	16
28	Chaz Davies (Aprilia)	GBR	+1:20.058	-

World GP Championships
Final Standings
Top 12 and British

500CC

1	Valentino Rossi	ITA	355
2	Max Biaggi	ITA	215
3	Tohru Ukawa	JPN	209
4	Alex Barros	BRA	204
5	Carlos Checa	ESP	141
6	Norick Abe	JPN	129
7	Daijiro Katoh	JPN	117
8	Loris Capirossi	ITA	109
9	Kenny Roberts Jr	USA	99
10	Olivier Jacque	FRA	81
11	Shinya Nakano	JPN	68
12	Nobuatsu Aoki	JPN	63
14	Jeremy McWilliams	GBR	59

Constructors' Championship
1. Honda 390; 2. Yamaha 272; 3. Suzuki 143;
4. Proton KR 96; 5. Aprilia 33; 6. Kawasaki 4

250CC

1	Marco Melandri	ITA	298
2	Fonsi Nieto	ITA	241
3	Roberto Rolfo	ITA	219
4	Toni Elias	ESP	178
5	Sebastian Porto	ARG	172
6	Franco Battaini	ITA	142
7	Emilio Alzamora	ESP	120
8	Roberto Locatelli	ITA	119
9	Randy de Puniet	FRA	119
10	Naoki Matsudo	JPN	92
11	Alex Debon	ESP	72
12	Casey Stoner	USA	68
18	Leon Haslam	GBR	19
22	Jay Vincent	GBR	16

Constructors' Championship
1. Aprilia 382; 2. Honda 244;
3. Yamaha 211

125CC

1	Arnaud Vincent	FRA	273
2	Manuel Poggiali	SMR	254
3	Daniel Pedrosa	ESP	243
4	Lucio Cecchinello	ITA	180
5	Steve Jenkner	GER	168
6	Pablo Nieto	ESP	145
7	Simone Sanna	ITA	106
8	Masao Azuma	JPN	101
9	Alex de Angelis	ITA	87
10	Gino Borsoi	ITA	82
11	Mika Kallio	FIN	78
12	Joan Olive	ESP	76
29	Chaz Davies	GBR	6

Constructors' Championship
1. Aprilia 341; 2. Honda 285; 3. Gilera 254;
4. Derbi 79; 5. Italjet 32

S u p e r b i k e s

Spanish WSB
Valencia, March 10
RACE 1
23 laps, 92.115km

1	Troy Bayliss (Ducati)	AUS	36:51.963	25
2	Noriyuki Haga (Aprilia)	AUS	+3.176	20
3	Ben Bostrom (Ducati)	USA	+3.316	16
6	Neil Hodgson (Ducati)	GBR	+14.445	10
10	Chris Walker (Kawasaki)	GBR	+31.596	6
12	James Toseland (Ducati)	GBR	+36.270	4

RACE 2
20 laps, 80.100km

1	Troy Bayliss (Ducati)	AUS	32:03.384	25
2	Noriyuki Haga (Aprilia)	JPN	+1.178	20
3	Colin Edwards (Honda)	USA	+2.285	16
5	Neil Hodgson (Ducati)	GBR	+17.382	11
7	Chris Walker (Kawasaki)	GBR	+31.737	9
10	James Toseland (Ducati)	GBR	+38.211	6

Points after rd 1: Bayliss 50, Haga 40, Edwards & Bostrom 29

Australian WSB
Phillip Island, Mar 24
Both races: 22 laps, 97.790km
RACE 1

1	Troy Bayliss (Ducati)	USA	34:30.102	25
2	Colin Edwards (Honda)	AUS	+2.469	20
3	Ruben Xaus (Aprilia)	ESP	+10.060	16
5	Neil Hodgson (Ducati)	GBR	+21.218	11
8	James Toseland (Ducati)	GBR	+41.138	8
9	Chris Walker (Kawasaki)	GBR	+50.879	7

RACE 2

1	Troy Bayliss (Ducati)	AUS	34:35.633	25
2	Colin Edwards (Honda)	USA	+2.472	20
3	Ruben Xaus (Aprilia)	ESP	+9.682	16
4	Neil Hodgson (Ducati)	GBR	+18.913	13
7	James Toseland (Ducati)	GBR	+32.956	9
9	Chris Walker (Kawasaki)	GBR	+33.085	7

Points after rd 2: Bayliss 100, Edwards 69,Bostrom 53

South African WSB
Kyalami, Apr 7
Both races: 25 laps, 106.575km
RACE 1

1	Troy Bayliss (Ducati)	AUS	43:01.781	25
2	Colin Edwards (Honda)	USA	+4.119	20
3	Ruben Xaus (Ducati)	ESP	+6.536	16
5	Neil Hodgson (Ducati)	GBR	+16.824	11
6	James Toseland (Ducati)	GBR	+29.544	10
8	Chris Walker (Kawasaki)	GBR	+47.298	8

RACE 2

1	Troy Bayliss (Ducati)	AUS	42:57.014	25
2	Ruben Xaus (Ducati)	ESP	+2.673	20
3	Colin Edwards (Honda)	GBR	+6.390	16
4	Neil Hodgson (Ducati)	GBR	+6.774	13
8	James Toseland (Ducati)	GBR	+28.876	8
9	Chris Walker (Kawasaki)	GBR	+40.781	7

Points after rd 3: Bayliss 150, Edwards 105, Xaus 79

Japanese WSB
Sugo, Apr 21
Both races: 25 laps, 93.425km
RACE 1

1	Colin Edwards (Honda)	USA	37:24.515	25
2	Makoto Tamada (Honda)	JPN	+0.161	20
3	Noriyuki Haga (Aprilia)	JPN	+4.486	16
4	Neil Hodgson (Ducati)	GBR	+12.255	13
9	James Toseland (Ducati)	GBR	+29.082	7
11	Chris Walker (Kawasaki)	GBR	+31.022	5

RACE 2

1	Makoto Tamada (Honda)	JPN	37:26.628	25
2	Colin Edwards (Honda)	USA	+3.297	20
3	Neil Hodgson (Ducati)	GBR	+3.469	16
11	James Toseland (Ducati)	GBR	+33.424	5
13	Chris Walker (Kawasaki)	GBR	+34.621	3

Points after rd 4: Bayliss 174, Edwards 150, Hodgson 98

Italian WSB
Monza, May 12
Both races: 104.274km, 18 laps
RACE 1

1	Troy Bayliss (Ducati)	AUS	32:34.429	25
2	Neil Hodgson (Ducati)	GBR	+0.259	20
3	Colin Edwards (Honda)	USA	+0.576	16
5	James Toseland (Ducati)	GBR	+18.860	11
NC:	Chris Walker GBR			

RACE 2

1	Troy Bayliss (Ducati)	AUS	32:51.693	25
2	Colin Edwards (Honda)	USA	+2.226	20
3	Noriyuki Haga (Aprilia)	JPN	+2.267	16
4	Neil Hodgson (Ducati)	GBR	+2.291	13
10	Chris Walker (Kawasaki)	GBR	+34.622	6

Points after rd 5: Bayliss 224, Edwards 186, Hodgson 131

British WSB
Silverstone, May 26
Both races: 101.880km, 20 laps
RACE 1

1	Colin Edwards (Honda)	USA	43:27.508	25
2	Noriyuki Haga (Aprilia)	JPN	+7.358	20
3	Neil Hodgson (Ducati)	GBR	+32.990	16
6	Mark Heckles (Honda)	GBR	+1:01.128	10
9	Shane Byrne (Ducati)	GBR	+1:15.226	7
10	James Toseland (Ducati)	GBR	+1:23.670	6
12	Michael Rutter (Ducati)	GBR	+1:28.844	4
14	Chris Walker (Kawasaki)	GBR	+2:00.294	2
16	Dean Ellison (Ducati)	GBR	+1 lap	-

RACE 2

1	Troy Bayliss (Ducati)	AUS	41:20.474	25
2	Colin Edwards (Honda)	USA	+4.909	20
3	Ruben Xaus (Ducati)	ESP	+16.656	16
4	Chris Walker (Kawasaki)	GBR	+58.435	13
5	Shane Byrne (Ducati)	GBR	+1:01.066	11
6	Neil Hodgson (Ducati)	GBR	+1:11.981	10
9	James Toseland (Ducati)	GBR	+1:24.886	7

NC: Richards, Rutter, Heckles, Ellison & Hislop all GBR
Points after rd 6: Bayliss 260, Edwards 231, Hodgson 157, Haga 129, Bostrom 119, Xaus 120

German WSB
Lausitzring   June 9
Both Races: 24 laps, 102.360km
RACE 1

1	Troy Bayliss (Ducati)	AUS	40:06.073	25
2	Colin Edwards (Honda)	USA	+0.651	20
3	Ruben Xaus (Ducati)	ESP	+18.966	16
7	James Toseland (Ducati)	GBR	+40.514	9
17	Mark Heckles (Honda)	GBR	+1 lap	-

RACE 2

1	Troy Bayliss (Ducati)	AUS	40:09.633	25
2	Colin Edwards (Honda)	USA	+1.650	20
3	Ruben Xaus (Ducati)	ESP	+5.065	16
7	James Toseland (Ducati)	GBR	+31.380	9
8	Neil Hodgson (Ducati)	GBR	+38.343	8
9	Chris Walker (Kawasaki)	GBR	+54.252	7
17	Mark Heckles (Honda)	GBR	+1:41.574	-

Points after rd 7: *Bayliss 310, Edwards 271, Hodgson 165, Haga 153, Xaus 152, Bostrom 143*

San Marino WSB
Misano   June 23
Both Races: 25 laps, 101.500km
RACE 1

1	Troy Bayliss (Ducati)	AUS	40:04.994	25
2	Colin Edwards (Honda)	USA	+2.906	20
3	Neil Hodgson (Ducati)	GBR	+14.095	16
7	Chris Walker (Kawasaki)	GBR	+47.899	9
8	James Toseland (Ducati)	GBR	+49.885	8
19	Mark Heckles (Honda)	GBR	+1 lap	-

RACE 2

1	Troy Bayliss (Ducati)	AUS	40:07.599	25
2	Colin Edwards (Honda)	USA	+3.329	20
3	Noriyuka Haga (Aprilia)	JPN	+8.447	16
4	Neil Hodgson (Ducati)	GBR	+14.089	13
8	Chris Walker (Kawasaki)	GBR	+44.766	8

Points after round 8: *Bayliss 360, Edwards 311, Hodgson 194, Haga 182, Bostrom 165, Xaus 152*

United States WSB
Laguna Seca   July 14
Both Races: 28 laps, 101.080km
RACE 1

1	Troy Bayliss (Ducati)	AUS	40:18.943	25
2	Ruben Xaus (Ducati)	ESP	+0.339	20
3	Colin Edwards (Honda)	USA	+2.051	16
5	Neil Hodgson (Ducati)	GBR	+4.104	11
9	James Toseland (Ducati)	GBR	+26.437	7
11	Chris Walker (Kawasaki)	GBR	+40.945	5
20	Mark Heckles (Honda)	GBR	+1 lap	-

RACE 2

1	Colin Edwards (Honda)	USA	40:14.793	25
2	Troy Bayliss (Ducati)	AUS	+1.086	20
3	Neil Hodgson (Ducati)	GBR	+1.672	16
6	James Toseland (Ducati)	GBR	+25.747	10
10	Chris Walker (Kawasaki)	GBR	+47.673	6
20	Mark Heckles (Honda)	GBR	+ 1 lap	-

Points after round 9: *Bayliss 405, Edwards 352, Hodgson 221, Haga 182, Bostrom 184, Xaus 172, Toseland 124*

European WSB
Brands Hatch   July 28
Both Races: 25 laps, 105.525km
RACE 1

1	Colin Edwards (Honda)	USA	36:27.555	25
2	Neil Hodgson (Ducati)	GBR	+1.173	20
3	Troy Bayliss (Ducati)	AUS	+10.327	16
6	Chris Walker (Kawasaki)	GBR	+26.496	10
9	James Toseland (Ducati)	GBR	+32.322	7
10	Shane Byrne (Ducati)	GBR	+32.634	6
14	Dean Ellison (Ducati)	GBR	+48.785	2
17	Mark Heckles (Honda)	GBR	+1:07.542	-
20	Glen Richards (Kawasaki)	GBR	+1:25.120	-

RACE 2

1	Colin Edwards (Honda)	USA	36:27.655	25
2	Troy Bayliss (Ducati)	AUS	+2.326	20
3	Neil Hodgson (Ducati)	GBR	+2.748	16
8	Chris Walker (Kawasaki)	GBR	+21.924	8
9	Michael Rutter (Ducati)	GBR	+24.708	7
10	Shane Byrne (Ducati)	GBR	+29.830	6
14	Glen Richards (Kawasaki)	GBR	+46.794	2
20	Mark Heckles (Honda)	GBR	+1:08.833	-

Points after round 10: *Bayliss 441, Edwards 402, Hodgson 257, Haga 206, Bostrom 206, Xaus 193*

German WSB
Oscherleben   Sep 1
Both Races: 28 laps, 102.676km
RACE 1

1	Colin Edwards (Honda)	USA	40:55.744	25
2	Troy Bayliss (Ducati)	AUS	+1.741	20
3	Neil Hodgson (Ducati)	GBR	+4.317	16
6	James Toseland (Ducati)	GBR	+30.228	10
9	Chris Walker (Kawasaki)	GBR	+42.727	7
15	Mark Heckles (Honda)	GBR	+1 lap	1

RACE 2

1	Colin Edwards (Honda)	USA	40:56.724	25
2	Troy Bayliss (Ducati)	AUS	+3.861	20
3	Neil Hodgson (Ducati)	GBR	+7.023	16
8	James Toseland (Ducati)	GBR	+32.391	8
15	Chris Walker (Kawasaki)	GBR	+1 lap	1
16	Mark Heckles (Honda)	GBR	+1 lap	-

Points after round 11: *Bayliss 481, Edwards 452, Hodgson 289, Haga 228, Bostrom 229, Xaus 204, Toseland 149*

Dutch WSB
Assen   Sep 8
Both Races: 16 laps, 96.432km
RACE 1

1	Colin Edwards (Honda)	USA	32:58.601	25
2	Troy Bayliss (Ducati)	AUS	+3.606	20
3	Noriyuki Haga (Aprilia)	JPN	+5.351	16
6	James Toseland (Ducati)	GBR	+19.592	10
17	Mark Heckles (Honda)	GBR	+1 lap	-

NC: Chris Walker & Neil Hodgson both GBR

RACE 2

1	Colin Edwards (Honda)	USA	32:59.881	25
2	Pierfrancesco Chili (Ducati)	ITA	+7.506	20
3	James Toseland (Ducati)	GBR	+11.042	16
4	Neil Hodgson (Ducati)	GBR	+18.090	13
7	Chris Walker (Kawasaki)	GBR	+25.886	9
15	Mark Heckles (Honda)	GBR	+1:13.524	1

Points after round 12: *Edwards 502, Bayliss 501, Hodgson 302, Haga 254, Bostrom 248, Xaus 217, Toseland 175*

Italian WSB

Imola   Sep 30
Both Races: 21 laps, 103.593km

RACE 1

1	Colin Edwards (Honda)	USA	38:17.324	25
2	Troy Bayliss (Ducati)	AUS	+0.514	20
3	Ruben Xaus (Ducati)	ESP	+8.651	16
4	Neil Hodgson (Ducati)	GBR	+20.395	13
6	James Toseland (Ducati)	GBR	+37.490	10
11	Chris Walker (Kawasaki)	GBR	+53.456	5
20	Mark Heckles (Honda)	GBR	+2:14.047	-

RACE 2

1	Colin Edwards (Honda)	USA	38:13.128	25
2	Troy Bayliss (Ducati)	AUS	+0.980	20
3	Ruben Xaus (Ducati)	ESP	+6.183	16
5	Neil Hodgson (Ducati)	GBR	+27.403	11
6	James Toseland (Ducati)	GBR	+34.187	10
12	Chris Walker (Kawasaki)	GBR	+1:23.214	4

NC: Mark Heckles GBR

World Superbikes
Final Standings

1	Colin Edwards (Honda) USA	552
2	Troy Bayliss (Ducati) AUS	541
3	Neil Hodgson (Ducati) GBR	326
4	Noriyuki Haga (Aprilia) JPN	278
5	Ben Bostrom (Ducati) USA	261
6	Ruben Xaus (Ducati) ESP	249
7	James Toseland (Ducati) GBR	195
8	Pierfrancesco Chili (Ducati) ITA	167
9	Chris Walker (Kawasaki) GBR	152
10	Gregorio Lavilla (Suzuki) ESP	130
11	Broc Parkes (Parmalat) AUS	77
12	Juan Borja (Ducati) ESP	74
13	Lucio Pedercini (Ducati) ITA	71
14	Hitoyasu Izutsu (Kawasaki) JPN	62
15	Marco Borciani (Ducati) ITA	55
16	Steve Martin (Ducati) AUS	52
17	Eric Bostrom (Kawasaki) USA	49
18	Makoto Tamada (Honda) JPN	45
19	Mauro Sanchini (Kawasaki) ITA	41
20	Alessandro Antonello (Ducati) ITA	38
21	Shane Byrne (Ducati) GBR	30
22	Peter Goddard (Benelli) AUS	23
23	Akira Yanagawa (Kawasaki) JPN	20
24	Aaron Yates (Suzuki) USA	17
25	Serafino Foti (Ducati) ITA	17
26	Nicky Hayden (Honda) USA	16
27	Wataru Yoshikawa (Yamaha) JPN	16
28	Mark Heckles (Honda) GBR	15
29	Takeshi Tshujimura (Yamaha) JPN	12
30	Michael Rutter (Ducati) GBR	11
31	Ivan Clementi (Kawasaki) ITA	11
32	Doug Chandler (Ducati) USA	10
33	Mathew Mladin (Suzuki) AUS	6
34	Alessandro Valia (Ducati) ITA	4
	Alexander Hofmann (Kawasaki) GER	4
36	Michele Malatesta (Ducati) ITA	3
37	Bertrand Stey (Honda) FRA	3
38	Dean Ellison (Ducati) GBR	2
	Glen Richards (Kawasaki) GBR	2
40	Jeronimo Vidal (Honda) ESP	1
41	Yuichi Takeda (Honda) JPN	1

Manufacturers

1. Ducati 575; 2. Honda 557;
3. Aprilia 278; 4. Kawasaki 208;
5. Suzuki 147; 6. Benelli 23; 7 Yamaha 16

British Superbikes
Final Standings

1	Steve Hislop (Ducati)	416
2	Sean Emmett (Ducati)	379
3	Michael Rutter (Ducati)	357
4	Shane Byrne (Ducati)	283
5	Steve Plater (Yamaha)	270
6	John Reynolds (Suzuki)	253

Sidecars

Valencia
March 10
1	Abbott/Biggs (Yamaha)	GBR	30:52.318	25
2	Steinhausen/Hopkinson (Suzuki)	GER	+1.850	20
3	Klaffenbock/Parzer (Yamaha)	AUT	+21.973	16

Kyalami
Apr 7
1	Webster/Woodhead (Suzuki)	GBR	35:02.112	25
2	Klaffenbock/Parzer (Yamaha)	AUT	+4.980	20
3	Steinhausen/Hopkinson (Suzuki)	GER	+22.134	16

Monza
May 12
1	Klaffenbock/Parzer (Yamaha)	AUT	25:37.255	25
2	Webster/Woodhead (Suzuki)	GBR	+0.299	20
3	Abbott/Biggs (Yamaha)	GBR	+21.416	16

Silverstone
May 26
1	Abbott/Biggs (Yamaha)	GBR	27:34.060	25
2	Hanks/Biggs (Yamaha)	GBR	+21.986	20
3	Steinhausen/Hopkinson (Suzuki)	GER	+39.728	16

Lausitzring
June 9
1	Steinhausen/Hopkinson (Yamaha)	GER	27:34.060	25
2	Hanks/Biggs (Yamaha)	GBR	+21.986	20
3	Schlosser/Hanni (Suzuki)	GER	+39.728	16

Misano
June 23
1	Abbott/Biggs (Yamaha)	GBR	34:19.837	25
2	Schlosser/Hanni (Suzuki)	GER	+4-818	20
3	Steinhausen/Hopkinson (Yamaha)	GER	+16.391	16

Brands Hatch
June 28
1	Webster/Woodhead (Suzuki)	GBR	29:24.446	25
2	Hanks/Biggs (Yamaha)	GBR	+14.830	20
3	Klaffenbock/Parzer (Yamaha)	GER	+20.042	16

Oschersleben
Sep 1
1	Webster/Woodhead (Suzuki)	GBR	34:53.827	25
2	Klaffenbock/Parzer (Yamaha)	GER	+8.504	20
3	Hanks/Biggs (Yamaha)	GBR	+10.795	16

Assen
Sep 8
1	Webster/Woodhead (Suzuki)	GBR	28:47.023	25
2	Klaffenbock/Parzer (Yamaha)	GER	+5.980	20
3	Hanks/Biggs (Yamaha)	GBR	+14.848	16

Imola
Sep 29
1	Klaffenbock/Parzer (Yamaha)	GER	26:02.699	20
2	Webster/Woodhead (Suzuki)	GBR	+0.379	25
3	Steinhausen/Hopkinson (Yamaha)	GER	+3.703	16

Final Standing
1. Abbott/Biggs GBR 151 (3 wins)
2. Steinhausen/Hopkinson GER 151 (1 win)
3. Klaffenbock/Parzer AUT 146
4. Webster/Woodhead GBR 145 (4 wins)
5. Hanks/Biggs GBR 145

Supersport

World Championship

Final Standing
1	Fabien Foret (Honda)	FRA	186
2	Katsuaki Fujiwara (Suzuki)	JPN	181
3	Stephane Chambon (Suzuki)	FRA	162
4	Paolo Casoli (Yamaha)	ITA	128
5	Andrew Pitt (Kawasaki)	AUS	126
6	Christian Kellner (Yamaha)	GER	94
7	Chris Vermeulen (Honda)	AUS	90
8	Jorg Teuchert (Yamaha)	GER	90
9	Iain MacPherson (Honda)	GBR	83
10	James Whitham (Yamaha)	GBR	80

Trials

World Championship
Final Standing
1	Dougie Lampkin (Montesa)	GBR	298
2	Takahisa Fujinami (Honda)	JPN	266
3	Albert Cabestany (Beta)	ESP	213
6	Graham Jarvis (Sherco)	GBR	193
14	Steve Colley (GAS)	GBR	44
17	Sam Connor (GAS)	GBR	29

World Indoor Championship
Final Standings
1	Albert Cabestany (Beta)	ESP	167
2	Dougie Lampkin (Montesa)	GBR	152
3	Adam Raga (GAS)	ESP	146
7	Steve Colley (GAS)	GBR	27

Motocross

World Championships

Final Standings

500CC

1	Stefan Everts (Yamaha)	BEL	268
2	Joel Smets (KTM)	BEL	229
3	Javier Garcia Vico (KTM)	ESP	225
10	James Noble (Honda)	GBR	222
13	Christian Burnham (Honda)	GBR	75
20	Mark Jones (Honda)	GBR	39
38	Mark Hucklebridge (VOR)	GBR	6

250CC

1	Mickael Pichon (Suzuki)	FRA	288
2	Joshua Coppins (Honda)	NZL	222
3	Pit Beirer (Honda)	GER	205
4	James Dobb (KTM)	GBR	177
7	Gordon Crockard (KTM)	IRL	143
11	Paul Cooper (Honda)	GBR	101
17	Mark Eastwood (Honda)	GBR	80
24	Justin Morris (Yamaha)	GBR	18
26	Jason Higgs (Yamaha)	GBR	16

125CC

1	Mickael Maschio (Kawasaki)	FRA	225
2	Steve Ramon (KTM)	BEL	221
3	Patrick Caps (KTM)	BEL	197
10	Stephen Sword (KTM)	GBR	96
21	Billy MacKenzie (Yamaha)	GBR	48
26	James Dobb (KTM)	GBR	25
31	Tom Church (KTM)	GBR	14

Sidecars

1	Sergis/Rasmanis (BSU)	LAT	662
2	Williemsen/Sabbe (VMC)	NED	494
3	Van Werven/Piccart (BSU)	NED	434
6	Brown/Peters (VMC)	GBR	332
18	Lyne/Sabbe (Zabel)	GBR	118

Motor Racing

Poor old Bernie Ecclestone (and doesn't it feel good to say that); having for years argued that a strong Ferrari team would mean a strong Formula One championship, look what's happened now he's got his wish. Arguably, the least interesting F1 season in history.

Michael Schumacher won 11 of the 17 races (taking his GP record to 64 wins), secured the drivers' title by July 21st (his third in a row), and finished the season 67 points clear of his Ferrari teammate Rubens Barrichello, to collect his fifth drivers' title and equal the record of the Argentinian Juan-Manuel Fangio. Ferrari won the constructors' championship by 129 points (their fourth in a row), and the only spark of interest (and it was a pretty small one) was trying to work out which of the two Ferrari drivers was really the quickest.

The tone was set in Austria when Barrichello, who was leading the race, was given instructions from the Ferrari team to allow Schumacher to pass. It had happened before, but it didn't make the tactic any more acceptable. "We have always had this philosophy - some people like it, some people don't," said Schumacher, who conceded the top spot on the podium to his teammate, as the Austrian crowd booed.

Barrichello, who had just signed a new contract with Ferrari, was philosophical and Schumacher offered the Brazilian some consolation. "Hopefully, we can secure the championship and then go racing," he said, and that's what happened, in a manner of speaking. There were six races after the French Grand Prix; and three were won by Schumacher and three by Barrichello, but were they really "going racing", as Schumacher had suggested, or were they continuing the orchestration begun at the A1-Ring?

There was no doubt what occurred at Indianapolis, where 140,000 US fans turned out for the US Grand Prix only to see the race leader Schumacher slow after the final bend to allow Barrichello to pass and win the race. The 10 points ensuring that the Brazilian was certain to finish runner-up in the championship.

The American audience were drop-jawed in disbelief; if this is F1, they must have thought, I'll go and give CART racing another try. Strangely, all the brilliant minds at Ferrari, couldn't work out that equation. If a race ain't worth winning, it ain't worth watching.

For Ecclestone, who has a very well-honed marketing brain, this was merely added ammunition for his call for a radical overhaul of the sport. It was only the third US GP since that country was re-introduced into F1 racing, and the crowd was already 70,000 fewer than in 2000. The man who had championed Ferrari's cause for so many years knew it was time to put the brakes on, and a post-season pow-wow was arranged at the Hilton Heathrow.

The new proposals included single-lap qualifying, limited tyre changes, and a new points scale, rewarding eight drivers (10, 8, 6, 5, 4, 3, 2, 1) rather than just six (10, 6, 4, 3, 2, 1). But the loudest applause from outside the hotel came with the announcement that team rules which interfere with the race results are banned. In theory, Rule 149, as it became, was vital to bring credibility back to the sport. In practice, though, it's another matter. You can prevent instructions during a race, but how do you police the rule if teams agree a strategy beforehand. Of course, you can't, and the rule therefore operates only as a cosmetic measure. It will, though, eliminate farcical finishes like those at the A1-Ring and Indianapolis, which is something.

The world rallying championship almost mirrored the F1 season with Marcus Gronholm winning the title with Schumacher-like ease, and his Peugeot teammate Richard Burns placing a distance second. But that's about as far as the comparisons go. Burns, the 2001 world champion, admitted that both derive motivation from trying to beat the other. "It's nothing personal, you know: we both want to win, that's all," said the Andorra-based Englishman, who considered that the rivalry was actually beneficial to the Peugeot team.

Cristiano da Matta won the ChampCar Series (CART to you and me), with Scot Dario Franchitti in fourth place. For most of the autumn, the rumours were rife that Ecclestone was about to make a takeover bid for CART and turn the series into a feeder championship for F1.

The rumours were triggered by an amendment to CART's stockholder rights made on September 12th which allowed one investor (Gerald Forsythe) to extend his share ownership to 23%. Ecclestone was expected to follow up with a bid for a majority share in the company, but the bid didn't materialise.

2003 F1 Teams

Ferrari
Michael Schumacher GER
Rubens Barrichello BRA

Williams-BMW
Ralf Schumacher GER
Juan-Pablo Montoya COL

McLaren-Mercedes
David Coulthard GBR
Kimi Raikkonen FIN

Renault
Jarno Trulli ITA
Fernando Alonso ESP

Sauber-Petronas
Nick Heidfeld GER
Heinz-Harald Frentzen GER

Jordan-Cosworth
Giancarlo Fisichella ITA
Ralph Firman GBR

Jaguar
Mark Webber AUS
Antonio Pizzonia BRA

BAR-Honda
Jacques Villeneuve CAN
Jenson Button GBR

Minardi-Cosworth
Justin Wilson GBR
Jos Verstappen NED

Toyota F1
Olivier Panis FRA
Cristiano da Matta BRA

Formula One

Australian Grand Prix

Melbourne, Mar 3
Laps: 58 x 5.303km   Total distance: 307.574km
1 Michael Schumacher (Ferrari) GER   1:35:36.792
                                            (193.011kph)
2 Juan Pablo Montoya (Williams) COL   +18.627
3 Kimi Raikkonen (McLaren) FIN   +25.066
4 Eddie Irvine (Jaguar) GBR   +1 lap
5 Mark Webber (Minardi) AUS   +2 laps
6 Mika Salo (Toyota) FIN   +2 laps
Pole Position: R Barrichello
Fastest Lap: K Raikkonen 1:28.541

WORLD CHAMPIONSHIP STANDINGS
Drivers: M Schumacher 10, Montoya 6,
Raikkonen 4, Irvine 3, Webber 2, Salo 1
Constructors: Ferrari 10, Williams 6, McLaren 4,
Jaguar 3, Minardi 2, Toyota 1

Malaysian Grand Prix

Sepang, Mar 17
Laps: 56 x 5.543km   Total distance: 310.408km
1 Ralf Schumacher (Williams) GER   1:34:12.912
                                            (197.680kph)
2 Juan Pablo Montoya (Williams) COL   +39.699
3 Michael Schumacher (Ferrari) GER   +1:01.794
4 Jenson Button (Renault) GBR   +1:09.766
5 Nick Heidfeld (Sauber) GER   +1 lap
6 Felipe Massa (Sauber) BRA   +1 lap
Pole Position: M Schumacher
Fastest Lap: J P Montoya 1:38.049
Drivers: M Schumacher 14, Montoya 12,
R Schumacher 10, Raikkonen 4, Button & Irvine 3,
Heidfeld & Webber 2, Massa & Salo 1
Constructors: Williams 22, Ferrari 14, McLaren 4,
Jaguar, Renault & Sauber 3, Minardi 2, Toyota 1

Brazilian Grand Prix

Interlagos, Mar 31
Laps: 71 x 4.309km   Total distance: 305.909km
1 Michael Schumacher (Ferrari) GER   1:31:43.663
                                            (200.098kph)
2 Ralf Schumacher (Williams) GER   +0.588
3 David Coulthard (McLaren) GBR   +59.110
4 Jenson Button (Renault) GBR   +1:06.883
5 Juan Pablo Montoya (Williams) COL   +1:07.563
6 Mika Salo (Toyota) FIN   +1 lap
Pole Position: J P Montoya
Fastest Lap: J P Montoya 1:16.079
Drivers: M Schumacher 24, R Schumacher 16,
Montoya 14, Button 6, Coulthard & Raikkonen 4, Irvine 3,
Heidfeld, Salo & Webber 2, Massa 1
Constructors: Williams 30, Ferrari 24, McLaren 8,
Renault 6, Jaguar & Sauber 3, Minardi &Toyota 2

San Marino Grand Prix

Imola, Apr 14
Laps: 62 x 4.933km   Total distance: 305.609km
1 Michael Schumacher (Ferrari) GER   1:29:10.789
                                            (205.613kph)
2 Rubens Barrichello (Ferrari) BRA   +17.907
3 Ralf Schumacher (Williams) GER   +19.755
4 Juan Pablo Montoya (Williams) COL   +44.725
5 Jenson Button (Renault) GBR   +1:23.395
6 David Coulthard (McLaren) GBR   +1 lap
Pole Position: M Schumacher
Fastest Lap: R Barrichello 1:24.170
Drivers: M Schumacher 34, R Schumacher 20,
Montoya 17, Button 8, Barrichello 6, Coulthard 5,
Raikkonen 4, Irvine 3, Heidfeld, Salo & Webber 2,
Massa 1
Constructors: Ferrari 40, Williams 37, McLaren 9,
Renault 8, Jaguar & Sauber 3, Minardi & Toyota 2

Spanish Grand Prix

Barcelona, Apr 28
Laps: 65 x 4.730km   Total distance: 307.327km
1 Michael Schumacher (Ferrari) GER   1:30:29.981
                                            (202.753kph)
2 Juan Pablo Montoya (Williams) COL   +35.629
3 David Coulthard (McLaren) GBR   +42.623
4 Nick Heidfeld (Sauber) GER   +1:06.696
5 Felipe Massa (Sauber) BRA   +1:18.973
6 Heinz-Harald Frentzen (Arrows) GER   +1:20.429
Pole Position: M Schumacher
Fastest Lap: M Schumacher 1:20.355
Drivers: M Schumacher 44, Montoya 23,
R Schumacher 20, Coulthard 9, Button 8, Barrichello 6,
Heidfeld 5, Raikkonen 4, Irvine & Massa 3, Salo &
Webber 2, Frentzen1
Constructors: Ferrari 50, Williams 43, McLaren 13,
Renault & Sauber 8, Jaguar 3, Minardi & Toyota 2,
Arrows 1

Austrian Grand Prix

A1-Ring, May 12
Laps: 71 x 4.326km   Total distance: 307.146km
1 Michael Schumacher (Ferrari) GER   1:33:51.562
                                            (196.344kph)
2 Rubens Barrichello (Ferrari) BRA   +0.182
3 Juan Pablo Montoya (Williams) COL   +17.730
4 Ralf Schumacher (Williams) GER   +18.448
5 Giancarlo Fisichella (Jordan) ITA   +49.965
6 David Coulthard (McLaren) GBR   50.672
Pole Position: Barrichello
Fastest Lap: M Schumacher 1:09.298
Drivers: M Schumacher 54, Montoya 27, R Schumacher
23, Barrichello 12, Coulthard 10, Button 8, Heidfeld 5,
Raikkonen 4, Irvine & Massa 3, Salo, Fisichella &
Webber 2
Constructors: Ferrari 66, Williams 50, McLaren 14,
Renault & Sauber 8, Jaguar 3, Jordan, Minardi &
Toyota 2, Arrows 1

Monaco Grand Prix

Monte Carlo, May 26

Laps: 78 x 3.370km   Total distance: 262.860km

1	David Coulthard (McLaren) GBR	1:45:39.055
		(149.280kph)
2	Michael Schumacher (Ferrari) GER	+1.049
3	Ralf Schumacher (Williams) GER	+1:17.449
4	Jarno Trulli (Renault) ITA	+1 lap
5	Giancarlo Fisichella (Jordan) ITA	+1 lap
6	Heinz-Harald Frentzen (Arrows) GER	+1 lap

Pole Position: Montoya

Fastest Lap: Barrichello 1:18.023

Drivers: M Schumacher 60, R Schumacher & Montoya 27, Coulthard 20, Barrichello 12, Button 8, Heidfeld 5, Fisichella & Raikonnen 4, Irvine & Massa & Trulli 3, Frentzen & Salo & Webber 2

Constructors: Ferrari 72, Williams 54, McLaren 24, Renault 11, Sauber 8, Jordan 4, Jaguar 3, Arrows & Minardi & Toyota 2

Canadian Grand Prix

Montreal, June 9

Laps: 70 x 4.361km   Total distance: 305.270km

1	Michael Schumacher (Ferrari) GER	1:33:36.111
		(195.682kph)
2	David Coulthard (McLaren) GBR	+1.132
3	Rubens Barrichello (Ferrari) BRA	+7.082
4	Kimi Raikkonen (McLaren) FIN	+37.563
5	Giancarlo Fisichella (Jordan) ITA	+42.812
6	Jarno Trulli (Renault) ITA	+48.948

Pole Position: Montoya

Fastest Lap: Montoya 1:15.960

Drivers: M Schumacher 70, R Schumacher & Montoya 27, Coulthard 26, Barrichello 16, Button 8, Raikonnen 7, Fisichella 6, Heidfeld 5, Trulli 4, Irvine & Massa 3, Frentzen & Salo & Webber 2

Constructors: Ferrari 86, Williams 54, McLaren 33, Renault 12, Sauber 8, Jordan 6, Jaguar 3, Arrows & Minardi & Toyota 2

European Grand Prix

Nürburgring, June 23

Laps: 60 x 5.146km   Total distance: 308.743km

1	Rubens Barrichello (Ferrari) BRA	1:35:07.426
		(194.742kph)
2	Michael Schumacher (Ferrari) GER	+0.294
3	Kimi Raikkonen (McLaren) FIN	+46.435
4	Ralf Schumacher (Willliams) GER	+1:06.963
5	Jenson Button (Renault) GBR	+1:16.944
6	Felipe Massa (Sauber) BRA	+1 lap

Pole Position: Montoya

Fastest Lap: M Schumacher 1:32.226

Drivers: M Schumacher 76, R Schumacher 30, Montoya 27, Coulthard & Barrichello 26, Raikonnen 11, Button 10, Fisichella 6, Heidfeld 5, Massa & Trulli 4, Irvine 3, Frentzen & Salo & Webber 2

Constructors: Ferrari 102, Williams 57, McLaren 37, Renault 14, Sauber 9, Jordan 6, Jaguar 3, Arrows & Minardi & Toyota 2

British Grand Prix

Silverstone, July 7

Laps: 60 x 5.141km   Total distance: 308.356km

1	Michael Schumacher (Ferrari) GER	1:31:45.015
		(201.649kph)
2	Rubens Barrichello (Ferrari) BRA	+14.578
3	Juan Pablo Montoya (Williams) COL	+31.661
4	Jacques Villeneuve (BAR) CAN	+1 lap
5	Olivier Panis (BAR) FRA	+1 lap
6	Nick Heidfeld (Sauber) GER	+1 lap

Pole Position: Montoya

Fastest Lap: Barrichello 1:23.083

Drivers: M Schumacher 86, Barrichello 32, Montoya 31, R Schumacher 30, Coulthard 26, Raikonnen 11, Button 10, Fisichella & Heidfeld 6, Massa & Trulli 4, Irvine & Villeneuve 3, Frentzen & Panis & Salo & Webber 2

Constructors: Ferrari 118, Williams 61, McLaren 37, Renault 14, Sauber 10, Jordan 6, BAR 5, Jaguar 3, Arrows & Minardi & Toyota 2

French Grand Prix

Magny-Cours, July 21

Laps: 72 x 4.251km   Total distance: 305.886km

1	Michael Schumacher (Ferrari) GER	1:32:09.837
		(199.136kph)
2	Kimi Raikkonen (McLaren) FIN	+1.104
3	David Coulthard (McLaren) GBR	+31.975
4	Juan Pablo Montoya (Williams) COL	+40.675
5	Ralf Schumacher (Williams) GER	+41.772
6	Jenson Button (Renault) GBR	+1 lap

Pole Position: Montoya

Fastest Lap: Coulthard 1:15.045

Drivers: M Schumacher 96, Montoya 34, Barrichello & R Schumacher 32, Coulthard 30, Raikonnen 17, Button 11, Fisichella & Heidfeld 6, Massa & Trulli 4, Irvine & Villeneuve 3, Frentzen & Panis & Salo & Webber 2

Constructors: Ferrari 128, Williams 66, McLaren 47, Renault 15, Sauber 10, Jordan 6, BAR 5, Jaguar 3, Arrows & Minardi & Toyota 2

German Grand Prix

Hockenheim, July 28

Laps: 67 x 4.574km   Total distance: 306.458km

1	Michael Schumacher (Ferrari) GER	1:27:52.078
		(209.263kph)
2	Juan Pablo Montoya (Williams) COL	+10.503
3	Ralf Schumacher (Williams) GER	+14.466
4	Rubens Barrichello (Ferrari) BRA	+23.195
5	David Coulthard (McLaren) GBR	+1 lap
6	Nick Heidfeld (Sauber) GER	+1 lap

Pole Position: M Schumacher

Fastest Lap: M Schumacher 1:16.462

Drivers: M Schumacher 106, Montoya 40, R Schumacher 36, Barrichello 35, Coulthard 32, Raikonnen 17, Button 11, Heidfeld 7, Fisichella 6, Massa & Trulli 4, Irvine & Villeneuve 3, Frentzen & Panis & Salo & Webber 2

Constructors: Ferrari 141, Williams 76, McLaren 49, Renault 15, Sauber 11, Jordan 6, BAR 5, Jaguar 3, Arrows & Minardi & Toyota 2

Hungarian Grand Prix

Hungaroring, Aug 28
Laps: 77 x 3.975km   Total distance: 306.069km
1   Rubens Barrichello (Ferrari) BRA   1:41:49.001
                                                    (180.365kph)
2   Michael Schumacher (Ferrari) GER   +0.434
3   Ralf Schumacher (Williams) GER   +13.356
4   Kimi Raikkonen (McLaren) FIN   +29.479
5   David Coulthard (McLaren) GBR   +37.800
6   Giancarlo Fisichella (Jordan) ITA   +1:08.804
Pole Position: Barrichello
Fastest Lap: M Schumacher 1:16.207
Drivers: *M Schumacher 112, Barrichello 45, Montoya &*
R Schumacher 40, Coulthard 34, Raikonnen 20, Button 11,
Fisichella & Heidfeld 7, Massa & Trulli 4, Irvine &
Villeneuve 3, Frentzen & Panis & Salo & Webber 2
Constructors: *Ferrari 157, Williams 80, McLaren 54,*
Renault 15, Sauber 11, Jordan 7, BAR 5, Jaguar 3,
Arrows & Minardi & Toyota 2

Belgian Grand Prix

Spa-Francochamps, Sep 1
Laps: 44 x 6.963km   Total distance: 306.355km
1   Michael Schumacher (Ferrari) GER   1:21:20.634
                                                    (225.970kph)
2   Rubens Barrichello (Ferrari) BRA   +1.977
3   Juan Pablo Montoya (Williams) COL   +18.445
4   David Coulthard (McLaren) GBR   +19.358
5   Ralf Schumacher (Williams) GER   +56.440
6   Eddie Irvine (Jaguar) GBR   +1:17.370
Pole Position: M Schumacher
Fastest Lap: M Schumacher 1:47.176
Drivers: *M Schumacher 122, Barrichello 51, Montoya 44,*
R Schumacher 42, Coulthard 37, Raikonnen 20, Button 11,
Fisichella & Heidfeld 7, Massa & Trulli & Irvine 4,
Villeneuve 3, Frentzen & Panis & Salo & Webber 2
Constructors: *Ferrari 173, Williams 86, McLaren 57,*
Renault 15, Sauber 11, Jordan 7, BAR 5, Jaguar 4,
Arrows & Minardi & Toyota 2

Italian Grand Prix

Monza, Sep 15
Laps: 53 x 5.793km   Total distance: 306.719km
1   Rubens Barrichello (Ferrari) BRA   1:16:19.982
                                                    (241.090kph)
2   Michael Schumacher (Ferrari) GER   +0.255
3   Eddie Irvine (Jaguar) GBR   +52.579
4   Jarno Trulli (Renault) ITA   +58.219
5   Jenson Button (Renault) GBR   +1:07.770
6   Olivier Panis (BAR) FRA   +1:08.491
Pole Position: Montoya
Fastest Lap: Barrichello 1:23.657
Drivers: *M Schumacher 128, Barrichello 61, Montoya 44,*
R Schumacher 42, Coulthard 37, Raikonnen 20, Button 13,
Irvine 8, Fisichella & Heidfeld & Trulli 7, Massa 4, Panis &
Villeneuve 3, Frentzen & Salo & Webber 2
Constructors: *Ferrari 189, Williams 86, McLaren 57,*
Renault 20, Sauber 11, Jaguar 8, Jordan 7, BAR 6,
Arrows & Minardi & Toyota 2

US Grand Prix

Indianapolis, Sep 29
Laps: 73 x 4.192km   Total distance: 306.016km
1   Rubens Barrichello (Ferrari) BRA   1:31:07.934
                                                    (201.476kph)
2   Michael Schumacher (Ferrari) GER   +0.011
3   David Coulthard (McLaren) GBR   +7.799
4   Juan-Pablo Montoya (Williams) COL   +9.911
5   Jarno Trulli (Renault) ITA   +56.847
6   Jacques Villeneuve (BAR) CAN   +58.212
Pole Position: M Schumacher
Fastest Lap: Barrichello 1:12.738
Drivers: *M Schumacher 134, Barrichello 71, Montoya 47,*
R Schumacher 42, Coulthard 41, Raikonnen 20, Button 13,
Trulli 9, Irvine 8, Fisichella & Heidfeld 7, Massa &
Villeneuve 4, Panis 3, Frentzen & Salo & Webber 2
Constructors: *Ferrari 205, Williams 89, McLaren 61,*
Renault 22, Sauber 11, Jaguar 8, Jordan & BAR 7,
Arrows & Minardi & Toyota 2

Japanese Grand Prix

Suzuka, Oct 13
Laps: 53 x 5.864   Total distance: 310.582km
1   Michael Schumacher (Ferrari) GER   1:26:59.698
                                                    (212.645kph)
2   Rubens Barrichello (Ferrari) BRA   +0.506
3   Kimi Raikkonen (McLaren) FIN   +23.292
4   Juan-Pablo Montoya (Williams) COL   +36.275
5   Takuma Sato (Jordan) JPN   +1:22.694
6   Jenson Button (Renault) GBR   +1 lap
Pole Position: M Schumacher
Fastest Lap: M Schumacher 1:36.125
See over for final standings

Driver's Championship

Final Standings

1	Michael Schumacher GER (Ferrari)	144
2	Rubens Barrichello BRA (Ferrari)	77
3	Juan Pablo Montoya COL (Williams/BMW)	50
4	Ralf Schumacher GER (Williams/BMW)	42
5	David Coulthard GBR (McLaren/Mercedes)	41
6	Kimi Raikkonen FIN (McLaren/Mercedes)	24
7	Jenson Button GBR (Renault)	14
8	Jarno Trulli ITA (Renault)	9
9	Eddie Irvine GBR (Jaguar)	8
10	Nick Heidfeld GER (Sauber/Petronas)	7
11	Giancarlo Fisichella ITA (Benetton/Renault)	7
12	Jacques Villeneuve CAN (BAR/Honda)	4
13	Felipe Massa BRA (Sauber/Petronas)	4
14	Olivier Panis FRA (BAR Honda)	3
15	Takuma Sato JPN (Jordan/Honda)	2
16	Mark Webber AUS (Minardi/Asiatech)	2
17	Mika Salo FIN (Toyota)	2
18	Heinz-Harald Frentzen GER (Arrows/Cosworth)	2

Constructors' Final Standings

1. Ferrari 221; 2. Williams BMW 92
3. McLaren Mercedes 65; 4. Renault 23;
5. Sauber Petronas 11; 6. Jordan Honda 9;
7. Jaguar 8; 8. BAR Honda 7;
9. Minardi Asiatech 2; 10. Toyota 2;
11. Arrows Cosworth 2

Formula 3000

Round 1

Interlagos, March 30
1	Rodrigo Sperafico (Durango) BRA	53:24.481
2	Mario Haberfield (Astromega) BRA	+0.738
3	Ricardo Mauricio (Red Bull) BRA	+3.900

Round 2

Imola, April 13
1	Sebastien Bourdais (Super Nova) FRA	51:39.076
2	Rodrigo Sperafico (Durango) BRA	+1.185
3	Giorgio Pantano (Coloni)	+12.641

Round 3

Barcelona, April 27
1	Giorgio Pantano (Coloni) ITA	51:44.572
2	Tomas Enge (Arden) CZE	+0.988
3	Sebastien Bourdais (Super Nova) FRA	+8.159

Round 4

A1-Ring, May 11
1	Tomas Enge (Coca-Cola Racing) CZE	48:53.862
2	Bjorn Wirdheim (Arden) SWE	+3.716
3	Mario Haberfield (Astromega) BRA	+4.867

Round 5

Monte Carlo, May 25
1	Sebastien Bourdais (Super Nova) FRA	1:07:40.545
2	Patrick Friesacher (Red Bull) AUT	+18.426
3	Tomas Enge (Arden) CZE	+27.629

Round 6

Nürburgring, June 22
1	Sebastien Bourdais (Super Nova) FRA	54:55.289
2	Ricardo Sperafico (Petrobras) BRA	+3.768
3	Antonio Pizzonia (Petrobas) BRA	+30.762

Round 7

Silverstone, July 6
1	Tomas Enge (Arden) CZE	49:45.388
2	Sebastien Bourdais (Super Nova) FRA	+12.916
3	Ricardo Sperafico (Petrobras) BRA	+17.600

Round 8

Magny-Cours, July 20
1	Tomas Enge (Arden) CZE	54:58.076
2	Sebastien Bourdais (Super Nova) FRA	+1.137
3	Giorgio Pantano (Coloni) ITA	+1.958

Round 9

Hockenheim, July 27
1	Giorgio Pantano (Coloni) ITA	50:00.768
2	Bjorn Wirdheim (Arden) SWE	+8.776
3	Rodrigo Sperafico (Durango) BRA	+23.483

Round 10

Hungaroring, Aug 17
1	Tomas Enge (Arden) CZE	59:24.642
2	Enrico Toccacelo (Coloni) ITA	+1.187
3	Giorgio Pantano (Coloni) ITA	+2.709

Round 11

Spa-Francorchamps, Aug 31
1	Giorgio Pantano (Coloni) ITA	47:06.609
2	Sebastien Bourdais (Super Nova) FRA	+0.426
3	Ricardo Sperafico (Petrobras) BRA	+1.071

Round 12

Monza, Sep 15
1	Bjorn Wirdheim (Arden) SWE	44:57.538
2	Antonio Pizzonia (Petrobras) BRA	+1.580
3	Tomas Enge (Arden) CZE	+2.308

FINAL STANDINGS

1	Sebastien Bourdais (Super Nova)	FRA	56
2	Giorgio Pantano (Coloni)	ITA	54
3	Tomas Enge (Arden)	CZE	50
4	Björn Wirdheim (Arden)	SWE	29
5	Ricardo Sperafico (Petrobras)	BRA	22
6	Rodrigo Sperafico (Durango)	BRA	20

ChampCar Series

Round 1
Monterrey, Mexico, Mar 10
85 laps of 3.386km

1	Cristiano da Matta	BRA	1:58:30.642	21
2	Dario Franchitti	GBR	+1.679	16
3	Christian Fittipaldi	BRA	+3.244	14

Round 2
Long Beach, California, Apr 14
90 laps of 3.167km

1	Michael Andretti	USA	2:02:14.542	21
2	Jimmy Vasser	USA	+0.466	17
3	Max Papis	ITA	+4.698	14
9	Dario Franchitti	GBR	+11.460	4

Points standing: *Da Matta 27, Andretti & Jourdain 22, Franchitti 20*

Round 3
Motegi Twin Ring, Japan, Apr 26
201 laps of 2.491km

1	Bruno Junqueira	BRA	2:00:05.882	21
2	Alex Tagliani	CAN	+12.282	16
3	Dario Franchitti	GBR	+1 lap	14

Points standing: *Franchitti 34, Jourdain 32, Da Matta 27, Tagliani 26, Junqueira 25, Andretti 22*

Round 4
Milwaukee, Wisconsin, June 2
250 laps of 1.661km

1	Paul Tracy	CAN	1:59:03.089	21
2	Adrian Fernandez	MEX	+0.747	17
3	Max Papis	ITA	+1.775	14
12	Dario Franchitti	GBR	+62 laps	1

Points standing: *Jourdain 42, Franchitti 35, Papis & Tracy 32, Da Matta 29, Andretti 28*

Round 5
Laguna Seca, California   June 9
201 laps of 3.602km

1	Cristiano da Matta	BRA	1:55:28.745	22
2	Christian Fittipaldi	BRA	+19.087	16
3	Kenny Brack	SWE	+19.410	14
19	Dario Franchitti	GBR	+87 laps	-

Points standing: *Da Matta 51, Jourdain 46, Fittipaldi 43, Junqueiro 38, Franchitti 35, Papis & Tracy 32*

Round 6
Portland International Raceway, June 16
110 laps of 3.169km

1	Cristiano da Matta	BRA	2:03:19.113	23
2	Bruno Junqueira	BRA	+0.625	16
3	Dario Franchitti	GBR	+7.761	14

Points standing: *Da Matta 74, Junqueiro & Jourdain 54, Franchitti 49, Fittipaldi 43, Carpentier 38, Andretti 34*

Round 7
Chicago Motor Speedway, June 30
250 laps of 1.656km

1	Cristiano da Matta	BRA	2:07:00.698	21
2	Bruno Junqueira	BRA	+0.639	16
3	Dario Franchitti	GBR	+3.444	14

Points standing: *Da Matta 95, Junqueiro 70, Franchitti 64, Jourdain 57, Fittipaldi 43, Dixon 42, Carpentier 38*

Round 8
Toronto, July 7
112 laps of 2.824km

1	Cristiano da Matta	BRA	2:06:19.372	23
2	Kenny Brack	SWE	+4.398	16
3	Christian Fittipaldi	BRA	+11.357	14
13	Dario Franchitti	GBR	+11 laps	-

Points standing: *Da Matta 118, Junqueiro 70, Franchitti 64, Jourdain 58, Fittipaldi 57, Dixon 52, Brack 48*

Round 9
Cleveland, Ohio, July 14
115 laps of 3.389km

1	Patrick Carpentier	CAN	2:00:05.785	21
2	Michael Andretti	USA	+17.069	16
3	Paul Tracy	CAN	+28.295	14
14	Dario Franchitti	GBR	+ 46 laps	-

Points standing: *Da Matta 120, Junqueiro 70, Franchitti 64, Carpentier & Jourdain 62, Brack 60, Fittipaldi 58*

Round 10
Vancouver, July 28
100 laps of 2.866km

1	Dario Franchitti	GBR	1:59:25.063	20
2	Paul Tracy	CAN	+1.239	18
3	Tony Kanaan	BRA	+2.363	14

Points standing: *Da Matta 122, Franchitti 84, Junqueiro & Jourdain 74, Carpentier 72, Tracy 68, Andretti 60*

Round 11
Lexington, Ohio, Aug 11
92 laps of 3.634km

1	Patrick Carpentier	CAN	1:56:17.573	23
2	Christian Fittipaldi	BRA	+3.213	16
3	Michael Andretti	USA	+4.733	14
17	Dario Franchitti	GBR	+54 laps	-

Points standing: *Da Matta 122, Carpentier 95, Junqueiro 86, Franchitti 84, Jourdain 76, Fittipaldi & Andretti 74*

Round 12
Elkhart Lake, Wisconsin, Aug 18
60 laps of 6.515km

1	Cristiano da Matta	BRA	1:56:43.030	21
2	Alex Tagliani	CAN	+0.805	16
3	Bruno Junqueira	BRA	+1.530	15
12	Dario Franchitti	GBR	+17 laps	1

Points standing: *Da Matta 143, Junqueiro & Carpentier 101, Franchitti 85, Fittipaldi 82, Tagliani & Jourdain 80, Andretti 77*

Round 13
Montreal, Aug 25
80 laps of 4.360km

1	Dario Franchitti	GBR	1:59:40.938	21
2	Cristiano da Matta	BRA	+2.588	18
3	Tony Kanaan	BRA	+4.612	14

Points standing: *Da Matta 161, Franchitti 106, Junqueiro & Carpentier 101, Fittipaldi & Jourdain 88, Andretti 82*

Round 14

Denver, Sep 1
100 laps of 2.651km

1	Bruno Junqueira	BRA	1:49:22.547	22
2	Scott Dixon	NZL	+0.282	16
3	Cristiano da Matta	BRA	+8.191	14
18	Dario Franchitti	GBR	+100 laps	-

Points standing: *Da Matta 175, Junqueiro 123, Franchitti 106, Carpentier 101, Fittipaldi 96, Jourdain 92, Tracy 86, Tagliani 83*

Round 15

Rockingham Speedway, Corby, Sep 14
211 laps of 2.380km

1	Dario Franchitti	GBR	1:58:44.754	20
2	Cristiano da Matta	BRA	+0.986	16
3	Patrick Carpentier	CAN	+2.785	14

Points standing: *Da Matta 191, Junqueiro 133, Franchitti 126, Carpentier 115, Fittipaldi 98, Jourdain 94, Tracy 86, Andretti 85, Tagliani 83*

Round 16

Miami, Oct 6
105 laps of 2.232km

1	Cristiano da Matta	BRA	2:07:09.003	21
2	Christian Fittipaldi	BRA	+0.734	16
3	Jimmy Vasser	USA	+1.343	14
10	Dario Franchitti	GBR	+2 laps	3

Points standing: *Da Matta 212, Junqueiro 143, Franchitti 129, Carpentier 115, Fittipaldi 114, Jourdain 102, Tagliani 95, Andretti 90, Tracy 87*

Round 17

Surfers Paradise, Australia, Oct 27
40 laps of 4.498km

1	Mario Dominguez	MEX	2:00:06.524	20
2	Patrick Carpentier	CAN	+2.177	16
3	Paul Tracy	CAN	+2.549	14
7	Dario Franchitti	GBR	+9.940	6

Points standing: *Da Matta 219, Junqueiro 144, Franchitti 135, Carpentier 131, Fittipaldi 116, Jourdain 105, Tagliani 103, Andretti 94, Vasser 91*

Round 18

Fontana, California, Nov 3
250 laps of 3.265km

1	Jimmy Vasser	USA	2:33:42.977	21
2	Michael Andretti	USA	+0.400	16
3	Patrick Carpentier	CAN	+1.794	14
10	Dario Franchitti	GBR	+8 laps	3

Points standing: *Da Matta 221, Junqueiro 148, Carpentier 145, Franchitti 138, Fittipaldi 122, Vasser 112, Andretti 110, Tagliani 108, Jourdain 105*

Round 19

Mexico City, Nov 17
73 laps of 4.426km

1	Kenny Brack	SWE	1:56:48.475	20
2	Cristiano da Matta	BRA	+3.987	16
3	Bruno Junqueiro	BRA	+5.073	16
5	Dario Franchitti	GBR	+12.548	10

ChampCar World Series

Drivers Championship
Final Standings

1	Cristiano da Matta	BRA	237
2	Bruno Junqueiro	BRA	164
3	Patrick Carpentier	CAN	157
4	Dario Franchitti	GBR	148
5	Christian Fittipaldi	BRA	122
6	Kenny Brack	SWE	114
7	Jimmy Vasser	USA	114
8	Alex Tagliani	CAN	111
9	Michael Andretti	USA	110
10	Michael Jourdain jr	MEX	105
11	Paul Tracy	CAN	101
12	Tony Kanaan	BRA	99
13	Scott Dixon	AUS	97
14	Adrian Fernandez	MEX	59
15	Tora Takagi	JPN	53
16	Oriol Servia	ESP	44
17	Shinji Nakano	JPN	43
18	Mario Dominguez	MEX	37
19	Max Papis	ITA	32
20	Townsend Bell	USA	19
21	Darren Manning	GBR	4
22	Andre Lotterer	GER	1

Rookie Of The Year
Final Standings
1. Mario Dominguez MEX
2. Townsend Bell USA
3. Darren Manning GBR

Manufacturers' Cup
Final Standings
1. Toyota 333pts
2. Honda 282
3. Ford-Cosworth 259

Constructors' Cup
Final Standings
1. Lola 401pts
2. Reynard 235

"We need to get our act together. We haven't got a very good act at the moment. It's nobody's fault. You can't blame Ferrari for winning. They've all got the same regulations. The trouble is that the technicians have got in front of the drivers. I mean truly it's not sort of decrying what Michael and the other drivers do but certainly their lives are a lot easier than they should be. I watched the on-board camera with Michael and he was sitting there like he was going to the shops"
Bernie Ecclestone.

"I could save Formula One. All I need is a fire hose and access to the Terminal Four Heathrow Hilton conference room today where the whole power-crazy bunch will be working out how to stuff each other, yet still come out looking like responsible custodians of one of the world's biggest sports"
Damon Hill.

"He is getting to be an old man now. He is getting past it"
Rubens Barrichello on Eddie Irvine.

"I may be older than Rubens but I'll never be as ugly"
Irvine recycling Winston Churchill.

Le Mans 24 Hours

Circuit de la Sarthe   June 15-16
Circuit length: 13.61km

	Drivers	Entrant	Category	Car	Laps
1	Biela/Kristensen/Pirro	Audi Sport Team GER	LMP900	Audi R8	375
2	Capello/Herbert/Pescatori	Audi Sport Team GER	LMP900	Audi R8	374
3	Krumm/Peter/Werner	Audi Sport Team GER	LMP900	Audi R8	372
4	Wallace/Leitzinger/Van der Poele	Team Bentley GBR	LM GTP	Bentley Exp	362
5	Beretta/Lamy/Comas	Playstation Team Oreca FRA	LMP900	Oreca Dallara	359
6	Sarrazin/Montagny/Minassian	Playstation Team Oreca FRA	LMP900	Oreca Dallara	359
7	Ara/Dalmas/Katoh	Team Goh JPN	LMP900	Audi R8	358
8	Lammers/Hillebrand/Coronel	Racing For Holland NED	LMP900	Dome S101	351
9	Taylor/Angelelli/Tinseau	Team Cadillac USA	LMP900	Cadillac Northstar	345
10	Boullion/Lagorce/Bourdais	Pescarolo Sport FRA	LMP900	Corvette C5-R	335

R a l l y i n g

World Championship

Rallye Automobile Monte Carlo
Jan 17-20
1 Sebastien Loeb (Citroen) FRA	3:58:44.8
2 Tommi Makinen (Mitsubishi) FIN	+45.9
3 Carlos Sainz (Ford) ESP	+2:01.6

Swedish Rally
Jan 31-Feb 3
1 Marcus Grönholm (Peugeot) FIN	3:07:28.6
2 Harri Rovanperä (Peugeot) FIN	+1:24.5
3 Carlos Sainz (Ford) ESP	+2:25.8

Tour de Corse
Mar 7-10
1 Gilles Panizzi (Peugeot) FRA	3:54:40.3
2 Marcus Grönholm (Peugeot) FIN	+40.5
3 Richard Burns (Peugeot) GBR	+52.4

Rally Catalunya
Mar 22-24
1 Gilles Panizzi (Peugeot) FRA	3:34:09.0
2 Richard Burns (Peugeot) GBR	+37.3
3 Philippe Bugalski (Citroen) FRA	+1:13.5

Rally of Cyprus
April 19-21
1 Marcus Gronholm (Peugeot) FIN	4:21:25.7
2 Richard Burns (Peugeot) GBR	+56.8
3 Tommi Makinen (Subaru) FIN	+59.0

Argentina Rally
May 16-19
1 Carlos Sainz (Ford) ESP	4:08:09.1
2 Petter Solberg (Subaru) NOR	+4.0
3 Colin McRae (Ford) GBR	+2:19.1

Acropolis Rally
June 13-16
1 Colin McRae (Ford) GBR	4:27:43.8
2 Marcus Grönholm (Peugeot) FIN	+24.5
3 Carlos Sainz (Ford) ESP	+1:45.6

Safari Rally
July 11-14
1 Colin McRae (Ford) GBR	7:58:28.0
2 Harri Rovanpera (Peugeot) FIN	+2:50.9
3 Thomas Radstrom (Citroen) SWE	+18:38.6

Rally Finland
Aug 8-11
1 Marcus Grönholm (Peugeot) FIN	3:17:52.5
2 Richard Burns (Subaru) GBR	+1:27.3
3 Petter Solberg (Subaru) NOR	+2:49.6

Rally of Germany
Aug 22-25
1 Sebastien Loeb (Citroen) FRA	3:47:17.3
2 Richard Burns (Peugeot) GBR	+14.3
3 Marcus Grönholm (Peugeot) FIN	+1:19.1

San Remo Rally
Sep 19-22
1 Giles Panizzi (Peugeot) FRA	4:10:15.6
2 Marcus Grönholm (Peugeot) FIN	+20.9
3 Petter Solberg (Subaru) NOR	+1:06.4

Rally New Zealand
Oct 3-6
1 Marcus Grönholm (Peugeot) FIN	3:58:45.4
2 Harri Rovanperä (Peugeot) FIN	+3:47.6
3 Tommi Makinen (Subaru) FIN	+4:26.3

Rally Australia
Oct 31-Nov 3
1 Marcus Grönholm (Peugeot) FIN	3:35:56.5
2 Harri Rovanperä (Peugeot) FIN	+57.3
3 Petter Solberg (Subaru) NOR	+1:28.7

Rally of Great Britain
Nov 14-17
1 Petter Solberg (Subaru) NOR	3:30:36.4
2 Markko Märtin (Ford) EST	+24.4
3 Carlos Sainz (Ford) ESP	+1:35.7

DRIVERS' CHAMPIONSHIP
Final Standings
1 Marcus Gronholm (Peugeot) FIN	77
2 Richard Burns (Peugeot) GBR	34
3 Colin McRae (Ford) GBR	33
4 Carlos Sainz (Peugeot) ESP	32
5 Gilles Panizzi (Peugeot) FRA	31
6 Harri Rovanperä (Peugeot) FIN	30
7 Petter Solberg (Subaru) NOR	27
8 Tommi Mäkinen (Subaru) FIN	19
9 Sebastien Loeb (Citroen) FRA	18
10 Markko Martin (Ford) EST	14

MANUFACTURERS' CHAMPIONSHIP
Final Standings
1. Peugeot 163; 2. Ford 94; 3. Subaru 54;
4=. Mitsubishi, Skoda & Hyundai 9

Netball

International Matches

Australia & Barbados in England

Manchester, Mar 5
Australia 82   Barbados 23
Sheffield, Mar 8
England 69   Barbados 33
Brighton, Mar 15
Australia 56   England 44

New Zealand in Jamaica

Kingston, Mar 3
Jamaica 44   New Zealand 46
Kingston, Mar 4
Jamaica 53   New Zealand 44
Kingston, Mar 6
Jamaica 42   New Zealand 44

Barbados in New Zealand

Jun 29, Invercargill
New Zealand 88   Barbados 27
July 1, Wellington
New Zealand 87   Barbados 35
July 3, Auckland
New Zealand 84   Barbados 22

South Africa in New Zealand

Nov 1, Auckland
New Zealand 71   South Africa 33
Nov 2, Christchurch
New Zealand 86   South Africa 37

English Leagues

Fisher & Paykel Super Cup

		P	W	D	L	PF	PA	Pts
1	Birmingham Blaze	5	4	0	1	270	248	22
2	Northern Thunder	5	4	0	1	253	210	20
3	London Tornadoes	5	4	0	1	263	229	20
4	London Hurricanes	5	2	0	3	235	242	12
5	Bath Force	5	1	0	4	207	245	9
6	Northern Flames	5	0	0	5	218	271	2

Teams receive five points for a win and two points for a defeat of five goals or fewer.

CLASSIFICATION MATCHES

5th/6th Place play-off
Northern Flames 49   Bath Force 35

3rd/4th Place Play-off
London Hurricanes 51   London Tornadoes 45

Final
Northern Thunder 51   Birmingham Blaze 38

English Counties League 2001-2002

Division 1

		P	W	D	L	F	A	Pts	Av
1	Essex Metro	7	7	0	0	438	242	35	1.810
2	Derbyshire	7	6	0	1	457	360	31	1.269
3	Middlesex	7	5	0	2	399	302	28	1.321
4	Bedfordshire	7	3	0	4	319	355	18	0.899
5	Surrey	6	3	0	3	343	342	17	1.003
6	Manchester	6	2	0	4	343	342	15	1.003
7	Kent	7	1	0	6	277	370	10	0.749
8	Hampshire North	7	0	0	7	180	443	2	0.406

Orienteering

European Championships

Sumeg, Hungary, Sep 23-30

Men

Short Race (3.20km)

1	Emil Wingstedt	SWE	13:26.1
2	Hakan Petersson	SWE	13:33.9
3	Yuri Omeltchenko	UKR	13:37.8
6	Jamie Stevenson	GBR	13:40.3
27	Daniel Marston	GBR	14:41.7
32	Jon Duncan	GBR	14:46.9

Middle Distance Race (5.20km)

1	Mikhail Mamleev	RUS	24:49
2	Yuri Omeltchenko	UKR	25:26
3	Jamie Stevenson	GBR	25:56
47	Daniel Marston	GBR	31:02
52	Jon Duncan	GBR	33:39

Classic Race (12.0km)

1	Thomas Bührer	SUI	81:18
2	Bjornar Valstad	NOR	82:20
2	Emil Wingstedt	SWE	82:20
14	Jon Duncan	GBR	85:38
23	Jamie Stevenson	GBR	88:28
32	Oli Johnson	GBR	90:56
44	Daniel Marston	GBR	95:34

Relay

1	Finland	134:58

(Jani Lakanen/Pasi Ikonen/Mats Haldin)

2	Sweden	138:28
3	Denmark	138:39
18	Great Britain	145:35

(Jon Duncan/Daniel Marston/Jamie Stevenson)

Women

Short Race (2.85km)

1	Vroni König-Salmi	SUI	13:53.1
2	Elisabeth Ingvaldsen	NOR	14:02.7
3	Anne Hausken	NOR	14:11.3
17	Sarah Rollins	GBR	15:16.9
33	Helen Bridle	GBR	16:05.2
41	Hannah Wootton	GBR	16:33.7

Middle Distance Race (4.5km)

1	Gunilla Svärd	SWE	26:02
2	Brigitte Wolf	SUI	26:25
3	Birgitte Huseby	NOR	26:35
18	Heather Monro	GBR	29:00
35	Helen Hargreaves	GBR	30:50
37	Helen Bridle	GBR	30:53
52	Hannah Wootton	GBR	37:55

Classic Race (9.7km)

1	Simone Luder	SUI	52:01
2	Hanne Staff	NOR	53:16
3	Birgitte Huseby	NOR	55:06
5	Heather Monro	GBR	55:39
21	Sarah Rollins	GBR	61:58
31	Helen Hargreaves	GBR	63:30

Relay

1	Norway	112:48

(Elisabeth Ingvaldsen/Birgitte Huseby/Hanne Staff)

2	Switzerland	115:08
3	Lithuania	115:17
17	Great Britain	134:09

(Sarah Rollins/Hannah Wootton/Heather Monro)

World Rankings

British/Irish shown in top 50

Men

1	Fredrik Löwegren	SWE	5391
2	Pasi Ikonen	FIN	5354
3	Holger Hott Johansen	NOR	5353
4	Michael Mamleev	RUS	5346
5	Mats Haldin	FIN	5330
6	Jani Lakanen	FIN	5318
7	Marian Davidik	SVK	5263
8	Thomas Bührer	SUI	5262
9	Yuri Omeltchenko	UKR	5259
10	Valentin Novikov	RUS	5254
27	Jamie Stevenson	GBR	5115
44	Jon Duncan	GBR	4977

Women

1	Simone Luder	SUI	5866
2	Vroni Koenig-Salmi	SUI	5550
3	Karin Hellman	SWE	5515
4	Hanne Staff	NOR	5474
5	Katarina Allberg	SWE	5442
6	Gunilla Svärd	SWE	5417
7	Anette Granstedt	SWE	5413
8	Emma Engstrand	SWE	5380
9	Heather Monro	GBR	5311
10	Karin Schmalfeld	GER	5268
37	Hannah Wootton	GBR	4917
48	Sarah Rollins	GBR	4800

Rowing

World records in rowing don't have much credibility for lakes are not like tracks, or even pools, for they vary enormously. They are shallow, deep, broad, narrow, tidal even, and they don't measure the wind properly either. So, you can record best times, but you shouldn't call them world records.

Matt Pinsent and James Cracknell, being articulate and intelligent human beings, would probably not disagree with a word of that. They went to Seville not to break a world record anyway, but to be crowned the best coxless pair in the world and, in particular, to redress the balance with the Australians Drew Ginn and James Tompkins, who had beaten them twice in three days, in the World Cup at Lucerne in July, to supplant them in the world pecking order.

For Cracknell and Pinsent, the feeling was a familiar one. In the last Olympic year, as half of the coxless four, they had crumpled twice on the same lake in the same month and in the same competition. That didn't make it any less of a shock when it happened this time, for in two short seasons in the pair Cracknell and Pinsent had assumed a mantle similar to that worn by Pinsent and Redgrave in the same event in earlier illustrious times.

Before Sydney, the coxless four had to dig deep into their psyches to discover how much losing meant, and how much they didn't want it to happen at the Olympics. They got the analytical process right, and found the answer, and won the gold medal. For Cracknell and Pinsent, the process was similar, the final World Cup spurned in order to resolve the performance issues in training. "Being beaten was not the hardest thing to take from that weekend. It was travelling home knowing that we didn't deserve to win," said Cracknell.

Cracknell attributed a significant part of the failure in Lucerne to the fact that they had lacked the courage in the final to row their own race, allowing the Croatians to set the pace. There were other issues between them about whether Pinsent held back too much in training, and Cracknell went in the opposite direction. Motivation became a vital issue, and one suspects that Steve Redgrave, who drew so many remarkable performances from Pinsent over 10 years on the water, will have had an input.

In Seville, all the questions were answered, loudly and assertively. The pace set by Cracknell and Pinsent in the final was blistering. At 500m, they were two seconds clear of the Skelin brothers; at halfway, the lead was over five seconds. It was as if someone had dared them to go as fast as they could. Over the third 500m, they were only the fifth fastest boat, but they were still over three seconds clear of the Yugoslavians, who had shot their bolt anyway. The South Africans Ramon di Clemente and Donovan Cech were almost as impressive over the last 500m as the Britons were over the first 500m, but it was all too late.

Seville Coxless Pair

Italicised figures are the split times for each 500m
with the ranking for each split given in brackets

		Lane	500m (pos)	1000m (pos)	1500m (pos)	2000m (pos)
1	**Pinsent/Cracknell GBR**	4	**1:30.86 (1)**	**3:05.54 (1)**	**4:41.81 (1)**	**6:14.27 (1)**
	Split times (ranking)			*1:34.68 (1)*	*1:36.27 (5)*	*1:32.46 (4)*
2	**Di Clemente/Cech RSA**	5	**1:33.50 (3)**	**3:10.04 (3)**	**4:47.29 (5)**	**6:15.60 (2)**
				1:36.14 (3)	*1:37.25 (6)*	*1:28.31 (1)*
3	**Skelin/Skelin CRO**	2	**1:33.07 (2)**	**3:09.14 (2)**	**4:45.27 (3)**	**6:15.97 (3)**
				1:36.07 (2)	*1:36.13 (4)*	*1:30.70 (3)*
4	**Ginn/Tomkins AUS**	3	**1:34.51 (5)**	**3:10.97 (5)**	**4:45.56 (4)**	**6:16.02 (4)**
				1:36.46 (4)	*1:34.59 (2)*	*1:30.06 (2)*
5	**Visacki/Stojic YUG**	6	**1:33.99 (4)**	**3:10.56 (4)**	**4:45.00 (2)**	**6:21.32 (5)**
				1:36.57 (5)	*1:34.04 (1)*	*1:36.32 (5)*
6	**Michalek/Imre CZE**	1	**1:35.49 (6)**	**3:12.49 (6)**	**4:48.19 (6)**	**6:21.73 (6)**
				1:37.00 (6)	*1:35.30 (3)*	*1:43.54 (6)*

It was an astonishing row which had brought Cracknell his sixth world title and Pinsent his 11th. Since winning his first world title in 1991, Pinsent has remained unbeaten in world championships, his four coxless pairs with Redgrave followed by four victories with the coxless four, and now three with Cracknell (including a formidable double of coxed and coxless pairs in 2001). If you count in the three Olympic titles over the same period, Pinsent's winning streak in global events rivals anyone competing in any sport. And of course, as if that were not enough, Cracknell and Pinsent also broke the world record in Seville, and it would be curmudgeonly of us not to give them credit for that too, even if world records don't really exist...

Britain won two other gold medals in Seville, but neither came in Olympic events. The victory of the coxed four, stroked by Steve Trapmore, had considerably more merit than the victory of Naomi Ashcroft and Leonie Barron in the lightweight pairs, for only four boats contested that discipline. With the Olympic classes now so dominant in the world championships, the coxless four earned more plaudits for second than either of the non-Olympic winners, Joshua West, Steve Williams, Toby Garbett and Rick Dunn just failing to catch the German boat. There were two further bronze medals for Britain, both coming in the lightweight coxless pairs (men and women), neither of which is an Olympic class. Ireland's Sam Lynch, too, while celebrating the retention of his lightweight sculls title, must rue the day that it was dropped from the Games.

The Boat Race does not usually shift the hairs on the back of anyone's neck, except perhaps for the rowers in the years the boats sank. Yet, the 148th edition was thrill-a-minute stuff with Olympic rower Sebastian Mayer's collapse at Barnes Bridge generally accepted as the reason for Cambridge's narrow defeat. "I went over my limits, whereas the others stayed within their limits. I couldn't have done any more. I can live with what I did," said Mayer, responding to criticism from the Cambridge coach Robin Williams.

World Championships

Seville, Sep 15-22
Crews are listed in order from bow to stroke, with the cox
signified by an asterisk.

Men

Single Sculls
1 Marcel Hacker GER   6:36.33
2 Iztok Cop SLO   6:39.00
3 Olaf Tufte NOR   6:39.45

Double Sculls
1 Haller/Peto HUN   6:05.74
2 Abbagnale/Berra ITA   6:06.93
3 Willms/Hajek GER   6:07.77
6 Wells/Lawson GBR   6:16.54

Quad Sculls
1 Germany   5:39.57
Bertram/Volkert/Geisler/Sens
2 Poland   5:40.43
Bronikowski/Kolbowicz/Kruszkowski/Korol
3 Italy   5:43.62
Righetti/Ragazzi/Galtarossa/Raineri

Coxless Pairs
1 Cracknell/Pinsent GBR   6:14.27
2 Di Clemente/Cech RSA   6:15.60
3 S Skelin/N Skelin CRO   6:15.97

Coxed Pairs
1 Germany   6:47.93
Krisch/Werner/Müller-Gattermann*
2 USA   6:50.60
Beery/Schmunk/Manion*
3 Australia   6:53.77
Laurich/Jahrling/Toon*

Coxless Four
1 Germany   5:41.35
Thormann/Dienstbach/Stüer/Heidicker
2 Great Britain   5:41.60
Williams/West/Garbett/Dunn
3 Italy   5:44.12
N Mornati/Leonardo/Carboncini/C Mornati

Coxed Four
1 Great Britain   6:06.70
Stallard/Trapmore/Fieldhouse/West/Cormack*
2 Germany   6:08.88
Landgraf/Zobelt/Broer/Rogge/Lier*
3 Croatia   6:10.54
Boraska/Martinov/Jukic/Saraga/Travas*

Eight
1 Canada   5:26.92
Swick/Light/Rutledge/Hamilton/Stankevicius/
Hoskins/Creek/Powell/Price*
2 Germany   5:28.16
Schulte/Englemann/Diessner/Koltzk/Doberschütz/
Schnabel/Siemes/Ruhe/Thiede*
3 USA   5:29.27
Torgerson/Klugh/ Hansen/Moser/Wherley/Müller/
Volpenheim/Watling/Cipollone*
6 Great Britain   5:35.78
Partridge/Ouseley/Devlin/Hodge/Burch/
Simmons/Bourne-Taylor/Van Maltzahn/Rudge*

Lightweight Single Sculls
1 Sam Lynch IRL   6:49.86
2 Stefano Basalini ITA   6:51.29
3 Steve Tucker USA   6:52.94

Lightweight Double Sculls
1 Luini/Pettinari ITA   6:10.80
2 Kucharski/Sycz POL   6:13.50
3 Rasmussen/Hansen DEN   6:14.82
Male/Kay GBR 3rd in B Final
Coakley/Byrne IRL 2nd in C Final

Lightweight Quad Sculls
1 Italy   5:51.89
Federici/Gilardoni/Moncada/Mannucci
2 Spain   5:54.23
Martin/Aguirre/Loriente/Dominguez
3 Netherlands   5:54.59
Blankert/De Loos/Van Der Linde/Bosma
4 Great Britain   5:55.03
Wakefield/Mackworth-Praed/Lee/Beechy

Lightweight Coxless Pair
1 Yantani/Cerda CHI   6:29.97
2 Gaddi/Sancassini ITA   6:31.94
3 Kittoe/English GBR   6:34.40

Lightweight Coxless Four
1 Denmark   5:47.21
Kristensen/Ebert/Moelvig/Ebbesen
2 Italy   5:49.41
Bertini/Amarante/Amitrano/Atunes
3 Canada   5:50.55
Vandor/Brambell/Mandick/Hassett
Great Britain 6th in B Final
Webb/Hunter/Hennessy/Warnock

Lightweight Eight
1 Italy   5:35.05
Scala/Lodigiani/Del Gaudio/Moriconi/Paniccia/
Grande/Fraquelli/Pasqualini/Di Palma*
2 Germany   5:36.51
Raeder/Achtruth/Fauck/Drews/Puetz/
Hobein/Johannesmeier/Dahlke/Derderding*
3 USA   5:38.21
Blackmore/Feins/Cashman/Liverman/Miller/
Douglas/Paradiso/Smith/McManus*
5 Great Britain   5:44.60
Bates/Ireland/Strange/Jones/Johnstone/
Haining/Miles/West/Haddow*

Women

Single Sculls
1 Rumyana Neykova BUL   7:07.71
2 Ekaterina Karsten BLR   7:11.74
3 Katrin Stomporowski GER   7:12.07
Elise Laverick GBR 1st in B Final

Double Sculls
1 G & C Evers-Swindell NZL   6:38.78
2 Merk/Fedotova RUS   6:41.06
3 Sancassini/Bascelli ITA   6:41.65
4 Houghton/Flood GBR   6:44.27

Quad Sculls
1 Germany   6:12.95
  Waleska/Scholz/Lutze/El Qalqili-Kowalski
2 Denmark   6:16.84
  Jespersen/Lauritzen/Pedersen/Nielsen
3 Belarus   6:18.12
  Zakharevskaya/Berazniova/Karsten/Mariya
5 Great Britain   6:20.15
  Mowbray/Winckless/Grainger/Romero

Coxless Pairs
1 Andrunache/Susanu ROM 6:53.80
2 Cook/Clark CAN   6:57.08
3 Bichyk/Helakh BLR   6:59.21
Gough/Carslake GBR 1st in C Final

Coxless Four
1 Australia   6:26.11
  Larsen/Winter/Sattin/Roberts
2 Canada   6:28.32
  MacLeod/De Jong/Marquardt/Van Roessel
3 China   6:31.28
  Zhao/Yang/Cong/Feng

Eight
1 USA   6:04.25
  Johnson/Pierce/Davies/Urtasun/Martern/
  Cox/Mickelson/MacKenzie/Whipple*
2 Australia   6:05.10
  Winter/Lutz/Wilson/Robinson/Taylor/
  Sattin/Roberts/Larsen/Bilson*
3 Germany   6:05.19
  Pyritz/Tucholke/Holthaus/Pyritz/Zimmermann/
  Schmidt/Wech/Günther/Ruppel*

Lightweight Single Sculls
1 Viktoriya Dimitrova BUL 7:28.89
2 Lisa Marie Schlenker USA 7:30.56
3 M-T Mas de Xaxars ESP 7:31.21
Kirsten McClelland-Brooks GBR 5th in B Final

Lighweight Double Sculls
1 Causby/Halliday AUS 6:52.84
2 Radünzel/Blasberg GER 6:53.56
3 Casey/Langlands GBR 6:55.28

Lightweight Quad Sculls
1 Australia   6:29.55
  Van Der Walle/Houston/Bennett/Every
2 Netherlands   6:30.01
  Pikkemaat/Ter Beek/Van Os/Klinkers
3 USA   6:32.48
  Finke/Cromwell/Borkhuis/Campanella
5 Great Britain   6:39.39
  Eastman/Rooks/Nitsch/Birch

Lightweight Coxless Pairs
1 Ashcroft/Barron GBR 7:29.91
2 Rodriguez/Godoy CHI 7:41.21
3 Almuedo/Casanueva ESP 7:47.26
4 boats only

Seville Medal Table

		G	S	B	Ttl
1	Germany	5	4	3	12
2	Italy	3	4	3	10
3	Great Britain	3	1	2	6
4	Australia	3	1	1	5
5	Bulgaria	2	-	-	2
6	USA	1	2	4	7
7	Canada	1	2	1	3
8	Denmark	1	1	1	3
9	China	1	1	-	2
10	Hungary	1	-	-	1
10	Ireland	1	-	-	1
10	New Zealand	1	-	-	1
10	Romania	1	-	-	1
14	Poland	-	2	-	2
15	Belarus	-	1	2	3
15	Spain	-	1	2	3
17	Netherlands	-	1	1	2
18	Russia	-	1	-	1
18	Slovenia	-	1	-	1
18	South Africa	-	1	-	1
21	Croatia	-	-	2	2
22	China	-	-	1	1
22	Norway	-	-	1	1

World Cup Series
Hazewinkel Regatta
June 14-16

Men
Single Sculls
1 Marcel Hacker   GER 6:48.11
2 Olaf Karl Tufte   NOR 6:51.53
3 Vaclav Chapula   CZE 6:51.61
Double Sculls
1 Haller/Petoe   HUN 6:18.03
2 Dolecek/Synek   CZE 6:20.29
3 Schmidt/Rohnert   GER 6:20.70
Quad Sculls
1 Ukraine   5:47.29
2 Poland   5:47.70
3 Italy   5:49.28
Coxless Pair
1 Cracknell/Pinsent GBR 6:28.97
2 Kirchoff/Landvoigt GER 6:30.40
3 Di Clemente/Cech RSA 6:30.73
Coxless Four
1 Great Britain 5:55.58
  West/Williams/Garbett/Dunn
2 Italy   5:55.83
3 Germany   5:57.60
Eight
1 Germany   5:33.04
2 Ronaia   5:33.28
3 Egypt   5:35.85

Lightweight Single Sculls

1	Michal Vabrousek	CZE	7:08.82
2	Zhu Zhi Fu	CHN	7:10.00
3	Ingo Sascha Euler	GER	7:11.68

Hugh Mackworth-Praed GBR 1st in B Final
Nick Wakefield GBR 2nd in B Final
Alasdair Stuart GBR 3rd in B Final

Lightweight Double Sculls

1	Luini/Pettinari	ITA	6:20.23
2	Ording/Brehmer	GER	6:22.28
3	Rasmussen/Quist	DEN	6:24.82

Lee/Beechey GBR 5th in B Final

Lightweight Coxless Pair

1	Kittoe/English	GBR	6:51.85
2	Hilckmann/Van Breda	NED	6:52.61
3	Westra/Van Eupen	NED	6:55.50
4	Ireland/Strange	GBR	6:56.04
6	Currie/Hunter	GBR	7:03.84

Lightweight Coxless Four

1	Denmark	5:57.17
2	Australia	5:58.22
3	Austria	6:00.57
5	Great Britain	6:03.52

Warnock/Hennessy/Webb/Hunter

Women

Single Sculls

1	Ekaterina Karsten	BLR	7:32.10
2	Miroslava Knapkova	CZE	7:34.60
3	Yulya Levina	RUS	7:36.60

Rebecca Romero GBR 2nd in B Final

Double Sculls

1	Houghton/Flood	GBR	6:57.51
2	Lutze/El Qalqili	GER	6:58.91
3	Kulifai/Barz	HUN	7:00.29

Quad Sculls

1	Ukraine	6:21.06
2	Germany	6:24.85
3	Great Britain	6:26.04

Laverick/Winckless/Grainger/Mowbray

Lightweight Single Sculls

1	Marit van Eupen	NED	7:54.26
2	Brooks McClelland	GBR	7:59.22
3	Daniela Nachazelova	CZE	8:02.48

Lightweight Double Sculls

1	Raduenzel/Blasberg	GER	7:03.06
2	Casey/Langlands	GBR	7:06.96
3	Elander/Daugaard	DEN	7:08.55

Lucerne Regatta

July 12-14

Men

Single Sculls

1	Marcel Hacker	GER	6:51.78
2	Olaf Karl Tufte	NOR	6:53.42
3	Iztop Cop	SLO	6:55.32

Double Sculls

1	Petoe/Haller	HUN	6:22.55
2	Dolecek/Synek	CZE	6:24.42
3	Willms/Hajek	GER	6:27.62

Quad Sculls

1	Italy	5:44.89
1	Ukraine	5:44.89
3	Poland	5:46.95

Coxless Pair

1	Ginn/Tompkins	AUS	6:30.02
2	Cracknell/Pinsent	GBR	6:33.36
3	Skelin/Skelin	CRO	6:33.44

Coxless Four

1	Germany	5:59.46
2	Italy	6:02.41
3	Slovenia	6:03.88
6	Great Britain	6:10.44

Devlin/Hodge/Burch/Simmons

Eight

1	USA	5:28.68
2	Germany	5:29.80
3	Canada	5:30.61

Lightweight Single Sculls

1	Sam Lynch	IRL	7:00.24
2	Tamas Varga	HUN	7:01.66
3	Daisaku Takeda	JPN	7:02.22

Lightweight Double Sculls

1	Luini/Pettinari	ITA	6:20.95
2	Ording/Brehmer	GER	6:22.53
3	Chevel/Moiseyev	RUS	6:25.61
5	Male/Kay	GBR	6:28.59

Lightweight Quad Sculls

1	Spain	5:58.10
2	Great Britain	5:58.77

Wakefield/Mackworth-Praed/Lee/Beechey

3	Netherlands	5:59.00

Lightweight Coxless Pair

1	Towey/O'Connor	IRL	6:33.82
2	Gaddi/Sancassani	ITA	6:35.29
3	Cerda/Yantani	CHI	6:36.34
5	Kittoe/English	GBR	6:41.81

Lightweight Coxless Four

1	Canada	5:55.51
2	Italy	5:57.42
3	Austria	5:57.48
6	Great Britain	6:03.48

Warnock/Hennessy/Webb/Hunter

Women

Single Sculls

1	Roumania Neykova	BUL	7:26.20
2	Katrin Stomporowski	GER	7:29.99
3	Miroslava Knapkova	CZE	7:32.37

Guin Batten GBR 3rd in B Final
Rebecca Romero GBR 5th in B Final

Double Sculls

1	Flood/Houghton	GBR	7:05.64
2	Paplavskaya/Sakickiene	LTU	7:06.73
3	Schmude/Huth	GER	7:08.43

Quadruple Sculls

1	Ukraine	6:14.03
2	Germany	6:15.24
3	USA	6:20.60
5	Great Britain	6:24.55

Laverick/Winckless/Grainger/Mowbray

Coxless Pair

1	Andrunache/Susanu	ROM	7:12.96
2	Geyser/Orsmond	RSA	7:18.56
3	Helakh/Bichyk	BLR	7:18.94

Carslake/Gough GBR 2nd in B Final

Eight

1	Germany	6:06.99
2	Romania	6;10.28
3	Australia	6:14.38

Lightweight Single Sculls
1 Kirsten Maclelland-Brooks GBR 7:59.22
2 Mirna Rajle CRO 7:47.87
3 Monica Stan ROM 7:50.84
Lightweight Double Sculls
1 Raduenzel/Blasberg GER 6:59.24
2 Casey/Langlands GBR 7:02.32
3 Van Eupen/Poot NED 7:04.12
Boyle/Jennings IRL 4th in B Final
Lightweight Quad Sculls
1 Great Britain 6:40.36
 Rooks/Eastman/Nitsch/Birch
2 Netherlands 6:42.13
3 Denmark 6:45.26
Only three boats

Munich Regatta
Aug 2-4
Men
Single Sculls
1 Marcel Hacker GER 6:46.66
2 Olaf Karl Tufte NOR 6:48.27
3 Iztop Cop SLO 6:50.45
Simon Cottle GBR 5th in B Final
Double Sculls
1 Dolecek/Synek CZE 6:15.74
2 Haller/Petoe HUN 6:15.79
3 Jones/Hardcastle AUS 6:18.16
Wells/Lawson GBR 1st in B Final
Quad Sculls
1 Ukraine 5:53.43
2 Belarus 5:54.12
3 Germany 5:54.41
Coxless Pair
1 Skelin/Skelin CRO 6:30.57
2 Michalek/Imre CZE 6:31.68
3 Stojic/Visacki YUG 6:35.68
Fieldhouse/Marrtin GBR 3rd in B Final
Coxless Four
1 Germany 5:52.43
2 Great Britain 5:53.81
 West/Williams/Garbett/Dunn
3 Slovenia 5:56.79
Eight
1 Germany 5:35.37
2 Australia 5:38.21
3 Russia 5:41.84
6 Great Britain 5:45.90
 Devlin/Hodge/Partridge/Simmons/Burch/Ouseley/
 Bourne-Taylor/Von Maltzahn/Rudge*
Lightweight Single Sculls
1 Sam Lynch IRL 6:56.65
2 MIchal Vabrousek CZE 6:57.97
3 Ingo Sascha Euler GER 7:00.79
Lightweight Double Sculls
1 Ording/Brehmer GER 6:19.30
2 Stewart/Karrasch AUS 6:21.15
3 Rasmussen/Hansen DEN 6:21.85
5 Male/Kay GBR 6:25.07
Lightweight Coxless Four
1 Denmark 5:58.15
2 Australia 5:59.84
3 Austria 6:01.88
Great Britain 2nd in B Final
Webb/Hunter/Hennessy/Warnock

Women
Single Sculls
1 Katrin Stomporowski GER 7:27.16
2 Miroslava Knapova CZE 7:30.67
3 Yulya Leviina RUS 7:31.18
6 Guin Batten GBR 7:42.93
Elise Laverick GBR 5th in B Final
Double Sculls
1 Evers-Swindell/Evers-Swindell NZL 6:55.91
2 Poplavskaya/Sackickiene RUS 6:57.48
3 Merk/Fedotova RUS 6:57.81
4 Houghton/Flood GBR 6:58.25
Quad Sculls
1 Ukraine 6:26.93
2 Australia 6:29.54
3 Great Britain 6:29.75
 Mowbray/Winckless/Grainger/Romero
Coxless Pair
1 Andrunache/Susanu ROM 7:07.84
2 Bichyk/Helakh BLR 7:10.39
3 Cook/Clark CAN 7:13.41
Eight
1 Germany 6:06.99
2 Romania 6:10.28
3 Australia 6:14.38
Lightweight Single Sculls
1 Daniele Nachazelova CZE 7:42.00
2 Kirsten van der Kolk NED 7:43.71
3 Mirna Rajle CRO 7:45.64
Lightweight Double Sculls
1 Causby/Halliday AUS 6:57.63
2 Van Eupen/Poot NED 6:59.78
3 Casey/Langlands GBR 7:02.22
Lightweight Quad Sculls
1 Australia 6:36.26
2 Netherlands 6:38.31
3 Denmark 6:41.12
4 Great Britain 6:42.41
 Rooks/Hall/Nitsch/Birch
Lightweight Coxless Pair
1 Ashcroft/Barron GBR 7:31.41
2 Petoe Saarine/Petoe HUN 7:44.75
3 Almuedo/Casanueva ESP 7:44.91
Four entries only
Lightweight Single Sculls
1 Kirsten McClelland-Brooks GBR 7:47.72
2 Mirna Rajle CRO 7:47.87
3 Monica Stan ROM 7:50.84
Lightweight Double Sculls
1 Raduenzel/Blasberg GER 6:59.24
2 Casey/Langlands GBR 7:02.32
3 Van Eupen/Poot NED 7:04.12
Lightweight Quad Sculls
1 Great Britain 6:40.36
Rooks/Eastman/Nitsch/Birch
2 Netherlands 6:42.13
3 Denmark 6:45.26
3 entries only

World Cup Final Standings

1. Germany 209; 2 Great Britain 103; 3. Italy 74;
4. Czech Rep 69; 5 Australia 68; 6. Ukraine 57;
7. Romania 55; 8. Belarus 53; 9. Denmark 51;
9. France 51

University Boat Races
Putney to Mortlake, Mar 23

CAMBRIDGE BEAT OXFORD
Distance: ⅔ length
Times (Cambridge first)
Mile: 3:38 - 3:37
Hammersmith Bridge: 6:23.5 - 6:23
Chiswick Steps: 10:12 - 10:11
Barnes Bridge 13:57.5 - 13:57
Finish: 16:54 - 16:56
Oxford: Robin Bourne-Taylor, Ben Burch
(President), Bas Dixon, Andrew Dunn, Gerritjan
Eggenkamp, Luke McGee, Dan Perkins, Matt Smith,
Pete Hackworth*
Cambridge: Sam Brooks, Rick Dunn, Lukas Hirst,
James Livingston, Sebastian Mayer, Tom Stallard
(President), Stu Welch, Josh West, Eleanor Griggs*

Reserve Race
Isis *(Oxford)* beat Goldie *(Cambridge)* by 2¼ lengths

Women's Race
Henley, Mar 24
Oxford bt Cambridge by 2 lengths (6:02)

Women's Henley
June 22-23
Single Sculls
Guin Batten (Thames) bt E Butler-Stoney (Wallingford)
4½ lengths; 6:16
Double Sculls
Loughborough bt Henley RC
1½ length; 5:44
Quad Sculls
University of London bt Upper Thames
4 lengths; 5:23
Coxless Pair
Osiris BC bt ULBC/Thames RC
2 lengths; 5:57
Coxed Four
Kingston bt Hereford
2½ lengths; 5:36
Coxless Four
Oxford Brookes University bt Kingston *rowed over*
Eight
Thames/Wallingford/Globe/Loughborough bt Tideway
3 lengths; 5:03
Lightweight Single Sculls
N Ashcroft (UT) bt L Hampton (NCRA)
2 lengths; 6:34
Lightweight Double Sculls
Thames/MAA bt NCRA
½ length; 5:45
Lightweight Quad Sculls
Marlow/TSS/UTRC/NCRA bt Lagan Scullers Belfast
2 lengths; 5:21
Lightweight Coxless Pair
Nottingham University bt Thames RC
1½ lengths; 6:09
Lightweight Coxless Four
Thames Tradesmen bt Norwich
4 lengths; 5:44

Henley Regatta
July 3-7
All events for men, except where stated
TEMPLE CUP - Eights
Harvard University (USA) bt Oxford Brookes University
Distance: ¾ Length; Time: 7:02
WYFOLD CUP - Coxless Fours
Aberdeen BC bt London Rowing Club
5 Lengths; 7:38
PRINCESS ELIZABETH CUP - Eights
Abingdon School bt St Paul's School
1¾ lengths; 7:00
STEWARDS' CUP - Coxless Fours
Danmarks Rocenter DEN bt Gorge Rowing Centre CAN
1¼ lengths; 7:01
DOUBLE SCULLS CUP
Vieilledent/Hardy FRA bt Haller/Petoe HUN
4 lengths; 7:32
BRITANNIA CUP - Coxed Fours
Harvard University B bt Harvard University A
1¾ lengths. 7:30
VISITORS' CUP - Coxless Fours
Oxford Brookes/Imperial College bt Cambridge University
2½ lengths; 7:20
DIAMOND SCULL - Single Sculls
Pete Wells bt Matthew Langridge
easily; 8:30
GRAND CHALLENGE CUP - Eights
Victoria/Victoria Uni CAN bt Dortmund/Munster GER
½ length; 6:20
SILVER GOBLETS & NICKALLS CUP - Coxless Pairs
Cracknell/Pinsent bt Clemente/Cech RSA
½ length; 7:35
PRINCESS ROYAL CUP - Single Sculls, women
Rumyana Neykova BUL bt Katrin R-Stomporowski GER
easily; 9:03
FAWLEY CUP - Coxless Fours
Leander/Evesham bt Windsor Boys' School
½ length; 7:32
PRINCE PHILIP CUP - Coxed Fours
Moseley/Oxford Brookes bt Cambridge University
2½ lengths; 7:20
THAMES CHALLENGE CUP - Eights
Leander bt Notts CRC
3 lengths; 6:50
QUEEN MOTHER CHALLENGE CUP - Coxless Fours
Leander/University of London bt Leander/Moseley
sculled over
MEN'S QUADRUPLE SCULLS
Tideway Scullers bt Leander
1¾ ; 7:26
WOMEN'S QUADRUPLE SCULLS
Marlow/Leander bt Leander/Tideway
easily; 8:07
REMENHAM CHALLENGE CUP - Women's Eights
Oxford Brookes bt Tideway Scullers
2¾ ; 7:44
THE LADIES' CHALLENGE CUP - Eights
Harvard University USA bt Molesey BC
2¾ ; 6:30

Rugby League

When British Olympic teams go to Australia, they allow six weeks acclimatisation. When England cricket teams tour down under, there's always two or three weeks before the first Test. When British Rugby League teams visit Australia, they have six days. For 24 hours on a plane, 11 time zones and 11,000 miles, somebody should have told them it wasn't enough, and pointed to the scoreline of the first Ashes Test a years earlier when the visiting Australians had suffered a shock defeat by adopting a similar strategy. The amnesiac officials were soon appraised, the British team losing by a record score of 64-10 to a rampant Australian team. Furthermore, as one reporter curtly stated, the scoreline did not flatter the winners either.

That was about as low as the year went, and arguably it couldn't have gone much lower. The Australian journey was, presumably, about money, for Rugby League is usually short of a few bob. The price was credibility, and it was a high price to pay, for in a sport where there are only three viable nations, to discount one of them doesn't leave a lot.

Fortunately, the three-Test tour of the UK by New Zealand in the autumn offered the opportunity for some serious face-saving. The British team did not have to fly anywhere; most of them only had to travel a few miles; and the time zone stayed resolutely the same. Even so, they still lost the First Test 30-16 to a New Zealand team which had (very sensibly) given itself three weeks flight recovery time.

The Second Test could have handed the Kiwis the series. "We couldn't afford to lose, could we?," said Andy Farrell, captaining Britain for a record 20th time. That they did not lose was in no small part due to the efforts of Farrell, who made 16 tackles without missing one, ran the ball 28 times, and kicked the 76th minute goal which brought the scores level at 14-all. They still made Paul Sculthorpe man-of-the-match, but even the British coach David Waite, who shouldn't be seen to show favours, thought it was the wrong call.

The draw meant the Lions couldn't win the series, but they could still lose it. The final Test at the McAlpine Stadium was a rare moment of joy for the national side as, for the first time in nine meetings over nine long years, they defeated a New Zealand Test team. Even when the Lions had taken their lead to 16-6 with less than 15 minutes left, the Kiwis, orchestrated by the man-of-the-series Stacey Jones, still hammered at the Lions defence, and though one try was conceded the Lions hung on.

In club competitions, Bradford Bulls beat Newcastle to become world club champions, but couldn't match St Helens in the Grand Final while Wigan, the third best team in the land, won the Challenge Cup.

Internationals

GB in Australia
One-off Test
Aussie Stadium, Sydney, July 12
AUSTRALIA 64   **GREAT BRITAIN 10**
Tries: Hill 2, Lockyer 2   Pratt, Sinfield
McKenna, Mason, Tallis
Timmins, Buderus
Tuqiri, Tahu
Goals: Johns 10   Sculthorpe
Australia: Lockyer; Tuqiri, Timmins, McKenna, Tahu;
Barrett, Johns*; Webcke, Buderus, Ryles, Tallis,
Simpson, Hill
Subs: Stevens, Menzies, Tate, Mason
Great Britain: Radlinski; Johnson, Wellens, Senior,
Pratt; Sculthorpe, Sheridan; O'Connor, Cunningham,
McDermott, Peacock, Fielden, Farrell*
Subs: Gleeson, Newton, Joynt, Sinfield
Attendance: 31,844
Referee: Russell Smith

New Zealand in GB
First Test
Ewood Park, Blackburn, Nov 9
GREAT BRITAIN (10) 16   **NEW ZEALAND (6) 30**
Tries: Pryce, Peacock   Jones, Vagana 2
Faa'fili 3
Goals: Farrell 4   Swain 3
Great Britain: Connolly, Pryce, Gleeson, Senior, Pratt,
Sinfield, Deacon, Fielden, Cunningham, McDermott,
Farrell*, Morley, Forshaw
Subs: Gilmour, Joynt, Anderson, Peacock
New Zealand: Paul, Faa'fili, Vagana, Toopi, Meli,
Hohaia, Jones*, Rauhihi, Swain, Seu Seu, Lauiti'iti,
Kearney, Guttenbeil
Subs: Betham, Solomona, Swann, Puletua
Attendance: 16,654
Referee: Steve Clark (Australia)

Second Test
McAlpine Stadium, Huddersfield, Nov 16
GREAT BRITAIN (6) 14   **NEW ZEALAND (10) 14**
Tries: Pryce, Gleeson   Meli, Kearney
Wiki
Goals: Farrell 3   Swain
Great Britain: Connolly, Pryce, Gleeson, Senior,
Gilmour, Sculthorpe, Deacon, O'Connor, Lowes, Fielden,
Peacock, Farrell*, Forshaw
Subs: Sinfield, Horne, Anderson, Orr
New Zealand: R Paul, Faa'fili, Vagana, Toopi, Meli,
Hohaia, Jones*, Seu Seu, Swain, Rauhihi, Wiki, Kearney,
Guttenbeil.
Subs: Puletua, Lauiti'iti, Betham, Swann
Referee: Steve Clark (Australia)

Third Test
JJB Stadium, Wigan, Nov 23
GREAT BRITAIN (8) 16   **NEW ZEALAND (0) 10**
Tries: Senior, Gleeson   Jones, Lauiti'iti
Sculthorpe
Goals: Farrell 2   Jones
Great Britain: Connolly; Pryce, Gleeson, Senior,
Gilmour; Sculthorpe, Deacon; Fielden, Lowes,
McDermott, Morley, Farrell*, Forshaw
Subs: Orr, Peacock, Anderson, Horne
New Zealand: Vaealiki; Fa'afili, Vagana, Hoppe, Meli;
Hohaia, Jones*; Seu Seu, Swain, Rauhihi, Wiki,
Guttenbeil, Betham
Subs: Solomona, Lauiti'iti, Puletua, Swann
Attendance: 22,247
Referee: Steve Clark (Australia)

Other NZ Tour Matches
The Boulevard, Hull, Oct 22
HULL 11   **NEW ZEALAND 28**

Knowsley Road, Oct 25
ST HELENS 26   **NEW ZEALAND 38**

Griffin Park, Brentford, Oct 30
ENGLAND A 12   **NEW ZEALAND 34**

Millennium Stadium, Nov 2
WALES 22   **NEW ZEALAND 50**

Other Internationals
Glen Mills, USA, Mar 16
USA 24   **IRELAND 22**

Glen Mills, USA, June 1
USA 26   **JAPAN 10**

Moscow, Sep 13
RUSSIA 54   **USA 10**

Wellington, Oct 12
NEW ZEALAND 24   **AUSTRALIA 34**

Churchill Park, Lautoka, Nov 9
FIJI 8   **ENGLAND A 44**

Suva, Nov 13
FIJI 18   **ENGLAND A 12**

Perpignan, France, Nov 30
FRANCE 10   **NEW ZEALAND 36**

British Results

Super League

		P	W	D	L	F	A	Pts
1	St Helens	28	23	0	5	927	522	46
2	Bradford	28	23	0	5	910	519	46
3	Wigan	28	19	1	8	817	475	39
4	Leeds	28	17	0	11	865	700	34
5	Hull FC	28	16	0	12	742	674	32
6	Castleford	28	14	2	12	736	615	30
7	Widnes	28	14	1	13	590	716	29
8	London	28	13	1	14	661	635	27
9	Halifax	28	8	0	20	558	856	16
10	Warrington	28	7	0	21	483	878	14
11	Wakefield	28	5	2	21	566	899	12
12	Salford	28	5	1	22	490	856	11

Play-offs
Week 1
Sep 27
Leeds 36   Hull 22
Sep 28
Wigan 26   Castleford 14
Hull and Castleford eliminated, winners play off to meet the loser of the 1-2 match

Week 2
Oct 4
Wigan 41   Leeds 18
Oct 5
St Helens 26   Bradford 28
Bradford go directly to the Grand Final

Week 3
Oct 11
St Helens 24   Wigan 8

Grand Final
Old Trafford, Oct 19
Bradford Bulls (8) 18   St Helens (12) 19
Tries: Naylor, Paul,   Bennett, Long, Gleeson
Withers
PG: Deacon 3   Long 3
DG: Long
Bradford: Withers, Vaikona, Naylor, Costin, Vainikolo, Paul, Deacon, Vagana, Lowes, Fielden, Gartner, Peacock, Forshaw
Subs: McDermott, Pryce, Anderson, Gilmour
St Helens: Wellens, Stewart, Gleeson, Newlove, Albert, Sculthorpe, Long, Britt, Cunningham, Ward, Jonkers, Bennett, Joynt
Subs: Stankevitch, Higham, Shiels, Hoppe.
Attendance: 61,138
Referee: Russell Smith (Castleford)

Challenge Cup Final
Millennium Stadium, Cardiff, April 27
St Helens 12   Wigan 21
Tries: Albert, Gleeson   Dallas, Lam, Connolly
Sculthorpe
Goals: Farrell 4
Drop goal: Lam
St Helens: Wellens, Stewart, Newlove, Gleeson, Albert, Martyn, Long, Britt, Cunningham, Shiels, Joynt, Jonkers, Sculthorpe *Subs:* Higham, Stankevitch, Hoppe, Ward
Bradford: Radlinski, Johnson, Connolly, Ainscough, Dallas, O'Neill, Lam, O'Connor, Newton, C. Smith, Cassidy, Furner, Farrell.
Subs Carney, Hodgson, M. Smith, Bibey
Attendance: 62,140
Referee: Stuart Cummings (Widnes)

Northern Ford Premiership

	P	W	D	L	PF	PA	Pts
Huddersfield	27	26	1	0	1156	256	53
Leigh	27	21	1	5	1021	426	43
Rochdale	27	19	1	7	809	582	39
Hull KR	27	18	1	8	715	468	37
Featherstone	27	18	1	8	836	604	37
Doncaster	27	16	1	10	741	603	33
Batley	27	16	1	10	658	666	33
Whitehaven	27	15	1	11	647	600	31
Oldham	27	13	3	11	748	553	29
Dewsbury	27	14	1	12	723	616	29
Workington	27	13	0	14	677	677	26
Sheffield	27	13	0	14	597	648	26
Barrow	27	12	1	14	707	670	25
Keighley	27	7	0	20	488	906	14
Swinton	27	6	1	20	473	918	13
Chorley Lynx	27	5	0	22	477	994	10
Hunslet	27	3	1	23	438	954	7
Gateshead	27	0	1	26	338	1108	1

Play-offs
Elimination Semi-finals
Sep 15
Hull KR 11   Oldham 19
Featherstone 42   Whitehaven 14
Doncaster 14   Batley 27
Preliminary Semi-finals
Sep 22
Featherstone 30   Batley 32
Rochdale 6   Oldham 20
Grand Final Play-off
Sep 22
Huddersfield 36   Leigh 10
Minor Semi-final
Sep 29
Batley 26   Oldham 16
Major Semi-final
Oct 7
Leigh 35   Batley 28

Grand Final
Halton Stadium, Oct 12
Huddersfield 38   Leigh 16

Australian League

NRL Premiership

NZ Warriors	24	17	0	7	688	454	38
Newcastle Knights	24	17	0	7	724	498	38
Brisbane Broncos	24	16	1	7	672	425	37
Sydney C Roosters	24	15	1	8	621	405	35
Cronulla Sharks	24	15	0	9	653	597	34
Parramatta Eels	24	10	2	12	531	440	26
St George-Illawarra	24	9	3	12	632	546	25
Canberra Raiders	24	10	1	13	471	641	25
Northern Eagles	24	10	0	14	503	740	24
Melbourne Storm	24	9	1	14	556	586	23
North Queensland	24	8	0	16	496	803	20
Penrith Panthers	24	7	0	17	546	654	18
West Tigers	24	7	0	17	498	642	18
South Sydney	24	5	0	19	385	817	12
Canterbury Bulldogs*	24	20	1	3	707	435	8

* Canterbury had 34 points earned prior to round 24 deducted following a salary cap breach

Play-offs

First Qualifying Final (4th v 5th)
Sydney Roosters 32   Cronulla Sharks 20
Second Qualifying Final (3rd v 6th)
Brisbane Broncos 24   Parramatta Eels 14
Third Qualifying Final (2nd v 7th)
Newcastle Knights 22   St Georges-Illawarra 26
Fourth Qualifying Final (1st v 8th)
NZ Warriors 36   Canberra Raiders 20
The two lowest -ranked losing teams from the qualifying finals are eliminated; the two highest ranked winning teams go directly to the preliminary finals

Semi-finals
St Georges-Illawarra 24   Cronulla Sharks 40
Sydney Roosters 38   Newcastle 12
The two losing semi-final teams are eliminated

First Preliminary Final
Brisbane Broncos 12   Sydney Roosters 16
Second Preliminary Final
NZ Warriors 16   Cronulla Sharks 10

Grand Final

Telstra Stadium, Sydney, Oct 6
Sydney Roosters 30   NZ Warriors 8
Tries: Hegarty   *Jones*
Wing, Fitzgibbon
Flannery, Fletcher
Goals: Fitzgibbon 5   *Cleary 2*
Attendance: 80,130

"We don't have to watch the Australians play, we've done our homework before we get here. We are very confident that we have prepared properly for the challenge, and we can rise to it. If I didn't think we could win I wouldn't be here"

David Waite, GB coach, prior to the Test against Australia which Britain lost by a record 64-10 score.

"It was on the flight that I began to question whether I was making the right decision. By the time I arrived in Sydney I knew it wasn't right, and it was then I decided I wanted to come home. I got off the plane, immediately made my decision to come back, and booked myself on the next available flight to England"

Craig Poucher, who didn't join the London Broncos at their Australian training camp.

World Club Challenge

McAlpine Stadium, Huddersfield, Feb 1
Bradford Bulls (26) 41   Newcastle Knights (14) 26
Tries: Paul 2, Withers 2   *Johns 2, Smith*
Gartner, Vainikolo   *Gidley, Buderus*
Goals: Deacon 8   *Johns 3*
DG: Deacon
Bradford: Withers, Vaikona, Naylor, Gilmour, Vainikolo, R Paul*, Deacon, McDermott, Lowes, Vagana, Peacock, Gartner, Forshaw *Subs:* Anderson, Fielden, Pryce, Costin
Newcastle: O'Davis, Gidley, Gidley, Hughes, Smith, Rudder, Johns*, Perry, Buderus, Parsons, Simpson, Abraham, Peden *Subs:* Jobson, Newton, Morris, O'Brien
Attendance: 21,113
Referee: Stuart Cummings (Widnes)

Rugby Union

I t was only to be expected that in the Six Nations decider between France and England in Paris in March, one team played expansive, imaginative rugby, while the other adopted an aggressive defensive strategy and tackled like demons. What what less expected was the showboaters were the English and the demons were the French.

The demons won by focusing on the base of the English scrum, turning over English ball, and hassling Jonny Wilkinson, who for the rest of the season was regarded as the lynch-pin of the English game, but not that day. It was, unbelievably, the seventh time in seven seasons that England had failed to win the Grand Slam by losing a single match. Since the Grand Slam win in 1995, three times in succession (1996-1998) England had lost to France; were beaten by Wales at Wembley in 1999; Scotland at Murrayfield in 2000; and Ireland at Lansdowne Road in 2001. Those last three games were the final matches in the respective seasons.

For Woodward, who at this point must have felt a slight numbing, it was the fourth straight championship in which his England team had started favourite and had lost the crucial match. And it goes without saying that the losses were all away from home; at fortress Twickenham, England do not lose any more.

So it was in the autumn, when New Zealand, Australia and South Africa made their regular incursions into the northern hemisphere. England has sent a second team to Argentina in the summer, always a risky thing to do, but the makeweights had raised their game and narrowly won the solitary Test. It all contributed to the morale of the England camp.

Saturday, November 9th though, wasn't just about England. It turned out to be a seminal day in northern hemisphere rugby. Pride of place must go the Irish, who defeated Australia for the first time in 23 years, with a display of intense and passionate rugby in a Lansdowne Road mudbath. Ireland were inspired by Brian O'Driscoll and bolstered by the immaculate kicking of Ronan O'Gara, whose six penalties secured the win.

At Twickenham, on the same afternoon, England took on about half the might of New Zealand, in a classic encounter. Out-muscled by the English pack in the first half, the New Zealanders had slumped to a 31-14 deficit with two quick English tries at the beginning of the second. The All Black revival largely concerned Jonah Lomu, whose career has been stop-start since his awesome international arrival in 1995. Lomu scored twice to set up a dramatic finale, and with the scores at 31-28 in the final minute and All Black Ben Blair haring for the line a try seemed certain. Ben Cohen's last-gasp tackle saved England's day. "I wouldn't have played for England again if I'd missed that," said Cohen.

The third match that afternoon was in Marseille and had few epic qualities, the French easily better than a South African side, which like New Zealand, was short of senior players, but unlike the All Blacks, was not able to mask the fact. It made it, though, three victories for the north over the south on an extraordinary day.

A week later, England defeated Australia, too, in another fabulous match that went to the wire. South Africa followed, but that was much less edifying. In a crudely physical game, the South Africans targeted the English halfbacks, in particular, and were very fortunate to have just the one player removed from the field of play. The England players kept their nerve and ran out 53-3 winners, which was all the South Africans deserved.

Scotland generally struggled throughout the year, finishing down the pack in the Six Nations, then losing a summer international against Canada. Their finest hour came against South Africa at Murrayfield in November, when they scored a shock win. But the perspective changed slightly after Twickenham.

The Welsh had a dreadful Six Nations, England put 50 points past them and they were reliant only on the Italians to give them any sense of self-respect. The coach, Graham Henry resigned halfway through the championship, under fire from all quarters of Welsh rugby. Had the dour New Zealander just smiled occasionally, he would have won a few friends. As it was, he left with none.

"It is safe to say that if Woodward had been in charge of one of the southern hemisphere sides and had failed four years in a row in the Tri-Nations, he would no longer be in a job"
Will Carling.

"I will never win an Oscar now but even if I did I would swap it for one sip of champagne from the Heineken Cup"
Richard Harris, late Munster fan.

"There are two types of rugby internationals, piano players and piano shifters; Willie [John McBride] and I were piano shifters..."
Colin 'Pinetree' Meads, who played for the All Blacks 133 times between 1957 and 1971.

"I find it sad to see Welsh rugby in such decline because in the Sixties and Seventies they were real tough buggers; a pack of coal-miners who emerged from under the ground for a bit of sport in the fresh air"
Colin Meads, on Wales.

"They also go through all these rigmaroles, warm-ups and warm-downs; before a match, I liked to sit in the dressing room and sulk. The only warm-up I ever did was the Haka"
Colin Meads, on modern methods.

Six Nations

Murrayfield, Feb 2
SCOTLAND (3) 3   **ENGLAND (12) 29**
Tries: Robinson 3, Tindall,
       Cohen
Cons: Wilkinson 2, Hodgson
Pen: Hodge   Wilkinson
Scotland: Metcalfe; Laney, McLaren, Townsend,
Paterson; Hodge, Redpath; Smith (Graham 63), Bulloch,
Stewart, Murray, Grimes, White, Pountney*, Taylor
England: Robinson; Healey, Greenwood,
Tindall (Balshaw 73), Cohen; Wilkinson (Hodgson 84),
Bracken (Duncombe 41); Rowntree, Thompson, White
(Leonard 76), Johnson*, Kay (Grewcock 69), Hill, Back,
Worsley
Referee: *S Walsh NZL*
Attendance: *67,500*

Stade de France, Feb 2
FRANCE (19) 33   **ITALY (12) 12**
Try: Traille, Betsen
Conv: Merceron
Pens: Merceron 7   *Dominguez 4*
France: Jeanjean (Garbajosa 53); Rougerie, Marsh,
Traille, Bory; Merceron, Michalak (Albouy 80); Crenca,
Bru (Ibañez 59), De Villiers, Auradou (Pelous 59), Privat,
Betsen, Magne*, Hall
Italy: Vaccari (Mirco Bergamasco 72); Dallan, Martin, C
Stoica, Pedrazzi (Mirco Bergamasco 46-50); Dominguez,
Troncon; Lo Cicero (De Carli 27-30, 56), Moscardi,
Muraro (Moreno 56), Checchinato (Giacheri 80), Dellapè,
Mauro Bergamasco (Persico 80), Bortolami, Phillips
Referee: *A Lewis IRL*
Attendance: *65,000*

Lansdowne Road, Feb 3
IRELAND (24) 54   **WALES (3) 10**
Tries: Murphy 2   *S Jones*
O'Connell, Hickie
Gleeson, O'Gara
Cons: Humphreys 2   *S Jones*
O'Gara
Pens: Humphreys 6   *S Jones*
Ireland: Dempsey; Murphy, O'Driscoll, Maggs, Hickie
(Henderson 74); Humphreys (O'Gara 74), Stringer
(Easterby 76); Clohessy (Wallace 72), Sheahan (Byrne 72),
Hayes; Galwey* (Gleeson 72), O'Connell (Longwell 31),
Easterby, Wallace, Foley
Wales: Morgan; James, Robinson (Marinos 9), Harris,
Morgan; Jones, Howley (Peel 56); John (Jones 56),
McBryde (B Williams 69), Anthony, C Quinnell, Wyatt
(Gough 6), Budgett, M Williams, S Quinnell*
Referee: *P De Luca ARG*
Attendance: *48,800*

Millennium Stadium, Feb 16
WALES (19) 33   **FRANCE (24) 37**
Tries: C Quinnell, Budgett   *Marsh 2, Rougerie*
Morgan
Cons: S Jones 3   *Merceron 2*
Pens: S Jones 4   *Merceron 4*
DG: *Merceron*
Wales: Morgan; James, Shanklin, Marinos
(R Williams 70), Morgan; Jones, Howley; John (Jones
48), McBryde (B Williams 62), Anthony, C Quinnell
(Gough 67), Moore, Budgett, M Williams, S Quinnell*
France: Brusque; Rougerie, Traille, Marsh,
Garbajosa; Merceron, Mignoni; Crenca (Millhoud 80),
Ibanez* (Bruno 65), De Villiers, Privat (Pelous 59),
Brouzet, Betsen, S Hall (A Audebert 68), I Harinordoquy
Referee: *David McHugh IRL*
Attendance: *50,000*

Twickenham, Feb 16
ENGLAND (31) 45   **IRELAND (6) 11**
Tries: Greenwood 2   *O'Gara*
Wilkinson, Cohen
Worsley, Kay
Cons: Wilkinson 6
Pen: Wilkinson   *Humphreys 2*
England: Robinson; Healey (Balshaw 61),
Greenwood, Tindall, Cohen; Wilkinson
(Hodgson 78), Bracken (Duncombe 78);
Rowntree (Leonard 17), Thompson, Vickery,
Johnson* (Grewcock 61), Kay, Hill (Moody 61), Back,
Worsley
Ireland: Dempsey; Murphy (Henderson 9, O'Gara 40),
Maggs, O'Driscoll, Hickie; Humphreys, Stringer; Clohessy
(Wallace 79), Sheahan (Byrne 53), Hayes, Galwey*
(Longwell 58) O'Kelly, Miller (Easterby 56), Wallace,
Foley
Referee: *P Marshall AUS*

Stadio Flaminio, Feb 17
ITALY (9) 12   **SCOTLAND (9) 29**
Tries: *Townsend, Laney*
Cons;   *Laney 2;*
Pens: Dominguez 4   *Laney 5*
Italy: Vaccari (Martin 69); Pedrazzi, Mirco Bergamasco,
Stoica, Dallan; Dominguez (Pez 80), Troncon;
Pucciariello (Moreno 52), Moscardi*, De Carli (Lo Cicero
60), Dellape (Giacheri 63), Checchinato, Bortolami,
Mauro Bergamasco, Phillips (Persico 80)
Scotland: Laney; Metcalfe, McLaren,Henderson,
Paterson; Townsend, Redpath*; Smith, Bulloch, Stewart
(Graham 59), Murray, Grimes, White, Mower (Leslie 69),
Taylor
Referee: *K Deaker NZL*
Attendance: *25,000*

Millennium Stadium, Mar 2
WALES (23) 44   **ITALY (13) 20**
Tries: Morgan, James   *Checchinato, Mazzariol*
Williams, Quinnell
Marinos
Cons: Jones 5   *Pez, Peens*
Pens: Jones 3   *Pez, Peens*
Wales: Morgan (Harris 59); James, Shanklin (R Williams 23), Marinos, Morgan; Jones, Howley (Peel 52); Thomas, McBryde (B Williams 60), Anthony (John 77), Gough (Wyatt 52), A Moore, Budgett, M Williams, S Quinnell* (B Sinkinson 63)
Italy: Peens; Pedrazzi (Benatti 67), Mirco Bergamasco, Stoica, Mazzucato; Pez (Raineri 64), Troncon; De Carli (Lo Cicero 48), Moscardi*, Perugini (Pucciariello 69), Bortolami (Phillips 60), Giacheri, Persico, Mauro Bergamasco (Mazzariol 65), Checchinato
Referee: C White ENG
Attendance: 58,346

Stade de France, Mar 2
FRANCE (17) 20   **ENGLAND (7) 15**
Tries: Merceron   *Robinson, Cohen*
Harinordoquy
Cons: Merceron 2   *Wilkinson*
Pens: Merceron 2   *Wilkinson*
FRANCE: Brusque; Rougerie (Pelous 60), Marsh, Traille, Bory; Merceron, Galthié* (Mignioni 66); Crenca, Ibanez (Azam 79), De Villiers, Auradou, Brouzet, Betsen (Martin 56-60), Magne, Harinordoquy (Martin 78)
ENGLAND: Robinson; Healey, Tindall (Paul 40), Greenwood, Cohen; Wilkinson, Bracken; Rowntree (Leonard 74), Thompson (West 74), Vickery, Johnson*, Kay (Grewcock 74), Hill, Back (Corry 47), Worsley
Referee: A Watson RSA
Attendance: 79,502

Lansdowne Road, Mar 2
IRELAND (22) 43   **SCOTLAND (12) 22**
Tries: O'Driscoll 3   *Leslie*
Horgan, S Easterby
Cons: Humphries 2   *Laney*
O'Gara
Pens: Humphries 4   *Laney 5*
Ireland: Dempsey; Horgan, O'Driscoll, Maggs, Hickie; Humpheys (O'Gara, 78), Stringer (Easterby 79); Clohessy (Wallace 78), Sheahan (Byrne 37), Hayes, Galwey* (Longwell 69), O'Kelly, Miller (Easterby 46), Wallace, Foley
Scotland: Laney; Metcalfe (Kogan 69), McLaren, Henderson, Paterson; Townsend, Redpath*; Smith, Bulloch, Stewart (Graham 62), Murray, Grimes, White (Leslie 56), Pountney, Taylor
Referee: N Whitehouse WAL
Attendance: 52,000

Lansdowne Road, Mar 23
IRELAND (19) 32   **ITALY (0) 17**
Tries: Kelly 2, Hickie   *Bergamasco, De Carli*
Con: O'Gara   *Dominguez 2*
Pens: Humphries 4
O'Gara
DG: *Peens*
Ireland: Dempsey; Kelly, O'Driscoll, Horgan, Hickie (Howe 80); Humphreys*, Stringer; Clohessy (Wallace 76), Byrne, Hayes, Longwell, O'Kelly (O'Connell 70), Easterby, Wallace, Foley
Italy: Peens; Mazzucato, Stoica, Raineri, Dallan; Dominguez, Troncon; De Carli, Moscardi*, Perugini (Pucciariello 27), Bortolami (Dellape 60), Giacheri, Persico, Bergamasco, Phillips (De Rossi 69)
Sin-Bin: Perugini (24-34), De Carli (45-50)
Referee: R Dixon SCO
Attendance: 48,898

Twickenham, Mar 23
ENGLAND (19) 50   **WALES (3) 10**
Tries: Greenwood   *Harris*
Wilkinson, Luger 2
Stimpson
Conv: Wilkinson 5   *Harris*
Pens: Wilkinson 4   *Harris*
DG: Wilkinson
England: Healey; Cohen, Tindall; (Stimpson 63), Greenwood, Luger; Wilkinson, Bracken (Dawson 59); Rowntree, Thompson; (West 74), White, Grewcock, Kay, Moody, Back*, Hill; (Worsley 80)
Wales: Morgan; James, G Thomas (R Williams 48), Marinos, Morgan; Harris, Howley (Peel 59); I Thomas, McBryde (B Williams 65), Anthony, Moore, Wyatt; (Llewellyn 54), Budgett, M Williams (Charvis 50), S Quinnell
Referee: A Cole AUS
Attendance: 75,000

Murrayfield, Mar 23
SCOTLAND (3) 10   **FRANCE (10) 22**
Try: Redpath   *Marsh 2, Galthié*
Conv: Laney   *Merceron 2*
Pen: Laney   *Merceron*
Scotland: Laney; Metcalfe, McLaren (Logan 78), J Leslie, Paterson; Townsend, Redpath*; Smith, Bulloch (Russell 75), M Stewart (Graham 62), Murray (Grimes 65), White, M Leslie, Pountney, Taylor
France: Brusque (Marlu 51); Rougerie, Marsh, Traille, Bory; Merceron, Galthié*; Crenca, Ibanez, Poux (Marconnet 65), Pelous (Privat 68), Brouzet, Betsen (Martin 78), Magne, Harinordoquy
Referee: A Rolland IRL
Attendance: 65,562

Stadio Flaminio, April 8
ITALY (3) 9   **ENGLAND (24) 45**
Tries: *Greenwood 2, Cohen*
                         Robinson, Dallaglio
                         Healey
Cons: *Wilkinson 5*
Pens: Dominguez 3   *Wilkinson*
Italy: Peens (Pez 74); Mazzucato, Stoica (Mazzantini 80), Raineri (Zanoletti 49), Dallan; Dominguez, Troncon; De Carli, Moscardi* (Moretti 74), Pucciariello (Nieto 59), Bortolami, Giacheri (Dellape 59), Persico, Bergamasco, Phillips (De Rossi 49)
England: Robinson; Luger, Tindall (Hodgson 77), Greenwood, Cohen (Healey 69); Wilkinson, Bracken (Dawson 56); Rowntree (Leonard 56), Thompson (West 73), White, Grewcock (Johnson 56), Kay, Moody, Back* (Dallaglio 56), Hill
Referee: M Lawrence RSA

Millennium Stadium, April 8
WALES (9) 22   **SCOTLAND (15) 27**
Tries: R Williams   *Bulloch 2*
Cons: Jones   *Laney*
Pens: Jones 5   *Laney 4, Hodge*
Wales: Morgan; R Williams, Taylor (Swansea), Marinos (Harris 44), Morgan (James 71); Jones; Howley (Peel 66); I Thomas (John 57), B Williams (McBryde 44), Anthony, Gough, Moore (Wyatt 12), Budgett (G Thomas h-t), M Williams, Charvis*
Scotland: Laney (Hodge 80); Logan (Metcalfe 60), McLaren, Leslie, Paterson; Townsend (Castres), Redpath*; Smith, Bulloch (Russell 75), Stewart (Graham h-t), Murray, White (Grimes 58), M Leslie (Petrie 71), Pountney, Taylor
Referee: J Jutge FRA
Attendance: 72,000

Stade de France, April 8
FRANCE (28) 44   **IRELAND (5) 5**
Tries: Betsen 2,   *Wood*
Brusque 2, Rougerie
Cons: Merceron 2
Pens: Merceron 4
Gelez
France: Brusque; Rougerie, Traille, Marsh, Bory (Marlu 76); Merceron (Gelez 76), Galthié* (Mignoni 76); Crenca, Ibanez (Azam 76), De Villiers (Poux 64), Pelous, Brouzet (Auradou 73), Betsen, Magne (Martin 76), Harinordoquy
Ireland: Dempsey; Horgan, O'Driscoll, Henderson, Hickie; Humphreys (O'Gara 49); Stringer; Clohessy (Wallace 63), Wood*, Hayes, Longwell (O'Connell 64), O'Kelly, S Easterby, D Wallace (Gleeson 49), Foley
Referee: P O'Brien NZL
Attendance: 78,000

Final Six-Nations Table

		P	W	D	L	PF	PA	Diff	Pts
1	France	5	5	0	0	156	75	81	10
2	England	5	4	0	1	184	53	131	8
3	Ireland	5	3	0	2	145	138	7	6
4	Scotland	5	2	0	3	91	128	-37	4
5	Wales	5	1	0	4	119	188	-69	2
6	Italy	5	0	0	5	70	183	-113	0

> **"I don't like the French. There's no harm in that is there?"**
>
> Patrick Clohessy, Ireland prop.

> **"He gave me his `eyebrows look' and said `fine' then walked away"**
>
> Clive Woodward, the England caoch describing Martin Johnson's reaction to being relegated to the bench.

> **"I suppose the key for me in dealing in any kind of people is to realise that I'm not dealing with a ball"**
>
> Johnny Wilkinson.

> **"He is not a player who purposely goes out on the pitch to be violent and cause damage to other players, other than in the true spirit of the game"**
>
> Neil Back, on his Leicester and England teammate Johnson. With friends like that...

Other Internationals

England Matches

Buenos Aires, June 22

ARGENTINA (12) 18   ENGLAND (3) 26
Tries: Kay, Christophers
Cons: Hodgson 2
Pens: Hodgson 3, Stimpson
England: Horak; Christophers, B Johnson, Appleford,
Stimpson; Hodgson, Gomersall; Vickery*, Thompson,
Flatman, Kay, Codling, Moody, Sanderson, Worsley
Argentina: Corelto; Camardon, Orengo, Contepomi,
Albanese; Quesada, Pichot*; Hasan Jalil, Mendez,
Reggiardo, Alvarez Kairelis, Fernandez Lobbe, Martin,
Phelan, Longo Elia
Subs: Giannantonio, Grau, Ledesma Arocena, Ostiglia
Referee: A Rolland IRL

Twickenham, Nov 9

ENGLAND (17) 31   NEW ZEALAND (14) 28
Tries: Cohen, Moody   Lomu 2, Lee, Howlett
Con: Wilkinson 2   Blair 2, Mehrtens 2
Pens: Wilkinson 3
DG: Wilkinson
England: Robinson; Simpson-Daniel, Tindall, Greenwood,
Cohen; Wilkinson, Dawson; Vickery, Thompson, Woodman,
Grewcock, M Johnson*, Hill, Moody, Dallaglio
Subs: Kay, Back, Healey, B Johnson
New Zealand: Blair; Lomu, Umaga, Lowen, Howlett;
Spencer, Devine; McDonnell, Hore, Meeuws, Robinson,
Williams, Holah, Randall*, Broomhall
Subs: Lee, Mehrtens, Mika, Robinson
Referee: J Kaplan RSA
Attendance: 75,000

Twickenham, Nov 16

ENGLAND (16) 32   AUSTRALIA (13) 31
Tries: Cohen 2   Flatley 2, Sailor
Con: Wilkinson 2   Burke 2
Pens: Wilkinson 6   Burke 4
England: Robinson; Simpson-Daniel, Tindall, Greenwood,
Cohen; Wilkinson, Dawson; Leonard, Thompson, Vickery,
Kay, M Johnson*, Back, Moody, Hill
Subs: Dallaglio, Healey
Australia: Burke; Sailor, Herbert, Flatley, Mortlack;
Larkham, Gregan*; Noriega, Paul, Young, Harrison,
Vickerman, Cockbain, Smith, Kefu
Subs: Giffin, Giteau, Croft, Darwin, Freier
Referee: P Honiss NZL
Attendance: 75,000

Twickenham, Nov 23

ENGLAND (18) 53   SOUTH AFRICA (3) 3
Tries: Greenwood 2
Back, Dallaglio, Hill
Cohen, penalty try
Cons: Wilkinson, Dawson
Gomersall 2, Stimpson 2
Pens: Wilkinson 2
England: Robinson; Cohen, Tindall, Greenwood,
Christophers; Wilkinson, Dawson; Leonard, Thompson,
Vickery, Kay, M Johnson*, Back, Moody, Hill
Subs: Dallaglio, Gomersall, Grewcock, Healey, Stimpson
South Africa: Greeff; Paulse, Fleck, James, Lombard;
Pretorius, Conradie; Carstens, Dalton, Roux, Labuschagne,
Venter, Krige*, Wannenburg, Van Niekirk
Subs: Jacobs, Van Biljon, Jordaan, Russell, Van der Linde
Sent off: Labuschagne 23
Referee: P O'Brien NZL
Attendance: 75,000

Scotland Matches

Thunderbird Stadium, Vancouver, June 15

CANADA (13) 26   SCOTLAND (15) 23
Tries: Murphy, Thiel   Blair, Taylor
                          Paterson
Cons: Barker 2   Laney
Pens: Barker 4   Laney 2
Canada: Stanley; Fauth, Witkowski, Cannon, Asselin;
Barker, Williams; Snow, Dunkley, Thiel, Charron*, James,
Baugh, Banks, Murphy
Subs; Knaggs, Nichols, Wirachowski, Yukes
Scotland: Metcalfe; Paterson, Craig, Laney, Kerr; Hodge,
Blair; Smith, Bullock, Stewart, Hines, Grimes*, Taylor,
White, Petrie
Subs: Jacobsen, McFadyen, Brotherstone, Hinshelwood
Referee: D McHugh IRL
Attendance: 5,274

Balboa Park, San Francisco, June 22

USA (13) 23   SCOTLAND (29) 65
Tries: Keyter   Hodge 2, Paterson 2
Timoteo   Hines, Kerr, Laney
                      Craig, Henderson, White
Cons: Wilfley 2   Laney 6
Pens: Wilfley 3   Laney
USA: Buchholz; Timoteo, Wilfley, Eloff, Keyter; Hercus,
Dalzell; Dorsey, Khasigian, MacDonald, Gross, Reed,
Satchwell, Schubert, Hodges*
Subs; Nagica, Anderson, Hodgson, Kjar, McGarry
Scotland: Metcalfe; Paterson, Craig, Laney, Kerr; Hodge,
Blair; Jacobsen, Bullock, Stewart, Hines, Grimes*,
McFadyen, White, Taylor
Subs: Di Rollo, Hall, Smith, Burns, Henderson, Scott
Referee: P Deluca ITA
Attendance: 2,400

Murrayfield, Nov 9
SCOTLAND (18) 37   **ROMANIA (3) 10**
Tries: Moffatt   *Tofan*
Pountney, Grimes
Leslie, Paterson
Cons: Laney 3
Pens: Laney 2   *Tofan*
                    Tofan
Scotland: Moffatt; Walker, Craig, Laney, Paterson; Ross, Redpath*; Douglas, Bullock, Smith, Grimes, Murray, Taylor, Leslie, Pountney
Subs: Hines, Petrie, Hinshelwood, Scott, Stewart, Townsend
Romania: Brezoianu; Teodorescu, Maftei, Gontineac*, Ghioc; Tofan, Mitu; Balan, Tincu, Dima, Petre, Petrechei, Chiriac, Corodeanu, Petrache
Subs: Dragnea, Sarbu, Socaciu, Toderasc
Referee: *A Turner RSA*
Attendance: *34,413*

Murrayfield, Nov 16
SCOTLAND (6) 21   **SOUTH AFRICA (6) 6**
Tries: Walker
Pountney
Cons: Laney
Pens: Laney 3   *James 2*
Scotland: Moffatt; Walker, Craig, Laney, Paterson; Ross, Redpath*; Douglas, Bullock, Smith, Grimes, Murray, Pountney, Leslie, Taylor
Subs: Hines, Hilton, Hinshelwood, Townsend
South Africa: Greeff; Paulse, Fleck, Jacobs, Lombard; James, Conradie; Carstens, Van Biljon, Roux, Labuschagne, Wentzel, Uys, Krige*, Van Niekirk
Subs: Venter, Pretorius, Van Der Linde
Referee: *N Williams WAL*
Attendance: *58,225*

Murrayfield, Nov 24
SCOTLAND (18) 36   **FIJI (12) 22**
Tries: Craig 3   *Ligairi, Naevo*
Laney, Grimes
Cons: Laney
Pens: Laney 3   *Narruhn 4*
Scotland: Hinshelwood; Walker, Craig, Laney, Paterson; Townsend, Redpath*; Douglas, Bullock, Smith, Grimes, White, Pountney, Taylor, Petrie
Subs: Moffatt, Hines, Ross, Beveridge, M Leslie, Scott
Fiji: Nariva; Ligairi, Ruivadra, Baikeinuku, Lasagavibau; Narruhn, Rauluni; Cavubati, Smith*, Rasila, Naevo, Raiwalui, Koyamaibole, Vuivau, Naivaluwaga
Subs: Serevi, Gadolo, Katalau, Leawere, Satala
Referee: *M Lawrence RSA*
Attendance: *37,351*

Wales Matches

Vodacom Park, Bloemfontein, June 8
SOUTH AFRICA (15) 34   **WALES (11) 19**
Tries: Matfield   *C Morgan, Williams*
Rautenbach, Joubert
penalty try, Skinstad
Cons: Pretorius 3
Pens: Pretorius   *S Jones 2*
DG: *S Jones*
South Africa: Loubscher; Terblanche, Snyman, Joubert, Paulse; Pretorius, Conradie; Human, Dalton, Meyer, Labuschagne, Matfield, Britz, Venter, Skinstad*
Subs: Jacobs, Rautenbach, Le Roux, Russell, Van Niekirk
Wales: K Morgan; R Williams, Taylor, Marinos, C Morgan; Jones, Peel; Thomas, McBryde, Evans, Llewellyn, S Williams, Owen, M Williams, Charvis*
Subs: M Davies, Madden, Parks, Powell, Shanklin, Sidoli, N Jenkins
Referee: *K Deaker NZL*
Attendance: *34,000*

Newlands, Cape Town, June 15
SOUTH AFRICA (8) 19   **WALES (3) 8**
Tries: Davidson   *Charvis*
Russell
Pens: Pretorius 3   *S Jones*
South Africa: Russell; Terblanche, Joubert, Barry, Paulse; Pretorius, Conradie; Human, Dalton, Meyer, Labuschagne, Davids, Venter, Krige, Skinstad*
Subs: Davidson, Rautenbach, Le Roux, Louw
Wales: K Morgan; R Williams, Taylor, Marinos, C Morgan; Jones, Peel; Thomas, McBryde, Evans, Llewellyn, S Williams, Owen, M Williams, Charvis*
Subs: M Davies, Powell, Shanklin, Sidoli, G Thomas, N Jenkins
Referee: *T Spreadbury ENG*
Attendance: *40,547*

Wrexham, Nov 1
WALES (12) 40   **ROMANIA (0) 3**
Tries: M Jones
Quinnell, penalty try
Thomas
Cons: S Jones 4
Pens: S Jones 4   *Tofan*
Wales: R Williams; Thomas, Shanklin, Parker, M Jones; N Jenkins, Peel; G Jenkins, Davies, Madden, Sidoli, S Williams, Owen, Charvis*, Quinnell
Subs: C Morgan, G Thomas, Evans, S Jones, Lewis, Llewellyn
Romania: Dumbrava; Picoiu, Gontineac*, Brezoianu; Ghioc; Tofan, Mitu; Florea, Mavrodin, Toderasc, Socol, Cristian, Corodeanu, Petrache, Tonita
Subs: Chiriac, Colyuneac, Dragos Dima, Lungu, Constantin, Podea
Referee: *J Jutge FRA*
Attendance: *9448*

Millennium Stadium, Cardiff, Nov 9
WALES (27) 58   FIJI (0) 14
Tries: M Jones 2   Serevi, Ligairi
Parker, G Williams
penalty try, Charvis
G Thomas
Cons: S Jones 3   Little, Serevi
Pens: S Jones 5   Tofan
Wales: R Williams; G Thomas, Shanklin, Parker, M Jones;
S Jones, Peel; I Thomas, Davies, Evans, Sidoli, Llewellyn,
D Jones, M Williams, Charvis*
Subs: Harris, Madden, Parks, Robinson, S Williams
Fiji: Narruhn; Ligairi, Rabeni, Baikeinuku, Lasagavibau;
Little, Rauluni; Cavubati, Smith*, Nyholt, Naevo, Raiwalui,
Doviverata, Naivaluwaga, Vuivau
Subs: Serevi, Nasagavesi
Referee: S Dickinson AUS
Attendance: 35,000

Millennium Stadium, Cardiff, Nov 16
WALES (22) 32   CANADA (12) 21
Tries: Robinson
McBryde
Cons: Jones 2
Pens: Jones 6   Barker 6
DG: Williams
Wales: R Williams; G Thomas, Robinson, Parker, M Jones;
S Jones, Peel; I Thomas, McBryde, Evans, Cooper,
Llewellyn, D Jones, M Williams, Charvis*
Subs: Harris, Owen, Powell, Quinnell
Canada: Stanley; Fauth, Witkowski, Cannon, Asselin;
Barker, Williams; Snow, Dunkley, Thiel, James, Tait, Banks,
Van Staveren, Murphy
Subs: Carlson, Cudmore, Di Girolomo, Fairhurst, Tkachuk
Referee: G De Santis ITA
Attendance: 30,000

Millennium Stadium, Cardiff, Nov 23
WALES (10) 17   NEW ZEALAND (9) 43
Tries: Robinson   Howlett 2, King
penalty try   Meeuws
Cons: Jones   Mehrtens 4
Pens: Jones   Mehrtens 5
Wales: R Williams; G Thomas, Robinson, Parker, M Jones;
S Jones, Peel; I Thomas, McBryde, Evans, Sidoli,
Llewellyn, D Jones, M Williams, Charvis*
Subs: Harris, Owens, James, G Jenkins
New Zealand: Blair; Lomu, Umaga, King, Howlett;
Mehrtens, Devine; Hayman, Mealamu, Woodcock,
Robinson, Williams, Braid, Randall*, So'oialo
Subs: Holah, Steinmetz, Meeuws, Mika
Referee: T Henning RSA
Attendance: 72,500

Ireland Matches

Dunedin, June 15
NEW ZEALAND (10) 15   IRELAND (3) 6
Tries: Kay, Christophers
Cons: Hodgson 2
Pens: Hodgson 3, Stimpson
New Zealand: MacDonald; Ralph, Umaga, Mauger,
Howlett; Mehrtens, Marshall; Hewett, Hammett, Somerville,
Jack, Maxwell, McCaw, Thorne*, Robertson
Subs: McDonnell, Gibson, Lomu
Ireland: Dempsey; Murphy, Kelly, O'Driscoll, Bishop;
O'Gara, Stringer; Hayes, Wood*, Corrigan, Longwell,
O'Connell, Easterby, Gleeson, Foley
Subs: Humphreys, O'Kelly
Referee: J Jutge FRA
Attendance: 30,200

Auckland, June 22
NEW ZEALAND (13) 40   IRELAND (3) 8
Tries: MacDonald 2   Longwell
Holah, Kelleher, Ralph
Cons: Mehrtens 3
Pens: Mehrtens 3
DG: O'Driscoll
New Zealand: MacDonald; Ralph, Robinson, Mauger,
Lomu; Mehrtens, Marshall; Hewett, Hammett, Somerville,
Jack, Maxwell, McCaw, Thorne*, Robertson
Subs: Howlett, Holah, Maling, McDonnell, Gibson, Kelleher
Ireland: Dempsey; Murphy, Kelly, O'Driscoll, Bishop;
O'Gara, Stringer; Hayes, Wood*, Corrigan, Longwell,
O'Kelly, Easterby, Gleeson, Foley
Subs: Byrne, Humphreys, Wallace, Cullen, Quinlan
Referee: T Henning RSA

Limerick, Sep 7
IRELAND (32) 39   ROMANIA (3) 8
Tries: Henderson   Maftei
Hayes, O'Driscoll
Gleeson, penalty try
Cons: O'Gara 3
Humphreys
Pens: O'Gara 2   Toffe
Ireland: Dempsey; Kelly, Maggs, O'Driscoll, Hickie;
O'Gara, Stringer; Hayes, Byrne, Corrigan, Longwell,
O'Kelly, Easterby, Gleeson, Foley*
Subs: Costello, Easterby, Henderson, Humphreys
Romania: Brezoianu; Vioreanu, Maftei, Gontineac*, Sauan;
Tofan, Sarbu; Dumitru, Mavrodin, Tuncu, Dragomir, Petre,
Chiriac, Manta, Petrache
Subs: Petrechei, Picoiu, Podea, Toderasc, Tudosa, Vusec
Referee: G de Santis ITA
Attendance: 8,000

Krasnoyarsk, Sep 21
RUSSIA (0) 3   **IRELAND (18) 35**
Tries: *Dempsey 2*
                          Wood, O'Kelly
Cons: *O'Gara 3*
Pens: Pieterse   *O'Gara 3*
Russia: Zakarlyuk; Kuzin, Dymchenko, Korobeinikov
(Pieterse 68), Sergeev; Rachkov, Motorin, Zykov,
Volschenk (Khrokin 62), Grachev, Sergeev, Phedchenko,
Hendriks (Nikolaichuk 62), Romak, Shukailov (Uambaev 73)
Ireland: Dempsey; Kelly (Henderson, 18-20), O'Driscoll,
Maggs, Hickie; O'Gara (Humphreys 75), Stringer (Easterby
75), O'Kelly, Hayes (Wallace 70), Wood* (Byrne 75),
Corrigan, Longwell, O'Kelly, Easterby (Quinlan 70),
Gleeson, Foley
Referee: *J Jutge FRA*
Attendance: *15,000*

Lansdowne Road, Sep 28
IRELAND (42) 63   **GEORGIA (0) 14**
Tries: O'Driscoll 2   *Katsadze, Khamashuridze*
Hickie, Maggs, Dempsey
S Easterby, Quinlan
G Easterby
Cons: O'Gara 5   *Jimsheladze 2*
Humphreys 2
Pens: O'Gara 3
Ireland: Dempsey; Kelly, O'Driscoll, Maggs, Hickie; O'Gara,
Stringer; Corrigan, Byrne, Hayes, Longwell, O'Kelly,
Easterby, Gleeson, Foley*
Subs: Sheahan, Wallace, Cullen, Quinlan, G Easterby,
Humphreys, Henderson
Georgia: Khamashuridze; Urjukashvili, Zibzibadze, Alania,
Khekhelashvili; Jimsheladze, Abusseridze; Shvelidze,
Guiorgadze, Tsabadze, Nadiradze, Didebulidze*,
Bolghashvili, Chkhaidze, Zedguinidze
Subs: Mtiulishvili, Ratianidze, Mtchedlishvili, Gundishvili,
Barkalaia, Katsadze, Lovadze.
Referee: *J Jutge FRA*
Attendance: *15,000*

Lansdowne Road, Nov 9
IRELAND (12) 18   **AUSTRALIA (3) 9**
Pens: O'Gara 6   *Burke 3*
Ireland: Dempsey; Horgan, O'Driscoll*, Maggs, Hickie;
O'Gara, Stringer; Corrigan, Byrne, Hayes, Longwell,
O'Kelly, Costello, Gleeson, Foley
Australia: Burke; Staniforth, Mortlock, Herbert, Sailor;
Larkham, Gregan*; Noriega, Freier, Stiles, Finegan, Giffin,
Cockbain, Smith, Tefu
Referee: *S Walsh NZL*
Attendance: *49,000*

Lansdowne Road, Nov 17
IRELAND (39) 64   **FIJI (3) 17**
Tries: Maggs 3   *Doviverata*
Murphy 2, Dawson
Foley, O'Driscoll
Bishop
Cons: Humphreys 5   *Serevi, Little*
Pens: Humphreys 3   *Little*
Ireland: Murphy; Bishop, O'Driscoll*, Maggs, Horgan;
Humphreys, Easterby; Hayes, Sheahan, Horan, O'Kelly,
Cullen, Dawson, Quinlan, Foley
Subs: D'Arcy, Miller, Corrigan, O'Driscoll
Fiji: Serevi; Ligairi, Satala, Baikeinuku, Lasagavibau; Little,
Rauluni; Cavubati, Smith*, Nyholt, Naevo, Raiwalui,
Doviverata, Vuivau, Koyamaibole
Subs: Narruhn, Rawaga, Nasagavesi, Naivaluwaga
Referee: *N Whitehouse WAL*

Lansdowne Road, Nov 23
IRELAND (10) 16   **ARGENTINA (7) 7**
Tries: Dempsey   *Martin*
Cons: O'Gara   *Contepomi*
Pens: O'Gara 3
Ireland: Dempsey; Bishop, O'Driscoll*, Maggs, Horgan;
O'Gara, Stringer; Corrigan, Byrne, Hayes, Longwell,
O'Kelly, Costello, Gleeson, Foley
Subs: Cullen, Horan, Quinlan
Argentina: Corleto; Camardon, Orengo, Arbizu*, Albanese;
Contepomi, Pichot; Hasan Jalil, Arocena, Reggiardo,
Kairelis, Fernandez Lobbe, Martin, Phlean, Longo Elia
Subs: Durand, Fernandez Miranda Sporleder
Referee: *C White ENG*
Attendance: *40,000*

Tri-Nations Series

Wellington, July 13
NEW ZEALAND 12   **AUSTRALIA 6**
Pens: Mehrtens 4   *Burke 2*
New Zealand: Cullen; Howlett, Robinson, Mauger,
Ralph; Mehrtens, Marshall; Hewett, Hammett, Somerville,
Jack, Maling, Thorne*, Robertson, McCaw
Australia: Latham; Tune, Burke, Herbert, Mortlock;
Larkham, Gregan*; Young, Paul, Noriega, Sharpe,
Harrison, Finegan, Kefu, Smith
Referee: J Kaplan RSA

Wellington, July 20
NEW ZEALAND 41   **SOUTH AFRICA 20**
Tries: Howlett   *Greeff, Joubert*
Hammett, Thorne
Marshall, Robertson
Cons: Mehrtens 2   *Pretorius 2*
Pens: Mehrtens 3   *Pretorius*
DG: Mahrtens   *Greeff*
New Zealand: Cullen; Howlett, Robinson, Mauger,
Ralph; Mehrtens, Marshall; Hewett, Hammett, Somerville,
Jack, Maling, Thorne*, Robertson, McCaw
South Africa: Greeff; Terblanche, Joubert, Barry, Hall;
Pretorius, Conradie; Sephaka, Dalton, Meyer,
Labuschagne, Matfield, Krige*, Skinstad, Van Niekerk
Referee: S Dickinson AUS

Brisbane, July 27
AUSTRALIA 38   **SOUTH AFRICA 27**
Tries: Latham 2   *Joubert 2, Skinstad*
Tune, Mortlock   *Russell*
Cons: Burke 3   *Pretorius 2*
Pens: Burke 3   *Pretorius*
Mortlock
Australia: Latham; Tune, Burke, Herbert, Mortlock;
Larkham, Gregan*; Young, Paul, Noriega, Sharpe,
Harrison, Finegan, Kefu, Smith
South Africa: Greeff; Terblanche, Joubert, Barry,
Paulse; Pretorius, Conradie; Sephaka, Dalton,
Rautenbach, Labuschagne, Matfield, Krige*, Skinstad,
Van Niekerk
Referee: S Lander ENG

Sydney, August 3
AUSTRALIA 16   **NEW ZEALAND 14**
Tries: Sharpe, Rogers   *McCaw*
Pens: Burke 2   *Mehrtens 3*
Australia: Latham; Tune, Burke, Herbert, Mortlock;
Larkham, Gregan*; Young, Paul, Noriega, Sharpe,
Harrison, Finegan, Kefu, Smith
New Zealand: Cullen; Howlett, Umaga, Mauger, Ralph;
Mehrtens, Marshall; Hewett, Willis, Somerville, Jack,
Maling, Thorne*, Robertson, McCaw
Referee: A Watson RSA

Durban, Aug 10
SOUTH AFRICA 23   **NEW ZEALAND 30**
Tries: De Kock   *MacDonald, penalty try*
Pretorius   *Howlett, Mauger*
Cons: Pretorius 2   *Mehrtens 2*
Pens: Pretorius 2   *Mehrtens 2*
DG: Pretorius
South Africa: Greeff; Paulse, Joubert, Barry, Hall;
Pretorius, De Kock; Sephaka, Dalton, Meyer,
Labuschagne, Venter, Krige*, Skinstad, Van Niekerk
New Zealand: MacDonald; Howlett, Umaga, Mauger,
Ralph; Mehrtens, Marshall; Hewett, Willis, Somerville,
Jack, Maling, Thorne*, Robertson, McCaw
Referee: D McHugh IRL

Johannesburg, August 17
SOUTH AFRICA 33   **AUSTRALIA 31**
Tries: Paulse 2   *Rogers, Kefu*
Russell, Van Kierkerk   *Cannon*
Greeff
Cons: Greeff 4   *Burke 2*
Pens: *Burke 3*
DG: *Gregan*
South Africa: Greeff; Paulse, Joubert, Barry, Hall;
Russell, De Kock; Sephaka, Dalton, Meyer,
Labuschagne, Venter, Krige*, Skinstad, Van Niekerk
Australia: Latham; Tune, Burke, Herbert, Mortlock;
Larkham, Gregan*; Young, Paul, Darwin, Sharpe,
Harrison, Finegan, Kefu, Smith
Referee: P O'Brien NZL

Final Table

	P	W	D	L	PF	PA	B*	Pts
New Zealand	4	3	0	1	97	65	3	15
Australia	4	2	0	2	91	86	3	11
South Africa	4	1	0	3	103	140	3	7

*Bonus Points

Heineken Cup

Quarter-finals
Stade Jean Bouin, Paris Jan 26
Stade Français 14   Munster 16

Castres, Jan 26
Castres 22   Montferrand 21

Recreation Ground, Jan 27
Bath 10   Llanelli 27

Welford Rd, Jan 27
Leicester 29   Leinster 18

Semi-finals
Beziers, Apr 27
Castres 17   Munster 25

City Ground, Nottingham, Apr 28
Leicester 13   Llanelli 12

Final
Millennium Stadium, May 25
LEICESTER 15   MUNSTER 9
Tries: Murphy
Healey
Conv: Stimpson
PG: Stimpson   O'Gara 3
Leicester: Stimpson; Murphy, Smith (Gelderbloom 76), Kafer, Tuilagi; Healey, Hamilton (Ellis 52); Rowntree (Freshwater 74), West, Garforth, Johnson*, Kay, Moody, Corrie, Back
Munster: Crotty (Staunton 65); O'Neill, Henderson (Mullins 67), Holland, Kelly; O'Gara, Stringer; Clohessy (Horan 61), Sheahan (Blaney 17-28), Hayes, Galwey*, O'Connell (O'Driscoll 61), Quinlan, Foley (Williams 53), Wallace
Referee: J Jutge FRA

Parker Pen Shield

Semi-finals
Oxford, Apr 27
London Irish 27   Pontypridd 33

Northampton, Apr 28
Gloucester 27   Sale 28

Final
Kassam Stadium, Oxford, May 26
Sale 25   Pontypridd 22
Tries: Shaw   Davies
Hanley, Harris
Cons: Hodgson 2
PG: Hodgson 2   Davey 4
Sale: Robinson; Cueto, Shaw, Deane (Harris 67), Hanley (Baxendell 11-20); Hodgson, Redpath*; Yates, Marais (Titterell 66), Turner, Lines, Jones, Sanderson (Black 30-39), Angelsea, Pinkerton
Pontypridd: Davey; Wyatt, Parker, Bryant, Johnston; Sweeney, John*, Jenkins, Davies (Rees 79), Bell, Cockbain, Sidoli, Kelly (Remnant 75), Owen
Referee: A Lewis IRL

The Celtic League

Semi-finals
Munster 15   Ulster 9
Leinster 35   Glasgow 13

Final
Lansdowne Road, Dec 15
Leinster 24   Munster 20
Tries: D'Arcy   O'Neill, Foley
Horgan
Cons: Spooner   O'Gara
PG: Spooner 4   O'Gara
Leinster: Dempsey; Hickie, B O'Driscoll, Horgan, D'Arcy; Spooner, O'Meara; Corrigan*, Byrne, Wallace, Cullen (Casey 59), O'Kelly, Miller, Costello, Gleeson
Munster: Crotty (Mullins 3-10, 64); O'Neill, Kelly (Hegarty 26-33), Henderson (Holland 58), Horgan; O'Gara, Prendergast; Horan, Sheahan, Clohessy (Cahill 61), Galwey* (McMahon 74), O'Connell (M O'Driscoll 74), Quinlan, Foley, Williams
Referee: N Whitehouse WAL

British/Irish Club Rugby

Zurich Premiership 2001-02

		P	W	D	L	PF	PA	B	Pts
1	Leicester	22	18	0	4	658	349	11	83
2	Sale	22	14	1	7	589	517	11	69
3	Gloucester	22	14	0	8	692	485	12	68
4	London Irish	22	11	3	8	574	465	7	57
5	Northampton	22	12	1	9	490	458	6	56
6	Newcastle	22	12	1	9	490	458	6	56
7	Wasps	22	12	0	10	519	507	6	54
8	Bristol	22	9	1	12	591	632	12	50
9	Harlequins	22	5	3	14	434	507	9	35
10	Saracens	22	7	0	15	425	671	6	34
11	Bath	22	7	0	15	311	524	5	33
12	Leeds	22	6	0	16	406	654	4	28

B=Bonus points; 4 points for a win; 2 points for a draw; 1 point for losing a match by 7 points or less; 1 point for scoring 4 tries or more

Championship Play-off

Quarter-Finals
Leicester, May 18
Leicester 13   Bristol 27

Gloucester, May 18
Gloucester 60   Newcastle 9

Reading, May 19
London Irish 14   Northampton 38

Sale, May 19
Sale 43   Wasps 27

Semi-Finals
Bristol, June 1
Bristol 32   Northampton 24

Sale, June 2
Sale 11   Gloucester 33

ZURICH CHAMPIONSHIP FINAL
Twickenham, June 8
Gloucester 28   Bristol 23

National League Division 1

		P	W	D	L	PF	PA	Pts
1	Rotherham	26	24	0	2	1099	325	120
2	Worcester	26	23	0	3	941	364	108
3	Exeter	26	19	1	6	707	448	92
4	Coventry	26	16	3	7	730	559	82
5	London Welsh	26	15	0	11	580	557	69
6	Bedford	26	12	3	11	654	600	68
7	Otley	26	11	1	14	601	675	56
8	Birmingham S	26	10	1	15	432	626	52
9	Wakefield	26	9	2	15	514	607	47
10	Rugby Lions	26	9	1	16	518	668	47
11	Moseley	26	9	1	16	448	695	46
12	Manchester	26	8	0	18	381	758	36
13	Henley	26	6	1	19	449	767	33
14	Bracknell	26	4	0	22	418	823	26

The Powergen Cup

Final
Twickenham, Apr 20
London Irish 38   **Northampton 7**
Tries: Appleford 2   *Cohen*
Bishop 2, Horak
Conv: Everitt 5   *Grayson*
PG: Everitt

London Irish: Horak; Sackey, Appleford, Venter (Hoadley 76), Bishop; Everitt (Brown 80), Martens (Edwards 57); Worsley, Drotske (Kirke 46), Hardwick (Halford 46), Strudwick*, Williams (Delaney 73), Halvey (Cockle 76), Sheasby, Danaher (Hardwick 64-69)
Northampton: Beal; Moir (Brooks 40), Jorgensen, Leslie (Tucker 76), Cohen; Grayson, Dawson; Smith, Thompson (Richmond 51), Stewart (Morris 51), Ackermann (Phillips 57, Stewart 64-69), Brouzet, Blowers, Seely, Pountney*
Referee: S Lander ENG

BT Scotland Premiership

		P	W	D	L	PF	PA	B	Pts
1	Hawick	18	15	1	2	505	284	10	72
2	Boroughmuir	18	15	0	3	488	291	11	71
3	Heriot's FP	18	10	0	8	501	330	10	50
4	Aberdeen GSFP	18	9	0	9	369	393	8	44
5	Glasgow Hawks	18	8	0	10	379	371	9	41
6	Melrose	18	9	0	9	325	439	5	41
7	Stirling County	18	8	0	10	345	385	7	39
8	Currie	18	7	0	11	393	459	9	37
9	Gala	18	6	2	10	314	433	4	32

BT Cellnet Cup

Final
Murrayfield, April 20
Hawick 20   **Glasgow Hawks 17**
Tries: Turnbull   *Adams, Leighton*
Walker
Cons: Stenhouse 2   *Little*
DG: Douglas
Stenhouse

Hawick: Turnbull (Hames 99); Walker, Douglas, Houston, Bruce (Murray 76); Stenhouse, Reid* (Irving 73); Edwards (Gillie 65), Howe (M Landels 47), Dunlea, MacLeod, Elliot, D Landels (Imray 73, Parker 95), Martin, Deans
Glasgow Hawks: Little; Adams (Hawkes 71), Morrison (Gordon 66), Leighton, Philip; Duffy (Hodgkinson 74), Sinclair (Francis 80); McIntyre (MacNeil 94), Docherty* (Horton 71), Murray (Mories 96), Smith, Hutton, Maxton, McKay, Sitch
Referee: C Muir SCO
Hawick won after extra time

Welsh/Scottish League

		P	W	D	L	PF	PA	T	Pts
1	Llanelli	20	15	0	5	583	402	60	**45**
2	Newport	20	14	1	5	576	415	68	**43**
3	Neath	20	14	0	6	616	366	64	**42**
4	Cardiff	20	13	1	6	498	404	56	**40**
5	Swansea	20	11	0	9	451	404	42	**33**
6	Edinburgh	20	10	2	8	498	512	55	**32**
7	Pontypridd	20	9	0	11	441	440	41	**27**
8	Glasgow	20	8	1	11	475	527	50	**25**
9	Bridgend	20	7	1	12	498	545	46	**22**
10	Ebbw Vale	20	5	0	15	407	609	36	**15**
11	Caerphilly	20	1	0	19	379	798	40	**3**

T = tries

The Principality Cup
Final
Millennium Stadium, May 18
Pontypridd 20   **Llanelli 17**
Tries: Davey   *L Davies*
PG: Davey 5   *S Jones 3*
DG: *S Jones*
Pontypridd: Davey; Wyatt, Parker, Bryant, Nuthall; Sweeney, John*; Jenkins, Davies, Bell (Cronk 25-26), Cockbain, Sidoli, Kelly (Harris 60), Owen, Parks
Llanelli: B Davies; M Jones, Cardey (Boobyer 81), L Davies (Bowen 47), Finau; S Jones, G Easterby (Peel 47); Madden, McBryde, J Davies (Booth 72), Cooper, Wyatt (Gross 72), Hodges, Quinnell*, S Easterby
Referee: G Simmonds WAL

Irish Interprovincial
Championship

		P	W	D	L	PF	PA	B	Pts
1	Leinster	3	2	1	0	86	35	2	**12**
2	Ulster	3	2	0	1	50	66	0	**8**
3	Munster	3	1	1	1	64	48	1	**7**
4	Cannacht	3	0	0	3	56	107	1	**1**

AIB All Ireland Division 1

		P	W	D	L	PF	PA	B	Pts
1	Cork Constitution	15	11	2	2	314	191	4	**52**
2	Shannon	15	11	1	3	359	209	5	**51**
3	Clontarf	15	10	1	4	354	225	5	**47**
4	Garryowen	15	9	2	4	357	259	5	**45**
5	St Mary's College	15	9	1	5	298	285	5	**43**
6	UCD	15	8	1	6	358	379	5	**39**
7	Galwegians	15	8	0	7	322	306	4	**36**
8	Terenure College	15	8	0	7	294	294	4	**36**
9	Blackrock College	15	6	1	8	357	339	8	**34**
10	Dungannon	15	6	1	8	283	305	6	**32**
11	Ballymena	15	6	0	9	259	281	6	**30**
12	Buccaneers	15	5	2	8	297	288	5	**29**
13	Lansdowne	15	5	1	9	272	308	5	**27**
14	Co Carlow	15	5	1	9	259	283	4	**26**
15	DLSP	15	4	0	11	251	407	5	**21**
16	Young Munster	15	2	0	13	209	384	4	**12**

Division 1 Play-offs
Semi-finals
Shannon 15   Clontarf 12
Cork Constitution 43   Garryowen 17

All Ireland League Final
Lansdowne Road, May 4
Cork Constitution 17   **Shannon 21**
Tries: Kelly   *McMahon, Lacey*
J Sheahan
Cons: O Meara 2   *Cregan*
Pens: O'Meara   *Cregan 2*
DG: *McNamara*
Cork: Walsh; Dillon, Kelly, Cian Mahoney, Horgan; Conor Mahoney, O'Meara; I Murray, F Sheahan, J O'Driscoll, D O'Callaghan, M O'Driscoll, J Sheahan, U O'Callaghan, J Murray
Shannon: Lacey; Cregan, Lawlor, Thompson, M McNamara; N McNamara, Hegarty; Horan, Blaney, J Hayes, Buckley (Galwey 55), T Hayes, A Quinlan, D Quinlan, McMahon
Referee: A Rolland IRL

Women's Rugby

World Cup

Barcelona, May 13-25
At the group phase, the teams are allocated according to seedings based on the 1998 World Cup, which were:
1 New Zealand; 2 USA; 3 England; 4 Canada; 5 Scotland; 6 Spain; 7 France; 8 Australia; 9 Wales; 10 Kazakhstan; 11 Japan; 12 Samoa; 13 Ireland; 14 Italy; 15 Holland; 16 Germany
The first phase is not a full round robin with each team only playing two other teams in the group. The teams that won two matches progressed directly to the semi-finals.

First Phase

Group A
New Zealand 117 Germany 0; Australia 30 Wales 0; Wales 77 Germany 0; New Zealand 36 Australia 3
Group B
USA 87 Netherlands 0; France 31 Kazakhstan 12; Kazakhstan 37 Netherlands 10; France 21 USA 9
Group C
England 63 Italy 9; Spain 66 Japan 0; Italy 30 Japan 3; England 13 Spain 5
Group D
Canada 45 Ireland 0; Scotland 13 Samoa 3; Samoa 22 Ireland 0; Canada 11 Scotland 0

Second Phase

Classification Round
Ireland 18 Germany 0; Japan 37 Netherlands 3; Wales 35 Italy 3; Samoa 9 Kazakhstan 5; Australia 17 USA 5; Scotland 23 Spain 16

Place Play-offs
15/16th Place

Netherlands 20	Germany 19

13/14th Place

Ireland 23	Japan 3

11/12th Place

Kazakhstan 20	Italy 3

9/10th Place

Samoa 17	Wales 14

7/8th Place

USA 23	Spain 5

5/6th Place

Australia 30	Scotland 0

Semi-finals

New Zealand 30	France 0
England 53	Canada 10

Bronze Medal match

France 41	Canada 7

Final

Olympic Stadium, Barcelona, May 25
NEW ZEALAND 19   ENGLAND 9
Tries: Hirovanaa
Waaka
PG: Wilson 2, Myers   Rae 2
DG: Rae
New Zealand: Wilson; Kahura, Rush, Shortland (Myers 66), Marsh; Richards, Hirovanna; Sheck (Vaaga 52), Palmer*, Luia'ana, Codling, Heighway, Waaka, Martin, Lili'a (Robinson 75)
England: George*; Crawford, Jupp, Rudge (De Baise 73), Day; Rae (Appleby 56-61), Japp; Edwards (O'Reilly 53), Garnett, Huxford, Henderson, Andrews (Burns 75), Phillips (Clayton 63), Frost, Stevens
***Referee:** G de Santis ITA*

Sailing

The British Challenge may not have made much of an impact in the Louis Vuitton Challenge (full details of that and the America's Cup itself will be in the next edition), but if they made it an Olympic class, the odds are surely that British sailors would make an instant impression. At world championships throughout the year, British boats qualified for Olympic places in seven of the 11 classes, and with some considerable style.

Ben Ainslie had the America's Cup as his ambition until January, when he jumped ship for a tilt at the Olympic Finn class. Ainslie had been working out with the US OneWorld team, but the mast was his office rather than the helm and as good as Ainslie is at checking the winds, the Olympic Laser champion wanted his hand on the wheel, or the rudder at least.

When he was back in control, Ainslie showed just how remarkable a sailor he is, winning the Finn Gold Cup, the world title for the class, just seven months after saying his farewells to the OneWorld team. It doesn't make him a heavyweight yet, for Ainslie needs more consistency and more weight, checking in at several pounds under the optimum weight of 97-98kg. As Ainslie was only an 80kg stripling when he won the Olympic Laser title, it has necessitated some serious protein intake.

Iain Percy, the reigning Olympic Finn champion, has a naturally larger frame than Ainslie, but their ambitions would balance out on the scales. It took Percy only 10 months from his first serious competition to win the world Star title in California, with some assistance from crewman Steve Mitchell, a former Etchells world champion. Percy differs from Ainslie in demeanour, as well as build, exuding confidence where Ainslie exudes (if it's possible) just diffidence. Their contrasting styles made the Olympic experience in Sydney even more of a compelling ride. Athens is beginning to look like another irresistible draw.

Which leaves only one British Olympic champion off the pace, for Shirley Robertson, of Europe class fame in Sydney, still has the marry the perfect team for a Yngling (the new and almost unpronounceable class) bid in Athens. As well, we should mention Paul Goodison in the Laser class and the glorious British revolution in Mistral racing, led by Dominic Tidey, Nick Dempsey (who led the world rankings at year end) and Natasha Sturges. Then there's Ellen McArthur, but we gave her a box *(see right)* and, to show that we go beyond a nationalistic brief, Robert Scheidt, whose achievement in recording a sixth world Laser title was immense.

More McArthur
Route Du Rhum
St Malo - Guadeloupe (Pointe-a-Pitre)
Nov 8-23
Monohull 60ft
1st Kingfisher - Ellen McArthur

Olympic Classes

Top British/Irish shown and other top-20 placings

470 World Championships

Cagliari, Sardinia, Sept 2-11

Men

1	Cooke/Nicholas	NZL	60
2	Kosmatopoulos/Trigonis	GRE	65
3	Martinez/Cantero	ESP	69
8	Rogers/Glanfield	GBR	104

Women

1	Bekatorou/Tsoulfa	GRE	40
2	Westerhof/Matthijsse	NED	61
3	Petitjean/Douroux	FRA	61
21	Lucas/Heeley	GBR	139

470 European Championships

Tallin, Estonia, July 25-Aug 3

Men

1	Charbonnier/Christidis	FRA	58
2	Kosmatopoulos/Trigonis	GRE	65
3	Rogers/Glanfield	GBR	69
8	Vials/Harvey	GBR	88
20	Plummer/Hawkley	GBR	170

Women

1	Bekatorou/Tsoulfa	GRE	49
2	Ilienko/Krutskikh	RUS	66
3	Westerhof/Matthijsse	NED	87
9	Bassadone/Hopson	GBR	145
13	Lucas/Heeley	GBR	164
20	Gibson/Clark	GBR	204

49er World Championship

Kaneohe, Hawaii, June 14-22

Men

1	Martinez/Fernandez	ESP	32
2	Draper/Hiscocks	GBR	40
3	Brotherton/Asquith	GBR	45
7	Richardson/Greenhalgh	GBR	63
17	Rice/Hillary	GBR	

49er European Championship

Grimstad, Norway, July 27-Aug 2

Men

1	Martinez/Fernandez	ESP	26
2	Draper/Hiscocks	GBR	29
3	Sundby/Bovim	NOR	35
7	Richardson/Greenhalgh	GBR	58
11	Brotherton/Asquith	GBR	73

Europe Class World Championship

Hamilton, Canada, Aug 21-Sep 3

Women

1	Sarah Blanck	AUS	33
2	Siren Sundby	NOR	45
3	Petra Niemann	GER	46
7	Maria Coleman	IRL	84
26	Kirsty Bonar	GBR	166

Europe Class European Championship

Nieuwpoort, Belgium, July 10-18

Women

1	Sari Multala	FIN	9
2	Trine Julie Abrahamsen	DEN	23
3	Sarah Mackay	NZL	33

(non-championship)

4	Siren Sundby	NOR	39
6	Maria Coleman	IRL	50
16	Debbie Winstanley	GBR	96

Finn World Cup

Piraeus, Greece, July 20-28

Men

1	Ben Ainslie	GBR	
2	Mateus Kusznierewicz	POL	
3	Emilios Papathanasiou	GRE	
9	Andrew Simpson	GBR	
12	Charlie Cumbley	GBR	

Finn European Championship

Cesme, Turkey, July 5-13

Men

1	Ben Ainslie	GBR	33
2	Luca Devoti	ITA	43
3	Karlo Kuret	CRO	51
6	Andrew Simpson	GBR	70
11	Charlie Cumbley	GBR	116
17	Chris Brittle	GBR	143

Laser World Championship

Hyannis YC, Cape Cod, USA, Sep 9-18

Men

1	Robert Scheidt	BRA	25
2	Karl Suneson	SWE	40
3	Paul Goodison	GBR	51
6	Edward Wright	GBR	86
13	Mark Howard	GBR	118

Note: This was Scheidt's sixth world title.

Laser European Championship

Vallensbaek, Denmark, July 12-20

Men

1	Karl Suneson	SWE	39
2	Fredrik Lassenius	SWE	45
3	Paul Goodison	GBR	48
8	Edward Wright	GBR	74
13	Dan Holman	GBR	83

Mistral World Championship

Pattaya, Thailand, Dec 4-15

Men

1	Gal Friedman	ISR	33.00
2	Ricardo Santos	BRA	45.00
3	Julien Bontemps	FRA	50.00
5	Dominic Tidey	GBR	63.00
7	Nick Dempsey	GBR	77.00

Women

1	Barbara Kendall	NZL	26.00
2	Alessandro Sensini	ITA	34.00
3	Faustine Merret	FRA	46.10
5	Natasha Sturges	GBR	61.00
11	Bryony Shaw	GBR	115.00

Mistral European Championships
Neusiedlersee, Austria, Sep 4-15
Men

1	Alexandre Guyader	FRA	54
2	Gal Friedman	ISR	55
3	Nicolas Beudou	FRA	68
6	Nick Dempsey	GBR	92
14	Dominic Tidey	GBR	147

Women

1	Alessandra Sensini	ITA	53
2	Natasha Sturges	GBR	56
3	Lisa Vidal	FRA	63
13	Bryony Shaw	GBR	143

Star World Championship
California Yacht Club, Aug 14-25
Men

1	Percy/Mitchell	GBR	11
2	Grael/Ferreira	BRA	18
3	Rohart/Adde	FRA	29
9	Mansfield/Collins	IRL	65

Star European Championship
Genoa, Italy, Oct 4-11
Men

1	Loof/Ekstrom	SWE	15
2	Reynolds/Sperry	USA	21
3	Holm/Leifelt	DEN	28
4	Pickel/Kolb	GER	28
5	Percy/Mitchell	GBR	30
12	Mansfield/Collins	IRL	55

Tornado World Championship
Marthas Vineyard, USA, Sep 21-28
Men

1	Bundock/Forbes	AUS	16
2	Backes/Voiron	FRA	19
3	Booth/Dercksen	NED	28
13	McMillan/Bulkeley	GBR	89
14	Styles/May	GBR	100
15	Wilson/Howden	GBR	105

Tornado European Championship
Vilamoura, Portugal, May 4-11
Men

1	Backes/Voiron	FRA	23
2	Booth/Dercksen	NED	38
3	Karsenbarg/Heemskerk	NED	64
8	Styles/May	GBR	90
10	Wilson/Howden	GBR	98
19	MacMillan/Bulkeley	GBR	138
20	Lovegrove/Sellars	GBR	142

Yngling World Championship
Brunnen, Switzerland, July 19-26
Women

1	Azon/Tutzo/Azon	ESP	43
2	Schumann/Bulle/Lippert	GER	52
3	Alison/Icyda/Leech	USA	54
16	Robertson/Leask/Ayton	GBR	93

Athens
Olympic Qualification

World Championships placings throughout 2002 earned Olympic qualification by nation for the 2004 Olympics as listed below.

49er
Spain, Great Britain, Ukraine, Italy, Denmark, Netherlands

Finn
Great Britain, Poland, Croatia, Spain, Belgium, Germany, France, Brazil, Ireland

Yngling
Spain, Germany, USA, Bermuda, Denmark

Star
Great Britain, Brazil, France, USA, Bermuda

Europe
Australia, Norway, Germany, Finland, Czech Republic, Netherlands, Ireland, Poland, China

470 Men
New Zealand, Spain, Israel, Australia, USA, Portugal, Great Britain, Italy, Japan, Argentina

470 Women
Netherlands, France, Russia, Germany, Spain, Israel

Laser
Brazil, Sweden, Great Britain, Italy, Australia, South Africa, Belgium, Finland, Canada, Croatia, Spain, Austria, Slovenia, Turkey

Tornado
Australia, France, Austria, Argentina, Sweden

Mistral Men
Israel, Brazil, France, Great Britain, Argentina, Portugal, New Zealand, Poland, Ukraine, Spain, Hungary, Netherlands

Mistral Women
New Zealand, Italy, France, Great Britain, Germany, China, Spain, Poland, Hong Kong, Switzerland

World Rankings

As at Dec 16, 2002
British/Irish rankings shown if top 20

470

Men

1	Wilmot/Page	AUS	4873
2	Kosmatopoulos/Trigonis	GRE	4811
3	Braslavets/Matviyenko	UKR	4769
4	Rogers/Glanfield	GBR	4618
19	Vials/Harvey	GBR	4038

Women

1	Bekatorou/Tsoulfa	GRE	4866
2	Armstrong/Stowell	AUS	4778
3	Rothweiler/Leu	GER	4668
18	Bassadone/Hopson	GBR	3827

49er

Men

1	Martinez/Fernandez	ESP	4789
2	Rodion/Leonchuk	UKR	4620
3	Lopez Vazquez/De la Plaza	ESP	4596
4	Brotherton/Asquith	GBR	4559
5	Draper/Hiscocks	GBR	4532
7	Richardson/Greenhalgh	GBR	4445

Europe

Women

1	Sari Multala	FIN	4967
2	Carolijn Brouwer	NED	4818
3	Maria Coleman	IRL	4738
20	Debbie Winstanley	GBR	3845

Finn

Men

1	Emilios Papathanasiou	GRE	4685
2	Karlo Kuret	CRO	4630
3	Mateusz Kusznierewicz	POL	4583
4	Andrew Simpson	GBR	4529
7	Chris Brittle	GBR	4096
12	Charlie Cumbley	GBR	3940
14	Ben Ainslie	GBR	3920
18	David Mellor	GBR	3794

Laser

Men

1	Paul Goodison	GBR	4966
2	Kalle Suneson	SWE	4903
3	Robert Scheidt	BRA	4746
5	Ed Wright	GBR	4710

Mistral

Men

1	Nick Dempsey	GBR	4467
2	Gal Friedman	ISR	4441
3	Ricardo Santos	BRA	4406
5	Dominic Tidey	GBR	4377

Women

1	Natsha Sturges	GBR	4430
2	Anna Graczyk	POL	4390
3	Agata Brygoza	POL	4338
8	Bryony Shaw	GBR	4156

Star

Men

1	Reynolds/Liljedahl	USA	4890
2	Percy/Mitchell	GBR	4859
3	Mansfield/Collins	IRL	4701

Tornado

Men

1	Bundock/Forbes	AUS	4890
2	Hagara/Steinacher	AUT	4886
3	Booth/Derecksen	NED	4734
4	Styles/May	GBR	4674
6	McMillan/Bulkeley	GBR	4385
9	Wilson/Howden	GBR	4264
17	Lovegrove/Sellars	GBR	3856

Yngling

Women

1	Azon Canalda/Tutzo/Garcia	ESP	4228
2	Dennison/Herbert/Aders	AUS	3966
3	Thies/De Jong/Bes	NED	3843
11	Robertson/Leask/Aytons	GBR	3090
16	Johnson/Line/Norris	GBR	2553

Skiing

No one came even close to Stephan Eberharter in the World Cup season. With Hermann Maier unable to effect a miracle recovery from the broken leg sustained in a motorbike accident (it sounded for a while as if he might), Eberharter had the speed disciplines to himself, and the 32-year-old duly mopped up the downhill titles at Wengen, Kitzbühel, St Moritz and Altenmarkt. The Austrian won a total of 10 races throughout the season, stood on the podium on 17 occasions and never once placed outside the top 10. In the World Cup, Eberharter finished top of the overall standings, won the downhill, and super G events, and finished third in the giant slalom. He won an Olympic gold medal as well *(see Winter Olympics section)* and probably should have retired, because it's hard to better sensational...but he didn't. Being a skiing champion in Austria is a bit like being Jonathan Ross in Britain, it's just limelight, limelight, limelight, and that's very seductive.

Michaela Dorfmeister won the overall women's World Cup title, making it a very good season all round for Austria. However, with Croatia's Janica Kostelic ruled out of the World Cup season recovering from knee surgery, Dorfmeister's success was not quite as lustrous as it might have been.

No success for British skiers with Alain Baxter struggling all winter to get the skis right. So discouraged was the Scot at one point that the British Ski and Snowboard Federation offered to help raise funds to release the skier from his contract with Head skis. Baxter declined the offer and, as we've written elsewhere, it proved (notwithstanding the subsequent drugs positive) to be the right decision. For most of his season though, the World Cup successes of the previous winter earlier, when he placed 11th in the slalom standings, must have felt worlds away.

Emma Carrick-Anderson completed her 11th season on the circuit, and the considerable promise remains unrealised. Amazingly, though, she is still only 27. Chemmy Alcott competed in her first World Cup, but her best result came in the World Junior Championships, where she finished fourth in the combination. And a second Baxter broke through, Alain's younger brother Noel earning selection for the Winter Olympic team, but that's another tale on another page.

> **"You have to be aggressive and attack in such a situation. I felt like a German soldier ready for battle in 1941"**
>
> Ivica Kostelic, explaining how he felt at the top of the slope before a race, as quoted in the Croatian weekly *Nacional*. The magazine also published comments from a year-old interview with Kostelic in which the skier also suggested that Hitler was more humane than Stalin, and Nazism was better than Communism.
>
> Oh dear.

Alpine

World Cup Final
Altenmarkt, Austria, , Mar 6-10

MEN
Downhill
1 Hannes Trinkl AUT 1:41.80
2 Hermann Maier AUT 1:42.07
3 Florian Eckert GER 1:42.26
DNF: Finlay Mickel GBR

Super G
1 Didier Cuche SUI 1:25.53
2 Fritz Strobl AUT 1:25.88
3 Alessandro Fattori ITA 1:26.14

Giant Slalom
1 Michael Von Gruenigen SUI 2:23.80
2 Benny Raich AUT 2:41.25
3 Stephan Eberharter AUT 2:41.69

Slalom
1 Ivica Kostelic CRO 1:37.92
2 Bode Miller USA 1:38.15
3 Jean-Pierre Vidal FRA 1:39.00

WOMEN
Downhill
1 Michaela Dorfmeister AUT 1:40.09
2 Renate Goetschl AUT 1:40.28
3 Selina Heregger AUT 1:40.29

Super G
1 Michaela Dorfmeister AUT 1:27.87
2 Alexandra Meissnitzer AUT 1:28.53
3 Hilde Gerg GER 1:29.37

Giant Slalom
1 Sonja Nef SUI 2:42.96
2 Anna Ottosson SWE 2:43.80
3 Tanja Poutiainen FIN 2:44.49

Slalom
1 Janica Kostelic CRO 1:54.66
2 Anja Paerson SWE 1:55.23
3 Ylva Nowen SWE 1:55.38

World Cup
MEN - FINAL STANDINGS
Overall
1 Stephan Eberharter AUT 1702
2 Kjetil Andre Aamodt NOR 1096
3 Didier Cuche SUI 1064
4 Bode Miller USA 952
5 Fritz Strobl AUT 846
78 Alain Baxter GBR 54
139 Finlay Mickel GBR 6

Downhill
1 Stephan Eberharter AUT 810
2 Fritz Strobl AUT 520
3 Kristian Ghedina ITA 381
53 Finlay Mickel GBR 6

Super G
1 Stephan Eberharter AUT 470
2 Didier Cuche SUI 426
3 Josef Strobl AUT 326

Giant Slalom
1 Frederic Covili FRA 471
2 Benny Raich AUT 429
3 Stephan Eberharter AUT 422

Slalom
1 Ivica Kostelic CRO 611
2 Bode Miller USA 560
3 Jean-Pierre Vidal FRA 456
28 Alain Baxter GBR 54

WOMEN
Overall
1 Michaela Dorfmeister AUT 1271
2 Renate Goetschl AUT 931
3 Sonja Nef SUI 904
4 Hilde Gerg GER 847
5 Anja Paerson SWE 840
117 Emma Carrick-Anderson GBR 3

Downhill
1 Isolde Kostner ITA 568
2 Michaela Dorfmeister AUT 469
3 Corinne Rey Bellet SUI 414

Super G
1 Hilde Gerg GER 355
2 Alexandra Meissnitzer AUT 248
3 Michaela Dorfmeister AUT 212

Giant Slalom
1 Sonja Nef SUI 676
2 Anja Paerson SWE 408
3 Michaela Dorfmeister AUT 341

Slalom
1 Laure Pequegnot FRA 597
2 Kristina Koznick USA 518
3 Anja Paerson SWE 480
117 Emma Carrick-Anderson GBR 3

World Junior Championships
Tarvisio/Sella Nevea/Ravascletto, Italy, Mar 3-6
Championships relocated from Narvik due to weather conditions

MEN
Downhill
1 Adam Cole USA 1:26.85
2 Mario Scheiber AUT 1:27.23
3 Aksel-Lund Svindal NOR 1:27.26
48 James Barcock GBR 1:31.24

Super G
1 Peter Fill ITA 1:25.02
2 Aksel-Lund Svindal NOR 1:25.52
2 Peter Struger AUT 1:25.52
53 James Barcock GBR 1:31.09

Giant Slalom
Event cancelled

Slalom
1 Steven Nyman USA 1:30.46
2 Marc Berthod SUI 1:30.73
3 Aksel-Lund Svindal NOR 1:31.37
33 James Barcock GBR 1:36.98

Combined
1 Aksel-Lund Svindal NOR
2 Steven Nyman USA
3 Alexander Koll AUT
24 James Barcock GBR

WOMEN
Downhill
1 Julia Mancusa USA 1:29.81
2 Astrid Vierthaler AUT 1:29.95
3 Nicole Hosp AUT 1:30.56
12 Chemmy Alcott GBR 1:32.44

Super G
1 Maria Riesch GER 1:27.54
2 Daniela Mueller AUT 1:28.55
3 Kelly Vanderbeek CAN 1:28.64

Giant Slalom
1 Julia Mancuso USA 1:52.15
2 Jessica Kelley USA 1:52.27
3 Florence Roujas FRA 1:52.32
13 Chemmy Alcott GBR 1:54.12

Slalom
1 Veronika Zuzulova SVK 1:36.54
2 Maria Riesch GER 1:36.68
3 Sandra Gini SUI 1:36.89
22 Chemmy Alcott GBR 1:39.89

Combined
1 Julia Mancusa USA
2 Tanya Buehler SUI
3 Daniela Mueller AUT
4 Chemmy Alcott GBR

Nordic Combined

World Cup
Final Standings
1 Ronny Ackermann GER 2000
2 Felix Gottwald AUT 1901
3 Samppa Lajunen FIN 1738
4 Jaakko Tallus FIN 1125
5 Daito Takahashi JPN 1101
6 Todd Lodwig USA 1033
7 Mario Stecher AUT 952
8 Bill Deming USA 817
9 Christoph Bieler AUT 810
10 Hannu Manninen FIN FIN

Cross-country

World Cup
MEN
Overall Standings
1 Per Elofsson SWE 780
2 Thomas Alsgaard NOR 777
3 Anders Aukland NOR 545
Sprint Standings
1 Trond Iverson NOR 328
2 Jens Arne Svartedal ITA 300
3 Cristian Zorzi ITA 264

WOMEN
Overall Standings
1 Bente Skari NOR 877
2 Katerina Neumannova CZE 763
3 Stefano Belmondo ITA 760
Sprint Standings
1 Bente Skari NOR 319
2 Anita Moen NOR 307
3 Katerina Neumannova CZE 293

Ski-jumping

World Cup
Final Overall Standings
1 Adam Malysz POL 1475
2 Sven Hannewald GER 1259
3 Matti Hautemaeki FIN 1048
4 Andreas Widhoelzl AUT 874
5 Martin Schmitt GER 795
6 Martin Hoellwarth AUT 737
7 Simon Ammann SUI 628
8 Martin Koch AUT 561
9 Stephan Hocke GER 508

Freestyle

World Cup
Final Standings
MEN
Overall
1 Tomas Kraus CZE 100
2 Scott Bellavance CAN 96
3 Isodor Gruener AUT 96
Aerials
1 Eric Bergoust USA 392
2 Alexei Grichin BLR 376
3 Ales Valenta CZE 364
Dual Moguls
1 Richard Gay FRA 264
2 Garth Hager USA 236
3 Stephane Rochon CAN 188
Moguls
1 Scott Bellavance 96
2 Toby Dawson USA 88
3 Travis Cabral USA 86

WOMEN
Overall
1 Veronika Bauer CAN 100
2 Magdalena Jonsson SWE 100
3 Margarita Marbler AUT 96
Aerials
1 Alla Tsuper BLR 492
2 Jacqui Cooper AUS 428
3 Deidra Dionne CAN 420
Dual Moguls
1 Christine Gerg GER 232
2 Kari Traa NOR 212
3 Tami Bradley CAN 204
Moguls
1 Margarita Marbler AUT 192
2 Shannon Bahrke USA 192
3 Kari Traa NOR 180

Snowboarding

World Cup
Final Standings
MEN
Overall
1 Jasey Jay Anderson CAN 792
2 Mathieu Bozzetto FRA 719
3 Nicolas Huet FRA 622
Giant Slalom
1 Dejan Kosir SLO 1000
2 Markus Ebner GER 800
3 Stephen Copp SWE 600
Parallel Giant Slalom
1 Dejan Kosir SLO 7510
2 Mathieu Bozzetto FRA 5552
3 Siegfried Grabner AUT 5420

Parallel Slalom
1 Mathieu Bozzetto FRA 4250
2 Nicolas Huet FRA 4000
3 Dejon Kosir SLO 3260
Parallel
1 Mathieu Bozzetto FRA 2530
2 Dejon Kosir SLO 1920
3 Felix Stadler AUT 1880
Snowboard Cross
1 Jasey Jay Anderson CAN 4700
2 Drew Neilson CAN 4090
3 Aymerick Mermoz FRA 3510
Halfpipe
1 Jan Michaelis GER 5080
2 Risto Mattila FIN 3660
3 Antti Autti FIN 2436
Big Air
1 Andreas Jakobsson SWE 1000
2 Bjoern Lindgren SWE 1000
3 Sami Tuoriniemi FIN 820

WOMEN
Overall
1 Karine Ruby FRA 999
2 Doresia Krings AUT 655
3 Doris Guenther AUT 591
Giant Slalom
1 Steffi von Siebenthal SUI 1000
2 Heidi Renoth GER 800
3 Lisa Kosglow USA 600
Parallel Giant Slalom
1 Isabelle Blanc FRA 6270
2 Doris Guenther AUT 5770
3 Karine Ruby FRA 5690
Parallel Slalom
1 Karine Ruby FRA 5200
2 Heidi Renoth GER 3620
3 Isabelle Blanc FRA 3080
Parallel
1 Ursula Bruhin SUI 3200
2 Nicolien Sauerbreij NED 2700
3 Isabelle Blanc FRA 1900
Snowboard Cross
1 Doresia Krings AUT 4130
2 Marie Laissus FRA 4110
3 Ursula Fingerlos AUT 3820
Halfpipe
1 Nicola Pederzolli AUT 6620
2 Sabine Wehr-Hasler GER 4570
3 Valerie Bourdier FRA 3380
4 Lesley McKenna GBR 2700
Big Air
1 Steffi von Siebenthal SUI 6620
2 Sabine Wehr-Hasler GER 4570
3 Valerie Bourdier FRA 3380

S n o o k e r

Napoleon Hill came out with a fair amount of old rubbish in his lifetime. "I have proved, times too numerous to enumerate, to my own satisfaction at least, that every human brain is both a broadcasting and a receiving station for vibrations of thought frequency," he once said, stopping the world's scientists in their tracks. "If you do not conquer self, you will be conquered by self," he said another time, and the world's psychologists, as one, said, "Y'what?"

Peter Ebdon, though, will not have a word said against the aphorisms of Hill. Quite the opposite, for Ebdon's own philosophy was shaped and formed by Hill's best selling book 'Think And Grow Rich' to such an extent that he was intending to give one to every child when he returned to his old school, Highbury Grove, for the annual prize-giving shortly after the world championships.

Presumably those pupils who want to become snooker champions will devour every word of Hill's prose, for look where it's taken Ebdon to. Not only has it brought him a world title, but taught him to play the oboe and know lots about horse breeding. All that just by understanding that the brain is a "broadcasting and receiving station for thought frequency".

The talents which brought him the world title could be defined in language alien to Hill by its simplicity; Ebdon played thoughtful and intelligent snooker and kept focused. He needed all his concentration against Stephen Hendry for the final went to the 35th frame, as key earlier shots were missed. In the last frame, Ebdon was always dominant. At 63-14, and the witching hour reached, Ebdon escaped a snooker, potted red and brown to extend the lead, and Hendry, waving goodbye to a record eighth title, respectfully downed tools.

It had been a wonderful final, watched at its climax by eight million BBC viewers. It had been a wonderful tournament, with a record 67 century breaks, 16 of which belonged to Hendry, a record for any ranking tournament, and which took the phlegmatic Scot to a century of world championship centuries.

Ronnie O'Sullivan had lasted longer than most first-time champions (none has retained the title in 14 tries) reaching the semi-final stage and raising the stakes with some ill-timed comments about the Doyle camp which could only motivate Hendry. "It added great tension to the occasion. It was a grudge match but what better than a grudge match," said O'Sullivan, who may reflect that what is better than a grudge match is a match you win. As always, O'Sullivan beats himself better than anyone else can. Maybe Ebdon should send him a copy of Napoleon Hill's book. Or maybe not.

Off the table, there was something close to a mood of reconciliation amongst the warring bodies of the sport, with the commercial activities handed over to World Snooker Ltd and the WPBSA board unanimously re-elected at the AGM.

World Championship

Crucible Theatre, Sheffield   Apr 20-May 6

ROUND 1	ROUND 2	Q-FINALS	S-FINALS	FINAL

Ronnie O'Sullivan (2) 10
Drew Hendry (Q) 5

Ronnie O'Sullivan 13
Robert Milkins 2

Fergal O'Brien (16) 8
Robert Milkins (Q) 10

Ronnie O'Sullivan 13
Stephen Lee 11

Paul Hunter (9) 9
Quinten Hann (Q) 10

Quinten Hann 3
Stephen Lee 13

Stephen Lee (8) 10
Chris Small (Q) 2

Ronnie O'Sullivan 13
Stephen Hendry 17

Stephen Hendry (5) 10
Shaun Murphy (Q) 4

Stephen Hendry 13
Anthony Davies 3

Alan McManus (12) 7
Anthony Davies (Q) 13

Stephen Hendry 13
Ken Doherty 12

Mark King (13) 10
David Gray (Q) 5

Mark King 12
Ken Doherty 13

Ken Doherty (4) 10
Stuart Bingham (Q) 8

| Stephen Hendry | 17 |
| **Peter Ebdon** | **18** |

John Higgins (3) 10
James Wattana (Q) 1

John Higgins 13
Graeme Dott 2

Graeme Dott (14) 10
Robin Hull (Q) 6

John Higgins 7
Matthew Stevens 13

Jimmy White (11) 10
Dominic Dale (Q) 2

Jimmy White 3
Matthew Stevens 13

Matthew Stevens (6)10
Mike Dunn (Q) 6

Matthew Stevens 16
Peter Ebdon 17

Peter Ebdon (7) 10
Michael Judge (Q) 4

Peter Ebdon 13
Joe Perry 7

Joe Swail (10) 6
Joe Perry (Q) 10

Peter Ebdon 13
Anthony Hamilton 6

Dave Harold (15) 6
Anthony Hamilton (Q) 10

Anthony Hamilton 13
Mark Williams 9

Mark Williams (1) 10
John Parrott (Q) 7

Final Frame Scores-Ebdon 1st: (65) 94-0, (100) 140-0, 73-13, 71-16, 0-126 (126), 40-73, 4-119 (116), 36-65, (134) 134-0, (56) 56-67, (52) 68-9, 70-68 (68), 77-14, (56) 69-13, 4-70, (89) 89-33, (68) 69-32, 0-126 (104), 0-108 (108), 21-66, 36-89 (68), 67-43, 0-110, 0-97 (93), 1-127 (63,55), 58-65, (103) 103-22, 62-26, 30-74 (58), (73) 73-21, (111) 111-0, 39-78 (67), (85) 85-4, (51) 52-62, (59) 72-14

Highest breaks: 145 Matthew Stevens; 141 Stephen Hendry; 138 Peter Ebdon
In total there were 67 century breaks, a championship record. Hendry hit 16, another record.
Prize Money: Winner-£260,000; Runner-up-£152,000; Losing semi-finalists-£76,000; Losing quarter-finalists-£38,000; Last 16-£21,000

Major Tournaments 2001-2002

Date	Tournament (1st prize)	Venue	Winner	Score	Runner-up
Aug 11-19	Champions Cup (£100,000)	Brighton Centre	**John Higgins**	7-4	Mark Williams
Sep 18-23	Scottish Masters (£63,000)	Thistle Hotel, Glasgow	**John Higgins**	9-6	Ronnie O'Sullivan
Sep 29-Oct 7	British Open (£92,500)	Newcastle	**John Higgins**	9-6	Graeme Dott
Oct 12-21	LG Cup (£82,500)	Guild Hall, Preston	**Stephen Lee**	9-4	Peter Ebdon
Nov 23-Dec 1	European Open (£44,000)	Malta	**Stephen Hendry**	9-3	Joe Perry
Dec 3-12	UK Champs (£100,000)	Barbican Centre, York	**Ronnie O'Sullivan**	10-1	Ken Doherty
Jan 23-27	Welsh Open (£82,000)	Cardiff	**Paul Hunter**	9-7	Ken Doherty
Feb 3-10	The Masters (£190,000)	Wembley	**Paul Hunter**	10-9	Mark Williams
Feb 23-Mar 2	China Open (£62,500)	Shanghai	**Mark Williams**	9-8	Anthony Hamilton
Mar 3-10	Thailand Masters (£67,500)	Bangkok	**Mark Williams**	9-4	Stephen Lee
Mar 19-24	Irish Masters (£62,000)	Dublin	**John Higgins**	10-3	Peter Ebdon
Apr 6-14	Scottish Open (£82,500)	Aberdeen	**Stephen Lee**	9-2	David Gray

Women's Events

World Championship
Swindon/Sheffield, Apr 21-28
Final
Kelly Fisher ENG bt Lisa Quick ENG 4-1

EUROPEAN CHAMPIONSHIP
Kalisz, Poland, May 29-June 8
Final
Kelly Fisher ENG bt Wendy Jans BEL 5-0

WELSH MASTERS
Cardiff, Jan 26
Final
Kelly Fisher ENG bt Wendy Jans BEL 4-0

UK CHAMPIONSHIP
York, Dec 12, 2001
Final
Kelly Fisher ENG bt Lynette Horsburgh ENG 4-1

BELGIAN 147 OPEN
Bruges, Nov 24, 2001
Final
Kelly Fisher ENG bt Lynette Horsburgh ENG 4-0

BRITISH OPEN
Newcastle, Oct 1, 2001
Final
Kelly Fisher ENG bt Lynette Horsburgh ENG 4-0

"I think it is a great idea to talk during sex, so long as it's about snooker"

Steve Davis on life's priorities.

"I don't trust them. Leaving their camp is one reason why I have done so well. Maybe there are other players who would do better if they left Doyle, but I don't think they have the bottle to."

Ronnie O'Sullivan, explaining why he left Ian Doyle's management team. His comments were perfectly timed to turn his world championship semi-final against Stephen Hendry (still with Doyle) into a 'Grudge Match'.

World Rankings

Rankings apply throughout the 2002-2003 season

1	(2)	Ronnie O'Sullivan ENG	50,024
2	(1)	Mark Williams WAL	46,785
3	(7)	Peter Ebdon ENG	44,652
4	(3)	John Higgins SCO	44,334
5	(4)	Ken Doherty IRL	43,479
6	(5)	Stephen Hendry SCO	42,128
7	(8)	Stephen Lee ENG	39,669
8	(6)	Matthew Stevens WAL	32,879
9	(9)	Paul Hunter ENG	31,309
10	(11)	Jimmy White ENG	28,934
11	(13)	Mark King ENG	27,432
12	(14)	Graeme Dott SCO	27,159
13	(27)	Joe Perry ENG	26,969
14	(25)	Quinten Hann AUS	26,232
15	(12)	Alan McManus SCO	25,740
16	(10)	Joe Swail NIR	24,879
17	(19)	Anthony Hamilton ENG	23,836
18	(22)	John Parrott ENG	23,488
19	(30)	David Gray ENG	22,868
20	(20)	Dominic Dale WAL	22,674
21	(15)	Steve Davis ENG	22,615
22	(18)	Drew Henry SCO	22,541
23	(16)	Fergal O'Brien IRL	22,408
24	(28)	Michael Judge NIR	22,018
25	(21)	Steve Davis ENG	21,775
26	(31)	Anthony Davies WAL	21,053
27	(17)	Marco Fu HKG	20,293
28	(29)	Tony Drago MLT	19,779
29	(24)	Chris Small SCO	19,423
30	(23)	Nigel Bond ENG	19,038
31	(61)	Allister Carter ENG	18,539
32	(32)	James Wattana THA	18,371
33	(54)	Robert Milkens ENG	18,073
34	(40)	Shokat Ali PAK	17,921
35	(45)	Michael Holt ENG	17,519
36	(34)	Patrick Wallace NIR	17,404
37	(34)	Mark Davis ENG	16,910
38	(38)	Alfred Burden ENG	16,698
39	(86)	Robin Hull FIN	16,528
40	(26)	Billie Snaddon SCO	16,403
41	(41)	Marcus Campbell SCO	16,062
42	(33)	Brian Morgan ENG	16,033
43	(48)	Ian McCulloch ENG	15,958
44	(36)	Jamie Burnett SCO	15,230
45	(35)	Terry Murphy NIR	15,083
46	(37)	Gary Wilkinson ENG	15,076
47	(50)	Jonathan Birch ENG	15,014
48	(49)	David Roe ENG	14,898
49	(47)	Dave Finbow ENG	14,765
50	(43)	Bradley Jones ENG	14,699
51	(85)	Barry Hawkins ENG	14,649
52	(52)	Stephen Maguire SCO	14,419
53	(95)	Marc Selby ENG	14,395
54	(39)	Darren Morgan WAL	14,377
55	(42)	Jimmy Michie ENG	14,286
56	(82)	Barry Pinches ENG	13,846
57	(44)	Stuart Bingham ENG	13,735
58	(55)	Stuart Pettman ENG	13,715
59	(65)	Bjorn Haneveer BEL	13,566
60	(72)	Mike Dunn ENG	13,342
61	(46)	Andy Hicks ENG	13,231
62	(51)	Nick Dyson ENG	13,063
63	(63)	Gerard Greene NIR	12,815
64	(87)	Nick Walker ENG	11,958
65	(57)	Paul Davies WAL	11,839
66	(64)	Rod Lawler ENG	11,552
67	(75)	Euan Henderson SCO	11,397
68	(88)	Anthony Bolsover ENG	11,295
69	(66)	Paul Wykes ENG	10,825
70	(67)	Adrian Gunnell ENG	10,680
71	(93)	Andrew Higginson ENG	10,676
72	(169)	Sean Murphy ENG	10,583
73	(53)	Gary Ponting ENG	10,399
74	(59)	Peter Lines ENG	10,363
75	(70)	Kristjan Helgason ISL	10,352
76	(58)	Lee Walker ENG	10,252
77	(78)	Alain Robidoux CAN	10,037
78	(71)	Neal Foulds ENG	9,958
79	(77)	Matthew Couch ENG	9,942
80	(69)	Wayne Brown ENG	9,921
81	(84)	Jason Prince NIR	9,908
82	(89)	Sean Storey ENG	9,685
83	(97)	Troy Shaw ENG	9,650
84	(96)	Tony Jones ENG	9,624
85	(56)	Jason Ferguson ENG	9,533
86	(62)	Steve James ENG	9,281
87	(80)	Hugh Abernethy SCO	9,212
88	(321)	Rory McLeod ENG	9,083
89	(73)	Martin Dziewialtowski SCO	9,064
90	(73)	Joe Johnson ENG	8,872
91	(76)	John Reid ENG	8,683
92	(74)	Phaitoon Phonbun THA	8,644
93	(113)	Craig Butler ENG	8,633
94	(290)	Luke Fisher ENG	8,558
95	(231)	Stephen Kershaw ENG	8,533
96	(98)	Nicolas Pierce ENG	8,507
97	(105)	Jeff Cundy ENG	8,443
98	(180)	Paul S Davison ENG	8,283
99	(-)	Andrew Norman ENG	8,233
100	(92)	Mark Gray ENG	7,891

Speed Skating

Inevitably, the world championships in Heerenveen in March fell in the shadow of the Olympic Games in Salt Lake City. No less than 16 of the Olympic medallists were absent from the world championships, although this in part is explained by the fact that the sprinters have their own world championships. At least the two most successful from Salt Lake stood their ground; Germany's Claudia Pechstein and Dutchman Jochem Uytdehaage won two titles apiece at the Games, each breaking the world record in both their finals.

Pechstein, who had eclipsed her compatriot Anni Friesinger in the US, could not sustain the performance level in Heerenveen, winning only the 5000m and finishing in third place overall, Friesinger taking the all around honours this time. Uytdehaage, though, coasted to another success.

The 26-year-old Dutchman has made a rapid rise in the sport, only coming to international notice in 2001 when he was a shock winner of the Dutch all-around championships. The Utrecht skater went on place fourth in that season's European championships, and rank 10th in the world championships. For this season, though, there has been another quantum leap in performance.

On home ice, it was another Dutchman who came closest to causing an upset in the world event, with Gianni Romme, himself a world all-around champion in 2000, failing by just fractions to match Uytdehaage over the 5000m distance. In the longer race, though, Uytdehaage was unpressed to win by seven seconds. Perhaps the best measure of the Olympic champions two distance wins in Heerenveen, though, was that the winning times for the 5000m and 10,000m were respectively 16 and 31 seconds slower than those needed to take the gold medals in Salt Lake City.

Friesinger may play the glamour card, pose topless for German magazines, market her own line of jewellery, that sort of thing, but she can skate a bit too. Victories in the 1500m and 3000m helped Friesinger to retain the title she won a year earlier in Bucharest; the magazines will no doubt want more pictures now.

		Long Track World Records, Set in 2001/2002			
MEN	1000m	1:07.18	Gerard van Velde	NED	Salt Lake City, Feb 16
	1500m	1:43.95	Derek Parra	USA	Salt Lake City, Feb 19
	5000m	6:14.66	Jochem Uytedhaage	NED	Salt Lake City, Feb 9
	10000m	12:58.92	Jochem Uytedhaage	NED	Salt Lake City, Feb 22
WOMEN	1000m	1:13.83	Chris Witty	USA	Salt Lake City, Feb 17
	1500m	1:54.02	Anni Freisinger	GER	Salt Lake City, Feb 20
	3000m	3:57.70	Claudia Pechstein	GER	Salt Lake City, Feb 10
	5000m	**6:46.91**	Claudia Pechstein	GER	Salt Lake City, Feb 23

Long Track

There is no British participation in any of the Long Track events.

World All-Around Championships
Heerenveen, Netherlands
Mar 15-17

Men

All-Around (Overall)
1 Jochem Uytdehaage NED 152.483
2 Dmitry Shepel RUS   153.116
3 Derek Parra USA   153.661

500m
1 Petter Andersen NOR   36.39
1 Dmitry Shepel RUS   36.39
3 Derek Parra USA   36.47

1500m
1 Dmitry Shepel RUS   1:48.44
2 Derek Parra USA   1:48.56
3 Dustin Molicki CAN   1:49.49

5000m
1 Jochem Uytdehaage NED 6:30.27
2 Gianni Romme NED   6:30.40
3 Carl Verheijen NED   6:32.50

10,000m
1 J Uytdehaage NED   13:27.25
2 Carl Verheijen NED   13:34.30
3 Pawel Jan Zygmunt POL 13:35.18

Women

All-Around (Overall)
1 Anni Friesinger GER   162.260
2 Cindy Klassen CAN   162.472
3 Claudia Pechstein GER 163.114

500m
1 Jennifer Rodriguez USA 38.59
2 Cindy Klassen CAN   39.16
3 Anni Friesinger GER   39.45

1500m
1 Anni Friesinger GER   1:56.43
2 Cindy Klassen CAN   1:56.88
3 Jennifer Rodriguez USA 1:57.71

3000m
1 Anni Friesinger GER   4:08.02
2 Claudia Pechstein GER 4:09.32
3 Cindy Klassen CAN   4:11.20

5000m
1 Claudia Pechstein GER 7:01.31
2 Cindy Klassen CAN   7:04.86
3 Anni Friesinger GER   7:06.64

World Sprint Championships
Hamar, Norway   *Jan 19-20*
Final Standings

Men
1 Jeremy Wotherspoon CAN 139.820
2 Casey Fitzrandolph USA 140.605
3 Michael Ireland CAN   140.830

Women
1 Catriona Lemay Doan CAN 152.680
2 Andrea Nuyt NED   153.420
3 Anzhelika Kotyuga BLR 153.635

European Championships
Erfurt, Germany   *Jan 4-6*

Men

Overall
1 Jochem Uytdehaage NED 155.466
2 Carl Verheijen NED   156.532
3 Dmitry Shepel RUS   156.768

500m
1 Petter Andersen NOR   36.630
2 Christian Breuer GER   36.730
3 Andre Vreugdenhil BEL 37.150

1500m
1 Petter Andersen NOR   1:49.73
2 Dmitry Shepel RUS   1:51.06
3 Vesa Rosendahl FIN   1:51.50

5000m
1 Carl Verheijen NED   6:37.54
2 Jochem Uytdehaage NED 6:37.63
3 Bart Veldkamp BEL   6:40.12

10,000m
1 Frank Dittrich GER   13:33.61
2 Pawel Zygmunt POL   13:40.77
3 Carl Verheijen NED   13:40.85

Women

Overall
1 Anni Friesinger GER   164.220
2 Claudia Pechstein GER 165.587
3 Renate Groenewold NED 166.729

500m
1 Anni Friesinger GER   39.670
2 Claudia Pechstein GER 40.160
3 Tonny de Jong NED   40.170

1500m
1 Anni Friesinger GER   1:58.73
2 Claudia Pechstein GER 2:00.78
3 Varvara Barysheva RUS 2:00.87

3000m
1 Anni Friesinger GER   4:12.33
2 Renate Groenewold NED 4:13.27
3 Claudia Pechstein GER 4:13.58

5000m
3 Claudia Pechstein GER 7:09.04
1 Anni Freisinger GER   7:09.19
2 Renate Groenewold NED 7:13.85

World Cup

Men

500m
1 Jeremy Wotherspoon USA 630
2 Toyoki Takeda JPN   550
3 Casey Fitzrandolph USA 535

1000m
1 Jeremy Wotherspoon USA 450
2 Jan Bos NED   390
3 Adne Søndral NOR   383

1500m
1 Adne Søndral NOR   374
2 Erben Wennemars NED   340
3 Derek Parra USA   328

5000m/10,000m
1 Gianni Romme NED   460
2 Bob de Jong NED   340
3 Carl Verheijen NED   291

Women

500m
1 Catriona Lemay Doan CAN 780
2 Svetlana Zhurova RUS   550
3 Sabine Völker GER   525

1000m
1 Sabine Völker GER   510
2 Jennifer Rodriguez USA 435
3 Aki Tonoike JPN   335

1500m
1 Anni Freisinger GER   500
2 Claudia Pechstein GER 360
3 Cindy Klassen CAN   330

3000m/5000m
1 Anni Freisinger GER   500
2 Claudia Pechstein GER 420
3 Maki Tabata JPN   305

Short Track

World Championships

Montreal   Apr 5-7
The top seven women/eight men
(after the 500m, 1000m & 1500m)
qualify for the 3000m.

MEN

Overall

1	Kim Dong-Sung KOR	136
2	Ahn Hyun-Soo KOR	42
3	Fabio Carta ITA	34
22	Leon Flack GBR	
34	Nicky Gooch GBR	

500m

1	Kim Dong-Sung KOR	41.930
2	Fabio Carta ITA	42.044
3	Ron Biondo USA	42.195

Gooch elim 1st rd; Flack elim 2nd rd

1000m

1	Kim Dong-Sung KOR	1:31.361
2	Ahn Hyun-Soo KOR	1:31.435
3	Eric Bedard CAN	1:31.632

Gooch elim 1st rd; Flack elim 2nd rd

1500m

1	Kim Dong-Sung KOR	2:21.736
2	Jon Guilmette CAN	2:31.595
3	Rusty Smith USA	2:31.706

Flack elim 1st rd; Gooch elim s-f

3000m

1	Kim Dong-Sung KOR	5:19.041
2	Ahn Hyun-Soo KOR	5:19.170
3	Fabio Carta ITA	5:20.145

5000m Relay

1	Korea	7:10.751
2	Canada	7:10.756
3	China	7:11.330

GBR elim heats

Women

Overall

1	Yang Yang (A) CHN	105
2	Ko Gi-Hyun KOR	63
3	Evgenia Radanova BUL	55
13	Joanna Williams GBR	
24	Sarah Lindsay GBR	

500m

1	Yang Yang (A) CHN	44.460
2	Evgenia Radanova BUL	44.586
3	Wang Chunlu CHN	44.676

Lindsay elim 1st rd; Williams elim q-f

1000m

1	Yang Yang (A) CHN	1:34.732
2	Ko Gi-Hyun KOR	1:34.734
3	Evgenia Radanova BUL	1:35.185

Lindsay elim 1st rd; Williams elim q-f

1500m

1	Yang Yang (A) CHN	2:31.630
2	Ko Gi-Hyun KOR	2:21.666
3	A Goulet-Nadon CAN	2:32.234

Williams elim s-finals

3000m

1	Choi Eun-Kyung KOR	5:17.678
2	Evgenia Radanova BUL	5:22.718
3	Ko Gi-Hyun KOR	5:34.285

3000m Relay

1	Korea	4:18.599
2	China	4:19.516
3	Canada	4:19.587

World Team Championships

Milwaukee   Mar 24-25

Final Standings

Men

1. China 36; 2. Canada 34;
3. Korea 34

Women

1. Korea 36; 2. China 35;
3. Canada 30

No British participation

European Championships

Grenoble, France   Jan 11-13

Men

Overall

1	Fabio Carta ITA	115
2	Nicola Rodigari ITA	81
3	Bruno Loscos FRA	42
10	Leon Flack GBR	
17	Nicky Gooch GBR	
21	Dave Allardice GBR	

500m

1	Nicola Rodigari ITA	43.010
2	Nicola Franceschina ITA	43.057
3	Fabio Carta ITA	43.889

Allardice elim rd 1; Gooch elim rd 2;
Flack elim rd 4

1000m

1	Fabio Carta ITA	1:32.915
2	Bruno Loscos FRA	1:33.192
3	Nicola Rodigari ITA	1:33.204

Gooch elim rd 3
Flack & Allardice elim rd 2

1500m

1	Fabio Carta ITA	2:20.849
2	Nicola Rodigari ITA	2:21.041
3	Nicola Franceschina ITA	2:22.392

Flack & Allardice elim rd 2;
Gooch elim rd 1

3000m

1	Fabio Carta ITA	5:03.098
2	Bruno Loscos FRA	5:06.567
3	Nicola Rodigari ITA	5:09.385

5000m Relay

1	Italy	7:20.752
2	Belgium	7:22.452
3	Germany	7:33.232

DSQ Great Britain

Women

Overall

1	Evgenia Radanova BUL	136
2	Mara Zini ITA	60
3	Joanna Williams GBR	55
8	Sarah Lindsay GBR	
18	Debbie Palmer GBR	

500m

1	Evgenia Radanova BUL	45.565
2	Mara Zini ITA	45.673
3	Marta Capurso ITA	45.767

Palmer GBR rd 1; Williams GBR rd 2;
Lindsay elim rd 3

1000m

1	Evgenia Radanova BUL	1:38.167
2	Joanna Williams GBR	1:38.626
3	Katia Zini ITA	1:38.711

Palmer elim rd 1; Lindsay elim rd 3

1500

1	Evgenia Radanova BUL	2:48.183
2	Joanna Williams GBR	2:48.658
3	Mara Zini ITA	2:72.720

Lindsay & Palmer GBR elim rd 2

3000m

1	Evgenia Radanova BUL	6:14.786
2	Mara Zini ITA	6:15.037
3	Joanna Williams GBR	6:15.149

3000m Relay

1	Italy	4:29.255
2	Bulgaria	4:31.030
3	Germany	4:31.885

World Cup

Final Standings

Men's Overall

1	Kim Dong-Sung KOR	99
2	Lee Seung-Jae KOR	92
3	Li Jiajun CHN	90
14	Nicky Gooch GBR	34
17	Leon Flack GBR	31
29	Dave Allardice GBR	19

Women's Overall

1	Yang Yang (A) CHN	99
2	Evgenia Radanova BUL	88
3	Yang Yang (S) CHN	87
8	Joanne Williams GBR	62
10	Sarah Lindsay GBR	62
17	Debbie Palmer GBR	35

British Champions

2001-2002

Men

500m: Leon Flack
1000m: Leon Flack
1500m: Nicky Gooch
3000m: Leon Flack

Women

500m: Sarah Lindsay
1000m: Sarah Lindsay
1500m: Sarah Lindsay

Speedway

World Championship - Grand Prix

Germany GP
Berlin   *May 5*
Standings: 1. Tomasz Gollob POL 25;
2. Henrik Gustafsson SWE 20; 3. Nicki Pedersen DEN 18;
4. Tony Rickardsson SWE; 5. Peter Karlsson SWE 15

Great Britain GP
Millennium Stadium   *June 9*
Standings: 1. Tony Rickardsson SWE 25; 2. Jason
Crump AUS 20; 3. Tomasz Gollob POL 18; 4. Niklas
Klingberg SWE 16; 5. Ryan Sullivan AUS 15

Denmark GP
Vojens   *July 28*
Standings: 1. Tony Rickardsson SWE 25;
2. Jason Crump AUS 20; 3. Leigh Adams AUS 18;
4. Tomasz Gollob POL 16; 5. Niklas Klingberg AUS 15

Czech Republic GP
Prague   *Aug 18*
Standings: 1. Billy Hamill USA 25; 2. Tony Rickardsson
SWE 20; 3. Jason Crump AUS 20 18; 4. Tomasz Gollob
POL 16; 5. Ryan Sullivan AUS 15

Poland GP
Bydgoszcz   *Sep 8*
Standings: 1. Jason Crump AUS 25;
2. Tony Rickardsson SWE 20; 3. Mikael Karlsson SWE 18;
4. Billy Hamill USA 16; 5. Rune Holta NOR 15

Sweden GP
Stockholm   *Sep 29*
Standings: 1. Jason Crump AUS 25;
2. Mikael Karlsson SWE 20; 3. Ryan Sullivan AUS 18;
4. Mark Loram GBR 16; 5. Tony Rickardsson SWE 15

World Championship Final Standings:

1	Tony Rickardsson SWE	121
2	Jason Crump AUS	113
3	Tomasz Gollob POL	89
4	Ryan Sullivan AUS	80
5	Leigh Adams AUS	69
6	Billy Hamill USA	61
7	Mikael Karlsson SWE	59
8	Todd Wiltshire AUS	56
9	Mark Loram GBR	54
10	Niklas Klingberg SWE	54

Elite League

Final Standings

	P	W	D	L	B*	Pts
Oxford	32	20	5	7	13	58
Poole	32	21	2	9	13	57
Coventry	32	21	2	9	11	55
Ipswich	32	17	2	13	7	43
Peterborough	30	12	6	16	7	33
King's Lynn	32	12	1	19	7	32
Eastbourne	32	11	3	18	7	32
Wolverhampton	32	12	0	20	4	28
Belle Vue	30	7	1	22	1	16

* Bonus points

Premier League

Final Standings

Newcastle	28	20	1	7	12	53
Hull	28	17	3	8	13	50
Sheffield	28	18	0	10	11	47
Isle of Wight	28	18	0	19	11	47
Swindon	28	16	3	9	10	45
Workington	28	16	2	10	8	42
Exeter	28	13	2	13	8	36
Edinburgh	28	13	1	14	8	35
Reading	28	12	3	13	6	33
Arena Essex	28	12	1	15	5	30
Stoke	28	13	1	14	3	30
Berwick	28	10	1	17	4	25
Glasgow	28	10	0	18	3	23
Trelawny	28	6	1	21	2	15
Newport	28	6	1	21	1	14

Conference League

Final Standings

Sheffield	14	11	0	3	7	29
Somerset	14	10	0	4	6	26
Boston	14	8	1	5	4	21
Rye House	14	7	1	6	4	19
Buxton	14	6	0	8	2	14
Peterborough	14	5	0	9	4	14
Newport	14	4	0	10	1	9
Mildenhall	14	4	0	10	0	8

Squash

Had the sport managed another year without a men's World Open, Scotsman turned Englishman Peter Nicol would have equalled Geoff Hunt's achievement of holding the title for four straight years. The difference between them, of course, being that Hunt had actually had to defend his title on an annual basis. Nicol won his solitary title in 1999, and sat back and waited for the sport to give him a chance to defend it.

So, for three years, Nicol could continue to call himself world champion, and capitalise on his standing commercially. Moreover, as he was world number one for a substantial part of the three years, few people were saying he didn't deserve the accolade. When a World Open did finally arrive, at Antwerp in December, Nicol had just celebrated an uninterrupted year at the top of the rankings and was a pretty warm favourite. But he couldn't even manage two titles in a row. Maybe it was all that waiting.

The crunch match for Nicol was probably one that he won. Against Anthony Ricketts in the quarter-final he was stretched to the limit, before winning in five games. In the same round David Palmer cruised past the Scot Martin Heath in just 46 minutes; Nicol was on court for exactly twice as long.

By his own admission, he was ill-prepared for the championships, not allowing a foot injury to properly recover, opting instead to play in the Canadian Classic in Toronto. Nicol won that event, but paid the price in Antwerp.

It was another migrant (the sport is full of them), who drew the curtains on Nicol's championship. John White changed allegiances from Australia to Scotland and it is quite possible that a number of Scottish officials afforded themselves a wry smile when the player who abandoned them was beaten by the one who had embraced them. White's win was emphatic.

In the final, White came up against David Palmer, an Australian based in Antwerp. Palmer had enjoyed some good fortune when his semi-final opponent Jonathon Power was forced to retire through a racket injury to his eye. White started with a vengeance against Palmer, taking the first two games, but the Australian (the one who stayed Aussie) had the greater durability and took the title in five games. He will not want to wait for three years to defend it.

Sarah Fitz-Gerald won the women's World Open. Her first title was in 1996, and this was her fifth. In the final, the Australian defeated Natalie Pohrer who may well be the first American to reach a World Open final (male or female). However, as Pohrer (Née Grainger) has also held South African and English eligibility in the past four years, it is fair to say that the Americans couldn't take too much credit for the achievement.

Jahangir Khan, who once won six World Open titles, was elected president of the World Squash Federation in 2002. After some insecure years, let's hope that Jahangir presides over an era of certainty.

Men's World Open

Antwerp   Dec 8-14

1st Round
Peter Nicol ENG (1) bt Gavin Jones WAL (Q)
15-4 15-8 15-7
Davide Bianchetti ITA (Q) bt Derek Ryan IRL
15-11 15-13 15-7
Alex Gough WAL (16) bt Lee Drew ENG
15-11 12-15 15-7 15-12
Mansoor Zaman PAK (21) bt Scott Handley ENG
15-6 13-15 10-15 15-13 15-5 ret.
Ong Beng Hee MAS (7) bt Mikkel Korsbjerg DEN
15-7 15-11 15-13
Wael El Hindi EGY (30) bt Tommy Berden NED
15-12 13-15 15-12 9-15 15-9
Anthony Rickets AUS (9) bt Jean-Michel Arcucci FRA
15-5 15-10 15-9
Nick Matthew ENG (32) bt Peter Genever ENG
15-2 17-16 15-11
Stewart Boswell AUS (4) Mohammed Abbas EGY
15-6 15-1 15-6
Shahid Zaman PAK (28) bt Liam Kenny IRL
17-14 15-7 15-6
Simon Parke ENG (26) bt Jan Koukal CZE (Q)
15-11 15-7 17-15
John White SCO (5) bt Alex Stait ENG (Q)
15-6 15-8 15-9
Stefan Casteleyn BEL (24) bt Ben Howell ENG (Q)
15-10 8-15 15-7 15-11
Mark Chaloner ENG (10) bt Mohammed A Hafiz EGY
15-10 17-15 15-9
Nick Taylor ENG (17) Lars Harms SUI
15-6 15-9 11-15 7-15 15-11
Olli Tuominen FIN (18) bt Cameron White AUS
15-7 15-2 17-14
Martin Heath SCO (11) bt Cameron Pilley AUS (Q)
15-7 9-15 15-6 15-7
Lee Beachill ENG (8) bt Ajaz Azmat PAK
15-6 15-4 15-8
Viktor Berg CAN bt Renan Lavigne FRA (20)
15-12 7-15 15-13 15-13
Amr Shabana EGY (15) bt Ben Garner ENG
15-11 15-9 15-10
Graham Ryding CAN (23) bt Rodney Durbach RSA
14-17 10-15 15-13 15-12 15-5
David Evans WAL (29) bt Mika Monto FIN (Q)
15-10 11-15 15-5 15-7
David Palmer AUS (3) bt Shahier Razik CAN
15-7 15-4 15-12
Stephen Meads ENG (31) bt Mohammed Azlan Iskander
MAS w/d
Karim Darwish EGY (12) bt Jonathan Kemp ENG
15-11 15-13 15-3
Omar Elborolossy EGY (22) bt Bradley Ball ENG
15-10 10-15 15-3 15-8
Thierry Lincou FRA (6) bt Andrew Whipp ENG (Q)
15-12 15-9 15-11
Gregory Gaulthier FRA (25) bt Del Harris ENG
12-15 15-10 15-2 9-15 15-8
Chris Walker ENG (14) bt Mike Corren AUS
15-13 15-9 15-9

Tim Garner ENG bt Glenn Keenan AUS
15-6 15-14 15-6
Jonathon Power CAN (2) bt Farrukh Zaman PAK
15-8 15-10 15-5

2nd Round
Peter Nicol bt Davide Bianchetti 15-8 15-4 15-13
Mansoor Zaman bt Alex Gough 4-15 16-17 15-12
17-14 15-7
Ong Beng Hee bt Wael El Hindi 17-14 10-15 9-15
15-4 15-10
Anthony Rickets bt Nick Matthew 15-10 15-13 15-5
Stewart Boswell bt Shahid Zaman 15-7 15-9 15-4
Simon Parke bt Joseph Kniepp 9-15 17-15 15-7
13-15 15-11
John White bt Stefan Casteleyn 17-15 15-10 15-12
Mark Chaloner bt Nick Taylor 17-15 15-9 15-10
Martin Heath bt Olli Tuominen 9-15 12-15 15-9
15-5 15-13
Lee Beachill bt Viktor Berg 15-9 15-6 15-2
Amr Shabana bt Graham Ryding 15-12 15-13 15-11
David Palmer bt David Evans 13-15 15-12 8-15
15-7 15-12
Karim Darwish bt Stephen Meads 8-15 15-9 15-8 15-4
Thierry Lincou bt Omar Elborolossy 15-12 13-15
15-10 15-11
Chris Walker bt Gregory Gaulthier 14-17 15-8 15-4
5-15 15-8
Jonathon Power bt Tim Garner 15-4 15-3 15-4

3rd Round
Peter Nicol bt Mansoor Zaman 15-8 15-8 15-11
Anthony Ricketts bt Ong Beng Hee 15-8 15-8 15-5
Simon Parke bt Stewart Boswell 7-15 15-13 5-15 17-15
15-12
John White bt Mark Chaloner 15-9 15-13 10-15 15-9
Martin Heath bt Lee Beachill 15-10 6-15 15-12 7-1 ret.
David Palmer bt Amr Shabana 6-15 15-11 15-3 15-11
Thierry Lincou bt Karim Darwish 15-9 3-15 15-6 15-12
Jonathon Power bt Chris Walker 12-15 15-5 15-3 15-7

Quarter-Finals
David Palmer bt Martin Heath 15-9 15-11 15-10
Jonathon Power bt Thierry Lincou 15-8 15-4 15-8
John White bt Simon Parke 16-17 15-10 15-6 15-7
Peter Nicol bt Anthony Ricketts 12-15 15-12 11-15
15-10 15-8

Semi-Finals
John White bt Peter Nicol 15-9 15-7 15-10
David Palmer bt Jonathon Power 13-15 10-10 ret.

Final
David Palmer bt John White
13-15 12-15 15-6 15-14 15-11

World Rankings

Men

As at Feb 1, 2003

		Average Pts
1	Peter Nicol ENG	1275.000
2	Jonathon Power CAN	1208.594
3	David Palmer AUS	1034.375
4	John White SCO	687.188
5	Stewart Boswell AUS	624.219
6	Thierry Lincou FRA	462.656
7	Anthony Ricketts AUS	400.781
8	Lee Beachill ENG	361.406
9	Ong Beng Hee MAS	311.719
10	Martin Heath SCO	304.688
11	Karim Darwish EGY	301.944
12	Chris Walker ENG	277.344
13	Mark Chaloner ENG	271.875
14	Amr Shabana EGY	257.031
15	Mansoor Zaman PAK	232.813
16	Joseph Kniepp AUS	231.406
17	Alex Gough WAL	225.278
18	Simon Parke ENG	203.472
19	Nick Taylor ENG	193.472
20	Oamr Elborolossy EGY	186.875
21	Paul Price AUS	185.938
22	David Evans WAL	179.375
23	Graham Ryding CAN	179.306
24	Nick Matthew ENG	174.219
25	Renan Lavigne FRA	173.750

Women

As at Feb 1, 2003

1	Sarah Fitz-Gerald AUS	1772.500
2	Carol Owens NZL	1692.188
3	Natalie Pohrer USA	1402.143
4	Linda Charman ENG	985.471
5	Rachel Grinham AUS	859.700
6	Vanessa Atkinson NED	859.105
7	Tania Bailey ENG	855.575
8	Cassie Jackman ENG	752.500
9	Rebecca Macree ENG	617.227
10	Natalie Grinham AUS	558.278
11	Fiona Geaves ENG	515.475
12	Stephanie Brind ENG	498.262
13	Jenny Tranfield ENG	464.889
14	Omneya Abdel Kawy EGY	436.114
15	Suzanne Horner ENG	412.184
16	Pamela Nimmo SCO	406.763
17	Vicky Botwright ENG	391.976
18	Shelley Kitchen NZL	334.881
19	Ellen Petersen DEN	286.647
20	Annelize Naude NED	263.263
21	Madeline Perry IRL	243.053
22	Isabelle Stoehr FRA	226.176
23	Engy Kheirallah EGY	213.824
24	Latasha Khan USA	209.167
25	Rebecca Chui HKG	201.806

Women's World Open

Qatar   Oct 28-Nov 2

1st round

Sarah Fitz-Gerald AUS (1) bt Heidi Mather AUS (Q)
9-3 9-1 9-2

Omneya Abdel Kawy EGY (13) bt Sharon Wee MAS
9-1 9-0 9-1

Vanessa Atkinson NED (5) bt Madeleine Perry IRL
9-1 9-3 9-5

Ellen Petersen DEN (16) bt Wendy Maitland SCO (Q)
8-10 6-9 9-5 9-2 9-5

Linda Charman ENG (4) bt Vicky Lankester ENG (Q)
9-2 9-1 9-2

Isabelle Stoehr FRA bt Pamela Nimmo SCO (11)
9-2 9-6 9-5

Tania Bailey ENG (8) bt Kim Hannes BEL (Q)
9-1 9-0 9-1

Annelize Naude NED bt Vicky Botwright ENG (12)
9-7 9-5 9-5

Fiona Geaves ENG (9) bt Dominique L-Walter ENG (Q)
9-0 9-0 9-0

Rachel Grinham AUS (6) bt Engy Kheirallah EGY
9-2 10-8 9-3

Shelley Kitchen NZL (14) bt Rebecca Chiu HKG
9-2 9-5 10-8

Natalie Pohrer ENG (3) bt Latasha Khan USA
9-1 9-0 9-0

Jenny Tranfield ENG (15) bt Kate Allison ENG (Q)
9-5 9-7 9-0

Stephanie Brind ENG bt Maha Zein EGY
9-4 9-2 9-0

Natalie Grinham AUS (10) bt Lara Petera NZL (Q)
9-4 9-1 9-7

Carol Owens NZL bt Cheryl Beaumont ENG (Q)
9-2 9-3 9-1

2nd Round

Sarah Fitz-Gerald bt Omneya Abdel Kawy 9-6 9-1 9-5
Vanessa Atkinson bt Ellen Petersen 9-4 9-0 9-3
Linda Charman bt Isabelle Stoehr 9-0 9-3 9-2
Tania Bailey bt Annelize Naude 9-3 9-2 9-1
Rachel Grinham bt Fiona Geaves 9-3 9-4 10-9
Natalie Pohrer bt Shelley Kitchen 9-4 9-2 9-3
Jenny Tranfield bt Stephanie Brind 9-1 9-10 9-7 9-0
Carol Owens bt Natalie Grinham 9-4 9-3 9-4

Quarter-finals

Sarah Fitz-Gerald bt Vanessa Atkinson 9-5 9-1 9-6
Linda Charman bt Tania Bailey 2-9 9-5 9-4 7-9 9-1
Natalie Pohrer bt Rachel Grinham 6-9 9-7 9-5 4-9 10-8
Carol Owens bt Jenny Tranfield 9-1 9-0 9-1

Semi-finals

Sarah Fitz-Gerald bt Linda Charman 9-2 1-9 9-4 9-3
Natalie Pohrer bt Carol Owens 5-9 2-9 9-5 9-1 10-8

Final

Sarah Fitz-Gerald bt Natalie Pohrer 10-8 9-3 7-9 9-7

Women's World Team Championship

Odense, Oct 13-19 (seedings in brackets)

Pool A Table

1 Australia (1)	4	4	0	12:0	36:0	325:59
2 South Africa (8)	4	3	1	8:4	24:16	259:251
3 Canada (9)	4	2	0	7:5	22:16	259:222
4 Spain (17)	4	1	3	2:10	8:31	178:317
5 India (16)	4	0	4	1:11	8:35	194:336

Pool B Table

1 England (2)	3	3	0	9:0	27:1	250:69
2 Malaysia (7)	3	2	1	6:3	19:22	209:165
3 Germany (10)	3	1	2	2:7	9:22	149:229
4 Ireland (15)	3	0	3	1:8	5:25	99:244

Pool C Table

1 New Zealand (3)	4	4	0	11:1	34:3	320:113
2 Netherlands (6)	4	3	1	9:3	27:12	294:197
3 France (14)	4	2	2	4:8	14:26	220:280
4 Denmark (11)	4	1	3	4:8	14:24	192:258
5 Japan (18)	4	0	4	2:10	8:32	140:318

Pool D Table

1 Egypt (4)	4	4	0	11:1	34:7	348:172
2 Scotland (5)	4	3	1	10:2	32:8	324:179
3 Hong Kong (13)	4	2	2	5:7	16:23	206:259
4 USA (12)	4	1	3	4:8	15:25	223:283
5 Austria (19)	4	0	4	0:12	2:36	133:341

Places 17 to 19 are decided by a round robin play-off; the remaining places are determined by knock-out draws

Places 17-19
Japan 3 India 0; Japan 3 Austria 0;
India 3 Austria 0

Places 9-16
Canada 2 USA 1; Hong Kong 2 Spain 1;
Ireland 2 France 1; Germany 2 Denmark 1

Places 13-16
USA 1 Spain 2; France 2 Denmark 1

Places 14-15
USA 2 Denmark 1

Places 13-14
France 2 Spain 1

Places 9-12
Canada 3 Hong Kong 0; Germany 2 Ireland 1

Places 11-12
Hong Kong 2 Ireland 1

Places 9-10
Canada 2 Germany 1

Quarter-Finals
Australia 3 Scotland 0; Egypt 2 Malaysia 1
New Zealand 2 South Africa 1; England 3 Netherlands 0

Places 5-8
Scotland 3 Malaysia 0; Netherlands 3 South Africa 0

Places 7-8
Malaysia 3 South Africa 0

Places 5-6
Netherlands 3 Scotland 0

Semi-Finals
Australia 3 Egypt 0; England 2 New Zealand 1

Third Place Match
New Zealand 2 Egypt 1

FINAL
Australia 2 England 1

European Team Championships

Boblingen, May 1-4

Men

Semi-finals
France 4 Wales 0
England 3 Netherlands 1

Final
England 2 France 2
(Walker lost to Lincou; Chaloner bt Lavigne;
Beachill bt Gaulthier; Harris lost to Arcucci)
England took the title 8:7 on games

Women

Semi-finals
England 3 Denmark 0
Scotland 2 Germany 1

Final
England 3 Scotland 0
(Campion bt Nimmo; Charman bt Macfie;
Brind bt Maitland)

British Open

National Squash Centre, Apr 10-15

Men

Quarter-finals
Peter Nicol ENG (1) bt Chris Walker ENG (8)
15-8 15-11 15-8
Thierry Lincou FRA (4) bt Martin Heath SCO
15-13 11-15 15-7 15-10
Jonathon Power CAN (3) bt Lee Beachill ENG
15-8 15-10 15-10
John White SCO (6) bt Alex Gough WAL
15-13 15-8 15-9

Semi-finals
Peter Nicol bt Thierry Lincou 15-6 15-9 17-14
John White bt Jonathon Power 11-15 15-13 15-12
9-15 15-13

Final
Peter Nicol bt John White 15-9 15-8 15-8

Women

Quarter-finals
Sarah Fitz-Gerald AUS (1) bt Jenny Tranfield ENG
9-5 9-1 9-1
Vanessa Atkinson NED (9) bt Fiona Geaves ENG (4)
2-9 9-4 9-3 7-9 9-1
Cassie Campion ENG (3) bt Rachel Grinham AUS (7)
9-4 10-8 9-4
Tania Bailey ENG (15) bt Carol Owens NZL (2)
9-2 9-7 9-2

Semi-finals
Sarah Fitz-Gerald bt Vanessa Atkinson
9-2 9-4 9-5
Tania Bailey bt Cassie Campion
9-2 3-9 9-4 3-9 9-7

Final
Sarah Fitz-Gerald bt Tania Bailey 9-3 9-0 9-0

Other Major Events

US Open
Sheraton Hotel, Boston, Jan 6-9
This was the postponed 2001 event
Final
Peter Nicol ENG (1) bt Jonathon Power CAN (2)
15-7 15-5 15-6

AON Women's Texas Open
Houston, Feb 28-Mar 3
Final
Carol Owens NZL (1) bt Cassie Campion ENG (2)
8-10 9-4 6-9 9-4 9-3

Pakistan Open
Fortress Stadium, Lahore, Mar 23-27
Final
Jonathon Power CAN (3) bt Peter Nicol ENG (1)
15-10 13-15 15-10 15-14

Grand Prix Finals
Doha, Apr 23-28
Men's Final
Jonathon Power CAN (4) bt Stewart Boswell AUS (6)
15-10 15-7 8-15 15-13
Women's Final
Sarah Fitz-Gerald AUS (1) bt Carol Owens NZL (2)
6-9 5-9 9-5 9-7 9-4

World Invitation Doubles
Sportcity, Manchester, Apr 16-19
Men's Doubles Final
Palmer/Price AUS (2) bt Chaloner/Johnson ENG (1)
15-7 17-15
Women's Doubles Final
Grinham/Grinham AUS (3/4) bt Campion/Charman ENG (1)
15-10 15-12
Mixed Doubles Final
Walker/Geaves ENG (2) bt Taylor/Botwright ENG (1)
15-17 15-8 15-10

Australian Open
Adelaide, June 27-30
Men's Final
Stewart Boswell AUS (2) bt Anthony Ricketts AUS (3)
13-15 9-15 15-9 15-2 15-11
Women's Final
Sarah Fitz-Gerald AUS (1) bt Laura Keating AUS (2)
9-0 9-2 9-0

US Open
Sheraton Hotel, Boston, Sep 11-15
Final
David Palmer AUS (3) bt Stewart Boswell AUS (5)
15-13 15-10 15-11

MILO SA Open
Johannesburg, Oct 17-20
Final
David Palmer AUS (1) bt John White SCO (2)
9-15 15-12 15-12 9-15 15-12

Qatar Classic
Doha, Oct 28-Nov 2
Final
Peter Nicol ENG (1) bt David Palmer AUS (2)
15-9 13-15 15-6 13-15 15-7

YMG Canadian Classic
Toronto, Nov 10-14
Final
Jonathon Power CAN (2) bt Peter Nicol ENG (1)
15-8 15-3 16-17 15-7

World Junior Championships
Chennai, Dec 10-14 (selected result)
Final
James Willstrop ENG (1) bt Peter Barker ENG (2)
9-0 9-3 9-1

Swimming

As the third most important swimming competition on the planet, it could be regarded as unfortunate that the British presence at the European championships in Berlin was a nominal one, a handful of second-string divers metaphorically carrying the flag. Because of a regrettable clash of dates, British swimmers were away, enjoying relative success in Manchester, at an event which holds far more domestic kudos than the European event, but which is always weaker in depth.

Absence from Berlin, however, did not make the British heart grow fonder of Europe. If we are to judge from the comments of the British chief coach, Bill Sweetenham, it was quite the opposite for, as five world records were broken in the German capital, Sweetenham launched into a dubious diatribe. When asked whether the current situation was like the old days of the East German system, Sweetenham replied, "You can't say with any certainty but the feeling within the coaching fraternity of the clean nations is that some of the others have got their hands in the cookie jar, and those cookies are getting more and more advanced. When you bring in things like gene therapy, the list is endless."

So what was Sweetenham implying? That the records set in Berlin were questionable and that they were the product of corrupt regime? But what regime was that? The five records were set by swimmers from four countries; Germany, Sweden, Ukraine and Poland, and we are still searching for the common thread between them. Undoubtedly there were those surprised by the renaissance of Franziska van Almsick, who broke her own world record in the 200m freestyle, but it was a record she had set as a 16-year-old in Rome eight years ago, and Van Almisck has had time on her side in her comeback.

Anna-Karin Kammerling of Sweden, Oleg Lisogor of Ukraine and Otylia Jedrzejczak of Poland also broke individual world records in Berlin; the first two coming in the relatively undeveloped 50m events (fly and breast) which should not be a surprise to Sweetenham as Zoe Baker, a swimmer he has hardly publicly endorsed, also broke a 50m record in Manchester, that of the women's breaststroke. Jedrzejczak's record came in the 200m fly and though unexpected, the Pole hardly mutilated the old record shaving just three hundredths of a second from the time Susie O'Neill set at the Sydney Olympics.

O'Neill, in case you missed it, swam for Australia. So does Ian Thorpe, who broke his own world record in the 400m at Manchester, while they were record-breaking in Berlin. To our knowledge, Sweetenham has never mentioned "Cookie Jar" and O'Neill or Thorpe in the same sentence. Nor should he, for there is no evidence that either took performance-enhancing drugs, which is exactly the same case as those who broke world records in Berlin.

If the bad news about Sweetenham is that he doesn't always speak as intelligently as you might hope, the good news is that he is leaps and bounds ahead of the previous performance director of British swimming Deryk Snelling, whose record was so poor that the Andorran Swimming Federation would look elsewhere.

Sweetenham started with that advantage (rule one in coaching always take over from a duffer), and the results have been forthcoming, most notably in the Commonwealth Games. Even before the Games, though, Sweetenham appeared to have changed the morale of British swimming, most simply by embracing the ethic of hard graft, and acknowledging the power of pure ambition. At times, his comments veer towards psycho-babble, particularly with regard to Baker and Mark Foster, but those close to the performance director have no doubt that his heart is in the right place.

Short course events have taken second place with Sweetenham, who insisted that the Britons selected for the European event in Riesa should not taper down, but stay in hard training coming into the competition. Sweetenham may see it as second division swimming, but we should not disregard the achievement of James Hickman who won his fourth straight world short course 200m butterfly title in Moscow in April. Hickman won his first title in Gothenburg in 1997, his second in Hong Kong two years later, and his third in Athens in 2000. Hickman may never win a world long course title, but the Leeds swimmer's record in the little pools is peerless.

World Long Course (50m) Records

Set In 2002

Men

400m Free	**Ian Thorpe** AUS	3:40.08	July 30	Manchester
200m Back	**Aaron Piersol** USA	1:55.15	March 20	Minneapolis
50m Breast	**Oleg Lisogor** UKR	27.18	August 2	Berlin
200m Breast	**Kosuke Kitajima** JPN	2:09.97	October 2	Busan, Korea
400m IM	**Michael F Phelps** USA	4:11.09	August 15	Fort Lauderdale
4x100m Medley	**USA**	3:33.48	August 29	Yokohama
	Piersol/Hansen/Phelps/Lezak			

Women

200m Free	**Franziska van Almsick** GER	1:56.64	August 3	Berlin
100m Back	**Natalie Coughlin** USA	59.58	August 13	Fort Lauderdale
50m Breast	**Zoe Baker** GBR	30.57	July 30	Manchester
50m Fly	**Anna-Karin Kammerling** SWE	25.57	July 30	Berlin
200m Fly	**Otylia Jedrzejczak** POL	2:05.78	August 4	Berlin
4x100m Free	**Germany**	3:36.00	July 29	Berlin
	Meissner/Dallmann/Volker/Van Almsick			

European Championships

Berlin   *July 25-Aug 4*

World Records are shown in bold

Men

50m Free
1 Bartosz Kizierowski POL   22.18
2 Lorenzo Vismara ITA   22.26
3 Oleksander Volynets UKR   22.31

100m Free
1 P vd Hoogenband NED   47.86
2 Alexander Popov RUS   48.94
3 Duje Draganja CRO   49.31

200m Free
1 P vd Hoogenband NED   1:44.89
2 Emiliano Brembilla ITA   1:46.94
3 Massi Rosolino ITA   1:47.98

400m Free
1 Emiliano Brembilla ITA   3:46.60
2 Massi Rosolino ITA   3:48.70
3 Dragos Coman ROM   3:48.78

800m Free
1 Dragos Coman ROM   8:04.34
2 Christian Minotti ITA   8:04.46
3 Jorg Hoffmann GER   8:04.56

1500m Free
1 Yuri Prilukov RUS   15:03.88
2 Cristian Minotti ITA   15:04.16
3 Igor Chervynsky UKR   15:07.65

50m Back
1 Thomas Rupprath GER   25.05
2 Stev Theloke GER   25.12
3 Bartosz Kizierowski POL   25.52

100m Back
1 Stev Theloke GER   54.42
2 Markus Rogan AUT   54.54
3 Pierre Roger FRA   54.89

200m Back
1 Gordan Kozulj CRO   1:58.70
2 Markus Rogan AUT   1:58.83
3 Marko Strahija CRO   1:58.89

50m Breast
1 Oleg Lisogor UKR   **27.18**
2 Mihaly Flaskay HUN   27.51
3 Karoly Guttler HUN   27.85

100m Breast
1 Oleg Lisogor UKR   1:00.29
2 Roman Sloudnov RUS   1:00.72
3 Hugues Duboscq FRA   1:01.04

200m Breast
1 Davide Rummolo ITA   2:11.37
2 Yohan Bernard FRA   2:11.77
3 Roman Sloudnov RUS   2:11.82

50m Fly
1 Jere Hard FIN   23.50
2 Thomas Rupprath GER   23.78
3 Lars Frolander SWE   23.85

100m Fly
1 Thomas Rupprath GER   51.94
2 Andry Serdinov UKR   52.17
3 Denis Sylantyev UKR   52.36

200m Fly
1 Franck Esposito FRA   1:55.18
2 Denis Sylantyev UKR   1:55.42
3 Anatoli Poliakov RUS   1:55.62

200m IM
1 Jani Sievinen FIN   1:59.30
2 Alessio Boggiatto ITA   1:59.83
3 Markus Rogan AUT   2:00.50

400m IM
1 Alessio Boggiatto ITA   4:13.19
2 Istvan Bathazi HUN   4:17.33
3 Nicolas Rostoucher FRA   4:19.19

4x100m Free
1 Germany   3:17.67
2 Sweden   3:17.75
3 Italy   3:18.20

4x200m Free
1 Italy   7:12.18
2 Germany   7:17.59
3 Greece   7:20.67

4x100m Medley
1 Russia   3:36.21
2 France   3:36.55
3 Germany   3:37.05

Women

50m Free
1 Therese Alshammar SWE   24.84
2 Martina Moravcova SVK   25.09
3 Aleksandra Herasimenia BLR 25.24

100m Free
1 Franziska van Almsick GER 54.39
2 Martina Moravcova SVK   54.61
3 Elena Popchenko BLR   54.62

200m Free
1 F Van Almsick GER   **1:56.64**
2 Camelia Potec ROM   1:57.80
3 Elena Popchenko BLR   1:57.91

400m Free
1 Yana Klockkova UKR   4:07.10
2 Eva Risztov HUN   4:07.24
3 Camelia Potec ROM   4:09.49

800m Free
1 Jana Henke GER   8:23.83
2 Eva Risztov HUN   8:28.06
3 Hannah Stockbauer GER   8:30.97

50m Back
1 Nina Zhivanevskaya ESP   28.58
2 Sandra Volker GER   28.81
3 Aleksandra Herasimenia BLR 28.86

100m Back
1 Stanislav Komarova RUS   1:01.40
2 Sandra Volker GER   1:01.42
3 Antje Buschschulte GER   1:01.56

200m Back
1 Stanislav Komarova RUS   2:09.49
2 Nina Zhivanevskaya ESP   2:10.27
3 Irina Amshennikova UKR   2:11.59

50m Breast
1 Emma Igelstrom SWE   31.17
2 Svitlana Bondarenko UKR   31.77
3 Elena Bogomazova RUS   32.10

100m Breast
1 Emma Igelstrom SWE   1:07.87
2 Svitlana Bondarenko UKR   1:09.28
3 Elena Bogomazova RUS   1:09.53

200m Breast
1 Mirna Jukic AUT   2:25.83
2 Anne Poleska GER   2:27.37
3 Emma Igelstrom SWE   2:27.61

50m Fly
1 A-K Kammerling SWE   25.57
2 Daniela Samulski GER   26.86
3 Chantal Groot NED   26.91

100m Fly
1 Martina Moravcova SVK   57.20
2 Otylia Jedrzejczak POL   57.97
3 A-K Kammerling SWE   58.94

200m Fly
1 Otylia Jedrzejczak POL   2:05.78
2 Eva Risztov HUN   2:08.24
3 Annika Mehlhorn GER   2:09.37

200m IM
1 Yana Klochkova UKR   2:11.59
2 Hanna Scherba BLR   2:13.04
3 Alenka Kejzar SLO   2:14.24

400m IM
1 Yana Klochkova UKR   4:35.10
2 Eva Risztov HUN   4:36.17
3 Nicole Hetzer GER   4:42.22

4x100m Free
1 Germany   **3:36.00**
2 Sweden   3:40.66
3 Netherlands   3:41.98

4x200m Free
1 Germany   7:59.07
2 Spain   8:05.83
3 Sweden   8:08.46

4x100m Medley
1 Germany   4:01.54
2 Sweden   4:06.15
3 Ukraine   4:06.22

Diving

Results from qualifying in italics

Men

1m Springboard
1 Nicola Marconi ITA   390.81
2 Jose Miguel Gil ESP   385.86
3 Christian Loeffler GER   377.94
16 Blake Aldridge GBR   *303.15*

3m Springboard
1 Dmitri Sautin RUS   495.45
2 Andreas Wels GER   463.59
3 Vassilly Lissovsky RUS   456.06
17 Blake Aldridge GBR   *334.17*

10m Platform
1 Dmitri Sautin RUS   495.45
2 Andreas Wels GER   463.59
3 Vassilly Lissovsky RUS   456.06
8 Gareth Brown GBR   363.06
13 Gareth Jones GBR   *272.94*

Women

1m Springboard
1	Heike Fischer GER	308.58
2	Vera Ilyina RUS	307.53
3	Natalia Oumyskova RUS	285.03
7	*Rebecca Burrows GBR*	*237.39*
11	*Rosie Whiting GBR*	*207.60*

3m Springboard
1	Yulia Pakhalina RUS	329.94
2	Ditte Kotzian GER	319.08
3	Conny Schmalfuss GER	295.29
11	Tandi Gerrard GBR	238.56
15	*Sarah Soo GBR*	*227.40*

10m Platform
1	Anke Piper GER	337.05
2	Tania Cagnotto ITA	331.32
3	Olga Leonova UKR	321.93
12	Monique McCarroll GBR	264.66

Synchronised Swimming

Solo
1	Virginie Dedieu FRA	99.100
2	Anastasia Davydova RUS	97.900
3	Gemma Mengual ESP	97.100

Duet
1	Davydova/Ermakova RUS	99.300
2	Mengual/Tirados ESP	97.900
3	Dedieu/Glez FRA	96.600

Team
1	Russia	99.000
2	Spain	98.100
3	Italy	96.400

Open Water

Men

5km
1	Luca Baldini ITA	55:35.6
2	Thomas Lurz GER	56:24.5
3	Stefano Rubaudo ITA	56:26.9

25km
1	Yury Kudinov RUS	5:09:47.4
2	Gilles Rondy FRA	5:18:02.0
3	David Meca ESP	5:18:27.1

Women

5km
1	Viola Valli ITA	1:00:25.9
2	Hanna Miluska SUI	1:00:27.3
3	Nadine Pastor GER	1:00:28.3

25km
1	Edith Van Dijk NED	5:27:34.0
2	O Shalyguina RUS	5:34:47.9
3	Natalia Pankina RUS	5:34:51.4

Medal Table

All disciplines

1	Germany	12	11	9	32
2	Russia	10	5	8	23
3	Italy	7	7	4	18
4	Ukraine	5	4	6	15
5	Sweden	4	3	4	10
6	Netherlands	3	0	2	5
7	France	2	3	4	9
8	Poland	2	1	1	4
9	Finland	2	0	0	2
10	Spain	1	5	2	8
11	Austria	1	2	1	4
12	Slovakia	1	2	0	3
13	Romania	1	1	2	4
14	Croatia	1	0	2	3
15	Hungary	0	6	1	7
16	Belarus	0	1	4	5
17	Switzerland	0	1	0	1
18	Greece	0	0	1	1
19	Slovenia	0	0	1	1

World Cup 2001-2002
Final Standings
Men: 1 Ed Moses USA 1048;
2 Oleg Lisogor UKR 1039; 3 Roman Sloudnov RUS 1025
Women: 1 Martina Moravcova SVK 1027;
2 Yana Klochkova UKR 1024; 3 Emma Igelström SWE 1016

Pan Pacific Championships

Yokohama, Aug 24-29

Men

50m Free: Jason Lezak USA 22.18
100m Free: Ian Thorpe AUS 48.84
200m Free: Ian Thorpe AUS 1:44.75
400m Free: Ian Thorpe AUS 3:45.28
800m Free: Grant Hackett AUS 7:44.78
1500m Free: Grant Hackett AUS 14:41.65
100m Back: Aaron Piersol USA 54.22
200m Back: Aaron Piersol USA 1:56.88
100m Breast: Kosuke Kitajima JPN 1:00.36
200m Breast: Brendan Hansen USA 2:11.80
100m Fly: Ian Crocker USA 52.45
200m Fly: Tom Malchow USA 1:55.21
200m IM: Michael Phelps USA 1:59.70
400m IM: Michael Phelps USA 4:12.48
4x100m Free: Australia 3:15.15
4x200m Free: Australia 7:09.00
4x100m Medley: USA **3:33.48**

Women

50m Free: Jenny Thompson USA 25.13
100m Free: Natalie Coughlin USA 53.99
200m Free: Lindsay Benko USA 1:58.74
400m Free: Diana Munz USA 4:09.50
800m Free: Diana Munz USA 8:30.45
1500m Free: Diana Munz USA 16:07.86
100m Back: Natalie Coughlin USA 59.72
200m Back: Margaret Hoelzer USA 2:11.00
100m Breast: Amanda Beard USA 1:08.22
200m Breast: Amanda Beard USA 2:26.31
100m Fly: Natalie Coughlin USA 57.88
200m Fly: Petria Thomas AUS 2:08.31
200m IM: Tomoko Hagiwara JPN 2:13.42
400m IM: Jennifer Reilly AUS 4:40.84
4x100m Free: Australia 3:39.78
4x200m Free: USA 7:56.96
4x100m Medley: Australia 4:00.50

World Short Course Championships

Moscow, Apr 3-7

Men

50m Free
1 Jose Martin Meolans ARG   21.36
2 Mark Foster GBR   21.44
3 Oleksandr Volinets UKR   21.55

100m Free
1 Ashley Callus AUS   46.99
2 Jose Martin Meolans ARG   47.09
3 Salim Iles ALG   47.66

200m Free
1 Klete Keller USA   1:44.36
2 Gustavo Borges BRA   1:45.67
3 Mark Johnston CAN   1:45.88

400m Free
1 Grant Hackett AUS   3:38.29
2 Kvetoslav Svoboda CZE   3:41.97
3 Chad Carvin USA   3:43.55

1500m Free
1 Grant Hackett AUS   14:33.94
2 Chris Thompson USA   14:39.43
3 Christian Minotti ITA   14:45.41

50m Back
1 Matt Welsh AUS   23.66
2 Peter Marshall USA   24.04
3 Toni Helbig GER   24.17

100m Back
1 Matt Welsh AUS   51.26
2 Aaron Peirsol USA   51.71
3 Peter Marshall USA   51.84

200m Back
1 Aaron Peirsol USA   **1:51.17**
2 Marko Strahija CRO   1:53.08
3 Blaz Medvesek SLO   1:53.66

50m Breast
1 Oleg Lisogor UKR   26.42
2 Jose Couto POR   27.22
3 Eduardo Fischer BRA   27.26

100m Breast
1 Oleg Lisogor UKR   58.33
2 Kosuke Kitajima JPN   59.10
3 Jarno Pihlava FIN   59.22

200m Breast
1 Jim Piper AUS   2:07.16
2 David Denniston USA   2:07.42
3 Jarno Pihlava FIN   2:07.61

50m Fly
1 Geoff Huegill AUS   22.89
2 Adam Pine AUS   23.29
3 Mark Foster GBR   23.36

100m Fly
1 Geoff Huegill AUS   50.95
2 Adam Pine AUS   51.27
3 Igor Martchenko RUS   51.41
5 James Hickman GBR   51.61

200m Fly
1 James Hickman GBR   1:53.14
2 Justin Norris AUS   1:54.07
3 Ioan Gherghel ROM   1:54.16

100m IM
1 Peter Mankoc SLO   52.90
2 Jani Sievinen FIN   53.78
3 Jakob Andersen DEN   54.31

200m IM
1 Jani Sievinen FIN   1:55.45
2 Peter Mankoc SLO   1:56.13
3 Thomas Wilkins USA   1:57.34

400m IM
1 Thomas Wilkins USA   4:04.82
2 Brian Johns CAN   4:06.85
3 Jacob Carstensen DEN   4:08.92

4x100m Free
1 USA   3:10.84
2 Sweden   3:11.14
3 Russia   3:11.24

4x200m Free
1 Australia   7:00.36
2 Russia   7:05.36
3 USA   7:08.73

4x100m Medley
1 USA   3:29.00
2 Australia   3:29.35
3 Russia   3:30.21

Women

50m Free
1 Therese Alshammar SWE   24.16
2 Alison Sheppard GBR   24.28
3 Tammie Stone USA   24.65

100m Free
1 Therese Alshammar SWE   52.89
2 Martina Morovcova SVK   52.96
3 Xu Yanvei CHN   53.35
6 Alison Sheppard GBR   53.91

200m Free
1 Lindsay Benko USA   **1:54.04**
2 Yang Yu CHN   1:55.34
3 Xu Yanvei CHN   1:55.63

400m Free
1 Yana Klochkova UKR   4:01.26
2 Chen Hua CHN   4:03.81
3 Rachel Komisarz USA   4:06.30

800m Free
1 Chen Hua CHN   8:16.34
2 Irina Oufimtseva RUS   8:21.91
3 Flavia Rigamonti SUI   8:23.38

50m Back
1 Jennifer Carroll CAN   27.38
2 Haley Cope USA   27.44
3 Diana MacManus USA   27.60

100m Back
1 Haley Cope USA   59.07
2 Ilona Hlavackova CZE   59.13
3 Diana MacManus USA   59.45

200m Back
1 Lindsay Benko USA   2:04.97
2 Reiko Nakamura JPN   2:07.30
3 Irina Amshennikova UKR   2:07.71

50m Breast
1 Emma Igelstrom SWE   **29.96**
2 Luo Xuejuan CHN   30.17
3 Zoe Baker GBR   30.56

100m Breast
1 Emma Igelstrom SWE   1:05.38
2 Sarah Poewe RSA   1:06.16
3 Luo Xuejuan CHN   1:06.36
Elim s-f: Zoe Baker GBR

200m Breast
1 Qi Hui CHN   2:20.91
2 Emma Igelstrom SWE   2:21.30
3 Mirna Jukic AUT   2:21.63

50m Fly
1 A-K Kammerling SWE   25.55
2 Petria Thomas AUS   26.36
3 Vered Borochovski ISR   26.38

100m Fly
1 Martina Moravcova SVK   57.04
2 Petria Thomas AUS   57.91
3 A-K Kammerling SWE   58.12

200m Fly
1 Petria Thomas AUS   2:05.76
2 Yang Yu CHN   2:06.10
3 Mary De Scenza USA   2:06.17

100m IM
1 Martina Moravcova SVK   59.91
2 Gabrielle Rose USA   1:00.68
3 Alison Sheppard GBR   1:00.88

200m IM
1 Yana Klochkova UKR   2:08.82
2 Gabrielle Rose USA   2:09.77
3 Oxana Verevka RUS   2:11.25

400m IM
1 Yana Klochkova UKR   4:30.63
2 Alenka Kejzar SLO   4:35.44
3 Georgina Bardach ARG   4:36.36

4x100m Free
1 Sweden   3:35.09
2 Australia   3:35.97
3 China   3:36.18

4x200m Free
1 China   **7:46.30**
2 USA   7:47.55
3 Australia   7:49.50

4x100m Medley
1 Sweden   **3:55.78**
2 USA   3:57.17
3 China   3:57.29

Medal Table

		G	S	B	Tot
1	Australia	10	7	2	18
2	USA	8	9	9	26
3	Sweden	7	2	1	10
4	Ukraine	5	0	2	7
5	China	3	4	5	12
6	Slovakia	2	1	0	3
7	Great Britain	1	2	3	6
8	Finland	1	1	2	4
9	Argentina	1	1	1	3
9	Canada	1	1	1	3
9	Slovenia	1	1	1	3
12	Russia	0	2	3	5
13	Czech Rep	0	2	0	2
13	Japan	0	2	0	2

1 silver/1 bronze: Austria, Brazil
1 silver: Croatia, Portugal, S Africa
2 bronzes: Denmark
1 bronze: Algeria, Germany, Israel, Italy, Romania, Switzerland

SWIMMING

European Short Course Championships
Riesa, Germany, Dec 12-15

Men

50m Free

1	Stefan Nystrand SWE	21.55
2	Lorenzo Vismara ITA	21.66
3	Rolandas Gimbutis LTU	21.74

100m Free

1	Lorenzo Vismara ITA	47.33
2	Jere Hard FIN	48.15
3	Johan Kenkhuis NED	48.23

Elim Heat: Simon Burnett GBR

200m Free

1	Emiliano Brembilla ITA	1:45.39
2	Kvetoslav Svoboda CZE	1:45.45
3	Matteo Pelliciari ITA	1:45.79
6	Simon Burnett GBR	1:45.88

Elim heat: Gavin Meadows GBR

400m Free

1	Emiliano Brembilla ITA	3:40.60
2	Yuri Prilukov RUS	3:41.90
3	A Oikonomou GRE	3:44.68

Elim heat: David Davies GBR

1500m Free

1	Yuri Prilukov RUS	14:35.06
2	David Davies GBR	14:42.51
3	Christian Minotti ITA	14:51.43

50m Back

1	Thomas Rupprath GER	23.66
2	Stev Theloke GER	24.29
3	Darius Grigalionis LTU	24.62

Elim heat: Steve Parry GBR

100 Back

1	Thomas Rupprath GER	51.51
2	Stev Theloke GER	51.71
3	Orn Arnarson ISL	51.91

200m Back

1	Orn Arnarson ISL	1:54.00
2	Stephen Parry GBR	1:54.11
3	Gordan Kozulj CRO	1:54.50

50m Breast

1	Oleg Lisogor UKR	26.94
2	Mark Warnecke GER	27.15
3	Jens Kruppa GER	27.36

100m Breast

1	Oleg Lisogor UKR	59.09
2	Hugues Duboscq FRA	59.18
3	Jarno Pihlava FIN	59.49

Elim heat: David Bartlett GBR

200m Breast

1	Davide Rummolo ITA	2:07.70
2	Maxim Podoprigora AUT	2:09.87
3	Richard Bodor HUN	2:10.62

Elim heat: Turner, Bartlett GBR

50m Fly

1	Jere Hard FIN	23.47
2	Milos Milosevic CRO	23.62
3	Igor Marchenko RUS	23.75

Elim s-f: James Hickman GBR

100m Fly

1	Thomas Rupprath GER	50.77
2	Andry Serdinov UKR	51.57
3	Igor Marchenko RUS	51.61
4	James Hickman GBR	51.66

200m Fly

1	Stephen Parry GBR	1:52.91
2	James Hickman GBR	1:23.73
3	Ioan Gherghel ROM	1:55.49

100m IM

1	Peter Mankoc SLO	53.05
2	Jani Sievinen FIN	53.58
3	Oleg Lisogor UKR	53.65

Elim heat: Adrian Turner GBR

200m IM

1	Jani Sievinen FIN	1:55.47
2	Tamas Kerekjarto HUN	1:56.07
3	Peter Mankoc SLO	1:56.28

400m IM

1	Alessio Boggiatto ITA	4:07.44
2	Jacob Carstensen DEN	4:08.80
3	Laszlo Cseh HUN	4:08.96
7	Adrian Turner GBR	4:14.51

Elim heat: David Davies GBR

4x50m Free Relay

1	Netherlands	1:26.41
2	Italy	1:26.63
3	Ukraine	1:26.83

Elim heat: Great Britain
Hickman/Parry/Meadows/Burnett

4x50m Medley Relay

1	Germany	**1:34.72**
2	Finland	1:35.69
3	Ukraine	1:36.46

DQ heat: Great Britain
Parry/Turner/Hickman/Burnett

Women

50m Free

1	Alison Sheppard GBR	24.20
2	A Herasimenia BLR	24.74
3	A-K Kammerling SWE	24.98

Elim s-f: Rosalind Brett GBR

100m Free

1	Martina Moravcova SVK	53.66
1	Elena Popshanka BLR	53.66
3	Petra Dallmann GER	54.03
4	Alison Sheppard GBR	54.04

Elim s-f: Rosalind Brett GBR

200m Free

1	Alena Popchanka BLR	1:55.91
2	Solenne Figues FRA	1:56.26
3	Josefin Lillhage SWE	1:56.57

Elim heat: Melanie Marshall GBR

400m Free

1	Eva Risztov RUS	4:01.95
2	Yana Klochkova UKR	4:04.50
3	Hannah Stockbauer GER	4:07.48
4	Kerianne Payne GBR	4:09.19

800m Free

1	Eva Risztov HUN	8:14.72
2	Flavia Rigamonti SUI	8:16.62
3	Hannah Stockbauer GER	8:20.92
5	Kerianne Payne GBR	8:25.87

50m Back

1	Antje Buschschulte GER	27.62
2	Ilona Hlavackova CZE	27.75
3	Janine Pietsch GER	27.88

Elim s-f: Price, Marshall GBR

100m Back

1	Antje Buschschulte GER	58.60
2	Ilona Hlavackova CZE	59.61
3	Sarah Price GBR	59.83

Elim s-f: Melanie Marshall GBR

200m Back

1	Sarah Price GBR	2:05.19
2	A Buschschulte GER	2:06.26
3	S Komorova RUS	2:07.57
6	Karen Lee GBR	2:10.27

50m Breast

1	Emma Igelstrom SWE	30.89
2	Sarah Poewe GER	30.90
3	Janne Schafer GER	31.12

Elim heat: Amy Konowalik GBR

100m Breast

1	Sarah Poewe GER	1:06.67
2	Mima Jukic AUT	1:07.11
3	Agnes Kovacs HUN	1:07.97

Elim heat: Amy Konowalik GBR

200m Breast

1	Mirna Juric AUT	2:21.66
2	Sarah Poewe GER	2:21.99
3	Anne Poleska GER	2:23.51

Elim heat: Amy Konowalik GBR

50m Fly

1	A-K Kammerling SWE	25.78
2	Lena Hallander SWE	26.74
3	Vered Borochovski ISR	26.87

Elim semi-final: Rosalind Brett GBR

100m Fly

1	Martina Moravcova SLO	56.82
2	A-K Kammerling SWE	57.94
3	Mette Jacobsen DEN	59.09

200m Fly

1	Eva Risztov HUN	2:07.19
2	Mette Jacobsen DEN	2:08.30
3	Roser Vives ESP	2:08.40

Elim heat: Rosalind Brett GBR

100m IM

1	Martina Moravcova SVK	1:00.21
2	Alison Sheppard GBR	1:00.99
3	Alenka Kejzar SLO	1:01.43

200m IM

1	Yana Klochkova UKR	2:08.28
2	Alenka Kejzar SLO	2:09.33
3	Hanna Shcherba BLR	2:10.23

400m IM

1	Yana Klochkova UKR	4:29.81
2	Eva Risztov HUN	4:33.09
3	Alenka Kejzar SLO	4:33.80

4 x 50m Free Relay

1	Sweden	1:38.65
2	Belarus	1:39.03
3	Germany	1:39.56
6	Great Britain	1:41.08

Sheppard/Brett/Marshall/Price

4 x 50m Medley Relay

1	Sweden	1:48.42
2	Germany	1:49.25
3	Netherlands	1:50.56
4	Great Britain	1:51.54

Price/Sheppard/Brett/Marshall

Commonwealth Trials & British LC Championships

Manchester, Apr 10-15

MEN

50m Free
1	Mark Foster	Bath Uni	22.51
2	Matthew Kidd	Leatherhead	22.77
3	Chris Cozens	Loughborough Uni	23.17

100m Free
1	Matthew Kidd	Leatherhead	50.20
2	Chris Cozens	Loughborough Uni	50.50
3	Adam Ruckwood	BHMM/PBEM	50.56

200m Free
1	James Salter	Edinburgh	1:49.26
2	David Carry	Aberdeen	1:50.80
3	Adam Faulkner	Nova Centurion	1:50.88

400m Free
1	Graeme Smith	Manchester A	3:50.64
2	James Salter	Edinburgh	3:51.71
3	Adam Faulkner	Nova Centurion	3:54.18

1500m Free
1	Graeme Smith	Manchester A	15:14.34
2	Adam Faulkner	Nova Centurion	15:19.64
3	Andrew Jameson	Aberdeen	15:38.18

50m Back
1	Adam Ruckwood	BHMM/PBEM	26.38
1	Martin Harris	Tower Hamlets	26.38
3	Gregor Tait	Edinburgh	26.51

100m Back
1	Gregor Tait	Edinburgh	55.98
2	Adam Ruckwood	BHMM/PBEM	56.33
3	Simon Burnett	Wycombe	56.80

200m Back
1	Gregor Tait	Edinburgh	2:00.02
2	Simon Militis	Portsmouth N	2:00.59
3	James Goddard	Stockport	2:00.69

50m Breast
1	Darren Mew	Bath Uni	27.64
2	James Gibson	Loughborough Uni	27.69
3	Adam Whitehead	Coventry	28.38

100m Breast
1	James Gibson	Loughborough Uni	1:00.69
2	Darren Mew	Bath Uni	1:01.14
3	Adam Whitehead	Coventry	1:01.72

200m Breast
1	Ian Edmond	Edinburgh	2:14.23
2	Robin Francis	Bath Uni	2:15.03
3	Adam Whitehead	Coventry	2:16.15

50m Fly
1	Mark Foster	Bath Uni	23.88
2	James Hickman	Leeds	24.72
3	Cameron Black	First Aqua	24.87

100m Fly
1	James Hickman	Leeds	53.41
2	Todd Cooper	Stirling Swim	54.09
3	Steve Parry	Manchester A	54.74

200m Fly
1	Steve Parry	Manchester A	1:57.64
2	James Hickman	Leeds	1:58.21
3	Todd Cooper	Stirling Swim	2:00.92

200m IM
1	Robin Francis	Bath Uni	2:03.05
2	Adrian Turner	Salford	2:03.52
3	David Carry	Aberdeen	2:04.46

400m IM
1	Robin Francis	Bath Uni	4:21.27
2	Simon Militis	Portsmouth N	4:22.96
3	Adrian Turner	Salford	4:23.29

WOMEN

50m Free
1	Alison Sheppard	Milngavie & B	25.10
2	Rosalind Brett	Loughborough Uni	25.73
3	Melanie Marshall	Loughborough Uni	25.91

100m Free
1	Melanie Marshall	Loughborough Uni	55.78
2	Karen Pickering	Ipswich	55.79
3	Karen Legg	Ferndown	55.99

200m Free
1	Karen Pickering	Ipswich	1:59.94
2	Karen Legg	Ferndown	2:00.15
3	Janine Belton	Loughborough Uni	2:01.33

400m Free
1	Rebecca Cooke	Glasgow	4:13.27
2	Karen Legg	Ferndown	4:17.31
3	Karen Nisbett	Leeds	4:17.72

800m Free
1	Rebecca Cooke	Glasgow	8:35.75
2	Nathalie Brown	Southend	8:43.42
3	Caroline Saxby	WEVE/DAQE	8:45.85

50m Back
1	Sarah Price	Barnet Copthall	29.35
2	Melanie Marshall	Loughborough Uni	29.75
3	Zoe Cray	Ipswich	29.98

100m Back
1	Sarah Price	Barnet Copthall	1:01.51
2	Joanne Fargus	Bath Uni	1:02.46
3	Katy Sexton	Portsmouth N	1:02.91

200m Back
1	Sarah Price	Barnet Copthall	2:10.78
2	Joanne Fargus	Bath Uni	2:12.83
3	Katy Sexton	Portsmouth N	2:13.73

50m Breast
1	Zoe Baker	Sheffield	31.33
2	Heidi Earp	Nova Centurion	32.83
3	Kate Haywood	Lincoln Vulcans	32.86

100m Breast
1	Kirsty Balfour	Edinburgh	1:10.24
2	Heidi Earp	Nova Centurion	1:10.29
3	Kate Haywood	Lincoln Vulcans	1:10.49

200m Breast
1	Jaime King	Bath Uni	2:29.52
2	Heidi Earp	Nova Centurion	2:29.89
3	Kirsty Balfour	Edinburgh	2:30.81

50m Fly
1	Rosalind Brett	Loughborough Uni	27.25
2	Julie Douglas	Loughborough Uni	27.99
3	Kerry Martin	Stirling Swim	28.05

100m Fly
1	Georgina Lee	Camphill Ed	1:00.29
2	Margaretha Pedder	Portsmouth N	1:01.46
3	Caroline Smart	PORS/THTW	1:01.66

200m Fly
1	Georgina Lee	Camphill Ed	2:10.59
2	Margaretha Pedder	Portsmouth N	2:12.15
3	Caroline Smart	PORS/THTW	2:13.54

200m IM
1	Kathryn Evans	Nova Centurion	2:17.35
2	Joanne Mullins	Orpington OJ	2:17.57
3	Holly Fox	Glasgow	2:18.78

400m IM
1	Holly Fox	Glasgow	4:50.34
2	Rebecca Cooke	Glasgow	4:52.45
3	Rebecca Shaw	LDSE/AIRE	4:52.55

British SC Championships

Cambridge, Sep 12-15

MEN				WOMEN			
50m Free				**50m Free**			
1 Mark Foster	Bath Uni	22.36		1 Alison Sheppard	MBS Swim Team	24.53	
100m Free				**100m Free**			
1 Matthew Bowe	Bath Uni	50.15		1 Alison Sheppard	MBS Swim Team	54.38	
200m Free				**200m Free**			
1 James Salter	Edinburgh	1:48.01		1 Karen Pickering	Ipswich	1:57.56	
400m Free				**400m Free**			
1 Adam Faulkner	Nova Centurion	3:46.14		1 Rebecca Cooke	Glasgow	4:08.58	
1500m Free				**800m Free**			
1 David Davies	Cardiff	14:54.60		1 Rebecca Cooke	Glasgow	8:27.66	
50m Back				**50m Back**			
1 Steve Parry	Manchester A	25.39		1 Sarah Price	Barnet Copthall	28.69	
100m Back				**100m Back**			
1 Steve Parry	Manchester A	53.15		1 Sarah Price	Barnet Copthall	1:00.15	
200m Back				**200m Back**			
1 Steve Parry	Manchester	1:54.49		1 Sarah Price	Barnet Copthall	2:07.59	
50m Breast				**50m Breast**			
1 Darren Mew	Bath Uni	27.77		1 Rachel Genner	Coventry	32.37	
100m Breast				**100m Breast**			
1 Darren Mew	Bath Uni	1:00.26		1 Kate Haywood	Lincoln Vulcans	1:10.23	
200m Breast				**200m Breast**			
1 Adrian Turner	Salford	2:12.07		1 Kirsty Balfour	Edinburgh	2:28.38	
50m Fly				**50m Fly**			
1 James Hickman	Leeds	24.18		1 Rosalind Brett	Loughborough Uni	27.56	
100m Fly				**100m Fly**			
1 James Hickman	Leeds	51.74		1 Rosalind Brett	Loughborough	1:00.30	
200m Fly				**200m Fly**			
1 James Hickman	Leeds	1:53.91		1 Terri Dunning	Birmingham	2:14.47	
100m IM				**100m IM**			
1 Adrian Turner	Salford	56.52		1 Alison Sheppard	MBS Swim Team	1:01.86	
200m IM				**200m IM**			
1 Steve Parry	Manchester A	1:59.50		1 Alex Savage	Ferndown	2:16.03	
400m IM				**400m IM**			
1 Steve Parry	Manchester A	4:13.09		1 Rebecca Cooke	Glasgow	4:45.04	

"Frankly, it's a bloody disgrace. The Prime Minister is preparing to host a reception this month to say well done to all the athletes in England who did well at the Commonwealth Games, and at the same time the Government are cutting the budget. It's a nonsense"

David Sparkes, chief executive of the Amateur Swimming Association.

"Not worth spending any more of my time on"

Bill Sweetenham, talking of Mark Foster and Zoe Baker.   Baker is the current world record holder and Commonweealth champion at 50m breaststroke, while Foster has won more major championship medals than any Briton in history.

"Sometimes, when the alarm goes off, I feel like I want to turn over and curl up, but you will never get anywhere like that. You have to go"

Stephanie Proud, 14-year-old swimming prodigy.

Table Tennis

European Championships
Zagreb, Croatia, Mar 30-Apr 7
Only British/Irish results shown in early rounds

Men's Singles
1st Qualifying Round
Teodor Yordanov BUL bt Darryl Strong IRL 4-0
Adam Robertson WAL bt Ricardo Oliveiro POR 4-0
Agon Saiti MKD bt Owen Griffiths WAL 4-0
Vladimir Ivanek UKR bt Niall Cameron SCO 4-0
Gavin Rumgay SCO bt John Bowe IRL 4-1
2nd Qualifying Round
Adam Robertson WAL bt Ron Davidovitz ISR 4-0
Vitaly Levshin UKR bt Stewart Crawford SCO 4-2
Artis Kopeika LAT bt Gavin Rumgay SCO 4-2
Round 1
Andrew Baggaley ENG bt Peter Fazekas HUN 4-0
Lucjan Blaszczyk POL bt Adam Robertson WAL 4-0
Matthew Syed ENG bt Yaldiz Gurhan RUS 4-1
Alex Perry ENG bt Sharon Yanic ISR 4-1
Trinko Keen NED bt Ryan Jenkins WAL 4-3
Gareth Herbert ENG bt Adam Lindner HUN 4-3
Geir Erlandsen NOR bt Terry Young ENG 4-1
Round 2
Robert Gardos AUT bt Matthew Syed ENG 4-1
Slobodan Grujic YUG bt |Andrew Baggaley ENG 4-1
Fredrik Hakansson SWE bt Gareth Herbert ENG 4-1
Kalinikos Kreanga GRE bt Alex Perry ENG 4-0
Semi-finals
Kalinikos Kreanga GRE bt Zoran Primorac CRO 4-3
Timo Boll GER bt Weerner Schlager AUT 4-3
Final
Timo Boll GER bt Kalinikos Kreanga GRE 4-3

Women's Singles
Qualifying Round
Stephanie Matthews SCO bt Roza Moiseyeva AZE 4-0
Nicola Bentley SCO bt Inta Laudupe LAT 4-2
Elda Stafala bt Gillian Edwards SCO 4-3
Claire Bentley SCO bt Maja Veskovska MKD 4-2
Olga Pritula ISR bt Catherine Davies WAL 4-0
Round 1
Andrea Mayrhofer AUT bt Kate Stewart ENG 4-1
Renata Strbikova CZE bt Bethan Daunton WAL 4-0
Silvija Erdelji YUG bt Stephanie Matthews SCO 4-0
Galia Dvorak ESP bt Helen Lower GBR 4-0
Alba Prades ESP bt Georgina Walker ENG 4-0
Ana Gogorita ROM bt Nicola Bentley SCO 4-0
Ruta Garkauskaite LTU bt Siwan Davies WAL 4-0
Marie Olsson SWE bt Katy Parker ENG 4-1
Peggy Regenwetter LUX bt Nicola Deaton ENG 4-0
Nicole Struse GER bt Claire Bentley SCO 4-0
Semi-finals
Ni Xia Lian LUX bt Csilla Batorfi HUN 4-1
Krisztine Toth HUN bt Tamara Boros CRO 4-2
Final
Ni Xia Lian LUX bt Krisztina Toth HUN 4-1

Men's Doubles
1st Qualifying Round
Andreoli/Lucesoli ITA bt Karlovic/Crawford CRO/SCO 3-0
2nd Qualifying Round
Rumgay/Cameron SCO bt Rasanen/Lundstrom FIN 3-1
Ciociu/Simon ROM bt Horvat/Griffiths /WAL 3-0
Round 1
Chmyrev/Fadeev SLO bt Rumgay/Cameron SCO 3-1
Samsanov/Saive BLR/BEL bt Jenkins/Robertson WAL 3-2
Baggaley/Herbert ENG bt Saive/Podpinka BEL 3-2
Perry/Young ENG bt Nekhviaqdovich/Chumakou BLR 3-0
Round 2
Hielscher/Wosik GER bt Perry/Young ENG 3-1
Legout/Quentel FRA bt Baggaley/Herbert ENG 3-1
Semi-final
Boll/Fejer-Konnerth GER bt Keen/Heister NED 4-2
Blaszczyk/Krzeszewski POL bt Chila/Eloi FRA 4-1
Final
Boll/Fejer-Konnerth GER bt Blaszczyk/Krzeszewski POL 4-0

Women's Doubles
Qualifying Round
Stankute/Kardauskaite LTU bt Edwards/Matthews SCO 3-1
Davies/Davies WAL bt Gjoka/Shaqiri ALB 3-0
Boros/Steff CRO/ bt Deaton/Lower ENG 3-0
Detrigne/Opdencamp BEL bt Stewart/Walker ENG 3-2
Pavlovich/Kostromina BLR bt Bentley/Bentley SCO 3-0
Round 1
Struse/Wosik GER bt Davies/Davies WAL 3-0
Semi-finals
Boros/Steff CRO/ROM bt Ganina/Palina SVK 4-1
Pavlovich/Kostromina BLR bt Garkauskaite/Pruisene LTU 4-0
Final
Boros/Steff CRO/ROM bt Pavlovich/Kostromina BLR 4-3

Mixed Doubles
Qualifying Round
Mohler/Wuest SUI bt Griffiths/Davies WAL 3-2
Cameron/Bentley SCO bt Cravcenko/Mittel AND
Round 1
Molin/Jonsson SWE bt Young/Parker ENG 3-1
Hielscher/Hain-Hofman GER bt Perry/Lower ENG 3-2
Juzbasic/Bakula CRO bt Rumgay/Edwards SCO 3-0
Blaszczyk/Ni POL/LUX bt Cameron/Bentley SCO 3-0
Carneros/Dvorak ESP bt Robertson/Davies WAL 3-0
Pazsy/Lovas HUN bt Baggaley/Walker ENG 3-1
Fadeev/Krekina SLO bt Crawford/Bentley SCO 3-0
Jenkins/Daunton WAL bt Tokic/Halas SVK 3-2
Wang/Svensson NOR/SWE bt Herbert/Deaton ENG 3-0
Round 2
Chen/Pavlovich AUT/BLR bt Jenkins/Daunton WAL 3-0
Semi-finals
Blaszczyk/Ni POL/LUX bt Schlager/Liu AUT 4-1
Karakasevic/Garkauskaite YUG/LTU bt Chen/Pavlovich AUT/BLR 4-0
Final
Blaszczyk/Ni POL/LUX bt Karakasevic/Garkauskaite YUG/LTU 4-0

Men's Team
Semi-finals
Germany bt France 3-2
Sweden bt Austria 3-1
Final
Sweden bt Germany 3-2

England matches
England 3 Italy 1; England 0 Croatia 3
England 0 Russia 3; England 0 Poland 3
Final England placing 16th

Wales matches
Wales 3 Ireland 1; Wales 3 Scotland 1
Wales 3 Ukraine 2; Wales 0 Romania 3
Wales 1 Finland 3
Final Wales placing 28th

Scotland matches
Scotland 2 Ireland 3; Scotland 1 Wales 3
Scotland 0 Switzerland 3; Scotland 3 Iceland 2
Final Scotland placing 35th

Ireland matches
Ireland 3 Scotland 2; Ireland 1 Wales 3
Ireland 2 Macedonia 3; Ireland 3 Albania 0
Final Ireland placing 42nd

Women's Team
Semi-finals
Croatia 3 Yugoslavia 2
Luxembourg 3 Belarus 2
Final
Croatia 3 Luxembourg 2

England matches
England 3 Norway 1; England 3 FYR Macedonia 0
England 3 Turkey 1; England 3 Estonia 1
Final England placing 25th; promoted from Division II to Division I (NB: highest division is Super League)

Wales matches
Wales 3 Bosnia 2; Wales 2 Turkey 3
Wales 3 Norway 2; Wales 2 Moldova 3
Final Wales placing 31st

Scotland matches
Scotland 0 Switzerland 3; Scotland 3 Albania 0
Scotland 1 Estonia 3; Scotland 1 Latvia 3
Scotland 1 Bosnia 3
Final Scotland placing 36th

English National Championships
MEN'S SINGLES
Final
Andrew Baggaley (Buckinghamshire) bt Alex Perry (Devonshire) 11-5 17-19 11-9 11-5 11-9
WOMEN'S SINGLES
Final
Nicola Deaton (Derbyshire) bt Helen Lower (Staffordshire) 11-8 11-5 11-9 11-9
MEN'S DOUBLES
Final
Gareth Herbert (Berkshire)/Andrew Baggaley (Buckinghamshire) bt Alan Cooke/Bradley Billington (Derbyshire) 12-10 6-11 9-11 12-10 11-6.
WOMEN'S DOUBLES
Final
Nicola Deaton (Derbyshire)/Helen Lower (Staffordshire) bt Kate Steward (Somerset)/Georgina Walker (Nottinghamshire) 11-7 9-11 13-11 11-6

World Rankings
As at Jan 1, 2003
British/Irish shown if in top 250

	MEN	
1	Timo Boll GER	2295
2	Ma Lin CHN	2294
3	Wang Liqin CHN	2184
4	Werner Schlager AUT	2175
5	Chuan Chih-Yuan TPE	2145
6	Kong Linghui CHN	2113
7	Vladimir Samsonov BLR	2089
8	Kalinikos Kreanga GRE	2063
9	Jean-Michel Saive BEL	2006
10	Wang Hao CHN	2004
86	Matthew Syed ENG	1420
148	Gareth Herbert ENG	1190
169	Alex Perry ENG	1154
197	Colum Slevin IRL	1080
206	Andrew Baggaley ENG	1063
227	Ryan Jenkins WAL	1032

	WOMEN	
1	Zhang Yining CHN	2340
2	Wang Nan CHN	2294
3	Lin Ling HKG	2072
4	Niu Jianfeng CHN	2068
5	Tamara Boros CRO	2060
6	Li Nan CHN	1995
7	Mihaela Steff ROM	1960
8	Li Jia Wei SIN	1953
9	Guo Yue CHN	1936
10	Li Ju CHN	1924
205	Nicola Deaton ENG	1046
226	Bethen Daunton WAL	1015

Tennis

As theories go, the Williams share-out was a plausible enough one. After all, Venus had stepped out for the French Open final at Roland Garros looking as miserable as sin, lending substance to the idea that it was Serena's turn. But was it Serena's turn or just Serena's day? Well, all theories must withstand more than a single examination, and little more than three months later, that particular conspiracy theory had been blown apart.

Serena beat her sister in the finals of Wimbledon and the US Open as well at Roland Garros. Moreover, the younger sister did not lose a set, and arguably her easiest victory came at Flushing Meadow. Thankfully, there was no sisterly divide, and the titles went to the best player, Serena, who completed the first hattrick of Grand Slam titles, man or woman, since Steffi Graf six years earlier.

Serena's physical capabilities had been evident since she won her first Grand Slam at Flushing Meadow in 1999. We can claim a little prescience here too as we asserted, on these pages, that "everything was within her reach". For the following two seasons, however, Serena mental abilities were repeatedly called into question. Although she was the most powerful striker of the ball on the circuit, Serena would be as profligate with her poor shots, as she was wondrous with her good ones. Not until two years later at Flushing Meadow did she reach her second Grand Slam final, and she lost to her sister.

The upgrade has been a mental one; the realisation perhaps that her remarkable physique gives her a huge advantage over most of the women. Perhaps only her sister and Capriati, on a going day, can come close to matching her for power, while the likes of Henin, Clijsters and even Mauresmo, must spend hours on the practise courts, trying to evolve new stategies to comabt their relative weaknesses.

For the immediate future, there is no apparent threat to Serena's dominance. The 2003 Australian Open has given her a fourth title in a row, and William Hill is prepared to offer only 9/2 against her completing the full set this year and matching Maureen Connolly, Margaret Court and Steffi Graf, the only players in history to achieve the 'Golden Slam'. Indeed, were she to win seven straight titles, that would be the best sequence ever, for Connolly and Court only managed six, and Graf just five.

The only succour for the rest of the women's game, is that Serena's muscular frame may not be designed for longevity in the sport. Or, it may be that Puma will not come up with enough money when her new

> **"There's no point in looking back. I've got a great life ahead of me"**
>
> Martina Hingis, not quite announcing her retirement.

deals runs out in December 2003. Or, she may just get bored and go off and run her own fashion house. Any of those things may happen, but don't count on it.

Pete Sampras was the story in the men's game. Having written him off after he won his seventh Wimbledon title in 2000 (didn't everyone?), and seen him relagated to a miserable Court 2 appearance at SW19 this year (have they no respect at the All England club?) the old groaner came back to win a fifth US Open, 12 years after he won his first. We put this 14th Grand Slam win almost entirely down to Greg Rusedski who told Sampras he was past it. Good old Greg, you know how to play the mind games.

Rusedski didn't have much of a year himself, a solitary ATP victory in January followed by a second round defeat in the Australian Open at the hands of Tim Henman.

Henman had his usual year, reaching the semi-final of Wimbledon and failing to get past the fourth round of any of the other Slam tournaments. Henman was walloped by the Australian Lleyton Hewitt at Wimbledon, who is currently the best player in the world by some way. As the Australian is seven years Henman's junior, it doesn't bode well for the Englishman in terms of future Grand Slam titles, the chances of which must be slim to none.

British tennis did have a Wimbledon winner, but they don't make the over-45 doubles tournament the back-page lead. Colin Dowdeswell and Buster Mottram were the champions; their win coming 20 years after Mottram had reached the 4th round of the men's singles. It was the best British performance of that year, and was not equalled by a British man for another 10 years, nor surpassed till Henman. If he does end his career without a Grand Slam, Henman should still receive great credit for changing the benchmark of success for the British game. Will it be back where it was when he goes, though?

"I tricked her at Wimbledon. I'm not going to tell you how, but my trainers and I totally had her surprised"

Serena Williams, on the secret tactics which out-foxed her sister at Wimbledon.

"Your confidence is low"

Gary Richardson, BBC reporter, to Anna Kournikova.

"You don't know my confidence is low. It's not..."

Kournikova, to Richardson.

"He's a step and a half slow coming into the net. He's just not the same player. I lost the match rather than he won the match. I'd be surprised if he wins his next match against Haas. To be honest with you, I'd be very surprised. I don't really see it. The movement is not the same and the fitness is not the same"

Greg Rusedski, on Pete Sampras, after losing to the American in the US Open. Sampras went on to win the tournament.

Grand Slam Events

Wimbledon
June 24-July 7

Men's Doubles
Semi-Finals
Bjorkman/Woodbridge SWE/AUS bt Johnson Palmer
USA 7-5 4-6 6-7(3) 7-5 6-2
Knowles/Nestor BAH/CAN bt B Bryan/M Bryan USA
6-4 7-6(5) 7-6(4)
Final
Bjorkman/Woodbridge bt Knowles/Nestor
6-1 6-2 6-7(7) 7-5

Women's Doubles
Semi-Finals
S Williams/V Williams USA bt Kournikova/Rubin
RUS/USA 6-7(3) 6-0 6-3
Ruano-Pascual/Suarez ESP/ARG bt Black/Likhovtseva
ZIM/RUS 6-3 3-6 6-4
Final
S Williams/V Williams bt Ruano-Pascual/Suarez 6-2 7-5

Mixed Doubles
Semi-Finals
Ullyett/Hantuchova ZIM/SVK bt Koenig/Callens RSA/BEL
6-3 3-6 6-2
Bhupati/Likhovtseva IND/RUS bt Johnson/Po-Messerli
USA 6-4 1-6 6-3
Final
Bhupati/Likhovtseva bt Ullyett/Hantuchova 6-2 1-6 6-1

Australian Open
Melbourne Park, Jan 14-27

Men's Doubles
Semi-Finals
Llodra/Santoro FRA bt Boutter/Clement FRA
6-3 3-6 12-10
Knowles/Nestor BAH/CAN bt Johnson/Palmer USA
6-1 6-4
Final
Knowles/Nestor bt Llodra/Santoro 7-6(4) 6-3

Women's Doubles
Semi-Finals
Hingis/Kournikova SUI/RUS bt Raymond/Stubbs
USA/AUS 6-7(5) 6-1 6-0
Hantuchova/Sanchez-Vicario SVK/ESP bt
Martinez/Serna ESP 6-0 6-2
Final
Hingis/Kournikova bt Hantuchova/Sanchez-Vicario
6-2 6-7(4) 6-1

Mixed Doubles
Semi-Finals
Ullyett/Hantuchova ZIM/SVK bt Bhupati/Likhovtseva
IND/RUS 3-6 6-4 7-6(10-6)
Etlis/Suarez ARG bt Hill/Vis AUS/NED 3-6 6-4 7-6(7)
Final
Ullyett/Hantuchova bt Etlis/Suarez 6-3 6-2

French Open
May 27-June 9

Men's Doubles
Semi-Finals
Haarhuis/Kafelnikov NED/RUS bt Bhupathi/Mirnyi
IND/BLR 6-7(1) 7-5 6-2
Knowles/Nestor BAH/CAN bt Cibulec/Paes CZE/IND
7-6(5) 7-5
Final
Haarhuis/Kafelnikov bt Knowles/Nestor 7-5 6-4

Women's Doubles
Semi-Finals
Raymond/Stubbs USA/AUS bt Fugiwara/Sugiyama JPN
6-1 6-7(5) 6-2
Ruano-Pascual/Suarez ESP/ARG bt Arendt/Huber
USA/RSA 6-0 6-4
7-6(5) 7-5
Final
Ruano-Pascual/Suarez bt Raymond/Stubbs 6-4 6-2

Mixed Doubles
Semi-Finals
Knowles/Bovina BAH/RUS bt Palmer/Sanchez-Vicario
USA/ESP 6-3 6-3
Black/Black ZIM bt Srebotnik/B Bryan SLO/USA
3-6 6-3 6-4
Final
Black/Black bt Bovina/Knowles 6-3 6-3

US Open
Aug 26-Sep 8

Men's Doubles
Semi-Finals
Bhupathi/Mirnyi IND/BLR bt Bryan/Bryan USA
6-3 3-6 6-3
Novak/Stepanek CZE bt Bjorkman/Woodbridge
SWE/AUS 6-2 7-6(4)
Final
Bhupathi/Mirnyi bt Novak/Stepanek 6-3 3-6 6-4

Women's Doubles
Semi-Finals
Dementieva/Husarova RUS/SVK bt Black/Likhovtseva
ZIM/RUS 7-5 6-1
Ruano-Pascual/Suarez ESP/ARG bt Petrova/Pratt
RUS/AUS 6-1 6-3
Final
Ruano-Pascual/Suarez bt Dementieva/Husarova 6-2 6-1

Mixed Doubles
Semi-Finals
Srebotnik/B Bryan SLO/USA bt Callens/Koenig BEL/RSA
6-4 3-6 7-6 (10-4)
Raymond/M Bryan USA bt Morariu/Gimelstob USA
6-3 6-3
Final
Raymond/M Bryan bt Srebotnik/B Bryan 7-6(9) 7-6(1)

Wimbledon

Men's Singles

FIRST ROUND

Lleyton Hewitt AUS (1) bt Jonas Bjorkman SWE
6-4 7-5 6-1

Gregory Carraz FRA (Q) bt Cecil Mamiit USA
6-2 6-4 6-7(5) 7-5

Julian Knowle AUT bt Michael Llodra FRA
3-6 6-4 6-3 3-6 6-3

Jarkko Nieminen FIN (32) bt Alan Mackin GBR (W)
7-6(5) 6-3 6-3

Gaston Gaudio ARG (24) bt Juan Pablo Guzman ARG (Q)
6-3 6-4 6-3

Mikhail Youzhny RUS bt Brian Vahaly USA (L)
6-3 1-6 6-3 6-2 *(Vahaly replaced Karol Kucera)*

Marc Rosset SUI bt Jose Acasuso ARG 6-3 7-6(4) 6-1

Nicolas Escude FRA (16) bt Alex Bogdanovic GBR (W)
4-6 6-4 6-4 6-4

Juan Carlos Ferrero ESP (9) bt Neville Godwin RSA
6-7(5) 6-3 6-3 6-3

Jeff Morrison USA (L) bt Noam Okun ISR
6-3 7-6(3) 6-2 *(Morrison replaces Haas)*

Michael Chang USA bt Lars Burgsmuller GER
6-3 7-6(4) 6-4

Sjeng Schalken NED (18) bt Kristian Pless DEN 6-3 6-3 7-5

Fabrice Santoro FRA (25) bt Agustin Calleri ARG
2-6 7-6(4) 6-4 4-6 6-3

Adrian Voinea ROM bt Nicolas Coutelot FRA 7-6(4) 6-1 6-3

Jan Vacek CZE bt Jerome Golmard FRA 6-2 7-6(6) 3-2 ret.

Mario Ancic CRO (Q) bt **Roger Federer SUI (7)**
6-3 7-6(2) 6-3

Tim Henman GBR (4) bt Jean-Francois Bachelot FRA (Q)
6-1 6-3 6-2

Scott Draper AUS (Q) bt Cristiano Caratti ITA (Q)
6-3 4-6 6-4 7-5

Wayne Ferreira RSA bt Albert Portas ESP
7-6(5) 6-3 6-7(4) 6-3

Ivan Ljubicic CRO (30) bt Ramon Delgado PAR
6-2 6-4 7-5

Raemon Sluiter NED bt Tommy Robredo ESP (20)
6-1 6-4 6-4

Radek Stepanek CZE (Q) bt Cyril Saulnier FRA (Q)
7-5 6-2 7-6(5)

Michel Kratochvil SUI bt Nikolay Davydenko RUS
6-4 6-2 6-4

Irakli Labadze GEO bt **Younes El Aynaoui MAR (13)**
4-6 7-6(4) 6-3 7-6(2)

Guillermo Canas ARG (10) bt Michael Kohlmann GER
7-5 6-4 6-4

Feliciano Lopez ESP bt Konstantinos Economidis GRE (Q)
6-3 3-6 4-6 7-6(2) 11-9

Sargis Sargsian ARM bt Fernando Vicente ESP
4-6 7-6(3) 6-3 6-2

Rainer Schuettler GER bt Hicham Arazi MAR 7-6(3) 6-4 6-4

Stefan Koubek AUT (31) bt Justin Bower RSA (Q)
6-3 3-6 6-2 4-6 6-3

Andre Sa BRA bt Anthony Dupuis FRA 6-3 4-6 6-4 5-7 6-3

Alexander Waske GER (Q) bt Andrea Gaudenzi ITA
7-6(4) 7-6(3) 6-7(2) 6-1

Flavio Saretta BRA bt **Thomas Johansson SWE (8)**
6-7(2) 6-4 7-6(4) 3-6 12-10

Yevgeny Kafelnikov RUS (5) bt Dominik Hrbaty SVK
6-1 7-6(4) 7-6(7)

Nicolas Thomann FRA (Q) bt Markus Hipfl AUT
6-1 7-6(3) 3-6 4-6 11-9

Vince Spadea USA bt Magnus Larsson SWE
3-6 7-6(4) 6-7(2) 6-4 6-1

Xavier Malisse BEL (27) bt Galo Blanco ESP 6-3 6-3 6-3

Greg Rusedski GBR (23) bt (Q)Jurgen Melzer AUT
6-1 6-4 7-5

Lee Hyung-Taik Lee KOR (Q) bt Andrei Stoliarov RUS
6-3 6-2 4-6 4-6 6-2

Alberto Martin ESP bt Stefano Galvani ITA 6-4 7-6(3) 6-4

Andy Roddick USA (11) bt Bohdan Ulihrach CZE
6-1 3-1 ret.

Thomas Enqvist SWE (14) bt Arvind Parmar GBR (W)
6-1 6-4 6-4

Mark Philippoussis AUS (W) bt Julien Boutter FRA
6-3 3-6 6-1 6-2

Nicolas Kiefer GER bt Juan Balcells ESP
6-3 2-6 5-7 7-5 6-3

Fernando Gonzalez CHI bt Juan Ignacio Chela ARG (19)
6-3 3-6 1-6 7-5 6-3

James Blake USA (29) bt Mariano Zabaleta ARG
6-2 6-2 ret.

Richard Krajicek NED bt Franco Squillari ARG
6-2 7-5 7-6(5)

Paradorn Srichaphan THA bt Jack Brasington USA (Q)
6-4 6-3 3-6 5-7 6-4

Andre Agassi USA (3) bt Harel Levy ISR 6-0 6-4 6-4

Pete Sampras USA (6) bt Martin Lee GBR 6-3 7-6(1) 6-3

George Bastl SUI (L) bt Denis Golovanov RUS (L)
6-4 6-2 7-6(5) *(Bastl replaces Felix Mantilla and
Golovanov replaces James Auckland)*

Paul-Henri Mathieu FRA (W) bt Francisco Clavet ESP
6-4 7-5 6-3

David Nalbandian ARG (28) bt David Sanchez ESP
6-4 6-3 4-6 7-5

Taylor Dent USA bt Max Mirnyi BLR (21) 4-6 6-4 7-6(3) 6-4

Jan-Michael Gambill USA bt Nicolas Massu CHI
6-3 7-6(9) 6-3

Wayne Arthurs AUS bt Michael Russell USA 6-4 6-4 6-3

Jiri Novak CZE (12) bt Fernando Meligeni BRA
2-6 6-0 6-4 6-4

Andrei Pavel ROM (15) bt Kenneth Carlsen DEN
6-4 6-1 3-6 6-3

Karol Beck SVK (Q) bt Alexandre Simoni BRA
6-7(3) 4-6 7-6(5) 6-2 6-2

Barry Cowan GBR (W) bt Attila Savolt HUN
6-7(3) 6-3 6-3 6-3

Nicolas Lapentti ECU (22) bt Jamie Delgado GBR (W)
6-3 6-2 6-7(6) 4-6 7-5

Todd Martin USA (26) bt Davide Sanguinetti ITA
6-3 6-4 7-6(1)

Arnaud Clement FRA bt Albert Montanes ESP
6-3 6-4 6-0

Olivier Rochus BEL bt Christophe Rochus BEL
6-2 3-6 7-6(6) 6-0

Marat Safin RUS (2) bt Cedric Pioline FRA
7-6(7) 6-2 6-3

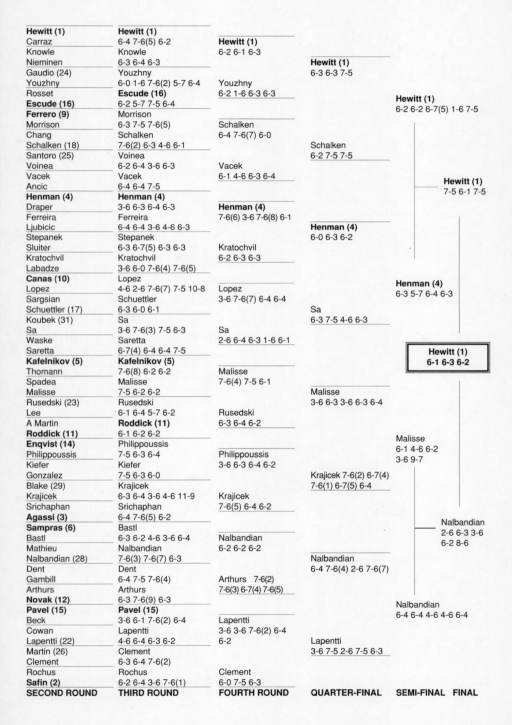

SECOND ROUND

Hewitt (1)
Carraz
Knowle
Nieminen
Gaudio (24)
Youzhny
Rosset
Escude (16)
Ferrero (9)
Morrison
Chang
Schalken (18)
Santoro (25)
Voinea
Vacek
Ancic
Henman (4)
Draper
Ferreira
Ljubicic
Stepanek
Sluiter
Kratochvil
Labadze
Canas (10)
Lopez
Sargsian
Schuettler (17)
Koubek (31)
Sa
Waske
Saretta
Kafelnikov (5)
Thomann
Spadea
Malisse
Rusedski (23)
Lee
A Martin
Roddick (11)
Enqvist (14)
Philippoussis
Kiefer
Gonzalez
Blake (29)
Krajicek
Srichaphan
Agassi (3)
Sampras (6)
Bastl
Mathieu
Nalbandian (28)
Dent
Gambill
Arthurs
Novak (12)
Pavel (15)
Beck
Cowan
Lapentti (22)
Martin (26)
Clement
Rochus
Safin (2)

THIRD ROUND

Hewitt (1)
6-4 7-6(5) 6-2
Knowle
6-3 6-4 6-3
Youzhny
6-0 1-6 7-6(2) 5-7 6-4
Escude (16)
6-2 5-7 7-5 6-4
Morrison
6-3 7-5 7-6(5)
Schalken
7-6(2) 6-3 4-6 6-1
Voinea
6-2 6-4 3-6 6-3
Vacek
6-4 6-4 7-5
Henman (4)
3-6 6-3 6-4 6-3
Ferreira
6-4 6-4 3-6 4-6 6-3
Stepanek
6-3 6-7(5) 6-3 6-3
Kratochvil
3-6 6-0 7-6(4) 7-6(5)
Lopez
4-6 2-6 7-6(7) 7-5 10-8
Schuettler
6-3 6-0 6-1
Sa
3-6 7-6(3) 7-5 6-3
Saretta
6-7(4) 6-4 6-4 7-5
Kafelnikov (5)
7-6(8) 6-2 6-2
Malisse
7-5 6-2 6-2
Rusedski
6-1 6-4 5-7 6-2
Roddick (11)
6-1 6-2 6-2
Philippoussis
7-5 6-3 6-4
Kiefer
7-5 6-3 6-0
Krajicek
6-3 6-4 3-6 4-6 11-9
Srichaphan
6-4 7-6(5) 6-2
Bastl
6-3 6-2 4-6 3-6 6-4
Nalbandian
7-6(3) 7-6(7) 6-3
Dent
6-4 7-5 7-6(4)
Arthurs
6-3 7-6(9) 6-3
Pavel (15)
3-6 6-1 7-6(2) 6-4
Lapentti
4-6 6-4 6-3 6-2
Clement
6-3 6-4 7-6(2)
Rochus
6-2 6-4 3-6 7-6(1)

FOURTH ROUND

Hewitt (1)
6-2 6-1 6-3
Youzhny
6-2 1-6 6-3 6-3
Schalken
6-4 7-6(7) 6-0
Vacek
6-1 4-6 6-3 6-4
Henman (4)
7-6(6) 3-6 7-6(8) 6-1
Kratochvil
6-2 6-3 6-3
Lopez
3-6 7-6(7) 6-4 6-4
Sa
2-6 6-4 6-3 1-6 6-1
Malisse
7-6(4) 7-5 6-1
Rusedski
6-3 6-4 6-2
Philippoussis
3-6 6-3 6-4 6-2
Krajicek
7-6(5) 6-4 6-2
Nalbandian
6-2 6-2 6-2
Arthurs 7-6(2)
7-6(3) 6-7(4) 7-6(5)
Lapentti
3-6 3-6 7-6(2) 6-4
6-2
Clement
6-0 7-5 6-3

QUARTER-FINAL

Hewitt (1)
6-3 6-3 7-5
Schalken
6-2 7-5 7-5
Henman (4)
6-0 6-3 6-2
Sa
6-3 7-5 4-6 6-3
Malisse
3-6 6-3 3-6 6-3 6-4
Krajicek 7-6(2) 6-7(4)
7-6(1) 6-7(5) 6-4
Nalbandian
6-4 7-6(4) 2-6 7-6(7)
Lapentti
3-6 7-5 2-6 7-5 6-3

SEMI-FINAL

Hewitt (1)
6-2 6-2 6-7(5) 1-6 7-5
Henman (4)
6-3 5-7 6-4 6-3
Malisse
6-1 4-6 6-2
3-6 9-7
Nalbandian
6-4 6-4 4-6 4-6 6-4

FINAL

Hewitt (1)
6-2 6-2 6-7(5) 1-6 7-5

Hewitt (1)
7-5 6-1 7-5

Malisse
6-1 4-6 6-2
3-6 9-7

Nalbandian
2-6 6-3 3-6
6-2 8-6

**Hewitt (1)
6-1 6-3 6-2**

Wimbledon

Women's Singles

FIRST ROUND

Venus Williams USA (1) bt Jane O'Donoghue GBR (W)
6-1 6-1

Virginia Ruano Pascual ESP bt Angelika Roesch GER
6-2 6-4

Maureen Drake CAN bt Marie-Gaianeh Mikaelian SUI
6-3 6-3

Jill Craybas USA bt Paola Suarez ARG (28)
6-4 5-7 7-5

Patty Schnyder SUI (17) bt Tatiana Perebiynis UKR (Q)
3-6 7-6(3) 7-5

Conchita Martinez ESP bt Celine Beigbeder FRA 6-1 6-0

Wynne Prakusya INA bt Jana Nejedly CAN 6-0 6-2

Lisa Raymond USA (16) bt Katarina Srebotnik SLO
6-4 6-2

Silvia Farina Elia ITA (10) bt Amy Frazier USA
7-5 4-6 6-4

Barbara Rittner GER bt Jennifer Hopkins USA
6-0 5-7 6-3

Emmanuelle Gagliardi SUI bt Hannah Collin GBR (W)
6-1 6-7(1) 6-2

Magdalena Maleeva BUL (19) bt Rachel Viollet GBR
6-1 6-0

Amanda Coetzer RSA (32) bt Zsofia Gubacsi HUN
6-3 6-2

Elena Baltacha GBR (W) bt Maria Vento-Kabchi VEN (Q)
6-4 6-4

Elena Likhovtseva RUS bt Roberta Vinci ITA (Q)
6-3 6-2

Kim Clijsters BEL (5) bt Samantha Reeves USA
6-2 7-6(5)

Monica Seles USA (4) bt Eva Bes ESP 6-0 6-0

Rossana Neffa-De Los Rios PAR bt Adriana Gersi CZE
6-3 7-5

Virginie Razzano FRA bt Anne Keothavong GBR (W)
6-3 7-6(5)

Ai Sugiyama JPN (27) bt Zuzana Ondraskova CZE (Q)
6-1 6-2

Tamarine Tanasugarn THA (20) bt Maria Sanchez Lorenzo
ESP 6-4 6-4

Jana Kandarr GER bt Tathiana Garbin ITA 7-6(4) 6-3

Meilen Tu USA bt Marissa Irvin USA 7-6(0) 6-2

Angelique Widjaja INA bt **Anna Smashnova ISR (15)**
6-3 6-2

Elena Dementieva RUS (12) bt Bianka Lamade GER
6-4 6-3

Emilie Loit FRA bt Janet Lee TPE 6-4 6-4

Vera Zvonareva RUS bt Antonella Serra-Zanetti ITA (Q)
6-3 6-2

Iva Majoli CRO (23) bt Tina Pisnik SLO 6-3 6-4

Barbara Schett AUT (29) bt Cara Black ZIM 6-2 6-2

Myriam Casanova SUI (Q) bt Henrieta Nagyova SVK
7-5 6-4

Denisa Chladkova CZE bt Martina Muller GER
6-3 7-5

Justine Henin BEL (6) bt Brie Rippner USA
6-2 6-7(4) 6-1

Sandrine Testud FRA (8) bt Anca Barna GER
6-7(3) 6-4 6-1

Mary Pierce FRA bt Alicia Molik AUS
6-4 4-6 8-6

Marlene Weingartner GER bt Natasha Zvereva BLR (W)
4-6 6-3 6-2

Laura Granville USA (Q) bt Nicole Pratt AUS (31)
7-5 7-5

Anastasia Myskina RUS (18) bt Eva Dyrberg DEN
2-6 6-1 7-5

Greta Arn GER bt Irina Selyutina KAZ
6-4 6-3

Rita Grande ITA bt Magui Serna ESP 6-1 6-3

Amelie Mauresmo FRA (9) bt Iveta Benesova CZE (Q)
6-1 5-7 6-2

Meghann Shaughnessy USA (13) bt Lucie Ahl GBR (Q)
6-2 6-2

Miriam Oremans NED bt Alexandra Fusai FRA (Q)
6-2 6-4

Eleni Daniilidou GRE bt Jelena Kostanic CRO
6-2 6-3

Saori Obata JPN bt Alexandra Stevenson USA (24)
6-1 6-3

Daja Bedanova CZE (26) bt Seda Noorlander NED
6-1 6-2

Selima Sfar TUN bt Kristina Brandi USA 6-3 6-3

Marta Marrero ESP bt Alina Jidkova RUS
6-0 7-6(5)

Jennifer Capriati USA (3) bt Janette Husarova SVK
6-1 6-4

Jelena Dokic YUG (7) bt Elena Tatarkova UKR (Q)
7-6(4) 6-4

Kveta Hrdlickova CZE bt Stephanie Foretz FRA
3-6 6-4 6-3

Tatiana Poutchek BLR bt Angeles Montolio ESP
6-4 6-3

Nathalie Dechy FRA (25) bt Mariana Diaz-Oliva ARG
6-2 6-3

Anne Kremer LUX (22) bt Gala Leon Garcia ESP
6-4 6-4

Maja Matevzic SLO bt Julie Pullin GBR (W)
6-7(4) 6-1 6-4

Martina Sucha SVK bt Lilia Osterloh USA
6-2 6-1

Daniela Hantuchova SVK (11) bt Cristina Torrens Valero
ESP 6-3 6-2

Iroda Tulyaganova UZB (14) bt Silvija Talaja CRO
2-6 6-2 6-4

Chanda Rubin USA bt Asa Svensson SWE 6-3 6-1

Elena Bovina RUS bt Adriana Serra Zanetti ITA
7-6(4) 7-6(3)

Tatiana Panova RUS (21) bt Anna Kournikova RUS
6-1 4-6 6-4

Clarisa Fernandez ARG (30) bt Ludmila Cervanova SVK
6-3 6-3

Els Callens BEL bt Barbara Schwartz AUT
3-6 6-4 6-2

Francesca Schiavone ITA bt Petra Mandula HUN
6-4 6-3

Serena Williams USA (2) bt Evie Dominikovic AUS
6-1 6-1

SECOND ROUND	THIRD ROUND	FOURTH ROUND	QUARTER-FINAL	SEMI-FINAL	FINAL

V Williams (1)
Ruano Pascual
Drake
Craybas
Schnyder (17)
Martinez
Prakusya
Raymond (16)
Farina Elia (10)
Rittner
Gagliardo
Maleeva (19)
Coetzer (32)
Baltacha
Likhovtseva
Clijsters (5)
Seles (4)
Neffa-De Los Rios
Razzano
Sugiyama (27)
Tanasugarn (20)
Kandarr
Tu
Widjaja
Dementieva (12)
Loit
Zvonareva
Majoli (23)
Schett (29)
Casanova
Chladkova
Henin (6)
Testud (8)
Drake
Weingartner
Granville
Myskina (18)
Arn
Grande
Mauresmo (9)
Shaughnessy (13)
Oremans
Daniilidou
Obata
Bedanova (26)
Sfar
Marrero
Capriati (3)
Dokic (7)
Hrdlickova
Poutchek
Dechy (25)
Kremer (22)
Matevzic
Sucha
Hantuchova (11)
Tulyaganova (14)
Rubin
Bovina
Panova
Fernandez (30)
Callens
Schiavone
S Williams (2)

THIRD ROUND
V Williams (1)
6-3 6-1
Drake
6-2 6-2
Martinez
6-1 6-3
Raymond
6-4 2-6 6-1
Farina Elia
6-3 6-2
Maleeva
6-4 6-3
Baltacha
5-7 6-4 6-2
Likhovtseva
7-6(5) 6-2
Seles (4)
6-4 6-0
Sugiyama
6-2 6-1
Tanasugarn
6-3 6-3
Tu
7-6(2) 7-5
Dementieva (12)
6-1 7-5
Majoli
7-6(5) 6-2
Casanova
6-3 3-6 6-3
Henin (6)
6-2 7-5
Pierce
6-3 6-4
Granville
6-3 6-4
Myskina
6-4 6-3
Mauresmo (9)
6-4 6-2
Oremans
7-5 6-3
Daniilidou
6-2 6-2
Bedanova
6-3 6-2
Capriati (3)
6-2 6-1
Dokic (7)
6-0 4-6 8-6
Dechy
6-3 6-2
Matevzic
6-2 1-6 6-2
Hantuchova (11)
6-2 4-6 6-3
Rubin
6-3 6-1
Panova
6-7(2) 6-3 6-2
Callens
2-6 6-3 6-4
S Williams (2)
6-3 6-3

FOURTH ROUND
V Williams (1)
5-7 6-2 6-1
Raymond
2-6 6-3 6-2
Maleeva
7-6(2) 6-4
Likhovtseva
6-4 7-6(2)
Seles (4)
4-6 6-1 6-4
Tanasugarn
6-2 3-6 6-0
Dementieva (12)
7-5 6-2
Henin (6)
6-4 6-4
Granville
3-6 6-4 6-1
Mauresmo (9)
6-4 6-2
Daniilidou
7-6(5) 6-4
Capriati (3)
6-4 6-2
Dokic (7)
7-5 6-2
Hantuchukova (11)
6-4 6-4
Rubin
6-4 6-1
S Williams (2)
7-6(5) 7-6(2)

QUARTER-FINAL
V Williams (1)
6-1 6-2
Likhovtseva
6-3 6-4
Seles (4)
6-2 6-2
Henin (6)
7-6(4) 7-6(5)
Mauresmo (9)
6-2 6-2
Capriati (3)
6-4 6-2
Hantchukova (11)
6-4 7-5
S Williams (2)
6-3 6-3

SEMI-FINAL
V Williams (1)
6-2 6-0
V Williams (1)
6-3 6-2
Henin (6)
7-5 7-6(4)
Mauresmo (9)
6-3 6-2
S Williams (2)
6-2 6-1

FINAL
S Williams (2)
7-6(4) 6-3

Australian Open
Men's Singles
FIRST ROUND

Alberto Martin ESP bt **Lleyton Hewitt AUS (1)**
1-6 6-1 6-4 7-6(4)

Michel Kratochvil SUI bt Fernando Meligeni BRA
6-4 6-1 6-2

Marcelo Rios CHI bt Jaymon Crabb AUS (W)
6-2 6-0 5-7 6-4

Karol Kucera SVK bt Sjeng Schalken NED (27)
6-1 6-4 1-6 6-1

Nicolas Lapentti ECU (23) bt Axel Pretzsch GER
7-5 4-6 6-0 6-0

Jose Acasuso ARG bt Jan Vacek CZE
3-6 1-6 6-4 7-6(5) 6-1

Gaston Gaudio ARG bt Jack Brasington USA (Q)
6-4 7-6(3) 7-5

Arnaud Clement FRA (15) bt Flavio Saretta BRA
6-4 7-6(5) 6-4

Roger Federer SUI (11) bt Michael Chang USA
6-4 6-4 6-3

Attila Savolt HUN bt Olivier Patience FRA (Q)
6-3 3-6 6-3 3-6 6-4

Rainer Schuettler GER bt Paul-Henri Mathieu FRA (W)
2-6 6-1 4-6 6-1 6-4

Carlos Moya ESP (17) bt Agustin Calleri ARG
2-6 6-7(3) 6-4 7-6(4) 0-1 ret.

Xavier Malisse BEL (29) bt Tomas Behrend GER (Q)
6-4 6-4 7-5

Todd Martin USA bt Andre Sa BRA 6-4 6-3 7-5

Jean-Francois Bachelot FRA (Q) bt Stefano Galvani ITA
(Q) 6-2 7-5 7-5

Tommy Haas GER (7) bt Andrei Stoliarov RUS 6-1 6-3 6-1

Byron Black ZIM (Q) bt Irakli Labadze GEO (L)
4-6 4-6 6-3 6-3 7-5

Albert Costa ESP bt Felix Mantilla ESP 2-6 6-2 6-3 6-4

Alexandre Simoni BRA bt Ota Fukarek CZE
4-6 7-5 6-2 6-7(3) 7-5

Andrei Pavel ROM (25) bt Franco Squillari ARG
6-4 6-3 3-6 6-2

Wayne Ferreira RSA bt Jan-Michael Gambill USA (19)
6-2 6-4 7-6(6)

David Nalbandian ARG bt Daniel Vacek CZE
7-6(0) 3-6 6-3 6-3

Ivan Ljubicic CRO bt Bohdan Ulihrach CZE
6-7(4) 1-6 6-4 7-6(7) 9-7

Andy Roddick USA (13) bt Mariano Zabaleta ARG
6-3 5-7 6-3 6-3

Marat Safin RUS (9) bt Anthony Dupuis FRA 7-5 6-4 6-2

Christophe Rochus BEL bt Raemon Sluiter NED (Q)
4-6 6-3 6-4 6-2

Mikhail Youzhny RUS bt Michael Llodra FRA
6-7(2) 6-2 6-2 6-3

Mardy Fish USA (Q) bt Fabrice Santoro FRA (20)
6-2 1-6 6-4 6-1

Nicolas Escude FRA (30) bt Todd Reid AUS (W)
1-6 6-1 6-4 6-4

Alex Calatrava ESP bt Olivier Rochus BEL (Q)
6-3 3-6 6-3 3-6 6-3

Juan Ignacio Chela ARG bt Noam Okun ISR (Q)
6-2 6-7(5) 6-3 6-1

Pete Sampras USA (8) bt Jarkko Nieminen FIN
6-3 6-3 6-4

Sebastien Grosjean FRA (5) bt Juan Balcells ESP
6-2 2-6 7-6(5) 7-6(2)

Francisco Clavet ESP bt Martin Lee GBR 7-6(3) 6-1 6-0

Andrea Gaudenzi ITA bt Richard Fromberg AUS (W)
1-6 6-0 7-5 6-3

Jiri Novak CZE (26) bt Nicolas Kiefer GER 6-1 6-0 6-4

Albert Portas ESP (18) bt Andrew Ilie AUS
6-7(3) 7-6(6) 6-2 6-0

Dominik Hrbaty SVK bt Lars Burgsmuller GER
3-6 2-6 6-3 6-3 7-5

Jerome Golmard FRA bt Wayne Arthurs AUS
7-6(4) 7-5 7-6(5)

Goran Ivanisevic CRO (10) bt Martin Damm CZE
4-6 7-5 7-6(4) 6-4

James Blake USA bt **Alex Corretja ESP (14)**
5-7 7-6(6) 6-3 6-2

Stefan Koubek AUT bt Cyril Saulnier FRA (Q)
0-6 1-6 7-6(6) 6-4 8-6

Kristian Pless DEN bt Max Mirnyi BLR 3-6 6-3 6-4 6-3

Hicham Arazi MAR (22) bt Ivo Heuberger SUI
6-4 6-2 4-6 7-6(1)

Tommy Robredo ESP (32) bt Michael Russell USA
6-7(5) 6-3 6-3 6-4

Fernando Gonzalez CHI (Q) bt Sargis Sargsian ARM
6-1 6-3 7-6(5)

Alex Kim USA (Q) bt Davide Sanguinetti ITA 3-6 6-2 6-3 6-4

Yevgeny Kafelnikov RUS (4) bt Michael Kohlmann GER
(Q) 6-3 6-3 6-2

Tim Henman GBR (6) bt Todd Larkham AUS (W)
7-5 6-2 6-2

Vladimir Voltchkov BLR bt Cecil Mamiit USA (Q)
3-6 6-3 6-3 6-3

Mark Philippoussis AUS bt Galo Blanco ESP 6-3 6-4 7-5

Greg Rusedski GBR (28) bt Scott Draper AUS (W)
7-6(8) 6-3 7-5

Thomas Enqvist SWE (24) bt Nicolas Thomann FRA (Q)
2-6 6-3 6-1 6-2

Jonas Bjorkman SWE bt Nicolas Massu CHI 6-4 ret.

Ramon Delgado PAR bt Albert Montanes ESP
7-5 6-7(5) 4-6 6-4 6-1

Guillermo Canas ARG (12) bt Paradorn Srichaphan THA
(W) 6-1 6-1 6-4

Thomas Johansson SWE (16) bt Jacobo Diaz ESP
6-1 3-6 7-6(2) 6-4

Markus Hipfl AUT bt Nikolay Davydenko RUS
6-1 6-4 3-6 6-4

Fernando Vicente ESP bt Kenneth Carlsen DEN
2-6 2-6 6-4 6-4 10-8

Younes El Aynaoui MAR (21) bt Jiri Vanek CZE 6-3 6-3 6-3

Andreas Vinciguerra SWE (31) bt Federico Luzzi ITA
6-2 6-2 7-6(3)

Taylor Dent USA (W) bt Michal Tabara CZE 6-2 6-1 6-2

Adrian Voinea ROM bt David Sanchez ESP
5-7 6-2 7-6(5) 6-2

Julien Boutter FRA bt **Gustavo Kuerten BRA (2)**
3-6 4-6 7-5 6-3 6-3

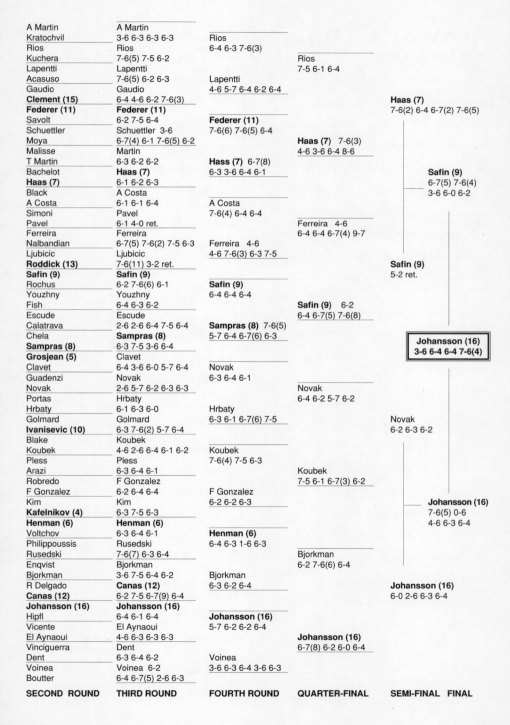

SECOND ROUND

A Martin
Kratochvil
Rios
Kuchera
Lapentti
Acasuso
Gaudio
Clement (15)
Federer (11)
Savolt
Schuettler
Moya
Malisse
T Martin
Bachelot
Haas (7)
Black
A Costa
Simoni
Pavel
Ferreira
Nalbandian
Ljubicic
Roddick (13)
Safin (9)
Rochus
Youzhny
Fish
Escude
Calatrava
Chela
Sampras (8)
Grosjean (5)
Clavet
Guadenzi
Novak
Portas
Hrbaty
Golmard
Ivanisevic (10)
Blake
Koubek
Pless
Arazi
Robredo
F Gonzalez
Kim
Kafelnikov (4)
Henman (6)
Voltchov
Philippoussis
Rusedski
Enqvist
Bjorkman
R Delgado
Canas (12)
Johansson (16)
Hipfl
Vicente
El Aynaoui
Vinciguerra
Dent
Voinea
Boutter

THIRD ROUND

A Martin — 3-6 6-3 6-3 6-3
Rios — 7-6(5) 7-5 6-2
Lapentti — 7-6(5) 6-2 6-3
Gaudio — 6-4 4-6 6-2 7-6(3)
Federer (11) — 6-2 7-5 6-4
Schuettler 3-6 — 6-7(4) 6-1 7-6(5) 6-2
Martin — 6-3 6-2 6-2
Haas (7) — 6-1 6-2 6-3
A Costa — 6-1 6-1 6-4
Pavel — 6-1 4-0 ret.
Ferreira — 6-7(5) 7-6(2) 7-5 6-3
Ljubicic — 7-6(11) 3-2 ret.
Safin (9) — 6-2 7-6(6) 6-1
Youzhny — 6-4 6-3 6-2
Escude — 2-6 2-6 6-4 7-5 6-4
Sampras (8) — 6-3 7-5 3-6 6-4
Clavet — 6-4 3-6 6-0 5-7 6-4
Novak — 2-6 5-7 6-2 6-3 6-3
Hrbaty — 6-1 6-3 6-0
Golmard — 6-3 7-6(2) 5-7 6-4
Koubek — 4-6 2-6 6-4 6-1 6-2
Pless — 6-3 6-4 6-1
F Gonzalez — 6-2 6-4 6-4
Kim — 6-3 7-5 6-3
Henman (6) — 6-3 6-4 6-1
Rusedski — 7-6(7) 6-3 6-4
Bjorkman — 3-6 7-5 6-4 6-2
Canas (12) — 6-2 7-5 6-7(9) 6-4
Johansson (16) — 6-4 6-1 6-4
El Aynaoui — 4-6 6-3 6-3 6-3
Dent — 6-3 6-4 6-2
Voinea 6-2 — 6-4 6-7(5) 2-6 6-3

FOURTH ROUND

Rios — 6-4 6-3 7-6(3)
Lapentti — 4-6 5-7 6-4 6-2 6-4
Federer (11) — 7-6(6) 7-6(5) 6-4
Hass (7) — 6-7(8) 6-3 3-6 6-4 6-1
A Costa — 7-6(4) 6-4 6-4
Ferreira 4-6 — 4-6 7-6(3) 6-3 7-5
Safin (9) — 6-4 6-4 6-4
Sampras (8) 7-6(5) — 5-7 6-4 6-7(6) 6-3
Novak — 6-3 6-4 6-1
Hrbaty — 6-3 6-1 6-7(6) 7-5
Koubek — 7-6(4) 7-5 6-3
F Gonzalez — 6-2 6-2 6-3
Henman (6) — 6-4 6-3 1-6 6-3
Bjorkman — 6-3 6-2 6-4
Johansson (16) — 5-7 6-2 6-2 6-4
Voinea — 3-6 6-3 6-4 3-6 6-3

QUARTER-FINAL

Rios — 7-5 6-1 6-4
Haas (7) 7-6(3) — 4-6 3-6 6-4 8-6
Ferreira 4-6 — 6-4 6-4 6-7(4) 9-7
Safin (9) 6-2 — 6-4 6-7(5) 7-6(8)
Novak — 6-4 6-2 5-7 6-2
Koubek — 7-5 6-1 6-7(3) 6-2
Bjorkman — 6-2 7-6(6) 6-4
Johansson (16) — 6-7(8) 6-2 6-0 6-4

SEMI-FINAL

Haas (7) — 7-6(2) 6-4 6-7(2) 7-6(5)
Safin (9) — 5-2 ret.
Novak — 6-2 6-3 6-2
Johansson (16) — 7-6(5) 0-6 4-6 6-3 6-4

FINAL

Safin (9) — 6-7(5) 7-6(4) 3-6 6-0 6-2
Johansson (16) — 6-0 2-6 6-3 6-4

Johansson (16) — 3-6 6-4 6-4 7-6(4)

Australian Open
Women's Singles
FIRST ROUND

Jennifer Capriati USA (1) bt Silvija Talaja CRO
6-4 6-1

Meilen Tu USA bt Joannette Kruger RSA
7-6(2) 6-0

Eleni Daniilidou GRE bt Rita Kuti Kis HUN
4-6 7-6(2) 6-4

Tatiana Panova RUS (29) bt Alicia Molik AUS
1-6 6-3 10-8

Rita Grande ITA (20) ITA bt Clarisa Fernandez ARG (Q)
7-6(4) 6-4

Kristie Boogert NED (Q) bt Gloria Pizzichini ITA (Q)
6-3 6-3

Svetlana Kuznetsova RUS (Q) bt Cho Yoon-Jeong KOR
(W) 6-3 2-6 6-4

Iroda Tulyagonova UZB (16) bt Maria Emilia Salerni ARG
(Q) 6-3 6-4

Meghann Shaughnessy USA (10) bt Alexandra Stevenson
USA 6-7(5) 6-2 7-5

Bryanne Stewart AUS (W) bt Jana Nejedly CAN 6-4 6-4

Antonella Serra-Zanetti ITA (Q) bt Elena Bovina RUS
6-2 6-2

Marlene Weingartner GER bt Angeles Montolio ESP (19)
6-3 6-3

Tamarine Tanasugarn THA (25) bt Selima Sfar TUN
6-4 6-3

Petra Mandula HUN bt Anca Barna GER 6-4 6-4

Katarina Srebotnik SLO bt Anna Smashnova ISR
6-2 6-2

Amelie Mauresmo FRA (7) bt Janet Lee TPE 6-1 6-0

Kim Clijsters BEL (4) bt Christina Wheeler AUS (W)
6-2 6-1

Barbara Schwartz AUT bt Eva Dyrberg DEN (Q)
6-1 6-4

Cindy Watson AUS (W) bt Maria Jose Martinez ESP
6-3 6-3

Emmanuelle Gagliardi SUI bt Elena Likhovtseva RUS (30)
6-1 6-7(7) 8-6

Ai Sugiyama JPN (24) bt Rachel McQuillan AUS
6-7(7) 6-3 6-3

Tina Pisnik SLO bt Marion Bartoli FRA (W)
6-3 4-6 9-7

Janette Husarova SVK bt Pavlina Nola NZL (L)
6-1 6-0

Iva Majoli CRO bt **Arantxa Sanchez Vicario ESP (14)**
6-4 7-5

Elena Dementieva RUS (12) bt Alina Jidkova RUS
6-3 6-2

Anastasia Myskina RUS bt Wynne Prakusya INA
6-7(3) 6-2 6-2

Maria Elena Camerin ITA bt Saori Obata JPN
7-5 6-4

Magui Serna ESP bt Amanda Grahame AUS (W)
6-3 6-3

Martina Muller GER bt Paolo Suarez ARG (27) 6-3 6-4

Nicole Pratt AUS bt Zsofia Gubacsi HUN
6-7 (6) 6-2 6-3

Marta Marrero ESP bt Adriana Gersi CZE 6-4 6-2

Justine Henin BEL (6) bt Anna Kournikova RUS
6-2 7-5

Conchita Martinez ESP bt Lina Krasnoroutskaya RUS (33)
3-6 6-3 2-0 ret.

Asa Svensson SWE bt Evie Dominikovic AUS
6-3 6-2

Martina Sucha SVK bt Gala Leon Garcia ESP
1-6 6-2 6-4

Mariana Diaz Oliva ARG bt Cristina Torrens Valero ESP
7-5 6-4

Amy Frazier USA bt Henrieta Nagyova SVK (22)
7-5 6-4

Adriana Serra-Zanetti ITA bt Virginia Ruano Pascual ESP
6-2 2-6 7-5

Jennifer Hopkins USA bt Irina Selyutina KAZ 6-2 0-6 6-2

Silvia Farina Elia ITA (11) bt Lilia Osterloh USA
6-4 3-6 6-4

Amanda Coetzer RSA (15) bt Miriam Oremans NED
6-1 6-1

Rossana Neffa-De Los Rios PAR bt Elena Tatarkova UKR
(Q) 6-3 6-2

Nuria Llagostera Vives ESP bt Jana Kandarr GER
6-0 6-1

Barbara Schett AUT (17) bt Andrea Glass GER 6-2 6-4

Anne Kremer LUX (28) bt Denisa Chladkova CZE
6-3 6-4

Barbara Rittner GEER bt Eva Bes ESP 6-3 6-4

Greta Arn GER (Q) bt Samantha Stosur AUS (W)
6-2 4-6 6-2

Martina Hingis SUI (3) bt Virginie Razzano FRA
6-2 6-2

Monica Seles USA (8) bt Patty Schnyder USA 6-1 6-2

Cara Black ZIM bt Emilie Loit FRA 7-5 6-3

Jelena Kostanic CRO (Q) bt Samantha Reeves USA
6-0 6-7(6) 6-3

Francesca Schiavone ITA (31) bt Aniko Kapros HUN
4-6 6-3 8-6

Daja Bedanova CZE (21) bt Tatiana Poutshek BLR
6-1 6-2

Ana Isabel Medina Garrigues ESP bt Bahia Mouhtassine
MAR (Q) 6-2 4-6 6-1

Blanka Lamade GER bt Celine Beigbeder FRA
5-7 7-5 6-2

Nathalie Dechy FRA bt **Sandrine Testud FRA (9)**
7-5 4-6 6-3

Magdalena Maleeva BUL (13) bt Marie-Galane Mikaelian
SUI 6-3 6-4

Kveta Hrdlickova bt Shinobu Asagoe JPN
4-6 6-3 6-2

Jill Craybas USA bt Mary Pierce FRA (W) 4-0 ret.

Lisa Raymond USA (18) bt Seda Noorlander NED
6-0 6-1

Daniela Hantchukova SVK bt Maja Matevkic SLO
6-3 6-1

Tathiana Garbin ITA bt Marissa Irvin USA 6--0 6-3

Kristina Brandi USA bt Ludmila Cervanova SVK
6-3 4-6 6-0

Venus Williams USA (2) bt Ansley Cargill USA (Q)
6-2 6-2

SECOND ROUND	THIRD ROUND	FOURTH ROUND	QUARTER-FINAL	SEMI-FINAL	FINAL
Capriati (1)	**Capriati (1)** 6-1 6-3				
Tu		**Capriati (1)** 6-2 3-6 6-1			
Daniilidou	Daniilidou 6-2 4-6 6-0		**Capriati (1)** 6-3 7-6(9)		
Panova					
Grande	Grande 7-6(5) 7-5	Grande 6-3 5-7 6-4		**Capriati (1)** 6-2 6-2	
Boogert					
Kuznetsova	**Tulyagonova (16)** 6-4 6-1				
Tulyagonova (16)					
Shaughnessy (9)	**Shaughnessy (9)** 6-2 6-0	Weingartner 6-2 3-6 6-3			
Stewart					
Serra-Zanetti	Weingartner 6-4 6-2		**Mauresmo (7)** 6-0 4-6 7-5		
Weingartner					
Tanasugarn	Tanasugarn 2-6 6-2 6-2	**Mauresmo (7)** 7-6(3) 6-1			
Mandula					
Srebotnik	**Mauresmo (7)** 7-5 6-3			**Capriati (1)** 7-5 3-6 6-1	
Mauresmo (7)					
Clijsters (4)	**Clijsters (4)** 6-1 6-1	**Clijsters (4)** 6-1 6-2			
Schwartz					
Watson	Watson 3-6 7-5 6-2		**Clijsters (4)** 6-0 6-2		
Gagliardi					
Sugiyama	Sugiyama 7-6(2) 6-0	Husarova 6-2 6-3			
Pisnik					
Husarova	Husarova 6-4 6-3			**Clijsters (4)** 6-2 6-3	
Majoli					
Dementieva (12)	**Dementieva (12)** 6-4 6-2	**Dementieva (12)** 6-1 6-2			
Myskina					
Camerin	Serna 6-3 6-3		**Henin (6)** 6-0 6-3		
Serna					
Muller	Pratt 6-1 6-2	**Henin (6)** 6-4 6-0			
Pratt					
Marrero	**Henin (6)** 6-3 3-6 6-1			**Capriati (1)** 4-6 7-6(7) 6-2	
Henin (6)					
Martinez	Svensson 6-4 6-1	Sucha 6-0 6-4			
Svensson					
Sucha	Sucha 6-1 7-5		Serra-Zanetti 6-1 7-5		
Diaz Oliva					
Frazier	Serra-Zanetti 6-3 7-6(5)	Serra-Zanetti 6-2 4-6 6-4			
Serra-Zanetti					
Hopkins	**Farina Elia (11)** 6-2 6-0			Hingis (3) 6-2 6-3	
Farina Elia (11)					
Coetzer (15)	**Coetzer (15)** 6-3 6-1	**Coetzer (15)** 6-3 6-3			
Neff-De Los Rios					
Llagostera Vivas	Schett 6-2 1-6 6-2		Hingis (3) 6-1 6-0		
Schett					
Kremer	Rittner 6-1 6-4	Hingis (3) 6-1 6-0			
Rittner					
Arn	**Hingis (3)** 61 6-2			**Hingis (3)** 4-6 6-1 6-4	
Hingis (3)					
Seles (8)	**Seles (8)** 6-1 6-1	Seles (8) 6-4 6-4			
Black					
Kostanic	Schiavone 6-1 6-2		Seles (8) 4-2 ret.		
Schiavone					
Bedanova	Medina Garrigues 6-4 6-2	Medina Garrigues 6-3 6-2			
Medina Garrigues					
Lamade	Dechy 6-2 6-7(4) 6-1			Seles (8) 6-7(4) 6-2 6-3	
Dechy					
Maleeva (13)	**Maleeva (13)** 6-4 7-5	**Maleeva (13)** 7-5 6-1			
Hrdlickova					
Craybas	Raymond 6-3 6-3		**V Williams (2)** 6-0 6-3		
Raymond					
Hantchukova	Hantchukova 6-0 6-2	**V Williams (2)** 6-0 6-3			
Garbin					
Brandi	**V Williams (2)** 3-6 6-0 6-4				
V Williams (2)					

French Open
Men's Singles
FIRST ROUND

Lleyton Hewitt AUS (1) bt Andre Sa BRA 7-5 6-4 7-5

Andrei Stoliarov RUS bt Jonas Bjorkman SWE
1-6 6-4 6-4 7-5

Sebastien De Chaunac FRA (W) bt Michael Chang USA
4-6 4-6 6-4 6-2 6-4

Sjeng Schalken NED (30) bt Ivan Miranda PER (Q)
7-6(2) 6-0 6-1

Carlos Moya ESP (17) bt Ramon Delgado PAR 6-3 6-2 6-2

Mark Philippoussis AUS bt Julien Varlet FRA (Q)
1-6 6-7(5) 6-4 7-6(3) 6-3

Alex Calatrava ESP bt Nicolas Kiefer GER 6-3 6-0 6-4

Guillermo Canas ARG (15) bt Karol Kucera SVK
6-7(3) 6-4 6-2 6-2

Andrea Gaudenzi ITA bt **Pete Sampras USA (12)**
3-6 6-4 6-2 7-6(3)

Jack Brasington USA (Q) Federico Luzzi ITA 6-2 6-2 7-5

Nikolay Davydenko RUS bt Giorgio Galimberti ITA
6-7(4) 6-4 6-1 6-3

Albert Costa ESP (20) bt Richard Gasquet FRA (W)
3-6 6-0 6-4 6-3

Fernando Meligeni BRA bt Nicolas Escude FRA (27)
6-4 6-2 0-6 6-4

Fernando Gonzalez CHI bt Scott Draper AUS (W)
6-2 7-6(9) 6-3

Davide Sanguinetti ITA bt Julian Knowle AUT
6-3 4-6 7-5 6-3

Gustavo Kuerten BRA (7) bt Ivo Heuberger SUI 7-5 6-2 6-2

Tommy Haas GER (3) bt Michal Tabara CZE 6-3 7-5 6-4

Feliciano Lopez ESP bt Didac Perez ESP (Q)
4-6 6-4 6-2 4-6 6-4

Amir Hadad ISR (Q) bt Christophe Rochus BEL
6-1 6-2 6-7(4) 6-2

Jarkko Nieminen FIN bt Nicolas Lapentti ECU (28)
6-3 6-4 7-6(5)

Andrei Pavel ROM (22) bt Martin Lee GBR
6-1 5-4 ret

Michel Kratochvil SUI bt Dominik Hrbaty SVK
6-0 6-7(6) 6-3 6-3

Albert Montanes ESP bt Anthony Dupuis FRA
6-7(3) 6-4 3-6 6-2 7-5

Younes El Aynaoui MAR (16) bt Jan-Michael Gambill USA
3-6 6-3 6-4 3-6 6-4

Thomas Johansson SWE (9) bt Franco Squillari ARG
6-2 7-6(6) 6-2

Arnaud Clement FRA bt Julien Benneteau FRA (W)
6-0 6-1 6-4

Todd Martin USA bt Martin Vassallo Arguello ARG (Q)
6-2 7-5 3-6 4-6 7-5

Alex Corretja ESP (18) bt Bohdan Ulihrach CZE 6-1 6-4 6-1

Fernando Vicente ESP bt Ivan Ljubicic CRO (32)
4-6 6-1 7-6(7) 4-6 6-3

Alberto Martin ESP bt Robby Ginepri USA 7-6(5) 6-2 6-3

Mariano Zabaleta ARG bt Jan Vacek CZE
6-1 3-6 6-3 6-4

Yevgeny Kafelnikov RUS (5) bt Tomas Behrend GER (Q)
6-3 6-2 3-6 6-7(3) 6-1

Hicham Arazi MAR bt **Roger Federer SUI (8)**
6-3 6-2 6-4

Mariano Puerta ARG (Q) bt Kristian Pless DEN
6-3 1-6 7-6(5) 5-7 6-3

Irakli Labadze GEO bt Julien Boutter FRA
7-6(4) 5-7 6-7(6) 6-3 9-7

Gaston Gaudio ARG (31) bt Juan Balcells ESP
6-4 6-2 7-5

Rainer Schuettler GER (24) bt Stefano Galvani ITA
7-6(4) 2-6 7-6(3) 6-1

Guillermo Coria ARG bt Sargis Sargsian ARM
6-2 7-5 6-0

Nicolas Coutelot FRA bt Stefan Koubek AUT 6-4 6-4 6-4

Juan Carlos Ferrero ESP (11) bt Jean-Rene Lisnard FRA
6-1 7-6(1) 6-3

Jiri Novak CZE (14) bt Mikhail Youzhny RUS
6-3 6-4 7-6(5)

Jens Knippschild GER (Q) bt Hyung-Taik Lee KOR
6-4 1-6 3-6 7-6(3) 6-1

Paul-Henri Mathieu FRA (W) bt Wayne Ferreira RSA
6-4 6-7(1) 5-7 6-2 6-0

Fabrice Santoro FRA (23) bt Magnus Norman SWE
6-2 5-7 3-6 6-4 6-4

Tommy Robredo ESP (25) bt Harel Levy ISR
6-1 6-0 1-0 ret

Oleg Ogorodov UZB (Q) bt Markus Hipfl AUT
6-7(8) 6-1 2-6 7-5 9-7

David Sanchez ESP bt Jose Acasuso ARG
6-4 7-5 6-4

Andre Agassi USA (4) bt Eric Prodon FRA (Q)
6-3 6-3 6-1

Tim Henman GBR (6) bt Galo Blanco ESP
6-4 6-3 7-6(6)

Xavier Malisse BEL bt Alexander Popp GER (Q)
6-4 6-1 4-6 6-1

Albert Portas ESP bt Andrew Ilie AUS 7-6(4) 6-3 6-4

Cecil Mamiit USA bt Max Mirnyi BLR (26)
6-3 6-4 5-7 6-4

Adrian Voinea ROM bt Juan Ignacio Chela ARG (21)
7-6(9) 7-5 4-6 7-6(7)

Vincent Spadea USA bt Cedric Pioline FRA
4-6 6-4 6-4 3-6 6-4

James Blake USA bt Lars Burgsmuller GER 6-2 2-1 ret

Sebastien Grosjean FRA (10) bt Francisco Clavet ESP
7-6(0) 7-6(2) 3-6 6-3

Wayne Arthurs AUS bt **Andy Roddick USA (13)**
4-6 7-6(14) 4-6 7-5 6-3

Arnaud Di Pasquale FRA bt Michael Russell USA
6-4 6-0 4-6 6-1

Paradorn Srichaphan THA bt Raemon Sluiter NED
5-7 6-2 6-7(5) 6-4 6-4

Thomas Enqvist SWE (19) bt Edgardo Massa ARG (Q)
4-6 4-6 6-3 6-2 6-4

David Nalbandian ARG (29) bt Agustin Calleri ARG
6-2 5-7 6-2 6-4

Flavio Saretta BRA bt Oliver Marach AUT (Q)
6-2 6-2 4-6 6-7(5) 6-4

Olivier Rochus BEL bt Attila Savolt HUN
6-4 7-6(0) 6-2

Marat Safin RUS (2) bt Michael Llodra FRA (W)
6-4 2-6 7-6(7) 6-4

SECOND ROUND

Hewitt (1)
Stoliarov
De Chaunac (W)
Schalken
Moya
Philippoussis
Calatrava
Canas (15)
Gaudenzi
Brasington
Davydenko
A Costa
Meligeni
F Gonzalez
Sanguinetti
Kuerten (7)
Haas (3)
Lopez
Hdad (Q)
Nieminen
Pavel
Kratochvil
Montanes
El Aynaoui (16)
Johansson (9)
Clement
T Martin
Corretja
Vicente
A Martin
Zabaleta
Kafelnikov (5)
Arazi
Puerta
Labadze
Gaudio
Schuettler
Coria
Coutelot
Ferrero (11)
Novak (14)
Knippschild
Mathieu
Santoro
Robredo
Ogorodov
Sanchez
Agassi (4)
Henman (6)
Malisse
Portas
Mamiit
Voinea
Spadea
Blake
Grosjean (10)
Arthurs
Di Pascuale
Srichapan
Enqvist
Nalbandian
Saretta
Rochus
Safin (2)

THIRD ROUND

Hewitt (1)
4-6 7-6(5) 6-0 7-5
Schalken
6-0 6-2 7-6(3)
Moya
6-2 7-6(7) 7-6(9)
Canas
3-6 6-1 6-2 6-0
Gaudenzi
6-3 7-6(0) 6-1
A Costa
7-5 7-6(4) 6-2
F Gonzalez
6-2 3-6 6-1 6-2
Kuerten (7)
6-7(0) 6-2 4-6 6-4 6-3
Haas (3)
6-3 6-4 6-4
Nieminen
6-7(4) 6-4 6-4 7-5
Pavel
6-3 6-1 6-3
Montanes
7-5 7-6(2) 6-4
Clement
7-6(4) 6-1 6-3
Corretja
6-2 6-3 7-5
Vicente
6-4 6-3 6-3
Zabaleta
7-6(4) 2-6 6-4 7-6(4)
Arazi
6-1 6-2 6-1
Gaudio
6-1 6-2 6-7(9) 6-4
Coria
6-4 6-2 6-3
Ferrero (11)
6-2 5-7 1-6 6-2 6-0
Novak (14)
6-1 6-2 7-5
Mathieu
7-5 6-1 1-6 6-4
Robredo
6-3 4-6 6-1 6-2
Agassi (4)
4-6 6-2 6-1 ret.
Malisse
6-2 3-6 7-6(4) 6-3
Portas
3-6 6-3 6-4 6-4
Spadea
6-4 4-6 2-6 7-6(4) 8-6
Grosjean (10)
6-4 3-6 6-2 7-5
Di Pascuale
7-6(4) 6-3 6-2
Srichapan
6-4 1-6 7-5 6-3
Nalbandian
6-3 6-4 6-0
Safin (2)
4-6 6-2 3-6 6-3 6-3

FOURTH ROUND

Hewitt (1)
6-1 7-5 6-7(3) 6-1

Canas (15)   4-6
7-6(1) 6-7(2) 6-1 6-2

A Costa
7-6(2) 6-1 7-5

Kuerten (7)
6-3 2-6 7-6(6) 6-4

Haas (3)
6-3 7-5 2-6 6-4

Pavel
6-1 1-6 6-4 6-3

Corretja
6-1 6-2 4-6 5-7 8-6

Zabaleta
4-6 6-3 6-4 6-3

Gaudio
6-2 4-6 6-4 3-1 ret.

Ferrero (11)
6-2 6-3 6-3

Mathieu
6-4 6-4 6-3

Agassi (4)
6-2 6-4 6-2

Malisse
6-2 6-3 7-6(3)

Grosjean (10)
6-2 7-6(5) 6-7(5) 6-4

Di Pascuale
6-4 6-3 6-3

Safin (2)
6-3 6-3 3-6 6-4

QUARTER-FINAL

Canas (15)
6-7(1) 7-6(13) 6-4
6-3

A Costa
6-4 7-5 6-4

Pavel
6-1 7-6(9) 6-4

Corretja
6-3 6-2 7-5

Ferrero (11)
6-7(3) 6-1 6-7(5)
6-2 6-4

Agassi (4)
4-6 3-6 6-3 6-3 6-3

Grosjean (10)
6-2 7-5 6-3

Safin (2)
3-6 6-4 6-3 6-2

SEMI-FINAL

A Costa
7-5 3-6 6-7(3) 6-4 6-0

A Costa
6-3 6-4 3-6
6-3

Corretja
7-6(5) 7-5 7-5

Ferrero (11)
6-3 5-7 7-5 6-3

Ferrero (11)
6-3 6-2 6-4

Safin (2)
6-3 6-2 6-2

FINAL

A Costa
6-1 6-0 4-6 6-3

French Open
Women's Singles
FIRST ROUND

Jennifer Capriati USA (1) bt Marissa Irvin USA
6-3 6-4

Amy Frazier USA bt Meilen Tu USA 6-4 6-0

Angelique Widjaja bt Jill Craybas USA 2-6 7-5 6-1

Evie Dominikovic AUS bt Alexandra Stevenson USA (28)
6-3 6-2

Patty Schnyder SUI (20) bt Milagros Sequera VEN (Q)
6-3 6-2

Tathiana Garbin ITA bt Silvija Talaja CRO 7-6(5) 6-4

Christina Wheeler AUS (W) bt Anna Kournikova RUS
6-4 6-3

Iroda Tulyaganova UZB (14) bt Eva Dyrberg DEN
7-6(8) 6-3

Conchita Martinez Granados ESP (Q) bt **Meghann
Shaughnessy USA (12)** 7-6(8) 6-3

Katarina Srebotnik SLO bt Gala Leon Garcia ESP
6-3 6-4

Emilie Loit FRA bt Alicia Molik AUS 6-2 3-6 7-5

Shinobu Asagoe JPN (Q) bt Anastasia Myskina RUS (19)
3-6 6-2 7-5

Martina Muller GER bt Amanda Coetzer RSA (30)
6-2 6-2

Elena Likhovtseva RUS bt Fabiola Zuluaga COL
7-5 6-4

Conchita Martinez ESP bt Maria Elena Camerin ITA
6-3 6-3

Jelena Dokic YUG (7) bt Emmanuelle Gagliardi SUI
6-4 6-2

Serena Williams USA (3) bt Martina Sucha SVK 6-3 6-0

Dally Randriantefy MAD (Q) bt Miriam Oremans NED
6-0 6-3

Janette Husarova SVK bt Alexandra Fusai FRA (W)
6-2 3-6 7-5

Ai Sugiyama JPN (26) bt Marion Bartoli FRA (W)
6-3 4-6 7-5

Francesca Schiavone ITA bt Anna Smashnova ISR (21)
6-4 6-2

Marie-Gaiane Mikaelian SUI bt Rita Kuti Kis HUN (Q)
4-6 6-0 6-1

Vera Zvonareva RUS (Q) bt Maja Matevzic SLO
6-4 7-6(7)

Marta Marrero ESP bt **Arantxa Sanchez Vicario ESP (15)**
6-0 6-1

Silvia Farina Elia ITA (9) bt Elena Bovina RUS 3-6 6-2 6-4

Tina Pisnik SLO bt Kveta Hrdlickova CZE 2-6 6-3 6-4

Jana Kandarr GER bt Laurence Andretto FRA (W)
6-3 6-0

Tamarine Tanasugarn THA (17) bt Denisa Chladkova CZE
6-3 6-2

Cristina Torrens Valero ESP (32) bt Magdalena
Grzybowska POL 6-2 6-1

Mary Pierce FRA (W) bt Irina Selyutina KAZ 7-5 7-5

Virginie Razzano FRA bt Henrieta Nagyova SVK
6-3 1-6 6-4

Aniko Kapros HUN bt **Justine Henin BEL (5)**
4-6 6-1 6-0

Paola Suarez ARG bt **Sandrine Testud FRA (8)**
2-6 7-5 6-1

Maria Goloviznina RUS (Q) bt Barbara Schwartz AUT
2-6 7-5 5-2 ret

Iveta Benesova CZE (Q) bt Jennifer Hopkins USA
7-6(3) 6-4

Nathalie Dechy FRA (27) bt Nuria Llagostera Vives ESP
(Q) 6-1 3-6 6-0

Eva Bes ESP bt Lisa Raymond USA (24) 6-4 6-3

Virginia Ruano Pascual ESP bt Stephanie Foretz FRA
6-2 6-4

Nicole Pratt AUS bt Magui Serna ESP
2-6 7-5 6-1

Amelie Mauresmo FRA (10) bt Camille Pin FRA (W)
6-2 6-1

Elena Dementieva RUS (13) bt Adriana Gersi CZE
7-5 6-3

Asa Svensson SWE bt Selima Sfar TUN
6-0 6-2

Rossana Neffa De Los Rios PAR bt Greta Arn GER
6-3 6-4

Anne-Gaelle Sidot FRA (W) bt Magdalena Maleeva BUL
(22) 6-2 6-4

Jelena Kostanic CRO bt Daja Bedanova CZE (25)
2-6 6-3 6-2

Clarisa Fernandez ARG bt Lubomira Bacheva BUL (Q)
7-5 6-1

Eleni Daniilidou GRE bt Celine Beigbeder FRA
6-3 6-1

Kim Clijsters BEL (4) bt Tatiana Poutchek BLR
3-6 6-3 8-6

Monica Seles USA (6) bt Angeles Montolio ESP
6-7(4) 6-3 6-0

Barbara Rittner GER bt Petra Mandula HUN
6-3 4-6 6-0

Ludmila Cervanova SVK bt Lilia Osterloh USA
6-4 6-4

Iva Majoli CRO (29) bt Kristina Brandi USA 6-4 6-3

Tatiana Panova RUS (18) bt Seda Noorlander NED
6-1 4-6 6-2

Mirjana Lucic CRO (Q) bt Stephanie Cohen Aloro FRA (W)
6-3 6-3

Adriana Serra Zanetti ITA bt Jana Nejedly CAN
6-1 6-2

Daniela Hantuchova SVK (11) bt Cara Black ZIM
6-2 6-3

Barbara Schett AUT (16) bt Marlene Weingartner GER
6-2 2-6 6-0

Chanda Rubin USA bt Cho Yoon-Jeong KOR 6-3 6-0

Samantha Reeves USA bt Zsofia Gubacsi HUN
6-1 6-1

Anne Kremer LUX (23) bt Janet Lee TPE
6-1 7-6(5)

Rita Grande ITA (31) bt Mariana Diaz Oliva ARG
6-4 6-4

Alina Jidkova RUS bt Saori Obata JPN
0-6 6-2 6-0

Wynne Prakusya INA bt Anca Barna GER
1-6 7-5 6-1

Venus Williams USA (2) bt Bianka Lamade GER
6-3 6-3

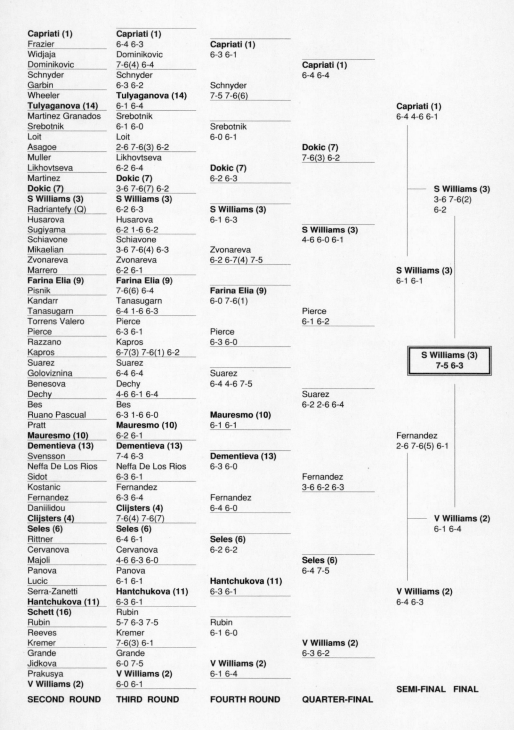

SECOND ROUND	THIRD ROUND	FOURTH ROUND	QUARTER-FINAL	SEMI-FINAL	FINAL

Capriati (1)
Frazier
Widjaja
Dominikovic
Schnyder
Garbin
Wheeler
Tulyaganova (14)
Martinez Granados
Srebotnik
Loit
Asagoe
Muller
Likhovtseva
Martinez
Dokic (7)
S Williams (3)
Radriantefy (Q)
Husarova
Sugiyama
Schiavone
Mikaelian
Zvonareva
Marrero
Farina Elia (9)
Pisnik
Kandarr
Tanasugarn
Torrens Valero
Pierce
Razzano
Kapros
Suarez
Goloviznina
Benesova
Dechy
Bes
Ruano Pascual
Pratt
Mauresmo (10)
Dementieva (13)
Svensson
Neffa De Los Rios
Sidot
Kostanic
Fernandez
Daniilidou
Clijsters (4)
Seles (6)
Rittner
Cervanova
Majoli
Panova
Lucic
Serra-Zanetti
Hantchukova (11)
Schett (16)
Rubin
Reeves
Kremer
Grande
Jidkova
Prakusya
V Williams (2)

Capriati (1)
6-4 6-3
Dominikovic
7-6(4) 6-4
Schnyder
6-3 6-2
Tulyaganova (14)
6-1 6-4
Srebotnik
6-1 6-0
Loit
2-6 7-6(3) 6-2
Likhovtseva
6-2 6-4
Dokic (7)
3-6 7-6(7) 6-2
S Williams (3)
6-2 6-3
Husarova
6-2 1-6 6-2
Schiavone
3-6 7-6(4) 6-3
Zvonareva
6-2 6-1
Farina Elia (9)
7-6(6) 6-4
Tanasugarn
6-4 1-6 6-3
Pierce
6-3 6-1
Kapros
6-7(3) 7-6(1) 6-2
Suarez
6-4 6-4
Dechy
4-6 6-1 6-4
Bes
6-3 1-6 6-0
Mauresmo (10)
6-2 6-1
Dementieva (13)
7-4 6-3
Neffa De Los Rios
6-3 6-1
Fernandez
6-3 6-4
Clijsters (4)
7-6(4) 7-6(7)
Seles (6)
6-4 6-1
Cervanova
4-6 6-3 6-0
Panova
6-1 6-1
Hantchukova (11)
6-3 6-1
Rubin
5-7 6-3 7-5
Kremer
7-6(3) 6-1
Grande
6-0 7-5
V Williams (2)
6-0 6-1

Capriati (1)
6-3 6-1
Schnyder
7-5 7-6(6)
Srebotnik
6-0 6-1
Dokic (7)
6-2 6-3
S Williams (3)
6-1 6-3
Zvonareva
6-2 6-7(4) 7-5
Farina Elia (9)
6-0 7-6(1)
Pierce
6-3 6-0
Suarez
6-4 4-6 7-5
Mauresmo (10)
6-1 6-1
Dementieva (13)
6-3 6-0
Fernandez
6-4 6-0
Seles (6)
6-2 6-2
Hantchukova (11)
6-3 6-1
Rubin
6-1 6-0
V Williams (2)
6-1 6-4

Capriati (1)
6-4 6-4
Dokic (7)
7-6(3) 6-2
S Williams (3)
4-6 6-0 6-1
Pierce
6-1 6-2
Suarez
6-2 2-6 6-4
Fernandez
3-6 6-2 6-3
Seles (6)
6-4 7-5
V Williams (2)
6-3 6-2

Capriati (1)
6-4 4-6 6-1
S Williams (3)
3-6 7-6(2)
6-2
S Williams (3)
6-1 6-1
Fernandez
2-6 7-6(5) 6-1
V Williams (2)
6-4 6-3

S Williams (3)
3-6 7-6(2)
6-2

V Williams (2)
6-1 6-4

S Williams (3)
7-5 6-3

US Open
Men's Singles
FIRST ROUND

Lleyton Hewitt AUS (1) bt Nicolas Coutelot FRA 6-2 6-3 6-3

Noam Okun ISR (Q) bt Igor Kunitchin RUS (Q)
6-7(4) 6-4 6-4 6-3

Nikolay Davydenko RUS bt Radoslav Lukaev BUL (Q)
6-4 1-6 6-4 6-2

James Blake USA (25) bt Brian Vahaly USA (W)
6-7(3) 6-3 6-3 7-6(5)

Marcelo Rios CHI (22) bt Jonas Bjorkman SWE
1-6 6-2 6-4 6-1

Robin Soderling SWE (Q) bt Lars Burgsmuller GER (L)
7-6(7) 6-0 6-4

John van Lottum NED (Q) bt Luis Horna PER
6-4 7-6(3) 4-6 6-4

Jiri Novak CZE (14) bt Richard Krajicek NED 6-1 5-4 Ret

Fernando Vicente ESP bt Jarkko Nieminen FIN (34)
1-6 6-3 6-0 6-2

Mardy Fish USA (W) bt Lee Hyung-Taik KOR
7-6(6) 4-6 6-3 6-3

Hicham Arazi MAR bt Olivier Rochus BEL 6-2 6-2 6-4

Younes El Aynaoui MAR (20) bt Jeff Morrison USA
6-7(6) 6-3 6-2 7-5

Tommy Robreto ESP (31) bt Mariano Zabaleta ARG
6-2 6-7(3) 7-5 4-6 7-6(5)

Fernando Meligeni BRA bt Agustin Calleri ARG
3-6 7-6(5) 6-4 6-4

Wayne Ferreira RSA bt Jan Vacek CZE 6-3 6-4 7-5

Albert Costa ESP (8) bt Magnus Norman SWE
6-2 6-4 3-6 6-3

Yevgeny Kafelnikov RUS (4) bt Davide Sanguinetti ITA
6-2 7-5 3-6 6-4

Dominik Hrbaty SVK bt Mario Ancic CRO (L)
4-6 6-3 7-6(3) 5-7 3-2 Ret.

Anthony Dupuis FRA bt Andrea Gaudenzi ITA
6-3 6-3 4-2 Ret.

Max Mirnyi BLR (32) bt Attila Savolt HUN
7-6(4) 7-5 0-1 Ret.

Xavier Malisse BEL (19) bt Albert Montanes ESP
7-5 6-2 6-2

Vincent Spadea USA bt Jerome Golmard FRA
4-6 2-6 6-1 6-3 6-2

Michael Chang USA bt Francisco Clavet ESP
7-6(6) 3-6 6-4 7-6(3)

Roger Federer SUI (13) bt Jiri Vanek CZE 6-1 6-3 4-6 7-5

Carlos Moya ESP (9) bt Adrian Voinea ROM
3-6 6-4 6-3 7-6(4)

Jan-Michael Gambill USA bt Julian Knowle AUT
6-1 2-1 Ret

Feliciano Lopez ESP bt Andre Sa BRA 7-5 7-6(1) 6-3

Gaston Gaudio ARG (21) bt Todd Martin USA
6-2 6-3 0-6 7-5

Harel Levy ISR bt Andrei Pavel ROM (30)
1-6 7-6(7) 4-6 6-3 6-4

Ramon Delgado PAR bt Alex Bogomolov Jr USA (W)
6-3 6-7(6) 0-6 6-4 7-5

Justin Gimelstob USA (W) bt Edwin Kempes NED (Q)
6-4 3-6 6-3 6-7(4) 6-3

Andre Agassi USA (6) bt Robby Ginepri USA 6-3 6-3 6-3

Tim Henman GBR (5) bt Tuomas Ketola FIN (Q)
6-1 6-1 6-1

Dick Norman BEL (Q) bt Bohdan Ulirach CZE
4-6 4-6 6-4 7-6(5) 6-4

Michael Llodra FRA bt Jose Acasuso ARG 6-1 6-2 6-2

Juan I Chela ARG (26) bt Felix Mantilla ESP
6-2 7-6(4) 6-2

Alex Corretja ESP (18) bt Irakli Labadze GEO
6-3 6-4 6-2

Ivo Heuberger SUI (Q) bt Slimane Saoudi FRA (Q)
6-4 2-6 7-5 3-6 7-6(3)

Raemon Sluiter NED bt Taylor Dent USA
3-6 6-3 6-0 1-6 6-3

Andy Roddick USA (11) bt Martin Verkerk NED (Q)
7-6(2) 6-3 6-4

Greg Rusedski GBR (33) bt Alex Kim USA (W)
6-1 4-6 7-6(1) 6-3

Paradorn Srichaphan THA bt Prakash Amritraj USA (W)
6-1 6-3 6-0

Kristian Pless DEN bt Eric Taino USA 6-7(5) 6-3 6-2 6-1

Pete Sampras USA (17) bt Albert Portas ESP 6-1 6-4 6-4

Thomas Enqvist SWE (29) bt Matias Boeker USA (W)
6-2 6-3 7-6(3)

Alberto Martin ESP bt Michel Kratochvil SUI
5-7 6-4 6-3 7-6(6)

Karol Kucera SVK bt Radek Stepanek CZE
6-7 6-4 2-6 6-2 6-1

Tommy Haas GER (3) bt David Sanchez ESP
7-6(1) 3-6 3-6 6-4 7-5

Juan Carlos Ferrero ESP (7) bt Wayne Arthurs AUS
7-6(4) 7-6(2) 3-6 7-5

Gaston Etlis ARG (Q) bt Bjorn Rehnquist SWE (Q)
6-3 6-4 7-6(3)

Kenneth Carlsen DEN bt Flavio Saretta BRA
7-6(2) 4-6 6-4 5-7 7-6(4)

Fernando Gonzalez CHI (28) bt Paul-Henri Mathieu FRA
2-6 7-6(1) 3-6 6-4 6-4

Jean-Rene Lisnard FRA (Q) bt Rainer Schuettler GER (23)
3-6 6-7(2) 6-4 4-0 ret

Guillermo Coria ARG bt Alexander Waske GER (Q)
7-6(4) 7-5 6-2

Arnaud Clement FRA bt Stefan Koubek AUT
6-3 4-7 5-6 6-3

Sebastien Grosjean FRA (10) bt Marc Rosset SUI
6-1 3-6 6-1 6-4

Sargis Sargsian ARM bt **David Nalbandian ARG (16)**
6-1 6-4 6-4

Alexander Popp GER bt Andreas Vinciguerra SWE
7-6(4) 7-6(10) 6-2

Ivan Ljubicic CRO bt Fabrice Santoro FRA
7-6(3) 6-4 6-7(2) 7-5

Sjeng Schalken NED (24) bt Mark Philippoussis AUS
6-7(1) 4-6 6-3 5-3 Ret

Nicolas Massu CHI bt Nicolas Lapentti ECU (27)
6-4 6-3 6-7(8) 7-5

Jurgen Melzer AUT bt Jack Brasington USA (W) 6-3 7-5 6-3

Gustavo Kuerten BRA bt Julien Boutter FRA
3-6 7-6(5) 6-1 6-0

Marat Safin RUS (2) bt Nicolas Kiefer GER
6-3 4-6 4-6 6-4 7-6(4)

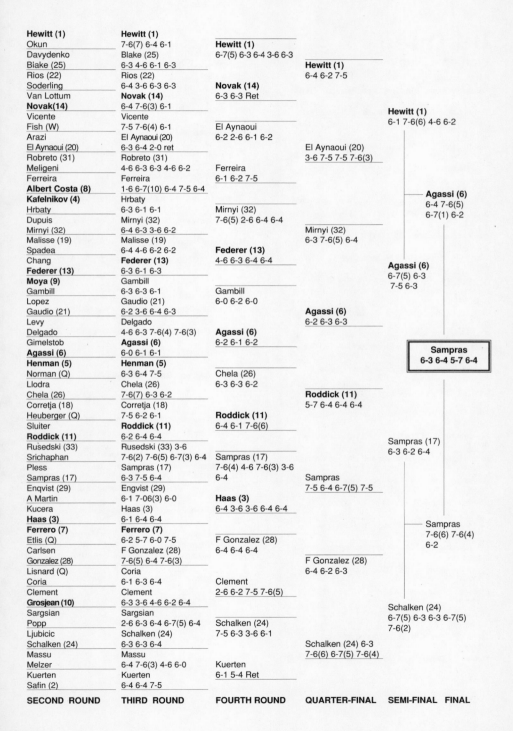

SECOND ROUND

Hewitt (1)
Okun
Davydenko
Biake (25)
Rios (22)
Soderling
Van Lottum
Novak(14)
Vicente
Fish (W)
Arazi
El Aynaoui (20)
Robreto (31)
Meligeni
Ferreira
Albert Costa (8)
Kafelnikov (4)
Hrbaty
Dupuis
Mirnyi (32)
Malisse (19)
Spadea
Chang
Federer (13)
Moya (9)
Gambill
Lopez
Gaudio (21)
Levy
Delgado
Gimelstob
Agassi (6)
Henman (5)
Norman (Q)
Llodra
Chela (26)
Corretja (18)
Heuberger (Q)
Sluiter
Roddick (11)
Rusedski (33)
Srichaphan
Pless
Sampras (17)
Enqvist (29)
A Martin
Kucera
Haas (3)
Ferrero (7)
Etlis (Q)
Carlsen
Gonzalez (28)
Lisnard (Q)
Coria
Clement
Grosjean (10)
Sargsian
Popp
Ljubicic
Schalken (24)
Massu
Melzer
Kuerten
Safin (2)

THIRD ROUND

Hewitt (1) — 7-6(7) 6-4 6-1
Blake (25) — 6-3 4-6 6-1 6-3
Rios (22) — 6-4 3-6 6-3 6-3
Novak (14) — 6-4 7-6(3) 6-1
Vicente — 7-5 7-6(4) 6-1
El Aynaoui (20) — 6-3 6-4 2-0 ret
Robreto (31) — 4-6 6-3 6-3 4-6 6-2
Ferreira — 1-6 6-7(10) 6-4 7-5 6-4
Hrbaty — 6-3 6-1 6-1
Mirnyi (32) — 6-4 6-3 3-6 6-2
Malisse (19) — 6-4 4-6 6-2 6-2
Federer (13) — 6-3 6-1 6-3
Gambill — 6-3 6-3 6-1
Gaudio (21) — 6-2 3-6 6-4 6-3
Delgado — 4-6 6-3 7-6(4) 7-6(3)
Agassi (6) — 6-0 6-1 6-1
Henman (5) — 6-3 6-4 7-5
Chela (26) — 7-6(7) 6-3 6-2
Corretja (18) — 7-5 6-2 6-1
Roddick (11) — 6-2 6-4 6-4
Rusedski (33) 3-6 — 7-6(2) 7-6(5) 6-7(3) 6-4
Sampras (17) — 6-3 7-5 6-4
Engvist (29) — 6-1 7-06(3) 6-0
Haas (3) — 6-1 6-4 6-4
Ferrero (7) — 6-2 5-7 6-0 7-5
F Gonzalez (28) — 7-6(5) 6-4 7-6(3)
Coria — 6-1 6-3 6-4
Clement — 6-3 3-6 4-6 6-2 6-4
Sargsian — 2-6 6-3 6-4 6-7(5) 6-4
Schalken (24) — 6-3 6-3 6-4
Massu — 6-4 7-6(3) 4-6 6-0
Kuerten — 6-4 6-4 7-5

FOURTH ROUND

Hewitt (1) — 6-7(5) 6-3 6-4 3-6 6-3
Novak (14) — 6-3 6-3 Ret
El Aynaoui — 6-2 2-6 6-1 6-2
Ferreira — 6-1 6-2 7-5
Mirnyi (32) — 7-6(5) 2-6 6-4 6-4
Federer (13) — 4-6 6-3 6-4 6-4
Gambill — 6-0 6-2 6-0
Agassi (6) — 6-2 6-1 6-2
Chela (26) — 6-3 6-3 6-2
Roddick (11) — 6-4 6-1 7-6(6)
Sampras (17) — 7-6(4) 4-6 7-6(3) 3-6 6-4
Haas (3) — 6-4 3-6 3-6 6-4 6-4
F Gonzalez (28) — 6-4 6-4 6-4
Clement — 2-6 6-2 7-5 7-6(5)
Schalken (24) — 7-5 6-3 3-6 6-1
Kuerten — 6-1 5-4 Ret

QUARTER-FINAL

Hewitt (1) — 6-4 6-2 7-5
El Aynaoui (20) — 3-6 7-5 7-5 7-6(3)
Mirnyi (32) — 6-3 7-6(5) 6-4
Agassi (6) — 6-2 6-3 6-3
Roddick (11) — 5-7 6-4 6-4 6-4
Sampras — 7-5 6-4 6-7(5) 7-5
F Gonzalez (28) — 6-4 6-2 6-3
Schalken (24) 6-3 — 7-6(6) 6-7(5) 7-6(4)

SEMI-FINAL

Hewitt (1) — 6-1 7-6(6) 4-6 6-2
Agassi (6) — 6-7(5) 6-3 7-5 6-3
Sampras (17) — 6-3 6-2 6-4
Schalken (24) — 6-7(5) 6-3 6-3 6-7(5) 7-6(2)

FINAL

Agassi (6) — 6-4 7-6(5) 6-7(1) 6-2
Sampras — 7-6(6) 7-6(4) 6-2

Sampras
6-3 6-4 5-7 6-4

SECOND ROUND   THIRD ROUND   FOURTH ROUND   QUARTER-FINAL   SEMI-FINAL   FINAL

US Open
Women's Singles

FIRST ROUND

Serena Williams USA (1) bt Corina Morariu USA (W) 6-2 6-3

Dinara Safina RUS bt Rita Grande ITA 7-6(5) 6-1

Iroda Tulyaganova UZB bt Adriana Serra Zanetti ITA 6-0 6-0

Nathalie Dechy FRA (26) bt Maja Matevzic SLO 6-3 7-6(4)

Daja Bedanova CZE (20) bt Alina Jidkova RUS 6-1 6-3

Elena Likhovtseva RUS bt Ally Baker USA (W) 4-6 6-2 7-6(3)

Denisa Chladkova CZE (Q) bt Meilen Tu USA 6-0 6-4

Anastasia Myskina RUS (15) bt Marta Marrero ESP 4-6 6-4 6-0

Daniela Hantuchova SVK (11) bt Nicole Pratt AUS 6-2 6-1

Virginie Razzano FRA bt Mariana Diaz Oliva ARG 7-5 6-1

Katarina Srebotnik SLO Laura Granville USA 6-3 6-4

Iva Majoli CRO (24) bt Ashley Harkleroad USA (W) 6-3 6-2

Tamarine Tanasugarn THA (27) Barbara Rittner GER 6-4 6-7(4) 6-2

Bea Bielik USA (W) Renata Voracova CZE 6-4 6-4

Cara Black ZIM bt Maria Emilia Salerni ARG 6-3 6-7(8) 6-4

Justine Henin BEL (8) bt Samantha Reeves USA 6-1 6-2

Lindsay Davenport USA (4) bt Eva Dyrberg DEN 6-2 6-1

Petra Mandula HUN bt Miriam Oremans NED 4-6 6-4 6-2

Rossana Neffa De Los Rios PAR Ludmila Cervanova SVK 6-1 6-4

Marion Bartoli FRA (Q) bt Arantxa Sanchez Vicario ESP 6-3 6-1

Svetlana Kuznetsova RUS bt Anne Kremer LUX (19) 7-6(3) 6-2

Janette Husarova SVK bt Maria Geznenge BUL (Q) 6-0 7-5

Els Callens BEL bt Tathiana Garbin ITA 6-0 2-6 6-1

Silvia Farina Elia ITA (13) bt Brie Rippner USA (Q) 6-1 6-4

Elena Dementieva RUS (12) bt Saori Obata JPN 6-2 6-4

Francesca Schiavone ITA bt Ansley Cargill USA (Q) 3-6 6-1 6-1

Fabiola Zuluaga COL (Q) bt Sarah Taylor USA 6-3 4-6 6-2

Tatiana Panova RUS (22) bt Lilia Osterloh USA 6-1 6-1

Stephanie Foretz FRA bt Alexandra Stevenson USA (31) 6-4 5-7 6-4

Angelique Widjaja INA bt Anna Kournikova RUS 6-3 6-0

Elena Bovina RUS bt Clarisa Fernandez ARG 7-6(5) 7-6(6)

Jelena Dokic YUG (5) bt Greta Arn GER 6-2 6-2

Kim Clijsters BEL (7) bt Conchita Martinez Granados ESP 6-1 6-0

Mashona Washington USA (W) bt Gala Leon Garcia ESP 6-4 6-3

Vera Zvonareva RUS bt Emmanuelle Gagliardi SUI 6-3 6-3

Henrieta Nagyova SVK bt Eleni Daniilidou GRE (28) 7-5 4-6 7-5

Patty Schnyder SUI (23) bt Nadia Petrova RUS 7-6(6) 5-7 6-2

Martina Sucha SVK bt Adriana Gersi CZE 6-1 5-7 6-0

Cristina Torrens Valero ESP bt Angelika Roesch GER 7-6(1) 6-3

Amelie Mauresmo FRA (10) bt Iveta Benesova CZE (Q) 6-3 6-2

Magdalena Maleeva BUL (16) bt Kveta Hrdlickova CZE 6-3 3-6 7-5

Emilie Loit FRA bt Shinobu Asagoe JPN 6-4 7-6(9)

Amy Frazier USA bt Virginia Ruano Pascual ESP 6-3 6-3

Ai Sugiyama JPN (18) bt Mi-Ra Jeon KOR (Q) 6-3 6-3

Meghann Shaughnessy USA (30) bt Wynne Prakusya INA 6-3 6-4

Conchita Martinez ESP bt Marlene Weingartner GER 6-2 6-1

Tina Pisnik SLO bt Sandra Cacic USA 6-2 6-2

Jennifer Capriati USA (3) bt Bethanie Mattek USA (Q) 6-0 6-0

Monica Seles USA (6) bt Zsofia Gubacsi HUN 6-3 6-3

Barbara Schwartz AUT bt Silvija Talaja CRO 6-3 6-3

Cho Yoon-Jeong KOR (Q) bt Magui Serna ESP 6-3 6-4

Paola Suarez ARG (32) bt Mary Pierce FRA 7-6(3) 6-3

Anna Smashnova ISR (17) bt Marie-Gaianeh Mikaelian SUI 7-6(1) 6-4

Amanda Coetzer RSA bt Tatiana Poutchek BLR 7-6(3) 7-6(7)

Antonella Serra Zanetti ITA (Q) bt Angeles Montolio ESP 1-6 6-2 6-4

Martina Hingis SUI (9) bt Marissa Irvin USA 6-3 5-7 6-4

Chanda Rubin USA (14) bt Jill Craybas USA 6-1 6-3

Anca Barna GER bt Alexandra Podkolzina USA 6-1 6-2

Myriam Casanova SUI bt Jelena Kostanic CRO 6-4 6-3

Lisa Raymond USA (21) bt Jennifer Hopkins US 6-4 6-3

Barbara Schett AUT (29) bt Asa Svensson SWE 6-3 6-2

Martina Muller GER bt Maret Ani EST (Q) 6-2 6-2

Alicia Molik AUS bt Patricia Wartusch AUT 6-2 6-2

Venus Williams USA (2) bt Mirjana Lucic CRO (Q) 6-4 6-0

S Williams (1)
Safina
Tulyagonova
Dechy (26)
Bedanova
Likhovtseva
Chladkova
Myskina (15)
Hantchukova (11)
Razzano
Srebotnik
Majoli (24)
Tanasugarn
Bielik
Black
Henin (8)
Davenport (3)
Mandula
Neffa De Los Rios
Bartoli
Kuznetsova
Husarova
Callens
Farina Elia
Dementieva (12)
Schiavone
Zuluaga
Panova (22)
Foretz
Widjaja
Bovina
Dokic (5)
Clijsters (7)
Washington
Zvonareva
Nagyova
Schnyder (23)
Sucha
Torrens Valero
Mauresmo (10)
Maleeva (16)
Loit
Frazier
Sugiyama (18)
Shaughnessy (30)
Martinez
Pisnik
Capriati (3)
Seles (6)
Schwartz
Cho
Suarez (32)
Smashnova (17)
Coetzer
Serra-Zanetti
Hingis (9)
Rubin (14)
Barna
Casanova
Raymond (21)
Schett (29)
Muller
Molik
V Williams (2)

SECOND ROUND

S Williams (1)
6-0 6-1
Dechy
6-1 3-6 7-6(1)
Bedanova
7-6(2) 2-6 6-3
Myskina (15)
3-6 7-5 6-1
Hantchukova (11)
6-3 6-2
Majoli
6-4 6-4
Bielik
6-4 6-2
Henin (8)
6-3 6-2
Davenport (3)
6-4 6-2
Bartoli
3-6 6-2 6-2
Kuznetsova
2-6 6-3 6-2
Farina Elia (13)
6-2 6-2
Schiavone
7-6(7) 6-3
Panova (22)
5-7 7-5 6-4
Foretz
7-5 6-1
Bovina
6-3 6-2
Clijsters (7)
6-1 7-6(1)
Zvonareva
6-1 6-0
Schnyder (23)
6-3 6-3
Mauresmo (10)
7-6(3) 6-2
Maleeva
4-6 6-3 7-5
Frazier
6-4 6-2
Shaughnessy
6-3 6-2
Capriati (3)
6-4 6-2
Seles (6)
1-6 7-6(5) 6-2
Cho
6-4 6-4
Coetzer
6-2 6-4
Hingis (9)
6-4 6-1
Rubin (14)
6-4 6-1
Raymond
6-4 6-2
Muller
5-7 6-2 7-5
V Williams (2)
6-1 6-2

THIRD ROUND

S Williams (1)
6-1 6-1
Bedanova
6-3 3-6 6-2
Hantchukova (11)
6-3 6-1
Henin (8)
7-5 6-1
Davenport (3)
6-3 6-1
Farina Elia (13)
6-2 6-3
Schiavone
3-6 6-4 6-3
Bovina
6-3 6-2
Clijsters (7)
1-6 7-5 6-4
Mauresmo (10)
6-1 6-4
Frazier
3-6 6-2 6-2
Capriati (3)
6-2 6-2
Seles (6)
6-1 5-7 6-3
Hingis (9)
6-3 6-4
Rubin (14)
7-6(2) 6-4
V Williams (2)
6-1 6-2

FOURTH ROUND

S Williams (1)
6-1 6-1
Hantchukova
6-1 3-6 7-6(4)
Davenport (3)
6-3 6-1
Bovina
7-6(4) 6-4
Mauresmo (10)
4-6 6-3 7-5
Capriati (3)
6-1 6-3
Seles (6)
6-4 6-2
V Williams (2)
6-2 4-6 7-5

QUARTER-FINAL

S Williams (1)
6-2 6-2
Davenport (3)
3-6 6-0 6-2
Mauresmo (10)
4-6 7-6(5) 6-3
V Williams (2)
6-2 6-3

SEMI-FINAL

S Williams (1)
6-3 7-5
S Williams (1)
6-4 6-3
V Williams (2)
6-3 5-7 6-4

FINAL

ATP Tour 2002

Date	Tournament	Singles Final		Doubles Final		Prize Money (US$)
Dec 31 Jan 6	Qatar ExxonMobil Open Doha, Qatar (HO)	**El Aynaoui** Mantilla	4-6 6-2 6-2	**Johnson/Palmer** Novak/Rikl	6-3 7-6	$1,000,000
Dec 31 Jan 6	TATA Open Chennai, India (HO)	**Canas** Srichaphan	6-4 7-6	**Bhupati/Paes** Cibulec/Fukarek	5-7 6-2 7-5	$400,000
Dec 31 Jan 6	AAPT Championships Adelaide (HO)	**Henman** Philippoussis	6-4 6-7 6-3	**W Black/Ullyett** M Bryan/B Bryan	7-5 6-2	$357,000
Jan 7 Jan 13	Heineken Open Auckland (HO)	**Rusedski** Golmard	6-7 6-4 7-5	**Bjorkman/Woodbridge** Garcia/Suk	7-6 7-6	$357,000
Jan 7 Jan 13	adidas International Sydney (HO)	**Federer** Ignacio	6-3 6-3	**Johnson/Palmer** Eagle/Stolle	6-4 6-4	$381,000
Jan 14 Jan 27	**Australian Open** Melbourne (H)	**Johansson** Safin	3-6 6-4 6-4 7-6	**Knowles/Nestor** Santoro/Llodra	7-6 6-3	AUS$16,500,00
Jan 28 Feb 3	Milan Indoors Milan (CI)	**Sanguinetti** Federer	7-6 4-6 6-1	**Braasch/Olhovsky** Boutter/Mirnyi	3-6 7-6 (12-10)	$381,000
Jan 28 Feb 3	ATP World Doubles Challenge, Bangalore			**Ferreira/Leach** Pala/Vizner	6-7 7-6 6-4 6-4	$350,000
Feb 11 Feb 17	Open 13 Marseille (HI)	**Enqvist** Escude	6-7 6-3 6-1	**Clement/Escude** Boutter/Mirnyi	6-4 6-3	$500,000
Feb 11 Feb 17	Chevrolet Cup Vina del Mar (CLO)	**Gonzalez** Lapentti	6-3 6-7 7-6	**Etlis/Rodriguez** Arnold/Lobo	6-3 6-4	$381,000
Feb 11 Feb 17	Copenhagen Open Copenhagen (HI)	**Burgsmuller** Larsson	6-3 6-3	**Knowle/Kohlmann** Novak/Stepanek	7-6 7-5	$381,000
Feb 18 Feb 24	Kroger/St Jude Memphis (HI)	**Roddick** Blake	6-4 3-6 7-5	**MacPhie/Zimonjic** B Bryan/M Bryan	6-3 3-6 (10-4)	$725,000
Feb 18 Feb 24	World Tennis Rotterdam (HI)	**Escude** Henman	3-6 7-6 6-4	**Federer/Mirnyi** Knowles/Nestor	4-6 6-3 (10-4)	$713,000
Feb 18 Feb 24	Copa AT&T Buenos Aires (CL)	**Massu** Calleri	2-6 7-6 6-2	**Etlis/Rodriguez** Aspelin/Kratzmann	3-6 6-3 (10-4)	$425,000
Feb 25 Mar 3	Dubai Tennis Open Dubai (HO)	**Santoro** El Aynaoui	6-4 3-6 6-3	**Knowles/Nestor** Eagle/Stolle	3-6 6-3 (13-11)	$925,000
Feb 25 Mar 3	Abierto Mexicano Pegase, Acapulco (CL)	**Moya** Meligeni	7-6 7-6	**B Bryan/M Bryan** Damm/Riki	6-3 3-6 (10-2)	$725,000
Feb 25 Mar 3	Sybase Open, San José, California (HI)	**Hewitt** Agassi	4-6 7-6 7-6	**Black/Ullyett** De Jager/Koenig	6-3 4-6 (10-5)	$400,000
Mar 4 Mar 10	Franklin Templeton Scottsdale, AZ (HO)	**Agassi** Balcells	6-2 7-6	**B Bryan/M Bryan** Knowles/Nestor	7-5 7-6	$400,000
Mar 4 Mar 10	Citrix Tennis C'ships Delray Beach, FL (HO)	**Sanguinetti** Roddick	6-4 4-6 6-4	**Damm/Suk** Adams/Ellwood	6-3 6-7 (10-5)	$400,000
Mar 11 Mar 17	Tennis Masters Series Indian Wells, CA(HO)	**Hewitt** Henman	6-1 6-2	**Knowles/Nestor** Federer/Mirnyi	6-4 6-4	$2,950,000

Dates	Tournament	Winner/Runner-up	Score	Doubles	Score	Prize
Mar 18 Mar 30	The Ericsson Open Miami (HO)	**Agassi** Federer	6-3 6-3 3-6 6-4	**Knowles/Nestor** Johnson/Palmer	6-3 3-6 6-1	$3,575,000
Apr 8 Apr 14	Grand Prix Hassan II Casablanca (CL)	**El Aynaoui** Canas	3-6 6-3 6-2	**Huss/Wakefield** Garcia/Lobo	6-4 6-2	$400,000
Apr 8 Apr 14	Estoril Open Estoril (CL)	**Nalbandian** Nieminen	6-4 7-6	**Braasch/Olhovsky** Aspelin/Kratzmann	6-3 6-3	$525,000
Apr 15 Apr 21	Monte Carlo Open Monaco (CL)	**Ferrero** Moya	7-5 6-3 6-4	**Bjorkman/Woodbridge** Haarhuis/Kafelnikov	6-3 3-6 (10-7)	$2,950,000
Apr 22 Apr 28	Open Seat Godo 2001 Barcelona (CLI)	**Gaudio** Costa	6-4 6-0 6-2	**Hill/Vacek** Arnold/Etlis	6-4 6-4	$955,000
Apr 22 Apr 28	US Men's Clay Court Champs, Houston (CLI)	**Roddick** Sampras	7-6 6-3	**Fish/Roddick** Gambill/Oliver	6-4 6-4	$400,000
Apr 29 May 5	BMW Open Munich (CL)	**El Aynaoui** Schuettler	6-4 6-4	**Luxa/Stepanek** Pala/Vizner	6-0 6-7 (11-9)	$381,000
Apr 29 May 5	Mallorca Open Mallorca (CL)	**Gaudio** Nieminen	6-2 6-3	**Bhupati/Paes** Knowles/Kohlmann	6-2 6-4	$381,000
May 6 May 12	Tennis Masters Series Rome (CL)	**Agassi** Haas	6-3 6-3 6-0	**Damm/Suk** Black/Ullyett	7-5 7-5	$2,578,000
May 13 May 19	Tennis Masters Series Hamburg (CL)	**Federer** Safin	6-1 6-3 6-4	**Bhupati/Gambill** Bjorkman/Woodbridge	6-2 6-4	$2,578,000
May 20 May 26	Raiffeisen Grand Prix St Polton, Austria (CLI)	**N Lapentti** Vicente	7-5 6-4	**Pala/Rikl** M Bryan/Hill	7-5 6-4	$381,000
May 20 May 26	World Team Cup Düsseldorf (CL)	**Argentina 3** Russia 0	*(Canas/Arnold/Etlis)* *(Safin/Kafelnikov/Cherkasov)*			$2,100,000
May 27 June 9	**French Open** Roland Garros (CL)	**Costa** Ferrero	6-1 6-0 4-6 6-3	**Haarhuis/Kafelnikov** Knowles/Nestor	7-5 6-4	4,284,000
Jun 10 Jun 16	Stella Artois Champs London (G)	**Hewitt** Henman	4-6 6-1 6-4	**Black/Ullyett** Bhupati/Mirnyi	7-5 6-3	$761,000
Jun 10 Jun 16	Gerry Weber Open Halle (G)	**Kafelnikov** Kiefer	2-6 6-4 6-4	**Prinosil/Rikl** Bjorkman/Woodbridge	4-6 7-6 7-5	$951,000
Jun 17 Jun 23	The Nottingham Open Nottingham (G)	**Bjorkman** Arthurs	6-2 6-7 6-2	**M Bryan/Knowles** Johnson/Palmer	0-6 7-6 6-4	$381,000
Jun 17 Jun 23	Heineken Trophy 's-Hertogenbosch (G)	**Schalken** Clement	3-6 6-3 6-2	**Damm/Suk** Haarhuis/MacPhie	7-6 6-7 6-4	$381,000
Jun 24 Jul 7	**The Championships** Wimbledon (G)	**Hewitt** Nalbandian	6-1 6-3 6-2	**Bjorkman/Woodbridge** Knowles/Nestor	6-1 6-2 6-7 7-5	£4,369,650
Jul 8 Jul 14	Swedish Open Bastad (CL)	**Moya** El Aynaoui	6-3 2-6 7-5	**Bjorkman/Woodbridge** Hanley/Hill	7-6 6-4	$381,000
Jul 8 Jul 14	UBS Open Gstaad, Switzerland (CL)	**Corretja** Gaudio	6-3 7-6 7-6	**Eagle/Rikl** Bertolini/Brandi	7-6 6-4	$600,000
Jul 8 Jul 14	Miller Lite Champs Rhode Island (G)	**Dent** Blake	6-1 4-6 6-4	**B Bryan/M Bryan** Melzer/Popp	7-5 6-3	$375,000
Jul 15 Jul 21	Mercedes Cup Stuttgart (CL)	**Youzhny** Canas	6-3 3-6 3-6 6-4 6-4	**Eagle/Rikl** Adams/Etlis	6-3 6-4	$500,000

Jul 15 Jul 21	Energis Dutch Open Amsterdam (CL)	**Chela** Costa	6-1 7-6	**Coetzee/Haggard** Sa/Simoni	7-6 6-3	$381,000
Jul 15 Jul 21	Croatia Open Umag (CL)	**Moya** Ferrer	6-2 6-3	**Cermak/Knowle** Ljubicic/Zovko	6-4 6-4	$381,000
Jul 22 Jul 28	Generali Open Kitzbuhel, Austria (CL)	**Corretja** Ferrero	6-4 6-1 6-3	**Koenig/Shimada** Arnold/Corretja	7-6 6-4	$880,000
Jul 22 Jul 28	Mercedes-Benz Cup Los Angeles, CA (HO)	**Agassi** Gambill	6-2 6-4	**Grosjean/Kiefer** Gimelstob/Llodra	6-4 6-4	$400,000
Jul 22 Jul 28	Idea Prokom Open Sopot, Poland (CL)	**Acasuso** Squillari	2-6 6-1 6-3	**Cermak/Friedl** Coetzee/Healey	7-5 7-5	$381,000
Jul 29 Aug 2	Masters Canada Toronto (HO)	**Canas** Roddick	6-4 7-5	**B Bryan/M Bryan** Knowles/Nestor	4-6 7-6 6-3	$2,950,000
Aug 5 Aug 11	Masters Cincinnati (HO)	**Moya** Hewitt	6-4 7-6	**Blake/Martin** Bhupati/Mirnyi	7-5 6-3	$2,950,000
Aug 12 Aug 18	RCA Championships Indianapolis (HO)	**Rusedski** Mantilla	6-7 6-4 6-4	**Knowles/Nestor** Bhupati/Mirnyi	7-5 6-7 6-4	$800,000
Aug 12 Aug 18	Legg Mason Classic Washington DC (HO)	**Blake** Srichipan	1-6 7-6 6-4	**Black/Ullyett** B Bryan/M Bryan	3-6 6-3 7-5	$800,000
Aug 19 Aug 25	The Hamlet Cup Long Island (HO)	**Srichapan** Chela	6-3 3-6 6-2	**Bhupati/M Bryan** Pala/Vizner	6-3 6-4	$480,000
Aug 26 Sep 8	**US Open** Flushing Meadow (HO)	**Sampras** Agassi	6-2 6-4 5-7 6-4	**Bhupati/Mirnyi** Novak/Stepanek	6-3 3-6 6-4	$8,087,100
Sep 9 Sep 15	Gelsor Open Bucharest (CL)	**Ferrer** Acasuso	7-6 7-6	**Knippschild/Nyborg** Benfele-Alvarez/Schneiter	6-3 6-3	$381,000
Sep 9 Sep 15	President's Cup Tashkent (HO)	**Kafelnikov** Voltchkov	7-6 7-5	**Adams/Koenig** Sluiter/Verkerk	6-2 7-5	$550,000
Sep 9 Sep 15	Brazil Open Salvador, Brazil (CL)	**Kuerten** Coria	6-7 7-5 7-6	**Humphries/Merklein** Kuerten/Sa	6-3 7-6	$571,000
Sep 23 Sep 29	International Series Palermo (CL)	**Gonzalez** Acasuso	5-7 6-3 6-1	**Arnold/Lobo** Cermak/Friedl	6-4 4-6 6-2	$381,000
Sep 23 Sep 29	Salem Open Hong Kong (HO)	**Ferrero** Moya	6-3 1-6 7-6	**Gambill/Oliver** Arthurs/Kratzmann	6-7 6-4 7-6	$400,000
Sep 30 Oct 6	Japan Open Tokyo (HO)	**Carlsen** Norman	7-6 6-3	**Coetzee/Haggard** Gambill/Oliver	7-6 6-4	$800,000
Sep 30 Oct 6	Kremlin Cup Moscow (CI)	**Mathieu** Schalken	4-6 6-2 6-0	**Federer/Mirnyi** Eagle/Stolle	6-4 7-6	$1,000,000
Oct 7 Oct 13	CA Tennis Trophy Vienna (HI)	**Federer** Novak	6-4 6-1 3-6 6-4	**Eagle/Stolle** Novak/Stepanek	6-4 6-3	$765,000
Oct 7 Oct 13	Grand Prix de Lyon Lyon (CI)	**Mathieu** Kuerten	4-6 6-3 6-1	**Black/Ullyett** Knowles/Nestor	6-4 3-6 7-6	$761,000
Oct 14 Oct 20	Masters Series Stuttgart (HI)	**Agassi** Novak	w/o	**Knowles/Nestor** Bhupati/Mirnyi	6-3 5-7 6-0	$2,578,000
Oct 21 Oct 27	Swiss Open Basel (CI)	**Nalbandian** Gonzalez	6-4 6-3 6-2	**B Bryan/M Bryan** Knowles/Nestor	7-6 7-5	$1,000,000

Oct 21	Swedish Open	**Srichapan**	6-7 6-0 6-3	**Black/Ullyett**	6-4 2-6 7-6	$650,000
Oct 27	Stockholm (HI)	Rios	6-2	Arthurs/Hanley		
Oct 21	St Petersburg Open	**Grosjean**	7-5 6-4	**Adams/Palmer**	7-6 6-3	$1,000,000
Oct 27	St Petersburg (CI)	Youzhny		Labadze/Safin		
Oct 28	Masters Paris	**Safin**	7-6 6-0 6-4	**Escude/Santoro**	6-3 7-6	$2,828,000
Nov 3	(CI)	Hewitt		Kuerten/Pioline		
Nov 3	Masters Cup	**Hewitt**	7-5 7-5 2-6			$3,700,000
Nov 9	Shanghai (HI)	Ferrero	2-6 6-4			

*Legend: H = Hard; CL = Clay; G = Grass; C = Carpet; I = Indoors   * Not ATP Tour event*

2002 ATP Champions Race

The Champions Race is based on performances in ATP tour events in the calendar year. This differs from the ATP Entry system which is a 12-month rolling system and is used to determine seedings for ATP events.

1	Lleyton Hewitt AUS	902
2	Andre Agassi USA	684
3	Marat Safin RUS	569
4	Juan Carlos Ferrero ESP	553
5	Carlos Moya ESP	544
6	Roger Federer SUI	518
7	Jiri Novak CZE	467
8	Tim Henman GBR	443
9	Andy Roddick USA	424
10	Albert Costa ESP	416

Men's Rankings (Entry List)

As at December 31, 2002
British shown if in top 500

1	Lleyton Hewitt	AUS	4485		56	Nicolas Massu	CHI	680
2	Andre Agassi	USA	3395		57	Taylor Dent	USA	672
3	Marat Safin	RUS	2845		58	Fernando Vicente	ESP	671
4	Juan Carlos Ferrero	ESP	2740		59	David Ferrer	ESP	643
5	Carlos Moya	ESP	2630		60	David Sanchez	ESP	642
6	Roger Federer	SUI	2590		61	Alberto Martin	ESP	640
7	Jiri Novak	CZE	2335		62	Feliciano Lopez	ESP	633
8	Tim Henman	GBR	2215		63	Radek Stepanek	CZE	633
9	Albert Costa	ESP	2070		64	Olivier Rochus	BEL	624
10	Andy Roddick	USA	2045		65	Kenneth Carlsen	DEN	621
11	Tommy Haas	GER	2020		66	Andre Sa	BRA	607
12	David Nalbandian	ARG	1775		67	Vincent Spadea	USA	586
13	Pete Sampras	USA	1735		68	Adrian Voinea	ROM	579
14	Thomas Johansson	SWE	1725		69	Michel Kratochvil	SUI	570
15	Guillermo Canas	ARG	1725		70	Anthony Dupuis	FRA	566
16	Paradorn Srichaphan	THA	1646		71	Raemon Sluiter	NED	558
17	Sebestien Grosjean	FRA	1640		72	Nicolas Kiefer	GER	550
18	Fernando Gonzalez	CHI	1636		73	Vladimir Voltchkov	BLR	550
19	Alex Corretja	ESP	1555		74	Fernando Meligeni	BRA	538
20	Sjeng Schalken	NED	1525		75	Bohdan Ulihrach	CZE	530
21	Gaston Gaudio	ARG	1490		76	Lars Burgsmuller	GER	525
22	Younes El Aynaoui	MAR	1435		77	Julien Boutter	FRA	513
23	Juan Ignacio Chela	ARG	1240		78	Albert Montanes	ESP	501
24	Marcelo Rios	CHI	1230		79	Franco Squillari	ARG	494
25	Xavier Malisse	BEL	1225		80	Mark Philippoussis	AUS	490
26	Andrei Pavel	ROM	1225		81	Nikolay Davydenko	RUS	487
27	Yevgeny Kafelnikov	RUS	1190		82	Kristian Pless	DEN	486
28	James Blake	USA	1170		83	Karol Kucera	SVK	483
29	Nicolas Lapentti	ECU	1090		84	Mardy Fish	USA	481
30	Tommy Robredo	ESP	1050		85	Luis Horna	PER	473
31	Greg Rusedski	GBR	1010		86	Martin Verkerk	NED	468
32	Mikhail Youzhny	RUS	995		87	Lee Hyung-Taik	KOR	463
33	Rainer Schuettler	GER	980		88	Albert Portas	ESP	450
34	Nicolas Escude	FRA	960		89	Mario Ancic	CRO	448
35	Fabrice Santoro	FRA	955		90	Hicham Arazi	MAR	443
36	Paul-Henri Mathieu	FRA	952		91	Jurgen Melzer	AUT	441
37	Gustovo Kuerten	BRA	935		92	Flavio Saretta	BRA	438
38	Arnaud Clement	FRA	925		93	Irakli Labadze	GEO	427
39	Wayne Ferreira	RSA	875		94	Olivier Mutis	FRA	415
40	Jarkko Nieminen	FIN	875		95	Attila Savolt	HUN	414
41	Jose Acasuso	ARG	868		96	Dick Norman	BEL	411
42	Jan-Michael Gambill	USA	825		97	Jeff Morrison	USA	406
43	Max Mirnyi	BLR	810		98	Arnaud Di Pasquale	FRA	398
44	Thomas Enqvist	SWE	810		99	Jerome Golmard	FRA	395
45	Guillermo Coria	ARG	778		100	Robby Ginepri	USA	392
46	Davide Sanguinetti	ITA	773		*Also*			
47	Todd Martin	USA	755		170	Arvind Parmar	GBR	214
48	Jonas Bjorkman	SWE	745		203	Martin Lee	GBR	163
49	Ivan Ljubicic	CRO	735		310	Jamie Delgado	GBR	87
50	Agustin Calleri	ARG	730		340	Alan Mackin	GBR	79
51	Dominik Hrbaty	SVK	726		394	Mark Hilton	GBR	62
52	Wayne Arthurs	AUS	720		447	Miles Maclagan	GBR	50
53	Mariano Zabaleta	ARG	711		455	Barry Cowan	GBR	47
54	Stefan Koubek	AUT	685		459	Alex Bogdanovic	GBR	46
55	Felix Mantilla	ESP	680		483	Lee Childs	GBR	42

Earnings Lists

	Men	US$		Women	US$
1	Lleyton Hewitt AUS	4,619,386	1	Serena Williams USA	3,935,668
2	Juan Carlos Ferrero ESP	2,761,498	2	Venus Williams USA	2,583,571
3	Andre Agassi USA	2,186,006	3	Jennifer Capriati USA	2,217,939
4	Roger Federer SUI	1,995,027	4	Kim Clijsters BEL	1,754,376
5	Yevgeny Kafelnikov RUS	1,778,810	5	Martina Hingis SUI	1,467,584
6	Carlos Moya ESP	1,772,314	6	Justine Henin BEL	1,213,093
7	Marat Safin RUS	1,719,408	7	Daniela Hantuchova SVK	1,188,379
8	Jiri Novak CZE	1,454,130	8	Monica Seles USA	1,096,630
9	Albert Costa ESP	1,434,439	9	Amelie Mauresmo FRA	1,073,807
10	Sebastien Grosjean FRA	1,331,157	10	Jelena Dokic YUG	918,633
11	Guillermo Canas ARG	1,276,617	11	Elena Dementieva RUS	844,325
12	Pete Sampras USA	1,222,999	12	Lindsay Davenport USA	805,191
13	Tim Henman GBR	1,194,899	13	Paola Suarez ARG	797,503
14	Tommy Haas GER	1,163,569	14	Lisa Raymond USA	738,157
15	Andy Roddick USA	1,060,878	15	Virginia Ruano-Pascual ESP	637,418
16	Thomas Johansson SWE	1,028,691	16	Magdalena Maleeva BUL	615,813
17	Max Mirnyi BLR	975,672	17	Janette Husarova SVK	599,021
18	David Nalbandian ARG	914,882	18	Patty Schnyder SUI	591,655
19	Sjeng Schalken NED	888,581	19	Silvia Farina-Elia ITA	568,322
20	Fabrice Santoro FRA	810,555	20	Elena Likhovtseva RUS	551,692
21	Younes El Aynaoui MAR	800,977	21	Anastasia Mystina RUS	545,661
22	Jonas Bjorkman SWE	798,909	22	Anna Kournikova RUS	515,635
23	Alex Corretja ESP	780,986	23	Chandra Rubin USA	507,966
24	Fernando Gonzalez CHI	735,682	24	Arantxa Sanchez-Vicario ESP	441,378
25	Daniel Nestor CAN	719,026	25	Cara Black ZIM	417,763
26	Mark Knowles BAH	709,149	26	Ai Sugiyama JPN	416,408
27	James Blake USA	678,026	27	Amanda Coetzer RSA	415,386
28	Paradorn Srichaphan THA	651,089	28	Elena Bovina RUS	407,495
29	Andrei Pavel ROM	646,098	29	Anna Pistolesi ISR	392,911
30	Nicolas Escude FRA	617,075	30	Meghann Shaughnessy USA	389,311
31	Gaston Gaudio ARG	610,684	31	Iva Majoli CRO	381,574
32	Arnaud Clement FRA	606,035	32	Rennae Stubbs AUS	371,921
33	Rainer Schuettler GER	586,434	33	Tatiana Panova RUS	366,491
34	Nicolas Lapentti ECU	580,135	34	Nathalie Dechy FRA	352,830
35	Xavier Malisse BEL	570,952	35	Katarina Srebotnik SLO	352,136
36	Tommy Robredo ESP	552,493	36	Alexandra Stevenson USA	338,933
37	Juan Ignacio Chela ARG	548,780	37	Conchita Martinez ESP	329,316
38	Jan-Michael Gambill USA	546,618	38	Daja Bedanova CZE	322,927
39	Marcelo Rios CHI	506,160	39	Sandrine Testud FRA	308,400
40	Mahesh Bhupathi IND	489,224	40	Barbara Schett AUT	290,021
41	Todd Woodbridge AUS	447,377	41	Tamarine Tanasugarn THA	285,955
42	Radek Stepanek CZE	444,793	42	Anne Kremer LUX	282,858
43	Gustavo Kuerten BRA	441,974	43	Clarisa Fernandez ARG	271,415
44	Ivan Ljubicic CRO	434,942	44	Elena Daniilidou GRE	263,730
45	Mikhail Youzhny RUS	434,142	45	Rita Grande ITA	261,135
46	Nicolas Kiefer GER	418,187	46	Iroda Tulyaganova UZB	258,539
47	Thomas Enqvist SWE	417,962	47	Magui Serna ESP	256,198
48	Mike Bryan USA	411,864	48	Francesca Schiavone ITA	245,088
49	Wayne Ferreira RSA	409,125	49	Nicole Pratt AUS	244,476
50	Paul-Henri Mathieu FRA	406,768	50	Emmanuelle Gagliardi SUI	236,579

WTA Tour 2002

Date	Tournament	Singles Final		Doubles Final		Prize Money
Dec 31 Jan 7	Australian Hardcourt Gold Coast (HO)	**V Williams** Henin	7-5 6-2	**Henin/Shaughnessy** Carlsson/Oremans	6-1 7-6(6)	$170,000
Dec 31 Jan 7	ABS Bank Classic Auckland (HO)	**Samshnova** Panova	6-2 6-2	**Arendt/Huber** Hredlickova/Nagyova	7-5 6-4	$140,000
Jan 7 Jan 13	adidas International Sydney (HO)	**Hingis** Shaughnessy	6-2 6-2	**Raymond/Stubbs** Hingis/Kournikova	w/o	$585,000
Jan 7 Jan 13	Tasmanian International Hobart (HO)	**Sucha** Medina Garrigues	7-6(7) 6-1	**Garbin/Grande** Barclay/Wheeler	6-2 7-6(3)	$110,000
Jan 7 Jan 13	Canberra Classic Gold Coast (HO)	**Smashnova** Tanasugarn	7-5 7-6(2)	**De Villiers/Selyutina** Reeves/Serra-Zanetti	6-2 6-3	$110,000
Jan 14 Jan 27	**Australian Open** Melbourne (HO)	**Capriati** Hingis	4-6 7-6(7) 6-2	**Kournikova/Hingis** Hantchukova/Sanchez-Vicario	6-2 6-7(4) 6-1	$16,500,00 ($AUS)
Jan 28 Feb 3	Pan Pacific Open Tokyo (CL)	**Hingis** Seles	7-6(6) 4-6 6-3	**Raymond/Stubbs** Callens/Vinci	6-1 6-1	$1,224,000
Feb 4 Feb 10	Open Gaz de France Paris (CI)	**V Williams** Dokic	w/o	**Dechy/Tu** Dementieva/Husarova	w/o	$585,000
Feb 11 Feb 17	Qatar Open Doha, Qatar (HO)	**Seles** Tanusugarn	7-6(6) 6-3	**Husarova/Sanchez-Vicario** Fusai/Vis	6-3 6-3	$170,000
Feb 11 Feb 17	Proximus Diamond Antwerp (CI)	**V Williams** Henin	6-3 5-7 6-3	**Maleeva/Schnyder** Dechy/Tu	6-3 6-7(3) 6-3	$585,000
Feb 18 Feb 24	Dubai Championships Dubai (HO)	**Mauresmo** Testud	6-4 7-6(3)	**Rittner/Vento-Kabchi** Testud/Vinci	6-3 6-2	$585,000
Feb 18 Feb 24	Copa Colsanitas Bogotá (CL)	**Zuluaga** Srebotnik	6-1 6-4	**Ruano-Pascual/Suarez** Krizan/Srebotnik	6-2 6-1	$170,000
Feb 18 Feb 24	US Indoors Memphis (HI)	**Raymond** Stevenson	4-6 6-3 7-6(9)	**Sugiyama/Tatarkova** Lee/Prakusya	6-4 2-6 6-0	$170,000
Feb 25 Mar 3	State Farm Classic Scottsdale, AZ (HO)	**S Williams** Capriati	6-2 4-6 6-4	**Raymond/Stubbs** Black/Likhovtseva	6-3 5-7 7-6(4)	$585,000
Feb 25 Mar 3	Mexicano Pegaso Acapulco, Mexico (CL)	**Srebotnik** Suarez	6-7(1) 6-4 6-2	**Ruano-Pascual/Suarez** Krizan/Srebotnik	7-5 6-1	$170,000
Mar 4 Mar 17	Tennis Masters Indian Wells, CA (HO)	**Hantuchova** Hingis	6-3 6-4	**Raymond/Stubbs** Ruano-Pascual/Suarez	7-6(4) 6-7(4) 6-3	$2,100,000
Mar 18 Mar 31	Nasdaq100 Open Miami, Florida (HO)	**S Williams** Capriati	7-5 7-6(4)	**Sanchez-Vicario/Tauziat** Raymond/Stubbs	6-0 6-4	$2,820,000
Apr 1 Apr 7	Porto Open Oporto, Portugal (CL)	**Montolio** Serna	6-1 2-6 7-5	**Black/Selyutina** Boogert/Serna	7-6(6) 6-4	$140,000
Apr 1 Apr 7	Sarasota Open Florida (CL)	**Dokic** Panova	6-2 6-2	**Dokic/Likhovtseva** Callens/Martinez	6-7(5) 6-3 6-3	$140,000
Apr 8 Apr 14	Bausch & Lomb Chps Amelia Island, FL (CLI)	**V Williams** Henin	2-6 7-5 7-6(5)	**Sancez-Vic./Hantuchova** Salerni/Svensson	6-4 6-2	$585,000

Dates	Tournament	Singles	Score	Doubles	Score	Prize
Apr 9 / Apr 15	Estoril Open Portugal (CL)	**Serna** Barna	6-4 6-2	**Bovina/Gubacsi** Rittner/Vento-Kabchi	6-3 6-1	$140,000
Apr 15 / Apr 21	Family Circle Cup Charleston, SC (CL)	**Majoli** Schnyder	7-6(5) 6-4	**Raymond/Stubbs** Fusai/Vis	6-4 3-6 7-6(4)	$1,224,000
Apr 15 / Apr 21	Budapest Open (CL)	**Muller** Casanova	6-2 3-6 6-4	**Barclay/Loit** Bovina/Gubacsi	4-6 6-3 6-3	$110,000
Apr 29 / May 5	Betty Barclay Cup Hamburg (CL)	**Clijsters** V Williams	1-6 6-3 6-4	**Hingis/Schett** Hantuchova/Sanchez-Vicario	6-1 6-1	$585,000
Apr 29 / May 5	Croatian Open Bol, Croatia (CL)	**Svensson** Majoli	6-3 4-6 6-1	**Garbin/Widjaja** Bovina/Nagyova	7-5 3-6 6-4	$170,000
May 6 / May 12	Eurocard German Open Berlin (CL)	**Henin** S Williams	6-2 1-6 7-6(5)	**Dementieva/Husarova** Hantuchova/Sanchez-Vic.	0-6 7-6(3) 6-2	$1,224,000
May 6 / May 12	J & S Cup Warsaw (CL)	**Bovina** Nagyova	6-3 6-1	**Kostanic/Nagyova** Koulikovskaya/Talaja	6-1 6-1	$170,000
May 13 / May 19	Masters Rome (CL)	**S Williams** Henin	7-6(6) 6-4	**Ruano-Pascual/Suarez** Martinez/Tarabini	6-1 2-6 6-4	$1,224,000
May 20 / May 26	Strasbourg International (CL)	**Farina Elia** Dokic	6-4 3-6 6-3	**Hopkins/Kostanic** Dhenin/Matevzic	0-6 6-4 6-4	$170,000
May 20 / May 26	Madrid Open (CL)	**Seles** Rubin	6-4 6-2	**Navratilova/Zvereva** Neffa-De Los Rios/Sanchez-Vicario	6-2 6-3	$170,000
May 27 / Jun 9	**French Open** Roland Garros (CL)	**S Williams** V Williams	7-5 6-3	**Ruano Pascual/Suárez** Raymond/Stubbs	6-4 6-2	5,220,000
Jun 10 / Jun 16	DFS Classic Birmingham (G)	**Dokic** Myskina	6-2 6-3	**Asagoe/Callens** Po-Messerli/Tauziat	6-4 6-3	$170,000
Jun 10 / July 16	Tashkent Open Uzbekistan (HO)	**Mikaelian** Poutchek	6-4 6-4	**Perebiynis/Poutchek** Buric/Fokina	7-5 6-2	$140,000
Jun 10 / July 16	Wien Energei GP Vienna (CL)	**Smashnova** Tulyaganova	6-4 6-1	**Mandula/Wartusch** Schwatrz/Woehr	6-2 6-4	$140,000
Jun 18 / Jun 24	Britannia Asset Chps Eastbourne (G)	**Rubin** Myskina	6-1 6-3	**Raymond/Stubbs** Black/Likhovtseva	6-7(5) 7-6(6) 6-2	$585,000
Jun 18 / Jun 24	Ordina Open 's-Hertogenbosch (G)	**Daniilidou** Dementieva	3-6 6-2 6-3	**Barclay/Muller** Lamade/Maleeva	6-4 7-5	$170,000
Jun 25 / July 9	**The Championships** Wimbledon (G)	**S Williams** V Williams	7-6(4) 6-3	**Williams/Williams** Ruano-Pascual/Suarez	6-2 7-5	£3,707,390
July 8 / July 14	Palermo International Palermo (CL)	**Diaz-Oliva** Zvoroneva	6-7(6) 6-1 6-3	**Koulikovskaya/Syssoeva** Bacheva/Roesch	6-4 6-3	$110,000
July 8 / July 14	French Community Chps Brussels (CL)	**Casanova** Sanchez-Vicario	4-6 6-2 6-1	**Schwatrz/Woehr** Garbin/Sanchez-Vicario	6-2 0-6 6-4	$140,000
Jul 8 / Jul 14	Grand Prix de S.A.R. Casablanca (CL)	**Wartusch** Koukalova	5-7 6-3 6-3	**Mandula/Wartusch** Dulko/Martinez Granados	6-2 6-1	$110,000
Jul 22 / Jul 28	Bank of the West Classic, Stanford (HO)	**V Williams** Cllijsters	6-3 6-3	**Raymond/Stubbs** Husarova/Martinez	6-1 6-1	$585,000
Jul 22 / Jul 28	Idea Prokom Open Sopot, Poland (CL)	**Safina** Nagyova	6-3 4-0 ret.	**Kuznetsova/Sanchez-V.** Koulikovskaya/Syssoeva	6-2 6-2	$300,000

Date	Tournament	Winner	Finalist	Score	Doubles Winners	Doubles Finalists	Score	Prize
Jul 29 Aug 4	Acura Classic San Diego (HO)	**V Williams** Dokic		6-7(6) 7-6(2) 6-0	**Dementieva/Husarova** Hantuchova/Sugiyama		6-2 6-4	$750,000
Aug 5 Aug 11	Nordic Light Open Helsinki (CL)	**Kuznetsova** Chladkova		0-6 6-3 7-6(2)	**Kuznetsova/Sanchez V.** Bes/Martinez		6-3 6-7(5) 6-3	$110,000
Aug 5 Aug 11	JPMorgan Chase Open Los Angeles (HO)	**Rubin** Davenport		5-7 7-6(5) 6-3	**Clijsters/Dokic** Hantuchova/Sugiyama		6-3 6-3	$585,000
Aug 12 Aug 18	Coupe Rogers AT&T Montreal (HO)	**Mauresmo** Capriati		6-4 6-1	**Ruano-Pascual/Suarez** Fjiwara/Sugiyama		6-4 7-6(3)	$1,224,000
Aug 19 Aug 25	Pilot Pen Tennis New Haven, USA (HO)	**V Williams** Davenport		7-5 6-0	**Hantuchova/Sanchez-Vic.** Garbin/Husarova		6-3 1-6 7-5	$585,000
Aug 26 Sep 8	**US Open** Flushing Meadow (HO)	**S Williams** V Williams		6-4 6-3	**Ruano-Pascual/Suarez** Dementieva/Husarova		6-2 6-1	$8,087,100
Sep 9 Sep 15	Brazil Open, Bahia (HO)	**Mskyina** Daniilidou		6-3 0-6 6-2	**Ruano-Pascual/Suarez** Loit/Neffa de los Rios		6-4 6-1	$650,000
Sep 9 Sep 15	Big Island Chps Waikoloa, Hawaii (HO)	**Black** Raymond		7-6(2) 6-4	**Tu/Vento-Kabchi** De Villiers/Selyutina		1-6 6-2 6-3	$140,000
Sep 9 Sep 15	SVW Polo Open Shanghai (HO)	**Smashnova** Kournikova		6-2 6-3	**Kournikova/Lee** Fujiwara/Sugiyama		7-5 6-3	$140,000
Sep 16 Sep 22	Toyota Princess Cup Tokyo (HO)	**S Williams** Clijsters		2-6 6-3 6-3	**Kuznetsova/Sanchez-Vic.** Mandula/Wartusch		6-2 6-4	$585,000
Sep 16 Sep 22	Challenge Bell Quebec City (HI)	**Bovina** Mikaelian		6-3 6-4	**Salerni/Zuluaga** Reeves/Steck		4-6 6-3 7-5	$170,000
Sep 23 Sep 29	Sparkassen Cup IGP Leipzig (CI)	**S Williams** Myskina		6-3 6-2	**Stevenson/S Williams** Husarova/Suarez		6-3 7-5	$585,000
Sep 23 Sep 29	Wismilak International Bali, Indonesia (HO)	Kuznetsova Martinez		3-6 7-6(4) 7-5	**Black/Ruano-Pascual** Sanchez-Vicario/Kuznetsova		6-2 6-3	$170,000
Sep 30 Oct 6	Japan Open Tokyo (HO)	**Craybas** Talaja		2-6 6-4 6-4	**Asagoe/Miyagi** Kuznetsova/Sanchez-Vicario		6-4 4-6 6-4	$170,000
Sep 30 Oct 6	Kremlin Cup Moscow (CL)	**Maleeva** Davenport		5-7 6-3 7-6(4)	**Dementieva/Husarova** Dokic/Petrova		2-6 6-3 7-6(7)	$1,224,000
Oct 7 Oct 13	Porsche Grand Prix Filderstadt, GER (HI)	**Clijsters** Hantuchova		4-6 6-3 6-4	**Davenport/Raymond** Shaughnessy/Suarez		6-2 6-4	$585,000
Oct 14 Oct 20	Eurotel Slovack Indoor Bratislava (HI)	**Matevzic** Benesova		6-0 6-1	**Matevzic/Nagyova** Dechy/Tu		6-2 6-2	$110,000
Oct 14 Oct 20	Swisscom Challenge Zurich (HI)	**Schnyder** Davenport		6-7(5) 7-6(8) 6-3	**Bovina/Henin** Dokic/Petrova		6-2 7-6(2)	$1,224,000
Oct 21 Oct 27	Generali Linz, Austria (HI)	**Henin** Stevenson		6-3 6-0	**Dokic/Petrova** Fujiwara/Sugiyama		6-3 6-2	$585,000
Oct 21 Oct 27	Seat Open Luxembourg (HI)	**Clijsters** Maleeva		6-1 6-2	**Clijsters/Husarova** Hrdlickova/Rittner		4-6 6-3 7-5	$170,000
Nov 4 Nov 10	Home Depot Chps Los Angeles (HI)	**Clijsters** S Williams		7-5 6-3	**Dementieva/Husarova** Black/Likhovtseva		4-6 6-4 6-3	$3,000,000
Nov 4 Nov 10	Volvo Open Pattaya City	**Widjaja** Cho		6-2 6-4	**Liggan/Voraceva** Krasnoroutskaya/Panova		7-5 7-6(7)	$110,000

Women's Rankings

As at December 31, 2002
British shown if in top 500

1	Serena Williams	USA	6080.00		56	Cara Black	ZIM	629.75
2	Venus Williams	USA	5140.00		57	Jill Craybas	USA	623.25
3	Jennifer Capriati	USA	3796.00		58	Emelie Loit	FRA	619.75
4	Kim Clijsters	BEL	3557.00		59	Henrieta Nagyova	SVK	602.50
5	Justine Henin-Hardenne	BEL	3218.00		60	Adriana Serra Zanetti	ITA	589.75
6	Amelie Mauresmo	FRA	3068.00		61	Emmanuelle Gagliardi	SUI	582.50
7	Monica Seles	USA	2952.00		62	Anca Barna	GER	575.75
8	Daniela Hantuchova	SVK	2667.75		63	Denisa Chladkova	CZE	572.50
9	Jelena Dokic	YUG	2506.00		64	Martina Sucha	SVK	562.25
10	Martina Hingis	SUI	2348.00		65	Virginia Ruano Pascual	ESP	562.00
11	Anastasia Myskina	RUS	1908.00		66	Barbara Rittner	GER	551.00
12	Lindsay Davenport	USA	1795.00		67	Els Callens	BEL	521.75
13	Chandra Rubin	USA	1752.00		68	Dinara Safina	RUS	520.25
14	Magdalena Maleeva	BUL	1701.00		69	Martina Muller	GER	515.50
15	Patty Schnyder	SUI	1644.00		70	Jelena Kostanic	CRO	513.00
16	Anna Pistolesi	ISR	1616.50		71	Tathiana Garbin	ITA	512.50
17	Silvia Farina Elia	ITA	1596.00		72	Angelique Widjaja	INA	511.00
18	Alexandra Stevenson	USA	1444.00		73	Meilen Tu	USA	510.75
19	Elena Dementieva	RUS	1426.00		74	Silvija Talaja	CRO	500.25
20	Nathalie Dechy	FRA	1295.00		75	Fabiola Zuluaga	COL	497.25
21	Amanda Coetzer	RSA	1220.00		76	Virginie Razzano	FRA	491.25
22	Eleni Danilidou	GRE	1192.75		77	Marissa Irvin	USA	485.50
23	Tatiana Panova	RUS	1177.00		78	Asa Svensson	SWE	480.00
24	Ai Sugiyama	JPN	1173.00		79	Cristina Torrens Valero	ESP	472.75
25	Anne Kremer	LUX	1151.75		80	Stephanie Foretz	FRA	469.25
26	Elena Bovina	RUS	1137.00		81	Angelika Roesch	GER	466.00
27	Paola Suarez	ARG	1091.00		82	Iveta Benesova	CZE	459.50
28	Tamarine Tanasugarn	THA	1056.00		83	Cho Yoon-Jeong	KOR	455.00
29	Lisa Raymond	USA	1048.75		84	Patricia Wartusch	AUT	451.25
30	Meghann Shaughnessy	USA	1046.00		85	Alina Jidkova	RUS	444.75
31	Clarisa Fernandez	ARG	1016.25		86	Sarah Taylor	USA	441.25
32	Iva Majoli	CRO	1007.00		87	Marta Marrero	ESP	436.50
33	Janette Husarova	SVK	978.00		88	Rossana Neffa De Los Rios	PAR	421.00
34	Conchita Martinez	ESP	967.00		89	Mariana Diaz Oliva	ARG	407.75
35	Anna Kournikova	RUS	960.00		90	Petra Mandula	HUN	407.50
36	Katarina Srebotnik	SLO	944.50		91	Greta Arn	GER	400.50
37	Daja Bedanova	CZE	939.00		92	Antonella Serra Zanetti	ITA	397.75
38	Sandrine Testud	FRA	901.00		93	Dally Randriantefy	MAD	389.25
39	Amy Frazier	USA	871.75		94	Alicia Molik	AUS	384.00
40	Barbara Schett	AUT	860.00		95	Flavia Pennetta	ITA	380.50
41	Francesca Schiavone	ITA	847.00		96	Shinobu Asagoe	JPN	377.75
42	Elena Likhovtseva	RUS	842.75		97	Marlene Weingartner	GER	377.00
43	Svetlana Kuznetsova	RUS	818.00		98	Conchita Martinez Granados	ESP	374.50
44	Marie-Gaianeh Mikaelian	SUI	782.75		99	Maureen Drake	CAN	373.75
45	Vera Zvonareva	RUS	748.25		100	Tatiana Poutchek	BLR	370.25
46	Rita Grande	ITA	725.75		*Aslo*			
47	Tina Pisnik	SLO	715.75		157	Elena Baltacha	GBR	201.25
48	Nicole Pratt	AUS	714.25		191	Julie Pullin	GBR	166.25
49	Laura Granville	USA	712.75		204	Lucie Ahl	GBR	153.00
50	Magui Serna	ESP	700.75		236	Anne Keothavong	GBR	120.25
51	Maja Matevzic	SLO	696.75		286	Jane O'Donoghue	GBR	77.50
52	Mary Pierce	FRA	679.00		327	Hannah Collin	GBR	58.25
53	Arantxa Sanchez Vicario	ESP	668.00		367	Helen Crook	GBR	48.25
54	Myriam Casanova	SUI	665.50		403	Lorna Woodroffe	GBR	39.00
55	Iroda Tulyaganova	UZB	641.00		415	Rachel Viollet	GBR	37.00
					439	Joanne Moore	GBR	32.25

Davis Cup

World Group Qualifying Round
NIA, Birmingham, Sep 20-22
Great Britain bt Thailand 3-2
*Tim Henman GBR bt Danai Udomchoke THA 4-6 6-3 6-2
6-2; Paradorn Srichaphan THA bt Martin Lee GBR
6-0 7-6(2) 6-2; Henman/Maclagan bt Srichaphan/Udomchoke
6-7(4) 6-4 7-5 6-2; Henman bt Srichaphan 6-3 6-2 6-3;
Udomchoke bt Arvind Parmar 6-3 6-1*

World Group

First Round
Feb 8-10
France bt Netherlands 3-2
Czech Rep bt Brazil 4-1
Spain bt Morocco 3-2
USA bt Slovak Republic 5-0
Russia bt Switzerland 3-2
Sweden bt Great Britain 3-2
*Tim Henman GBR bt Jonas Bjorkman SWE 6-4 7-5 4-6
7-5; Thomas Enqvist SWE bt Greg Rusedski GBR
7-6(3) 7-6(5) 6-2; Henman/Rusedski bt Bjorkman/Johansson
7-6(1) 2-6 6-7(4) 6-3 6-3; Enqvist bt Henman 6-4 6-2 6-4;
Johansson bt Rusedski 4-6 6-3
7-5 6-4*
Croatia bt Germany 4-1
Argentina bt Australia 5-0

Quarter-finals
Apr 5-7
France bt Czech Republic 3-2
USA bt Spain 3-1
Russia bt Sweden 4-1
Argentina bt Croatia 3-2

Semi-finals
Sep 20-22
France bt USA 3-2
Russia bt Argentina 3-2

FINAL
Paris, Nov 29-Dec 1
France bt Australia 3-2
*Safin RUS bt Mathieu FRA 6-4 3-6 6-1 6-4; Grosjean
FRA bt Kafelnikov RUS 7-6(3) 6-3 6-0; Escude/Santoro
FRA bt Kafelnikov/Safin 6-3 3-6 5-7 6-3 6-4; Safin bt
Grosjean 6-3 6-2 7-6(11); Youzhny RUS bt Mathieu 3-6
2-6 6-3 7-5 6-4*

Fed Cup

Eur-African Group IIA

Round Robin
Pretoria, Apr 9
Great Britain bt Malta 3-0
*Rachel Viollet GBR bt Sarah Wetz MLT 6-0 6-2
Lucie Ahl GBR bt Rosanne Dimech MLT 6-1 6-2
Baltacha/Pullin GBR bt Dimech/Wetz MLT 6-0 6-1*

Pretoria, Apr 13
Great Britain bt Norway 3-0
*Elena Baltacha GBR bt Anette Aksdal NOR 6-0 6-1
Julie Pullin GBR bt Ina Sartz NOR 6-3 6-0
Ahl/Viollet GBR bt Aksadal/Sartz NOR 6-0 6-0*

Quarter-final
Pretoria, Apr 13
Great Britain bt Lithuania 2-0
*Elena Baltacha GBR bt Lina Stanciute LTU
4-6 6-2 6-2
Lucie Ahl GBR bt Edita Liachovicuite LTU
6-3 6-1*

**Great Britain promoted to Euro/African Group IIA
for 2003**

World Group

1st Round
Austria bt USA 3-2
Croatia bt Czech Republic 3-2
Spain bt Hungary 4-1
Germany bt Russia 3-2
Slovak Republic bt Switzerland 3-2
France bt Argentina 3-2
Italy bt Sweden 5-0
Belgium bt Australia 3-1

Quarter-finals
Austria bt Croatia 4-1
Spain bt Germany 5-1
Slovak Republic bt France 4-1
Italy bt Belgium 4-1

Semi-finals
Spain bt Austria 3-2
Slovak Republic bt Italy 3-1

FINAL
Gran Canaria, Nov 2-3
Slovak Republic bt Spain 3-1
*Conchita Martinez ESP bt Janette Husarova SVK
6-4 7-6(6)
Daniela Hantchukova SVK bt Magui Serna ESP 6-2 6-1
Hantchukova SVK bt Martinez ESP 6-7(8) 7-5 6-4
Husarova SVK bt Arantxa Sanchez-Vicario ESP 6-0 6-2*

Triathlon

The world championships has never been a problem for the British men; Spencer Smith once and Simon Lessing four times bringing home the bacon. It's been very different for the British women who have been baconless since the championships began in 1989.

It was probably inevitable that the British duck was broken by an athlete who has spent rather more of her time in Australia than in the UK. Leanda Cave was born in Lincolnshire, represents Wales (her mother was born in Rhyl), but can pronounce Wagga Wagga properly, having spent 14 years down under.

Cave only returned to the UK fold in 2000, and the world championships at Edmonton a year later was her first major championships as a British triathlete. Although she was the first UK athlete home in Canada, Cave was only 17th, and notwithstanding progress through the World Cup season, was very much an outsider for the title in Cancun.

Cave was sixth leaving the water and only seven seconds adrift of the race leader Nicole Hackett, as good a swim as she had put together all year. Staying with the lead pack on the bike, Cave was content to settle in behind Barb Lindquist, who at one point held a lead of 30 seconds during the 10km run. But on the fourth and final lap, Cave quickly regained the ground on the tiring American, drawing away on the final stages to win by about 60 metres.

Nor did the British successes stop there, for Michelle Dillon, having taken the word crawl literally during the swimming stage, was absolutely brilliant on the run, posting the third fastest time of the day and taking the bronze medal behind Cave and Lindquist. Dillon, need we remind you, represented Australia in the 10,000m at the 1994 Commonwealth Games.

Which gives us a tidy link to the men's race and Britain's third medal, courtesy of Andrew Johns, who was born in Peterborough but bred in Australia (is there no end to it?). Since he moved the Britain in 1998, Johns has been the most consistent of triathletes, twice winning the European title (in 1998 and 2000), on the podium in 13 World Cup races, and three times placing in the top 10 at the world championships. This was his best result yet, Johns handling the difficult conditions (32 degrees) well to finish third to the Spaniard Ivan Rana.

In the hierarchy of sporting championships, the world duathlon has a fairly lowly ranking. We probably should not have highlighted that, for there was a British winner (and one who has never held an Australian passport). Tim Don, who won the world junior title in 1998, has found his progress in the senior ranks hampered by injuries, and if his duathlon victory in Alpharetta, a month before finishing 30th in the world championships, did not count for much, he did at least have the world number one, Greg Bennett, a second behind him.

World Championships

Cancun, Mexico, Nov 9-10
1.5km swim, 40km bike, 10km run

Elite Men

1	Ivan Rana	ESP	1:50:41
2	Peter Robertson	AUS	1:51:07
3	Andrew Johns	GBR	1:51:17
4	Greg Bennett	AUS	1:51:27
5	Vladimir Polikarpenko	UKR	1:51:37
17	Marc Jenkins	GBR	1:53:10
24	Richard Stannard	GBR	1:53:46
30	Tim Don	GBR	1:54:21

Elite Women

1	Leanda Cave	GBR	2:01:31
2	Barb Lindquist	USA	2:01:41
3	Michelle Dillon	GBR	2:02:11
4	Michellie Jones	GBR	2:02:25
5	Nicole Hackett	AUS	2:02:35
17	Andrea Whitcombe	GBR	2:04:50

Junior Men

1	Terenzo Bozzone	NZL	56:00
2	David Hauss	FRA	56:03
3	Tyler Butterfield	BER	56:04
7	Oliver Freeman	GBR	56:05

Junior women

1	Marion Lorblanchet	FRA	1:01:19
2	Wendy de Boer	NED	1:01:20
3	Elizabeth May	LUX	1:01:46
9	Helen Tucker	GBR	1:02:37

European Championships

Gyor, Hungary, July 6-7

Men

1	Ivan Rana ESP	1:47:46
2	Filip Ospaly CZE	1:47:48
3	Petzold Maik GER	1:47:50
6	Marc Jenkins GBR	1:48:24
7	Richard Stannard GBR	1:48:47
8	Paul Amey GBR	1:48:51
19	David Haines GBR	1:50:44
24	Stuart Hayes GBR	1:51:24
34	Richard Allen GBR	1:52:38

Women

1	Kathleen Smets BEL	1:59:06
2	Leanda Cave GBR	1:59:09
3	Christiane Pilz GER	1:59:25
10	Andrea Whitcombe GBR	2:00:25
11	Julie Dibens GBR	2:01:09
12	Michelle Dillon GBR	2:01:17
20	Anneliese Heard GBR	2:02:37
31	Jodie Swallow GBR	2:05:39

World Long Distance Championships

Nizza, Sep 22

Men

1	Cyrille Neveu	FRA	6:19:45
2	Torbjorn Sindballe	DEN	6:22:05
3	Rutger Beke	BEL	6:22:52

Women

1	Ines Estedt	GER	7:06:43
2	Kathleen Smet	BEL	7:11:55
3	Virginia Berasategui	ESP	7:14:18

World Rankings

As at Dec 5, 2002
British/Irish shown if in top 100

Men

1	Greg Bennett	AUS	5069
2	Ivan Rana	ESP	4699
3	Andrew Johns	GBR	4583
4	Chris Hill	AUS	4557
5	Peter Robertson	AUS	4193
6	Martin Krnavek	CZE	4059
7	Hamish Carter	NZL	3961
8	Bevan Docherty	NZL	3839
9	Dimitry Gaag	KAZ	3800
10	Vladimir Polikarpenko	UKR	3746
11	Craig Watson	NZL	3643
12	Miles Stewart	AUS	3583
13	Kris Gemmell	NZL	3528
14	Simon Whitfield	CAN	3370
15	Filip Ospaly	CZE	3283
16	Hunter Kemper	USA	3178
17	Shane Reed	NZL	3175
18	Marc Jenkins	GBR	2935
19	Stephane Poulat	FRA	2916
20	Rasmus Henning	DEN	2839
26	Tim Don	GBR	2420
46	Paul Amey	GBR	1749
47	Richard Stannard	GBR	1744
50	Simon Lessing	GBR	1663
88	Stuart Hayes	GBR	927

Women

1	Siri Lindley	USA	6112
2	Barbara Lindquist	USA	5778
3	Loretta Harrop	AUS	4806
4	Michellie Jones	AUS	4651
5	Kathleen Smet	BEL	4552
6	Nicole Hackett	AUS	4425
7	Leanda Cave	GBR	4053
8	Laura Reback	USA	3983
9	Jill Savege	CAN	3934
10	Sheila Taormina	USA	3865
11	Carol Montgomery	CAN	3700
12	Michelle Dillon	GBR	3619
13	Carla Moreno	BRA	3596
14	Liz Blatchford	AUS	3442
15	Sandra Soldan	BRA	3260
16	Sharon Donnelly	CAN	3249
17	Machiko Nakanishi	JPN	3112
18	Christiane Pilz	GER	3053
19	Anja Dittmer	GER	2946
20	Lenka Radova	CZE	2932
22	Andrea Whitcombe	GBR	2433
46	Stephanie Forrester	GBR	1535
58	Jessica Harrison	GBR	1290
76	Julie Dibens	GBR	973
85	Annie Emmerson	GBR	863

World Cup

All British athletes who completed an event are listed

Round 1

Geelong, Australia, April 14

Men

1	Peter Robertson	AUS	1:51:33.8
2	Courtney Atkinson	AUS	1:51:58.4
3	Hamish Carter	NZL	1:52:01.1

Women

1	Loretta Harrop	AUS	2:01:35.5
2	Barb Lindquist	USA	2:02:09.8
3	Siri Lindley	USA	2:03:05.9
7	Leanda Cave	GBR	2:04:55.7

Round 2

St Petersburg, Florida, USA, Apr 27

Men

1	Sylvain Dodet	FRA	1:53:35
2	Shane Reed	NZL	1:53:48
3	Greg Bennett	AUS	1:53:59
15	Simon Lessing	GBR	1:54:58
18	Richard Allen	GBR	1:55:17
35	David Haines	GBR	1:57:48

Women

1	Michellie Jones	AUS	2:01:57
2	Sheila Toarmina	USA	2:02:40
3	Barbara Lindquist	USA	2:02:59
31	Jessica Harrison	GBR	2:11:43

Round 3

Ishigaki, Japan, May 19

Men

1	Peter Robertson	AUS	1:49:23
2	Ivan Rana	ESP	1:49:45
3	Kris Gemmell	NZL	1:49:55

Women

1	Barbara Lindquist	USA	1:56:53
2	Lorette Harrop	AUS	1:57:29
3	Nicole Hackett	AUS	1:58:29

Round 4

Gamagori, Japan, June 9

Men

1	Greg Bennett	AUS	1:49:30
2	Bevan Docherty	NZL	1:50:00
3	Chris Hill	AUS	1:50:13

Women

1	Loretta Harrop	AUS	1:57:55
2	Nicole Hackett	AUS	1:58:35
3	Barbara Lindquist	USA	1:58:40

Round 5

Edmonton, July 14

Men

1	Simon Whitfield	CAN	1:49.07
2	Greg Bennett	AUS	1:49.18
3	Hamish Carter	NZL	1:49.24
4	Simon Lessing	GBR	1:49:44
5	Paul Amey	GBR	1:49:52

Women

1	Siri Lindley	USA	2:01.33
2	Barbara Lindquist	USA	2:01.42
3	Sheila Taormina	USA	2:01.55

Round 6

Corner Brook, Newfoundland, July 21

Men

1	Simon Whitfield	CAN	1:53:35
2	Hunter Kemper	USA	1:53:39
3	Bevan Docherty	NZL	1:53:58

Women

1	Siri Lindley	USA	2:05:43
2	Jill Savage	CAN	2:06:13
3	Kathleen Smet	BEL	2:06:32

Round 7

Tiszaujvaros, Hungary, July 28

Men

1	Craig Walton	AUS	1:45:03
2	Vladimir Polikarpenko	UKR	1:45:32
3	Martin Krnavek	CZE	1:45:51

Women

1	Siri Lindley	USA	1:57:05
2	Lenka Radova	CZE	1:57:16
3	Tracy Hargreaves-Looze	AUS	1:57:24
14	Jessica Harrison	GBR	1:58:32

Round 8

Lausanne, Aug 31

Men

1	Filip Ospaly	CZE	1:52:06
2	Greg Bennett	AUS	1:52:12
3	Andrew Johns	GBR	1:52:40
9	Tim Don	GBR	1:53:18
16	Marc Jenkins	GBR	1:53:34
20	Richard Stannard	GBR	1:53:45
23	Stuart Hayes	GBR	1:54:12

Women

1	Siri Lindley	USA	2:02:42
2	Jill Savege	CAN	2:02:57
3	Kathleen Smet	BEL	2:03:08
4	Leanda Cave	GBR	2:04:08
5	Andrea Whitcombe	GBR	2:04:31
7	Michelle Dillon	GBR	2:05:11
10	Julie Dibens	GBR	2:05:35
14	Jessica Harrison	GBR	2:06:08
25	Tanya Allen	GBR	2:07:50
29	Annie Emmerson	GBR	2:08:51

Round 9

Hamburg, Sep 7

Men

1	Greg Bennett	AUS	1:47:04
2	Andrew Johns	GBR	1:47:33
3	Cedric Deanaz	FRA	1:47:35
8	Marc Jenkins	GBR	1:48:12
12	Tim Don	GBR	1:48:29

Women

1	Jill Savege	CAN	1:57:54
2	Siri Lindley	USA	1:57:56
3	Carla Moreno	BRA	1:58:05
4	Michelle Dillon	GBR	1:58:39
5	Leanda Cave	GBR	1:59:11

Round 10
Nizza, Sep 21
Men

1	Miles Stewart	AUS	1:48:57
2	Filip Ospaly	CZE	1:49:01
3	Vladimir Polikarpenko	UKR	1:49:13
4	Tim Don	GBR	1:49:23
10	Marc Jenkins	GBR	1:50:02
12	Richard Stannard	GBR	1:50:07
13	Stuart Hayes	GBR	1:50:12
36	Richard Allen	GBR	1:52:15

Women

1	Sheila Taormina	USA	2:02:04
2	Carla Moreno	BRA	2:02:30
3	Michelle Dillon	GBR	2:02:49
6	Andrea Whitcombe	GBR	2:03:18
7	Leanda Cave	GBR	2:03:33
13	Julie Dibens	GBR	2:04:35
18	Jessica Harrison	GBR	2:05:00

Round 11
Makuhari, Japan, Oct 6
Men

1	Miles Stewart	GBR	1:48:23
2	Hamish Carter	NZL	1:48:27
3	Juraci Moreira	BRA	1:48:29

Women

1	Jill Savege	CAN	2:01:32
2	Nicole Hackett	AUS	2:01:52
3	Liz Blatchford	AUS	2:02:20

Round 12
Funchal, Madeira, Oct 12
Men

1	Ivan Rana	ESP	1:46:11
2	Marc Jenkins	GBR	1:46:14
3	Jose Merchan	ESP	1:46:18
18	Richard Stannard	GBR	1:47:50
34	Andrew Johns	GBR	1:50:00

Women

1	Andrea Whitcombe	GBR	1:59:16
2	Lenka Radova	CZE	1:59:34
3	Marian Lorblanchet	FRA	1:59:43
10	Jessica Harrison	GBR	2:01:35

The Royal Windsor Triathlon
Windsor, June 16
Men

1	Richard Allen	GBR	1:50:16
2	Spencer Smith	GBR	1:51:09
3	Andrew Johns	GBR	1:53:41

Women

1	Heather Williams	GBR	2:11:26
2	Andrea Whitcombe	GBR	2:12:19
3	Kristine Semple	GBR	2:20:32

The London Triathlon
Docklands, Aug 11
Men

1	Simon Lessing	GBR	1:46:39
2	Hamish Carter	NZL	1:47:27
3	Stuart Hayes	GBR	1:47:43

Women

1	Michelle Dillon	GBR	2:03:36
2	Annie Emmerson	GBR	2:03:59
3	Andrea Whitcombe	GBR	2:04:59

Hawaii Ironman
Kona, Hawaii, Oct 20
2.4m swim, 112m bike, 26.2m run
Men

1	Tim De Boom	U.S	8:29:56
2	Peter Reid	CAN	8:33:06
3	Cameron Brown	NZL	8:35:34

Women

1	Natascha Badmann	SUI	9:07:54
2	Nina Kraft	GER	9:14:24
3	Lori Bowden	CAN	9:22:27

World Duathlon Championships
Alpharetta, Georgia, USA, Oct 19-20
10km run, 40km cycle, 5km run
Men

1	Tim Don	GBR	1:45:28
2	Greg Bennett	AUS	1:45:29
3	Luca Barzaghi	ITA	1:45:34

Women

1	Corine Raux	FRA	1:57:36
2	Erika Csomor	HUN	1:57:50
3	Edwidge Pitel	FRA	1:58:02
4	Annie Emerson	GBR	1:58:21
5	Michelle Dillon	GBR	1:58:30
8	Andrea Whitcombe	GBR	1:59:36

World Aquathon Championships
Cancun, Mexico, Nov 3
2.5km run - 750m swim - 2.5km run
Men

1	Kris Gemmell	NZL	
2	Andrey Glushchenko	UKR	
3	Filip Ospaly	CZE	

Women

1	Sandra Soldan	BRA	
2	Jill Savege	CAN	
3	Lenka Radova	CZE	

No times available for this event

Volleyball

World Indoor Championships, Men

Buenos Aires, Cordoba, Sante Fe & Salta, Sep 28-Oct 12

First Round
Pool A
Argentina bt Australia 3-1; Portugal bt China 3-1;
Portugal bt Australia 3-1; Argentina bt China 3-1;
China bt Australia 3-1; Argentina bt Portugal 3-1

Table		Matches	Sets		Points	
	Pts	W-L	W-L	Ratio	W-L	Ratio
1 **Argentina**	6	3-0	9-3	3.000	312-289	1.080
2 **Portugal**	5	2-1	7-5	1.400	286-267	1.071
3 **China**	4	1-2	5-7	0.714	270-282	0.957
4 **Australia**	3	0-3	3-9	0.333	282-312	0.904

Pool B
Italy bt Croatia 3-0; Poland bt Canada 3-1;
Poland bt Italy 3-2; Canada bt Croatia 3-1;
Italy bt Canada 3-0; Poland bt Croatia 3-0

Table						
1 **Poland**	6	3-0	9-3	3.000	282-254	1.110
2 **Italy**	5	2-1	8-3	2.667	255-228	1.118
3 **Canada**	4	1-2	4-7	0.571	251-261	0.962
4 **Croatia**	3	0-3	1-9	0.111	202-247	0.818

Pool C
France bt Tunisia 3-1; Bulgaria bt Russia 3-0;
France bt Russia 3-1; Bulgaria bt Tunisia 3-1;
France bt Bulgaria 3-2; Russia bt Tunisia 3-0

Table						
1 **France**	6	3-0	9-4	2.250	289-265	1.091
2 **Bulgaria**	5	2-1	8-4	2.000	292-257	1.136
3 **Russia**	4	1-2	4-6	0.667	222-221	1.005
4 **Tunisia**	3	0-3	2-9	0.222	214-274	0.781

Pool D
Japan bt Kazakhstan 3-1; Yugoslavia bt Spain 3-1;
Spain bt Japan 3-2; Yugoslavia bt Kazakhstan 3-0;
Yugoslavia bt Japan 3-0; Spain bt Kazakhstan 3-1

Table						
1 **Yugoslavia**	6	3-0	9-1	9.000	246-188	1.309
2 **Spain**	5	2-1	7-6	1.167	293-287	1.021
3 **Japan**	4	1-2	5-7	0.714	269-274	0.982
4 **Kazakhstan**	3	0-3	2-9	0.222	218-277	0.787

Pool E
Brazil bt Venezuela 3-0; USA bt Egypt 3-1;
USA bt Brazil 3-2; Venezuela bt Egypt 3-0;
Brazil bt Egypt 3-0; USA bt Venezuela 3-0

Table						
1 **USA**	6	3-0	9-3	3.000	300-277	1.083
2 **Brazil**	5	2-1	8-3	2.667	268-230	1.165
3 **Venezuela**	4	1-2	3-6	0.500	205-215	0.953
4 **Egypt**	3	0-3	1-9	0.111	197-248	0.794

Pool F
Netherlands bt Greece 3-0; Cuba bt Czech Rep 3-1;
Greece bt Cuba 3-0; Netherlands bt Czech Rep 3-2;
Netherlands bt Cuba 3-1; Czech Rep bt Greece 3-2

Table						
1 **Netherlands**	6	3-0	9-3	3.000	273-240	1.137
2 **Greece**	4	1-2	5-6	0.833	226-246	0.919
3 **Czech Rep**	4	1-2	6-8	0.750	311-309	1.006
4 **Cuba**	4	1-2	4-7	0.571	245-260	0.942

Second Round
Pool G
Italy bt Bulgaria 3-2; Argentina bt Japan 3-2;
Italy bt Japan 3-1; Argentina bt Bulgaria 3-1;
Japan bt Bulgaria 3-2; Argentina bt Italy 3-1

Table						
1 **Argentina**	6	3-0	9-4	2.250	308-271	1.137
2 **Italy**	5	2-1	7-6	1.167	305-292	1.045
3 **Japan**	4	1-2	6-8	0.750	301-320	0.941
4 **Bulgaria**	3	0-3	5-9	0.556	296-327	0.905

Pool H
Portugal bt Spain 3-2; Russia bt Poland 3-2;
Russia bt Spain 3-2; Portugal bt Poland 3-1;
Russia bt Portugal 3-0; Poland bt Spain 3-1

Table						
1 **Russia**	6	3-0	9-4	2.250	299-263	1.137
2 **Portugal**	5	2-1	6-6	1.000	272-278	0.978
3 **Poland**	4	1-2	6-7	0.857	299-292	1.024
4 **Spain**	3	0-3	5-9	0.556	284-321	0.885

Pool J
Brazil bt Czech Rep 3-0; France bt Netherlands 3-0;
Brazil bt France 3-0; Netherlands bt Czech Rep 3-2;
Brazil bt Netherlands 3-0; France bt Czech Rep 3-1

Table						
1 **Brazil**	6	3-0	9-0	MAX	225-181	1.243
2 **France**	5	2-1	6-4	1.500	238-216	1.102
3 **Netherlands**	4	1-2	3-8	0.375	230-257	0.895
4 **Czech Rep**	3	0-3	3-9	0.333	249-288	0.865

Pool K
Yugoslavia bt Greece 3-0; USA bt China 3-0;
Yugoslavia bt China 3-0; Greece bt USA 3-2;
Greece bt China 3-2; Yugoslavia bt USA 3-1

Table						
1 **Yugoslavia**	6	3-0	9-1	9.000	246-210	1.171
2 **Greece**	5	2-1	6-6	1.000	255-253	1.008
3 **USA**	4	1-2	6-6	1.000	271-268	1.011
4 **China**	3	0-3	1-9	0.111	208-249	0.835

Quarter-finals
France bt Australia 3-1
Russia bt Greece 3-0
Brazil bt Italy 3-2
Yugoslavia bt Portugal 3-0

5th-8th Place Play-offs
Argentina bt Greece 3-0
Italy bt Portugal

7th/8th Place Play-off
Greece bt Portugal 3-2

5th/6th Place Play-off
Italy bt Argentina 3-2

Semi-finals
Russia bt France 3-2
Brazil bt Yugoslavia 3-1
Bronze Medal Match
France bt Yugoslavia 3-0

FINAL
Brazil bt Russia 3-2

Final Standings: 1 Brazil; 2 Russia; 3 France;
4 Yugoslavia; 5 Italy; 6 Argentina; 7 Greece; 8 Portugal;
9-12 Japan, Netherlands, Poland, USA; 13-16 Bulgaria,
China, Czech Rep, Spain; 17-18 Canada, Venezuela;
19-24 Australia, Croatia, Cuba, Egypt, Tunisia,
Kazakhstan

World Indoor Championships, Women

Berlin, Stuttgart, Bremen, Liepzig, Dresden, Riesa, Schwerin, Munster, Aug 30-Sep 15

First Round

Pool A
Italy bt Japan 3-0; Germany bt Czech Rep 3-2;
Bulgaria bt Mexico 3-0; Germany bt Japan 3-1;
Italy bt Mexico 3-0; Bulgaria bt Czech Rep 3-0;
Japan bt Mexico 3-0; Bulgaria bt Germany 3-0;
Italy bt Czech Rep 3-0; Japan bt Bulgaria 3-1;
Czech Rep bt Mexico 3-2; Italy bt Germany 3-0;
Czech Rep bt Japan 3-1; Italy bt Bulgaria 3-0;
Germany bt Mexico 3-0

Table

		Pts	W-L	W-L	Ratio		W-L	Ratio
1	Italy	10	5-0	15-0	MAX		382-288	1.326
2	Bulgaria	8	3-2	10-6	1.667		368-339	1.086
3	Germany	8	3-2	9-9	1.000		429-403	1.065
4	Japan	7	2-3	8-10	0.800		402-401	1.002
5	Czech Rep	7	2-3	8-12	0.667		435-464	0.938
6	Mexico	5	0-5	2-15	0.133		294-415	0.708

Pool B
Netherlands bt Romania 3-1; Canada bt Egypt 3-0;
Korea bt Cuba 3-2; Netherlands bt Egypt 3-0;
Cuba bt Canada 3-2; Korea bt Romania 3-1;
Cuba bt Netherlands 3-0; Korea bt Canada 3-0;
Romania bt Egypt 3-0; Korea bt Netherlands 3-0;
Cuba bt Egypt 3-0; Romania bt Canada 3-0;
Korea bt Egypt 3-0; Cuba bt Romania 3-0;
Netherlands bt Canada 3-0

Table

1	Korea	10	5-0	15-3	5.000	425-334	1.272
2	Cuba	9	4-1	14-5	2.800	436-356	1.225
3	Netherlands	8	3-2	9-7	1.286	373-336	1.110
4	Romania	7	2-3	8-9	0.889	383-376	1.019
5	Canada	6	1-4	5-12	0.417	339-377	0.899
6	Egypt	5	0-5	0-15	-	198-375	0.528

Pool C
Kenya bt Puerto Rico 3-1; USA bt Argentina 3-0;
Russia bt Dominican Rep 3-1; Argentina bt Kenya 3-0;
USA bt Russia 3-2; Puerto Rico bt Dominican Rep 3-0;
Puerto Rico bt Argentina 3-2; USA bt Dominican Rep 3-0;
Russia bt Kenya 3-0; Dominican Rep bt Kenya 3-0;
Russia bt Argentina 3-0; USA bt Puerto Rico 3-0;
USA bt Kenya 3-0; Russia bt Puerto Rico 3-0;
Dominican Rep bt Argentina 3-0

Table

1	USA	10	5-0	15-2	7.500	408-334	1.222
2	Russia	9	4-1	14-4	3.500	424-296	1.432
3	Puerto Rico	8	3-2	9-9	1.000	364-404	0.901
4	Dominican	7	2-3	7-9	0.778	350-369	0.949
5	Argentina	6	1-4	5-12	0.417	348-387	0.899
6	Kenya	5	0-5	1-15	0.067	290-394	0.736

Pool D
Brazil bt Poland 3-0; China bt Australia 3-0;
Greece bt Thailand 3-0; China bt Brazil 3-1;
Poland bt Thailand 3-0; Greece bt Australia 3-1;
China bt Thailand 3-1; Brazil bt Australia 3-0;
Greece bt Poland 3-2; Brazil bt Greece 3-0;
Thailand bt Australia 3-1; China bt Poland 3-0;
Brazil bt Thailand 3-0; Greece bt China 3-0;
Poland bt Australia 3-0

Table

1	Brazil	9	4-1	13-3	4.333	389-320	1.216
2	China	9	4-1	12-5	2.400	407-336	1.211
3	Greece	9	4-1	12-6	2.000	412-400	1.030
4	Poland	7	2-3	8-9	0.889	383-388	0.987
5	Thailand	6	1-4	4-13	0.308	343-397	0.864
6	Australia	5	0-5	2-15	0.133	324-417	0.777

Second Round

Pool E
Cuba bt Greece 3-1; Russia bt Italy 3-2;
Russia bt Greece 3-0; Cuba bt Italy 3-1;
Italy bt Greece 3-0; Russia bt Cuba 3-1

Table

1	Russia	6	3-0	9-3	3.000	285-239	1.192
2	Cuba	5	2-1	7-5	1.400	270-277	0.975
3	Italy	4	1-2	6-6	1.000	275-263	1.046
4	Greece	3	0-3	1-9	0.111	196-247	0.794

Pool F
China bt Bulgaria 3-0; Korea bt Puerto Rico 3-0;
China bt Puerto Rico 3-0; Bulgaria bt Korea 3-1;
Bulgaria bt Puerto Rico 3-0; Korea bt China 3-0

Table

1	Korea	5	2-1	7-3	2.333	231-206	1.121
2	China	5	2-1	6-3	2.000	216-172	1.256
3	Bulgaria	5	2-1	6-4	1.500	228-204	1.118
4	Puerto Rico	3	0-3	0-9	-	132-225	0.587

Pool G
USA bt Brazil 3-0; Netherlands bt Germany 3-1;
Brazil bt Germany 3-0; USA bt Netherlands 3-2;
Brazil bt Netherlands 3-1; USA bt Germany 3-0

Table

1	**USA**	6	3-0	9-2	4.500	260-231	1.126
2	**Brazil**	5	2-1	6-4	1.500	233-221	1.054
3	**Netherlands**	4	1-2	6-7	0.857	271-288	0.941
4	**Germany**	3	0-3	1-9	0.111	227-251	0.904

Final Round
Quarter-finals
Russia bt Bulgaria 3-0
Italy bt Korea 3-0
USA bt Cuba 3-0
China bt Brazil 3-2

5th-8th Place Play-offs
Cuba bt Bulgaria 3-2
Korea bt Brazil 3-2

7th/8th Place Play-off
Brazil bt Bulgaria 3-0

5th/6th Place Play-off
Cuba bt Korea 3-2

Semi-finals
USA bt Russia 3-2
Italy bt China 3-1

Bronze Medal Match
Russia bt China 3-1

FINAL
Italy bt USA 3-2

Final Standings: 1 Italy; 2 USA; 3 Russia; 4 China; 5 Cuba; 6 Korea; 7 Brazil; 8 Bulgaria; 9 Netherlands; 10-12 Germany, Greece, Puerto Rico; 13-16 Dominican Rep; Japan, Poland, Romania; 17-20 Argentina, Canada, Czech Rep, Thailand; 21-24 Australia, Egypt, Kenya, Mexico

Beach Volleyball

World Tour Ranking
End of season

Men
1	Baracetti/Conde	ARG	2030
2	Araujo/Benjamin	BRA	1964
3	Ricardo/Loiola	BRA	1820
4	Laciga/Laciga	SUI	1700
5	Child/Heese	CAN	1540
6	Wong/Metzger	USA	1510
7	Emanuel/Tande	BRA	1500
8	Kjemperud/Hoidalen	NOR	1320
9	Heuscher/Kobel	SUI	1194
10	Para/Harley	BRA	1148

Women
1	Walsh/May	USA	3070
2	Behar/Shelda	BRA	2740
3	Pottharst/Cook	AUS	2370
4	McPeak/Youngs	USA	2310
5	Ana Paula/Minello	BRA	2280
6	Perrotta/Gattelli	ITA	1640
7	Barros/Pires	BRA	1630
8	Alexandra/Monica	BRA	1400
9	Leenstra/Kadijk	MED	1390
10	Pohl/Rau	GER	1200

Weightlifting

World Championships
Warsaw, Nov 23-26
The scores shown in kgs are for snatch/clean & jerk, followed by the total. Where totals are equal, higher ranking is given to the lifter with the lighter body weight

Men

56kg

1 Wu Meijin CHN		287.5
2 Yang Chin Yi CHN		277.5
3 Adrian Jigau ROM		277.5

Incomplete results for class

62kg

1 Im Yong-Su KOR	140.0/175.0	315.0
2 Le Maosheng CHN	140.0/170.0	310.0
3 Stefan Georgiev BUL	137.5/172.5	310.0

69kg

1 Zhang Guozheng CHN	155.0/192.5	347.5
2 Chen Chufu CHN	157.5/187.5	345.0
3 Sbai Youssef TUN	152.5/182.5	335.0
23 Wayne Healey IRL	100.0/135.0	235.0

77kg

1 Georgi Markov BUL	170.0/200.0	370.0
2 Oleg Perepetchonov RUS	165.0/202.5	367.5
3 Barkah Hossein IRI	165.0/200.0	365.0

85kg

1 Zlatan Vanev BUL	167.5/217.5	385.0
2 George Asanidze GEO	177.5/207.5	385.0
3 Ruslan Novikov BLR	172.5/207.5	380.0

94kg

1 Nizami Pashaev AZE	177.5/215.0	392.5
2 Milen Dobrev BUL	175.0/212.5	387.5
3 Oliver Caruso GER	180.0/207.5	387.5
13 Paul Supple GBR	152.5/182.5	335.0

105kg

1 Denis Gotfrid UKR	190.0/230.0	420.0
2 Alan Tsagaev BUL	185.0/232.5	417.5
3 Vladimir Smortchkov RUS	197.5/220.0	417.5

+105kg

1 Hossein Rezazedah IRI	210.0/262.5	472.5
2 Damian Damianov BUL	205.0/245.0	450.0
3 Artem Udachin UKR	200.0/240.0	440.0

Women

48kg

1 Wang Mingjuan CHN	92.5/115.0	207.5
2 Nurcan Taylor TUR	87.5/105.0	192.5
3 I Dragneva-Rifatova BUL	82.5/100.0	182.5

53kg

1 Ri Song-Hui KOR	97.5/127.5	225.0
2 Li Xuejiu CHN	95.0/127.5	222.5
3 Udomporn Polsak THA	95.0/120.0	215.0
15 Joanne Calvino GBR	60.0/77.5	137.5

58kg

1 Song Zhijuan CHN	100.0/120.0	230.0
2 Wandee Kameaim THA		212.5
3 Chariklia Kastritsi GRE		210.0
5 Michaela Breeze GBR		205.0

Incomplete results for class

63kg

1 Liu Xia CHN	107.5/135.0	242.5
2 Anastasia Tsakiri GRE	105.0/135.0	240.0
3 Gergana Kirilova BUL	102.5/122.5	225.0

69kg

1 Pawina Thongsuk	12.5/147.5	260.0
2 Valentina Popova RUS	115.0/142.5	257.5
3 Nahla Mohamed EGY	110.0/135.0	245.0

75kg

1 Svetlana Haribova RUS	117.5/145.0	262.5
2 Sun Ruiping CHN	115.0/145.0	260.0
3 Ludmila Arefieva RUS	112.5/125.0	237.5

+75kg

1 Agata Wrobel POL	125.0/162.5	287.5
2 Albina Khomich RUS	132.5/150.0	282.5
3 Tang Gonghong CHN	117.5/160.0	277.5

European Championships

Antalya, Turkey, April 22-28

<table>
<tr><td colspan="4">

Men

56kg
</td></tr>
<tr><td>1</td><td>Vitali Derbenev BLR</td><td>125.0/152.5</td><td>277.5</td></tr>
<tr><td>2</td><td>Sedat Artune TUR</td><td>122.5/145.0</td><td>267.5</td></tr>
<tr><td>3</td><td>Igor Grabueca MLD</td><td>122.5/145.0</td><td>267.5</td></tr>
</table>

Men

56kg
1	Vitali Derbenev BLR	125.0/152.5	277.5
2	Sedat Artune TUR	122.5/145.0	267.5
3	Igor Grabueca MLD	122.5/145.0	267.5

62kg
1	Leonidas Sabanis GRE	140.0/165.0	305.0
2	Stefan Georgiev BUL	130.0/167.5	297.5
3	Olexander Lykhvald UKR	132.5/160.0	292.5
	John Lubin GBR	107.5/-	-

69kg
1	Galabin Boevski BUL	160.0/190.0	350.0
2	Giorgios Tzelilis GRE	150.0/182.5	332.5
3	Reyham Arabacioglu TUR	150.0/180.0	330.0

77kg
1	Georgi Markov BUL	167.5/200.0	367.5
2	Vasil Vanev BUL	155.0/207.5	362.5
3	Mehmet Yilmaz TUR	165.0/195.0	360.0
12	Shaun Trebilcock GBR	120.0/155.0.	275.0

85kg
1	George Asanidze GEO	175.0/205.0	380.0
2	Mariusz Rytkowski POL	172.5/207.5	380.0
3	Aslanbek Ediev RUS	165.0/202.5	367.5

94kg
1	Alexei Petrov RUS	185.0/215.0	400.0
2	Milen Dobrev BUL	182.5/215.0	397.5
3	Nizami Pashaev AZE	180.0/215.0	395.0
11	Peter May GBR	160.0/187.5	347.5

105kg
1	Alan Konstantinovich BUL	185.0/235.0	420.0
2	Denis Gotfrid UKR	187.5/230.0	417.5
3	Bunyami Sudas TUR	185.0/232.5	417.5
15	Delroy McQueen GBR	155.0/205.0	360.0
16	Cheema Gurbinder GBR	155.0/190.0	345.0

+105kg
1	Ronny Weller GER	202.5/247.5	450.0
2	Pavel Najdek POL	185.0/245.0	430.0
3	Alexei Kolokoltsev UKR	187.5/240.0	427.5
14	Giles Greenwood GBR	165.0/197.5	362.5

Women

48kg
1	Elena Zinovieva UKR	80.0/97.5	177.5
2	Svetlana Ulyanova RUS	77.5/95.0	172.5
3	Nurcan Taylan TUR	77.5/90.0	167.5

53kg
1	Aylin Dasdelen TUR	92.5/112.5	205.0
2	Emine Bilgin TUR	80.0/105.0	185.0
3	Aniko Ajkai HUN	75.0/105.0	180.0
8	Kirstie Law GBR	65.0/80.0	145.0

58kg
1	A Klejnovska POL	90.0/123.0	212.5
2	Neli Simova BUL	87.5/117.5	205.0
3	Henrietta Raki HUN	92.5/112.5	205.0
6	Michaela Breeze GBR	85.0/107.5	192.5

63kg
1	Natalia Skakun UKR	105.0/135.0	240.0
2	Anastasia Tsakiri GRE	105.0/135.0	240.0
3	Gergana Kirilova BUL	97.5/120.0	217.5
9	Annette Campbell GBR	80.0/100.0	180.0

69kg
1	Valentina Popova RUS	112.5/140.0	252.5
2	Svetlana Habirova RUS	107.5/140.0	247.5
3	Maria Tatsi GRE	90.0/122.5	212.5
12	Sharon Oakley GBR	80.0/100.0	180.0
13	Juliana Auguste GBR	72.5/90.0	162.5

75kg
1	Sule Sahbaz TUR	112.5/132.5	245.0
2	Aysel Ozgur TUR	110.0/130.0	240.0
3	Ilona Danko HUN	107.5/127.5	235.0
9	Rachel Clark GBR	85.0/100.0	185.0
10	Kerri Ann Wotenick GBR	72.5/87.5	160.0

+75kg
1	Agata Wrobel POL	127.5/155.0	282.5
2	Viktoria Varga HUN	120.0/155.0	275.0
3	Albina Khomich RUS	125.0/145.0	270.0

W r e s t l i n g

Freestyle

World Championships, Men
Tehran, Sep 5-7

55kg
1 Rene Montero Rosales   CUB
2 Namik Abdellaev   AZE
3 Alexander Zakharuk   UKR

60kg
1 Aram Markaryan   ARM
2 Purevbaatar Oyunbuleg   MGL
3 Mohammad Talee   IRI

66kg
1 Elbrus Tedeev   UKR
2 Ali Reza Dabir   IRI
3 Zaur Botaev   RUS

74kg
1 Mehdi Hajizadeh Jouibari   IRI
2 Magomed Isagaschiev   RUS
3 Volodymyr Syrotyn   UKR
21 Nat Ackerman   GBR

84kg
1 Adam Saitev   RUS
2 Yoel Romero Palacio   CUB
3 Majid Khodaee   IRI

96kg
1 Eldari Kurtanidze   GEO
2 Alireza Heydari   IRI
3 Vadim Tasoev   UKR

120kg
1 David Musulbes   RUS
2 Alexis Rodriguez Valera   CUB
3 Aydin Polatci   TUR

European Championships, Men
Baku, May 1-4

55kg
1 Nazim Alidyanov   AZE
2 Ghenadi Tulbea   MDA
3 Alexander Kontoev   RUS

60kg
1 Arif Kama   TUR
2 Vasyl Fedorishin   UKR
3 Arif Abdullaev   AZE
8 Paul Stridgeon   GBR

66kg
1 Zaur Botaev   RUS
2 Elman Asgarov   AZE
3 Nicolai Paslar   BUL

74kg
1 Arpad Ritter   HUN
2 Mourad Gaidarov   BLR
3 Magomed Isagaschiev   RUS
19 Nat Ackerman   GBR

84kg
1 Sazhid Sazhidov   RUS
2 Beibulat Musaev   BLR
3 Revaz Mindorashvili   GEO

96kg
1 K Kuramagomedov   RUS
2 Eldari Kurtanidze   GEO
3 Fatih Cakiroglu   TUR
5 Johannes Roussow   GBR

120kg
1 David Musulbes   RUS
2 David Otiasvili   GEO
3 Zekeriya Gueclue   TUR

World Cup, Men
Spokane, USA, Apr 6-7

55kg: Stephen Abas USA
60kg: Guivi Sissaouri CAN
66kg: Bae Jin-Kuk KOR
74kg: Joe Williams USA
84kg: Khadshimourad Gatsalov RUS
97kg: Georgi Gogchelidze RUS
120kg: Kerry McCoy USA

World Championships, Women
Chalkida, Greece, Nov 2-3

48kg
1 Brigitte Wagner   GER
2 Inga Karamtshakova   RUS
3 Ida Hellstrom   SWE

51kg
1 Sofia Poubouridou   GRE
2 Chiharu Icho   JPN
3 Natalya Golts   RUS

55kg
1 Saori Yoshida   JPN
2 Tina George-Wilson   USA
3 Ida-Theres Karlsson   SWE

59kg
1 Alena Kartakhova   RUS
2 Lotta Andersson   SWE
3 Mabel Fonseca Ramirez   CUB

63kg
1 Kaori Icho   JPN
2 Sara Eriksson   SWE
3 Lene Aanes   NOR

67kg
1 Katerina Burmistrova   UKR
2 Lise Golliot-Legrand   FRA
3 Kristie Marano   USA

72kg
1 Kyoko Hamaguchi   JPN
2 Xu Wang   CHN
3 Edyta Witkowski   POL

European Championships, Women
Seinaejoki, Finland, Apr 11-14

48kg
1 Inga Karamtshakova   RUS
2 Brigitte Wagner   GER
3 A Berthenet-Hidalgo   FRA

51kg
1 Olga Smirnova   RUS
2 Ida Hellstroem   SWE
3 Innessa Rebar   UKR

55kg
1 Tatiana azereva   UKR
2 Ida-Theres Karlsson   SWE
3 Gudrun Hoeie   NOR

59kg
1 Sara Eriksson   SWE
2 Monika Michalik   POL
3 Christina Oertli   GER

63kg
1 Malgorzata Bassa   POL
2 Lene Aanes   NOR
3 Daria Nazarova   RUS

67kg
1 Lise Golliot-Legrand   FRA
2 Anita Schaetzle   GER
3 Anna Shamova   RUS

72kg
1 Svetlana Martinenko   RUS
2 Nina Englich   GER
3 Svetlana Sayenko   UKR

World Cup, Women
Cairo, Oct 19-20

48kg: Misato Shimizu JPN
51kg: Natayla Golts RUS
55kg: Seiko Yamamoto JPN
59kg: Rena Iwama II JPN
63kg: Kaori Icho JPN
67kg: Katerina Burmistrova UKR
72kg: Kyoko Hamaguchi JPN

Greco-Roman

World Championships

Moscow, Sep 20-22
Greco-Roman wrestling is men only; there are no British greco-roman wrestlers

55kg
1 Gaider Mamedaliev   RUS
2 Neps Gukulov   TKM
3 Hassan Rangraz   IRI
60kg
1 Armen Nazarian   BUL
2 Wlodzimierz Zawadzki   POL
3 Roberto Monzon   CUB
66kg
1 Jimmy Samuelsson   SWE
2 Farid Mansurov   AZE
3 Manuchari Kvirkvelia   GEO
74kg
1 Varteres Samourgashev   RUS
2 Badri Khasaia   GEO
3 Filiberto Ascuy   CUB
84kg
1 Ara Abrahamian   SWE
2 Alexander Menshikov   RUS
3 Mohamed Abd El Fatah   EGY
96kg
1 Mehmet Oezal   TUR
2 Karam Ibragim   EGY
3 Ali Mollov   BUL
120kg
1 Dremiel Byers   USA
2 Mihaly Deak Bardos   HUN
3 Youri Patrikeev   RUS

European Championships

Seinaejoki, Apr 11-14

55kg
1 Renat Birkkinin   RUS
2 Tanyo Tenev   BUL
3 Dariusz Jablonski   POL
60kg
1 Armen Nazarian   BUL
2 Rustem Mambetov   RUS
3 Djamel Ainaoui   FRA
66kg
1 Seref Eroglu   TUR
2 Manuchari Kvirkvelia   GEO
3 Michael Beilin   ISR
74kg
1 Badri Khasia   GEO
2 Varteres Samourgashev   RUS
3 Marko Yli-Hannuksela   FIN
85kg
1 Hamza Yerlikaya   TUR
2 Ara Abrahamian   SWE
3 Vyatcheslav Makarenko   BLR
96kg
1 Georgi Kogouashvili   RUS
2 Sergei Lishtvan   BLR
3 David Saldadze   UKR
120kg
1 Youri Patrikeev   RUS
2 Mihaly Deak Bardos   HUN
3 Juha Ahokas   FIN

World Cup

Cairo, Oct 19-20

55kg: Erkan Yildirim TUR
60kg: James Gruenwald USA
66kg: Selcuk Cebi TUR
74kg: Mahmut Altay TUR
84kg: Nazmi Avluca TUR
96kg: Karam Ibragim EGY
120kg: Yekta Guel TUR

E x t r a s

Aussie Rules

Grand Final
Melbourne CG   Sep 28
COLLINGWOOD 9:12   66
BRISBANE LIONS 10:15 **75**
Goals
*Collingwood: Rocca 4, Fraser 3,
Lockyer 1, Buckley 1
Brisbane: Lynch 4, Hart 1, Black 1,
McRae 1, Brown 1, Voss 1,
Akermanis 1*

Attendance: 91,817

Gaelic Football

All-Ireland Final
Croke Park   Sep 22
Armagh 1:12 **15** Kerry 0:14 **14**

Greyhound Racing

Derby Final
Wimbledon, June 1 (480m)
1 (5)	Allen Gift	16/1
2 (6)	Call Me Baby	8/1
3 (1)	Crack Him Out	9/4
4 (4)	Blue Gooner	5/1
5 (3)	Pilot Alert	2/1F
6 (2)	Windgap Java	5/1
*Time: 29.06
Trainer: Claude Gardiner*

Handball

European Championships
MEN
Sweden, Jan 25-Feb 3
Semi-finals
Denmark 23   Germany 28
Sweden 33   Iceland 22
Bronze Medal Match
Denmark 29   Iceland 22
Final
Germany 31   Sweden 33
WOMEN
Denmark, Dec 6-15
Semi-finals
Denmark 22   Russia 18
France 16   Norway 21
Bronze Medal Match
Russia 22   France 27
Final
Denmark 25   Norway 22

Hurling

All-Ireland Final
Croke Park   Sep 8
Clare 0:19 **19** Kilkenny 2:20 **26**

K a r a t e

World Championships
Madrid, Nov 21-24
MEN'S KATA
Team
1. Japan; 2. Spain; 3 Croatia
Individual
1. Takashi Katada JPN

MEN'S KUMITE
Team
1. Spain; 2. England; 3. Iran
Individual
-60kg: 1. Damien Dovy BEN; 3.
Paul Newby ENG
-65kg: 1. George Kotaka USA
-70kg: 1. Giuseppe di Domenico ITA
-75kg: 1. Ivan Leal Reglero ESP
-80kg: 1. Yann Baillon FRA
+80kg: 1. Leon Walters ENG
Open: 1. Pedrag Stojadinov YUG

WOMEN'S KATA
Team
1. France; 2. Japan; 3 Italy/Spain
Individual
1. Atsuko Wakai JPN

WOMEN'S KUMITE
Team
1. Spain; 2. France;
3. Turkey/England
Individual
-53kg: 1. Kora Knuehmann GER
-60kg: 1. Nathalie Leroy FRA
+60kg: 1. Elisa Au USA
Open: 1. Snezana Peric YUG

Lacrosse

World Championships
Men
Perth, Australia, July 5-14
Semi-finals
USA 18   Iroquois 8
Canada 15   Australia 14
Bronze Medal Game
Australia 12   Iroquois 11
Final
USA 18   Canada 15
Final placings
1. USA; 2. Canada; 3. Australia;
4. Iroquois; 5. Japan; 6. England;
7. Scotland; 8. Germany;
9. Sweden; 10. Czech Republic;
11. South Korea; 12. Wales

Pool

World 8-Ball Championships
Blackpool, May 24-June 1
Men
Singles
Jason Twist ENG bt
Yannick Beaufils 11-9
Team
Wales bt England 8-6
Women
Singles
Sue Thompson ENG bt
Lisa Quick ENG 8-3
Team
England bt South Africa 8-1

Powerboating

World Class 1 Championship
Final Standing
1 Spirit Of Norway
Bjorn Gjelsten/Steve Curtis
NOR/GBR 131 pts

Racquets

British Open
Queen's Club, Jan 30-Feb 10
Men's Final
Harry Foster bt M Hubbard
16/13 15/12 18/17 10/15 15/1

Real Tennis

World Championship
The men's world title was awarded to Robert Fahey AUS after James Male GBR declined to play the match scheduled for the Royal Melbourne Tennis club in February.

Shooting

World Championships
Lahti, Finland, July 7-12
Where scores are equal, placings are decided by shoot-offs. British shown if in top 50.

MEN
10m Running Target
1	Dmitri Lykin RUS	684.9
2	Yang Ling CHN	684.9
3	Adam Saathoff USA	681.1

10m Running Target Mixed
1	Jozsef Sike HUN	390
2	Michael Jakosits GER	387
3	Adam Saathoff USA	387

300m Rifle 3 Positions
1	Rajmond Debevec SLO	1168
2	Eric Uptagrafft USA	1165
3	Thomas Jerabek CZE	1163

300m Rifle Prone
1	Norbert Sturny SUI	597
2	Thomas Jerabek CZE	597
3	Michael Larsson SWE	597

300m Standard Rifle 3x20
1	Marcel Buerge SUI	589
2	Milan Mach CZE	585
3	Arild Roeyseth NOR	583

50m Running Target
1	Maxim Stepanov RUS	592
2	Lubos Racansky CZE	592
3	Jozsef Sike HUN	591

50m Running Target Mixed
1	Jozsef Skie HUN	395
2	Emil Andersson SWE	394
3	Lubomir Pelanch SVK	392

10m Air Pistol
1	Mikhail Nestruev RUS	685.3
2	Anrija Zlatic YUG	683.9
3	Franck Dumoulin FRA	683.4
19	Mick Gault GBR	578
41	Nick Baxter GBR	573

10m Air Rifle
1	Jason Parker USA	699.9
2	Li Jie CHN	699.9
3	Eugeni Aleinikov RUS	699.1

25m Centre Fire Pistol
1	Park Byung-Taek KOR	590
2	Mikhail Nestruev RUS	589
3	Lee Sang Hak KOR	586
45	Peter Flippant GBR	569

Double Trap
1	Daniele di Spigno ITA	188
2	Walton Eller USA	187/14
3	Joonas Olkkonen FIN	187/13
4	Richard Faulds GBR	187/7
33	John Bellamy GBR	131
41	George Digweed GBR	124

50m Pistol
1	Tan Zongliang CHN	662.7
2	Martin Tenk CZE	660.3
3	Vladimir Gontcharov RUS	657.7

50m Rifle 3 Positions
1	Marcel Buerge SUI	1258
2	K Prikhodtchenko RUS	1255.4
3	Peter Sidi HUN	1250.7

50m Rifle Prone
1	Matthew Emmons USA	699.7
2	Rajmond Debevec SLO	698.8
3	Espen Berg-Knutsen NOR	698.3
37	Michael Babb GBR	587

25m Rapid Fire Pistol
1	Marco Spangenberg GER	690.9
2	Ralf Schumann GER	690.9
3	Niki Marty SUI	688.3

Skeet
1	Harald Jensen NOR	147/4
2	Valeri Shomin RUS	147/3
3	Ennio Falco ITA	146
7	Richard Brickell GBR	121
9	Drew Harvey GBR	120

25m Standard Pistol
1	Rene Vogn DEN	580
2	Alexander Danilov ISR	580
3	Giovanni Bossi AUT	579

Trap
1	Khaled Almudhaf KUW	146
2	MIchael Diamond AUS	144
3	Giovanni Pellielo ITA	119

WOMEN
10m Running Target
1	Xu Xuan CHN	391
2	Wang Xia CHN	381
3	Natalya Kovalenko KAZ	380

10m Running Target Mixed
1	Audrey Soquet FRA	390
2	Qui Zhiqi CHN	385
3	Wang Xia CHN	383

300m Rifle Prone
1	Charlotte Jakobsen DEN	594
2	Estelle Preti SUI	593
3	Lindy Hansen NOR	590
18	Mary Pugsley GBR	575

300m Standard Rifle 3x20
1	Charlotte Jakobsen DEN	588
2	Helena Juppala FIN	584
3	Karin Hansen DEN	579

10m Air Pistol
1	Olena Kostevych UKR	485.2
2	Nino Salukvadze GEO	484.9
3	Olga Kousnetsova RUS	484.8

10m Air Rifle
1	Katerina Kurkova CZE	502.1
2	Du Li CHN	500.9
3	Sonja Pfeilschifter GER	500.3
29	Louise Minett GBR	393

Double Trap
1	Lin Yi Chun TPE	143
2	Wang Jing Lin CHN	142/4
3	Son Hye Kyoung KOR	142/3

Skeet
1	Diana Igaly HUN	98
2	Andrea Stranovska SVK	95
3	Elena Little GBR	92
20	Susan Bramley GBR	64
32	Pinky Legrelle GBR	60

25m Pistol
1	Munkbayer Dorisuren GER	689.9
2	Irada Ashumova AZE	687.3
3	Chen Ying CHN	687.2

50m Rifle 3 Positions
1	Petra Horneber GER	675.5
2	Natalia Kalnish UKR	674.1
3	Martina Prekel GER	673

50m Rifle Prone
1	Olga Dovgun KAZ	597
2	Wang Xian CHN	593
3	Natalia Kalnish UKR	591
30	Ann Roberts GBR	585
35	Sheena Sharp GBR	584

Trap
1	Elena Tkach RUS	93
2	Daina Gudzinevicuite LTU	92
3	Wang Yujin CHN	91

Water Skiing

World Barefoot Championships
Wallsee, Austria, Aug 20-25
British shown if in top 10

MIXED TEAM
1 USA
2 South Africa
3 Australia
6 Great Britain

MEN
Slalom
1 Keith Stonge USA
2 Jason Lee USA
3 Ron Scarpa USA
5 David Small GBR
Jumps
1 David Small GBR
2 Massi Colosio ITA
3 Brett New AUS
Tricks
1 Patrick Wehner FRA
2 Keith Stonge USA
3 David Small GBR
Overall
1 David Small GBR
2 Keith Stonge USA
3 Patrick Wehner FRA

WOMEN
Slalom
1 Nadine de Villiers RSA
2 Rachel George USA
3 Gizella Halasz AUS
Jump
1 Nadine de Villers RSA
2 Rachel George USA
3 Kirsten Gronvik NOR
Tricks
1 Nadine de Villers RSA
2 Rachel George USA
3 Gizella Halasz AUS
Overall
1 Nadine de Villiers RSA
2 Rachel George USA
3 Gizella Halasz AUS

World Cableski Championships
Alfsee-Rieste, Germany, Sep 7-8

MIXED TEAM
1 Belarus
2 Germany
3 Slovakia
5 Great Britain

MEN
Slalom
1 Alexander Grew GER
1 Alois Krenn AUT
3 Simon Herrmann GER
Tricks
1 Aleksai Zernosek BLR
2 Vichaslau Durnov BLR
3 Yuri Rickter BLR
19 Stuart Marston GBR
Jump
1 Thomas Bauer GER
2 Manfred Hintringer AUT
3 Daniel Resl CZE
8 Stuart Marston GBR
Overall
1 Aleksai Zernosek BLR
2 Andreas Pape GER
3 Miroslav Hribik SVK
8 Stuart Marston GBR

WOMEN
Slalom
1 Lisa Adams GBR
2 Nadine Wich GER
3 Bronislav Machova BLR
Tricks
1 Olga Pavlova BLR
2 Julia Meier-Gromyko BLR
3 Irina Tourets BLR
Jump
1 Irina Tourets BLR
2 Julia Meier-Gromyko BLR
3 Olga Pavlova BLR
Overall
1 Irina Tourets BLR
2 Julia Meier-Gromyko BLR
3 Olga Pavlova BLR

EAME Tournament Championships
(Europe-Africa-Middle East)
Roquebrune, France, Sep 18-22

MEN
Tricks
1 Oleg Deviatovski BLR	11040
2 Nicolas Le Forestier FRA	10820
3 Aleksei Zernosek BLR	10410
7 Thomas Asher GBR	9420
8 Jason Seels GBR	9130

Slalom
1 Thomas Degasperi ITA
2 Glenn Campbell GBR
3 Fabrizio Ciappone ITA
6 Jeremy Newby-Ricci GBR
9 William Asher GBR
Jumps
Distance given for Final
1 Jochen Luers GER	68.8m
2 Jesper Cassoe DEN	67.0m
3 Jason Seels GBR	66.5m
5 Thomas Asher GBR	63.5m
9 Damian Sharman GBR	58.4m

Overall
1 Oleg Deviatovski BLR	2608.70
2 Jason Seels GBR	2535.92
3 Aleksei Zernosek BLR	2502.49
4 Thomas Asher GBR	2324.39

WOMEN
Tricks
1 Elena Milakova RUS	7250
2 Clementine Lucine FRA	7200
3 Anais Amade FRA	7060

Slalom
1 Cristina Muggiasca Buros SUI
2 Geraldine Jamin FRA
3 Irene Reinstaller ITA
7 Sarah Gatty Saunt GBR
Jumps
1 Elena Milakova RUS	50.1m
2 Anais Amade FRA	48.6m
3 Clementine Lucine FRA	48.5m

Overall
1 A Andriopoulou GRE	2705.98
2 Elena Milakova RUS	2637.27
3 Anais Amade FRA	2595.75
9 Maria Toms GBR	1949.84

The Archive

**A sport by sport
listing of past champions
and records**

AMERICAN FOOTBALL

SUPER BOWL

Season	Date	Winner	Runner-up	Score	Venue	Attendance	MVP	Team-Pos
I	15.1.67	Green Bay	Kansas City	35-10	Los Angeles	61,946	Bart Starr (GB-QB)	
II	14.1.68	Green Bay	Oakland	33-14	Miami	75,546	Bart Starr (GB-QB)	
III	12.1.69	New York Jets	Baltimore	16-7	Miami	75,389	Joe Namath (NY-QB)	
IV	11.1.70	Kansas City	Minnesota	23-7	New Orleans	80,582	Len Dawson (KC-QB)	
V	17.1.71	Baltimore	Dallas	16-13	Miami	79,204	Chuck Howley (D-LB)	
VI	16.1.72	Dallas	Miami	24-3	New Orleans	81,023	Roger Staubach (D-QB)	
VII	14.1.73	Miami	Washington	14-7	Los Angeles	90,182	Jake Scott (M-S)	
VIII	31.1.74	Miami	Minnesota	24-7	Houston	71,882	Larry Csonka (M-RB)	
IX	12.1.75	Pittsburgh	Minnesota	16-6	New Orleans	80,997	Franco Harris (P-RB)	
X	18.1.76	Pittsburgh	Dallas	21-7	Miami	80,187	Lynn Swann (P-WR)	
XI	9.1.77	Oakland	Minnesota	32-14	Pasadena	103,438	Fred Biletnikoff (O-WR)	
XII	15.1.78	Dallas	Denver	27-10	New Orleans	75,583	White & Martin (Da-DT/DE)	
XIII	21.1.79	Pittsburgh	Dallas	35-31	Miami	79,484	Terry Bradshaw (P-QB)	
XIV	20.1.80	Pittsburgh	Los Angeles	31-19	Pasadena	103,985	Terry Bradshaw (P-QB)	
XV	25.1.81	Oakland	Philadelphia	27-10	New Orleans	76,135	Jim Plunkett (O-QB)	
XVI	24.1.82	San Francisco	Cincinnati	26-21	Pontiac	81,270	Joe Montana (SF-QB)	
XVII	30.1.83	Washington	Miami	27-17	Pasadena	103,667	John Riggins (W-RB)	
XVIII	22.1.84	LA Raiders	Washington	38-9	Tampa	72,920	Marcus Allen (LA-RB)	
XIX	20.1.85	San Francisco	Miami	38-16	Stanford	84,059	Joe Montana (SF-QB)	
XX	26.1.86	Chicago	New England	46-10	New Orleans	73,818	Richard Dent (CH-DE)	
XXI	25.1.87	New York Gts	Denver	39-20	Pasadena	101,063	Phil Simms (NY-QB)	
XXII	13.1.88	Washington	Denver	42-10	San Diego	73,302	Doug Williams (W-QB)	
XXIII	22.1.89	San Francisco	Cincinnati	20-16	Miami	75,129	Jerry Rice (SF-WR)	
XXIV	28.1.90	San Francisco	Denver	55-10	New Orleans	72,919	Joe Montana (SF-QB)	
XXV	27.1.91	New York Gts	Buffalo	20-19	Tampa	73,813	Ottis Anderson (NY-RB)	
XXVI	26.1.92	Washington	Buffalo	37-24	Minneapolis	63,130	Mark Rypien (W-QB)	
XXVII	31.1.93	Dallas	Buffalo	52-17	Pasadena	98,374	Troy Aikman (D-QB)	
XXVIII	30.1.94	Dallas	Buffalo	30-13	Atlanta	72,817	Emmitt Smith (D-RB)	
XXIX	29.1.95	San Francisco	San Diego	49-28	Miami	74,107	Steve Young (S-QB)	
XXX	28.1.96	Dallas	Pittsburgh	27-17	Arizona	76,347	Larry Brown (D-CB)	
XXXI	26.1.97	Green Bay	New England	35-21	New Orleans	72,301	Desmond Howard (GB-WR)	
XXXII	25.1.98	Denver	Green Bay	31-24	San Diego	68,912	Terrell Davis (D-RB)	
XXXIII	31.1.99	Denver	Atlanta	34-19	Miami	74,803	John Elway (D-QB)	
XXXIV	30.1.00	St Louis	Tennessee	23-16	Atlanta	72,625	Kurt Warner (S-QB)	
XXXV	28.1.01	Baltimore	N York Giants	34-7	Tampa Bay	71,921	Ray Lewis (B-LB)	
XXXVI	3.2.02	New Orleans	NE Patriots	20-17	St Louis Rams	72,922	Tom Brady (NE-QB)	

WORLD BOWL

1991	London Monarchs 21	Barcelona Dragons 0	Wembley Stadium, London
1992	Sacramento Surge 21	Orlando Thunder 17	Olympic Stadium, Montreal
1995	Frankfurt Galaxy 26	Amsterdam Admirals 22	Olympic Stadium, Amsterdam
1996	Scottish Claymores 32	Frankfurt Galaxy 27	Murrayfield, Edinburgh
1997	Barcelona Dragons 38	Rhein Fire 24	Olympic Stadium, Barcelona
1998	Rhein Fire 34	Frankfurt Galaxy 10	Waldstadion, Frankfurt
1999	Frankfurt Galaxy 38	Barcelona Dragons 24	Rheinstadion, Dusseldorf
2000	Rhein Fire 13	Scottish Claymores 10	Waldstadion, Frankfurt
2001	Berlin Thunder 24	Barcelone Dragons 17	Amsterdam ArenA
2002	Berlin Thunder 26	Rhein Fire 20	Rheinstadion, Dusseldorf

ANGLING

WORLD FRESHWATER CHAMPIONS

Year	Individual	Team
1957	Mandelli ITA	Italy
1958	Garroit BEL	Belgium
1959	Robert Tesse FRA	France
1960	Robert Tesse FRA	Belgium
1961	Ramon Legogue FRA	East Germany
1962	Raimondo Tedasco ITA	Italy
1963	William Lane ENG	France
1964	Joseph Fontanet FRA	France
1965	Robert Tesse FRA	Romania
1966	Henri Guiheneuf FRA	France
1967	Jacques Isenbaert BEL	Belgium
1968	Gunter Grebenstein FRG	France
1969	Robin Harris ENG	Netherlands
1970	Marcel Van den Eynde BEL	Belgium
1971	Dino Bassi ITA	Italy
1972	Hubert Levels HOL	France
1973	Pierre Michiels BEL	Belgium
1974	Aribert Richter FRG	France
1975	Ian Heaps ENG	France
1976	Dino Bassi ITA	Italy
1977	Jean Mainil BEL	Luxembourg
1978	Jean-Pierre Fourgeat FRA	France
1979	Gerard Heulard FRA	France
1980	Wolf-Rudiger Kremkus FRG	West Germany
1981	Dave Thomas ENG	France
1982	Kevin Ashurst ENG	Netherlands
1983	Wolf-Rudiger Kremkus FRG	Belgium
1984	Bobby Smithers IRE	Luxembourg
1985	Dave Roper ENG	England
1986	Lud Wever HOL	Italy
1987	Clive Branson WAL	England
1988	Jean-Pierre Fougeat FRA	England
1989	Tom Pickering ENG	Wales
1990	Bob Nudd ENG	France
1991	Bob Nudd ENG	England
1992	David Wesson AUS	Italy
1993	Mario Barros POR	Italy
1994	Bob Nudd ENG	England
1995	Paul Jean FRA	France
1996	Alan Scotthorne ENG	Italy
1997	Alan Scotthorne ENG	Italy
1998	Alan Scotthorne ENG	England
1999	Bob Nudd ENG	Spain
2000	Jacopo Falsini ITA	Italy
2001	Umberto Ballabeni ITA	England
2002	Juan Blasco ESP	Spain

NATIONAL LEAGUE CHAMPIONS

The National League began in 1906, results from 1960

Year	Individual	Team
1960	K Smith	King's Lynn
1961	J Blakey	Coventry
1962	V Baker	Lincoln
1963	R Sims	Northampton N
1964	C Burch	Kidderminster
1965	D Burr	Rugby
1966	R Jarvis	Boston
1967	E Townsin	Derby Railway
1968	D Groom	Leighton Buzz
1969	R Else	Stoke
1970	B Lakey	Cambridge
1971	R Harris	Leicester
1972	P Coles	Birmingham
1973	A Wright	Grimsby
1974	P Anderson	Leicester
1975	M Hoad-Reddick	Birmingham
1976	N Wells	Birmingham
1977	R Foster	Coventry
1978	D Harris	Coleshill
1979	M Cullen	Barnsley
1980	P Burrell	Notts
1981	D Steer	Essex
1982	A Mayer	Rotherham
1983	D Howl	Notts
1984	C Gregg	Coleshill
1985	B Oliver	ABC
1986	M Stabler	I Walton, Staffs
1987	J Robinson	Nottingham
1988	S Hall	Redditch
1989	B Wickens	Reading
1990	S Cheetham	Trevs
1991	P Hargreaves	I Walton
1992	K Gregory	Nottingham
1993	S Canty	Liverpool
1994	S Ellis	Highfield
1995	S Tyler	Barnsley
1996	R Mitchell	Scunthorpe
1997	A Whiteley	Barnsley
1998	M Runacres	Southport
1999	G Frith	Redditch
2000	T Flannery	Daiwa Gordon
2001	D Vincent	Clegg Ossett
2002	M Evans	Redditch

WORLD FLY FISHING CHAMPIONS

Year	Individual	Team
1981	C Wittkamp HOL	Netherlands
1982	Viktor Diez ESP	Italy
1983	S Fernandez ESP	Italy
1984	Tony Pawson ENG	Italy
1985	Leslaw Frasik POL	Poland
1986	Slivoj Svoboda TCH	Italy
1987	Brian Leadbetter ENG	England
1988	John Pawson ENG	England
1989	Wladislaw Trzebuinia POL	Poland
1990	Franciszek Szajnik POL	Czechoslovakia
1991	Brian Leadbetter ENG	New Zealand
1992	Pierluigi Coccito ITA	Italy
1993	Russell Owen WAL	England
1994	Pascal Cognard FRA	Czech Republic
1995	Jeremy Herrmann ENG	England
1996	Pierluigi Coccito ITA	Czech Republic
1997	Pascal Cognard FRA	France
1998	Tomas Starychfojtu CZE	Czech Republic
1999	Ross Stewart AUS	Australia
2000	Pascal Cognard FRA	France
2001	Vladimir Sedivy CZE	France
2002	Jerome Brossutti FRA	France

ARCHERY

TARGET WORLD CHAMPIONS (OLYMPIC)

Year	Men's Individual	Women's Individual	Men's Team	Women's Team
1931	Michael Sawicki POL	Janina Kurkowska POL	France	Poland
1932	Laurent Reth BEL	Janina Kurkowska POL	Poland	Poland
1933	Don Mackenzie USA	Janina Kurkowska POL	Belgium	Poland
1934	Henry Kjellson SWE	Janina Kurkowska POL	Sweden	Poland
1935	Adrien Van Kolen BEL	Ina Catani SWE	Czechoslovakia	Great Britain
1936	Emil Heilborn SWE	Janina Kurkowska POL	Czechoslovakia	Poland
1937	Georges DeRons BEL	Ingo Simon GBR	Poland	Great Britain
1938	Frantisek Hadas TCH	Nora Weston Martyr GBR	Czechoslovakia	Poland
1939	Roger Beday FRA	Janina Kurkowska POL	France	Poland
1946	Einar Tang-Holbek DEN	Nilla de Wharton Burr GBR	Denmark	Great Britain
1947	Hans Deutgen SWE	Janina Kurkowska POL	Czechoslovakia	Denmark
1948	Hans Deutgen SWE	Nilla de Wharton Burr GBR	Sweden	Czechoslovakia
1949	Hans Deutgen SWE	Barbara Waterhouse GBR	Czechoslovakia	Great Britain
1950	Hans Deutgen SWE	Jean Lee USA	Denmark	Finland
1952	Stellan Andersson SWE	Jean Lee USA	Sweden	USA
1953	Bror Lundgren SWE	Jean Richards USA	Sweden	Finland
1955	Nils Andersson SWE	Katarzyna Wisniowska POL	Sweden	Great Britain
1957	Oziek Smathers USA	Carole Meinhart USA	USA	USA
1958	Stig Thysell SWE	Sigrid Johansson SWE	Finland	USA
1959	James Caspers USA	Ann Weber Hoyt USA	USA	USA
1961	Joe Thornton USA	Nancy Vonderheide USA	USA	USA
1963	Charles Sandin USA	Victoria Cook USA	USA	USA
1965	Matti Haikonen FIN	Maire Lindholm FIN	USA	USA
1967	Ray Rogers USA	Maria Maczynska POL	USA	Poland
1969	Hardy Ward USA	Dorothy Lidstone CAN	USA	Soviet Union
1971	John Williams USA	Emma Gapchenko URS	USA	Poland
1973	Viktor Sidoruk URS	Linda Myers USA	USA	Soviet Union
1975	Darrell Pace USA	Zebiniso Rustamova URS	USA	Soviet Union
1977	Richard McKinney USA	Luann Ryon USA	USA	USA
1979	Darrell Pace USA	Kim Jin-Ho KOR	USA	Korea
1981	Kyosti Laasonen FIN	Natalya Butuzova URS	USA	Soviet Union
1983	Richard McKinney USA	Kim Jin-Ho KOR	USA	Korea
1985	Richard McKinney USA	Irina Soldatova URS	Korea	Soviet Union
1987	Vladimir Echeev URS	Ma Xiaojun CHN	West Germany	Soviet Union
1989	Stanislaw Zabrodsky URS	Kim Soo-Nyung KOR	Korea	Korea
1991	Simon Fairweather AUS	Kim Soo-Nyung KOR	Korea	Korea
1993	Park Kyung-Mo KOR	K Hyo-Jung KOR	France	Korea
1995	Lee Kyung-Chul KOR	Natalya Valeeva MLD	Korea	Korea
1997	Kim Kyung-Ho KOR	Kim Du-Ri KOR	Korea	Korea
1999	Hong Sung-Chil KOR	Lee Fon-Kung KOR	Italy	Italy
2001	Jung Ki-Yeon KOR	Park Sung-Hyun KOR	Korea	China

INDOOR WORLD CHAMPIONS

Year	Men's Olympic Team	Men's Compound Team	Women's Olympic Team	Women's Compound Team
1991	Sebastian Flute FRA -	Joe Asay USA -	Natalya Valeeva URS -	Lucia Panico ITA
1993	Gennady Mitrofanov RUS -	Kirk Ethridge USA	Jennifer O'Donnell USA -	Inga Low USA -
1995	Magnus Pettersson SWE USA	Michael Hendrikse USA USA	Natalya Valeeva MLD Ukraine	Glenda Penaz USA USA
1997	Chung Jae-Hun KOR Korea	Dee Wilde USA Sweden	Tetyana Muntyan UKR Germany	Valerie Fabre FRA USA
1999	Magnus Pettersson SWE Australia	James Butts USA USA	Natalia Valeeva ITA France	Ashley Kamuf USA France
2001	Michele Frangilli ITA USA	Morgan Lundin SWE Italy	Natalia Valeeva ITA Russia	Mary Zorn USA USA

ASSOCIATION FOOTBALL

WORLD CUP FINALS

Year	Winners	Runners-up	Venue	Attendance
1930	**Uruguay 4** *Dorado, Cea, Iriarte, Castro*	**Argentina 2** *Peucelle, Stabile*	Montevideo, Uruguay	90,000
1934	**Italy 2** *Orsi, Schiavio*	**Czechoslovakia 1** * *Puc*	Rome, Italy	55,000
1938	**Italy 4** *Colaussi (2), Piola (2)*	**Hungary 2** *Titkos, Sarosi*	Paris, France	50,000
1950	**Uruguay 2** *Schiaffino, Ghiggia*	**Brazil 1** ** *Friaca*	Rio de Janeiro, Brazil	199,854
1954	**West Germany 3** *Morlock, Rahn (2)*	**Hungary 2** *Puskas, Czibor*	Berne, Switzerland	55,000
1958	**Brazil 5** *Vava (2), Pele (2), Zagalo*	**Sweden 2** *Liedholm, Simonsson*	Stockholm, Sweden	49,737
1962	**Brazil 3** *Amarildo, Zito, Vava*	**Czechoslovakia 1** *Masopust*	Santiago, Chile	69,068
1966	**England 4** *Hurst (3), Peters*	**West Germany 2** * *Haller, Weber*	London, England	93,000
1970	**Brazil 4** *Pele, Gerson, Jairzinho, Carlos Alberto*	**Italy 1** *Boninsegna*	Mexico City, Mexico	110,000
1974	**West Germany 2** *Breitner (pen), Müller*	**Holland 1** *Neeskens (pen)*	Munich, West Germany	77,833
1978	**Argentina 3** *Kempes (2), Bertoni*	**Holland 1** * *Nanninga*	Buenos Aires, Argentina	77,000
1982	**Italy 3** *Rossi, Tardelli, Altobelli*	**West Germany 1** *Breitner*	Madrid, Spain	92,000
1986	**Argentina 3** *Brown, Valdano, Burruchaga*	**West Germany 2** *Rummenigge, Völler*	Mexico City, Mexico	114,580
1990	**West Germany 1** *Brehme (pen)*	**Argentina 0**	Rome, Italy	73,603
1994	**Brazil 0** *Brazil won 3-2 on penalties*	**Italy 0** *	Los Angeles, USA	94,194
1998	**France 3** *Zidane 2, Petit*	**Brazil 0**	Paris, France	75,000
2002	**Brazil 2** *Ronaldo 2*	**Germany 0**	Yokohama, Japan	69,029

* after extra time
** deciding match of final pool

ASSOCIATION FOOTBALL

EUROPEAN CHAMPIONSHIP FINALS

1960	**Soviet Union 2** *Metreveli, Ponedelnik*	**Yugoslavia 1** * *Galic*	Paris, France	17,966
1964	**Spain 2** *Pereda, Marcellino*	**Soviet Union 1** *Khusainov*	Madrid, Spain	105,000
1968	**Italy 1** *Domenghini*	**Yugoslavia 1** * *Dzajic*	Rome, Italy	85,000
Replay	**Italy 2** *Riva, Anastasi*	**Yugoslavia 0**	Rome, Italy	50,000
1972	**West Germany 3** *G Müller (2), Wimmer*	**Soviet Union 0**	Brussels, Belgium	43,437
1976	**Czechoslovakia 2** *Svehlik, Dobias* *(Czechoslovakia won 5-4 on penalties)*	**West Germany 2** * *D Muller, Holzenbein*	Belgrade, Yugoslavia	45,000
1980	**West Germany 2** *Hrubesch (2)*	**Belgium 1** *Van der Eycken*	Rome, Italy	47,864
1984	**France 2** *Platini, Bellone*	**Spain 0**	Paris, France	47,000
1988	**Holland 2** *Gullit, Van Basten*	**Soviet Union 0**	Munich, Germany	72,308
1992	**Denmark 2** *Jensen, Vilfort*	**Germany 0**	Gothenburg, Sweden	37,800
1996	**Germany 2** *Bierhoff (2)*	**Czech Republic 1*** *Berger (pen)*	London, England	76,000
2000	**France 2** *Wiltord, Trezeguet*	**Italy 1*** *Delvecchio*	Rotterdam, Netherlands	50,000

*after extra time   **deciding match of final pool   ***after sudden death extra time (Golden Goal)*

EUROPEAN CHAMPIONS CUP

Year	Winner	Runner-up
1956	**Real Madrid** 4	Reims 3
1957	**Real Madrid** 2	Fiorentina 0
1958	**Real Madrid** 3	AC Milan 2 *(aet)*
1959	**Real Madrid** 2	Reims 0
1960	**Real Madrid** 7	Eintracht Frankfurt 3
1961	**Benfica** 3	Barcelona 2
1962	**Benfica** 5	Real Madrid 3
1963	**AC Milan** 2	Benfica 1
1964	**Internazionale** 3	Real Madrid 1
1965	**Internazionale** 1	Benfica 0
1966	**Real Madrid** 2	Partizan Belgrade 1
1967	**Celtic** 2	Internazionale 1
1968	**Manchester Utd** 4	Benfica 1 *(aet)*
1969	**AC Milan** 4	Ajax 1
1970	**Feyenoord** 2	Celtic 1 *(aet)*
1971	**Ajax** 2	Panathinaikos 0
1972	**Ajax** 2	Internazionale 0
1973	**Ajax** 1	Juventus 0
1974	Bayern Munich 1	Atletico Madrid 1
	Bayern Munich 4	Atletico Madrid 0
1975	**Bayern Munich** 2	Leeds Utd 0
1976	**Bayern Munich** 1	St Etienne 0
1977	**Liverpool** 3	B Moenchengladbach 1
1978	**Liverpool** 1	FC Brugge 0
1979	**Nottingham Forest** 1	Malmo 0
1980	**Nottingham Forest** 1	Hamburg 0
1981	**Liverpool** 1	Real Madrid 0
1982	**Aston Villa** 1	Bayern Munich 0
1983	**Hamburg** 1	Juventus 0

Year	Winner	Runner-up
1984	**Liverpool** 1	Roma 1
	(aet: Liverpool won 4-2 on penalties)	
1985	**Juventus** 1	Liverpool 0
1986	**Steaua Bucharest** 0	Barcelona 0
	(aet: Steaua won 2-0 on penalties)	
1987	**Porto** 2	Bayern Munich 1
1988	**PSV Eindhoven** 0	Benfica 0
	(aet: PSV won 6-5 on penalties)	
1989	**AC Milan** 4	Steaua Bucharest 0
1990	**AC Milan** 1	Benfica 0
1991	**Red Star Belgrade** 0	Marseille 0
	(aet: Red Star won 5-3 on penalties)	
1992	**Barcelona** 1	Sampdoria 0 *(aet)*
1993	Marseille* 1	**AC Milan** 0
1994	**AC Milan** 4	Barcelona 0
1995	**Ajax** 1	AC Milan 0
1996	**Juventus** 1	Ajax 1
	(aet: Juventus won 4-2 on penalties)	
1997	**Borussia Dortmund** 3	Juventus 1
1998	**Real Madrid** 1	Juventus 0
1999	**Manchester Utd** 2	Bayern Munich 1
2000	**Real Madrid** 3	Valencia 0
2001	**Bayern Munich** 1	Valencia 1
	(aet; Bayern Munich won 5-4 on penalties)	
2002	**Real Madrid** 2	Bayer Leverkusen 1

* subsequently stripped of title

ASSOCIATION FOOTBALL

INTER-CITIES FAIRS CUP

Year	Winners	Score		Runners-up
1958	Barcelona	2-2	6-0	London
1960	Barcelona	0-0	4-1	Birmingham City
1961	Roma	2-2	2-0	Birmingham City
1962	Valencia	6-2	1-1	Barcelona
1963	Valencia	1-2	2-0	Dynamo Zagreb
1964	Zaragoza	2-1*		Valencia
1965	Ferencvaros	1-0*		Juventus
1966	Barcelona	0-1	4-2	Zaragoza
1967	Dynamo Zagreb	2-0	0-0	Leeds United
1968	Leeds United	1-0	0-0	Ferencvaros
1969	Newcastle United	3-0	2-3	Ujpest Dozsa
1970	Arsenal	1-3	3-0	Anderlecht
1971	Leeds United	2-2	1-1	Juventus

Over one leg only

UEFA CUP

1972	Tottenham H	2-1	1-1	Wolverhampton
1973	Liverpool	3-0	0-2	M'gladbach
1974	Feyenoord	2-0	2-2	Tottenham H
1975	M'gladbach	1-0	1-1	Twente E
1976	Liverpool	3-2	1-1	F C Brugge
1977	Juventus	1-0	1-2*	Athletic Bilbao
1978	PSV Eindhoven	3-0	0-0	Bastia
1979	M'gladbach	1-0	1-1	Red Star B
1980	E'tracht Frankfurt	1-0	2-3*	M'gladbach
1981	Ipswich Town	3-0	2-4	AZ 67 Alkmaar
1982	IFK Gothenburg	1-0	3-0	SV Hamburg
1983	Anderlecht	1-0	1-1	Benfica
1984	Tottenham H	1-1	1-1**	Anderlecht
1985	Real Madrid	3-0	0-1	Videoton
1986	Real Madrid	5-1	0-2	Cologne
1987	IFK Gothenburg	1-0	1-1	Dundee Utd
1988	Bayer Leverkusen	0-3	3-0**	Espanyol
1989	Napoli	2-1	3-3	VFB Stuttgart
1990	Juventus	3-1	0-0	Fiorentina
1991	Internazionale	2-0	0-1	AS Roma
1992	Ajax	2-2	0-0*	Torino
1993	Juventus	3-1	3-0	B Dortmund
1994	Internazionale	1-0	1-0	Salzburg
1995	Parma	1-0	1-1	Juventus
1996	Bayern Munich	2-0	3-1	Bordeaux
1997	Schalke	1-0	0-1**	Internazionale
1998	Internazionale	3-0		Lazio
1999	Parma	3-0		Marseille
2000	Galatasaray	0-0**		Arsenal
2001	Liverpool	5-4***		Alaves
2002	Feyenoord	3-2		B Dortmund

From 1998, the final over one leg only
* won on away goals ** won on penalties
*** won on Golden Goal extra-time

EUROPEAN CUP WINNERS' CUP

Year	Winners	Runner-up
1961	Fiorentina 2	Rangers 0 *(1st Leg)*
	Fiorentina 2	Rangers 1 *(2nd Leg)*
1962	Atletico Madrid 1	Fiorentina 1
	Atletico Madrid 3	Fiorentina 0
1963	Tottenham H 5	Atletico Madrid I
1964	Sporting Lisbon 3	MTK Budapest 3 *(aet)*
	Sporting Lisbon 1	MTK Budapest 0
1965	West Ham Utd 2	Munich 1860 0
1966	B Dortmund 2	Liverpool 1 *(aet)*
1967	Bayern Munich 1	Rangers 0 *(aet)*
1968	AC Milan 2	Hamburg 0
1969	Slovan Bratislava 3	Barcelona 2
1970	Manchester City 2	Gornik Zabrze 1
1971	Chelsea 1	Real Madrid 1 (aet)
	Chelsea 2	Real Madrid 1 (aet)
1972	Rangers 3	Dynamo Moscow 2
1973	AC Milan 1	Leeds Utd 0
1974	Magdeburg 2	AC Milan 0
1975	Dynamo Kiev 3	Ferencvaros 0
1976	Anderlecht 4	West Ham U 2
1977	Hamburg 2	Anderlecht 0
1978	Anderlecht 4	Austria/WAC 0
1979	Barcelona 4	Fort. Dusseldorf 3 *(aet)*
1980	Valencia 0	Arsenal 0
	(aet: Valencia won 5-4 on penalties)	
1981	Dynamo Tblisi 2	Carl Zeiss Jena 1
1982	Barcelona 2	Standard Liege 1
1983	Aberdeen 2	Real Madrid 1 *(aet)*
1984	Juventus 2	Porto 1
1985	Everton 3	Rapid Vienna 1
1986	Dynamo Kiev 3	Atletico Madrid 0
1987	Ajax 1	Lokomotiv Leipzig 0
1988	Mechelen 1	Ajax 0
1989	Barcelona 2	Sampdoria 0
1990	Sampdoria 2	Anderlecht 0
1991	Manchester Utd 2	Barcelona 1
1992	Werder Bremen 2	Monaco 0
1993	Parma 3	Antwerp 1
1994	Arsenal 1	Parma 0
1995	Real Zaragoza 2	Arsenal 1
1996	PSG 1	Rapid Vienna 0
1997	Barcelona 1	Paris St Germain 0
1998	Chelsea 1	VFB Stuttgart 0
1999	Lazio 2	Mallorca 1

Competition terminated 1999 to make way for expanded Champions League and UEFA Cup.

ASSOCIATION FOOTBALL

DIVISION 1

	Winners	Pts	Runners-up	Pts
1888-89	Preston NE	40	Aston Villa	29
1889-90	Preston NE	33	Everton	31
1890-91	Everton	29	Preston NE	27
1891-92	Sunderland	42	Preston NE	37
1892-93	Sunderland	48	Preston NE	37
1893-94	Aston Villa	44	Sunderland	38
1894-95	Sunderland	47	Everton	42
1895-96	Aston Villa	45	Derby County	41
1896-97	Aston Villa	47	Sheffield Utd	36
1897-98	Sheffield Utd	42	Sunderland	37
1898 99	Aston Villa	45	Liverpool	43
1899-00	Aston Villa	50	Sheffield Utd	48
1900-01	Liverpool	45	Sunderland	43
1901-02	Sunderland	44	Everton	41
1902-03	Sheffield Wed	42	Aston Villa	41
1903-04	Sheffield Wed	47	Man City	44
1904-05	Newcastle Utd	48	Everton	47
1905-06	Liverpool	51	Preston NE	47
1906-07	Newcastle Utd	51	Bristol City	48
1907-08	Man Utd	52	Aston Villa	43
1908-09	Newcastle Utd	53	Everton	46
1909-10	Aston Villa	53	Liverpool	48
1910-11	Man Utd	52	Aston Villa	51
1911-12	Blackburn Rvrs	49	Everton	46
1912-13	Sunderland	54	Aston Villa	50
1913-14	Blackburn Rvrs	51	Aston Villa	44
1914-15	Everton	46	Oldham Athletic	45
1919-20	West Brom Alb	60	Burnley	51
1920-21	Burnley	59	Man City	54
1921-22	Liverpool	57	Tottenham	51
1922-23	Liverpool	60	Sunderland	54
1923-24	Huddersfield T	57	Cardiff City	57
1924-25	Huddersfield T	58	West Brom Alb	56
1925-26	Huddersfield T	57	Arsenal	52
1926-27	Newcastle Utd	56	Huddersfield T	51
1927-28	Everton	53	Huddersfield T	51
1928-29	Sheffield Wed	52	Leicester City	51
1929-30	Sheffield Wed	60	Derby County	50
1930-31	Arsenal	66	Aston Villa	59
1931-32	Everton	56	Arsenal	54
1932 33	Arsenal	58	Aston Villa	54
1933-34	Arsenal	59	Huddersfield T	56
1934-35	Arsenal	58	Sunderland	54
1935-36	Sunderland	56	Derby County	48
1936-37	Man City	57	Charlton Ath	54
1937-38	Arsenal	52	Wolverhampton	51
1938-39	Everton	59	Wolverhampton	55
1946-47	Liverpool	57	Man Utd	56
1947-48	Arsenal	59	Man Utd	52
1948-49	Portsmouth	58	Man Utd	53
1949-50	Portsmouth	53	Wolverhampton	53
1950-51	Tottenham H	60	Man Utd	56
1951-52	Man Utd	57	Tottenham H	53
1952-53	Arsenal	54	Preston NE	54
1953 54	Wolverhampton	57	West Brom Alb	53
1954-55	Chelsea	52	Wolverhampton	48
1955-56	Man Utd	60	Blackpool	49
1956-57	Man Utd	64	Tottenham	56
1957-58	Wolverhampton	64	Preston NE	59
1958-59	Wolverhampton	61	Man Utd	55
1959-60	Burnley	55	Wolverhampton	54
1960-61	Tottenham H	66	Sheffield Wed	58
1961-62	Ipswich Town	56	Burnley	53
1962-63	Everton	61	Tottenham	55
1963-64	Liverpool	57	Man Utd	53
1964-65	Man Utd	61	Leeds United	61
1965-66	Liverpool	61	Leeds United	55
1966-67	Man Utd	60	Nottingham F	56
1967-68	Man City	58	Man Utd	56
1968 69	Leeds Utd	67	Liverpool	61
1969-70	Everton	66	Leeds Utd	57
1970-71	Arsenal	65	Leeds Utd	64
1971-72	Derby County	58	Leeds Utd	57
1972-73	Liverpool	60	Arsenal	57
1973-74	Leeds Utd	62	Liverpool	57
1974-75	Derby County	53	Liverpool	51
1975-76	Liverpool	60	QPR	59
1976-77	Liverpool	57	Man City	56
1977-78	Nottingham F	64	Liverpool	57
1978-79	Liverpool	68	Nottingham F	60
1979-80	Liverpool	60	Man Utd	58
1980-81	Aston Villa	60	Ipswich Town	56
1981-82	Liverpool	87	Ipswich Town	83
1982-83	Liverpool	82	Watford	71
1983-84	Liverpool	80	Southampton	77
1984-85	Everton	90	Liverpool	77
1985-86	Liverpool	88	Everton	86
1986-87	Everton	86	Liverpool	77
1987-88	Liverpool	90	Man Utd	81
1988-89	Arsenal	76	Liverpool	76
1989-90	Liverpool	79	Aston Villa	70
1990-91	Arsenal	83	Liverpool	76
1991-92	Leeds Utd	82	Man Utd	78

PREMIER LEAGUE

	Winners	Pts	Runners-up	Pts
1992-93	Man Utd	84	Aston Villa	74
1993-94	Man Utd	92	Blackburn	84
1994-95	Blackburn	89	Man Utd	88
1995-96	Man Utd	82	Newcastle Utd	78
1996-97	Man Utd	75	Newcastle Utd	68
1997-98	Arsenal	78	Man Utd	77
1998-99	Man Utd	79	Arsenal	78
1999-00	Man Utd	91	Arsenal	73
2000-01	Man Utd	80	Arsenal	70
2001-02	Arsenal	87	Liverpool	80

ASSOCIATION FOOTBALL

FA CUP

Scorers from first Wembley final (1923) onwards

Year	Winners	Runners-up
1872	**Wanderers** 1	Royal Engineers 0
1873	**Wanderers** 2	Oxford University 0
1874	**Oxford University** 2	Royal Engineers 0
1875	Royal Engineers 1	Old Etonians 1*
	Royal Engineers 2	Old Etonians 0
1876	Wanderers 1	Old Etonians 1
	Wanderers 3	Old Etonians 0
1877	**Wanderers** 2	Oxford University 1*
1878	**Wanderers** 3	Royal Engineers 1
1879	**Old Etonians** 1	Clapham Rovers 0
1880	**Clapham Rovers** 1	Oxford University 0
1881	**Old Carthusians** 3	Old Etonians 0
1882	**Old Etonians** 1	Blackburn Rovers 0
1883	**Blackburn Olympic** 2	Old Etonians 1*
1884	**Blackburn Rovers** 2	Queen's Park 1
1885	**Blackburn Rovers** 2	Queen's Park 0
1886	Blackburn Rovers 0	WBA 0
	Blackburn Rovers 2	WBA 0
1887	**Aston Villa** 2	WBA 0
1888	**WBA** 2	Preston North End 1
1889	**Preston North End** 3	Wolverhampton Wdrs 0
1890	**Blackburn Rovers** 6	Sheffield Wednesday 1
1891	**Blackburn Rovers** 3	Notts County 1
1892	**WBA** 3	Aston Villa 0
1893	**Wolv'hampton W** 1	Everton 0
1894	**Notts County** 4	Bolton Wanderers 1
1895	**Aston Villa** 1	WBA 0
1896	**Sheffield Wed** 2	Wolverhampton Wdrs 1
1897	**Aston Villa** 3	Everton 2
1898	**Nottingham Forest** 3	Derby County 1
1899	**Sheffield United** 4	Derby County 1
1900	**Bury** 4	Southampton 0
1901	Tottenham Hotspur 2	Sheffield United 2
	Tottenham Hotspur 3	Sheffield United 1
1902	Sheffield United 1	Southampton 1
	Sheffield United 2	Southampton 1
1903	**Bury** 6	Derby County 0
1904	**Manchester City** 1	Bolton Wanderers 0
1905	**Aston Villa** 2	Newcastle United 0
1906	**Everton** 1	Newcastle United 0
1907	**Sheffield Wed** 2	Everton 1
1908	**Wolv'hampton W** 3	Newcastle United 1
1909	**Manchester United** 1	Bristol City 0
1910	Newcastle United 1	Barnsley 1
	Newcastle United 2	Barnsley 0
1911	Bradford City 0	Newcastle United 0
	Bradford City 1	Newcastle United 0
1912	Barnsley 0	WBA 0
	Barnsley 1	WBA 0*
1913	**Aston Villa** 1	Sunderland 0
1914	**Burnley** 1	Liverpool 0
1915	**Sheffield United** 3	Chelsea 0
1920	**Aston Villa** 1	Huddersfield Town 0*
1921	**Tottenham Hotspur** 1	Wolverhampton Wdrs 0
1922	**Huddersfield Town** 1	Preston North End 0
1923	**Bolton Wanderers** 2	West Ham United 0
	Jack, JR Smith	

Year	Winners	Runners-up
1924	**Newcastle United** 2	Aston Villa 0
	Harris, Seymour	
1925	**Sheffield United** 1	Cardiff City 0
	Tunstall	
1926	**Bolton Wanderers** 1	Manchester City 0
	Jack	
1927	**Cardiff City** 1	Arsenal 0
	Ferguson	
1928	**Blackburn Rovers** 3	Huddersfield Town 1
	Roscamp (2), McLean	*Jackson*
1929	**Bolton Wanderers** 2	Portsmouth 0
	Butler, Blackmore	
1930	**Arsenal** 2	Huddersfield Town 0
	James, Lambert	
1931	**WBA** 2	Birmingham City 1
	WG Richardson (2)	*Bradford*
1932	**Newcastle United** 2	Arsenal 1
	Allen (2)	*John*
1933	**Everton** 3	Manchester City 0
	Stein, Dean, Dunn	
1934	**Manchester City** 2	Portsmouth 1
	Tilson (2)	*Rutherford*
1935	**Sheffield Wed** 4	WBA 2
	Rimmer (2), Hooper,	*Boyes, Sandford*
	Palethorpe	
1936	**Arsenal** 1	Sheffield United 0
	Drake	
1937	**Sunderland** 3	Preston North End 1
	Gurney, Carter	*F O'Donnell*
	Burbanks	
1938	**Preston North End** 1	Huddersfield Town 0*
	Mutch (pen)	
1939	**Portsmouth** 4	Wolverhampton Wdrs 1
	Parker (2), Barlow,	*Dorsett*
	Anderson	
1946	**Derby County** 4	Charlton Athletic 1*
	Stamps (2), Doherty,	*H Turner*
	H Turner (og)	
1947	**Charlton Athletic** 1	Burnley 0*
	Duffy	
1948	**Manchester United** 4	Blackpool 2
	Rowley (2), Pearson,	*Shimwell (pen),*
	Mortensen	
	Anderson,	
1949	**Wolv'hampton W** 3	Leicester City 1
	Pye (2), Smyth	*Griffiths*
1950	**Arsenal** 2	Liverpool 0
	Lewis (2)	
1951	**Newcastle United** 2	Blackpool 0
	Milburn (2)	
1952	**Newcastle United** 1	Arsenal 0
	G Robledo	
1953	**Blackpool** 4	Bolton Wanderers 3
	Mortensen (3), Perry	*Lofthouse, Moir, Bell*
1954	**WBA** 3	Preston North End 2
	Allen (2,1 pen)	*Morrison, Wayman*
	Griffin	
1955	**Newcastle United** 3	Manchester City 1
	Milburn, Mitchell,	*Johnstone*
	Hannah	

ASSOCIATION FOOTBALL

1956 **Manchester City** 3 Birmingham City 1
Hayes, Dyson, *Kinsey*
Johnstone

1957 **Aston Villa** 2 Manchester United 1
McParland (2) *Taylor*

1958 **Bolton Wanderers** 2 Manchester United 0
Lofthouse (2)

1959 **Nottingham Forest** 2 Luton Town 1
Dwight, Wilson *Pacey*

1960 **Wolv'hampton Wdrs** 3 Blackburn Rovers 0
McGrath (og), Deeley (2)

1961 **Tottenham Hotspur** 2 Leicester City 0
Smith, Dyson

1962 **Tottenham Hotspur** 3 Burnley 1
Greaves, Smith, *Robson*
Blanchflower (pen)

1963 **Manchester United** 3 Leicester City 1
Herd (2), Law *Keyworth*

1964 **West Ham United** 3 Preston North End 2
Sissons, Hurst, Boyce *Holden, Dawson*

1965 **Liverpool** 2 Leeds United 1*
Hunt, St John *Bremner*

1966 **Everton** 3 Sheffield Wednesday 2
Trebilcock (2), Temple *McCalliog, Ford*

1967 **Tottenham Hotspur** 2 Chelsea 1
Robertson, Saul *Tambling*

1968 **WBA** 1 Everton 0*
Astle

1969 **Manchester City** 1 Leicester City 0
Young

1970 Chelsea 2 Leeds United 2*
Houseman, *Charlton, Jones*
Hutchinson
Chelsea 2 Leeds United 1*
Osgood, Webb *Jones*

1971 **Arsenal** 2 Liverpool 1*
Kelly, George *Heighway*

1972 **Leeds United** 1 Arsenal 0
Clarke

1973 **Sunderland** 1 Leeds United 0
Porterfield

1974 **Liverpool** 3 Newcastle United 0
Keegan (2), Heighway

1975 **West Ham United** 2 Fulham 0
A Taylor (2)

1976 **Southampton** 1 Manchester United 0
Stokes

1977 **Manchester United** 2 Liverpool 1
Pearson, J Greenhoff *Case*

1978 **Ipswich Town** 1 Arsenal 0
Osborne

1979 **Arsenal** 3 Manchester United 2
Talbot, Stapleton, *McQueen, McIlroy*
Sunderland

1980 **West Ham United** 1 Arsenal 0
Brooking

* after extra time

1981 Tottenham Hotspur 1 Manchester City 1*
Hutchison (og) *Hutchison*
Tottenham Hotspur 3 Manchester City 2
Villa (2), Crooks *Mackenzie,*
Reeves (pen)

1982 Tottenham Hotspur 1 QPR 1*
Hoddle *Fenwick*
Tottenham Hotspur 1 QPR 0
Hoddle (pen)

1983 Manchester United 2 Brighton & Hove Alb 2*
Stapleton, Wilkins *Smith, Stevens*
Manchester United 4 Brighton & Hove Alb 0
Robson (2), Whiteside,
Muhren (pen)

1984 **Everton** 2 Watford 0
Sharp, Gray

1985 **Manchester United** 1 Everton 0*
Whiteside

1986 **Liverpool** 3 Everton 1
Rush (2), Johnston *Lineker*

1987 **Coventry City** 3 Tottenham Hotspur 2*
Bennett, Houchen, *C Allen, Mabbutt*
Mabbutt (og)

1988 **Wimbledon** 1 Liverpool 0
Sanchez

1989 **Liverpool** 3 Everton 2*
Aldridge, Rush (2) *McCall (2)*

1990 Manchester United 3 Crystal Palace 3*
Pemberton (og), *O'Reilly, I Wright (2)*
Hughes (2)
Manchester United 1 Crystal Palace 0
Martin

1991 **Tottenham Hotspur** 2 Nottingham Forest 1*
Stewart, Walker (og) *Pearce*

1992 **Liverpool** 2 Sunderland 0
Thomas, Rush

1993 Arsenal 1 Sheffield Wednesday 1*
Wright *Hirst*
Arsenal 2 Sheffield Wednesday 1*
Wright, Linighan *Waddle*

1994 **Manchester United** 4 Chelsea 0
Cantona 2 (2 pens)
Hughes, McClair

1995 **Everton** 1 Manchester United 0
Rideout

1996 **Manchester United** 1 Liverpool 0
Cantona

1997 **Chelsea** 2 Middlesbrough 0
Di Matteo, Newton

1998 **Arsenal** 2 Newcastle 0
Overmars, Anelka

1999 **Manchester United** 2 Newcastle 0
Sheringham, Scholes

2000 **Chelsea** 1 Aston Villa 0
Di Matteo

2001 **Liverpool** 2 Arsenal 1
Owen 2 *Ljungberg*

2002 **Arsenal** 2 Chelsea 0
Parlour, Ljungberg

ASSOCIATION FOOTBALL

LEAGUE CUP

Played as a two-leg final until 1966

1961	**Aston Villa**	0-2 3-0	Rotherham Utd
1962	**Norwich City**	3-0 1-0	Rochdale
1963	**Birmingham City**	3-1 0-0	Aston Villa
1964	**Leicester City**	1-1 3-2	Stoke City
1965	**Chelsea**	3-2 0-0	Leicester City
1966	**WBA**	1-2 4-1	West Ham United

1967 **QPR** 3 WBA 2
1968 **Leeds United** 1 Arsenal 0
1969 **Swindon Town** 3 Arsenal 1*
1970 **Manchester City** 2 WBA 1*
1971 **Tottenham Hotspur** 2 Aston Villa 0
1972 **Stoke City** 2 Chelsea 1
1973 **Tottenham Hotspur** 2 Norwich City 0
1974 **Wolverhampton W** 2 Manchester City 1
1975 **Aston Villa** 1 Norwich City 0
1976 **Manchester City** 2 Newcastle Utd 1*
1977 Aston Villa 1 Everton1*
    Aston Villa 3 Everton 2*
1978 Nottingham Forest 0 Liverpool 0*
    Nottingham Forest 1 Liverpool 0*
1979 **Nottingham Forest** 3 Southampton 2
1980 **Wolverhampton W** 1 Nottingham Forest 0
1981 Liverpool 1 West Ham Utd 1*
    Liverpool 2 West Ham Utd 1

MILK CUP

1982 **Liverpool** 3 Tottenham Hotspur 1*
1983 **Liverpool** 2 Manchester Utd 1*
1984 Liverpool 0 Everton 0*
    Liverpool 1 Everton 0
1985 **Norwich City** 1 Sunderland 0
1986 **Oxford Utd** 3 QPR 0

LITTLEWOODS CUP

1987 **Arsenal** 2 Liverpool 1
1988 **Luton Town** 3 Arsenal 2
1989 **Nottingham Forest** 3 Luton Town 1
1990 **Nottingham Forest** 1 Oldham Athletic 0

RUMBELOWS LEAGUE CUP

1991 **Sheffield Wed** 1 Manchester Utd 0
1992 **Manchester Utd** 1 Nottingham Forest 0

COCA-COLA CUP

1993 **Arsenal** 2 Sheffield Wed 1
1994 **Aston Villa** 3 Manchester Utd 1
1995 **Liverpool** 2 Bolton Wanderers 1
1996 **Aston Villa** 3 Leeds Utd 0
1997 Leicester City 1 Middlesbrough 1*
    Leicester City 1 Middlesbrough 0*
1998 **Chelsea** 2 Middlesbrough 0*

WORTHINGTON CUP

1999 **Tottenham H** 1 Leicester City 0
2000 **Leicester City** 2 Tranmere Rovers 1
2001 **Liverpool** 1 Birmingham City 1*
    Liverpool won 5-4 on penalties
2002 **Blackburn** 2 Tottenham H 1
* After extra time

ASSOCIATION FOOTBALL

SCOTTISH LEAGUE

Year	Winners	Runner-up
1890-91	**Dumbarton/Rangers**	
1891-92	**Dumbarton**	Celtic
1892-93	**Celtic**	Rangers
1893-94	**Celtic**	Hearts
1894-95	**Hearts**	Celtic
1895-96	**Celtic**	Rangers
1896-97	**Hearts**	Hibernian
1897-98	**Celtic**	Rangers
1898-99	**Rangers**	Hearts
1899-00	**Rangers**	Celtic
1900-01	**Rangers**	Celtic
1901-02	**Rangers**	Celtic
1902-03	**Hibernian**	Dundee
1903-04	**Third Lanark**	Hearts
1904-05	**Celtic**	Rangers
1905-06	**Celtic**	Hearts
1906-07	**Celtic**	Dundee
1907-08	**Celtic**	Falkirk
1908-09	**Celtic**	Dundee
1909-10	**Celtic**	Falkirk
1910-11	**Rangers**	Aberdeen
1911-12	**Rangers**	Celtic
1912-13	**Rangers**	Celtic
1913-14	**Celtic**	Rangers
1914-15	**Celtic**	Hearts
1915-16	**Celtic**	Rangers
1916-17	**Celtic**	Morton
1917-18	**Rangers**	Celtic
1918-19	**Celtic**	Rangers
1919-20	**Rangers**	Celtic
1920-21	**Rangers**	Celtic
1921-22	**Celtic**	Rangers
1922-23	**Rangers**	Airdrieonians
1923-24	**Rangers**	Airdrieonians
1924-25	**Rangers**	Airdrieonians
1925-26	**Celtic**	Airdrieonians
1926-27	**Rangers**	Motherwell
1927-28	**Rangers**	Celtic
1928-29	**Rangers**	Celtic
1929-30	**Rangers**	Motherwell
1930-31	**Rangers**	Celtic
1931-32	**Motherwell**	Rangers
1932-33	**Rangers**	Motherwell
1933-34	**Rangers**	Motherwell
1934-35	**Rangers**	Celtic
1935-36	**Celtic**	Rangers
1936-37	**Rangers**	Aberdeen
1937-38	**Celtic**	Hearts
1938-39	**Rangers**	Celtic
1946-47	**Rangers**	Hibernian
1947-48	**Hibernian**	Rangers
1948-49	**Rangers**	Dundee
1949-50	**Rangers**	Hibernian
1950-51	**Hibernian**	Rangers
1951-52	**Hibernian**	Rangers
1952-53	**Rangers**	Hibernian
1953-54	**Celtic**	Hearts
1954-55	**Aberdeen**	Celtic
1955-56	**Rangers**	Aberdeen
1956-57	**Rangers**	Hearts
1957-58	**Hearts**	Rangers
1958-59	**Rangers**	Hearts
1959-60	**Hearts**	Kilmarnock
1960-61	**Rangers**	Kilmarnock
1961-62	**Dundee**	Rangers
1962-63	**Rangers**	Kilmarnock
1963-64	**Rangers**	Kilmarnock
1964-65	**Kilmarnock**	Hearts
1965-66	**Celtic**	Rangers
1966-67	**Celtic**	Rangers
1967-68	**Celtic**	Rangers
1968-69	**Celtic**	Rangers
1969-70	**Celtic**	Rangers
1970-71	**Celtic**	Aberdeen
1971-72	**Celtic**	Aberdeen
1972-73	**Celtic**	Rangers
1973-74	**Celtic**	Hibernian
1974-75	**Rangers**	Hibernian
1975-76	**Rangers**	Celtic
1976-77	**Celtic**	Rangers
1977-78	**Rangers**	Aberdeen
1978-79	**Celtic**	Rangers
1979-80	**Aberdeen**	Celtic
1980-81	**Celtic**	Aberdeen
1981-82	**Celtic**	Aberdeen
1982-83	**Dundee Utd**	Celtic
1983-84	**Aberdeen**	Celtic
1984-85	**Aberdeen**	Celtic
1985-86	**Celtic**	Hearts
1986-87	**Rangers**	Celtic
1987-88	**Celtic**	Hearts
1988-89	**Rangers**	Aberdeen
1989-90	**Rangers**	Aberdeen
1990-91	**Rangers**	Aberdeen
1991-92	**Rangers**	Hearts
1992-93	**Rangers**	Aberdeen
1993-94	**Rangers**	Aberdeen
1994-95	**Rangers**	Motherwell
1995-96	**Rangers**	Celtic
1996-97	**Rangers**	Celtic
1997-98	**Celtic**	Rangers
1998-99	**Rangers**	Celtic
1999-00	**Rangers**	Celtic
2000-01	**Celtic**	Rangers
2001-02	**Celtic**	Rangers

ASSOCIATION FOOTBALL

SCOTTISH FA CUP

1874	**Queen's Park** 2	Clydesdale 0	
1875	**Queen's Park** 3	Renton 0	
1876	Queen's Park 1	Third Lanark 1	
	Queen's Park 2	Third Lanark 0	
1877	Vale of Leven 0	Rangers 0	
	Vale of Leven 1	Rangers 1	
	Vale of Leven 3	Rangers 2	
1878	**Vale of Leven** 1	Third Lanark 0	
1879	**Vale of Leven** 1	Rangers 1	

Leven awarded Cup, Rangers refused replay

1880	**Queen's Park** 3	Thornliebank 0	
1881	Queen's Park 2	Dumbarton 1	

Abandoned due to pitch invasion

	Queen's Park 3	Dumbarton 1	
1882	Queen's Park 2	Dumbarton 2	
	Queen's Park 4	Dumbarton 1	
1883	Dumbarton 2	Vale of Leven 2	
	Dumbarton 2	Vale of Leven 1	
1884	**Queen's Park**		

Queen's Park awarded Cup as Vale of Leven did not appear

1885	Renton 0	Vale of Leven 0	
	Renton 3	Vale of Leven 1	
1886	**Queen's Park** 3	Renton 1	
1887	**Hibernian** 2	Dumbarton 1	
1888	**Renton** 6	Cambuslang 1	
1889	Third Lanark 3	Celtic 1	

Abandoned due to snowstorm

	Third Lanark 2	Celtic 1	
1890	Queen's Park 1	Vale of Leven 1	
	Queen's Park 2	Vale of Leven 1	
1891	**Hearts** 1	Dumbarton 0	
1892	Celtic 1	Queen's Park 0	

Abandoned due to pitch invasion

1892	**Celtic** 1	Queen's Park 0	
1893	Queen's Park 0	Celtic 1	

Abandoned due to frost

	Queen's Park 2	Celtic 1	
1894	**Rangers** 3	Celtic 1	
1895	**St Bernard's** 2	Renton 1	
1896	**Hearts** 3	Hibernian 1	
1897	**Rangers** 5	Dumbarton 1	
1898	**Rangers** 2	Kilmarnock 0	
1899	**Rangers** 2	Rangers 0	
1900	**Celtic** 4	Queen's Park 3	
1901	**Hearts** 4	Celtic 3	
1902	**Hibernian** 1	Celtic 0	
1903	Rangers 1	Hearts 1	
	Rangers 0	Hearts 0	
	Rangers 2	Hearts 0	
1904	**Celtic** 3	Rangers 2	
1905	Third Lanark 0	Rangers 0	
	Third Lanark 3	Rangers 0	
1906	**Hearts** 1	Third Lanark 0	
1907	**Celtic** 3	Hearts 0	
1908	**Celtic** 5	St Mirren 1	
1909	Celtic 2	Rangers 2	
	Celtic 1	Rangers 1	

Cup not awarded, riot

1910	Dundee 2	Clyde 2	
	Dundee 0	Clyde 0	
	Dundee 2	Clyde 1	
1911	Celtic 0	Hamilton Academicals 0	
	Celtic 2	Hamilton Academicals 0	
1912	**Celtic** 2	Clyde 0	
1913	**Falkirk** 2	Raith Rovers 0	
1914	Celtic 0	Hibernian 0	
	Celtic 4	Hibernian 1	
1920	**Kilmarnock** 3	Albion Rovers 2	
1921	**Partick Thistle** 1	Rangers 0	
1922	**Morton** 1	Rangers 0	
1923	**Celtic** 1	Hibernian 0	
1924	**Airdrieonians** 2	Hibernian 0	
1925	**Celtic** 2	Dundee 1	
1926	**St Mirren** 2	Celtic 0	
1927	**Celtic** 3	East Fife 1	
1928	**Rangers** 4	Celtic 0	
1929	**Kilmarnock** 2	Rangers 0	
1930	Rangers 0	Partick Thistle 0	
	Rangers 2	Partick Thistle 1	
1931	Celtic 2	Motherwell 2	
	Celtic 4	Motherwell 2	
1932	Rangers 1	Kilmarnock 1	
	Rangers 3	Kilmarnock 0	
1933	**Celtic** 1	Motherwell 0	
1934	**Rangers** 5	St Mirren 0	
1935	**Ranger** 2	Hamilton Academicals 1	
1936	**Rangers** 1	Third Lanark 0	
1937	**Celtic** 2	Aberdeen 1	
1938	East Fife 1	Kilmarnock 1	
	East Fife 4	Kilmarnock 2	
1939	**Clyde** 4	Motherwell 0	
1947	**Aberdeen** 2	Hibernian 1	
1948	Rangers 1	Morton 1	
	Rangers 1	Morton 0	
1949	**Rangers** 4	Clyde 1	
1950	**Rangers** 3	East Fife 0	
1951	**Celtic** 1	Motherwell 0	
1952	**Motherwell** 4	Dundee 0	
1953	Rangers 1	Aberdeen 1	
	Rangers 1	Aberdeen 0	
1954	**Celtic** 2	Aberdeen 1	
1955	Clyde 1	Celtic 1	
	Clyde 1	Celtic 0	
1956	**Hearts** 3	Celtic 1	
1957	Falkirk 1	Kilmarnock 1	
	Falkirk 2	Kilmarnock 1	
1958	**Clyde** 1	Hibernian 0	
1959	**St Mirren** 3	Aberdeen 1	
1960	**Rangers** 2	Kilmarnock 0	
1961	Dunfermline 0	Celtic 0	
	Dunfermline 2	Celtic 0	
1962	**Rangers** 2	St Mirren 0	
1963	Rangers 1	Celtic 1	
	Rangers 3	Celtic 0	
1964	**Rangers** 3	Dundee 1	
1965	**Celtic** 3	Dunfermline 2	
1966	Rangers 0	Celtic 0	
	Rangers 1	Celtic 0	

Year	Winners	Runners-up
1967	Celtic 2	Aberdeen 0
1968	Dunfermline 3	Hearts 1
1969	Celtic 4	Rangers 1
1970	Aberdeen 3	Celtic 1
1971	Celtic 1	Rangers 1
	Celtic 2	Rangers 1
1972	Celtic 6	Hibernian 1
1973	Rangers 3	Celtic 2
1974	Celtic 3	Dundee United 0
1975	Celtic 3	Airdrieonians 1
1976	Rangers 3	Hearts 1
1977	Celtic 1	Rangers 0
1978	Rangers 2	Aberdeen 1
1979	Rangers 0	Hibernian 0
	Rangers 0	Hibernian 0
	Rangers 3	Hibernian 2
1980	Celtic 1	Rangers 0*
1981	Rangers 0	Dundee United 0
	Rangers 4	Dundee United 1
1982	Aberdeen 4	Rangers 1*
1983	Aberdeen 1	Rangers 0*
1984	Aberdeen 2	Celtic 1*
1985	Celtic 2	Dundee United 1
1986	Aberdeen 3	Hearts 0
1987	St Mirren 1	Dundee United 0*
1988	Celtic 2	Dundee United 1
1989	Celtic 1	Rangers 0
1990	Aberdeen 0	Celtic 0
Aberdeen won 9-8 on penalties		
1991	Motherwell 4	Dundee United 3*
1992	Rangers 2	Airdrieonians 1
1993	Rangers 2	Aberdeen 1
1994	Dundee United 1	Rangers 0
1995	Celtic 1	Airdrieonians 0
1996	Rangers 5	Hearts 1
1997	Kilmarnock 1	Falkirk 0
1998	Hearts 2	Rangers 1
1999	Rangers 1	Celtic 0
2000	Rangers 4	Aberdeen 0
2001	Celtic 3	Hibernian 0
2002	Rangers 3	Celtic 2

* After extra time

SCOTTISH LEAGUE CUP

Year	Winners	Runners-up
1946-47	Rangers 4	Aberdeen 0
1947-48	East Fife 0	Falkirk 0*
	East Fife 4	Falkirk 1
1948-49	Rangers 2	Raith Rovers 0
1949-50	East Fife 3	Dunfermline A 0
1950-51	Motherwell 3	Hibernian 0
1951-52	Dundee 3	Rangers 2
1952-53	Dundee 2	Kilmarnock 0
1953-54	East Fife 3	Partick Thistle 2
1954-55	Hearts 4	Motherwell 2
1955-56	Aberdeen 2	St Mirren 1
1956-57	Celtic 0	Partick Thistle 0*
	Celtic 3	Partick Thistle 0
1957-58	Celtic 7	Rangers 1
1958-59	Hearts 5	Partick Thistle 1
1969-60	Hearts 2	Third Lanark 1
1960-61	Rangers 2	Kilmarnock 0
1961-62	Rangers 1	Hearts 1*
	Rangers 3	Hearts 1
1962-63	Hearts 1	Kilmarnock 0
1963-64	Rangers 5	Morton 0
1966-65	Rangers 2	Celtic 1
1965-66	Celtic 2	Rangers 1
1966-67	Celtic 1	Rangers 0
1967-68	Celtic 5	Dundee 3
1968-69	Celtic 6	Hibernian 2
1969-70	Celtic 1	St.Johnstone 0
1970-71	Rangers 1	Celtic 0
1971-72	Partick Thistle 4	Celtic 1
1972-73	Hibernian 2	Celtic 1
1973-74	Dundee 1	Celtic 0
1974-75	Celtic 6	Hibernian 3
1975-76	Rangers 1	Celtic 0
1976-77	Aberdeen 2	Celtic 1
1977-78	Rangers 2	Celtic 1
1978-79	Rangers 2	Aberdeen 1
1979-80	Dundee United 0	Aberdeen 0
	Dundee United 3	Aberdeen 0**
1980-81	Dundee United 3	Dundee 0**
1981-82	Rangers 2	Dundee United 1
1982-83	Celtic 2	Rangers 1
1983-84	Rangers 3	Celtic 2*
1984-85	Rangers 1	Dundee United 0
1985-86	Aberdeen 3	Hibernian 0
1986-87	Rangers 2	Celtic 1
1987-88	Rangers 3	Aberdeen 3*
Rangers won 5-3 on penalties		
1988-89	Rangers 3	Aberdeen 2
1989-90	Aberdeen 2	Rangers 1*
1990-91	Rangers 2	Celtic 1*
1991-92	Hibernian 2	Dunfermline 0
1992-93	Rangers 2	Aberdeen 1
1993-94	Rangers 2	Hibernian 1
1994-95	Raith Rovers 2	Celtic 2
Raith won 6-5 on penalties		
1995-96	Aberdeen 2	Dundee 0
1996-97	Stranraer 1	St Johnstone 0
1997-98	Celtic 3	Dundee United 0
1998-99	Rangers 2	St Johnstone 1
1999-00	Celtic 2	Aberdeen 0
2000-01	Celtic 3	Kilmarnock 0
2001-02	Rangers 4	Ayr 0

* after extra time ** Played at Dens Park, Dundee

ATHLETICS

WORLD RECORDS

Men

100m	9.78	(+2.0)	Tim Montgomery	USA	Paris	September 14, 2002
200m	19.32	(+0.4)	Michael Johnson	USA	Atlanta	August 1, 1996
400m	43.18		Michael Johnson	USA	Seville	August 26, 1999
800m	1:41.11		Wilson Kipketer	DEN	Cologne	August 24, 1997
1000m	2:11.96		Noah Ngeny	KEN	Rieti	September 5, 1999
1500m	3:26.00		Hicham El Guerrouj	MAR	Rome	July 14, 1998
Mile	3:43.13		Hicham El Guerrouj	MAR	Rome	July 7, 1999
2000m	4:44.79		Hicham El Guerrouj	MAR	Berlin	September 7, 1999
3000m	7:20.67		Daniel Komen	KEN	Rieti	September 1, 1996
5000m	12:39.36		Haile Gebrselassie	ETH	Helsinki	June 13, 1998
10,000m	26:22.75		Haile Gebrselassie	ETH	Hengelo	June 1, 1998
Marathon	2:05:38		Khalid Khannouchi	MAR	London	April 14, 2002
3000msc	7:53.17		Brahim Boulami	MAR	Zurich	August 16, 2002
110mh	12.91	(+0.5)	Colin Jackson	GBR	Stuttgart	August 20, 1993
400mh	46.78		Kevin Young	USA	Barcelona	August 6, 1992
High Jump	2.45m		Javier Sotomayor	CUB	Salamanca	July 27, 1993
Pole Vault	6.14m A		Sergey Bubka	UKR	Sestriere	July 31, 1994
Long Jump	8.95m	(+0.3)	Mike Powell	USA	Tokyo	August 30, 1991
Triple Jump	18.29m	(+1.3)	Jonathan Edwards	GBR	Gothenburg	August 7, 1995
Shot	23.12m		Randy Barnes	USA	Los Angeles	May 20, 1990
Discus	74.08m		Jürgen Schult	GER	Neubrandenburg	June 6, 1986
Hammer	86.74m		Yury Sedykh	URS	Stuttgart	August 30, 1986
Javelin	98.48m		Jan Zelezny	CZE	Jena	May 25, 1996
Decathlon	9026		Roman Sebrle	CZE	Götzis	May 27 2001
4x100m	37.40		United States		Barcelona/Stuttgart	8.8.92/21.8.93
4x400m	2:54.20		United States (Young/Pettigrew/Washington/Johnson)		New York	July 22, 1998
20km Walk	1:17:25.6		Bernardo Segura	MEX	Bergen	May 7, 1994
50km Walk	3:40:57.9		Thierry Toutain	FRA	Héricourt	September 29, 1996

Women

100m	10.49	(0.0)	Florence Griffith-Joyner	USA	Indianapolis	July 16, 1988
200m	21.34	(+1.3)	Florence Griffith-Joyner	USA	Seoul	September 29, 1988
400m	47.60		Marita Koch	GDR	Canberra	October 6, 1985
800m	1:53.28		Jarmila Kratochvilova	TCH	Munich	July 26, 1983
1000m	2:28.98		Svetlana Masterkova	RUS	Brussels	August 23, 1996
1500m	3:50.46		Qu Yunxia	CHN	Beijing	September 11, 1993
Mile	4:12.56		Svetlana Masterkova	RUS	Zürich	August 14, 1996
2000m	5:25.36		Sonia O'Sullivan	IRL	Edinburgh	July 8, 1994
3000m	8:06.11		Wang Junxia	CHN	Beijing	September 13, 1993
5000m	14:28.09		Jiang Bo	CHN	Shanghai	October 23, 1997
10,000m	29:31.78		Wang Junxia	CHN	Beijing	September 8, 1993
Marathon	2:17:18		Paula Radcliffe	GBR	Chicago	October 13, 2002
3000msc	9:16.51		Alesya Turova	TUR	Gdansk	July 27, 2002
100mh	12.21	(+0.7)	Yordanka Donkova	BUL	Stara Zagora	August 20, 1988
400mh	52.61		Kim Batten	USA	Gothenburg	August 11, 1994
High Jump	2.09m		Stefka Kostadinova	BUL	Rome	August 30, 1987
Pole Vault	4.81m		Stacy Dragila	USA	Palo Alto	June 9, 2001
Long Jump	7.52m	(+1.4)	Galina Chistyakova	URS	Leningrad	June 11, 1988
Triple Jump	15.50m		Inessa Kravets	UKR	Gothenburg	August 10, 1994
Shot	22.63m		Natalya Lisovskaya	URS	Moscow	June 7, 1987
Discus	76.80m		Gabriele Reinsch	GER	Neubrandenburg	July 9, 1988
Hammer	76.07m		Michaela Melinte	ROM	Rüdlingen	July 1, 2001
Javelin	71.45m		Osleidys Menéndez	CUB	Réthymno	July 28, 2000
Heptathlon	7291		Jackie Joyner-Kersee	USA	Seoul	September 24, 1988
4x100m	41.37		East Germany		Canberra	October 6, 1985
4x400m	3:15.17		Soviet Union		Seoul	October 1, 1988
20km Walk	1:26:52.3		Olimpiada Ivanova	RUS	Brisbane	September 6, 2001

A = Record set at altitude

ATHLETICS

BRITISH RECORDS
Men

100m	9.87	Linford Christie	Stuttgart	August 15, 1993
	9.87	Dwain Chambers	Paris	September 14, 2002
200m	19.87 A*	John Regis	Sestriere	July 31, 1994
300m	31.56	Doug Walker	Gateshead	July 19, 1998
400m	44.36	Iwan Thomas	Birmingham	July 13, 1997
600m	1:14.95	Steve Heard	Haringey	July 14, 1991
800m	1:41.73 **	Sebastian Coe	Florence	June 10, 1981
1000m	2:12.18	Sebastian Coe	Oslo	July 11, 1981
1500m	3:29.67	Steve Cram	Nice	July 16, 1985
Mile	3:46.32	Steve Cram	Oslo	July 27, 1985
2000m	4:51.39	Steve Cram	Budapest	August 4, 1985
3000m	7:32.79	Dave Moorcroft	Crystal Palace	July 17, 1982
2 Miles	8:13.51	Steve Ovett	Crystal Palace	September 15, 1978
5000m	13:00.41	Dave Moorcroft	Oslo	July 7, 1982
10,000m	27:18.14	Jon Brown	Brussels	August 28, 1998
20,000m	57:28.7	Carl Thackery	La Flèche	March 31, 1990
1 Hour	20,855m	Carl Thackery	La Flèche	March 31, 1990
Half-marathon	60:09	Paul Evans	Marrakesh	January 15, 1995
25,000m	1:15:22.6	Ron Hill	Bolton	July 21, 1965
30,000m	1:31:30.4	Jim Alder	Crystal Palace	September 5, 1970
Marathon	2:07:13	Steve Jones	Chicago	October 20, 1985
2000msc	5:19.86	Mark Rowland	Crystal Palace	August 28, 1988
3000msc	8:07.96	Mark Rowland	Seoul	September 30, 1988
110mh	12.91 (+0.5)	Colin Jackson	Stuttgart	August 20, 1993
200mh	22.63	Colin Jackson	Cardiff	June 1, 1991
400mh	47.82	Kriss Akabusi	Barcelona	August 6, 1992
High Jump	2.37m	Steve Smith	Seoul	September 20, 1992
	2.37m	Steve Smith	Stuttgart	August 22, 1993
Pole Vault	5.80m	Nick Buckfield	Haniá	May 27, 1998
Long Jump	8.27m	Chris Tomlinson	Tallahassee	April 13, 2002
Triple Jump	18.29m (+1.3)	Jonathan Edwards	Gothenburg	August 7, 1995
Shot	21.68m	Geoff Capes	Cwmbran	May 18, 1980
Discus	66.64m	Perris Wilkins	Edgbaston	June 6, 1998
Hammer	77.54m	Martin Girvan	Wolverhampton	May 12, 1994
Javelin	91.46m	Steve Backley	Auckland	January 25, 1992
Decathlon	8847	Daley Thompson	Los Angeles	August 9, 1994
20km Walk	1:22:03	Ian McCombie	Seoul	April 27, 1988
50km Walk	3:51:37	Chris Maddocks	Burrator	October 28, 1990
4x100m	37.73	Great Britain	Seville	August 29, 1999
		Gardener/Campbell/Devonish/Chambers		
4x200m	1:21.29	Great Britain	Birmingham	June 23, 1989
4x400m	2:56.60	Great Britain	Atlanta	August 3, 1996
		Thomas/Baulch/Richardson/Black		
4x800m	7:03.89 WR	Great Britain	Crystal Palace	August 30, 1982
		Elliot/Cook/Cram/Coe		
4x1500m	14:56.8	Great Britain	Bourges	June 23, 1979
4x1 Mile	16:21.1	British Milers' Club Team	Oxford	July 10, 1993

* A=Record set at altitude
** Time taken from photo-electric cell

ATHLETICS

BRITISH RECORDS
Women

Event	Record	Athlete	Venue	Date
100m	11.10	Kathy Cook	Rome	September 5, 1981
200m	22.10	Kathy Cook	Los Angeles	August 9, 1984
300m	35.46	Kathy Cook	Crystal Palace	August 18, 1984
400m	49.43	Kathy Cook	Los Angeles	August 6, 1984
600m	1:26.18	Diane Modahl	Crystal Palace	August 22, 1987
800m	1:56.21	Kelly Holmes	Monaco	September 9, 1995
1000m	2:32.55	Kelly Holmes	Leeds	June 15, 1995
1500m	3:58.07	Kelly Holmes	Sheffield	June 29, 1997
Mile	4:17.57	Zola Budd	Zurich	August 21, 1985
2000m	5:26.93	Yvonne Murray	Edinburgh	July 8, 1994
3000m	8:26.97	Paula Radcliffe	Rome	June 29, 2001
5000m	14:31.42	Paula Radcliffe	Manchester	July 28, 2002
10,000m	30:01.09	Paula Radcliffe	Munich	August 6, 2002
20,000m	1:15:46	Carolyn Hunter-Rowe	Barry	March 6, 1994
1 Hour	16,364m	Alison Fletcher	Bromley	September 3, 1997
Half-marathon	1:07:07	Paula Radcliffe	South Shields	October 22, 2000
Marathon	2:18:18	Paula Radcliffe	Chicago	Oct 13, 2002
3000msc	9:52.71	Tara Krzywicki	Glasgow	July 1, 2001
100mh	12.80	Angie Thorp	Atlanta	July 31, 1996
400mh	52.74	Sally Gunnell	Stuttgart	August 19, 1993
High Jump	1.95m	Diana Davies	Oslo	June 26, 1982
		Susan Jones	Bremen	June 24, 2001
Pole Vault	4.40m	Janine Whitlock	Birmingham	July 14, 2001
Long Jump	6.90m	Beverly Kinch	Helsinki	August 14, 1983
Triple Jump	15.15m	Ashia Hansen	Fukuoka	September 13, 1997
Shot	19.36m	Judy Oakes	Gateshead	August 14, 1988
Discus	67.48m	Meg Ritchie	Walnut	April 26, 1981
Hammer	68.15m	Lorraine Shaw	Nice	March 17, 2001
Javelin	59.50m	Karen Martin	Cosford	July 14, 1999
Heptathlon	6831	Denise Lewis	Talence	July 30, 2000
5000m Walk	22:01.53	Lisa Kehler	Birmingham	July 26, 1998
10km Walk	45:18.8	Vicky Lupton	Watford	September 2, 1995
20km Walk	1:56:59	Cath Reader	Loughborough	October 21,1995
4x100m	42.43	Great Britain	Moscow	August 1, 1980
		Oakes/Cook/Callender/Lannaman		
4x200m	1:31.57	Great Britain	Crystal Palace	August 20, 1977
4x400m	3:22.01	Great Britain	Atlanta	August 3, 1996
		Hansen/Smith/Gunnell/Keough		
4x800m	8:19.9	Great Britain	Sheffield	June 5, 1992

ATHLETICS

WORLD CHAMPIONSHIPS

1983 Helsinki; 1987 Rome;
1991 Tokyo; 1993 Stuttgart; 1995
Gothenburg; 1997 Athens; 1999
Seville; 2001 Edmonton

Men

100m

1983 **Carl Lewis** USA
1987 **Carl Lewis** USA*
1991 **Carl Lewis** USA
1993 **Linford Christie** GBR
1995 **Donovan Bailey** CAN
1997 **Maurice Greene** USA
1999 **Maurice Greene** USA
2001 **Maurice Greene** USA
*Won by Ben Johnson, later
stripped of title for drug-taking

200m

1983 **Calvin Smith** USA
1987 **Calvin Smith** USA
1991 **Michael Johnson** USA
1993 **Frankie Fredericks** NAM
1995 **Michael Johnson** USA
1997 **Ato Boldon** TRI
1999 **Maurice Greene** USA
2001 **Kostas Kenteris** GRE

400m

1983 **Bert Cameron** JAM
1987 **Thomas Schonlebe** GDR
1991 **Antonio Pettigrew** USA
1993 **Michael Johnson** USA
1995 **Michael Johnson** USA
1997 **Michael Johnson** USA
1999 **Michael Johnson** USA
2001 **Avard Moncur** BAH

800m

1983 **Willi Wulbeck** FRG
1987 **Billy Konchellah** KEN
1991 **Billy Konchellah** KEN
1993 **Paul Ruto** KEN
1995 **Wilson Kipketer** DEN
1997 **Wilson Kipketer** DEN
1999 **Wilson Kipketer** DEN
2001 **André Bucher** SUI

1500m

1983 **Steve Cram** GBR
1987 **Abdi Bile** Som
1991 **Noureddine Morceli** ALG
1993 **Noureddine Morceli** ALG
1995 **Noureddine Morceli** ALG
1997 **Hicham El Guerrouj** MAR
1999 **Hicham El Guerrouj** MAR
2001 **Hicham El Guerrouj** MAR

5000m

1983 **Eamonn Coghlan** IRE
1987 **Said Aouita** MAR
1991 **Yobes Ondieki** KEN
1993 **Ismael Kirui** KEN
1995 **Ismael Kirui** KEN
1997 **Daniel Komen** KEN
1999 **Salah Hissou** MAR
2001 **Richard Lima** KEN

10,000m

1983 **Alberto Cova** ITA
1987 **Paul Kipkoech** KEN
1991 **Moses Tanui** KEN
1993 **Haile Gebrselassie** ETH
1995 **Haile Gebrselassie** ETH
1997 **Haile Gebrselassie** ETH
1999 **Haile Gebrselassie** ETH
2001 **Charles Kamathr** KEN

Marathon

1983 **Rob de Castella** AUS
1987 **Douglas Wakiihuri** KEN
1991 **Hiromi Taniguchi** JPN
1993 **Mark Plaatjes** USA
1995 **Martin Fiz** ESP
1997 **Abel Antón** ESP
1999 **Abel Antón** ESP
2001 **Gezahegne Abera** ETH

3000m Steeplechase

1983 **Patriz Ilg** FRG
1987 **Francesco Panetta** ITA
1991 **Moses Kiptanui** KEN
1993 **Moses Kiptanui** KEN
1995 **Moses Kiptanui** KEN
1997 **Wilson Kipketer Boit** KEN
1999 **Christopher Koskei** KEN
2001 **Reuben Kosgei** KEN

110m Hurdles

1983 **Greg Foster** USA
1987 **Greg Foster** USA
1991 **Greg Foster** USA
1993 **Colin Jackson** GBR
1995 **Allen Johnson** USA
1997 **Allen Johnson** USA
1999 **Colin Jackson** GBR
2001 **Allen Johson** USA

400m Hurdles

1983 **Edwin Moses** USA
1987 **Edwin Moses** USA
1991 **Samuel Matete** ZAM
1993 **Kevin Young** USA
1995 **Derrick Adkins** USA
1997 **Stéphane Diagana** FRA
1999 **Fabrizio Mori** ITA
2001 **Felix Sanchez** DOM

High Jump

1983 **Genn Avdeyenko** URS
1987 **Patrik Sjoberg** SWE
1991 **Charles Austin** USA
1993 **Javier Sotomayor** CUB
1995 **Troy Kemp** BAH
1997 **Javier Sotomayor** CUB
1999 **Vyacheslav Voronin** RUS
2001 **Martin Buss** GER

Pole Vault

1983 **Sergey Bubka** URS
1987 **Sergey Bubka** URS
1991 **Sergey Bubka** URS
1993 **Sergey Bubka** UKR
1995 **Sergey Bubka** UKR
1997 **Sergey Bubka** UKR
1999 **Maksim Tarasov** RUS
2001 **Dmitri Markov** AUS

Long Jump

1983 **Carl Lewis** USA
1987 **Carl Lewis** USA
1991 **Mike Powell** USA
1993 **Mike Powell** USA
1995 **Ivan Pedroso** CUB
1997 **Ivan Pedroso** CUB
1999 **Ivan Pedroso** CUB
2001 **Ivan Pedroso** CUB

Triple Jump

1983 **Zdzislaw Hoffmann** POL
1987 **Khristo Markov** BUL
1991 **Kenny Harrison** USA
1993 **Mike Conley** USA
1995 **Jonathan Edwards** GBR
1997 **Yoelbi Quesada** CUB
1999 **Charles Friedek** GER
2001 **Jonathan Edwards** GBR

Shot

1983 **Edward Sarul** POL
1987 **Werner Günthör** SUI
1991 **Werner Günthör** SUI
1993 **Werner Günthör** SUI
1995 **John Godina** USA
1997 **John Godina** USA
1999 **CJ Hunter** USA
2001 **John Godina** USA

Discus

1983 **Imrich Bugar** TCH
1987 **Jürgen Schult** GDR
1991 **Lars Riedel** GER
1993 **Lars Riedel** GER
1995 **Lars Riedel** GER
1997 **Lars Riedel** GER
1999 **Anthony Washington** USA
2001 **Lars Riedel** GER

Hammer

1983 **Sergey Litvinov** URS
1987 **Sergey Litvinov** URS
1991 **Yuriy Sedykh** URS
1993 **Andrey Abduvalyev** TJK
1995 **Andrey Abduvalyev** TJK
1997 **Heinz Weis** GER
1999 **Karsten Kobs** GER
2001 **Szymon Ziolkowskr** POL

Javelin

1983 **Detlef Michel** GDR
1987 **Seppo Räty** FIN
1991 **Kimmo Kinnunen** FIN
1993 **Jan Zelezny** CZE
1995 **Jan Zelezny** CZE
1997 **Marius Corbett** RSA
1999 **Aki Parviainen** FIN
2001 **Jan Zelezny** CZE

ATHLETICS

Decathlon
1983 **Daley Thompson** GBR
1987 **Torsten Voss** GDR
1991 **Dan O'Brien** USA
1993 **Dan O'Brien** USA
1995 **Dan O'Brien** USA
1997 **Tomás Dvorák** CZE
1999 **Tomás Dvorák** CZE
2001 **Tomás Dvorák** CZE

20km Walk
1983 **Ernesto Canto** MEX
1987 **Maurizio Damilano** ITA
1991 **Maurizio Damilano** ITA
1993 **Valentin Massana** ITA
1995 **Michele Didoni** ITA
1997 **Daniel Garcia** MEX
1999 **Ilya Markov** RUS
2001 **Roman Rasskazov** RUS

50km Walk
1983 **Ronald Weigel** GDR
1987 **Hartwig Gauder** GDR
1991 **Aleksandr Potashov** URS
1993 **Jesús Angel Garcia** ESP
1995 **Valentin Kononen** FIN
1997 **Robert Korzeniowski** POL
1999 **German Skurygin** RUS
2001 **Robert Korzeniowski** POL

4x100m Relay
1983 **USA**
1987 **USA**
1991 **USA**
1993 **USA**
1995 **Canada**
1997 **Canada**
1999 **USA**
2001 **USA**

4x400m Relay
1983 **Soviet Union**
1987 **USA**
1991 **Great Britain**
1993 **USA**
1995 **USA**
1997 **USA**
1999 **USA**
2001 **USA**

Women

100m
1983 **Marlies Gohr** GDR
1987 **Silke Gladisch** GDR
1991 **Katrin Krabbe** GER
1993 **Gail Devers** USA
1995 **Gwen Torrence** USA
1997 **Marion Jones** USA
1999 **Marion Jones** USA
2001 **Z Pintusevich-Block** UKR

200m
1983 **Marita Koch** GDR
1987 **Silke Gladisch** GDR
1991 **Katrin Krabbe** GER
1993 **Merlene Ottey** JAM
1995 **Merlene Ottey*** JAM
1997 **Zhanna Pintusevich** UKR
1999 **Inger Miller** USA
2001 **Marion Jones** USA
* Gwen Torrence finished first, but
was disqualified for running out of
her lane

400m
1983 **Jarmila Kratochvilova** TCH
1987 **Olga Bryzgina** URS
1991 **Marie-José Pérec** FRA
1993 **Jearl Miles** USA
1995 **Marie-José Pérec** FRA
1997 **Cathy Freeman** AUS
1999 **Cathy Freeman** AUS
2001 **Amy Thiam Mbcke** SEN

800m
1983 **Jarmila Kratochvilova** TCH
1987 **Sigrun Wodars** GDR
1991 **Lilia Nurutdinova** URS
1993 **Maria Mutola** MOZ
1995 **Ana Quirot** CUB
1997 **Ana Quirot** CUB
1999 **Ludmila Formanova** CZE
2001 **Maria Mutola** MOZ

1500m
1983 **Mary Decker** USA
1987 **Tatyana Samolenko** URS
1991 **Hassiba Boulmerka** ALG
1993 **Liu Dong** CHN
1995 **Hassiba Boulmerka** ALG
1997 **Carla Sacramento** POR
1999 **Svetlana Masterkova** RUS
2001 **Gabriela Szabo** ROM

3000m*
1983 **Mary Decker** USA
1987 **Tatyana Samolenko** URS
1991 **Tatyana Dorovskikh**** URS
1993 **Qu Yunxia** CHN
* Superseded by the 5000m
** née Samolenko

5000m
1995 **Sonia O'Sullivan** IRL
1997 **Gabriela Szabo** ROM
1999 **Gabriela Szabo** ROM
2001 **Olga Yegorova** RUS

10,000m
1987 **Ingrid Kristiansen** NOR
1991 **Liz McColgan** GBR
1993 **Wang Junxia** CHN
1995 **Fernanda Ribeiro** POR
1997 **Sally Barsosio** KEN
1999 **Gete Wami** ETH
2001 **Derartu Tulu** ETH

Marathon
1983 **Grete Waitz** NOR
1987 **Rosa Mota** POR
1991 **Wanda Panfil** POL
1993 **Junko Asari** JPN
1995 **Manuela Machado** POR
1997 **Hiromi Suzuki** JPN
1999 **Yong Song-ock** PRK
2001 **Lidia Simon** ROM

100m Hurdles
1983 **Bettine Jahn** GDR
1987 **Ginka Zagorcheva** BUL
1991 **Ludmila Narozhilenko** URS
1993 **Gail Devers** USA
1995 **Gail Devers** USA
1997 **Ludmila Engquist**** SWE
1999 **Gail Devers** USA
2001 **Anjanette Kirkland** USA
** née Narozhilenko

400m hurdles
1983 **Yekaterina Fesenko** URS
1987 **Sabine Busch** GDR
1991 **Tatyana Ledovskaya** URS
1993 **Sally Gunnell** GBR
1995 **Kim Batten** USA
1997 **Nezha Bidouane** MAR
1999 **Daimi Pernia** CUB
2001 **Nezha Bidouane** MAR

High Jump
1983 **Tamara Bykova** URS
1987 **Stefka Kostadinova** BUL
1991 **Heike Henkel** GER
1993 **Ioamnet Quintero** CUB
1995 **Stefka Kostadinova** BUL
1997 **Hanne Haugland** NOR
1999 **Inga Babakova** UKR
2001 **Hestrie Kloete** RSA

Pole Vault
1999 **Stacy Dragila** USA
2001 **Stacy Dragila** USA

Long Jump
1983 **Heike Daute** GDR
1987 **Jackie Joyner-Kersee** USA
1991 **Jackie Joyner-Kersee** USA
1993 **Heike Drechsler** GER
1995 **Fiona May** ITA
1997 **Lyudmila Galkina** RUS
1999 **Niurka Montalvo** ESP
2001 **Fiona May** ITA

Triple Jump
1993 **Ana Biryukova** RUS
1995 **Inessa Kravets** UKR
1997 **Sárka Kaspárková** CZE
1999 **Paraskevi Tsiamita** GRE
2001 **Tatyana Lebedeva** RUS

Shot
1983 **Helena Fibingerova** TCH
1987 **Natalya Lisovskaya** URS
1991 **Zhihong Huang** CHN
1993 **Zhihong Huang** CHN
1995 **Astrid Kumbernuss** GER
1997 **Astrid Kumbernuss** GER
1999 **Astrid Kumbernuss** GER
2001 **Yanina Korolchik** BLR

ATHLETICS

Discus
1983 **Martina Opitz** GDR
1987 **Martina Hellmann*** GDR
1991 **Tsvetanka Khristova** BUL
1993 **Olga Burova** RUS
1995 **Ellina Svereva** BLR
1997 **Beatrice Faumuina** NZL
1999 **Franka Dietzsch** GER
2001 **Natalya Sadova** RUS
* née Opitz

Hammer
1999 **Michaela Melinte** ROM
2001 **Yipsi Moreno** CUB

Javelin
1983 **Tiina Lillak** FIN
1987 **Fatima Whitbread** GBR
1991 **Xu Demei** CHN
1993 **Trine Hattestad** NOR
1995 **Natalya Shikolenko** BLR
1997 **Trine Hattestad** NOR
1999 **Mirela Manjani-Tzelili** GRE
2001 **Osleidys Menéndez** CUB

Heptathlon
1983 **Ramona Neubert** GDR
1987 **Jackie Joyner-Kersee** USA
1991 **Sabine Braun** GER
1993 **Jackie Joyner-Kersee** USA
1995 **Ghada Shouaa** SYR
1997 **Sabine Braun** GER
1999 **Eunice Barber** FRA
2001 **Yelena Prokhorova** RUS

10km Walk
1987 **Irina Strakhova** URS
1991 **Alina Ivanova** URS
1993 **Sari Essayah** FIN
1995 **Irina Stankina** RUS
1997 **Annarita Sidoti** ITA

20km Walk
1999 **Liu Hongyu** CHN
2001 **Olimpiada Ivanova** RUS

4x100m Relay
1983 **East Germany**
1987 **USA**
1991 **Jamaica**
1993 **Russia**
1995 **USA**
1997 **USA**
1999 **Bahamas**
2001 **USA**

4x400m Relay
1983 **East Germany**
1987 **East Germany**
1991 **Soviet Union**
1993 **USA**
1995 **USA**
1997 **Germany**
1999 **Russia**
2001 **Jamaica**

WORLD CROSS-COUNTRY CHAMPIONS

From 1998, the championships also incorporated a short race (over 4km for both men and women). The results are given with the traditional races first, the short races below.

Year	Men	Women
1973	**Pekka Paivarinto** FIN	**Paola Cacchi** ITA
1974	**Eric de Beck** BEL	**Paola Cacchi** ITA
1975	**Ian Stewart** SCO	**Julie Brown** USA
1976	**Carlos Lopes** POR	**Carmen Valero** ESP
1977	**Leon Schots** BEL	**Carmen Valero** ESP
1978	**John Treacy** IRL	**Grete Waitz** NOR
1979	**John Treacy** IRL	**Grete Waitz** NOR
1980	**Craig Virgin** USA	**Grete Waitz** NOR
1981	**Craig Virgin** USA	**Grete Waitz** NOR
1982	**Mohamed Kedir** ETH	**Maricica Puica** ROM
1983	**Bekele Debele** ETH	**Grete Waitz** NOR
1984	**Carlos Lopes** POR	**Maricica Puica** ROM
1985	**Carlos Lopes** POR	**Zola Budd** ENG
1986	**John Ngugi** KEN	**Zola Budd** ENG
1987	**John Ngugi** KEN	**Annette Sergent** FRA
1988	**John Ngugi** KEN	**Ingrid Kristiansen** NOR
1989	**John Ngugi** KEN	**Annette Sergent** FRA
1990	**Khalid Skah** MAR	**Lynn Jennings** USA
1991	**Khalid Skah** MAR	**Lynn Jennings** USA
1992	**John Ngugi** KEN	**Lynn Jennings** USA
1993	**William Sigei** KEN	**Albertina Dias** POR
1994	**William Sigei** KEN	**Helen Chepngeno** KEN
1995	**Paul Tergat** KEN	**Derartu Tulu** ETH
1996	**Paul Tergat** KEN	**Gete Wami** ETH
1997	**Paul Tergat** KEN	**Derartu Tulu** ETH
1998	**Paul Tergat** KEN	**Sonia O'Sullivan** IRL
	John Kibowen KEN	**Sonia O'Sullivan** IRL
1999	**Paul Tergat** KEN	**Gete Wami** ETH
	Benjamin Limo KEN	**Jackline Maranga** KEN
2000	**Mohammed Mourhit** BEL	**Derartu Tulu** ETH
	John Kibowen KEN	**Kutre Dulecha** ETH
2001	**Mohammed Mourhit** KEN	**Paula Radcliffe** GBR
	Enock Koech KEN	**Gete Wami** ETH
2002	**Kenenisa Bekele** ETH	**Paula Radcliffe** GBR
	Kenenisa Bekele	**Edith Masai** KEN

ATHLETICS

BOSTON MARATHON

The oldest of the major marathons, Boston was first
run in 1897 although at just under 40km. It was run
over the full distance for the first time in 1927

1975	Bill Rogers USA	Liane Winger FRG
1976	Jack Fultz USA	Kim Merritt USA
1977	Jerome Drayton CAN	Miki Gorman USA
1978	Bill Rogers USA	Gayle Barron USA
1979	Bill Rogers USA	Joan Benoit USA
1980	Bill Rodgers USA	Jacqui Gareau CAN
1981	Toshihiko Seko JPN	Allison Roe NZL
1982	Alberto Salazar USA	Charlotte Teske FRG
1983	Greg Meyer USA	Joan Benoit USA
1984	Geoff Smith GBR	Lorraine Moller NZL
1985	Geoff Smith GBR	Lisa Weidenbach USA
1986	Rob de Castella AUS	Ingrid Kristiansen NOR
1987	Toshihiko Seko JPN	Rosa Mota POR
1988	Ibrahim Hussein KEN	Rosa Mota POR
1989	Abebe Mekonnen ETH	I Kristiansen NOR
1990	Gelindo Bordin ITA	Rosa Mota POR
1991	Ibrahim Hussein KEN	Wanda Panfil POL
1992	Ibrahim Hussein KEN	Olga Markova RUS
1993	Cosmas N'Deti KEN	Olga Markova RUS
1994	Cosmas N'Deti KEN	Uta Pippig GER
1995	Cosmas N'Deti KEN	Uta Pippig GER
1996	Moses Tanui KEN	Uta Pippig GER
1997	Lameck Aguta KEN	Fatuma Roba ETH
1998	Moses Tanui KEN	Fatuma Roba ETH
1999	Joseph Chebet KEN	Fatuma Roba ETH
2000	Elijah Lagat KEN	Catherine Ndereba KEN
2001	Lee Bong-Ju KOR	Catherine Ndereba
2002	Rodgers Rop KEN	Catherine Ndereba

LONDON MARATHON

Year	Men	Women
1981	Dick Beardsley USA* & Inge Simonsen NOR*	Joyce Smith GBR
1982	Hugh Jones GBR	Joyce Smith GBR
1983	Mike Gratton GBR	Grete Waitz NOR
1984	Charlie Spedding GBR	Ingrid Kristiansen NOR
1985	Steve Jones GBR	I Kristiansen NOR
1986	Toshihiko Seko JPN	Grete Waitz NOR
1987	Hiromi Taniguchi JPN	I Kristiansen NOR
1988	H Jorgensen DEN	I Kristiansen NOR
1989	Doug Wakiihuri KEN	Veronique Marot GBR
1990	Allister Hutton GBR	Wanda Panfil POL
1991	Yakov Tolstikov URS	Rosa Mota POR
1992	Antonio Pinto POR	Katrin Dörre GER
1993	Eamonn Martin GBR	Katrin Dörre GER
1994	Dionicio Ceron MEX	Katrin Dörre GER
1995	Dionicio Ceron MEX	Malgorzata Sobanska POL
1996	Dionicio Ceron MEX	Liz McColgan GBR
1997	Antonio Pinto POR	Joyce Chepchumba KEN

1998	Abel Anton ESP	Catherine McKiernan IRL
1999	Abdel El Mouaziz MAR	Joyce Chepchumba KEN
2000	Antonio Pinto POR	Tegla Loroupe KEN
2001	Abdel El Mouaziz MAR	Derartu Tulu ETH
2002	Khalid Khannouchi USA	Paula Radcliffe GBR

NEW YORK MARATHON

Year	Men	Women
1976	Bill Rodgers USA	Miki Gorman USA
1977	Bill Rodgers USA	Miki Gorman USA
1978	Bill Rodgers USA	Grete Waitz NOR
1979	Bill Rodgers USA	Grete Waitz NOR
1980	Alberto Salazar USA	Grete Waitz NOR
1981	Alberto Salazar USA	Allison Roe NZL**
1982	Alberto Salazar USA	Grete Waitz NOR
1983	Rod Dixon NZL	Grete Waitz NOR
1984	Orlando Pizzolato ITA	Grete Waitz NOR
1985	Orlando Pizzolato ITA	Grete Waitz NOR
1986	Gianni Poli ITA	Grete Waitz NOR
1987	Ibrahim Hussein KEN	Priscilla Welch GBR
1988	Steve Jones GBR	Grete Waitz NOR
1989	Juma Ikangaa TAN	Ingrid Kristiansen NOR
1990	Doug Wakiihuri KEN	Wanda Panfil POL
1991	Salvador Garcia MEX	Liz McColgan GBR
1992	Willie Mtolo RSA	Lisa Ondieki AUS
1993	Andres Espinoza MEX	Uta Pippig GER
1994	German Silva MEX	Tecla Lorupe KEN
1995	German Silva MEX	Tecla Lorupe KEN
1996	Giacomo Leone ITA	Anuta Catuna ROM
1997	John Kagwe KEN	F Rochat-Moser SUI
1998	John Kagwe KEN	Franca Fiacconi ITA
1999	Joseph Chebet KEN	Adriana Fernandez MEX
2000	Abdel El Mouaziz MAR	Ludmila Petrova RUS
2001	Tesfaye Jifar ETH	Margaret Okayo KEN
2002	Rodgers Rop KEN	Joyce Chepchumba KEN

* Dead-heated
** The course used in 1981-1983 was found to be
155m short and the world bests of Salazar and Roe
were invalidated

BADMINTON

WORLD CHAMPIONS
MEN'S SINGLES
1977 Flemming Delfs DEN
1980 Rudy Hartono INA
1983 Icuk Sugiarto INA
1985 Hang Jian CHN
1987 Yang Yang CHN
1989 Yang Yang CHN
1991 Zhao Jianhua CHN
1993 Joko Suprianto INA
1995 Heryanto Arbi INA
1997 Peter Rasmussen DEN
1999 Sun Jun CHN
2001 Hendrawan INA

WOMEN'S SINGLES
1977 Lene Köppen DEN
1980 Wiharjo Verawaty INA
1983 Li Lingwei CHN
1985 Han Aiping CHN
1987 Han Aiping CHN
1989 Li Lingwei CHN
1991 Tang Jiuhong CHN
1993 Susi Susanti INA
1995 Ye Zhaoying CHN
1997 Ye Zhaoying CHN
1999 Camilla Martin DEN
2001 Gong Ruina CHN

MEN'S DOUBLES
1977 Wahjudi/Tjun INA
1980 Chandra/Christian INA
1983 Fladberg/Hellerdie DEN
1985 Park Joo-Bong/Kim Moon-Soo KOR
1987 Li Yongbo/Tian Bingye CHN
1989 Li Yongbo/Tian Bingye CHN
1991 Park Joo-Bong/Kim Moon-Soo KOR
1993 Subagja/Gunawan INA
1995 Mainaky/Subagja INA
1997 Sigit/Wijaya INA
1999 Ha/Kim KOR
2001 Haryanto/Gunawan INA

WOMEN'S DOUBLES
1977 Tuganoo/Vero JPN
1980 Perry/Webster GBR
1983 Lin Ying/Wu Dixie CHN
1985 Han Aiping/Li Lingwei CHN
1987 Lin Ying/Guan Weizhen CHN
1989 Lin Ying/Guan Weizhen CHN
1991 Gan Weizhen/Nong Qunha CHN
1993 Nong Qunha/Zhou Lei CHN
1995 Gil/Jang KOR
1997 Ge/Gu CHN
1999 Ge/Gu CHN
2001 Huang/Gao CHN

MIXED DOUBLES
1977 Stovgaard/Köppen DEN
1980 Christian/Wogoeno INA
1983 Kihlström/Perry SWE/GBR
1985 Park Joo-bong/Yoo Sang-hee KOR
1987 Wang Pengrin/Shi Fagying CHN
1989 Park Joo-Bong/Chung Myung-Hee KOR
1991 Park Joo-Bong/Chung Myung-Hee KOR
1993 Lund/Bengtsson DEN/SWE
1995 Lund/Thomsen DEN
1997 Liu/Ge CHN
1999 Kim/Ra KOR
2001 Zhang/Gao CHN

SUDIRMAN CUP (Team)
1989 Indonesia
1991 & 93 Korea
1995, 97 & 99 China
2001 Indonesia

THOMAS CUP (Men's Team)
1949, 52 & 55 Malaya
1958, 61 & 64 Indonesia
1967 Malaysia
1970, 73, 76 & 79 Indonesia
1982 China
1984 Indonesia
1986, 88 & 90 China
1992 Malaysia
1994, 96, 98 & 2000 Indonesia
2002 Malaysia

UBER CUP (Women's Team)
1957, 59 & 63 United States
1966, 69 & 73 Japan
1975 Indonesia
1978 & 81 Japan
1984, 86, 88, 90 & 92 China
1994 & 96 Indonesia
1998, 2000 & 2002 China

EUROPEAN CHAMPIONS
MEN'S SINGLES
1976 Flemming Delfs DEN
1978 Flemming Delfs DEN
1980 Flemming Delfs DEN
1982 Jens Peter Nierhoff DEN
1984 Morten Frost DEN
1986 Morten Frost DEN
1988 Darren Hall ENG
1990 Steve Baddeley ENG
1992 Paul-Eric Høyer-Larsen DEN
1994 Paul-Eric Høyer-Larsen DEN
1996 Paul-Eric Høyer-Larsen DEN
1998 Peter Gade Christensen DEN
2000 Peter Gade Christensen DEN
2002 Peter Rasmussen DEN

WOMEN'S SINGLES
1978 Lene Köppen DEN
1980 Liselotte Blumer SWE
1982 Lene Köppen DEN
1984 Helen Troke ENG
1986 Helen Troke ENG
1988 Kirsten Larsen DEN
1990 Pernille Nedergaard DEN
1992 Pernille Nedergaard DEN
1994 Lim Xiaoqing SWE
1996, 98 & 2000 Camilla Martin DEN
2002 Jie Yao NED

420

BASEBALL

WORLD SERIES

	Winners	Runners-up	Score
1903	Boston Red Sox (AL)	Pittsburgh Pirates (NL)	5-3
1904	No Series		
1905	New York Giants (NL)	Philadelphia Athletics (AL)	4-1
1906	Chicago White Sox (AL)	Chicago Cubs (NL)	4-2
1907	Chicago Cubs (NL)	Detroit Tigers (AL)	4-0 with 1 tie
1908	Chicago Cubs (NL)	Detroit Tigers (AL)	4-1
1909	Pittsburgh Pirates (NL)	Detroit Tigers (AL)	4-3
1910	Philadelphia Athletics (AL)	Chicago Cubs (NL)	4-1
1911	Philadelphia Athletics (AL)	New York Giants (NL)	4-2
1912	Boston Red Sox (AL)	New York Giants (NL)	4-3 with 1 tie
1913	Philadelphia Athletics (AL)	New York Giants (NL)	4-1
1914	Boston Braves (NL)	Philadelphia Athletics (AL)	4-0
1915	Boston Red Sox (AL)	Philadelphia Phillies (NL)	4-1
1916	Boston Red Sox (AL)	Brooklyn Dodgers (NL)	4-1
1917	Chicago White Sox (AL)	New York Giants (NL)	4-2
1918	Boston Red Sox (AL)	Chicago Cubs (NL)	4-2
1919	Cincinnati Reds (NL)	Chicago White Sox (AL)	5-3
1920	Cleveland Indians (AL)	Brooklyn Dodgers (NL)	5-2
1921	New York Giants (NL)	New York Yankees (AL)	5-3
1922	New York Giants (NL)	New York Yankees (AL)	4-0 with 1 tie
1923	New York Yankees (AL)	New York Giants (NL)	4-2
1924	Washington Senators (AL)	New York Giants (NL)	4-3
1925	Pittsburgh Pirates (NL)	Washington Senators (AL)	4-3
1926	St Louis Cardinals (NL)	New York Yankees (AL)	4-3
1927	New York Yankees (AL)	Pittsburgh Pirates (NL)	4-0
1928	New York Yankees (AL)	St Louis Cardinals (NL)	4-0
1929	Philadelphia Athletics (AL)	Chicago Cubs (NL)	4-1
1930	Philadelphia Athletics (AL)	St Louis Cardinals (NL)	4-2
1931	St Louis Cardinals (NL)	Philadelphia Athletics (AL)	4-3
1932	New York Yankees (AL)	Chicago Cubs (NL)	4-0
1933	New York Giants (NL)	Washington Senators (AL)	4-1
1934	St Louis Cardinals (NL)	Detroit Tigers (AL)	4-3
1935	Detroit Tigers (AL)	Chicago Cubs (NL)	4-2
1936	New York Yankees (AL)	New York Giants (NL)	4-2
1937	New York Yankees (AL)	New York Giants (NL)	4-1
1938	New York Yankees (AL)	Chicago Cubs (NL)	4-0
1939	New York Yankees (AL)	Cincinnati Reds (NL)	4-0
1940	Cincinnati Reds (NL)	Detroit Tigers (AL)	4-3
1941	New York Yankees (AL)	Brooklyn Dodgers (NL)	4-1
1942	St Louis Cardinals (NL)	New York Yankees (AL)	4-1
1943	New York Yankees (AL)	St Louis Cardinals (NL)	4-1
1944	St Louis Cardinals (NL)	St Louis Browns (AL)	4-2
1945	Detroit Tigers (AL)	Chicago Cubs (NL)	4-3
1946	St Louis Cardinals (NL)	Boston Red Sox (AL)	4-3
1947	New York Yankees (AL)	Brooklyn Dodgers (NL)	4-3
1948	Cleveland Indians (AL)	Boston Braves (NL)	4-2
1949	New York Yankees (AL)	Brooklyn Dodgers (NL)	4-1
1950	New York Yankees (AL)	Philadelphia Phillies (NL)	4-0
1951	New York Yankees (AL)	New York Giants (NL)	4-2
1952	New York Yankees (AL)	Brooklyn Dodgers (NL)	4-3
1953	New York Yankees (AL)	Brooklyn Dodgers (NL)	4-2
1954	New York Giants (NL)	Cleveland Indians (AL)	4-0
1955	Brooklyn Dodgers (NL)	New York Yankees (AL)	4-3
1956	New York Yankees (AL)	Brooklyn Dodgers (NL)	4-3
1957	Milwaukee Braves (NL)	New York Yankees (AL)	4-3
1958	New York Yankees (AL)	Milwaukee Braves (NL)	4-3
1959	Los Angeles Dodgers (NL)	Chicago White Sox (AL)	4-2
1960	Pittsburgh Pirates (NL)	New York Yankees (AL)	4-3

Year	Winners	Runners-up	Score
1961	New York Yankees (AL)	Cincinnati Reds (NL)	4-1
1962	New York Yankees (AL)	San Francisco Giants (NL)	4-3
1963	Los Angeles Dodgers (NL)	New York Yankees (AL)	4-0
1964	St Louis Cardinals (NL)	New York Yankees (AL)	4-3
1965	Los Angeles Dodgers (NL)	Minnesota Twins (AL)	4-3
1966	Baltimore Orioles (AL)	Los Angeles Dodgers (NL)	4-0
1967	St Louis Cardinals (NL)	Boston Red Sox (AL)	4-3
1968	Detroit Tigers (AL)	St Louis Cardinals (NL)	4-3
1969	New York Mets (NL)	Baltimore Orioles (AL)	4-1
1970	Baltimore Orioles (AL)	Cincinnati Reds (NL)	4-1
1971	Pittsburgh Pirates (NL)	Baltimore Orioles (AL)	4-3
1972	Oakland Athletics (AL)	Cincinnati Reds (NL)	4-3
1973	Oakland Athletics (AL)	New York Mets (NL)	4-3
1974	Oakland Athletics (AL)	Los Angeles Dodgers (NL)	4-1
1975	Cincinnati Reds (NL)	Boston Red Sox (AL)	4-3
1976	Cincinnati Reds (NL)	New York Yankees (AL)	4-0
1977	New York Yankees (AL)	Los Angeles Dodgers (NL)	4-2
1978	New York Yankees (AL)	Los Angeles Dodgers (NL)	4-2
1979	Pittsburgh Pirates (NL)	Baltimore Orioles (AL)	4-3
1980	Philadelphia Phillies (NL)	Kansas City Royals (AL)	4-2
1981	Los Angeles Dodgers (NL)	New York Yankees (AL)	4-2
1982	St Louis Cardinals (NL)	Milwaukee Brewers (AL)	4-3
1983	Baltimore Orioles (AL)	Philadelphia Phillies (NL)	4-1
1984	Detroit Tigers (AL)	San Diego Padres (NL)	4-1
1985	Kansas City Royals (AL)	St Louis Cardinals (NL)	4-3
1986	New York Mets (NL)	Boston Red Sox (AL)	4-3
1987	Minnesota Twins (AL)	St Louis Cardinals (NL)	4-3
1988	Los Angeles Dodgers (NL)	Oakland Athletics (AL)	4-1
1989	Oakland Athletics (AL)	San Francisco Giants (NL)	4-0
1990	Cincinnati Reds (NL)	Oakland Athletics (AL)	4-0
1991	Minnesota Twins (AL)	Atlanta Braves (NL)	4-3
1992	Toronto Blue Jays (AL)	Atlanta Braves (NL)	4-2
1993	Toronto Blue Jays (AL)	Philadelphia Phillies (NL)	4-2
1994	No Series		
1995	Atlanta Braves (NL)	Cleveland Indians (AL)	4-2
1996	New York Yankees (AL)	Atlanta Braves (NL)	4-2
1997	Florida Marlins (NL)	Cleveland Indians (AL)	4-3
1998	New York Yankees (AL)	San Diego Padres (NL)	4-0
1999	New York Yankees (AL)	Atlanta Braves (NL)	4-0
2000	New York Yankees (AL)	New York Mets (NL)	4-1
2001	Arizona Diamondbacks (NL)	New York Yankees (AL)	4-3
2002	Anaheim Angels (AL)	San Francisco Giants (NL)	4-3

BASKETBALL

WORLD CHAMPIONSHIPS, MEN

1950 **Argentina**
1954 **USA**
1959 **Brazil**
1963 **Brazil**
1967 **USSR**
1970 **Yugoslavia**
1974 **USSR**
1978 **Yugoslavia**
1982 **USSR**
1986 **USA**
1990 **Yugoslavia**
1994 **USA**
1998 **Yugoslavia**
2002 **Yugoslavia**

WORLD CHAMPIONSHIPS, WOMEN

1953 **USA**
1957 **USA**
1959 **USSR**
1964 **USSR**
1967 **USSR**
1971 **USSR**
1975 **USSR**
1979 **USA**
1983 **USSR**
1986 **USA**
1990 **USA**
1994 **Brazil**
1998 **USA**
2002 **USA**

NATIONAL (EBBA) CUP WINNERS

Year	Winners	Runner-up	Score
1936	**Hoylake YMCA**	London Polytechnic	32-21
1937	**Hoylake YMCA**	Latter Day Saints	23-17
1938	**Catford Saints**	Rochdale Greys	61-47
1939	**Catford Saints**	Rochdale Greys	53-41
1940	**Birmingham Inst**	Central YMCA	35-30
1947	**Carpathians**	Birmingham D'bran	48-25
1948	**Latter Day Saints**	Latvian Society	39-30
1949	**Latter Day Saints**	Birmingham D'bran	44-35
1950	**Latter Day Saints**	USAF Burtonwood	43-32
1951	**Birmingham D'bran**	London Polytechnic	34-33
1952	**London Poly**	Birmingham D'bran	40-29
1953	**London Poly**	Birmingham D'bran	55-46
1954	**London Poly**	Nottingham YMCA	98-53
1955	**London Poly**	Birmingham D'bran	58-54
1957	**Central YMCA**	London Polytechnic	63-51
1958	**Central YMCA**	East Ham	48-40
1959	**Aspley OB**	Birmingham D'bran	58-39
1960	**Central YMCA**	London Polytechnic	95-62
1961	**London University**	Central YMCA	68-59
1962	**Central YMCA**	RAE Eagles	87-47
1963	**Central YMCA**	London University	70-69
1964	**Central YMCA**	London University	78-56
1965	**Aldershot Warriors**	Oxford University	79-63
1966	**Oxford University**	Aldershot Warriors	91-70
1967	**Central YMCA**	Vauxhall Motors	64-62
1968	**Oxford University**	Aldershot Warriors	61-59
1969	**Central YMCA**	Aldershot Warriors	70-62
1970	**Liverpool Police**	Oxford University	73-67
1971	**Manchester Uni**	Sutton	88-81
1972	**Avenue (Leyton)**	Cambridge	58-66
1973	**London Latvian SK**	Sutton	70-69
1974	**Sutton & C Palace**	All Stars	120-100
1975	**All Stars**	Sutton & C Palace	82-81
1976	**Crystal Palace**	All Stars	108-88
1977	**Crystal Palace**	All Stars	91-90
1978	**Crystal Palace**	Coventry	89-87
1979	**Doncaster**	Crystal Palace	73-71
1980	**Crystal Palace**	Doncaster	97-67
1981	**Crystal Palace**	Doncaster	91-74
1982	**Solent**	Doncaster	127-91
1983	**Solent**	Birmingham	98-97
1984	**Solent**	Leicester	86-67
1985	**Kingston**	Manchester United	103-98
1986	**Kingston**	Solent	113-82
1987	**Kingston**	Portsmouth	95-87
1988	**Kingston**	Portsmouth	90-84
1989	**Bracknell**	Manchester	87-75
1990	**Kingston**	Sunderland	103-78
1991	**Sunderland**	Leicester	88-81
1992	**Kingston**	Thames Valley	90-71
1993	**Guildford**	Worthing	82-72
1994	**Worthing**	Thames Valley	92-83
1995	**Sheffield Sharks**	Thames Valley	89-66
1996	**London Towers**	Sheffield Sharks	70-58
1997	**Leopards**	Sheffield Sharks	87-79
1998	**Thames Valley**	Leicester Tigers	82-78
1999	**Sheffield Sharks**	Leopards	67-65
2000	**Sheffield Sharks**	Manchester Giants	89-80
2001	**Leicester Riders**	London Leopards	84-82
2002	**Chester Jets**	Birmingham Bullets	112-105

LEAGUE CHAMPIONS - MEN

Year	Winners	Runners-up
1972-73	**Avenue (Leyton)**	Liverpool
1973-74	**Crystal Palace**	Islington
1974-75	**Islington**	Crystal Palace
1975-76	**Crystal Palace**	Islington
1976-77	**Crystal Palace**	Manchester
1977-78	**Crystal Palace**	Milton Keynes
1978-79	**Doncaster**	Crystal Palace
1979-80	**Crystal Palace**	Doncaster
1980-81	**Birmingham**	Crystal Palace
1981-82	**Crystal Palace**	Solent
1982-83	**Crystal Palace**	Sunderland
1983-84	**Solent**	Crystal Palace
1984-85	**Kingston**	Manchester United
1985-86	**Manchester United**	Kingston
1986-87	**Portsmouth**	Kingston
1987-88	**Portsmouth**	Kingston
1988-89	**Glasgow**	Livingston
1989-90	**Kingston**	Sunderland
1990-91	**Kingston**	Sunderland

BASKETBALL

1991-92	**Kingston**	Thames Valley
1992-93	**Worthing**	Thames Valley
1993-94	**Thames Valley**	Worthing
1994-95	**Sheffield Sharks**	Thames Valley
1995-96	**London Towers**	Sheffield
1996-97	**Leopards**	London Towers
1997-98	**Gtr London Leopards**	Birmingham Bullets
1998-99	**Sheffield Sharks**	Manchester Giants
1999-00	**Manchester Giants**	Birmingham Bullets
2000-01	**Leicester Riders**	Sheffield Sharks
2001-02	**Chester Jets**	Sheffield Sharks

LEAGUE CHAMPIONS - WOMEN

Year	Winners	Runners-up
1975-76	**Tigers (Herts)**	Cleveland E
1976-77	**Tigers (Herts)**	Southgate
1977-78	**Cleveland E**	Tigers (Herts)
1978-79	**Cleveland E**	Tigers (Herts)
1979-80	**Tigers**	Cleveland E
1980-81	**Southgate**	Crystal Palace
1981-82	**Southgate**	Northampton
1982-83	**Southgate**	Northampton
1983-84	**Northampton**	Nottingham
1984-85	**Northampton**	Crystal Palace
1985-86	**Crystal Palace**	Northampton
1986-87	**Northampton**	Crystal Palace
1987-88	**Northampton**	Stockport
1988-89	**Northampton**	London YMCA
1989-90	**Northampton**	Sheffield
1990-91	**Sheffield**	London YMCA
1991-92	**Sheffield**	Thames Valley
1992-93	**Sheffield**	Northampton
1993-94	**Sheffield**	Northampton
1994-95	**Sheffield**	Barking & Dagenham
1995-96	**Sheffield Hatters**	Birmingham
1996-97	**Sheffield Hatters**	Thames Valley Ladies
1997-98	**Sheffield Hatters**	Thames Valley Ladies
1998-99	**Sheffield Hatters**	Rhondda Rebels
1999-00	**Sheffield Hatters**	Spelthorne Acers
2000-01	**Sheffield Hatters**	Rhonnda Rebels
2001-02	**Sheffield Hatters**	Rhonnda Rebels

NATIONAL LEAGUE (preceded NBA)

1938	**Goodyears**
1939	**Firestones**
1940	**Firestones**
1941	**Oshkosh**
1942	**Oshkosh**
1943, 44 & 45	**Fort Wayne Pistons**
1946	**Rochester Royals**
1947	**Chicago Stags**
1948	**Minneapolis Lakers**
1949	**Anderson Packers**

NBA

1947	**Philadelphia Warriors**
1948	**Baltimore Bullets**
1949	**Minneapolis Lakers**
1950	**Minneapolis Lakers**
1951	**Rochester Royals**
1952	**Minneapolis Lakers**
1953	**Minneapolis Lakers**
1954	**Minneapolis Lakers**
1955	**Syracuse Nationals**
1956	**Philadelphia Warriors**
1957	**Boston Celtics**
1958	**St Louis Hawks**
1959	**Boston Celtics**
1960	**Boston Celtics**
1961	**Boston Celtics**
1962	**Boston Celtics**
1963	**Boston Celtics**
1964	**Boston Celtics**
1965	**Boston Celtics**
1966	**Boston Celtics**
1967	**Philadelphia 76ers**
1968	**Boston Celtics**
1969	**Boston Celtics**
1970	**New York Knicks**
1971	**Milwaukee Bucks**
1972	**Los Angeles Lakers**
1973	**New York Knicks**
1974	**Boston Celtics**
1975	**Golden State Warriors**
1976	**Boston Celtics**
1977	**Portland Trail Blazers**
1978	**Washington Bullets**
1979	**Seattle Supersonics**
1980	**Los Angeles Lakers**
1981	**Boston Celtics**
1982	**Los Angeles Lakers**
1983	**Philadelphia 76ers**
1984	**Boston Celtics**
1985	**Los Angeles Lakers**
1986	**Boston Celtics**
1987	**Los Angeles Lakers**
1988	**Los Angeles Lakers**
1989	**Detroit Pistons**
1990	**Detroit Pistons**
1991	**Chicago Bulls**
1992	**Chicago Bulls**
1993	**Chicago Bulls**
1994	**Houston Rockets**
1995	**Houston Rockets**
1996-98	**Chicago Bulls**
1999	**San Antonio Spurs**
2000	**Los Angeles Lakers**
2001	**Los Angeles Lakers**
2002	**Los Angeles Lakers**

BASKETBALL

NBA LEADING SCORERS

1950	George Mikan (Mn)	1865
1951	George Mikan (Mn)	1932
1952	Paul Arizin (Ph)	1674
1953	Neil Johnston (Ph)	1564
1954	Neil Johnston (Ph)	1759
1955	Neil Johnston (Ph)	1631
1956	Bob Pettit (St L)	1849
1957	Paul Arizin (Ph)	1817
1958	George Yardley (Dt)	2001
1959	Bob Pettit (St L)	2105
1960	Wilt Chamberlain (Ph)	2707
1961	Wilt Chamberlain (Ph)	3033
1962	Wilt Chamberlain (Ph)	4029
1963	Wilt Chamberlain (SF)	3586
1964	Wilt Chamberlain (SF)	2948
1965	Wilt Chamberlain (SF/Ph)	2534
1966	Wilt Chamberlain (Ph)	2649
1967	Rick Barry (SF)	2775
1968	Dave Bing (Dt)	2142
1969	Elvin Hayes (SD)	2327
1970	Jerry West (LA)	2309
1971	Lew Alcindor (MI) *	2596
1972	Kareem Abdul-Jabbar (MI)	2822
1973	Nate Archibald (KC/Om)	2719
1974	Bob McAdoo (Bf)	2261
1975	Bob McAdoo (Bf)	2831
1976	Bob McAdoo (Bf)	2427
1977	Pete Maravich (NO)	2273
1978	George Gervin (SA)	2232
1979	George Gervin (SA)	2365
1980	George Gervin (SA)	2585
1981	Adrian Dantley (Ut)	2452
1982	George Gervin (SA)	2551
1983	Alex English (Dn)	2326
1984	Adrian Dantley (Ut)	2418
1985	Bernard King (NY)	1809
1986	Dominique Wilkins (At)	2366
1987	Michael Jordan (Ch)	3041
1988	Michael Jordan (Ch)	2868
1989	Michael Jordan (Ch)	2633
1990	Michael Jordan (Ch)	2753
1991	Michael Jordan (Ch)	2580
1992	Michael Jordan (Ch)	2404
1993	Michael Jordan (Ch)	2541
1994	David Robinson (SA)	2383
1995	Shaquille O'Neal (Orl)	2315
1996	Michael Jordan (Ch)	2491
1997	Michael Jordan (Ch)	2431
1998	Michael Jordan (Ch)	2357
1999	Shaquille O'Neal (LA) **	1289
2000	Shaquille O'Neal (LA)	2344
2001	Jerry Stackhouse (Dt)	2380
2002	Paul Pierce (Bo)	2144

* took name of Kareem Abdul-Jabbar

** season latestarting through players' strike

BILLIARDS

WORLD CHAMPIONS

English unless otherwise stated

Men

1870	**William Cook**
1870	**John Roberts jnr**
1870	**Joseph Bennett**
1871	**John Roberts jnr**
1871	**William Cook**
1875	**John Roberts jnr**
1880	**Joseph Bennett**
1885	**John Roberts jnr**
1889	**Charles Dawson**
1901	**H W Stevenson**
1901	**Charles Dawson**
1901	**H W Stevenson**
1903	**Charles Dawson**
1908	**Melbourne Inman**
1909	**H W Stevenson**
1910	**H W Stevenson**
1911	**H W Stevenson**
1912	**Melbourne Inman**
1913	**Melbourne Inman**
1914	**Melbourne Inman**
1919	**Melbourne Inman**
1920	**Willie Smith**
1921	**Tom Newman**
1922	**Tom Newman**
1923	**Willie Smith**
1924	**Tom Newman**
1925	**Tom Newman**
1926	**Tom Newman**
1927	**Tom Newman**
1928	**Joe Davis**
1929	**Joe Davis**
1930	**Joe Davis**
1932	**Joe Davis**
1933	**Walter Lindrum** AUS
1934	**Walter Lindrum** AUS
1951	**Clark McConachy** NZL
1968	**Rex Williams**
1971	**Leslie Driffield**
1971	**Rex Williams**
1980	**Fred Davis**
1982	**Rex Williams**
1983	**Rex Williams**
1984	**Mark Wildman**
1985	**Ray Edmonds**
1986	**Robbie Foldvari** AUS
1987	**Norman Dagley**
1988	**Norman Dagley**
1989	**Mike Russell**
1991	**Mike Russell**
1992	**Geet Sethi** IND
1993	**Geet Sethi** IND
1994	**Peter Gilchrist**
1995	**Geet Sethi** IND
1996	**Mike Russell**
1998	**Geet Sethi** IND
2001	**Peter Gilchrist**
2002	**Mike Russell**

Women

2000	**Emma Bonney**
2001	**Kelly Fisher**
2002	**Emma Bonney**

BOBSLEIGH/LUGE/SKELETON

BOBSLEIGH

Year	Two-man	Four-man
1930	No event	Italy
1931	Killian/Huber GER	Germany
1933	Papana/Hubert ROM	No event
1934	Frim/Dumitrescu ROM	Germany
1935	Capadrutt/Diener SUI	Germany
1937	McEnvoy/Black GBR	Great Britain
1938	Fischer/Thielacke GER	Great Britain
1939	Lundnen/Kuffer BEL	Switzerland
1947	Feierabend/Waser SUI	Switzerland
1949	Endrich/Waller SUI	USA
1950	Feierabend/Waser SUI	USA
1951	Osterl/Nieberl FRG	W Germany
1953	Endrich/Stoeckli SUI	USA
1954	Scheibmeier/Zambelli ITA	Switzerland
1955	Feierabend/Warburton SUI	Switzerland
1957	Monti/Alvera ITA	Switzerland
1958	Monti/Alvera ITA	W Germany
1959	Monti/Alvera ITA	USA
1961	Monti/Siorpaes ITA	Italy
1962	Ruatti/De Lorenzo ITA	W Germany
1963	Monti/Siorpaes ITA	Italy
1965	Nash/Dixon GBR	Canada
1966	Monti/Siorpaes ITA	*
1967	Thaler/Durnthaler AUT	**
1969	de Zordo/Frassinelli ITA	W Germany
1970	Floth/Bader FRG	Italy
1971	Gaspari/Armano ITA	Switzerland
1973	Zimmerer/Utzshneider FRG	Switzerland
1974	Zimmerer/Utzshneider FRG	W Germany
1975	Alvera/Perruquet ITA	Switzerland
1977	Hiltebrand/Meier SUI	E Germany
1978	Schärer/Benz SUI	E Germany
1979	Schärer/Benz SUI	W Germany
1981	Germeshausen/Gerhardt GDR	E Germany
1982	Schärer/Benz SUI	Switzerland
1983	Pichler/Leuthold SUI	Switzerland
1985	Hoppe/Schauerhammer GDR	E Germany
1986	Hoppe/Schauerhammer GDR	Switzerland
1987	Pichler/Poltera SUI	Switzerland
1989	Hoppe/Musiol GDR	Switzerland
1990	Weder/Gerber SUI	Switzerland
1991	Lochner/Zimmermann GER	Germany
1993	Langen/Joechel GER	Switzerland
1995	Langen/Hampel GER	Germany
1996	Langen/Zimmermann GER	Germany
1997	Götschi/Acklin SUI	Germany
1999	Huber/Ranzi ITA	France
2000	Langen/Zimmerman GER	Germany
2001	Langen/Jakobs GER	Germany

* Not decided due to fatal accident
** Not decided due to thaw

LUGE

	Men	Women
1955	Anton Salvesen NOR	Karla Kienzl AUT
1956	-	Maria Isser AUT
1957	Hans Schaller FRG	M Semczyszak POL
1958	Jerzy Wojnar POL	-
1959	Herbert Thaler AUT	Elly Lieber AUT
1960	Helmuth Berndt FRG	Maria Isser AUT
1961	Jerzy Wojnar POL	Elisab. Nagele SUI
1962	Thomas Kohler GDR	Ilse Geisler GDR
1963	Fritz Nachmann FRG	Ilse Geisler GDR
1965	Hans Plenk FRG	O Enderlein GDR
1967	Thomas Kohler GDR	O Enderlein GDR
1969	Josef Feistmantl AUT	Petra Tierlich GDR
1970	Josef Fendt FRG	Barbara Piecha POL
1971	Karl Brunner ITA	E Demleitner FRG
1973	Hans Rinn GDR	M Schumann GDR
1974	Josef Fendt FRG	M Schumann GDR
1975	Wolfram Fiedler GDR	M Schumann GDR
1977	Hans Rinn GDR	M Schumann GDR
1978	Paul Hildgartner ITA	Vera Sosulya URS
1979	Detlef Gunther GDR	Mel Sollmann GDR
1981	Sergey Danilin URS	Mel Sollmann GDR
1983	Miroslav Zajonc CAN	Steffi Martin GDR
1985	Michael Walter GDR	Steffi Martin GDR
1987	Markus Prock AUT	C Schmidt GDR
1989	Georg Hackl FRG	Susi Erdmann GDR
1990	Georg Hackl FRG	G Kohlisch GDR
1991	Arnold Huber ITA	Susi Erdmann GDR
1993	Wendel Suckow USA	G Weissensteiner ITA
1995	Armin Zöggeler ITA	Gabi Kohlisch GER
1996	Markus Prock AUT	Jana Bode GER
1997	Georg Hackl GER	Susi Erdmann GER
1999	Armin Zöggeler ITA	S Wiedermann GER
2000	Jens Müller GER	Sylke Otto GER
2001	Armin Zöggeler ITA	Sylke Otto GER

MEN'S TWO-SEATER

1955	Hans Krausner/Herbert Thaler AUT
1957	Josef Strillinger/Fritz Nachmann FRG
1958	Josef Strillinger/Fritz Nachmann FRG
1960	Reinhold Frosch/Ewald Walch AUT
1961	Roman Pichler/Raimondo Prinoth ITA
1962	Giovanni Graber/Gianp'lo Ambrosi ITA
1963	Ryszard Pedrak/Lucjan Kudzia POL
1965	Wolfgang Scheidel/Thomas Kohler GDR
1967	Klaus Bonsack/Thomas Kohler GDR
1969	Manfred Schmid/Ewald Walch AUT
1970	Manfred Schmid/Ewald Walch AUT
1971	Paul Hildgartner/Walter Plaikner ITA
1973	Horst Hornlein/Reinhard Bredow GDR
1974	Bernd Hann/Ulrich Hann GDR
1975	Bernd Hann/Ulrich Hann GDR
1977	Hans Rinn/Norbert Hahn GDR
1978	Dainis Bremse/Aigars Krikis URS
1979	Hans Brandner/Balthasar Schwarm FRG
1981	Bernd Hann/Ulrich Hann GDR
1983	Jorg Hoffmann/Jochen Pietzsch GDR
1985	Jorg Hoffmann/Jochen Pietzsch GDR

BOBSLEIGH/LUGE/SKELETON

1987   **Jorg Hoffmann/Jochen Pietzsch** GDR
1989   **Stefan Krausse/Jan Behrendt** GDR
1990   **Hansjorg Raffl/Norbert Huber** ITA
1991   **Stefan Krausse/Jan Behrendt** GER
1993   **Stefan Krausse/Jan Behrendt** GER
1995   **Stefan Krausse/Jan Behrendt** GER
1996   **Tobias Schiegl/Markus Schiegl** AUT
1997   **Tobias Schiegl/Markus Schiegl** AUT
1999   **Patric Leitner/Alexander Reisch** GER
2000   **Patric Leitner/Alexander Reisch** GER
2001   **Andre Florschütz/Torsten Wustlich** GER

SKELETON
1998 onwards

	Men	Women
1998	**Willi Schneider GER**	
1999	**Jim Shea** USA	
2000	**Gregor Staehli** SUI	**Steffi Hanzlik GER**
2001	**Martin Rettl** AUT	**Maya Pedersen SUI**

BOWLS

World Outdoor Championships - Men

	Singles	Pairs	Triples	Fours	Team
1966	David Bryant ENG	Kelly/Palm AUS	Australia	New Zealand	Australia
1972	Malwyn Evans WAL	Delgado/Liddell HKG	United States	England	Scotland
1976	Doug Watson RSA	Watson/Moseley RSA	South Africa	South Africa	South Africa
1980	David Bryant ENG	Sandercock/Reuben RSA	England	Hong Kong	England
1984	Peter Belliss NZL	Adrain/Arculli SCO/USA	Ireland	England	Scotland
1988	David Bryant ENG	Brassey/Belliss NZL	New Zealand	Ireland	England
1992	Tony Allcock ENG	Corsie/Marshall SCO	Israel	Scotland	Scotland
1996	Tony Allcock ENG	Henry/Allen IRE	Scotland	England	Scotland
2000	Jeremy Henry IRE	Sneddon/Marshall SCO	New Zealand	Wales	Australia

World Outdoor Championships - Women

	Singles	Pairs	Triples	Fours	Team
1969	Gladys Doyle PNG	McDonald/Cridlan RSA	South Africa	South Africa	South Africa
1973	Elsie Wilkie NZL	Lucas/Jenkinson AUS	New Zealand	New Zealand	New Zealand
1977	Elsie Wilke NZL	Wong/Chok HKG	Wales	Australia	Australia
1981	Norma Shaw ENG	Bell/Allely IRE	Hong Kong	England	England
1985	Merle Richardson AUS	Richardson/Craig AUS	Australia	Scotland	Australia
1988	Janet Ackland WAL	Johnston/Nolan IRE	Australia	Australia	England
1992	Margaret Johnston IRE	Johnston/Nolan IRE	Scotland	Scotland	Scotland
1996	Carmelita Anderson NFI	Johnston/Nolan IRE	South Africa	Australia	South Africa
2000	Margaret Johnston IRE	Letham/Lindores SCO	New Zealand	New Zealand	England

World Indoor Championships - Men

	Singles	Pairs		Singles	Pairs
1979	David Bryant ENG	No event	1991	Richard Corsie SCO	Bryant/Allcock ENG
1980	David Bryant ENG	No event	1992	Ian Schuback AUS	Bryant/Allcock ENG
1981	David Bryant ENG	No event	1993	Richard Corsie SCO	Smith/Thomson ENG
1982	John Watson SCO	No event	1994	Andy Thomson ENG	Curtis/Schuback AUS
1983	Bob Sutherland SCO	No event	1995	Andy Thomson ENG	Marshall/Corsie SCO
1984	Jim Baker IRE	No event	1996	David Gourlay jnr SCO	Kirkow/Schubank AUS
1985	Terry Sullivan WAL	No event	1997	Hugh Duff SCO	King/Allcock ENG
1986	Tony Allcock ENG	Bryant/Allcock ENG	1998	Paul Foster SCO	Corsie/Robertson SCO
1987	Tony Allcock ENG	Bryant/Allcock ENG	1999	Alex Marshall SCO	Rees/Price WAL
1988	Hugh Duff SCO	Schuback/Yates AUS	2000	Robert Weale WAL	Gourlay/Marshall SCO
1989	Richard Corsie SCO	Bryant/Allcock ENG	2001	Paul Foster SCO	Gillett/McMahon ENG
1990	John Price WAL	Bryant/Allcock ENG	2002	Tony Allcock ENG	Duff/Foster SCO

English Bowling Association Championships
First competition 1905 - results from 1985 only

	Singles	Pairs	Triples	Fours
1985	Roy Keating Devon	Haxby Road Yorks	Clevedon Somerset	Aldershot Essex
1986	Wynne Richards Surrey	Owton Lodge Durham	Poole Park Dorset	Stony Stratford Bucks
1987	David Holt Lancs	Bolton Lancs	Worcester County	Aylesbury Tn Bucks
1988	Richard Bray Cornwall	Leicester	Belgrave Leics	Summertown Oxon
1989	John Ottaway Norfolk	Essex County	Southbourne Sussex	Blackheath & G Kent
1990	Tony Allcock Gloucs	Wymondham D Norfolk	Cheltenham Gloucs	Bath Avon
1991	Tony Allcock Gloucs	Wigton Cumbria	Wigton Cumbria	Wokingham Berks
1992	Stephen Farish Cumbria	Blackheath & G Kent	Chandos Pk Bucks	Bournemouth Hants
1993	John Wickham Devon	Erdington Ct Warwicks	Preston Sussex	Reading Berks
1994	Kevin Morley Notts	Pontelan North'berland	Torquay Devon	Cheltenham Gloucs
1995	John Leeman Durham	Swindon W Wiltshire	Cheltenham Gloucs	Hollingbury Pk Sussex
1996	John Ottaway Norfolk	Bank Ho Hotel Worcs	Brit Cellophane S'erset	March Cons Cambs B
1997	Richard Brittan Warwick B	Dorchester Dorset	Wigton Cumbria	Swindon West Wilts
1998	Grant Burgess	Stoke Stafford	Bolton Lancs	Banbury Boro Oxon
1999	Nicky Brett Hunts	Northampton	Hampshire	Buckinghamshire
2000	John Ottaway Norfolk	Cumbria	Northumberland	Lancashire
2001	Gordon Charlton	March Conservative	Siemens	South Derbyshire
2002	Martyn Sekyar Hants	Gilt Edge	Banbury	Siemens

BOXING

WORLD CHAMPIONS - UNDISPUTED

HEAVYWEIGHT
1882 **John L Sullivan** USA
1892 **James J Corbett** USA
1897 **Bob Fitzsimmons** GBR
1899 **James J Jeffries** USA
1905 **Marvin Hart** USA
1906 **Tommy Burns** CAN
1908 **Jack Johnson** USA
1915 **Jess Willard** USA
1919 **Jack Dempsey** USA
1926 **Gene Tunney** USA
1930 **Max Schmeling** GER
1932 **Jack Sharkey** USA
1933 **Primo Carnera** ITA
1934 **Max Baer** USA
1935 **James J Braddock** USA
1937 **Joe Louis** USA
1949 **Ezzard Charles** USA
1951 **Jersey Joe Walcott** USA
1952 **Rocky Marciano** USA
1956 **Floyd Patterson** USA
1959 **Ingemar Johansson** SWE
1960 **Floyd Patterson** USA
1962 **Sonny Liston** USA
1964 **Cassius Clay** USA
1970 **Joe Frazier** USA
1973 **George Foreman** USA
1974 **Muhammed Ali** USA
1978 **Leon Spinks** USA
1987 **Mike Tyson** USA
1999 **Lennox Lewis** GBR

CRUISERWEIGHT
1988 **Evander Holyfield** USA

LIGHT HEAVYWEIGHT
1903 **Jack Root** AUT
1903 **George Gardner** IRL
1903 **Bob Fitzsimmons** GBR
1905 **Jack O'Brien** USA
1912 **Jack Dillon** USA
1916 **Battling Levinsky** USA
1920 **Georges Carpentier** FRA
1922 **Battling Siki** SEN
1923 **Mike McTigue** IRL
1925 **Paul Berlenbach** USA
1926 **Jack Delaney** CAN
1927 **Jim Slattery** USA
1927 **Tommy Loughran** USA
1930 **Jim Slattery** USA
1930 **Maxie Rosenbloom** USA
1934 **Bob Olin** USA
1935 **John Henry Lewis** USA
1939 **Melio Bettina** USA
1939 **Billy Conn** USA
1941 **Anton Christoforidis** GRE
1941 **Gus Lesnevich** USA
1948 **Freddie Mills** GBR

1950 **Joey Maxim** USA
1952 **Archie Moore** USA
1962 **Harold Johnson** USA
1963 **Willie Pastrano** USA
1965 **José Torres** PUR
1966 **Dick Tiger** NGR
1968 **Bob Foster** USA
1983 **Michael Spinks** USA
1999 **Roy Jones** USA

MIDDLEWEIGHT
1891 **Jack Dempsey** IRL
1891 **Bob Fitzsimmons** GBR
1898 **Tommy Ryan** USA
1907 **Stanley Ketchel** USA
1908 **Billy Papke** USA
1908 **Stanley Ketchel** USA
1910 **Billy Papke** USA
1911 **Cyclone Thompson** USA
1913 **Frank Klaus** USA
1913 **George Chip** USA
1914 **Al McCoy** USA
1917 **Mike O'Dowd** USA
1920 **Johnny Wilson** USA
1923 **Harry Greb** USA
1926 **Tiger Flowers** USA
1926 **Mickey Walker** USA
1931 **Gorilla Jones** USA
1932 **Marcel Thil** FRA
1941 **Tony Zale** USA
1947 **Rocky Graziano** USA
1948 **Tony Zale** USA
1948 **Marcel Cerdan** ALG
1949 **Jake la Motta** USA
1951 **Sugar Ray Robinson** USA
1951 **Randolph Turpin** GBR
1951 **Sugar Ray Robinson** USA
1953 **Carl 'Bobo' Olsen** HAW
1955 **Sugar Ray Robinson** USA
1957 **Gene Fullmer** USA
1957 **Sugar Ray Robinson** USA
1957 **Carmen Basilio** USA
1958 **Sugar Ray Robinson** USA
1960 **Paul Pender** USA
1961 **Terry Downes** GBR
1962 **Paul Pender** USA
1963 **Dick Tiger** NGR
1963 **Joey Giardello** USA
1965 **Dick Tiger** NGR
1966 **Emile Griffith** USA
1968 **Nino Benvenuti** ITA
1970 **Carlos Monzon** ARG
1976 **Carlos Monzon** ARG
1977 **Rodrigo Valdez** COL
1978 **Hugo Corro** ARG
1979 **Vito Antuofermo** ITA
1980 **Alan Minter** GBR
1980 **Marvin Hagler** USA

JUNIOR MIDDLEWEIGHT
1962 **Denny Moyer** USA
1963 **Ralph Dupas** USA
1963 **Sandro Massinghi** ITA
1965 **Nino Benvenuti** ITA
1966 **Kim Ki-soo** KOR
1968 **Sandro Massinghi** ITA
1969 **Freddie Little** USA
1970 **Carmelo Bossi** ITA
1971 **Koichi Wajima** JPN
1974 **Oscar Albarado** USA
1975 **Koichi Wajima** JPN

WELTERWEIGHT
1892 **Billy Smith** CAN
1894 **Tommy Ryan** USA
1896 **Charles 'Kid' McCoy** USA
1898 **Mysterious Billy Smith**
1900 **Rube Ferns** USA
1900 **Matty Matthews** USA
1901 **Rube Ferns** USA
1901 **Joe Walcott** BAR
1904 **Dixie Kid** USA
1905 **Joe Walcott** BAR
1906 **Honey Mellody** USA
1907 **Mike 'Twin' Sullivan** USA
1915 **Ted Kid Lewis** GBR
1916 **Jack Britton** USA
1917 **Ted Kid Lewis** GBR
1919 **Jack Britton** USA
1922 **Micky Walker** USA
1926 **Pete Latzo** USA
1927 **Joe Dundee** ITA
1929 **Jackie Fields** USA
1930 **Jack Thompson** USA
1930 **Tommy Freeman** USA
1931 **Jack Thompson** USA
1931 **Lou Broulliard** CAN
1932 **Jackie Fields** USA
1933 **Young Corbett III** ITA
1933 **Jimmy McLarnin** IRL
1934 **Barney Ross** USA
1934 **Jimmy McLarnin** IRL
1935 **Barney Ross** USA
1938 **Henry Armstrong** USA
1940 **Fritzie Zivic** USA
1941 **Freddie Cochrane** USA
1946 **Marty Servo** USA
1946 **Sugar Ray Robinson** USA
1951 **Johnny Bratton** USA
1951 **Kid Gavilan** CUB
1954 **Johnny Saxton** USA
1955 **Tony de Marco** USA
1955 **Carmen Basilio** USA
1956 **Johnny Saxton** USA
1956 **Carmen Basilio** USA
1958 **Virgil Atkins** USA
1958 **Don Jordon** DOM
1960 **Benny Kid Paret** CUB
1961 **Emile Griffith** USA

BOXING

1961 **Benny Kid Paret** CUB
1962 **Emile Griffith** USA
1963 **Louis Rodriguez** CUB
1963 **Emile Griffith** USA
1966 **Curtis Cokes** USA
1969 **Jose Napoles** CUB
1970 **Billy Backus** USA
1971 **Jose Napoles** CUB
1981 **Sugar Ray Leonard** USA
1985 **Don Curry** USA
1986 **Lloyd Honeyghan** GBR

JUNIOR WELTERWEIGHT
1922 **Pinky Mitchell** USA
1926 **Mushy Callahan** USA
1930 **Jackie Kid Berg** GBR
1931 **Tony Canzoneri** USA
1932 **Johnny Jaddick** USA
1933 **Battling Shaw** MEX
1933 **Tony Canzoneri** USA
1933 **Barney Ross** USA
1946 **Tippy Larkin** USA
1959 **Carlos Ortiz** PUR
1960 **Duilio Loi** ITA
1962 **Eddie Perkins** USA
1962 **Duilio Loi** ITA
1963 **Roberto Cruz** PHI
1963 **Eddie Perkins** USA
1965 **Carlos Hernandez** VEN
1966 **Sandro Lopopolo** ITA
1967 **Paul Fujii** USA

LIGHTWEIGHT
1896 **George Lavigne** USA
1899 **Frank Erne** SUI
1902 **Joe Gans** USA
1908 **Battling Nelson** DEN
1910 **Ad Wolgast** USA
1912 **Willie Ritchie** USA
1914 **Freddie Welsh** GBR
1917 **Benny Leonard** USA
1925 **Jimmy Goodrich** USA
1925 **Rocky Kansas** USA
1926 **Sammy Mandell** USA
1930 **Al Singer** USA
1930 **Tony Canzoneri** USA
1933 **Barney Ross** USA
1935 **Tony Canzoneri** USA
1936 **Lou Ambers** USA
1938 **Henry Armstrong** USA
1939 **Lou Ambers** USA
1940 **Lew Jenkins** USA
1941 **Sammy Angott** USA
1942 **Beau Jack** USA
1943 **Bob Montgomery** USA
1943 **Sammy Angott** USA
1944 **Juan Zurita** MEX
1945 **Ike Williams** USA
1951 **Jimmy Carter** USA
1952 **Lauro Salas** MEX

1952 **Jimmy Carter** USA
1954 **Paddy de Marco** USA
1954 **Jimmy Carter** USA
1955 **Wallace Bud Smith** USA
1956 **Joe Brown** USA
1962 **Carlos Ortiz** PUR
1965 **Ismael Laguna** PAN
1965 **Carlos Ortiz** PUR
1968 **Carlos Teo Cruz** DOM
1969 **Mando Ramos** USA
1970 **Ismael Laguna** PAN
1978 **Roberto Duran** PAN

JUNIOR LIGHTWEIGHT
1921 **Johnny Dundee** ITA
1923 **Jack Bernstein** USA
1923 **Johnny Dundee** ITA
1924 **Kid Sullivan** USA
1925 **Mike Ballerino** USA
1925 **Tod Morgan** USA
1929 **Benny Bass** USA
1931 **Kid Chocolate** CUB
1933 **Frankie Klick** USA
1959 **Harold Gomes** USA
1960 **Flash Elorde** PHI
1967 **Yoshiaki Numata** JPN
1967 **Hiroshi Kobayashi** JPN

FEATHERWEIGHT
1892 **George Dixon** CAN
1897 **Solly Smith** USA
1898 **Dave Sullivan** IRL
1898 **George Dixon** CAN
1900 **Terry McGovern** USA
1901 **Young Corbett** USA
1904 **Abe Attell** USA
1912 **Johnny Kilbane** USA
1923 **Eugene Criqui** FRA
1923 **Johnny Dundee** ITA
1925 **Louis Kid Kaplan** USA
1927 **Benny Bass** USA
1928 **Tony Canzoneri** USA
1928 **Andre Routis** FRA
1929 **Battling Battalino** USA
1933 **Freddie Miller** USA
1936 **Petey Sarron** USA
1937 **Henry Armstrong** USA
1938 **Joey Archibald** USA
1946 **Willie Pep** USA
1948 **Sandy Saddler** USA
1949 **Willie Pep** USA
1950 **Sandy Saddler** USA
1957 **Hogan Kid Bassey** NGR
1959 **Davey Moore** USA
1963 **Sugar Ramos** CUB
1964 **Vicente Saldivar** MEX

JUNIOR FEATHERWEIGHT
1922 **Jack Kid Wolfe** USA
1923 **Carl Duane** USA

BANTAMWEIGHT
1890 **George Dixon** CAN
1899 **Terry McGovern** USA
1901 **Harry Forbes** USA
1903 **Frankie Neil** USA
1904 **Joe Bowker** GBR
1905 **Jimmy Walsh** USA
1910 **Johnny Coulon** CAN
1914 **Kid Williams** DEN
1917 **Pete Herman** USA
1920 **Joe Lynch** USA
1921 **Pete Herman** USA
1921 **Johnny Buff** USA
1922 **Joe Lynch** USA
1924 **Abe Goldstein** USA
1924 **Eddie Martin** USA
1925 **Charley Rosenberg** USA
1929 **Al Brown** PAN
1936 **Tony Marino** USA
1936 **Sixto Escobar** PUR
1937 **Harry Jeffra** USA
1938 **Sixto Escobar** PUR
1940 **Lou Salica** USA
1942 **Manuel Ortiz** USA
1947 **Harold Dade** USA
1947 **Manuel Ortiz** USA
1950 **Vic Toweel** RSA
1952 **Jimmy Carruthers** AUS
1954 **Robert Cohen** ALG
1956 **Mario D'Agata** ITA
1957 **Alphonse Halimi** ALG
1959 **Joe Becerra** MEX
1962 **Eder Jofre** BRA
1965 **Fighting Harada** JPN
1968 **Lionel Rose** AUS
1969 **Ruben Olivares** MEX
1970 **Chucho Castillo** MEX
1971 **Ruben Olivares** MEX
1972 **Rafael Herrera** MEX
1972 **Enrique Pinder** PAN

FLYWEIGHT
1916 **Jimmy Wilde** GBR
1923 **Pancho Villa** PHI
1925 **Fidel La Barba** USA
1937 **Benny Lynch** GBR
1938 **Peter Kane** GBR
1943 **Jackie Paterson** GBR
1948 **Rinty Monaghan** GBR
1950 **Terry Allen** GBR
1950 **Dado Marino** HAW
1952 **Yoshio Shirai** JPN
1954 **Pascual Perez** ARG
1960 **Pone Kingpetch** THA
1962 **Fighting Harada** JPN
1963 **Pone Kingpetch** THA
1963 **Hiroyuki Ebihara** JPN
1964 **Pone Kingpetch** THA
1965 **Salvatore Burruni** ITA

BOXING

WORLD CHAMPIONS - DISPUTED

HEAVYWEIGHT

WBA

1958 Virgil Atkins USA
1965 Ernie Terrell USA
1968 Jimmy Ellis USA
1978 Muhammad Ali USA
1979 John Tate USA
1980 Mike Weaver USA
1982 Mike Dokes USA
1983 Gerrie Coetzee RSA
1984 Greg Page USA
1985 Tony Tubbs USA
1986 Tim Witherspoon USA
1986 James Smith USA
1987 Mike Tyson USA
1990 J 'Buster' Douglas USA
1990 Evander Holyfield USA
1992 Riddick Bowe USA
1993 Evander Holyfield USA
1994 Michael Moorer USA
1994 George Foreman USA
1995 Bruce Seldon USA
1996 Mike Tyson USA
1996 Evander Holyfield USA
1999 Lennox Lewis GBR
2000 Evander Holyfield USA
2001 John Ruiz USA

WBC

1978 Ken Norton USA
1978 Larry Holmes USA
1984 Tim Witherspoon USA
1984 Pinklon Thomas USA
1986 Trevor Berbick JAM
1989 Mike Tyson USA
1990 J 'Buster' Douglas USA
1990 Evander Holyfield USA
1992 Riddick Bowe USA
1992 Lennox Lewis GBR
1994 Oliver McCall USA
1995 Frank Bruno GBR
1996 Mike Tyson USA
1997 Lennox Lewis GBR
2001 Hasim Rahman USA
2001 Lennox Lewis GBR

IBF

1984 Larry Holmes USA
1985 Michael Spinks USA
1987 Tony Tucker USA
1989 J 'Buster' Douglas USA
1990 Evander Holyfield USA
1992 Riddick Bowe USA
1993 Evander Holyfield USA
1994 Michael Moorer USA
1994 George Foreman USA
1995 Francois Botha* RSA

1996 Michael Moorer USA
1997 Evander Holyfield USA
1999 Lennox Lewis GBR
2001 Hasim Rahman USA
2001 Lennox Lewis GBR
*Stripped of title - tested positive

CRUISERWEIGHT

WBA

1982 Ossie Ocasio PUR
1984 Piet Crous RSA
1985 Dwight Muh'd Qawi USA
1986 Evander Holyfield USA
1989 Taoufik Belbouli FRA
1989 Robert Daniels USA
1991 Bobby Cruz USA
1993 Orlin Norris USA
1995 Nate Miller USA
1997 Fabrice Tiozzo FRA
2000 Virgil Hill USA
2002 Jean-Marc Mormeck FRA

WBC

1979 Marvin Camel USA
1980 Carlos de Leon PUR
1982 S T Gordon USA
1983 Carlos de Leon PUR
1985 Alfonso Ratliff USA
1985 Bernard Benton USA
1986 Carlos de Leon PUR
1988 Evander Holyfield USA
1989 Carlos de Leon PUR
1990 Massimiliano Duran ITA
1991 Anaclet Wamba FRA
1996 Marcelo Dominguez ARG
1998 Juan Carlos Gomez CUB

IBF

1983 Marvin Camel USA
1984 Lee Roy Murphy USA
1986 Rickey Parkey USA
1987 Evander Holyfield USA
1989 Glenn McCrory GBR
1990 Jeff Lampkin USA
1991 James Warring USA
1992 Alfred Cole USA
1996 Adolpho Washington USA
1997 Uriah Grant JAM
1997 Imamu Mayfield USA
1998 Arthur Williams USA
1999 Vassily Jirov USA

LIGHT-HEAVYWEIGHT

WBA

1971 Vicente Rondon VEN
1974 Victor Galindez ARG
1978 Mike Rossman USA
1979 Victor Galindez ARG

1979 Marvin Johnson USA
1980 Eddie Mustafa Mh'd USA
1981 Michael Spinks USA
1986 Marvin Johnson USA
1987 Leslie Stewart JAM
1987 Virgil Hill USA
1991 Thomas Hearns USA
1992 Iran Barkley USA
1992 Virgil Hill USA
1997 D Michalczewski GER
1997 Louis Del Valle USA
1998 Roy Jones USA
2001 Bruno Girard FRA

WBC

1974 John Conteh GBR
1977 Miguel Cuello ARG
1978 Mate Parlov YUG
1978 Marvin Johnson USA
1979 Matthew Saad Mh'd USA
1981 Dwight Muh'd Qawi USA
1985 JB Williamson USA
1986 Dennis Andries GBR
1987 Thomas Hearns USA
1988 Donny Lalonde CAN
1988 Sugar Ray Leonard USA
1989 Dennis Andries GBR
1989 Jeff Harding AUS
1990 Dennis Andries GBR
1991 Jeff Harding AUS
1994 Mike McCallum JAM
1995 Fabrice Tiozzo FRA
1996 Roy Jones USA
1997 Montell Griffin USA
1997 Roy Jones USA
1998 Graciano Rocchigiani ITA
1999 Roy Jones USA

IBF

1985 Slobodan Kacar YUG
1986 Bobby Czyz USA
1987 P Charles Williams USA
1993 Henry Maske GER
1996 Virgil Hill USA
1997 D Michalczewski GER
1997 William Guthrie USA
1998 Reggie Johnson USA
1999 Roy Jones USA

SUPER-MIDDLEWEIGHT

WBA

1984 Park Chong-Pal KOR
1988 F Obelmejias VEN
1989 Baek In-Chul KOR
1990 Christophe Tiozzo FRA
1991 Victor Cordoba PAN
1992 Michael Nunn USA
1994 Steve Little USA
1994 Frank Liles USA

1999 **Byron Mitchell** USA
2000 **Bruno Girard** FRA
2001 **Byron Mitchell** USA

WBC
1988 **Sugar Ray Leonard** USA
1990 **Mauro Galvano** ITA
1992 **Nigel Benn** GBR
1996 **Sugarboy Malinga** RSA
1996 **Vincenzo Nardiello** ITA
1996 **Robin Reid** GBR
1997 **Sugarboy Malinga** RSA
1998 **Richie Woodhall** GBR
1999 **Marcus Beyer** GER
2000 **Glenn Catley** GBR
2000 **Dingaan Thobela** RSA
2000 **Dave Hilton** CAN
2001 **Eric Lucas** CAN

IBF
1984 **Murray Sutherland** CAN
1988 **Grac Rocchigiani** FRG
1990 **Lindell Holmes** USA
1991 **Darrin van Horn** USA
1992 **Iran Barkley** USA
1993 **James Toney** USA
1994 **Roy Jones** USA
1997 **Charles Brewer** USA
1998 **Sven Ottke** GER

MIDDLEWEIGHT
WBA
1987 **Sambu Kalambay** ZAI
1989 **Mike McCallum** USA
1992 **Reggie Johnson** USA
1994 **John D Jackson** USA
1994 **Jorge Castro** ARG
1995 **Shinji Takehara** JPN
1996 **William Joppy** USA
1997 **Julio Cesar Green** DOM
1998 **William Joppy** USA
2001 **Felix Trinidad** USA
2001 **Bernard Hopkins** USA
2001 **William Joppy** USA

WBC
1974 **Rodrigo Valdez** COL
1987 **Sugar Ray Leonard** USA
1987 **Thomas Hearns** USA
1988 **Iran Barkley** USA
1989 **Roberto Duran** PAN
1990 **Julian Jackson** USA
1993 **Gerald McClellan** USA
1995 **Julian Jackson** USA
1995 **Quincy Taylor** USA
1996 **Keith Holmes** USA
1998 **Hassine Cherifi** FRA
1999 **Keith Holmes** USA
2001 **Bernard Hopkins** USA

IBF
1987 **Frank Tate** USA
1988 **Michael Nunn** USA
1991 **James Toney** USA
1993 **Roy Jones** USA
1994 **Bernard Hopkins** USA
1998 **Robbie Allen** USA
1999 **Bernard Hopkins** USA

SUPER-WELTERWEIGHT
WBA
1975 **Yuh Jae-Do** KOR
1976 **Koichi Wajima** JPN
1976 **Jose Duran** ESP
1976 **Angel Castellini** ARG
1977 **Eddie Gazo** NCA
1978 **Masashi Kudo** JPN
1979 **Ayube Kalule** UGA
1981 **Sugar Ray Leonard** USA
1981 **Tadashi Mihara** JPN
1982 **Davey Moore** USA
1983 **Roberto Duran** PAN
1984 **Mike McCallum** JAM
1988 **Julian Jackson** USA
1991 **Gilbert Dele** FRA
1991 **Vinny Pazienza** USA
1992 **Cesar Vasquez** ARG
1992 **Vinny Pazienza** USA
1992 **Julio Cesar Vasquez**ARG
1995 **Pernell Whitaker** USA
1995 **Carl Daniels** USA
1995 **Julio C'r Vasquez** ARG
1996 **Laurent Boudouani** FRA
1999 **David Reid** USA
2000 **Felix Trinidad** PUR
2001 **Fernando Vargas** USA
2002 **Oscar de la Hoya** USA

WBC
1975 **Miguel de Oliviera** BRA
1975 **Elisha Obed** BAH
1976 **Eckhard Dagge** FRG
1977 **Rocky Mattioli** ITA
1979 **Maurice Hope** GBR
1981 **Wilfred Benitez** USA
1982 **Thomas Hearns** USA
1986 **Duane Thomas** USA
1987 **Lupe Aquino** MEX
1988 **Gianfranco Rosi** ITA
1988 **Don Curry** USA
1989 **Rene Jacquot** FRA
1989 **John Mugabi** UGA
1990 **Terry Norris** USA
1993 **Simon Brown** JAM
1994 **Terry Norris** USA
1995 **Luis Santana** DOM
1995 **Terry Norris** USA
1997 **Keith Mullings** USA
1999 **Javier Castillejo** ESP
2001 **Oscar de le Hoya** USA

IBF
1984 **Mark Medal** USA
1984 **Carlos Santos** PUR
1986 **Buster Drayton** USA
1987 **Matthew Hilton** CAN
1988 **Robert Hines** USA
1989 **Darrin Van Horn** USA
1989 **Gianfranco Rosi** ITA
1994 **Vincent Pettway** USA
1996 **Terry Norris** USA
1997 **Raul Marquez** USA
1997 **Luis Ramon Campas** MEX
1999 **Fernando Vargas** USA
2000 **Felix Trinidad** PUR
2001 **Ronald Wright** USA

WELTERWEIGHT
WBA
1975 **Angel Espada** PUR
1976 **Pipino Cuevas** MEX
1980 **Thomas Hearns** USA
1983 **Don Curry** USA
1987 **Mark Breland** USA
1987 **Marlon Starling** USA
1988 **Tomas Molinares** COL
1989 **Mark Breland** USA
1990 **Aaron Davis** USA
1991 **Meldrick Taylor** USA
1992 **Crisanto Espana** VEN
1994 **Ike Quartey** GHA
1998 **James Page** USA
2001 **Andrew Lewis** GUY
2002 **Ricardo Mayorga** NCA

WBC
1975 **John H Stracey** GBR
1976 **Carlos Palomino** MEX
1979 **Wilfred Benitez** USA
1979 **Sugar Ray Leonard** USA
1980 **Roberto Duran** PAN
1980 **Sugar Ray Leonard** USA
1983 **Milton McCrory** USA
1987 **Lloyd Honeyghan** GBR
1987 **Jorge Vaca** MEX
1988 **Lloyd Honeyghan** GBR
1989 **Marlon Starling** USA
1990 **Maurice Blocker** USA
1991 **Simon Brown** JAM
1991 **Buddy McGirt** USA
1993 **Pernell Whitaker** USA
1997 **Oscar De La Hoya** USA
1999 **Felix Trinidad** PUR
       Vacant
2000 **Shane Mosley** USA
2002 **Vernon Forrest USA**

IBF
1984 **Don Curry** USA
1987 **Lloyd Honeyghan** GBR
1988 **Simon Brown** JAM

BOXING

1991 **Buddy McGirt** USA
1992 **Felix Trinidad** PUR
Vacant
2001 **Vernon Forrest** USA
2002 **Michele Piccirillo** ITA

SUPER-LIGHTWEIGHT
WBA
1968 **Nicolino Loche** ARG
1972 **Alfonso Frazer** PAN
1972 **Antonio Cervantes** COL
1976 **Wilfred Benitez** USA
1977 **Antonio Cervantes** COL
1980 **Aaron Pryor** USA
1984 **Johnny Bumphus** USA
1984 **Gene Hatcher** USA
1985 **Ubaldo Sacco** ARG
1986 **Patrizio Oliva** ITA
1987 **Juan Martin Coggi** ARG
1990 **Loreto Garza** USA
1991 **Edwin Rosario** PUR
1992 **Morris East** PHI
1993 **Juan Martin Coggi** ARG
1994 **Frankie Randall** USA
1996 **Juan Martin Coggi** ARG
1996 **Frankie Randall** USA
1997 **Khalid Rahilou** FRA
1998 **Sharmba Mitchell** USA
2001 **Kostya Tszyu** AUS
2002 **Diobelys Hurtado** CUB
2002 **Vivian Harris** GUY

WBC
1968 **Pedro Adigue** PHI
1970 **Bruno Acari** ITA
1974 **Perico Fernandez** ESP
1975 **Saensak Muangsurin**THA
1976 **Miguel Velasquez** ESP
1976 **Saensak Muangsurin**THA
1978 **Kim Sang-Hyun** KOR
1980 **Saoul Mamby** USA
1982 **Leroy Haley** USA
1983 **Bruce Curry** USA
1984 **Billy Costello** USA
1985 **Lonnie Smith** USA
1986 **Tsuyoshi Hamada** JAP
1986 **Rene Arredondo** MEX
1987 **Rene Arredondo** MEX
1988 **Roger Mayweather** USA
1989 **Julio Cesar Chavez** MEX
1994 **Frankie Randall** USA
1994 **Julio Cesar Chavez** MEX
1996 **Oscar De La Hoya** USA
1998 Vacant
1999 **Kostya Tszyu** AUS

IBF
1983 **Aaron Pryor** USA
1986 **Gary Hinton** USA

1986 **Joe Louis Manley** USA
1987 **Terry Marsh** GBR
1988 **James Buddy McGirt**USA
1988 **Meldrick Taylor** USA
1990 **Julio Cesar Chavez** MEX
1991 **Rafael Pineda** COL
1992 **Pernell Whitaker** USA
1993 **Charles Murray** USA
1994 **Jake Rodriguez** USA
1995 **Konstantin Tszyu** RUS
1997 **Vince Phillips** USA
1999 **Terron Millett** USA
2000 **Zab Judah** USA
2001 **Kostya Tszyu** AUS

LIGHTWEIGHT
WBA
1970 **Ken Buchanan** GBR
1972 **Roberto Duran** PAN
1979 **Ernesto Espana** VEN
1980 **Hilmer Kenty** USA
1981 **Sean O'Grady** USA
1981 **Claude Noel** TRI
1981 **Arturo Frias** USA
1982 **Ray Mancini** USA
1984 **Livingstone Bramble**USA
1986 **Edwin Rosario** PUR
1987 **Julio Cesar Chavez** MEX
1989 **Edwin Rosario** PUR
1990 **Juan Nazario** PUR
1990 **Pernell Whitaker** USA
1992 **Joey Gamache** USA
1992 **Tony Lopez** USA
1993 **Dingaan Thobela** RSA
1993 **Orzoubek Nazarov** RUS
1998 **Jean Baptiste Mendy** FRA
1999 **Julien Lorcy** FRA
1999 **Stefano Zoff** ITA
1999 **Gilbert Serrano** VEN
2000 **Takanori Hatekeyama** JPN
2001 **Julien Lorcy** FRA
2001 **Raul Balbi** ARG
2002 **Leonard Dorin** ROM

WBC
1971 **Pedro Carrasco** ESP
1972 **Mando Ramos** USA
1972 **Chango Carmona** MEX
1972 **Rodolfo Gonzalez** MEX
1974 **Guts Ishimatsu** JPN
1976 **Esteban de Jesus** PUR
1979 **Jim Watt** GBR
1981 **Alexis Arguello** NCA
1983 **Edwin Rosario** PUR
1984 **Jose Luis Ramirez** MEX
1985 **Hector Camacho** PUR
1987 **Jose Luis Ramirez** MEX
1988 **Julio Cesar Chavez** MEX
1989 **Pernell Whitaker** USA

1992 **Miguel Gonzalez** MEX
1996 **Jean-B Mendy** FRA
1997 **Steve Johnson** USA
1998 **Cesar Bazan** MEX
1999 **Stevie Johnson** USA
2000 **Jose Luis Castillo** MEX
2002 **Floyd Mayweather** USA

IBF
1984 **Charlie Brown** USA
1984 **Harry Arroyo** USA
1985 **Jimmy Paul** USA
1986 **Greg Haugen** USA
1987 **Vinny Pazienza** USA
1988 **Greg Haugen** USA
1989 **Pernell Whitaker** USA
1992 **Tracy Spann** USA
1993 **Freddie Pendleton** USA
1994 **Rafael Ruelas** USA
1995 **Phillip Holliday** RSA
1997 **Shane Mosley** USA
1999 **Paul Spadafora** USA

SUPER-FEATHERWEIGHT
WBA
1971 **Alfredo Marcano** VEN
1972 **Ben Villaflor** PHI
1973 **Kuniaki Shibata** JPN
1973 **Ben Villaflor** PHI
1976 **Sam Serrano** PUR
1980 **Yasutsune Uehara** JPN
1981 **Sam Serrano** PUR
1983 **Roger Mayweather** USA
1984 **Rocky Lockridge** USA
1985 **Wilfredo Gomez** PUR
1986 **Alfredo Layne** PAN
1986 **Brian Mitchell** RSA
1991 **Joey Gamache** USA
1991 **Genaro Hernandez** USA
1995 **Choi Yong-Soo** KOR
1998 **Takanori Hatekayama** JPN
1999 **Lavka Sim** MGL
1999 **Jong Kwon-baek** KOR
2000 **Joel Casamayor** USA
2002 **Acelino Freitas** BRA

WBC
1969 **Rene Barrientos** PHI
1970 **Yoshiaki Numata** JPN
1971 **Ricardo Arredondo** MEX
1974 **Kuniaki Shibata** JPN
1975 **Alfredo Escalera** PUR
1978 **Alexis Arguello** NCA
1980 **Rafael Limon** MEX
1981 **Cornelius Edwards** UGA
1981 **Rolando Navarette** PHI
1982 **Rafael Limon** MEX
1982 **Bobby Chacon** USA
1983 **Hector Camacho** PUR

BOXING

1984 **Julio Cesar Chavez** MEX	1974 **Bobby Chacon** USA	1998 **Enrique Sanchez** MEX
1988 **Azumah Nelson** GHA	1975 **Ruben Olivares** MEX	1998 **Carlos Barreto** VEN
1994 **Jesse James Leija** MEX	1975 **David Kotey** GHA	1999 **Nestor Garza** MEX
1995 **Gabe Ruelas** USA	1976 **Danny Lopez** USA	2000 **Clarence Adams** USA
1995 **Azumah Nelson** GHA	1980 **Salvador Sanchez** MEX	2001 **Yober Ortega** VEN
1997 **Genaro Hernandez** USA	1982 **Juan Laporte** PUR	2002 **Y Sithyodthong** THA
1998 **Floyd Mayweather** USA	1984 **Wilfredo Gomez** PUR	2002 **Osamu Sato** JPN
2002 **S Singmanassak** THA	1984 **Azumah Nelson** GHA	2002 **Salim Medjkoune** FRA
	1988 **Jeff Fenech** AUS	
IBF	1990 **Marcos Villasana** MEX	**WBC**
1984 **Yuh Hwan-Kil** KOR	1991 **Paul Hodkinson** GBR	1976 **Rigoberto Riasco** PAN
1985 **Lester Ellis** AUS	1993 **Gregorio Vargas** MEX	1976 **Royal Kobayashi** JPN
1985 **Barry Michael** AUS	1993 **Kevin Kelley** USA	1976 **Yum Dong-Kyun** KOR
1987 **Rocky Lockridge** USA	1995 **Alejandro Gonzalez** MEX	1977 **Wilfredo Gomez** PUR
1988 **Tony Lopez** USA	1995 **Manuel Medina** MEX	1983 **Jaime Garza** USA
1989 **Juan Molina** PUR	1995 **Luisito Espinosa** PHI	1984 **Juan Meza** MEX
1990 **Tony Lopez** USA	1999 **Naseem Hamed** GBR	1985 **Lupe Pintor** MEX
1991 **Brian Mitchell** RSA	2000 **Guty Espadas** MEX	1986 **Samart Payakarun** THA
1993 **John John Molina** PUR	2001 **Erik Morales** MEX	1987 **Jeff Fenech** AUS
1995 **Eddie Hopson** USA	2002 **Marco A Barrera** MEX	1988 **Daniel Zaragoza** MEX
1995 **Tracy Patterson** USA	2002 **Erik Morales** MEX	1990 **Paul Banke** USA
1995 **Arturo Gatti** CAN		1990 **Pedro Decima** ARG
1998 **Roberto Garcia** USA	**IBF**	1991 **Kiyoshi Hatanaka** JPN
1999 **Diego Corrales** USA	1984 **Oh Min-Keum** KOR	1991 **Daniel Zaragoza** MEX
2000 **Steve Forbes** USA	1985 **Chung Ki-Young** KOR	1992 **Thierry Jacob** FRA
	1986 **Antonio Rivera** PUR	1992 **Tracy Patterson** USA
	1988 **Calvin Grove** USA	1994 **Hector A Sanchez** DOM
FEATHERWEIGHT	1988 **Jorge Paez** MEX	1995 **Daniel Zaragoza** MEX
WBA	1991 **Troy Dorsey** USA	1997 **Erik Morales** MEX
1968 **Raul Rojas** USA	1991 **Manuel Medina** MEX	2000 **Willie Jorin** USA
1968 **Shozo Saijyo** JPN	1993 **Tom Johnson** USA	2002 **Oscar Larios** MEX
1971 **Antonio Gomez** VEN	1997 **Naseem Hamed** GBR	
1972 **Ernesto Marcel** PAN	1997 **Hector Lizarraga** MEX	**IBF**
1974 **Ruben Olivares** MEX	1998 **Manuel Medina** MEX	1983 **Bobby Berna** PHI
1974 **Alexis Arguello** NCA	1999 **Cesar Soto** MEX	1984 **Suh Seung-Il** KOR
1977 **Rafael Ortega** PAN	1999 **Paul Ingle** GBR	1985 **Kim Ji-Won** KOR
1977 **Cecilio Lastra** ESP	2000 **Mbulelo Botile** RSA	1987 **Lee Seung-Hoon** KOR
1978 **Eusebio Pedroza** PAN	2001 **Frankie Toledo** USA	1988 **Jose Sanabria** VEN
1985 **Barry McGuigan** IRL	2001 **Manuel Medina** MEX	1989 **Fabrice Benichou** FRA
1986 **Steve Cruz** USA	2002 **Johnny Tapia** USA	1990 **Welcome Ncita** RSA
1987 **Toni Esparragoza** VEN		1992 **Kennedy McKinney** USA
1991 **ParkYoung-Kyun** KOR		1994 **Vuyani Bungu** RSA
1992 **Wilfredo Vazquez** COL	**SUPER BANTAMWEIGHT**	1999 **Benedict Ledwaba** RSA
1992 **Park Young-Kyun** KOR	**WBA**	2001 **Manny Pacquiao** PHI
1993 **Eloy Rojas** VEN	1977 **Hong Soo-Hwan** KOR	
1996 **Wilfredo Vazquez** COL	1978 **Ricardo Cardona** COL	
1998 **Fred Norwood** USA	1980 **Leo Randolph** USA	**BANTAMWEIGHT**
1998 **Antonio Cermeno** VEN	1980 **Sergio Palma** ARG	**WBA**
1999 **Freddie Norwood** USA	1982 **Leo Cruz** DOM	1973 **Romeo Anaya** MEX
2000 **Derrick Gainer** USA	1984 **Loris Stecca** ITA	1973 **Arnold Taylor** RSA
	1984 **Victor Callejas** PUR	1974 **Hong Soo-Hwan** KOR
	1987 **Louis Espinoza** USA	1975 **Alfonso Zamora** MEX
WBC	1987 **Julio Gervacio** DOM	1977 **Jorge Lujan** PAN
1968 **Howard Winstone** GBR	1988 **Bernardo Pinango** VEN	1980 **Julian Solis** PUR
1968 **Jose Legra** CUB	1988 **Juan Jose Estrada** MEX	1980 **Jeff Chandler** USA
1969 **Johnny Famechon** FRA	1989 **Jesus Salud** USA	1984 **Richard Sandoval** USA
1970 **Vicente Saldivar** MEX	1990 **Luis Mendoza** COL	1986 **Gaby Canizales** USA
1970 **Kuniaki Shibata** JPN	1991 **Raul Perez** MEX	1986 **Bernardo Pinango** VEN
1972 **Clemente Sanchez** MEX	1992 **Wilfredo Vasquez** PUR	1987 **Takuya Muguruma** JPN
1972 **Jose Legra** CUB	1995 **Antonio Cermeno** VEN	1987 **Park Chang-Young** KOR
1973 **Eder Jofre** BRA		

BOXING

1987 Wilfredo Vasquez PUR
1988 Khaokor Galaxy THA
1988 Moon Sung-Kil KOR
1989 Khaokor Galaxy THA
1989 Luisito Espinosa PHI
1991 Israel Contreras VEN
1992 Eddie Cook USA
1992 Jorge Julio COL
1993 Junior Jones USA
1994 John M Johnson USA
1994 Doarung PetroleumTHA
1995 Veeraphol Sahaprom THA
1996 Nana Konadu THA
1996 Daorung C Siriwat THA
1998 Nana Konadu THA
1998 Johnny Tapia USA
1999 Paulie Ayala USA
2001 Eidy Moya VEN
2002 Johnny Bredahl DEN

WBC
1973 Rafael Herrera MEX
1974 Rodolfo Martinez MEX
1976 Carlos Zarate MEX
1979 Lupe Pintor MEX
1983 Alberto Davila USA
1985 Daniel Zaragoza MEX
1985 Miguel Lora COL
1988 Raul Perez MEX
1991 Greg Richardson USA
1991 Joichiro Tatsuyoshi JPN
1992 Victor Rabanales MEX
1993 Byun Jong-Il KOR
1993 Yasuei Yakushiji JPN
1995 Wayne McCullough IRL
1996 Siri Singmanassak THA
1997 Joichiro Tatsuyoshi JPN
1999 Veeraphol Sahaprom THA

IBF
1984 Satoshi Shingaki JPN
1985 Jeff Fenech AUS
1987 Kelvin Seabrooks USA
1988 Orlando Canizales USA
1995 Harold Maestre COL
1995 Mbulelo Botile RSA
1997 Tim Austin USA

SUPER FLYWEIGHT
WBA
1981 Gustavo Ballas ARG
1981 Rafael Pedroza PAN
1982 Jiro Watanabe JPN
1984 Khaosai Galaxy THA
1992 Katsuya Onizuka GBR
1994 Hyung Chui-Lee KOR
1995 Alimi Goitea VEN
1996 Yokthai Sit-Oar THA
1997 Satoshi Iida JPN

1999 Jesus Rojas VEN
1999 Hideki Todaka JPN
2000 Leo Gomez VEN
2001 Celes Kobayashi JPN
2002 Alexander Munoz VEN

WBC
1980 Rafael Orono VEN
1981 Kim Chul-Ho KOR
1982 Rafael Orono VEN
1983 Payao Poontarat THA
1984 Jiro Watanabe JPN
1986 Gilberto Roman MEX
1987 Santos Laciar ARG
1987 Jesus Rojas COL
1988 Gilberto Roman MEX
1989 Nana Yaw Konadu GHA
1990 Moon Sung-Kil KOR
1993 Jose Luis Bueno MEX
1994 Hiroshi Kawashima JPN
1996 Gerry Penalosa PHI
1998 Cho In-Joo KOR
2000 Masanori Tokuyama JPN

IBF
1983 Chun Joo-Do KOR
1985 Ellyas Pical INA
1986 Cesar Polanco DOM
1986 Chang Tae-Il KOR
1987 Ellyas Pical INA
1989 Juan Polo Perez COL
1990 Robert Quiroga USA
1993 Julio Cesar Borboa MEX
1994 Harold Grey USA
1995 Carlos Salazar ARG
1996 Harold Grey USA
1996 Danny Romero USA
1997 Johnny Tapia USA
1999 Mark Johnson USA
2000 Felix Machado VEN

FLYWEIGHT
WBA
1966 Horacio Accavallo ARG
1969 Hiroyuki Ebihara JPN
1969 Bernabe Villacampo PHI
1970 B Chartvanchai THA
1970 Masao Ohba JPN
1973 Chartchai Chionoi THA
1974 Susumu Hanagata JPN
1975 Erbito Salavarria PHI
1976 Alfonso Lopez PAN
1976 Guty Espadas MEX
1978 Betulio Gonzalez VEN
1979 Luis Ibarra PAN
1980 Kim Tae-Shik KOR
1980 Shoji Oguma JPN
1980 Peter Mathebula RSA
1981 Santos Laciar ARG

1981 Luis Ibarra PAN
1981 Juan Herrera MEX
1982 Santos Laciar ARG
1985 Hilario Zapata PAN
1987 Fidel Bassa COL
1989 Jesus Rojas VEN
1990 Lee Yul-Woo KOR
1990 Yukihito Tamakama JPN
1991 Elvis Alvarez COL
1991 Kim Yong-Kang KOR
1992 Aqueles Guzman VEN
1992 David Griman VEN
1994 Saensor Ploenchit THA
1996 Jose Bonilla VEN
1998 Hugo Soto ARG
1998 Mauricio Pastrana COL
1999 Leo Gamez VEN
2000 Sornpichai
        Kratchingdaeng THA
2001 Eric Morel PUR

WBC
1966 Walter McGowan GBR
1966 Chartchai Chionoi THA
1969 Efren Torres MEX
1970 Chartchai Chionoi THA
1970 Erbito Salavarria PHI
1972 Venice Borkorsor THA
1973 Betulio Gonzalez VEN
1974 Shoji Oguma JPN
1975 Miguel Canto MEX
1979 Park Chan-Hee KOR
1981 Antonio Avelar MEX
1982 Prudencio Cardona COL
1982 Freddie Castillo MEX
1982 Eleoncio Mercedes DOM
1983 Charlie Magri GBR
1983 Frank Cedeno PHI
1984 Koji Kobayashi JPN
1984 Gabriel Bernal MEX
1984 Sot Chitalada THA
1988 Kim Yong-Kang KOR
1989 Sot Chitalada THA
1991 M Kittikasem THA
1992 Yuri Arbachakov RUS
1997 Chatchai Sasakul THA
1998 Manny Pacquio PHI
1999 Medgoen Singsurat THA
2000 Malcolm Tunacao PHI
2001 Pongsaklek
        Wongjongkam THA
IBF
1983 Kwon Soon-Chun KOR
1985 Chung Chong-Kwan KOR
1986 Chung Bi-Won KOR
1986 Shin Hi-Sup KOR
1987 Dodie Penalosa PHI
1987 Choi Chang-Ho KOR
1988 Rolando Bohol PHI

1988 **Duke McKenzie** GBR
1989 **Dave McAuley** GBR
1992 **Rodolfo Blanco** COL
1992 **P Sitbangprachan** THA
1994 **Francisco Tejedor** COL
1995 **Danny Romero** USA
1996 **Mark Johnson** USA
1999 **Irene Pacheco** COL

LIGHT FLYWEIGHT
WBA
1975 **Jaime Rios** PAN
1976 **Juan Jose Guzman** DOM
1976 **Yoko Gushiken** JPN
1981 **Pedro Flores** MEX
1981 **Kim Hwan-Jin** KOR
1981 **Katsuo Takashiki** JPN
1983 **Lupe Madera** MEX
1984 **Francisco Quiroz** DOM
1985 **Joey Olivo** USA
1985 **Yuh Myung-Woo** KOR
1992 **Hiroki Ioka** JPN
1992 **Yuh Myung-Woo** KOR
1993 **Leo Gamez** VEN
1995 **Hiyong Choi** KOR
1996 **Carlos Murillo** PAN
1996 **Keiji Yamaguchi** JPN
1996 **Pichit Chor Siriwat** THA
2000 **Beibis Mendoza** COL
2001 **Rosenda Alvarez** NCA

WBC
1975 **Franco Udella** ITA
1975 **Luis Estaba** VEN
1978 **Freddie Castillo** MEX
1978 **Netrnoi Vorasingh** THA
1978 **Kim Sung-Kun** KOR
1980 **Shigeo Nakajima** JPN
1980 **Hilario Zapata** PAN
1982 **Amado Ursua** MEX
1982 **Tadashi Tomori** JPN
1982 **Hilario Zapata** PAN
1983 **Chang Jung-Koo** KOR
1988 **German Torres** MEX
1989 **Lee Yul-Woo** KOR
1989 **Humberto Gonzalez** MEX
1990 **Rolando Pascua** PHI
1991 **Melchor Cob Castro** MEX
1991 **Humberto Gonzalez** MEX
1993 **Michael Carbajal** USA
1994 **Humberto Gonzalez** MEX
1995 **Saman Sorjaturong** THA
1999 **Choi Yo-Sam** KOR
2002 **Jorge Arce** MEX

IBF
1983 **Dodie Penalosa** PHI
1986 **Choi Chong-Hwan** KOR
1988 **Tacy Macalos** PHI

1989 **M Kittikasem** THA
1990 **Michael Carbajal** USA
1991 **Welcome Ncita** RSA
1992 **Michael Carbajal** USA
1994 **Humberto Gonzalez** MEX
1995 **Saman Sorjaturong** THA
1996 **Michael Carbajal** USA
1997 **Mauricio Pastrana** COL
1998 Vacant
1999 **Will Grigsby** USA
1999 **Ricardo Lopez** MEX
2002 **Miguel Barrera** COL

STRAWWEIGHT
WBA
1988 **Leo Gamez** DOM
1989 **Kim Bong-Jun** KOR
1991 **Choi Hi-Yong** KOR
1992 **Hideyuki Ohashi** JPN
1993 **Chana Porpaoin** THA
1995 **Rosendo Alvarez** NCA
1998 **Ricardo Lopez** MEX
1999 **Noel Arambulet** VEN
2000 **Joma Gamboa** PHI
2000 **Keitaro Hoshino** JPN
2001 **Chana Porpaoin** THA
2001 **Yukata Niide** JPN
2002 **Keitaro Hoshino** JPN
2002 **Noel Ambulent** VEN

WBC
1987 **Lee Kyung-Yung** KOR
1988 **Hiroki Ioka** JPN
1988 **Napa Kiatwanchai** THA
1989 **Choi Jeum-Hwan** KOR
1990 **Hideyuki Ohashi** JPN
1990 **Ricardo Lopez** MEX
2000 **Jose Antonio Aguirre** MEX

IBF
1988 **Sam Sithnaruepol** THA
1989 **Nico Thomas** INA
1989 **Eric Chavez** PHI
1990 **F Lookmingkwan** THA
1992 **Manuel Melchor** PHI
1992 **Ratanopol Sorvorapin** THA
1998 **Zolani Lepethelo** RSA
2001 **Robert Leyva** MEX

BOXING

WORLD AMATEUR CHAMPIONS

SUPER-HEAVYWEIGHT (+91kg)
1982 Tyrell Biggs USA
1983 Tyrell Biggs USA
1986 Teofilio Stevenson CUB
1989 Roberto Baladao CUB
1991 Roberto Baladao CUB
1993 Roberto Baladao CUB
1995 Aleksey Lezin RUS
1997 George Kandelaki GEO
1999 Siren Samil TUR
2001 Ruslan Chagaev UZB

HEAVYWEIGHT (-91KG)
1974 Teofilio Stevenson CUB
1978 Teofilio Stevenson CUB
1982 Aleksandr Lagubkin URS
1983 Willie De Witt CAN
1986 Felix Savon CUB
1989 Felix Savon CUB
1993 Felix Savon CUB
1995 Felix Savon CUB
1997 Felix Savon CUB
1999 Michael Bennett USA
2001 Odlanier Fonte Solis CUB

LIGHT-HEAVYWEIGHT (-81kg)
1974 Mate Parlov YUG
1978 Sixto Soria CUB
1982 Pablo Romero CUB
1983 Pablo Romero CUB
1986 Pablo Romero CUB
1989 Henry Maske GDR
1991 Torsten May GER
1993 Ramon Garbey CUB
1995 Antonio Tarver USA
1997 Aleksandr Labziak RUS
1999 Michael Simms USA
2001 Yevgeny Makarenko RUS

MIDDLEWEIGHT (-75kg)
1974 Rufat Riskiyev URS
1978 Jose Gomez CUB
1982 Bernando Comas CUB
1983 Bernando Comas CUB
1986 Darin Allen USA
1989 Andrey Kurnyavka URS
1991 Tommaso Russo ITS
1993 Ariel Hernandez CUB
1995 Ariel Hernandez CUB
1997 Zsolt Erdei HUN
1999 Utkirbeck Haydarov UZB
2001 Andrei Gogolev RUS

LIGHT-MIDDLEWEIGHT (-71kg)
1974 Rolando Garbey CUB
1978 Viktor Savchenko URS
1982 Aleksandr Koshkin URS
1983 Shawn O'Sullivan CAN

1986 Angel Espinosa CUB
1989 Israel Akopkokhyan URS
1991 Juan Lemus CUB
1993 Francisc Vastag ROM
1995 Francisc Vastag ROM
1997 Alfredo Duvergel CUB
1999 Marin Simion ROM
2001 Damien Echemendia Austin CUB

WELTERWEIGHT (-67kg)
1974 Emilio Correa CUB
1978 Valery Rachkov URS
1982 Mark Breland USA
1983 Mark Breland USA
1986 Kenneth Gould USA
1989 Francisc Vastag ROM
1991 Juan Hernandez CUB
1993 Juan Hernandez CUB
1995 Juan Hernandez CUB
1997 Oleg Saitov RUS
1999 Juan Hernandez CUB
2001 Loren Armientieros Aragon CUB

LIGHT-WELTERWEIGHT (-63.5kg)
1974 Ayub Kalule UGA
1978 Valery Lvov URS
1982 Carlos Garcia CUB
1983 Carlos Garcia CUB
1986 Vasily Shishov URS
1989 Igor Ruzhnikov URS
1991 Konstantin Tszyu URS
1993 Hector Vinent CUB
1995 Hector Vinent CUB
1997 Dorel Simion ROM
1999 Mahammat Abdullaev UZB
2001 Martinez Biongenes Luna CUB

LIGHTWEIGHT (-60kg)
1974 Vasily Solomin URS
1978 Andeh Davidson NGR
1982 Angel Herrera CUB
1983 Pernell Whitaker USA
1986 Adolfo Horta CUB
1989 Julio Gonzalez CUB
1991 Marco Rudolph GER
1993 Damian Austin CUB
1995 Leonard Doroftei ROM
1997 Aleksandr Maletin RUS
1999 Mario Kindelan CUB
2001 Mario Kindelan CUB

FEATHERWEIGHT (-57kg)
1974 Howard Davis USA
1978 Angel Herrera CUB
1982 Adolfo Horta CUB
1983 Adolfo Horta CUB

1986 Kelcie Banks USA
1989 Airat Khamatov URS
1991 Kirkor Kirkorov BUL
1993 Serafim Todorov BUL
1995 Serafim Todorov BUL
1997 Istvan Kovacs HUN
1999 Ricardo Juarez USA
2001 Palyani Ramazan TUR

BANTAMWEIGHT (-54kg)
1974 Wilfredo Gomez PUR
1978 Adolfo Horta CUB
1982 Floyd Favors USA
1983 Floyd Favors USA
1986 Moon Sung-Kil KOR
1989 Enrique Carrion CUB
1991 Serafim Todorov BUL
1993 Alexander Hristov BUL
1995 Raimkul Malachbekov RUS
1997 Raimkul Malachbekov RUS
1999 Raicu Crinu ROM
2001 Guiller Ortiz Rigondeaux CUB

FLYWEIGHT (-51kg)
1974 Douglas Rodriguez CUB
1978 Henryk Srednicki POL
1982 Yury Aleksandrov URS
1983 Steve McCrory USA
1986 Pedro Reyes CUB
1989 Yury Arbachakov URS
1991 Istvan Kovacs HUN
1993 Waldemar Font CUB
1995 Zoltan Lunke GER
1997 Manuel Mantilla CUB
1999 Bulat Jumadilov KZK
2001 Jerome Thomas FRA

LIGHT-FLYWEIGHT (-48kg)
1974 Jorge Hernandez CUB
1978 Stephen Muchoki KEN
1982 Ismail Mustafov BUL
1983 Rafael Saiz CUB
1986 Juan Torres CUB
1989 Eric Griffin USA
1991 Eric Griffin USA
1993 Nshan Muntjian ARM
1995 Daniel Petrov BUL
1997 Maikro Romero CUB
1999 Brian Viloria USA
2001 Yan Varela Barteleny CUB

CANOEING

WORLD CHAMPIONS
SPRINT
Annually except Olympic years

Men
K1 200
1994 Sergey Kalesnik BLR
1995 Piotr Markiewicz POL
1997 Vince Fehervari HUN
1998 Michael Kolganov ISR
1999 Michael Kolganov ISR
2001 Ronald Rauhe GER
2002 Ronald Rauhe GER

K1 500
1989 Martin Hunter AUS
1990 Sergey Kalesnik URS
1991 Renn Crichlow CAN
1993 Mikko Kolehmainen FIN
1994 Zsombor Borhi HUN
1995 Piotr Markiewicz POL
1997 Botond Storcz HUN
1998 Akos Vereckei HUN
1999 Akos Vereckei HUN
2001 Akos Vereckei HUN
2002 Nathan Baggaley AUS

K1 1000
1989 Zsolt Gyulay HUN
1990 Knut Holmann NOR
1991 Knut Holmann NOR
1993 Knut Holmann NOR
1994 Clint Robinson AUS
1995 Knut Holmann NOR
1997 Botond Storcz HUN
1998 Lutz Liwowski GER
1999 Lutz Liwowski GER
2001 B Amir-Tahmasseb FRA
2002 Erik Veras-Larsen NOR

K2 200
1994 Friemuth/Wysocki GER
1995 Bonomi/Scarpa ITA
1997 Fehervari/Hegedus HUN
1998 Fehervari/Hegedus HUN
1999 Fehervari/Hegedus HUN
2001 Duonela/Balciunas LTU
2002 Duonela/Balciunas LTU

K2 500
1989 Bluhm/Gutsche GDR
1990 Kalesnik/Tishchenko URS
1991 Roman/Sánchez ESP
1993 Bluhm/Gutsche GER
1994 Bluhm/Gutsche GER
1995 Bonomi/Scarpa ITA
1997 Trim/Collins AUS
1998 Riszdorfer/Baca SVK
1999 Twardowski/Wysocki POL
2001 Rauhe/Wieskoetter GER
2002 Rauhe/Wieskoetter GER

K2 1000
1989 Bluhm/Gutsche GDR
1990 Bluhm/Gutsche GDR
1991 Bluhm/Gutsche GDR
1993 Bluhm/Gutsche GER
1994 Staal/Nielsen DEN
1995 Rossi/Scarpa ITA
1997 Rossi/Negri ITA
1998 Rossi/Negri ITA
1999 Riszdorfer/Baca SVK
2001 Larsen/Fjeldheim NOR
2002 Oskarsson/Nilsson SWE

K4 200
1994 Russia
1995 Hungary
1997 Russia
1998 Hungary
1999 Hungary
2001 Hungary
2002 Slovakia

K4 500
1989 Soviet Union
1990 Soviet Union
1991 Germany
1993 Russia
1994 Russia
1995 Russia
1997 Hungary
1998 Germany
1999 Russia
2001 Russia
2002 Slovakia

K4 1000
1989 Hungary
1990 Hungary
1991 Hungary
1993 Germany
1994 Russia
1995 Germany
1997 Germany
1998 Germany
1999 Hungary
2001 Germany
2002 Slovakia

C1 200
1994 Nikolay Buhalov BUL
1995 Nikolay Buhalov BUL
1997 Bela Belicza HUN
1998 Martin Doktor CZE
1999 Maxim Opalev RUS
2001 Dmitro Sablin UKR
2002 Maxim Opalev RUS

C1 500
1989 Mikhail Slivinsky URS
1990 Mikhail Slivinsky URS
1991 Mikhail Slivinsky URS
1993 Nikolay Buhalov BUL

1994 Nikolay Buhalov BUL
1995 Nikolay Buhalov BUL
1997 Martin Doktor CZE
1998 Maxim Opalev RUS
1999 Maxim Opalev RUS
2001 Maxim Opalev RUS
2002 Maxim Opalev RUS

C1 1000
1989 Ivan Klementyev URS
1990 Ivan Klementyev URS
1991 Ivan Klementyev EUN
1993 Ivan Klementyev RUS
1994 Ivan Klementyev RUS
1995 Imre Pulai HUN
1997 Andreas Dittmer GER
1998 Steve Giles CAN
1999 Maxim Opalev RUS
2001 Andreas Dittmer GER
2002 Andreas Dittmer GER

C2 200
1994 Masojkov/Dovgalionok BLR
1995 Kolonics/Horváth HUN
1997 Zereske/Gille GER
1998 Zereske/Gille GER
1999 Fomitchev/Artemida RUS
2001 Jedraszko/Baraszkiewicz POL
2002 Rojas/Balceiro CUB

C2 500
1989 Zhuravsky/Reneysky URS
1990 Zhuravsky/Reneysky URS
1991 Paliza/Szabó HUN
1993 Kolonics/Horváth HUN
1994 Andreiev/Obreja ROM
1995 Kolonics/Horváth HUN
1997 Kolonics/Horváth HUN
1998 Kolonics/Horváth HUN
1999 Jedraszko/Baraszkiewicz POL
2001 Rojas/Pereira CUB
2002 Rojas/Balceiro CUB

C2 1000
1989 Fredriksen/Nielsson DEN
1990 Papke/Spelly GDR
1991 Papke/Spelly GER
1993 Nielsson/Fredericksen DEN
1994 Dittmer/Kirchbach GER
1995 Kolonics/Horváth HUN
1997 Kirchbach/Roder GER
1998 Kovalev/Kostoglod RUS
1999 Kovalev/Kostoglod RUS
2001 Kobierski/Sliwinski POL
2002 Kobierski/Sliwinski POL

CANOEING

C4 200
1994 Russia
1995 Hungary
1997 Belarus
1998 Czech Republic
1999 Hungary
2001 Hungary
2002 Russia

C4 500
1989 Soviet Union
1990 Soviet Union
1991 Soviet Union
1993 Hungary
1994 Hungary
1995 Hungary
1997 Hungary
1998 Hungary
1999 Russia
2001 Romania
2002 Romania

C4 1000
1989 Soviet Union
1990 Soviet Union
1991 Soviet Union
1993 Hungary
1994 Hungary
1995 Romania
1997 Romania
1998 Hungary
1999 Russia
2001 Hungary
2002 Poland

Women
K1 200
1994 Rita Koban HUN
1995 Rita Koban HUN
1997 Caroline Brunet CAN
1998 Caroline Brunet CAN
1999 Caroline Brunet CAN
2001 Karen Furneaux CAN
2002 Teresa Portela ESP

K1 500
1989 Katrin Borchert GDR
1990 Josefa Idem ITA
1991 Katrin Borchert GER
1993 Birgit Schmidt GER
1994 Birgit Schmidt GER
1995 Rita Koban HUN
1997 Caroline Brunet CAN
1998 Caroline Brunet CAN
1999 Caroline Brunet CAN
2001 Josefa Idem ITA
2002 Katalin Kovacs HUN

K1 1000
1997 Caroline Brunet CAN
1998 Josefa Idem ITA
1999 Caroline Brunet CAN

2001 Josefa Idem ITA
2002 Katalin Kovacs HUN

K2 200
1994 Koban/Laky HUN
1995 Kennedy/Gibeau CAN
1997 Fischer/Schuck GER
1998 Gibeau/Furneaux CAN
1999 Aramburu/Manchon ESP
2001 Molanes/Manchon ESP
2002 Molanes/Manchon ESP

K2 500
1989 Nothnagel/Singer GDR
1990 Portwich/Von Seck GDR
1991 Portwich/Von Seck GER
1993 Olsson/Andersson SWE
1994 Urbanczyk/Hajcel POL
1995 Portwich/Schuck GER
1997 Fischer/Schuck GER
1998 Borchert/Wood AUS
1999 Sokolowska/Pastuszka
     POL
2001 Szabo/Bota HUN
2002 Szabo/Bota HUN

K2 1000
1997 Fischer/Bednar GER
1998 Wood/Bochert AUS
1999 Wood/Bochert AUS
2001 Mucke/Opgen-Rhein GER
2002 Szabo/Bota HUN

K4 200
1994 Hungary
1995 Canada
1997 Germany
1998 Hungary
1999 Hungary
2001 Hungary
2002 Hungary

K4 500
1989 East Germany
1990 East Germany
1991 Germany
1993 Germany
1995 Germany
1997 Germany
1998 Germany
1999 Hungary
2001 Hungary
2002 Hungary

K4 1000
2001 Hungary
2002 Poland

CANOEING

SLALOM

(Held since 1949, alternate years, full list for men's K1, others from varying dates)

Men

K1

1949 **Othmar Eiterer** AUT
1951 **Hans Frühwirth** AUT
1953 **Walter Kirschnaum** FRG
1955 **Sigi Holzhauer** FRG
1957 **Manfred Vogt** GDR
1959 **Paul Farrant** GBR
1961 **Eberhard Gläser** GDR
1963 **Jürgen Bremer** GDR
1965 **Kurt Presslmayr** AUT
1967 **Jürgen Bremer** GDR
1969 **Claude Peschier** FRA
1971 **Siegbert Horn** GDB
1973 **Norbert Sattler** AUT
1975 **Siegbert Horn** GDR
1977 **Albert Venn** GBR
1979 **Peter Fauster** AUT
1981 **Richard Fox** GBR
1983 **Richard Fox** GBR
1985 **Richard Fox** GBR
1987 **Tony Prijon** GER
1989 **Richard Fox** GBR
1991 **Shaun Pearce** GBR
1993 **Richard Fox** GBR
1995 **Oliver Fix** GER
1997 **Thomas Becker** GER
1999 **David Ford** CAN
2002 **Fabien Lefevre** FRA

K1 Team

1979 **Great Britain**
1981 **Great Britain**
1983 **Great Britain**
1985 **Great Britain**
1987 **Great Britain**
1989 **Yugoslavia**
1991 **France**
1993 **Great Britain**
1995 **Germany**
1997 **Great Britain**
1999 **Germany**
2002 **Germany**

C1

1979 **Jon Lugbill** USA
1981 **Jon Lugbill** USA
1983 **Jon Lugbill** USA
1985 **David Hearn** USA
1987 **Jon Lugbill** USA
1989 **Jon Lugbill** USA
1991 **Martin Lang** GER
1993 **Martin Lang** GER
1995 **David Hearn** USA
1997 **Michal Martikan** SVK
1999 **Emmanuel Brugvin** FRA
2002 **Michal Martikan** SVK

C1 Team

1979 **USA**
1981 **USA**
1983 **USA**
1985 **USA**
1987 **USA**
1989 **USA**
1991 **USA**
1993 **Slovenia**
1995 **Germany**
1997 **Slovakia**
1999 **Poland**
2002 **Czech Republic**

C2

1979 **Welsnik/Czupryna** GER
1981 **Garvis/Garvis** USA
1983 **Haller/Haller** USA
1985 **Küppers/Impelmann** FRG
1987 **Calori/Calori** FRA
1989 **Hemmer/Loose** FRG
1991 **Adisson/Forgues** FRA
1993 **Simek/Rohan** CZE
1995 **Kolomanski/Staniszewski**
POL
1997 **Adisson/Forgues** FRA
1999 **Jiras/Mader** CZE
2002 **Hochschorner/Hochschorner**
SVK

C2 Team

1989 **France**
1991 **France**
1993 **Czech Republic**
1995 **Czech Republic**
1997 **France**
1999 **Czech Republic**
2002 **France**

Women

K1

1979 **Cathy Hearn** USA
1981 **Ulrike Deppe** FRG
1983 **Liz Sharman** GBR
1985 **Margit Messelhauser** FRG
1987 **Liz Sharman** GBR
1989 **Myriam Jerusalmi** FRA
1991 **Elisabeth Micheler** GER
1993 **Myriam Jerusalmi** FRA
1995 **Lynn Simpson** GBR
1997 **Brigitte Guibal** FRA
1999 **Stepanka Hilgertova** CZE
2002 **Rebecca Giddens** USA

K1 Team

1989 **France**
1991 **France**
1993 **France**
1995 **Germany**
1997 **France**
1999 **Germany**
2002 **France**

CRICKET

ENGLAND v AUSTRALIA

	W	L	D
1876-77	1	1	0
1878-79	0	1	0
1880	1	0	0
1881-82	0	2	2
1882	0	1	0
1882-83	2	2	0
1884	1	0	2
1884-85	3	2	0
1886	3	0	0
1886-87	2	0	0
1887-88	1	0	0
1888	2	1	0
1890	2	0	0
1891-92	1	2	0
1893	1	0	2
1894-95	3	2	0
1896	2	1	0
1897-98	1	4	0
1899	0	1	4
1901-02	1	4	0
1902	1	2	2
1903-04	3	2	0
1905	2	0	3
1907-08	1	4	0
1909	1	2	2
1911-12	4	1	0
1912	1	0	2
1920-21	0	5	0
1921	0	3	2
1924-25	1	4	0
1926	1	0	4
1928-29	4	1	0
1930	1	2	2
1932-33	4	1	0
1934	1	2	2
1936-37	2	3	0
1938	1	1	2
1946-47	0	3	2
1948	0	4	1
1950-51	1	4	0
1953	1	0	4
1954-55	3	1	1
1956	2	1	2
1958-59	0	4	1
1961	1	2	2
1962-63	1	1	3
1964	0	1	4
1965-66	1	1	3
1968	1	1	3
1970-71	2	0	4
1972	2	2	1
1974-75	1	4	1
1975	0	1	3
1976-77	0	1	0
1977	3	0	2
1978-79	5	1	0
1979-80	0	3	0
1980	0	0	1
1981	3	1	2
1982-83	1	2	2
1985	3	1	2
1986-87	2	1	2
1987-88	0	0	1
1989	0	4	2
1990-91	0	3	2
1993	1	4	1
1994-95	1	3	1
1997	2	3	1
1998-99	1	3	1
2001	1	4	0
2002-03	1	4	0
Total	**95**	**125**	**86**

ENGLAND v S AFRICA

	W	L	D
1888-89	2	0	0
1891-92	1	0	0
1895-96	3	0	0
1898-99	2	0	0
1905-06	1	4	0
1907	1	0	2
1909-10	2	3	0
1912	3	0	0
1913-14	4	0	1
1922-23	2	1	2
1924	3	0	2
1927-28	2	2	1
1929	2	0	3
1930-31	0	1	4
1935	0	1	4
1938-39	1	0	4
1947	3	0	2
1948-49	2	0	3
1951	3	1	1
1955	3	2	0
1956-57	2	2	1
1960	3	0	2
1964-65	1	0	4
1965	0	1	2
1994	1	1	1
1995-96	0	1	4
1998	2	1	2
1999-2000	1	2	2
Total	**50**	**23**	**47**

ENGLAND v W INDIES

	W	L	D
1928	3	0	0
1929-30	1	1	2
1933	2	0	1
1934-35	1	2	1
1939	1	0	2
1947-48	0	2	2
1950	1	3	0
1953-54	2	2	1
1957	3	0	2
1959-60	1	0	4

1963	1	3	1
1966	1	3	1
1967-68	1	0	4
1969	2	0	1
1973	0	2	1
1973-74	1	1	3
1976	0	3	2
1980	0	1	4
1980-81	0	2	2
1984	0	5	0
1985-86	0	5	0
1988	0	4	1
1989-90	1	2	1
1991	2	2	1
1993-94	1	3	1
1997-98*	1	3	2
2000	3	1	1
Total	**31**	**52**	**43**

* Draws include one Test abandoned

ENGLAND v NEW ZEALAND

	W	L	D
1929-30	1	0	3
1931	1	0	2
1932-33	0	0	2
1937	1	0	2
1946-47	0	0	1
1949	0	0	4
1950-51	1	0	1
1954-55	2	0	0
1958	4	0	1
1958-59	1	0	1
1962-63	3	0	0
1965	3	0	0
1965-66	0	0	3
1969	2	0	1
1970-71	1	0	1
1973	2	0	1
1974-75	1	0	1
1977-78	1	1	1
1978	3	0	0
1983	3	1	0
1983-84	0	1	2
1986	0	1	2
1987-88	0	0	3
1990	1	0	2
1994	1	0	2
1996-97	2	0	1
1999	1	2	1
Total	**37**	**6**	**39**

ENGLAND v SRI LANKA

	W	L	D
1981-82	1	0	0
1984	0	0	1
1988	1	0	0
1991	1	0	0
1992-93	0	1	0
1998	0	1	0
2000-01	2	1	0

2002	1	0	1
Total	**6**	**3**	**2**

ENGLAND v INDIA

	W	L	D
1932	1	0	0
1933-34	2	0	1
1936	2	0	1
1946	1	0	2
1951-52	1	1	3
1952	3	0	1
1959	5	0	0
1961-62	0	2	3
1963-64	0	0	5
1967	3	0	0
1971	0	1	2
1972-73	1	2	2
1974	3	0	0
1976-77	3	1	1
1979	1	0	3
1979-80	1	0	0
1981-82	0	1	5
1982	1	0	2
1984-85	2	1	2
1986	0	2	1
1990	1	0	2
1992-93	0	3	0
1996	1	0	2
2001	0	1	2
2002	1	1	2
Total	**33**	**16**	**42**

ENGLAND v PAKISTAN

	W	L	D
1954	1	1	2
1961-62	1	0	2
1962	4	0	1
1967	2	0	1
1968-69	0	0	3
1971	1	0	2
1972-73	0	0	3
1974	0	0	3
1977-78	0	0	3
1978	2	0	1
1982	2	1	0
1983-84	0	1	2
1987	0	1	4
1987-88	0	1	2
1992	1	2	2
1996	0	2	1
2000	1	0	2
2001	1	1	0
Total	**16**	**10**	**34**

ENGLAND v ZIMBABWE

	W	L	D
1996-97	0	0	2
2000	1	0	1
Total	**1**	**0**	**3**

CRICKET

WORLD CUP

1975	West Indies
1979	West Indies
1983	India
1987	Australia
1992	Pakistan
1995	Sri Lanka
1999	Australia

COUNTY CHAMPIONSHIP

1864	Surrey
1865	Nottinghamshire
1866	Middlesex
1867	Yorkshire
1868	Nottinghamshire
1869	Nottinghamshire & Yorkshire (shared)
1870	Yorkshire
1871	Nottinghamshire
1872	Nottinghamshire
1873	Gloucestershire & Nottinghamshire (shared)
1874	Gloucestershire
1875	Nottinghamshire
1876	Gloucestershire
1877	Gloucestershire
1878	Undecided
1879	Lancashire & Nottinghamshire (shared)
1880	Nottinghamshire
1881	Lancashire
1882	Lancashire & Nottinghamshire (shared)
1883	Nottinghamshire
1884	Nottinghamshire
1885	Nottinghamshire
1886	Nottinghamshire
1887	Surrey
1888	Surrey
1889	Lancashire, Nottinghamshire & Surrey (shared)
1890	Surrey
1891	Surrey
1892	Surrey
1893	Yorkshire
1894	Surrey
1895	Surrey
1896	Yorkshire
1897	Lancashire
1898	Yorkshire
1899	Surrey
1900	Yorkshire

1901	Yorkshire
1902	Yorkshire
1903	Middlesex
1904	Lancashire
1905	Yorkshire
1906	Kent
1907	Nottinghamshire
1908	Yorkshire
1909	Kent
1910	Kent
1911	Warwickshire
1912	Yorkshire
1913	Kent
1914	Surrey
1915-1918	Not held
1919	Yorkshire
1920	Middlesex
1921	Middlesex
1922	Yorkshire
1923	Yorkshire
1924	Yorkshire
1925	Yorkshire
1926	Lancashire
1927	Lancashire
1928	Lancashire
1929	Nottinghamshire
1930	Lancashire
1931	Yorkshire
1932	Yorkshire
1933	Yorkshire
1934	Lancashire
1935	Yorkshire
1936	Derbyshire
1937	Yorkshire
1938	Yorkshire
1939	Yorkshire
1940-1945	Not held
1946	Yorkshire
1947	Middlesex
1948	Glamorgan
1949	Middlesex & Yorkshire (shared)
1950	Lancashire & Surrey (shared)
1951	Warwickshire
1952	Surrey
1953	Surrey
1954	Surrey
1955	Surrey
1956	Surrey
1957	Surrey
1958	Surrey
1959	Yorkshire
1960	Yorkshire
1961	Hampshire
1962	Yorkshire
1963	Yorkshire
1964	Worcestershire
1965	Worcestershire

1966	Yorkshire
1967	Yorkshire
1968	Yorkshire
1969	Glamorgan
1970	Kent
1971	Surrey
1972	Warwickshire
1973	Hampshire
1974	Worcestershire
1975	Leicestershire
1976	Middlesex
1977	Kent & Middlesex (shared)
1978	Kent
1979	Essex
1980	Middlesex
1981	Nottinghamshire
1982	Middlesex
1983	Essex
1984	Essex
1985	Middlesex
1986	Essex
1987	Nottinghamshire
1988	Worcestershire
1989	Worcestershire
1990	Middlesex
1991	Essex
1992	Essex
1993	Middlesex
1994	Warwickshire
1995	Warwickshire
1996	Leicestershire
1997	Glamorgan
1998	Leicestershire
1999	Surrey
2000	Surrey*; Northamptonshire
2001	Yorkshire; Sussex
2002	Surrey; Essex

*Since 2000, championship split into two divisions

CRICKET

C & G TROPHY
(Gillette Cup 1963-80, NatWest Trophy 1981-2000)
1963 **Sussex** beat Worcestershire by 14 runs
1964 **Sussex** beat Warwickshire by 8 wkts
1965 **Yorkshire** beat Surrey by 175 runs
1966 **Warwickshire** beat Worcestershire by 5 wkts
1967 **Kent** beat Somerset by 32 runs
1968 **Warwickshire** beat Sussex by 4 wkts
1969 **Yorkshire** beat Derbyshire by 69 runs
1970 **Lancashire** beat Sussex by 6 wkts
1971 **Lancashire** beat Kent by 24 runs
1972 **Lancashire** beat Warwickshire by 4 wkts
1973 **Gloucestershire** beat Sussex by 40 runs
1974 **Kent** beat Lancashire by 4 wkts
1975 **Lancashire** beat Middlesex by 7 wkts
1976 **Northants** beat Lancashire by 4 wkts
1977 **Middlesex** beat Glamorgan by 5 wkts
1978 **Sussex** beat Somerset by 5 wkts
1979 **Somerset** beat Northamptonshire by 45 runs
1980 **Middlesex** beat Surrey by 7 wkts
1981 **Derbyshire** beat Northants fewer wkts lost
(scores level)
1982 **Surrey** beat Warwickshire by 9 wkts
1983 **Somerset** beat Kent by 24 runs
1984 **Middlesex** beat Kent by 4 wkts
1985 **Essex** beat Nottinghamshire by 1 run
1986 **Sussex** beat Lancashire by 7 wkts
1987 **Nottinghamshire** beat Northants by 3 wkts
1988 **Middlesex** beat Worcestershire by 3 wkts
1989 **Warwickshire** beat Middlesex by 4 wkts
1990 **Lancashire** beat Northamptonshire by 7 wkts
1991 **Hampshire** beat Surrey by 4 wkts
1992 **Northants** beat Leicestershire by 8 wkts
1993 **Warwickshire** beat Sussex by 5 wkts
1994 **Worcestershire** beat Warwickshire by 8 wkts
1995 **Warwickshire** beat Northants by 4 wkts
1996 **Lancashire** beat Essex by 129 runs
1997 **Essex** beat Warwickshire by 9 wkts
1998 **Essex** beat Leicester by 192 runs
1999 **Gloucestershire** beat Somerset by 50 runs
2000 **Gloucestershire** beat Warwickshire by 22
runs on the Duckworth/Lewis method
2001 **Somerset** beat Leicestershire by 41 runs
2002 **Yorkshire** bt Somerset by 6 wkts

SUPER CUP
1972 **Leicestershire** beat Yorkshire by 5 wkts
1973 **Kent** beat Worcestershire by 39 runs
1974 **Surrey** beat Leicestershire by 27 runs
1975 **Leicestershire** beat Middlesex by 5 wkts
1976 **Kent** beat Worcestershire by 43 runs
1977 **Gloucestershire** beat Kent by 64 runs
1978 **Kent** beat Derbyshire by 6 wkts
1979 **Essex** beat Surrey by 35 runs
1980 **Northants** beat Essex by 6 runs
1981 **Somerset** beat Surrey by 7 wkts
1982 **Somerset** beat Nottinghamshire by 9 wkts
1983 **Middlesex** beat Essex by 4 runs
1984 **Lancashire** beat Warwickshire by 6 wkts
1985 **Leicestershire** beat Essex by 5 wkts

1986 **Middlesex** beat Kent by 2 runs
1987 **Yorkshire** beat Northants fewer wkts lost
(scores level)
1988 **Hampshire** beat Derbyshire by 7 wkts
1989 **Nottinghamshire** beat Essex by 3 wkts
1990 **Lancashire** beat Worcestershire by 69 runs
1991 **Worcestershire** beat Lancashire by 65 runs
1992 **Hampshire** beat Kent by 41 runs
1993 **Derbyshire** beat Lancashire by 6 runs
1994 **Warwickshire** beat Worcestershire by 6 wkts
1995 **Lancashire** beat Kent by 35 runs
1996 **Lancashire** beat Northants by 31 runs
1997 **Surrey** beat Kent by 8 wkts
1998 **Lancashire** beat Derby by 9 wkts
1999 **Gloucestershire** beat Yorkshire by 124 runs
2000 **Gloucestershire** beat Glamorgan by 7 wkts
2001 **Surrey** beat Gloucestershire by 47 runs
2002 **Warwickshire** bt Essex bt 5 wkts

AXA LIFE LEAGUE
(John Player League 1969-86,
Refuge Assurance League 1987-91,
no sponsor 1992)
1969 **Lancashire**
1970 **Lancashire**
1971 **Worcestershire**
1972 **Kent**
1973 **Kent**
1974 **Leicestershire**
1975 **Hampshire**
1976 **Kent**
1977 **Leicestershire**
1978 **Hampshire**
1979 **Somerset**
1980 **Warwickshire**
1981 **Essex**
1982 **Sussex**
1983 **Yorkshire**
1984 **Essex**
1985 **Essex**
1986 **Hampshire**
1987 **Worcestershire**
1988 **Worcestershire**
1989 **Lancashire**
1990 **Derbyshire**
1991 **Nottinghamshire**
1992 **Middlesex**
1993 **Glamorgan**
1994 **Warwickshire**
1995 **Kent**
1996 **Surrey**
1997 **Warwickshire**
1998 **Lancashire**

CGU NATIONAL LEAGUE
	Division One	Division Two
1999	**Lancashire Lightning**	Sussex
2000	**Gloucestershire Gladiators**	Surrey
2001	**Kent Spitfires**	Glamorgan
2002	**Glamorgan Dragons**	Gloucestershire

CURLING

WORLD CHAMPIONSHIPS

	Men	Venue (s)	Women	Venue (s)
1959	Canada	Falkirk & Edinburgh	-	-
1960	Canada	Falkirk & Edinburgh	-	-
1961	Canada	Ayr, Kirkaldy, Perth & Edinburgh	-	-
1962	Canada	Falkirk & Edinburgh	-	-
1963	Canada	Perth, Scotland	-	-
1964	Canada	Calgary, Canada	-	-
1965	USA	Perth	-	-
1966	Canada	Vancouver, Canada	-	-
1967	Scotland	Perth	-	-
1968	Canada	Pointe Claire, Canada	-	-
1969	Canada	Perth	-	-
1970	Canada	Uttica, USA	-	-
1971	Canada	Megeve, France	-	-
1972	Canada	Regina, Canada	-	-
1973	Sweden	Regina	-	-
1974	USA	Berne, Switzerland	-	-
1975	Switzerland	Perth	-	-
1976	USA	Duluth, USA	-	-
1977	Sweden	Karlstad, Sweden	-	-
1978	USA	Winnipeg, Canada	-	-
1979	Norway	Berne	Switzerland	Perth
1980	Canada	Moncton, Canada	Canada	Perth
1981	Switzerland	London, Canada	Sweden	Perth
1982	Canada	Garmisch, Germany	Denmark	Geneva, Switzerland
1983	Canada	Regina	Switzerland	Moose Jaw, Canada
1984	Norway	Duluth	Canada	Perth
1985	Canada	Glasgow, Scotland	Canada	Jonkoping, Sweden
1986	Canada	Toronto, Canada	Canada	Kelowna, Canada
1987	Canada	Vancouver	Canada	Chicago, USA
1988	Norway	Lausanne, Switzerland	Germany	Glasgow
1989	Canada	Milwaukee, USA	Canada	Milwaukee*
1990	Canada	Vasteras, Sweden	Norway	Vasteras, Sweden
1991	Scotland	Winnipeg	Norway	Winnipeg
1992	Switzerland	Garmisch	Sweden	Garmisch
1993	Canada	Geneva	Canada	Geneva
1994	Canada	Obertsdorf	Canada	Obertsdorf
1995	Canada	Brandon	Sweden	Brandon
1996	Canada	Hamilton	Canada	Hamilton
1997	Sweden	Berne	Canada	Berne
1998	Canada	Kamloops, Canada	Sweden	Kamloops
1999	Scotland	St John, Canada	Sweden	St John
2000	Canada	Braehead, Glasgow	Canada	Braehead
2001	Sweden	Lausanne, Switzerland	Canada	Lausanne
2002	Canada	Brunswick, North Dakota, USA	Scotland	Brunswick

* Championships played together for the first time

CYCLING

World Champions

Men

Track - men's amateur races ceased in 1991, professional races in 1992, to be replaced by Open events, which are listed first. Pro records follow.

SPRINT
1993	Gary Neiwand AUS
1994	Martin Nothstein USA
1995	Darryn Hill AUS
1996	Florian Rousseau FRA
1997	Florian Rousseau FRA
1998	Florian Rousseau FRA
1999	Laurent Gane FRA
2000	Jan Van Eijden GER
2001	Arnaud Tournant FRA
2002	Sean Eadie AUS

INDIVIDUAL PURSUIT
1993	Graeme Obree GBR
1994	Chris Boardman GBR
1995	Graeme Obree GBR
1996	Chris Boardman GBR
1997	Philippe Ermenault FRA
1998	Philippe Ermenault FRA
1999	Robert Bartko GER
2000	Jens Lehmann GER
2001	Alexandre Symonenko UKR
2002	Brad McGee AUS

TEAM PURSUIT
1993	Australia
1994	Germany
1995	Australia
1996	Italy
1997	Italy
1998	Ukraine
1999	Germany
2000	Germany
2001	Ukraine
2002	Australia

POINTS RACE
1993	Etienne de Wilde BEL
1994	Bruno Risi SUI
1995	Silvio Martinello ITA
1996	Juan Llaneras ESP
1997	Silvio Martinello ITA
1998	Juan Llaneras ESP
1999	Bruno Risi SUI
2000	Juan Llaneras Rosello ESP
2001	Bruno Risi SUI
2002	Chris Newton GBR

KEIRIN
1993	Gary Neiwand AUS
1994	Martin Nothstein USA
1995	Frédéric Magne FRA
1996	Martin Nothstein USA
1997	Frédéric Magne FRA
1998	Jens Fiedler GER
1999	Jens Fiedler GER
2000	Frédéric Magne FRA
2001	Ryan Bayley AUS
2002	Jobie Dajka AUS

KILOMETRE TIME TRIAL
1993	Florain Rousseau FRA
1994	Florian Rousseau FRA
1995	Shane Kelly AUS
1996	Shane Kelly AUS
1997	Shane Kelly AUS
1998	Arnaud Tournant FRA
1999	Arnaud Tournant FRA
2000	Arnaud Tournant FRA
2001	Arnaud Tournant FRA
2002	Chris Hoy GBR

MADISON
1995	Martinello/Villa ITA
1996	Martinello/Villa ITA
1997	Alzamora/Llaneras ESP
1998	De Wilde/Gilmour BEL
1999	Galvez/Llaneras ESP
2000	Steinweg/Weispfennig GER
2001	Neuville/Sassone FRA
2002	Neuville/Perque FRA

TEAM SPRINT
1995	Germany
1996	Australia
1997	France
1998	France
1999	France
2000	France
2001	France
2002	Great Britain

INDIVIDUAL TIME TRIAL
1994	Chris Boardman GBR
1995	Miguel Induráin ESP
1996	Alex Zülle SUI
1997	Laurent Jalabert FRA
1998	Abraham Olano ESP
1999	Jan Ullrich GER
2000	Sergey Gontchar UKR
2001	Jan Ullrich GER
2002	Santiago Botero COL

ROAD RACE
1994	Luc Leblanc FRA
1995	Abraham Olano ESP
1996	Johan Museeuw BEL
1997	Laurent Brochard FRA
1998	Oscar Camenzind SUI
1999	Oscar Freire ESP
2000	Romans Vainsteins LAT
2001	Oscar Freire ESP
2002	Mario Cipollini ITA

MOTOR PACED
1993	Jens Veggerby DEN
1994	Carsten Podlesch GER

TANDEM
1993	Paris/Chiappa ITA
1994	Colas/Magné FRA

PROFESSIONAL SPRINT
1970	Gordon Johnson AUS
1971	Leijin Loevesijn NED
1972	Robert van Lancker BEL
1973	Robert van Lancker BEL
1974	Peder Pedersen DEN
1975	John Nicnholon AUS
1976	John Nicnholon AUS
1977	Koichi Nakano JPN
1978	Koichi Nakano JPN
1979	Koichi Nakano JPN
1980	Koichi Nakano JPN
1981	Koichi Nakano JPN
1982	Koichi Nakano JPN
1983	Koichi Nakano JPN
1984	Koichi Nakano JPN
1985	Koichi Nakano JPN
1986	Koichi Nakano JPN
1987	Noboyuki Tawara JPN
1988	Stephen Pate AUS
1989	Claudio Golinelli ITA
1990	Michael Hubner GDR
1991	Carey Hall AUS*
1992	Michael Hubner GER

failed a drugs test title left vacant

PROFESSIONAL 5KM PURSUIT
First held in 1939
1970	Hugh Porter GBR
1971	Dirk Baert BEL
1972	Hugh Porter GBR
1973	Hugh Porter GBR
1974	Roy Schuiten NED
1975	Roy Schuiten NED
1976	Francesco Moser ITA
1977	Gregor Braun FRG
1978	Gregor Braun FRG
1979	Bert Osterbosch NED
1980	Tony Doyle GBR
1981	Alain Bondue FRA
1982	Alain Bondue FRA
1983	Steele Bishop AUS
1984	Hans-Henrik Oersted DEN
1985	Hans-Henrik Oersted DEN
1986	Tony Doyle GBR
1987	Hans-Henrik Oersted DEN
1988	Lech Piasecki POL
1989	Colin Sturgess GBR
1990	Vyacheslav Yekimov URS
1991	Francis Moreau FRA
1992	Mike McCarthy USA

CYCLING

PROFESSIONAL POINTS PACE
1980 **Stan Tourne** BEL
1981 **Urs Freuler** SUI
1982 **Urs Freuler** SUI
1983 **Urs Freuler** SUI
1984 **Urs Freuler** SUI
1985 **Urs Freuler** SUI
1986 **Urs Freuler** SUI
1987 **Urs Freuler** SUI
1988 **Daniel Wyder** SUI
1989 **Urs Freuler** SUI
1990 **Laurent Blondl** FRA
1991 **Vyacheslav Yekimov** URS
1992 **Bruno Risi** SUI

PROFESSIONAL KEIRIN
1980 **Danny Clark** AUS
1981 **Danny Clark** AUS
1982 **Gordon Singleton** Can
1983 **Urs Freuler** SUI
1984 **Robert Dill-Bundi** SUI
1985 **Urs Freuler** SUI
1986 **Michel Vaarten** BEL
1987 **Harurni Honda** Jap
1988 Claudio Golinelli ITA*
1989 **Claudio Golinelli** ITA
1990 **Michael Hubner** GDR
1991 **Michael Hubner** GER
1992 **Michael Hubner** GER
*failed drugs test title left vacant

PRO MOTOR PACED
First held 1895
1970 **Ehrenfried Rudolph** FRG
1971 **Theo Verschueren** BEL
1972 **Theo Verschueren** BEL
1973 **Cees Stam** NED
1974 **Cees Stam** NED
1975 **Dieter Kemper** FRG
1976 **Wilfried Peffgen** FRG
1977 **Cees Stam** NED
1978 **Wilfried Peffgen** FRG
1979 **Martin Venix** NED
1980 **Wilfried Peffgen** FRG
1981 **Rene Kos** NED
1982 **Martin Venix** NED
1983 **Bruno Vicini** ITA
1984 **Horst Schotz** FRG
1985 **Bruno Vicini** ITA
1986 **Bruno Vicini** ITA
1987 **Max Hurtzler** SUI
1988 **Danny Clark** AUS
1989 **Giovanni Renosto** ITA
1990 **Walter Brugna** ITA
1991 **Danny Clark** AUS
1992 **Peter Steiger** SUI

PROFESSIONAL ROAD RACE
First held 1927
1970 **Jean-Pierre Monsere** BEL
1971 **Eddy Merckx** BEL
1972 **Marino Basso** ITA
1973 **Felice Gimondi** ITA
1974 **Eddy Merckx** BEL
1975 **Hennie Kuiper** NED
1976 **Freddy Maertens** BEL
1977 **Francesco Moser** ITA
1978 **Gerrie Knetemann** NED
1979 **Jan Raas** NED
1980 **Bernard Hinault** FRA
1981 **Freddy Maertens** BEL
1982 **Giuseppe Saronni** ITA
1983 **Greg LeMond** USA
1984 **Claude Criquielion** BEL
1985 **Joop Zoetemelk** NED
1986 **Moreno Argentin** ITA
1987 **Stephen Roche** IRE
1988 **Maurizio Fondriest** ITA
1989 **Greg LeMond** USA
1990 **Rudy Dhaenens** BEL
1991 **Gianni Bugno** ITA
1992 **Gianni Bugno** ITA
1993 **Lance Armstrong** USA
1994 **Luc Leblanc** FRA
1995 **Abraham Olano** ESP
1996 **Johan Museeuw** BEL

Women

SPRINT
First held 1958
1969 **Galina Tsareva** URS
1970 **Galina Tsareva** URS
1971 **Galina Tsareva** URS
1972 **Galina Yermolayeva** URS
1973 **Sheila Young** USA
1974 **Tamara Piltsikova** URS
1975 **Sue Novarra** USA
1976 **Sheila Young** USA
1977 **Galina Tsareva** URS
1978 **Galina Tsareva** URS
1979 **Galina Tsareva** URS
1980 **Sue Reber-Novarra** USA
1981 **Sheila Ochowitz-Young** USA
1982 **Connee Paraskevin** USA
1983 **Connee Paraskevin** USA
1984 **Connee Paraskevin** USA
1985 **Isabelle Nicoloso** FRA
1986 **C Rothenburger** GDR
1987 **Erika Salumyae** URS
1989 **Erika Salumyae** URS
1990 **C Young-Paraskevin** USA
1991 **Ingrid Haringa** NED
1993 **Tanya Dubnikoff** CAN
1994 **Galina Enioukina** RUS
1995 **Félicia Ballanger** FRA
1996 **Félicia Ballanger** FRA
1997 **Félicia Ballanger** FRA
1998 **Félicia Ballanger** FRA
1999 **Félicia Ballanger** FRA
2000 **Natalia Markovnichenko** BLR
2001 **Svetlana Grankovskaia** RUS
2002 **Natalia Tsylinskaya** BLR

3KM PURSUIT
1970 **Tamara Garkushina** URS
1971 **Tamara Garkushina** URS
1972 **Tamara Garkushina** URS
1973 **Tamara Garkushina** URS
1974 **Tamara Garkushina** URS
1975 **K van Oosten-Hage** NED
1976 **K van Oosten-Hage** NED
1977 **Vera Kuznetsova** URS
1978 **K van Oosten-Hage** NED
1979 **K van Oosten-Hage** NED
1980 **Nadezhda Kibardina** URS
1981 **Nadezhda Kibardina** URS
1982 **Rebecca Twigg** USA
1983 **Connie Carpenter** USA
1984 **Rebecca Twigg** USA
1985 **Rebecca Twigg** USA
1986 **Jeannie Longo** FRA
1987 **Rebecca Twigg** USA
1988 **Jeannie Longo** FRA
1989 **Jeannie Longo** FRA
1990 **L van Moorsel** NED
1991 **Petra Rossner** GER
1993 **Rebecca Twigg** USA
1994 **Marion Clignet** FRA
1995 **Rebecca Twigg** USA
1996 **Marion Clignet** FRA
1997 **Judith Arndt** GER
1998 **Lucy T Sharman** AUS
1999 **Marion Clignet** FRA
2000 **Yvonne McGregor** GBR
2001 **L Zijlaard-Van Moorsel** NED
2002 **L Zijlaard-Van Moorsel**

500M TIME TRIAL
1995 **Félicia Ballanger** FRA
1996 **Félicia Ballanger** FRA
1997 **Félicia Ballanger** FRA
1998 **Félicia Ballanger** FRA
1999 **Félicia Ballanger** FRA
2000 **Natalia Markovnichenko** BLR
2001 **Nancy Contreras Reyes** MEX
2002 **Natalia Tsylinskaya** BLR

30KM POINTS
1987 **Sally Hodge** GBR
demonstration event
1989 **Jeannie Longo** FRA
1990 **Karen Nedliday** NZL
1991-94 **Ingrid Haringa** NED
1995 **Svet. Samokhvalova** RUS
1996 **S Samokhvalova** RUS
1997 **Natalia Karimova** RUS
1998 **Feodora Ruano** ESP
1999 **Marion Clignet** FRA
2000 **Marion Clignet** FRA
2001 **Olga Slioussareva** RUS
2002 **Olga Slioussareva** RUS

CYCLING

ROAD RACE
First held 1958

1970	**Anna Konkina** URS
1971	**Anna Konkina** URS
1972	**Genevieve Gambillon** FRA
1973	**Nicole Vandenbroeck** BEL
1974	**Genevieve Gambillon** FRA
1975	**Trijntje Fopma** NED
1976	**K van Oosten-Hage** NED
1977	**Josiane Bost** FRA
1978	**Beate Habetz** FRG
1979	**Petra de Bruin** NED
1980	**Beth Heiden** USA
1981	**Ute Enzenauer** FRG
1982	**Mandy Jones** GBR
1983	**Marianne Berglund** SWE
1985	**Jeannie Longo** FRA
1986	**Jeannie Longo** FRA
1987	**Jeannie Longo** FRA
1989	**Jeannie Longo** FRA
1990	**Catherine Marsal** FRA
1991	**L van Moorsel** NED
1993	**L Van Moorsel** NED
1994	**Monica Valvik** NOR
1995	**Jeannie Longo** FRA
1996	**Barbara Heeb** SUI
1997	**A Cappellotto** ITA
1998	**Diana Ziluite** LTU
1999	**Edita Pucinskaite** LTU
2000	**Zinaida Stahurskaia** BLR
2001	**Rasa Polikeviciute** LTU
2002	**Susanne Ljungskog** SWE

INDIVIDUAL TIME TRIAL

1994	**Karen Kurreck** USA
1995	**Jeannie Longo** FRA
1996	**Jeannie Longo** FRA
1997	**Jeannie Longo** FRA
1998	**Leontien van Moorsel** NED
1999	**L Zijlaard-van Moorsel**
2000	**Mari Holden** USA
2001	**Jeannie Longo-Ciprelli** FRA
2002	**Zoulfia Zabirova** RUS

WOMEN'S 50 KM TEAM TRIAL

1987	**Soviet Union**
1988	**Italy**
1989	**Soviet Union**
1990	**Netherlands**
1991	**France**
1992	**USA**
1993	**Russia**
1994	**Russia**

Grands Tours
TOUR DE FRANCE

1903	**Maurice Garin** FRA
1904	**Henri Cornet** FRA
1905	**Louis Trousselier** FRA
1906	**Rene Pottier** FRA
1907	**Lucien Petit-Breton** FRA
1908	**Lucien Petit-Breton** FRA
1909	**Francois Faber** LUX
1910	**Octave Lapize** FRA
1911	**Gustave Garrigou** FRA
1912	**Odile Defraye** BEL
1913	**Philippe Thys** BEL
1914	**Philippe Thys** BEL
1919	**Firmin Lambot** BEL
1920	**Philippe Thys** BEL
1921	**Leon Scieur** BEL
1922	**Firmin Lambot** BEL
1923	**Henri Pelissier** FRA
1924	**Ottavio Bottecchia** ITA
1925	**Ottavio Bottecchia** ITA
1926	**Lucien Buysse** BEL
1927	**Nicholas Frantz** LUX
1928	**Nicholas Frantz** LUX
1929	**Maurice De Waele** BEL
1930	**Andre Leducq** FRA
1931	**Antonin Magne** FRA
1932	**Andre Leducq** FRA
1933	**Georges Speicher** FRA
1934	**Antonin Magne** FRA
1935	**Romain Maes** BEL
1936	**Sylvere Maes** BEL
1937	**Roger Lapebie** FRA
1938	**Gino Bartali** ITA
1939	**Sylvere Maes** BEL
1947	**Jean Robic** FRA
1948	**Gino Bartali** ITA
1949	**Fausto Coppi** ITA
1950	**Ferdinand Kubler** SUI
1951	**Hugo Koblet** SUI
1952	**Fausto Coppi** ITA
1953	**Louison Bobet** FRA
1954	**Louison Bobet** FRA
1955	**Louison Bobet** FRA
1956	**Roger Walkowiak** FRA
1957	**Jacques Anquetil** FRA
1958	**Charly Gaul** LUX
1959	**Federico Bahamontes** ESP
1960	**Gastone Nencini** ITA
1961	**Jacques Anquetil** FRA
1962	**Jacques Anquetil** FRA
1963	**Jacques Anquetil** FRA
1964	**Jacques Anquetil** FRA
1965	**Felice Gimondi** ITA
1966	**Lucien Aimar** FRA
1967	**Roger Pingeon** FRA
1968	**Jan Janssen** HOL
1969	**Eddy Merckx** BEL
1970	**Eddy Merckx** BEL
1971	**Eddy Merckx** BEL
1972	**Eddy Merckx** BEL
1973	**Luis Ocana** ESP
1974	**Eddy Merckx** BEL
1975	**Bernard Thevenet** FRA
1976	**Lucien van Impe** BEL
1977	**Bernard Thevenet** FRA
1978	**Bernard Hinault** FRA
1979	**Bernard Hinault** FRA
1980	**Joop Zoetemelk** HOL
1981	**Bernard Hinault** FRA
1982	**Bernard Hinault** FRA
1983	**Laurent Fignon** FRA
1984	**Laurent Fignon** FRA
1985	**Bernard Hinault** FRA
1986	**Greg LeMond** USA
1987	**Stephen Roche** IRE
1988	**Pedro Delgado** ESP
1989	**Greg LeMond** USA
1990	**Greg LeMond** USA
1991	**Miguel Induráin** ESP
1992	**Miguel Induráin** ESP
1993	**Miguel Induráin** ESP
1994	**Miguel Induráin** ESP
1995	**Miguel Induráin** ESP
1996	**Bjarne Riis** DEN
1997	**Jan Ullrich** GER
1998	**Marco Pantani** ITA
1999	**Lance Armstrong** USA
2000	**Lance Armstrong** USA
2001	**Lance Armstrong** USA
2002	**Lance Armstrong** USA

GIRO d'ITALIA

1909	**Luigi Ganna** ITA
1910	**Carlo Galetti** ITA
1911	**Carlo Galetti** ITA
1912	**Atala** (team event only)
1913	**Carlo Oriani** ITA
1914	**Alfonso Calzolari** ITA
1919	**Costante Girardengo** ITA
1920	**Gaetano Belloni** ITA
1921	**Giovanni Brunero** ITA
1922	**Giovanni Brunero** ITA
1923	**Costante Girardengo** ITA
1924	**Giuseppe Enriri** ITA
1925	**Alfredo Binda** ITA
1926	**Giovanni Brunero** ITA
1927	**Alfredo Binda** ITA
1928	**Alfredo Binda** ITA
1929	**Alfredo Binda** ITA
1930	**Luigi Marchisio** ITA
1931	**Francesco Camusso** ITA
1932	**Antonio Pesenti** ITA
1933	**Alfredo Binda** ITA
1934	**Learro Guerra** ITA
1935	**Vasco Bergamaschi** ITA
1936	**Gino Bartali** ITA
1937	**Gino Bartali** ITA
1938	**Giovanni Valetti** ITA
1939	**Giovanni Valetti** ITA
1940	**Fausto Coppi** ITA
1946	**Gino Bartali** ITA
1947	**Fausto Coppi** ITA
1948	**Fiorenzo Magni** ITA
1949	**Fausto Coppi** ITA

CYCLING

1950	**Hugo Koblet** SUI		1947	**Edward Van Dijck** BEL
1951	**Fiorenzo Magni** ITA		1948	**Bernardo Ruiz** ESP
1952	**Fausto Coppi** ITA		1950	**Emilio Rodriguez** ESP
1953	**Fausto Coppi** ITA		1955	**Jean Dotto** FRA
1954	**Carlo Cleriri** SUI		1956	**Angelo Conterno** ITA
1955	**Fiorenzo Magni** ITA		1957	**Jesus Lorono** ESP
1956	**Charly Gaul** LUX		1958	**Jean Stablinski** FRA
1957	**Gastone Nenrini** ITA		1959	**Antonio Suarez** ESP
1958	**Errole Baldini** ITA		1960	**Frans De Mulder** BEL
1959	**Charly Gaul** LUX		1961	**Angelo Soler** ESP
1960	**Jacques Anquetil** FRA		1962	**Rudi Altig** GER
1961	**Arnaldo Pambianco** ITA		1963	**Jacques Anquetil** FRA
1962	**Franco Balmamion** ITA		1964	**Raymond Poulidor** FRA
1963	**Franco Balmamion** ITA		1965	**Rolf Wolfshohl** GER
1964	**Jacques Anquetil** FRA		1966	**Francesco Gabica** ESP
1965	**Vittorio Adorni** ITA		1967	**Jan Janssen** NED
1966	**Gianni Motta** ITA		1968	**Felice Gimondi** ITA
1967	**Felice Gimondi** ITA		1969	**Roger Pingeon** FRA
1968	**Eddy Merckx** BEL		1970	**Luis Ocaña** ESP
1969	**Felice Gimondi** ITA		1971	**Ferdi Bracke** BEL
1970	**Eddy Merckx** BEL		1972	**José Manuel Fuente** ESP
1971	**Gosta Pettersson** SWE		1973	**Eddy Merckx** BEL
1972	**Eddy Merckx** BEL		1974	**José Manuel Fuente** ESP
1973	**Eddy Merckx** BEL		1975	**Augustin Tamames** ESP
1974	**Eddy Merckx** BEL		1976	**José Pesarrodona** ESP
1975	**Fausto Bertoglio** ITA		1977	**Freddy Maertens** BEL
1976	**Felice Gimondi** ITA		1978	**Bernard Hinault** FRA
1977	**Michel Pollentier** BEL		1979	**Joop Zoetemelk** NED
1978	**Johan De Muynck** BEL		1980	**Faustino Ruperez** ESP
1979	**Giuseppe Saronni** ITA		1981	**Giovanni Battaglin** ITA
1980	**Bernard Hinault** FRA		1982	**Marino Lejaretta** ESP
1981	**Giovani Battaglin** ITA		1983	**Bernhard Hinault** FRA
1982	**Bernard Hinault** FRA		1984	**Eric Caritoux** FRA
1983	**Guiseppe Saronni** ITA		1985	**Pedro Delgado** ESP
1984	**Francesco Moser** ITA		1986	**Alvaro Pino** ESP
1985	**Bernard Hinault** FRA		1987	**Luis Herrera** COL
1986	**Roberto Visentini** ITA		1988	**Sean Kelly** IRL
1987	**Stephen Roche** IRE		1989	**Pedro Delgado** ESP
1988	**Andy Hampsten** USA		1990	**Marco Giovanetti** ITA
1989	**Laurent Fignon** FRA		1991	**Melchior Mauri** ESP
1990	**Gianni Bugno** ITA		1992	**Tony Rominger** SUI
1991	**Franco Chioccioli** ITA		1993	**Tony Rominger** SUI
1992	**Miguel Induráin** ESP		1994	**Tony Rominger** SUI
1993	**Miguel Induráin** ESP		1995	**Laurent Jalabert** FRA
1994	**Evgeny Berzin** RUS		1996	**Alex Zulle** SUI
1995	**Tony Rominger** SUI		1997	**Alex Zulle** SUI
1996	**Pavel Tonkov** RUS		1998	**Abraham Olano** ESP
1997	**Ivan Gotti** ITA		1999	**Jan Ullrich** GER
1998	**Marco Pantani** ITA		2000	**Roberto Heras** ESP
1999	**Ivan Gotti** ITA		2001	**Angel Casero** ESP
2000	**Stefano Garzelli** ITA		2002	**Aitor Gonzalez** ESP
2001	**Gilberto Simoni** ITA			
2002	**Paolo Savoldelli** ITA			

VUELTA DE ESPANA

1935	**Gustave Deloor** BEL
1936	**Gustave Deloor** BEL
1941	**Julian Berrendero** ESP
1942	**Julian Berrendero** ESP
1945	**Delio Rodriguez** ESP
1946	**Dalmacio Langarica** ESP

DARTS

WORLD PROFESSIONAL CHAMPIONS

Year	Winner	Runner-up	Score
1978	Leighton Rees	John Lowe	11-7
1979	John Lowe	Leighton Rees	5-0
1980	Eric Bristow	Bobby George	5-3
1981	Eric Bristow	John Lowe	5-3
1982	Jocky Wilson	John Lowe	5-3
1983	Keith Deller	Eric Bristow	6-5
1984	Eric Bristow	Dave Whitcombe	7-1
1985	Eric Bristow	John Lowe	6-2
1986	Eric Bristow	Dave Whitcombe	6-0
1987	John Lowe	Eric Bristow	6-4
1988	Bob Anderson	John Lowe	6-4
1989	Jocky Wilson	Eric Bristow	6-4
1990	Phil Taylor	Eric Bristow	6-1
1991	Dennis Priestley	Eric Bristow	6-0
1992	Phil Taylor	Mike Gregory	6-5
1993	John Lowe	Alan Warriner	6-3
1994*	John Part	Bobby George	6-0
	Dennis Priestley	Phil Taylor	6-1
1995	Richie Burnett	Raymond Barneveld	6-3
	Phil Taylor	Rod Harrington	6-2
1996	Steve Beaton	Richie Burnett	6-3
	Phil Taylor	Dennis Priestley	6-4
1997	Les Wallace	Marshall James	6-3
	Phil Taylor	Dennis Priestley	6-3
1998	Ray Barneveld	Richie Burnett	6-5
	Phil Taylor	Dennis Priestley	6-0
1999	Ray Barneveld	Ronnie Baxter	6-5
	Phil Taylor	Peter Manley	6-2
2000	Ted Hankey	Ronnie Baxter	6-0
	Phil Taylor	Dennis Priestley	7-3
2001	John Walton	Ted Hankey	6-2
	Phil Taylor	John Part	7-0
2002	Tony David	Mervyn King	6-4
	Phil Taylor	Peter Manley	7-0

*BDO version is given first, WDC version second

WORLD MASTERS

1974	Cliff Inglis ENG
1975	Alan Evans WAL
1976	John Lowe ENG
1977	Eric Bristow ENG
1978	Ronnie Davis ENG
1979	Eric Bristow ENG
1980	John Lowe ENG
1981	Eric Bristow ENG
1982	Dave Whitcombe ENG
1983	Eric Bristow ENG
1984	Eric Bristow ENG
1985	Dave Whitcombe ENG
1986	Bob Anderson ENG
1987	Bob Anderson ENG
1988	Bob Anderson ENG
1989	Peter Evison ENG
1990	Phil Taylor ENG
1991	Rod Harrington ENG
1992	Dennis Priestley ENG
1993	Steve Beaton ENG

| 1994 | Richie Burnett ENG |

NEWS OF THE WORLD

Competition terminated when paper withdrew its support in 1991. (British unless stated)

1948	Harry Leadbetter
1949	Jack Boyce
1950	Dixie Newberry
1951	Harry Perryman
1952	Tommy Gibbons
1953	Jimmy Carr
1954	Oliver James
1955	Tom Reddington
1956	Trevor Peachey
1957	Alwyn Mullins
1958	Tommy Gibbons
1959	Albert Welch
1960	Tom Reddington
1961	Alec Adamson
1962	Eddie Brown
1963	Robbie Rumney
1964	Tom Barrett
1965	Tom Barrett
1966	Wilf Ellis
1967	Wally Seaton
1968	Bill Duddy
1969	Barry Twomlow
1970	Henry Barney
1971	Dennis Filkins
1972	Brian Netherton
1973	Ivor Hodgkinson
1974	Peter Chapman
1975	Derek White
1976	Bill Lennard
1977	Mick Norris
1978	Stefan Lord SWE
1979	Bobby George
1980	Stefan Lord SWE
1981	John Lowe
1982	Roy Morgan
1983	Eric Bristow
1984	Eric Bristow
1985	Dave Lee
1986	Bobby George
1987	Mike Gregory
1988	Mike Gregory
1989	Dave Whitcombe
1990	Paul Cook

EQUESTRIANISM

JUMPING

WORLD CHAMPIONSHIP - MEN

Year	Rider	Horse
1953	**Francisco Goyoago** ESP	Quorum
1954	**Hans Gunter Winkler** FRG	Halla
1955	**Hans Gunter Winkler** FRG	Halla
1956	**Raimondo d'Inzeo** ITA	Merano
1960	**Raimondo d'Inzeo** ITA	Gowran Girl
1966	**P Jonqueres d'Oriola** FRA	Pomone B
1970	**David Broome** GBR	Beethoven
1974	**Hartwig Steenken** FRG	Simona
1978	**Gerd Wiltfang** FRG	Roman
1982	**Norbert Koof** FRG	Fire II
1986	**Gail Greenhough** CAN	Mr T
1990	**Eric Navet** FRA	Quito de Baussy
1994	**Franke Sloothaak** GER	San Patrignano Weihaiwej
1998	**Rodrigo Pessoa** BRA	Gandini Lianos
2002	**Dermott Lennon** IRL	Liscalgot

WORLD CHAMPIONSHIP - WOMEN

1965	**Marion Coakes** GBR	Stroller
1970	**Janou Lefebvre** FRA	Rocket
1974	**Janou Tissot** FRA (née Lefebvre)	Rocket

VOLVO WORLD CUP

1979	**Hugo Simon** AUT	Gladstone
1980	**Conrad Homfeld** USA	Balbuco
1981	**Michael Matz** USA	Jet Run
1982	**Melanie Smith** USA	Calypso
1983	**Norman Dello Joio** USA	I Love You
1984	**Mario Deslauriers** CAN	Aramis
1985	**Conrad Homfeld** USA	Abdullah
1986	**Leslie Burr-Lenehan** USA	McLain
1987	**Katharine Burdsall** USA	The Natural
1988	**Ian Millar** CAN	Big Ben
1989	**Ian Millar** CAN	Big Ben
1990	**John Whitaker** GBR	Milton
1991	**John Whitaker** GBR	Milton
1992	**Thomas Fruhmann** AUT	Bockmann's Genius
1993	**Ludger Beerbaum** GER	Almox Ratina Z
1994	**Jos Lansink** HOL	Bollvorm's Libero H
1995	**Nick Skelton** GBR	Midnight Madness
1996	**Hugo Simon** AUT	E T FRH
1997	**Hugo Simon** AUT	E T FRH
1998	**Jos Lansink** NED	Nissan Calvaro Z
1999	**Rodrigo Pessoa** BRA	Baloubet du Roi
2000	**Rodrigo Pessoa** BRA	Baloubet du Roi
2001	**Markus Fuchs** SUI	Tinka's Boy
2002	**Otto Becker** GER	Dobel's Cento

THREE-DAY EVENTING

WORLD CHAMPIONSHIPS - INDIVIDUAL

1966	**Carlos Moratorio** ARG	Chalon
1970	**Mary Gordon-Watson** GBR	Cornishman V
1974	**Bruce Davidson** USA	Irish Cap
1978	**Bruce Davidson** USA	Might Tango
1982	**Lucinda Green** GBR	Regal Realm
1986	**Virginia Leng** GBR	Priceless
1990	**Blyth Tait** NZL	Messiah
1994	**Vaughan Jefferis** NZL	Bounce
1998	**Blyth Tait** NZL	Ready Teddy
2002	**Jean Teulere** FRA	Espoir de la Mare

BADMINTON HORSE TRIALS

Year	Rider	Horse
1949	**John Shedden** GBR	Golden Willow
1950	**Tony Collings** GBR	Remus
1951	**Hans Schwarzenbach** SUI	Vae Victus
1952	**Mark Darley** IRE	Emily Little
1953	**Lawrence Rook** GBR	Starlight
1954	**Margaret Hough** GBR	Bambi
1955	**Frank Weldon** GBR	Kilbarry
1956	**Frank Weldon** GBR	Kilbarry
1957	**Sheila Willcox** GBR	High and Mighty
1958	**Sheila Willcox** GBR	High and Mighty
1959	**Sheila Waddington** GBR (née Willcox)	Airs and Graces
1960	**Bill Roycroft** AUS	Our Solo
1961	**Lawrence Morgan** AUS	Salad Days
1962	**A Drummond-Hay** GBR	Merely-a-Monarch
1963	**Susan Fleet** GBR	Gladiator
1964	**James Templer** GBR	M'Lord Connolly
1965	**Eddie Boylan** IRE	Durlas Eile
1966	Not held	
1967	**Celia Ross-Taylor** GBR	Jonathan
1968	**Jane Bullen** GBR	Our Nobby
1969	**Richard Walker** GBR	Pasha
1970	**Richard Meade** GBR	The Poacher
1971	**Mark Phillips** GBR	Great Ovation
1972	**Mark Phillips** GBR	Great Ovation
1973	**Lucinda Prior-Palmer** GBR	Be Fair
1974	**Mark Phillips** GBR	Columbus
1975	Cancelled after dressage	
1976	**Lucinda Prior-Palmer** GBR	Wideawake
1977	**Lucinda Prior-Palmer** GBR	George
1978	**Jane Holderness-Roddam** (née Bullen) GBR	Warrior
1979	**Lucinda Prior-Palmer** GBR	Killaire
1980	**Mark Todd** NZL	Southern Comfort
1981	**Mark Phillips** NZL	Lincoln
1982	**Richard Meade** GBR	Speculator lil
1983	**Lucinda Green** GBR (née Prior-Palmer)	Regal Realm
1984	**Lucinda Green** GBR	Beagle Bay
1985	**Virginia Holgate** GBR	Priceless
1986	**Ian Stark** GBR	Sir Wattie
1987	Not held	
1988	**Ian Stark** GBR	Sir Wattie
1989	**Virginia Leng** GBR (née Holgate)	Master Craftsman
1990	**Nicola McIrvine** GBR	Middle Road
1991	**Rodney Powell** GBR	The Irishman
1992	**Mary Thompson** GBR	King William
1993	**Virginia Leng** GBR	Welton Houdini
1994	**Mark Todd** NZL	Horton Point
1995	**Bruce Davidson** USA	Eagle Lion
1996	**Mark Todd** NZL	Bertie Blunt
1997	**David O'Connor** USA	Custom Made

EQUESTRIANISM

1998	**Chris Bartle** GBR	Word Perfect II
1999	**Ian Stark** GBR	Jaybee
2000	**Mary King** GBR	Star Appeal
2001	Cancelled due to foot and mouth	
2002	**Pippa Funnell** GBR	Supreme Rock

BURGHLEY HORSE TRIALS

Year	Rider	Horse
1962	**Anneli Drummond-Hay** GBR	Golden Willow
1963	**Harry Freeman-Jackson** IRL	St Finbar
1964	**Richard Meade** GBR	Barberry
1965	**Jeremy Beale** GBR	Victoria Bridge
1967	**Lorna Sutherland** GBR	Popadom
1968	**Sheila Wilcox** GBR	Fair and Square
1969	**Gillian Watson** GBR	Shaitan
1970	**Judy Bradwell** GBR	Don Camillo
1972	**Janet Hodgson** GBR	Larkspur
1973	**Mark Phillips** GBR	Maid Marion
1975	**Aly Pattinson** GBR	Carawich
1976	**Jane Holderness-Roddam** GBR	
		Warrior
1977	**Lucinda Prior-Palmer** GBR	George
1978	**Lorna Clarke** GBR	Greco
1979	**Andrew Hoy** AUS	Davy
1980	**Richard Walker** GBR	John of Gaunt
1981	**Lucinda Prior-Palmer** GBR	Beagle Bay
1982	**Richard Walker** GBR	Ryan's Cross
1983	**Ginny Holgate** GBR	Priceless
1984	**Ginny Holgate** GBR	Night Cap
1986	**Ginny Leng*** GBR	Murphy Himself
1987	**Mark Todd** NZL	Wilson Fair
1988	**Jane Thelwall** GBR	King's Jester
1990	**Mark Todd** NZL	Face The Music
1991	**Mark Todd** NZL	Welton Greylag
1992	**Charlotte Hollingsworth** GBR	The Cool Customer
1993	**Stephen Bradley** USA	Sassy Reason
1994	**William Fox-Pitt** GBR	Chaka
1995	**Andrew Nicholson** NZL	Buckley Province
1996	**Mary King** GBR	Star Appeal
1997	**Mark Todd** NZL	Broadcast News
1998	**Blythe Tait** NZL	Chesterfield
1999	**Mark Tood** NZL	Diamond Hall Red
2000	**Andrew Nicholson** NZL	Mr Smiffy
2001	**Blythe Tait** NZL	Ready Teddy
2002	**William Fox-Pitt** GBR	Highland Lad

* née Holgate

DRESSAGE

WORLD CHAMPIONSHIPS - INDIVIDUAL

1966	**Josef Neckermann** FRG	Mariano
1970	**Yelena Petuchkova** URS	Pepel
1974	**Reiner Klimke** FRG	Mehmed
1978	**Christine Stückelberger** SUI	Granat
1982	**Reiner Klimke** FRG	Ahlerich
1986	**Anne Grethe Jensen** DEN	Marzog
1990	**Nicole Uphoff** FRG	Rembrandt
1994	**Isabell Werth** GER	Gigolo
1998	**Isabell Werth** GER	Gigolo
2002	**Nadine Capellmann** GER	Farbenfroh

FENCING

World Champions

MEN'S FOIL	MEN'S EPEE	MEN'S SABRE
1921 -	Lucien Gaudin FRA	-
1922 -	Raoul Herde NOR	Adrianus de Jong HOL
1923 -	Wouter Brouwer HOL	Adrianus de Jong HOL
1925 -	-	János Garay HUN
1926 Giorgio Chiavacci ITA	Georges Tainturier FRA	Sándor Gambos HUN
1927 Oreste Puliti ITA	Georges Buchard FRA	Sándor Gambos HUN
1929 Oreste Puliti ITA	Philippe Cattiau FRA	Gyula Glykais HUN
1930 Giulio Gaudini ITA	Philippe Cattiau FRA	György Piller HUN
1931 Rene Lemoine FRA	Georges Buchard FRA	György Piller HUN
1933 Gioacch'o Guaragna ITA	Georges Buchard FRA	Endre Kabos HUN
1934 Giulio Gaudini ITA	Pál Dunay HUN	Endre Kabos HUN
1935 shared by four men	Hans Drakenberg SWE	Aladár Gerevich HUN
1937 Gustavo Marzi ITA	Bernard Schmetz FRA	Pál Kovács HUN
1938 Gioacch'o Guaragna ITA	Michel Pécheux FRA	Aldo Montano ITA
1947 Christian d'Oriola FRA	Edouard Artigas FRA	Aldo Montano ITA
1949 Christian d'Oriola FRA	Dario Mangiarotti ITA	Gastone Daré FRA
1950 Renzo Nostino ITA	Mogens Luchow DEN	Jean Levavasseur FRA
1951 Manlio Di Rosa ITA	Edoardo Mangiarotti ITA	Aladar Gerevich HUN
1953 Christian d'Oriola FRA	Jozsef Sakovics HUN	Pál Kovács HUN
1954 Christian d'Oriola FRA	Edoardo Mangiarotti ITA	Rudolf Kárpáti HUN
1955 Jozsef Gyuricza HUN	Giorgio Anglesio ITA	Aladár Gerevich HUN
1957 Mihaly Fülöp HUN	Armand Mouyal FRA	Jerzy Pawlowski POL
1958 Giancarlo Bergamini ITA	Bill Hoskyns GBR	Yakov Rylsky URS
1959 Allan Jay GBR	Bruno Khabarov URS	Rudolf Kárpáti HUN
1961 Ryszard Parulski POL	Jack Guittet FRA	Yakov Rylsky URS
1962 German Sveshnikov URS	Istvan Kausz HUN	Zoltan Horvath HUN
1963 Jean-Cl'de Magnan FRA	Roland Losert AUT	Yakov Rylsky URS
1965 Jean-Cl'de Magnan FRA	Zoltan Nemere HUN	Jerzy Pawlowski POL
1966 German Sveshnikov URS	Aleksey Nikanchikov URS	Jerzy Pawlowski POL
1967 Viktor Putyatin URS	Aleksey Nikanchikov URS	Mark Rakita URS
1969 Friedrich Wessel FRG	Bogdan Andrzejewski POL	Viktor Sidiak URS
1970 Friedrich Wessel FRG	Aleksey Nikanchikov URS	Tibor Pézsa HUN
1971 Vasiliy Stankovich URS	Grigoriy Kriss URS	Michele Maffei ITA
1973 Christian Noël FRA	Rolf Edling SWE	Mario Aldo Monttano ITA
1974 Aleks'dr Romankov URS	Rolf Edling SWE	Mario Aldo Monttano ITA
1975 Christian Noël FRA	Alexander Pusch FRG	Vladimir Nazlimov URS
1977 Aleks'dr Romankov URS	Johan Harmenberg SWE	Pál Gerevich HUN
1978 Didier Flament FRA	Alexander Pusch FRG	Viktor Krovopuskov URS
1979 Aleks'dr Romankov URS	Philippe Riboud FRA	Vladimir Nazlimov URS
1981 Vladimir Smirnov URS	Zoltan Szekely HUN	Mariusz Wodke POL
1982 Aleks'dr Romankov URS	Jenö Pap HUN	Viktor Krovopuskov URS
1983 Aleks'dr Romankov URS	Ellmar Bormann FRG	Vasiliy Etropolski BUL
1985 Mauro Numa ITA	Philippe Boisse FRA	Gyorgy Nebald HUN
1986 Andrea Borella ITA	Philippe Riboud FRA	Sergey Mindirgassov URS
1987 Mathias Gey FRG	Volker Fischer FRG	Jean François Lamour FRA
1989 Alexander Koch FRG	Manuel Pereira ESP	Grigoriy Kirienko URS
1990 Philippe Omnès FRA	Thomas Gerull FRG	György Nébald HUN
1991 Ingo Weissenborn GER	Andrey Shuvalov URS	Grigory Kirienko URS
1993 Alexander Koch GER	Pavel Kolobkov RUS	Grigory Kirienko RUS
1994 Rolando Tuckers CUB	Pavel Kolobkov RUS	Felix Becker GER
1995 Dmitri Chevtchenko RUS	Eric Srecki FRA	Grigory Kirienko RUS
1997 Sergey Golubitsky UKR	Eric Srecki FRA	Stanislav Pozdniakov RUS
1998 Sergey Golubitsky UKR	Hugues Obry FRA	Luigi Tarantino ITA
1999 Sergey Golubitsky UKR	Arnd Schmitt GER	Damien Touya FRA
2001 Salvatore Sanzo ITA	Paolo Milanoli ITA	Stanislav Pozdniakov RUS
2002 Simone Vanni ITA	Pavel Kolobkov RUS	Stanislav Pozdniakov RUS

FENCING

World Champions

WOMEN'S FOIL

1929	**Helene Mayer** GER
1930	**Jenny Addam** BEL
1931	**Helene Mayer** GER
1933	**Gwen Nelligan** GBR
1934	**Ilona Elek** HUN
1935	**Ilona Elek** HUN
1937	**Helene Mayer** GER
1938	**Marie Sediva** CZE
1947	**Ellen Müller-Preiss** AUT
1949	**Ellen Müller-Preiss** AUT
1950	**Ellen Müller-Preiss** AUT
	Renée Garilhe FRA
	Title shared
1951	**Ilona Elek** HUN
1953	**Irene Camber** ITA
1954	**Karen Lachman** DEN
1955	**Lidia Domolki** HUN
1957	**Aleksandra Zabelina** URS
1958	**Valentina Kiselyeva** URS
1959	**Yelina Yefimova** URS
1961	**Heidi Schmid** FRG
1962	**Olga Szabo-Orban** ROM
1963	**Ildiko Rejto** HUN
1965	**Galina Gorokhova** URS
1966	**Tatyana Samusenko** URS
1967	**Aleksandra Zabelina** URS
1969	**Yelena Novikova** URS
1970	**Galina Gorokhova** URS
1971	**Marie-Chantal Demaille** FRA
1973	**Valentina Nikonova** URS
1974	**Ildiko Bobis** HUN
1975	**Ecaterina Stahl** ROM
1977	**Valentina Sidorova** URS
1978	**Valentina Sidorova** URS
1979	**Cornelia Hanisch** FRG
1981	**Cornelia Hanisch** FRG
1982	**Naila Giliazova** URS
1983	**Dorina Vaccaroni** ITA
1985	**Cornelia Hanisch** FRG
1986	**Anja Fichtel** GER
1987	**Elisabeta Tufan** ROM
1989	**Olga Velichko** URS
1990	**Anja Fichtel** GER
1991	**Giovanna Trillini** ITA
1993	**Fracesca Bortolozzi** ITA
1994	**Reka Szabo-Lazar** ROM
1995	**Laura Badea** ROM
1997	**Giovanna Trillini** ITA
1998	**Sabine Bau** GER
1999	**Valentina Vezzali** ITA
2001	**Valentina Vezzali** ITA
2002	**Svetlana Bojko** RUS

WOMEN'S EPEE

1989	**Anja Straub** SUI
1990	**Taime Chappe** CUB
1991	**Marianne Horvath** HUN
1991	**Marianne Horvath** HUN
1993	**Oksana Yermakova** EST
1994	**Laura Chiesa** ITA
1995	**Joanna Jakimiuk** POL
1997	**Miraide Garcia** CUB
1998	**Laura Flessel** FRA
1999	**Laura Flessel-Colovic** FRA
2001	**Claudia Bokel** GER
2002	**Hee Hyun** KOR

WOMEN'S SABRE

1999	**Elena Jemaeva** AZE
2001	**Anne-Lise Tauya** FRA
2002	**Tan Xue** CHN

FENCING

World Champions

	Men			Women		
	Team Foil	Team Epée	Team Sabre	Team Foil	Team Epée	Team Sabre
1929	Italy	-	-	-	-	-
1930	Italy	Belgium	Hungary	-	-	-
1931	Italy	Italy	Hungary	-	-	-
1932	-	-	-	Denmark	-	-
1933	Italy	Italy	Hungary	Hungary	-	-
1934	Italy	France	Hungary	Hungary	-	-
1935	Italy	France	Hungary	Hungary	-	-
1936	-	-	-	West Germany	-	-
1937	Italy	Italy	Hungary	Hungary	-	-
1938	Italy	France	Italy	-	-	-
1947	France	France	Italy	Denmark	-	-
1948	-	-	-	Denmark	-	-
1949	Italy	Italy	Italy	-	-	-
1950	Italy	Italy	Italy	France	-	-
1951	France	France	Hungary	France	-	-
1952	-	-	-	Hungary	-	-
1953	France	Italy	Hungary	Hungary	-	-
1954	Italy	Italy	Hungary	Hungary	-	-
1955	Italy	Italy	Hungary	Hungary	-	-
1956	-	-	-	Soviet Union	-	-
1957	Hungary	Italy	Hungary	Italy	-	-
1958	France	Italy	Hungary	Soviet Union	-	-
1959	Soviet Union	Hungary	Poland	Hungary	-	-
1961	Soviet Union	Soviet Union	Poland	Soviet Union	-	-
1962	Soviet Union	France	Poland	Hungary	-	-
1963	Soviet Union	Poland	Poland	Soviet Union	-	-
1965	Soviet Union	France	Soviet Union	Soviet Union	-	-
1966	Soviet Union	France	Hungary	Soviet Union	-	-
1967	Romania	Soviet Union	Soviet Union	Hungary	-	-
1969	Soviet Union	Soviet Union	Soviet Union	Romania	-	-
1970	Soviet Union	Hungary	Soviet Union	Soviet Union	-	-
1971	France	Hungary	Soviet Union	Soviet Union	-	-
1973	Soviet Union	West Germany	Hungary	Hungary	-	-
1974	Soviet Union	Sweden	Soviet Union	Soviet Union	-	-
1975	France	Sweden	Soviet Union	Soviet Union	-	-
1977	West Germany	Sweden	Soviet Union	Soviet Union	-	-
1978	Poland	Hungary	Hungary	Soviet Union	-	-
1979	Soviet Union	Soviet Union	Soviet Union	Soviet Union	-	-
1981	Soviet Union	Soviet Union	Hungary	Soviet Union	-	-
1982	Soviet Union	France	Hungary	Italy	-	-
1983	West Germany	France	Soviet Union	Italy	-	-
1985	Italy	West Germany	Soviet Union	West Germany	-	-
1986	Italy	West Germany	Soviet Union	Soviet Union	-	-
1987	West Germany	Soviet Union	Soviet Union	Hungary	-	-
1989	Soviet Union	Italy	Soviet Union	West Germany	Hungary	-
1990	Italy	Italy	Soviet Union	Italy	West Germany	-
1991	Cuba	Soviet Union	Hungary	Italy	Hungary	-
1993	Germany	Italy	Hungary	Germany	Hungary	-
1994	Italy	France	Russia	Romania	Spain	-
1995	Cuba	Germany	Italy	Italy	Hungary	-
1997	France	Cuba	France	Italy	Hungary	-
1998	Poland	Hungary	Hungary	Italy	France	-
1999	France	Germany	France	Germany	Hungary	Italy
2001	France	Hungary	Russia	Italy	Russia	Russia
2002	Germany	France	Russia	Russia	Hungary	Russia

GOLF

THE OPEN

1860	**Willie Park Snr** GBR	174	Prestwick	1926	**Bobby Jones** (am) USA	291	Royal Lytham
1861	**Tom Morris Snr** GBR	163	Prestwick	1927	**Bobby Jones** (am) USA	285	St Andrews
1862	**Tom Morris Snr** GBR	163	Prestwick	1928	**Walter Hagen** USA	292	Sandwich
1863	**Willie Park Snr** GBR	168	Prestwick	1929	**Walter Hagen** USA	292	Muirfield
1864	**Tom Morris Snr** GBR	167	Prestwick	1930	**Bobby Jones** (am) USA	291	Hoylake
1865	**Andrew Strath** GBR	162	Prestwick	1931	**Tommy Armour** USA	296	Carnoustie
1866	**Willie Park Snr** GBR	169	Prestwick	1932	**Gene Sarazen** USA	283	Prince's
1867	**Tom Morris Snr** GBR	170	Prestwick	1933	**Densmore Shute** USA	292*	St Andrews
1868	**Tom Morris Jnr** GBR	157	Prestwick	1934	**Henry Cotton** GBR	283	Sandwich
1869	**Tom Morris Jnr** GBR	154	Prestwick	1935	**Alfred Perry** GBR	283	Muirfield
1870	**Tom Morris Jnr** GBR	149	Prestwick	1936	**Alfred Padgham** GBR	287	Hoylake
1872	**Tom Morris Jnr** GBR	166	Prestwick	1937	**Henry Cotton** GBR	290	Carnoustie
1873	**Tom Kidd** GBR	179	St Andrews	1938	**Reg Whitcombe** GBR	295	Sandwich
1874	**Mungo Park** GBR	159	Musselburgh	1939	**Dick Burton** GBR	290	St Andrews
1875	**Willie Park Snr** GBR	166	Prestwick	1946	**Sam Snead** USA	290	St Andrews
1876	**Bob Martin** GBR	176	St Andrews	1947	**Fred Daly** GBR	293	Hoylake
1877	**Jamie Anderson** GBR	160	Musselburgh	1948	**Henry Cotton** GBR	284	Muirfield
1878	**Jamie Anderson** GBR	157	Prestwick	1949	**Bobby Locke** RSA	283*	Sandwich
1880	**Jamie Anderson** GBR	169	St Andrews	1950	**Bobby Locke** RSA	279	Troon
1880	**Robert Ferguson** GBR	162	Musselburgh	1951	**Max Faulkner** GBR	285	Portrush
1881	**Robert Ferguson** GBR	170	Prestwick	1952	**Bobby Locke** RSA	287	Royal Lytham
1882	**Robert Ferguson** GBR	171	St Andrews	1953	**Ben Hogan** USA	282	Carnoustie
1883	**Willie Fernie** GBR	158*	Musselburgh	1954	**Peter Thomson** AUS	283	Royal Birkdale
1884	**Jack Simpson** GBR	160	Prestwick	1955	**Peter Thomson** AUS	281	St Andrews
1885	**Bob Martin** GBR	171	St Andrews	1956	**Peter Thomson** AUS	286	Hoylake
1886	**David Brown** GBR	157	Musselburgh	1957	**Bobby Locke** RSA	279	St Andrews
1887	**Willie Park Jnr** GBR	161	Prestwick	1958	**Peter Thomson** AUS	278*	Royal Lytham
1888	**Jack Burns** GBR	171	St Andrews	1959	**Gary Player** RSA	284	Muirfield
1889	**Willie Park Jnr** GBR	155*	Musselburgh	1960	**Kel Nagle** AUS	278	St.Andrews
1890	**John Ball** (am) GBR	164	Prestwick	1961	**Arnold Palmer** USA	284	Royal Birkdale
1891	**Hugh Kirkaldy** GBR	166	St Andrews	1962	**Arnold Palmer** USA	276	Troon
1892	**Harold Hilton** (am) GBR	305	Muirfield	1963	**Bob Charles** NZL	277*	Royal Lytham
1893	**Will Auchterlonie** GBR	322	Prestwick	1964	**Tony Lema** USA	279	St Andrews
1894	**John H Taylor** GBR	326	Sandwich	1965	**Peter Thomson** AUS	285	Royal Birkdale
1895	**John H Taylor** GBR	322	St Andrews	1966	**Jack Nicklaus** USA	282	Muirfield
1896	**Harry Vardon** GBR	316*	Muirfield	1967	**Rob. de Vicenzo** ARG	278	Hoylake
1897	**Harold Hilton** (am) GBR	314	Hoylake	1968	**Gary Player** RSA	289	Carnoustie
1898	**Harry Vardon** GBR	307	Prestwick	1969	**Tony Jacklin** GBR	280	Royal Lytham
1899	**Harry Vardon** GBR	310	Sandwich	1970	**Jack Nicklaus** USA	283*	St Andrews
1900	**John H Taylor** GBR	309	St Andrews	1971	**Lee Trevino** USA	278	Royal Birkdale
1901	**James Braid** GBR	309	Muirfield	1972	**Lee Trevino** USA	278	Muirfield
1902	**Sandy Herd** GBR	307	Hoylake	1973	**Tom Weiskopf** USA	276	Troon
1903	**Harry Vardon** GBR	300	Prestwick	1974	**Gary Player** RSA	282	Royal Lytham
1904	**Jack White** GBR	296	Sandwich	1975	**Tom Watson** USA	279*	Carnoustie
1905	**James Braid** GBR	318	St Andrews	1976	**Johnny Miller** USA	279	Royal Birkdale
1906	**James Braid** GBR	300	Muirfield	1977	**Tom Watson** USA	268	Turnberry
1907	**Arnaud Massy** FRA	312	Hoylake	1978	**Jack Nicklaus** USA	281	St Andrews
1908	**James Braid** GBR	291	Prestwick	1979	**Seve Ballesteros** ESP	283	Royal Lytham
1909	**John H Taylor** GBR	295	Deal	1980	**Tom Watson** USA	271	Muirfield
1910	**James Braid** GBR	299	St Andrews	1981	**Bill Rogers** USA	276	Sandwich
1911	**Harry Vardon** GBR	303	Sandwich	1982	**Tom Watson** USA	284	Troon
1912	**Edward Ray** GBR	295	Muirfield	1983	**Tom Watson** USA	275	Royal Birkdale
1913	**John H Taylor** GBR	304	Hoylake	1984	**Seve Ballesteros** ESP	276	St Andrews
1914	**Harry Vardon** GBR	306	Prestwick	1985	**Sandy Lyle** GBR	282	Sandwich
1920	**George Duncan** GBR	303	Deal	1986	**Greg Norman** AUS	280	Turnberry
1921	**Jock Hutchinson** USA	296*	St Andrews	1987	**Nick Faldo** GBR	279	Muirfield
1922	**Walter Hagen** USA	300	Sandwich	1988	**Seve Ballesteros** ESP	273	Royal Lytham
1923	**Arthur Havers** GBR	295	Troon	1989	**Mark Calcavecchia** USA	275*	Troon
1924	**Walter Hagen** USA	301	Hoylake	1990	**Nick Faldo** GBR	270	St Andrews
1925	**Jim Barnes** USA	300	Prestwick	1991	**Ian Baker-Finch** AUS	272	Royal Birkdale

GOLF

THE OPEN

1992	Nick Faldo GBR	272	Muirfield
1993	Greg Norman AUS	267	Sandwich
1994	Nick Price ZIM	268	Turnberry
1995	John Daly USA	282*	St Andrews
1996	Tom Lehman USA	271	Royal Lytham
1997	Justin Leonard USA	272	Royal Troon
1998	Mark O'Meara USA	280*	Birkdale
1999	Paul Lawrie GBR	290*	Carnoustie
2000	Tiger Woods USA	269	St Andrews
2001	David Duval USA	274	Royal Lytham
2002	Ernie Els RSA	278*	Muirfield

US OPEN

Year	Winner (USA unless stated)	Score	Venue
1895	Horace Rawlins	173	Newport
1896	James Foulis	152	Shinnecock Hs
1897	Joe Lloyd	162	Chicago
1898	Willie Smith	315	Baltimore
1900	Harry Vardon GBR	313	Chicago
1901	Willie Anderson	331*	Myopia Hunt
1902	Laurie Auchterlonie	307	Garden City
1903	Willie Anderson	307*	Baltusrol
1904	Willie Anderson	303	Glen View
1905	Willie Anderson	314	Myopia Hunt
1906	Alex Smith	295	Onwentsia
1907	Alex Ross	302	Philadelphia
1908	Fred McLeod	322*	Myopia Hunt
1909	George Sargent	290	Englewood
1910	Alex Smith	298*	Philadelphia
1911	John McDermott	307*	Chicago
1912	John McDermott	294	Buffalo
1913	Francis Ouimet (am)	304*	Brookline
1914	Walter Hagen	290	Midlothian
1915	Jerome Travers (am)	297	Baltusrol
1916	Charles Evans Jnr (am)	286	Minikahda
1919	Walter Hagen	301*	Brae Burn
1920	Edward Ray GBR	295	Inverness
1921	Jim Barnes	289	Columbia
1922	Gene Sarazen	288	Skokie
1923	Bobby Jones (am)	296*	Inwood
1924	Cyril Walker	297	Oakland Hills
1925	Willie Macfarlane	291*	Worcester
1926	Bobby Jones (am)	293	Scioto
1927	Tommy Armour	301 *	Oakmont
1928	Johnny Farrell	294*	Olympia Flds
1929	Bobby Jones (am)	294*	Winged Foot
1930	Bobby Jones (am)	287	Interlachen
1931	Billy Burke	292*	Inverness
1932	Gene Sarazen	286	Fresh Meadow
1933	Johnny Goodman (am)	287	North Shore
1934	Olin Dutra	293	Merion
1935	Sam Parks Jnr	299	Oakmont
1936	Tony Manero	282	Baltusrol
1937	Ralph Guldahl	281	Oakland Hills
1938	Ralph Guldahl	284	Cherry Hills
1939	Byron Nelson	284*	Philadelphia
1940	Lawson Little	287*	Canterbury
1941	Craig Wood	284	Colonial
1946	Lloyd Mangrum	284*	Canterbury
1947	Lew Worsham	282*	St Louis

1948	Ben Hogan	276	Riviera
1949	Cary Middlecoff	286	Medinah
1950	Ben Hogan	287*	Merion
1951	Ben Hogan	287	Oakland Hills
1952	Julius Boros	281	Northwood
1953	Ben Hogan	283	Oakmont
1954	Ed Furgol	284	Baltusrol
1955	Jack Fleck	287*	Olympic
1956	Cary Middlecoff	281	Oak Hill
1957	Dick Mayer	282*	Inverness
1958	Tommy Bolt	283	Southern Hills
1959	Billy Casper	282	Winged Foot
1960	Arnold Palmer	280	Cherry Hills
1961	Gene Littler	281	Oakland Hills
1962	Jack Nicklaus	283*	Oakmont
1963	Julius Boros	293*	Brookline
1964	Ken Venturi	278	Congressional
1965	Gary Player RSA	282*	Bellerive
1966	Billy Casper	278*	Olympic
1967	Jack Nicklaus	275	Baltusrol
1968	Lee Trevino	275	Oak Hill
1969	Orville Moody	281	Champions
1970	Tony Jacklin GBR	281	Hazeltine
1971	Lee Trevino	280*	Merion
1972	Jack Nicklaus	290	Pebble Beach
1973	Johnny Miller	279	Oakmont
1974	Hale Irwin	287*	Winged Foot
1975	Lou Graham	287	Medinah
1976	Jerry Pate	277	Atlanta
1977	Hubert Green	278	Southern Hills
1978	Andy North	285	Cherry Hills
1979	Hale Irwin	284	Inverness
1980	Jack Nicklaus	272	Baltusrol
1981	David Graham AUS	273	Merion
1982	Tom Watson	282	Pebble Beach
1983	Larry Nelson	280	Oakmont
1984	Fuzzy Zoeller	276*	Winged Foot
1985	Andy North	279	Oakland Hills
1986	Raymond Floyd	279	Shinnecock Hls
1987	Scott Simpson	277	Olympic Club
1988	Curtis Strange	278	Brookline
1989	Curtis Strange	278	Oak Hill
1990	Hale Irwin	280*	Medinah
1991	Payne Stewart	282*	Hazeltine
1992	Tom Kite	285	Monterey
1993	Lee Janzen	272	Baltusrol
1994	Ernie Els RSA	279	Oakmont
1995	Corey Pavin	280	Shinnecock Hls
1996	Steve Jones	278	Oakland Hills
1997	Ernie Els RSA	280	Congressional
1998	Lee Janzen	280	Olympic Club
1999	Payne Stewart	279	Pinehurst
2000	Tiger Woods	272	Pebble Beach
2001	Retief Goosen RSA	276*	Southern Hills
2002	Tiger Woods USA	277	Bethpage

* after play off

GOLF

US MASTERS
(US unless stated)

Year	Winners	Score
1934	Horton Smith	284
1935	Gene Sarazen	282*
1936	Horton Smith	285
1937	Byron Nelson	283
1938	Henry Picard	285
1939	Ralph Guldahl	279
1940	Jimmy Demaret	280
1941	Craig Wood	280
1942	Byron Nelson	280*
1946	Herman Keiser	282
1947	Jimmy Demaret	281
1948	Claude Harmon	279
1949	Sam Snead	282
1950	Jimmy Demaret	283
1951	Ben Hogan	280
1952	Sam Snead	286
1953	Ben Hogan	274
1954	Sam Snead	289*
1955	Cary Middlecoff	279
1956	Jack Burke Jnr	289
1957	Doug Ford	282
1958	Arnold Palmer	284
1959	Art Wall Jnr	284
1960	Arnold Palmer	282*
1961	Gary Player RSA	280
1962	Arnold Palmer	280*
1963	Jack Nicklaus	286
1964	Arnold Palmer	276
1965	Jack Nicklaus	271
1966	Jack Nicklaus	288*
1967	Gay Brewer	280
1968	Bob Goalby	277
1969	George Archer	281
1970	Billy Casper	279*
1971	Charles Coody	279
1972	Jack Nicklaus	286
1973	Tommy Aaron	283
1974	Gary Player RSA	278
1975	Jack Nicklaus	276
1976	Raymond Floyd	271
1977	Tom Watson	276
1978	Gary Player RSA	277
1979	Fuzzy Zoeller	280*
1980	S Ballesteros ESP	275
1981	Tom Watson	280
1982	Craig Stadler	284*
1983	S Ballesteros ESP	280
1984	Ben Crenshaw	277
1985	Bernh. Langer FRG	282
1986	Jack Nicklaus	279
1987	Larry Mize	285*
1988	Sandy Lyle GBR	281
1989	Nick Faldo GBR	283*
1990	Nick Faldo GBR	278*
1991	Ian Woosnam GBR	277
1992	Fred Couples	275
1993	Bernh. Langer GER	277
1994	J-M Olazábal ESP	279
1995	Ben Crenshaw	274
1996	Nick Faldo GBR	276
1997	Tiger Woods	270
1998	Mark O'Meara	279
1999	J-M Olazábal ESP	280
2000	Vijay Singh FIJ	278
2001	Tiger Woods	272
2002	Tiger Woods	276

US PGA

Year	Winner	Score
1916	Jim Barnes	1 up
1919	Jim Barnes	6 & 5
1920	Jock Hutchison	1 up
1921	Walter Hagen	3 & 2
1922	Gene Sarazen	4 & 3
1923	Gene Sarazen	38th
1924	Walter Hagen	2 up
1925	Walter Hagen	6 & 5
1926	Walter Hagen	5 & 3
1927	Walter Hagen	1 up
1928	Leo Diegel	6 & 5
1929	Leo Diegel	6 & 4
1930	Tommy Armour	1 up
1931	Tom Creavy	2 & 1
1932	Olin Dutra	4 & 3
1933	Gene Sarazen	5 & 4
1934	Paul Runyan	38th
1935	Johnny Revolta	5 & 4
1936	Densmore Shute	3 & 2
1937	Densmore Shute	37th
1938	Paul Runyan	8 & 7
1939	Henry Picard	37th
1940	Byron Nelson	1 up
1941	Vic Ghezi	38th
1942	Sam Snead	2 & 1
1944	Bob Hamilton	1 up
1945	Byron Nelson	4 & 3
1946	Ben Hogan	6 & 4
1947	Jim Ferrier	2 & 1
1948	Ben Hogan	7 & 6
1949	Sam Snead	3 & 2
1950	Chandler Harper	4 & 3
1951	Sam Snead	7 & 6
1952	Jim Turnesa	1 up
1953	Walter Burkemo	2 & 1
1954	Chick Harbert	4 & 3
1955	Doug Ford	4 & 3
1956	Jack Burke	3 & 2
1957	Lionel Hebert	2 & 1
1958	Dow Finsterwald	276
1959	Bob Rosburg	277
1960	Jay Hebert	281
1961	Jerry Barber	277*
1962	Gary Player RSA	278
1963	Jack Nicklaus	279
1964	Bobby Nichols	271
1965	Dave Marr	280
1966	Al Geiberger	280
1967	Don January	281*
1968	Julius Boros	281
1969	Raymond Floyd	276
1970	Dave Stockton	279
1971	Jack Nicklaus	281
1972	Gary Player RSA	281
1973	Jack Nicklaus	277
1974	Lee Trevino	276
1975	Jack Nicklaus	276
1976	Dave Stockton	281
1977	Lanny Wadkins	282*
1978	John Mahaffey	276*
1979	David Graham AUS	272*
1980	Jack Nicklaus	274
1981	Larry Nelson	273
1982	Raymond Floyd	272
1983	Hal Sutton	274
1984	Lee Trevino	273
1985	Hubert Green	278
1986	Bob Tway	276
1987	Larry Nelson	287*
1988	Jeff Sluman	272
1989	Payne Stewart	276
1990	Wayne Grady AUS	282
1991	John Daly	276
1992	Nick Price ZIM	278
1993	Paul Azinger	272
1994	Nick Price ZIM	269
1995	Steve Elkington AUS	267
1996	Mark Brooks	277*
1997	Davis Love III	269
1998	Vijay Singh	271
1999	Tiger Woods	277
2000	Tiger Woods	270*
2001	David Toms	265
2002	Rich Beem	278

* after play off

GOLF

WORLD MATCHPLAY

Year	Winner	Runner-up	Score
1964	**Arnold Palmer** USA	Neil Coles ENG	2&1
1965	**Gary Player** RSA	Peter Thomson AUS	3&2
1966	**Gary Player** RSA	Jack Nicklaus USA	6&4
1967	**Arnold Palmer** USA	Peter Thomson AUS	1 up
1968	**Gary Player** RSA	Bob Charles NZL	1 up
1969	**Bob Charles** NZL	Gene Littler USA	37th
1970	**Jack Nicklaus** USA	Lee Trevino USA	2&1
1971	**Gary Player** RSA	Jack Nicklaus USA	5&4
1972	**Tom Weiskopf** USA	Lee Trevino USA	4&3
1973	**Gary Player** RSA	G Marsh AUS	40th
1974	**Hale Irwin** USA	Gary Player RSA	3&1
1975	**Hale Irwin** USA	Al Geiberger USA	4&2
1976	**David Graham** AUS	Hale Irwin USA	38th
1977	**Graham Marsh** AUS	Ray Floyd USA	5&3
1978	**Isao Aoki** JPN	Simon Owen NZL	3&2
1979	**Bill Rogers** USA	Isao Aoki JPN	1 up
1980	**Greg Norman** AUS	Sandy Lyle SCO	1 up
1981	**S Ballesteros** ESP	Ben Crenshaw USA	1 up
1982	**S Ballesteros** ESP	Sandy Lyle SCO	37th
1983	**Greg Norman** AUS	Nick Faldo ENG	3&2
1984	**S Ballesteros** ESP	B Langer FRG	2&1
1985	**S Ballesteros** ESP	B Langer FRG	6&5
1986	**Greg Norman** AUS	Sandy Lyle SCO	2&1
1987	**Ian Woosnam** WAL	Sandy Lyle SCO	1 up
1988	**Sandy Lyle** SCO	Nick Faldo ENG	2&1
1989	**Nick Faldo** ENG	Ian Woosnam WAL	1 up
1990	**Ian Woosnam** WAL	Mark McNulty ZIM	4&2
1991	**S Ballesteros** ESP	Nick Price ZIM	3&2
1992	**Nick Faldo** ENG	Jeff Sluman USA	8&7
1993	**Corey Pavin** USA	Nick Faldo ENG	1 up
1994	**Ernie Els** RSA	C Montgomerie SCO	4&2
1995	**Ernie Els** RSA	Steve Elkington AUS	3&1
1996	**Ernie Els** RSA	Vijay Singh FIJ	3&2
1997	**Vijay Singh** FIJ	Ernie Els RSA	1 hole
1998	**Mark O'Meara** USA	Tiger Woods USA	1 hole
1999	**C Montgomerie** SCO	Mark O'Meara USA	3&2
2000	**Lee Westwood** ENG	C Montgomerie SCO	38th
2001	**Ian Woosnam** WAL	P Harrington IRL	2&1
2002	**Ernie Els** RSA	Sergio Garcia ESP	2&1

WORLD CUP OF GOLF

Year	Winner	Score
1953	**Argentina** (de Vicenzo & Cerda)	287
1954	**Australia** (Thomson & Nagle)	556
1955	**USA** (Furgol & Harbert)	560
1956	**USA** (Hogan & Snead)	567
1957	**Japan** (Nakamura & Ono)	557
1958	**Ireland** (Bradshaw & O'Connor)	579
1959	**Australia** (Nagle & Thomson)	563
1960	**USA** (Palmer & Snead)	565
1961	**USA** (Demaret & Snead)	560
1962	**USA** (Palmer & Snead)	557
1963	**USA** (Nicklaus & Palmer)	482
1964	**USA** (Nicklaus & Palmer)	554
1965	**South Africa** (Henning & Player)	571
1966	**USA** (Nicklaus & Palmer)	548
1967	**USA** (Nicklaus & Palmer)	557
1968	**Canada** (Balding & Knudson)	569
1969	**USA** (Moody & Trevino)	552
1970	**Australia** (Devin & Graham)	544
1971	**USA** (Nicklaus & Trevino)	555
1972	**Taiwan** (Hsieh & Lu)	438
1973	**USA** (Miller & Nicklaus)	558
1974	**South Africa** (Cole & Hayes)	554
1975	**USA** (Graham & Miller)	554
1976	**Spain** (Ballesteros & Pinero)	574
1977	**Spain** (Ballesteros & Garrido)	591
1978	**USA** (Mahaffey & North)	564
1979	**USA** (Mahaffey & Irwin)	575
1980	**Canada** (Halidorson & Nelford)	572
1982	**Spain** (Canizares & Pinero)	563
1983	**USA** (Caldwell & Cook)	565
1984	**Spain** (Canizares & Rivero)	414
1985	**Canada** (Halidorson & Barr)	559
1987	**Wales** (Woosnam & Llewellyn)	574
1988	**USA** (Crenshaw & McCumber)	560
1989	**Australia** (Fowler & Grady)	278
1990	**Germany** (Langer & Giedeon)	556
1991	**Sweden** (Forsbrand & Johansson)	563
1992	**USA** (Couples & Love III)	548
1993	**USA** (Couples & Love III)	556
1994	**USA** (Couples & Love III)	536
1995	**USA** (Couples & Love III)	543
1996	**South Africa** (Els & Westner)	547
1997	**Ireland** (Harrington & McGinley)	545
1998	**England** (Faldo & Carter)	568
1999	**USA** (Woods/O'Meara)	545
2001	**South Africa** (Els/Goosen)	264
2002	**Japan** (Maruyama/Izawa)	252

GOLF

RYDER CUP

Year	Venue	Winner	Score
1927	Worcester, Massachusetts	**USA**	9.5-2.5
1929	Moortown, Yorkshire	**GBR**	7-5
1931	Scioto, Ohio	**USA**	9-3
1933	Southport & Ainsdale, Lancs	**GBR**	6.5-5.5
1935	Ridgewood, New Jersey	**USA**	9-3
1937	Southport & Ainsdale, Lancs	**USA**	8-4
1947	Portland, Oregon	**USA**	11-1
1949	Ganton, Yorkshire	**USA**	7-5
1951	Pinehurst, North Carolina	**USA**	9.5-2.5
1953	Wentworth, Surrey	**USA**	6.5-5.5
1955	Thunderbird G&CC, C'fornia	**USA**	8-4
1957	Lindrick, Yorkshire	**GBR**	7.5-4.5
1959	Eldorado CC, California	**USA**	8.5-3.5
1961	Royal Lytham, Lancs	**USA**	14.5-9.5
1963	Atlanta, Georgia	**USA**	23-9
1965	Royal Birkdale, Lancs	**USA**	19.5-12.5
1967	Houston, Texas	**USA**	23.5-8.5
1969	Royal Birkdale, Lancs	Drawn	16-16
1971	St Louis, Missouri	**USA**	18.5-13.5
1973	Muirfield, Scotland	**USA**	19-13
1975	Laurel Valley, Pennsylvania	**USA**	21-11
1977	Royal Lytham, Lancs	**USA**	12.5-7.5
1979	Greenbrier, West Virginia	**USA**	17-11
1981	Walton Heath, Surrey	**USA**	18.5-9.5
1983	PGA National, Florida	**USA**	14.5-13.5
1985	The Belfry, Sutton Coldfield	**Europe**	16.5-11.5
1987	Muirfield Village, Ohio	**Europe**	15-13
1989	The Belfry, Sutton Coldfield	Drawn	14-14
1991	Kiawah Island, S Carolina	**USA**	14.5-13.5
1993	The Belfry, Sutton Coldfield	**USA**	15-13
1995	Oak Hill CC, Rochester, NY	**Europe**	14.5-13.5
1997	Valderrama, Spain	**Europe**	14.5-13.5
1999	Brookline, Massachusets	**USA**	14.5-13.5
2001	Cancelled due to terrorist attacks in the USA		
2002	The Belfry, Sutton Coldfield	**Europe**	15.5-12.5

GYMNASTICS

ARTISTIC

From 2002, apparatus world
championships held separately
from all-around and team
championships

Men

ALL-AROUND

1983	**Dmitri Bilozerchev** URS
1985	**Yuri Korolev** URS
1987	**Dmitri Bilozerchev** URS
1989	**Igor Korobchinski** URS
1991	**Grigori Misutin** URS
1993	**Vitali Scherbo** BLR
1994	**Ivan Ivankov** BLR
1995	**Li Xiaoshuang** CHN
1997	**Ivan Ivankov** BLR
1999	**Nikolay Krukov** RUS
2001	**Jing Feng** CHN

FLOOR

1983	**Tong Fei** CHN
1985	**Tong Fei** CHN
1987	**Lou Yun** CHN
1989	**Igor Korobchinski** URS
1991	**Igor Korobchinski** URS
1993	**Grigori Misutin** URS
1994	**Vitali Scherbo** BLR
1995	**Vitali Scherbo** BLR
1996	**Vitali Scherbo** BLR
1997	**Alexei Nemov** RUS
1999	**Alexei Nemov** RUS
2001	**Jordan Jovtchev** BUL
2002	**Marian Dragulescu** ROM

POMMEL HORSE

1983	**Dmitri Bilozerchev** URS
1985	**Valentin Mogilni** URS
1987	**Dmitri Bilozerchev** URS
	Borkai HUN
1989	**Valentin Mogilni** URS
1991	**Valeri Belenki** URS
1993	**Pae Gil-Su** KOR
1994	**Marius Urzica** ROM
1995	**Li Donghua** SUI
1996	**Pae Gil-Su** KOR
1997	**Valeri Belenki** GER
1999	**Alexei Nemov** RUS
2001	**Marius Urzica** ROM
2002	**Marius Urzica** ROM

RINGS

1983	**Dmitri Bilozerchev** URS
	Koji Gushiken JPN
1985	**Li Ning** CHN/**Korolev** URS
1987	**Yuri Korolev** URS
1989	**Andreas Aguilar** FRA
1991	**Grigori Misutin** URS
1993	**Yuri Chechi** ITA
1994	**Yuri Chechi** ITA
1995	**Yuri Chechi** ITA
1996	**Yuri Chechi** ITA

1997	**Yuri Chechi** ITA
1999	**Dong Zhen** CHN
2001	**Jordan Jovtchev** BUL
2002	**Szilveszter Csollany** HUN

VAULT

1983	**Artur Akopian** URS
1985	**Tong Fei** CHN
1987	**S Kroll** GDR/**Lou Yun** CHN
1989	**Jörg Behrendt** GDR
1991	**Yu Ok-Yul** KOR
1993	**Vitaly Scherbo** BLR
1994	**Vitaly Scherbo** BLR
1995	**Alexei Nemov** RUS
	Grigori Misutin RUS
1996	**Alexei Nemov** RUS
1997	**Sergei Fedorchenko** KZK
1999	**Li Xiaoping** CHN
2001	**Marian Dragulescu** ROM
2002	**Li Xiaopeng** CHN

PARALLEL BARS

1983	**Artemov** URS/**Lou** CHN
1985	**Kroll** GDR/**Mogilni** URS
1987	**Vladimir Artemov** URS
1989	**Li Jing** CHN/**Artemov** URS
1991	**Li Jing** CHN
1993	**Vitali Scherbo** BLR
1994	**Liping Huang** CHN
1995	**Vitali Scherbo** BLR
1996	**Rustam Cahripov** UKR
1997	**Zhang Jinjing** CHN
1999	**Lee Joo-Hyung** KOR
2001	**Sean Townsend** USA
2002	**Li Xiaopeng** CHN

HIGH BAR

1983	**Dmitri Bilozerchev** URS
1985	**Tong Fei** CHN
1987	**Dmitri Bilozerchev** URS
1989	**Li Chunyang** CHN
1991	**Li Chunyang** CHN
	Ralf Büchner GER
1993	**Sergei Charkov** RUS
1994	**Vitali Scherbo** BLR
1995	**Andreas Wecker** GER
1996	**Jesus Carballo** ESP
1997	**Jani Tanskanen** FIN
1999	**Jesus Caballo** ESP
2001	**Vlasios Maras** GRE
2002	**Vlasios Maras** GRE

TEAM

1983	**China**
1985	**Soviet Union**
1987	**Soviet Union**
1989	**Soviet Union**
1991	**Soviet Union**
1993	no competition
1994	**China**
1995	**China**
1996	no competition

1997	**China**
1999	**China**
2001	**Belarus**

Women

ALL-AROUND

1983	**Natalia Yurchenko** URS
1985	**Oksana Omelianchik** URS
	Yelena Sushnova URS
1987	**Aurelia Dobre** ROM
1989	**S'lana Boguinskaya** URS
1991	**Kim Zmeskal** USA
1993	**Shannon Miller** USA
1994	**Shannon Miller** USA
1995	**Lilia Podkopayeva** UKR
1997	**Svetlana Khorkina** RUS
1999	**Maria Olaru** ROM
2001	**Svetlana Khorkina** RUS

VAULT

1983	**Boriana Stoyanova** BUL
1985	**Yelena Sushnova** URS
1987	**Yelena Sushnova** URS
1989	**Olessia Dudnik** URS
1991	**Lavinia Milosovici** ROM
1993	**Yelena Puskin** BLR
1994	**Gina Gogean** ROM
1995	**Lilia Podkopayeva** UKR
	Simona Amanar ROM
1996	**Gina Gogean** ROM
1997	**Simona Amanar** ROM
1999	**E Zamolodchikova** RUS
2001	**Svetlana Khorkina** RUS
2002	**E Zamolodchikova** RUS

UNEVEN BARS

1983	**Maxi Gnauck** GDR
1985	**Gabriela Fahnrich** GDR
1987	**Daniela Silivas** ROM
	D Thümmler GDR
1989	**Fan Di** CHN
	Daniela Silivas ROM
1991	**Kim Gwang-suk** KOR
1993	**Shannon Miller** USA
1994	**Li Luo** CHN
1995	**Svetlana Khorkina** RUS
1996	**Svetlana Khorkina** RUS
	Yelena Piskun BLR
1997	**Svetlana Khorkina** RUS
1999	**Svetlana Khorkina** RUS
2001	**Svetlana Khorkina** RUS
2002	**Courtney Kupets** USA

GYMNASTICS

BEAM
1983 **Olga Mostepanova** URS
1985 **Daniela Silivas** ROM
1987 **Aurelia Dobre** ROM
1989 **Daniela Silivas** ROM
1991 **S'lana Boguinskaya** URS
1993 **Lavinia Milosovici** ROM
1994 **Shannon Miller** USA
1995 **Mo Huilan** CHN
1996 **Dina Kochetkova** RUS
1997 **Gina Gogean** ROM
1999 **Ling Jie** CHN
2001 **Andreea Raducan** ROM
2002 **Ashley Postell** USA

FLOOR
1983 **Ekaterina Szabo** ROM
1985 **Oksana Omelianchik** URS
1987 **Yelena Sushnova** URS
     Daniela Silivas ROM
1989 **Daniela Silivas** ROM
     S'lana Boguinskaya URS
1991 **Bontas** ROM
     Chusovitina URS
1993 **Shannon Miller** USA
1994 **Dina Kochetkova** RUS
1995 **Gina Gogean** ROM
1996 **Gina Gogean** ROM
     Kui Yuanyuan CHN
1997 **Gina Gogean** ROM
1999 **Andreea Raducan** ROM
2001 **Andreea Raducan** ROM
2002 **Elena Gomez** ESP

TEAM
1983 **Soviet Union**
1985 **Soviet Union**
1987 **Romania**
1989 **Soviet Union**
1991 **Soviet Union**
1993 no competition
1994 **Romania**
1995 **Romania**
1996 no competition
1997 **Romania**
1999 **Romania**
2001 **Romania**

HOCKEY

WORLD CUP

	Men		Women
1971	Pakistan	1974	Netherlands
1973	Netherlands	1976	West Germany
1975	India	1978	Netherlands
1978	Pakistan	1981	West Germany
1982	Pakistan	1983	Netherlands
1986	Australia	1986	Netherlands
1990	Netherlands	1990	Netherlands
1994	Pakistan	1994	Australia
1998	Netherlands	1998	Australia
2002	Germany	2002	Argentina

EUROPEAN CUP

	Men	Women
1970	West Germany	-
1974	Spain	-
1978	West Germany	-
1983	Netherlands	Netherlands (1984)
1987	Netherlands	Netherlands
1991	Germany	England
1995	Germany	Netherlands
1999	Germany	Netherlands

CHAMPIONS TROPHY

	Men	Women
1978	Pakistan	-
1980	Pakistan	-
1981	Netherlands	-
1982	Netherlands	-
1983	Australia	-
1984	Australia	-
1985	Australia	-
1986	West Germany	-
1987	West Germany	Netherlands
1988	West Germany	-
1989	Australia	South Korea
1990	Australia	-
1991	Germany	Australia
1992	Germany	-
1993	Australia	Australia
1994	Pakistan	
1995	Germany	Australia
1996	Netherlands	
1997	Germany	Australia
1998	Netherlands	
1999	Australia	Australia
2000	Netherlands	Netherlands
2001	Germany	Argentina
2002	Netherlands	China

EUROPEAN CLUB CHAMPIONS CUP

MEN

1969-70	Club Egara de Terrasa ESP
1971-75	Frankfurt 1880 FRG
1976-78	Southgate ENG
1979	Klein Zwitserland NED
1980	Slough ENG
1981	Klein Zwitserland NED
1982-83	Dynamo Alma-Ata URS
1984	TG 1846 Frankental FRG

1985	Atletico Terrasa ESP
1986	Kampong, Utrecht NED
1987	Bloemendaal NED
1988-95	Uhlenhorst Mülheim FRG
1996	SV Kampong NED
1997	HGC Wasenaar NED
1998	Athletic Terrassa ESP
1999	's-Hertogenbosch NED
2000	Club an der Alster GER
2001	Bloemendaal NED
2002	Der Alster GER

WOMEN

1974	Harvestehuder, Hamburg FRG
1976-82	Amsterdam NED
1983-87	HGC Wassenaar NED
1988-90	Amsterdam NED
1991	HGC Wassenaar NED
1992	Amsterdam NED
1993	Russelsheimer GER
1994	HGC Wassenaar NED
1995-96	S V Kampong NED
1997	Berliner GER
1998	Russelsheimer GER
1999	Rott Weiss GER
2000	's Hertogenbosch NED
2001	's Hertogenbosch NED
2002	's Hertogenbosch NED

NATIONAL LEAGUE

	Men	Women
1989	Southgate	-
1990	Hounslow	Slough
1991	Havant	Slough
1992	Havant	Slough
1993	Hounslow	Ipswich
1994	Havant	Leicester
1995	Teddington	Slough
1996	Cannock	Hightown
1997	Reading	Slough
1998	Cannock	Slough
1999	Cannock	Slough
2000	Cannock	Hightown
2001	Surbiton	Slough
2002	Reading	Slough

HOCKEY

NATIONAL CUP

Year	Winner	Runner-up
1972-3	Hounslow	-
1974-5	Southgate	-
1976	Nottingham	-
1977	Slough	-
1978	Guildford	-
1979	Slough	Chelmsford
1980	Slough	Norton
1981	Slough	Sutton Coldfield
1982	Southgate	Slough
1983	Neston	Slough
1984	East Grinstead	Sheffield
1985	Southgate	Ipswich
1986	Southgate	Slough
1987	Southgate	Ealing
1988	Southgate	Ealing
1989	Hounslow	Ealing
1990	Havant	Sutton Coldfield
1991	Hounslow	Sutton Coldfield
1992	Hounslow	Hightown
1993	Hounslow	Leicester
1994	Teddington	Slough
1995	Guildford	Hightown
1996	Reading	Ipswich
1997	Teddington	Hightown
1998	Cannock	Clifton
1999	Reading	Slough
2000	Reading	Clifton
2001	Guildford	Slough
2002	Cannock	Ipswich

HORSE RACING

THE DERBY

*filly

Year	Winner	Jockey
1780	Diomed	Sam Arnull
1781	Young Eclipse	Charles Hindley
1782	Assassin	Sam Arnull
1783	Saltram	Charles Hindley
1784	Sergeant	Sam Arnull
1785	Aimwell	Charles Hindley
1786	Noble	J White
1787	Sir Peter Teazle	Sam Arnull
1788	Sir Thomas	William South
1789	Skyscraper	Sam Chifney
1790	Rhadamanthus	John Arnull
1791	Eager	Matt Stephenson
1792	John Bull	Frank Buckle
1793	Waxy	Bill Clift
1794	Daedalus	Frank Buckle
1795	Spread Eagle	Anthony Wheatley
1796	Didelot	John Arnull
1797	(unnamed colt)	John Singleton
1798	Sir Harry	Sam Arnull
1799	Archduke	John Arnull
1800	Champion	Bill Clift
1801	Eleanor*	John Saunders
1802	Tyrant	Frank Buckle
1803	Ditto	Bill Clift
1804	Hannibal	Bill Arnull
1805	Cardinal Beaufort	Denni Fitzpatrick
1806	Paris	John Shepherd
1807	Election	John Arnull
1808	Pan	Frank Collinson
1809	Pope	Tom Goodison
1810	Whalebone	Bill Clift
1811	Phantom	Frank Buckle
1812	Octavius	Bill Arnull
1813	Smolensko	Tom Goodison
1814	Blucher	Bill Arnull
1815	Whisker	Tom Goodison
1816	Prince Leopold	Will Wheatley
1817	Azor	Jem Robinson
1818	Sam	Sam Chifney jr
1819	Tiresias	Bill Clift
1820	Sailor	Sam Chifney jr
1821	Gustavus	Sam Day
1822	Moses	Tom Goodison
1823	Emilius	Frank Buckle
1824	Cedric	Jem Robinson
1825	Middleton	Jem Robinson
1826	Lapdog	George Dockeray
1827	Mameluke	Jem Robinson
1828	Cadland	Jem Robinson
1829	Frederick	John Forth
1830	Priam	Sam Day
1831	Spaniel	WillWheatley
1832	St Giles	Bill Scott
1833	Dangerous	Jem Chapple
1834	Plenipotentiary	Patrick Conolly
1835	Mundig	Bill Scott
1836	Bay Middleton	Jem Robinson
1837	Phosphorus	George Edwards
1838	Amato	Jim Chapple
1839	Bloomsbury	Sim Templeman
1840	Little Wonder	William MacDonald
1841	Coronation	Patrick Conolly
1842	Attila	Bill Scott
1843	Cotherstone	Bill Scott
1844	Orlando	Nat Flatman
1845	Merry Monarch	Foster Bell
1846	Pyrrhus the First	Sam Day
1847	Cossack	Sim Templeman
1848	Surplice	Sim Templeman
1849	The Flying Dutchman	Charlie Marlow
1850	Voltigeur	Job Marson
1851	Teddington	Job Marson
1852	Daniel O'Rourke	Frank Butler
1853	West Australian	Frank Butler
1854	Andover	Alfred Day
1855	Wild Dayrell	Robert Sherwood
1856	Ellington	Tom Aldcroft
1857	Blink Bonny*	Jack Charlton
1858	Beadsman	John Wells
1859	Musjid	John Wells
1860	Thormanby	Harry Custance
1861	Kettledrum	Ralph Bullock
1862	Caractacus	John Parsons
1863	Macaroni	Tom Challoner
1864	Blair Athol	Jim Snowden
1865	Gladiateur	Harry Grimshaw
1866	Lord Lyon	Harry Custance
1867	Hermit	John Daley
1868	Blue Gown	John Wells
1869	Pretender	John Osborne
1870	Kingcraft	Tom French
1871	Favonius	Tom French
1872	Cremorne	Charlie Maidment
1873	Doncaster	Fred Webb
1874	George Freder'k	Harry Custance
1875	Galopin	Jack Morris
1876	Kisber	Charlie Maidment
1877	Silvio	Fred Archer
1878	Sefton	Harry Constable
1879	Sir Bevys	George Fordham
1880	Bend Or	Fred Archer
1881	Iroquois	Fred Archer
1882	Shotover*	Tom Cannon
1883	St Blaise	Charlie Wood
1884	St Gatien	Charlie Wood
	Harvester d/h	Sam Loates
1885	Melton	Fred Archer
1886	Ormonde	Fred Archer
1887	Merry Hampton	Jack Watts
1888	Ayrshire	Fred Barrett
1889	Donovan	Tommy Loates
1890	Sainfoin	Jack Watts
1891	Common	George Barrett
1892	Sir Hugo	Fred Allsopp
1893	Isinglass	Tommy Loates
1894	Ladas	Jack Watts
1895	Sir Visto	Sam Loates

HORSE RACING

Year	Winner	Jockey
1896	Persimmon	Jack Watts
1897	Galtee More	Charlie Wood
1898	Jeddah	Otto Madden
1899	Flying Fox	Morny Cannon
1900	Diamond Jubilee	Herbert Jones
1901	Volodyovski	Lester Reiff
1902	Ard Patrick	Skeets Martin
1903	Rock Sand	Danny Maher
1904	St Amant	Kempton Cannon
1905	Cicero	Danny Maher
1906	Spearmint	Danny Maher
1907	Orby	Johnny Reiff
1908	Signorinetta*	Billy Bullock
1909	Minoru	Herbert Jones
1910	Lemberg	Bernard Dillon
1911	Sunstar	George Stern
1912	Tagalie*	Johnny Reiff
1913	Aboyeur	Edwin Piper
1914	Durbar II	Matt MacGee
1915	Pommern	Steve Donoghue
1916	Fifinella*	Joe Childs
1917	Gay Crusader	Steve Donaghue
1918	Gainsborough	Joe Childs
1919	Grand Parade	Fred Templeman
1920	Spion Kop	Frank O'Neill
1921	Humorist	Steve Donoghue
1922	Captain Cuttle	Steve Donoghue
1923	Papyrus	Steve Donoghue
1924	Sansovino	Tommy Weston
1925	Manna	Steve Donoghue
1926	Coronach	Joe Childs
1927	Call Boy	Charlie Elliott
1928	Fellstead	Harry Wragg
1929	Trigo	Joe Marshall
1930	Blenheim	Harry Wragg
1931	Cameronian	Freddie Fox
1932	April the Fifth	Fred Lane
1933	Hyperion	Tommy Weston
1934	Windsor Lad	Charlie Smirke
1935	Bahram	Freddie Fox
1936	Mahmoud	Charlie Smirke
1937	Mid-day Sun	Michael Beary
1938	Bois Roussel	Charlie Elliott
1939	Blue Peter	Eph Smith
1940	Pont l'Eveque	Sam Wragg
1941	Owen Tudor	Billy Nevett
1942	Watling Street	Harry Wragg
1943	Straight Deal	Tommy Carey
1944	Ocean Swell	Billy Nevett
1945	Dante	Billy Nevett
1946	Airborne	Tommy Lowrey
1947	Pearl Diver	George Bridgland
1948	My Love	Rae Johnstone
1949	Nimbus	Charlie Elliott
1950	Galcador	Rae Johnstone
1951	Arctic Prince	Charlie Spares
1952	Tulyar	Charlie Smirke
1953	Pinza	Gordon Richards
1954	Never Say Die	Lester Piggott
1955	Phil Drake	Freddie Palmer
1956	Lavandin	Rae Johnstone
1957	Crepello	Lester Piggott
1958	Hard Ridden	Charlie Smirke
1959	Parthia	Harry Carr
1960	St Paddy	Lester Piggott
1961	Psidium	Roger Poincelet
1962	Larkspur	Neville Sellwood
1963	Relko	Yves St-Martin
1964	Santa Claus	Scobie Breasley
1965	Sea Bird II	Pat Glennon
1966	Charlottown	Scobie Breasley
1967	Royal Palace	George Moore
1968	Sir Ivor	Lester Piggott
1969	Blakeney	Ernie Johnson
1970	Nijinsky	Lester Piggott
1971	Mill Reef	Geoff Lewis
1972	Roberto	Lester Piggott
1973	Morston	Eddie Hide
1974	Snow Knight	Brian Taylor
1975	Grundy	Pat Eddery
1976	Empery	Lester Piggott
1977	The Minstrel	Lester Piggott
1978	Shirley Heights	Greville Starkey
1979	Troy	Willie Carson
1980	Henbit	Willie Carson
1981	Shergar	Walter Swinburn
1982	Golden Fleece	Pat Eddery
1983	Teenoso	Lester Piggott
1984	Secreto	Christy Roche
1985	Slip Anchor	Steve Cauthen
1986	Shahrastani	Walter Swinburn
1987	Reference Point	Steve Cauthen
1988	Kahyasi	Ray Cochrane
1989	Nashwan	Willie Carson
1990	Quest For Fame	Pat Eddery
1991	Generous	Alan Munro
1992	Dr Devious	John Reid
1993	Commander in Chief	Mick Kinane
1994	Erhaab	Willie Carson
1995	Lammtarra	Water Swinburn
1996	Shaamit	Michael Hills
1997	Benny The Dip	Willie Ryan
1998	High-Rise	Olivier Peslier
1999	Oath	Kieren Fallon
2000	Sinndar	Johnny Murtagh
2001	Galileo	Mick Kinane
2002	High Chaparral	Johnny Murtagh

1000 GUINEAS

(since 1950)

Year	Winner	Jockey
1950	Camaree	Rae Johnstone
1951	Belle Of All	Gordon Richards
1952	Zabara	Ken Gethin
1953	Happy Laughter	Manny Mercer
1954	Festoon	Scobie Beasley
1955	Meld	Harry Carr
1956	Honeylight	Edgar Britt
1957	Rose Royal II	Charlie Smirke
1958	Bella Paola	Serge Boullenger
1959	Petite Etoile	Doug Smith

Year	Winner	Jockey
1960	Never Too Late	Roger Poincelet
1961	Sweet Solera	Bill Rickaby
1962	Abermaid	Bill Williamson
1963	Hula Dancer	Roger Poincelet
1964	Pourparler	Garnie Bougoure
1965	Night Off	Bill Williamson
1966	Glad Rags	Paul Cook
1967	Fleet	George Moore
1968	Caergwrle	Sandy Barclay
1969	Full Dress II	Ron Hutchinson
1970	Humble Duty	Lester Piggott
1971	Altesse Royale	Yves St-Martin
1972	Waterloo	Eddie Hide
1973	Mysterious	Geoff Lewis
1974	Highclere	Joe Mercer
1975	Nocturnal Spree	Johnny Roe
1976	Flying Water	Yves St-Martin
1977	Mrs McArdy	Eddie Hide
1978	Enstone Spark	Ernie Johnson
1979	One in a Million	Joe Mercer
1980	Quick As Lightning	Brian Rouse
1981	Fairy Footsteps	Lester Piggott
1982	On The House	John Reid
1983	Ma Biche	Freddie Head
1984	Pebbles	Philip Robinson
1985	Oh So Sharp	Steve Cauthen
1986	Midway Lady	Ray Cochrane
1987	Miesque	Freddie Head
1988	Ravinella	George Moore
1989	Musical Bliss	Walter Swinburn
1990	Salsabil	Willie Carson
1991	Shadayid	Willie Carson
1992	Hatoof	Walter Swinburn
1993	Sayyedati	Walter Swinburn
1994	Las Meninas	John Reid
1995	Harayir	Richard Hills
1996	Bosra Sham	Pat Eddery
1997	Sleepytime	Kieren Fallon
1998	Cape Verdi	Frankie Dettori
1999	Wince	Kieren Fallon
2000	Lahan	Richard Hills
2001	Ameerat	Philip Robinson
2002	Kazzia	Frankie Dettori

2000 GUINEAS

(since 1950)

Year	Winner	Jockey
1950	Palestine	Charlie Smirke
1951	Ki Ming	Charlie Elliott
1952	Thunderhead II	Roger Poincelet
1953	Nearula	Edgar Britt
1954	Darius	Manny Mercer
1955	Our Babu	Doug Smith
1956	Gilles De Retz	Frank Barlow
1957	Crepello	Lester Piggott
1958	Pall Mall	Doug Smith
1959	Taboun	George Moore
1960	Martial	Ron Hutchinson
1961	Rockavon	Norman Stirk
1962	Privy Councillor	Bill Rickaby

Year	Winner	Jockey
1963	Only For Life	Jimmy Lindley
1964	Baldric II	Bill Pyers
1965	Niksar	Duncan Keith
1966	Kashmir II	Jimmy Lindley
1967	Royal Palace	George Moore
1968	Sir Ivor	Lester Piggott
1969	Right Tack	Geoff Lewis
1970	Nijinsky	Lester Piggott
1971	Brigadier Gerard	Joe Mercer
1972	High Top	Willie Carson
1973	Mon Fils	Frankie Durr
1974	Nonoalco	Yves St-Martin
1975	Bolkonski	Gianfranco Dettori
1976	Wollow	Gianfranco Dettori
1977	Nebbiolo	Gabriel Curran
1978	Roland Gardens	Frankie Durr
1979	Tap On Wood	Steve Cauthen
1980	Known Fact	Willie Carson
1981	To-Agori-Mou	Greville Starkey
1982	Zino	Freddie Head
1983	Lomond	Pat Eddery
1984	El Gran Senor	Pat Eddery
1985	Shadeed	Lester Piggott
1986	Dancing Brave	Greville Starkey
1987	Don't Forget Me	Willie Carson
1988	Doyoun	Walter Swinburn
1989	Nashwan	Willie Carson
1990	Tirol	Mick Kinane
1991	Mystiko	Michael Roberts
1992	Rodrigo de Triano	Lester Piggott
1993	Zafonic	Pat Eddery
1994	Mister Baileys	Jason Weaver
1995	Pennekamp	Thierry Jarnet
1996	Mark Of Esteem	Frankie Dettori
1997	Entrepreneur	Mick Kinane
1998	King Of Kings	Mick Kinane
1999	Island Sands	Frankie Dettori
2000	King's Best	Kieren Fallon
2001	Golan	Kieren Fallon
2002	Rock Of Gibraltar	Johnny Murtagh

THE OAKS

(Since 1950)

Year	Winner	Jockey
1950	Asmena	Rae Johnstone
1951	Neasham Belle	Stan Clayton
1952	Frieze	Edgar Britt
1953	Ambiguity	Joe Mercer
1954	Sun Cap	Rae Johnstone
1955	Meld	Harry Carr
1956	Sicarelle	Freddie Palmer
1957	Carrozza	Lester Piggott
1958	Bella Paola	Max Garcia
1959	Petite Etoile	Lester Piggott
1960	Never Too Late	Roger Poincelet
1961	Sweet Solera	Bill Rickaby
1962	Monade	Yves St-Martin
1963	Noblesse	Garnie Bougoure
1964	Homeward Bound	Greville Starkey
1965	Long Look	Jack Purtell
1966	Valoris	Lester Piggott

HORSE RACING

Year	Winner	Jockey
1967	Pia	Eddie Hide
1968	La Lagune	Gerard Thiboeuf
1969	Sleeping Partner	John Gorton
1970	Lupe	Sandy Barclay
1971	Altesse Royale	Geoff Lewis
1972	Ginevra	Tony Murray
1973	Mysterious	Geoff Lewis
1974	Polygamy	Pat Eddery
1975	Juliette Marny	Lester Piggott
1976	Pawneese	Yves St-Martin
1977	Dunfermline	Willie Carson
1978	Fair Salinia	Greville Starkey
1979	Scintillate	Pat Eddery
1980	Bireme	Willie Carson
1981	Blue Wind	Lester Piggott
1982	Time Charter	Billy Newnes
1983	Sun Princess	Willie Carson
1984	Circus Plume	Lester Piggott
1985	Oh So Sharp	Steve Cauthen
1986	Midway Lady	Ray Cochrane
1987	Unite	Walter Swinburn
1988	Diminuendo	Steve Cauthen
1989*	Snow Bride	Steve Cauthen
1990	Salsabil	Willie Carson
1991	Jet Ski Lady	Christy Roche
1992	User Friendly	George Duffield
1993	Intrepidity	Michael Roberts
1994	Balanchine	Frankie Dettori
1995	Moonshell	Frankie Dettori
1996	Lady Carla	Pat Eddery
1997	Reams Of Verse	Kieren Fallon
1998	Shahtoush	Mick Kinane
1999	Ramruna	Kieren Fallon
2000	Love Divine	Richard Quinn
2001	Imagine	Mick Kinane
2002	Kazzia	Frankie Dettori

* Aliysa (Walter Swinburn) won, but was disq after a drugs test

1969	Intermezo	Ron Hutchinson
1970	Nijinsky	Lester Piggott
1971	Athens Wood	Lester Piggott
1972	Boucher	Lester Piggott
1973	Peleid	Frankie Durr
1974	Bustino	Joe Mercer
1975	Bruni	Tony Murray
1976	Crow	Yves St-Martin
1977	Dunfermline*	Willie Carson
1978	Julio Mariner	Eddie Hide
1979	Son of Love	Alain Lequeux
1980	Light Cavalry	Joe Mercer
1981	Cut Above	Joe Mercer
1982	Touching Wood	Paul Cook
1983	Sun Princess*	Willie Carson
1984	Commanche Run	Lester Piggott
1985	Oh So Sharp*	Steve Cauthen
1986	Moon Madness	Pat Eddery
1987	Reference Point	Steve Cauthen
1988	Minster Son	Willie Carson
1989	Michelozo	Steve Cauthen
1990	Snurge	Richard Quinn
1991	Toulon	Pat Eddery
1992	User Friendly*	George Duffield
1993	Bob's Return	Philip Robinson
1994	Moonax	Pat Eddery
1995	Classic Cliche	Frankie Dettori
1996	Shantou	Frankie Dettori
1997	Silver Patriarch	Pat Eddery
1998	Nedawi	John Reid
1999	Mutafaweq	Frankie Dettori
2000	Millenary	Richard Quinn
2001	Milan	Mick Kinane
2002	Bollin Eric	Kevin Darley

ST LEGER
(since 1950)

Year	Winner	Jockey
1950	Scratch II	Rae Johnstone
1951	Talma II	Rae Johnstone
1952	Tulyar	Charlie Smirke
1953	Premonition	Eph Smith
1954	Never Say Die	Charlie Smirke
1955	Meld*	Harry Carr
1956	Cambremer	Freddie Palmer
1957	Ballymoss	Tommy Burns
1958	Alcide	Harry Carr
1959	Cantelo*	Eddie Hide
1960	St Paddy	Lester Piggott
1961	Aurelius	Lester Piggott
1962	Hethersett	Harry Carr
1963	Ragusa	Garnie Bougoure
1964	Indiana	Jimmy Lindley
1965	Provoke	Joe Mercer
1966	Sodium	Frankie Durr
1967	Ribocco	Lester Piggott
1968	Ribero	Lester Piggott

GRAND NATIONAL

Year	Winnner	Jockey
1836	The Duke	N/A
1837	The Duke	Mr Potts*
1838	Sir William	T Oliver
1839	Lottery	J Mason
1840	Jerry	Brethertorf
1841	Charity	H Powell
1842	Gay Lad	T Oliver
1843	Vanguard	T Oliver
1844	Discount	Crickmere
1845	Cureall	B Loft
1846	Pioneer	W Taylor
1847	Matthew	D Wynne
1848	Chandler	J Little*
1849	Peter Simple	Cunn'ham
1850	Abd-el-Kader	C Green
1851	Abd-el-Kader	T Abbott
1852	Miss Mowbray	Goodman'
1853	Peter Simple	T Oliver
1854	Bourton	J Tasker
1855	Wanderer	J Hanlon
1856	Freetrader	G Stevens
1857	Emigrant	C Boyce
1858	Little Charley	W Archer
1859	Half Caste	C Green
1860	Anatis	Pickernell*
1861	Jealousy	J Kendall
1862	Huntsman	Lamplugh
1863	Emblem	G Stevens
1864	Emblematic	G Stevens
1865	Alcibiade	Coventry*
1866	Salamander	Goodman'
1867	Cortolvin	J Page
1868	The Lamb	G Ede*
1869	The Colonel	G Stevens
1870	The Colonel	G Stevens
1871	The Lamb	Pickernell*
1872	Casse Tete	J Page
1873	Disturbance	Rich'dson*
1874	Reugny	Rich'dson*
1875	Pathfinder	Pickernell*
1876	Regal	J Cannon
1877	Austerlitz	F Hobson*
1878	Shifnal	J Jones
1879	The Liberator	G More*
1880	Empress	T Beasley*
1881	Woodbrook	T Beasley*
1882	Seaman	Manners*
1883	Zoedone	G Kinsky*
1884	Voluptuary	T Wilson*
1885	Roquefort	T Wilson*
1886	Old Joe	T Skelton
1887	Gamecock	B Daniels
1888	Playfair	Mawson
1889	Frigate	T Beasley*
1890	Ilex	Night'gall
1891	Come Away	HBeasley*
1892	Father O'Flynn	R Owen*
1893	Cloister	B Dollery
1894	Why Not	Night'gall
1895	Wild Man from Borneo	J Widger*
1896	The Soarer	Campbell*
1897	Manifesto	Kavanagh
1898	Drogheda	J Gourley
1899	Manifesto	Will'mson
1900	Ambush II	Anthony
1901	Grudon	Night'gall
1902	Shannon Lass	D Read
1903	Drumcree	Woodland
1904	Moifaa	A'Birch
1905	Kirkland	T Mason
1906	Ascetic's Silver	Hastings*
1907	Eremon	A Newey
1908	Rubio	H Bletsoe
1909	Lutteurill	Parfrement
1910	Jenkinstown	Chadwick
1911	Glenside	Anthony*
1912	Jerry M	E Piggott
1913	Covertcoat	Woodland
1914	Sunloch	W Smith
1915	Ally Sloper	JAnthony*
1916	Vermouth	J Reardon
1917	Ballymacad	T Driscoll
1918	Poethlyn	E Piggott
1919	Poethlyn	E Piggott
1920	Troytown	JAnthony*
1921	Shaun Spadah	D Rees
1922	Music Hall	B Rees
1923	Sergeant Murphy	T Bennett*
1924	Master Robert	B Trudgill
1925	Double Chance	J Wilson*
1926	Jack Horner	Watkinson
1927	Sprig	T Leader
1928	Tipperary Tim	B Dutton*
1929	Gregalach	B Everett
1930	Shaun Goilin	Cullinan
1931	Grakle	B Lyall
1932	Forbra	J Hamey
1933	Kellsboro' Jack	Williams
1934	Golden Miller	G Wilson
1935	Reynoldstown	F Furlong*
1936	Reynoldstown	F Walwyn*
1937	Royal Mail	Williams
1938	Battleship	B Hobbs
1939	Workman	T Hyde
1940	Bogskar	M Jones
1946	Lovely Cottage	B Petre*
1947	Caughoo	Dempsey
1948	Sheila's Cottage	Thompson
1949	Russian Hero	McMorrow
1950	Freebooter	J Power
1951	Nickel Coin	J Bullock
1952	Teal	Thompson
1953	Early Mist	B Marshall
1954	Royal Tan	B Marshall
1955	Quare Times	P Taaffe
1956	E.S.B.	D Dick
1957	Sundew	F Winter
1958	Mr. What	Freeman
1959	Oxo	Scudamore
1960	Merryman II	G Scott
1961	Nicolaus Silver	B Beasley
1962	Kilmore	F Winter
1963	Ayala	P Buckley
1964	Team Spirit	Robinson
1965	Jay Trump	T Smith*
1966	Anglo	T Norman
1967	Foinavon	Buck'ham
1968	Red Alligator	B Fletcher
1969	Highland Wedding	E Harty
1970	Gay Trip	P Taaffe
1971	Specify	J Cook
1972	Well To Do	G Thorner
1973	Red Rum	B Fletcher
1974	Red Rum	B Fletcher
1975	L'Escargot	Carberry
1976	Rag Trade	J Burke
1977	Red Rum	T Stack
1978	Lucius	B Davies
1979	Rubstic	M Barnes
1980	Ben Nevis	Fenwick*
1981	Aldaniti	Champion
1982	Grittar	Saunders*
1983	Corbiere	B De Haan
1984	Hallo Dandy	Doughty
1985	Last Suspect	H Davies
1986	West Tip	Dunwoody
1987	Maori Venture	S Knight
1988	Rhyme'N Reason	B Powell
1989	Little Polveir	J Frost
1990	Mr Frisk	Armytage*
1991	Seagram	N Hawke
1992	Party Politics	Llewellyn
1993	Not Run**	
1994	Miinnehoma	Dunwoody
1995	Royal Athlete	J Titley
1996	Rough Quest	Fitzgerald
1997	Lord Gyllene	A Dobbin
1998	Earth Summit	Llewellyn
1999	Bobbyjo	P Carberry
2000	Papillon	R Walsh
2001	Red Marauder	R Guest
2002	Bindaree	J Culloty

* amateur jockey

** false start, but many continued to race. Esha Ness won; the race subsequently declared void.

ICE HOCKEY

WORLD CHAMPIONS

Year	Winner	Runner-up
1920	Canada	USA
1924	Canada	USA
1928	Canada	Sweden
1930	Canada	Germany
1931	Canada	USA
1932	Canada	USA
1933	USA	Canada
1934	Canada	USA
1935	Canada	Switzerland
1936	Great Britain	Canada
1937	Canada	Gt Britain
1938	Canada	Gt Britain
1939	Canada	USA
1947	Czechoslov'a	Sweden
1948	Canada	Czech'kia
1949	Czechoslov'a	Canada
1950	Canada	USA
1951	Canada	Sweden
1952	Canada	USA
1953	Sweden	WGermany
1954	Soviet Union	Canada
1955	Canada	USSR
1956	Soviet Union	USA
1957	Sweden	USSR
1958	Canada	USSR
1959	Canada	USSR
1960	USA	Canada
1961	Canada	Czech'kia
1962	Sweden	Canada
1963	Soviet Union	Sweden
1964	Soviet Union	Sweden
1965	Soviet Union	Czech'kia
1966	Soviet Union	Czech'kia
1967	Soviet Union	Sweden
1968	Soviet Union	Czech'kia
1969	Soviet Union	Sweden
1970	Soviet Union	Sweden
1971	Soviet Union	Czech'kia
1972	Czechoslov'a	USSR
1973	Soviet Union	Sweden
1974	Soviet Union	Czech'kia
1975	Soviet Union	Czech'kia
1976	Czechoslov'a	USSR
1977	Czechoslov'a	Sweden
1978	Soviet Union	Czech'kia
1979	Soviet Union	Czech'kia
1981	Soviet Union	Sweden
1982	Soviet Union	Czech'kia
1983	Soviet Union	Czech'kia
1985	Czechoslov'a	Canada
1986	Soviet Union	Sweden
1987	Sweden	USSR
1989	Soviet Union	Canada
1990	Soviet Union	Sweden
1991	Sweden	Canada
1992	Sweden	Finland
1993	Russia	Sweden
1994	Canada	Finland
1995	Finland	Sweden
1996	Czech Rep	Canada
1997	Canada	Sweden
1998	Sweden	Finland
1999	Czech Rep	Finland
2000	Czech Rep	Slovakia
2001	Czech Rep	Finland
2002	Slovakia	Russia

STANLEY CUP

Year	Winner
1939-40	New York Rangers
1940-41	Boston Bruins
1941-42	Toronto Maple Leafs
1942-43	Detroit Red Wings
1943-44	Montreal Canadiens
1944-45	Toronto Maple Leafs
1945-46	Montreal Canadiens
1946-47	Toronto Maple Leafs
1947-48	Toronto Maple Leafs
1948-49	Toronto Maple Leafs
1949-50	Detroit Red Wings
1950-51	Toronto Maple Leafs
1951-52	Detroit Red Wings
1952-53	Montreal Canadiens
1953-54	Detroit Red Wings
1954-55	Detroit Red Wings
1955-56	Montreal Canadiens
1956-57	Montreal Canadiens
1957-58	Montreal Canadiens
1958-59	Montreal Canadiens
1959-60	Montreal Canadiens
1960-61	Chicago Blackhawks
1961-62	Toronto Maple Leafs
1962-63	Toronto Maple Leafs
1963-64	Toronto Maple Leafs
1964-65	Montreal Canadiens
1965-66	Montreal Canadiens
1966-67	Toronto Maple Leafs
1967-68	Montreal Canadiens
1968-69	Montreal Canadiens
1969-70	Boston Bruins
1970-71	Montreal Canadiens
1971-72	Boston Bruins
1972-73	Montreal Canadiens
1973-74	Philadelphia Flyers
1974-75	Philadelphia Flyers
1975-76	Montreal Canadiens
1976-77	Montreal Canadiens
1977-78	Montreal Canadiens
1978-79	Montreal Canadiens
1979-80	New York Islanders
1980-81	New York Islanders
1981-82	New York Islanders
1982-83	New York Islanders
1983-84	Edmonton Oilers
1984-85	Edmonton Oilers
1985-86	Montreal Canadiens
1986-87	Edmonton Oilers
1987-88	Edmonton Oilers
1988-89	Calgary Flames
1989-90	Edmonton Oilers
1990-91	Pittsburgh Penguins
1991-92	Pittsburgh Penguins
1992-93	Montreal Canadiens
1993-94	New York Rangers
1994-95	New Jersey Devils
1995-96	Colorado Avalanche
1996-97	Detroit Red Wings
1997-98	Detroit Red Wings
1998-99	Dallas Stars
1999-00	New Jersey Devils
2000-01	Colorado Avalanche
2001-02	Detroit Red Wings

ICE SKATING

WORLD CHAMPIONS

	Men	Women	Pairs	Ice Dancing
1886	G Fuchs GER	-	-	-
1887	G Hügel AUT	-	-	-
1898	H Grenander SWE	-	-	-
1899	G Hügel AUT	-	-	-
1900	G Hügel AUT	-	-	-
1901-05	U Salchow SWE	-	-	-
1906	G Fuchs GER	M Syers GBR	-	-
1907	U Salchow SWE	M Syers GBR	-	-
1908	U Salchow SWE	L Kronberger HUN	Hübler/Berger GER	-
1909	U Salchow SWE	L Kronberger HUN	Johnson/Johnson GBR	-
1910	U Salchow SWE	L Kronberger HUN	Hübler/Burger GER	-
1911	U Salchow SWE	L Kronberger HUN	Eilers/Jakobsson FIN	-
1912	F Kachler AUT	O M Horvath HUN	Johnson/Johnson GBR	-
1913	F Kachler AUT	O M Horvath HUN	Englemann/Mejstrick AUT	-
1914	G Sandahl SWE	O M Horvath HUN	Eilers/Jakobsson FIN	-
1922	G Grafstrom SWE	H Planck AUT	Engelmann/Berger AUT	-
1923	F Kachler AUT	H Planck AUT	Jakobsson/Jakobsson FIN	-
1924	G Grafstrom SWE	H Planck AUT	Englenmann/Berger AUT	-
1925	W Böckl AUT	H Jaross AUT	Jaross/Wrede AUT	-
1926	W Böckl AUT	H Jaross AUT	Joly/Brunet FRA	-
1927	W Böckl AUT	S Henie NOR	Jaross/Wrede AUT	-
1928	W Böckl AUT	S Henie NOR	Joly/Brunet FRA	-
1929	G Grafstrom SWE	S Henie NOR	Scholz/Kaiser AUT	-
1930	K Schäfer AUT	S Henie NOR	A Brunet/P Brunet FRA	-
1931	K Schäfer AUT	S Henie NOR	Rotter/Szollas HUN	-
1932	K Schäfer AUT	S Henie NOR	A Brunet/P Brunet FRA	-
1933	K Schäfer AUT	S Henie NOR	Rotter/Szollas HUN	-
1934	K Schäfer AUT	S Henie NOR	Rotter/Szollas HUN	-
1935	K Schäfer AUT	S Henie NOR	Rotter/Szollas HUN	-
1936	K Schäfer AUT	S Henie NOR	Herber/Baier GER	-
1937	F Kaspar AUT	C Colledge GBR	Herber/Baier GER	-
1938	F Kaspar AUT	M Taylor GBR	Herber/Baier GER	-
1939	G Sharp GBR	M Taylor GBR	Herber/Baier GER	-
1947	H Gerschwiler SUI	B Ann Scott CAN	Lannoy/Baugniet BEL	-
1948	R Button USA	B Ann Scott CAN	Lannoy/Baugniet BEL	-
1949	R Button USA	A Vrzanova TCH	Kekesy/Kiraly HUN	-
1950	R Button USA	A Vrzanova TCH	K Kennedy/P Kennedy USA	-
1951	R Button USA	J Altwegg GBR	R Falk/P Falk FRG	-
1952	R Button USA	J du Bief FRA	R Falk/P Falk FRG	Westwood/Demmy GBR
1953	H A Jenkins USA	T Albright USA	J Nicks/J Nicks GBR	Westwood/Demmy GBR
1954	H A Jenkins USA	G Busch FRG	Dafoe/Bowden CAN	Westwood/Demmy GBR
1955	H A Jenkins USA	T Albright USA	Dafoe/Bowden CAN	Westwood/Demmy GBR
1956	H A Jenkins USA	C Heiss USA	Schwarz/Oppelt AUT	Weight/Thomas GBR
1957	D Jenkins USA	C Heiss USA	Wagner/Paul CAN	Markham/Jones GBR
1958	D Jenkins USA	C Heiss USA	Wagner/Paul CAN	Markham/Jones GBR
1959	D Jenkins USA	C Heiss USA	Wagner/Paul CAN	Denny/Jones GBR
1960	A Giletti FRA	C Heiss USA	Wagner/Paul CAN	Denny/Jones GBR
1962	D Jackson CAN	S Dijkstra NED	Jelinek/Jelinek CAN	Romanova/Roman TCH
1963	D McPherson CAN	S Dijkstra NED	Kilius/Bäumler FRG	Romanova/Roman TCH
1964	Schnelidorfer FRG	S Dijkstra NED	Kilius/Bäumler FRG	Romanova/Roman TCH
1965	A Calmat FRA	P Burka CAN	Belousova/Protopopov URS	Romanova/Roman TCH
1966	E Danzer AUT	P Fleming USA	Belousova/Protopopov URS	Towler/Ford GBR
1967	E Danzer AUT	P Fleming USA	Belousova/Protopopov URS	Towler/Ford GBR
1968	E Danzer AUT	P Fleming USA	Belousova/Protopopov URS	Towler/Ford GBR
1969	T Wood USA	G Seyfert GDR	Rodnina/Ulanov URS	Towler/Ford GBR
1970	T Wood USA	G Seyfert GDR	Rodnina/Ulanov URS	Pakhomova/Gorshkov URS
1971	O Nepela TCH	B Schuba AUT	Rodnina/Ulanov URS	Pakhomova/Gorshkov URS
1972	O Nepela TCH	B Schuba AUT	Rodnina/Ulanov URS	Pakhomova/Gorshkov URS
1973	O Nepela TCH	K Magnussen CAN	Rodnina/Zaitsev URS	Pakhomova/Gorshkov URS

ICE SKATING

1974	J Hoffmann GDR	C Errath GDR	Rodnina/Zaitsev URS	Pakhomova/Gorshkov URS
1975	S Volkov URS	D De Leeuw NED	Rodnina/Zaitsev URS	Moiseyeva/Minenkov URS
1976	J Curry GBR	D Hamill USA	Rodnina/Zaitsev URS	Pakhomova/Gorshkov URS
1977	V Kovalyev URS	L Fratianne USA	Rodnina/Zaitsev URS	Moiseyeva/Minenkov URS
1978	C Tickner USA	A Potzsch GDR	Rodnina/Zaitsev URS	Linichuk/Karponosov URS
1979	V Kovalyev URS	L Fratianne USA	Babilonia/Gardner USA	Linichuk/Karponosov URS
1980	J Hoffmann GDR	A Potzsch GDR	Tcherkasova/Shakrai URS	Regoczy/Sallay HUN
1981	S Hamilton USA	D Biellmann SUI	Vorobyeva/Lissovsky URS	Torvill/Dean GBR
1982	S Hamilton USA	E Zayak USA	Baess/Theirbach GDR	Torvill/Dean GBR
1983	S Hamilton USA	R Sumners USA	Valova/Vasilyev URS	Torvill/Dean GBR
1984	S Hamilton USA	K Witt GDR	Underhill/Martini CAN	Torvill/Dean GBR
1985	A Fadeyev URS	K Witt GDR	Valova/Vasilyev URS	Bestiaminova/Bukin URS
1986	B Boitano USA	D Thomas USA	Gordyeva/Grinkov URS	Bestiaminova/Bukin URS
1987	B Orser CAN	K Witt GDR	Gordyeva/Grinkov URS	Bestiaminova/Bukin URS
1988	B Boitano USA	K Witt GDR	Valova/Vasilyev URS	Bestiaminova/Bukin URS
1989	K Browning CAN	M Ito JPN	Gordyeva/Grinkov URS	Klimova/Ponomarenko URS
1990	K Browning CAN	J Trenary USA	Gordyeva/Grinkov URS	Klimova/Ponomarenko URS
1991	K Browning CAN	K Yamaguchi JPN	Mishkutienok/Dmitryev CIS	I & P Duchesnay FRA
1992	V Petrenko UKR	K Yamaguchi JPN	Mishkutienok/Dmitryev CIS	Klimova/Ponomar'ko URS
1993	K Browning CAN	O Baiul UKR	Brasseur/Eisler CAN	Usova/Zhulin RUS
1994	Elvis Stojko CAN	Y Sato JPN	Shishkova/Naumov RUS	Gritschuk/Platov RUS
1995	Elvis Stojko CAN	Lu Chen CHN	Kovarikova/Novotny TCH	Gritschuk/Platov RUS
1996	Todd Eldredge USA	Michelle Kwan USA	Eltsova/Bouchkov RUS	Gritschuk/Platov RUS
1997	Elvis Stojko CAN	Tara Lipinski USA	Wötzel/Steuer GER	Gritschuk/Platov RUS
1998	Alexei Yagudin RUS	Michelle Kwan USA	Bereznaya/Sikhuralidze RUS	Krylova/Ovsyannikov RUS
1999	Alexei Yagudin RUS	M Butyrskaya RUS	Bereznaya/Sikhuralidze RUS	Krylova/Ovsyannikov RUS
2000	Alexei Yagudin RUS	Michelle Kwan USA	Petrova/Tikhonov RUS	Anissina/Peizerat FRA
2001	Evgeni Plushenko RUS	Michelle Kwan USA	Sale/Pelletier CAN	Fusar-Poli/Margaglio ITA
2002	Alexei Yagudin RUS	Irina Slutskaya RUS	Xue Shen/Hongbo Xiao CHN	Lobacheva/Averbukh RUS

ICE SKATING

BRITISH CHAMPIONS (FROM 1972)

Year				
1972	J Curry	M McLean	McCafferty/Taylforth	Green/Watts
1973	J Curry	J Scott	Sessions/Harrison	Green/Watts
1974	J Curry	G Keddie	McCafferty/Taylforth	Green/Watts
1975	J Curry	K Richardson	Taylforth/Taylforth	Green/Watts
1976	R Cousins	K Richardson	Lindsey/Beckwith	Thompson/Maxwell
1977	R Cousins	K Richardson	Lindsey/Beckwith	Thompson/Maxwell
1978	R Cousins	D Cottrill	Garland/Daw	Torvill/Dean
1979	R Cousins	K Richardson	Garland/Daw	Torvill/Dean
1980	C Howarth	K Wood	Garland/Daw	Torvill/Dean
1981	M Pepperday	D Cottrill	Garland/Jenkins	Torvill/Dean
1982	M Pepperday	K Wood	Garland/Jenkins	Torvill/Dean
1983	M Pepperday	S A Jackson	Garland/Jenkins	Torvill/Dean
1984	S Pickavance	S A Jackson	Cushley/Cushley	Barber/Slater
1985	S Pickavance	J Conway	Peake/Naylor	Jones/Askham
1986	P Robinson	J Conway	Peake/Naylor	Jones/Askham
1987	P Robinson	J Conway	Peake/Naylor	Jones/Askham
1988	C Newberry	J Conway	Peake/Naylor	Jones/Askham
1989	S Cousins	E Murdoch	Peake/Naylor	Burton/Place
1990	S Cousins	J Conway	Peake/Naylor	Hall/Bloomfield
1991	S Cousins	J Conway	Pritchard/Briggs	Bruce/Place
1992	S Cousins	C von Saher	Pearce/Shorten	Humphreys/Lanning
1993	S Cousins	S Main	Mednick/Briggs	Torvill/Dean
1994	S Cousins	J Arrowsmith	Rogers/Aldred	Fitzgerald/Kyle
1995	S Cousins	S Main	Rogers/Aldred	Humphreys/Askew
1996	N Wilson	J Arrowsmith	Rogers/Aldred	Humphreys/Askew
1997	S Cousins	J. Arrowsmith	Polulischenko/Seabrook	Clements/Shortland
1998	C Shorten	S Main	Polulischenko/Seabrook	Clements/Shortland
1999	N Wilson	T Sear	Kemp/Thomas	Keeble/Zalewski
2000	A Street	Z Jones	Sfikas/Seabrook	Humphreys/Baranov
2001	M Davies	Z Jones	Sfikas/Seabrook	Humphreys/Baranov

JUDO

WORLD CHAMPIONS

Men

-60kg

1979	Thierry Ray	FRA
1981	Yasuhiko Moriwaki	JPN
1983	Khazret Tletseri	URS
1985	Shinji Hosokawa	JPN
1987	Kim Jae-yup	KOR
1989	Amiran Totikashvilli	URS
1991	Tadanori Koshino	JPN
1993	Ryuki Sonoda	JPN
1995	Nikolai Ojeguine	RUS
1997	Tadahiro Nomura	JPN
1999	Manuolo Poulet	CUB
2001	Anis Lounifi	TUN

-65kg

1979	Nikolay Soludukhin	URS
1981	Katsu. Kashiwazaki	JPN
1983	Nikolay Soludukhin	URS
1985	Yuri Sokolov	URS
1987	Yosuke Yamamoto	JPN
1989	Drago Becanovic	YUG
1991	Udo Quellmalz	GER
1993	Yukimasa Nakamura	JPN
1995	Udo Quellmalz	GER
1997	Kim Hyuk	KOR

-66kg

1999	Larbi Benbouaoud	FRA
2001	Arash Miresmaeli	IRI

-71kg

1979	Kyoto Katsuki	JPN
1981	Park Chong-hak	KOR
1983	Hidetoshi Nakanishi	JPN
1985	Ahn Byeong-kuen	KOR
1987	Mike Swain	USA
1989	Toshihiko Koga	JPN
1991	Toshihiko Koga	JPN
1993	Hoon Chung	KOR
1995	Daisuke Hideshima	JPN
1997	Kenzo Nakamura	JPN

-73kg

1999	Jimmy Pedro	USA
2001	Vitali Makakrov	RUS

-78kg

1979	Shozo Fujii	JPN
1981	Neil Adams	GBR
1983	Nobutoshi Hikage	JPN
1985	Nobutoshi Hikage	JPN
1987	Hirotaka Okada	JPN
1989	Kim Byung-ju	KOR
1991	Daniel Lascau	GER
1993	Ki-Young Chun	KOR
1995	Toshihiko Toga	JPN
1997	Cho In-chul	KOR

-81kg

1999	Graeme Randall	GBR
2001	In-Chui Cho	KOR

-86kg

1979	Detlef Ultsch	GDR
1981	Bern'd Tchoullouyan	FRA
1983	Detlef Ultsch	GDR
1985	Peter Seisenbacher	AUT
1987	Fabien Canu	FRA
1989	Fabien Canu	FRA
1991	Hirotaka Okada	JPN
1993	Yoshio Nakamura	JPN
1995	Jeon Ki-Young	KOR
1997	Jeon Ki-Young	KOR

-90kg

1999	Hidehiko Yoshida	JPN
2001	Frédéric Demontfocon	FRA

-95kg

1979	Tengiz Khubuluri	URS
1981	Tengiz Khubuluri	URS
1983	Valeriy Divisenko	URS
1985	Hitoshi Sugai	JPN
1987	Hitoshi Sugai	JPN
1989	Koba Kurtanidze	URS
1991	Stephane Traineau	FRA
1993	Antal Kovacs	HUN
1995	Pawel Nastula	POL
1997	Pawel Nastula	POL

-100kg

1999	Kosei Inoue	JPN
2001	Kosei Inoue	JPN

+95kg

1979	Yasuhiro Yamashita	JPN
1981	Yasuhiro Yamashita	JPN
1983	Yasuhiro Yamashita	JPN
1985	Cho Yong-chul	KOR
1987	Grigory Vertichev	URS
1989	Naoya Ogawa	JPN
1991	Sergey Kosorotov	RUS
1993	David Douillet	FRA
1995	David Douillet	FRA
1997	David Douillet	FRA

+100kg

1999	Shinichi Shinohara	JPN
2001	Alexandre Mikhylin	RUS

Open

1979	Sumio Endo	JPN
1981	Yasuhiro Yamashita	JPN
1983	Hitoshi Saito	JPN
1985	Yoshimi Masaki	JPN
1987	Naoya Ogawa	JPN
1989	Naoya Ogawa	JPN
1991	Naoya Ogawa	JPN
1993	Rafael Kubacki	POL
1995	David Douillet	FRA
1997	Rafael Kubacki	POL
1999	Shinichi Shinohara	JPN
2001	Alexandre Mikhylin	RUS

JUDO

Women

-48kg
1980 **Jane Bridge** GBR
1982 **Karen Briggs** GBR
1984 **Karen Briggs** GBR
1986 **Karen Briggs** GBR
1987 **Zhangyun Li** CHN
1989 **Karen Briggs** GBR
1991 **Cécile Nowak** FRA
1993 **Ryoko Tamura** JPN
1995 **Ryoko Tamura** JPN
1997 **Ryoko Tamura** JPN
1999 **Ryoko Tamura** JPN
2001 **Ryoko Tamura** JPN

-52kg
1980 **Edith Hrovat** AUT
1982 **Loretta Doyle** GBR
1984 **Kaori Yamaguchi** JPN
1986 **Dominique Brun** FRA
1987 **Sharon Rendle** GBR
1989 **Sharon Rendle** GBR
1991 **Alessandra Giungi** ITA
1993 **Rodriguez Verdecia** CUB
1995 **Marie-Claire Restoux** FRA
1997 **Marie-Claire Restoux** FRA
1999 **Noriko Narasaki** JPN
2001 **Sun-Hui Kye** PRK

-56kg
1980 **Gerda Winklbauer** AUT
1982 **Beatrice Rodriguez** FRA
1984 **Ann-Maria Burns** USA
1986 **Ann Hughes** GBR
1987 **Catherine Arnaud** FRA
1989 **Catherine Arnaud** FRA
1991 **Miriam Blasco** ESP
1993 **Nicola Fairbrother** GBR
1995 **Driulis Gonzalez** CUB
1997 **Isabel Fernandez** ESP
1999 **Driulis Gonzalez** CUB

-57kg
2001 **Yuris Leidis Lupetey** CUB

-61 kg
1980 **Anita Staps** HOL
1982 **Martine Rothier** FRA
1984 **Natasha Hernandez** VEN
1986 **Diane Bell** GBR
1987 **Diane Bell** GBR
1989 **Catherine Fleury** FRA
1991 **Fraucke Eickoff** GER
1993 **Gella Vandecaveye** BEL
1995 **Jung Sung-Sook** KOR
1997 **Séverine Vandenhende** FRA
1999 **Kaiko Maeda** JPN

-63kg
2001 **Gella Vandecaveye** BEL

-66kg
1980 **Edith Simon** AUT
1982 **Brigitte Deydier** FRA
1984 **Brigitte Deydier** FRA
1986 **Brigitte Deydier** FRA
1987 **Alexandra Schreiber** FRG
1989 **Emanuela Pierantozzi** ITA
1991 **Emanuela Pierantozzi** ITA
1993 **Cho Min-Sun** KOR
1995 **Cho Min-Sun** KOR
1997 **Kate Howey** GBR
1999 **Sibelius Veranes** CUB

-70kg
2001 **Masae Ueno** JPN

-72kg
1980 **Jocelyne Triadou** FRA
1982 **Barbara Classen** FRG
1984 **Ingrid Berghmans** BEL
1986 **Irene de Kok** HOL
1987 **Irene de Kok** HOL
1989 **Ingrid Berghmans** BEL
1991 **Kim Mi-jung** KOR
1993 **Chunhui Leng** CHN
1995 **Castellana Luna** CUB
1997 **Noriko Anno** JPN
1999 **Noriko Anno** JPN

-78kg
2001 **Noriko Anno** JPN

+72kg
1980 **Margarita de Cal** ITA
1982 **Natalina Lupino** FRA
1984 **Maria-Teresa Motta** ITA
1986 **Gao Fengliang** CHN
1987 **Gao Fengliang** CHN
1989 **Gao Fengliang** CHN
1991 **Moon Ji-yoon** KOR
1993 **Johanna Hagn** GER
1995 **Angelique Seriese** BEL
1997 **Christine Cicot** FRA
1999 **Beate Maksymov** POL

+78kg
2001 **Hua Yuan** CHN

Open
1980 **Ingrid Berghmans** BEL
1982 **Ingrid Berghmans** BEL
1984 **Ingrid Berghmans** BEL
1986 **Ingrid Berghmans** BEL
1987 **Gao Fengliang** CHN
1989 **Estella Rodriguez** CUB
1991 **Zhuang Xiaoyan** CHN
1993 **Beata Maksymow** POL
1995 **Monique Van Der Lee** NED
1997 **Daina Beltran** CUB
1999 **Daina Beltran** CUB
2001 **Seline Lebrun** FRA

MODERN PENTATHLON

World Champions

Men

Year	Individual	Team
1949	**Tage Bjurefelt** SWE	**Sweden**
1950	**Lars Hall** SWE	**Sweden**
1951	**Lars Hall** SWE	**Sweden**
1953	**Gábor Benedek** HUN	**Sweden**
1954	**Björn Thofelt** SWE	**Hungary**
1955	**Konstantin Salnikov** URS	**Hungary**
1957	**Igor Novikov** URS	**Soviet Union**
1958	**Igor Novikov** URS	**Soviet Union**
1959	**Igor Novikov** URS	**Soviet Union**
1961	**Igor Novikov** URS	**Soviet Union**
1962	**Eduards Dobnikov** URS	**Soviet Union**
1963	**András Balczó** HUN	**Hungary**
1965	**András Balczó** HUN	**Hungary**
1966	**András Balczó** HUN	**Hungary**
1967	**András Balczó** HUN	**Hungary**
1969	**András Balczó** HUN	**Soviet Union**
1970	**Peter Kelemen** HUN	**Hungary**
1971	**Boris Onischenko** URS	**Soviet Union**
1973	**Pavel Lednev** URS	**Soviet Union**
1974	**Pavel Lednev** URS	**Soviet Union**
1975	**Pavel Lednev** URS	**Hungary**
1977	**Janusz Pyciak-Peciak** POL	**Poland**
1978	**Pavel Lednev** URS	**Poland**
1979	**Robert Nieman** USA	**USA**
1981	**Janusz Pyciak-Peciak** POL	**Poland**
1982	**Daniele Masala** ITA	**Soviet Union**
1983	**Anatoly Starostin** URS	**Soviet Union**
1985	**Attila Mizsér** HUN	**Soviet Union**
1986	**Carlo Massullo** ITA	**Italy**
1987	**Joël Bouzou** FRA	**Hungary**
1989	**László Fábián** HUN	**Hungary**
1990	**Gianluca Tiberti** ITA	**Soviet Union**
1991	**Arkadiusz Skrzypaszek** POL	**Unified Team**
1993	**Richard Phelps** GBR	**Hungary**
1994	**Dmitri Svatkovsky** RUS	**France**
1995	**Dmitri Svatkovsky** RUS	**Italy**
1997	**Sebastien Deleigne** FRA	**Hungary**
1998	**Sebastien Deleigne** FRA	**Mexico**
1999	**Gabor Balogh** HUN	**Hungary**
2000	**Andrejus Zadneprovskis** LTU	**USA**
2001	**Gabor Balogh** HUN	**Hungary**
2002	**Michal Sedlecky** CZE	**Hungary**

Women

Year	Individual	Team
1981	**Anne Ahlgren** SWE	**Great Britain**
1982	**Wendy Norman** GBR	**Great Britain**
1983	**Lynn Chernobrywy** CAN	**Great Britain**
1984	**Svetlana Yakovleva** URS	**Soviet Union**
1985	**Barbara Kotowska** POL	**Poland**
1986	**Irina Kiselyeva** URS	**Soviet Union**
1987	**Irina Kiselyeva** URS	**Soviet Union**
1988	**Dorata Idzi** POL	**Poland**
1989	**Lori Norwood** USA	**Poland**
1990	**Eva Fjellerup** DEN	**Poland**
1991	**Eva Fjellerup** DEN	**Poland**
1992	**Iwona Kowalewska** POL	**Poland**
1993	**Eva Fjellerup** DEN	**Italy**
1994	**Eva Fjellerup** DEN	**Italy**
1995	**Kerstin Danielsson** SWE	**Hungary**
1996	**Janna Dolgacheva** BLR	**Russia**
1997	**Elizaveta Suvorova** RUS	**Italy**
1998	**Anna Sulima** POL	**Poland**
1999	**Zsuszanna Voros** HUN	**Russia**
2000	**Pernille Svarre** DEN	**Poland**
2001	**Stephanie Cook** GBR	**Great Britain**
2002	**Bea Simoka** HUN	**Hungary**

MOTOR CYCLING

Grand Prix

125cc	250cc	500cc
1949 Nello Pagani ITA	Bruno Ruffo ITA	Leslie Graham GBR
1950 Bruno Ruffo ITA	Dario Ambrosini ITA	Umberto Masetti ITA
1951 Carlo Ubbiali ITA	Bruno Ruffo ITA	Geoff Duke GBR
1952 Cecil Sandford GBR	Enrico Lorenzetti ITA	Umberto Masetti ITA
1953 Werner Haas FRG	Werner Haas FRG	Geoff Duke GBR
1954 Rupert Hollaus AUT	Werner Haas FRG	Geoff Duke GBR
1955 Carlo Ubbiali ITA	Herman Muller FRG	Geoff Duke GBR
1956 Carlo Ubbiali ITA	Carlo Ubbiali ITA	John Surtees GBR
1957 Tarquinio Provini ITA	Cecil Sandford GBR	Libero Liberati ITA
1958 Carlo Ubbiali ITA	Tarquinio Provini ITA	John Surtees GBR
1959 Carlo Ubbiali ITA	Carlo Ubbiali ITA	John Surtees GBR
1960 Carlo Ubbiali ITA	Carlo Ubbiali ITA	John Surtees GBR
1961 Tom Phillis AUS	Mike Hailwood GBR	Gary Hocking ZIM
1962 Luigi Taveri SUI	Jim Redman ZIM	Mike Hailwood GBR
1963 Hugh Anderson NZL	Jim Redman ZIM	Mike Hailwood GBR
1964 Luigi Taveri SUI	Phil Read GBR	Mike Hailwood GBR
1965 Hugh Anderson NZL	Phil Read GBR	Mike Hailwood GBR
1966 Luigi Taveri SUI	Mike Hailwood GBR	Giacomo Agostini ITA
1967 Bill Ivy GBR	Mike Hailwood GBR	Giacomo Agostini ITA
1968 Phil Read GBR	Phil Read GBR	Giacomo Agostini ITA
1969 Dave Simmonds GBR	Kel Caruthers AUS	Giacomo Agostini ITA
1970 Dieter Braun FRG	Rod Gould GBR	Giacomo Agostini ITA
1971 Angel Nieto ESP	Phil Read GBR	Giacomo Agostini ITA
1972 Angel Nieto ESP	Jarno Saarinen FIN	Giacomo Agostini ITA
1973 Kent Andersson SWE	Dieter Braun FRG	Phil Read GBR
1974 Kent Andersson SWE	Walter Villa ITA	Phil Read GBR
1975 Paolo Pileri ITA	Walter Villa ITA	Giacomo Agostini ITA
1976 Pier-Paolo Bianchi ITA	Walter Villa ITA	Barry Sheene GBR
1977 Pier-Paolo Bianchi ITA	Mario Lega ITA	Barry Sheene GBR
1978 Eugenio Lazzarini ITA	Kork Ballington RSA	Kenny Roberts USA
1979 Angel Nieto ESP	Kork Ballington RSA	Kenny Roberts USA
1980 Pier-Paolo Bianchi ITA	Anton Mang FRG	Kenny Roberts USA
1981 Angel Nieto ESP	Anton Mang FRG	Marco Lucchinelli ITA
1982 Angel Nieto ESP	Jean-Louis Tournadre FRA	Franco Uncini ITA
1983 Angel Nieto ESP	Carlos Lavado VEN	Freddie Spencer USA
1984 Angel Nieto ESP	Christian Sarron FRA	Eddie Lawson USA
1985 Fausto Gresini ITA	Freddie Spencer USA	Freddie Spencer USA
1986 Luca Cadalora ITA	Carlos Lavado VEN	Eddie Lawson USA
1987 Fausto Gresini ITA	Anton Mang FRG	Wayne Gardner AUS
1988 Jorge Martinez ESP	Sito Pons ESP	Eddie Lawson USA
1989 Alex Criville ESP	Sito Pons ESP	Eddie Lawson USA
1990 Loris Capirossi ITA	John Kocinski USA	Wayne Rainey USA
1991 Loris Capirossi ITA	Luca Cadalora ITA	Wayne Rainey USA
1992 Alessandro Gramigni ITA	Luca Cadalora ITA	Wayne Rainey USA
1993 Dirk Raudies GER	Loris Capirossi ITA	Kevin Schwantz USA
1994 Kazuto Sakata JPN	Massimiliano Biaggi ITA	Michael Doohan AUS
1995 Haruchika Aoki JPN	Massimiliano Biaggi ITA	Michael Doohan AUS
1996 Haruchika Aoki JPN	Massimiliano Biaggi ITA	Michael Doohan AUS
1997 Valentino Rossi ITA	Massimiliano Biaggi ITA	Michael Doohan AUS
1998 Kazuto Sakata JPN	Loris Capirossi ITA	Michael Doohan AUS
1999 Emilio Alzamora ESP	Valentino Rossi ITA	Alex Criville ESP
2000 Roberto Locatelli ITA	Olivier Jacque FRA	Kenny Roberts Jr USA
2001 Manuel Poggiali SMR	Daijiro Katoh JPN	Valentino Rossi ITA
2002 Arnaud Vincent FRA	Marco Melandri ITA	Valentino Rossi ITA

Superbikes

World Champions

1988 **Fred Merkel** USA
1989 **Fred Merkel** USA
1990 **Raymond Roche** FRA
1991 **Doug Polen** USA
1992 **Doug Polen** USA
1993 **Scott Russell** USA
1994 **Carl Fogarty** GBR
1995 **Carl Fogarty** GBR
1996 **Troy Corser** AUS
1997 **John Kocinski** USA
1998 **Carl Fogarty** GBR
1999 **Carl Fogarty** GBR
2000 **Colin Edwards** USA
2001 **Troy Bayliss** AUS
2002 **Colin Edwards** USA

Race Wins

59	**Carl Fogarty** GBR
31	**Colin Edwards** USA
27	**Doug Polen** USA
23	**Raymond Roche** FRA
	Troy Corser AUS
22	**Troy Bayliss** AUS
16	**Giancarlo Falappa** ITA
14	**Pierfrancesco Chili** ITA
	Scott Russell USA
	John Kocinski USA
13	**Aaron Slight** NZL
12	**Noriuki Haga** JPN
11	**Stephane Mertens** BEL
10	**Fabrizio Pirovano** ITA

Wins in a Season

17	**Doug Polen** 1991
14	**Troy Bayliss*** 2002
13	**Carl Fogarty** 1995
11	**Carl Fogarty** 1993
	Carl Fogarty 1999
	Colin Edwards 2002
10	**Carl Fogarty** 1994
9	**Scott Russell** 1994
	John Kocinski 1997
8	**Raymond Roche** 1990

* Baylis won 14 races, but did not win the title.

Manufacturers

1988 **Honda**
1989 **Honda**
1990 **Honda**
1991 **Ducati**
1992 **Ducati**
1993 **Ducati**
1994 **Ducati**
1995 **Ducati**
1996 **Ducati**
1997 **Honda**
1998 **Ducati**
1999 **Ducati**
2000 **Ducati**
2001 **Ducati**
2002 **Ducati**

MOTOR RACING

FORMULA 1 CHAMPIONS

Year	Winning Driver	Car	Runner up	Winning Constructor
1950	**Giuseppe Farina** ITA	Alfa Romeo	Juan Manuel Fangio ARG	-
1951	**Juan Manuel Fangio** ARG	Alfa Romeo	Alberto Ascari ITA	-
1952	**Alberto Ascari** ITA	Ferrari	Giuseppe Farina ITA	-
1953	**Alberto Ascari** ITA	Ferrari	Juan Manuel Fangio ARG	-
1954	**Juan Manuel Fangio** ARG	Maserati/Mercedes	Jose Gonzalez ARG	-
1955	**Juan Manuel Fangio** ARG	Mercedes-Benz	Stirling Moss GBR	-
1956	**Juan Manuel Fangio** ARG	Lancia-Ferrari	Stirling Moss GBR	-
1957	**Juan Manuel Fangio** ARG	Maserati	Stirling Moss GBR	-
1958	**Mike Hawthorn** GBR	Ferrari	Stirling Moss GBR	Vanwall
1959	**Jack Brabham** AUS	Cooper-Climax	Tony Brooks GBR	Cooper-Climax
1960	**Jack Brabham** AUS	Cooper-Climax	Bruce McLaren NZL	Cooper-Climax
1961	**Phil Hill** USA	Ferrari	Wolfgang von Trips FRG	Ferrari
1962	**Graham Hill** GBR	BRM	Jim Clark GBR	BRM
1963	**Jim Clark** GBR	Lotus-Climax	Graham Hill GBR	Lotus-Climax
1964	**John Surtees** GBR	Ferrari	Graham Hill GBR	Ferrari
1965	**Jim Clark** GBR	Lotus-Climax	Graham Hill GBR	Lotus-Climax
1966	**Jack Brabham** AUS	Brabham-Repco	John Surtees GBR	Brabham-Repco
1967	**Denny Hulme** NZL	Brabham-Repco	Jack Brabham AUS	Brabham-Repco
1968	**Graham Hill** GBR	Lotus-Ford	Jackie Stewart GBR	Lotus-Ford
1969	**Jackie Stewart** GBR	Matra-Ford	Jacky Ickx BEL	Matra-Ford
1970	**Jochen Rindt** AUT	Lotus-Ford	Jacky Ickx BEL	Lotus-Ford
1971	**Jackie Stewart** GBR	Tyrrell-Ford	Ronnie Peterson SWE	Tyrrell-Ford
1972	**Emerson Fittipaldi** BRA	Lotus-Ford	Jackie Stewart GBR	Lotus-Ford
1973	**Jackie Stewart** GBR	Tyrrell-Ford	Emerson Fittipaldi BRA	Lotus-Ford
1974	**Emerson Fittipaldi** BRA	McLaren-Ford	Clay Regazzoni SUI	McLaren-Ford
1975	**Niki Lauda** AUT	Ferrari	Emerson Fittipaldi BRA	Ferrari
1976	**James Hunt** GBR	McLaren-Ford	Niki Lauda AUT	Ferrari
1977	**Niki Lauda** AUT	Ferrari	Jody Scheckter RSA	Ferrari
1978	**Mario Andretti** USA	Lotus-Ford	Ronnie Peterson SWE	Lotus-Ford
1979	**Jody Scheckter** RSA	Ferrari	Gilles Villeneuve CAN	Ferrari
1980	**Alan Jones** AUS	Williams-Ford	Nelson Piquet BRA	Williams-Ford
1981	**Nelson Piquet** BRA	Brabham-Ford	Carlos Reutemann ARG	Williams-Ford
1982	**Keke Rosberg** FIN	Williams-Ford	Pironi FRA and Watson GBR	Ferrari
1983	**Nelson Piquet** BRA	Brabham-BMW	Alain Prost FRA	Ferrari
1984	**Niki Lauda** AUT	McLaren-TAG	Alain Prost FRA	McLaren-TAG
1985	**Alain Prost** FRA	McLaren-TAG	Michele Alboreto ITA	McLaren-TAG
1986	**Alain Prost** FRA	McLaren-TAG	Nigel Mansell GBR	Williams-Honda
1987	**Nelson Piquet** BRA	Williams-Honda	Nigel Mansell GBR	Williams-Honda
1988	**Ayrton Senna** BRA	McLaren-Honda	Alain Prost FRA	McLaren-Honda
1989	**Alain Prost** FRA	McLaren-Honda	Ayrton Senna BRA	McLaren-Honda
1990	**Ayrton Senna** BRA	McLaren-Honda	Alain Prost FRA	McLaren-Honda
1991	**Ayrton Senna** BRA	McLaren-Honda	Nigel Mansell GBR	McLaren-Honda
1992	**Nigel Mansell** GBR	Williams-Renault	Ricardo Patrese ITA	Williams-Renault
1993	**Alain Prost** FRA	Williams-Renault	Ayrton Senna BRA	Williams-Renault
1994	**Michael Schumacher** GER	Benetton-Ford	Damon Hill GBR	Williams-Renault
1995	**Michael Schumacher** GER	Benetton-Renault	Damon Hill GBR	Benetton-Renault
1996	**Damon Hill** GBR	Williams-Renault	Jacques Villeneuve CAN	Williams-Renault
1997	**Jacques Villeneuve** CAN	Williams-Renault	Heinz-Harald Frentzen GER	Williams-Renault
1998	**Mika Hakkinen** FIN	McLaren-Mercedes	Michael Schumacher GER	McLaren-Mercedes
1999	**Mika Hakkinen** FIN	McLaren-Mercedes	Eddie Irvine GBR	Ferrari
2000	**Michael Schumacher** GER	Ferrari	Mika Hakkinen FIN	Ferrari
2001	**Michael Schumacher** GER	Ferrari	David Coulthard GBR	Ferrari
2002	**Michael Schumacher** GER	Ferrari	Rubens Barrichello BRA	Ferrari

MOTOR RACING

INDY CAR CHAMPIONS

Year	Winner (USA unless stated)
AAA	
1950	Henry Banks
1951	Tony Bettenhausen
1952	Chuck Stevenson
1953	Sam Hanks
1954	Jimmy Bryan
1955	Bob Sweikert
USAC	
1956	Jimmy Bryan
1957	Jimmy Bryan
1958	Tony Bettenhausen
1959	Rodger Ward
1960	AJ Foyt Jnr
1961	AJ Foyt Jnr
1962	Rodger Ward
1963	AJ Foyt Jnr
1964	AJ Foyt Jnr
1965	Mario Andretti
1966	Mario Andretti
1967	AJ Foyt Jnr
1968	Bobby Unser
1969	Mario Andretti
1970	Al Unser
1971	Joe Leonard
1972	Joe Leonard
1973	Roger McCluskey
1974	Bobby Unser
1975	AJ Foyt Jnr
1976	Gordon Johncock
1977	Tom Sneva
1978	Tom Sneva
1979	AJ Foyt Jnr
CART	
1979	Rick Mears
1980	Johnny Rutherford
1981	Rick Mears
1982	Rick Mears
1983	Al Unser
1984	Mario Andretti
1985	Al Unser
1986	Bobby Rahal
1987	Bobby Rahal
1988	Danny Sullivan
1989	Emerson Fittipaldi BRA
1990	Al Unser Jnr
1991	Michael Andretti
IndyCar	
1992	Bobby Rahal
1993	Nigel Mansell GBR
1994	Paul Tracy CAN
1995	Jacques Villeneuve CAN
PPG Cart	
1996	Jimmy Vasser
1997	Alex Zanardi ITA
1998	Alex Zanardi ITA
1999	Juan Montoya BRA
2000	Gil de Ferran BRA
2001	Gil de Ferran BRA
2002	Cristiana da Matta BRA

LE MANS

Year	Drivers	Car
1949	Chinetti ITA/Selsdon GBR	Ferrari
1950	Rosier/Rosier FRA	Talbot-Lago
1951	Walker/Whitehead GBR	Jaguar
1952	Lang/Riess FRG	Mercedes-Benz
1953	Rolt/Hamilton GBR	Jaguar
1954	Gonzalez ARG/Trintignant FRA	Ferrari
1955	Hawthorn/Bueb GBR	Jaguar
1956	Flockhart/Sanderson GBR	Jaguar
1957	Flockhart/Bueb GBR	Jaguar
1958	Gendebien BEL/Hill USA	Ferrari
1959	Shelby/Salvadori GBR	Aston Martin
1960	Gendebien/Frere BEL	Ferrari
1961	Gendebien BEL/Hill USA	Ferrari
1962	Gendebien BEL/Hill USA	Ferrari
1963	Scarfiotti/Bandini ITA	Ferrari
1964	Guichet FRA/Vaccarella ITA	Ferrari
1965	Rindt AUT/Gregory USA	Ferrari
1966	Amon/McLaren NZL	Ford
1967	Gurney/Foyt USA	Ford
1968	Rodriguez MEX/Bianchi BEL	Ford
1969	Ickx BEL/Oliver GBR	Ford
1970	Herrmann FRG/Attwood GBR	Porsche
1971	Marko AUT/van Lennep HOL	Porsche
1972	Pescarolo FRA/Hill GBR	Matra-Simca
1973	Pescarolo/Larrousse FRA	Matra-Simca
1974	Pescarolo/Larrousse FRA	Matra-Simca
1975	Ickx BEL/Bell GBR	Mirage-Ford
1976	Ickx BEL/van Lennep HOL	Porsche
1977	Ickx BEL/Barth FRG/Haywood USA	Porsche
1978	Jaussaud/Pironi FRA	Renault Alpine
1979	Ludwig FRG/Whittington USA/ Whittington USA	Porsche
1980	Jaussaud/Rondeau FRA	Rondeau-Ford
1981	Ickx BEL/Bell GBR	Porsche
1982	Ickx BEL/Bell GBR	Porsche
1983	Schuppan/Haywood/Holbert	Porsche
1984	Ludwig FRG/Pescarolo FRA	Porsche
1985	Ludwig/Winter FRG/Barillo ITA	Porsche
1986	Stuck FRG/Bell GBR/Holbert USA	Porsche
1987	Stuck/Bell/Holbert	Porsche
1988	Lammers HOL/Dumfries GBR/ Wallace GBR	Jaguar
1989	Mass/Reuter FRG/Dickens SWE	Mercedes
1990	Nielsen DEN/Brundle GBR/Cobb USA	Jaguar
1991	Herbert GBR/Gachot BEL/ Wendler GER	Mazda
1992	Warwick/Blundell GBR/Dalmas FRA	Peugeot
1993	Bouchut/Helary FRA	Peugeot
1994	Dalmas FRA/Haywood USA/ Baldi ITA	Porsche
1995	Dalmas FRA/Lehto FIN	McLaren
1996	Jones/Reuter/Wurtz	Porsche
1997	Alboreto/Johansson/Kristensen	Joest
1998	McNish/Ortelli/Aiello	Porsche AG
1999	Martini/Dalmas/Winkelhock	BMW
2000	Biela/Kristensen/Pirro	Audi
2001	Biela/Kristensen/Pirro	Audi
2002	Biela/Kristensen/Pirro	Audi

MOTOR RACING

World Rally Champions

There was no drivers championship until 1977

Year	Driver	Manufacturer
1968	-	Ford
1969	-	Ford
1970	-	Porsche
1971	-	Alpine-Renault
1972	-	Lancia
1973	-	Alpine-Renault
1974	-	Lancia
1975	-	Lancia
1976	-	Lancia
1977	Sandro Munari ITA	Fiat
1978	Markku Alen FIN	Fiat
1979	Bjorn Waldgard SWE	Ford
1980	Walter Rohrl FRG	Fiat
1981	Ari Vatanen FIN	Talbot
1982	Timo Salanen FIN	Audi
1983	Hannu Mikkola FIN	Lancia
1984	Stig Blomqvist SWE	Audi
1985	Timo Salanen FIN	Peugeot
1986	Juha Kankkunen FIN	Peugeot
1987	Juha Kankkunen FIN	Lancia
1988	Mikki Biasion ITA	Lancia
1989	Mikki Biasion ITA	Lancia
1990	Carlos Sainz ESP	Lancia
1991	Juha Kankkunen FIN	Lancia
1992	Carlos Sainz ESP	Lancia
1993	Juha Kankkunen FIN	Toyota
1994	Didier Auriol FRA	Toyota
1995	Colin McRae GBR	Subaru
1996	Tommi Makinen FIN	Subaru
1997	Tommi Makinen FIN	Subaru
1998	Tommi Makinen FIN	Subaru
1999	Tommi Makinen FIN	Subaru
2000	Marcus Gronholm FIN	Peugeot
2001	Richard Burns GBR	Subaru
2002	Marcus Gronholm FIN	Peugeot

NETBALL

World Champions

1963	Australia
1967	Australia
1971	New Zealand
1975	Australia
1979*	Australia / New Zealand / Trinidad
1983	Australia
1987	New Zealand
1991	Australia
1995	Australia
1999	Australia

* Title shared

ROWING

WORLD CHAMPIONS
Olympic year championships not included

Men

SINGLE SCULLS
1962	**Vyacheslav Ivanov** URS
1966	**Don Spero** USA
1970	**Alberto Demiddi** ARG
1974	**Wolfgang Honig** GDR
1975	**Peter-Michael Kolbe** FRG
1977	**Joachim Dreifke** GDR
1978	**Peter-Michael Kolbe** FRG
1979	**Pertti Karppinen** FIN
1981	**Peter-Michael Kolbe** FRG
1982	**Rodiger Reiche** GDR
1983	**Peter-Michael Kolbe** FRG
1985	**Pertti Karppinen** FIN
1986	**Peter-Michael Kolbe** FRG
1987	**Thomas Lange** GDR
1989	**Thomas Lange** GDR
1990	**Juri Jaanson** URS
1991	**Thomas Lange** GER
1993	**Derek Porter** CAN
1994	**Andre Willms** GER
1995	**Iztok Cop** SLO
1997	**James Kovan** USA
1998	**Rob Waddell** NZL
1999	**Rob Waddell** NZL
2001	**Olaf Tufte** NOR
2002	**Marcel Hacker** GER

DOUBLE SCULLS
1962	**René Duhamel/Bernard Monnereau** FRA
1966	**Melchior Borgin/Martin Studach** SUI
1970	**Jorgen Engelbrech/Niels Secher** DEN
1974	**Christof Kreuziger/Hans-Uirich Schmied** GDR
1975	**Alf Hansen/Frank Hansen** NOR
1977	**Chris Baillieu/Michael Hart** GBR
1978	**Alf Hansen/Frank Hansen** NOR
1979	**Alf Hansen/Frank Hansen** NOR
1981	**Klaus Kroppelien/Joachim Dreifke** GDR
1982	**Alf Hansen/Rolf Thorsen** NOR
1983	**Thomas Lange/Uwe Heppner** GDR
1985	**Thomas Lange/Uwe Heppner** GDR
1986	**Alberto Belgori/Igor Pescialli** ITA
1987	**Vasil Radeyev/Danatyl Yordanov** BUL
1989	**Lars Bjøness/Rol Bent Thorsen** NOR
1990	**Christophe Zerbst/Arnold Jonke** AUT
1991	**Henk-Jan Zwolle/Nicolaas Rienks** NED
1993	**Yves Lamargue/Samuel Barathay** FRA
1994	**Lars Bjøness/Rol Bent Thorsen** NOR
1995	**L Christiansen/M Halabo-Hansen** DEN
1997	**Stephan Volkert/Andreas Hajek** GER
1998	**Stephan Volkert/Andreas Hajek** GER
1999	**Luka Spik/Iztok Cop** SLO
2001	**Akos Haller/Tibor Peto** HUN
2002	**Akos Haller/Tibor Peto** HUN

QUAD SCULLS
1974	**East Germany**
1975	**East Germany**
1977	**East Germany**
1978	**East Germany**
1979	**East Germany**
1981	**East Germany**
1982	**East Germany**
1983	**West Germany**
1985	**Canada**
1986	**Soviet Union**
1987	**Soviet Union**
1989	**Romania**
1990	**Soviet Union**
1991	**Soviet Union**
1993	**Germany**
1994	**Italy**
1995	**Italy**
1997	**Italy**
1998	**Italy**
1999	**Germany**
2001	**Germany**
2002	**Germany**

COXLESS PAIR
1962	**Dieter Bender/Gunther Zumkeller** FRG
1966	**Peter Gorny/Werner Klatt** GDR
1970	**Peter Gorny/Werner Klatt** GDR
1974	**Bernd Landvoig/Jörg Landvoigt** GDR
1975	**Bernd Landvoig/Jörg Landvoigt** GDR
1977	**Vitaliy Yeliseyev/Aleksandr Kulagin** URS
1978	**Bernd Landvoig/Jörg Landvoigt** GDR
1979	**Bernd Landvoig/Jörg Landvoigt** GDR
1981	**Yuriy Pimenov/Nikolay Pimenov** URS
1982	**Magnus Grepperud/Sverre Loken** NOR
1983	**Carl Ertel/Ulf Sauerbrey** GDR
1985	**Nikolay Pimenov/Yury Pimenov** URS
1986	**Nikolay Pimenov/Yury Pimenov** URS
1987	**Andrew Holmes/Steven Redgrave** GBR
1989	**Thomas Jung/Uwe Kellner** GDR
1990	**Thomas Jung/Uwe Kellner** GDR
1991	**Steven Redgrave/Matthew Pinsent** GBR
1993	**Steven Redgrave/Matthew Pinsent** GBR
1994	**Steven Redgrave/Matthew Pinsent** GBR
1995	**Steven Redgrave/Matthew Pinsent** GBR
1997	**Michel Andrieux/J-Christophe Rolland** FRA
1998	**Robert Sens/Detlewf Kirchoff** GER
1999	**Drew Ginn/James Tompkins** AUS
2001	**James Cracknell/Matthew Pinsent** GBR
2002	**James Cracknell/Matthew Pinsent** GBR

COXED PAIR
1962	**West Germany**
1966	**Netherlands**
1970	**Romania**
1974	**Soviet Union**
1975	**East Germany**
1977	**Bulgaria**
1978	**East Germany**
1979	**East Germany**
1981	**Italy**
1982	**Italy**
1983	**East Germany**
1985	**Italy**

ROWING

1986	Great Britain
1987	Italy
1989	Italy
1990	Italy
1991	Italy
1993	Great Britain
1994	Croatia
1995	Italy
1997	USA
1998	Australia
1999	USA
2001	Great Britain
2002	Germany

COXLESS FOUR

1962	West Germany
1966	East Germany
1970	East Germany
1974	East Germany
1975	East Germany
1977	East Germany
1978	Soviet Union
1979	East Germany
1981	Soviet Union
1982	Switzerland
1983	West Germany
1985	West Germany
1986	USA
1987	East Germany
1989	East Germany
1990	Australia
1991	Australia
1993	France
1994	Italy
1995	Italy
1997	Great Britain
1998	Great Britain
1999	Great Britain
2001	Great Britain
2002	Germany

COXED FOUR

1962	West Germany
1966	East Germany
1970	West Germany
1974	East Germany
1975	Soviet Union
1977	East Germany
1978	East Germany
1979	East Germany
1981	East Germany
1982	East Germany
1983	New Zealand
1985	Soviet Union
1986	East Germany
1987	East Germany
1989	Romania
1990	East Germany
1991	Germany
1993	Romania
1994	Romania

1995	USA
1997	France
1998	Australia
1999	USA
2001	France
2002	Great Britain

EIGHTS

1962	West Germany
1966	West Germany
1970	East Germany
1974	USA
1975	East Germany
1977	East Germany
1981	Soviet Union
1982	New Zealand
1983	New Zealand
1985	Soviet Union
1986	Australia
1987	USA
1989	West Germany
1990	West Germany
1991	Germany
1993	Germany
1994	USA
1995	Germany
1997	USA
1998	USA
1999	USA
2001	Romania
2002	Canada

LIGHTWEIGHT SINGLE SCULLS

1974	William Belden USA
1975	Reto Wyss SUI
1977	Reto Wyss SUI
1978	José Antonio Montosa ESP
1979	William Belden USA
1981	Scott Roop USA
1982	Raimund Haberl AUT
1983	Bjarne Eltang DEN
1985	Ruggero Verroca ITA
1986	Peter Antonie AUS
1987	Willem Van Belleghem BEL
1989	Frans Goebel NED
1990	Frans Goebel NED
1991	Niall O'Toole IRL
1993	Peter Haining GBR
1994	Peter Haining GBR
1995	Peter Haining GBR
1997	Karsten Nielsen DEN
1998	Stefano Basalini ITA
1999	Karsten Nielsen DEN
2001	Sam Lynch IRL
2002	Sam Lynch IRL

LIGHTWEIGHT DOUBLE SCULLS

1978	Bornick/Gilje NOR
1979	Bornick/Gilje NOR
1981	Esposito/Verroca ITA
1982	Esposito/Verroca ITA
1983	Esposito/Verroca ITA

ROWING

1985	**Crispon/Renault** FRA
1986	**Smith/Whitwell** GBR
1987	**Gandola/Calabrese** ITA
1989	**Schmölzer/Rantasa** AUT
1990	**Peterson/Dreher** USA
1991	**Von Warburg/Buchheit** GER
1993	**Lynagh/ Hick** AUS
1994	**Esposito/Crispi** ITA
1995	**Geir/Geir** SUI
1997	**Kucharski/Sycz** POL
1998	**Kucharski/Sycz** POL
1999	**Krispi/Pettinari** ITA
2001	**Luini/Pettinari** ITA
2002	**Luini/Pettinari** ITA

LIGHTWEIGHT QUAD SCULLS

1989	**West Germany**
1990	**Italy**
1991	**Australia**
1993	**-**
1994	**Austria**
1995	**Austria**
1997	**Italy**
1998	**Italy**
1999	**Italy**
2001	**Italy**
2002	**Italy**

LIGHTWEIGHT COXLESS PAIR

1993	**Spain**
1994	**Italy**
1995	**Italy**
1997	**Switzerland**
1998	**France**
1999	**Italy**
2001	**Ireland**
2002	**Chile**

LIGHTWEIGHT COXLESS FOURS

1974	**Australia**
1975	**France**
1977	**France**
1978	**Switzerland**
1979	**Great Britain**
1981	**Australia**
1982	**Italy**
1983	**Spain**
1985	**West Germany**
1986	**Italy**
1987	**West Germany**
1989	**West Germany**
1990	**West Germany**
1991	**Great Britain**
1993	**USA**
1994	**Denmark**
1995	**Italy**
1997	**Italy**
1998	**Denmark**
1999	**Denmark**
2001	**Austria**
2002	**Denmark**

LIGHTWEIGHT EIGHTS

1974	**USA**
1975	**West Germany**
1977	**Great Britain**
1978	**Great Britain**
1979	**Spain**
1981	**Denmark**
1982	**Italy**
1983	**Spain**
1985	**Italy**
1986	**Italy**
1987	**Italy**
1989	**Italy**
1990	**Italy**
1991	**Italy**
1993	**Canada**
1994	**Great Britain**
1995	**Denmark**
1997	**Australia**
1998	**Germany**
1999	**USA**
2001	**France**
2002	**Italy**

Women

SINGLE SCULLS

1974	**Christine Scheiblich** GDR
1975	**Christine Scheiblich** GDR
1977	**Christine Scheiblich** GDR
1978	**Christine Hann (nee Scheiblich)** GDR
1979	**Sandra Toma** ROM
1981	**Sandra Toma** ROM
1982	**Irina Fettisova** URS
1983	**Jutta Hampe** GDR
1985	**Cornelia Linse** GDR
1986	**Jutta Hampe** GDR
1987	**Magdalena Georgeyeva** BUL
1989	**Elisabeta Lipa** ROM
1990	**Birgit Peter** GDR
1991	**Silken Laumann** CAN
1993	**Jana Thieme** GER
1994	**Trine Hansen** DEN
1995	**Maria Brandin** SWE
1997	**Ekaterina Khodotovich** BLR
1998	**Irina Fedotova** RUS
1999	**Ekaterina Karsten** BLR
2001	**Katrin Stomporowski** GER
2002	**Rumyana Neykova** BUL

DOUBLE SCULLS

1974	**Yelena Antonova/Galina Yermoleyeva** URS
1975	**Yelena Antonova/Galina Yermoleyeva** URS
1977	**Anke Borchmann/Roswietha Zobelt** GDR
1978	**Svetla Otzetova/Zdravka Yordanova** BUL
1979	**Cornelia Linse/Heidi Westphal** GDR
1981	**Margarita Kokarevitha/Antonina Makhina** URS
1982	**Yelena Braticko/Antonina Makhina** URS
1983	**Jutta Scheck/Martina Schroter** GDR
1985	**Sylvia Schurabe/Martina Schroter** GDR
1986	**Sylvia Schurabe/Beate Schramm** GDR
1987	**Steska Madina/Violeta Ninova** BUL

ROWING

1989	Jana Sorgers/Beate Schramm GDR
1990	Kathrin Boron/Beate Schramm GDR
1991	Kathrin Boron/Beate Schramm GER
1993	Philippa Baker/Brenda Lawson NZL
1994	Philippa Baker/Brenda Lawson NZL
1995	Marnie McBean/Kathleen Heddle CAN
1997	Kathrin Boron/Meike Evers GER
1998	Jana Thieme/Kathrin Boron GER
1999	Jana Thieme/Kathrin Boron GER
2001	Kerstin Kowalski/Kathrin Boron GER
2002	Georgina and Caroline Evers-Swindell NZL

QUAD SCULLS

1974	East Germany
1975	East Germany
1977	East Germany
1978	Bulgaria
1979	East Germany
1981	Soviet Union
1982	Soviet Union
1983	East Germany
1985	East Germany
1986	East Germany
1987	East Germany
1989	East Germany
1990	East Germany
1991	Germany
1993	China
1994	Germany
1995	Germany
1997	Germany
1998	Germany
1999	Germany
2001	Germany
2002	Germany

COXLESS PAIRS

1974	Marilena Ghita/Cornelia Neascu ROM
1975	Sabine Dahne/Angelika Noack GDR
1977	Sabine Dahne/Angelika Noack GDR
1978	Cornelia Bugel/Ute Steindorf GDR
1979	Cornelia Bugel/Ute Steindorf GDR
1981	Sigrid Anders/Iris Rudolph GDR
1982	Silvia Frohlich/Marita Sandig GDR
1983	Silvia Frohlich/Marita Sandig GDR
1985	Rodica Arba/Elena Florea ROM
1986	Rodica Arba/Olga Homeghi ROM
1987	Rodica Arba/Olga Homeghi ROM
1989	Kathrin Haaker/Judith Zeidler GDR
1990	Stefanie Werremeier/Ingeburg Althoff FRG
1991	Marnie McBean/Kathleen Heddle CAN
1993	Christine Gosse/Helene Cortin FRA
1994	Christine Gosse/Helene Cortin FRA
1995	Megan Still/Kate Slatter AUS
1997	Emma Robinson/Alison Korn CAN
1998	Emma Robinson/Alison Korn CAN
1999	Emma Robinson/Theresa Luke CAN
2001	Georgeta Damian/Viorica Susanu ROM
2002	Georgeta Andrunache/Viorica Susanu ROM

COXED FOUR
Discontinued since 1987

1974	East Germany
1975	East Germany
1977	East Germany
1978	East Germany
1979	Soviet Union
1981	Soviet Union
1982	Soviet Union
1983	Soviet Union
1985	East Germany
1986	Romania
1987	Romania

COXLESS FOUR

1986	USA
1989	East Germany
1990	Romania
1991	Canada
1993	China
1994	Netherlands
1995	USA
1997	Great Britain
1998	Ukraine
1999	Belarus
2001	Australia
2002	Australia

EIGHTS

1974	East Germany
1975	East Germany
1977	East Germany
1978	Soviet Union
1979	Soviet Union
1981	Soviet Union
1983	Soviet Union
1985	Soviet Union
1986	Soviet Union
1987	Soviet Union
1989	Romania
1990	Romania
1991	Canada
1993	Romania
1994	Germany
1995	USA
1997	Romania
1998	Romania
1999	Romania
2001	Australia
2002	USA

LIGHTWEIGHT SINGLE SCULLS

1985	Adair Ferguson AUS
1986	Maria Sava ROM
1987	Magdalena Georgieva BUL
1989	Kris Karlson USA
1990	Mette Jenson DEN
1991	Philippa Baker NZL
1993	Michelle Darvill CAN
1994	Constanta Pipota ROM
1995	Regina Joyce AUS
1997	Sarah Garner USA

ROWING

1998 **Pia Vogel** SUI
1999 **Pia Vogel** SUI
2001 **Sinead Jennings** IRL
2002 **Viktoriya Dimitrova** BUL

LIGHTWEIGHT DOUBLE SCULLS
1985 **Lin Clark/Beryl Crockford** GBR
1986 **Chris Ernst/Cary Beth Sands** USA
1987 **Stefka Madina/Violeta Ninova** BUL
1989 **Cary Beth Sands/Kris Karlson** USA
1990 **Ulla Jensen/Regitze Siggaard** DEN
1991 **Christiane Weber/Claudia Waldi** GER
1993 **Collen Miller/Wendy Wiebe** CAN
1994 **Collen Miller/Wendy Wiebe** CAN
1995 **Collen Miller/Wendy Wiebe** CAN
1997 **Michelle Darvill/Angelika Brand** GER
1998 **Christine Collins/Sarah Garner** USA
1999 **Constanta Burcica/Camelia Macovicuic** ROM
2001 **Janet Radunzel/Claudia Blasberg** GER
2002 **Sally Ann Causby/Amber Jae Halliday** AUS

RUGBY LEAGUE

WORLD CUP

	Winner	Venue
1954	Great Britain	France
1957	Australia	Australia
1960	Great Britain	England
1968	Australia	Aus/Nzl
1970	Australia	England
1972	Great Britain	France
1975*	Australia	Worldwide
1977	Australia	Aus/Nzl
1988	Australia	N Zealand
1992	Australia	England
1995	Australia	Eng/Wal
2000	Australia	UK/Irl/Fra

* World Chps played home & away

WORLD CLUB

1997	Brisbane Broncos
2000	Melbourne Storm
2001	St. Helens
2002	Braford Bulls

LEAGUE CHAMPIONS

1973-74	Salford
1974-75	St. Helens
1975-76	Salford
1976-77	Featherstone Rovers
1977-78	Widnes
1978-79	Hull Kingston Rovers
1979-80	Bradford Northern
1980-81	Bradford Northern
1981-82	Leigh
1982-83	Hull
1983-84	Hull Kingston Rovers
1984-85	Hull Kingston Rovers
1985-86	Halifax
1986-87	Wigan
1987-88	Widnes
1988-89	Widnes
1989-90	Wigan
1990-91	Wigan
1991-92	Wigan
1992-93	Wigan
1993-94	Wigan
1994-95	Wigan
1995-96	Wigan

SUPER LEAGUE

1996	St. Helens Saints
1997	Bradford Bulls

GRAND FINAL

1998	Wigan Warriors
1999	St Helens
2000	St Helens
2001	Bradford Bulls
2002	St Helens

PREMIERSHIP TROPHY

1975	Leeds
1976	St. Helens
1977	St. Helens
1978	Bradford Northern
1979	Leeds
1980	Widnes
1981	Hull Kingston Rovers
1982	Widnes
1983	Widnes
1984	Hull Kingston Rovers
1985	St. Helens
1986	Warrington
1987	Wigan
1988	Widnes
1989	Widnes
1990	Widnes
1991	Hull
1992	Wigan
1993	St. Helens
1994	Wigan
1995	Wigan
1996	Wigan
1996	Wigan
1997	Wigan Warriors

Discontinued in 1997

CHALLENGE CUP

1897	Batley
1899	Oldham
1900	Swinton
1901	Batley
1902	Broughton Rangers
1903	Halifax
1904	Halifax
1905	Warrington
1906	Bradford
1907	Warrington
1908	Hunslet
1909	Wakefield Trinity
1910	Leeds
1911	Broughton Rangers
1912	Dewsbury
1913	Huddersfield
1914	Hull
1915	Huddersfield
1920	Huddersfield
1921	Leigh
1922	Rochdale Hornets
1923	Leeds
1924	Wigan
1925	Oldham
1926	Swinton
1927	Oldham
1928	Swinton
1929	Wigan
1930	Widnes
1931	Halifax
1932	Leeds
1933	Huddersfield
1934	Hunslet
1935	Castleford
1936	Leeds
1937	Widnes
1938	Salford
1939	Halifax
1941	Leeds
1942	Leeds
1943	Dewsbury
1944	Bradford Northern
1945	Huddersfield
1946	Wakefield Trinity
1947	Bradford Northern
1948	Wigan
1949	Bradford Northern
1950	Warrington
1951	Wigan
1952	Workington Town
1953	Huddersfield
1954	Warrington
1955	Barrow
1956	St. Helens
1957	Leeds
1958	Wigan
1959	Wigan
1960	Wakefield Trinity
1961	St. Helens
1962	Wakefield Trinity
1963	Wakefield Trinity
1964	Widnes
1965	Wigan
1966	St. Helens
1967	Featherstone Rovers
1968	Leeds
1969	Castleford
1970	Castleford
1971	Leigh
1972	St. Helens
1973	Featherstone Rovers
1974	Warrington
1975	Widnes
1976	St. Helens
1977	Leeds
1978	Leeds
1979	Widnes
1980	Hull Kingston Rovers
1981	Widnes
1982	Hull
1983	Featherstone Rovers
1984	Widnes
1985	Wigan
1986	Castleford
1987	Halifax
1988	Wigan
1989, 90 & 91	Wigan
1992	Wigan
1993	Wigan
1994	Wigan
1995	Wigan
1996	St. Helens
1997	St. Helens
1998	Sheffield Eagles
1999	Leeds Rhinos
2000	Bradford Bulls
2001	St Helens
2002	Wigan

RUGBY UNION

WORLD CUP
1987 Eden Park, Auckland
New Zealand 29   France 9
1991 Twickenham
Australia 12   England 6
1995 Ellis Park, Johannesburg
South Africa 15   New Zealand 12 aet
1999 Millennium Stadium, Cardiff
Australia 35   France 12

Lions v South Africa
1910 **Lions 10** South Africa 14
    Lions 8 South Africa 3
    Lions 5 South Africa 21
1924 **Lions 3** South Africa 7
    Lions 0 South Africa 17
    Lions 3 South Africa 3
1938 **Lions 12** South Africa 26
    Lions 3 South Africa 19
    Lions 21 South Africa 16
1955 **Lions 23** South Africa 22
    Lions 9 South Africa 25
    Lions 9 South Africa 6
    Lions 8 South Africa 22
1962 **Lions 3** South Africa 3
    Lions 0 South Africa 3
    Lions 3 South Africa 8
    Lions 14 South Africa 34
1968 **Lions 20** South Africa 25
    Lions 6 South Africa 6
    Lions 6 South Africa 11
    Lions 6 South Africa 19
1974 **Lions 12** South Africa 3
    Lions 28 South Africa 9
    Lions 26 South Africa 9
    Lions 13 South Africa 13
1980 **Lions 22** South Africa 26
    Lions 19 South Africa 26
    Lions 10 South Africa 12
    Lions 17 South Africa 13
1997 **Lions 25** South Africa 16
    Lions 18 South Africa 15
    Lions 16 South Africa 35

Lions v New Zealand
1930 **Lions 6** New Zealand 3
    Lions 10 New Zealand 13
    Lions 10 New Zealand 15
    Lions 8 New Zealand 22
1950 **Lions 9** New Zealand 9
    Lions 0 New Zealand 8
    Lions 3 New Zealand 6
    Lions 8 New Zealand 11
1959 **Lions 17** New Zealand 18
    Lions 8 New Zealand 11
    Lions 8 New Zealand 22
    Lions 9 New Zealand 6
1966 **Lions 3** New Zealand 20
    Lions 12 New Zealand 16
    Lions 6 New Zealand 19
    Lions 11 New Zealand 24
1971 **Lions 9** New Zealand 3
    Lions 12 New Zealand 22
    Lions 13 New Zealand 3
    Lions 14 New Zealand 14
1977 **Lions 12** New Zealand 16
    Lions 13 New Zealand 9
    Lions 7 New Zealand 19
    Lions 9 New Zealand 10
1983 **Lions 12** New Zealand 16
    Lions 0 New Zealand 9
    Lions 8 New Zealand 15
    Lions 6 New Zealand 38
1993 **Lions 18** New Zealand 20
    Lions 20 New Zealand 7
    Lions 13 New Zealand 30

Lions v Australia
1930 **Lions 5** Australia 6
1950 **Lions 19** Australia 6
    Lions 24 Australia 3
1959 **Lions 17** Australia 6
    Lions 24 Australia 3
1966 **Lions 11** Australia 8
    Lions 31 Australia 0
1989 **Lions 12** Australia 30
    Lions 19 Australia 12
    Lions 19 Australia 18
2001 **Lions 29** Australia 13
    Lions 14 Australia 35
    Lions 23 Australia 29

FOUR/FIVE/SIX NATIONS
1883 **England**
1884 **England**
1886 **England & Scotland**
1887 **Scotland**
1890 **England & Scotland**
1891 **Scotland**
1892 **England**
1893 **Wales**
1894 **Ireland**
1895 **Scotland**
1896 **Ireland**
1899 **Ireland**
1900 **Wales**
1901 **Scotland**
1902 **Wales**
1903 **Scotland**
1904 **Scotland**
1905 **Wales**
1906 **Ireland & Wales**
1907 **Scotland**
1908 **Wales**
1909 **Wales**
1910 **England**
1911 **Wales**
1912 **England & Ireland**
1913 **England**
1914 **England**
1920 **England, Wales & Scotland**
1921 **England**
1922 **Wales**

RUGBY UNION

FIVE/FIVE/SIX NATIONS (cont)

1923	England
1924	England
1925	Scotland
1926	Scotland & Ireland
1927	Scotland & Ireland
1928	England
1929	Scotland
1930	England
1931	Wales
1932	England Ireland & Wales
1933	Scotland
1934	England
1935	Ireland
1936	Wales
1937	England
1938	Scotland
1939	England Ireland & Wales
1947	Wales & England
1948	Ireland
1949	Ireland
1950	Wales
1951	Ireland
1952	Wales
1953	England
1954	England Wales & France
1955	Wales & France
1956	Wales
1957	England
1958	England
1959	France
1960	France & England
1961	France
1962	France
1963	England
1964	Scotland & Wales
1965	Wales
1966	Wales
1967	France
1968	France
1969	Wales
1970	Wales & France
1971	Wales
1973	Five way tie
1974	Ireland
1975	Wales
1976	Wales
1977	France
1978	Wales
1979	Wales
1980	England
1981	France
1982	Ireland
1983	France & Ireland
1984	Scotland
1985	Ireland
1986	France & Scotland
1987	France
1988	Wales & France
1989	France

1990	Scotland
1991	England
1992	England
1993	France
1994	Wales
1995	England
1996	England
1997	France
1998	France
1999	Scotland
2000	England
2001	England
2002	France

EUROPEAN CUP

1996-97	Brive 28	Leicester 9	
1997-98	Bath 19	Brive 18	
1998-99	Ulster 21	Colombiers 6	
1999-00	Northampton 9	Munster 8	
2000-01	Leicester 34	Stade Francais 30	
2001-02	Leicester 15	Munster 9	

ENGLISH LEAGUE CHAMPIONS

1987-88	Leicester
1988-89	Bath
1989-90	Wasps
1990-91	Bath
1991-92	Bath
1992-93	Bath
1993-94	Bath
1994-95	Leicester
1995-96	Bath
1996-97	Wasps
1997-98	Newcastle
1998-99	Leicester
1999-00	Leicester
2000-01	Leicester
2001-02	Leicester

WELSH LEAGUE CHAMPIONS

1990-91	Neath
1991-92	Swansea
1992-93	Llanelli
1993-94	Swansea
1994-95	Cardiff
1995-96	Neath
1996-97	Pontypridd
1997-98	Swansea
1998-99	Llanelli

WELSH / SCOTTISH LEAGUE

1999-00	Cardiff
2000-01	Swansea
2001-02	Llanelli

RUGBY UNION

SCOTTISH LEAGUE CHAMPIONS

1973-74	**Hawick**
1974-75	**Hawick**
1975-76	**Hawick**
1976-77	**Hawick**
1977-78	**Hawick**
1978-79	**Heriots FP**
1979-80	**Gala**
1981-82	**Hawick**
1982-83	**Gala**
1983-84	**Hawick**
1984-85	**Hawick**
1985-86	**Hawick**
1986-87	**Hawick**
1987-88	**Kelso**
1988-89	**Kelso**
1989-90	**Melrose**
1990-91	**Boroughmuir**
1991-92	**Melrose**
1992-93	**Melrose**
1993-94	**Melrose**
1994-95	**Stirling County**
1995-96	**Melrose**
1996-97	**Melrose**
1997-98	**Watsonians**
1998-99	**Heriots FP**
1999-00	**Heriots FP**
2000-01	**Hawick**
2001-02	**Hawick**

ALL-IRELAND LEAGUE CHAMPIONS

1990-91	**Cork Constitution**
1991-92	**Garryowen**
1992-93	**Young Munster**
1993-94	**Garryowen**
1994-95	**Shannon**
1995-96	**Shannon**
1996-97	**Shannon**
1997-98	**Shannon**
1998-99	**Garryowen**
1999-00	**St Mary's**
2000-01	**Cork Constitution**
2001-02	**Cork Constitution**

POWERGEN CUP

Formerly Pilkingtopn Cup

	Winner	Runner-up
1972	**Gloucester** 17	Moseley 6
1973	**Coventry** 27	Bristol 15
1974	**Coventry** 26	London Scottish 6
1975	**Bedford** 28	Rosslyn Park 12
1976	**Gosforth** 23	Rosslyn Park 14
1977	**Gosforth** 27	Waterloo 11
1978	**Gloucester** 6	Leicester 3
1979	**Leicester** 15	Moseley 12
1980	**Leicester** 21	London Irish 9
1981	**Leicester** 22	Gosforth 15
1982	**Gloucester & Moseley** Shared 12-12 aet	
1983	**Bristol** 28	Leicester 22
1984	**Bath** 10	Bristol 9
1985	**Bath** 24	London Welsh 15
1986	**Bath** 25	Wasps 17
1987	**Bath** 19	Wasps 12
1988	**Harlequins** 28	Bristol 22
1989	**Bath** 10	Leicester 6
1990	**Bath** 48	Gloucester 6
1991	**Harlequins** 25	Northampton 13 aet
1992	**Bath** 15	Harlequins 12 aet
1993	**Leicester** 23	Harlequins 16
1994	**Bath** 21	Leicester 9
1995	**Bath** 36	Wasps 16
1996	**Bath** 16	Leicester 15
1997	**Leicester** 9	Sale 3
1998	**Saracens** 48	Wasps 18
1999	**Wasps** 29	Newcastle 19
2000	**Wasps** 31	Northampton 23
2001	**Newcastle** 30	Harlequins 27
2002	**London Irish** 38	Northampton 7

SWALEC CUP

1972	**Neath** 15	Llanelli 9
1973	**Llanelli** 30	Cardiff 7
1974	**Llanelli** 12	Aberavon 10
1975	**Llanelli** 15	Aberavon 6
1976	**Llanelli** 15	Swansea 4
1977	**Newport** 16	Cardiff 15
1978	**Swansea** 13	Newport 9
1979	**Bridgend** 18	Pontypridd 12
1980	**Bridgend** 15	Swansea 9
1981	**Cardiff** 14	Bridgend 6
1982	**Cardiff** 12*	Bridgend 12
1983	**Pontypool** 18	Swansea 6
1984	**Cardiff** 24	Neath 19
1985	**Llanelli** 15	Cardiff 14
1986	**Cardiff** 28	Newport 21
1987	**Cardiff** 16	Swansea 15 aet
1988	**Llanelli** 28	Neath 13
1989	**Neath** 14	Llanelli 13
1990	**Neath** 16	Bridgend 10
1991	**Llanelli** 24	Pontypool 9
1992	**Llanelli** 16	Swansea 7
1993	**Llanelli** 21	Neath 18
1994	**Cardiff** 15	Llanelli 8
1995	**Swansea** 17	Pontypridd 12
1996	**Pontypridd** 29	Neath 22
1997	**Cardiff** 33	Swansea 26
1998	**Llanelli** 19	Ebbw Vale 12
1999	**Swansea** 37	Llanelli 10
2000	**Llanelli** 22	Swansea 12

Principality Cup

2001	**Neath** 8	Newport 13
2002	**Pontypridd** 20	Llanelli 17

* won on most tries

SAILING

America's Cup Winners

Year	Winning boat (skipper)	Score	Challenger
1870	**Magic** (Andrew Comstock)	-	Cambria GBR
1871	**Columbia** (Nelson Comstoek)	4-1	Livonia GBR
	Sappho (Sam Greenwood)		
1876	**Madeleine** (Josephus Williams)	2-0	Countess Dufferin CAN
1881	**Mischief** (Nathaniel Clock)	2-0	Atalanta CAN
1885	**Puritan** (Aubrey Crocker)	2-0	Genesta GBR
1886	**Mayflower** (Martin Stone)	2-0	Galatea GBR
1887	**Volunteer** (Henry Haff)	2-0	Thistle GBR
1893	**Vigilant** (William Hansen)	3-0	Valkyrie II GBR
1895	**Defender** (Henry Haff)	3-0	Valkyrie lil GBR
1899	**Columbia** (James Barr)	3-0	Shamrock GBR
1901	**Columbia** (James Barr)	3-0	Shamrock II GBR
1903	**Reliance** (James Barr)	3-0	Shamrock lil GBR
1920	**Resolute** (Charles Adams)	3-2	Shamrock IV GBR
1930	**Enterprise** (Harold Vanderbilt)	4-0	Shamrock V GBR
1934	**Rainbow** (Harold Vanderbilt)	4-2	Endeavour GBR
1937	**Ranger** (Harold Vanderbilt)	4-0	Endeavour II GBR
1958	**Columbia** (Briggs Cunningham)	4-0	Sceptre GBR
1962	**Weatherly** (Emil MosbacherJr)	4-1	Gretel AUS
1964	**Constellation** (Bob Bavier Jr)	4-0	Sovereign GBR
1967	**Intrepid** (Emil Mosbacher Jr)	4-0	Dame Pattie AUS
1970	**Intrepid** (Bill Ficker)	4-1	Gretel II AUS
1974	**Courageous** (Ted Hood)	4-0	Southern Cross AUS
1977	**Courageous** (Ted Turner)	4-0	Australia AUS
1980	**Freedom** (Dennis Conner)	4-1	Australia AUS
1983	**Australia II** (John Bertrand)	4-3	Liberty USA
1987	**Stars & Stripes** (Dennis Conner)	4-0	Kookaburra lil AUS
1988	**Stars & Stripes** (Dennis Conner)	2-0	New Zealand NZL
1992	**America 3** (Bill Koch)	4-1	Il Moro di Venezia ITA
1995	**Black Magic I** (Russell Coutts)	5-0	Young America USA
2000	**Team New Zealand** (Coutts)	5-0	Prada ITA

All winning boats from USA, except Australia II in 1983 and Black Magic I (New Zealand) in 1995

Admiral's Cup Winners

1957	**Great Britain**	1977	**Great Britain**	1997	**USA**
1959	**Great Britain**	1979	**Australia**	1999	**Netherlands**
1961	**USA**	1981	**Great Britain**	2001	Did not take place
1963	**Great Britain**	1983	**West Germany**		
1965	**Great Britain**	1985	**West Germany**		
1967	**Australia**	1987	**New Zealand**		
1969	**USA**	1989	**Great Britain**		
1971	**Great Britain**	1991	**France**		
1973	**West Germany**	1993	**Germany**		
1975	**Great Britain**	1995	**Italy**		

SKIING

World Champions

There is no World Championship in Olympic years.

MEN'S DOWNHILL

1950	Zeno Colo ITA
1954	Christian Pravda AUT
1958	Toni Sailer AUT
1962	Karl Schranz AUT
1966	Jean-Claude Killy FRA
1970	Bernard Russi SUI
1974	David Zwilling AUT
1978	Josef Walcher AUT
1982	Harti Weirather AUT
1985	Pirmin Zurbriggen SUI
1987	Peter Müller SUI
1989	Hansjörg Tauscher FRG
1991	Franz Heinzer SUI
1993	Urs Lehmann SUI
1996	Patrick Ortlieb AUT
1997	Bruno Kernan SUI
1999	Hermann Maier AUT
2001	Hannes Trinkl AUT

MEN'S SUPER G

1987	Pirmin Zurbriggen SUI
1989	Martin Hangl SUI
1991	Stefan Eberharter AUT
1993	race cancelled
1996	Atle Skaardal NOR
1997	Atle Skaardal NOR
1999	Hermann Maier AUT
2001	Daron Rahlves USA

MEN'S GIANT SLALOM

1950	Zeno Colo ITA
1954	Stein Eriksen NOR
1958	Toni Sailer AUT
1962	Egon Zimmermann AUT
1966	Guy Périllat FRA
1970	Karl Schranz AUT
1974	Gustavo Thoeni ITA
1978	Ingemar Stenmark SWE
1982	Steve Mahre USA
1985	Markus Wasmaier FRG
1987	Pirmin Zurbriggen SUI
1989	Rudolf Nierlich AUT
1991	Rudolf Nierlich AUT
1993	Kjetil Andre Aamodt NOR
1996	Alberto Tomba ITA
1997	Michael von Grünigen SUI
1999	Lasse Kjus NOR
2001	MichaelvonGruenigen SUI

MEN'S SLALOM

1950	Georges Schneider SUI
1954	Stein Eriksen NOR
1958	Josef Rieder AUT
1962	Charles Bozon FRA
1966	Carlo Senoner ITA
1970	Jean-Noël Augert FRA
1974	Gustavo Thoeni ITA
1978	Ingemar Stenmark SWE
1982	Ingemar Stenmark SWE
1985	Jonas Nilsson SWE
1987	Frank Wörndl FRG
1989	Rudolf Nierlich AUT
1991	Marc Girardelli AUT
1993	Kjetil Andre Aamodt NOR
1996	Alberto Tomba ITA
1997	Tom Stiansen NOR
1999	Kalle Palander FIN
2001	Mario Matt AUT

MEN'S COMBINED

1954	Stein Eriksen NOR
1958	Toni Sailer AUT
1962	Karl Schranz AUT
1966	Jean-Claude Killy FRA
1970	Bill Kidd USA
1974	Franz Klammer AUT
1978	Andreas Wenzel LIE
1982	Michel Vion FRA
1985	Pirmin Zurbriggen SUI
1987	Marc Girardelli LUX
1989	Marc Girardelli LUX
1991	Stefan Eberharter AUT
1993	Lasse Kjus NOR
1996	Marc Girardelli LUX
1997	Kjetil Andre Aamodt NOR
1999	Kjetil Andre Aamodt NOR
2001	Kjetil Andre Aamodt NOR

WOMEN'S DOWNHILL

1950	Trude B-Jochum AUT
1954	Ida Schöpfer SUI
1958	Lucille Wheeler CAN
1962	Christl Haas AUT
1966	Marielle Goitschel FRA
1970	Annerösli Zyrd SUI
1974	Annemarie Moser-Pröll AUT
1978	Annemarie M-Pröll AUT
1982	Gerry Sorensen CAN
1985	Michela Figini SUI
1987	Maria Walliser SUI
1989	Maria Walliser SUI
1991	Petra Kronberger AUT
1993	Kate Pace CAN
1996	Picabo Street USA
1997	Hilary Lindh USA
1999	Renate Goetschl AUT
2001	Michaela Dorfmeister AUT

WOMEN'S SUPER G

1987	Maria Walliser FRG
1989	Ulrike Maier AUT
1991	Ulrike Maier AUT
1993	Katja Seizinger GER
1996	Isolde Kostner ITA
1997	Isolde Kostner ITA
1999	Alex Meissnitzer AUT
2001	Corinne Rey Bellet SUI

WOMEN'S GIANT SLALOM

1950	Dagmar Rom AUT
1954	Lucienne Schmitt FRA
1958	Lucille Wheeler CAN
1962	Marinne Jahn AUT
1966	Marielle Goitschel FRA
1970	Betsy Clifford CAN
1974	Fabienne Serrat FRA
1978	Maria Epple FRG
1982	Erika Hess SUI
1985	Diann Roffe USA
1987	Vreni Schneider SUI
1989	Vreni Schneider SUI
1991	Pernilla Wiberg SWE
1993	Carole Merle FRA
1996	Deborah Compagnoni ITA
1997	Deborah Compagnoni ITA
1999	Alex Meissnitzer AUT
2001	Sonja Nef SUI

WOMEN'S SLALOM

1950	Dagmar Rom AUT
1954	Trude Klecker AUT
1958	Inger Björnbakken NOR
1962	Marinne Jahn AUT
1966	Annie Famose FRA
1970	Ingrid Lafforgue FRA
1974	Hanni Wenzel LIE
1978	Lea Sölkner AUT
1982	Erika Hess SUI
1985	Perrine Pelen FRA
1987	Erika Hess SUI
1989	Mateja Svet YUG
1991	Vreni Schneider SUI
1993	Karin Buder AUT
1996	Pernilla Wiberg SWE
1997	Deborah Compagnoni ITA
1999	Zali Steggal AUS
2001	Sonja Nef SUI

WOMEN'S COMBINED

1954	Ida Schöpfer SUI
1958	Frieda Dänzer SUI
1962	Marielle Goitschel FRA
1966	Marielle Goitschel FRA
1970	Michele Jacot FRA
1974	Fabienne Serrat FRA
1978	Annemarie M-Pröll AUT
1982	Erika Hess SUI
1985	Erika Hess SUI
1987	Erika Hess SUI
1989	Tamara McKinney USA
1991	Chantal Bournissen SUI
1993	Miriam Vogt GER
1996	Pernilla Wiberg SWE
1997	Renate Goetschl AUT
1999	Pernilla Wiberg SWE
2001	Martina Ertl GER

SKIING

World Cup winners

MEN'S OVERALL
1967 Jean-Claude Killy FRA
1968 Jean-Claude Killy FRA
1969 Karl Schranz AUT
1970 Karl Schranz AUT
1971 Gustavo Thoeni ITA
1972 Gustavo Thoeni ITA
1973 Gustavo Thoeni ITA
1974 Piero Gros ITA
1975 Gustavo Thoeni ITA
1976 Ingemar Stenmark SWE
1977 Ingemar Stenmark SWE
1978 Ingemar Stenmark SWE
1979 Ingemar Stenmark SWE
1980 Andreas Wenzel LIE
1981 Phil Mahre USA
1982 Phil Mahre USA
1983 Phil Mahre USA
1984 Pirmin Zurbriggen SUI
1985 Marc Girardelli LUX
1986 Marc Girardelli LUX
1987 Pirmin Zurbriggen SUI
1988 Pirmin Zurbriggen SUI
1989 Marc Girardelli LUX
1990 Pirmin Zurbriggen SUI
1991 Marc Girardelli LUX
1992 Paul Accola SUI
1993 Marc Girardelli LUX
1994 Kjetil Andre Aamodt NOR
1995 Alberto Tomba ITA
1996 Lasse Kjus NOR
1997 Luc Alphand FRA
1998 Hermann Maier AUT
1999 Lasse Kjus NOR
2000 Hermann Maier AUT
2001 Hermann Maier AUT

MEN'S DOWNHILL
1967 Jean-Claude Killy FRA
1968 Gerhard Nenning AUT
1969 Karl Schranz AUT
1970 Schranz/Cordin both AUT
1971 Bernhard Russi SUI
1972 Bernhard Russi SUI
1973 Roland Collombin SUI
1974 Roland Collombin SUI
1975 Franz Klammer AUT
1976 Franz Klammer AUT
1977 Franz Klammer AUT
1978 Franz Klammer AUT
1979 Peter Muller SUI
1980 Peter Muller SUI
1981 Harti Weirather AUT
1982 Podborski/Muller CAN/SUI
1983 Franz Klammer AUT
1984 Urs Raber SUI
1985 Helmut Hohlfehner AUT
1986 Peter Wirnsberger AUT
1987 Pirmin Zurbriggen SUI
1988 Pirmin Zurbriggen SUI

1989 Marc Girardelli LUX
1990 Helmut Hohlflehner AUT
1991 Franz Heinzer SUI
1992 Franz Heinzer SUI
1993 Franz Heinzer SUI
1994 Marc Girardelli LUX
1995 Luc Alphand FRA
1996 Luc Alphand FRA
1997 Luc Alphand FRA
1998 Andreas Schifferer AUT
1999 Lasse Kjus NOR
2000 Hermann Maier AUT
2001 Hermann Maier AUT

MEN'S SUPER G
1986 Markus Wasmeier FRG
1987 Pirmin Zurbriggen SUI
1988 Pirmin Zurbriggen SUI
1989 Pirmin Zurbriggen SUI
1990 Pirmin Zurbriggen SUI
1991 Franz Heinzer SUI
1992 Paul Accola SUI
1993 Kjetil Andre Aamodt NOR
1994 Jan Einar Thorsen NOR
1995 Peter Runggaldier ITA
1996 Atle Skaardal NOR
1997 Luc Alphand FRA
1998 Hermann Maier AUT
1999 Hermann Maier AUT
2000 Hermann Maier AUT
2001 Hermann Maier AUT

MEN'S GIANT SLALOM
1967 Jean-Claude Killy FRA
1968 Jean-Claude Killy FRA
1969 Karl Schranz AUT
1970 Gustavo Thoeni ITA
1971 Thoeni ITA/Russel FRA
1972 Gustavo Thoeni ITA
1973 Hans Hinterseer AUT
1974 Piero Gros ITA
1975 Ingemar Stenmark SWE
1976 Ingemar Stenmark SWE
1977 Heini Hemmi SUI
1978 Ingemar Stenmark SWE
1979 Ingemar Stenmark SWE
1980 Ingemar Stenmark SWE
1981 Ingemar Stenmark SWE
1982 Phil Mahre USA
1983 Phil Mahre USA
1984 Ingemar Stenmark SWE
1985 Marc Girardelli LUX
1986 Joel Gaspoz SUI
1987 Pirmin Zurbriggen SUI
1988 Alberto Tomba ITA
1989 Ole Christ'n Furuseth NOR
1990 Ole Christ'n Furuseth NOR
1991 Alberto Tomba ITA
1992 Alberto Tomba ITA
1993 Kjetil Andre Aamodt NOR
1994 Christian Mayer AUT

1995 Alberto Tomba ITA
1996 Michael von Grünigen SUI
1997 Michael von Grünigen SUI
1998 Hermann Maier AUT
1999 Michael von Grünigen SUI
2000 Hermann Maier AUT
2001 Hermann Maier AUT

MEN'S SLALOM
1967 Jean-Claude Killy FRA
1968 Domeng Giovanoli SUI
1969 Augert/Matt/Penz/Russel
1970 Russel/Penz both FRA
1971 Jean-Noel Augert FRA
1972 Jean-Noel Augert FRA
1973 Gustavo Thoeni ITA
1974 Gustavo Thoeni ITA
1975 Ingemar Stenmark SWE
1976 Ingemar Stenmark SWE
1977 Ingemar Stenmark SWE
1978 Ingemar Stenmark SWE
1979 Ingemar Stenmark SWE
1980 Ingemar Stenmark SWE
1981 Ingemar Stenmark SWE
1982 Phil Mahre USA
1983 Ingemar Stenmark SWE
1984 Marc Girardelli LUX
1985 Marc Girardelli LUX
1986 Rok Petrovic YUG
1987 Bojan Krizaj YUG
1988 Alberto Tomba ITA
1989 Armin Bittner FRG
1990 Armin Bittner FRG
1991 Marc Girardelli LUX
1992 Alberto Tomba ITA
1993 Tomas Fogdoe SWE
1994 Alberto Tomba ITA
1995 Alberto Tomba ITA
1996 Sébastien Amiez FRA
1997 Thomas Sykora AUT
1998 Thomas Sykora AUT
1999 T Stangassinger AUT
2000 Kjetil Andre Aamodt NOR
2001 Benjamin Raich AUT

WOMEN'S OVERALL
1967 Nancy Greene USA
1968 Nancy Greene USA
1969 Gertrud Gabl AUT
1970 Michele Jacot FRA
1971 Annemarie Moser-Pröll AUT
1972 Annemarie Moser-Pröll
1973 Annemarie Moser-Pröll
1974 Annemarie Moser-Pröll
1975 Annemarie Moser-Pröll
1976 Rosi Mittermaier FRG
1977 Lise-Marie Morerod SUI
1978 Hanni Wenzel LIE
1979 Annemarie Moser-Pröll
1980 Hanni Wenzel LIE

SKIING

1981	**Marie-Therese Nadig** SUI
1982	**Erika Hess** SUI
1983	**Tamara McKinney** USA
1984	**Erika Hess** SUI
1985	**Michela Figini** SUI
1986	**Maria Walliser** SUI
1987	**Maria Walliser** SUI
1988	**Michela Figini** SUI
1989	**Vreni Schneider** SUI
1990	**Petra Kronberger** AUT
1991	**Petra Kronberger** AUT
1992	**Petra Kronberger** AUT
1993	**Anita Wachter** AUT
1994	**Vreni Schneider** SUI
1995	**Vreni Schneider** SUI
1996	**Katja Seizinger** GER
1997	**Pernilla Wiberg** SWE
1998	**Katja Seizinger** GER
1999	**Alex Meissnitzer** AUT
2000	**Renate Götschl** AUT
2001	**Janica Kostelic** CRO

WOMEN'S DOWNHILL

1967	**Marielle Goitschel** FRA
1968	**Isabelle Mir** FRA &
	Olga Pall AUT
1969	**Wiltrud Drexel** AUT
1970	**Isabelle Mir** FRA
1971	**Annemarie Moser-Pröll**
1972	**Annemarie Moser-Pröll**
1973	**Annemarie Moser-Pröll**
1974	**Annemarie Moser-Pröll**
1975	**Annemarie Moser-Pröll**
1976	**Brigitte H-Totschnig** AUT
1977	**Brigitte H-Totschnig** AUT
1978	**Annemarie Moser-Pröll**
1979	**Annemarie Moser-Pröll**
1980	**Marie-Therese Nadig** SUI
1981	**Marie-Therese Nadig** SUI
1982	**C Gros-Gaudenier** FRA
1983	**Doris De Agostini** SUI
1984	**Maria Walliser** SUI
1985	**Michela Figini** SUI
1986	**Maria Walliser** SUI
1987	**Michela Figini** SUI
1988	**Michela Figini** SUI
1989	**Michela Figini** SUI
1990	**K Gütensohn-Knopl** FRG
1991	**Chantal Bournissen** SUI
1992	**Katja Seizinger** GER
1993	**Katja Seizinger** GER
1994	**Katja Seizinger** GER
1995	**Picabo Street** USA
1996	**Picabo Street** USA
1997	**Renate Götschl** AUT
1998	**Katja Seizinger** GER
1999	**Renate Götschl** AUT
2000	**Regina Haeusl** GER
2001	**Isolde Kostner** ITA

WOMEN'S SUPER G

1986	**Marina Kiehl** FRG
1987	**Maria Walliser** SUI
1988	**Michela Figini** SUI
1989	**Carole Merle** FRA
1990	**Carole Merle** FRA
1991	**Carole Merle** FRA
1992	**Carole Merle** FRA
1993	**Carole Merle** FRA
1994	**Katja Seizinger** GER
1995	**Katja Seizinger** GER
1996	**Katja Seizinger** GER
1997	**Hilde Gerg** GER
1998	**Katja Seizinger** GER
1999	**Alex Meissnitzer** AUT
2000	**Renate Götschl** AUT
2001	**Regine Cavagnoud** FRA

WOMEN'S GIANT SLALOM

1967	**Nancy Greene** USA
1968	**Nancy Greene** USA
1969	**Marilyn Cochran** USA
1970	**Michelle Jacot** FRA
	Francoise Macchi FRA
1971	**Annemarie Moser-Pröll**
1972	**Annemarie Moser-Pröll**
1973	**Monica Kaserer** AUT
1974	**Hani Wenzel** LIE
1975	**Annemarie Moser-Pröll**
1976	**Lise-Marie Morerod** SWE
1977	**Lise-Marie Morerod** SWE
1978	**Lise-Marie Morerod** SWE
1979	**Christa Kinshoffer** FRG
1980	**Hanni Wenzel** LIE
1981	**Tamara McKinney** USA
1982	**Irene Epple** FRG
1983	**Tamara McKinney** USA
1984	**Erika Hess** SUI
1985	**Michela Figini** SUI &
	Marina Kiehl FRG
1986	**Vreni Schneider** SUI
1987	**Maria Walliser** SUI &
	Vreni Schneider SUI
1988	**Mateja Svet** YUG
1989	**Vreni Schneider** SUI
1990	**Anita Wachter** AUT
1991	**Vreni Schneider** SUI
1992	**Carole Merle** FRA
1993	**Carole Merle** FRA
1994	**Anita Wachter** AUT
1995	**Vreni Schneider** SUI
1996	**Martina Ertl** GER
1997	**Deborah Compagnoni** ITA
1998	**Martina Ertl** GER
1999	**Alex Meissnitzer** AUT
2000	**Michaela Dorfmeister** AUT
2001	**Sonja Nef** SUI

WOMEN'S SLALOM

1967	**Marielle Goitschel** FRA &
	Annie Famose FRA
1968	**Marielle Goitschel** FRA
1969	**Gertrud Gabl** AUT
1970	**Ingrid Laforgue** FRA
1971	**Britt Laforgue** FRA &
	Betsy Clifford CAN
1972	**Britt Laforgue** FRA
1973	**Patricia Emonet** FRA
1974	**Christa Zechmeister** FRG
1975	**Lise-Marie Morerod** SWE
1976	**Rosi Mittermaier** GER
1977	**Lise-Marie Morerod** SWE
1978	**Hanni Wenzel** LIE
1979	**Regina Sackl** AUT
1980	**Perrine Pelen** FRA
1981	**Erika Hess** SUI
1982	**Erika Hess** SUI
1983	**Erika Hess** SUI
1984	**Tamara McKinney** USA
1985	**Erika Hess** SUI
1986	**Roswitha Steiner** AUT
1987	**CorinneSchmidhauser**SUI
1988	**Roswitha Steiner** AUT
1989	**Vreni Schneider** SUI
1990	**Vreni Schneider** SUI
1991	**Petra Kronberger** AUT
1992	**Vreni Schneider** SUI
1993	**Vreni Schneider** SUI
1994	**Vreni Schneider** SUI
1995	**Vreni Schneider** SUI
1996	**Elfi Eder** AUT
1997	**Pernilla Wiberg** SWE
1998	**Ylva Nowén** SWE
1999	**Sabine Egger** AUT
2000	**Michaela Dorfmeister** AUT
2001	**Janica Kostelic** CRO

SNOOKER

WORLD CHAMPIONS

The World Championship took place up to 1952 when a disagreement caused the professional players to organise their own match-play tournament which ended in 1957. The World Championship was not staged again until 1964 when it was revived on a challenge basis. In 1969 it adopted the knockout format.

All players British unless otherwise stated

1927	Joe Davis	20-11	Tom Dennis
1928	Joe Davis	16-13	Fred Lawrence
1929	Joe Davis	19-14	Tom Dennis
1930	Joe Davis	25-12	Tom Dennis
1931	Joe Davis	25-21	Tom Dennis
1932	Joe Davis	30-19	Clark McConachy NZL
1933	Joe Davis	25-18	Willie Smith
1934	Joe Davis	25-23	Tom Newman
1935	Joe Davis	25-20	Willie Smith
1936	Joe Davis	34-27	Horace Lindrum AUS
1937	Joe Davis	32-29	Horace Lindrum AUS
1938	Joe Davis	37-24	Sidney Smith
1939	Joe Davis	43-30	Sidney Smith
1940	Joe Davis	37-36	Fred Davis
1946	Joe Davis	78-67	Horace Lindrum AUS
1947	W Donaldson	82-63	Fred Davis
1948	Fred Davis	84-61	Walter Donaldson
1949	Fred Davis	80-65	Walter Donaldson
1950	W Donaldson	51-46	Fred Davis
1951	Fred Davis	58-39	Walter Donaldson
1952	Horace Lindrum AUS	94-49	Clark McConachy NZL

Professional Match-Play Championship

1952	Fred Davis	38-35	Walter Donaldson
1953	Fred Davis	37-34	Walter Donaldson
1954	Fred Davis	39-21	Walter Donaldson
1955	Fred Davis	37-34	John Pulman
1956	Fred Davis	38-35	John Pulman
1957	John Pulman	39-34	Jackie Rea

Challenge Matches

1964	John Pulman	19-16	Fred Davis
1964	John Pulman	40-33	Rex Williams
1965	John Pulman	37-36	Fred Davis
1965	John Pulman	25-22	Rex Williams
1965	John Pulman	39-12	F van Rensburg RSA
1966	John Pulman	5-2	Fred Davis
1968	John Pulman	39-34	Eddie Charlton AUS

Knock-out

1969	John Spencer	37-34	Gary Owen
1970	Ray Reardon	37-33	John Pulman
1971*	John Spencer	37-29	Warren Simpson AUS
1972	Alex Higgins	37-32	John Spencer
1973	Ray Reardon	38-32	Eddie Charlton AUS
1974	Ray Reardon	22-12	Graham Miles
1975	Ray Reardon	31-30	Eddie Charlton AUS
1976	Ray Reardon	27-16	Alex Higgins
1977	John Spencer	25-21	Cliff Thorburn CAN
1978	Ray Reardon	25-18	Perrie Mans RSA
1979	Terry Griffiths	24-16	Dennis Taylor
1980	Cliff Thorburn CAN	18-16	Alex Higgins
1981	Steve Davis	18-12	Doug Mountjoy
1982	Alex Higgins	18-15	Ray Reardon
1983	Steve Davis	18-6	Cliff Thorburn CAN
1984	Steve Davis	18-16	Jimmy White
1985	Dennis Taylor	18-17	Steve Davis
1986	Joe Johnson	18-12	Steve Davis
1987	Steve Davis	18-14	Joe Johnson
1988	Steve Davis	18-11	Terry Griffiths
1989	Steve Davis	18-3	John Parrott
1990	Stephen Hendry	18-12	Jimmy White
1991	John Parrott	18-11	Jimmy White
1992	Stephen Hendry	18-14	Jimmy White
1993	Stephen Hendry	18-5	Jimmy White
1994	Stephen Hendry	18-17	Jimmy White
1995	Stephen Hendry	18-9	Nigel Bond
1996	Stephen Hendry	18-12	Peter Ebdon
1997	Ken Doherty	18-12	Stephen Hendry
1998	John Higgins	18-12	Ken Doherty
1999	Stephen Hendry	18-11	Mark Williams
2000	Mark Williams	18-16	Matthew Stevens
2001	RonnieO'Sullivan	18-14	John Higgins
2002	Peter Ebdon	18-17	Stephen Hendry

* Played November 1970

SQUASH

WORLD AMATEUR CHAMPIONSHIP

1967 **Geoff Hunt** AUS
1969 **Geoff Hunt** AUS
1971 **Geoff Hunt** AUS
1973 **Cameron Nancarrow** AUS
1976 **Kevin Shawcross** AUS
1977 **Maqsood Ahmed** PAK
1979 **Jahangir Khan** PAK
1981 **Steve Bowditch** AUS
1983 **Jahangir Khan** PAK
1985 **Jahangir Khan** PAK

The World Amateur was gradually replaced by the World Open as squash became more professional

WORLD OPEN
Men

1976 **Geoff Hunt** AUS
1977 **Geoff Hunt** AUS
1979 **Geoff Hunt** AUS
1980 **Geoff Hunt** AUS
1981 **Jahangir Khan** PAK
1982 **Jahangir Khan** PAK
1983 **Jahangir Khan** PAK
1984 **Jahangir Khan** PAK
1985 **Jahangir Khan** PAK
1986 **Ross Norman** NZL
1987 **Jansher Khan** PAK
1988 **Jahangir Khan** PAK
1989 **Jansher Khan** PAK
1990 **Jansher Khan** PAK
1991 **Rodney Martin** AUS
1992 **Jansher Khan** PAK
1993 **Jansher Khan** PAK
1994 **Jansher Khan** PAK
1995 **Jansher Khan** PAK
1996 **Jansher Khan** PAK
1997 **Rodney Eyles** AUS
1998 **Jonathon Power** CAN
1999 **Peter Nicol** GBR
2002 **David Palmer** AUS

BRITISH OPEN
Men

1930 **Don Butcher** GBR
1931 **Don Butcher** GBR
1932 **Abdelfattah Amr Bey** EGY
1933 **Abdelfattah Amr Bey** EGY
1934 **Abdelfattah Amr Bey** EGY
1935 **Abdelfattah Amr Bey** EGY
1936 **Abdelfattah Amr Bey** EGY
1937 **Abdelfattah Amr Bey** EGY
1938 **James Dear** GBR
1946 **Mahmoud Karim** EGY
1947 **Mahmoud Karim** EGY
1948 **Mahmoud Karim** EGY
1949 **Mahmoud Karim** EGY
1950 **Hashim Khan** PAK
1951 **Hashim Khan** PAK
1952 **Hashim Khan** PAK
1953 **Hashim Khan** PAK

1954 **Hashim Khan** PAK
1955 **Hashim Khan** PAK
1956 **Roshan Khan** PAK
1957 **Hashim Khan** PAK
1958 **Azam Khan** PAK
1959 **Azam Khan** PAK
1960 **Azam Khan** PAK
1961 **Azam Khan** PAK
1962 **Mohibullah Khan** PAK
1963 **Abdelfattah Abou Taleb** EGY
1964 **Abdelfattah Abou Taleb**
1965 **Abdelfattah Abou Taleb**
1966 **Abdelfattah Abou Taleb**
1967 **Jonah Barrington** GBR
1968 **Jonah Barrington** GBR
1969 **Geoff Hunt** AUS
1970 **Jonah Barrington** GBR
1971 **Jonah Barrington** GBR
1972 **Jonah Barrington** GBR
1973 **Jonah Barrington** GBR
1974 **Geoff Hunt** AUS
1975 **Qamar Zaman** PAK
1976 **Geoff Hunt** AUS
1977 **Geoff Hunt** AUS
1978 **Geoff Hunt** AUS
1979 **Geoff Hunt** AUS
1980 **Geoff Hunt** AUS
1981 **Geoff Hunt** AUS
1982 **Jahangir Khan** PAK
1983 **Jahangir Khan** PAK
1984 **Jahangir Khan** PAK
1985 **Jahangir Khan** PAK
1986 **Jahangir Khan** PAK
1987 **Jahangir Khan** PAK
1988 **Jahangir Khan** PAK
1989 **Jahangir Khan** PAK
1990 **Jahangir Khan** PAK
1991 **Jahangir Khan** PAK
1992 **Jansher Khan** PAK
1993 **Jansher Khan** PAK
1994 **Jansher Khan** PAK
1995 **Jansher Khan** PAK
1996 **Jansher Khan** PAK
1997 **Jansher Khan** PAK
1998 **Peter Nicol** GBR
1999 **Jonathon Power** CAN
2000 **David Evans** WAL
2001 **David Palmer** AUS
2002 **Peter Nicol** ENG

SQUASH

WORLD OPEN

Women

1976	**Heather McKay** AUS
1979	**Heather McKay** AUS
1981	**Rhonda Thorne** AUS
1983	**Vicki Cardwell** AUS
1985	**Susan Devoy** NZL
1987	**Susan Devoy** NZL
1989	**Martine Le Moignan** GBR
1990	**Susan Devoy** NZL
1991	**Susan Devoy** NZL
1992	**Susan Devoy** NZL
1993	**Michelle Martin** AUS
1994	**Michelle Martin** AUS
1995	**Michelle Martin** AUS
1996	**Sarah Fitz-Gerald** AUS
1997	**Sarah Fitz-Gerald** AUS
1998	**Sarah Fitz-Gerald** AUS
1999	**Cassie Campion** GBR
2000	**Carol Owens** AUS
2001	**Sarah Fitz-Gerald** AUS
2002	**Sarah Fitz-Gerald** AUS

BRITISH OPEN

Women

1922	**Joyce Cave** GBR
1922	**Sylvia Huntsman** GBR
1923	**Nancy Cave** GBR
1924	**Joyce Cave** GBR
1925	**Cecily Fenwick** GBR
1926	**Cecily Fenwick** GBR
1928	**Joyce Cave** GBR
1929	**Nancy Cave** GBR
1930	**Nancy Cave** GBR
1931	**Cecily Fenwick** GBR
1932	**Susan Noel** GBR
1933	**Susan Noel** GBR
1934	**Susan Noel** GBR
1934	**Margot Lumb** GBR
1935	**Margot Lumb** GBR
1936	**Margot Lumb** GBR
1937	**Margot Lumb** GBR
1938	**Margot Lumb** GBR
1939	**Margot Lumb** GBR
1947	**Joan Curry** GBR
1948	**Joan Curry** GBR
1949	**Joan Curry** GBR
1950	**Janet Morgan** GBR
1951	**Janet Morgan** GBR
1952	**Janet Morgan** GBR
1953	**Janet Morgan** GBR
1954	**Janet Morgan** GBR
1955	**Janet Morgan** GBR
1956	**Janet Morgan** GBR
1957	**Janet Morgan** GBR
1958	**Janet Morgan** GBR
1959	**Janet Morgan** GBR
1960	**Sheila Macintosh** GBR
1961	**Fran Marshall** GBR

1962	**Heather Blundell** AUS
1963	**Heather Blundell** AUS
1964	**Heather Blundell** AUS
1965	**Heather Blundell** AUS
1966	**Heather McKay** AUS
1967	**Heather McKay** AUS
1968	**Heather McKay** AUS
1969	**Heather McKay** AUS
1970	**Heather McKay** AUS
1971	**Heather McKay** AUS
1972	**Heather McKay** AUS
1973	**Heather McKay** AUS
1974	**Heather McKay** AUS
1975	**Heather McKay** AUS
1976	**Heather McKay** AUS
1977	**Heather McKay** AUS
1978	**Susan Newman** AUS
1979	**Barbara Wall** AUS
1980	**Vicki Hoffman** AUS
1981	**Vicki Hoffman** AUS
1982	**Vicki Cardwell** (née Hoffman) AUS
1983	**Vicki Cardwell** AUS
1984	**Susan Devoy** NZL
1985	**Susan Devoy** NZL
1986	**Susan Devoy** NZL
1987	**Susan Devoy** NZL
1988	**Susan Devoy** NZL
1989	**Susan Devoy** NZL
1990	**Susan Devoy** NZL
1991	**Lisa Opie** GBR
1992	**Susan Devoy** NZL
1993	**Michelle Martin** AUS
1994	**Michelle Martin** AUS
1995	**Michelle Martin** AUS
1996	**Michelle Martin** AUS
1997	**Michelle Martin** AUS
1998	**Michelle Martin** AUS
1999	**Leilani Joyce** NZL
2000	**Leilani Joyce** NZL
2001	**Sarah Fitz-Gerald** AUS
2002	**Sarah Fitz-Gerald** AUS

SPEED SKATING

SHORT TRACK WORLD CHAMPIONS

Year	Venue	Men	Women
1976	Champaign	**Alan Rattray** USA	**Celeste Chlapaty** USA
1977	Grenoble	**Gaetan Boucher** CAN	**Brenda Webster** CAN
1978	Solihull	**James Lynch** AUS	**Sarah Doctor** USA
1979	Quebec	**Hiroshi Toda** JPN	**Sylvie Daigle** CAN
1980	Milan	**Gaetan Boucher** CAN	**Miyoshi Kato** JPN
1981	Meudon	**Benoit Baril** CAN	**Miyoshi Kato** JPN
1982	Moncton	**Guy Daignault** CAN	**Maryse Perreault** CAN
1983	Tokyo	**Louis Grenier** CAN	**Sylvie Daigle** CAN
1984	Peterborough	**Guy Daignault** CAN	**Mariko Kinoshita** JPN
1985	Amsterdam	**Toshinobu Kawai** JPN	**Eiko Shishii** JPN
1986	Chamonix	**Tatsuyoshi Ishihara** JPN	**Bonnie Blair** USA
1987	Montreal	**Toshinobu Kawai** JPN/**Michel Daignault** CAN	**Eiko Shishii** JPN
1988	St Louis	**Peter van de Velde** NED	**Sylvie Daigle** CAN
1989	Solihull	**Michel Daignault** CAN	**Sylvie Daigle** CAN
1990	Amsterdam	**Lee Joon-Ho** KOR	**Sylvie Daigle** CAN
1991	Sydney	**Wilf O'Reilly** GBR	**Nathalie Lambert** CAN
1992	Denver	**Kim Ki-Hoon** KOR	**Kim So-Hee** KOR
1993	Beijing	**Marc Gagnon** CAN	**Nathalie Lambert** CAN
1994	Guildford	**Marc Gagnon** CAN	**Nathalie Lambert** CAN
1995	Gjøvik	**Chae Ji-Hoon** KOR	**Chun Lee-Kyung** KOR
1996	The Hague	**Marc Gagnon** CAN	**Chun Lee-Kyung** KOR
1997	Nagano	**Kim Dong-Sung** KOR	**Chun L-Kyung** KOR/**Yang Yang (A)** CHN
1998	Vienna	**Marc Gagnon** CAN	**Yang Yang (A)** CHN
1999	Sofia	**Li Jiajun** CHN	**Yang Yang (A)** CHN
2000	Sheffield	**Rioung Min** KOR	**Yang Yang (A)** CHN
2001	Jeonju City	**Li Jiajun** CHN	**Yang Yang (A)** CHN
2002	Montreal	**Kim Dong-Sung** KOR	**Yang Yang (A)** CHN

BRITISH CHAMPIONS

Abbreviations: ALD=Aldwych, ALT=Altrincham, MOH=Mohawks, NOT=Nottingham

Year	Venue	Men	Women
1981	Streatham	not held	**Lisa Harrold** NOT
1982	Birmingham	**Gary Rudd** ALD	**Lisa Harrold** NOT
1983	Nottingham	**Wilf O'Reilly** MOH/**Gary Rudd** ALD	**Caron New** MOH
1984	Peterborough	**Wilf O'Reilly** MOH	**Amanda Worth** NOT
1985	Richmond	**Wilf O'Reilly** MOH	**Nicola Bell** NOT
1986	Peterborough	**Wilf O'Reilly** MOH	**Nicola Bell** NOT
1987	Solihull	**Wilf O'Reilly** MOH	**Amanda Worth** NOT
1988	Richmond	**Wilf O'Reilly** MOH	**Caron New** MOH
1989	Richmond	**Wilf O'Reilly** MOH	**Alyson Birch** ALT
1990	Humberside	**Stuart Horsepool** NOT	**Alyson Birch** ALT
1991	Richmond	**Wilf O'Reilly** MOH	**Debbie Palmer** ALD
1992	Humberside	**Matthew Jasper** NOT	**Debbie Palmer** ALD
1993	Humberside	**Nicky Gooch** ALD	**Debbie Palmer** ALD
1994	Humberside	**Nicky Gooch** ALD	**Debbie Palmer** ALD
1995	Guildford	**Matthew Jasper** NOT	**Debbie Palmer** ALD
1996	Guildford	**Nicky Gooch** ALD	**Debbie Palmer** ALD
1997	Guildford	**Nicky Gooch** ALD	**Debbie Palmer** ALD
1998	Guildford	**Nicky Gooch** ALD	**Debbie Palmer** ALD
2002	Nottingham	**Leon Flack**	**Sarah Lindsay**

SWIMMING

WORLD CHAMPIONS

Men

50m Freestyle
1986 Tom Jager USA
1991 Tom Jager USA
1994 Alexander Popov RUS
1998 Bill Pilczuk USA
2001 Anthony Ervin USA

100m Freestyle
1973 Jim Montgomery USA
1975 Andrew Coan USA
1978 David McCagg USA
1982 Jorg Woithe GDR
1986 Matt Biondi USA
1991 Matt Biondi USA
1994 Alexander Popov RUS
1998 Alexander Popov RUS
2001 Anthony Ervin USA

200m Freestyle
1973 Jim Montgomery USA
1975 Tim Shaw USA
1978 William Forrester USA
1982 Michael Gross FRG
1986 Michael Gross FRG
1991 Giorgio Lamberti ITA
1994 Antti Kasvio FIN
1998 Michael Klim AUS
2001 Ian Thorpe AUS

400m Freestyle
1973 Rick DeMont USA
1975 Tim Shaw USA
1978 Vladimir Salnikov URS
1982 Vladimir Salnikov URS
1986 Rainer Henkel FRG
1991 Jörg Hoffmann GER
1994 Kieren Perkins AUS
1998 Ian Thorpe AUS
2001 Ian Thorpe AUS

800m Free
2001 Ian Thorpe AUS

1500m Freestyle
1973 Steve Holland AUS
1975 Tim Shaw USA
1978 Vladimir Salnikov URS
1982 Vladimir Salnikov URS
1986 Rainer Henkel FRG
1991 Jörg Hoffmann GER
1994 Kieren Perkins AUS
1998 Grant Hackett AUS
2001 Grant Hackett AUS

50m Back
2001 Randall Bal USA

100m Backstroke
1973 Roland Matthes GDR
1975 Roland Matthes GDR
1978 Robert Jackson USA
1982 Dirk Richter GDR
1986 Igor Polyanski URS
1991 Jeff Rouse USA
1994 Martin Lopez-Zubero ESP
1998 Lenny Krayzelburg USA
2001 Matt Welsh AUS

200m Backstroke
1973 Roland Matthes GDR
1975 Zoltan Verraszto HUN
1978 Jesse Vassallo USA
1982 Rick Carey USA
1986 Igor Polyanski URS
1991 Martin Zubero ESP
1994 Vladimir Selkov RUS
1998 Lenny Krayzelburg USA
2001 Aaron Peirsol USA

50m Breaststroke
2001 Oleg Lisogor UKR

100m Breaststroke
1973 John Hencken USA
1975 David Wilkie GBR
1978 Walter Kusch GDR
1982 Steve Lundquist USA
1986 Victor Davis CAN
1991 Norbert Rosza HUN
1994 Norbert Rosza HUN
1998 Fred Deburghgraeve BEL
2001 Roman Sloudnov RUS

200m Breaststroke
1973 David Wilkie GBR
1975 David Wilkie GBR
1978 Nick Nevid USA
1982 Victor Davis CAN
1986 Josef Szabó HUN
1991 Mike Barrowman USA
1994 Norbert Rosza HUN
1998 Kurt Grote USA
2001 Brendan Hansen USA

50m Butterfly
2001 Geoff Huegill AUS

100m Butterfly
1973 Bruce Robertson CAN
1975 Greg Jagenburg USA
1978 Joe Bottom USA
1982 Matt Gribble USA
1986 Pablo Morales USA
1991 Anthony Nesty SUR
1994 Rafal Szukala POL
1998 Michael Klim AUS
2001 Lars Frolander SWE

200m Butterfly
1973 Robin Backhaus USA
1975 William Forrester USA
1978 Mike Bruner USA
1982 Michael Gross FRG
1986 Michael Gross FRG
1991 Melvin Stewart USA
1994 Denis Pankratov RUS

1998 Denis Silantiev RUS
2001 Michael Phelps USA

200m Individual Medley
1973 Gunnar Larsson SWE
1975 András Hargitay HUN
1978 Graham Smith CAN
1982 Alexsei Sidorenko URS
1986 Tamás Darnyi HUN
1991 Tamás Darnyi HUN
1994 Jani Sievinen FIN
1998 Marcel Wouda NED
2001 Massi Rosolino ITA

400m Individual Medley
1973 András Hargitay HUN
1975 András Hargitay HUN
1978 Jesse Vassallo USA
1982 Ricardo Prado BRA
1986 Tamás Darnyi HUN
1991 Tamás Darnyi HUN
1994 Tom Dolan USA
1998 Tom Dolan USA
2001 Alessio Boggiatto ITA

4x100m Freestyle Relay
1973 United States
1975 United States
1978 United States
1982 United States
1986 United States
1991 United States
1994 United States
1998 United States
2001 Australia

4x200m Freestyle Relay
1973 United States
1975 West Germany
1978 United States
1982 United States
1986 East Germany
1991 Germany
1994 Sweden
1998 Australia
2001 Australia

4x100m Medley Relay
1973 United States
1975 United States
1978 United States
1982 United States
1986 United States
1991 United States
1994 United States
1998 Australia
2001 Australia

1m Springboard
1991 Edwin Jongejans NED
1994 Evan Stewart ZIM
1998 Zhuocheng Yu CHN
2001 Feng Wang CHN

SWIMMING

3m Springboard
1973 **Phil Boggs** USA
1975 **Phil Boggs** USA
1978 **Phil Boggs** USA
1982 **Greg Louganis** USA
1986 **Greg Louganis** USA
1991 **Kent Ferguson** USA
1994 **Zhuocheng Yu** CHN
1998 **Dmitri Sautin** RUS
2001 **Dmitri Sautin** RUS

10m Platform
1973 **Klaus Dibiasi** ITA
1975 **Klaus Dibiasi** ITA
1978 **Greg Louganis** USA
1982 **Greg Louganis** USA
1986 **Greg Louganis** USA
1991 **Sun Shuwei** CHN
1994 **Dmitri Sautin** RUS
1998 **Dmitri Sautin** RUS
2001 **Liang Tian** CHN

3m Springboard Synchro
1998 **Xu/Yu** CHN
2001 **Peng/Wang** CHN

Platform Synchro
1998 **Sun/Tian** CHN
2001 **Tian/Hu** CHN

Water Polo
1973 **Hungary**
1975 **Soviet Union**
1978 **Italy**
1982 **Soviet Union**
1986 **Yugoslavia**
1991 **Yugoslavia**
1994 **Italy**
1998 **Spain**
2001 **Spain**

Women

50m Freestyle
1986 **Tamara Costache** ROM
1991 **Zuang Yong** CHN
1994 **Jingyi Le** CHN
1998 **Amy Van Dyken** USA
2001 **Inge de Bruijn** NED

100m Freestyle
1973 **Kornelia Ender** GDR
1975 **Kornelia Ender** GDR
1978 **Barbara Krause** GDR
1982 **Birgit Meineke** GDR
1986 **Kristin Otto** GDR
1991 **Nicole Haislett** USA
1994 **Jingyi Le** CHN
1998 **Jenny Thompson** USA
2001 **Inge de Bruijn** NED

200m Freestyle
1973 **Keena Rothhammer** USA
1975 **Shirley Babashoff** USA
1978 **Cynthia Woodhead** USA
1982 **A Verstappen** NED
1986 **Heike Friedrich** GDR
1991 **Hayley Lewis** AUS
1994 **F van Almsick** GER
1998 **Claudia Poll** CRC
2001 **Giaan Rooney** AUS

400m Freestyle
1973 **Heather Greenwood** USA
1975 **Shirley Babashoff** USA
1978 **Tracey Wickham** AUS
1982 **Carmela Schmidt** GDR
1986 **Heike Friedrich** GDR
1991 **Janet Evans** USA
1994 **Aihua Yang** CHN
1998 **Yan Chen** CHN
2001 **Yana Klochkova** UKR

800m Freestyle
1973 **Novella Calligaris** ITA
1975 **Jenny Tunrall** AUS
1978 **Tracey Wickham** AUS
1982 **Kim Lineham** USA
1986 **Astrid Strauss** GDR
1991 **Janet Evans** USA
1994 **Janet Evans** USA
1998 **Brooke Bennett** USA
2001 **Hannah Stockbauer** GER

1500m Freestyle
2001 **Hannah Stockbauer** GER

50m Backstroke
2001 **Haley Cope** USA

100m Backstroke
1973 **Ulrike Richter** GDR
1975 **Ulrike Richter** GDR
1978 **Linda Jezek** USA
1982 **Kristin Otto** GDR
1986 **Betsy Mitchell** USA
1991 **Krisztina Egerszegi** HUN
1994 **Cihong He** CHN
1998 **Lea Maurer** USA
2001 **Natalie Coughlin** USA

200m Backstroke
1973 **Melissa Belote** USA
1975 **Birgit Treiber** GDR
1978 **Linda Jezek** USA
1982 **Cornelia Sirch** GDR
1986 **Cornelia Sirch** GDR
1991 **Krisztina Egerszegi** HUN
1994 **Cihong He** CHN
1998 **Roxanna Maracineanu** FRA
2001 **Diana Mocanu** ROM

50m Breaststroke
2001 **Xuej Uan Luo** CHN

100m Breaststroke
1973 **Renate Vogel** GDR
1975 **Hannelore Anke** GDR
1978 **Yulia Bogdanova** URS

1982 **Ute Geweniger** GDR
1986 **Sylvia Gerasch** GDR
1991 **Linley Frame** AUS
1994 **Samantha Riley** AUS
1998 **Kristy Kowal** USA
2001 **Xuej Uan Luo** CHN

200m Breaststroke
1973 **Renate Vogel** GDR
1975 **Hannelore Anke** GDR
1978 **Lina Kachushite** URS
1982 **Svetlana Varganova** URS
1986 **Silke Horner** GDR
1991 **Yelena Volkova** URS
1994 **Samantha Riley** AUS
1998 **Agnes Kovacs** HUN
2001 **Agnes Kovacs** HUN

50m Fly
2001 **Inge de Bruijn** NED

100m Butterfly
1973 **Kornelia Ender** GDR
1975 **Kornelia Ender** GDR
1978 **Mary Pennington** USA
1982 **Mary Meagher** USA
1986 **Kornelia Gressler** GDR
1991 **Qian Hong** CHN
1994 **Limin Liu** CHN
1998 **Jenny Thompson** USA
2001 **Petria Thomas** AUS

200m Butterfly
1973 **Rosemarie Kother** GDR
1975 **Rosemarie Kother** GDR
1978 **Tracy Caulkins** USA
1982 **Ines Geissler** GDR
1986 **Mary Meagher** USA
1991 **Summer Sanders** USA
1994 **Limin Liu** CHN
1998 **Susan O'Neill** AUS
2001 **Petria Thomas** AUS

200m Individual Medley
1973 **Angela Hubner** GDR
1975 **Kathy Heddy** USA
1978 **Tracy Caulkins** USA
1982 **Petra Schneider** GDR
1986 **Kristin Otto** GDR
1991 **Lin Li** CHN
1994 **Lu Bin** CHN
1998 **Yanyan Wu** CHN
2001 **Martha Bowen** USA

400m Individual Medley
1973 **Gudrun Wegner** GDR
1975 **Ulrike Tauber** GDR
1978 **Tracy Caulkins** USA
1982 **Petra Schneider** GDR
1986 **Kathleen Nord** GDR
1991 **Lin Li** CHN
1994 **Guohong Dai** CHN
1998 **Yan Chen** CHN

SWIMMING

2001 **Yana Klochkova** UKR

4x100m Freestyle Relay
1973 & 75 **East Germany**
1978 **United States**
1982 **East Germany**
1986 **East Germany**
1991 **United States**
1994 **China**
1998 **United States**
2001 **Germany**

4x200m Freestyle Relay
1986 **East Germany**
1991 **Germany**
1994 **China**
1998 **Germany**
2001 **Great Britain**

4x100m Medley Relay
1973 & 75 **East Germany**
1978 **United States**
1982 **East Germany**
1986 **East Germany**
1991 **United States**
1994 **China**
1998 **United States**
2001 **Australia**

1m Springboard
1991 **Gao Min** CHN
1994 **Lixia Chen** CHN
1998 **Irina Lashko** RUS
2001 **Blythe Hartley** CAN

3m Springboard
1973 **Christine Kohler** GDR
1975 **Irina Kalinina** URS
1978 **Irina Kalinina** URS
1982 **Megan Neyer** USA
1986 **Gao Min** CHN
1991 **Gao Min** CHN
1994 **Shuping Tan** CHN
1998 **Yulia Pakhalina** RUS
2001 **Jingjing Guo** CHN

10m Platform Diving
1973 **Ulrike Knape** SWE
1975 **Janet Ely** USA
1978 **Irina Kalinina** URS
1982 **Wendy Wyland** USA
1986 **Lin Chen** CHN
1991 **Fu Mingxia** CHN
1994 **Fu Mingxia** CHN
1998 **Olena Zhupyna** UKR
2001 **Mian Xu** CHN

3m Springboard Synchro
1998 **Lashko/Pakhalina** RUS
2001 **Wu/Guo** CHN

10m Platfrom Synchro
1998 **Zhupyna/Serbina** UKR
2001 **Duan/Sang** CHN

Synchronised Swimming

Solo
1973 **Teresa Anderson** USA
1975 **Gail Buzonas** USA
1978 **Helen Vandenburg** CAN
1982 **Tracie Ruiz** USA
1986 **Carolyn Waldo** CAN
1991 **Sylvie Frechette** CAN
1994 **Becky Dyroen Lance** USA
1998 **Olga Sedakova** RUS
2001 **Olga Brousnikina** RUS

Duet
1973 **Anderson/Johnson** USA
1975 **Curren/Norrish** USA
1978 **Calkins/Vandenburg** CAN
1982 **Hambrook/Kryczka** CAN
1986 **Cameron/Waldo** CAN
1991 **Josephson/Josephson** USA
1994 **Lancer/Sidduth** USA
1998 **Sedakova/Brousnikina** RUS
2001 **Tachibana/Takeda** JPN

Team
1973 **United States**
1975 **United States**
1978 **United States**
1982 **Canada**
1986 **Canada**
1991 **United States**
1994 **United States**
1998 **Russia**
2001 **Russia**

Water Polo
1986 **Australia**
1991 **Netherlands**
1994 **Hungary**
1998 **Italy**
2001 **Italy**

TABLE TENNIS

WORLD CHAMPIONS

Men's Singles

1926	Roland Jacobi HUN
1928	Zoltan Mechlovits HUN
1929	Fred Perry GBR
1930	Viktor Barna HUN
1931	Miklos Szabados HUN
1932	Viktor Barna HUN
1933	Viktor Barna HUN
1934	Viktor Barna HUN
1935	Viktor Barna HUN
1936	Stanislav Kolar TCH
1937	Richard Bergmann AUT
1938	Bohumil Vana TCH
1939	Richard Bergmann AUT
1947	Bohumil Vana TCH
1948	Richard Bergmann GBR
1949	Johnny Leach GBR
1950	Richard Bergmann GBR
1951	Johnny Leach GBR
1952	Hiroji Satoh JPN
1953	Ferenc Sidó HUN
1954	Ichiro Ogimura JPN
1955	Toshiaki Tanaka JPN
1956	Ichiro Ogimura JPN
1957	Toshiaki Tanaka JPN
1959	Jung Kuo-tuan CHN
1961	Chuang Tse-tung CHN
1963	Chuang Tse-tung CHN
1965	Chuang Tse-tung CHN
1967	Nobuhiko Hasegawa JPN
1969	Shigeo Ito JPN
1971	Stellan Bengtsson SWE
1973	Hsi En-ting CHN
1975	Istvan Jonyer HUN
1977	Mitsuru Kohno JPN
1979	Seiji Ono JPN
1981	Guo Yuehua CHN
1983	Guo Yuehua CHN
1985	Jiang Jialiang CHN
1987	Jiang Jialiang CHN
1989	Jan-Ove Waldner SWE
1991	Jorgen Persson SWE
1993	Jean-Philippe Gatien FRA
1995	Kong Linghui CHN
1997	Jan-Ove Waldner SWE
1999	Liu Goulilang CHN
2001	Wang Liqim CHN

Men's Team 1975 onwards

1975	China
1977	China
1979	Hungary
1981	China
1983	China
1985	China
1987	China
1989	Sweden
1991	Sweden
1993	Sweden
1995	China
1997	China
1999	China
2001	China

Men's Doubles From 1969

1969	Alser/Johansson SWE
1971	Jonyer/Klampar HUN
1973	Bengtsson/Johansson SWE
1975	Gergely/Jonyer HUN
1977	Li/Liang CHN
1979	Surbek/Stipancic YUG
1981	Cai/Li CHN
1983	Surbeh/Kalinic YUG
1985	Applegren/Carlsson SWE
1987	Chen/Wei CHN
1989	Rosskopf/Fetzner FRG
1991	Karlsson/von Scheele SWE
1993	Wang/Lu CHN
1995	Wang/Lu CHN
1997	Kong/Liu CHN
1999	Kong/Liu CHN
2001	Wang/Yen CHN

Women's Singles

1926	Maria Mednyanszky HUN
1928	Maria Mednyanszky HUN
1929	Maria Mednyanszky HUN
1930	Maria Mednyanszky HUN
1931	Maria Mednyanszky HUN
1932	Anna Sipos HUN
1933	Anna Sipos HUN
1934	Marie Kettnerova TCH
1935	Marie Kettnerova TCH
1936	Ruth Aarons USA
1937	Ruth Aarons USA and Trudi Pritzi AUT*
1938	Trudi Pritzi AUT
1939	Vlasta Depetrisova TCH
1947	Gizi Farkas HUN
1948	Gizi Farkas HUN
1949	Gizi Farkas HUN
1950	Angelica Rozeanu ROM
1951	Angelica Rozeanu ROM
1952	Angelica Rozeanu ROM
1953	Angelica Rozeanu ROM
1954	Angelica Rozeanu ROM
1955	Angelica Rozeanu ROM
1956	Tomi Okawa JPN
1957	Fujie Eguchi JPN
1959	Kimiyo Matsuzaki JPN
1961	Chiu Chunghui CHN
1963	Kimiyo Matsuzaki JPN
1965	Naoko Fukazu JPN
1967	Sachiko Morisawa JPN
1969	Toshiko Kowada JPN
1971	Lin Huiching CHN
1973	Hu Yu-lan CHN
1975	Pak Yung-sun KOR
1977	Pak Yung-sun KOR
1979	Ge Xinai CHN
1981	Tong Ling CHN
1983	Cao Yanhua CHN
1985	Cao Yanhua CHN
1987	He Zhili CHN
1989	Qiao Hong CHN
1991	Deng Yaping CHN
1993	Hyun Jung Hwa CHN
1995	Deng Yaping CHN
1997	Deng Yaping CHN
1999	Wang Nan CHN
2001	Wang Nan CHN

* Finalists. Title was left vacant

Women's Team From 1977

1977	China
1979	China
1981	China
1983	China
1985	China
1987	China
1989	China
1991	Korea
1993	China
1995	China
1997	China
1999	China
2001	China

Women's Doubles 1969 on

1969	Grinberg/Rudnova URS
1971	Cheng/Lin CHN
1973	Alexandru ROM/Hamada JPN
1975	Alexandru/Takashima
1977	Pak/Yang CHN
1979	Zhang/Zhang CHN
1981	Zhang/Cao CHN
1983	Shen/Dai CHN
1985	Dai/Geng CHN
1987	Yang/Hyun KOR
1989	Qiao/Deng CHN
1991	Chen/Gao CHN
1993	Liu/Qiao CHN
1995	Deng/Lui CHN
1997	Deng/Yang CHN
1999	Wang/Li CHN
2001	Wang/Li CHN

TABLE TENNIS

Mixed Doubles From 1965

Year	Winners	Country
1965	**Kimura/Seki**	JPN
1967	**Hasegawa/Yamanaka**	JPN
1969	**Hasegawa/Kono**	JPN
1971	**Chang/Lin**	CHN
1973	**Liang/Li**	CHN
1975	**Gomozkov/Ferdman**	URS
1977	**Secretin/Bergeret**	FRA
1979	**Liang/Ge**	CHN
1981	**Xie/Huang**	CHN
1983	**Guo/Ni**	CHN
1985	**Cai/Cao**	CHN
1987	**Hui/Geng**	CHN
1989	**Yoo/Hyun**	KOR
1991	**Wang/Liu**	CHN
1993	**Wang/Liu**	CHN
1995	**Wang/Liu**	CHN
1997	**Liu/Wang**	CHN
1999	**Ma/Zhang**	CHN
2001	**Qin/Yang**	CHN

TENNIS

WIMBLEDON

Men's Singles

1877	**Spencer Gore** GBR
1878	**Frank Hadow** GBR
1879	**Rev John Hartley** GBR
1880	**Rev John Hartley** GBR
1881	**William Renshaw** GBR
1882	**William Renshaw** GBR
1883	**William Renshaw** GBR
1884	**William Renshaw** GBR
1885	**William Renshaw** GBR
1886	**William Renshaw** GBR
1887	**Herbert Lawford** GBR
1888	**Ernest Renshaw** GBR
1889	**William Renshaw** GBR
1890	**Willoughby Hamilton** GBR
1891	**Wilfred Baddeley** GBR
1892	**Wilfred Baddeley** GBR
1893	**Joshua Pim** GBR
1894	**Joshua Pim** GBR
1895	**Wilfred Baddeley** GBR
1896	**Harold Mahoney** GBR
1897	**Reginald Doherty** GBR
1898	**Reginald Doherty** GBR
1899	**Reginald Doherty** GBR
1900	**Reginald Doherty** GBR
1901	**Arthur Gore** GBR
1902	**Lawrence Doherty** GBR
1903	**Lawrence Doherty** GBR
1904	**Lawrence Doherty** GBR
1905	**Lawrence Doherty** GBR
1906	**Lawrence Doherty** GBR
1907	**Norman Brookes** AUS
1908	**Arthur Gore** GBR
1909	**Arthur Gore** GBR
1910	**Tony Wilding** NZL
1911	**Tony Wilding** NZL
1912	**Tony Wilding** NZL
1913	**Tony Wilding** NZL
1914	**Norman Brookes** AUS
1919	**Gerald Patterson** AUS
1920	**Bill Tilden** USA
1921	**Bill Tilden** USA
1922	**Gerald Patterson** AUS
1923	**William Johnston** USA
1924	**Jean Borotra** FRA
1925	**Rene Lacoste** FRA
1926	**Jean Borotra** FRA
1927	**Henri Cochet** FRA
1928	**Rene Lacoste** FRA
1929	**Henri Cochet** FRA
1930	**Bill Tilden** USA
1931	**Sidney Wood** USA
1932	**Ellsworth Vines** USA
1933	**Jack Crawford** AUS
1934	**Fred Perry** GBR
1935	**Fred Perry** GBR
1936	**Fred Perry** GBR
1937	**Donald Budge** USA
1938	**Donald Budge** USA

1939	**Bobby Riggs** USA
1946	**Yvon Petra** FRA
1947	**Jack Kramer** USA
1948	**Bob Falkenburg** USA
1949	**Ted Schroeder** USA
1950	**Budge Patty** USA
1951	**Dick Savitt** USA
1952	**Frank Sedgman** AUS
1953	**Vic Seixas** USA
1954	**Jaroslav Drobny** EGY
1955	**Tony Trabert** USA
1956	**Lew Hoad** AUS
1957	**Lew Hoad** AUS
1958	**Ashley Cooper** AUS
1959	**Alex Olmedo** USA
1960	**Neale Fraser** AUS
1961	**Rod Laver** AUS
1962	**Rod Laver** AUS
1963	**Chuck McKinley** USA
1964	**Roy Emerson** AUS
1965	**Roy Emerson** AUS
1966	**Manuel Santana** ESP
1967	**John Newcombe** AUS
1968	**Rod Laver** AUS
1969	**Rod Laver** AUS
1970	**John Newcombe** AUS
1971	**John Newcombe** AUS
1972	**Stan Smith** USA
1973	**Jan Kodes** TCH
1974	**Jimmy Connors** USA
1975	**Arthur Ashe** USA
1976	**Bjorn Borg** SWE
1977	**Bjorn Borg** SWE
1978	**Bjorn Borg** SWE
1979	**Bjorn Borg** SWE
1980	**Bjorn Borg** SWE
1981	**John McEnroe** USA
1982	**Jimmy Connors** USA
1983	**John McEnroe** USA
1984	**John McEnroe** USA
1985	**Boris Becker** FRG
1986	**Boris Becker** FRG
1987	**Pat Cash** AUS
1988	**Stefan Edberg** SWE
1989	**Boris Becker** FRG
1990	**Stefan Edberg** SWE
1991	**Michael Stich** GER
1992	**Andre Agassi** USA
1993	**Pete Sampras** USA
1994	**Pete Sampras** USA
1995	**Pete Sampras** USA
1996	**Richard Krajicek** NED
1997	**Pete Sampras** USA
1998	**Pete Sampras** USA
1999	**Pete Sampras** USA
2000	**Pete Sampras** USA
2001	**Goran Ivanisevic** CRO
2002	**Lleyton Hewitt** AUS

Women's Singles

1884	**Maud Watson** GBR
1885	**Maud Watson** GBR
1886	**Blanche Bingley** GBR
1887	**Lottie Dod** GBR
1888	**Lottie Dod** GBR
1889	**Blanche Hillyard** GBR
1890	**Helene Rice** GBR
1891	**Lottie Dod** GBR
1892	**Lottie Dod** GBR
1893	**Lottie Dod** GBR
1894	**Blanche Hillyard** GBR
1895	**Charlotte Cooper** GBR
1896	**Charlotte Cooper** GBR
1897	**Blanche Hillyard** GBR
1898	**Charlotte Cooper** GBR
1899	**Blanche Hillyard** GBR
1900	**Blanche Hillyard** GBR
1901	**Charlotte Sterry** GBR
1902	**Muriel Robb** GBR
1903	**Dorothea Douglass** GBR
1904	**Dorothea Douglass** GBR
1905	**May Sutton** USA
1906	**Dorothea Douglass** GBR
1907	**May Sutton** USA
1908	**Charlotte Sterry** GBR
1909	**Dora Boothby** GBR
1910	**D Lambert Chambers** GBR
1911	**D Lambert Chambers** GBR
1912	**Ethel Larcombe** GBR
1913	**D Lambert Chambers** GBR
1914	**D Lambert Chambers** GBR
1919	**Suzanne Lenglen** FRA
1920	**Suzanne Lenglen** FRA
1921	**Suzanne Lenglen** FRA
1922	**Suzanne Lenglen** FRA
1923	**Suzanne Lenglen** FRA
1924	**Kathleen McKane** GBR
1925	**Suzanne Lenglen** FRA
1926	**Kathleen Godfree** GBR
1927	**Helen Wills** USA
1928	**Helen Wills** USA
1929	**Helen Wills** USA
1930	**Helen Wills Moody** USA
1931	**Cilly Aussem** GER
1932	**Helen Wills Moody** USA
1933	**Helen Wills Moody** USA
1934	**Dorothy Round** GBR
1935	**Helen Wills Moody** USA
1936	**Helen Jacobs** USA
1937	**Dorothy Round** GBR
1938	**Helen Wills Moody** USA
1939	**Alice Marble** USA
1946	**Pauline Betz** USA
1947	**Margaret Osborne** USA
1948	**Louise Brough** USA
1949	**Louise Brough** USA
1950	**Louise Brough** USA
1951	**Doris Hart** USA
1952	**Maureen Connolly** USA

TENNIS

1953 Maureen Connolly USA	GBR	1957 Mulloy/Patty USA
1954 Maureen Connolly USA	1888 E & W Renshaw GBR	1958 Davidson/Schmidt SWE
1955 Louise Brough USA	1889 E & W Renshaw GBR	1959 Emerson/Fraser AUS
1956 Shirley Fry USA	1890 Pim/Stoker GBR	1960 Osuna/Ralston USA
1957 Althea Gibson USA	1891 H & W Baddeley GBR	1961 Emerson/Fraser AUS
1958 Althea Gibson USA	1892 Barlow/Lewis GBR	1962 Hewitt/Stolle AUS
1959 Maria Bueno BRA	1893 Pim/Stoker GBR	1963 Osuna/Palafox MEX
1960 Maria Bueno BRA	1894 H & W Baddeley GBR	1964 Hewitt/Stolle AUS
1961 Angela Mortimer GBR	1895 H & W Baddeley GBR	1965 Newcombe/Roche AUS
1962 Karen Susman USA	1896 H & W Baddeley GBR	1966 Fletcher/Newcombe AUS
1963 Margaret Smith AUS	1897 L & R Doherty GBR	1967 Hewitt/McMillan SAF
1964 Maria Bueno BRA	1898 L & R Doherty GBR	1968 Newcombe/Roche AUS
1965 Margaret Smith AUS	1899 L & R Doherty GBR	1969 Newcombe/Roche AUS
1966 Billie Jean King USA	1900 L & R Doherty GBR	1970 Newcombe/Roche AUS
1967 Billie Jean King USA	1901 L & R Doherty GBR	1971 Emerson/Laver AUS
1968 Billie Jean King USA	1902 Risely/Smith GBR	1972 Hewitt/McMillan SAF
1969 Ann Jones GBR	1903 L & R Doherty GBR	1973 Connors/Nastase USA
1970 Margaret Court AUS	1904 L & R Doherty GBR	1974 Newcombe/Roche AUS
1971 Evonne Goolagong AUS	1905 L & R Doherty GBR	1975 Gerulaitis/Mayer USA
1972 Billie Jean King USA	1906 Risely/Smith GBR	1976 Gottfried/Ramirez
1973 Billie Jean King USA	1907 Brookes/Wilding AUS/NZL	USA/MEX
1974 Chris Evert USA	1908 Ritchie/Wilding GBR/NZL	1977 Case/Masters AUS
1975 Billy Jean King USA	1909 Gore/Barrett GBR	1978 Hewitt /McMillan SAF
1976 Chris Evert USA	1910 Ritchie/Wilding GBR/NZL	1979 Fleming/McEnroe USA
1977 Virginia Wade GBR	1911 Decugis/Gobert GBR	1980 McNamara/McNamee AUS
1978 Martina Navratilova TCH	1912 Dixon/Barrett GBR	1981 Fleming/McEnroe USA
1979 Martina Navratilova TCH	1913 Dixon/Barrett GBR	1982 McNamara/McNamee AUS
1980 Evonne Cawley AUS	1914 Brookes/Wilding AUS/NZL	1983 Fleming/McEnroe USA
1981 Chris Evert Lloyd USA	1919 Wood/Thomas AUS	1984 Fleming/McEnroe USA
1982 Martina Navratilova USA	1920 Garland/Williams USA	1985 Gunthardt/Taróczy
1983 Martina Navratilova USA	1921 Lycett/Woosnam GBR	SUI/HUN
1984 Martina Navratilova USA	1922 Anderson/Lycett AUS/GBR	1986 Nystrom/Wilander SWE
1985 Martina Navratilova USA	1923 Godfree/Lycett GBR	1987 Flach/Seguso USA
1986 Martina Navratilova USA	1924 Hunter/Richards USA	1988 Flach/Seguso USA
1987 Martina Navratilova USA	1925 Borotra/Lacoste FRA	1989 Fitzgerald/Jarryd
1988 Steffi Graf FRG	1926 Brugnon/Cochet FRA	AUS/SWE
1989 Steffi Graf FRG	1927 Hunter/Tilden USA	1990 Leach/Pugh USA
1990 Martina Navratilova USA	1928 Brugnon/Cochet FRA	1991 Fitzgerald/Jarryd
1991 Steffi Graf GER	1929 Allison/Van Ryn USA	1992 McEnroe/Stich
1992 Steffi Graf GER	1930 Allison/Van Ryn USA	AUS/GER
1993 Steffi Graf GER	1931 Lott/Van Ryn USA	1993 Woodbridge/Woodforde
1994 Conchita Martinez ESP	1932 Borotra/Brugnon FRA	AUS
1995 Steffi Graf GER	1933 Borotra/Brugnon FRA	1994 Woodbridge/Woodforde
1996 Steffi Graf GER	1934 Lott/Stoefen USA	1995 Woodbridge/Woodforde
1997 Martina Hingis SUI	1935 Crawford/Quist AUS	1996 Woodbridge/Woodforde
1998 Jana Novotna CZE	1936 Hughes/Tuckey GBR	1997 Woodbridge/Woodforde
1999 Lindsay Davenport USA	1937 Budge/Mako USA	1998 Eltingh/Haarhuis NED
2000 Venus Williams USA	1938 Budge/Mako USA	1999 Bhupati/Paes IND
2001 Venus Williams USA	1939 Cooke/Riggs USA	2000 Woodbridge/Woodforde
2002 Serena Williams USA	1946 Brown/Kramer USA	2001 Johnson/Palmer USA
	1947 Falkenburg/Kramer USA	2002 Bjorkman/Woodbridge
Men's Doubles	1948 Bromwich/Sedgman AUS	SWE/AUS
1879 Erskine/Lawford GBR	1949 Gonzales/Parker USA	
1880 E & W Renshaw GBR	1950 Bromwich/Quist AUS	**Women's Doubles**
1881 E & W Renshaw GBR	1951 McGregor/Sedgman AUS	1913 McNair/Boothby GBR
1882 Hartley/Richardson GBR	1952 McGregor/Sedgman AUS	1914 Morton/Ryan USA
1883 Grinstead/WElldon GBR	1953 Hoad/Rosewall AUS	1919 Lenglen/Ryan FRA/USA
1884 E & W Renshaw GBR	1954 Hartwig/Rose AUS	1920 Lenglen/Ryan FRA/USA
1885 E & W Renshaw GBR	1955 Hartwig/Hoad AUS	1921 Lenglen/Ryan FRA/USA
1886 E & W Renshaw GBR	1956 Hoad/Rosewall AUS	1922 Lenglen/Ryan FRA/USA
1887 Bowes-Lyon/Wilberforce		

1923 **Lenglen/Ryan** FRA/USA	1988 **Graf/Sabatini** FRG/ARG	1992 **Suk/Savchenko** CZE/LAT
1924 **Wightman/Wills** USA	1989 **Novotna/Sukova** TCH	1993 **Woodforde/Navratilova**
1925 **Lenglen/Ryan** FRA/USA	1990 **Novotna/Sukova** TCH	AUS/USA
1926 **Browne/Ryan** USA	1991 **Savchenko/Zvereva** URS	1994 **Woodbridge/Sukova**
1927 **Wills/Ryan** USA	1992 **Fernandez/Zvereva**	AUS/CZE
1928 **Saunders/Watson** GBR	USA/BLR	1995 **Stark/Navratilova** USA
1929 **Mitchell/Watson** GBR	1993 **Fernandez/Zvereva**	1996 **Suk/Sukova** CZE
1930 **Wills Moody/Ryan** USA	1994 **Fernandez/Zvereva**	1997 **Suk/Sukova** CZE
1931 **Barron/Mudford** GBR	1995 **Novotna/Sanchez Vicario**	1998 **Mirnyi/Williams** BLR/USA
1932 **Metaxa/Sigart** FRA/BEL	CZE/ESP	1999 **Paes/Raymond** IND/USA
1933 **Mathieu/Ryan** FRA/USA	1996 **Hingis /Sukova** SUI/CZE	2000 **Johnson/Po** USA
1934 **Mathieu/Ryan** FRA/USA	1997 **Fernandez /Zvereva**	2001 **Friedl/Hantuchova**
1935 **James/Stammers** GBR	USA/BLR	CZE/SVK
1936 **James/Stammers** GBR	1998 **Hingis/Novotna** SUI/CZE	2002 **Bhupati/Likhovtseva**
1937 **Mathieu/Yorke** FRA/GBR	1999 **Davenport/Morariu** USA	IND/RUS
1938 **Fabyan/Marble** USA	2000 **V Williams/S Williams** USA	
1939 **Fabyan/Marble** USA	2001 **Raymond/Stubbs** USA/AUS	## US OPEN
1946 **Brough/Osborne** USA	2002 **V Williams/S Williams** USA	
1947 **Hart/Todd** USA		### Men's Singles
1948 **Brough/Du Pont** USA	**Mixed Doubles** since 1950	(First played 1881)
1949 **Brough/Du Pont** USA	1950 **Sturgess/Brough** RSA/USA	1946 **Jack Kramer** USA
1950 **Brough/Du Pont** USA	1951 **Sedgman/Hart** AUS/USA	1947 **Jack Kramer** USA
1951 **Fry/Hart** USA	1952 **Sedgman/Hart** AUS/USA	1948 **Ricardo Gonzales** USA
1952 **Fry/Hart** USA	1953 **Seixas/Hart** USA	1949 **Ricardo Gonzales** USA
1953 **Fry/Hart** USA	1954 **Seixas/Hart** USA	1950 **Arthur Larsen** USA
1954 **Brough/Du Pont** USA	1955 **Seixas/Hart** USA	1951 **Frank Sedgman** USA
1955 **Mortimer/Shilcock** GBR	1956 **Seixas/Fry** USA	1952 **Frank Sedgman** USA
1956 **Buxton/Gibson** GBR/USA	1957 **Rose/Hard** AUS/USA	1953 **Tony Trabert** USA
1957 **Gibson/Hard** USA	1958 **Howe/Coghlan** AUS	1954 **Vic Seixas** USA
1958 **Bueno/Gibson** BRA/USA	1959 **Laver/Hard** AUS/USA	1955 **Tony Trabert** USA
1959 **Arth/Hard** USA	1960 **Laver/Hard** AUS/USA	1956 **Ken Rosewall** AUS
1960 **Bueno/Hard** BRA/USA	1961 **Stolle/Turner** AUS	1957 **Malcolm Anderson** AUS
1961 **Hantze/Moffitt** USA	1962 **Fraser/Du Pont** AUS/USA	1958 **Ashley Cooper** AUS
1962 **Moffit/Susman** USA	1963 **Fletcher/Smith** AUS	1959 **Neale Fraser** AUS
1963 **Bueno/Hard** BRA/USA	1964 **Stolle/Turner** AUS	1960 **Neale Fraser** AUS
1964 **Smith/Turner** AUS	1965 **Fletcher/Smith** AUS	1961 **Roy Emerson** AUS
1965 **Bueno/Moffitt** BRA/USA	1966 **Fletcher/Smith** AUS	1962 **Rod Laver** AUS
1966 **Bueno/Richey** BRA/USA	1967 **Davidson/King** AUS/USA	1963 **Raphael Osuna** MEX
1967 **Casals/King** USA	1968 **Fletcher/Court** AUS	1964 **Roy Emerson** AUS
1968 **Casals/King** USA	1969 **Stolle/Jones** AUS/GBR	1965 **Manuel Santana** ESP
1969 **Court/Tegart** AUS	1970 **Nastase/Casals** ROM/USA	1966 **Fred Stolle** AUS
1970 **Casals/King** USA	1971 **Davidson/King** AUS/USA	1967 **John Newcombe** AUS
1971 **Casals/King** USA	1972 **Nastase/Casals** ROM/USA	1968 **Arthur Ashe** USA
1972 **King/Stove** USA/NED	1973 **Davidson/King** AUS/USA	Open **Arthur Ashe** USA
1973 **Casals/King** USA	1975 **Riessen/Court** USA/AUS	1969 **Stan Smith** USA
1974 **Goolagong/Michel**	1976 **Roche/Durr** AUS/FRA	Open **Rod Laver** AUS
AUS/USA	1977 **Hewitt/Stevens** RSA	1970 **Ken Rosewall** AUS
1975 **Kiyomura/S'matsu** JPN	1978 **McMillan/Stove** RSA/NED	1971 **Stan Smith** USA
1976 **Evert/Navratilova** USA/TCH	1979 **Hewitt/Stevens** RSA	1972 **Ilie Nastase** ROM
1977 **Cawley/Russell** AUS/USA	1980 **Austin/Austin** USA	1973 **John Newcombe** AUS
1978 **Reid/Turnbull** USA	1981 **McMillan/Stove** RSA/NED	1974 **Jimmy Connors** USA
1979 **King/Navratilova** USA/TCH	1982 **Curren/Smith** RSA/USA	1975 **Manuel Orantes** ESP
1980 **Jordan/Smith** USA	1983 **Lloyd/Turnbull** GBR/AUS	1976 **Jimmy Connors** USA
1981 **Navratilova/Shriver** USA	1984 **Lloyd/Turnbull** GBR/AUS	1977 **Guillermo Vilas** ARG
1982 **Navratilova/Shriver** USA	1985 **McNamee/N'lova** AUS/USA	1978 **Jimmy Connors** USA
1983 **Navratilova/Shriver** USA	1986 **Flach/Jordan** USA	1979 **John McEnroe** USA
1984 **Navratilova/Shriver** USA	1987 **Bates/Durie** GBR	1980 **John McEnroe** USA
1985 **Jordan/Smylie** USA/AUS	1988 **Stewart/Garrison** USA	1981 **John McEnroe** USA
1986 **Navratilova/Shriver** USA	1989 **Pugh/Novotna** USA/CZE	1982 **Jimmy Connors** USA
1987 **K-Kilsch/Sukova** FRG/TCH	1990 **Leach/Garrison** USA	1983 **Jimmy Connors** USA
	1991 **Fitzgerald/Smylie** AUS	1984 **John McEnroe** USA

1985	Ivan Lendl TCH
1986	Ivan Lendl TCH
1987	Ivan Lendl TCH
1988	Mats Wilander SWE
1989	Boris Becker FRG
1990	Pete Sampras USA
1991	Stefan Edberg SWE
1992	Stefan Edberg SWE
1993	Pete Sampras USA
1994	Andre Agassi USA
1995	Pete Sampras USA
1996	Pete Sampras USA
1997	Pat Rafter AUS
1998	Pat Rafter AUS
1999	Andre Agassi USA
2000	Marat Safin RUS
2001	Lleyton Hewitt AUS
2002	Pete Sampras USA

Women's Singles
(First played 1887)

1946	Pauline Betz USA
1947	Louise Brough USA
1948	Margaret Du Pont USA
1949	Margaret Du Pont USA
1950	Margaret Du Pont USA
1951	Maureen Connolly USA
1952	Maureen Connolly USA
1953	Maureen Connolly USA
1954	Doris Hart USA
1955	Doris Hart USA
1956	Shirley Fry USA
1957	Althea Gibson USA
1958	Althea Gibson USA
1959	Maria Bueno BRA
1960	Darlene Hard USA
1961	Darlene Hard USA
1962	Margaret Smith AUS
1963	Maria Bueno BRA
1964	Maria Bueno BRA
1965	Margaret Smith AUS
1966	Maria Bueno BRA
1967	Billie Jean King USA
1968	Margaret Court AUS
Open	Virginia Wade GBR
1969	Margaret Court AUS
Open	Margaret Court AUS
1970	Margaret Court AUS
1971	Billie Jean King USA
1972	Billie Jean King USA
1973	Margaret Court AUS
1974	Billie Jean King USA
1975	Chris Evert USA
1976	Chris Evert USA
1977	Chris Evert USA
1978	Chris Evert USA
1979	Tracy Austin USA
1980	Chris Evert Lloyd USA
1981	Tracy Austin USA
1982	Chris Evert Lloyd USA
1983	Martina Navratilova USA

1983	Martina Navratilova USA
1985	Hanna Mandlikova TCH
1986	Martina Navratilova USA
1987	Martina Navratilova USA
1988	Steffi Graf FRG
1989	Steffi Graf FRG
1990	Gabriela Sabatini ARG
1991	Monica Seles YUG
1992	Monica Seles YUG
1993	Steffi Graf GER
1994	Aranxta Sanchez ESP
1995	Steffi Graf GER
1996	Steffi Graf GER
1997	Martina Hingis SUI
1998	Lindsay Davenport USA
1999	Serena Williams USA
2000	Venus Williams USA
2001	Venus Williams USA
2002	Serena Williams USA

FRENCH OPEN

Men's Singles

1925	Rene Lacoste FRA
1926	Henri Cochet FRA
1927	Rene Lacoste FRA
1928	Henri Cochet FRA
1929	Rene Lacoste FRA
1930	Henri Cochet FRA
1931	Jean Borotra FRA
1932	Henri Cochet FRA
1933	Jack Crawford AUS
1934	Gottfried Von Cramm GER
1935	Fred Perry GBR
1936	Gottfried Von Cramm
1937	Henner Henkel GER
1938	Donald Budge USA
1939	Donald McNeill USA
1946	Marcel Bernard FRA
1947	Jozsef Asboth HUN
1948	Frank Parker USA
1949	Frank Parker USA
1950	Budge Patty USA
1951	Jaroslav Drobny EGY
1952	Jaroslav Drobny EGY
1953	Ken Rosewall AUS
1954	Tony Trabert USA
1955	Tony Trabert USA
1956	Lew Hoad AUS
1957	Sven Davidson SWE
1958	Mervyn Rose AUS
1959	Nicola Pietrangeli ITA
1960	Nicola Pietrangeli ITA
1961	Manuel Santana ESP
1962	Rod Laver AUS
1963	Roy Emerson AUS
1964	Manuel Santana ESP
1965	Fred Stolle AUS
1966	Tony Roche AUS
1967	Roy Emerson AUS

1968	Ken Rosewall AUS
1969	Rod Laver AUS
1970	Jan Kodes TCH
1971	Jan Kodes TCH
1972	Andres Gimeno ESP
1973	Ilie Nastase ROM
1974	Bjorn Borg SWE
1975	Bjorn Borg SWE
1976	Adriano Panatta ITA
1977	Guillermo Vilas ARG
1978	Bjorn Borg SWE
1979	Bjorn Borg SWE
1980	Bjorn Borg SWE
1981	Bjorn Borg SWE
1982	Mats Wilander SWE
1983	Yannick Noah FRA
1984	Ivan Lendl TCH
1985	Mats Wilander SWE
1986	Ivan Lendl TCH
1987	Ivan Lendl TCH
1988	Mats Wilander SWE
1989	Michael Chang USA
1990	Andres Gomez ECU
1991	Jim Courier USA
1992	Jim Courier USA
1993	Sergi Bruguera ESP
1994	Sergi Bruguera ESP
1995	Thomas Muster AUT
1996	Yevgeny Kafelnikov RUS
1997	Gustavo Kuerten BRA
1998	Carlos Moya ESP
1999	Andre Agassi USA
2000	Gustavo Kuerten BRA
2001	Gustavo Kuerten BRA
2002	Albert Costa ESP

Women's Singles

1925	Suzanne Lenglen FRA
1926	Suzanne Lenglen FRA
1927	Kea Bouman NED
1928	Helen Wills Moody FRA
1929	Helen Wills Moody FRA
1930	Helen Wills Moody USA
1931	Cilly Aussem GER
1932	Helen Moody USA
1933	Margaret Scriven GBR
1934	Margaret Scriven GBR
1935	Hilde Sperling GER
1936	Hilde Sperling GER
1937	Hilde Sperling GER
1938	Simone Mathieu FRA
1939	Simone Mathieu FRA
1946	Margaret Osborne USA
1947	Pat Todd USA
1948	Nelly Landry FRA
1949	Margaret Du Pont USA
1950	Doris Hart USA
1951	Shirley Fry USA
1952	Doris Hart USA
1953	Maureen Connolly USA
1954	Maureen Connolly USA

TENNIS

1955 Angela Mortimer GBR	1955 Ken Rosewall AUS	1957 Shirley Fry USA
1956 Althea Gibson USA	1956 Lew Hoad AUS	1958 Angela Mortimer GBR
1957 Shirley Bloomer GBR	1957 Ashley Cooper AUS	1959 Mary Reitano AUS
1958 Zsuzsi Kormoczy HUN	1958 Ashley Cooper AUS	1960 Margaret Smith AUS
1959 Christine Truman GBR	1959 Alex Olmedo USA	1961 Margaret Smith AUS
1960 Darlene Hard USA	1960 Rod Laver AUS	1962 Margaret Smith AUS
1961 Ann Haydon GBR	1961 Roy Emerson AUS	1963 Margaret Smith AUS
1962 Margaret Smith AUS	1962 Rod Laver AUS	1964 Margaret Smith AUS
1963 Lesley Turner AUS	1963 Roy Emerson AUS	1965 Margaret Smith AUS
1964 Margaret Smith AUS	1964 Roy Emerson AUS	1966 Margaret Smith AUS
1965 Lesley Turner AUS	1965 Roy Emerson AUS	1967 Nancy Richey USA
1966 Ann Jones GBR	1966 Roy Emerson AUS	1968 Billie Jean King USA
1967 Françoise Durr FRA	1967 Roy Emerson AUS	1969 Margaret Court AUS
1968 Nancy Richey USA	1968 Bill Bowrey AUS	1970 Margaret Court AUS
1969 Margaret Court AUS	1969 Rod Laver AUS	1971 Margaret Court AUS
1970 Margaret Court AUS	1970 Arthur Ashe USA	1972 Virginia Wade GBR
1971 Evonne Goolagong AUS	1971 Ken Rosewall AUS	1973 Margaret Court AUS
1972 Billie Jean King USA	1972 Ken Rosewall AUS	1974 Evonne Goolagong AUS
1973 Margaret Court AUS	1973 John Newcombe AUS	1975 Evonne Goolagong AUS
1974 Chris Evert USA	1974 Jimmy Connors USA	1976 Evonne Cawley AUS
1975 Chris Evert USA	1975 John Newcombe AUS	1977 Kerry Reid AUS
1976 Sue Barker GBR	1976 Mark Edmondson AUS	1977* Evonne Cawley AUS
1977 Mimi Jausovec YUG	1977 Roscoe Tanner USA	1978* Christine O'Neill AUS
1978 Virginia Ruzici ROM	1977* Vitas Gerulaitis USA	1979* Barbara Jordan USA
1979 Chris Evert Lloyd USA	1978* Guillermo Vilas ARG	1980* Hana Mandlikova TCH
1980 Chris Evert Lloyd USA	1979* Guillermo Vilas ARG	1981* Martina Navratilova USA
1981 Hana Mandlikova TCH	1980* Brian Teacher USA	1982* Chris Evert Lloyd USA
1982 Martina Navratilova USA	1981* Johan Kriek RSA	1983* Martina Navratilova USA
1983 Chris Evert Lloyd USA	1982* Johan Kriek RSA	1984* Chris Evert Lloyd USA
1984 Martina Navratilova USA	1983* Mats Wilander SWE	1985* Martina Navratilova USA
1985 Chris Evert Lloyd USA	1984* Mats Wilander SWE	1987 Hana Mandlikova TCH
1986 Chris Evert Lloyd USA	1985* Stefan Edberg SWE	1988 Steffi Graf FRG
1987 Steffi Graf FRG	1987 Stefan Edberg SWE	1989 Steffi Graf FRG
1988 Steffi Graf FRG	1988 Mats Wilander SWE	1990 Steffi Graf FRG
1989 Arantxa Sanchez V ESP	1989 Ivan Lendl TCH	1991 Monica Seles YUG
1990 Monica Seles YUG	1990 Ivan Lendl TCH	1992 Monica Seles YUG
1991 Monica Seles YUG	1991 Boris Becker GER	1993 Monica Seles YUG
1992 Monica Seles YUG	1992 Jim Courier USA	1994 Steffi Graf GER
1993 Steffi Graf GER	1993 Jim Courier USA	1995 Mary Pierce FRA
1994 Aranxta Sanchez V ESP	1994 Pete Sampras USA	1996 Monica Seles USA
1995 Steffi Graf GER	1995 Andre Agassi USA	1997 Martina Hingis SUI
1996 Steffi Graf GER	1996 Boris Becker USA	1998 Martina Hingis SUI
1997 Iva Majoli CRO	1997 Pete Sampras USA	1999 Martina Hingis SUI
1998 Arantxa Sanchez V ESP	1998 Petr Korda CZE	2000 Lindsay Davenport USA
1999 Steffi Graf GER	1999 Yevgeny Kafelnikov RUS	2001 Jennifer Capriati USA
2000 Mary Pierce FRA	2000 Andre Agassi USA	2002 Jennifer Capriati USA
2001 Jennifer Capriati USA	2001 Andre Agassi USA	*Championships held in December
2002 Serena Williams USA	2002 Thomas Johansson SWE	

AUSTRALIAN OPEN

Men's Singles

1946 John Bromwich AUS	
1947 Dinny Pails AUS	
1948 Adrian Quist AUS	
1949 Frank Sedgman AUS	
1950 Frank Sedgman AUS	
1951 Dick Savitt USA	
1952 Ken McGregor AUS	
1953 Ken Rosewall AUS	
1954 Mervyn Rose AUS	

Women's Singles

1946 Nancye Bolton AUS
1947 Nancye Bolton AUS
1948 Nancye Bolton AUS
1949 Doris Hart USA
1950 Louise Brough USA
1951 Nancye Bolton AUS
1952 Thelma Long AUS
1953 Maureen Connolly USA
1954 Thelma Long AUS
1955 Beryl Penrose AUS
1956 Mary Carter AUS

TENNIS

DAVIS CUP

1900	USA 3 British Isles 0	
1902	USA 3 British Isles 2	
1903	British Isles 4 USA 1	
1904	British Isles 5 Belgium 0	
1905	British Isles 5 USA 0	
1906	British Isles 5 Great Britain 0	
1907	Australasia 3 British Isles 2	
1908	Australasia 3 USA 2	
1909	Australasia 5 USA 0	
1911	Australasia 5 USA 0	
1912	British Isles 3 Australasia 2	
1913	USA 3 British Isles 2	
1914	Australasia 3 USA 2	
1919	Australasia 4 British Isles 1	
1920	USA 5 Australasia 0	
1921	USA 5 Japan 0	
1922	USA 4 Australasia 1	
1923	USA 4 Australasia 1	
1924	USA 5 Australasia 0	
1925	USA 5 France 0	
1926	USA 4 France 1	
1927	France 3 USA 2	
1928	France 4 USA 1	
1929	France 3 USA 2	
1930	France 4 USA 1	
1931	France 3 Great Britain 2	
1932	France 3 USA 2	
1933	Great Britain 3 France 2	
1934	Great Britain 4 USA 1	
1935	Great Britain 5 USA 0	
1936	Great Britain 3 France 2	
1937	USA 4 Great Britain 1	
1938	USA 3 Australia 2	
1939	Australia 3 USA 2	
1946	USA 5 Australia 0	
1947	USA 4 Australia 1	
1948	USA 5 Australia 0	
1949	USA 4 Australia 1	
1950	Australia 4 USA 1	
1951	Australia 3 USA 2	
1952	Australia 4 USA 1	
1953	Australia 3 USA 2	
1954	United States 3 Australia 2	
1955	Australia 5 USA 0	
1956	Australia 5 USA 0	
1957	Australia 3 USA 2	
1958	USA 3 Australia 2	
1959	Australia 3 USA 2	
1960	Australia 4 Italy 1	
1961	Australia 5 Italy 0	
1962	Australia 5 Mexico 0	
1963	USA 3 Australia 2	
1964	Australia 3 USA 2	
1965	Australia 4 Spain 1	
1966	Australia 4 India 1	
1967	Australia 4 Spain 1	
1968	USA 4 Australia 1	
1969	USA 5 Romania 0	
1970	USA 5 West Germany 0	
1971	USA 3 Romania 2	
1972	USA 3 Romania 2	
1973	Australia 5 USA 0	
1974	South Africa beat India by walkover	
1975	Sweden 3 Czechoslovakia 2	
1976	Italy 4 Chile 1	
1977	Australia 3 Italy 1	
1978	USA 4 Great Britain 1	
1979	USA 5 Italy 0	
1980	Czechoslovakia 4 Italy 1	
1981	USA 3 Argentina 1	
1982	USA 4 France 1	
1983	Australia 3 Sweden 2	
1984	Sweden 4 USA 1	
1985	Sweden 3 West Germany 2	
1986	Australia 3 Sweden 2	
1987	Sweden 5 India 0	
1988	West Germany 4 Sweden 1	
1989	West Germany 3 Sweden 2	
1990	USA 3 Australia 2	
1991	France 3 USA 1	
1992	USA 3 Switzerland 1	
1993	Germany 4 Australia 1	
1994	Sweden 4 Russia 1	
1995	USA 3 Russia 2	
1996	France 3 Sweden 2	
1997	Sweden 5 USA 0	
1998	Sweden 4 Italy 1	
1999	Australia 3 France 2	
2000	Spain 3 Australia 1	
2001	France 3 Australia 2	
2002	Russia 3 France 2	

TENNIS

FED CUP

The Federation Cup began in 1963. In 1995, the Cup became the Fed Cup and adopted a similar format to the Davis Cup

1963 Queen's, London
USA 2 Australia 1
1964 Germantown CC, Philadelphia
Australia 2 USA 1
1965 Kooyong Tennis Club, Melbourne
Australia 2 USA 1
1966 Press Sporting Club, Turin
USA 3 Germany 0
1967 Blau Weiss Club, Berlin
USA 2 Great Britain 0
1968 Stade Roland Garros, Paris
Australia 3 Netherlands 0
1969 Athens Tennis Club
USA 2 Australia 1
1970 Freiburg Tennis Club
Australia 3 Germany 0
1971 Perth, Australia
Australia 3 Great Britain 0
1972 Ellis Park, Johannesburg
South Africa 2 Great Britain 1
1973 Bad Homberg, Germany
Australia 3 South Africa 0
1974 Tennis Club of Naples
Australia 2 USA 1
1975 Aixoise CC, France
Czechoslovakia 3 Australia 0
1976 The Spectrum, Philadelphia
USA 2 Australia 1
1977 Devonshire Park, Eastbourne
USA 2 Australia 1
1978 Kooyong Stadium, Melbourne
USA 2 Australia 1
1979 RSHE de Campo, Madrid
USA 3 Australia 0
1980 Rot-Weiss TC, Berlin
USA 3 Australia 0
1981 Tamagawa-en RC, Tokyo
USA 3 Great Britain 0
1982 Decathlon Club, Santa Clara, CA
USA 3 West Germany 0
1983 Albisguetli TC, Zurich
Czechoslovakia 2 West Germany 1
1984 Esporte Clube Pinheiros, Sao Paulo
Czechoslovakia 2 Australia 1
1985 Nagoya Green TC, Japan
Czechoslovakia 2 USA 1
1986 Stvanice Stadium, Prague
USA 3 Czechoslovakia 0
1987 Hollyburn CC, Vancouver
West Germany 2 USA 1
1988 Flinders Park, Melbourne
Czechoslovakia 2 Soviet Union 1
1989 Ariake TC, Tokyo
USA 3 Spain 0
1990 Peachtree World of Tennis, Atlanta
USA 2 Soviet Union 1

1991 City of Nottingham TC
Spain 2 USA 1
1992 Waldstadion, Frankfurt
Germany 2 Spain 1
1993 Waldstadion, Frankfurt
Spain 3 Australia 0
1994 Waldstadion, Frankfurt
Spain 3 USA 0
1995 Club Tenis de Valencia
Spain 3 USA 2
1996 Atlantic City Convention Centre
USA 3 Spain 0
1997 Brabanthallen, 's-Hertogenbosch
France 4 Netherlands 1
1998 Geneva
Spain 3 Switzerland 2
1999 Stanford University, California
USA 4 Russia 1
2000 Las Vegas
USA 5 Spain 0
2001 Madrid
Belgium 2 Russia 1
2002 Gran Canaria
Slovak Rep 3 Spain 1

TRIATHLON

TRIATHLON
Men
1989	Mark Allen	USA
1990	Greg Welch	AUS
1991	Miles Stewart	AUS
1992	Simon Lessing	GBR
1993	Spencer Smith	GBR
1994	Spencer Smith	GBR
1995	Simon Lessing	GBR
1996	Simon Lessing	GBR
1997	Chris McCormack	AUS
1998	Simon Lessing	GBR
1999	Dimitry Gaag	KZK
2000	Olivier Marceau	FRA
2001	Peter Robertson	AUS
2002	Ivan Rana	ESP

Women
1989	Erin Baker	NZL
1990	Karen Smyers	USA
1991	Joanne Ritchie	CAN
1992	Michellie Jones	AUS
1993	Michellie Jones	AUS
1994	Emma Carney	AUS
1995	Karen Smyers	USA
1996	Jackie Gallagher	AUS
1997	Emma Carney	AUS
1998	Joanne King	AUS
1999	Loretta Harrop	AUS
2000	Nicole Hackett	AUS
2001	Siri Lindley	USA
2002	Leanda Cave	GBR

LONG DISTANCE TRIATHLON

Men
1994	Rob Barel	NED
1995	Simon Lessing	GBR
1996	Greg Welch	AUS
1997	Luc Van Lierde	BEL
1998	Luc Van Lierde	BEL
1999	Peter Sandvang	DEN
2000	Peter Sandvang	DEN
2001	Peter Sandvang	DEN
2002	Marc Ruhe	LIE

Women
1994	Isabelle Mouthon	FRA
1995	Jenny Rose	NZL
1996	Karen Smyers	USA
1997	Ines Estedt	GER
1998	Rina Hill	AUS
1999	Suzanne Nielsen	DEN
2000	Isabelle Mouthon	FRA
2001	Lisbeth Kristensen	DEN
2002	Marianne Vlasveld	NED

DUATHLON

Men
From 1993 onwards
1993	Greg Welch	AUS
1994	Norman Stadler	GER
1995	Oscar Galindez	ARG
1996	Andrew Noble	AUS
1997	Jonathon Hall	AUS
1998	Yann Million	FRA
1999	Yann Million	FRA
2000	Benny Vansteelant	BEL
2001	Benny Vansteelant	BEL
2002	Tim Don	GBR

Women
1993	Carol Montgomery	CAN
1994	Irma Heeren	NED
1995	Natascha Badman	SUI
1996	Jackie Gallagher	AUS
1997	Irma Heeren	NED
1998	Irma Heeren	NED
1999	Jackie Gallagher	AUS
2000	Steph Forrester	SCO
2001	Erika Csomor	HUN
2002	Corinne Raux	FRA

VOLLEYBALL

Indoor World Champions

	Men	Women
1949	Soviet Union	-
1952	Soviet Union	Soviet Union
1956	Czechoslovakia	Soviet Union
1960	Soviet Union	Soviet Union
1962	Soviet Union	Japan
1966	Czechoslovakia	Japan
1970	East Germany	Soviet Union
1974	Poland	Japan
1978	Soviet Union	Cuba
1982	Soviet Union	China
1986	USA	China
1990	Italy	Soviet Union
1994	Italy	Cuba
1998	Italy	Cuba
2002	Brazil	Italy

World Cup

	Men	Women
1965	Soviet Union	-
1969	East Germany	-
1973	-	Soviet Union
1977	Soviet Union	Japan
1981	Soviet Union	China
1985	USA	China
1989	Cuba	Cuba
1991	Unified Team	Cuba
1995	Italy	Cuba
1999	Cuba	Russia

World Grand Champions Cup

1993	Italy	Cuba
1997	Brazil	Russia
2001	Cuba	China

Obituary

Jeff Astle (football) In 361 appearances for West Bromwich Albion, Astle scored 174 goals, and in the year the Baggies won the FA Cup, 1968, became the first-ever player to score in every round. Ironically, though, he will doubtless be best remembered for a goal he missed. It was for England against Brazil in the 1970 World Cup and would have leveled the scores at one apiece. Astle, plagued by injury, retired in 1974, but 20 years later was back in the public eye with a comedy singing spot on the Fantasy Football tv programme. Astle died in January from a degenerative brain disease of which a contributory cause, according to the coroner, could have been the heading of a football. Astle was 59.

Charles Benson (journalism) For 30 years, and alongside Peter O'Sullivan and Clive Graham, Benson worked as a racing correspondent for the Daily Express. He died of cancer in June, aged 66.

John Bromley (television) From journalistic roots, Bromley moved into television in 1964. During 25 years with Independent Television, Bromley was responsible for World Of Sport, The Big Match, On the Ball and Saint and Greavsie, amongst others. He became controller of sport at London Weekend, and in 1981 was made chairman of the ITV sports network committee. After his retirement in 1989, the much-loved Bromley (or Brommers, as he was universally known) worked as a TV consultant. He was also a press attache for the 1996 British Olympic team in Atlanta, doubling up as social secretary for the press corps, or so it seemed. He died, from cancer in February, aged 68.

David Brooks (rugby union) Manager of the British Lions when they toured South Africa in 1968, Brooks later became president of the RFU. He died in January, aged 77.

Joyce Cooper (swimming) For six years, from 1927 to 1933, not an international championship passed without Cooper amongst the medals. Her best haul was at the Empire Games in Hamilton, Canada in 1930, when she won four gold medals; her titles coming in the 110yds and 440yds freestyle, the 110yds backstroke and the freestyle relay. Two years earlier, Cooper had won three medals, though no titles, at the Amsterdam Olympic Games, an achievement that probably surpassed her title-spree in Canada. Cooper also broke the world record for the 150yds backstroke, perhaps the only world record ever achieved at the Hornsey Baths in north London. She died, in July, aged 93.

Jack Fairman (motor racing) In partnership with a young Stirling Moss, Fairman made his name in endurance racing, most famously at the Montlhery circuit, near Paris, where he shared the driving in a Jaguar XK120 which covered 16,852 miles in seven days and nights. In 1953, when past his 40th birthday, Fairman made his debut in Formula One, but had no success in his 12 Grand Prix starts. He died in February, aged 88.

George Francis (boxing) Francis shaped the careers of Frank Bruno and John Conteh and, 21 years apart, took them both to world titles. As a coach, Francis concentrated on having his charges as fit as possible, and for Bruno, who was never a masterful boxer, in particular, it made the difference between success and failure. With Conteh, Francis instilled discipline, and their relationship was the defining period of his coaching career. Francis died in October, taking his own life. He was 73.

Sir Arthur Gold (athletics) As a high jumper, Gold was always struggling at international level, though he compensated with longevity, still competing at club level at the age of 43. His career as an administrator took off in 1965 when he was appointed honorary secretary of the Amateur Athletic Association. Over the course of the next 40 years, in that role, as president of the European Association, and eventually as chairman of the British Olympic Association, Gold was a doughty and opinionated presence. A fierce campaigner against drugs in sport, he retired from the BOA post in 1992. Gold died in May, aged 85.

Dick Hern (horse racing) Major Dick Hern trained the winners of 17 Classics, including the three Derby winners Troy, Henbit and Nashwan, all ridden to victory by Willie Carson. However, it was Brigadier Gerard, the 1971 2000 Guineas winner, who earned the reputation as his most popular horse. Hern, who had coached the 1952 British showjumping team to Olympic gold, was also for many years the Queen's trainer. However, in 1989 that association came to an end, and Hern was forced out of his stables at West Isley, in circumstances that left many in the sport feeling that Hern had been shabbily treated. Hern finally retired from training at the end of the 1997 Flat season. He died in May, aged 81.

Ben Hollioake (cricket) Born in Australia, Hollioake made his international debut for his adopted country in the same year as his elder brother Adam. Of the two, the younger brother was considered to have the greater talent, Adam the greater tenacity. In his first one-day international, against Australia at Lord's, the 19-year-old Ben struck 63 runs from 48 balls and was hailed as the new Ian Botham. Yet, though he played in another 19 one-day international and two full Tests, he did not fulfil his considerable potential. Ben Hollioake died in March, killed in a car crash while at his parents home in Perth, Australia. He was 24.

Geoffrey Howard (cricket) For 15 years, Howard was secretary of Lancashire County Cricket Club. While in that position he also managed MCC tours abroad, most notably the 1954-55 trip to Australia, with an England team captained by Len Hutton, which won the Ashes series. Howard died in November, aged 93.

Ian Hutchinson (football) In 144 matches for Chelsea, Hutchinson scored 58 goals, but none was as important as the goal which secured a replay against Leeds in the 1970 FA Cup Final. Hutchinson was also responsible for the winner in the second game at Manchester when his long throw-in (he was one of the first to acquire the skill) was eventually nodded in by David Webb. Hutchinson was forced into retirement at the age of 27 through injury. He died, after a long illness in September, aged 54.

Ron Jacobs (rugby union) Between 1956 and 1964 Jacobs won 29 caps for England at loose-head prop, and twice captained his country. In 1957, he was a member of the team which won England its first post-war Grand Slam. Jacobs stayed involved with the sport after he stopped playing and in the 1983-84 season was elected president of the RFU. He died in November, aged 74.

Stan Lynn (football) Lynn played at left back in the Aston Villa team which thwarted the ambitions of Manchester United in the 1957 FA Cup Final. Villa won that match 2-1, the defeat costing United a famous Double. A year later, Lynn became the first full-back to score a hattrick, when he put three past Sunderland at Villa Park, two of the goals being penalties. He died in April, aged 73.

Sir Bert Millichip (football) For 15 years, Millichip was chairman of the Football Association, his period in charge including some of the most difficult times for the sport in its long history. Millichip also carried out a variety of functions for UEFA over 20 years and was knighted for his services to the sport. He died in December, aged 88.

Charlie Mitten (football) Mitten was a traditional left-winger, who had played in Manchester United's Cup-winning side in 1948. Two years later, to the anger of his manager Matt Busby, Mitten signed to play for Sante Fe, an Colombian side. When he returned to England, Mitten was banned by FIFA as Colombia were not at that stage members of the world governing body. Mitten also played for Fulham and Mansfield Town and managed Newcastle. He died in January, aged 80.

Dick Moore (cricket) On a heady day in July 1937, Moore scored 316 runs for Hampshire against Warwickshire, to set a club record that still stands. Moore scored over 6000 runs for his county, but never played for England. Moore died in March, aged 88.

Geoffrey Page (rowing) For almost 35 years, Page covered rowing for the Sunday Telegraph and, since 1984, for the Daily Telegraph too. Page, himself, rowed at international level, winning a silver medal in the eights at the 1954 Commonwealth Games. He died in April, aged 72.

Umer Rashid (cricket) A left-arm spinner with Sussex, Rashid drowned in Grenada while on a pre-season tour in April. His brother Burhan died in the same incident and it was reported that Umer was trying to save his brother. Umer Rashid was 26.

Arthur Rowley (football) Rowley holds the record for the most goals scored in English League football, 434 coming in 619 appearances. His most prolific period was with Leicester City; eight years at the East Midlands club bringing him 265 goals in 303 games (including 16 hattricks). He left Leicester to become player-manager at Shrewsbury town, where his trusty left foot was largely responsible for 38 goals in just 43 games. Rowley subsequently managed Sheffield United briefly before spending six years with Southend United. He died in December, aged 76.

Dick Saunders (horse racing) Riding the 7-1 favourite Grittar to victory in 1982 made the 48-year-old Saunders the oldest jockey in history to be successful in the Grand National. It was his first and only ride in the race. Saunders died in January, aged 68.

Harry Sharratt (football) One of the most popular amateur players of the fifties, the Bishop Auckland goalkeeper was once booked for building a snowman in his goalmouth. Sharratt was on the winning side in three FA Amateur Cup Finals. He died in August, aged 72.

Crew Stoneley (athletics) Stoneley ran the opening leg of the 400m relay team which took the silver medal at the 1932 Los Angeles Olympics. Tommy Hampson, Lord Burghley and Godfrey Rampling made up the team. Stoneley's chances of an Olympic reprise in 1936 were frustrated by a military posting - he went on to become a brigadier. Of the 1932 team, only Rampling competed in Berlin, and the team won gold. Stoneley died in August, aged 91.

Albert Stubbins (football) It cost Liverpool £13,000 to secure the services of Stubbins from Newcastle in 1946. The striker quickly became an Anfield favourite, helping the club to the first post-war championship title in 1947. Stubbins went on to play 180 games and score 83 goals for Liverpool, before retiring from League football in 1953. His picture would later appear on the cover of the Beatle's LP Sergeant Pepper's Lonely Hearts Club Band. Stubbins died in December, aged 83.

Rob Walker (motor racing) From its modest base at Dorking, Surrey, Walker Racing achieved landmark victories in Formula One, being the first and the last 'privateer' to win a Grand Prix. Walker's most celebrated years were from 1958-62 with Stirling Moss at the wheel of Walker's cars, but Jochen Rindt, Jo Siffert and, ultimately, Graham Hill all drove for the Surrey team. Walker died in April, aged 84.

Nick Whitehead (athletics) At the Rome Olympics, in 1960, Whitehead ran the anchor leg of the 4x100m relay team which won the bronze medal. Later he became the British team manager for six years, from 1978-84, and a director of the National Coaching Federation and deputy director of the Sports Council for Wales. He died, of cancer, in October, aged 69.

Sir Walter Winterbottom (football) Though never successful with England at World Cup level, Winterbottom's record as manager of the England over a 15-year period, was 78 wins and only 27 defeats from 137 games. His early England teams included such folk heroes as Stanley Matthews and Tom Finney, and by the time he bowed out in 1962, the luminaries of the team included Jimmy Greaves and Johnny Haynes. Winterbottom was also in charge in 1953 when the Hungarians inflicted 6-3 and 7-1 defeats on England, something of a rude awakening for the nation. After leaving the FA, Winterbottom became an executive director of the Sports Council. He died in February, aged 89.

Kenneth Wolstenholme (football) On the most day in English football, Wolstenholme signed off the match with the most famous phrase. "There are people on the pitch, they think it's all over...it is now," as Geoff Hurst scored his third and England's fourth goal to wrap up victory in the 1966 World Cup Final. Wolstenholme commented on over 2000 matches, including 23 FA Cup Finals and five World Cups in a television career that spanned from the post-war years until 1971, when he was effectively supplanted by a young David Coleman. Wolstenholme died in March, aged 81.

Overseas

Roone Artledge (USA, television)
Artledge was in charge of ABC Sports coverage of every Olympic Games from 1964 to 1988. He died of cancer in December, aged 71.

Alexander de Merode (Belgium, administrator) From its inception in 1967, de Merode was president of the medical commission of the IOC. Though a lawyer by qualification, de Merode was obliged to become a scientist by profession, and at times the demands of his position would have strained even the most eminent of biochemists. He died in November, aged 68.

Hansie Cronje (South Africa, cricket)
An immensely influential of his country for 53 of his 68 Test matches, with 3,714 runs (at an average of 36.41). that would have been Cronje's epitaph, but he was implicated in the match-fixing scandal that erupted in 2000 and though he denied fixing matches, Cronje admitted to receiving substantial sums from bookmakers, and encouraging teammates to underperform. He was subsequently banned from cricket for life. Cronje died in June, when a cargo plane he was travelling in, crashed into a mountain. He was 32.

Willie Davenport (USA, athletics) At the Mexico Olympic Games in 1968, Davenport won the 100m hurdles in 13.33, the fastest-ever automatic time. A year later, he equalled the hand-timed record as well. Davenport competed in three summer Games as a hurdler and in 1980 at Lake Placid was part of the US four-man bobsleigh team. He died in June, from a heart attack suffered at Chicago's O'Hare airport. He was 59.

Ben Eastman (USA, athletics) In 1932, Eastman knocked a full second off the world 440yds record, with a time of 46.4. Two months later, he set a world record for the 880yds as well, and the Californian would have been favourite for whichever of those races he opted for at the Los Angeles Olympics later that year. Eastman chose the shorter distance but finished second to the unsung Pennsylvanian Bill Carr, who broke Eastman's record in the final. Britain's Tommy Hampson won the 800m, breaking Eastman's other world record in the process, but two years later the Californian reclaimed the world record, but never made a second Olympic Games. Eastman died in October, aged 91.

Manfred Ewald (Germany, politics)
Head of East German sport (the DTB) from 1961 to 1988, which included the years, from roughly 1968 onwards, when the country's high-level performers were systematically doped. In 2000, Ewald was given a 22-month suspended sentence after being convicted of causing harm to 142 former sportswomen, by imposing a regimen of performance-enhancing drugs on them. He died, of pneumonia, in October, aged 76.

Kim Gallagher (USA, athletics)
Gallagher overcame anaemia, chronic fatigue and ovarian surgery to win bronze medals in the 800m in successive Olympic Games, in 1984 and 1988. She died, of a stroke, in November, aged 38.

Bob Hayes (USA, athletics) After watching Hayes win the 100m in Tokyo at the 1964 Olympics, even Jesse Owens was convinced he had seen the greatest sprinter ever. Hayes won that final in 10 seconds flat and by over two metres. It was his 49th successive victory. In the relay, his performance was, if anything, even more impressive, the American four metres down from the Frenchman Jocelyn Delecour at the final handover. Hayes was estimated to have run the last 100m in 8.9 seconds. He broke the tape three metres ahead of Delecour, and the Americans had also broken the world record. Hayes, only 21, retired as an athlete, signing up as a pro footballer with Dallas Cowboys. Hayes was also credited with revolutionising the NFL, so quick that he forced defences to rethink their strategies. Hayes, who served 10 months in jail for drug offences in 1979, died in September. He was 59.

Warren Jones (Australia, sailing) Jones was credited with being the driving force behind the successful Americas Cup campaign of Australia II at Newport, Rhode Island in 1983, when the cup was finally wrested from the grip of the USA. He died in April, aged 65.

Dick Lane (USA am. football) In his first season in the NFL in 1952, Lane broke the record for interceptions, his tally of 14 still the best today. Known as 'Night Train'', Lane would instill fear in the opposition with a tackling technique that would drag the receiver down by his head and neck. The technique of head-hunting was eventually outlawed, but Lane remained a dominant force at cornerback. He died from a heart attack in January, aged 73.

Audrey Mestre (France, diver) In an attempt on the world no-limit freediving record of 171 metres, in the waters off the Dominican Republic in July, the Frenchwoman died. Maestre was 28.

Carl 'Bobo' Olson (USA, boxing) In March 1953, Olson met Randolph Turpin for the vacant world middleweight title, defeating the Englishman after 15 rounds on points. Olson, of Swedish parentage, defended the title successfully three times, before losing it to middleweight legend Sugar Ray Robinson. In three title contests against Robinson, Olson always came second best. He died in January, aged 73.

Ben Plucknett (USA, athletics) Had the Americans not boycotted the 1980 Olympics, Plucknett would have been on the team. Instead, his fame now resides in the circumstances surrounding his two world records in 1981; rejected by the IAAF as he had previously tested positive for steroids, but ratified by the US governing body. Plucknett died of a brain aneurism in November, aged 48.

Franziska Rochat-Moser (athletics) The 1997 winner of the New York Marathon and the Swiss record hold for the distance died from injuries sustained in an alpine climbing accident in March. She was 35.

Juan Schiaffino (Uruguay, football) It was Schiaffino's goal which brought the scores level in the 1950 World Cup Final. The 200,000 ardent Brazilians fans were silenced when the Uruguayan scored in the second half, and 14 minutes later Ghiggia scored the Uruguayan winner. Schiaffino died in November. He was 77.

Jack Shea (USA, speed skating) Shea won the Olympic speed skating titles at 500m and 1500m at his home rink in Lake Placid in the 1932 Winter Olympics. The American chose not to defend those titles in Germany four years later, in the light of the anti-semitic policies of Hitler's Germany. Shea's son, Jim Shea snr, competed in the nordic events at the 1964 Winter Games and his grandson, Jim jr, won the men's skeleton at Salt Lake City, just a month after his grandfather died, from injuries sustained in a road accident. He was 91.

Sam Snead (USA, golf) Snead could never quite complete the set of Majors for though he won three Masters' titles, three US PGA titles, and one Open Championship (from just two tries) he was never able to win the US Open, finishing second on four occasions. He was also a Ryder Cup player on eight occasions and won a total of 164 tour events. A naturally gifted player, Snead's longevity in the game was often ascribed to the fact that he did not adopt a punishing practice schedule. As if to prove a point, in 1979 he became the first player in an official event to shoot his age with a round of 66 in the Quad City Open. Snead was 67. When he retired from the US Tour in the same year, Snead was active in creating the Seniors' Tour. He died from a stroke in May, aged 90.

Sohn Kee-Chung (Korea, athletics) At the Berlin Olympics, when still only 21, Sohn won the marathon, but not running under his own name. As Korea was under Japanese hegemony, he was given a Japanese name, Kitei Son, and the Japanese flag flew at the medal presentation. Fifty-two years later, Sohn carried the torch into the Olympic stadium at the start of the Seoul Olympics. It was an emotional postscript. Sohn died in November, aged 88.

Johnny Unitas (USA, am. football) When he retired in 1974, Unitas held 22 NFL records, and still no quarterback has matched his achievement of completing at least one touchdown pass in 47 straight games. In 1970, 15 years after he first played as a professional, Unitas finally lead the Baltimore Colts to victory in the Super Bowl. A year earlier, Unitas had been voted the greatest quarterback of all time. Unitas died from a heart attack in September. He was 69.

Vava (Brazil, football) Edvaldo Isidio Neto first played for his country as an amateur in the 1952 Olympics, but it was as the thrustful centre-forward in the 1958 and 1962 Brazil teams, that Vava enjoyed his greatest successes. Not originally a first choice in 1958, Vava played in just five matches but scored six goals, two against Sweden in the final, won 5-2 by the Brazilians. Four years later Vava would against score in the final, against the Czechs, as Brazil added another World Cup title. Vava died in January, from heart problems, aged 67.

Fritz Walter (Germany, football) The Hungarians were the warm favourites for the 1954 World Cup, but in front of 64,000 spectators in Berne, Walter led the German team to a surprise victory in the final. Thereafter, Walter, one of six players from the Kaiserslautern club including his brother Otto, was known as 'The Hero of Berne'. For the West Germans, the World Cup win signalled their rehabilitation into world sport. Walter was also in the World Cup team four years later, in Sweden, but the Germans lost to the host nation in the semi-finals. Walter died in June, ,aged 81.

Mamo Wolde (athletics) Following the two victories of Abebe Bikila in the Olympic marathon, Wolde made it a hattrick for Ethiopian athletes when he won the marathon by over three minutes in the rarified air of Mexico City. Four years later in Munich, Wolde took the bronze medal. An Ethiopian hero then, Wolde's life took a very different course in 1992 when he was held in prison for nine years, as a suspect of, and eventually, controversially, convicted of murder. He served nine years in jail, released only a few months before he died in March. He was 69.

Calendar

January

1	Cricket	N Zealand v India, 3rd ODI Christchurch, New Zealand
1-5	Darts	PDC World Championships Circus Tavern, Purfleet
1-5	Tennis	ATP Event Adelaide, Australia ATP Event Chennai, India ATP Event Doha, Qatar
1-5	Tennis	WTA Event Gold Coast, Australia WTA Event Auckland, New Zealand
2-6	Cricket	England v Australia, 5th Test Sydney, Australia
2-6	Cricket	S Africa v Pakistan, 2nd Test Cape Town
3-5	Speed Skating	European Long Track Chps Heerenveen, Netherlands
4	Athletics	Great North Cross Country Newcastle
4	Cricket	New Zealand v India, 4th ODI Queenstown
4-5	Am Football	Wild Card Weekend USA
4-5	Skiing	Alpine World Cup, women Berchtesgaden, Germany
4-5	Skiing	Alpine World Cup, men Kranjska Gora, Slovenia
4-6	Football	Scottish Cup 2nd rd
4-6	Football	FA Cup 3rd rd
4-12	Darts	BDO World Championships Lakeside CC, Frimley Green
5-26	Bowls	World Indoor Championships Hopton-on-Sea, Norfolk
6	Skiing	Alpine World Cup, men Hinterstoder, Austria
6-12	Golf	Mercedes Championships Kapalua, Hawaii
6-12	Tennis	WTA Event Sydney WTA Event Hobart, Tasmania WTA Event Canberra
7-8	Football	Worthington Cup s-fs 1st leg
8	Cricket	England v Bradman XI Bowral, Australia
8	Cricket	New Zealand v India, 5th ODI Wellington
9	Cricket	Australia v Sri Lanka, ODI Sydney
9-12	Golf	South African Airways Open Erinvale GC, Cape Town
10-11	Rugby Union	Heineken Cup Pool matches
10-12	Rugby Union	PP Challenge Cup q-f 1st legs
11	Athletics	IAAF Cross-country Belfast
11	Cricket	England v Australia, ODI (VB) Hobart
11	Cricket	New Zealand v India, 6th ODI Auckland
11	Motor Cycling	GP of Sheffield - Indoor Trials
11-12	Am Football	Divisional Play-offs
11-12	Skiing	Alpine World Cup Chamonix, France
11-12	Skiing	Alpine World Cup Innsbruck, Austria
11-21	Sailing	Louis Vuitton Cup final Auckland
12	Basketball	Men's National Cup final NIA, Birmingham
12-19	Snowboarding	World Championship Kreischberg, Austria
13	Cricket	England v Sri Lanka, ODI (VB) Sydney
13-19	Golf	Sony Open in Hawaii Honolulu
13-26	Tennis	Australian Open Flinders Park, Melbourne
14	Cricket	New Zealand v India, ODI Hamilton
14	Skiing	Alpine World Cup Adelboden, Switzerland
15	Cricket	Australia v Sri Lanka, ODI (VB) Brisbane
16-19	Golf	SA PGA Championship Houghton GC, Johannesburg
17	Cricket	England v Sri Lanka, ODI (VB) Adelaide
17-18	Bobsleigh	World Cup, women Igls, Austria
17-18	Swimming	World Cup (short course) Paris
17-19	Rugby Union	PP Challenge Cup q-f 2nd leg
17-19	Skiing	Alpine World Cup, women Cortina d'Ampezzo, Italy
17-19	Skiing	Alpine World Cup, men Wengen, Switzerland
17-19	Speed Skating	European Short Track Chps St Petersburg, Russia
18	Rugby Union	Heineken Cup Pool matches
18	Skiing	Freestyle World Cup Laax, Switzerland
18-19	Bobsleigh	World Cup, men St Moritz, Switzerland
18-19	Speed Skating	World Sprint Chps, Long Track Calgary, Canada
19	Am Football	Conference Championships
19	Athletics	IAAF Cross-country Seville, Spain
19	Cricket	England v Australia, ODI (VB) Adelaide
20-26	Golf	Phoenix Open Scottsdale, Arizona

20-26	Ice Skating	European Figure Skating Chps Malmo, Sweden
20-Feb 3	Handball	Men's World Championships Lisbon, Portugal
21	Cricket	Australia v Sri Lanka, ODI (VB) Melbourne
21-22	Swimming	World Cup (short course) Stockholm
21-24	Skeleton	European Championship St Moritz, Switzerland
22	Football	Worthington Cup s-f 2nd leg
22-26	Motor Rallying	Monte Carlo Rally
22-26	Snooker	Welsh Open Cardiff
23	Cricket	VB Series Final 1 Sydney
23-26	Golf	Caltex Masters Singapore
23-26	Squash	Greenwich Open, women New York
24-26	Skiing	Alpine World Cup, men Austria
25-26	Football	Scottish Cup 3rd rd
25-27	Football	FA Cup 4th rd
25-26	Bobsleigh	European Championship,men Winterberg, Germany
25	Cricket	VB Series Final 2 Melbourne
25	Rugby Union	Powergen Cup quarter-finals
25-26	Golf	LPGA Skins Game Hawaii
25-26	Skiing	Alpine World Cup, women Maribor, Slovenia
25-26	Swimming	World Cup (short course) Berlin
26	Am Football	Super Bowl XXXVII San Diego, USA
26	Athletics	IAAF Cross-country Tourcoing, France
26	Athletics	Osaka Marathon
27	Cricket	VB Series Final 3 Adelaide
27-Feb 2	Golf	Bob Hope Chrysler Classic California
27-Feb 2	Tennis	ATP Event Bogota, Colombia ATP Event Milan ATP Event Bogota
27-Feb 2	Tennis	WTA Event Tokyo
28	Skiing	Alpine World Cup, men Schladming, Austria
29-Feb 1	Skeleton	World Cup Altenberg, Germany
29-Feb 2	Skiing	Freestyle World Chps Deer Valley, USA
30-Feb 2	Golf	Heineken Classic Royal Melbourne GC

February

1-2	Cycling	Cyclo-cross World Chps Monopoli, Italy
2	Athletics	Norwich Union Indoor Glasgow, Scotland
2	Athletics	Sparkassen Cup - Indoor Stuttgart
2-16	Skiing	Alpine World Championships St Moritz, Switzerland
2-7	Snooker	Masters Wembley
3-9	Golf	AT&T National Pro-Am Poppy Hills, CA, USA
3-9	Tennis	WTA, Open Gaz de France Paris WTA Event Hyderabad, India
4-5	Football	Scottish League Cup s-f
5	Athletics	Indoor Meeting Dortmund, Germany
5-9	Motor Rallying	Swedish Rally
6-9	Golf	ANZ Championship NSW GC, Sydney
6-9	Hockey	Indoor World Cup Leipzig, Germany
7	Athletics	Milrose Games - Indoor Mtg New York
7-8	Bobsleigh	World Cup, men Calgary, Canada
7-9	Speed Skating	World Long Track Chps Gothenburg, Sweden
7-9	Speed Skating	World Cup, Short Track Salt Lake City, USA
7-9	Tennis	Australia v GB, Davis Cup Sydney (Clay)
8	Athletics	UK World X-Country Trials 1 Nottingham
8	Motor Cycling	GP of Torino - Indoor Trials Italy
8-9	Judo	EJU 'Super A' Tournament Paris
9	Athletics	IAAF Cross-country Loule, Portugal
9	Athletics	Flanders - Indoor Meeting Ghent, Belgium
9	Cricket	World Cup, Group B S Africa v W Indies Sri Lanka v N Zealand
10	Cricket	World Cup, Group A Zimbabwe v Namibia
10-16	Golf	Buick Invitational San Diego, California
10-16	Squash	British National Chps Manchester
10-16	Tennis	ATP Event Vina Del Mar ATP Event Marseille ATP Event San Jose, USA

10-16	Tennis	WTA Diamond Games, GSI Antwerp, Belgium WTA Tour, Qatar Open Doha, Qatar
11-16	Badminton	All England Open NIA, Birmingham
11	Cricket	World Cup Bangladesh v Canada, Gp B Australia v Pakistan Gp A
11-16	Skeleton	World Championship Nagano, Japan
12	Football	England v Australia Upton Park
12	Football	Scotland v Ireland Hampden Park
12	Football	Yugoslavia v Azerbaijan Group 9, Euro 2004 qualifier
12	Cricket	World Cup India v Netherlands, Gp A S Africa v Kenya, Gp B
12-15	Triathlon	Winter World Championship Oberstaufen, Germany
13	Cricket	World Cup Zimbabwe v England, Gp A W Indies v N Zealand, Gp B
13-16	Golf	Johnnie Walker Classic Perth, Australia
14	Cricket	World Cup S Lanka v Bangladesh, Gp B
14	Rugby League	World Club Cup Chp St Helens v Sydney Roosters Reebok stadium, Bolton
14-15	Skiing	Freestyle World Cup Inawashiro, Japan
14-16	Cycling	Track World Cup 1 Moscow
14-16	Diving	Grand Prix 1 Adelaide
14-16	Speed Skating	World Cup, Short Track Chicoutimi, Canada
15-17	Football	FA Cup 5th rd
15	Athletics	European Indoor Cup Leipzig, Germany
15-23	Bobsleigh	World Championship, men Lake Placid, USA
15	Cricket	World Cup Australia v India, Gp A Kenya v Canada, Gp B
15	Rugby Union	Six Nations England v France Italy v Wales
15-Mar 1	Sailing	Americas Cup Auckland
16	Athletics	IAAF Cross-country Diekirch, Luxembourg
16	Athletics	IAAF Cross-country Chiba, Japan
16	Cricket	World Cup S Africa v N Zealand, Gp B England v Netherlands, Gp A
16	Cricket	World Cup Pakistan v Namibia, Group A
16	Rugby Union	Six Nations Scotland v Ireland
17-23	Golf	Nissan Open Pacific Palisades, Cal

17-23	Luge	World Championships Sigulda, Latvia
17-23	Tennis	ATP Event Buenos Aires ATP Event Rotterdam ATP Event Memphis
17-23	Tennis	WTA, Dubai Duty Free Open Dubai, UAE WTA Event Bogota, Colombia WTA Event Memphis, Tennessee
18	Football	UEFA Champions League Group A Leverkusen v Newcastle Barcelona v Internazionale Group B Roma v Valencia Arsenal v Ajax
18	Athletics	Indoor Meeting Stockholm
18	Cricket	World Cup W Indies v Bangladesh, Gp B
18-Mar 1	Skiing	Cross-Country World Chps Val di Fiemme, Italy
19	Football	UEFA Champions League Group C Real Madrid v B Dortmund AC Milan v Lokomotiv Moscow Group D Basel v D La Coruna Manchester Utd v Juventus
19	Cricket	World Cup England v Namibia, Gp A Zimbabwe v India, Gp A Sri Lanka v Canada, Gp B
20	Cricket	World Cup Australia v Netherlands, Gp A
20	Football	UEFA Cup 4th rd, 1st leg Slavia Prague v Besiktas Hertha Berlin v Boavista Malaga v AEK Athens Wisla Krakow v Lazio Anderlecht v Panithinaikos Celtic v Stuggart Porto v Denizlispor Auxerre v Liverpool
20-23	Golf	Carlsberg Malaysian Open Kuala Lumpur
20-Mar 2	Skiing	Ski Jumping World Chps Val di Fiemme, Italy
21	Athletics	Norwich Union Indoor GP Birmingham
21	Cricket	World Cup New Zealand v Kenya, Gp B
21	Motor Cycling	GP of Pesaro - Indoor Trials Italy
21	Rugby League	Super League starts St Helens v Bradford
21-28	Skiing	Nordic Combined World Chps Val di Fiemme, Italy
22	Athletics	English National X Country Parliament Hill, London

22	Cricket	World Cup S Africa v Bangladesh, Gp B England v Pakistan, Gp A
22	Rugby Union	Six Nations Wales v England Italy v Ireland
22-23	Football	Scottish Cup 4th rd
22-23	Judo	EJU 'Super A' Tournament Munich
22-23	Judo	EJU 'Super A' Tournament Hamburg, Germany
23	Athletics	Gaz de France - Indoor Mtg Lievin, France
23	Cricket	World Cup India v Namibia, Gp A W Indies v Canada, Gp B
23	Rugby Union	Six Nations France v Scotland
24	Cricket	World Cup Sri Lanka v Kenya, Gp B Zimbabwe v Australia, Gp A
24	Netball	England v New Zealand MEN Arena, Manchester
24-28	Squash	Tournament of Champions New York
24-30	Tennis	ATP Event Copenhagen ATP Event Dubai ATP Event Acapulco
24-30	Tennis	WTA Tour Acapulco
24-Mar 2	Golf	Chrysler Classic of Tucson Arizona, USA
24-Mar 2	Tennis	WTA State Farm Classic Scottsdale, Arizona
25	Football	UEFA Champions League Group C L Moscow v AC Milan B Dortmund v Real Madrid Group D Juventus v Manchester Utd D La Coruna v Basel
25	Cricket	World Cup Pakistan v Netherlands, Gp A
26	Cricket	World Cup N Zealand v Bangladesh, Gp B England v India, Gp A
26	Football	UEFA Champions League Group B Valencia v Roma Ajax v Arsenal Group A Newcastle v Leverkusen Internazionale v Barcelona
26-Mar 2	Golf	WGC-Accenture Match Play Carlsbad, California
26-Mar 2	Rallying	Anatolian Rally Turkey
26	Netball	England v New Zealand NEC, Birmingham
27	Cricket	World Cup South Africa v Canada, Gp B Australia v Namibia, Gp A

27	Football	UEFA Cup 4th rd 2nd leg Besiktas v Slavia Prague Boavista v Hertha Berlin AEK Athens v Malaga Lazio v Wisla Krakow Panathinaikos v Anderlecht Stuttgart v Celtic Denizlispor v Porto Liverpool v Auxerre
28	Athletics	LBBW - Indoor Meeting Karlsruhe, Germany
28	Cricket	World Cup Zimbabwe v Netherlands, Gp A Sri Lanka v West Indies, Gp B
28-Mar 2	Ice Skating	Grand Prix Final St Petersburg, Russia
28	Netball	England v New Zealand London Arena

March

1-2	Athletics	Norwich Union Trials NIA, Birmingham
1-2	Bobsleigh	World Championship, women Winterberg, Germany
1	Boxing	John Ruiz v Roy Jones WBA heavyweight title Las Vegas
1	Cricket	World Cup Kenya v Bangladesh, Gp B Pakistan v India, Gp A
1-2	Rugby League	Challenge Cup 5th rd
1	Rugby Union	Powergen Cup semi-finals
1-2	Skiing	Freestyle World Cup Voss, Norway
1-2	Table Tennis	English National Chps
2	Football	Worthington Cup final Millennium Stadium
2	Athletics	Athina 2003 - Indoor Meeting Athens
2-Apr 13	Athletics	Flora 1000 Mile Challenge London
2	Cricket	World Cup Australia v England, Group A,
2	Cycling	Road World Cup, women Australia
2	Motor Cycling	World Superbikes Valencia, Spain
3	Cricket	World Cup N Zealand v Canada, Gp B S Africa v Sri Lanka, Gp B Namibia v Holland, Gp A
3-9	Golf	Ford Championship Miami, Florida
3-9	Tennis	ATP Event Scottsdale
3-9	Tennis	ATP Event Delray Beach, Florida
3-16	Tennis	WTA, Pacific Life Open Indian Wells, California
4	Cricket	World Cup West Indies v Kenya, Gp B Zimbabwe v Pakistan, Gp A

4-9	Archery	World Indoor Championships Nimes, France
6-9	Golf	Dubai Desert Classic United Arab Emirates
6-9	M Pentathlon	World Cup Hermosillio Sonora, Mexico
7	Cricket	World Cup, Super Six 1st Pool A v 1st Pool B 2nd Pool A v 2nd Pool B
7-9	Diving	Grand Prix 4 Electrostal, Russia
8-9	Football	FA Cup quarter-finals
8	Athletics	UK World X Country Trials 2 Brighton
8	Cricket	World Cup, Super Six 3rd Pool A v 3rd Pool B
8	Rugby Union	Six Nations Scotland v Wales Ireland v France
9	Motor Racing	F1 - Australian GP Melbourne
9	Rugby Union	Six Nations England v Italy
10	Cricket	World Cup, Super Six 2nd Pool A v 1st Pool B
10-16	Golf	The Honda Classic Palm Beach, Florida
10-16	Tennis	Masters Series Event Indian Wells, USA
11	Football	UEFA Champions League Group A Internazionale v Newcastle Barcelona v B Leverkusen Group B Arsenal v Roma Ajax v Valencia
11	Cricket	World Cup, Super Six 1st Pool A v 3rd Pool B
11	Horse Racing	Smurfit Champion Hurdle Cheltenham
12	Football	UEFA Champions League Group C B Dortmund v Lokomotiv Real Madrid v AC Milan Group D Juventus v D La Coruna Manchester United v Basel
12	Cricket	World Cup, Super Six 3rd Pool A v 2nd Pool B
12	Horse Racing	Champion Chase Cheltenham
13	Football	UEFA Cup q-f 1st legs
13-16	Golf	Qatar Masters Doha GC LPGA Welch's/Fry's Chp Tucson, Arizona
13	Horse Racing	Tote Cheltenham Gold Cup
14	Cricket	World Cup, Super Six 2nd Pool A v 3rd Pool B
14	Motor Cycling	GP of Nice - Indoor Trials
14-16	Athletics	World Indoor Championships NIA, Birmingham
14-16	Speed Skating	World Single Distance Chps Long Track Berlin
15	Basketball	BBL Trophy Final Sheffield
15	Cricket	World Cup, Super Six 3rd Pool A v 1st Pool B 1st Pool A v 2nd Pool B
15-16	Rugby League	Challenge Cup Quarter-Finals
15-16	Speed Skating	World Short Track Team Chps Sofia, Bulgaria
16	Football	Scottish League Cup final
17-23	Golf	Bay Hill Invitational Orlando, Florida
17-30	Tennis	Masters Series Event Miami
17-30	Tennis	WTA NASDAQ-100 Open Miami, Florida
18	Football	UEFA Champions League Group C L Moscow v Real Madrid AC Milan v B Dortmund Group D Basel v Juventus D La Coruna v Man Utd
18-23	Badminton	Sudirman Cup Eindhoven, Netherlands
18	Cricket	World Cup Semi-final St. George's Pk Port Elizabeth
19	Football	UEFA Champions League Group A Newcastle United v Barcelona B Leverkusen v Internazionale Group B Roma v Ajax Valencia v Arsenal
20	Football	UEFA Cup q-f, 2nd legs
20	Cricket	World Cup Semi-final Kingsmead, Durban
20-23	Golf	LPGA PING Banner Health Moon Valley CC, Phoenix, Az Madeira Island Open Santo da Serra, Madeira
20	Horse Racing	Flat Racing season starts
21-23	Cycling	Track World Cup Aguascalientes, Mexico
21-23	Speed Skating	World Short Track Chps Warsaw, Poland
22	Cycling	Primavera Rosa Women's World Cup
22	Cycling	Milan-San Remo Men's World Cup
22	Horse Racing	Lincoln Handicap Doncaster
22	Rugby Union	Six Nations England v Scotland Wales v Ireland
22-23	Football	Scottish Cup 5th rd
23	Cricket	World Cup Final The Wanderers, Jo'burg
23	Motor Racing	F1 Grand Prix Sepang, Malaysia
23	Rugby Union	Six Nations Italy v France
24-30	Golf	The Players Championship Ponte Vedra, Florida
24-30	Ice Skating	World Figure Skating Chps Washington DC

25-30	Snooker	Irish Masters Dublin
27-30	Golf	LPGA Nabisco Championship Mission Hills CC Rancho Mirage, California
27-30	Squash	Texas Open Dallas
29	Football	Euro 2004 Qualifiers Group 1 Cyprus v Israel France v Malta Group 2 Bosnia v Luxembourg Romania v Denmark Group 3 Belarus v Moldova Netherlands v Czech Rep Poland v Hungary Group 5 Germany v Lithuania Scotland v Iceland Group 6 Armenia v Northern Ireland Ukraine v Spain Group 7 Liechtenstein v England FYR Macedonia v Slovakia Group 8 Croatia v Belgium Group 9 Italy v Finland Wales v Azerbaijan Group 10 Albania v Russia Georgia v Rep of Ireland
29	Gymnastics	Great Britain v Spain Artistic Aldershot
29	Rowing	Head of the River River Thames
29	Rugby Union	Six Nations France v Wales Scotland v Italy
29-30	Athletics	World Cross-country Chps Lausanne, Switzerland
29-Apr 6	Table Tennis	European Championships Courmayeur, Italy
30	Cycling	Castilla y Leon Women's World Cup
30	Motor Cycling	World Superbikes Phillip Island, Australia
30	Motor Cycling	Motocross Grand Prix Bellpuig, Spain
30	Rugby Union	Six Nations Ireland v England
31-Apr 6	Golf	BellSouth Classic Duluth, Georgia, USA
31	Tennis	Davis Cup round
31-Apr 6	Tennis	WTA Event Sarasota, Florida WTA Event Casablanca, Morocco

April

1-7	Ice Hockey	2003 IIHF World Women's Championship Beijing, China
2	Football	Euro 2004 Qualifiers Group 1 Israel v France Slovenia v Cyprus Group 2 Denmark v Bosnia Luxembourg v Norway Group 3 Czech Rep v Austria Moldova v Netherlands Group 4 Hungary v Sweden Poland v San Marino Group 5 Lithuania v Scotland Group 6 Northern Ireland v Greece Spain v Armenia Group 7 England v Turkey Slovakia v Liechtenstein Group 8 Croatia v Andorra Estonia v Bulgaria Group 9 Serbia-Montenegro v Wales Group 10 Albania v Rep of Ireland Georgia v Switzerland
3-6	Ice Skating	World Synchro Skating Chps Ottawa, Canada
3-6	Squash	Irish Open Dublin
4	Horse Racing	Martell Melling Chase Aintree
4	Motor Racing	F1 Brazilian GP Interlagos
4-6	Golf	LPGA Office Depot Chp Tarzana, California
4-6	Gymnastics	European Rhythmic Chps Riesa, Germany
5	Horse Racing	Martell Grand National Aintree
5	Motor Cycling	GP of Bangor - Trials Northern Ireland
5	Rugby Union	Powergen Cup Final Twickenham
5-13	Curling	World Championships Winnipeg, Canada
5-13	Snooker	Scottish Event Edinburgh
6	Cycling	Tour of Flandres Men's World Cup Belgium
6	Football	LDV Vans Trophy final Millennium Stadium
6	Hockey	EHA Women's Cup final Milton Keynes
6	Motor Cycling	Grand Prix Suzuka, Japan

6	**Rowing**	The Boat Race
		Putney-Mortlake
7-13	**Tennis**	ATP Event
		Casablanca, Morocco
7-13	**Tennis**	ATP & WTA Event
		Estoril, Portugal
7-13	**Tennis**	WTA Family Circle Cup
		Charleston, South Carolina
8-9	**Football**	UEFA Champions League
		quarter-final first leg
9	**Ice Hockey**	Stanley Cup play-offs begin
9-13	**Motor Rallying**	New Zealand Rally
12-13	**Squash**	English Open
		London
10	**Football**	UEFA Cup semi-final first leg
10-13	**Golf**	US Masters
		Augusta, Georgia
11-13	**Cycling**	Track World Cup
		Cape Town, South Africa
11-13	**Rugby Union**	Heineken Cup quarter-finals
12	**Horse Racing**	Scottish Champion Hurdle
		Ayr
12-13	**Judo**	British Open
		Crystal Palace
12-13	**Rugby League**	Challenge Cup Semi-Finals
12-13	**Rugby Union**	Parker Pen Challenge Cup
		semi-finals first leg
12-20	**Weightlifting**	European Championships
		Loutraki, Greece
13	**Athletics**	Flora London Marathon
		Blackheath-The Mall
13	**Athletics**	Rotterdam Marathon
13	**Cycling**	Paris-Roubaix
		Men's World Cup
13	**Hockey**	EHA Men's Cup final
		Milton Keynes
13-14	**Football**	FA Cup semi-finals
13-20	**Ice Hockey**	World Championships Div I
		Zagreb, Croatia
13	**Triathlon**	ITU World Cup
		Ishigaki, Japan
14-20	**Golf**	US Tour, The Heritage
		Hilton Head Island, SC
14-20	**Tennis**	Masters Series Event
		Monte Carlo
14-20	**Tennis**	WTA Bausch & Lomb Chps
		Amelia Island, Florida
		WTA Budapest Grand Prix
		Budapest
17-19	**Golf**	LPGA Takefuji Classic
		Las Vegas, Nevada
17-19	**Golf**	Algarve Open de Portugal
		Vale do Lobo, Portugal
18-20	**Canoeing**	Flatwater World Cup
		Curitiba, Brazil
18-21	**Cricket**	County Championship begins
19	**Football**	Scottish Cup semi-finals
19-May 5	**Snooker**	World Championship
		The Crucible, Sheffield
20	**Athletics**	Boston Marathon
20	**Cycling**	Amstel Gold Race
		Men & Women's World Cup
		Netherlands
20	**Motor Racing**	F1 San Marino GP
		Imola

21-27	**Golf**	Shell Houston Open
		Redstone GC, Houston
21-27	**Tennis**	ATP Event
		Barcelona
		ATP Event
		Houston
21-27	**Tennis**	Fed Cup round
22-23	**Football**	UEFA Champions League
		quarter-final second leg
22-27	**Squash**	PSA Masters, men
		Doha, Qatar
23	**Cycling**	La Flèche Wallonne
		Women's World Cup
		Belgium
23-27	**Bowls**	WIBC Championships
		Belfast
23-27	**Squash**	WISPA Grand Prix Finals
		Doha, Qatar
24	**Football**	UEFA Cup semi-final 2nd leg
24-27	**Golf**	Canarias Open de España
		Tenerife, Spain
24-27	**Mod Pen**	World Cup, Women
		Szekesfehervar, Hungary
		World Cup, Men
		Berlin
25-27	**Golf**	LPGA Chick-fil-A Charity Chp
		Stockbridge, Georgia
26-27	**Basketball**	NBL Finals
26	**Horse Racing**	attheraces Gold Cup
		Sandown Park
26	**Rugby League**	Challenge Cup Final
		Millennium Stadium
26	**Triathlon**	World Cup
		St. Anthony's, USA
26-27	**Rugby Union**	PP Challenge Cup s-f 2nd leg
26-27	**Rugby Union**	Heineken Cup semi-finals
26-May 11	**Ice Hockey**	World Championship
		Finland
27	**Cricket**	National Cricket League begins
27	**Cycling**	Liège-Bastogne-Liège
		Men's World Cup
27	**Motor Cycling**	World Superbikes
		Sugo, Japan
27	**Motor Cycling**	Grand Prix
		Welkom, South Africa
28-May 4	**Golf**	HP Classic of New Orleans
		New Orleans, Louisiana
28-May 4	**Tennis**	ATP Event
		Mallorca
		ATP Event
		Munich
28-May 4	**Tennis**	WTA J&S Cup
		Warsaw
		WTA Croatian Bol Open
		Bol
30	**Football**	Euro 2004 Qualifiers
		Group 1
		Malta v Slovenia
		Group 4
		Latvia v San Marino
		Group 8
		Andorra v Estonia
30	**Football**	Scotland v Austria
		Hampden Park, Glasgow

May

1-4	**Equestrianism**	Badminton Horse Trials
1-4	**Golf**	LPGA Michelob Light Open Williamsburg, Virginia
1-4	**Golf**	Italian Open
1-4	**Squash**	European Team Chps Nottingham
1-4	**Wrestling**	European Freestyle Chps Riga, Latvia
2-4	**Canoeing**	Flatwater World Cup Hazewinkel, Belgium
2-4	**Diving**	Grand Prix 6 Victoria, Canada
3	**Football**	End of Nationwide season
3	**Horse Racing**	2000 Guineas Newmarket
3-4	**Gymnastics**	European Team Chps Artistic & Rhythmic Moscow
3-4	**Gymnastics**	British Championships Sports Acrobatics Fenton Manor, Stoke on Trent
3-4	**Netball**	Super Cup - Weekend 1
4	**Basketball**	BBL Championship Final NIA, Birmingham
4	**Horse Racing**	1000 Guineas Newmarket
4	**Motor Racing**	F1 Catalunyan GP Barcelona
5	**Football**	FA Women's Cup final
5	**Athletics**	Grand Prix I Belem, Brazil
5-11	**Golf**	Wachovia Championship Charlotte, North Carolina
5-11	**Tennis**	Masters Series Event Rome
5-11	**Tennis**	WTA German Open Berlin
5-15	**Sailing**	Mistral European Chp Mondello, Sicily
6-7	**Football**	UEFA Champions League semi-final 1st legs
7-11	**Rallying**	Rally Argentina
8-11	**Diving**	Grand Prix 7 The Woodlands, Texas
8-11	**Equestrianism**	Nations Cup Super League showjumping La Baule, France
8-11	**Golf**	LPGA Asahi Ryokuken Chp North Augusta
8-11	**Golf**	International Open The Belfry, Sutton Coldfield
8-11	**Mod Pen**	World Cup, Men Budapest
9-11	**Karate**	EKF European Chps Bremen, Germany
10	**Athletics**	Grand Prix I Osaka, Japan
10	**Football**	FA Vase final
10	**Football**	End of Premiership season
10	**Rugby Union**	Zurich Premiership final day
10-11	**Canoeing**	Slalom World Cup Penrith, Australia
10-11	**Netball**	Super Cup - Weekend 2
10-June 1	**Cycling**	Giro d'Italia
11	**Football**	Nationwide League play-offs semi-finals first leg
11	**Motor Cycling**	Grand Prix Jerez de la Frontera, Spain
12-18	**Badminton**	World Championships NIA, Birmingham
12-18	**Golf**	Byron Nelson Championship Las Colinas, Irving, Texas
12-18	**Tennis**	Masters Series Event Hamburg, Germany
12-18	**Tennis**	WTA Italia Masters Rome
13-14	**Football**	UEFA Champions League semi-final second leg
14	**Football**	Nationwide League play-offs semi-finals 2nd leg
15	**Athletics**	Super Grand Prix Doha, Qatar
15-18	**Golf**	Deutsche Bank Open Gut Kaden, Hamburg
15-18	**Judo**	European Championships Athens, Greece
15-18	**Squash**	Seattle Open, women
16-18	**Cycling**	Track World Cup Sydney
16-18	**Diving**	Grand Prix 8 Mexico City
17	**Athletics**	Grand Prix I Portland, Oregon
17	**Football**	FA Cup final Millennium Stadium
17	**Horse Racing**	Juddmonte Lockinge Stakes Newbury
17	**Motor Cycling**	GP of Kiefersfelden - Trials Germany
17	**Rugby Union**	Zurich Championship q-f
17	**Speedway**	Grand Prix, round 1 Chorzow, Poland
17-18	**Canoeing**	Slalom World Cup Guang Zhou, China
17-18	**Netball**	Super Cup - Weekend 3
18	**Football**	FA Trophy final
18	**Motor Cycling**	World Superbikes 4 Monza, Italy
18	**Motor Cycling**	Motocross Grand Prix St Jean d'Angely, France
18	**Motor Racing**	F1 Austrian GP A1-Ring
18	**Rugby Union**	Zurich Championship q-fs
19-25	**Golf**	Bank of America Colonial Fort Worth, Texas
19-25	**Table Tennis**	World Championships Paris
19-25	**Tennis**	ATP Event St Pölten, Austria
19-25	**Tennis**	WTA Event Strasbourg, France WTA Open de España Madrid
21	**Football**	UEFA Cup Final Olimpico Stadium, Seville
22	**Football**	South-Africa v England, Durban

22-25	Equestrianism	Nations Cup Super League showjumping Rome
22-25	Golf	Volvo PGA Championship Wentworth Club, Surrey
22-25	Golf	LPGA Corning Classic Corning, New York
22-26	Cricket	England v Zimbabwe, 1st Test Lord's
23	Rugby Union	Parker Pen Challenge Cup Final
23-25	Canoeing	Flatwater World Cup Szeged, Hungary
23-25	Wrestling	Greco-Roman European Chps Belgrade, Yugoslavia
24	Athletics	Super Grand Prix Eugene, Oregon
24	Football	Third Division Play-off Final Millennium Stadium
24	Rowing	Copenhagen Regatta
24	Rugby Union	Heineken Cup Final Lansdowne Road, Dublin
24-25	Cycling	Mountain Bike Cross-Country World Cup St. Wendel, Germany
24-25	Netball	Super Cup - Weekend 4
25	Football	Second Division Play-off Final Millennium Stadium
25	Motor Cycling	Grand Prix Le Mans, France
26	Football	First Division Play-off Final Millennium Stadium
26-June 1	Golf	Memorial Tournament Dublin, Ohio, USA
26-June 8	Tennis	French Open Roland Garros, Paris
28	Football	Champions League Final Old Trafford
29-June 1	Equestrianism	Nations Cup Super League Showjumping St Gallen, Switzerland
29-June 1	Golf	The Wales Open Newport
29-June 1	Mod Pen	World Cup, Women Warsaw
30-June 1	Golf	LPGA Kellogg-Keebler Stonebridge CC, Aurora, Ill
30-June 1	Rowing	World Cup Milan
30-June 2	Canoeing	Wildwater European Chps Karlovy Vary, Czech Republic
30-June 2	Squash	Heliopolis Open, women Cairo, Egypt
31	Football	Scottish Cup final Hampden Park, Glasgow
31	Cycling	World Cup of Montreal Women
31	Cycling	Mountain Bike World Cup X-C, DHL Fort William
31	Netball	Super Cup Finals
31	Rugby Union	Zurich Championship s-f
31	Speedway	Grand Prix, round 2 Stockholm

June

1	Athletics	Grand Prix I Hengelo, Netherlands
1	Motor Cycling	Motocross Grand Prix Montevarchi, Italy
1	Motor Cycling	World Superbikes Oschersleben, Germany
1	Motor Racing	F1 Monaco GP
1	Rugby Union	Zurich Championship s-f
1-12	Netball	England Tour of New Zealand
2-8	Golf	Kemper Open Potomac, Maryland, USA
3	Athletics	Grand Prix II
4-8	Rallying	Acropolis Rally Greece
4-8	Squash	Hurghada International Egypt
5-8	Golf	British Masters Forest of Arden, Warwickshire
5-8	Golf	McDonald's LPGA Wilmington, Delaware
5-9	Cricket	England v Zimbabwe, 2nd Test Chester-le-Street
5-12	Sailing	Finn European Championship Langedrag, Sweden
6	Horse Racing	Vodafone Coronation Cup Epsom
6	Horse Racing	Vodafone Oaks Epsom
6-14	Sailing	Tornado European Chp Calgiari, Sardinia
7	Athletics	Grand Prix I Seville, Spain
7	Football	Euro 2004 Qualifier Group 1 Israel v Slovenia Malta v Cyprus Group 2 Denmark v Norway Romania v Bosnia Group 3 Belarus v Netherlands Moldova v Austria Group 4 Hungary v Latvia San Marino v Sweden Group 5 Iceland v Faroe Islands Scotland v Germany Group 6 Spain v Greece Ukraine v Armenia Group 7 FYRMacedoniavLiechtenstein Slovakia v Turkey Group 8 Bulgaria v Belgium Estonia v Andorra Group 9 Finland v Serbia-Montenegro Group 10 Rep of Ireland v Albania Switzerland v Russia

7	**Horse Racing**	Vodafone Derby Epsom
7	**Rugby Union**	South Africa v Scotland Durban
7	**Rugby Union**	Australia v Ireland Perth, Australia
7	**Rugby Union**	Zurich Championship Final Twickenham
7-8	**Cycling**	Mountain Bike World Cup DHL, Alpe D'Huez, France
8	**Athletics**	Grand Prix I Moscow
8	**Motor Cycling**	Motocross Grand Prix Gorna Rosica, Bulgaria
8	**Motor Cycling**	Grand Prix Mugello, Italy
9-15	**Tennis**	ATP Event Halle, Germany
9-15	**Tennis**	Stella Artois, men Queens Club, London
9-15	**Tennis**	WTA DFS Classic Birmingham WTA Wien Grand Prix Vienna
10	**Athletics**	Grand Prix II Bratislava, Slovak Republic
10-11	**Cricket**	C & G Trophy quarter-finals
11	**Football**	Euro 2004 Qualifiers Group 2 Luxembourg v Denmark Norway v Romania Group 3 Austria v Belarus Czech Rep v Moldova Group 4 San Marino v Hungary Sweden v Poland Group 5 Faroe Islands v Germany Lithuania v Iceland Group 6 Greece v Ukraine N Ireland v Spain Group 7 England v Slovakia Turkey v FYR Macedonia Group 8 Belgium v Andorra Estonia v Croatia Group 9 Finland v Italy Azerbaijan v Serbia-M'negro Group 10 Rep of Ireland v Georgia Switzerland v Albania
12	**Athletics**	Super Grand Prix Ostrava, Czech Republic
12-15	**Golf**	US Open Matteson, Illinois
12-15	**Golf**	St Omer Open St Omer, France
13-15	**Golf**	Giant Eagle LPGA Classic Vienna, Ohio, USA
13-24	**Cricket**	Twenty-20 Cup round-robin

14	**Rugby Union**	South Africa v Scotland Johannesburg
14	**Rugby Union**	New Zealand v England Wellington
14	**Rugby Union**	Australia v Wales Sydney
14	**Speedway**	Grand Prix, round 3 Cardiff
15	**Athletics**	Grand Prix I Lille, France
15	**Motor Cycling**	World Superbikes Silverstone
15	**Motor Cycling**	Grand Prix Catalunya
15	**Motor Racing**	F1 Montreal GP
15	**Triathlon**	ITU World Cup Gamagori, Japan
16-22	**Golf**	Buick Classic Harrison, New York
16-22	**Tennis**	ATP & WTA Event S-Hertogenbosch, Netherl'ds
16-22	**Tennis**	Nottingham Open, men
16-22	**Tennis**	WTA Brittanic Asset Chps Eastbourne
17	**Cricket**	England v Pakistan, ODI NW Challenge Old Trafford
17-22	**Equestrianism**	Nations Cup Super League showjumping Aachen, Germany
17-20	**Horse Racing**	Royal Ascot Meeting
18-22	**Rallying**	Cyprus Rally
19-22	**Golf**	Wegmans Rochester LPGA Pittsford, New York
19-22	**Golf**	The Diageo Championship Gleneagles, Perthshire
19-22	**Triathlon**	European Triathlon Chps Carlsbad, Czech Republic
20-22	**Canoeing**	Flatwater World Cup Duisburg, Germany
20	**Cricket**	England v Pakistan, ODI NW Challenge The Oval
20-22	**Rowing**	World Cup Munich
20-22	**Rowing**	Women's Henley
21	**Cricket**	England v Pakistan, ODI NW Challenge Lord's
21	**Motor Cycling**	GP of St Julia de Loria - Trials Spain
21	**Rugby Union**	South Africa v Argentina Port Elizabeth, South Africa
21	**Rugby Union**	Australia v England Melbourne
21	**Rugby Union**	New Zealand v Wales Hamilton, New Zealand
21-22	**Athletics**	European Cup, Super League Florence, Italy
21-22	**Athletics**	European Cup, 2nd League A Aarhus, Denmark
21-22	**Athletics**	European Cup, 2nd League B Istanbul, Turkey
21-22	**Athletics**	European Cup, 1st League B Valenje, Slovenia

21-22	Athletics	European Cup, 1st League A Lappeenranta, Finland
21-22	Canoeing	Marathon World Cup Bergen, Norway
22	Am Football	NFL Europe World Bowl Dusseldorf, Germany
22	Motor Cycling	World Superbikes Misano, San Marino
22	Triathlon	ITU World Cup Tongyeong, South Korea
23-29	Golf	FedEx St. Jude Classic Memphis, Tennessee, USA
23-July 6	Tennis	The Open Championships Wimbledon
24	Athletics	Grand Prix I Athens
25-29	Mod Pen	World Cup Usti Nad Laben, Czech Rep
26	Cricket	England v Zimbabwe, ODI NW Series Trent Bridge
26-29	Golf	Open de France Le Golf National, Paris
27	Athletics	Golden League Oslo, Norway
27-29	Diving	Grand Prix 9 Rome
27-29	Golf	Shoprite LPGA Classic Galloway, New Jersey
28	Cricket	England v South Africa, ODI NW Series The Oval
28	Greyhound R	Derby Final Wimbledon
28	Motor Cycling	GP of Benasque - Trials
28	Motor Cycling	Grand Prix Assen, Netherlands
28	Rowing	Amsterdam Regatta
28	Rugby Union	New Zealand v France Christchurch
28	Speedway	Grand Prix, round 4 Copenhagen
28	Triathlon	ITU World Cup Beijing
28-29	Cycling	Mountain Bike World Cup Mont-Sainte-Anne, Canada
29	Athletics	Grand Prix II Prague, Czech Rep
29	Cricket	Zimbabwe v S Africa, ODI NW Series Canterbury
29	Motor Racing	F1 German GP Nurburgring
30-July 6	Golf	100th Western Open Lemont, Illinois, USA

July

1	Athletics	Super Grand Prix Lausanne
1	Cricket	England v Zimbabwe, ODI NW Series Headingley
2-6	Rowing	Henley Regatta
3	Cricket	England v South Africa, ODI NW Series Old Trafford
3-6	Golf	Smurfit European Open The K Club, Dublin
3-6	Golf	US Women's Open North Plain, Oregon
4	Athletics	Golden League Paris
4-6	Canoeing	Flatwater World Cup Zagreb, Croatia
4-6	Gymnastics	Women's Artistic British Chps Spectrum Complex, Guildford
5	Cricket	Zimbabwe v South Africa ODI NW Series Cardiff
5	Horse Racing	Coral Eurobet Eclipse Stakes Sandown Park
5-6	Athletics	European Cup Cmbd Events Super League Bressanone, Italy
5-6	Canoeing	Slalom World Cup La Seu d'Urgell, Spain
5-6	Gymnastics	British Trampolining Chps NEC Arena, Birmingham
5-27	Cycling	Tour de France
6	Cricket	England v Zimbabwe, ODI NW Series Bristol
6	Motor Racing	F1 French GP Magny-Cours
6-11	Sailing	Europe Class European Chp Mallorca, Spain
6-16	Sailing	470 European Championship Brest, France
7	Athletics	Grand Prix I Zagreb, Croatia
7-13	Golf	Greater Milwaukee Open Brown Deer GC, Wisconsin
7-13	Tennis	ATP Event Bastad, Switzerland ATP Event Newport, USA ATP Event Gstaad, Switzerland
7-13	Tennis	WTA Internazionali Palermo Palermo, Italy WTA Porto Open Casablanca, Morocco
8	Athletics	Grand Prix II Nice, France
8	Cricket	England v South Africa, ODI NW Series Edgbaston
10-19	Archery	World Championships New York
10	Cricket	Zimbabwe v S Africa, ODI NW Series Rose Bowl

CALENDAR

10-13	Golf	The Barclays Scottish Open Loch Lomond, Glasgow
10	Horse Racing	Darley Cup Stakes Newmarket
11	Athletics	Golden League Rome
11-20	Netball	World Netball Championship Jamaica
12	Cricket	NW Series Final Lord's
12	Motor Cycling	GP of Sestriere - Trials Italy
12	Rugby Union	Tri Nations Series South Africa v Australia Cape Town
12	Speedway	Grand Prix, round 5 Krsko, Slovenia
12-13	Canoeing	Marathon European Chps Gdansk, Poland
12-13	Canoeing	Slalom World Cup Ljubljana/Tacen, Slovenia
12-13	Cycling	Mountain Bike World Cup Grouse Mountain, Canada
12-13	Fencing	British Championships Cosford
12-13	Rowing	World Cup Lucerne, Switzerland
13	Athletics	Super Grand Prix Gateshead
13	Motor Cycling	Grand Prix Donington Park
13	Motor Cycling	World Superbikes Laguna Seca, USA
13	Triathlon	World Cup Edmonton, Canada
13-20	Sailing	49er European Championship Laredo, Spain
13-27	Swimming	World Championships Barcelona
14-20	Golf	B.C. Open Endicott, New York
14-20	Mod Pen	World Championships Pesaro, Italy
14-20	Tennis	ATP Event Amsterdam ATP Event Stuttgart
14-20	Tennis	Federation Cup round
16-28	Shooting	European Championships Plzen, Czech Republic
17-20	Golf	Open Championship Royal St George's GC Sandwich, Kent
17-20	Golf	LPGA Big Apple Classic New Rochelle, New York
18-20	Rowing	National Championships Strathclyde
19	Athletics	Super Grand Prix Madrid
19	Cricket	Twenty-20 Cup s-fs & final Lord's
19	Motor Cycling	GP of Breal - Trials France
20	Motor Cycling	Motocross Grand Prix Park Extreme, Russia

20	Motor Racing	F1 British GP Silverstone
19	Rugby Union	Tri Nations Series South Africa v New Zealand Pretoria
20	Triathlon	ITU World Cup Corner Brook, Canada
21-27	Golf	Greater Hartford Open Cromwell, Connecticut
21-27	Tennis	ATP Event Umag, Croatia ATP Event Indianapolis, USA ATP Event Kitzbühel, Austria
21-27	Tennis	WTA Bank of the West Stanford, California
23-27	Equestrianism	Nations Cup Super League International Horse Show Hickstead
23-26	Golf	LPGA Evian Masters Evian-les-Bains
23-27	Rallying	ADAC Rallye Deutschland Germany
24-28	Cricket	England v South Africa 1st Test, Edgbaston
24-27	Golf	Nissan Irish Open Portmarnock GC, Dublin
25-27	Cycling	BMX World Championships Perth, Australia
25-Aug 2	Sailing	Laser European Chp Split, Croatia
26	Horse Racing	K George VI and QE Stakes Ascot
26	Rugby Union	Tri Nations Series Australia v N Zealand Sydney
27-Aug 2	Darts	Stan James World Matchplay Winter Gardens, Blackpool
27	Motor Cycling	Grand Prix Sachsenring, Germany
27	Motor Cycling	World Superbikes Brands Hatch
29-Aug 2	Horse Racing	Goodwood Meeting
28-Aug 3	Golf	Buick Open Grand Blanc, Michigan
28-Aug 3	Tennis	ATP Event Los Angeles ATP Event Washington
28-Aug 3	Tennis	ATP & WTA Event Sopot, Thailand
28-Aug 3	Tennis	WTA Acura Classic San Diego, California
29-Aug 5	Shooting	European Shotgun Chps Brno, Czech Republic
30-Aug 3	Cycling	Track World Championships Shenzhen, China
30	Horse Racing	Sussex Stakes Goodwood
31-Aug 3	Golf	Scandinavian Masters Malmo, Sweden
31-Aug 3	Golf	Women's British Open Royal Lytham and St. Annes
31-Aug 4	Cricket	England v S Africa, 2nd Test Lord's

August

1-3	Canoeing	Slalom World Cup Final Bratislava/Cunovo, Slovakia
2	Rugby Union	Tri Nations Series Australia v S Africa Brisbane
2-9	Sailing	Cowes Week
3	Cycling	HEW Cyclassics Cup Men's World Cup
3	Motor Racing	F1 German GP Hockenheim, Germany
3	Triathlon	ITU World Cup Tiszaujvaros, Hungary
3-8	Speedway	World Cup Vojens, Denmark
3-9	Orienteering	World Orienteering Chps Rapperswil, Jona, Switzerland
4-10	Golf	The International Castle Rock, Colorado
4-10	Tennis	Masters Series Montreal
4-10	Tennis	WTA JP Morgan Chase Open Los Angeles WTA Nordic Light Open Helsinki
5	Athletics	Super Grand Prix Stockholm
6-16	Bowls	EWBA Championships Leamington Spa
6-10	Equestrianism	Nations Cup Super League Dublin
6-10	Rallying	Neste Rally Finland
7	Cricket	C & G Trophy semi-final 1
7-10	Golf	Nordic Open Copenhagen
8	Athletics	Super Grand Prix Crystal Palace
8-10	Golf	LPGA Wendy's Chp Dublin, Ohio
9	Cricket	C & G Trophy semi-final 2
9	Cycling	San Sebastian Classic Men's World Cup
9	Rugby Union	Tri Nations Series N Zealand v S Africa Dunedin
10	Athletics	Golden League Berlin
10	Football	Charity Shield Millennium Stadium
10	Triathlon	ITU World Cup New York
11-17	Tennis	Masters Series Event Cincinnatti
11-17	Tennis	WTA Rogers AT&T Cup Toronto
13-17	Equestrianism	European Dressage Chps Hickstead
14-18	Cricket	England v S Africa, 3rd Test Trent Bridge
14-17	Equestrianism	Hickstead Derby Meeting
14-17	Golf	LPGA Jamie Farr Kroger Sylvania, Ohio
14-17	Golf	Russian Open Moscow
14-17	Golf	US PGA Championship Oak Hill CC, Rochester, NY
15	Athletics	Golden League Zurich
16	Football	Start of Premiership season
16-30	Bowls	EBA Championships Worthing
16-17	Canoeing	Marathon World Cup Tyn nad Vitavou, Czech Rep
16-24	Gymnastics	World Artistic Championships Anaheim, USA
16-24	Hockey	Champions Trophy, men Amstelveen, Netherlands
16	Rugby Union	Tri Nations Series New Zealand v Australia Auckland
17	Cycling	Road World Cup Züri Metzgete, Switzerland
17	Motor Cycling	Grand Prix Brno, Czech Republic
17	Triathlon	ITU World Cup Manchester
18	Athletics	Grand Prix I Helsinki
18-24	Golf	Reno-Tahoe Open Reno, Nevada
18-24	Tennis	ATP Event Long Island
18-24	Tennis	WTA Pilot Pen New Haven, Connecticut
19-21	Horse Racing	York Meeting
20	Football	Euro 2004 Qualifier Grp 5 Faroe Islands v Iceland
20	Football	Norway v Scotland Ullevaal stadium, Oslo
20-24	Equestrianism	European Showjumping Chps Donaueschingen, Germany
21-24	Golf	WGC - NEC Invitational Firestone CC, Akron, Ohio
21-25	Cricket	England v S Africa, 4th Test Headingley
23	Cycling	GP de Plouay Women's World Cup
23	Rugby Union	Wales v England Millennium Stadium
23	Speedway	Grand Prix, round 6 Gothenburg, Sweden
23-24	Cycling	Mountain Bike European Chps Graz, Austria
23-31	Athletics	World Championships Paris
24	Motor Racing	F1 Hungarian GP Hungaroring, Budapest
24	Rowing	World Championships Milan
25-31	Mod Pen	European Championships Madrid
25-Sep 1	Golf	Deutsche Bank U.S. Chp Norton, Massachusetts
25-Sep 7	Tennis	US Open Flushing Meadow, New York
28-31	Equestrianism	Nations Cup Super League Rotterdam
28-31	Golf	BMW Open Munich
30	Cricket	C& G Trophy final Lord's
30	Cycling	Rund um die Nürnberger Women's Road World Cup Germany
30	Rugby Union	France v England Marseille
30-Sep 1	Sailing	Star European Championship Cascais, Portugal
30	Triathlon	ITU World Cup Hamburg

September

1-7	Golf	Bell Canadian Open Ancaster, Ontario
3-7	Cycling	Mountain Bike World Chps Lugano, Switzerland
3-7	Rallying	Telstra Rally Australia
4-7	Canoeing	World Slalom Championships Augsburg, Germany
4-7	Equestrianism	Burghley Horse Trials
4-7	Golf	Omega European Masters Crans-sur-Sierre, Switzerland
4-8	Cricket	England v S Africa, 5th Test The Oval
5	Athletics	Golden League Brussels
5-14	Basketball	Men's European Chp Finals Sweden
6	Football	Euro 2004 Qualifiers Group 1 France v Cyprus Slovenia v Israel Group 2 Bosnia v Norway Romania v Luxembourg Group 3 Belarus v Czech Rep Netherlands v Austria Group 4 Latvia v Poland Sweden v San Marino Group 5 Iceland v Germany Scotland v Faroe Islands Group 6 Armenia v Greece Ukraine v Northern Ireland Group 7 Liechtenstein v Turkey FYR Macedonia v England Group 8 Andorra v Croatia Bulgaria v Estonia Group 9 Azerbaijan v Finland Italy v Wales Group 10 Georgia v Albania Rep of Ireland v Russia
6	Rugby Union	England v France Twickenham
6	Speedway	Grand Prix, round 7 Prague, Czech Republic
6	Triathlon	ITU World Cup Lausanne
6-28	Cycling	Vuelta a España
7	Cycling	Rotterdam Tour Women's World Cup
7	Motor Cycling	Grand Prix Estoril, Portugal
7	Motor Cycling	World Superbikes Assen, Netherlands
8-12	Equestrianism	Blenheim Horse Trials

8-14	Golf	John Deere Classic Deere Run Silvis, Illinois
8-14	Tennis	ATP Event Tashkent, Uzbekistan
8-14	Tennis	ATP Event Salvador ATP Event Bucharest, Romania
8-14	Tennis	WTA Wismilak International Bali, Indonesia
10	Football	Euro 2004 Qualifers Group 1 Israel v Malta Slovenia v France Group 2 Denmark v Romania Luxembourg v Bosnia Group 3 Czech Rep v Netherlands Moldova v Belarus Group 4 Latvia v Hungary Poland v Sweden Group 5 Germany v Scotland Group 6 Israel v Malta Northern Ireland v Armenia Spain v Ukraine Group 7 England v Liechtenstein Slovakia v FYR Macedonia Group 8 Andorra v Bulgaria Belgium v Croatia Group 9 Wales v Finland Serbia-Montenegro v Italy Group 10 Albania v Georgia Russia v Switzerland
10-14	Canoeing	World Flatwater Chps Gainesville, USA
10-17	Shooting	Shotgun World Chps Nicosia, Cyprus
11-14	Golf	Trophée Lancôme Saint-Nom-la-Bretèche, Paris
11-14	Judo	World Championships Osaka, Japan
11-25	Sailing	World Sailing Championships Cadiz, Spain
12-13	Athletics	World Athletics Final Monaco
12	Triathlon	ITU World Cup Nice
12-14	Golf	The Solheim Cup Barseback, Malmo, Sweden
13	Horse Racing	St Leger Stakes Doncaster
13-14	Cycling	Mountain Bike World Cup Kaprun, Austria
14	Hurling	All Ireland SHC Final Croke Park

14	Motor Racing	F1 Italian GP
		Monza, Italy
15	Tennis	Davis Cup 3rd round
15-21	Golf	Lumber Classic of Penn
		Farmington, PA
15-21	Tennis	WTA Polo Open
		Shanghai
15-21	Water Skiing	Tournament World Chps
		Clermont, Florida
17-20	Cricket	County Championship ends
17-21	Equestrianism	Horse of the Year Show
		NEC, Birmingham
18-21	Equestrianism	European Eventing Chps
		Punchestown
18-21	Golf	Linde German Masters
		Gut Lärchenhof, Cologne
19-28	Basketball	European Chp, Women
		Greece
19-21	Equestrianism	Nations Cup S League Final
		Barcelona
20	Motor Cycling	Grand Prix
		Jacarepagua, Rio
20	Speedway	Grand Prix, round 8
		Poland
20	Triathlon	ITU World Cup
		Madrid
21	Athletics	BUPA Great North Run
		Newcastle to South Shields
22-28	Golf	Valero Texas Open
		LaCantera GC, San Antonio
22-28	Tennis	ATP Event
		Hong Kong
		ATP Event
		Palermo, Italy
		ATP Event
		Shanghai
22-28	Tennis	WTA Sparkassen Cup GP
		Leipzig, Germany
24-28	Taekwondo	World Taekwondo Chps
		Garmisch, Germany
25-28	Golf	Links Championship
		St Andrews, etc
26-28	Golf	LPGA Safeway Classic
		Portland, Oregon
26-28	Horse Racing	Ascot Festival
27	Aussie Rules	Grand Final
		Melbourne
27	Motor Cycling	Trial des Nations
27	Motor Cycling	World Superbikes
		Imola, Italy
27-28	Canoeing	Marathon World Chps
		Valladolid, Spain
28	Athletics	Berlin Marathon
28	Gaelic Football	All Ireland SFC Final
		Croke Park
28	Motor Racing	F1 American GP
		Indianapolis
29-Oct 5	Tennis	ATP & WTA Event
		Tokyo
29-Oct 5	Tennis	ATP Event
		Toulouse, France
29-Oct 5	Tennis	ATP & WTA Event
		Moscow

October

1-5	Rallying	Rallye Sanremo
2-5	Golf	WGC-American Express Chp
		Capitol City Club, Atlanta
2-5	Wrestling	Greco-Roman World Chps
		Créteil, France
4	Athletics	World Half Marathon Chps
		Vilamoura, Portugal
4	Speedway	Grand Prix, round 9
		Hamar, Norway
4-12	Fencing	World Championships
		Havana, Cuba
5	Cycling	Paris-Tours
		Men's World Cup
5	Motor Cycling	Grand Prix
		Twin Ring Motegi, Japan
6-12	Golf	Las Vegas Invitational
		Nevada
6-12	Tennis	ATP Event
		Lyon, France
		ATP Event
		Vienna
6-12	Tennis	WTA Porsche Tennis GP
		Filderstadt, Germany
8-12	Cycling	Road World Championships
		Hamilton, Canada
9-12	Golf	Dutch Open
		Hilversum
10-12	Gymnastics	Artistic Grand Prix
		Glasgow
10-Nov 22	Rugby Union	World Cup
		Australia
11	Football	Euro 2004 Qaulifiers
		Group 1
		Cyprus v Slovenia
		France v Israel
		Group 2
		Bosnia v Denmark
		Norway v Luxembourg
		Group 3
		Austria v Czech Rep
		Netherlands v Moldova
		Group 4
		Hungary v Poland
		Sweden v Latvia
		Group 5
		Germany v Iceland
		Scotland v Lithuania
		Group 6
		Armenia v Spain
		Greece v Northern Ireland
		Group 7
		Turkey v England
		Group 8
		Belgium v Estonia
		Croatia v Bulgaria
		Group 9
		Italy v Azerbaijan
		Wales v Serbia-Montenegro
		Group 10
		Russia v Georgia
		Switzerland v Rep of Ireland

Rugby World Cup

Pool A

October 10	**Australia v Argentina**	Telstra Stadium, Sydney (20:00)
October 11	**Ireland v Romania**	Central Coast Stadium, Gosford (17:00)
October 14	**Argentina v Namibia**	Central Coast Stadium, Gosford (19:30)
October 18	**Australia v Romania**	Suncorp Stadium, Brisbane (16:00)
October 19	**Ireland v Namibia**	Aussie Stadium, Sydney (20:00)
October 22	**Argentina v Romania**	Aussie Stadium, Sydney (20:30)
October 25	**Australia v Namibia**	Adelaide Oval, Adelaide (15:30)
October 26	**Argentina v Ireland**	Adelaide Oval, Adelaide (18:00)
October 30	**Namibia v Romania**	York Park, Launceston (20:00)
November 1	**Australia v Ireland**	Telstra Dome, Melbourne (20:35)

Pool B

October 11	**France v Fiji**	Suncorp Stadium, Brisbane (19:30)
October 12	**Scotland v Japan**	Dairy Farmers Stadium, Townsville (20:00)
October 15	**Fiji v Spain or USA***	Suncorp Stadium, Brisbane (17:00)
October 18	**France v Japan**	Dairy Farmers Stadium, Townsville (19:00)
October 20	**Scotland v Spain or USA***	Suncorp Stadium, Brisbane (19:30)
October 23	**Fiji v Japan**	Dairy Farmers Stadium, Townsville (20:00)
October 25	**France v Scotland**	Telstra Stadium, Sydney (20:30)
October 27	**Japan v Spain or USA***	North Power Stadium, Gosford (19:30)
October 31	**France v Spain or USA***	WIN stadium, Wollongong (19:30)
November 1	**Scotland v Fiji**	Aussie stadium, Sydney (16:00)

Decided by repechage playoff finals in April

Pool C

October 11	**South Africa v Uruguay**	Subiaco Oval, Perth (20:00)
October 12	**England v Georgia**	Subiaco Oval, Perth (20:00)
October 15	**Samoa v Uruguay**	Subiaco Oval, Perth (20:00)
October 18	**South Africa v England**	Subiaco Oval, Perth (20:00)
October 19	**Georgia v Samoa**	Subiaco Oval, Perth (20:00)
October 24	**South Africa v Georgia**	Aussie Stadium, Sydney (20:00)
October 26	**England v Samoa**	Telstra Dome, Melbourne (20:30)
October 28	**Georgia v Uruguay**	Aussie Stadium, Sydney (19:30)
November 1	**South Africa v Samoa**	Suncorp Stadium, Brisbane (17:30)
November 2	**England v Uruguay**	Suncorp Stadium, Brisbane (17:30)

Pool D

October 11	**New Zealand v Italy**	Telstra Dome, Melbourne (14:30)
October 12	**Wales v Canada**	Telstra Dome, Melbourne (18:00)
October 15	**Italy v Tonga**	Canberra Stadium, Canberra (19:30)
October 17	**New Zealand v Canada**	Telstra Dome, Melbourne (19:30)
October 19	**Wales v Tonga**	Canberra Stadium, Canberra (18:00)
October 21	**Italy v Canada**	Canberra Stadium, Canberra (19:30)
October 24	**New Zealand v Tonga**	Suncorp Stadium, Brisbane (17:30)
October 25	**Italy v Wales**	Canberra Stadium, Canberra (18:30)
October 29	**Canada v Tonga**	WIN stadium, Wollongong (19:30)
November 2	**New Zealand v Wales**	Stadium Australia, Sydney (20:35)

Quarter-finals

November 8	**QF1: Winner D v Runner-Up C**	Telstra Dome, Melbourne (18:30)
	QF2: Winner A v Runner-Up B	Suncorp Stadium, Brisbane (20:00)
November 9	**QF3: Winner B v Runner-Up A**	Telstra Dome, Melbourne (18:30)
	QF4: Winner C v Runner-Up D	Suncorp Stadium, Brisbane (20:00)

Semi-finals

November 15	**Winner QF1 v Winner QF2**	Telstra Stadium, Sydney (20:00)
November 16	**Winner QF3 v Winner QF4**	Telstra Stadium, Sydney (20:00)
November 20	**3rd place play-off**	Telstra Stadium, Sydney (20:00)
November 22	**FINAL**	Telstra Stadium, Sydney (20:00)

12	Athletics	Chicago Marathon
12	Motor Cycling	Grand Prix Sepang, Malaysia
12	Motor Racing	F1 Japanese GP Suzuka, Japan
13-19	Golf	Chrysler Classic Greensboro Forest Oaks CC, N Carolina
13-19	Tennis	Masters Series Event Madrid
13-19	Tennis	WTA Swisscom Challenge Zurich WTA VUB Open 2002 Bratislava, Slovakia
15-19	Rallying	Tour de Corse
16-19	Golf	Cisco World Match Play Chp Wentworth Club, Surrey
16-19	Golf	Turespaña Mallorca Classic Pula GC, Majorca
17-19	Gymnastics	World Trampoline Chps Hanover, Germany
18-26	Baseball	World Series USA
18	Cycling	Giro di Lombardi Men's World Cup
18	Horse Racing	Dubai Champion Stakes Newmarket
18	Rugby League	Super League Grand Final Old Trafford
19	Athletics	Amsterdam Marathon
19	Motor Cycling	Grand Prix Phillip Island, Australia
19	Motor Cycling	World Superbikes Magny-Cours, France
19	Triathlon	ITU World Cup Madeira, Portugal
19-29	Gymnastics	World Rhythmic Chps Maastricht, Netherlands
20-26	Golf	FUNAI Classic Lake Buena Vista, Florida
20-26	Tennis	ATP Event Basel, Switzerland ATP Event St Petersburg, Russia ATP Event Stockholm
20-26	Tennis	WTA Generali Linz WTA Seat Open Luxembourg
22-26	Rallying	Rallye Costa Brava Spain
23-26	Golf	Telefonica Open de Madrid Club de Campo, Madrid
25	Judo	European Team Chps, women Bucharest, Romania
26	Triathlon	World Cup Rio, Brazil
27-Nov 2	Golf	Chrysler Championship Palm Harbor, Florida
27-Nov 2	Tennis	Masters Series Event Paris
27-Nov 2	Tennis	WTA Advanta Championships Philadelphia, Pennsylvania WTA Bell Challenge Quebec City, Canada
30-Nov 2	Golf	Volvo Masters Valderrama, Sotogrande

November

1	Baseball	World Cup Cuba
2	Athletics	New York City Marathon
2	Motor Cycling	Grand Prix Valencia
2	Triathlon	ITU World Cup Cancun, Mexico
3-9	Golf	The Tour Championship Houston, Texas
3-9	Tennis	ATP World Doubles Chp
3-9	Tennis	WTA Tour Championships Los Angeles WTA Volvo Women's Open Pattaya City, Thailand
5-9	Rallying	Network Q Rally England and Wales
10-16	Tennis	Masters Cup Houston
12-22	Weightlifting	World Championships Vancouver, Canada
13-16	Golf	WGC - EMC World Cup Kiawah Island, South Carolina
15-16	Football	Euro 2004 play-offs 1st leg
16	Motor Cycling	Trial des Nations - Indoor
16-17	Gymnastics	Northern European Chps Artistic Bells Sports Centre, Perth
16-30	Volleyball	World Cup, men Japan
17-30	Tennis	Federation Cup s-fs and final
18-19	Football	Euro 2004, play-offs 2nd leg
23	Triathlon	ITU World Cup Geelong, Australia
24	Tennis	Davis Cup Final
29-Dec 7	Hockey	Champions Trophy, women Sydney
29	Horse Racing	Hennessy Cognac Gold Cup Newbury
30	Football	EURO 2004 Finals draw Lisbon

December

6	Horse Racing	Tingle Creek Chase Sandown Park
6	Judo	European Team Chps, men Crystal Palace, London
6-7	Gymnastics	British Rhythmic Chps Burton-on-Trent
6-7	Triathlon	World Championships Queenstown, New Zealand
7	Athletics	Fukuoka Marathon Japan
13	Horse Racing	Triplepint Gold Cup Cheltenham
14	Athletics	European Cross Country Chps Edinburgh
18-22	Equestrianism	The Olympia International
26	Horse Racing	King George VI Chase Kempton Park
27	Horse Racing	Coral Welsh National Chepstow

Federations

AMERICAN FOOTBALL
World League of American Football
99 Kings Road
London SW3 4PA
Tel: 0207 225 3070
Website: www.nfleurope.com

NFL (USA)
Tel: 001 212 450 2000
Website: www.nfl.com

ANGLING
National Federation of Anglers
Halliday House, Egginton Junction
Nr Hilton, Derbyshire DE65 6GU
Tel: 01283 734735
Website: www.nfadirect.com

ARCHERY
Grand National Archery Society
Lilleshall National Sports Centre
Newport, Shropshire TF10 9AT
Tel: 01952 677888
Website: www.gnas.org

International Federation (FITA)
Tel: 0041 21 6143050
Website: www.archery.org

ASSOCIATION FOOTBALL
The Football Association
25 Soho Square
London W1D 4FA
Tel: 0207 745 4545
Website: www.the-fa.org

International Federation (FIFA)
Tel: 0041 1 384 9595
Website: www.fifa.com

European Federation (UEFA)
Tel: 0041 22 994 4444
Website: www.uefa.com

The Football League
Unit 5, Edward VII Quay
Navigation Way
Preston, Lancs PR2 2YF
Tel: 01772 325800

Website:
Nationwide:
www.football.nationwide.co.uk

Football Association of Wales
3 Westgate Street, Cardiff CF1 1DD
Tel: 02920 372325
Website: www.faw.org.uk

Scottish Football Association
Hampden Park
Glasgow G4 9AY
Tel: 0141 616 6000
Website: www.scottishfa.co.uk

N Ireland Association
20 Windsor Avenue,
Belfast BT9 6EG
Tel: 02890 669458
Websote: www.irishfa.com

Women's Football Association
25 Soho Square
London W1D 4FA
Tel: 0207 745 4545

ATHLETICS
UK Athletics
10 Harbourne Road
Edgbaston
Birmingham B15 3AA
Tel: 0121 456 5098
Website: www.ukathletics.net

International Federation (IAAF)
Tel: 00377 93 10 88 88
Website: www.iaaf.org

BADMINTON
Badminton Association of England
National Badminton Centre
Bradwell Road
Loughton Lodge
Milton Keynes MK8 9LA
Tel: 01908 268400
Website: www.baofe.co.uk

International Badminton Federation
Tel: 01242 234 904
Website: www.intbadfed.org

BASEBALL
Baseball Softball UK
Ariel House
74a Charlotte Street
London W1P 1LR
Tel: 0207 453 7055
website: www.baseballsoftballuk.com

International Baseball Association
Tel: 0041 21 318 8240
Website: www.baseball.ch

Major League (USA)
Tel: 001 212 931 7800
Website:
www.majorleaguebaseball.com

BASKETBALL
English Basketball Association
48 Bradford Road, Stanningley
Leeds LS28 6DF
Tel: 0870 774 4225
Website:
www.englandbasketball.co.uk

British Basketball League
Basketball House,Bickenhill Trading
Estate, Bickenhill Lane,
Birmingham, B37 7JQ
Tel: 0845 345 7890
Website: www.bbl.org.uk

National Basketball Association (USA)
Tel: 001 212 407 8000
Website: www.nba.com

BILLIARDS AND SNOOKER
World Snooker
2 Ground Floor, Albert House
111-117 Victoria Street,
Bristol BS1 6AX
Tel: 0117 317 8200
Website: www.worldsnooker.com/

BOBSLEIGH
British Bobsleigh Association
Albany House
5 New Street
Salisbury SP1 2PH
Tel: 01722 340014
Website: www.british-bobsleigh.com

International Federation (FIBT)
Via Piranesi, 44/B
20137 Milan, Italy
Tel: 0039 02 757 3319
Website: www.bobsleigh.com

BOWLS
English Bowling Association
Lyndhurst Road
Worthing BN11 2AZ
Tel: 01903 820222
Website: www.bowlsengland.com

World Bowls Board
Tel: 01903 247468

BOXING
Amateur Boxing Association
Crystal Palace Sports Centre
London SE19 2BB
Tel: 0208 778 0251

British Boxing Board of Control
Jack Petersen House
52A Borough High Street
London SE1 1XW
Tel: 0207 403 5879

CANOEING
British Canoe Union
John Dudderidge House
Adbolton Lane, West Bridgford
Nottingham NG2 5AS
Tel: 0115 982 1100
Website: www.bcu.org.uk

International Canoe Fed (FIC)
Tel: 0034 91 506 1150
Website: www.canoeicf.com

CRICKET
England and Wales Cricket Board
Lord's Cricket Ground
St John's Wood, London NW8 8QN
Tel: 0207 432 1200
Website: www.lords.org
General website (Cricinfo):
www-aus.cricket.org

CROQUET
The Croquet Association
Cheltenham Croquet Club, Old Bath
Road, Cheltenham, GL53 7DF
Tel: 01242 242 318
Website: www.croquet.org.uk

World Croquet Federation
Tel: 0061 3 6244 7863
Website: www.worldcroquet.u-
net.com

CURLING
English Curling Association
Tel: 01923 825004

Royal Caledonian (Scottish Ass)
Tel: 0131 333 3003

World Curling Federation
74 Tay Street
Perth PH2 8NN
Tel: 01738 451 630
Website:
www.worldcurlingfederation.org

CYCLING
British Cycling Federation
Stuart Street
Manchester M11 4DQ
Tel: 0870 871 2000
Website: www.bcf.uk.com

International Cycling Union (UCI)
Tel: 00 41 21 468 5811
Website: www.uci.ch

DARTS
British Darts Organisation
2 Pages Lane, Muswell Hill
London N10 1PS
Tel: 0208 883 5055
Website: www.bdodarts.com

Professional Darts Corporation
NAC, Stoneleigh Park, Kenilworth,
Warwickshire, CV8 2RF
Tel: 02476 693 335
Website: www.planetdarts.co.uk

EQUESTRIAN
British Equestrian Federation
National Agricultural Centre
Stoneleigh Park, Kenilworth
Warwickshire CV8 2LR
Tel: 02476 698871
Website: www.bef.co.uk

International Federation (FEI)
Tel: 0041 21 312 5656
Website: www.horsesport.org

FENCING
Amateur Fencing Association
1 Barons Gate, 33-35 Rothschild Rd
London W4 5HT
Tel: 0208 742 3032
Website: www.britishfencing.com

International Federation (FIE)
Tel: 0041 21 320 3115
Website:www.fie.ch

GOLF
European Golf Tour
Wentworth Drive, Virginia Water
Surrey GU25 4LX
Tel: 01344 840 400
Website: www.europeantour.com

Women's European Tour
The Tytherington Club
Dorchester Way, Tytherington
Macclesfield SK10 2JP
Tel: 01625 611444
Website: www.ladieseuropeantour
.com

US PGA Tour
Tel: 001 904 285 3700
Website: www.pgatour.com

US LPGA Tour
Tel: 001 386 274 6200
Website: www.lpga.com

GREYHOUND RACING
National Greyhound Racing Club
Twyman House, 16 Bonny Street
London NW1 9QD
Tel: 0207 267 9256
Website: www.thedogs.co.uk

GYMNASTICS
**British Amateur Gymnastics
Association**
Ford Hall
Lilleshall National Sports Centre
Newport TF10 9NB
Tel: 0845 129 7129
Website: www.baga.co.uk

International Federation (FIG)
Tel: 0041 32 494 6410
Website: www.fig-gymnastics.com

HANDBALL
**International Handball
Association**
Tel: 0041 61 228 9040

British Handball Federation
40 Newchurh Road, Rawtenstall,
Rossendale, Lancashire, BB4 7QX
Tel: 01706 229354
Website: www.englandhandball.com

HANG GLIDING
Hang Gliding and Paragliding
The Old School Room
Loughborough Road
Leicester LE4 5PJ
Tel: 0114 267 9227

HOCKEY
National Hockey Foundation
The Stadium, Silbury Boulevard
Milton Keynes MK9 1HA
Tel: 01908 544 644
Website: www.hockeyonline.co.uk

International Federation (FIH)
Tel: 00 32 2 219 4537
Website:www.fihockey.org

HORSE RACING
British Horse Racing Board
42 Portman Square
London W1H 6EN
Tel: 0207 396 0011
Website: www.bhb.co.uk/bhb/

ICE HOCKEY
British Ice Hockey Association
The Galleries of Justice
Shire Hall, The Lace Market
Nottingham NG1 1HN
Tel: 0115 915 9204
Website: www.icehockeyuk.co.uk

International Federation (IIHF)
Website: www.iihf.com

National Hockey League (NHL)
Tel: 001 212 789 2000
Website: www.nhl.com

ICE SKATING
National Ice Skating Assoc of UK
Lower Parliament Street
Nottingham NG1 1LA
Tel: 0115 988 8060
New website pending

International Skating Union (ISU)
Tel: 0041 21 612 6666
Website:www.isu.org

JUDO
British Judo Association
7A Rutland Street
Leicester LE1 1RB
Tel: 0116 255 9669
Fax: 0116 255 9660
Website: www.britishjudo.org.uk

International Judo Federation
Tel: 0082 2 3398 1017
Website: ww.ijf.org

KARATE
English Karate Governing Body
23 Sidlaws Road, Cove,
Farnborough GU14 9JL
Website: www.ekgb.org.uk

World Karate Federation (WFK)
Tel: 00 34 91 659 2256
Website: www.wkf.net

LACROSSE
English Lacrosse Association
26 Wood Street, Manchester
Tel: 0161 834 4582
Website: www.englishlacrosse.co.uk

LUGE
International Federation (FIL)
Tel: 0049 86 526 6960
Website: www.fil-luge.org

MODERN PENTATHLON
Modern Pentathlon Assoc of GB
Pentathlon House
1 Mount Pleasant, Tadley
Hampshire RG26 4JH
Tel: 0118 981 7181
Website: www.mpagb.org.uk

**International Union of Modern
Pentathlon**
Tel: 00377 97 77 85 55
Website: www.pentathlon.org

MOTOR CYCLING
Auto-Cycle Union
ACU House, Wood Street, Rugby
Warwickshire CV21 2YX
Tel: 01788 566 400

International Federation (FIM)
Tel: 0041 22 950 9500
Website:www.fim.ch

MOTOR SPORTS
RAC Motor Sports Association
Motor Sports House
Riverside Park
Colnbrook, Slough SL3 OHG
Tel: 01753 681736
Website: www.msauk.org

International Federation (FIA)
Tel: 00 33 1 43 12 44 55
Website:www.fia.com

NETBALL
All England Netball Association
Netball House
9 Paynes Park, Hitchin SG5 1EH
Tel: 01462 442344
Website: www.england-netball.co.uk

International Netball Fed (INF)
Tel: 0121 446 4451
Website: www.netball.org

OLYMPIC GAMES
International Olympic Committee
Chateau de Vidy
1007 Lausanne
Switzerland
Tel: 00 41 21 621 6111
Website: www.olympic.org

ORIENTEERING
British Orienteering Federation
Riversdale
Dale Road North, Darley Dale,
Matlock DE4 2HX
Tel: 01629 734042
Web: www.cix.co.uk/~bof/index.html

**International Orienteering
Federation (IOF)**
Tel: 00358 9 348 13112
Website:www.orienteering.org

POLO
Hurlingham Polo Association
Manor Farm, Little Coxwell
Faringdon
Oxon SN7 7LW
Tel: 01367 242828
Website: www.hpa-polo.co.uk

REAL TENNIS AND RACKETS
Tennis and Rackets Association
c/o The Queens Club
Palliser Road
West Kensington
London W14 9EQ
Tel: 0207 386 3447
Website: www.real-tennis.com

ROWING
Amateur Rowing Association
The Priory, 6 Lower Mall
Hammersmith
London W6 9DJ
Tel: 0208 237 6700
Website: www.ara-rowing.org

International Federation (FISA)
Tel: 0041 21 617 8373
Website:www.fisa.org

RUGBY LEAGUE
The Rugby Football League
Red Hall, Red Hall Lane
Leeds LS71 8NB
Tel: 0113 232 9111
Website: www.rfl.uk.com

RUGBY UNION
The Rugby Football Union
Rugby Road
Twickenham, Middx TW1 1DZ
Tel: 0208 892 8161
Website: www.rfu.com

Irish Rugby Football Union
62 Lansdowne Road
Ballsbridge
Dublin
Tel: 00 3531 647 3800
Website: www.irfu.ie

Scottish Rugby Union
7/9 Roseburn Street
Edinburgh EH12 5PJ
Tel: 0131 3372346
Website: www.sru.org.uk

Welsh Rugby Union
PO Box 22, Cardiff CF1 1JL
Tel: 02920 390111
Website: www.wru.co.uk

International Rugby Board (IRFB)
Tel: 00353 1 240 9200
Website: www.irfb.com

SAILING
Royal Yachting Association
RYA House, Romsey Road
Eastleigh
Hants SO50 9YA
Tel: 0845 345 0400
Website:www.rya.org.uk

International Federation (ISAF)
Tel: 02380 635 111
Website: www.sailing.org

SHOOTING
British Shooting Sports Council
PO Box 11
Bexhill-on-Sea TN40 1ZZ
Tel: 01424 217 031
Website: www.bssc.org.uk

International Federation (ISSF)
Tel: 0049 89 544 3550
Website: www.issf-shooting.org

SKIING
British Ski Federation
Hillend
Biggar Road
Midlothian EH10 7EF
Tel: 0131 445 7676
Web: www.ifyouski.com/bssf/

International Federation (FIS)
Tel: 00 41 33 244 6161
Website: www.fis-ski.com

SNOOKER
See Billiards

SPEEDWAY
British Speedway Promoters Association
Website: www.british-speedway.co.uk

SQUASH
Squash Rackets Association
National Squash Centre, Rawnsley Street, Manchester M11 3FF
Tel: 0161 231 4499
Website: www.englandsquash.com

World Squash Federation
Tel: 01424 429245
Website: www.worldsquash.org

SWIMMING
Amateur Swimming Association
Harold Fern House
Derby Square, Loughborough
Leics LE11 5AL
Tel: 01509 618700
Website: www.britishswimming.org

International Federation (FINA)
Tel: 0041 21 310 4710
Website: www.fina.org

TABLE TENNIS
English Table Tennis Association
Queensbury House
Havelock Road
Hastings TN34 1HF
Tel: 01424 722525
Website: www.etta.co.uk

International Table Tennis Federation
Tel: 00 41 21 340 7090
Website: www.ittf.com

TENNIS
Lawn Tennis Association
The Queens Club
Barons Court
West Kensington
London W14 9EG
Tel: 0207 381 7000
Website: www.lta.org.uk

International Tennis Federation
Tel: 0208 878 6464
Website: www.itftennis.com

International Men's Tennis (ATP)
Tel: 001 904 285 8000
Website: www.atptour.com

International Women's Tennis (WTA)
Tel: 001 727 895 5000
Website: www.wtatour.com

TENPIN BOWLING
British Tenpin Bowling Association
114 Balfour Road
Ilford
Essex IG1 4JD
Tel: 0208 478 1745
Website: www.btba.org.uk

TRAMPOLINING
See Gymnastics

TRIATHLON
British Triathlon Association
PO Box 25
Loughborough LE11 3WX
Tel: 01509 228 321
Website: www.britishtriathlon.org

International Triathlon Union
Website: www.triathlon.org

VOLLEYBALL
English Volleyball Association
27 South Road, West Bridgford
Nottingham NG2 7AG
Tel: 0115 981 6324
Website: www.volleyballengland.org

International Federation
Tel: 00 41 21 345 3535
Website: www.fivb.ch

WATER SKIING
British Water Ski Federation
The Tower, Thorpe Road, Chertsey,
Surrey KT16 8PH
Tel: 01932 570 885
Website: www.britishwaterski.co.uk

International Waterski Federation
Tel: 00 41 41 752 0095
Website: www.iwsf.com

WEIGHTLIFTING
British Amateur Weightlifters Association
131 Hurst Street
Oxford
OX4 1HE
Tel: 01865 200 339
Website: www.bawla.com

International Weightlifting Federation
Tel: 00 36 1 353 0530
Website: www.iwf.net

WRESTLING
BritishWrestling Association
12 Westwood Lame, Brimington,
Chesterfield S43 1PA
Tel: 01246 236 443
Website: www.britishwrestling.org

International Federation (FILA)
Website: www.fila-wrestling.org

Sports Internet Directory

The sports internet directory (SID) is a selection of key sites, categorised alphabetically. We have also listed in a separate box, the sites which are our favourites, which best meet the requirements of ease of access, are constantly updated and offer reliable information. The nature of the internet means that we can offer no guarantee that the sites will still be as good next week as they were last.

For information, the research for this directory was done on an Apple Mac G4(Dual 867MHz), using an ADSL connection.

Air Sports

International Federation
www.fai.org

UK Sky Diving
www.skygod.demon.co.uk

Paragliding
www.paragliding.net

American Football

National Football League (NFL)
www.nfl.com

Arizona Cardinals	www.azcardinals.com
Atlanta Falcons	www.atlantafalcons.com
Baltimore Ravens	www.ravenszone.com
Buffalo Bills	www.buffalobills.com
Carolina Panthers	www.panthers.com
Chicago Bears	www.chicagobears.com
Cincinnati Bengals	www.bengals.com
Cleveland Browns	www.clevelandbrowns.com
Dallas Cowboys	www.dallascowboys.com
Denver Broncos	www.denverbroncos.com
Detroit Lions	www.detroitlions.com
Green Bay Packers	www.packers.com
Houston Texans	www.houstontexans.com
Indianapolis Colts	www.colts.com
Jacksonville Jaguars	www.jaguars.com
Kansas City Chiefs	www.kcchiefs.com
Miami Dolphins	www.miamidolphins.com
Minnesota Vikings	www.vikings.com
New England Patriots	www.patriots.com
New Orleans Saints	www.neworleanssaints.com
New York Giants	www.giants.com
New York Jets	www.newyorkjets.com
Oakland Raiders	www.raiders.com
Philadelphia Eagles	www.philadelphiaeagles.com
Pittsburgh Steelers	www.steelers.com
San Diego Chargers	www.chargers.com
San Francisco 49ers	www.sf49ers.com
Seattle Seahawks	www.seahawks.com
St Louis Rams	www.stlouisrams.com
Tampa Bay Buccaneers	www.buccaneers.com
Tennessee Titans	www.titansonline.com
Washington Redskins	www.redskins.com

Superbowl
www.superbowl.com

NFL Europe
www.nfleurope.com

Amsterdam Admirals	www.admirals.nl
Barcelona Dragons	www.dragons.es
Berlin Thunder	www.berlin-thunder.de
Frankfurt Galaxy	www.frankfurt-galaxy.com
Rhein Fire	www.rhein-fire.de
Scottish Claymores	www.claymores.co.uk

Women's American Football
www.womensprofootball.com

College Football (NCAA)
www.ncaafootball.net

American Sports

Fox Sports
www.foxsports.com

ESPN
www.espn.go.com

CBS
www.sportsline.com

Angling

Federation of Fly Fishers
www.fedflyfishers.org

Coarse Fishing
www.matchangler.com

Scottish Angling
www.dholt.demon.co.uk/index.htm

General
www.fishing.co.uk/

Archery

International Target Federation (FITA)
www.archery.org

International Field Archery Association (IFAA)
www.archery-ifaa.org

European and Mediterranean Archery Union
www.emau.org

The Grand National Archery Society (UK)
www.gnas.org

Association Football

International Federation (FIFA)
www.fifa.com

European Federation (UEFA)
www.uefa.com

National Federations

England	www.the-fa.org
Scotland	www.scottishfa.co.uk
Wales	www.faw.org.uk
Northern Ireland	www.irishfa.com
Ireland	www.fai.ie

European Championship 2004
www.euro2004.com

English Premiership

Arsenal	www.arsenal.com
Aston Villa	www.avfc.co.uk
Blackburn Rovers	www.rovers.co.uk
Birmingham City	www.bcfc.com
Bolton Wanderers	www.bwfc.co.uk
Charlton Athletic	www.cafc.co.uk
Chelsea	www.chelseafc.co.uk
Everton	www.evertonfc.com
Fulham	www.fulhamfc.co.uk
Leeds United	www.leedsunited.com
Liverpool	www.liverpoolfc.tv
Manchester City	www.mcfc.co.uk
Manchester United	www.manutd.com
Middlesbrough	www.mfc.co.uk
Newcastle United	www.nufc.co.uk
Southampton	www.saintsfc.co.uk
Sunderland	www.safc.com
Tottenham Hotspur	www.spurs.co.uk
West Bromwich Albion	www.wba.co.uk
West Ham United	www.westhamunited.co.uk

English Division 1

Bradford City	www.bradfordcityfc.co.uk
Brighton & Hove Albion	www.seagulls.co.uk
Burnley	www.burnleyfootballclub.com
Coventry City	www.ccfc.co.uk
Crystal Palace	www.cpfc.co.uk
Derby County	www.dcfc.co.uk
Gillingham	www.gillinghamfootballclub.com
Grimsby Town	www.gtfc.co.uk
Ipswich Town	www.itfc.co.uk
Leicester City	www.lcfc.co.uk
Millwall	www.millwallfc.co.uk
Norwich City	www.canaries.co.uk

SID 5-Star Sites

news.bbc.co.uk

The vast resources at the BBC's disposal make this site invaluable. Regularly updated and offering extensive coverage of all major sports, this site is an ideal homepage.

www.runningstats.com

In the esoteric world of road running, this site does a brilliant job. Gives frequent and comprehensive results from worldwide events.

www.horseweb.de

A sport where regular information is almost impossible to find, but this site is a rare and welcome exception. In English and German, and updated daily.

www.uefa.com

In the build-up to EURO 2004, the UEFA site has comprehensive news for all European international sides, and loads of information for European club competitions.

Nottingham Forest	www.nottinghamforest.co.uk
Portsmouth	www.portsmouthfc.co.uk
Preston North End	www.pnefc.net
Reading	www.readingfc.co.uk
Rotherham United	www.themillers.co.uk
Sheffield United	www.sufc.co.uk
Sheffield Wednesday	www.swfc.co.uk
Stoke City	www.stokecityfc.co.uk
Walsall	www.saddlers.co.uk
Watford	www.watfordfc.com
Wimbledon	www.wimbledon-fc.co.uk
Wolverhampton W	www.wolves.co.uk

English Division 2

Barnsley	www.barnsleyfc.co.uk
Blackpool	www.blackpoolfc.co.uk
Brentford	www.brentfordfc.co.uk
Bristol City	www.bcfc.co.uk
Cardiff City	www.cardiffcityfc.co.uk
Chesterfield	www.chesterfield-fc.co.uk
Cheltenham Town	www.the-robins.co.uk
Colchester United	www.colchesterunited.net
Crewe Alexandra	www.crewealexfc.co.uk
Huddersfield Town	www.htafc.com
Luton Town	www.lutontown.co.uk
Mansfield Town	www.mansfieldtown.net
Northampton Town	www.ntfc.co.uk
Notts County	www.nottscountyfc.co.uk
Oldham Athletic	www.oldhamathletic.co.uk
Peterborough United	www.theposh.com
Plymouth Argyle	www.pafc.co.uk
Port Vale	www.port-vale.co.uk
Queen's Park Rangers	www.qpr.co.uk
Stockport County	www.stockportcounty.com
Swindon Town	www.swindonfc.co.uk
Tranmere Rovers	www.tranmererovers.co.uk
Wigan Athletic	www.wiganlatics.co.uk
Wycombe Wanderers	www.wycombewanderers.co.uk

English Division 3

Bournemouth	www.afcb.co.uk
Boston United	www.bostonunited.co.uk
Bristol Rovers	www.bristolrovers.co.uk
Bury	www.buryfc.co.uk
Cambridge United	www.cambridgeunited.com
Carlisle United	www.carlisleunited.co.uk
Darlington	www.darlingtonfc.net
Exeter City	www.exetercityfc.co.uk
Halifax Town	www.halifaxafc.net
Hartlepool United	www.hartlepoolunited.co.uk
Hull City	www.hullcityafc.net
Kidderminster Harriers	www.harriers.co.uk
Leyton Orient	www.leytonorient.com
Lincoln City	www.redimps.com
Macclesfield Town	www.mtfc.co.uk
Oxford United	www.oufc.co.uk
Rochdale	www.rochdaleafc.co.uk
Rushden & Diamonds	www.thediamondsfc.com
Scunthorpe United	www.scunthorpe-united.co.uk
Shrewsbury Town	www.shrewsburytown.co.uk
Southend United	www.southendunited.co.uk
Swansea City	www.swansfc.co.uk
Torquay United	www.torquayunited.com
Wrexham	www.wrexhamafc.co.uk
York City	www.ycfc.net

Scottish Premiership
www.scotprem.com

Aberdeen	www.afc.co.uk
Celtic	www.celticfc.co.uk
Dundee	www.dundeefc.co.uk
Dundee United	www.dundeeunitedfc.co.uk
Dunfermline	www.dunfermline-athletic.com
Hearts	www.heartsfc.co.uk
Hibernian	www.hibs.co.uk
Kilmarnock	www.kilmarnockfc.co.uk
Livingston	www.livingstonfc.co.uk
Motherwell	www.motherwellfc.co.uk
Rangers	www.rangers.co.uk
Partick Thistle	www.ptfc.co.uk

Other Sites

www.teamtalk.com
www.fourfourtwo.com
www.football365.com
www.worldsoccer.com
www.soccernet.com
www.planetfootball.com

Athletics

International Federation (IAAF)
www.iaaf.org

European Athletic Association (EAA)
www.eaa-athletics.ch

UK Athletics
www.ukathletics.net

Other Federations

Athletics Australian	www.athletics.org.au
Athletics Canadian	www.athleticscanada.com
French Federation	www.athle.org
German Federation	www.dlv-sport.de
US Track & Field	www.ustaf.com

Track Events (Golden League)

Golden Gala-Rome	www.goldengala.it/
Gaz de France-Paris	www.gazdefrance.com
Bislett Games-Oslo	www.bislettgames.com
Herculis-Monaco	www.herculis.com
Weltklasse-Zurich	www.weltklasse.ch
Van Damme-Brussels	www.memorialvandamme.be
ISTAF - Berlin	www.istaf.de

Road Running

Marathon Assoc	www.aims-association.org
London Marathon	www.london-marathon.co.uk
Rotterdam Marathon	www.rotterdammarathon.nl
Berlin Marathon	www.berlin-marathon.com
New York Marathon	www.nyrrc.org
Boston Marathon	www.bostonmarathon.org

Magazines

Track and Field News	www.trackandfieldnews.com
Runners' World	www.runnersworld.com
Running Stats	www.runningstats.com

Australian Rules Football

International AF Confederation
www.iafc.org.au

Australian Football League
www.afl.com.au

British ARF League
www.barfl.co.uk

Badminton

International Federation (IBF)
www.intbadfed.org

European Badminton Union (EBU)
www.eurobadminton.org/

National Federations
England   www.baofe.co.uk
Wales   www.welshbadminton.net
Scotland   www.scotbadminton.demon.
              co.uk

General Badminton Site
www.worldbadminton.net

Baseball

Major League Baseball
www.mlb.com

International Baseball Association
www.baseball.ch

British Baseball
www.baseballsoftballuk.com

Basketball

National Basketball Association (NBA)
www.nba.org

Women's NBA
www.wnba.com

International Basketball Federation (FIBA)
www.fiba.com

British Basketball League (BBL)
www.bbl.org.uk

English Basketball
www.basketballengland.org.uk/

General Site
www.britball.com

Biathlon

International Biathlon Union
www.ibu.at

Bobsleigh/Luge

International Bobsleigh Federation (FIBT)
www.bobsleigh.com

International Luge Federation
www.fil-luge.org

British Bobsleigh Association
british-bobsleigh.com

British Luge Association
www.gbla.org.uk

Bowls

English Bowling Association
www.bowlsengland.com

British Crown Green Bowling Association
www.bowls.org

Boxing

World Boxing Council
www.wbcboxing.com

International Boxing Federation
www.ibf-usba-boxing.com

World Boxing Organisation
www.wbo-int.com/

World Boxing Association
www.wbaonline.com

International Amateur Boxing Association
www.aiba.net/

Other Sites
www.usatoday.com/sports/boxing/news.htm
www.sportsline.com/u/boxing/
www.boxing-records.com
www.amateur-boxing.com

Canoeing

International Canoe Federation
www.canoeicf.com

European Canoe Association
www.canoe-europe.org

British Canoe Union
www.bcu.org.uk

Irish Canoe Union
www.irishcanoeunion.com

Precision (slalom newspaper)
www.canoekayak.com

Cricket

General Site
www.cricinfo.com

Wisden
www.wisden.co.uk

Channel 4
www.cricket4.com

Other Sites
www.cricketline.com

Croquet

World Croquet Federation
www.worldcroquet.u-net.com

Curling

World Curling Federation
www.worldcurlingfederation.org

Scottish Federation
www.scotcurl.co.uk

Canadian Federation
www.curling.ca

Cycling

International Cycling Union (UCI)
www.uci.ch

British Cycling Federation (BCF)
www.bcf.uk.com

Tour de France
www.letour.fr

Other Sites
www.cyclingnews.com
www.cyclingteams.com
www.cycling4all.com
www.descent-world.co.uk

Darts

International Darts Players Association
www.idpa.net/

Professional Darts Corporation
www.planetdarts.co.uk

British Darts Organisation (BDO)
www.bdodarts.com

Equestrianism

International Federation (FEI)
www.horsesport.org

British Equestrian Federation
www.equestrian.co.uk

British Show Jumping Association
www.bsja.co.uk

British Dressage
www.britishdressage.co.uk

Events
Badminton *www.badminton-horse.co.uk*
Burghley *www.burghley.co.uk*

Statistics Site
www.bcm.nl

Results Site
www.horseweb.de

Fencing

International Federation (FIE)
www.fie.ch

British Fencing Assocation
www.BritishFencing.com

Gaelic Sports

Gaelic Athletic Association
www.gaa.ie

Golf

US Men's Golf Tour
www.pgatour.com

European Men's Golf Tour
www.europeantour.com

US Women's Tour
www.lpga.com

European Women's Tour
www.ladieseuropeantour.com

English Golf Union (amateur)
www.englishgolfunion.org

US Golf Association (amateur)
www.usga.org
General Site
www.golf.com

Greyhound Racing

British Greyhound Racing Board
www.thedogs.co.uk

Magazine
www.greyhoundmonthly.com

Stud Directory
www.fredsharpe.freeserve.co.uk

Gymnastics

International Federation (FIG)
www.fig-gymnastics.com

European Gymnastics Union
www.gymnastics-ueg.org

British Gymnastics
www.baga.co.uk

US Gymnastics
www.usa-gymnastics.org

General Sites
www.gymmedia.com
www.gymn-forum.com

Rhythmic Gymnastics
www.rsg.net

Trampolining
welcome.to/trampolining

Handball

European Federation (EHF)
www.eurohandball.com

England Handball Association
www.englandhandball.com

Hockey

International Federation (FIH)
www.fihockey.org

English Hockey Association (EHA)
www.hockeyonline.co.uk

Australian Hockey
www.hockey.org.au

German Hockey
www.german-fieldhockey.de

General Site
www.fieldhockey.com

Horse Racing

British Horseracing Board
www.bhb.co.uk

Weatherbys
www.weatherbys-group.com

USA Jockey Club
www.jockeyclub.com

Breeders Cup
www.breederscup.com

Irish Racing
www.irish-racing.com

French Racing
www.france-galop.fr

Racecourses

Aintree	www.aintree.co.uk
Ascot	www.ascot.co.uk
Cheltenham	www.cheltenham.co.uk
Epsom	www.epsomderby.co.uk
Goodwood	www.goodwood.co.uk
Newbury	www.newbury-racecourse.co.uk
Newmarket	www.newmarketracecourses.co.uk
Sandown	www.sandown.co.uk
York	www.yorkraceourse.co.uk

General Sites
www.racingpost.co.uk
www.racenews.co.uk
www.racemeetings.co.uk

Ice Hockey

International Ice Hockey Federation (IIHF)
www.iihf.com

US National Hockey League
www.nhl.com

UK Ice Hockey (IHUK)
www.icehockeyuk.co.uk

English Ice Hockey Association
www.eiha.co.uk

General Site
www.azhockey.com

Ice Skating

International Federation (ISU)
www.isu.org

General Site
www.skatingsource.com

Judo

International Federation (IJF)
www.ijf.org

British Federation (BJF)
www.britishjudo.org.uk

Scottish Federation
www.scotjudo.org

Karate

International Federation
www.wkf.net

European Federation
www.eku.com

English Federation
www.ekgb.org.uk

Modern Pentathlon

International Federation (UIMP)
www.pentathlon.org

British Federation
www.mpagb.org.uk

Motor Cycling

International Federation
www.fim.ch

British Federation (ACU)
www.acu.org.uk

World Superbikes
www.superbike.it

Grand Prix Racing
www.motograndprix.com

Speedway
www.speedwaygp.com

General Site
www.europark.com

Motor Racing

International Federation
www.fia.com

Formula 1
www.formula-1.com
www.f1.racing-live.com/

RAC Motor Sports Association
www.msauk.org

Rallying
www.rally-live.com

US Championship Series (CART)
www.cart.com

Le Mans
www.club-arnage.com

Netball

International Federation (IFNA)
www.netball.org

All-England Assocation
www.england-netball.co.uk

New Zealand Association
www.netballnz.co.nz

Australian Association
www.netball.asn.au

Orienteering

International Federation (IOF)
www.orienteering.org

Polo

Hurlingham
www.hpa-polo.co.uk

Rackets

General Site
www.rackets.co.uk

Real Tennis

General Site
www.real-tennis.com

Rowing

International Federation (FISA)
www.worldrowing.com

British Federation (ARA)
www.ara-rowing.org

The Boat Race
www.theboatrace.org

Henley Regatta
henley.rowing.org.uk

General Site
users.ox.ac.uk/~quarrell/

Rugby League

National Rugby League - Australia
www.nrl.com.au

British Amateur Rugby League
www.barla.org.uk

Rugby Football League
www.rfl.uk.com

General Sites
rleague.com

Rugby Union

International Federation
www.irfb.com

National Governing Bodies

RFU (England)	www.rfu.com
Argentina	www.uar.com.ar
Australia	www.rugby.com.au
France	www.ffr.fr
Ireland	www.irfu.ie
Italy	www.federazioneitalianarugby.it
New Zealand	www.nzrugby.co.nz
Scotland	www.sru.org.uk
South Africa	www.sarugby.net
Wales	www.wru.co.uk

Six Nations
www.sixnationsweb.com

General Sites
www.rugbyrugby.com
www.planet-rugby.com
www.scrum.com

Sailing

International Federation (ISAF)
www.sailing.org

Royal Yachting Association
www.rya.org.uk

Cowes Week
www.cowesweek.co.uk

Shooting

International Federation
www.issf-shooting.org

British Small-Bore (NSRA)
www.nsra.co.uk

British Clay Pigeon (CPSA)
www.cpsa.co.uk

Skiing

InternationalFederation (FIS)
www.fis-ski.com

British Skiing
www.britski.org

World Cup
www.skiworldcup.org

Snooker

General Sites
www.worldsnooker.com
www.worldofsnooker.co.uk

Squash

International Federation (WSF)
www.squash.org

Women's Squash (wispa)
www.wispa.net

Men's Squash (PSA)
www.psa-squash.com

Swimming

International Federation (FINA)
www.fina.org

British Federation
www.britishswimming.org

US Federation
www.usa-swimming.org

Australian Federation
www.ausswim.telstra.com.au

British Diving
www.diving-gbdf.com

General Sites
www.swimnews.com
www.swiminfo.com

Table Tennis

International Federation
www.ittf.com

European Federation
www.ettu.org

English Federation
www.etta.co.uk

Taekwondo

International Federation
www.wtf.org

European Federation
www.etutaekwondo.org

Tenpin Bowling

International Federation (ETBF)
www.bowling-ez.com

British Federation
www.btba.org.uk

Tennis

International Federation (ITF)
www.itftennis.com

Men's Tennis (ATP)
www.atptennis.com
stevegtennis.com

Women's Tennis (WTA)
www.sanexwta.com
www.acemantennis.com

Lawn Tennis Association
www.lta.org.uk

Events

Wimbledon	www.wimbledon.org
Australian Open	www.ausopen.org
French Open	www.frenchopen.org
US Open	www.usopen.org
Davis Cup	www.daviscup.org
ATP Masters Series	www.masters-series.com

Triathlon

International Federation (ITU)
www.triathlon.org

European Federation (ETU)
www.etu.org

British Federation (BTA)
www.britishtriathlon.co.uk

General Site
www.triathletemag.com

Volleyball

International Federation
www.fivb.ch

General Site
www.v-spirit.com

Water Skiing

International Federation
www.iwsf.com

European/Middle East Federation
www.waterskieame.org

British Federation
www.britishwaterski.co.uk

General Site
www.planetwaterski.com

Weightlifting

International Federation
www.iwf.net

European Federation
www.tradecenter.sm/ewf/

British Federation
www.weights.demon.co.uk

Archive Site
www.iat.uni-leipzig.de/weight.htm

Wrestling

International Federation (FILA)
www.fila-wrestling.org

British Federation
www.britishwrestling.org

Newspapers

The Guardian: www.guardianunlimited.co.uk

Daily Telegraph: www.telegraph.co.uk

The Times: www.thetimes.co.uk

The Independent: www.independent.co.uk

New York Times: www.nytimes.com

LA Times: www.latimes.com

USA Today: www.usatoday.com

Sydney Morning Herald: www.smh.com.au

L'Equipe: www.lequipe.fr

Sports Bookshops

Sportpages: www.sportspages.co.uk

Sport Books Direct: www.sportsbooksdirect.co.uk

W H Smith: www.whsmith.co.uk

Sports Sponsorship

Sponsorship Online: www.sponsorshiponline.co.uk

Sports Councils

UK Sport: www.uksport.gov.uk

Sport England: www.sportengland.org

Northern Ireland SC: www.sportni.org

Sport Scotland: www.sportscotland.org.uk

SC for Wales: www.sports-council-wales-.co.uk

Olympics

International Olympic Committee: www.olympics.org

British Olympic Association: www.olympics.org.uk

Athens Olympic Games: www.athens2004.gr

Betting

William Hill: www.willhill.co.uk

Ladbrokes: www.ladbrokes.com

Tote (Pool Betting): www.tote.co.uk

IG Index (Spread Betting): www.igindex.co.uk

Betfair (Betting Exchange): www.betfair.com

Britodds (Comparative Prices): www.Britodds.com

Abbreviations

TIMES

Where a time is shown, hours minutes and seconds are separated by a colon. A full point is used only as a decimal point for parts of a second. eg 3 hours 23 minutes and 7.5 seconds is shown as 3:23:7.50

In cycling events, the time for each rider is shown as the difference between themselves and the winner, using either @ or + sign.

st   same time

OTHERS

WR   World Record
World records may also be shown in bold for some sports
ER   European Record
BR   British Record
jr   Junior
sn   Senior
w/o   Walk over
ret   Retired
aet   After extra time
s-f   Semi-final
q-f   Quarter-final
qfy   Qualifying

COUNTRIES

AFG	Afghanistan
AHO	Netherlands Antilles
ALB	Albania
ALG	Algeria
AND	Andorra
ANG	Anguilla
ANO	Angola
ANT	Antigua and Barbuda
ARG	Argentina
ARM	Armenia
ARU	Aruba
ASA	American Samoa
AUS	Australia
AUT	Austria
AZE	Azerbaijan
BAH	Bahamas
BAN	Bangladesh
BAR	Barbados
BDI	Burundi
BEL	Belgium
BEN	Benin
BER	Bermuda
BHU	Bhutan
BIH	Bosnia-Herzegovina
BIZ	Belize
BLR	Belarus
BOL	Bolivia
BOT	Botswana
BRA	Brazil
BRN	Bahrain
BRU	Brunei
BUL	Bulgaria
BUR	Burkina Faso
CAF	Central African Republic
CAM	Cambodia
CAN	Canada
CAY	Cayman Islands
CGO	Congo
CHI	Chile
CHN	People's Rep of China
CIV	Cote d'Ivoire
CKI	Cook Islands
CMR	Cameroon
COD	D R of Congo
COL	Colombia
COM	Comoros
CPV	Cape Verde
CRC	Costa Rica
CRO	Croatia
CUB	Cuba
CYP	Cyprus
CZE	Czech Republic
DEN	Denmark
DJI	Djibouti
DMN	Dominica
DOM	Dominican Republic
ECU	Equador
EGY	Egypt
ENG	England
ERI	Eritrea
ESA	El Salvador
ESP	Spain
EST	Estonia
ETH	Ethiopia
FIJ	Fiji
FIN	Finland
FKI	Falkland Islands
FRA	France
FRO	Faroe Islands
FSM	Federated States of Micronesia
GAB	Gabon
GAM	The Gambia
GBR	Great Britain and NI
GBS	Guinea-Bissau
GEO	Georgia
GER	Germany
GHA	Ghana
GIB	Gibraltar
GRE	Greece
GRN	Grenada
GUA	Guatemala
GUE	Guernsey
GUI	Guinea
GUM	Guam
GUY	Guyana
HAI	Haiti
HKG	Hong Kong
HON	Honduras
HUN	Hungary
INA	Indonesia
IND	India
IOM	Isle of Man
IRL	Ireland
IRI	Iran
IRQ	Iraq
ISL	Iceland
ISR	Israel
ISV	US Virgin Islands
ITA	Italy
IVB	British Virgin Islands
JAM	Jamaica
JER	Jersey
JOR	Jordan
JPN	Japan
KAZ	Kazakhstan
KEN	Kenya
KGZ	Kyrgyzstan
KIR	Kiribati
KOR	Korea
KSA	Saudi Arabia
KUW	Kuwait
LAO	Laos
LAT	Latvia
LBA	Libya
LBR	Liberia

LES	Lesotho	OMA	Oman	SUR	Surinam
LIE	Liechenstein	PAK	Pakistan	SVK	Slovak Republic
LTU	Lithuania	PLW	Palau	SWE	Sweden
LUX	Luxemburg	PAN	Panama	SWZ	Swaziland
MAC	Macedonia	PAR	Paraguay	SYR	Syria
MAD	Madagascar	PER	Peru	TAN	Tanzania
MAR	Morocco	PHI	Philippines	TCI	Turks and Caikos Islands
MAS	Malaysia	PNG	Papua New Guinea	TGA	Tonga
MAW	Malawi	POL	Poland	THA	Thailand
MDA	Moldova	POR	Portugal	TJK	Tadjikistan
MDV	Maldives	PRK	North Korea	TKM	Turkmenistan
MEX	Mexico	PUR	Puerto Rico	TOG	Togo
MKD	FYR of Macedonia	QAT	Qatar	TPE	Taiwan (Chinese Taipei)
MLI	Mali	ROM	Romania	TRI	Trinidad & Tobago
MLT	Malta	RSA	South Africa	TUN	Tunisia
MGL	Mongolia	RUS	Russia	TUR	Turkey
MNT	Montserrat	RWA	Rwanda	TUV	Tuvalu
MON	Monaco	SAM	Samoa	UAE	United Arab Emirates
MOZ	Mozambique	SCO	Scotland	UGA	Uganda
MRI	Mauritius	SEN	Senegal	UKR	Ukraine
MTN	Mauritania	SEY	Seychelles	URU	Uruguay
MYA	Myanmar	SIN	Singapore	USA	United States
NAM	Namibia	SKN	St Kitts and Nevis	UZB	Uzbekistan
NAU	Nauru	SLE	Sierra Leone	VAN	Vanuatu
NCA	Nicaragua	SLO	Slovenia	VIE	Vietnam
NED	Netherlands	SMR	San Marino	VEN	Venezuela
NEP	Nepal	SOL	Solomon Islands	VIN	St Vincent and the
NFI	Norfolk Islands	SOM	Somalia		Grenadines
NGR	Nigeria	SRI	Sri Lanka	WAL	Wales
NIG	Niger	STH	St Helena	YUG	Yugoslavia
NIR	Northern Ireland	STL	St Lucia	ZAM	Zambia
NOR	Norway	STP	Sao Tome and Principe	YEM	Yemen
NIU	Niue	SUD	Sudan	ZIM	Zimbabwe
NZL	New Zealand	SUI	Switzerland		